International Business

Environments and Operations

Global Edition
THIRTEENTH EDITION

John D. Daniels
University of Miami

Lee H. Radebaugh
Brigham Young University

Daniel P. Sullivan
University of Delaware

Boston Columbus Indianapolis New York San Francisco Upper Saddle River
Amsterdam Cape Town Dubai London Madrid Milan Munich Paris Montreal Toronto
Delhi Mexico City Sao Paulo Sydney Hong Kong Seoul Singapore Taipei Tokyo

Editorial Director: Sally Yagan
Editor in Chief: Eric Svendsen
Acquisitions Editor: Jennifer M. Collins
Senior Acquisitions Editor, Global Edition:
　Steven Jackson
Product Development Manager: Ashley Santora
Editorial Project Manager: Susan Abraham
Editorial Assistant: Meg O'Rourke
Director of Marketing: Patrice Lumumba Jones
Marketing Manager: Nikki Ayana Jones
Marketing Assistant: Ian Gold
Marketing Manager, International: Dean Erasmus
Senior Managing Editor: Judy Leale
Associate Production Project Manager: Ana Jankowski

Senior Operations Supervisor: Arnold Vila
Art Director: Mike Fruhbeis
Text Designer: Frubilicious Design Group
Manager, Visual Research: Beth Brenzel
Photo Researcher: Rachel Lucas
Manager, Rights and Permissions: Zina Arabia
Image Permission Coordinator: Joanne Dipel
Cover Designer: Jodi Notowitz
Cover Art: © photocreo/Fotolia
Editorial Media Project Manager: Denise Vaughn
Production Media Project Manager: Lisa Rinaldi
Full-Service Project Management: Integra
Cover Printer: Lehigh-Phoenix Color/
　Hagerstown

Pearson Education Limited
Edinburgh Gate
Harlow
Essex CM20 2JE
England

and Associated Companies throughout the world

Visit us on the World Wide Web at:
www.pearsoned.co.uk

© Pearson Education Limited 2011

The rights of John D. Daniels, Lee H. Radebaugh and Daniel P. Sullivan to be identified as authors of this work have been asserted by them in accordance with the Copyright, Designs and Patents Act 1988.

Authorised adaptation from the United States edition, entitled International Business: Environments and Operations,
13ᵗʰ edition, ISBN 978-0-13-21-2842-1 by John D. Daniels, Lee H. Radebaugh *and* Daniel P. Sullivan, *published by*
Pearson Education, publishing as Prentice Hall © 2011.

Credits and acknowledgments borrowed from other sources and reproduced, with permission, in this textbook appear on appropriate page within text.

Chapter opener photo credits: Ch. 1: Laszio Szirtesi/Shutterstock; Ch. 2: Modern Company for Development and Tourism Services (MCD); Ch. 3: Walter Bibikow/Photolibrary.com; Ch. 4: Dinodia/Photolibrary.com; Ch. 5: © David Sanger photography/Alamy; Ch. 6: Alan Kraft/Shutterstock; Ch. 7: AFP/Getty Images; Ch. 8: Junko Kimura/Getty Images; Ch. 9: Newscom; Ch. 10: Photolibrary.com; Ch. 11: © WiNG/Creative Common Attribution ShareAlike 3.0; Ch. 12: Photolibrary.com; Ch. 13: Alexander Korobov/Shutterstock; Ch. 14: Newscom; Ch. 15: APWide World Photos; Ch. 16: Gunnar Kullenberg/Photolibrary.com; Ch. 17: Adan Gregor/Shutterstock; Ch. 18: Newscom; Ch. 19: Scott Olson/Getty Images Editorial; Ch. 20: Anderson Ross/Getty Images, Inc. Blend Images.

ISBN 10: 0-273-75600-1
ISBN 13: 978-0-273-75600-2

British Library Cataloguing-in-Publication Data
A catalogue record for this book is available from the British Library

10 9 8 7 6 5 4 3 2 1
14 13 12 11

Typeset in 10/12 Palatino by Integra
Printed and bound by Courier/Kendallville in The United States of America

The publisher's policy is to use paper manufactured from sustainable forests.

brief contents

contents

chapter opening and closing cases

Master of Science in International Business Program and faculty director of the University of Colorado Denver CIBER.

special features

Looking to the Future

Does
Ge◉graphy Matter?

MAPS

Designed to help improve students' geographic literacy, the book's many maps add interest and illustrate facts and topics discussed in the text. Many case maps zero in on the case company's home country or market region to give students a close-up look at foreign locales. A complete atlas with index is available following Chapter 1.

preface

This textbook is one of the best-selling international business textbooks in both the United States and the rest of the world. Widely used in both undergraduate and MBA level courses, this text has had authorized translations into Spanish, Chinese, Thai, and Russian. This textbook set the global standard for studying the environments and operations of international business. The elements of success that have driven this performance anchor our efforts to make this edition the best version yet. We believe these efforts result in a textbook that provides you and your students the best possible understanding of what is happening and is likely to happen in the world of business.

New to this Edition:

- All cases have been updated to reflect the current global business environment.
- Nine entirely new cases.
- Expanded coverage of the emerging economies, especially the BRICs.
- Emerging factors influencing the value of a currency, especially with the rise in importance of the euro and the challenge of what to do with the Chinese yuan as the Chinese economy continues to grow.
- Updated and expanded Test Item File and PowerPoints.

Authoritative, Relevant, Current

Students, faculty, and managers praise this book for its compelling balance between rigorous, authoritative theory and meaningful practice within the context of a fresh, current analysis of the international business environment. Indeed, this book not only describes the ideas of international business but also uses contemporary examples, scenarios, and cases to make sense of what managers do and should do. We include multiple insights and real-world examples, which we base on our research, discussions with managers and other stakeholders, opinions of students and professors, and observations from traveling the world. We believe no other textbook comes close to successfully blending a comprehensive review of international business theory with exhaustive attention to what happens in the many parts of the global market. We're confident that this new edition, by making international business ideas and practices more meaningful than ever before, will give students a comprehensive, current view of international business in the twenty-first century.

Relevant Materials That Engage Students

AUTHOR-WRITTEN CASES

An enduring strength of this text is its in-depth case profiles of cutting-edge issues in international business. This edition introduces new cases and updates and revises the remaining. (Please see pages 19–22 for a complete list of cases.) We believe the cases set the standard for integration of theory and practice in an international business textbook on the following three levels:

1. *Level of Analysis*: Cases engage an extensive range of topics from environmental, institutional, country, industry, company, and individual perspectives. No one perspective dominates; all are represented and, hence, create a meaningful representation of the world of international business.

2. *Scope of Geographic Coverage*: Cases cover topics in settings that span the globe; no region is unaddressed, no major market is neglected.

3. *Scope of Company Coverage*: Cases look at various issues from a range of company perspectives, notably companies headquartered in all regions of the world, from large MNEs to small exporters, from old-line manufacturers to emergent cyber businesses, from companies that make products to those that deliver services.

Opening Business Case   Each chapter starts with a provocative case written to set the stage for the major issues covered in the chapter. Designed to grab the student's attention, these cases look at fascinating issues in a way that makes students want to understand the ideas and concepts of international business. These cases, by variously taking the point of view of individuals, companies, and institutions, give a great sense of the richness of the ensuing chapter. Material from the opening cases is then integrated with chapter discussions that we highlight in the text.

Closing Business Case   Each chapter closes with a rich, elaborate case that integrates the ideas and tools presented in the chapter. The closing cases aim to put the student into a situation that asks, given certain circumstances, what should be done. Called on to analyze issues and decisions for which the chapter prepares them, students can then grapple with many of the opportunities and challenges of international business.

New Cases in This Edition

We have extensively updated *all* the cases from the previous edition so that students will find them relevant and rigorous. In addition, we have included several entirely new cases:

- Chapter 5: Woolworths South Africa: Making Sustainability Sustainable
- Chapter 7: Protecting the Malaysian Automobile Industry
- Chapter 8: Vodafone Turns East
- Chapter 9: The Global Economic Crisis: Icelandic Saga
- Chapter 10: Welcome to the World of Sony—Unless the Yen Keeps Rising
- Chapter 11: Value Chains: Where, When, and Why
- Chapter 13: Burger King Beefs Up Global Operations
- Chapter 14: Will the Transatlantic Joint Venture of British Airways and American Airlines Fly?
- Chapter 19: Etihad—A New Airline Hedging Bets on Profitability

LOOKING TO THE FUTURE

Each chapter offers future scenarios that are important to managers, companies, or the world. The topic of each *Looking to the Future* feature alludes to ideas discussed in the chapter in a way that prompts students to engage their imagination about the future of the world.

POINT–COUNTERPOINT

To reinforce our strong applications orientation, we have included a separate feature in every chapter that brings to life a major debate in contemporary international business and globalization. We use a point–counterpoint style to highlight the diversity of perspectives that managers and policymakers use to make sense of vital issues. The give-and-take between two sides reinforces this textbook's effort to link theory and practice in ways that will undoubtedly energize class discussion.

GEOGRAPHY AND INTERNATIONAL BUSINESS

In appropriate chapters, we have added "Does Geography Matter?" sections. Some of the geographic variables we include to help explain the chapters' content are country location, location of population and population segments within countries, natural resources and barriers, climate, natural disasters, and country size.

NEW TOPICS AND CHAPTER CHANGES

Although it is a tired cliché, every instructor of international business knows the world is changing in many and often unpredictable ways. We wake up to the same challenges you do, trying to make sense of what we read, hear, and see in the global press. Our effort to make sense of this leads to an unconditional effort to improve and update the text to reflect the latest knowledge and practice of international business. Most notably, among the many changes in this edition are the following:

PART ONE: BACKGROUND FOR INTERNATIONAL BUSINESS

- Updated opening case, such as new map showing selected national sports and coverage of cultural impediments to sports' globalization (Chapter 1)
- Brought in globalization views of two Nobel economists, Robert Solow and George Akerlof about the disparity of rich and poor (Chapter 1)
- Added economic uncertainties (oil prices and economic recession), especially as they affect present and future globalization and business (Chapter 1)
- Included competitive improvement of emerging economy companies, such as the merger between Brazil's Perdigão and Sadia in the global food industry (Chapter 1)
- Revised the ending case, such as by inclusion of swine flu epidemic effects (Chapter 1)

PART TWO: COMPARATIVE ENVIRONMENTAL FRAMEWORKS

- Appended opening case, such as the Saudi 2008 royal decree allowing men and women to mix in the workplace (Chapter 2)
- Introduced concept of cultural friction (Chapter 2)
- Included latest OECD info on work-leisure trade-off (Chapter 2)
- Added ethnographic information comparing work motivation and customs in the United States, Dominican Republic, and Barbados (Chapter 2)
- Updated features, examples, and ending case (Chapter 2)
- Revised opening case to reflect recent events in China's development strategy (Chapter 3)
- Expanded discussion of the construct of political ideology (Chapter 3)
- Improved discussion of principles and practices of totalitarianism (Chapter 3)
- Revision of trends in democracy and freedom trends given consequences of global financial crisis (Chapter 3)

- Streamlined discussion of the rule of man versus the rule of law (Chapter 3)
- Updated profile of countries regulation of aspects of the day-to-day operations of businesses (Chapter 3)
- Update of top and bottom 10 countries regarding the ease of doing business (Chapter 3)
- Reset specification of strategic implications of global financial crisis to company operations (Chapter 3)
- Revised end of chapter case with emphasis on unfolding software piracy trends (Chapter 3)
- Extensively revised opening case, emphasizing the exhilarating comeback of emerging economies (Chapter 4)
- Updated economic statistics throughout chapter (Chapter 4)
- Extensive and thorough adjustment of chapter material to implication of global financial crisis (Chapter 4)
- Expanded discussion of inflation, with attention to chronic inflation, hyperinflation, deflation, and reflation (Chapter 4)
- Expanded discussion of unemployment, profile of U3 vs. U6 measurement standards (Chapter 4)
- Expanded coverage of pre-economics, with introduction of provocative point-counterpoint—"Is Growth Good?" (Chapter 4)
- Reset coverage of public debt to reflect debt implications of global financial crisis (Chapter 4)
- Introduction of the "Bottom of the Pyramid" framework in understanding the opportunity of poverty (Chapter 4)
- Improved discussion of the types of economic systems with greater consideration of features of a mixed economy (Chapter 4)
- Revised profile of the dynamics of economic transition, given the increasing involvement of national governments (Chapter 4)
- New section on the expanding role of the state in economic activity (Chapter 4)
- Revised consideration of economic freedom pushed back and the rise of mixed economy (Chapter 4)
- Revised profile of the means of economic transition (Chapter 4)
- Updated and revised profile of the BRIC phenomenon (Chapter 4)
- New opening case study on sustainabilty in Woolworths, a South African department store (Chapter 5)
- Impact of the global economic crisis on FDI (Chapter 5)
- Enhanced discussion of the role of stakeholders other than shareholders as sources of influence on corporate strategies and decisions (Chapter 5)
- Enhanced discussion of ethical behavior as influenced by global, regional, and national governments and NGOs (Chapter 5)
- Update of the results of legal and other action against the German company Siemens on corporate bribery as discussed in the Point-Counterpoint (Chapter 5)
- New discussion of the attitude of the Obama administration in the United States toward global warming and how to deal with the Kyoto Protocol (Chapter 5)
- Revision of closing case study to reflect changes in the operating environment (Chapter 5)

PART THREE: THEORIES AND INSTITUTIONS: TRADE AND INVESTMENT

- Strengthened discussion on specialization assumptions (Chapter 6)
- Updated examples, features, and trade figures (Chapter 6)
- Included effect of economic downturn on immigration (Chapter 6)
- Revised the opening and closing cases, such as with a new map showing LUKOIL's global operations (Chapter 6)
- New opening case on the Malaysian automobile industry (Chapter 7)
- Brought buy-local provisions up-to-date with examples of 2009 economic stimulus packages (Chapter 7)
- Discussed the subsidy effect by 12 countries in their automobile industries because of the global economic recession (Chapter 7)
- Updated examples and features (Chapter 7)
- Revised ending case, such as bringing in the more liberal U.S. commercial policies with Cuba (Chapter 7)
- Update of the opening case to reflect changes in the global auto industry resulting from the global economic crisis (Chapter 8)
- Discussion of the collapse of the Doha Round of trade negotiations in the WTO and the challenges in solving the problems between the developed and developing countries (Chapter 8)
- Update on the rise of bilateral and regional trade agreements and their challenge to global efforts (Chapter 8)
- Update on the challenges facing the EU due to expansion and the possible entry of Iceland, which is a direct result of the global financial crisis (Chapter 8)
- Update of the impact of the NAFTA agreement on Canada, the United States, and Mexico, as well as challenges facing NAFTA as it moves forward (Chapter 8)
- Updates of trends in other bilateral and regional trade groups in Latin America, Asia, and Africa (Chapter 8)
- The impact of the growth of the global economy and subsequent crash in 2007–2009 on commodity prices and commodity exporters, including the OPEC countries (Chapter 8)
- New closing case study discusses the increased competition within the telecommunication industry in China, brought about by the WTO (Chapter 8)

PART FOUR: WORLD FINANCIAL ENVIRONMENT

- Update of opening case to reflect the change in remittances due to the global financial crisis (Chapter 9)
- New table of more recent exchange rates and updating examples to reflect new currency values (Chapter 9)
- Change in the ranking of international banks in terms of foreign exchange trading, reflecting the changing landscape for international banking that emerged from the global financial crisis (Chapter 9)
- New platforms and institutions to trade foreign exchange, such as FXMarketSpace by CME and Reuters and the merger of the Philadelphia Stock Exchange with NASDAQ OMX (Chapter 9)
- Additional examples in the Point-Counterpoint discussion of currency speculation to illustrate the problems involved in currency speculation (Chapter 9)
- New closing case study discusses the global economic crisis and its impact on Icelandic bank Kaupthing (Chapter 9)

- Addition of the Fresco Group in El Salvador to illustrate the challenges of operating in a dollarized economy (Chapter 10)
- Discussion of the enhanced role of the SDR as a result of the global economic crisis and the desire of some countries to use the SDR rather than just the U.S. dollar as the major reserve asset for central banks (Chapter 10)
- Simplification of the discussion on exchange rate arrangements and a focus on fixed versus flexible exchange rates (Chapter 10)
- Update of the influence of the euro in the global economy and the challenge of having new countries adopt the euro (Chapter 10)
- Elimination of the closing case on the Chinese yuan and integration in the chapter of the discussion of the emerging role of the yuan in the global foreign exchange and capital markets (Chapter 10)
- Significant discussion on the impact of the global financial crisis on currency markets in general, and on the U.S. dollar, the euro, the Chinese yuan, and the Japanese yen (Chapter 10)
- New end-of-chapter case on the impact of the rising Japanese yen on corporate strategy, using Sony as an example of a Japanese company feeling the effects of the rising yen on performance and strategy (Chapter 10)

PART FIVE: GLOBAL STRATEGY, STRUCTURE, AND IMPLEMENTATION

- Improved coverage of industrial organization paradigm (Chapter 11)
- Streamlined profile of the five fundamental forces model (Chapter 11)
- Expanded discussion of the cost leadership and differentiation strategy in international markets (Chapter 11)
- Expanded specification of the value chain (Chapter 11)
- Updated profile of international labor costs and implications to location economics (Chapter 11)
- Linkage of international strategy trends and ideas from the Bottom of the Pyramid framework (Chapter 11)
- Introduction of economic cluster effects (Chapter 11)
- Expanded profile of the dynamic of change in competitive competencies, and position (Chapter 11)
- New end of chapter case, highlighting the dynamic of the value chain in different markets types (Chapter 11)
- Brought opening case up-to-date, such as new map showing Carrefour's priority among countries (Chapter 12)
- Updated examples and features (Chapter 12)
- Bolstered discussion of companies' uniqueness in optimizing locations (Chapter 12)
- Enhanced the trade-off between country similarity and market opportunity (Chapter 12)
- Put in CAGE (cultural, administrative, geographic, economic) distance framework (Chapter 12)
- New closing case on Burger King's international expansion, including map (Chapter 12)
- Revised discussion of the characteristics of exporters (Chapter 13)
- Improved coverage of export development perspectives, contrasting incremental internationalization and the born global phenomenon (Chapter 13)
- Streamlined profile of exporting pitfalls (Chapter 13)
- Expanded coverage of the import process (Chapter 13)

- Updated profile of the technology of trade (Chapter 13)
- Expanded coverage of the documentation demands of international trade (Chapter 13)
- New coverage of third party logistics and Baltic Dry Freight Index aspects of trade (Chapter 13)
- Streamlined coverage of countertrade (Chapter 13)
- New ending case on proposed joint venture among British Airways, American Airlines, and Iberia for North Atlantic traffic, including route maps (Chapter 14)
- Update, opening case, examples, and features (Chapter 14)
- Illustration of collaborative complexity with Boeing 787 (Dreamliner) example (Chapter 14)
- Included horizontal alliances as means of dealing with external groups, such as governments (Chapter 14)
- Added advantage of companies from developed countries' in making acquisitions during economic downturns (Chapter 14)
- Put in "rule of law" perception concerning appropriation (Chapter 14)
- Adjustments of organizational practices, and trends in response to global financial crisis throughout chapter (Chapter 15)
- Updated opening and closing cases (Chapter 15)
- Revised interpretation of forms of contemporary organization (Chapter 15)
- Consideration of unemployment pressures to understanding of organizational culture (Chapter 15)

PART SIX: MANAGING INTERNATIONAL OPERATIONS

- Added new pharmaceutical research directions in Point-Counterpoint sections (Chapter 16)
- Enhanced coverage of companies' fight against the gray market (Chapter 16)
- Updated cases, examples, and features and reversed opening and closing cases (Chapter 16)
- Brought in effect of packaging on country image differences (Chapter 16)
- Discussed efficiencies of small retailers in developing countries (Chapter 16)
- Showed how brand can overcome negativity of country-of-origin (Chapter 16)
- Update of the Samsonite opening case to reflect the downward impact of the global financial crisis on travel and the purchase of luggage as well as the strategy in penetrating foreign markets (Chapter 17)
- Discussion of new ISO quality standards (Chapter 17)
- Problem of maintaining quality control over global supply chains, especially in China, to ensure product safety (Chapter 17)
- Discussion of the impact of the global financial crisis on supply chain management (Chapter 17)
- Update of the Ventus case at the end of the chapter to reflect the impact of the global financial crisis on Ventus's call center business and its reliance on a weakening U.S. market (Chapter 17)
- Update of the legal action against the former CEO of Parmalat and what Parmalat is trying to do to remain in business (Chapter 18)
- Update of the implementation of International Financial Reporting standards worldwide (Chapter 18)
- Discussion of the tension between the U.S.-based Financial Accounting Standards Board and the International Accounting Standards Board, especially resulting from the global financial crisis and the priorities of the new Obama administration (Chapter 18)

- Debate over whether some U.S. companies should be allowed to use IFRS for listing in the United States (Chapter 18)
- Update on what the implementation of IFRS in the EU has done to the reported results of Swedish company, Ericsson (Chapter 18)
- Update of the opening case on what GPS Capital Markets Inc. has done to weather the storm from the global financial crisis and what it needs to do to remain competitive (Chapter 19)
- New data on capital structures from selected countries using Compustat Global (Chapter 19)
- Discussion of the impact of the global financial crisis on global debt and equity markets (Chapter 19)
- Discussion of the pressure by the OECD and individual countries to shut down some operations of tax haven countries where inappropriate and illegal financial transactions were taking place (Chapter 19)
- New closing case examines the hedging strategies UAE airline Etihad uses in the light of the fluctuating cost of aviation fuel (Chapter 19)
- Refined and expanded interpretation of the idea of globalizing your career reported in opening case (Chapter 20)
- Profile of emerging trends in expatriate processes given consequences of global financial crisis (Chapter 20)
- Discussion of growing trend toward younger and older expatriates
- Highlighting implications of changing workplace of globalization to third-country nationals (Chapter 20)
- Improved specification of the approaches to global staffing (Chapter 20)
- Better linkage of expatriate selection and personal characteristics (Chapter 20)
- Profile of changing compensation patterns (Chapter 20)
- Streamlined profile of relationship between labor and multinational enterprises (Chapter 20)

Engaging In-Text Learning Aids

We believe a powerful textbook must teach as well as present ideas. To that end, we use several in-text aids to make this book an effective learning tool. Most notably, each chapter uses all of the following features:

CHAPTER OBJECTIVES AND SUMMARY

Each chapter begins with learning objectives and ends with a summary that ties directly to the chapter material. This linkage helps students prepare for the major issues within each chapter, appreciate their general relationships, and reinforce the important lessons of the chapter material.

CONCEPT LINKS

Throughout each chapter, as warranted by discussion in the corresponding text, we highlight in the margin how ideas from previous chapters link to the ideas being discussed. This cumulative series of concept links helps the student build an understanding of the connections among concepts across chapters. This feature also facilitates student understanding when instructors do not assign all chapters.

CASE LINKS

Another effort to help students better interpret the connections among ideas and practices is our latest innovation. Specifically, as warranted by discussion in the corresponding text, we highlight with text shading and icons how those ideas being discussed elaborate ideas that were presented in the opening and closing cases of that chapter.

KEY TERMS AND POINTS: BOLDING, MARGINAL NOTES, AND GLOSSARY

Every chapter highlights key terms; each key term is put in bold print when it first appears. Key learning points are also highlighted in the adjoining margin. These terms and others are then assembled in an end-of-chapter list and into a comprehensive glossary at the end of the book.

CASE QUESTIONS

The closing case of each chapter stipulates several questions to guide how students apply what they have learned in the chapter to the reality of international business. We have found in our classes that the questions at the end of the case go a long way to putting the case into perspective for students. In addition, they make for great assignment activities, directing students to respond to questions with information presented in the specific case as well as the chapter.

POINT–COUNTERPOINT

This feature, as we have already discussed, is compelling not only for class discussion, but also for specific assignments. These assignments may include requiring students to take sides in debates or to apply arguments to specific countries.

Currency and Readability

We have always prided ourselves on being current in the research and examples we cite in the chapters. The 13th edition is no exception; in fact, we believe our coverage goes beyond that of any other IB text. If you examine the endnotes for any chapter, you will see that we include both classic and the most up-to-date materials from both scholarly treatises and the popular press. If you examine the list of companies in the "Company Index and Trademarks," you will see that our citations are numerous and include large and small firms from a variety of industries based in countries throughout the world. These citations illustrate to students the practical reality of the theories and alternative operations we describe.

We have made a special effort in this edition to improve the readability of the extensive materials we present. First, we make a point of putting authors' names (except for classics such as Adam Smith) only in the reference section rather than in the chapters' prose. We have simply seen too many students try to remember names rather than concepts. Second, we have engaged a copy editor to improve the language and flow of materials.

Acknowledgments

Every author relies on the comments, critiques, and insights of reviewers. It is a tough task that few choose to support. Therefore, we want to thank the following people for their insightful and helpful comments on the twelfth edition of

International Business: Environments and Operations, which helped guide us in preparing the thirteenth edition.

ERICA BERTE, Indiana University—Purdue University Columbus
SIMON BEST, St. Francis College
ROBERT BLANCHARD, Salem State University
LARRY CHASTEEN, Stephen F. Austin University
PRAKASH DHEERJYA, California State—Dominguez Hills
PHIL FIORAVANTE, Walsh College
JOSEPH GANITSKY, University of Miami
TARIQUE HOSSAIN, California State Polytechnic University
KONGHEE KIM, St. Cloud State University
DAVID KNIGHT, Brewton-Parker College
NADA KOBIESSI, Long Island University
SUT SAKCHUTCHAWAN, Waynesburg College
ROBERT VAMBERY, Ashland University
SIVAKUMAR VENKATARAMANY, Ashland University

In addition, we have been fortunate since the first edition to have colleagues who have been willing to make the effort to critique draft materials, react to coverage already in print, advise on suggested changes, and send items to be corrected. Because this is the culmination of several previous editions, we would like to acknowledge everyone's efforts. However, many more individuals than we can possibly list have helped us. To those who must remain anonymous, we offer our sincere thanks. In any event, special thanks go to the following faculty members who made detailed comments.

RON ABERNATHY, University of North Carolina, Greensboro
YUSAF AKBAR, Southern New Hampshire University
BRENT ALLRED, William & Mary
DAVID ASTLES, Sierra Nevada College
DR. JUAN BARRERA, Elmhurst College
DON BEEMAN, The University of Toledo
ERVIN BLACK, Brigham Young University
JEAN BODDEWYN, City University of New York
BRIGITTE BOJKOWSZKY, University of Missouri, St. Louis
MARY YOKO BRANNEN, San Jose State University
MICHAEL BARAN, South Puget Sound Community College
MARTIN BRESSLER, Houston Baptist University
BILL BRUNSEN, Eastern New Mexico University
MARK A. BUCHANAN, Boise State University
ROBERT BUZZELL, George Mason University
SANDRA CHRISTENSEN, Eastern Washington University
TREVA CLARK, York College of Pennsylvania
PHILLIP COHEN, San Jacinto College North Campus
MICHAEL B. CONNOLLY, University of Miami
ANGELICA CORTES, University of Texas Pan American
TIM CURRAN, University of South Florida, St. Petersburg
MADELINE DAMKAR, California State University, East Bay campus
ANNE DAVIS, University of St. Thomas
SHASHI DEWAN, Winona State University
DR. LAURA PORTOLESE DIAS, Shoreline Community College
MICHAEL FATHI, Georgia Southwestern State University

STANLEY E. FAWCETT, Brigham Young University
ADALBERTO FISCHMANN, Missouri Southern State University
STANLEY FLAX, St. Thomas University
JAN FLYNN, Georgia College & State University
TOM FOSTER, Brigham Young University
ELDRIDGE T. FREEMAN, JR., Chicago State University
RALPH GAEDEKE, California State University at Sacramento
ROBERTO P. GARCIA, Indiana University
MIKE GERINGER, California Polytechnic State University
DEBBIE GILLIARD, Metropolitan State College of Denver
LENORE GOLDBERG, Centenary College
J. TOMAS GOMEZ-ARIAS, Saint Mary's College of California
JORGE GONZALEZ, University of Wisconsin, Milwaukee
CHARLES M. GOODWIN, The State University of New York, Geneseo
KENNETH GRAY, Florida A&M University
DAVID GROSSMAN, Florida Southern College
URNESH C. GULATI, East Carolina College
JIAN (JAMES) GU, Salem State College
JAMES GUNN, Sage College of Albany
MICHAEL J. HAND, United States Department of Commerce
ALFRED J. HAGAN, Pepperdine University
DAVID HARRISON, University of South Carolina, Aiken
DONAL HEFFERNAN, Metropolitan State University
CHRISTINA HEISS, University of Missouri, Kansas City
FRED HOYT, Illinois Wesleyan University
PAUL HUDEC, Milwaukee School of Engineering
SAMIRA HUSSEIN, Johnson County Community College
RALPH F. JAGODKA, Mt. San Antonio Community College
R. BOYD JOHNSON, Indiana Wesleyan University
MERRILY KAUTT, University of Colorado at Denver
RAIHAN KHAN, The State University of New York, Oswego
KI HEE KIM, William Patterson University
SEUNG H. KIM, Saint Louis University
TUNGA KIYAK, Michigan State University
CHRISTOPHER KORTH, Western Michigan University
JEFFREY A. KRUG, Virginia Commonwealth University
SAL KUKALIS, California State University, Long Branch
SUMIT K. KUNDU, Florida International University
BRUCE KUSCH, Brigham Young University, Idaho
ANN LANGLOIS, Palm Beach Atlantic University
JOSEPH LEONARD, Miami Unviersity
DEBORAH LITVIN, Merrimack College
RONALD LOCKLIN, Boston University
VIONCE LUCHSINGER, University of Baltimore
DENISE LUETHGE, University of Michigan, Flint
WLLIAM MACHANIC, University of New Hampshire
BARBARA MACLEOD, Ohio Wesleyan University
CHARLES MAHONE, Howard University
RAJIV MALKAN, Montgomery College
ERIC MARTIN, Eastern Connecticut State University
DAVID MCARTHUR, Utah Valley State College

MARLEEN MCCORMICK, University of Colorado at Denver and Health Sciences Center

JOHN ROBERT MCINTYRE, Georgia Institute of Technology

BOB MCNEAL, Alabama State University

MOHAN MENON, University of South Alabama

SAEED MORTAZAVI, Humboldt State University

BEHNAM NAKHAI, Millersville University

VI NARAPAREDDY, University of Denver

LUCIARA NARDON, Vlerick Leuven Gent Management School

DENNIS NOAH, Towson University

MOONSONG DAVID OH, California State University at Los Angeles

JOSEPHINE OLSON, University of Pittsburgh

NORA PALUGOD, Richard Stockton College of New Jersey

NAMGYOO K. PARK, Korean Advanced Institute of Science and Technology

JAMIE PAURUS, Valley City State University

ANN PERRY, American University

DOUGLAS K. PETERSON, Indiana State University

LUCIE PFAFF, College of Mt. St. Vincent

JERRY PINOTTI, MacCormac College

MICHAEL J. PISANI, Central Michigan University

DANIEL POWROZNIK, Chesapeake College

ASEEM PRAKASH, University of Washington

CLINT RELYEA, Arkansas State University

CHRISTOPHER ROBERTSON, Northeastern University

JUAN ROBERTSON, Central Washington University Center

ROBERT ROBERTSON, Saint Leo University

FERNANDO ROBLES, George Washington University

AL ROSENBLOOM, Saint Xavier University

VARTAN SAFARIAN, Winona State University

SAEED SAMIEE, University of Tulsa

ROBERT SANFORD, Salem State College

JESSE SAUCEDO, Syracuse University

BILL SAWAYA, Brigham Young University

LARRY SCHRAMM, Oakland University

KRISTIE SEAWRIGHT, Brigham Young University

EUGENE SEELEY, Utah Valley State College

NASIR SHEIKH, Portland State University

MARK SIPPER, La Roche College

ROBERT SPOHR, Montcalm Community College

RICHARD A. STANFORD, Furman University

DAVID STEPHEN, University of Colorado, Denver

JOHN STOVALL, Georgia Southwestern State University

DANTE SUAREZ, Trinity University

PEGGY TAKAHASHI, University of San Francisco

S. PETER TAN, Parkland College

KYLE USREY, Whitworth University

RAY VALADEZ, Pepperdine University

LOUIS WATANABE, Bellevue Community College

GARY WATERS, Hawaii Pacific University

CAROL WELLS, California National University

LARRY WILCH, Bob Jones University

WILLIAM WISE, Metropolitan State College of Denver

ROBERT C. WOOD, San Jose State University

MARK WOODHULL, Schreiner University

CRAIG WOODRUFF, American Graduate School of International Management

ALAN WRIGHT, Henderson State University

WENDY WYSOCKI, Monroe County Community College

ANATOLY ZHUPLEV, Loyola Marymount University

We would also like to acknowledge people whom we interviewed in writing cases. These are Omar Aljindi (Java Lounge—Adjusting to Saudi Arabian Culture), Brenda Yester (Carnival Cruise Lines: Exploiting a Sea of Global Opportunity), Julio A. Ramirez (Burger King Beefs Up Global Operations), and Ali R. Manbien (GPS: In the Market for an Effective Hedging Strategy?). In addition, we would like to thank Manuel Serapio at the University of Colorado at Denver for his excellent case at the end of Chapter 17, Ventus and Business Process Outsourcing. Additionally, others who helped with administrative and research matters are Melanie Hunter, Hongbin Hu, Robert Walker, and Jordan Peterson.

It takes a dedicated group of individuals to take a textbook from final manuscript. We would like to thank our partners at Pearson for their tireless efforts in bringing the thirteenth edition of this book to fruition. Our thanks go to Editorial Director, Sally Yagan; Editor in Chief, Eric Svendsen; Acquisitions Editor, Jennifer M. Collins; Editorial Project Manager, Susie Abraham; Marketing Manager, Nikki Jones; Senior Managing Editor, Judy Leale; Project Manager, Production, Ana Jankowski; Project Specialist, Heather Johnson; and Ashley Santora.

Pearson gratefully acknowledges and thanks the following people for their work on the Global Edition:

DR. CAROLINE AKHRAS, Professor of Management, Department of Management and Marketing Faculty of Business Administration and Economics, Notre Dame University, Zouk Mosbeh, Lebanon.

DR. MARINA APAYDIN, Assistant Professor of Strategic Management Strategy and Entrepreneurship Unit, Department of Management, School of Business, The American University in Cairo, Cairo, Egypt.

ABHISHEK BHATI, Associate Dean (Business & IT), James Cook University Australia, Singapore.

SALINA DAUD, Universiti Tenaga Nasional, Malaysia.

DR. CLAUDIO DE MATTOS, Division of Marketing, International Business and Strategy Manchester Business School, The University of Manchester, Manchester, UK.

HADIA FAKHRELDIN, Lecturer, Business Administration Department, Faculty of Business Administration, Economics & Political Science, The British University in Egypt, Egypt.

Associate Professor Jens Graff, Solbridge International School of Business, Woosong University, South Korea.

DR. ELHAM S. HASHAM, Graduate Advisor, Notre Dame University, Lebanon.

BERSANT HOBDARI, Associate Professor, Department of International Economics and Management, Copenhagen Business School, Denmark.

HUGH HUTCHESON, FRM, Coordinator of the Advanced Financial Risk Management Programme and Visiting Faculty Member, Insurance and Risk Management Division, School of Economic & Business Sciences, University of the Witwatersrand Johannesburg, South Africa.

Roopali Khurana, Lecturer of Business Process Management and Business Statistics, Fontys University of Applied Sciences, The Netherlands. (See online supplementary case study on Spanish retailer Zara.)

Dr. Raj Komaran, Singapore Management University, Singapore.

John Luiz, Director of International Programmes, Wits Business School (University of the Witwatersrand), South Africa.

Teena Lyons.

Hendrik van Schaik, Lecturer, Department of Business Management, University of Johannesburg, South Africa.

Dr. Samir M. Youssef, Professor of International Business, American University in Cairo, Cairo, Egypt.

Dr. Ying Zhang, Department of Management, University of Strathclyde Business School, UK.

about the authors

From left to right: **Daniel Sullivan, Lee Radebaugh, John Daniels.**

Three respected and renowned scholars show your students how dynamic, how real, how interesting, and how important the study of international business can be.

John D. Daniels, the Samuel N. Friedland Chair of Executive Management at the University of Miami, received his Ph.D. at the University of Michigan. His dissertation won first place in the award competition of the Academy of International Business. Since then, he has been an active researcher and won a decade award from the *Journal of International Business Studies.* His articles have appeared in such leading journals as *Academy of Management Journal, Advances in International Marketing, California Management Review, Columbia Journal of World Business, International Marketing Review, International Trade Journal, Journal of Business Research, Journal of High Technology Management Research, Journal of International Business Studies, Management International Review, Multinational Business Review, Strategic Management Journal, Transnational Corporations,* and *Weltwirtschaftliches Archiv.* Professor Daniels recently co-edited with Jeffrey Krug three volumes, *Multinational Enterprise Theory,* and three volumes, *International Business and Globalization.* On its 30th anniversary, *Management International Review* referred to him as "one of the most prolific American IB scholars." He has also served as president of the Academy of International Business and dean of its Fellows. He also served as chairperson of the international division of the Academy of Management. Professor Daniels has worked and lived a year or longer in seven different countries, worked shorter stints in approximately 30 other countries on six continents, and traveled in many more. His foreign work has been a combination of private sector, governmental, teaching, and research assignments. He was formerly a faculty member at the Pennsylvania State University, director of the Center for International Business Education and Research (CIBER) at Indiana University, and holder of the E. Claiborne Robins Distinguished Chair at the University of Richmond.

Lee H. Radebaugh is the Kay and Yvonne Whitmore Professor International Business and Director of the Whitmore Global Management Center/CIBER at Brigham Young University. He received his M.B.A. and doctorate from Indiana University. He taught at Pennsylvania State University from 1972 to 1980. He also has been a visiting professor at Escuela de Administracion de Negocios para Graduados (ESAN) in Lima, Peru. In 1985, Professor Radebaugh was the James Cusator Wards visiting professor at Glasgow University, Scotland. His other books include *International Accounting and Multinational Enterprises* (John Wiley and Sons, 6th Edition) with S. J. Gray and Erv Black; *Introduction to Business: International Dimensions* (South-Western Publishing Company) with John D. Daniels; and seven books on Canada-U.S. trade and investment relations, with Earl Fry as co-editor. He has also published several other monographs and articles on international business and international accounting in journals such as the *Journal of Accounting Research, Journal of International Financial Management and Accounting, Journal of International Business Studies,* and the *International Journal of Accounting.* He is the former editor of the *Journal of International Accounting Research* and area editor of the *Journal of International Business Studies.* His primary teaching interests are international business and international accounting. Professor Radebaugh is an active member of the American Accounting Association, the European Accounting Association, the International Association of Accounting Education and Research, and the Academy of International Business, having served on several committees as the president of the International Section of the AAA and as the secretary treasurer of the AIB. He is a member of the Fellows of the Academy of International Business. He is also active with the local business community as past president of the World Trade Association of Utah and member of the District Export Council. In 2007, Professor Radebaugh received the Outstanding International Accounting Service Award of the International Accounting Section of the American Accounting Association, and in 1998, he was named International Person of the Year in the state of Utah and Outstanding International Educator of the International Section of the American Accounting Association.

Daniel P. Sullivan, Professor of International Business at the Alfred Lerner College of Business of the University of Delaware, received his Ph.D. from the University of South Carolina. He researches a range of topics, including globalization and business, international management, global strategy, competitive analysis, and corporate governance. His work on these topics has been published in leading scholarly journals, including the *Journal of International Business Studies, Management International Review, Law and Society Review,* and *Academy of Management Journal.* In addition, he serves on the editorial boards of the *Journal of International Business Studies* and *Management International Review.* Professor Sullivan has been honored for both his research and teaching, receiving grants and winning awards for both activities while at the University of Delaware and, his former affiliation, the Freeman School of Tulane University. He has been awarded numerous teaching honors at the undergraduate, M.B.A., and E.M.B.A. levels—most notably, he has been voted Outstanding Teacher by the students of 12 different Executive M.B.A. classes at the University of Delaware and Tulane University. Professor Sullivan has taught, designed, and administered a range of graduate, undergraduate, and nondegree courses on topics spanning globalization and business, international business operations, international management, strategic perspectives, executive leadership, and corporate strategy. In the

United States, he has delivered lectures and courses at several university sites and company facilities. In addition, he has led courses in several foreign countries, including China, Bulgaria, the Czech Republic, France, South Korea, Switzerland, Taiwan, and the United Kingdom. Finally, he has worked with many managers and consulted with several multinational enterprises on issues of international business.

Background for International Business

one

Globalization and International Business

PART ONE

Objectives

- To define *globalization* and *international business* and show how they affect each other

- To understand why companies engage in international business and why international business growth has accelerated

- To discuss globalization's future and the major criticisms of globalization

- To become familiar with different ways in which a company can accomplish its global objectives

- To apply social science disciplines to understanding the differences between international and domestic business

The world's a stage; each plays his part, and takes his share.

—*Dutch proverb*

CASE The Global Playground

You may not realize how avidly sports have entered the global arena.[1] Sports, according to one political historian, is now "the most globalized [legitimate] business in the world." Historically, the majority of players and teams in most sports competed only on their own home turf. There were, of course, some exceptions—notably the World Cup in soccer and the Grand Slams of tennis—but by and large, local fans used to be happy to cheer on local talent. Today, however, fans everywhere demand to see the best, and "best" has become a decidedly global standard.

How has sports managed to score so well with an international customer base? For one thing, satellite TV now brings live events from just about anywhere in the world to fans just about anywhere else in the world. Thus the key players in the sports-promotion business—team owners, league representatives, and sports associations—have broadened audience exposure, expanding fan bases and augmenting revenues, especially through advertising that cuts across national borders.

Likewise, because more fans expect to see the world's best teams and players, the search for talent has become a worldwide phenomenon. Today, for example, you can find U.S. and European professional basketball scouts in remote areas of Nigeria looking for tall youngsters who can be trained to play a sport that's been imported from half a world away.

THE INTERNATIONAL JOB MARKET

Fortunately for foreign talent scouts, today's top-notch players are willing to follow the money wherever it may take them. Take soccer—the world's most popular sport and one in which the Fédération Internationale de Football Association (FIFA) boasts more member countries than the United Nations. Many of the best Brazilian players now play for European teams with much higher payrolls than their Brazilian counterparts, and in just about every sport, top players play for pay in foreign countries. British soccer star David Beckham has played for professional teams in England, Spain, the United States, and Italy.

Interestingly, fans continue to follow national favorites even after they've taken their talents elsewhere. About 300 million Chinese tuned in to watch local basketball legend Yao Ming's first game in America's National Basketball Association (NBA). England's professional soccer league (Premiership) includes players from about 70 countries, which helps to increase the TV fan base outside England.

Many athletes, of course, join national teams for such international competitions as the Olympics and soccer's World Cup.

How the ATP Courts Worldwide Support

If you're a fan of individual sports, you've probably noticed that players are globe hoppers. Take tennis. Although its popularity has grown in many countries, no single country boasts enough interested fans to keep players at home for year-round competition. In any case, today's top-flight tennis pros come from every continent except Antarctica, and tennis fans everywhere want to see the top players compete on local courts. For 2009, the Association of Tennis Professionals (ATP) sanctioned 63 tournaments in 31 countries. It also requires member pros to play in a certain number of events—and thus stop over in a number of countries—to maintain international rankings.

Because no tennis pro can possibly play in every tournament, organizers must attract enough top draws to fill stadium seats and land lucrative TV contracts. Tournaments, therefore, compete for top-billed stars, not only with other tournaments but also with such regular international showcases as the Olympics and the Davis Cup. How do tournaments compete? Your first guess is probably right: on the basis of money. Prizes for two weeks' worth of expert serving and volleying can be extremely generous (about U.S. $7 million for the 2009 singles champions of the Australian Open).

Remember, too, that tournaments earn money through ticket sales, corporate sponsorship agreements, television contracts, and leasing of advertising space. The more people in the stadium and TV audience, the more sponsors and advertisers will pay to get their attention. Moreover, international broadcasts attract sponsorship from international companies. The sponsor list for the 2009 Australian Open tennis tournament included a South Korean automaker (Kia), a Dutch brewer (Heineken), a Swiss watchmaker (Rolex), a French personal care company (Garnier), and a U.S. financial firm (GE Money).

From National to International Sports Pastimes

Some countries have legally designated a national sport, and some others effectively have one. Map 1.1 shows a sample of these. However, other sports have sometimes replaced national sports in popularity, such as cricket's replacement of field hockey as India's most popular sport.

MAP 1.1 Examples of National Sports

Some 33 countries have either defined a national sport by law or de facto have a national sport. Some national sports are shared by more than one country, such as cricket by six former British colonies in the Caribbean. Some others have been established to protect an historical heritage, such as *tejo* in Colombia. Note also that Canada has two designations, one for winter and one for summer.

Source: The information on sports was taken from Wikipedia, http://en.wikipedia.org/wiki/National_sport (accessed March 3, 2009).

Note: Given that this is a Mercator projection, the scale approximates east-west distance at the equator; however, the farther you move from the equator, the more the east-west distance is distorted.

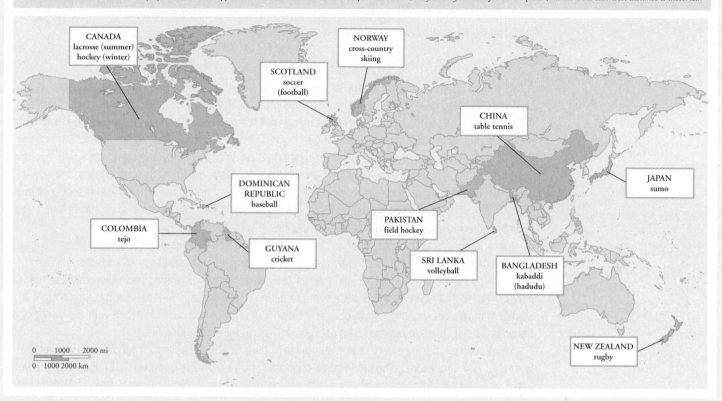

Further, the International Baseball Federation now has 112 member countries, even though baseball was popular only among North Americans for most of its history. As TV revenues flattened in North America, Major League Baseball (MLB) began broadcasting games to international audiences. Increased exposure not only broadened the global fan base, but it also showed youngsters all over the world how the game was played. As late as 1986, only 14 percent of MLB players were born outside the United States; by 2008, that number had climbed to 28 percent. The average MLB clubhouse is now a bastion of multilingual camaraderie, with players and coaches talking baseball in Spanish, Japanese, and Korean as well as English.

THE WIDE WORLD OF TELEVISED SPORTS

Not surprisingly, other professional sports groups have expanded their global TV coverage (and marketing programs). Most viewers of Stanley Cup hockey watch from outside North America. Fans watch National Association for Stock Car Auto Racing (NASCAR) races in more than 120 countries and NBA games in about 200. If you lived in the North African nation of Tunisia and enjoyed simultaneous access to multiple TV channels, you could watch more hours of NBA action than there are hours in the year.

And TV isn't the only means by which sports organizations are seeking foreign fan bases and players. For several years, the National Football League (NFL) of the United States sponsored a now-defunct professional league in Europe. It continues to underwrite flag-football programs in Chinese schools, and it will play some regular NFL games in Europe through 2011. With the growth of broadband, we'll soon enter the realm of thousand-channel TV, where we'll be able to tune into sporting events that currently appeal only to highly localized niche markets. How about Thai boxing or Japanese sumo wrestling?

The Top-Notch Pro as Upscale Brand

Relatedly, many top players (and teams) are effectively global brands. Golfer Tiger Woods, auto racer Kimi Raikkonen, and tennis star Maria Sharapova are so popular globally that companies within and outside the sports industry are willing to pay them millions of dollars for endorsing clothes, equipment, and other products. The photo shows David Beckham in an ad for Armani.

Promotion as Teamwork

A few teams, such as the New York Yankees in baseball, the New Zealand All Blacks in rugby, and Manchester United (Man U) in soccer also have enough brand-name cachet to sell clothing and other items to fans around the world. Just about every team can get something for the rights to use its logo, and some teams have enough name recognition to support global chains of retail outlets. Man U's Red Café sports-themed restaurants even thrive in such faraway markets as Singapore. Similarly, companies both sponsor and seek endorsements from well-known teams. Nike, for instance, the U.S. sports shoes and apparel giant, has fought hard to become the top sportswear and equipment supplier to European soccer teams. The success of this campaign has had such a big influence on Nike's international sales efforts that it now takes in more money abroad than in the United States.

Many nonsports companies, such as Canon (cameras, office equipment), Sharp (consumer electronics), and Carlsberg (beer), sponsor teams mainly to get corporate logos emblazoned on uniforms. Still others, such as United Airlines in Chicago, pay for the naming rights to arenas and other venues. And, of course, teams themselves can be attractive international investments. A Japanese investor bought the Seattle Mariners baseball team (U.S.A.), and the owner of a U.S. baseball team joined with the owner of a Canadian hockey team to buy the Liverpool Football Club of the United Kingdom.

What does all this mean to you as a sports fan? Chances are—especially if you're a male—you fantasized at one time about going pro in some sport, but you've probably given up that fantasy and settled into the role of spectator. Now that pro sports has become a global phenomenon (thanks to better communications), you can enjoy a greater variety—and a higher level of competition—than any generation before you.

English footballer David Beckham unveils a giant poster of himself advertising underwear for the Italian company, Armani, on the side of Selfridges department store on June 11, 2009 in London, England. The poster is the latest in a series of high-profile adverts in which David Beckham has modeled for Emporio Armani underwear.
Source: Oli Scarff/Getty Images, Inc.

That's the upside, but we must point out that people don't always take easily to another country's sport. Despite many efforts, cricket has never become popular in the United States, nor has American football built much fan base abroad. Cricket became popular in many countries during centuries of British colonialism, but it has made no recent inroads internationally. American football has never gained much popularity outside the United States. A former NFL lineman expressed a reason: that rules for American football and cricket are so complicated that one must learn them as children. However, basketball and soccer have traveled to new markets more easily because they are easier to understand.

Nor is everyone happy with the unbridled globalization of sports—or at least with some of the effects. Brazilian soccer fans lament the loss of their best players, such as Ronaldinho, and U.S. fans and public officials protested the sale of the MLB Seattle Mariners to a foreign investor. **⊙RN** Case Review Note

Introduction

In its broadest sense, **globalization** refers to the broadening set of interdependent relationships among people from different parts of a world that happens to be divided into nations. Also, the term sometimes refers to the integration of world economies through the reduction of barriers to the movement of trade, capital, technology, and people.[2]

Throughout recorded history, human contacts over ever-wider geographic areas have expanded the variety of available resources, products, services, and markets. We've altered the way we want and expect to live, and we've become more deeply affected (positively and negatively) by conditions outside of our immediate domains.

Our opening case shows how far-flung global contact allows the world's best sports talent to compete—regardless of nationality—and fans to watch them, from almost anywhere. The changes that have led firms to consider ever more distant places as sources of supplies and markets affect almost every industry and, in turn, consumers. Although we may not always know it, we commonly buy products from all over the world. "Made in" labels do not tell us everything about product origins. Today, so many different components, ingredients, and specialized business activities go into products that we're often challenged to say exactly where they were made.

Here's an interesting example. Although we tend to think of the Kia Sorento as a Korean car, the Japanese firm Matsushita furnishes one of the car's features—the CD player. It makes the optical-pickup units in China, sends them to Thailand to add electronic components, transports the semifinished product to Mexico for final assembly, and trucks completed CD players to a U.S. port. Finally, they're shipped to Korea, installed in Kia's vehicles, and then marketed around the world.[3]

WHAT IS *INTERNATIONAL BUSINESS*?

Globalization enables us to get more variety, better quality, or lower prices. Our daily meals, for instance, contain spices that aren't grown domestically and fresh produce that's out of season in one local climate or another. A Los Angeles restaurant calculated the distance traveled by the ingredients in just one of its main courses to be the equivalent of more than two and a half trips around the world.[4] Our cars, like a Kia Sorento equipped with a CD player, cost less than if all the parts were made and the labor performed in one place. Remember, too, that all of these connections between supplies and markets result from the activities of **international business,** which consists of all commercial transactions—including sales, investments, and transportation—that take place between two or more countries. Private companies undertake such transactions for profit; governments may undertake them either for profit or for political reasons.

International business consists of all commercial transactions between two or more countries.

- The goal of private business is to make profits.
- Government business may or may not be motivated by profit.

The Study of International Business   Why should we study international business? A simple answer is that international business comprises a large and growing portion of the world's total business. Today, global events and competition affect almost all companies, large and small, regardless of industry. This is the result of selling output to and securing supplies and resources from foreign countries, as well as competing against products and services from abroad. Thus most managers need to approach their operating strategies from an international standpoint. Recall the NBA teams in our opening case, which are looking globally for human resources—on-court talent—and additional markets that exist abroad. As a manager in almost any industry, you'll need to consider both (1) where to obtain the inputs you need of the required quality and at the best possible price and (2) where you can best sell the product or service that you've put together from those inputs.

Understanding the Environment/Operations Relationship   At the same time, you'll need to understand that the best way of doing business abroad may not be the same as the best way at home. Why? Basically, there are two reasons. First, when your company operates internationally, it will engage in *modes* of business (which we'll discuss shortly)—such as exporting and importing—that differ from those in which it engages domestically. Second, physical, social, and competitive conditions differ among countries and affect the optimum ways to conduct business. Thus companies operating internationally have more diverse and complex operating environments than those that conduct business only at home. Figure 1.1 outlines the complex set of relationships among conditions and operations that may occur when a firm decides to conduct some of its business on an international scale.

Even if you never have direct international business responsibilities, understanding some international business complexities may be useful to you. Companies' international operations and the governmental regulation of those operations affect overall national

Case Review Note

Studying international business is important because

- Most companies either are international or compete with international companies.
- Modes of operations may differ from those used domestically.
- The best way of conducting business may differ by country.
- An understanding helps you make better career decisions.
- An understanding helps you decide what governmental policies to support.

FIGURE 1.1   Factors in International Business Operations

The conduct of a company's international operations depends on two factors: its objectives and the means by which it intends to achieve them. Likewise, its operations affect, and are affected by, two sets of factors: physical/social and competitive.

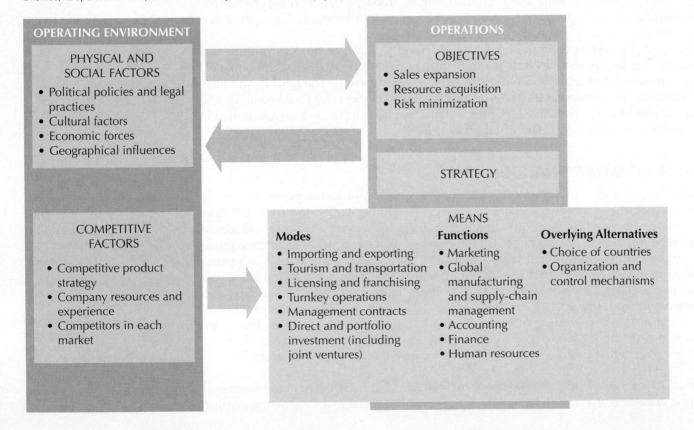

conditions—profits, employment security and wages, consumer prices, and national security. A better understanding of international business will help you make more informed operational and citizenry decisions, such as where you want to operate and what governmental policies you want to support.

The Forces Driving Globalization

Measuring globalization, especially for historical comparisons, is problematic. First, a country's interdependence must be measured indirectly.[5] Second, when national boundaries shift (consider the breakup of the former Soviet Union or the reunification of East and West Germany), domestic business transactions can become international transactions or vice versa.

Nevertheless, various reliable indicators assure us that globalization has been increasing, at least since the mid-twentieth century. Currently, about 25 percent of world production is sold outside its country of origin, as opposed to about 7 percent in 1950. Restrictions on imports have generally been decreasing, and output from foreign-owned investments as a percentage of world production has been increasing. In almost every year since World War II, world trade has grown more rapidly than world production. However, in recessionary periods such as 2008, global trade and investment contract even more than the global economy.

At the same time, however, globalization is less pervasive than you might suppose. Much of the world (especially rural Africa, Asia, and Latin America), for example, lacks the resources to establish more than the barest connection with anyone beyond the outskirts of their isolated spheres.[6] Only a few countries—mainly very small ones—either sell over half their production abroad or depend on foreign output for over half their consumption. What this means is that most of the world's goods and services are still sold in the countries in which they're produced. Moreover, the principal source of capital in most countries is domestic rather than international.[7]

Granted, these measurements address only *economic* aspects of global interdependence. Various studies have relied on different indicators for comparison.[8] One of the most comprehensive is the A.T. Kearney/Foreign Policy Globalization Index, which shows not only that some countries are more globalized than others but also that a given country may be highly globalized on one dimension and not on another. This index ranks 72 countries across four dimensions:

- *Economic*—international trade and investment
- *Technological*—Internet connectivity
- *Personal contact*—international travel and tourism, international telephone traffic, and personal transfers of funds internationally
- *Political*—participation in international organizations and government monetary transfers

In recent years, the index has ranked Singapore and Hong Kong as the most globalized countries and India and Iran as the least globalized. The ranking of the United States shows how globalization can differ by dimension: The United States ranks first on the technological scale but only 71st on the economic.[9]

FACTORS IN INCREASED GLOBALIZATION

What factors have contributed to the increased growth in globalization in recent decades? Most analysts cite the following seven factors:

1. Increase in and expansion of technology
2. Liberalization of cross-border trade and resource movements
3. Development of services that support international business

4. Growing consumer pressures

5. Increased global competition

6. Changing political situations

7. Expanded cross-national cooperation

Needless to say, these factors are interrelated, and each deserves a closer look.

Increase in and Expansion of Technology Many of the proverbial "modern marvels" and efficient means of production have come about from fairly recent advances in technology. Thus much of what we buy today did not exist a decade or two ago. There is also an increased demand because of rising productivity, which means, on average, that people produce and can buy more by working the same number of hours. Furthermore, more than half the scientists who have ever lived are alive today. One reason, of course, is population growth. But another reason is economic growth, which frees up a much larger portion of the total population to *develop* new products because a smaller portion of the population can *produce* what is demanded. As the base of our technology expands, new product development accelerates and we need more scientists and engineers to work on technical applications.

Advances in Communications and Transportation Strides in communications and transportation now permit us to learn about and want products and services developed in other parts of the world. Moreover, the costs of improved communications and transportation have risen more slowly in most years than costs in general. A three-minute phone call from New York to London that cost $10.80 in 1970 costs less than $0.20 today.

Innovations in transportation mean that more countries can compete for sales to a given market. For example, the sale of foreign-grown flowers in the United States used to be impractical; today, however, flowers from as far away as Ecuador, Israel, the Netherlands, and New Zealand compete with each other for the U.S. market because growers can ship flowers quickly and economically.

Or recall our opening case. Innovations in transportation and communications allow individual athletes and teams to go head to head at venues around the world and sports media to broadcast competitions to fans—and consumers—around the world. If it weren't for modern means of transportation, a tennis pro couldn't play in Monte Carlo right after finishing a tournament in Miami. And if it weren't for modern means of advertising to fans around the globe, the prize money wouldn't be big enough to induce players to do all that traveling.

Improved communications and transportation not only speed up interactions, they also enhance a manager's ability to oversee foreign operations. Thanks to the Internet, even small companies can reach global customers and suppliers. Atlanta's Randy Allgaier, for example, has established a partnership in Taiwan, which contracts a Chinese factory to manufacture lighting fixtures for him—all this without his need for costly on-site contact with people in either Taiwan or China.[10]

Liberalization of Cross-Border Trade and Resource Movements To protect its own industries, every country restricts the movement across its borders not only of goods and services but also of the resources—such as workers and capital—needed to produce them. Such restrictions, of course, set limits on international business activities, and because regulations can change at any time, they also contribute to a climate of uncertainty. Over time, however, most governments have reduced restrictions on international movements of products and services, primarily for three reasons:

1. Their citizens want a greater variety of goods and services at lower prices.

2. Competition spurs domestic producers to become more efficient.

3. They hope to induce other countries to lower their barriers in turn.

Development of Services That Support International Business Companies and governments have developed a variety of services that facilitate the conduct of international business. Take the sale of goods and services in a foreign country and currency. Today, because of bank credit agreements—clearing arrangements that convert one currency into another, and insurance that covers such risks as damage en route and nonpayment—most producers can be paid relatively easily for goods and services sold abroad. What happens, for instance, when Nike sells sportswear to a French soccer team? As soon as the shipment arrives at French customs (probably from somewhere in Asia), a bank in Paris can collect payment in euros from the soccer team and pay Nike in U.S. dollars through a U.S. bank.

Other supporting services encompass much more than finance, and they're far too numerous for the current discussion. We will, however, mention one. You can send letters and packages any place in the world by paying postage or a fee only in the country from which you mail them and only in the local currency, regardless of whether they pass through or over other countries.

Growing Consumer Pressures Not only do consumers know more now than previously about products and services available in other countries, but also many more of them can afford to buy products that were once considered luxuries. Today, we want more, newer, better products, and we want them more finely differentiated. As usually occurs, this greater affluence has been unevenly spread, both among and within countries as well as from one year to another, but more and more companies are now responding to those markets where incomes and consumption are growing most rapidly, such as China.

Greater affluence has also spurred companies to spend more heavily on research and development and to search worldwide—via the Internet, industry journals, trade fairs, and trips abroad—for innovations and products they can sell to ever-more-demanding consumers. By the same token, consumers are more proficient today at scouring the globe for better deals; U.S. consumers, for instance, regularly search the Internet for lower-priced prescription drugs available from abroad.

Increased Global Competition The pressures, both present and potential, of increased foreign competition can persuade companies to buy or sell abroad. For example, they might introduce products into markets where competitors are already gaining sales or seek supplies where competitors are getting cheaper or more attractive products or the means to produce them.

In recent years, many companies have merged or acquired firms to gain operating efficiencies that enable them to compete with or become global leaders. An example is the merger between the two Brazilian firms Perdigão and Sadia to become BRF-Brasil Foods, a major exporter of chilled and frozen foods.[11] In addition, so-called **born-global companies** start out with a global focus because of their founders' international experience[12] and because advances in communications give them a good idea of where global markets and supplies are.[13] Related to this, many new companies locate in areas where there are many competitors and suppliers—a situation known as **clustering**—which helps them to become quickly aware of foreign opportunities and to gain easier access to the resources needed to move internationally.[14]

Regardless of industry, firms have to become more global to compete; in today's business environment, failure to do so can be catastrophic. (Figure 1.2 shows this humorously.) Once a few companies have responded to foreign opportunities, others inevitably follow suit. *And* they learn from each other's foreign experiences. As our opening case suggests, for example, the early success of foreign-born baseball players in U.S. leagues undoubtedly spurred American basketball and football organizations to begin looking for and developing overseas talent.[15]

Case Review Note

FIGURE 1.2   International Business as a Two-Edged Sword

Although global competition promotes efficiency, it obliges both companies and their employees to spend time and effort on a greater range of activities.

Source: © 1998 The New Yorker Collection, Roz Chast, from cartoonbank.com. All rights reserved.

Changing Political Situations

A major reason for growth in international business is the end of the schism between the non-Communist world and what was once the Communist world. For nearly half a century after World War II, business between the two camps was minimal. Today, there are few countries that do business almost entirely within a political bloc.

Another political factor is the willingness of governments to support programs—such as improving airport and seaport facilities—that have fostered speed and cost efficiencies for delivering goods internationally. In addition, governments now provide an array of services to help domestic companies sell more abroad, such as collecting information about foreign markets, furnishing contacts with potential buyers abroad, and offering insurance against nonpayment in the home-country currency.

Expanded Cross-National Cooperation

Increasingly, governments have come to realize that their own interests can be addressed through international cooperation by means of treaties, agreements, and consultation. The willingness to pursue such policies is due largely to these three needs:

1. To gain reciprocal advantages
2. To attack problems jointly that one country acting alone cannot solve
3. To deal with areas of concern that lie outside the territory of any nation

Gain Reciprocal Advantages   Essentially, because companies don't want to be at a disadvantage when operating internationally, they petition their governments to act on their behalf. Thus governments join international organizations and sign treaties and agreements on a variety of commercial activities, such as transportation and trade. Treaties and agreements may be *bilateral* (involving only two countries) or *multilateral* (involving a few or many).

Countries sign treaties that allow each other's commercial ships and planes to use certain seaports and airports in exchange for reciprocal port use. They enact treaties that cover commercial-aircraft safety standards and flyover rights or treaties that protect property, such as foreign-owned investments, patents, trademarks, and copyrights.

Countries also enact treaties for reciprocal reductions of import restrictions (remaining prepared, of course, to retaliate when another party interferes with trade flows by raising trade barriers or cutting diplomatic ties).

Multinational Problem Solving Countries act to coordinate activities along mutual borders, building highways and railroads or hydroelectric dams that serve the interests of all parties. They also cooperate to solve problems that they either cannot or will not solve by themselves.

First, the resources needed to solve the problem may be too great for one country to manage; related to this, sometimes no single country is willing to pay for a project that will also benefit another country. Japan and the United States, for example, share the costs of ballistic-missile defense technology.[16] In any case, many problems are inherently global and can't be easily addressed by a single country. That's why we've seen the development of cooperative efforts to fight the spread of such diseases as malaria, to set warning systems against such natural disasters as tsunamis, and to take actions affecting environmental problems such as global warming.[17]

Second, one country's policies may affect those of others. Higher real-interest rates in one country, for example, can attract funds very quickly from individuals and companies in countries with lower rates, thus creating a shortage of investment funds in the latter. For instance, companies shift funds in response to slight interest rate changes. Similarly, companies may change suppliers in one country for those in another as costs change, thus contributing to unemployment in the country where they abandon suppliers.[18] To coordinate economic policies in these and other areas, economically important countries meet regularly to share information and pool ideas.[19]

Areas outside National Territories Three global areas belong to no single country: the noncoastal areas of the oceans, outer space, and Antarctica. Until their commercial viability was demonstrated, they excited little interest for either exploitation or multinational cooperation. The oceans, however, contain food and mineral resources, and they also constitute the surface over which much international commerce passes. Today, we need treaties to specify the amounts and methods of fishing to be allowed, to address questions of oceanic mineral rights (such as on oil resources below the Arctic Ocean),[20] and to deal with the confiscation of ships by pirates.[21]

Likewise, there's disagreement on the commercial benefits to be reaped from outer space. Commercial satellites, for example, pass over countries that receive no direct benefit from them but argue that they should. If that sounds a little far-fetched, remember that countries do charge foreign airlines for flying over their territories.[22]

Antarctica, with minerals and abundant sea life along its coast, attracts thousands of tourists each year, has a highway leading to the South Pole, and has thus been the subject of agreements to limit commercial exploitation. (The photo shows a group of flags at the South Pole.) However, there is still disagreement about Antarctica's development—how much there should be and who does it.

Much of the cooperation we've just described has been undertaken by international organizations, which we discuss in more detail in later chapters, especially in Chapter 8.

What's Wrong with Globalization?

Although we've discussed seven interrelated reasons for the increase in international business and globalization, we should remember that the consequences of the increase remain controversial. To thwart the globalization process, *antiglobalization* forces regularly protest international conferences—sometimes violently. There are

The photo shows flags at the South Pole in Antarctica, an area lying outside the confines of any country. Antarctica, one of the last frontiers of globalization, elicited little interest from governments until its commercial viability became apparent. Now, there is much concern about the development and what companies and countries will benefit from development.

Source: Frank Whitney/Getty Images, Inc.

many issues, but we focus on three: *threats to national sovereignty, growth and environmental stress,* and *growing income inequality and personal stress.* We revisit these in more depth in later chapters, and they furnish the issues for several of our Point-Counterpoint features.

THREATS TO NATIONAL SOVEREIGNTY

Critics of globalization claim

• Countries lose sovereignty.
• The resultant growth hurts the environment.
• Some people lose both relatively and absolutely.

You've probably heard the slogan "Think globally, act locally." In essence, it means that the accommodation of local interests should prevail over global interests. Some observers worry that the proliferation of international agreements, particularly those that undermine local restrictions on how goods are bought and sold, will diminish a nation's **sovereignty**—that is, a nation's freedom to "act locally" and without externally imposed restrictions.

The Question of Local Objectives and Policies   Countries seek to fulfill their citizens' economic, political, and social objectives by setting rules reflecting national priorities, such as those governing worker protection and environmental practices. However, some critics argue that individual countries' priorities are undermined by opening borders to trade. For example, if a country has stringent regulations on labor conditions and requires clean production methods, companies may produce where they can cut production costs because of less rigorous rules. The result may be that the strict country must forgo its priorities or face the downside of fewer jobs and tax receipts.

The Question of Small Economies' Overdependence   In addition, critics say that small economies depend so much on larger economies for supplies and sales that they are vulnerable to foreign demands. What sort of demands? These include everything from supporting certain positions at the United Nations to supporting a large economy's foreign military or economic actions. Nobel economist George Akerlof has added that consequences of this dependence are intensified by poor countries' inadequate administrative capacity to deal with globalization.[23] These countries are also concerned that large international companies are powerful enough to dictate their operating terms (say, by threatening to relocate), exploit legal loopholes to avoid political oversight and taxes, and counter the small economies' best interests by favoring their home countries' political and economic interests.

The Question of Cultural Homogeneity   Finally, critics charge that globalization homogenizes products, companies, work methods, social structures, and even language, thus undermining the cultural foundation of sovereignty. In Chapter 2, we'll see that, as international differences diminish, countries find it harder to maintain the traditional ways of life that unify and differentiate their cultures. Recall in our opening case that despite countries' designation of national sports to maintain tradition, some are losing out to imported sports anyway. Fundamentally, many critics feel helpless when it comes to stopping foreign incursion by such means as satellite television, print media, and Internet sites.[24]

CRN
Case Review Note

ECONOMIC GROWTH AND ENVIRONMENTAL STRESS

Much criticism of globalization revolves around issues of economic growth. According to one argument, as globalization brings growth, it consumes more nonrenewable natural resources and increases environmental damage—despoliation through toxic and pesticide runoffs into rivers and oceans, air pollution from factory and vehicle emissions, and deforestation that can affect weather and climate.

The Argument for Global Growth and Global Cooperation   Not everyone agrees with this antiglobalization conclusion. Others argue that globalization has positive results for both the sustenance of natural resources and the maintenance of an environmentally sound planet. Global cooperation, they say, fosters superior and uniform standards for combating environmental problems. Further, global competition encourages companies to seek resource-saving and environmentally friendly technologies, such as automobile engines that use less gas and emit fewer pollutants. However, unless the positive results of globalization outpace the negative consequences of growth, sustaining economic growth will remain a problem in the future.

The pursuit of global interests may even conflict with what a country's citizens think is best for themselves. Consider, for instance, the effect of global pressure on Brazil to curtail logging activity in the Amazon region to help protect the world's climate. Unemployed Brazilian workers have felt that job creation in the logging industry is more important than climate protection outside Brazil.

GROWING INCOME INEQUALITY AND PERSONAL STRESS

In measuring economic well-being, we must look not only at our absolute situations but also at how well we're doing compared to others. We generally don't find our economic status satisfactory unless we're doing better *and* keeping up with others.

Income Inequality   By various measurements, income inequality has been growing in a number of countries. Critics claim that globalization has affected this disparity by helping to develop a global superstar system, creating access to a greater supply of low-skilled and low-cost labor and speeding competition that leads to winners and losers.

The superstar system is especially apparent in sports, where global stars such as Tiger Woods and Oscar De La Hoya earn far more than the average professional players in their sports and far more than professionals in sports with a more limited worldwide following. This superstar system also carries over to other professions, such as business, where charismatic top people can command many times what others can.

Although globalization has brought unprecedented opportunities for organizations to profit by gaining additional sales and cheaper or better supplies, critics argue that profits have gone disproportionately to the top executives rather than to the rank and file. Nobel economist Robert Solow has supported this criticism by arguing that greater access to low-cost labor in poor countries has reduced the real wage growth of labor in rich countries.[25] Additionally, even if overall worldwide gains from globalization are positive, there are bound to be some losers in either an absolute or relative sense (who will probably become critics of globalization). The speed with which technology and competition are expanding globally is simply accelerating the number of winners and losers along with the relative positions of individuals, companies, and countries. For instance, recent shifts in manufacturing jobs from the United States to China and India have helped China and India grow more rapidly than the United States, thus lessening the U.S.'s *relative* economic leadership over those countries.[26] Likewise, some displaced workers have lost economic and social standing relative to workers whose jobs were not transferred abroad. The challenge, therefore, is to maximize the gains made possible by globalization while simultaneously minimizing the costs borne by the losers.

Personal Stress   There are also certain repercussions of globalization that we can't measure in strictly economic terms. What about the stress imposed on the people whose relative economic and social status suffer? What about stress for people who merely fear loss of their jobs?[27] There is in fact some evidence that the growth in globalization goes hand in hand not only with increased insecurity about job and social status but also with costly social unrest.[28] Further, although few of the world's problems are brand new, we may worry about them more now because globalized communications bring exotic sagas of misery into living rooms everywhere.[29]

Point ▶ ◀ Counterpoint

Is Offshoring Good Strategy?

Point   **Yes Offshoring** is the process of shifting production to a foreign country. *If offshoring succeeds in reducing costs, it's good.* This is happening with many companies in many industries. Most branded clothing companies offshore to have work done by cheaper sewing machine operators. Many investment companies are hiring back-office workers in poor countries to cut the cost of industry research; Fidelity has hired about 5,000 such workers in India. What good are cost savings? It's one of the things that you learn in your first business course: If you can cut your costs, you can cut your prices or improve your product. Let's look at a specific example. By offshoring work to India, Claimpower, a small medical-insurance billing company, cut costs, lowered the prices it charges doctors, and quadrupled its business in two years.[30]

What's the main complaint about offshoring? Too many domestic jobs end up abroad. As we discuss this, keep in mind that employment results from offshoring are difficult to isolate from other employment changes, such as those resulting from improvements in production technology or cyclical global recessions and economic expansions. However, I'll try to pinpoint direct results of offshoring.

Counterpoint   **No** Some things are good for some of the people some of the time, and that's *almost* the case with offshoring, which unfortunately is good for only a *few* people but not for *most*. I keep hearing about the cost savings, but when I buy goods or services, I rarely find anything that's cheaper than it used to be. Whether I'm buying a Ralph Lauren shirt, getting medical services from a doctor who is saving money by using Claimpower, or having Fidelity manage my assets, I have seen no price reductions for me. Further, Claimpower's growth had to be at the expense of other companies in the business, not because of growth in the economy.

I know of one study that took a close look at 17 high-income countries, and here's what it found: In aggregate, the percentage of national income going to labor did in fact go down between 2000 and 2007. And profits? The percentage of national income going to profits went up.[38]

Here's one of the key problems: When you replace jobs by offshoring, you're exchanging *good* jobs for *bad* ones. Most of the workers who wind up with the short end of the offshoring stick struggled for decades to get reasonable work hours and a few basic benefits, such as

IBM is a good example. Over 70 percent of its nearly 400,000 employees are based outside the United States. By shipping some of its programming work to China, IBM saves a tidy $40 an hour per worker—which comes out to $168 million a year.[31] Analysts agree that IBM's competitors in low-wage countries, such as Infosys from India, can underprice IBM with competitive products and services if IBM fails to offshore.[32] Moreover, when you become price competitive, you sell more at home and abroad, *create* jobs in the process, and improve the chances of survival.[33] In this case, IBM is actually saving jobs by offshoring. Again, it's basic business: Cost savings generate growth, and growth creates more jobs.[34]

And not just any jobs: This process lets companies create more *high-value* jobs at home—the ones performed by people like managers and researchers, who draw high salaries. When that happens, demand for qualified people goes up, and in the United States, that process has already resulted in more buying power as the percentage of white-collar and professional employees in the workforce has increased. These are *high-income* people, and more of them are employed as a result of sending *low-income* jobs to countries with lower labor costs.[35]

Further, offshoring is a natural extension of *outsourcing,* the process of companies contracting work to other companies so that they can concentrate on what they do best.[36] This contributes to making a company more efficient. What is the difference, then, of outsourcing to a domestic versus a foreign company?

Admittedly, workers do get displaced from offshoring, but *aggregate* employment figures show that these workers find other jobs the same as do workers who get displaced for other reasons. In a dynamic economy, people are constantly shifting jobs. So changing jobs because of outsourcing is no different from changing jobs for any other reason—say, because your company decided to invest in some laborsaving technology. In any case, because there are bound to be upper limits on the amount of outsourcing that a country can do, the direst predictions about job loss are exaggerated: There simply aren't enough unemployed people abroad who have the needed skills *and* who will work at a sufficiently low cost. In addition, offshoring isn't for all companies or all types of operations.

Take Delta Airlines, Farouk Systems, and SLM. They are bringing many operations *back* from abroad because of such factors as poor quality, consumer pressure, and concerns about competitive security. In fact, about a fifth of the companies that have gone to offshoring now say that the savings are less than they expected.[37] And that brings us back to what we said implicitly at the outset: Offshoring works when you cut operating costs *effectively*. ▶

health care and retirement plans. More important, their incomes allowed them to send their kids to college, and the result was an upwardly mobile—and productive—generation.

Now, many of these employees have worked long and loyally for their employers and what do they have to show for it in the offshoring era? Yes, I know the government subsidizes some health insurance costs, but very few of these displaced workers can come up with the required cost sharing of their health-care bills when they've lost their jobs.[39] On top of everything else, they may have no other usable skills, and at their ages, who's going to foot the bill for retraining them? The increase in what you call "high-value jobs" doesn't do *them* any good.

While offshoring may lead to short-term cost savings, many studies indicate that outsourcing (whether domestic or international) merely diverts companies' attention from taking steps to find innovative means of more efficient production, such as better operating techniques and more efficient machinery.[40] By concentrating on these latter alternatives, we may cut costs, increase production, and maintain the jobs that are going abroad.

And while we're on the subject of job "value," what kinds of jobs *are* we creating in poor countries? No doubt multinational enterprises (MNEs) pay workers in low-wage countries more than they could get otherwise, and I'll grant that some of these jobs—the white-collar and technical jobs—are pretty good. But for most people, the hours are long, the working conditions are barbaric, and the pay is barely enough to survive on. There is also little job security. As salaries creep up where companies are offshoring, the companies merely move to even cheaper places to get the job done. For instance, this is what happened to workers in the island country of Mauritius. As soon as Mauritians began to think that they might expect a better way of life, MNEs found workers elsewhere to do their sewing.[41]

Admittedly, in a dynamic economy, people have to change jobs more often than they would in a stagnant economy—*but not to the extent caused by offshoring*. I know that there's still some disagreement about the effects of offshoring on a country's employment rate. Researchers are still looking into the issue, but what they're finding are data like these: About 11 percent of U.S. jobs are at risk of being offshored—nearly 2 million of them in accounting-related fields alone.[42] So are we really creating higher-level jobs? Here's the bottom line: In countries like the United States, workers simply aren't equipped to handle the pace of change when it means that jobs can be exported faster than the average worker can retrain for different skills. ◀

Why Companies Engage in International Business

We've alluded to reasons why companies engage in international business. Basically, they're trying to create value for their organizations. We'll now focus on some of the specific ways in which firms can create value by going global. Start by taking another look at Figure 1.1 (page 50), where you'll see three major operating objectives that underlie the reasons for companies to engage in international business:

- Expanding sales
- Acquiring resources
- Minimizing risk

Normally, these three objectives guide all decisions about whether, where, and how to engage in international business. Let's examine each of them in more detail.

EXPANDING SALES

Case Review Note

Pursuing international sales usually increases the potential market and potential profits.

A company's sales depend on the desire and ability of consumers to buy its products or services. Obviously, there are more potential consumers and sales in the world than in any single country. Now, ordinarily, higher sales create value—but only if the costs of making the additional sales don't increase disproportionately. Recall, for instance, our opening case. Televising sports competitions to multiple countries increases costs only marginally, while generating advertising revenue in excess of these marginally increased costs. In fact, additional sales from abroad may enable a company to reduce its per-unit costs by covering its fixed costs—say, up-front research costs—over a larger number of sales. Because of lower unit costs, it can increase sales even more.

So increased sales are a major motive for a company's expansion into international markets, and in fact, many of the world's largest companies—including Volkswagen (Germany), Ericsson (Sweden), IBM (United States), Michelin (France), Nestlé (Switzerland), and Sony (Japan)—derive more than half their sales outside their home countries.[43] Bear in mind, however, that international business is not the purview only of large companies. In the United States, 97 percent of exporters are classified as small and mid-sized companies (SMMs).[44] Many small companies also depend on sales of components to large companies, which, in turn, install them in finished products slated for sale abroad.

ACQUIRING RESOURCES

Foreign sources may give companies

- Lower costs.
- New or better products.
- Additional operating knowledge.

Producers and distributors seek out products, services, resources, and components from foreign countries. Sometimes it's because domestic supplies are inadequate (as is the case with crude oil shipped to the United States). They're also looking for anything that will give them a competitive advantage. This may mean acquiring a resource that cuts costs; an example is Rawlings' reliance on labor in Costa Rica—a country that hardly plays baseball—to produce baseballs.[45]

Sometimes firms gain competitive advantage by improving product quality or by differentiating their products from those of competitors; in both cases, they're potentially increasing market share and profits. Most automobile manufacturers, for example, hire one of several automobile-design companies in northern Italy to help with styling.[46] Many companies establish foreign research-and-development (R&D) facilities to tap additional scientific resources.[47] This is especially important for companies based in countries with low technological capabilities.[48] Companies also learn while operating abroad. Avon, for instance, applies know-how from its Latin American marketing experience to help sell to the U.S. Hispanic market.[49]

MINIMIZING RISK

Operating in countries with different business cycles can minimize swings in sales and profits. The key is the fact that sales decrease or grow more slowly in a country that's in a recession and increase or grow more rapidly in one that's expanding economically. During 2008, for example, General Motors' U.S. sales fell 21 percent, but this was partially offset by its sales growth of 30 percent in Russia, 10 percent in Brazil, and 9 percent in India.[50] In addition, by obtaining supplies of products or components from different countries, companies may be able to soften the impact of price swings or shortages in any one country.

Finally, companies often go into international business for defensive reasons. Perhaps they want to counter competitors' advantages in foreign markets that might hurt them elsewhere. By operating in Japan, for instance, Procter & Gamble (P&G) delayed foreign expansion on the part of potential Japanese competitors by slowing their amassment of the necessary resources to expand into other international markets where P&G was active.

Similarly, British-based Natures Way Foods followed a customer, the grocery chain Tesco, into the U.S. market. In so doing, it not only expanded sales but also strengthened its relationship with Tesco, effectively reducing the risk that Tesco would find an alternative supplier who might then threaten Natures Way Foods' relationship with Tesco in the U.K. market.[51]

International operations may reduce operating risk by

- Smoothing sales and profits.
- Preventing competitors from gaining advantages.

Modes of Operations in International Business

When pursuing international business, an organization must decide on one of the suitable *modes of operations* included in Figure 1.1 (page 50). In the following sections, we discuss each of these modes in some detail.

MERCHANDISE EXPORTS AND IMPORTS

Exporting and importing are the most popular modes of international business, especially among smaller companies. **Merchandise exports** are tangible products—goods—that are sent *out* of a country; **merchandise imports** are goods brought *into* a country. Because we can actually *see* these goods as they leave and enter the country, we sometimes call them *visible exports* and *imports*. When an Indonesian plant sends athletic shoes to the United States, the shoes are exports for Indonesia and imports for the United States. For most countries, the export and import of goods are the major sources of international revenues and expenditures.

Merchandise exports and imports are usually a country's most common international economic transactions.

SERVICE EXPORTS AND IMPORTS

Note that the terms *export* and *import* often apply only to *merchandise*, not to *services*. When we refer to products that generate *nonproduct international earnings*, we use the terms **service exports** and **service imports.** The company or individual that provides the service and receives payment makes a *service export;* the company or individual that receives and pays for it makes a *service import*. Currently, services constitute the fastest growth sector in international trade. Service exports and imports take many forms, and in this section, we discuss the most important:

- Tourism and transportation
- Service performance
- Asset use

Service exports and imports are international nonproduct sales and purchases.

- Examples of services are travel, transportation, banking, insurance, and the use of assets such as trademarks, patents, and copyrights.
- Service exports and imports are very important for some countries.
- They include many specialized international business operating modes.

Tourism and Transportation Let's say that the Williams sisters, Venus and Serena, take Air France from the United States to Paris to play in the French Open tennis tournament.

Their tickets on Air France and travel expenses in France are service exports for France and service imports for the United States. Obviously, then, tourism and transportation are important sources of revenue for airlines, shipping companies, travel agencies, and hotels.

The economies of some countries depend heavily on revenue from these sectors. In Greece and Norway, for example, a significant amount of employment and foreign-exchange earnings comes from foreign cargo carried by Greek and Norwegian shipping lines. Tourism earnings are more important to the Bahamian economy than earnings from export merchandise. (As we'll see in our closing case, year-round good weather enables Caribbean countries to benefit from passengers arriving on cruise ships.)

Service Performance   Some services—including banking, insurance, rental, engineering, and management services—net companies earnings in the form of *fees*—payments for the performance of those services. On an international level, for example, companies may pay fees for engineering services rendered as so-called **turnkey operations,** which are often construction projects performed under contract and transferred to owners when they're operational. The U.S. company Bechtel currently has a turnkey contract in Egypt to build a nuclear plant to generate electricity.[52] Companies also pay fees for **management contracts**—arrangements in which one company provides personnel to perform general or specialized management functions for another. Disney receives such fees from managing theme parks in France and Japan.

Asset Use   When one company allows another to use its assets—such as trademarks, patents, copyrights, or expertise—under contracts known as **licensing agreements,** they receive earnings called *royalties.* For example, Adidas pays a royalty for the use of the Real Madrid football team's logo on hooded jackets it sells. **Royalties** also come from franchise contracts. **Franchising** is a mode of business in which one party (the *franchisor*) allows another (the *franchisee*) to use a trademark as an essential asset of the franchisee's business. As a rule, the franchisor (say, McDonald's) also assists continuously in the operation of the franchisee's business, perhaps by providing supplies, management services, or technology.

INVESTMENTS

Dividends and interest paid on foreign investments are also considered service exports and imports because they represent the use of assets (capital). The investments themselves, however, are treated in national statistics as different forms of service exports and imports. Note that *foreign investment* means ownership of foreign property in exchange for a financial return, such as interest and dividends, and it may take two forms: *direct* and *portfolio.*

Direct Investment   In **foreign direct investment (FDI),** sometimes referred to simply as *direct investment*, the investor takes a controlling interest in a foreign company. When, for example, a Japanese investor bought the Seattle Mariners, the baseball team became a Japanese FDI in the United States. Control need not be a 100 percent (or even a 50 percent) interest—if a foreign investor holds a minority stake and the remaining ownership is widely dispersed, no other owner may be efficient at countering the decisions of the foreign investor.

When two or more companies share ownership of an FDI, the operation is a **joint venture.** An example in our opening case is the joint ownership of Liverpool Football Club by owners of a U.S. baseball team and a Canadian hockey team.

Although the world's 100 largest international companies account for a high proportion of global output, the vast number of companies using FDI means that it's also common among smaller companies. Today, about 79,000 companies worldwide control about 790,000 FDIs in all industries.[53]

Portfolio Investment A **portfolio investment** is a *noncontrolling* financial interest in another entity. A portfolio investment usually takes one of two forms: stock in a company or loans to a company (or country) in the form of bonds, bills, or notes purchased by the investor. They're important for most companies with extensive international operations, and except for stock, they're used primarily for short-term financial gain—as a relatively safe means of earning more money on a firm's investment. To earn higher yields on short-term investments, companies routinely move funds from country to country.

Key components of portfolio investment are

- Noncontrolling interest of a foreign operation.
- Financial benefit (e.g., loans).

TYPES OF INTERNATIONAL ORGANIZATIONS

Basically, an "international company" is any company that operates internationally, but we have a variety of terms to designate different types of operations. Companies can work together on an international basis in any number of ways, including *joint ventures, licensing agreements, management contracts, minority ownership,* and *long-term contractual arrangements.* The term **collaborative arrangements** can be used to describe all of these types of operations. The term **strategic alliance** is sometimes used to mean the same thing, but it's often reserved to refer either to an agreement that's of critical importance to one or more partners or to an agreement that does not involve joint ownership.

Multinational Enterprises A **multinational enterprise (MNE)** takes a worldwide view of markets and production; in other words, it's willing to consider market and production locations anywhere in the world. The true MNE typically uses most of the modes of operations we've described in this chapter. However, because it isn't always easy to determine if a company really takes a "worldwide view," experts have devised some narrower definitions of an MNE. Some people argue, for instance, that an MNE must have direct investments in a minimum number of countries.

An MNE (sometimes called MNC or TNC) is a company that has a worldwide approach to markets and production or one with operations in more than one country.

Does Size Matter? Some definitions require a certain size—usually giant size. A small company, however, can take a worldwide view and adopt any of the operating modes that we've discussed, even while remaining within its resource capabilities. This is often the case with what we've called *born-global companies.* Of course, born-global companies usually start out as small companies, but if they are successful, they become large companies. VistaPrint is a good example. Founded in the late 1990s, it now maintains two-thirds of its workforce outside the United States, sells in 120 countries, and has a capitalization of over a billion U.S. dollars.[54]

MNCs and TNCs Today, most writers apply the term *MNE* to any company with operations in more than one country. This is the definition we use in this text. The term **multinational corporation or multinational company (MNC)** is often used as a synonym for MNE. At the United Nations, the term **transnational company (TNC)** is used interchangeably with MNE.

Why International Business Differs from Domestic Business

Now that we've explained the modes by which companies operate internationally, let's turn to the conditions in a company's *external environment* that may affect those operations. Smart companies don't form international strategies—or develop the means to implement them—without examining the dimensions of the external environment indicated in the

Managers in international business must understand social science disciplines and how they affect all functional business fields.

left-hand side of Figure 1.1 (page 50). As you can see, we've organized these dimensions, or factors, into the following categories:

- *Physical factors* (such as a country's geography) and *social factors* (such as its politics, law, culture, and economy)
- *Competitive factors* (such as the number and strength of a company's suppliers, customers, and rival firms)

In examining both categories, we delve into the realm of the *social sciences*, which is extremely helpful in explaining how external conditions affect patterns of behavior in different parts of the world.

PHYSICAL AND SOCIAL FACTORS

Physical and social factors can affect the ways in which companies produce and market products, staff operations, and even maintain accounts. In the following sections, we focus on five key factors: *geographic, political, legal, behavioral,* and *economic.* Remember that any of these factors may require companies, if they are to operate efficiently, to alter how they operate abroad compared to how they operate domestically.

Geographic Influences   Managers who are knowledgeable about geography are in a position to determine the location, quantity, quality, and availability of the world's resources, as well as the best way to exploit them. The uneven distribution of resources throughout the world accounts in large part for the fact that different products and services are produced in different parts of the world.

Again, take sports. Norway fares better in the Winter Olympics than in the Summer Olympics because of its climate, and except for the well-publicized Jamaican bobsled team (whose members actually lived in Canada), tropical countries don't even compete in the Winter Olympics. The reason East Africans tend to dominate distance races is, at least in part, that they can train at higher altitudes than most other runners.

Geographic barriers—mountains, deserts, jungles, and so forth—often affect communications and distribution channels in many countries. And the chance of natural disasters and adverse climatic conditions (hurricanes, floods, earthquakes, tsunamis) can make investments riskier in some areas than in others, while affecting global supplies and prices. (Again, we can look ahead to our ending case, which shows that cruise-line operators must adjust their ports-of-call when hurricanes threaten.)

Finally, population distribution and the impact of human activity on the environment may exert strong future influences on international business, particularly if ecological changes or regulations force companies to move or alter operations.

Political Policies   It should come as no surprise that a nation's political policies influence the ways in which international business takes place within its borders (indeed, *whether* it will take place). We can turn again to the sports arena to see how politics can affect international operations in any industry. Did you know that Cuba once had a minor-league baseball franchise? That arrangement went the way of diplomatic relations between Cuba and the United States back in the 1960s, but several Cuban baseball players are now members of professional U.S. teams. However, most of them had to defect from Cuba to play abroad.

Obviously, political disputes—particularly those that result in military confrontation—can disrupt trade and investment. Even conflicts that directly affect only small areas can have far-reaching effects. The terrorist bombing of a hotel in Indonesia, for instance, resulted in the loss of considerable tourist revenue and investment capital because both individuals and businesses abroad perceived Indonesia as too risky an environment for safe and profitable enterprises.

Natural conditions affect where different goods and services can be produced.

Case Review Note

Politics often determines where and how international business can take place.

Legal Policies Domestic and international laws play a big role in determining how a company can operate overseas. *Domestic law* includes both home- and host-country regulations on such matters as taxation, employment, and foreign-exchange transactions. Singapore law, for example, determines how the local Man U's Red Café is taxed, how its revenues can be converted from Singapore dollars to British pounds, and even which nationalities of people it employs. Meanwhile, British law determines how and when the earnings from Man U's Singapore operations are taxed in the United Kingdom.

International law—in the form of legal agreements between the two countries—determines how earnings are taxed by *both* jurisdictions. Mainly as a function of agreements reached in international forums, international law may also determine how (and whether) companies can operate in certain places. As we point out in our closing case, for example, international agreement permits ships' crews to move about virtually anywhere without harassment.

Finally, the ways in which laws are *enforced* also affect a firm's foreign operations. Most countries, for example, have joined in international treaties and enacted domestic laws dealing with the violation of trademarks, patented knowledge, and copyrighted materials. Many, however, do very little to enforce either the treaties or their own laws. That's why companies must make a point not only of understanding treaties and laws but also of determining how fastidiously they're enforced in different countries.

Behavioral Factors The related disciplines of anthropology, psychology, and sociology can help managers better understand values, attitudes, and beliefs in a foreign environment. In turn, such understanding can help managers make operational decisions in different countries.

Let's return once again to our opening case. We stressed that although professional sports are spreading internationally, the popularity of specific sports differs among countries. Interestingly, these differences affect the way in which the U.S. film industry treats sports as subject matter. As a rule, U.S. producers spare no expense to ensure that movies generate the greatest possible international appeal (and revenue). When it comes to sports-themed movies, however, they typically cut costs. Why? Because people in one country are usually lukewarm about other countries' sports, moviemakers see little point in spending extra money trying to attract foreign audiences and revenues with these films.[55]

While we're on the subject, we should point out that sports rules sometimes differ among countries. The Japanese *do* care about U.S. baseball, but Japanese culture values harmony more than U.S. culture does, and U.S. culture values competitiveness more than the Japanese culture does. This difference is reflected in different baseball rules: Whereas the best possible outcome of a baseball game in Japan is a tie, Americans prefer that a game be played out until there's a winner.

Economic Forces Economics explains why countries exchange goods and services, why capital and people travel among countries in the course of business, and why one country's currency has a certain value compared to another's. Recall from our opening case that the percentage of non-U.S.-born players on major-league rosters has been increasing. Players from the Dominican Republic form the largest share of non-U.S.-born players, but even though baseball is quite popular in the Dominican Republic, the idea of putting a major-league baseball team there simply isn't feasible. Why? Because too few Dominicans can afford the ticket prices necessary to support a team. Obviously, higher incomes in the United States and Canada permit higher baseball salaries that attract Dominican players to major-league teams.

Economics also helps explain why one country can produce goods or services less expensively than another. In addition, it provides the analytical tools to determine the impact of an international company's operations on the economies of both host and home countries, as well as the impact of the host country's economic environment on a foreign company.

Case Review Note

Case Review Note

Each country has its own laws regulating business. Agreements among countries set international law.

The interpersonal norms of a country may necessitate a company's alteration of operations.

Economics explains country differences in costs, currency values, and market size.

THE COMPETITIVE ENVIRONMENT

In addition to its physical and social environments, every globally active company operates within a competitive environment. Figure 1.1 (page 50) highlights the key competitive factors in the external environment of an international business—product strategy, resource base and experience, and competitor capability.

Competitive Strategy for Products   Most products compete by means of *cost* or *differentiation strategies*. A successful differentiation strategy usually takes one of two approaches:

- Developing a favorable *brand image,* usually through advertising or from long-term consumer experience with the brand; or

- Developing *unique characteristics,* such as through R&D efforts or different means of distribution.

A company's situation may differ among countries by

- Its competitive ranking.
- The competitors it faces.

Using either approach, a firm may mass-market a product or sell to a target market (the latter approach is called a *focus strategy*). Different strategies can be used for different products or for different countries, but a firm's choice of strategy plays a big part in determining how and where it will operate. Take Fiat, an Italian automobile brand that competes in most of the world largely with a cost strategy aimed at mass-market sales. This strategy has influenced Fiat to locate engine plants in China, where production costs are low, and to sell in India and Argentina, which are cost-sensitive markets.

Interestingly, Fiat also owns Ferrari, which competes with a focus strategy to very high-income consumers. Whereas the competitive characteristics of the U.S. market have not been conducive to a mass-market Fiat brand strategy, Fiat sells over a quarter of all its Ferraris in the United States.[56] With Fiat's investment in Chrysler, it plans to also sell the Fiat 500 (a sort of boutique car) with a focus strategy through Chrysler distributors, mainly on the U.S. East and West Coasts.

Company Resources and Experience   Other competitive factors are a company's size and resources compared to those of its competitors. A market leader, for example—say, Coca-Cola—has resources for much more ambitious international operations than a smaller competitor like Royal Crown. Royal Crown sells in about 60 countries, whereas Coca-Cola sells in over 200.

In large markets (such as the United States), as compared to small markets (such as Ireland), companies have to invest many more resources to secure national distribution. (And even then, they'll probably face more competitors: In a European country, for example, especially in retailing, a firm is likely to face three or four significant competitors, as opposed to the 10 to 20 it will face in the United States.)[57]

Conversely, a company's national market share and brand recognition have a bearing on how it can operate in a given country. A company with a long-standing dominant market position uses operating tactics quite different from those employed by a newcomer. Remember, too, that being a leader in one country doesn't guarantee being a leader anywhere else. In most markets, Coca-Cola is the leader, with Pepsi-Cola coming in a strong second; in India, however, Coke is number three, trailing both Pepsi and a locally owned brand called *Thums Up.*[58]

Competitors Faced in Each Market   Finally, success in a market (whether domestic or foreign) often depends on whether your competition is also international or local. Commercial aircraft makers Boeing and Airbus, for example, compete only with each other in every market they serve. Thus what they learn about each other in one country is useful in predicting the other's strategies elsewhere. In contrast, the British grocery chain Tesco faces different competition in almost every foreign market it enters.

Looking to the Future

Three Ways of Looking at Globalization

At this juncture, there's a good deal of difference of opinion on the future of international business and globalization. Basically, there are three major viewpoints:

- Further globalization is inevitable.
- International business will grow primarily along regional rather than global lines.
- Forces working against further globalization and international business will slow down the growth of both.

The view that globalization is inevitable reflects the premise that advances in transportation and communications are so pervasive that consumers everywhere will demand the best products for the best prices regardless of their origins. Those who hold this view also argue that because MNEs have so many international production and distribution networks in place, they'll pressure their governments to place fewer rather than more restrictions on the international movement of goods and the means of producing them.

Even if we accept this view, we must still meet at least one challenge to riding the wave of the future: Because the future is what we make of it, we must figure out how to spread the benefits of globalization equitably while minimizing the hardships placed on those parties—both people and companies—who suffer from increased international competition.

Not long ago, the *Wall Street Journal* posed one question to all living Nobel Prize winners in economics: "What is the greatest economic challenge for the future?" Several responses relate to globalization and international business. Robert Fogel said it's the problem of getting available technology and food to people who are needlessly dying. Both Vernon Smith and Harry Markowitz specified the need to bring down global trade barriers. Lawrence Klein called for "the reduction of poverty and disease in a peaceful political environment." John Nash felt we must address the problem of increasing the worldwide standard of living while the amount of the earth's surface per person is shrinking.[59] Clearly, each of these responses projects both challenges and opportunities for managers in the international arena.

The second view—that growth will be largely regional rather than global—is based on studies showing that almost all of the companies we think of as "global" conduct most of their business in home and neighboring countries.[60] In addition, most world trade is regional, and many treaties to remove trade barriers are regional agreements. Transport costs favor regional over global business. Further, regional sales may be sufficient for companies to gain scale economies to cover their fixed costs adequately. Nevertheless, regionalization of business activity may be merely a transition stage. In other words, companies may first promote international business in nearby countries and then expand their activities once they've reached certain regional goals.

The third view argues that the pace of globalization will slow down or may in fact already be in the process of collapse.[61] We've already had occasion to cite a few antiglobalization sentiments, and it's easy to see that some people are adamant and earnest in voicing their reservations. The crux of the antiglobalization movement is the belief that there's a growing schism between parties (including MNEs) who are thriving in a globalized environment and those who aren't. For example, during 2008, hungry people (those consuming less than 1,800 calories per day) rioted in over 30 countries as their numbers increased by about 100 million from the year before.[62]

Antiglobalists pressure governments to promote nationalism by raising barriers to trade and rejecting international organizations and treaties. Historically, such groups have often been successful (at least temporarily) in obstructing either technological or commercial advances that threatened their well-being. Recently, for example, antiglobalization interests in Australia and Austria succeeded in electing anti-immigration parties. In Brazil and South Africa, voters have authorized domestic companies to copy pharmaceuticals under global patent protection. Bolivia and Venezuela have nationalized some foreign investments, and the United States prevented China from purchasing a U.S. oil company. The sparring between pro- and antiglobalists is one of the reasons why the globalization process has so far progressed in fits and starts.

There are other uncertainties that may hamper globalization. First, there is the question of oil prices, which are important in determining the cost of international transportation. Between January and June of 2008, global oil prices rose 44 percent and then descended 74 percent by the end of the year.[63] Many U.S. companies, such as U.S. furniture manufacturers, responded by returning to U.S. production bases rather than facing transport cost uncertainty.[64] Second, the economic recession beginning in 2008 has led countries to employ measures to protect their own production and work forces.[65] Third, recent rises in safety concerns—property confiscation, terrorism, and the piracy of ships—may inhibit companies from venturing as much internationally.

Finally, there is a view that for globalization to succeed, efficient institutions with clear-cut mandates are necessary; however, there is concern that neither the institutions nor the people working in them can adequately handle the complexities of an interconnected world.[66]

Going Forward

Only time will tell, but one thing seems certain from everything we've read in this chapter: If a company wants to capitalize on international opportunities, it can't wait too long to see what happens on political and economic fronts. Investments in research, equipment, plants, and personnel training can take years to pan out. Forecasting foreign opportunities and risks is always a challenge, but by examining different ways in which the future may evolve, a company's management has a better chance of avoiding unpleasant surprises. That's why each chapter of this book includes a feature that shows how certain chapter topics can become subjects for looking into the future of international business. ■

CASE

Carnival Cruise Lines: Exploiting a Sea of Global Opportunity

I must go down to the seas again, for the call of the running tide

Is a wild call and a clear call that may not be denied

—John Masefield, The Seekers

In recent years, the call of the sea has spurred the cruise business.[67] Sea voyages, of course, have had an aura of mystique for centuries, but only in recent decades has the experience of the open sea and exotic ports of call been available to a mass market.

Historically, the recreational sea voyage was an essentially elitist endeavor. Certainly, members of the lower classes occasionally found themselves on the open sea, but usually as displaced job seekers or crew members aboard ships. In recent years, however, the cruise industry has undergone a sea of change of sorts, and the demographic groups it now targets include the working middle class as well as the idle rich.

What's a *Cruise*, and What Happened to the Cruise Industry?

A "cruise" is a sea voyage taken for pleasure (as opposed to, say, passage on a whaling ship, an assignment in the navy, or a ferry ride to get you from point A to point B). Typically, passengers enjoy cabin accommodations for the duration of a fixed itinerary that brings them back to their original point of embarkation.

There was a time when ships (called *passenger liners*) transported people across oceans and seas for business or pleasure, but the advent of transoceanic air service after World War II offered a speedier and less expensive alternative, and airlines captured passengers from ocean liners. The competitive balance tipped decisively in the 1960s, when advances in jet technology made air travel a viable option for a growing mass market of budget-minded international travelers. Converting more shipboard space to low-priced accommodations, shipping lines countered with the reminder that "getting there is half the fun," but one by one, they retired the great luxury liners that had plied the seas for decades.

The Contemporary Cruise Industry

Today, the cruise industry is dominated by three companies—Carnival, Royal Caribbean, and Star—which command a combined 91 percent of the market. By far, the largest of the three is

MAP 1.2 Where Carnival's Cruise Lines (Brands) Are Headquartered

Countries designated on the map denote headquarters locations of each company/brand (e.g., four lines operate out of North America and three out of the United Kingdom). Carnival has the most recognized brands in North America, the United Kingdom, Germany, France, Italy, and Spain—areas that account for 85 percent of the world's cruise-line passengers.

Source: Data come from Carnival Corporation/Corporate Information/Our Brands at http://phx.corporate-ir.net/phoenix.zhtml?c=200767&p=irol-products (accessed June 25, 2009).

Note: Given that this is a Mercator projection, the scale approximates east-west distance at the equator; however, the farther you move from the equator, the more the east-west distance is distorted.

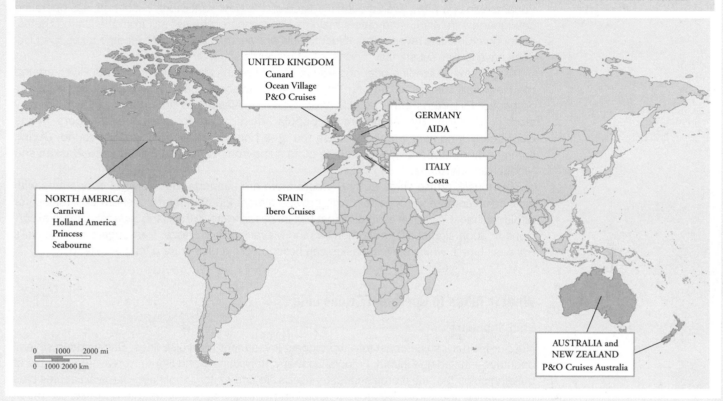

Carnival Corporation, which operates a number of lines that it calls *brands.* Map 1.2 shows the headquarters of these brands. Carnival offers cruises to every continent on the globe, including Antarctica.

Carnival Corporation was born when Ted Arison, a former partner in Norwegian Cruise Lines, saw an opportunity to expand mass-market sea travel by promoting the idea of the "Fun Ship" vacation—an excursion on a pleasure craft designed to be a little less formal and luxurious than the traditional ocean liner. The timing was right. Sea travel still projected a certain aura, and Arison found that he could buy a retired liner at a good price. Moreover, there were more people in the world who could afford an ocean-borne vacation. On top of everything else, a lot of these vacationers gravitated to holidays—group tours, theme-park visits, and sojourns in Las Vegas—that were compatible with the Fun Ship concept.

Arison bought a secondhand ship, refurbished it in bright colors, rigged it with bright lights, and installed discos and casinos. On its maiden voyage from Miami in 1972, the *Mardi Gras* ran aground with 300 journalists on board, but, fortunately, neither the ship nor Arison's business concept was severely damaged. Embarking from Miami to such destinations as Jamaica, Puerto Rico, and the U.S. Virgin Islands, the *Mardi Gras* soon became successful.

Over time, Arison added not only ships but also whole cruise lines to his fleet. Today, each brand operates primarily in a designated area of the world and is differentiated from other Carnival brands in two ways: (1) in terms of geographically pertinent themes (based in Italy, for instance, Costa boasts a Mediterranean flavor); and (2) in terms of cost per cruise (the cost per night on Cunard and Seabourne cruises is much higher than that on Carnival cruises).

Doing Business in International Waters

Given the nature of its business, it should come as no surprise that Carnival—indeed, the whole cruise-line industry—is international in scope. Take the nationality of competitors. Companies can obtain so-called *flags of convenience* from about 30 different countries. Here's how the process works. By registering as, say, a Liberian legal entity, a company can take advantage of lower taxes and less stringent employment rules. Legally, Carnival is a Panamanian company, even though it's listed on the New York Stock Exchange, has operating headquarters in Miami, and caters mainly to passengers who set sail from the United States. Although cruise-line revenue is subject to neither Panamanian nor U.S. income taxes, Carnival does have to pay substantial "port fees" wherever its ships drop anchor.

Only a few cruise-line offerings—such as excursions along the Mississippi River, around the Hawaiian Islands, or among the Galapagos Islands—can be characterized as purely domestic. Even trips from the U.S. West Coast to Alaska are "international" because they stop in Canada. By far the most popular destination for cruise passengers is the Caribbean/Bahamas, largely because the area boasts balmy weather year round. During summer months, Carnival shifts some of its ships from Caribbean/Bahamas to Alaskan and Mediterranean routes.

Obviously, cruise ships go only where there are seaports, but Carnival cooperates with (and owns some) tour operators who provide almost 2,000 different onshore excursions (for additional fees). Carnival estimates that half its passengers to the Caribbean take shore excursions to such sightseeing attractions as the Mayan ruins in Belize. Passengers on Carnival's Princess Lines, which serves Alaska, can helicopter to a glacier for a little dogsledding.

What It Takes to Operate a Cruise Line

Ship Shopping

Not surprisingly, ships constitute the biggest investment for cruise lines. Shipyards in several countries—including Finland, France, Germany, Italy, Japan, and South Korea—are capable of building ships that meet cruise-industry needs. To add to its global fleet, Carnival secures bids from all over the world. Because shipbuilding employs so many people and uses so much locally produced steel, governments often subsidize the industry—a practice that works to the benefit of the cruise-line industry by offering less expensive prices for ships. For instance, the Italian government awarded the shipyard Fincantieri about $50 million in subsidies to build five ships sold to Carnival for $2.5 billion for a 2010 and 2011 delivery.

Where to Find Able-Bodied Seamen

Shipping companies—including cargo and cruise lines—scour the world for crew members who not only can perform specialized tasks but who are properly certified (by international agreement, a registered crew member can enter virtually any port in the world). Cruise lines, of course, have special staffing needs—notably, crew who can interact with passengers. About a third of all the world's ship crews are from the Philippines, not only because of reasonable labor costs but because Filipinos are generally fluent in English. On a typical Carnival ship, crew members hail from over 100 countries, and Carnival maintains a range of employee-training programs, including instruction in English as a foreign language.

Casinos and Other Amenities

Although Carnival has thrived with the concept of informal cruises for a mass market, each of its cruises offers one or two formal nights per week; theme-based dinners centering on national cuisines; a variety of musical entertainment, games and contests; and spas and athletic facilities. Because cruises operate outside the jurisdiction of any national authority, they're not subject to any national laws restricting gambling. Casinos, therefore, are onboard fixtures.

Passengers can also shop for merchandise from all over the world. Indeed, art dealers occasionally hold shipboard auctions and seminars, and one dealer sells about

300,000 pieces of art per year on cruise ships. As you might expect, the pricier the cruise, the pricier the average objet d'art.

The Overseas Environment

Because Carnival operates around the world, it has the advantage of treating the whole world as a source of both customers and supplies. In addition, because its chief assets are ocean borne, Carnival can ship capital and other assets to places where they can best serve the company's needs. However, it's also vulnerable to a wide range of environmental disturbances. Let's take a look at a few of these.

Political Issues

After terrorists seized a cruise ship in the Mediterranean in 1985, the major cruise lines instituted a policy of strict security checks for boarding passengers. Even before 9/11, then, the cruise-line industry has had in place a security protocol that the airline industry didn't establish until afterward.

In the wake of 9/11, when cancellations started to exceed bookings, Carnival increased the number of U.S. ports from which its ships embarked so that passengers with a heightened fear of flying could reach points of departure by land. Carnival also redeploys cruises to avoid areas in which passengers might face danger from political upheaval or crime, such as suspending cruises to St. Croix in the U.S. Virgin Islands because of its high crime rate. Further, Carnival does not stop in Cuba, a popular tourist destination, because the U.S. government limits travel there by U.S. citizens.

Health Issues

In 2006, almost 700 people on a Carnival transatlantic cruise were stricken with a virus that caused diarrhea and vomiting, a type of outbreak that had occurred sporadically in the past. Cruise operators have found these outbreaks hard to control because of the close contact among people on board a ship. More than once, Carnival has had to take an infected ship out of service to eradicate all traces of the virus; the process involves sanitizing every object on board, down to the poker chips. When the H1N1 flu (swine flu) hit Mexico in 2009, Carnival modified itineraries temporarily to avoid Mexican ports.

Economic Issues

Buying a cruise is generally considered discretionary rather than priority spending. During recessions, people are more apt to take shorter cruises and to embark from nearby ports rather than flying to faraway points of departure. Interestingly, however, in comparison with other segments of the tourist industry, cruise lines have fared well during economic downturns. Why? This is due in part to their all-inclusive per diem prices that are often bargains when compared with the cost of travel to major cities and popular resorts. In addition, fixed cruise-line prices spare passengers the added risk of encountering unforeseen unfavorable exchange rates. Nevertheless, in 2009, Carnival offered discounts because of the global recession, which attracted more passengers but lower profits.

But there is some concern in the industry over uncertain gasoline prices and mortgage interest rates, which might leave more households with too little discretionary income for taking cruises. In addition, oil price increases have upped Carnival's fuel costs at a time when many potential passengers want lower prices.

The Weather

Whenever there are hurricanes, Carnival may have to cancel trips, switch embarkation points (e.g., from Galveston to Houston for six weeks in 2008 because of Hurricane Ike), or change destinations. Typically, passengers on canceled trips received full refunds and those on shortened cruises partial refunds.

Concluding Remarks

Overall, the outlook for Carnival and the cruise-line industry is sunny. With prospects for growing incomes (despite a global recession) in many countries (such as China), more people will have discretionary income to spend on tourism. Only 16 percent of the U.S. population has yet to take a cruise—a potential two-edged sword. On the one hand, this number indicates growth potential. On the other hand, people who have taken a cruise continue to be repeat customers, and the percentage of first-time customers is in fact declining. On the downside, then, industry observers worry that experienced cruisers will tire of visiting one port that's pretty much like another and that noncruisers will still prefer such destinations as resorts to ports of call. ■

QUESTIONS

1. What global forces have contributed to the growth of the cruise-line industry?
2. What specific steps has Carnival Cruise Lines taken to benefit from global social changes?
3. What are some of the national differences that affect the operations of cruise lines?
4. Although most cruise-line passengers are from the United States, the average number of annual vacation days taken by U.S. residents is lower than that of workers in most other high-income countries (13 days, compared with 42 in Italy, 37 in France, 35 in Germany, and 25 in Japan). How might cruise lines increase sales to people outside the United States?
5. What threats exist to the future performance of the cruise-line industry and, specifically, of Carnival Cruise Lines? If you were in charge of Carnival, how would you (a) try to prevent these threats from becoming reality and (b) deal with them if they were realized?
6. Discuss the ethics of cruise lines regarding the avoidance of taxes while buying ships built with governmental subsidies.

SUMMARY

- Globalization is the ongoing process that deepens and broadens the relationships and interdependence among countries. International business is a mechanism to bring about globalization.

- International business has been growing rapidly in recent decades because of technological expansion, the liberalization of government policies on cross-border movements (goods, services, and the resources to produce them), the development of institutions needed to support and facilitate international transactions, consumer pressures to buy foreign products and services, increased global competition, changing political situations, and cooperation in dealing with transnational problems and issues. Because of these factors, foreign countries increasingly are a source of both production and sales for domestic companies.

- Globalization has many critics who feel that it weakens national sovereignty, promotes growth that is detrimental to the earth's environment, and skews income distributions.

- Offshoring—the transferring of production abroad—is controversial in terms of who benefits when costs are reduced and whether the process exchanges good jobs for bad ones.

- Companies engage in international business to expand sales, to acquire resources, and to diversify or reduce their risks.

- A company can engage in international business through various operating modes, including exporting and importing merchandise and services, direct and portfolio investments, and collaborative arrangements with other companies.

- Multinational enterprises (MNEs) take a global approach to markets and production. Sometimes they are referred to as multinational corporations or companies (MNCs) or transnational companies (TNCs).

- When operating abroad, companies may have to adjust their usual methods of carrying out business. This is because foreign conditions often dictate a more suitable method, and the operating modes used for international business differ somewhat from those used on a domestic level.

- To operate within a company's external environment, its managers must have not only knowledge of business operations but also a working knowledge of the basic social sciences: geography, political science, law, anthropology, sociology, psychology, and economics.

- A company's competitive strategy influences how and where it can best operate. Likewise, from one country to another, a company's competitive situation may differ in terms of its relative strength and which competitors it faces.

- There is disagreement about the future of international business—that globalization is inevitable, that it will be primarily regional, and that the growth will slow.

KEY TERMS

born-global company (p. 53)
clustering (p. 53)
collaborative arrangement (p. 63)
foreign direct investment (FDI) (p. 62)
franchising (p. 62)
globalization (p. 49)
international business (p. 49)
joint venture (p. 62)
licensing agreement (p. 62)

management contract (p. 62)
merchandise export (p. 61)
merchandise import (p. 61)
multinational corporation
    or company (MNC) (p. 63)
multinational enterprise
    (MNE) (p. 63)
offshoring (p. 58)
portfolio investment (p. 63)

royalty (p. 62)
service export (p. 61)
service import (p. 61)
sovereignty (p. 56)
strategic alliance (p. 63)
transnational company
    (TNC) (p. 63)
turnkey operation (p. 62)

ENDNOTES

1   *Sources include the following:* George Vecsey, "When the Game Absorbs the Globe," *New York Times* (April 1, 2007): A+; Chris Isidore, "NFL Struggles to Win on the Road," CNNMoney.com (July 13, 2007), http://money.cnn.com/2007/07/13/commentary/sportsbiz/index.htm; "Percentage of Foreign-Born," *Dominican Today* (April 1, 2008), www.dominicantoday.com/dr/sports/2008/4/1; Simon Kuper, "Lost in Translation," *Financial Times* (February 2–3, 2008): p. life & arts 2; "Percentage of Foreign-Born Major League Baseball Players Drops," Dominican Today.com/dr/sports/2008/4/1 (accessed March 3, 2009); Steve McGrath, "Latest Private-Equity Triumph: U.K. Soccer," *Wall Street Journal* (February 7, 2007): C3; Matthew Graham, "Nike Overtakes Adidas in Football Field," *Financial Times* (August 19, 2004): 19; L. Jon Wertheim, "The Whole World Is Watching," *Sports Illustrated* (June 14, 2004): 73–86; Wertheim Jon, "Hot Prospects in Cold Places," *Sports Illustrated* (June 21, 2004): 63–66; Grant Wahl, "Football vs. Fútbol," *Sports Illustrated* (July 5, 2004): 69–72; Wahl, "On Safari for 7-Footers," *Sports Illustrated* (June 28, 2004): 70–73; André Richelieu, "Building the Brand Equity of Professional Sports Teams," Paper presented at the annual meeting of the Academy of International Business, Stockholm, Sweden (July 10–13, 2004); Brian K. White, "Seattle Mariners Justify Losing Streak as 'Cunning,'" GlossyNews.com (July 15, 2004) (accessed November 6, 2004); "Japanese Owners Don't Want MLB in Control of World Cup," SportsLine.com wire reports (July 8, 2004) (accessed November 6, 2004); Harald Dolles and Sten Söderman, *Globalization of Sports—The Case of Professional Football and Its International Challenges* (Tokyo: German Institute for Japanese Studies, working paper, May 1, 2005).

2   For a good discussion of the versatility of the term *globalization,* see Joyce S. Osland, "Broadening the Debate: The Pros and Cons of Globalization," *Journal of Management Inquiry* 10:2 (June 2003): 137–54.

3   Sarah McBride, "Kia's Audacious Sorento Plan," *Wall Street Journal* (April 8, 2003): A12.

4   Sara Dickerman, "Air Supply: How Many Frequent-Flier Miles Did Your Dinner Earn?" *New York Times Style Magazine* (Fall 2004): 30.

5   Günther G. Schulze and Heinrich W. Ursprung, "Globalisation of the Economy and the Nation State," *The World Economy* 22:3 (May 1999): 295–352.

6   Robert O. Keohane and Joseph S. Nye, Jr., "Globalization: What's New? What's Not?" *Foreign Policy* 118 (Spring 2000): 104–19.

7   Martin Wolf, "Economic Globalisation," *Financial Times* (January 23, 2003): The World: 2003, section iii: 3.

8   For example, see OECD, *Measuring Globalisation: OECD Economic Globalisation Indicators* (Paris: OECD, 2005); Pim Martens and Daniel Zywietz, "Rethinking Globalization: A Modified Globalization Index," *Journal of International Development* 18:3 (2006): 331–50.

9   "The Globalization Index," *Foreign Policy* (November–December 2007): 68–76.

10 Betty Liu, "Cross-Border Partnerships," *Financial Times* (March 14, 2003): 9.

11 Antonio Regalado and Lauren Etter, "Brazil Food Merger Creates Export Giant," *Wall Street Journal* (May 20, 2009): B2.

12 See Rodney C. Shrader, Benjamin M. Oviatt, and Patricia Phillips McDougall, "How New Ventures Exploit Trade-Offs among International Risk Factors: Lessons for the Accelerated Internationalization of the 21st Century," *Academy of Management Journal* 43:6 (2000): 1227–47; Ian Fillis, "The Internationalization Process of the Craft Microenterprise," *Journal of Developmental Entrepreneurship* 7:1 (2002): 25–43; Michael Copeland, "The Mighty Micro Multinational," *Business 2.0 Magazine* (July 28, 2006): n.p.

13 S. Tamer Cavusgil, "Extending the Reach of E-Business," *Marketing Management* (March–April 2002): 24–29.

14 Stephanie A. Fernhaber, Brett Anitra Gilbert, and Patricia P. McDougall, "International Entrepreneurship and Geographic Location: An Empirical Examination of New Venture Internationalization," *Journal of International Business Studies* 39:2 (2008): 267–90.

15 Dan McGraw, "The Foreign Invasion of the American Game," *The Village Voice* (May 28–June 3, 2003) (accessed June 4, 2007).

16 Kerry Gildea, "U.S., Japan Review Options for Future Sea-Based Missile Defense Work," *Defense Daily International* (July 12, 2002): 1–2.

17 Michael M. Phillips, "G-8 Nations Shape Plan to Fight Diseases," *Wall Street Journal* (February 13, 2006): A8.

18 Thomas L. Friedman, "Moving with the Herd," *Computerworld* (January 15, 2001): 41–43; Daniele Archiburgi and Bengt-Ake Lundvall, eds., *The Globalizing Learning Economy* (Oxford: Oxford University Press, 2001).

19 For a long time, the group was the *G7*, including Canada, France, Germany, Italy, Japan, United Kingdom, and United States; it became the *G8* when Russia started to attend meetings. There is also the *G20*, which includes the *G8* plus Argentina, Australia, Brazil, China, India, Indonesia, Mexico, Saudi Arabia, South Africa, South Korea, Turkey, and one seat for the European Union.

20 Guy Chazan, "Norwegian Oil Firm Goes to Energy's Last Frontier," *Wall Street Journal* (February 13, 2009): B1+.

21 Robert Wright, "Somali Pirates Seize Two Tankers," *Financial Times* (March 27, 2009): 2.

22 Susan Carey, "Calculating Costs in the Clouds," *Wall Street Journal* (March 6, 2007): B1+.

23 His views are discussed in Joellen Perry, "Nobel Laureates Say Globalization's Winners Should Aid Poor," *Wall Street Journal* (August 25, 2008): 2.

24 Lorraine Eden and Stefanie Lenway, "Introduction to the Symposium Multinationals: The Janus Face of Globalization," *Journal of International Business Studies* 32:3 (2001): 383–400.

25 His views are discussed in Joellen Perry, "Nobel Laureates Say Globalization's Winners Should Aid Poor," *Wall Street Journal* (August 25, 2008): 2.

26 Steve Lohr, "An Elder Challenges Outsourcing's Orthodoxy," *New York Times* (September 9, 2004): C1+; Paul A. Samuelson, "Where Ricardo and Mill Rebut and Confirm Arguments of Mainstream Economists Supporting Globalization," *Journal of Economic Perspectives* 18:3 (Summer 2004): 135–47.

27 An examination of this subject may be found in Arne Kalleberg, "Precarious Work, Insecure Workers: Employment Relations in Transition," *American Sociological Review* 74:1 (2009): 1–22.

28 Bernhard G. Gunter and Rolph van der Hoeven, "The Social Dimension of Globalization: A Review of the Literature," *International Labour Review* 143:1/2 (2004): 7–43.

29 Jagdish Bhagwati, "Anti-Globalization: Why?" *Journal of Policy Modeling* 26:4 (2004): 439–64.

30 Craig Karmin, "Offshoring Can Generate Jobs in the U.S.," *Wall Street Journal* (March 16, 2004): B1.

31 William M. Bulkeley, "IBM Documents Give Rare Look at 'Offshoring,'" *Wall Street Journal* (January 19, 2004): A1+; William M. Bulkeley, "IBM to Cut U.S. Jobs, Expand in India," *Wall Street Journal* (March 26, 2009): B1.

32 Richard Waters, "Big Blueprint for IBM," *Financial Times* (March 3, 2009): 14.

33 N. Gregory Mankiw and Phillip Swagel, "The Politics and Economics of Offshore Outsourcing," NBR Working Paper No. 12398 (July 2006); Kristien Coucke and Leo Sleuwaegen, "Offshoring as a Survival Strategy: Evidence from Manufacturing Firms in Belgium," *Journal of International Business Studies* 39:8 (2008): 1261–77.

34 Matthew J. Slaughter, "Globalization and Employment by U.S. Multinationals: A Framework and Facts," *Daily Tax Report* (March 26, 2004): 1–12.

35 Robert C. Feenstra and Gordon H. Hanson, "The Impact of Outsourcing and High-Technology Capital on Wages: Estimates for the United States, 1979–1990," *Quarterly Journal of Economics* 114:3 (1999): 907–40.

36 Alan S. Brown, "A Shift in Engineering Offshore," *Mechanical Engineering* 131:3 (2009): 24–29.

37 Timothy Aeppel, "Coming Home: Appliance Maker Drops China to Produce in Texas," *Wall Street Journal* (August 24, 2009): B1+; Linda Tucci, "Offshoring Has Long Way to Go," *CIO News Headlines* (June 2, 2005): n.p.; Alexandra Harney, "Travel Industry," *Financial Times* (September 2, 2004): 11; Paulo Prada and Niraj Sheth, "Delta Air Ends Use of India Call Centers," *Wall Street Journal* (April 18–19, 2009): B1+.

38 Marcus Walker, "Just How Good Is Globalization?" *Wall Street Journal* (January 25, 2007): A10, referring to data from Morgan Stanley Research.

39 Deborah Solomon, "Federal Aid Does Little for Free Trade's Losers," *Wall Street Journal* (March 1, 2007): A1+.

40 Paul Windrum, Andreas Reinstaller, and Christopher Bull, "The Outsourcing Productivity Paradox: Total Outsourcing, Organisational Innovation, and Long Run Productivity Growth," *Journal of Evolutionary Economics* 19:2 (2009): 197–232.

41 Carlos Tejada, "Paradise Lost," *Wall Street Journal* (August 14, 2003): A1+.

42 Alan S. Blinder, "Offshoring: The Next Industrial Revolution," *Foreign Affairs* 85:2 (March–April 2006): 113–22; David Wessel and Bob Davis, "Working Theory," *Wall Street Journal* (March 28, 2007): A1+ (discussing studies by Alan S. Binder); A. Hilsenrath, "Forrester Revises Loss Estimates to Overseas Jobs," *Wall Street Journal* (May 17, 2004): A8; J. Kirkegaard, "Offshoring, Outsourcing, and Production Relocation—Labor-Market Effects in the OECD Countries and Developing Asia," Working Paper No. 07–2 (Washington: Peterson Institute for International Economics, 2007).

43 United Nations Conference on Trade and Development, *World Investment Report 2001: Promoting Linkages* (New York and Geneva: United Nations, 2001): 90–92.

44 Karen E. Thuermer, "Small Business Takes to Export," *World Trade* 21:12 (2008): 40–43.

45 Phillip Hersh, "Sewing Circles," *Chicago Tribune* (July 15, 2003): n.p.

46 Bill Breen, "Driven by Design," *Fast Company* 117 (2007): 104–109.

47 Heather Berry, "Leaders, Laggards, and the Pursuit of Foreign Knowledge," *Strategic Management Journal* 27 (2006): 151–68.

48 Jaeyong Song and Jongtae Shin, "The Paradox of Technological Capabilities: A Knowledge Sourcing from Host Countries of Overseas R&D Operations," *Journal of International Business Studies* 39:2 (2008): 291–303.

49 Nery Ynclan, "Avon Is Opening the Door to Spanglish," *Miami Herald* (July 23, 2002): E1.

50 Sharon Terlep, "GM Sales Fell 11% in '08," *Wall Street Journal* (January 22, 2009): B3.

51 Jonathan Birchall, "Tesco to Bring Its Own Suppliers to US," *Financial Times* (November 24, 2006): 21.

52 "Contract Will Be Signed in April with Bechtel to Carry Out First Nuclear Plant," *Info—Prod Research* (March 30, 2009): n.p.

53 United Nations Conference on Trade and Development, *World Investment Report 2008: Transnational Corporations, and the Infrastructure Challenge* (New York and Geneva: United Nations, 2008): xvi.

54 Michael V. Copeland, "The Mighty Micro-Multinational," *Business 2.0* 7:6 (2006):106–115.

55 Linn Hirschberg, "Is the Face of America That of a Green Ogre?" *New York Times Magazine* (November 14, 2004): 90–94.

56 Gabriel Kahn, "How to Slow Down a Ferrari: Buy It," *Wall Street Journal* (May 8, 2007): B1+.

57 John Willman, "Multinationals," *Financial Times* (February 25, 2003): Comment & Analysis, ii.

58 Edward Luce, "Hard Sell to a Billion Consumers," *Financial Times* (April 25, 2002): 14.

59 David Wessel and Marcus Walker, "Good News for the Globe," *Wall Street Journal* (September 3, 2004): A7+.

60 Alan M. Rugman and Cecelia Brain, "Multinational Enterprises Are Regional, Not Global," *Multinational Business Review* 11:1 (2004): 3.

61 John Ralston Saul, "The Collapse of Globalism," *Harpers* (March 2004): 33–43; James Harding, "Globalisation's Children Strike Back," *Financial Times* (September 11, 2001): 4; Bob Davis, "Wealth of Nations," *Wall Street Journal* (March 29, 2004): A1; Harold James, *The End of Globalisation: Lessons from the Great Depression* (Cambridge, MA: Harvard University Press, 2001).

62 Alessandra Rizzo, "U.N.: World's Hungry Now at Historic Levels," *Miami Herald* (June 20, 2009): 10A, using data from the U.N. Food and Agricultural Organization.

63 "Historical Crude Oil Prices," InflationData.com, http://inflationdata.com/inflation_Rate/Historical_Oil_Prices_Table.asp (January 8, 2009) (accessed April 8, 2009).

64 Larry Rohter, "Shipping Costs Start to Crimp Globalization," *New York Times* (August 3, 2009): 1+.

65 John Miller, "Nations Rush to Establish New Barriers to Trade," *Wall Street Journal* (February 6, 2009): A1.

66 On the schism between those who thrive in a globalized environment and those who don't, see Jagdish Bhagwati, "Anti-Globalization: Why?" *Journal of Policy Modeling* 26:4 (2004): 439–64; Roger Sugden and James R. Wilson, "Economic Globalisation: Dialectics, Conceptualisation and Choice," *Contributions to Political Economy* 24:1 (2005): 13–32; J. Ørstrøm Møller, "Wanted: A New Strategy for Globalization," *The Futurist* (January–February 2004): 20–22.

67 *Sources include the following:* We'd like to acknowledge the invaluable assistance of Brenda Yester, vice president of Carnival Cruise Lines. Other sources include Pan Kwan Yuk, "Carnival Outlook Down on Discounts," *Financial Times* (March 25, 2009): 16; Tom Stieghorst, *McClatchy-Tribune Business News* (March 21, 2008): n.p.; "Carnival Cruise Lines; Carnival Experiencing Dramatic Increase on On-Line Shore Excursion Sales," *Entertainment & Travel* (March 26, 2008): 168; "The Wave Rolls On; Carnival Cruise Lines Reports Record Booking Week," *PR Newswire* (March 3, 2009): n.p.; Martha Brannigan, "Cruise Lines Aim for Wider Appeal," *Knight Ridder Tribune Business News* (March 14, 2007): 1; "Carnival Scrubs Ship after Virus Sickens Nearly 700 Passengers," *Wall Street Journal* (November 20, 2006): n.p.; Cruise Lines International Association, "Cruise Industry Overview," Marketing Edition 2006, www.cruising.org/press/overview%202006.cfm (accessed May 9, 2007); "Who's Who in Cruising," *Caterer and Hotelkeeper* (February 26, 2004): 77; Donald Urquhart, "Greed and Corruption Rooted in Flag of Convenience System," *The Business Times Singapore* (March 9, 2001): n.p.; "Fall 2003: Shipbuilding Back on Course?" www.CruiseIndustryNews.com-Cruise (accessed November 19, 2004); Daniel Grant, "Onboard Art," *American Artist* (March 2003): 18; Nicole Harris, "Ditching the Cruise Director," *Wall Street Journal* (April 22, 2004): D1+; Douglas Frantz, "Sovereign Islands," *Miami Herald* (February 19, 1999): A1+; Rana Foroohar et al., "The Road Less Traveled," *Newsweek* (May 26, 2003): 40; Cruise Lines International Association, "The Overview, Spring 2004," msword/reports/overviews/spring04OV.doc.

An Atlas

Satellite television transmission now makes it commonplace for us to watch events as they unfold in other countries. Transportation and communication advances and government-to-government accords have contributed to our increasing dependence on foreign goods and markets. As this dependence grows, updated maps are a valuable tool. They can show the locations of population, economic wealth, production, and markets; portray certain commonalities and differences among areas; and illustrate barriers that might inhibit trade. In spite of the usefulness of maps, a substantial number of people worldwide have a poor knowledge of how to interpret information on maps and even of how to find the location of events that affect their lives.

We urge you to use the following maps to build your awareness of geography.

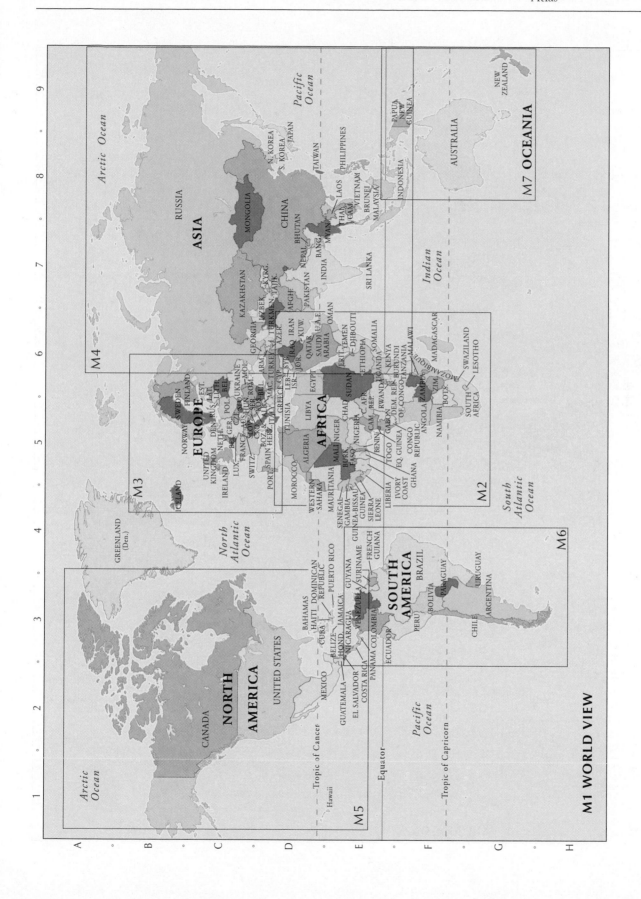

M1 WORLD VIEW

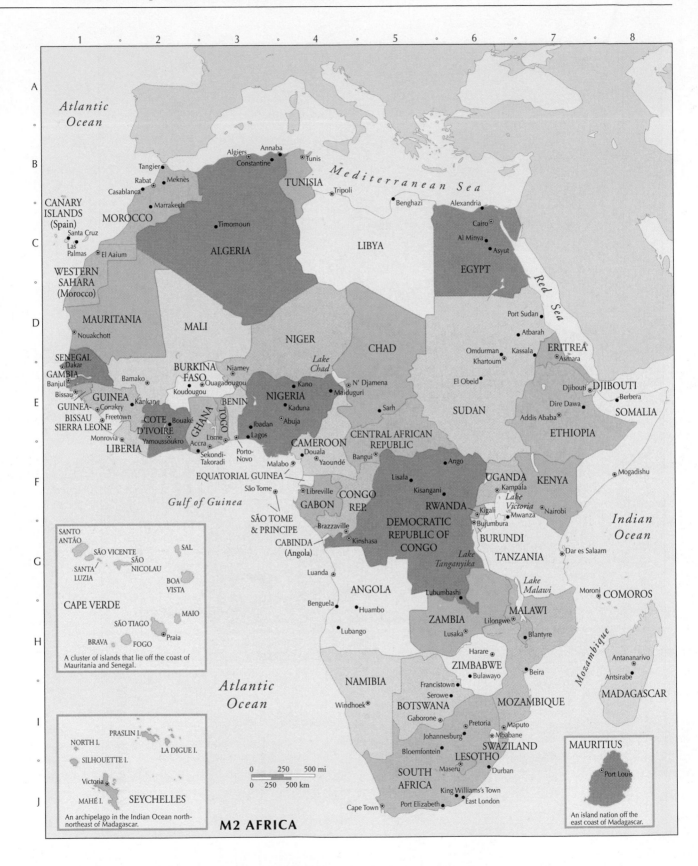

M2 AFRICA

M3 EUROPE

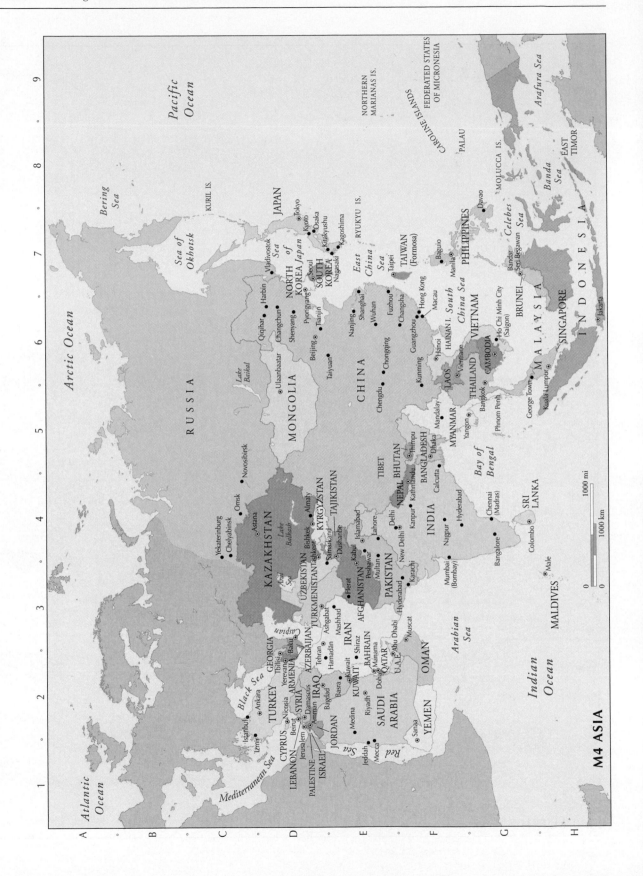

M4 ASIA

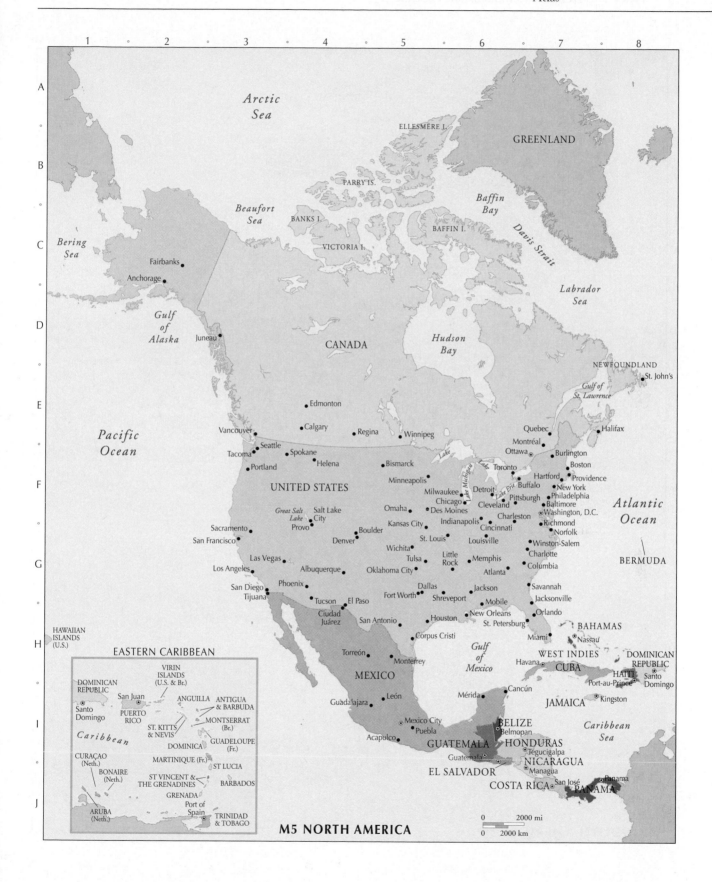

1   2   3   4   5   6   7   8

A

Arctic
Sea

ELLESMÈRE I.

GREENLAND

B

PARRY IS.

Beaufort
Sea

BANKS I.

Baffin
Bay

VICTORIA I.

BAFFIN I.

Davis Strait

C

Bering
Sea

Fairbanks

Anchorage

Labrador
Sea

D

Gulf
of
Alaska

Juneau

CANADA

Hudson
Bay

NEWFOUNDLAND

St. John's

Gulf of
St. Lawrence

E

Edmonton

Pacific
Ocean

Vancouver

Calgary

Regina

Winnipeg

Quebec

Halifax

Montréal

Seattle

Spokane

Ottawa

Burlington

Tacoma

Helena

Bismarck

Lake

Toronto

Boston

Portland

Lake Michigan

Buffalo

Hartford

Providence

F

UNITED STATES

Minneapolis

Milwaukee

Chicago

Detroit

Lake Erie

Pittsburgh

New York

Philadelphia

Cleveland

Baltimore

Great Salt
Lake

Salt Lake
City

Omaha

Des Moines

Charleston

Washington, D.C.

Atlantic
Ocean

Sacramento

Provo

Kansas City

Indianapolis

Cincinnati

Richmond

San Francisco

Boulder

St. Louis

Louisville

Norfolk

Denver

Wichita

Winston-Salem

Las Vegas

Tulsa

Little
Rock

Memphis

Charlotte

BERMUDA

G

Los Angeles

Albuquerque

Oklahoma City

Atlanta

Columbia

Phoenix

Dallas

Jackson

Savannah

San Diego

Fort Worth

Shreveport

Jacksonville

Tijuana

Tucson

El Paso

Mobile

Orlando

Ciudad
Juárez

San Antonio

New Orleans

St. Petersburg

BAHAMAS

Corpus Cristi

Houston

Miami

Nassau

H

HAWAIIAN
ISLANDS
(U.S.)

Torreón

Gulf
of
Mexico

WEST INDIES

DOMINICAN
REPUBLIC

EASTERN CARIBBEAN

Monterrey

Havana

CUBA

HAITI

Santo
Domingo

VIRIN
ISLANDS
(U.S. & Br.)

MEXICO

Mérida

Cancún

Port-au-Prince

DOMINICAN
REPUBLIC

San Juan

ANGUILLA

ANTIGUA
& BARBUDA

León

JAMAICA

Kingston

Santo
Domingo

PUERTO
RICO

MONTSERRAT
(Br.)

Guadalajara

I

Caribbean

ST. KITTS
& NEVIS

GUADELOUPE
(Fr.)

Mexico City

Puebla

BELIZE

Belmopan

Caribbean
Sea

DOMINICA

Acapulco

CURAÇAO
(Neth.)

MARTINIQUE (Fr.)

GUATEMALA

HONDURAS

BONAIRE
(Neth.)

ST VINCENT &
THE GRENADINES

ST LUCIA

Guatemala

Tegucigalpa

NICARAGUA

BARBADOS

EL SALVADOR

Managua

J

ARUBA
(Neth.)

GRENADA

Port of
Spain

TRINIDAD
& TOBAGO

COSTA RICA

San José

Panama

PANAMA

0   2000 mi

0   2000 km

M5 NORTH AMERICA

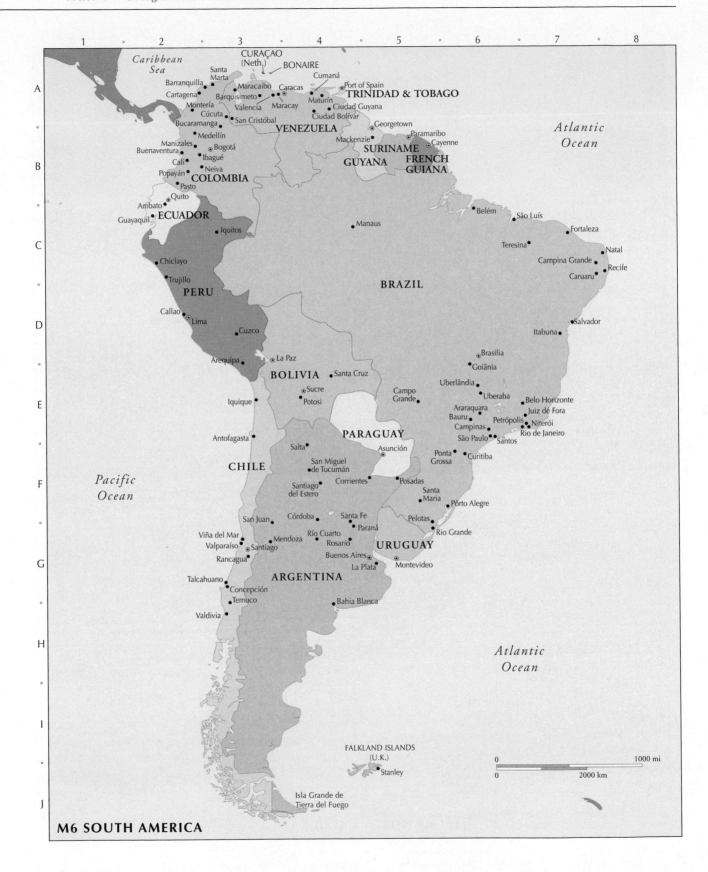

M6 SOUTH AMERICA

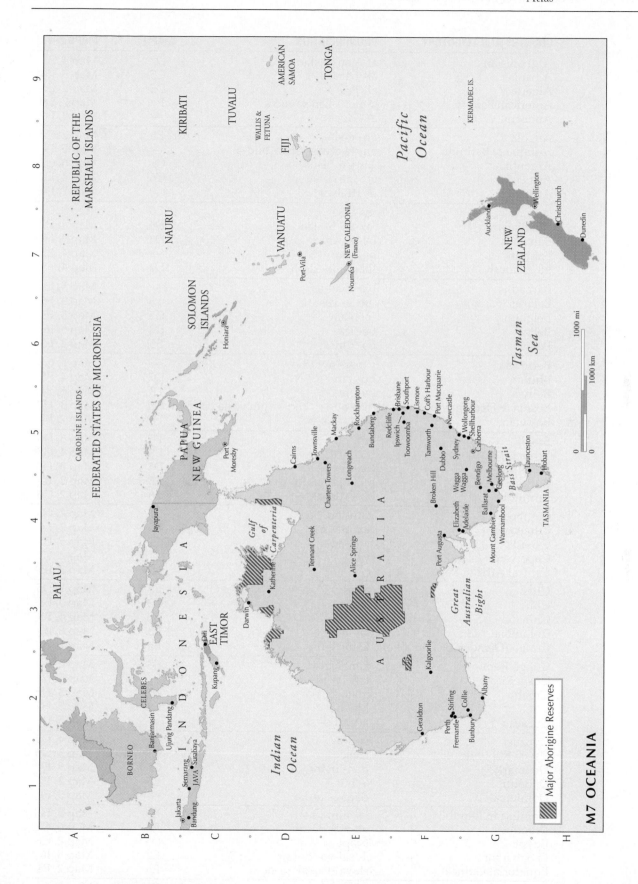

M7 OCEANIA

Major Aborigine Reserves

COUNTRY AND TERRITORY	PRONUNCIATION	MAP 1	MAPS 2–7
Afghanistan	af-´gan-ə-,stan	D7	Map 4, E3
Albania	al-´bā-nē-ə	C5	Map 3, I5
Algeria	al-´jir-ē-ə	D5	Map 2, C3
American Samoa	ə-mer´i-kən sə-mō´ə	F9	Map 7, D9
Andorra	an-´dȯr-ə	—	Map 3, H2
Angola	an-´gō-lə	E5	Map 2, G4
Antigua & Barbuda	an-´tē-g(w)ə / bär-´büd-ə	—	Map 5, I3
Argentina	,,är-jen-´tē-nə	G3	Map 6, G3
Armenia	är-´mē-ne-ə	C6	Map 4, D2
Australia	ȯ-´strāl-yə	G8	Map 7, E4
Austria	´ȯs-trē-ə	C5	Map 3, G4
Azerbaijan	´az-ər-´bī-jän	D6	Map 4, D2
Bahamas	bə-hä´-məz	D3	Map 5, H7
Bahrain	bä-´rān	—	Map 4, E2
Bangladesh	´bänJ-glə-´desh	D7	Map 4, F5
Barbados	bär-´b̄ād-əs	—	Map 5, J3
Belarus	´bē-lə-´rüs	C5	Map 3, F6
Belgium	´bel-jəm	C5	Map 3, F3
Belize	bə-´lēz	D2	Map 5, I6
Benin	bə-´nin	E5	Map 2, E3
Bermuda	(´)bər-´myüd-ə	—	Map 5, G8
Bhutan	bü-´tan	D7	Map 4, F5
Bolivia	bə-´liv-ē-ə	F3	Map 6, E4
Bosnia & Herzegovina	´bäz-nē-ə / ´hert-sə-gō-´vē-nə	D5	Map 3, H5
Botswana	bät-´swän-ə	F5	Map 2, I5
Brazil	brə-´zil	F3	Map 6, D6
Brunei	brōo-nī´	E8	Map 4, G7
Bulgaria	´bəl-´gar-ē-ə	D5	Map 3, H6
Burkina Faso	bu`r-´kē-nə-´fa`-sō	E5	Map 2, E2
Burundi	bu`-´rün-dē	E6	Map 2, G6
Cambodia	kam-´bd-ē-ə	E7	Map 4, G5
Cameroon	´kam-ə-´rün	E5	Map 2, F4
Canada	´kan-əd-ə	C2	Map 5, E5
Cape Verde Islands	´vard	—	Map 2, G1
Central African Rep.		E5	Map 2, E5
Chad	´chad	E5	Map 2, D5
Chile	´chil-ē	G3	Map 6, F3
China	´chī-nə	D8	Map 4, E5
Colombia	kə-´ləm-bē-ə	E3	Map 6, B3
Congo (Democratic Republic)	´känJ(´)gō	E5	Map 2, G5
Congo Republic	´känJ(´)gō	E5	Map 2, F4
Costa Rica	´käs-tə-´rē-kə	E2	Map 5, J7
Croatia	krō-´ā-sh(ē)ə	D5	Map 3, H5
Cuba	´kyü-bə	E3	Map 5, H7
Curaçao	´k(y)ür-ə-´sō	—	Map 5, J1
Cyprus	´sī-prəs	D6	Map 4, D2
Czech Republic	´chek	C5	Map 3, G5
Denmark	´den-´märk	C5	Map 3, E4
Djibouti	jə-´büt-ē	E6	Map 2, E7
Dominica	´däm-ə-´nē-kə	—	Map 5, I3
Dominican Republic	də-´min-i-kən	E3	Map 5, H8
Ecuador	´ek-wə-´dȯ(ə)r	E3	Map 6, C2
Egypt	´ē-jəpt	D5	Map 2, C6
El Salvador	el-´sal-və-´dȯ(ə)r	E2	Map 5, I6
Equatorial Guinea	ē-kwa´-tōr-ēal `gi-nē	E5	Map 2, F4
Eritrea	´er-ə-´trē-ə	E6	Map 2, E6
Estonia	e-´stō-nē-ə	C5	Map 3, E6

COUNTRY AND TERRITORY	PRONUNCIATION	MAP 1	MAPS 2–7
Ethiopia	´ē-thē-´ō-pē-ə	E6	Map 2, E7
Falkland Islands	´fȯ(l)-klənd	—	Map 6, J4
Fiji	´fē-jē	—	Map 7, D8
Finland	´fin-lənd	B5	Map 3, C6
France	´fran(t)s	C5	Map 3, G3
French Guiana	gē-´an-ə	E3	Map 6, B5
Gabon	ga-´bōⁿ	E5	Map 2, F4
Gambia	´gam-bē-ə	E4	Map 2, E1
Georgia	´jȯr-jə	C6	Map 4, D2
Germany	´jerm-(ə-)nē	C5	Map 3, F4
Ghana	´gän-ə	E5	Map 2, E2
Greece	´grēs	D5	Map 3, I6
Greenland	´grēn-lənd	A4	Map 5, E7
Grenada	grə-nā´də	—	Map 5, J3
Guatemala	´gwät-ə-´mäl-ə	E2	Map 5, I6
Guinea	´gin-ē	E4	Map 2, E1
Guinea-Bissau	´gin-ē-bis-´au˙	E4	Map 2, E1
Guyana	gī-´an-ə	E3	Map 6, B4
Haiti	´hāt-ē	E3	Map 5, H8
Honduras	hän-´d(y)u˙r-əs	E2	Map 5, I7
Hong Kong	´hänJ-´känJ	—	Map 4, F6
Hungary	´hənJ-g(ə)rē	C5	Map 3, G5
Iceland	´ī-slənd	B4	Map 3, B1
India	´in-dê-ə	D7	Map 4, F4
Indonesia	´in-də-´nē-zhə	E8	Map 4, H7; Map 7, B3
Iran	i-´rän	D6	Map 4, E3
Iraq	i-´räk	D6	Map 4, D2
Ireland	´ī(ə)r-lənd	C5	Map 3, F1
Israel	´iz-rē-əl	D6	Map 4, D2
Italy	´it-əl-ē	D6	Map 3, H4
Ivory Coast	ī´və-rē	E5	Map 2, E2
Jamaica	jə-´mā-kə	E3	Map 5, I7
Japan	jə-´pan	D8	Map 4, D7
Jordan	´jȯrd-ən	D6	Map 4, D2
Kazakhstan	kə-´zak-´stan	D7	Map 4, D4
Kenya	´ken-yə	E6	Map 7, F7
Kiribati	kîr-ì-bàs´	—	Map 7, B8
Korea, North	kə-´rē-ə	D8	Map 4, D7
Korea, South	kə-´rē-ə	D8	Map 4, D7
Kosovo	´Ko-sō-vō	C5	Map M3, H6
Kuwait	kə-´wāt	D6	Map 4, E2
Kyrgyzstan	kîr-gē-stän´	D7	Map 4, D4
Laos	´lau˙s	D7	Map 4, F5
Latvia	´lat-vē-ə	C5	Map 3, E6
Lebanon	´leb-ə-nən	D6	Map 4, D2
Lesotho	lə-´sō-(´)tō	F6	Map 2, J6
Liberia	lī-´bir-ē-ə	E5	Map 2, F2
Libya	´lib-ē-ə	D5	Map 2, C4
Liechtenstein	lìk´tən-stīn´	—	Map 3, G4
Lithuania	´lith-(y)ə-´wā-nē-ə	C5	Map 3, E6
Luxembourg	´lək-səm-´bərg	C5	Map 3, G3
Macedonia	´mas-ə-´dō-nyə	D6	Map 3, I6
Madagascar	´mad-ə-´gas-kər	F6	Map 2, I8
Malawi	mə-´lä-wē	F6	Map 2, H6

COUNTRY AND TERRITORY	PRONUNCIATION	MAP 1	MAPS 2–7
Malaysia	mə-ˈlā-zh(ē-)ə	E8	Map 4, G6
Maldives	môlˊdīvz	—	Map 4, H3
Mali	ˊmäl-ē	D5	Map 2, D2
Malta	ˊmȯl-tə	—	Map 3, J5
Marshall Islands	märˊshəl	—	Map 7, A8
Mauritania	ˊmȯr-ə-ˊtā-nē-ə	D5	Map 2, D1
Mauritius	mȯ-ˊrishˊəs	—	Map 2, J8
Mexico	ˊmek-si-ˊkō	D2	Map 5, I5
Micronesia	mīˊkrō-nēˊzhə	—	Map 7, A5
Moldova	mäl-ˊdō-və	D6	Map 3, G7
Mongolia	män-ˊgōl-yə	D8	Map 4, D5
Morocco	mə-ˊräk-(ˊ)ō	D5	Map 2, B2
Mozambique	ˊmō-zəm-ˊbēk	F6	Map 2, H6
Myanmar	ˊmyän-ˊmär	E7	Map 4, F5
Namibia	nə-ˊmib-ē-ə	F5	Map 2, I4
Naura	näˊ-ü-rü	—	Map 7, B7
Nepal	nə-ˊpȯl	D7	Map 4, E4
Netherlands	ˊneth-ər-lən(d)z	C5	Map 3, F3
New Caledonia	ˊkal-ə-ˊdō-nyə	—	Map 7, E7
New Zealand	ˊzē-lənd	G9	Map 7, H7
Nicaragua	ˊnik-ə-ˊräg-wə	E3	Map 5, I7
Niger	ˊnī-jər	E5	Map 2, D4
Nigeria	nī-ˊjir-ē-ə	E5	Map 2, E4
Norway	ˊnȯ(ə)r-ˊwā	C5	Map 3, D3
Oman	ō-ˊmän	E6	Map 4, F2
Pakistan	ˊpak-i-ˊstan	D7	Map 4, E3
Palau	pä-louˊ	—	Map 7, A3
Palestine	pa-lə-ˊstīn	—	Map 4, D1
Panama	ˊpan-ə-ˊmä	E3	Map 5, J8
Papua New Guinea	ˊpap-yə-wə	F9	Map 7, C5
Paraguay	ˊpar-ə-ˊgwī	F3	Map 6, E4
Peru	pə-ˊrü	F3	Map 6, D2
Philippines	ˊfil-ə-ˊpēnz	E8	Map 4, F7
Poland	ˊpō-lənd	D5	Map 3, F5
Portugal	ˊpōr-chi-gəl	D5	Map 3, I1
Puerto Rico	ˊpōrt-ə-ˊrē(ˊ)kō	E3	Map 5, I2
Qatar	ˊkät-ər	D6	Map 4, E2
Romania	rō-ˊä-nē-ə	D5	Map 3, H6
Russia	ˊrəsh-ə	C7	Map 3, D7; Map 4, C5
Rwanda	ruˋ-ˊän-də	E6	Map 2, F6
St. Kitts & Nevis	ˊkits / ˊnē-vəs	—	Map 5, I3
St. Lucia	sänt-ˊlü-shə	—	Map 5, I3
St. Vincent and the Grenadines	grènˊə-dēnzˊ	—	Map 5, J3
San Marino	sàn mə-rēˊnō	—	Map 3, H4
São Tomé and Príncipe	soun tōə-mèˊprēnˊ-sēpə	—	Map 2, F3
Saudi Arabia	ˊsauˋd-ē	E6	Map 4, E2
Senegal	ˊsen-i-ˊgˋl	E4	Map 2, D1
Serbia & Montenegro	ˊsər-bē-ə / ˊmän-tə-ˊnē-grō	D5	Map 3, H2
Seychelles	sā-shèlzˊ	—	Map 2, J1
Sierra Leone	sē-ˊer-ə-lē-ˊōn	E4	Map 2, E1
Singapore	ˊsinJ-(g)ə-ˊpō(ə)r	—	Map 4, H6
Slovakia	slō-ˊväk-ē-ə	C5	Map 3, G5
Slovenia	slō-ˊvēn-ē-ə	C5	Map 3, H5
Solomon Islands	ˊsäl-ə-mən	—	Map 7, C6
Somalia	sō-ˊmäl-ē-ə	E6	Map 2, F8

COUNTRY AND TERRITORY	PRONUNCIATION	MAP 1	MAPS 2–7
South Africa	´a-fri-kə	F6	Map 2, J5
Spain	´spāpn	C5	Map 3, I1
Sri Lanka	(´)srē-´länJ-kə	E7	Map 4, G4
Sudan	sü-´dan	E6	Map 2, E6
Suriname	su˙r-ə-´näm-ə	E3	Map 6, B5
Swaziland	´swäz-ē-´land	F6	Map 2, I6
Sweden	´swēd-ən	B5	Map 3, C5
Switzerland	´swit-sər-lənd	C5	Map 3, G4
Syria	´sir-ē-ə	D6	Map 4, D2
Taiwan	´tī-´wän	D8	Map 4, E7
Tajikistan	tä-´ji-ki-´stan	D7	Map 4, E4
Tanzania	´tan-zə-´nē-ə	F6	Map 2, G6
Thailand	´tī-land	E8	Map 4, F5
Togo	´tō(´)gō	E5	Map 2, E3
Tonga	´tän-gə	—	Map 7, D9
Trinidad & Tobago	´trin-ə-´dad / tə-´bā-(´)gō	—	Map 5, J3
Tunisia	t(y)ü-´nē-zh(ē-)ə	D5	Map 2, B4
Turkey	´tər-kē	D6	Map 4, D2
Turkmenistan	tûrk´-men-i-stàn´	D6	Map 4, D3
Tuvalu	tü´-vä-lü	—	Map 7, C9
Uganda	(y)ü-´gan-də	E6	Map 2, F6
Ukraine	yü-´krän	C6	Map 3, F7
United Arab Emirates	yoo-nī´tid à r´əb i-mîr´its	D6	Map 4, E2
United Kingdom	king´dəm	C5	Map 3, F2
United States	yu˙-´nīt-əd-´stāts	D2	Map 5, F5
Uruguay	´(y)u˙r-ə-gwī	G3	Map 6, G5
Uzbekistan	(´)u˙z-´bek-i-´stan	C6	Map 4, D3
Vanuatu	van-ə-´wät-(´)ü	—	Map 7, D7
Vatican City	vàt´ i-kən	—	Map 3, H4
Venezuela	´ven-əz(-ə)-´wā-lə	E3	Map 6, A4
Vietnam	vē-´et-´näm	E8	Map 4, G6
Western Sahara	sə-hâr´ə	D4	Map 2, C1
Yemen	´yem-ən	E6	Map 4, F2
Zambia	´zam-bē-ə	F5	Map 2, H5
Zimbabwe	zim-´bäb-wē	F6	Map 2, H6

two

The Cultural Environments Facing Business

Objectives

- To understand methods for learning about cultural environments

- To analyze the major causes of cultural difference and change

- To discuss behavioral factors influencing countries' business practices

- To understand cultural guidelines for companies that operate internationally

Follow and adjust to current customs in order to get along with others.

—Philippine proverb

converted revenue-generating space into an area for prayer. McDonald's dims its lights, closes its doors, and suspends service during the five times per day when Muslim men are called to prayer.

Of course, not all business-related adjustments are due to religious principles. In most cultures, personal interactions are often tricky. Here's an interesting example between Saudis and non-Saudis. British publisher Parris-Rogers International (PRI) dispatched two salesmen to Saudi Arabia. Because of being paid on commission, they moved aggressively, figuring they could make the same number of calls—and sales—per day as they made in Britain. Back home, they were used to punctual schedules, the undivided attention of potential clients, and conversations devoted only to business transactions. To them, time was money. In Saudi Arabia, however, they soon found that appointments seldom began on time and usually took place at local cafés over casual cups of coffee. As far as they were concerned, Saudis spent too much time in idle chitchat, and to make matters worse, they would turn their attention to personal acquaintances rather than continuing with business. Eventually, both salesmen began showing their irritation. Before long, their Saudi counterparts came to regard them as rude and impatient, and their employer had to recall them.

Foreign workers can also be traumatized by certain Saudi practices, especially when it comes to legal sanctions. Not only are there patrols to police female apparel, but people's hands and heads (151 of the latter in 2007) are occasionally cut off in public. Passersby are expected to observe the execution of these punishments, some of which are occasioned by crimes that don't constitute offenses in other countries, such as abandoning one's religion or practicing homosexuality.

Rules of behavior may also be hard to comprehend because of the ways in which religious and legal rules have been adapted to contemporary situations. Islamic law, for instance, forbids charging interest and selling accident insurance (strict doctrine holds that there are no accidents, only preordained acts of God). In the case of mortgages, the Saudi government gets around this proscription by offering interest-free loans. The solution seems to work well enough when the country is awash with oil revenue, but when oil prices fall, would-be homeowners must wait years for a loan. As for accident insurance, the government has simply eliminated the prohibition because Saudi businesses, like businesses everywhere, need the coverage.

Such flexibility is particularly common when dealing with foreigners and foreign companies. Saudis, for instance, are more lenient about visiting female executives than Saudi women in general. An example of this is disallowing Saudi women to work as flight attendants on Saudi Arabian Airlines (where they would have to work alongside men) while permitting women from other Arab countries to do so. In foreign investment compounds, where almost everyone is a foreigner, religious patrols make exceptions to most strict religious prescriptions.

Back at the Java Lounge, we're happy to report that business has been successful. This is primarily because its entrepreneurs spent the time and money to research their expectation that enough Saudis had become sufficiently westernized and affluent to frequent the restaurant. In fact, there are enough modernized high-income people in the country to sustain a market for Parisian haute couture. Even though Saudi Arabia prohibits fashion magazines and movies, this clientele knows what is and isn't fashionable, largely through growth in Internet usage and the ownership of forbidden satellite dishes in an estimated two-thirds of Saudi homes. Women buy items from designer collections, which they wear abroad or—when in Saudi Arabia—in front of husbands and other women. Underneath their *abayas,* they often sport expensive jewelry, makeup, and clothing. When traveling abroad, Saudi men also favor the latest high-end fashions.

The owners of the Java Lounge also realized that, as more Saudis interact with foreigners and the country strives for economic growth, there will be changes in domestic cultural and social values. These changes are particularly apparent in the book *Leaders of Saudi Arabia,* which highlights the backgrounds and philosophies of 140 Saudi leaders, both male and female. Bear in mind, however, that changes tend to be uneven, particularly differing among geographic areas of the country and among people of certain income and educational levels. As for the entrepreneurs of the Java Lounge, conditions have rewarded their foresight, but they remain carefully attuned to a variety of cultural and social norms that continue to characterize life in Saudi Arabia.

CRN
Case Review Note

Introduction

Our opening case shows how important it is for companies to understand and be sensitive to ever-changing operating environments. Figure 2.1 shows how **culture**—learned norms based on the values, attitudes, and beliefs of a group of people—is an integral part of a nation's operating environment. Culture is sometimes an elusive topic to study. Why? Because people belong to different groups, and each group comprises a culture. These groups are based on nationality, ethnicity, religion, gender, work organization, profession, age, political party membership, and income level. (You've undoubtedly heard the term *youth culture*, which refers to a group designated by age.) In this chapter, we emphasize the nature of *national cultures*; however, we also discuss other cultural memberships, especially as they differ from country to country.

Concept Check

In Chapter 1, we explain that *behavioral factors*, values, attitudes, and beliefs can be studied as keys both to cultural conditions and to ways of developing suitable business practices.

THE PEOPLE FACTOR

Business involves *people:* Every business employs, sells to, buys from, and is owned and regulated by people. International business, of course, involves people from different cultures. Every business function, therefore—managing a workforce, marketing and transporting output, purchasing supplies, dealing with regulators, securing funds—is subject to potential cultural differences.

Concept Check

Keep in mind our definition of **international business** in Chapter 1, where we stress that it involves "all commercial transactions"—sales, investments, transportation, and so forth.

Cultural Diversity   In Chapter 1, we explained that companies become international to create value for their organizations and observed that one means to this end is the acquisition of foreign assets, including knowledge-based resources. Another means of gaining global competitive advantage is fostering cultural diversity. By bringing together people of diverse backgrounds and experience, companies often gain a deeper knowledge about products and services and ways in which to produce and deliver them. At companies like PepsiCo and IBM, executives report that much of their recent growth has been a result of greater workforce diversity.[2] As we see in the next few sections, however, bringing together people with different backgrounds and perspectives is difficult.

Concept Check

Recall that in Chapter 1 we identify two means of gaining useful knowledge from overseas activities: (1) learning from foreign operating experiences and (2) tapping into foreign intellectual competencies.

Cultural Collision   **Cultural collision** occurs when divergent cultures come in contact. In international business, the major problems of *cultural collision* arise under two conditions:

- When a company implements practices that are less effective than intended
- When a company's employees encounter distress because of difficulty in accepting or adjusting to foreign behaviors

FIGURE 2.1   Cultural Factors Affecting International Business Operations

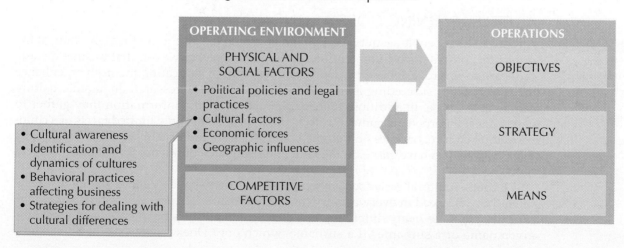

Sensitivity and Adjustment   An international firm doing business in another country must determine which of that nation's business practices differ from its own and then decide what adjustments, if any, are necessary if it is to operate efficiently. In this chapter, we start by examining *cultural awareness,* especially the need for building it. Then we discuss the causes of cultural differences, rigidities, and changes. Next, we describe the major behavioral factors that affect the conduct of international business. Finally, we take a look at the reasons why some businesses—and some individuals—do or don't adjust much to other cultures.

Cultural Awareness

Most cultural variables are universal. Every society, for example, has its own daily routines and rules, codes of social relations, language, and the show of emotions—even concepts of luck. The forms of these variables, however, differ from culture to culture, and not everyone responds to them in the same way even within a given culture. Every culture, for instance, features some form of dance, but types of dances vary among and within cultures, and in every culture there are some nondancers.[3]

Building your awareness of other cultures is not an easy task, and there's still no fool-proof method for doing so.[4] Travelers remark on cultural differences, experts write about them, and international businesspeople find they affect operations. Even so, people tend to disagree on just what they are, whether they're widespread or limited in scope, and whether they're deep seated or superficial.

Moreover, it's not easy to isolate culture from such factors as economic and political conditions. A survey, for instance, that measures people's risk-taking attitudes toward starting a new business may be influenced by current economic conditions rather than spurred by basic values and beliefs.

Some cultural differences, such as acceptable attire, are fairly obvious, and others aren't. Finally, people in every culture evince ingrained responses to given situations, and they often expect that people from other cultures will behave the same way they do. In our opening case, for example, PRI's British sales reps expected their potential Saudi customers to be punctual and to give them and the business details their undivided attention. In fact, their compensation system discouraged them from spending much time on each business transaction. Their Saudi counterparts, meanwhile, had no compulsion to wrap things up, regarded time spent in a café as worthwhile, and considered small talk a good way to identify good business partners. They regarded business dealings as less urgent than conversing with friends.

A LITTLE LEARNING GOES A LONG WAY

Although some people seem to have an innate ability to say and do the right thing at the right time, others offend unintentionally. Experts agree, however, that businesspeople can learn to improve awareness and sensitivity and, by educating themselves, enhance the likelihood of succeeding abroad. Gathering some basic research on another culture can be instructive. In addition, managers must assess the information they gather to determine if it perpetuates unwarranted stereotypes, covers only limited facets of a country and its culture, or relies on outdated data. They should also observe the behavior of those people who have garnered the kind of respect and confidence they themselves will need.

Of course, cultural variations are so numerous that managers cannot memorize everything they will need in every country (or, for that matter, in any one country). Consider, for example, how many different ways there are to address people. Should you use a given name or a surname? If a surname, which one? Does a wife take her husband's

---

Almost everyone agrees that national cultures differ, but they disagree on what the differences are.

Problem areas that can hinder managers' cultural awareness are

- Subconscious reactions to circumstances.
- The assumption that all societal subgroups are similar.

Case Review Note

Concept Check

We stress in Chapter 1 that understanding cultural values, attitudes, and beliefs is often crucial in deciding when and how to alter operations in foreign countries.

name? In addition, many languages have pronouns and verb forms (familiar and polite) that reflect status and how well people know each other. These can even vary among countries using the same language. While mistakes are sometimes humorous, they may at other times be perceived as the result of ignorance or rudeness, which may jeopardize a business deal. Fortunately, there are country guidebooks based on people's experiences, including those of successful international managers. You can also consult with knowledgeable people at home and abroad, whether in a governmental or private capacity.

There is, however, another side to the cultural coin: Too often when we can't explain some difference—say, why the Irish consume more cold cereal than the Spanish do—we tend to attribute it to culture without trying to understand it. (Perhaps the difference is simply that companies such as Kellogg's and General Mills have marketed their cereals more in Ireland.) Fortunately, we now have access to many recent studies on cross-cultural attitudes and practices that concern businesspeople.[5] Nevertheless, many attitudes, practices, and cultures remain unstudied.

Although we report major findings of studies throughout the chapter, we should emphasize a few common shortcomings:

1. Comparing countries by what people say can be risky. For one thing, responses (say, how satisfied they are with their working conditions) may be colored by the culture you're trying to understand. Some groups of people, for example, may be happiest when they're complaining, or they respond with what they think you want to hear.

2. When researchers are focused on national differences in terms of *averages*, they may overlook specific variations within countries and believe in unrealistic stereotypes. For example, if one hears that the average Scandinavian feels uncomfortable with bargaining, it could be a grave mistake to assume that the Ikea (Swedish) buyer does not expect to bargain on prices.[6] And, of course, personality differences make some people outliers in their own cultures, with no certainty that they'll eventually integrate and conform to cultural norms.[7]

3. Cultures evolve. Thus behavior reflecting "current" attitudes may well change in the future. Our opening case, for instance, details several ways in which Saudi attitudes toward women are changing. Interestingly, the Saudi government recently inaugurated a TV channel in which women with uncovered faces serve as anchors who interview men.

The Idea of a "Nation": Delineating Cultures

In the following section, we begin by showing why the idea of a "nation" is a useful but imperfect cultural reference when we're talking about international business. Then we explain why cultures develop and change. Finally, we discuss how language and religion influence culture.

THE NATION AS A POINT OF REFERENCE

Having said in Chapter 1 that international business includes all commercial transactions between two or more *nations*, we focus in this chapter on *national* cultures. The idea of a *nation* provides a workable definition of a *culture* because the basic similarity among people is often both the cause and effect of national boundaries. The laws governing business operations also apply primarily along national lines. Within its borders, a nation's people largely share such essential attributes as values, language, and race. There is a feeling of "we" that casts foreigners as "they." National identity is perpetuated through rites and symbols—flags, parades, rallies—and the preservation of national sites, documents, monuments, and museums promotes a common perception of history.

The nation is a useful definition of society because

- Similarity among people is a cause and an effect of national boundaries.
- Laws apply primarily along national lines.

Managers find country-by-country analysis difficult because

- Subcultures exist within nations.
- Similarities link groups from different countries.

Cultural value systems are set early in life but may change through

- Choice or imposition.
- Contact with other cultures.

The Nation as Cultural Mediator   Obviously, the existence of shared attributes doesn't mean that everyone in a country is alike. Nor does it suggest that each country is unique in all respects. In fact, nations usually include various subcultures, ethnic groups, races, and classes. However, a national culture must be flexible enough to accommodate the diversity. In fact, a nation legitimizes itself by mediating the diversity,[8] and nations that fail in this role often dissolve. The important thing is that every nation boasts certain human, demographic, and behavioral characteristics that constitute its national identity and affect the practices of any company that does business under its jurisdiction.

Nevertheless, certain cultural attributes can link groups from different nations more closely than groups within a given nation. No matter what country you're in, for instance, people in urban areas differ in certain attitudes from people in rural areas, and managers have different work attitudes than do production workers. Thus managers in Country A may hold work values more similar to those of managers in Country B than to those of production workers in Country A. As a consequence, when international businesspeople compare nations, they must be careful to examine *relevant groups*—differentiating, for example, between the typical attitudes of rural dwellers and those of urban dwellers, or those of young people versus old people.

HOW CULTURES FORM AND CHANGE

Culture is transmitted in various ways—from parent to child, teacher to pupil, social leader to follower, peer to peer. Developmental psychologists believe that by age 10 most children have acquired their basic value systems; i.e., they've developed concepts of evil versus good, dirty versus clean, ugly versus beautiful, unnatural versus natural, abnormal versus normal, paradoxical versus logical, and irrational versus rational.From this point on, these values are not easily changed.[9]

Sources of Change   Both individual and collective values and customs, however, may evolve over time. Examining this evolution may tell us something about the process by which a culture comes to accept (or reject) certain business practices, and this knowledge could be of use to international companies that would like to introduce changes into a culture. The important thing here is *change*, which may result from either *choice* or *imposition*.

Change by Choice   Change by choice may occur as a reaction to social and economic situations that present people with new alternatives. When, for example, rural people choose to accept factory jobs, they change some basic customs—notably, by working regular hours that don't allow the sort of work-time social interactions that farmwork allowed.

Change by Imposition   Change by imposition—sometimes called **cultural imperialism**—involves the imposed introduction into a culture of certain elements from an alien culture, such as the forced change in law by an occupying country which, over time, becomes part of the subject culture.

As a rule, contact among countries brings change—a process known as *cultural diffusion*. When this change results in mixing cultural elements, the process is known as *creolization*. (In many Asian countries, for example, ethnic Chinese embody a mixture of Chinese and local cultures).[10] Some groups and governments have tried to protect national cultures, but they have been less than fully successful because people travel and access foreign information through a variety of sources. The photo shows a group in the Czech Republic protesting the widespread acceptance of a cultural change.

Czech marchers dress as snowmen to protest the recent encroachment of Santa Claus, who is neither a part of the country's traditions nor the figure (the spirit of young Jesus) who traditionally brings gifts to children on Christmas.
Source: Hana Kalvachova/Getty Images, Inc.

LANGUAGE AS BOTH A DIFFUSER AND STABILIZER OF CULTURE

National boundaries and geographic obstacles limit people's contact with other cultures, and so does language. Map 2.2 shows the distribution of the world's major language groups. Not surprisingly, when people from different areas speak the same language, culture spreads more easily. That fact helps explain why there's greater cultural homogeneity among all English-speaking countries or among all Spanish-speaking countries than between English-speaking countries and Spanish-speaking countries.

> A common language within countries is a unifying force.

Our map, by the way, omits most of the world's approximately 6,000 languages because each is spoken by proportionately few people. When people understand only one language that has relatively few users—especially if they're concentrated in a small geographic area—they tend to cling to their culture because they have little meaningful contact with others.

Such languages as English, French, and Spanish have such widespread acceptance (they're prevalent in 44, 27, and 20 countries, respectively) that, as a rule, native speakers don't feel the same need to learn other languages as do speakers of languages that, like Finnish or Greek, are found in only limited geographic areas. Among nations that share a same language, commerce is easier because translating everything (which can be both time consuming and expensive) isn't necessary. Thus when people study second languages, they usually choose the ones that are most useful in interacting with other countries, especially in the realm of commerce.

Concept Check

As we observe in Chapter 1, improved communications and transportation are key factors in the increased international interactions that we know as **international business**.

Why English Travels So Well Take a look at Figure 2.2. The pie chart on the right shows portions of worldwide output by language. As you can see, English-speaking peoples account for over 40 percent of the world's production—a fact that goes a long way toward explaining why English is the world's most important *second* language. Remember, too, that MNEs—which are largely headquartered in English-speaking countries—decide on the language to use for communicating among employees in the different countries where they operate. Not surprisingly, it's usually English, both because they transfer many English-only speakers as managers abroad and because they need a common means for managers from different countries to communicate with each other.

MAP 2.2   Distribution of the World's Major Languages

The people of the world speak thousands of different languages, but only a few of them remain important in the dissemination of culture. A significant portion of the world, for example, speaks English, French, or Spanish. In those countries labeled "Regional," the predominant language is not dominant anywhere else; Japanese, for example, is dominant only in Japan. But take a look at China: It's the only place where people speak Mandarin, but it's important in international business because the population of China comprises a *lot* of people. The classification "Regional" actually takes in two categories: (1) countries in which the dominant language is not dominant anywhere else (e.g., Japan) and (2) countries in which several different languages are spoken (e.g., India).

Sources: www.udon.de/sprachk.htm. The number of native speakers is taken from *World Almanac and Book of Facts* (Mahwah, NJ: Primedia Reference, 2002).

Note: Given that this is a Mercator projection, the scale approximates east-west distance at the equator; however, the farther you move from the equator, the more the east-west distance is distorted.

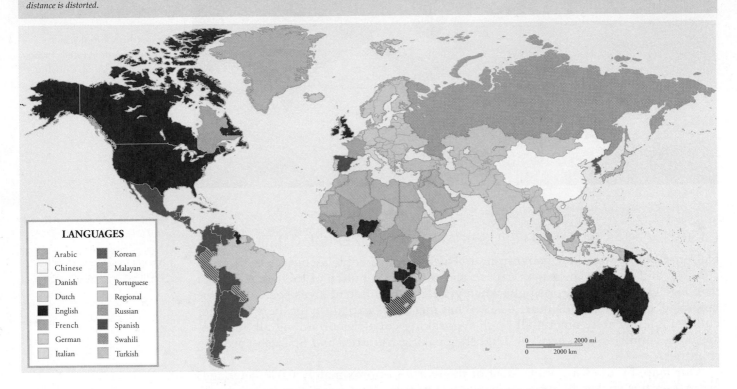

In addition, many MNEs from non-English-speaking countries—such as Nokia from Finland and Philips from the Netherlands—have adopted English as their operating language.[11] Thus you've probably heard that English is the "international language of business," but at least one prominent linguist predicts that monolingual English speakers will eventually experience more difficulty in communicating worldwide. Why? Because the percentage of people speaking English as a first language will decrease while the languages of such countries as China and India will grow very rapidly along with their economies.[12] As is so often the case, history may also have a thing or two to teach us in this matter: Latin once dominated as the language of scholarship and French as the language of diplomacy, but both have long since been supplanted.

Nevertheless, for some time now, English words—especially American-English words—have been entering into other languages. An estimated 20,000 English words, for example, have been integrated into the Japanese language. In part, English travels so well because the U.S. media are so influential in promoting U.S. lifestyles. Of course, the United States also originates a healthy percentage of new technology and new products. When, for example, a new U.S. product enters a foreign market, its vocabulary usually enters the language as well. Sometimes it enters in its good, old-fashioned English form. In a Spanish-speaking country, for instance, you might see a sign announcing that *Vendemos blue jeans de varios colores* ("We sell various colors of blue jeans"). At other times, the local language gives it an Anglicized twist. Thus Russians call tight denim pants *dzhinsi* (pronounced "jeansy"), and the French call a self-service restaurant *le self*. Finally, the intrusion of English into another language may result in the development of

FIGURE 2.2 Major Language Groups: Population and Output

Native speakers of just a handful of languages—notably English—account for much more of the world's economic output than their total numbers would indicate. Only 6% of the world's people speak English as a native language, for example, but they account for 42% of its economic output, which helps to explain the prevalence of English as a second language in conducting international business.

Sources: Data for the chart on the left is from the Central Intelligence Agency, *The World Factbook,* at www.cia.gov. Data for the chart on the right is calculated from GDP figures supplied by the World Development Indicators database, World Bank (September 2004), and country language figures supplied by Wikipedia, at en.wikipedia.org.

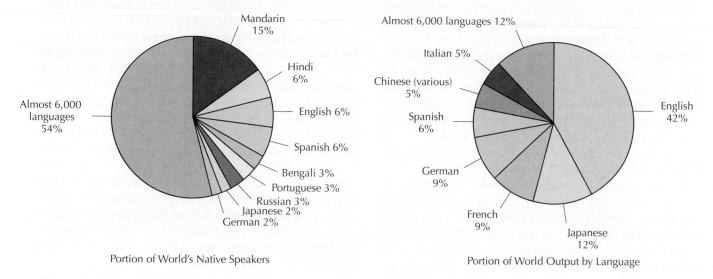

Portion of World's Native Speakers

Portion of World Output by Language

a hybrid tongue, such as "Spanglish" (Spanish and English) or "Chinglish" (Mandarin Chinese and English), which may ultimately become a distinct language.[13]

Note, however, that some countries, such as Finland, prefer to coin their own new words rather than accept Anglicized items into their vocabularies, and because many countries see language as an integral part of the culture, they regulate linguistic changes. In the business arena, for example, they may require that all public signs be in the local language.

RELIGION AS A CULTURAL STABILIZER

Map 2.3 shows the approximate distribution of the world's major religions. In many countries, the practice of religion has declined significantly; indeed, a few nations in northern Europe are sometimes called "post-Christian" societies. At the same time, religion has been a cultural stabilizer because centuries of profound religious influence continue to play a major role in shaping cultural values even in these societies.[14] Among people with strong religious convictions, the role of religion in shaping behavior is even stronger.

Many of these religions—Buddhism, Christianity, Hinduism, Islam, and Judaism—influence specific beliefs that may affect business, such as inhibiting the sale of certain products or the performance of work at certain times. McDonald's, for example, serves neither beef nor pork in India so as not to offend either its Hindu or Muslim populations, and El Al, the Israeli national airline, does not fly on Saturday, the Jewish Sabbath.

Of course, not all nations that practice the same religion impose the same constraints on business. In predominantly Muslim countries, for example, Friday is a day of worship and a non-workday. In Turkey (a secular Muslim country that adheres to the Christian work calendar to keep in step with European business activity), however, Friday is a workday. In places where rival religions or factions are vying for political control, the resulting strife can cause so much upheaval that business activity suffers, whether from property damage, broken supply chains, or breaches in connections with customers. Unfortunately, the problem is substantial. In recent years, religious-related violence has erupted in such countries as India, Iraq, Sudan, and Northern Ireland.

Many strong values are the result of a dominant religion.

Does Geography Matter? Where Birds of a Feather Flock Together

Some groups of people are more isolated from the rest of the world than others, sometimes because of natural barriers (rugged terrain and geographic remoteness) and sometimes by other barriers (unique languages, outmoded transportation and communications, xenophobia). Obviously, the more isolated people are, the less likely they are to influence and be influenced by other people. Historically, natural barriers—and natural advantages—have been quite important in determining where people do and don't live. Take a quick look at any map, for instance, and you'll see that a large portion of big cities are situated where waterways facilitated the interaction of people and interchange of goods.

On the one hand, although airplanes and communications systems have rendered many natural barriers less formidable, these barriers still play a role in determining which people are harder to get to know than others. In Papua New Guinea, for example, the mutual isolation of tribal groups has resulted in about 800 different languages and permitted little cultural diffusion. Similarly, natural conditions continue to affect physical cultures that people have developed, such as clothing for native Inuits of the Arctic being different from the attire typically worn on Brazil's beaches. The Inuit language, by the way, has more words for *snow* than any other language.

On the other hand, of course, some places have traditionally enjoyed more-than-average outside contact than others. As we saw in our opening case, the Saudi port of Jeddah, having long experienced more external contact than the rest of Saudi Arabia, has borrowed much more liberally from outside cultures.

Then there's the effect of *proximity* on cultural diffusion: Understandably, people generally have more contact with nearby groups than with those that are far away. Take a look, for instance, at Map 2.2. As you can see, most German-speaking countries, Arabic-speaking countries, and Spanish-speaking countries are more or less adjacent to each other. Likewise, Map 2.3 reveals that virtually all of the world's major religions—Christianity, Islam, and Buddhism—are geographically clustered. The notable exceptions to this rule have resulted from colonization and immigration. Both English and Spanish, for instance, spread to distant parts of the world during eras of European colonization.

Finally, cultural—and subcultural—clusters tend to confirm the old adage that "Birds of a feather flock together." Immigration patterns, for example, often reflect the tendency of people to go where they can find a subcultural support group. That's why there's a heavy concentration of Central American immigrants in the Los Angeles area. They feel comfortable locating there because, even if friends and family aren't already waiting, they'll find affinities in language, diet, and general customs. Globally, we find many such patterns, such as Hong Kong Chinese in Vancouver, Canada, and Algerians in Marseilles, France. ●

Behavioral Practices Affecting Business

Concept Check

In Chapter 1, we emphasize the importance of studying the *behavioral factors* that affect business conditions to help managers decide why and how they may need to alter operations in different countries.

It should come as no surprise that culture affects business practices—everything from decisions about what products to sell to decisions about organizing, financing, managing, and controlling operations. Attitudes and values constitute *cultural variables,* and both researchers and businesspeople define cultural variables differently, attaching different names to slightly different and sometimes overlapping concepts. Because of all these nuances in terms and concepts, there are thousands of possible ways of relating culture to business—far too many to cover in one chapter. Thus we'll settle for hitting the highlights—the factors that, according to both international managers and academic researchers, have the most effect on business practices in different countries. We also pursue the topic of cultural variables in later chapters.

ISSUES IN SOCIAL STRATIFICATION

Every culture values some people more highly than others, and such distinctions—or *social stratification*—dictate a person's class or status within that culture. In business, this practice may entail valuing members of managerial groups more highly than members of production groups. Your ranking is determined by two sets of factors: (1) those pertaining to you as an individual and (2) those pertaining to your affiliation with or membership in certain groups. Let's focus for a moment on this second set.

MAP 2.3 Distribution of the World's Major Religions

Most countries are home to people of various religious beliefs, but a nation's culture is typically influenced most heavily by a dominant religion. The practices of the dominant religion, for instance, often shape customary practices in legal and business affairs.

Source: The numbers for adherents are taken from *World Almanac and Book of Facts*, Center for the Study of Global Christianity, Gordon-Conwell Theological Seminary, World Christian Database, at www.worldchristiandatabase.org (accessed September 2005). Reprinted with permission.

Note: Given that this is a Mercator projection, the scale approximates east-west distance at the equator; however, the farther you move from the equator, the more the east-west distance is distorted.

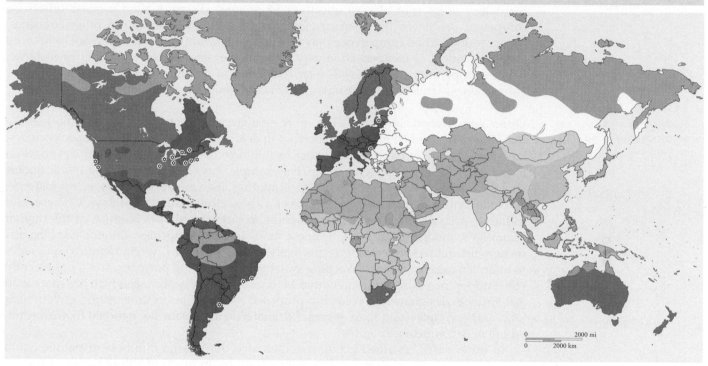

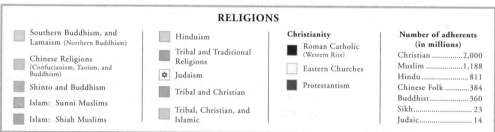

RELIGIONS

Southern Buddhism, and Lamaism (Northern Buddhism)	Hinduism	**Christianity**
Chinese Religions (Confucianism, Taoism, and Buddhism)	Tribal and Traditional Religions	Roman Catholic (Western Rite)
Shinto and Buddhism	✿ Judaism	Eastern Churches
Islam: Sunni Muslims	Tribal and Christian	Protestantism
Islam: Shiah Muslims	Tribal, Christian, and Islamic	

Number of adherents (in millions)

Christian	2,000
Muslim	1,188
Hindu	811
Chinese Folk	384
Buddhist	360
Sikh	23
Judaic	14

Ascribed and Acquired Memberships Affiliations determined by birth—known as **ascribed group memberships**—include those based on gender, family, age, caste, and ethnic, racial, or national origin. Other affiliations are called **acquired group memberships** and include those based on religion, political affiliation, and professional and other associations. For example, social stratification affects marketing inasmuch as most advertisers prefer spokespeople who appeal to their target audience.

Social stratification also affects employment practices. One study of hiring, promotion, compensation, and staff-reduction practices at a number of banks showed that employers differed by nationality on all four functions. When, for example, they needed to make staff reductions, British banks were most prone to save costs by discharging on a performance-to-salary basis (targeting, say, a middle-aged manager with a high salary and average performance), whereas German banks were more concerned with minimizing personal hardship (targeting younger managers, regardless of performance, because they could find new jobs more easily).[15]

In the following sections, we focus on some of the individual characteristics and group memberships that influence a person's social ranking from country to country. We also touch on two additional factors that are often important: *education* (especially

Group affiliations can be

- Ascribed or acquired.
- A reflection of class and status.

how much you have and where you got it) and *social connections* (who you know and in what places).[16]

Performance Orientation   In some nations, such as the United States, companies tend to base a person's eligibility for employment and promotion primarily on competence, thereby fostering work environments driven more by competition than by cooperation. In fact, some of these nations value competence so highly that they've actually taken regulatory steps (not always effective) to prevent discrimination against otherwise competent people on the basis of gender, race, age, and religion. In other countries, however, individual competence may be of secondary importance. A person's eligibility for employment or compensation may reflect some other factor. In Japan, for instance, where cooperation is stressed over competition in the workplace, seniority or "humaneness" (tolerance of mistakes) often carries significant weight.[17]

Open and Closed Societies   The more egalitarian, or "open," a society, the less the importance of ascribed group membership in determining rewards. In less open societies, however, laws may be designed either to reinforce or to undermine rigid stratification based on ascribed group membership. For example, laws requiring racial or ethnic quotas usually aim to weaken stratification by countering discrimination. Malaysia, for instance, has long maintained employment quotas for three ethnic groups—Malays, Chinese, and Indians—primarily to upgrade the economic position of Malays because, at the time of Malaysia's independence, the Chinese and Indian minorities dominated business ownership and the professions, respectively.[18] The Malaysian system requires companies to maintain expensive record-keeping systems of their hiring practices, and it has recently come under increasing criticism within Malaysia.[19] Likewise, Brazil, which has more than 300 terms to designate skin color, has proposed racial quotas in universities, government jobs, and even television soap operas.[20] (It plans no quotas for the national football team, where only competence counts.)

In other cases, ascribed group memberships deny large numbers of people equal access to the preparation needed to qualify for jobs. In much of sub-Saharan Africa, for instance, the literacy rate for women is much lower than that for men—in Niger and Mali, for example, 42 percent and 52 percent of the male literacy rate, respectively.[21]

Finally, even when individuals qualify for given positions and no legal barriers exist to hold them back, certain social obstacles—say, public opposition to the use of child labor in the employer's home country—may make a company wary of adopting certain practices in host countries. In some cases, opposition to certain groups may come from other workers, customers, local shareholders, or government officials. In addition, the old adage that "It's *who* you know, not *what* you know" has some validity just about everywhere. (This is a point we pursue in our chapter-ending case, which details a U.S. company's adventures in Uganda. Here, we'll see not only that effective opposition can come from small ad hoc groups, but also that the people you need to know can sometimes be found in unexpected places.)

Case Review Note

Gender-Based Groups   Country-specific differences in attitudes toward gender are sometimes quite pronounced. Some of these probably seem paradoxical, at least to the outsider.

Case Review Note

"When Jobs Are Scarce..." (I)   Countries differ in tradition and attitude toward gender equality.[22] Recall our opening case: Women in Saudi Arabia can't work in some professions, and there are more than 13 employed men for every employed woman. Compare that figure with the United States, where only 1.2 men are employed for every woman.[23] Here's another interesting statistic: In Lithuania, more than 50 percent of both males and females agreed with the following statement: "When jobs are scarce, men have a better right to a job than women." In Sweden and Iceland, the number was under 10 percent.[24]

In many parts of the world, however, barriers to gender-based employment practices are coming down, due to changes in both attitudes and work requirements. In the United States, one noticeable change in attitudes has been reflected in the number of people of one gender employed in occupations previously dominated by the other, such as the increase in male nurses.[25] Further, there's been a decrease in production jobs requiring brawn and an increase in jobs for people with specialized education, such as X-ray technology and psychiatric casework. With these shifts, the relative demand for female employees has increased.

Age-Based Groups All countries treat age groups differently, and each country expresses its attitudes toward age in different ways. All, for instance, enforce age-related laws such as statutes applying to employment, driving privileges, rights to obtain products and services (such as alcohol, cigarettes, certain pharmaceuticals, and bank accounts), and civic duty (voting, serving in the military or on juries). Sometimes the logic of these laws seems quite contradictory. In the United States, for example, people can vote, marry, drive, and die for their country before they can legally buy alcohol.

National differences—both in laws and customs, and especially in employment practices—can be substantial. Both Finland and the Netherlands, for example, enforce mandatory retirement ages, but with few exceptions (say, airline pilots), U.S. law specifically prohibits the practice. In Britain, age discrimination laws apply to everyone, regardless of age, whereas U.S. law is designed to protect only people over age 40.[26] Laws regulating product sales and promotion also vary. In parts of Switzerland, you can legally buy alcohol at age 14, whereas U.S. law puts the age at 21.[27] Not surprisingly, every country specifies an age at which people can be licensed to drive. U.S. advertisers bombard children with TV advertisements, but Sweden prohibits ads targeted to children.

"When Jobs Are Scarce..." (II) Finally, country differences in attitudes concerning age can affect business operations. When, for example, the proposition "When jobs are scarce, people should be forced to retire early" was put to people in different countries, almost three-quarters of Bulgarians agreed, but only 10 percent of Japanese.[28] Why the difference? For one thing, Japanese hold much more strongly to the assumption that there's a significant correlation between age and wisdom. That's why the seniority system, although now declining in importance, plays a key role in promotion and compensation decisions in Japan—much more so than in Western countries.[29] The United States, in contrast, is often characterized as a culture that favors youth. Indeed, U.S. TV writers claim that they can't find jobs after age 30, and there's a booming market for products designed to make people look younger.

Family-Based Groups In some cultures—say, much of Latin America—the most important group membership is the family. An individual's position in society at large depends heavily on the family's social status or "respectability" rather than on individual achievement. Because family ties are so strong, there may also be a tendency to cooperate more closely within the family unit than in other relationships. In such cultures, not surprisingly, small family-run companies are quite successful; conversely, however, they often encounter difficulties in growing because owners are reluctant to share responsibility with professional managers hired from outside the family. When its business culture is hampered by this state of affairs, a country (or region) may lack the indigenously owned *large-scale* operations that are usually necessary for long-term economic development.[30]

WORK MOTIVATION

Not surprisingly, motivated employees are normally more productive than those who aren't. On an aggregate basis, of course, this relationship between motivation and productivity influences companies' efficiency and countries' economic development positively.

Studies show substantial differences in how and why people in different nations are motivated to work, and we devote the following discussion to summarizing the major differences.

Materialism and Motivation   Max Weber observed when developing a theory, the *Protestant ethic*, that the predominantly Protestant countries were the most economically developed. He attributed this "ethic" to an outgrowth of the Protestant Reformation in sixteenth-century Europe, which reflects the belief that work is a pathway to salvation and that material success does not impede salvation.

The desire for material wealth is
- A prime motivation to work.
- Positive for economic development.

Although we no longer accept a strict distinction between Protestant and non-Protestant attitudes toward work and material gain, we do tend to adhere to the underlying values of Weber's concept: namely, that self-discipline, hard work, honesty, and a belief in a just world foster work motivation and, thus, economic growth.[31] As a matter of fact, evidence indicates a positive correlation between the intensity of religious belief per se (regardless of specific belief systems) and adherence to some attributes that lead to economic growth (say, confidence in the rule of law and belief in the virtue of thrift).[32] Moreover, there's strong evidence that the individual desire for material wealth is a prime incentive to perform the kind of work that leads to community-wide economic development.[33]

The Productivity/Leisure Trade-Off   Some cultures place less value on leisure time than others. As a result, people in such cultures work longer hours, take fewer holidays and vacations, and, in general, spend less time and money on leisure activities. In a study of the 30 OECD (fairly high-income) countries, France and the United States offer an example of contrast. Among the 30 countries, France has the longest mandated vacation (30 days), and the French spend the longest average time per day eating and drinking (135 minutes) and sleeping (530 minutes). In the United States, there is no mandated vacation, and Americans spend only an average of 74 minutes per day eating and drinking, and 518 minutes sleeping.[34] In the United States, there is still some disdain for people who fall on either end of the work/leisure spectrum: people of privilege who appear to contribute nothing to society and people who appear to be satisfied with a lifestyle that can be maintained by unemployment benefits. Americans, for instance, who give up work (primarily retirees) often complain that they're no longer allowed to contribute anything useful to society.

In parts of some poor countries, meanwhile, such as rural India, living "the simple life"—that is, without benefit of much material comfort—seems to be a desirable end in itself. When productivity gains afford them the choice, people tend to choose to take at least part of the gains in leisure rather than all of it in earnings to buy more.[35] By and large, however, most people today in most countries, whether rich or poor, regard personal economic advancement as a worthwhile goal in life (although certainly not the only goal).

People are more eager to work if
- Rewards for success are high.
- There is some uncertainty of success.

Expectation of Success and Reward   Two factors that motivate attitudes toward work are the perceived likelihood of success and the reward from success versus failure. Generally, people have little enthusiasm for efforts when the likelihood of success seems too easy or too difficult. Why? Because the probability of success on the one hand or failure on the other seems almost certain. Few of us, for instance, would care to run a race against either a snail or a racehorse; in either case, the outcome is too predictable. Our enthusiasm peaks when uncertainty of success is high—say, when we're challenged to race another human of roughly equal ability. Likewise, the reward for a successfully completed task—say, winning a fair footrace—may be high or low, and most of us usually work harder the more we expect that success will lead to a higher reward.

Success and Reward across Borders   Performed in different countries, the same tasks come with different probabilities of success, different rewards for success, and different consequences for failure. In cultures in which the probability of economic failure is almost certain and the perceived rewards of success are low, people tend— not surprisingly—to view work as necessary but unsatisfying, mainly because they foresee little benefit to themselves from their efforts. This attitude may prevail in harsh climates, in very poor areas, or in subcultures subject to discrimination. Likewise, if there is little difference in reward between working hard or not, there is less motivation to work hard. Take Cuba, for instance, where public policy allocates output from productive to unproductive workers; naturally, there's not much enthusiasm for work. We find the greatest enthusiasm for work when high uncertainty of outcome is combined with the likelihood of a positive reward for success and little or no reward for failure.[36]

Performance and Achievement: The Masculinity–Femininity Index   One study found significant differences among countries by using a so-called **masculinity–femininity index** to compare the attitudes of employees in 50 countries toward work and achievement. Employees with a high "masculinity score" admired successful work achievers, harbored little sympathy for the unfortunate, and preferred to be better than others rather than on a par with them. They shared a money-and-things orientation rather than a people orientation, a belief that it's better "to live to work" than "to work to live," and a preference for performance and growth over quality of life and the environment.[37]

Similarly, the degree to which individuals are assertive, confrontational, and aggressive in their relationships with others varies across borders. Such attitudinal differences help explain why an international company may encounter managers abroad who behave differently from what it expects or prefers. Let's say a company in a high-masculinity country, such as Austria, sets up operations in a high-femininity country such as Sweden. The typical purchasing manager in Sweden probably has a high need for smooth social relationships and prefers amiable and continuing relationships with suppliers to, say, immediate lower costs or faster delivery. The Swedish manager may also place such organizational goals as employee and social welfare ahead of a typical Austrian parent's goals of growth and efficiency.

Hierarchies of Needs   According to the **hierarchy-of-needs theory** of motivation, people try to fulfill lower-level needs before moving on to higher-level needs.[38] As you can see from Figure 2.3, the most basic needs are *physiological*—the needs for food, water, and sex. You have to satisfy (or nearly satisfy) such needs before *security* needs— such as the need for a safe physical and emotional environment—become a sufficiently powerful set of motivators. Then you must satisfy your security needs before triggering the motivational effect of *affiliation* or social needs (such as the need for peer acceptance). Once you've satisfied your affiliation needs, you'll be motivated to satisfy your *esteem* needs—the need to bolster your self-image through recognition, attention, and appreciation. The highest-order need calls for *self-actualization*—self-fulfillment or (to quote Robert Lewis Stevenson) "becom[ing] all that we are capable of becoming." Finally, note that the hierarchy-of-needs theory also implies that you'll typically work to satisfy a need, but once you've satisfied it, its value as a motivator diminishes.

> The ranking of needs may differ among countries.

What can the hierarchy-of-needs theory tell us about doing business in foreign countries? For one thing, research has shown that people in different countries not only attach different degrees of importance to different needs, but they also rank higher-order needs differently. The hierarchy-of-needs theory, then, can be helpful in differentiating among the reward preferences of employees in different countries. In very poor countries, for example, a company can motivate workers simply by providing enough compensation to satisfy their needs for food and shelter. Elsewhere, workers are motivated by other needs.

However, economics (even at low levels of income) cannot fully explain work motivation. For example, a long-term ethnographic study uncovered many differences among

FIGURE 2.3 The Hierarchy of Needs and Need-Hierarchy Comparisons

The pyramid on the left represents the five-level hierarchy of needs formulated by Maslow. The two block pyramids on the right (a, b) represent two different groups of people—say, the populations of two different countries. Note that the block representing affiliation needs (level 3) is wider in (b) than in (a); conversely, the block representing self-actualization needs (level 5) is wider in (a) than in (b). In other words, even if we rank various needs in the same order (or hierarchy), the people in one country may regard a given higher-order need as more important (wider) than do people in another country.

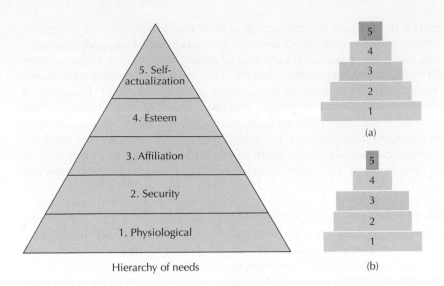

5. Self-actualization

4. Esteem

3. Affiliation

2. Security

1. Physiological

Hierarchy of needs

(a)

(b)

employees in a large U.S. airline's back-office tasks in the United States, the Dominican Republic, and Barbados. We'll mention just a few differences here. Whereas employees in the United States and the Dominican Republic saw the job as a stepping-stone to higher-level positions, few Barbadian employees wanted promotions because these would change their relationships with friends. U.S. workers usually dressed very casually because they would not be seen by outsiders in the back office, but Barbadians dressed up to be seen going to what was considered a prestige job. In fact, the company tried to save Barbadian employees time and money by offering its own bus transportation, but the employees preferred to be seen on the slower public transportation that required transfers in the city. The staff in Barbados was made up almost entirely of women, whose absenteeism and turnover were very low because Barbados has a history of working women. In the Dominican Republic, however, most female hires stayed on only until they married.[39]

RELATIONSHIP PREFERENCES

So far, we've discussed two categories of behavioral practices affecting business: social stratification systems and work motivation. Next, we discuss some of the values underlying such differences.

There are national variations in the preference for autocratic or consultative management.

Power Distance   From country to country, likely employee preferences differ in terms of interacting with bosses, subordinates, and peers. Considerable anecdotal evidence indicates that people perform better when the nature of their interactions fits their preferences. That's why companies are well advised to align management styles with employee preferences for interacting with superiors.

Power distance refers to the general relationship between superiors and subordinates. Where power distance is *high*, people prefer little consultation between superiors and subordinates. Employees usually prefer one of two management styles: *autocratic* (ruling with unlimited authority) or *paternalistic* (regulating conduct by supplying needs). Where power distance is *low*, they prefer "consultative" styles.[40] What might happen, therefore, if a Dutch company assigned domestic managers, who typically prefer low power distance, to improve productivity at a facility in Morocco, where workers typically prefer high power distance? The Dutch managers might consult with Moroccan subordinates in an attempt to improve employee productivity. Unfortunately, they may end up making subordinates feel so uncomfortable that performance deteriorates rather than improves.

Interestingly, employees who prefer an autocratic style of superior–subordinate relationship are also willing to accept decision making by a majority of subordinates. What they don't accept is interaction between superiors and subordinates in decision making. Clearly, worker-participation methods are likely to be more effective in some countries than in others.

Individualism versus Collectivism   **Individualism** is characterized by a preference for fulfilling leisure time and improving skills outside the organization. It also implies a low preference for receiving compensation in the form of benefits and a high preference for personal decision making and on-the-job challenges. **Collectivism,** in contrast, encourages dependence on the organization and a preference for thorough training, satisfactory workplace conditions, and good benefits. In countries typified by high individualism, self-actualization is a prime motivator because employees want challenges. In those characterized by high collectivism, the need for security—notably, the desire for a safe physical and emotional environment—is a prime motivator.[41]

> "Safe" work environments motivate collectivists. Challenges motivate individualists.

Degrees of individualism and collectivism also influence employee interactions. Japan, for instance, has a much more collectivist culture than does the United States, especially concerning the role of work groups. Consider, for example, Levi Strauss, which once introduced team-based production into several U.S. plants because overseas managers had observed high productivity when the system was used in Asia. Unfortunately, U.S. employees—especially the most skilled workers—detested the system, productivity went down, and Levi returned to a more individualistic system that was more suitable to its U.S. workforce.

Situational Differences: The Family   Applying any measure of *individualism versus collectivism* is a complex and imprecise process.[42] In some cases, for example, the preference for individualism may vary by situation. Although China and Mexico can be characterized as collectivist cultures, they differ from Japan to the extent that the preference for collectivism is based more on kinship relationships that do not carry over into the workplace.[43] In both China and Mexico, moreover, the concept of family includes not only the *nuclear family* (consisting of husband, wife, and minor children) but also the *vertically extended family* (including members of several generations) and perhaps the *horizontally extended family* as well (encompassing aunts, uncles, and cousins).

Such differences can affect business in a variety of ways:

1. The material rewards to be gained from individual work may be less motivating when rewards are divided among members of a group.

2. Because relocation means that family members must also find new jobs, a worker's geographic mobility is limited. Even when extended families don't live together, mobility may be reduced because people prefer to remain near relatives.

3. Interrelated familial roles may complicate purchasing decisions.

4. Security and social needs may be met more effectively at home than in the workplace.

RISK-TAKING BEHAVIOR

People in various cultures differ in their willingness to accept things the way they are and in their feelings about their control over their destinies. The following discussion examines four types of *risk-taking behavior* that reflect these attitudes: *uncertainty avoidance, trust, future orientation,* and *fatalism.*

> Nationalities differ in
> - Ease of handling uncertainties.
> - Degree of trust among people.
> - Future orientation.
> - Attitudes of self-determination and fatalism.

Uncertainty Avoidance   In countries where **uncertainty avoidance** is high, most employees prefer following set rules even if breaking them may be in the company's best interests. They also plan to stay with current employers for a long time, preferring the certainty of present positions over the uncertainty of potential advancement elsewhere.[44] When uncertainty avoidance is high, superiors may need to be more precise in their directions to subordinates, who typically don't want to determine for themselves what they need to do to advance the company's interests.

In the same countries, fewer consumers are prepared to risk being early adopters of products. Gillette, for example, depends heavily on introducing new products. Thus it may be wise for Gillette to enter markets like Denmark and the United Kingdom, which rate low on uncertainty avoidance, before venturing into Belgium and Portugal, which rate high.

Trust   Surveys measure *trust* among countries by asking respondents to evaluate such statements as "Most people can be trusted" and "You can't be too careful in dealing with people." Findings indicate substantial international differences. Many more Norwegians than Brazilians, for example, regard most people as trustworthy.[45] Where trust is high, the cost of doing business tends to be lower because managers don't spend much time fussing over every possible contingency and monitoring every action for compliance with certain business principles. Instead, they can spend time producing, selling, and innovating.[46]

Future Orientation   Cultures differ in their perceptions of the risks from delaying gratification by investing for the future. For example, **future orientation** (living for the future) is more pronounced in Switzerland, the Netherlands, and Canada than in Russia, Poland, and Italy.[47] In the former cultures, companies may find it easier to motivate workers through such delayed-compensation programs as retirement plans.

Fatalism   If people believe strongly in self-determination, they may be willing to work hard to achieve goals and take responsibility for performance. But if they're *fatalistic*—if they believe every event in life is inevitable—they're less likely to accept the basic cause-and-effect relationship between work and reward. In countries that rate high on fatalism, people do less planning for contingencies, such as buying insurance. Religious differences play a significant role in levels of fatalism in a culture. Conservative or fundamentalist Christian, Buddhist, Hindu, and Muslim groups, for instance, are more likely to view occurrences as "the will of God." For this reason, managers are less apt to sway them with cause-and-effect logic than by making personal appeals to them or offering them rewards for complying with requests.[48]

INFORMATION AND TASK PROCESSING

"Beauty," we're often told, "is in the eye of the beholder." So, apparently, are perceptions and judgments on cultural as well as personal levels. Both perception and judgment are based on what people perceive as accurate *information*, and different cultures handle information in different ways. The following discussion examines some of the ways in which different cultures perceive, obtain, and process information.

Perception of Cues   As a rule, we're selective in perceiving *cues*—features that inform us about the nature of something. We may identify things by means of any of our senses (sight, smell, touch, sound, or taste), and each sense can provide information in various ways; through vision, for example, we sense color, depth, and shape. The cues that people rely on differ among cultures. The reason is partly physiological. Genetic differences in eye pigmentation, for instance, allow some people to differentiate colors more precisely than others can.

Perceptual differences also reflect cultural factors. The richness of their descriptive vocabulary allows some people to note and express very subtle differences in color. This difference in perceptual faculties also allows some cultures to perceive certain subjects more precisely than others. Arabic, for example, has more than 6,000 different words for camels, their body parts, and the equipment associated with them,[49] and Arabic speakers can express nuances about camels that just about everybody else will probably overlook.

Obtaining Information: Low-Context versus High-Context Cultures Researchers classify some countries (including the United States and most of northern Europe) as **low-context cultures:** cultures in which people generally regard as relevant only firsthand information that bears directly on the subject at hand. Businesspeople spend little time on small talk and tend to get to the point. In **high-context cultures** (for example, most countries in southern Europe), people tend to regard seemingly peripheral information as pertinent and to infer meanings from things said either indirectly or casually.

When people from the two types of cultures have to deal with each other, those from low-context cultures may perceive those from high-context cultures as inefficient in their use of time. Conversely, people from high-context cultures may perceive those from low-context cultures as overly aggressive. Recall from our opening case, for example, the problems encountered (and largely caused) by the low-context approach of two sales reps from Great Britain in the high-context business environment of Saudi Arabia.

Information Processing Insofar as all cultures categorize, plan, and quantify, information processing is a universal activity. At the same time, however, every culture has its own systems for ordering and classifying information. In U.S. telephone directories, for instance, entries appear in alphabetical order by last (family) name. In Iceland, they're organized by first (given) names. (Icelandic last names are derived from the father's first name: Thus Jon, son of Thor, is Jon *Thorsson,* and his sister's last name is *Thorsdottir,* "daughter of Thor"). To perform efficiently and work amicably in a foreign environment, you need to understand such differences in processing systems. Perhaps more importantly, different processing systems create challenges in sharing global data. Even the use of global personnel directories is problematic because of different alphabets and alphabetizing systems.

Monochronic versus Polychronic Cultures Cultural differences also affect the degree of multitasking with which people are comfortable. According to some researchers, for example, northern European cultures are **monochronic:** People prefer to work sequentially, such as finishing transactions with one customer before dealing with another. Conversely, **polychronic** southern Europeans are more comfortable when working simultaneously on a variety of tasks, such as dealing immediately with multiple customers who need service.[50] Imagine the potential misconceptions if the two types of businesspeople try to get together: What if those from northern Europe perceive their southern European counterparts as uninterested in doing business with them because they don't bother to give them their undivided attention?

Idealism versus Pragmatism Whereas some cultures tend to focus first on the whole and then on the parts, others do the opposite. Consider the following example. When asked to describe an underwater scene in which one large fish was swimming among some smaller fish and other aquatic life, most Japanese first described the overall picture. Most Americans, however, first described the large fish.[51]

Similarly, some cultures prefer to establish overall principles before they try to resolve small issues—an approach sometimes labeled **idealism.** Cultures in which people focus more on details than on abstract principles are said to be characterized by **pragmatism.**

It helps managers to know whether cultures favor

- Focused or broad information.
- Sequential or simultaneous handling of situations.
- Handling principles or small issues first.

CRN
Case Review Note

These different approaches to information processing can affect business in a number of ways. In a culture of pragmatists (as in the United States), for example, labor negotiations tend to focus on well-defined issues—say, hourly pay increases for a specific bargaining unit. In an idealist culture like that of Argentina, labor disputes tend to blur the focus on specific demands as workers tend to rely first on mass action—such as general strikes or political activities—to publicize basic principles.

COMMUNICATIONS

Cross-border communications do not always translate as intended.

Thus far, we've seen how language affects culture—and international business. We now look at problems in *communications*—that is, problems in translating spoken and written language. These problems occur not only when you must shift from one language to another, but also when you must communicate with someone from another country with the same official language. Finally, we discuss communications that occur by means other than spoken and written language—by a so-called silent language.

Spoken and Written Language　Translating one language directly into another is not as straightforward as it may seem. Some words simply don't have direct translations. English, for example, has one word—*children*—that may mean either "young people" or "offspring." Spanish, however, has two words—*niños* and *hijos*—that distinguish between the two. The importance of language differences is shown humorously in Figure 2.4.

In addition, language, including common word meanings, is constantly evolving. Microsoft, for example, once purchased a thesaurus code for its Spanish version of Word, but by the time it had implemented the software, the connotations of many synonyms had shifted; some, in fact, were transformed into outright insults that alienated potential customers, such as referring to people of mixed race by using the Spanish word for *bastard*.[52] Remember, too, that in any language, words mean different things in different contexts. One U.S. company, for instance, once described itself as an "old friend" of China. Unfortunately, the Chinese word it chose for *old* meant "former" instead of "long-standing."[53]

FIGURE 2.4 Some Words Do Not Translate Exactly

When dealing across languages, it is useful to express things in more than one way to help ensure that all parties comprehend the same thing.

Source: The New Yorker (August 20, 2007).

"You'll have to phrase it another way. They have no word for 'fetch.'"

Finally, remember that grammar is complex and the seemingly slight misuse (or even placement) of a word can substantially change the meaning of an utterance. All of the following, each originally composed to assist English-speaking guests, have appeared on signs in hotels around the world:

FRANCE: "Please leave your values at the desk."

MEXICO (to assure guests about the safety of drinking water): "The manager has personally passed all the water served here."

JAPAN: "You are invited to take advantage of the chambermaid."

NORWAY: "Ladies are requested not to have children in the bar."

SWITZERLAND: "Because of the impropriety of entertaining guests of the opposite sex in the bedroom, it is suggested that the lobby be used for this purpose."

GREECE (at check-in line): "We will execute customers in strict rotation."

These examples offer a humorous look at language barriers that usually result only in a little embarrassment. Poor translations, however, can have much graver consequences. Inaccurate translations have caused structural collapses of buildings and airplane crashes, such as the collision of Air Kazakhstan and Saudi Arabian Air planes over India.[54] So choose your words carefully. Although there's no foolproof way of ensuring translations, experienced international businesspeople rely on such rules as the following:

- Get references for the people who will do your translating.

- Make sure your translator knows the technical vocabulary of your business.

- For written work, do *back translations:* Have one person, for example, go from English to French and a second from French back to English. If your final message says what you said originally, it's probably satisfactory.

- Use simple words whenever possible (such as *ban* instead of *interdiction*).

- Avoid slang. American slang, especially words or phrases originating from sports, like *off base, out in left field, threw me a curve,* and *ballpark figure,* are probably meaningless to most businesspeople outside the United States.

- When either you or your counterpart is dealing in a language other than your first language, clarify communications in several ways (repeat things in different words and ask questions) to ensure that all parties have the same interpretation.

- Recognize the need and budget from the start for the extra time needed for translation and clarification.

Be careful with humor. Although many jokes have universal appeal, a lot of humor does not. A Microsoft executive, for instance, once gave a speech to Indian executives in which he quipped that he really didn't have the qualifications to speak because he had never completed his MBA. The comment was badly received because Indians place high importance on education and on persevering rather than dropping out.[55]

Finally, even when all parties to a communication come from countries that share an official language, don't assume understanding will go smoothly. Table 2.1, for instance, lists just some of the approximately 4,000 words that have different meanings in British and American English. Here's a good example of what can go wrong. When Hershey's launched its Elegancita candy bar in Latin America, its expensive advertising campaign boasted about the *cajeta* in the product. Unfortunately, although *cajeta* means "goat's-milk caramel" in Mexico, in much of South America it's vulgar slang for a part of the female anatomy.[56]

TABLE 2.1   Dangers of Misspeaking the Language(s) of Business

Below are a couple of short lists containing words whose meanings are different in the United States and the United Kingdom—"two countries separated by a common language," as the British playwright G. B. Shaw once quipped. There are approximately 4,000 words with the potential to cause problems for people who—in theory—speak the same language.

United States	United Kingdom
turnover	*redundancy*
sales	*turnover*
inventory	*stock*
stock	*shares*
president	*managing director*
paperback	*limp cover*

Case Review Note

Silent Language   Of course, spoken and written language isn't our only means of communicating. In fact, we constantly exchange messages through a host of nonverbal cues that form what has been called a *silent language*.[57] Our opening case offers a good example. Recall that in the process of conducting market research for the Java Lounge, consultants selected the most promising interviewees by observing demeanor and certain physical cues.

Colors and sounds are also interesting aspects of a culture's "silent language." In most Western countries, for instance, black is associated with death. In parts of Asia, white has the same connotation; in various parts of Latin America, it's purple. For a product to succeed, its colors must obviously be consistent with the consumer's frame of reference. When, for example, United Airlines promoted a new passenger service in Hong Kong by giving white carnations to its best customers, the promotion backfired. Why? In Hong Kong, white carnations are given only in sympathy for a death in the family. On the spoken-language front, Motorola had difficulty assigning cell phone numbers in China because certain sounds in Mandarin came out wrong. If you give out a number ending in *54—7424*, for instance, you'll sound as if you're saying, "I die, my wife dies, my child dies."[58]

Silent language includes color associations, sense of appropriate distance, time and status cues, body language, and prestige.

Distance   Another aspect of silent language is the appropriate distance people maintain during conversations. In the United States, for example, the customary distance for a business discussion is 5 to 8 feet; for personal business, it's 18 inches to 3 feet.[59] When the distance is closer or farther than what's customary for them, people tend to feel uneasy. Thus U.S. managers conducting business in Latin America may find themselves constantly moving backward to avoid the closer conversational distance that their Latin American counterparts are trying to maintain because of their accustomed closer distance. At the end of the discussion, both parties may well feel uneasy about each other without realizing why.

Time and Punctuality   Perceptions of time and punctuality also affect unspoken cues that may create confusion internationally. U.S. businesspeople usually arrive early for business appointments, a few minutes late for dinner at someone's home, and a bit later still for large social gatherings. In another country, the concept of punctuality in any or all of these situations may be different. U.S. businesspeople in Latin America may consider it discourteous if their Latin American counterparts do not arrive at the stated time for a business meeting. Conversely, a Latin American host may find it equally discourteous if a U.S. guest arrives only a few minutes later than the stated time for dinner.

United States It's fine	**Germany** You lunatic	**Greece** An obscene symbol for a body orifice	**France** Zero or worthless	**Japan** Money, especially change

FIGURE 2.5 Body Language Is Not a Universal Language

The fine line between approval and put-down: Very few gestures have universal meanings. In the United States, you'd probably be safe in approving of another person's statement by forming an O with your thumb and index finger (the so-called high sign). In Germany, Greece, and France, however, you'd be expressing a very different opinion.

Source: The meanings have been taken from descriptions in Roger E. Axtell, *Gestures* (New York: John Wiley, 1998). Reprinted by permission of John Wiley & Sons, Inc.

Culturally speaking, there are different ways of looking at time. In English-speaking, Germanic, and Scandinavian countries, people tend to value time as a scarce commodity; if it's lost, it can't be recouped.[60] Thus they're prone not only to sticking to schedules but also to emphasizing short-term results, even if taking longer would yield better results.

In contrast, people who view time as an event prefer to take whatever time is necessary to complete the event. In one case, a U.S. company competing for a contract in Mexico with a French company drew up a presentation, confident that it would win on the basis of better technology. In fact, managers were so confident that they scheduled a tight, one-day meeting in Mexico City, allowing what they thought was plenty of time for the presentation and questions. Unfortunately, the Mexican team arrived one hour after the scheduled start. Then, when one member of the Mexican team was called out of the room for an urgent phone call, the whole group got upset when the U.S. team tried to proceed without him. The French team, in contrast, allocated two weeks for discussions and won the contract even though its technology was clearly less sophisticated.[61]

Body Language Body language, or *kinesics*—the way that people walk, touch, and move their bodies—also differs among cultures. Indeed, very few gestures are universal in meaning. A Greek, Turk, or Bulgarian, for example, indicates "yes" with a sideways movement of the head that resembles nothing so much as the shake of the head that means "no" in the United States and much of Europe. As Figure 2.5 shows, certain gestures may have several—even contradictory—meanings.

Prestige Another factor in silent language relates to a person's organizational position. A U.S. businessperson who places great faith in objects as cues to prestige may underestimate the status of foreign counterparts who don't value large, plush offices on high floors. A foreigner may underestimate U.S. counterparts who perform their own services, such as opening their own doors, fetching their own coffee, and answering unscreened phone calls.

Dealing with Cultural Differences

After a company has identified key cultural differences in the country where it intends to do business, must it alter its customary practices to succeed there? Can people actually overcome culturally related adjustment problems when working abroad? There are no easy answers to these questions, but the following discussion highlights some of the variables that affect *degrees* of successful adjustment. Basically, we can break down these variables into four issues:

1. The extent to which a culture is willing to accept the introduction of anything foreign
2. Whether key cultural differences are small or great

3. The ability of individuals to adjust to what they find in foreign cultures

4. The general management orientation of the company doing business in a foreign culture

In the following sections, we address each of these issues in some depth.

HOST SOCIETY ACCEPTANCE

Host cultures do not always expect foreigners to adjust to them.

Although our opening case illustrates the advantages of *adjusting* to a host country's culture, international companies sometimes succeed in introducing new products, technologies, and operating procedures with relatively little adjustment. How have they pulled off this feat? Primarily they have done so because the product, technology, or procedure they're introducing does not run counter to deep-seated attitudes or because the host culture is willing to accept the foreign product or practice as an agreeable trade-off. Bahrain, for instance, permits the sale of pork products (ordinarily prohibited by religious law) as long as transactions are limited to special grocery store departments in which Muslims can neither work nor shop. Bahrain does this because it needs the non-Muslim workers.

Sometimes the local society regards foreigners and domestic citizens differently. When staying overnight in Jeddah, for example, Western female flight attendants can wear the types of clothing publicly that local women cannot.[62] In other instances, local citizens may actually feel that their cultures are being mocked when foreigners bend over backwards to make adjustments.[63] But usually laws treat local and foreign citizens similarly.

DEGREE OF CULTURAL DIFFERENCES

Obviously, some countries are much like other countries, usually because they share many characteristics such as language, religion, geographic location, ethnicity, and level of economic development.

When doing business in a similar culture, companies

- Usually have to make fewer adjustments.
- May overlook subtle differences.

Cultural Distance   A Human Values study compared 43 societies on 405 cultural dimensions,[64] and by averaging the **cultural distance** separating countries on each dimension (say, the number of countries apart for Sweden and Spain on each dimension), researchers could determine the *cultural proximity* of two countries. On this scale, the United Kingdom is culturally close to the United States and China is culturally distant.

Map 2.4 identifies 58 countries according to the findings of a study by GLOBE (Global Leadership and Organizational Behavior Effectiveness) designed to cluster countries on a fairly specific dimension—namely, the values and attitudes of middle managers toward leadership characteristics. When a company moves into a foreign country that's culturally close rather than culturally distant, or when it moves within a cluster of culturally similar countries, it should expect to encounter fewer cultural differences and to face fewer cultural adjustments. An Ecuadorian company doing business in Colombia, for instance, should expect to make fewer adjustments than if it wanted to do business in Thailand.

Even within clusters, however, there may still be significant cultural differences that could affect business dealings. Moreover, managers may assume that closely clustered countries are more alike than they really are, and if they become too confident about the fit between their own and another nation, they may well overlook important subtleties. Women's roles and behavior, for example, differ substantially from one Arab country to another even though Arab countries overall are similar culturally.

Cultural Friction   Even if a home and host country have similar cultures, a business interaction may be viewed negatively—a situation called **cultural friction**—because of possible changes in power relationships and the sovereignty that sets countries apart.[65] Thus companies should also consider the host country's perception of their role in its market. Disney, for instance, had much more success in opening a theme park in Japan than in France, even though France is culturally closer to the United States than Japan. Why? On the one hand, the Japanese were more receptive to Disney for a variety of reasons: (1) Both Japanese children and adults, familiar with the *Mickey Mouse Club* on TV, perceived Mickey Mouse as a wholesome, nonthreatening figure; (2) the Japanese had a tradition of buying souvenirs on family excursions; and (3) Disney's reputation for supercleanliness and smiling faces fit well with Japanese preferences for harmony and order. The French, on the other hand, knew Mickey Mouse only as a comic book conniver who'd been reformulated for the French market. They regarded Disney souvenirs as tacky and policies requiring personnel to dress uniformly and smile mindlessly as violations of personal dignity.[66]

ABILITY TO ADJUST: CULTURE SHOCK

Firms operating internationally must send personnel abroad for both short and long periods of time. These personnel are subject to the laws where they go, as well as to potential exposure to certain foreign practices they may find traumatic. Recall, for example, the severe forms of capital and corporal punishment in Saudi Arabia to which we alluded in our opening case. In fact, there are cultural practices all over the world that many outsiders consider downright wrong, ranging from polygamy and child marriage to concubinage, slavery, and burning of widows. Both companies and individuals must decide if they're ready to carry on business in places that countenance such practices.

In addition, even in countries whose practices aren't necessarily traumatic to them, workers who go abroad often encounter something called **culture shock**—the frustration that results from having to absorb a vast array of new cultural cues and expectations. Even such seemingly simple tasks as using a different type of toilet or telephone, getting a driver's license, or finding where to buy specific merchandise can at first be taxing experiences.

| Some people get frustrated when entering a different culture.

According to some researchers, people working in a culture that's significantly different from their own may pass through certain stages in the process of adjustment. At first, much like tourists, they're delighted with quaint differences. Later, however, they grow depressed and confused (the *culture shock* phase), so their effectiveness in the foreign environment suffers. Fortunately for most people, culture shock begins to ebb after a month or two as they grow more comfortable.

Interestingly, some people experience culture shock when they go back home—a phenomenon known as **reverse culture shock.** What's happened? Basically, they've learned to accept the things they've encountered abroad—perhaps such seemingly simple things as more leisurely lunches—that were never common options back home.

COMPANY AND MANAGEMENT ORIENTATIONS

Whether and how much a company and its managers adapt to a foreign culture depends not only on the host-country culture but also on their own attitudes. The following sections discuss three such attitudes or orientations—polycentrism, ethnocentrism, and geocentrism.

Polycentrism   A *polycentric* organization or individual tends to believe that business units in different countries should act like local companies. Given the unique problems that many companies have heard about in foreign ventures, it's not surprising that many develop polycentric perspectives. In some respects, however, polycentrism may be an overly cautious response to cultural variety. How so? A firm whose outlook is too rigidly polycentric may shy away from certain countries or avoid transferring home-country practices or resources that will actually work well abroad.

| Polycentrist management is so overwhelmed by national differences that it won't introduce workable changes.

Look at it this way. To compete effectively, an international company—and its foreign units—must usually perform some functions differently from the competitors it encounters abroad in order to have an advantage over them. They may, for instance, need to sell new products or invent new ways to produce and market them. Because the

MAP 2.4
A Synthesis of
Country Clusters

As you can see, this map illustrates a key finding of the GLOBE study in the early 2000s of middle manager attitudes and values: namely, that managers in different countries share different ideas about the nature of *leadership*—ideas that, not surprisingly, tend to affect domestic business practices. Note that cluster labels (e.g., "Nordic Europe," "Confucian Asia") reflect the attitudes of *a majority of countries comprising each cluster.* Thus note the inclusion of Turkey—where Arabic is not the dominant language—in the "Arab" cluster and the inclusion of Costa Rica and Guatemala in the "Latin American" cluster even though attitudes there tend to be closer to those in countries grouped in the "Latin European" cluster.

Source: The map is prepared from data shown in Vipin Gupta, Paul J. Hanges, and Peter Dorfman, "Cultural Clusters: Methodology and Findings," *Journal of World Business* 37 (Spring 2002): 13. Reprinted with permission from Elsevier.

Note: Given that this is a Mercator projection, the scale approximates east-west distance at the equator; however, the farther you move from the equator, the more the east-west distance is distorted.

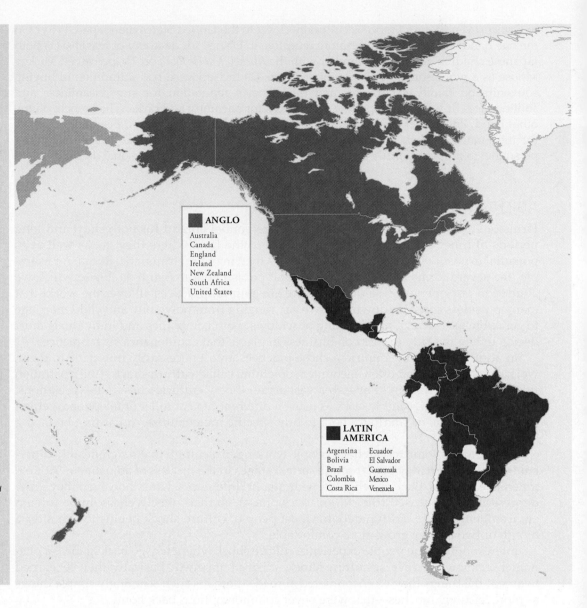

ANGLO

Australia
Canada
England
Ireland
New Zealand
South Africa
United States

LATIN AMERICA

Argentina   Ecuador
Bolivia   El Salvador
Brazil   Guatemala
Colombia   Mexico
Costa Rica   Venezuela

---

overly polycentric firm is less receptive to the idea of risking such innovation in an unfamiliar market, it may rely too heavily on imitation of proven host-country practices and, in the process, lose the innovative edge it has honed at home.

Ethnocentrist management overlooks national differences and

- Ignores important factors.
- Believes home-country objectives should prevail.
- Thinks change is easy.

Case Review Note

Ethnocentrism   *Ethnocentrism* reflects the conviction that one's own culture is superior to that of other countries. In international business, the term is usually applied to a company (or individual) strongly committed to the principle that what works at home will work abroad—so strongly committed that its overseas practices tend to ignore differences in cultures and markets.

Generally speaking, ethnocentrism may lead managers to adopt three different sets of practices:

1. Managers overlook important cultural factors because they've become accustomed to certain cause-and-effect relationships in the home country. Thus the British sales reps in our opening case wrongly assumed that by moving aggressively they could make the same number of calls and sales in Saudi Arabia as they made in Britain.

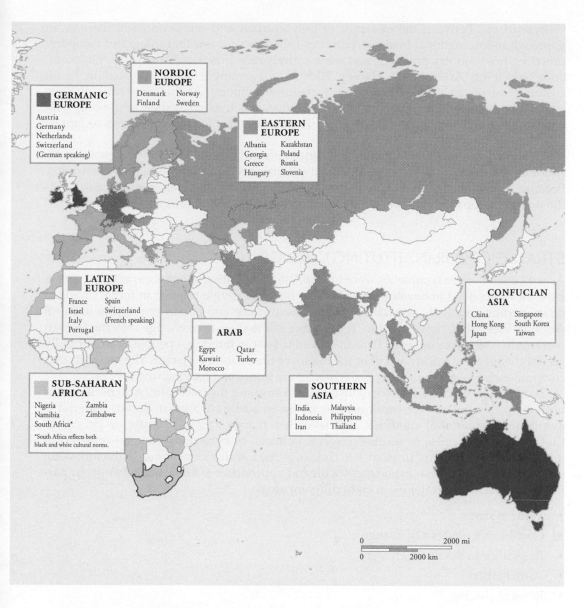

GERMANIC EUROPE
Austria
Germany
Netherlands
Switzerland
(German speaking)

NORDIC EUROPE
Denmark   Norway
Finland   Sweden

EASTERN EUROPE
Albania   Kazakhstan
Georgia   Poland
Greece   Russia
Hungary   Slovenia

LATIN EUROPE
France   Spain
Israel   Switzerland
Italy   (French speaking)
Portugal

ARAB
Egypt   Qatar
Kuwait   Turkey
Morocco

CONFUCIAN ASIA
China   Singapore
Hong Kong   South Korea
Japan   Taiwan

SUB-SAHARAN AFRICA
Nigeria   Zambia
Namibia   Zimbabwe
South Africa*
*South Africa reflects both
black and white cultural norms.

SOUTHERN ASIA
India   Malaysia
Indonesia   Philippines
Iran   Thailand

0   2000 mi
0   2000 km

2. Although it recognizes environmental differences, a firm still focuses on home-country objectives rather than those that fit with foreign-country or worldwide conditions. Because it doesn't perform as well as local competitors—and because it's probably encountering opposition to its practices in overseas markets—long-term competitiveness may suffer.

3. Although recognizing differences, a firm underestimates the complexity of introducing new management methods, products, or marketing means.

Before we go any further, we should point out that ethnocentrism isn't entirely an inappropriate way of looking at things. Obviously, much of what works at home will in fact work abroad. Recall also that concentrating on national differences in terms of *averages* overlooks specific variations within countries. By engaging in a focus strategy, a company may be able to sell to outliers even though the *average* consumer in the country has strong cultural biases against the product. Pursuing such a strategy, for example, you could sell meat products to the minority of Indians who eat meat regularly or on occasion. Likewise, a company may identify partners, suppliers, and employees among the minority of population whose attitudes don't fit the cultural average (there are always individualists in even the most collectivist societies).

Case Review Note

Geocentric management often uses business practices that are hybrids of home and foreign norms. Because people do not necessarily accept change readily, the management of change is important.

Geocentrism   Between the extremes of polycentrism and ethnocentrism, there is an approach to international business practices called *geocentrism* that integrates company practices, host-country practices, and some entirely new practices.[67] In our opening case, both Saks Fifth Avenue and Harvey Nichols, for example, have adjusted to Saudi customs (for instance, by setting aside women-only floors). At the same time, they've introduced home-country merchandising practices (such as what they sell) along with entirely new practices (such as providing drivers' lounges for the chauffeurs of female customers).

Geocentrism requires companies to balance informed knowledge of their own organizational cultures with both home- and host-country needs, capabilities, and constraints. Because it encourages innovation and improves the likelihood of success, geocentrism is the preferred approach for companies to succeed in foreign cultures and markets.

STRATEGIES FOR INSTITUTING CHANGE

As we've seen, when companies want to establish competitive advantages in foreign markets, they may need to develop new products (such as veggie burgers in India) or adjust their operating methods (separate workstations for male and female employees in Saudi Arabia). Inevitably, however, they'll introduce some degree of change into the foreign markets in which they operate. Thus they need to bear in mind that people don't normally accept change very readily, in either the home- or host-country market. The methods that companies choose for managing such changes are important for ensuring success.

Fortunately, we can gain a lot of insight by examining the international experiences of both for-profit and not-for-profit organizations. In addition, a great deal of material is available on potential methods and so-called *change agents*—people or processes that intentionally cause or accelerate social, cultural, or behavioral change—much of it dealing with overcoming resistance to change in the international arena. In the following sections, we discuss both experiences with and approaches to successful change. In particular, we focus on strategies in eight different areas:

- Value systems
- Cost-benefit analysis of change
- Resistance to too much change
- Participation
- Reward sharing
- Opinion leadership
- Timing
- Learning abroad

We conclude with a discussion on the importance of learning as a two-way process—one in which companies transfer knowledge to and from both domestic and foreign markets.

Value Systems   The more something contradicts our value system, the more difficulty we have accepting it. In Eritrea, for example, people eat a small amount of seafood compared with people in a lot of other countries. This is noteworthy because Eritrea has suffered several periods of agricultural famine in recent years but boasts a long coastline rich in seafood. In trying to persuade Eritrean adults to eat more seafood, however, the Eritrean government and the United Nations World Food Program have faced formidable opposition. There are religious taboos against eating fish without scales and insect-like sea creatures (including shrimp and crayfish), and most Eritreans have grown up believing that seafood has a foul taste. Among schoolchildren, however, whose value systems and habits were still flexible, officials faced little opposition.[73]

Point   Counterpoint

Does International Business Lead to Cultural Imperialism?

Point ▶ **Yes** The idea is pretty well accepted: International business influences globalization and globalization influences culture. Now, I have nothing against international business or globalization—at least part of it. What I don't like is *modern cultural imperialism*. What's *modern cultural imperialism?* It's what happens when the West, especially the United States, imposes its technical, political, military, and economic supremacy on developing countries.[68]

For years now, U.S. business has been in the business of exporting U.S. culture—mostly through tactics that are rarely in the best interests of the national cultures it's targeted for economic domination. Because U.S. companies nearly monopolize the international entertainment media, people all over the world are stuck with CNN, MTV, and the Disney Channel and bombarded with U.S. movies. Moreover, the same viewers are barraged with ads for the products—everything from nonnutritious soft drinks to obesity-creating fast foods—that pop up in the TV shows and movies they can't escape, even in the privacy of their own homes.

And what about the hordes of U.S. tourists who plop down more for a night's lodging in a developing country than the hotel maid makes in a year? If you ask them, they'll tell you they're just taking a look at how the other half lives, but the fact is, they're selling the U.S. lifestyle to a market that can't afford it and that's probably better off without a lot of it. Thanks to canned entertainment, nonstop advertising, and a sales force posing as tourists, culture shoppers in developing countries can sample U.S. possessions and practices to their hearts' content. Never mind that they come from a place—at least according to TV and the movies—that's populated mostly by the superwealthy and by cops and psychotic malcontents whose daily lives are taken up with bullet-spattered body parts, round-the-clock sex, and inane family relationships. The lifestyle is seductive and promotes everything that's "Made in the U.S.A." That's why people everywhere are starting to behave and even talk like fictional Americans—after all, everyday speech from Manila to Managua is now peppered with U.S. slang. Along the way, people are letting their own cultural identities slip away.

Once they have a foot in the door, Western companies barge in to exploit the demand that they've created, further destabilizing local cultures. In Mexico, Wal-Mart thinks nothing of putting up a superstore virtually next door to ancient ruins—and in the process, by the way, eradicating the nearby street market. What's more, because international companies tend to cluster in urban markets, they drag workers away from rural areas to work hours—under managers

Counterpoint ◀ **No** You imply that people in poor countries passively accept everything they see in movie theaters and on TV. They've turned their backs on a lot of products that international companies have promoted. Like most of us, they pick and choose.[70] You also imply that cultures in developing countries are the same. They aren't. They interpret what they see and hear—and what they buy—quite differently.

Like cultural purists everywhere, you've overlooked how cultural diffusion works. With contact, culture heads in both directions and evolves. Way back—say, between 100 BC and AD 400—about 50 Mediterranean languages disappeared when people took up reading and writing in Latin and Greek.[71] Today, of course, very few of us converse in Latin, but that doesn't mean it's completely disappeared; it's *evolved*—namely, into one of the "Romance" languages.

I agree that many languages are in trouble today, and it's important to study them while they're still around. But the thing to remember is this: Most of them are giving way to dominant languages in the countries where they are spoken, such as to Spanish, Mandarin, or Arabic. Of course, American English is seeping into other languages, but Americans have recently added a lot of foreign words as well. If you're a *macho* (Spanish) guy in charge of the whole *enchilada* (Spanish), for example, you're probably called the head *honcho* (Japanese).

Similarly, although U.S.-style fast food is almost everywhere, it has not entirely displaced local foods anywhere. When it comes to food, the result of international business is greater diversity for everybody. And what we're witnessing is not "cultural imperialism" but rather cultural *hybridization*. In most countries, U.S. hamburgers, Japanese sushi, Italian pizza, Mexican tacos, and Middle Eastern pita bread coexist with the local cuisine.

Also, just because people in developing countries have taken a liking to soft drinks and fast food doesn't mean they have scrapped their traditional values. Moreover, some evidence suggests that, although young people are most likely to adopt elements from a foreign culture, they tend to revert to traditional values and habits as they get older. If that's the case, it's hard to argue that they're spearheading any permanent changes in their local cultures.[72]

As people seek to fulfill different wants, they must make trade-offs. But, are people (and societies) worse off because they give up, say, lunch with the family to be able to afford certain consumer goods that will satisfy the whole family's needs? Globalization simply gives people more options. And as for the impact of tourism, that's also a two-edged sword. You say that its effect on host cultures is primarily who speak only English—that don't even allow time to go home for lunch.[69]

I admit, if a country is rich enough, it can afford to resist cultural exploitation. Canada, for instance, says no to foreign investment in culturally sensitive industries and makes sure there's Canadian content in local entertainment media. Finland discourages architecture that runs counter to tradition, and in France, the government discourages languages other than French and subsidizes a national motion picture industry. In the developing world, however, where there's precious little cash for fighting off cultural extinction, people are at the mercy of foreign culture brokers (not to mention local politicians who are too busy siphoning off every extra rupee and peso to protect their own personal way of life). ▶

negative, but quite often it has helped maintain certain features of a traditional culture, such as the revival of traditional Balinese dancing because tourists want to see it.

Let me close by saying that a successful business, whether locally or foreign owned, must accommodate itself sufficiently to the culture in which it operates. This may mean revising plans to respond to local demands. For instance, before Wal-Mart finalized its construction plans in Mexico, executives consulted with anthropologists, reduced the store's height, and decided on a stone facade in a subdued color. Now it can be seen only from atop the pyramids. And while we're on the subject, you also failed to mention that the so-called traditional street market in question was peddling imported plastic goods rather than indigenous Mexican handicrafts. ◀

Cost-Benefit Analysis of Change   Although some adjustments to foreign ways are inexpensive, others are quite costly. Some result in greatly improved sales or production performance, whereas others improve performance only marginally. Thus a company must consider the expected *cost-benefit relationship* of what it does abroad. On each December 12, for example, U.S.-based Cummins Engine shuts down its Mexican plant so workers may observe a religious holiday. Moreover, Cummins hosts a celebration for employees and families that includes a priest to offer the appropriate prayers. In this case, the cost to the employer is well worth the resulting renewal of employee commitment.

Resistance to Too Much Change   When the German magazine publisher Gruner + Jahr (G+J) bought U.S.-based *McCall's*, it immediately overhauled the magazine's format. The new owner changed editors, eliminated long stories and such features as advice columns, increased celebrity coverage, made layouts more robust, supplemented articles with sidebars, and refused discounts for big advertisers. Before long, morale declines led to increased employee turnover. More importantly, revenues fell because the change in format seemed too radical to advertisers.[74] According to most observers, G+J might have obtained more employee and advertiser acceptance had it phased in its plans for change a little more gradually.

Participation   One way to avoid problems like those encountered by G+J is to discuss proposed changes with stakeholders (employees, suppliers, customers, and the like) in advance. The company might perceive the strength of the resistance that it faces, stimulate stakeholders to recognize the need for change, and ease fears of the consequences of change. Employees, for instance, may at least be satisfied that management has listened to them, regardless of the decisions it ultimately makes.[75]

Companies sometimes make the mistake of thinking that stakeholder participation in decision making is effective only in countries with sufficiently educated people who are willing to speak up to make substantial contributions to the policy-making process. Anyone who's had to deal with foreign aid programs can tell you that participation can be extremely important even in countries where education levels are low and power distance and uncertainty avoidance high.

Reward Sharing   Sometimes a proposed change may have no foreseeable benefit for the people whose support must be obtained if it's to succeed. Production workers, for example, may have little incentive to try new work practices unless they see some more or less immediate benefit for themselves. What can an employer do? It might develop bonus or profit-sharing programs based on the new approach. In one case, a U.S.-Peruvian gold-mining venture won the support of skeptical Andean villagers by donating sheep.[76]

Opinion Leadership   By making use of local channels of influence, or *opinion leaders*, a firm may be able to facilitate the acceptance of change. Opinion leaders may emerge in unexpected places. When, for example, Ford wanted to instill U.S. production methods in a Mexican plant, managers relied on Mexican production workers, rather than on either Mexican or U.S. supervisors, to observe operations at U.S. plants. What was the advantage of this approach? The Mexican workers had more credibility than supervisors with the Mexican employees who would have to implement the new methods.[77] (Our closing case, which concerns a dam construction project in Uganda, tells the story of a fairly unusual opinion leader—one whose leadership techniques include the performance of elaborate religious rituals.)

CRN
Case Review Note

Timing   Many well-conceived changes fail simply because they're ill timed. A proposed laborsaving production method, for example, might under many circumstances make employees nervous about losing their jobs no matter how much management tries to reassure them. If, however, the proposal is made during a period of labor shortage, the firm is likely to encounter less fear and resistance.

In certain cases, of course, crisis precipitates the acceptance of change. In Turkey, for example, family members have traditionally dominated business organizations. Indeed, family members sometimes continue to exert substantial influence even after they no longer have any official responsibilities. In more and more instances, however, poor performance has stimulated a rapid change in this practice: Many families no longer "run" the business, but rather serve in "advisory capacities" (often on the board of directors).

Learning Abroad   Finally, remember that, as companies gain more experience in overseas operations, they may learn as well as impart valuable knowledge—knowledge that proves just as useful in the home country as in a host country. Such learning may concern any business function; however, access to researchers is a particularly potent advantage in operating abroad.

Looking to the
Future   What Will Happen to National Cultures?

Scenario 1: New Hybrid Cultures Will Develop and Personal Horizons Will Broaden

International contact is increasing at a rate few could have imagined a couple decades ago—a process that should lead to a certain mixing and greater similarity among national cultures. And at first glance, that's exactly what's happening.[78] The mixing seems evident when one sees, for example, a group of Japanese tourists listening to a Philippine band perform an American pop song in a British hotel in Indonesia. Likewise, combination languages such as "Spanglish" have emerged. The growing mix seems evident when one sees people in every corner of the world wearing

similar clothing and listening to international recording stars alongside other people wearing local styles and listening to local recording artists. Competitors headquartered in far-flung areas of the globe are increasingly copying each other's operating practices, thus creating a competitive work environment that's now more global than national. As companies and people get used to operating internationally, they should continue to become more confident in applying the benefits of cultural diversity and globally inspired operating procedures to explore new areas in both workplace productivity and consumer behavior.

We'll also see people taking advantage of greater mobility and, in the process, broadening their concepts

(continued)

of what it means to enjoy global citizenship.[79] Historically, for example, most people who immigrated to foreign countries were able to return to their homelands perhaps once in their lives. They were thus compelled to accept the cultures of their adopted countries, sacrificing much of their native cultural identity in the process. Today, however, immigrants, most of whom come to high-income countries from low-income countries to find work, often obtain dual citizenship and maintain contact with their native cultures through travel, direct-dial phone calls, and Internet communications. The important thing is that immigrants now tend to transfer culture in both directions, bringing greater cultural diversity to both host and home countries. There has also emerged a class of international managers whose traditional ties to specific cultures are much looser than those of most people. Educated in France, for instance, CEO Carlos Ghosn of Japan's Nissan and France's Renault is a Brazilian of Lebanese extraction.[80]

Scenario 2: Although the Outward Expressions of National Culture Will Continue to Become More Homogeneous, Distinct Values Will Tend to Remain Stable

Beneath the surface of the visual aspects of culture (including most of the elements that we touched on in the previous section), people continue to hold fast to some of the basic things that make national cultures different from one another. In other words, although certain material and even behavioral facets of cultures will become more universal, certain fundamental values and attitudes—for example, ways in which people cooperate, approach problem solving, and are motivated—will remain much the same. Religious differences, for instance, are as strong as ever, and language differences still bolster ethnic identities. What's important is that differences in these areas are still powerful enough to fragment the world culturally and to stymie the global standardization of products and operating methods.

Scenario 3: Nationalism Will Continue to Reinforce Cultural Identity

If people didn't perceive the *cultural* differences among themselves and others, they'd be less likely to regard themselves as distinct *national* entities. That's why appeals to cultural identity are so effective in mobilizing people to defend national identity. Typically, such efforts promote the "national culture" by reinforcing language and religion, subsidizing nationalistic programs and activities, and propagandizing against foreign influences on the national culture.

Scenario 4: Existing National Borders Will Shift to Accommodate Ethnic Differences

In several countries, we're seeing more evidence of subcultural power and influence. Why? Basic factors include immigration and the rise of religious fundamentalism. Equally important seems to be the growing desire among ethnic groups for independence from dominant groups where they reside. In recent years, for example, both Yugoslavia and Czechoslovakia have broken up for this reason, and in Sudan and Afghanistan, ethnic groups are currently pitted against one another in bloody wars. Meanwhile, some subcultures—such as the Inuits in the Arctic and the Kurds in the Middle East—simply resist identity by established national boundaries. Because they have less in common with their "countrymen" than with ethnic brethren in other countries, it's hard to assign them a national identity on the basis of geographic circumstances.

Regardless of the scenario that unfolds in any given arena, international businesspeople must learn to examine specific cultural differences if they hope to operate effectively in a foreign environment. In the future, analysis based only on national characteristics won't be sufficient; businesses will have to pay attention to all the other myriad factors that contribute to distinctions in values, attitudes, and behavior. ■

CASE

Charles Martin in Uganda: What to Do When a Manager Goes Native

James Green, a vice president at U.S.-based Hydro Generation (HG), pondered a specific question: Should he retain Charles Martin for the operation phase of a major dam project in Uganda?[81] (See Map 2.5 for the location of Uganda in Africa and of the dam project in Uganda.) Martin had already completed his assignments on the preliminary and construction phases of the project, and the results had been highly satisfactory—he'd finished every task on time and within budget.

MAP 2.5 Uganda

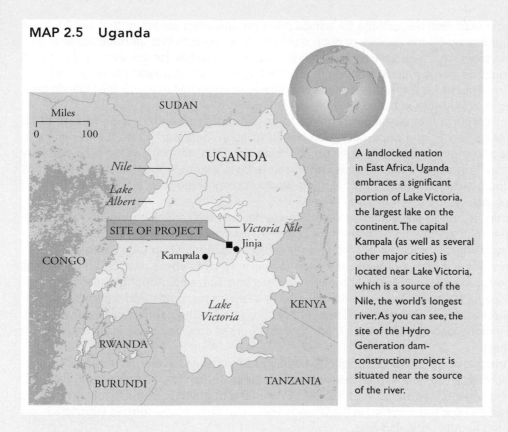

A landlocked nation in East Africa, Uganda embraces a significant portion of Lake Victoria, the largest lake on the continent. The capital Kampala (as well as several other major cities) is located near Lake Victoria, which is a source of the Nile, the world's longest river. As you can see, the site of the Hydro Generation dam-construction project is situated near the source of the river.

Green, however, was a little concerned with the *means* by which Martin tended to achieve his ends. In Green's opinion, Martin was too eager to accommodate Ugandan ways of doing business, some of which ran counter both to HG's organizational culture and to its usual methods of operating in foreign environments. In particular, Green worried that some of Martin's actions might have unforeseen repercussions for the company's presence in Uganda.

He also knew the philosophy and values of founder and current CEO Lawrence Lovell, who had been instrumental in shaping HG's mission and culture. A devout Christian and regular attendee of the National Prayer Breakfast, Lovell believed strongly that business activities, though secular, should embody Christian values. As a manager, he believed that subordinates should be given full responsibility for making and implementing decisions but that they should also be held accountable for the results.

Martin, however, wanted to stay in Uganda, and HG would be hard-pressed to find someone else with his combination of professional training, experience with HG, and familiarity with the host country. (Martin, although only 29, had already proved effective in using his knowledge of local development issues to disarm critics of the power plant.)

Hiring Martin as a project liaison specialist represented a new approach for HG. In this capacity, Martin had been given a threefold task:

1. To gain local support for the project by working with both Ugandan authorities in the capital of Kampala and villagers in the vicinity of the construction site
2. To set up an office and hire office personnel to take charge of local purchasing (including lower-level hiring), clearing incoming goods through customs, securing immigration permissions for foreigners attached to the project, overseeing the logistics of getting materials going from the airport in Kampala to the dam site, and keeping inventory and accounting records
3. To help foreign personnel (mainly engineers) get settled and feel comfortable living and working in Uganda

Martin was also responsible for establishing an operating structure that would spare incoming managers the hassles of such mundane start-up activities as obtaining licenses, installing telephones and utilities, and finding local people to hire for the wide range of jobs that would be needed. In addition, although HG specialized in power plants (it had built plants in 16 countries and retained ownership shares in about half of them), the Uganda project was its first African venture.

Dam construction anywhere requires huge amounts of capital, and projects often face opposition from groups acting on behalf of such local parties as the people who will need to move because of subsequent flooding. Thus, to forestall adverse publicity and, more importantly, activity that could lead to costly work stoppages, HG needed as many local allies as it could get. Getting (and keeping) them was another key facet of Martin's job.

Martin, although still young by most standards, was well suited to the Ugandan project. After high school, he'd entered the University of Wisconsin, where he became fascinated with Africa through a course in its precolonial history. Graduating with a major in African studies, he served with the Peace Corps in Kenya, where he worked with small business start-ups and took side trips to Ethiopia and Tanzania. Although he loved working in Kenya, Martin developed a disdain for the Western managers and workers who isolated themselves in expatriate ghettos and congregated in the capital's first-class hotels. His own creed became "Don't draw attention to yourself and, above all, learn and respect the culture."

At the end of his Peace Corps stint, Martin was determined to return to and work somewhere in Africa. After earning an MBA at the University of Maryland, he took a job with HG, where he worked for two years on project bidding and budgeting. Both when he was hired and when HG became involved in the Ugandan project, Martin made sure his superiors knew he wanted an African assignment.

Not surprisingly, HG saw the advantage of someone who possessed both a home-country corporate perspective and a knowledge of the host country's economics, politics, and culture. In Uganda, a country of about 25 million, English is the official language, but many people speak only an indigenous language—mainly Bantu or Nilotic languages. Although about two-thirds of Ugandans are Christians (about evenly split between Roman Catholics and Anglicans), there are large numbers of Muslims and adherents of various animistic religions.

Since gaining independence in 1962, Uganda has had a largely unhappy history. The ruthless dictatorship of Idi Amin included mass murder among its policies, and, more recently, Uganda has been forced to absorb huge numbers of refugees fleeing bloodshed in Rwanda, Zaire, and the Sudan. Nepotism is the norm, and the government is considered one of the most corrupt in the world. On the positive side, foreign companies that want to do business in Uganda aren't heavily regulated, and because few people have access to electricity, the Ugandan government strongly favored the HG power plant project.

Now, as the construction phase of the project was coming to an end, Green reviewed Martin's performance. Specifically, he was concerned not only about some of Martin's business practices but also about certain aspects of his lifestyle, not the least of which was his participation in local tribal rituals. HG had no formal guidelines on the lifestyles of expatriate managers in its employ, but the company culture tended to encourage standards of living that were consistent with the values of a prosperous international company. With what HG paid him, Martin could certainly afford to live in one of the upscale neighborhoods that were home to most foreign managers working in and around Kampala. Martin, however, preferred a middle-class Ugandan neighborhood and declined to frequent the places where fellow expatriates typically gathered, such as churches and clubs.

As far as Green was concerned, not only was Martin's lifestyle inconsistent with HG culture, but his preference for isolating himself from the expatriate community also made him of little use in helping colleagues adapt to the kind of life that would be comfortable for them in the alien environment of Uganda. With completion of the dam, foreign managers and engineers would be moving in with their families.

As for Martin's business-related practices, Green was ready to admit that business in Uganda usually moved at a leisurely pace. It could take months to get a phone installed, supplies delivered, or operating licenses issued. Martin, however, had quickly learned that he could speed things up by handing out tips in advance. Nor could Green argue that such payments were exorbitant: In a country where per capita GDP is about $1,300 a year, people tended to take what they could get.

It was also a fact of local life that unemployment was high and so-called job searches were generally conducted through word of mouth, especially among family members. Martin had developed the practice of mentioning openings to local people and then interviewing and hiring the relatives they recommended. In a country like Uganda, he reasoned, such family connections could come in handy. Hiring the niece of a high-ranking customs officer couldn't hurt when it came to getting import clearances.

To Green, however, although such practices were both normal and legal in Ugandan business dealings, they bordered on the unethical in a U.S. organization. He also worried about a variety of long-term practical consequences. For instance, what if word got out that HG was paying extra for everything (and, inevitably, it would)? Wouldn't *everyone* start to expect bonuses for every little service?

What's worse, if word reached the higher echelons of the Ugandan government, HG would probably find itself dealing with people in a position to demand large payments for such services as, say, not finding some excuse to hinder efficient operation of the project. Not only would these payments start to get costly, but they might be illegal under U.S. law. What about adverse international publicity that could negatively affect HG's operations in other countries?

Finally, Green wasn't comfortable with Martin's hiring practices. He had no reason to doubt the competence of any given hiree, but nepotism comes with risks. An employee's close connection with some government official, for example, might encourage the employee to participate more actively in the extortion process. What if a woman hired to work on import clearances decided to go into business with her uncle, the customs officer, to charge a little extra for every import approval? In addition, given Uganda's history of political instability, the company ran the risk that today's friends in high places might be tomorrow's enemies of the state.

Then there was the issue of the tribal rituals. The dam would displace about 700 villagers, and during early negotiations with the Ugandan government (and before Martin's transfer to Uganda), HG assembled a resettlement package that included the renovation of schools and health centers in the new location. HG executives understood that the package, valued at millions of dollars, was acceptable to the people who were affected. Shortly after Martin's arrival, however, two tribes living close to the Bujagali Falls site of the dam proclaimed the river home to sacred spirits. One leader likened the site to the tribe's Mecca.

As news of the claims reached the international press, worldwide support for the tribes began to grow. With permission from HG headquarters, Martin hired a specialist in African religions, who advised HG to work with the religious caretakers of the falls to find a solution. When contacted, the official caretaker revealed that, although the spirits could not be moved, they could be appeased at the right price. For a fee of $7,500, he sacrificed a sheep, two cows, four goats, and a slew of chickens, pinning them down on hot coals while 40 diviners prayed and danced. For the finale, blood was sprinkled on some sacred trees. Unfortunately, the spirits were not appeased. It seems that Martin had not participated in the ceremony. So Martin paid another fee of about $10,000 to repeat the ceremony, in which he took part, evidently appeasing the spirits.

Green was concerned about Martin's part in the second ceremony, which he himself considered pagan and probably a sham. Granted, Martin's participation had allowed work to continue, but Green worried that the episode could not only damage HG's image but could also offend Uganda's Christian majority and the many Christian missionaries in the country. On top of everything, Martin's participation might be construed in some quarters as a mockery of tribal customs, thereby contributing to a hostile environment for HG.

Having thoroughly considered the Charles Martin case, James Green now had to make decisions about staffing the operational phase of the project. He knew he needed to transfer a number of managers and engineers to Uganda, and he'd already begun interviewing some. But he was still left with one critical question: How much would the new expatriates benefit from the presence of an American who, like Martin, could be a valuable source of advice about Ugandan culture? And if he had to have someone in that role, was Martin still right for the part? ∎

QUESTIONS

1. Describe Ugandan cultural attributes that might affect the operations of a foreign company doing business there.
2. How would you describe the respective attitudes of Martin and Green: ethnocentric, polycentric, or geocentric? What factors do you suspect of having influenced their respective attitudes?
3. Who was right, Green or Martin, about Martin's more controversial actions in facilitating the project? How might things have turned out if Martin had not been a member of the project team?
4. In the next phase of the project—running the power plant—should HG employ someone whose main function is that of liaison between its corporate culture and the culture of its host country? If so, is Martin the right person for the job?

SUMMARY

- *Culture* includes norms based on learned attitudes, values, and beliefs. Almost everyone agrees that there are cross-country differences in culture, but most experts disagree as to exactly what they are.

- International companies and individuals must evaluate their business and personal practices to ensure that their behavior may fit with national norms.

- In addition to being part of a *national* culture, people are simultaneously part of other cultures, such as a professional or organizational culture.

- Distinct societies are often found within a given country. People also may have more in common with similar groups in foreign countries than with groups in their own countries.

- Cultural change may take place as a result of choice or imposition. Isolation from other groups, especially because of language, tends to stabilize cultures.

- People fall into social-stratification systems according to their *ascribed* and *acquired group memberships*. These memberships determine an individual's level of access to economic resources, prestige, social relations, and power. An individual's affiliations may determine his or her qualifications and access to certain jobs.

- Some people work far more than is necessary to satisfy their basic needs for food, clothing, and shelter. They're motivated to work for various reasons, including the preference for material possessions over leisure time, the belief that work will bring success and reward, and the desire for achievement.

- There are national differences in norms that influence people's behavior. Such norms determine whether they prefer autocratic or consultative working relationships, whether they prefer their activities to follow set rules, and how much they prefer to compete or cooperate with fellow workers.

- There are national differences in norms determining such behavioral factors as trust, belief in fate, and confidence in planning for the future.

- Failure to perceive subtle distinctions in culturally determined behavior can result in misunderstandings in international dealings.

- People communicate through spoken, written, and silent language—all governed by culturally determined cues. Cultural background also plays a major role in the ways in which people process information.

- Host cultures don't always expect foreign companies or individuals to conform to their norms. Sometimes they accommodate foreign companies, and sometimes they apply different standards to the behavior of foreigners.

- A company usually needs to make fewer adjustments when entering a culture that's similar to its own, but it must be quite careful to heed subtleties both in host-country behaviors and in host-country perceptions of foreigners' behaviors.

- People living and working in foreign environments should be sensitive to the dangers of excessive *polycentrism* and excessive *ethnocentrism*. Usually, *geocentrism* is a safer approach.

- In deciding whether to make changes in either home- or host-country operations, a company should consider several factors: the importance of the proposed changes to every party involved, the cost and benefit to the company of each proposed change, the value of opinion leaders in implementing the changes, and the timing of changes.

KEY TERMS

acquired group membership (p. 101)
ascribed group membership (p. 101)
cultural collision (p. 93)
cultural distance (p. 114)
cultural friction (p. 114)
cultural imperialism (p. 96)
culture (p. 93)
culture shock (p. 115)

future orientation (p. 108)
hierarchy-of-needs theory (p. 105)
high-context culture (p. 109)
idealism (p. 109)
individualism versus collectivism (p. 107)
low-context culture (p. 109)
masculinity–femininity index (p. 105)

monochronic (approach to multi-tasking) (p. 109)
polychronic (approach to multitasking) (p. 109)
power distance (p. 106)
pragmatism (p. 109)
reverse culture shock (p. 115)
uncertainty avoidance (p. 107)

ENDNOTES

1 *Sources include the following:* "First Coed University Inaugurated," *Miami Herald* (September 24, 2009): 13A; Abeer Allam, "Saudi Women Bridle at Business Rules," *Financial Times* (May 22, 2009): 4; Karen Elliott House, "Pressure Points," *Wall Street Journal* (April 10, 2007): A1+; Karen Elliot House, "For Saudi Women, a Whiff of Change," *Wall Street Journal* (April 7, 2007): A1+; Rachel Miller, "How to Exploit Pop around the Globe," *Marketing* (August 8, 2002): point-of-purchase section, 27; Roula Khalaf, "Saudi Women Carve a Place in the Future of Their Country," *Financial Times* (January 25, 2002): 3; Steve Jarvis, "Western-Style Research in the Middle East," *Marketing News* (April 29, 2002): International section, 37; Nadim Kawach, "Job Nationalisation to Gain Peace," *Financial Times Global News Wire* (July 12, 2002); John A. Quelch, "Does Globalization Have Staying Power?" *Marketing Management* 11:2 (March–April 2002): 18–27; "Andy Fry, Pushing into Pan Arabia," *Haymarket Publishing Services* (June 8, 2001): worldwide advertising section, 21; Ali Kanso, Abdul Karim Sinno, and William Adams, "Cross-Cultural Public Relations," *Competitiveness Review* 11:1 (2001): 65; Edward Pilkington, "Like Dallas Policed by the Taliban," *The Guardian* [London] (July 2, 2002): sec. G2, 2; Barbara Slavin, "U.S. Firms' Saudi Offices Face Manpower Issues," *USA Today* (May 13, 2002): 5A; Susan Taylor Martin, "Inside Saudi Arabia," *St. Petersburg* [FL] *Times* (July 21, 2002): 1A; Susan Taylor Martin, "Hanging Out at the Mall, Saudi Style," *St. Petersburg* [FL] *Times* (July 24, 2002): 8A; Colbert I. King, "When in Saudi Arabia . . . Do as Americans Do," *Washington Post* (February 2, 2002): A25; Donna Abu-Nasr, "Saudis Begin to Show Wear and Tear of Life under Feared Religious Police," *AP Worldstream* (April 28, 2002): n.p.; Cecile Rohwedder, "The Chic of Arabia," *Wall Street Journal* (January 23, 2004): A11+; Roula Khalaf, "Saudi's Grand Mufti Condemns Mixed Sexes at Economic Forum," *Financial Times* (January 22, 2004): 6; Joseph A. Kéchichian, "Jeddah Forum: A Step towards Reforms," *Gulf News* (January 22, 2004): n.p.; Parris-Rogers International (PRI) case in John D. Daniels and Lee H. Radebaugh, *International Business: Environments and Operations,* 9th ed. (Upper Saddle River, NJ: Prentice Hall, 2001): 45–46. We appreciate the help of Omar Aljindi, one of Java Lounge's owners, in providing information about the company's operations.

2 Jeanne Brett, Kristin Behfar, and Mary C. Kern, "Managing Multicultural Teams," *Harvard Business Review* 84 (November 2006): 84–91; Yaping Gong, "The Impact of Subsidiary Top Management Team National Diversity on Subsidiary Performance: Knowledge and Legitimacy Perspectives," *Management International Review* 46:6 (2006): 771–98; Carol Hymowitz, "Leadership," *Wall Street Journal* (November 14, 2005): R1.

3 David E. Brown, "Human Universals, Human Nature and Human Culture," *Daedalus* 133:4 (Fall 2004): 47–54.

4 Tomasz Lenartowicz and Kendall Roth, "The Selection of Key Informants in IB Cross-Cultural Studies," *Management International Review* 44:1 (2004): 23–51.

5 Three of the most significant are Geert Hofstede, *Cultures and Organizations: Software of the Mind* (New York, NY: McGraw-Hill, 1997), which explores attitudes in 50 countries, primarily those concerning workplace relationships; Ronald Inglehart, Miguel Basa–ez, and Alejandro Moreno, *Human Values and Beliefs: A Cross-Cultural Sourcebook* (Ann Arbor, MI: University of Michigan Press, 1998): analyzes political, religious, sexual, and economic norms in 43 countries; Robert J. House, Paul J. Hanges, Mansour Javidan, Peter W. Dorfman, and Vipin Gupta, eds., *Culture, Leadership, and Organizations* (Thousand Oaks, CA: Sage, 2004) examines leadership preferences in 59 countries.

6 Mary Lou Egan and Marc Bendick, Jr., "Combining Multicultural Management and Diversity into One Course on Cultural Competence," *Academy of Management Learning & Education* 7:3 (2008): 387–93.

7 Geert Hofstede and Robert R. McCrae, "Personality and Culture Revisited: Linking Traits and Dimensions of Culture," *Cross-Cultural Research* 38:1 (February 2004): 52–88.

8 Robert J. Foster, "Making National Cultures in the National Acumen," *Annual Review of Anthropology* 20 (1991): 235–60, discusses the concept and ingredients of a national culture.

9 Harry C. Triandis, "Dimensions of Cultural Variation as Parameters of Organizational Theories," *International Studies of Management and Organization* 12:4 (Winter 1982–1983): 143–44.

10 See Aihwa Ong, *Flexible Citizenship: The Cultural Logics of the Transnationality* (Durham, NC: Duke University Press, 1999); Leo Paul Dana, *Entrepreneurship in Pacific Asia* (Singapore: World Scientific, 1999).

11 Yadong Luo and Oded Shenkar, "The Multinational Corporation as a Multilingual Community: Language and Organization in a Global Context," *Journal of International Business Studies* 37 (2006): 321–39.

12 David Crystal, *English as a Global Language* (Cambridge: Cambridge University Press, 1997): 1–23; Jon Boone, "Native English Speakers Face Being Crowded Out of Market," *Financial Times* (February 15, 2006): 8.

13 Evelyn Nien-Ming Ch'ien, *Weird English* (Boston, MA: Harvard University, 2004).

14 Inglehart et al., *Human Values and Beliefs*, 21.

15 Michael Segalla, "National Cultures, International Business," *Financial Times* (March 6, 1998): mastering global business section, 8–10.

16 Fons Trompenaars, *Riding the Waves of Culture* (Burr Ridge, IL: Richard D. Irwin, 1994): 100–16.

17 "When Culture Masks Communication: Japanese Corporate Practice," *Financial Times* (October 23, 2000): 10; Robert House et al., "Understanding Cultures and Implicit Leadership Theories across the Globe: An Introduction to Project GLOBE," *Journal of World Business* 37 (2002): 3–10.

18 "Putting the Malaise into Malaysia," *Asia Times Readers Forum*, at forum.atimes.com/topic.asp?topic_ID=9002& whichpage=10 (accessed May 27, 2007).

19 John Burton, "Cracks Appear in Malaysia's Multi-ethnic Settlement," *Financial Times* (January 10, 2008): 11.

20 Larry Rohter, "Multiracial Brazil Planning Quotas for Blacks," *New York Times* (October 2, 2001): A3; "Out of Eden," *The Economist* (July 5, 2003): 31+.

21 *Women of the World 2005* (Washington, DC: Population Reference Bureau, 2005): 8.

22 Hayat Kabasakal and Muzaffer Bodur, "Arabic Cluster: A Bridge between East and West," *Journal of World Business* 37 (2002): 40–54.

23 Robert F. Szarfran, "Age-Adjusted Labor Force Participation Rates, 1960-2045," *Monthly Labor Review* 125:9 (2002): 25–38.

24 Inglehart et al., *Human Values and Beliefs*, question V128.

25 "The New Workforce," Economist.com (November 1, 2001) (accessed March 12, 2005).

26 "The Employers Forum on Age," *Legal: Europe*, at www.efa.org.uk/legal/europe.asp (accessed May 27, 2007); Cindy Wu, John J. Lawler, and Xiang Xi, "Overt Employment Discrimination in MNC Affiliates: Home-Country Cultural and Institutional Effects," *Journal of International Business Studies* 39:5 (2008): 772–94.

27 "Minimum Legal Ages for Alcohol Purchase or Consumption around the World," at www.geocities.jp/m_kato_clinic/mini-age-alcohol-eng-l.html (accessed May 28, 2007).

28 Inglehart et al., *Human Values and Beliefs*, questions V129.

29 Markus Pudalko, "The Seniority Principle in Japanese Companies: A Relic of the Past?" *Asia Pacific Journal of Human Resources* 44:3 (2006): 276–94.

30 Francis Fukuyama, *Trust: The Social Virtues and the Creation of Prosperity* (New York, NY: Free Press, 1995).

31 For a good overview of the literature on the Protestant ethic, see Harold B. Jones Jr., "The Protestant Ethic: Weber's Model and the Empirical Literature," *Human Relations* 50:7 (1997): 757–86.

32 Luigi Guiso, Paola Sapienza, and Luigi Zingales, "People's Opium? Religion and Economic Attitudes," *Journal of Monetary Economics* 50:1 (2003): 225–38.

33 See, for example, David S. Landes, *The Wealth and Poverty of Nations* (New York, NY: Norton, 1998).

34 David Gauthier-Villars, "France Wrests Title of Sleeping Giant," *Wall Street Journal* (May 5, 2009): A8.

35 David Gardner, "Indians Face 10m Rupee Question: Do You Sincerely Want to Be Rich?" *Financial Times* (July 15–16, 2000): 24.

36 Triandis, "Dimensions of Cultural Variation as Parameters of Organizational Theories," 159–60.

37 Hofstede, *Cultures and Organizations*.

38 Abraham Maslow, *Motivation and Personality* (New York, NY: Harper & Row, 1954).

39 Richard Metters, "A Case Study of National Culture and Offshoring Services," *International Journal of Operations & Production Management* 28:8 (2008): 727–47.

40 Hofstede, *Cultures and Organizations* 49–78; House et al., *Culture, Leadership, and Organizations*.

41 Hofstede, *Cultures and Organizations*.

42 Maxim Voronov and Jefferson A. Singer, "The Myth of Individualism-Collectivism: A Critical Review," *The Journal of Social Psychology* 142:4 (August 2002): 461–81.

43 See John J. Lawrence and Reh-song Yeh, "The Influence of Mexican Culture on the Use of Japanese Manufacturing Techniques in Mexico," *Management International Review* 34:1 (1994): 49–66; P. Christopher Earley, "East Meets West Meets Mideast: Further Explorations of Collectivistic and

Individualistic Work Groups," *Academy of Management Journal* 36:2 (1993): 319–46.

44 Hofstede, *Cultures and Organizations*.

45 Inglehart et al., *Human Values and Beliefs*, question V94.

46 Srilata Zaheer and Akbar Zaheer, "Trust across Borders," *Journal of International Business Studies*, 37:1 (2006): 21–29.

47 Examples in this section come from the GLOBE (Global Leadership and Organizational Behavior Effectiveness) project. See Bakacsi et al., "The Germanic Europe Cluster: Where Employees Have a Voice," *Journal of World Business* 37 (2002): 55–68; Jorge Correia Jesino, "Latin Europe Cluster: From South to North," *Journal of World Business* 37 (2002): 81–89.

48 Ping Ping Fu, Jeff Kennedy, Jasmine Tata, Gary Yuki, Michael Harris Bond, Tai-Kuang Peng, Ekkirala S. Srinivas, Jon P. Howell, Leonel Prieto, Paul Koopman, Jaap J. Boonstra, Selda Pasa, Marie-François Lacassagne, Hiro Higashide, and Adith Cheosakul, "The Impact of Societal Cultural Values and Individual Social Beliefs on the Perceived Effectiveness of Managerial Influence Strategies: A Meso Approach," *Journal of International Business Studies* 35:4 (2004): 284–304.

49 Benjamin Lee Whorf, *Language, Thought and Reality* (New York: Wiley, 1956): 13.

50 For an examination of subtle differences among northern European cultures, see Malene Djursaa, "North Europe Business Culture: Britain vs. Denmark and Germany," *European Management Journal* 12:2 (June 1994): 138–46.

51 Richard E. Nisbett et al., "Culture and Systems of Thought: Holistic versus Analytic Cognition," *Psychological Review* 108:2 (April 2001): 291–310.

52 Don Clark, "Hey, #@*% Amigo, Can You Translate the Word 'Gaffe'?" *Wall Street Journal* (July 8, 1996): B6.

53 René White, "Beyond Berlitz: How to Penetrate Foreign Markets through Effective Communications," *Public Relations Quarterly* 31:2 (Summer 1986): 15.

54 Mark Nicholson, "Language Error Was Cause of Indian Air Disaster," *Financial Times* (November 14, 1996): 1.

55 Manjeet Kripalani and Jay Greene, "Culture Clash," *Business Week* (February 14, 2005): 9.

56 Christina Hoag, "Slogan Could Offend Spanish Speakers," *Miami Herald* (March 8, 2005): C1+.

57 Much of the discussion on silent language is based on Edward T. Hall, "The Silent Language in Overseas Business," *Harvard Business Review* (May–June 1960). Hall identified five variables—time, space, things, friendships, and agreements—and was the first to use the term *silent language*.

58 Benjamin Fulford, "The China Factor," *Forbes* (November 13, 2000): 116–22.

59 Fulford, "The China Factor."

60 For an excellent explanation of four ways to view time, see Carol Saunders, Craig Van Slyke, and Douglas Vogel, "My Time or Yours? Managing Time Visions in Global Virtual Teams," *Academy of Management Executive* 18:1 (2004): 19–31. See also Lawrence A. Beer, "The Gas Pedal and the Brake: Toward a Global Balance of Diverging Cultural Determinants in Managerial Mindsets," *Thunderbird International Business Review* 45:3 (May–June 2003): 255–70.

61 Trompenaars, *Riding the Waves of Culture*, 130–31.

62 Daniel Pearl, "Tour Saudi Arabia: Enjoy Sand, Surf, His-and-Her Pools," *Wall Street Journal* (January 22, 1998): A1.

63 June N. P. Francis, "When in Rome? The Effects of Cultural Adaptation on Intercultural Business Negotiations," *Journal of International Business Studies* 22:3 (1991): 321–22.

64 Inglehart, *Human Values and Beliefs*, 16.

65 Oded Shenkar, Yadong Luo, and Orly Yeheskel, "From 'Distance' to 'Friction,' Substituting Metaphors and Redirecting Intercultural Research," *Academy of Management Review* 33:4 (2008): 905–23.

66 Mary Yoko Brannen, "When Mickey Loses Face: Recontextualization, Semantic Fit, and the Semiotics of Foreignness," *Academy of Management Review* 29:4 (2004): 593–616.

67 Mary Yoko Brannen and Yoko Salk, "Partnering across Borders: Negotiating Organizational Culture in a German-Japanese Joint Venture," *Human Relations* 53:4 (June 2000): 451–87; Baruch Shimoni and Harriet Bergman, "Managing in a Changing World: From Multiculturalism to Hybridization—The Production of Hybrid Management Culture in Israel, Thailand, and Mexico," *Academy of Management Perspectives* (August 2006): 76–89.

68 John Tomlinson, *Globalization and Culture* (Chicago: University of Chicago Press, 1999).

69 "In Mexico, Ancient Life vs. Wal-Mart," *Miami Herald* (September 6, 2004): 6A.

70 Nader Asgary and Alf H. Walle, "The Cultural Impact of Globalisation: Economic Activity and Social Change," *Cross Cultural Management* 9:3 (2000): 58–76; Tyler Cowen, *Creative Destruction: How Globalization Is Changing the World's Cultures* (Princeton, NJ: Princeton University Press, 2002): 128–52.

71 Clive Cookson, "Linguists Speak Out for the Dying Languages," *Financial Times* (March 26, 2004): 9.

72 Adrian Furnham and Stephen Bochner, *Culture Shock* (London: Methuen, 1986): 234.

73 Geraldine Brooks, "Eritrea's Leaders Angle for Sea Change in Nation's Diet to Prove Fish Isn't Foul," *Wall Street Journal* (June 2, 1994): A10.

74 Patrick M. Reilly, "Pitfalls of Exporting Magazine Formulas," *Wall Street Journal* (July 24, 1995): B1; James Bandler and Matthew Karnitschnig, "Lost in Translation," *Wall Street Journal* (August 19, 2004): A1+.

75 Mzamo P. Mangaliso, "Building Competitive Advantage from Ubuntu: Management Lessons from South Africa," *Academy of Management Executive* 15:3 (August 2001): 23–34.

76 Sally Bowen, "People Power Keeps Peru's Investors in Check," *Financial Times* (February 6, 1998): 6.

77 Roberto P. Garcia, "Learning and Competitiveness in Mexico's Automotive Industry: The Relationship between Traditional and World-Class Plants in Multination Firm Subsidiaries," unpublished Ph.D. dissertation (Ann Arbor, MI: University of Michigan, 1996).

78 Philippe Rosinski, *Coaching across Cultures: New Tools for Leveraging National, Corporate & Professional Differences* (London: Nicholas Brealey, 2003).

79 Aihwa Ong, *Flexible Citizenship: The Cultural Logics of Transnationality* (Durham, NC: Duke University Press, 1999).

80 James Mackintosh, "A Superstar Leader in an Industry of Icons," *Financial Times* (December 16, 2004): 10.

81 *Sources include the following:* Khadija Sharife, "Damnation for Africa's Big Dams?" *African Business* 352 (April 2009): 52–54; "Uganda Economy: Back to Basics," *EIU Newswire* (June 19, 2009): n.p.; "AES Begins Compensation for the Bujagali Project Affected Residents," *The Bujagali Power Project Update* 1:3 (October 2001): 1+; Deepak Gopinath, "The Divine Power of Profit," *Institutional Investor* 35:3 (March 2001): 39–45; Probe International home page, "World Bank Campaign," at www.probeinternational.org (accessed November 3, 2004); Taimur Ahmad, "We Are Devo," *Project Finance* 216 (April 2001): 39–44; "Give Us Freedom and Kampala: The Baganda on the March," *The Economist* (February 8, 2003): 64; "Uganda: Harnessing the Power of the Nile," IrinNews.org (March 21, 2003); Stephen Linaweaver, "A Case Study of the Bujagali Falls Hydropower Project, Uganda," Occasional Paper No. 42 (London: London School of Economics and Political Science, July 2002); "AAGM: Bujagali: A Dream That Ugandans Love to Hate," *Financial Times Information* (June 23, 2002); Charlotte Denny, "Nile Power Row Splits Uganda," *The Guardian* [London] (August 15, 2001), at www.guardian.co.uks; Marc Lacey, "Traditional Spirits Block a $500 Million Dam Plan in Uganda," *New York Times* (September 13, 2001): B1+; Mark Turner, "Uganda's Dam-Builders Search for Consensus," *Financial Times* (October 1, 2001): 15; "Appeasing the Spirits," *The Irish Times* (January 5, 2002): 62; "Face Music—History of Uganda," at www.music.ch/face/inform/history_uganda (accessed March 7, 2005); "Uganda," Lonely Planet World Guide, at www.lonelyplanet.com/destinations/africa/uganda/culture.htm (accessed March 7, 2005). The people in the case are fictitious, but some of the incidents are based on the experiences of U.S.-based AES Electric, Ltd., the world's largest independent power producer, which contracted with the Ugandan government to build a $520 million dam on the Bujagali Falls of the Nile River in 2001. Citing diminishing returns, AES withdrew from the project in 2003. The Blackstone Group announced in 2007 that it would resume the project.

three

The Political and Legal Environments Facing Business

Objectives

- To discuss the philosophy and practices of the political system

- To profile trends in contemporary political systems

- To explain the idea of political risk and describe approaches to managing it

- To discuss the philosophy and practices of the legal system

- To describe trends in contemporary legal systems

- To explain legal issues facing international companies

Every road has two directions.

—Russian proverb

CASE China—Complicated Risks, Big Opportunities

From 1949 to the late 1970s, China's was autarkic, championing a self-sufficient economy that relied entirely on its own resources. Communist Party leaders believed contact with foreigners would corrupt the nation's political structure and pollute its cultural life; hence, they prohibited foreign direct investment and restricted foreign trade.[1] Near the end of the 1970s, however, Chinese leadership began to rethink its economic strategy. Realizing by 1978 that it was lagging behind much of the world, China enacted the Law on Joint Ventures Using Chinese and Foreign Investment. This law effectively began China's reintegration into the global economy.

Since then, Chinese economic policy has been characterized by step-by-step liberalization and gradual entry into the world of foreign trade and investment. Unquestionably, the Communist Party maintains an absolute monopoly on political power. Today, however, free market principles shape the country's business environment. This transformation has yielded astonishing results. Over the past quarter century, no

MAP 3.1 China: The Inscrutable Market

With more than 1.3 billion consumers and a labor force of just over 800 million workers, China is attractive to foreign investors. One of every five people in the world lives in China, but the population is unevenly distributed: In fact, 50 percent of all Chinese live on 8.2 percent of the country's total land. Even so, maintaining centralized control over the nation's political and economic affairs has traditionally been almost impossible: The vast distances between seats of authority ensure that local officials are often free to run things the way they want to.

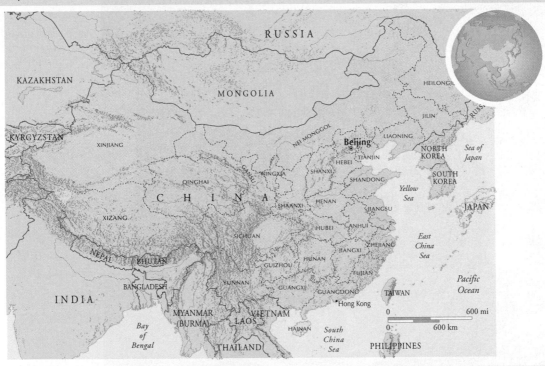

country has prospered more from globalization than China. Its companies have moved from woefully run state-owned enterprises to world-class multinationals, it has accumulated the greatest financial reserves in the world, and there is a growing sense that China's global ascendency is at hand.

THE SIREN CALL OF OPPORTUNITY

Compelling incentives attract investment to China. The 1980s witnessed a gold rush of investments by foreign companies, ranging from manufacturing ventures and export processing to licensing agreements and service relationships. This rush has run unabated for nearly 30 years. Despite the current global crisis, for instance, investment flows into China grew 23.6 percent in 2008. Total FDI in China—representing more than 600,000 ventures set up by companies from around the world—approached U.S. $900 billion.

Why have foreign companies rushed to China? Quite simply, they are racing to take advantage of stunning opportunities:

- *Market Potential.*   China, with a population of more than 1.3 billion people, has seen its economic growth move tens of millions from subsistence into the middle class. Hundreds of millions more, although poor, see a brighter future. Moreover, many domestic markets are still in the early- or mid-growth stage of the product life cycle.

- *Market Performance.*   Rapid economic development has catapulted China into one of the biggest economies of the world; it is trending to be the biggest within a decade. Growing income power increases consumer spending. During the industrialization of the United States and Great Britain in the nineteenth century, the real incomes per capita of their populations doubled in 50 years; China's did the same in nine years.

- *Infrastructure.*   China is in a multiyear program to build its infrastructure; it is investing trillions of dollars on highways, airports, seaports, waterways, dams, power plants, telecom grids, and communication networks.

- *Resources.*   China has a well-educated population and an immense pool of productive labor, yet its wage rates remain far below those in many other countries—roughly 1/3 of the Mexican and 1/25 of the U.S. wage rates.

- *Strategic Positioning.*   Many companies see investment and operation in China as fundamental elements of their global strategies. Like the United States a hundred years ago, China is on the rise; companies respond accordingly.

THE COMPLICATION OF REALITY

China's attractiveness is tarnished by an array of political and legal complications. Its unique political and legal systems make business operations a complex and often frustrating process. In short, the country currently practices a system of state capitalism whereby the government manipulates market activities to achieve political purposes. Consequently, foreign companies doing business in China may find themselves at a disadvantage. Although many stumbling blocks and systemic constraints are recent developments, all reflect the mix of ancient and contemporary political and legal forces that define the Chinese business environment.

Some observers argue that, when it comes to doing business in China, the number one rule is to throw away the rule book. Circumstances alert foreign investors to abandon the notion that Western ideas automatically work in China. In the West, for instance, a basic principle holds that you can form a corporation "for any valid business purpose." This principle does not exist in China. If you want to incorporate in China, the government wants to know—in excruciating detail—such basics as who you are, what you want to do, how do you plan to do it, how much you intend to invest, and how many jobs you will create.

Traditionally, centralized authority has determined the path and pace of economic development—a situation that is hardly unique to China. As they undergo their own transitions, many once-government-controlled economies around the world deal with legacies of centralized decision making. China, however, is a particularly tough case. According to aspiring foreign investors, China's political and legal systems foster time-consuming busywork. Moreover, it tends to stack the odds against foreigners who are bold enough to forge ahead in the face of an elaborate government structure and a fledgling legal system.[2]

POLITICS AND BUREAUCRACY

"If the great invention of European civilization was a legal system," quipped an observer, "then China's was bureaucracy." Frustrated investors blame China's treacherous business terrain on a bureaucratic system that relies on arbitrary agendas rather than objective standards to regulate activity. Those who believe that economics determines the most efficient means of generating prosperity see this as an illogical situation. Still, this circumstance is utterly logical to a Chinese leadership that sees state control of the country's business activity as the most reliable path toward harmonious prosperity.

Whereas Westerners are accustomed to the doctrine of the "rule of law," China has long relied on another: the "rule of man" and its premise that governance and rules of conduct are at the discretion of a single person, such as the reigning emperor, or a select group of persons, such as the Communist Party. In the 1940s, with the ascendancy of Mao Zedong and the Communist Party, a new centralized leadership took over an already complicated civil service system. It then added another layer of bureaucratic authority by superimposing the hierarchy of the Communist Party. The result was a regulatory system more byzantine than ever.

Today, foreign investors navigate complex political channels. Companies endure protracted negotiations (often spanning several years) in seeking permission to start local operations. At each stop of the long march, national, regional, and local officials demand explanations about how the investment encourages capital formation, promotes exports, creates jobs, and transfers technology.

Complicating this intricate process is the long-running conflict between central and local Chinese authorities. The vastness of the country means that local officials, whether headquartered in the smallest villags or the largest city, are often left to govern according to their own preferences. "The centre," notes one observer, often "has no control over the provinces. When it sends people to investigate illegal pirating of CDs, local governors block access to the factories." A sixteenth-century Chinese proverb, "The mightiest dragon cannot crush the local snake," captures the spirit of this power struggle. Essentially, even though the central government in Beijing may appear to be all powerful, its practical reach is limited by the politics of local fiefdoms.

THE LEGAL SYSTEM

China had no formal legal system in 1978 when it launched one of the greatest campaigns of legal reform in history. Progress has stabilized what had been an utterly unpredictable legal environment. Still, China faces challenges, including legislative gaps, hazy interpretation, lax enforcement, and philosophical disagreements.

"Chinese legislation is chock-full of ambiguities," says one Beijing-based lawyer, who thinks it will take 10 to 15 years to iron out many wrinkles. Some observers are a bit more pessimistic, comparing the state of the present Chinese legal system with that of the United States in the 1920s—an antiquated composite of statutes and legal codes that took more than 80 years to modernize.

Others note that, in the case of the Chinese system, even bigger problems reflect a difference in the conception of legality in a society. Western legal systems rest on the rule of law and its doctrine of legitimate laws executed by public officials who are held accountable for their just administration. In contrast, China practices the philosophy of the rule of man, seeing the right of the "man"—whether emperor, party, or local bureaucrat—to make decisions without concern for any system of checks and balances.

THE LEGALITY OF ILLEGALITY

China's legal practices, combined with the growing pains of fledgling legal institutions and political norms, create problems for foreign companies. A flashpoint of controversy is the protection of intellectual property—any product of someone's intellect that has commercial value such as patents, trademarks, and copyrights. Western companies complain that the relentless, widespread, and sophisticated theft of their intellectual property fuels China's economic surge.

In the United States, the FBI estimates that American companies lose up to U.S. $250 billion annually to counterfeiting, half of it because of China's illegal practices. Although impossible to pinpoint the extent of intellectual property violations in China, aggressive estimates attribute nearly a third of the Chinese economy to piracy. In frustration, the United States has accused the Chinese of counterfeiting (or pirating) software, videos, pharmaceuticals, and other goods—sometimes with the open encouragement of Chinese officials—and of falling short in punishing perpetrators.[3]

Meanwhile, on the city streets and country roads of China, counterfeiting is pervasive. What accounts for China's status as the world's premier number-one counterfeiter? Most analysts point to China's collectivist orientation, rule-of-man legacy, and dubious enforcement of loosely stipulated laws. These conditions have created an unprecedented political and legal morass. "We have never seen a problem of this size and magnitude in world history," notes one observer. "There's more counterfeiting going on in China now than we've ever seen anywhere."[4] The problem threatens to worsen. Government policies have "left a deep impression on companies that intellectual property is there for anyone to use it." Practically, China has excelled in producing high-quality knockoffs, or, as they say in Shanghai, "We can copy everything except your mother."[5]

WHERE TO NOW?

The siren call of opportunities in China continues to attract foreign firms. Still, would-be investors question how an opaque political system and an arbitrary legal system can possibly protect their commercial and property rights. Some believe that the influence of external institutions will spur China to improve the transparency of its business environment. For instance, managers note China's membership in the WTO, a global institution that sets rules for international trade. China's 2001 ascension to the WTO requires it to accept rules on all sorts of business matters, including tariffs, antidumping regulations, and protecting trademarks and copyrights. So far, China has formally complied with many WTO regulations, notably amending its legal code to conform to stipulations on issues ranging from trade and investment to intellectual property protection.

Still, problems persist, given China's sluggishness in enforcing its WTO obligations. Granted, signs of compliance are a step in the right direction, but on paper the laws and penalties are stiffer than in practice. The question now is: Will China actually enforce those laws? At this point, the data are not encouraging.

Frustration with China's performance on the protection of intellectual property provoked the United States to file complaints with the WTO about "inadequate enforcement." The United States argued that China's failure to curb piracy not only costs software, music, and book publishers billions of dollars in lost sales but also makes it unfairly hard for legitimate firms to operate in the Chinese market. Expressing "great regret and strong dissatisfaction at the decision," a Chinese official responded that the U.S. action was "not a sensible move."[6]

Despite a long list of political difficulties and legal disappointments, foreign investors keep heading to China. Perhaps driven by optimism, perhaps by confidence in continued progress, or perhaps by desperation to get a foot in the market, companies leave the sanctuary of predictable markets for the unique ways of the Middle Kingdom. Few doubt that once they cross the modern-day Rubicon, they  face the intriguing task of making sense of China's political and legal systems.

Introduction

Chapter 2 showed that the cultural issues facing international businesses differ from those facing domestic firms. This chapter carries the analysis forward, focusing on the fact that once a company leaves its home country, it operates in markets with different political and legal systems. Certainly, the market environments of some countries are similar (Australian companies will not find many surprises in New Zealand). In other cases, the differences are profound (an unprepared U.S. company will encounter shocks in Russia).

In both cases, political and legal factors shape the environment in which managers make decisions. Our opening case about China shows how a nation's political and legal environment forces companies to rethink the best ways to acquire resources, make investments, adapt operating modes, and manage risk. Figure 3.1 shows how political policies and legal practices are integral parts of a nation's operating environment. They shape the role of government in the society, reflect the prevailing political ideology, moderate the degree of political risks companies face, and pose legal conditionalities for a range of operational and strategic issues. Therefore, as we saw with respect to culture and its many applications to company conduct in foreign markets, political and legal influences are an integral part of a country's business environment.

FIGURE 3.1   Political and Legal Factors Influencing International Business Operations

In navigating among countries, firms study how the political and legal situations of various local environments converge and diverge. Determining where, when, and how to adjust business practices to local environments without undermining the basis for success is an enduring challenge of international business. The study of successful companies indicates that they begin with the realization that when it comes to politics and laws, countries' decidedly different ideas result in decidedly different political and legal environments. They then position themselves to compete by understanding these differences—rather than ignoring or, worse, resisting them. The conceptual perspectives and analytical tools that guide their understanding are the focus of this chapter.

The Political Environment

Our profile of China showed that its evolving political and legal systems have created a thriving business environment in which foreign investors can enter markets, establish operations, manage activities, and earn profits. Still, the Chinese political system imposes hardships, while its legal system complicates attempts to right wrongs. By no means is this situation unique to China. Rather, as this chapter explains, the interplay of political ideologies, conceptions of political freedoms, legacies of legality, presumptions of fairness, and the exercise of power make for challenging business environments.

Consider for a moment the case of Russia. Its economy has expanded rapidly; since 2000, growth has averaged more than 7 percent per year, and FDI has grown nearly 30-fold, reaching U.S. $80 billion in 2008. Even so, says an executive at Swedish retailer IKEA, the Russian political environment is "a bit of a roller coaster. . . . [Y]ou don't know exactly what will happen tomorrow."[7] The roster of horror stories features several well-known names. Products of technology firm Motorola were confiscated by import authorities, while the professional-services firm PriceWaterhouseCooper was charged with tax evasion on rather unconvincing evidence. On the whole, doing business in Russia means you'd better be "big enough to defend yourself against bureaucratic attacks [and] . . . ready to hold your nose when elections are rigged and political opposition is crushed."[8] Ironically, although Russian Prime Minister Vladimir Putin has promised a "dictatorship of the law," some see lawlessness on the upswing.[9]

Consequently, international firms evaluate, monitor, and forecast political environments. They study how government officials exercise authority, pass policies, regulate enterprise, and punish wrongdoers. They monitor how politicians are elected and replaced. They assess whether the rule of law or the rule of man prevails in the legal sytem. They gauge whether freedom is a practical ideal or a wishful abstraction.[10] And, on the basis of these insights, they forecast business scenarios. Engaging these issues—admittedly difficult and oftentimes puzzling—prepares managers to qualify the return on investments in terms of the riskiness of the political system.

No matter whether they target Afghanistan or Zimbabwe, managers begin the process of analysis by focusing on the nature of a country's **political system**—specifically, the structural dimensions and power dynamics of its prevailing government. The poltical system defines the institutions, organizations, and interest groups along with the political norms and rules that govern the activities of political actors. The purpose of any political system is straightforward: integrate different groups into a functioning, self-sustaining, and self-governing society. Correspondingly, the test of any political system is its ability to unite a society in the face of divisive viewpoints. Success supports peace and prosperity. Failure leads to instability, insurrection, and, ultimately, national disintegration.

> The fundamental goal of a political system is to integrate the elements of society.

> The test of a political system: uniting a society in the face of divisive viewpoints.

INDIVIDUALISM VERSUS COLLECTIVISM

Political systems across countries share similarities and demonstrate differences. Explaining the rhyme and reason of these characteristics has intrigued a long line of philosophers, beginning with Plato and Confucius and moving on to such thinkers as Machiavelli, Adam Smith, Jean-Jacques Rousseau, John Stuart Mill, and Milton Friedman. Although they span time and place, each has wrestled with enduring questions: How should society balance individual rights versus the needs of the community to develop a rational, righteous, and harmonious system? Should society guarantee individual freedom in the pursuit of economic self-interest? Does society fare better when individual rights are subordinated to collective goals? Should society champion equality or accept hierarchy? Are individual rights inalienable or conferred by the collective? Engaging these questions anchors interpretation of the political systems in terms **individualism** versus **collectivism.**

> **Concept Check**
>
> Chapter 2 showed that culture moderates the practices of international business. Many points of interpretation, both from an academic and managerial perspective, followed from the degree to which a country engages a collectivist or individualistic orientation.

Individualism   This doctrine emphasizes the primacy of individual freedom, self-expression, and personal independence—the principle that all men have "certain unalienable Rights, that among these are Life, Liberty and the pursuit of Happiness."[11] Individualism champions the exercise of one's ambitions and desires, while opposing most of the external interference posed by the political system that constrain individual choice. Furthermore, individualism presumes that the task of the political system is to develop a form of government that protects the liberty of individuals to act as they wish, as long their actions do not infringe on the liberties of others.

> Individualism refers to the primacy of the rights and role of the individual. Collectivism refers to the primacy of the rights and role of the group.

The business implications of individualism hold that each person commands the right to make economic decisions largely free of rules and regulations. Countries with an individualist orientation shape their marketplace with the idea of **laissez-faire.** Literally meaning "leave things alone," laissez-faire holds that government should not interfere in business affairs. Instead, agents behave and the market operates according to the neoliberal principles of market fundamentalism. Individuals are presumed to be self-regulating in promoting economic prosperity and growth, acting fairly and justly to maximize personal performance without threatening the welfare of society. Countries with individualistic orientation include the United States, Australia, the United Kingdom, Canada, Netherlands, and New Zealand.

Gaps between philosophical ideals and opportunistic behaviors often fan an adversarial relationship between governments and business in individualistic societies. Recent events dramatize this circumstance. The global economic crisis revealed that financial companies had opportunistically maximized their interests at the expense of society's welfare. Companies' support of deregulation, privatization, and trade liberalization—advocated with the goal of enhancing individual choice—destabilized the marketplace and jeopardized system sustainability. As a recourse, national governments worldwide instituted laws and regulations that addressed market inefficiencies (such as insufficient consumer knowledge or excessive producer power) that had distorted fair and just competition. In other words, the global credit crisis spurred governments to rein in the individualism of market fundamentalism in order to protect the welfare of the collective.

Collectivism This doctrine emphasizes the primacy of the collective—whether it is a group, party, class, society, nation, race, etc.—over the interest of the individual. No matter the importance of the individuals that comprise the group, ultimately the group as a whole is greater than the sum of its parts. Collectivism endorses the priority of the goals of the group; individuals, sometimes from birth, sometimes by subsequent socialization, define their identity accordingly. Collectivism integrates individuals into cohesive societies that accept the principle that, as Ayn Rand noted, "Collectivism requires self-sacrifice, the subordination of one's interests to those of others." Countries with a collectivistic orientation include Argentina, China, Vietnam, Japan, North Korea, Egypt, Brazil, and Mexico.

Collectivism in the business world holds that the ownership of assets, the structure of industries, the conduct of companies, and the actions of managers must improve the welfare of society. Business decisions are made by the group and, therefore, group members assume joint responsibility. Systems that feature a collectivist orientation hold that government intervenes in market situations to ensure that business practices benefit society—as our earlier reference to the implications of the global economic crisis exemplified. In many cases, governments in collectivist societies, such as Sweden, take actions that promote social equality, labor rights, balanced income distribution, and workplace democracy. In extreme cases, such as those of Venezuela or North Korea, political leaders may overrun personal privacy, control mass media, and profess the ideologies of harmony, consensus, and equality in their efforts to control the economy.

POLITICAL IDEOLOGY

Translating the implications of individualism and collectivism to the political system directs our attention to the construct of political ideology. In theory, an ideology is an integrated vision that defines a holistic conception of an abstract ideal and its normative thought processes. For example, the ideal of freedom carries with it several philosophical presumptions about corollary principles, doctrines, goals, practices, and symbols.

As such, a **political ideology** is the system of ideas that expresses the goals, theories, and aims of a sociopolitical program, thereby stipulating how society ought to function and outlining the methods by which it will work. In the United States, for example, the liberal principles of the Democratic Party and the conservative doctrine of the Republican Party define their respective political ideologies. In Japan, we find a similar situation with the two largest parties—the Liberal Democratic Party, defined by a conservative ideology, and the Democratic Party of Japan, championing social liberalism. In both countries, a particular party promotes an ideology that offers an integrated collection of political, economic, and cultural ideas for a certain social order based on its idealized sense of how society should work. Furthermore, beyond merely elucidating a vision of a better, brighter future, a political ideology specifies the means for achieving that ideal order.

In Japan and the United States, as in many other countries, there are other active political parties that list smaller memberships than the main factions. Consequently, most societies are pluralistic systems in which different groups champion competing political ideologies. **Pluralism** is not restricted to institutional demographics; it also arises when two or more groups in a country differ in terms of language (Belgium), class structure (the United Kingdom), ethnic background (South Africa), tribal legacy (Afghanistan), or religion (India). Far more common, though, are pluralistic systems marked by a diversity of formal groups advocating competing political ideologies.

Pluralism rests upon ideas drawn from the sociology of small groups. When translated to the level of a society, these ideas make sense of the relationships and interactions between and within groups as they champion and contest political ideologies. In a pluralistic society, government does not command the authority to act unilaterally. Rather, government's task is to balance the initiatives championed by the various groups. The fact that these groups anchor their agendas in different political ideologies calls upon the government to negotiate solutions. Consequently, ambiguity often marks decision making in pluralistic societies. The prevalence of pluralism requires managers understand the dynamic of interplay and its implications to the business environment.

Figure 3.2 outlines a **political spectrum** of the various forms of political ideologies. Spectrum analysis, by specifying a basic conceptual structure, guides the assessment of a complex issue—in this case, the issue of political ideology. Essentially, configuring ideologies along the central axis lets us model different political ideologies in relation to each other. The goal of relativity depends on specifying credible ideas to anchor the endpoints of the axis; reasonably set, one can then position alternative ideas.

The standard of "reasonably set" can prove treacherous. The world enjoys a rich menu of ideologies, including many that reference ideals of anarchism, conservatism, secularism, environmentalism, liberalism, feminism, nationalism, socialism, and theocracy. Interpretation of these choices is also moderated by cultural perspectives. From a Western perspective, for example, one commonly sees the endpoints defined as conservative versus liberal interpretations of democracy—i.e., Republican versus Democrat. Other endpoints command greater relevance in other contexts. For example, a political spectrum in an Islamic country is likely bounded by theocracy versus secularism to reflect the role of the clergy in the government. Alternatively, in the specific case of Taiwan, one could define the political spectrum in terms of parties that champion Chinese reunification versus those that endorse Taiwanese independence. Similarly, in the case of Canada, one could set the political spectrum to reflect the implications of the Quebec sovereignty movement.

Managers investing and operating internationally pay explicit attention to the freedoms, or lack thereof, that they command in exercising their options. And, as we shall see later in this chapter and in Chapter 4, the standards of political freedom and economic freedom bear decisively upon company practice and management action.

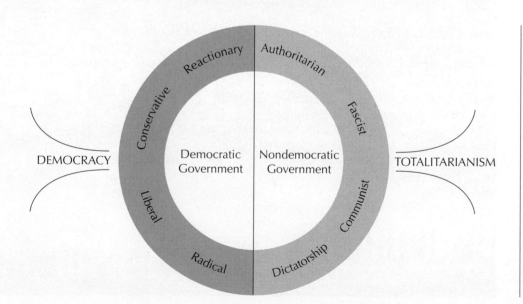

FIGURE 3.2   The Political Spectrum

In practice, purely democratic and totalitarian systems are extreme exceptions. Looking around the world, one finds that there are variations of each political ideology. For example, democratic systems range from radical on one side (advocates of extreme political reform) to reactionary (advocates of a return to past conditions). Likewise, totalitarian systems emphasize different degrees of state control; fascism aims to control people's minds, souls, and daily existence, whereas authoritarianism confines itself to political control of the state. Figure 3.2 communicates that the majority of political ideologies fall between democracy and totalitarianism.

Therefore, Figure 3.2 sets the political spectrum with democracy (and its call to safeguard freedom) anchoring one endpoint and totalitarianism (with its call to abolish freedom) the other.

The ideologies that fall between these endpoints in Figure 3.2 vary in their interpretation of the ideal of freedom. Liberal political ideologies, for instance, advocate the right of an individual to realize his or her own potential. In contrast, authoritarianism and fascism endorse collectivist ideals that call for subordinating individual freedoms to the welfare of society. Similar examples can be cited, but they would essentially reinforce the central point: Freedom is the distinguishing feature of political ideologies, with some emphasizing its primacy and others opposing it. Therefore, we profile the ideals and means of the two endpoints, democracy and totalitarianism.

Democracy   In the view of Abraham Lincoln, the sixteenth President of the United States, **democracy** is a government "of the people, by the people, and for the people." Modern-day democracies translate this ideology into the normative principles that all citizens are politically and legally equal; all are equally entitled to freedom of thought, opinion, belief, speech, and association; and all equally enjoy sovereign power over legislators and officials.

Practically speaking, a democracy is a political system that grants voters the power to alter the laws and structures of government, to make decisions (either directly or through representatives), and to participate directly in elections. These principles and practices enable a democracy to institutionalize political freedoms and civil liberties that, by emphasizing the role of individuals over the collective state, endorse the doctrine of individualism.

The scale and scope of modern society imposes limits on the practice of democracy. Most prominently, the population of most nations makes participation by all voters in the democratic process impossible. Therefore, many democratic countries practice various forms of representative democracy in which citizens elect representatives to act on their behalf. In some democracies, for instance the United States, citizens directly elect executives and lawmakers. In others, such as Japan, they vote for representatives or for a ruling party; the victorious party then selects the prime minister, who functions as chief executive of the country. There are hybrids of each form of democracy. Israel, for

Democracy calls for wide participation by citizens in a fair and just decision-making process.

Democracy and individualism are intrinsically related and mutually dependent; a democracy legitimates standards of individualism and individualism supports standards of democracy.

Here we have what appears to be an ordinary snapshot of grassroots democracy in Pretoria, South Africa, for the 2009 national election. However, one must be mindful that even though the right to vote is idealized as an inalienable human right, billions around the world have no option or, when offered the option to vote for one candidate, no real voice. For South Africans, non-whites could not vote in national elections until the abolition of apartheid in 1994. Hence the image of people patiently waiting in long lines in a dusty field on a hot day to express their opinion carries powerful meaning.
Source: Foto24/Gallo Images/Getty Images

example, has a parliamentary government like that of Japan, but Israelis vote directly for candidates running for prime minister.

Types of Democracy   There are five prominent types of democracy:

- In a *parliamentary democracy*, citizens exercise political power by electing representatives to a legislative branch of government called a *parliament*. The executive branch typically consists of a cabinet, headed by a prime minister who is regarded as the head of government. There is an independent judiciary but no formal separation of powers between the executive and legislative branches. Examples include India and Australia.

- A *liberal democracy* originates in a constitution that protects certain individual freedoms (such as freedom of speech, assembly, and religion) and certain individual liberties (such as the right to property and privacy). All citizens, both public and private, are treated equally before the law and receive due process under it. All liberal democracies, such as Japan or New Zealand, are representative democracies.

- A multiparty democracy defines the political system whereby three or more political parties, whether separately or as part of a coalition, govern. The multiparty system prevents the leadership of a single party from setting policy without negotiating compromises among the opposition parties. Canada, Germany, Italy, and Israel feature multiparty systems.

- A *representative democracy*, such as the United States, is one in which the people's elected representatives hold ultimate sovereignty. Representatives are charged with the responsibility of acting in the people's interest and not merely as their proxy representatives. In other words, officials represent voters and, while mindful of voter preferences, still command the authority to act as they see fit.

- A *social democracy* advocates the use of democratic means to achieve a gradual transition from capitalism to socialism. This view of democracy rests on the belief that society must regulate and reform capitalism to control its intrinsic tendency toward injustice and opportunism. The term *social democracy* is largely interchangeable with *democratic socialism*. Examples of social democracy are Norway and Sweden.

Notwithstanding nuances in terms and tenets, all democratic political systems accept the legitimacy of a relationship between a responsible citizenry and a responsive government. That encourages participation in the political process and guarantees fundamental freedoms and liberties. So defined, societies can then institute democratic governments "of the people, by the people, and for the people." Table 3.1 lists the principal means used to translate the democratic ideology into practice.

Assessing Democracy   The fundamental element of democracy is **freedom**—whether freedom of speech, freedom of association, freedom of belief, or freedom in any other part of life. The range of political ideologies in practice today champion different standards of political freedom. For instance, classical liberal philosophy holds that freedom is the absence of coercion of one man by his fellow man, jurisprudence holds that an individual has the right to determine one's own actions autonomously, and environmentalism advocates constraints on the use of ecosystems in any definition of freedom. Others take a more abstract approach discussing notions of positive freedom versus negative freedom (the former referring to the right to fulfill one's own potential, the latter referring to freedom from restraints).

This chapter follows the lead of Freedom House—a nonprofit organization dedicated to the principles of political and economic freedom—to define freedom. Freedom House specifies that "Freedom is possible only in democratic political systems

Types of democracies include:
- Parliamentarian Democracy
- Liberal Democracy
- Multiparty Democracy
- Representative Democracy
- Social Democracy

The defining feature of democracy is freedom. Factors for evaluating freedom include political rights and civil liberties.

TABLE 3.1 Fundamental Features of Democratic Political Systems

- Freedom of opinion, expression, press, religion, association, and access to information
- Exercise of citizen power and civic responsibility, either directly or through elected representatives
- Citizen equality in opportunity and treatment before the law
- Free, fair, and regular elections
- Majority rule coupled with protection of individual and minority rights
- Fair and independent court system charged with protecting individual rights and property
- Subordination of government to the rule of law

in which the governments are accountable to their own people; the rule of law prevails; and freedoms of expression, association, and belief, as well as respect for the rights of minorities and women, are guaranteed."[12]

Since 1972, Freedom House has published an annual assessment of the state of political and civil freedom in 193 countries and 15 selected territories.[13] It derives its measures of freedom from the Universal Declaration of Human Rights enacted by the United Nations in 1948.[14] Applying these measures to each country, it computes an aggregate ranking that shows the relative performance of a particular country regarding the central measure of freedom. Map 3.2 shows the worldwide distribution of freedom. A quick glance highlights three sets of countries:

- *A free country* exhibits elected officials and competitive parties in which the opposition plays an important role and possesses actual power. There is widespread consensus on the inalienable freedoms of expression, assembly, association, education, and religion.

Alternatives to democracy generally emphasize political and social stability at the expense of individual freedom and liberty.

Freedom House identifies three types of countries:

- *Free*
- *Partly free*
- *Not free*

MAP 3.2 Map of Freedom, 2009

If you live in a country classified as "free," you enjoy a high level of political rights and civil liberties. If your homeland is "not free," you enjoy very few rights and liberties. If you are a citizen of a "partly free" nation, your share of rights and liberties ranges anywhere from average to just below average.

Source: Freedom House, "Map of Freedom 2009," at www.freedomhouse.org.

Note: Given that this is a Mercator projection, the scale approximates east-west distance at the equator; however, the farther you move from the equator, the more the east-west distance is distorted.

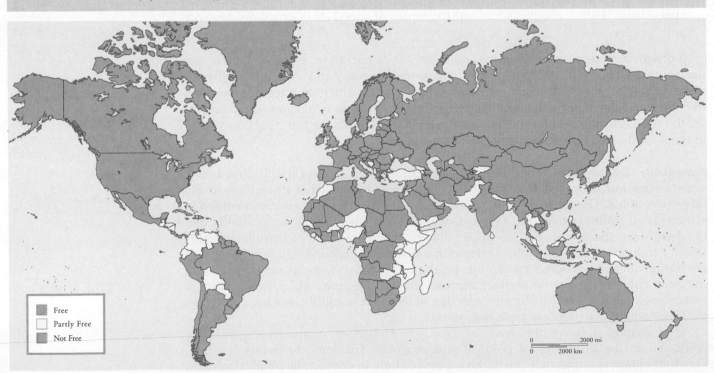

▦	Free
▢	Partly Free
▩	Not Free

- *A partly free country* exhibits limited political rights and civil liberties. This sort of nation is characterized by political corruption, violence and terrorism, one-party dominance, and military influence on politics; elections are unfair, and the government practices censorship and political terror, frustrates free association, and discriminates against minorities.

- *A not free country* represses or denies basic rights and civil liberties through a political system ruled by autocrats, military juntas, one-party dictatorships, or religious hierarchies. The government allows minimal to no exercise of political rights, relies on the rule of man as the basis of law, severely constrains religious and social freedoms, and controls most if not all business activity.

Totalitarianism A **totalitarian system** subordinates the individual to the interests of the collective. A single agent in whatever form—such as an individual, an assembly, a committee, a junta, or a party—monopolizes political power. The agent uses this power to regulate many, if not all, aspects of public and private life—including an individual's occupation, income level, personal interests, religion, and even family structure.[15] The ideological standards of totalitarianism require that the government eliminate dissent within the state. Ensuring unquestioning support for the official ideology is dependent on indoctrination, persecution, surveillance, propaganda, censorship, and violence. A totalitarian system, by default, tolerates no ideas, interests, or activities that run counter to the ideology of the state. In extreme situations, personal survival is linked to the survival of the ruling regime—a condition that forcibly merges the interests of individuals with those of the state. Totalitarian states fall into Freedom House's "Partly Free" and "Not Free" categories.

The dynamics of change in a totalitarian state help elaborate the means it uses to enforce its ideology. Totalitarianism rejects the existing form of society (prior to its replacement, or alternative, as practiced in other countries) as corrupt, immoral, and beyond reform or redemption. Instead, a single leader advocates a new society where wrongs will be corrected, injustice will be redressed, and harmony will prevail. The state then brings to bear propaganda, indoctrination, and incarceration to institute conformity by citizens. Control of the media enables the state to filter information; control of education enables the state to filter ideas; and control of the police enables the state to suppress dissent. The cumulative result is a "virtual mind prison" in which the leader and the state fuse together.[16]

Types of Totalitarianism The term *totalitarianism* is a catchall for several forms of political systems, including the following.

- *Authoritarianism:* In an authoritarian form of government, the regime tolerates no deviation from state ideology. Day-to-day life reflects obedience to state authority. Resistance incurs punishment. Unlike a totalitarian system that regulates the political, economic, and social structure of society, an authoritarian regime confines itself to political control of the state.

- *Fascism:* "The Fascist conception of the state," according to Benito Mussolini, a past fascist dictator of Italy, "is all-embracing; outside of it no human or spiritual value may exist, much less have any value." Thus understood, "Fascism is totalitarian and the Fascist State, as a synthesis and a unit which includes all values, interprets, develops, and lends additional power to the whole life of a people."[17] The fascist ideal is the control of people's minds, souls, and daily existence.

- *Secular totalitarianism:* In this system, a single political party forms a government in which only party members hold office, elections are controlled through unfair laws, dissent is tolerated as long as it does not challenge the state, and organized religions

Concept Check

Recall our discussion in Chapter 2 of "Behavioral Factors Affecting Business": It is important to remember that these variables change as people change—or as some authority aims to influence them. In an effort to shape people's behavior to support the interests of the state, totalitarian systems manipulate behavioral norms governing work motivation, risk taking, communication practices, and consumption preferences.

A totalitarian system consolidates power in a single agent who then controls political, economic, and social activities of the country.

Types of totalitarian systems include:

- Authoritarianism
- Fascism
- Secular totalitarianism Theocratic

are suppressed. In China, an example of this situation, the Communist Party wields sole power, permitting eight other parties to participate in state affairs but only under its recognized leadership and subject to its direction. Similar conditions prevail in Vietnam and Singapore. Usually, the secular totalitarian state does not prescribe an all-encompassing ideology; it grants individual freedoms so long as ensuing activities do not challenge its authority. The Communist Party insists that its approximately 74 million members (roughly 5 percent of the total population) be atheists, thereby preempting a competing ideology as well as reinforcing its secular orientation.

Religion exerts a strong influence on people's values. In Chapter 2, we note how it functions as a stabilizer of a country's **culture**. Similar forces are at play when countries mix religion and politics. The elements of religion that stabilize culture also regiment the political process.

- *Theocratic totalitarianism:* Under this system, government is an expression of the preferred deity, with leaders often claiming to represent the deity's interests on earth. Procedurally, the theocratic state follows ancient dogma in place of modern political or legal principles. Examples of religious leadership, such as the Taliban Party in Afghanistan and clergy in Iran, determine political processes and legal practices based on their interpretation of the Koran. Strict social regulation and gender regimentation typically ensue.

TRENDS IN POLITICAL SYSTEMS

The latter half of the twentieth century and the early twenty-first century have seen a steady expansion of nations instituting democratic political systems. The number of democratic countries grew from 22 of 154 (14 percent) in 1950 to 90 of 193 (47 percent) in 2008. The number of nations that made the transition from nondemocratic to democratic political systems, particularly during the 1970s and 1980s, gave rise to the so-called **third wave of democratization.**[18] Highlighted by the fall of the Berlin wall in 1989 and the ensuing collapse of the Communist Bloc, the swelling third wave of democratization gave rise to the notion of the so-called "end of history." This notion held that the democratic ideology, reinforced by the market fundamentalism of capitalism, represented the final stage of social development. Or, as its author reasoned, "What we may be witnessing is not just the end of the Cold War, or the passing of a particular period of post-war history, but the end of history as such: that is, the end point of mankind's ideological evolution and the universalization of Western liberal democracy as the final form of human government."[19]

The third wave of democratization was worldwide: Countries from Africa, Asia, Latin America, South America, and Eastern Europe abandoned totalitarian political systems. In their place emerged democracies based on greater individual freedoms and expanded civil liberties. Societies began building fairer civic institutions, independent media, objective judiciaries, and stronger property rights.[20] Today, as a result of the third wave of democratization, more people live in countries with elected democratic governments than at any time in history.

In profiling "The Forces Driving Globalization" in Chapter 1, we note the power of changing political situations. In particular, the past few decades have witnessed the spread of the ideology of democracy and the corresponding decline in totalitarianism. The acceptance of democracy and its advocacy of freedom have accelerated the pace of **international business.**

Engines of Democracy   Several engines powered the third wave of democratization. Most notably:

1. The failure of totalitarian regimes to deliver economic progress led to deepening legitimacy problems. Aggrieved citizens contested the right of political officials to govern. The fall of the Berlin Wall punctuated this epic change. As formerly Communist countries adopted democratic principles and practices, they weakened the links between new political practices and old economic habits.

2. Improved communications technology eroded totalitarian states' control of information. Democracy benefits from an informed public with easy access to media.

Images of resistance and rebellion had a snowball effect on the worldwide campaign for democratic reform. Today, expanding Internet access engages previously disenfranchised people worldwide. Access to the world beyond the village, earlier seen perhaps only when newspapers arrived in a bundle every few weeks or a neighbor returned from a trip, is now available through expanding wireless and satellite systems. Plugged into the Internet, more people access a growing smorgasbord of information. And, observed Thomas Jefferson, author of the Declaration of Independence and third President of the United States, "Information is the currency of democracy."

3. The data indicate that political freedom pays economic dividends.[21] The median per capita gross domestic product, a measure of the general standard of living, is almost seven times higher for the freest countries than for not free countries. In many countries, economic advances fostered the rise of a new middle class. Worldwide, the past 15 years have seen more than two billion people migrate from poverty to the middle class. Their prosperity supports the political stability and faith in the future that powers democracy.[22]

The march toward greater political freedoms and expansive civil liberties, beginning in the 1970s, fueled a belief in the inevitability of democracy—the so-called "end of history" phenomenon. This trend stabilized operating conditions for companies worldwide and supported common rules for international competition. The progressive democratization of the world, in turn, accelerated the globalization of business.

THE MOMENTUM OF DEMOCRACY

Democracy retains strong appeal worldwide. Surveys show that people in most countries want democracy. In addition, increasing wealth and education, along with an expanding middle class, have powered the march of democracy in every region in the world today. Nonetheless, trends raise troubling questions about the momentum of democracy. More pointedly, managers are qualifying their interpretation of political environments with the possibility that, rather than ending, "history" has just begun.

Former British Prime Minister Winston Churchill noted that "democracy is the worst form of government except all those other forms that have been tried from time to time."[23] Therefore, although seen as superior to its alternatives, democracy still exhibits imperfections. Some fledgling democracies that emerged in the past two decades, especially those in the former Soviet bloc countries, have struggled with domestic unrest and security threats; in consequence, managers grapple with the reappearance of strong state controls. The terrorist attacks of September 11, 2001, also reset interpretations of the standards of freedom. Resulting restrictions on freedoms raised questions about the legitimacy of leading democracies.

Finally, the global economic crisis, by threatening the rise of the middle class, threatens the spread of democracy. History shows that right-wing totalitarian movements have generally drawn their popular support from middle classes seeking to preserve the status quo. In addition, people falling back into poverty are politically hazardous. Left-wing totalitarianism has often developed from working class movements seeking to overthrow perceived oppressors. Consequently, the growing risk of a shrinking middle class in the face of the economic and political instability due to the global credit crisis threatens to undo recent progress.[24]

Disturbing Data   Longitudinal data confirms the slowing momentum of democracy. In 1987, there were 66 electoral democracies in the world; in 1997, there were 117; in 2006 there were 123; and by 2008, there were 119 (Figure 3.3).[25] The *Freedom in the World 2008*

FIGURE 3.3   Tracking
Electoral Democracies

The most recent Freedom House
*Annual Survey of Political Rights and
Civil Liberties* reports that there are
now 119 electoral democracies in
the world versus 66 in 1987. As you
can see, however, the democracy
curve starts to flatten out in the
mid-1990s and begins to decline in
2007. A downward turn would
signify a decline in democracy or,
put differently, an increase in
totalitarianism.

Source: Freedom House, "Freedom in the
World 2008," at www.freedomhouse.
org (accessed June 2009).

Freedom in the World: Electoral Democracies, 1989–2008

Number of Electoral Democracies

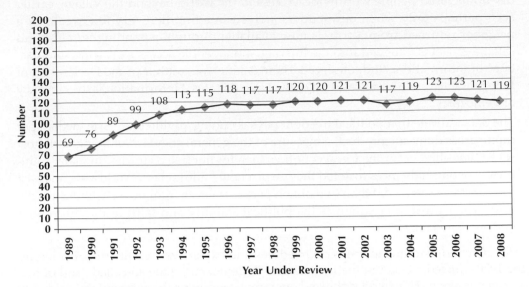

Percentage of Electoral Democracies

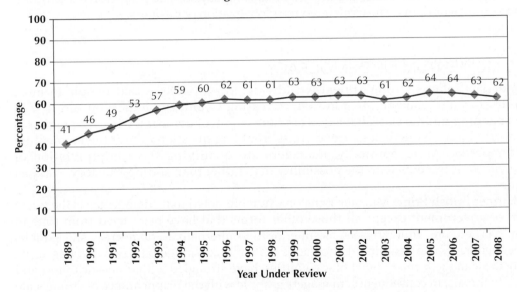

report warned: "This year's results show a profoundly disturbing deterioration of freedom worldwide. A number of countries that had previously shown progress toward democracy have regressed, while none of the most influential Not Free states showed signs of improvement. As the second consecutive year that the survey has registered a global decline in political rights and civil liberties, friends of freedom worldwide have real cause for concern." *Freedom in the World 2009* reports further deterioration. Freedom retreated in much of the world; 34 countries registered declines in the degree of freedom in their political systems while 14 showed improvements.[26] Worldwide, powerful regimes have imposed "forceful measures designed to suppress democratic reformers, international assistance to those reformers and ultimately the very idea of democracy itself."[27]

Other data corroborate this trend. The Economist Intelligence Unit studies the "texture of democracy," relying on 60 indicators that assess free elections, civil liberties, government functioning, political participation, and political culture in a country.[28] Assessing

165 countries, it found that about half of the world's democracies are "democracies" in name only; just 30 are "full democracies," while 50 are "flawed democracies." Of the remaining 85 countries, 36 are classified as "hybrid regimes" (those that mix democratic and totalitarian practices), and 51 are outright authoritarian regimes. Put differently, presently under 15% of humanity live in democracies, while 35% live in countries governed by authoritarian regimes. Regarding trends, the *Economist* reported that 68 countries had declining democracy scores between 2006 and 2008, 56 countries experienced improvements, and 43 countries were unchanged.[29]

Alternative Viewpoints The legitimacy of Western notions of democracy, when applied to societies that do not have the same level of comfort with its ideals and institutions, has come under question. Hu Jintao, China's president and Communist Party chief, speaks of "democracy" with a different meaning from the one understood by Westerners. In his view, calls for multiparty democracy are taboo, opposition cannot officially organize, reform must obey the "correct political orientation," and change must be in an "orderly" way that upholds the party's leadership.[30]

Similarly, Russian Prime Minister Vladimir Putin, proclaiming that "I am a true democrat," argues that his country's application of authoritarianism has been misinterpreted. He has criticized the West, charging that the "largest complexity today is that some of the participants in the international dialogue believe that their ideas [of democracy] are the ultimate truth."[31] Likewise, Brazil's President Luiz Inacio Lula da Silva says countries like the United States, United Kingdom, Germany, France, Canada, and Japan, the primary advocates of Western-style democracy, no longer speak for the world. He contends that these countries have lost the moral authority to solve the world's problems and dictate solutions to poorer countries.[32]

Alternative points of perspective, fortified by charges of hypocrisy against the United States (owing to its incursion in Iraq and Afghanistan, along with the implications of its antiterrorist activities to political freedoms and civil liberties), have raised an intricate question—namely, what constitutes democracy in action? Consequently, some wonder whether democracy, at least in the form advocated by the world's veteran democracies, has run its course as a preferred political system. If so, as we consider in our "Looking to the Future" insert, what, then, might become of democracy?

Looking to the Future — What Might Become of Democracy?

Routinely, managers wonder what a political map of the world will look like in the next decade. Will democracy continue to spread? Will totalitarianism make a comeback? Will new political ideologies arise? It is tempting to see these questions as academic exercises. The latest data, however, suggest that they are anything but. On a global scale, we see evidence of the slowing momentum of democracy, growing numbers of nations reducing political freedoms, and the resurgence of authoritarian ideologies.

These trends have ominous overtones. The number of "free" countries, after flatlining for nearly a decade, has begun falling—a fact that suggests the onset of what Freedom House director Jennifer Windsor calls a pattern of "freedom stagnation." "Although the past 30 years," she reports, "have seen significant gains for political freedom around the world, the number of 'Free' countries has remained largely unchanged since the high point in 1998. Our assessment points to a freedom stagnation that has developed in the last decade."[33] These trends are worldwide. Freedom has suffered setbacks in the Asia-Pacific region and declines in the Middle East, South America, Africa, and some of the nations of the former Soviet Union. These shifts raise the specter of a backlash against democracy.

Exceptions and Alternatives

Complicating matters is the reemergence of authoritarian regimes worldwide, notably those in Russia,

(continued)

Venezuela, and Iran. In 1991, following decades of Communist rule, Soviet President Mikhail Gorbachev began building democratic institutions and acquainting the country with the rudiments of political and economic freedom. Boris Yeltsin, the first president of Russia, continued along Gorbachev's path. Today, however, under Prime Minster Vladimir Putin, Russia suppresses many individual freedoms. In Venezuela, populist President Hugo Chávez, who has initiated a program to nationalize foreign-owned assets, has closed organizations, movements, and media that called for democracy. Meanwhile, Iran has institutionalized hostility toward personal freedom, corrupted the electoral process, and suppressed freedom of speech, and seems intent on enlisting other nations in its anti-democracy campaign.

At the same time, programs to build democratic states struggle. Spreading democracy in the Arab world, which is regularly rated the world's least-free region, has been a long-running goal of the United States. Progress has been limited. U.S. military involvement has raised questions about the legitimacy of democratic ideals throughout the region. In addition, faltering institutions and changes in political sentiments hinder the transition to democracy in several Islamic nations, including Bahrain, Egypt, Saudi Arabia, Jordan, and the Palestinian areas. Strong economies in the oil-rich Persian Gulf stall the spread of democracy, which, it appears, is not truly essential to economic prosperity. Consequently, some Arab leaders contend that the transition from totalitarianism to democracy is "a slow process."[34]

The historic reluctance of Islamic states to engage in democratic practice, in turn, introduces the "clash-of-civilizations" scenario. Irreconcilable cultural and religious differences between Islam and the West, goes this reasoning, will trigger a worldwide backlash against Western political ideals.[35] Some experts speculate that an epic collision between nations and groups of different civilizations will usher in a new political ideology.

Lastly, some link the decline of Western-styled democracy to the growing appeal of the distinct political ideals and attitudes of the so-called Beijing Consensus. A euphemism for the Chinese system of totalitarian democracy, this political ideology calls for a one-party system in which elected representatives, preapproved by the ruling party, oversee a nominal democratic system whose citizens, though granted the right to vote, cannot participate in decision making.[36] The Communist Party is still authoritarian, but it rules largely by consent, preferring persuasion to the iron fist. However, it is quick to suppress threats to its authority. China's remarkable economic performance over the past thirty years has helped legitimate its political ideology as a practical one-party alternative to liberal and multiparty democracies. This tendency has gained greater credibility given its strong economic performance, in the wake of the global economic crisis. Some argue that state control in the style of the Chinese, not free markets in the style of the United States, may represent the superior path toward economic prosperity and political harmony.

Where to Now?

The advent of "freedom stagnation" questions long-cherished and presumably inalienable ideals of democracy. Today, as some countries question democracy and other models emerge, people wonder what is to become of democracy. Will it persist in the form of liberal democracy, as in the United States, or will it transmute into a single-party system like that in China? Will totalitarianism triumph? Or will a "clash of civilizations" give rise to new ideas of freedom and liberty?

Whatever the question, history will no doubt play a part in the answer. The first and second waves of democratization (1828 to 1926 and 1943 to 1962, respectively) were each followed by periods of antidemocratic movements and freedom backlash. The end of the second wave, for instance, saw more than 20 countries revert from democracy to totalitarianism. Hence the question arises: Are we facing once again a cycle of transition, consolidation, and regression?[37]

Whatever the answer, few doubt that the political world has changed for managers. If democracy proves resilient, businesspeople must adjust operations to the growing pains of the countries that choose this ideology. If democracy takes a different path, they must rethink the conduct of business in a world that champions economic growth at the price of individual freedom. If democracy changes as civilizations clash, few signposts will remain standing. Finally, if democracy falters in the face of resurgent totalitarianism, managers face a future of control and coercion. ■

POLITICAL RISK

Discussion so far highlights the dynamism of the political environment. Complicating this tendency is the range of choices available to officials and voters in structuring the political system. Consequently, managers face unpredictability in the political environment. Furthermore, investing overseas exposes companies to the risks that arise from the political quirks of nations. This class of risk is commonly referred to as **political risk** and is defined as the potential loss arising from a change in government policy. More precisely, political risk is the likelihood that political decisions, events, or conditions will affect a country's business environment in ways that will cost investors some or all of the value of their investment or force them to accept lower rates of return. Table 3.2 identifies leading causes of political risks.

The global economic crisis has increased political risk in the world. The previous three decades or so had seen principles of globalization standardize the inconsistencies of politics across markets. Certainly, countries developed at different paces, but as each developed in terms of the apparent inevitability of globalization, managers could safely presume that laws of economics, not the quirks of politics, would shape local markets. The financial crisis has reset the equation; now, politics and political motivations influence the performance of global markets and the actions of international companies on a scale we have not seen in decades. If the global financial crisis continues to shake faith in democracy and free markets, politics and politicians will create complicated sets of political risks for foreign companies.

The evaluation of political risk often relies upon a macro-micro criterion. Macropolitical risks affect all participants in a given country, while micropolitical risks are project specific and usually affect specific companies. We follow this logic but refine it by distilling the macro-micro criterion into *systemic, procedural, distributive,* and *catastrophic* forms of political risks. We now profile each.

Systemic Political Risk   As a rule, a country's political processes do not treat foreign operations unfairly. If they did, few companies would hazard the investment. More often, the risks faced by investors—both domestic and foreign—result from shifts in

Concept Check

In Chapter 1, we note that interest groups in some countries fear that the globalization of the local business environment will weaken **national sovereignty**—that is, a nation's freedom from external control and right to act in its own interests. Here, we observe that this attitude itself contributes to political risk: Foreign companies and investors face greater problems when a host government becomes increasingly sensitive to aspects of its national sovereignty.

Political risk: the risk that political decisions or events in a country will negatively affect the profitability or sustainability of an investment.

The primary types of political risk, from least to most disruptive, are

- Systemic
- Procedural
- Distributive
- Catastrophic

TABLE 3.2   Types and Outcomes of Political Risk

Type	Outcome
Expropriation or nationalization	A government or political faction seizes a company's local assets. Compensation—if there is any—is usually trivial. More common in the 1960s and 1970s, expropriation is increasing in tandem with resurgent totalitarian political systems.
International war or civil strife	Military action damages or destroys a company's local assets.
Unilateral breach of contract	A government repudiates a contract negotiated with a foreign company. The company's profits are often reallocated to the host country. The foreign company also suffers when a government approves a local firm's repudiation of a contract.
Destructive government actions	By imposing unilateral trade barriers, say, in the form of revised local-content requirements, a government interferes with the transfer of goods or the distribution of goods to local consumers.
Harmful action against people	Action on the part of local agents say, kidnapping, extortion, or terrorist activities, targets local employees of a foreign company.
Restrictions on repatriation of profit	The host government arbitrarily limits the amount of gross profit that a foreign company can remit from its local operations.
Differing points of view	A government's interpretations of such issues as labor rights or environmental obligations create problems for a foreign company in its home market.
Discriminatory taxation policies	A foreign company is saddled with a higher tax burden than a local competitor or other foreign firm that is treated favorably because of its nationality.

public policy. New political leadership, for instance, may adopt policies that differ from its predecessor's—say, reducing the individual benefit of business activity by increasing tax rates in order to fund polices that support the welfare of society. In that case, new regulations will alter the macrobusiness environment for all companies.

At other times, a government may target public policy initiatives toward an economic sector that it sees dominated by foreign interests. In an effort to install what he calls a system of "Bolivarian socialism," for example, President Hugo Chávez of Venezuela has initiated a program to nationalize the local operations of foreign companies.[38] In both situations, politically driven change of macroeconomic and social policies creates *systemic risks*—risks that impact all firms that operate in the particular political system.

Case Review Note

Systemic changes do not necessarily create political risks that reduce potential profits. In fact, elections and policy shifts can create opportunities for foreign investors. In the 1990s, for example, a newly elected government in Argentina initiated a radical program to deregulate and privatize the country's state-centered economy. Investors who accepted the risk and pursued the resulting opportunities prospered as freer markets emerged in Argentina. Our opening case traces a similar market pattern and profit potential in China. Political change geared toward free market standards reduced the riskiness of the business environment, and moreover, change created opportunities. Still taking advantage of such opportunities, whether in China or many other countries, entails taking risks in environments where political and legal complications pose roadblocks to profitability.

Procedural Political Risk   Each day, people, products, and funds move from point to point in the global market. Each move creates a *procedural transaction* between the units involved, whether units of a company or units of a country. Political actions sometimes create frictions that interfere with these transactions. The repercussions, for example, of government corruption or a partisan judicial system can raise the costs of business. More specifically, corrupt officials might pressure a foreign firm to pay for special assistance to clear goods through customs or obtain a permit to open a factory. These sorts of politically motivated interference escalate expenses, thereby lowering rates of return.

Distributive Political Risk   Many countries see foreign investors as agents of prosperity. As foreign investors generate more profits in the local economy, the host country may begin to question the *distributive justice* of the rewards of operating in its market. In other words, as the business grows more successful, officials may question whether they are receiving their "fair" share of the growing profits. Far more often than not, political officials demand a greater share. Some then launch a campaign of creeping expropriation, whose goal is to appropriate gradually a greater share of the rewards—typically in ways that do not provoke the investor to depart. The tools of creeping expropriation takes various forms, including increases in tax rates on profits or increasing barriers to transferring personnel into or profits out of the country. Underlying the means of creeping expropriation is the gradual elimination of foreign companies' property rights.

A foreign firm may feel the pressure of distributive risk in subtle ways. Few people, for instance, think of the United States as a hotbed of distributive political risk. If you're in the cigarette business, however, you know that the United States has perhaps the highest degree of political risk in the world. The U.S. government has long battled cigarette makers (both domestic and foreign) on matters of taxation, regulation, business practice, and liability. In the process, it has imposed compliance costs and punitive fees in the hundreds of billions of dollars.

Catastrophic Political Risk   Catastrophic political risk includes random political developments that adversely affect the operations of every company in a country. Typically, it arises from flash points, such as ethnic discord, illegal regime change, civil disorder, or insurrection. It disrupts the business environment in a way that affects every firm in the country. If such disruptions spiral out of control, they devastate companies and countries.

Systemic political risks impact all firms.

The dynamic of distributive political risk is creeping expropriation, a gradual elimination of foreign companies' local property rights.

Catastrophic political risk can devastate companies and countries.

Point > Counterpoint

Should Political Risk Management Be an Active Strategy?

Point **Yes** I think we can agree on a few points. First, it's no secret that the actions of the host government can have a huge effect on the success of companies. Second, this means that every company doing business overseas faces political risk, and that's why companies must develop strategies for political risk management. Third, these strategies can take one of two approaches: active or passive. Naturally, those who advocate active political risk management believe it's the better way to go, and in my opinion, they're right. The more they consult experts who help them predict political problems, the better they are going to manage the corresponding risks.

Now, there's no denying that you may expose yourself to political risk whenever you take an active approach to managing overseas operations. This is why experienced overseas managers rely on not one, but two battle-tested tactics: They turn to statistical modeling to quantify the precise degree of political risk they're facing and they solicit the judgment of local experts to estimate the general degree of political risk they'll have to deal with in a given country.

Relying on either of these approaches endorses the assumption that neither positive nor negative political events in any country are independent or random events: They unfold in observable patterns that let managers make reasonable estimates of the odds of future events. That's why rigorous quantitative analysis and modeling aim to detect, measure, and predict future events that may pose political risk.

If you support active political risk management, you're assuming that if you measure the right set of discrete events, then you should be able not only to calculate the degree of political risk in a given country but also to estimate your odds of facing politically risky disruptions—civil strife, contract repudiation, financial control, regime change, ethnic tension, terrorism, and the like. Granted, this approach requires identifying valid indicators of political risk that can be measured reliably—for example, the number of generals in political power, the pace of urbanization, the frequency and nature of government crises, the degree of literacy, or ethno-lingual fractionalization. But once you have collected the data for the right set of measures, you can objectively estimate your exposure to political risk within a given country as well as across countries.

Political risk indicators have helped global companies monitor developments in individual countries as well as regional markets. Moreover, managers apply data they've collected in one country to benchmark analysis in another country that is experiencing similar processes of political

Counterpoint **No** Your proactive risk-management position fails to observe that many companies refrain from managing political risk directly—for all the right reasons. Instead, they treat political risk as an unpredictable hazard, reasoning that no model, regardless of how systematically it's been specified, can predict the degree of political risk in a country. Granted, models can extrapolate from economic, political, and social reports to generate meaningful insights about who may take office, what polices may be passed, and how these sorts of political events could affect the business environment. Ultimately, these insights make the political system and its risks understandable but by no means predictable.

These insights do not qualify as predictions precisely because of the intrinsic impossibility of reliably measuring uncertain situations. The political world is complex, its inalienable feature is ambiguity, and its tendency to change is high. Compounding these challenges is the range of variables that affect a country's political environment and, more difficultly, the many linkages among them. This situation becomes more difficult as companies head into emerging markets, each marked by its own political peculiarities. Collectively, no matter how powerful the spreadsheet or insightful the expert, the dimensions and evolving dynamic of a political environment defy specification. Rather, managing responsibly with politics and its risks in a foreign market demands resetting cognitive models so that one can deal with the conditions of unpredictable hazards.

Rejecting the hypothesis that one can predict political risk demands that managers find a cost-effective way to hedge their exposure. An approach based on risk management, not risk prediction, becomes the basis for protection. Typically, companies that favor passive risk management outsource the political risk-management process, largely because they reason that they're shielding themselves from political risk by buying political risk insurance. Consider the flexibility they give themselves through this approach. First, they have options to purchase coverage that protects operations from a wide array of political risks, including (but not limited to) government expropriation, involuntary abandonment, and damage to assets due to political violence. Second, they can purchase their political risk insurance from a variety of providers—government agencies, international organizations, and private companies. Here's a short list of leading insurers:

- *Overseas Private Investment Corporation (OPIC)* encourages U.S. investment projects overseas by offering political risk insurance, all-risk guarantees, and direct loans.

change. In sum, estimating political risk by means of cross-country, highly aggregated data is a powerful tool. Still, we don't go so far as to say that there are no limitations to what you can do with it. That's why some companies complement quantitative measures with in-depth, country-specific qualitative indicators of political risks.

How does this approach work? One tactic entails polling country experts to tap their judgments and insights. Of course, these people consider quantitative factors when assessing a nation's political conditions. The best ones, however, bring something personal to the table. They enrich analyses by adding their own expertise—their sense of how things work in the targeted host country—which involves certain subjective elements. Simply put, spreadsheet estimation, no matter how rigorous, no matter how extensive, can only carry analysis so far. Enriching interpretation requires perspectives and perceptions that intuitively understand the political drama and a country in ways that numbers may tap but never fully represent.

If you want to integrate this tactic into your overall risk-assessment strategy, you could begin by running standardized interviews with experts to identify and evaluate key factors in a country's political environment. A useful starting point is the Internet; entering the search string "political risk management" quickly generates leads to several resources. Consulting these then supports projecting likely scenarios and prudently assigning probabilities to outcomes and their implications—the hallmarks of effective political risk management. ▶

OPIC insurance protects U.S. overseas investment ventures against civil strife and other forms of violence, expropriation, and inconvertibility of currency. Recently, having reduced its role in the political insurance end of the business, OPIC now focuses on investments in emerging markets that fit U.S. foreign policy priorities.

- *Multilateral development banks (MDBs)* are international financial institutions (such as the African Development Bank, the Asian Development Bank, and the World Bank Group) that are funded and owned by member governments. Their goal is to promote progress in developing member countries by providing financial incentives, such as long-term below-market rates. By reducing the amount of company capital at risk, these financial incentives encourage firms to expand into politically risky environments.

- Several private insurance companies underwrite political risk protection—for a price. Many insurers cover "routine" political risks that involve property and income, such as contract repudiation and currency inconvertibility. Private insurers are reluctant to cover the risk of extraordinary circumstances such as political violence in the form of war or insurrection, as well as the risk of nationalization and expropriation of assets.

We have no quarrel with the notion that prediction and control are touchstones of competent management. Still, politics are anything but predictable and controllable. Hence, all things considered, it just makes better sense to avoid the delusion of active management and opt for the practicality of passivly managing political risk. ◀

The Legal Environment

Businesspeople champion consistency in laws from country to country. A uniform set of laws makes it easier to plan where to invest and, once there, how to run operations to comply with regulations. However, just as political ideologies differ from country to country, so do the principles and practices of the prevailing legal system. Consequently, how a country develops, interprets, and enforces its laws is a key aspect of the business environment. Done legitimately, consumers and companies can make lawful decisions that support peace and prosperity. Done arbitrarily, all suffer because "to distrust the judiciary," said Honoré de Balzac, "marks the beginning of the end of society."

LEGAL SYSTEMS

A legal system is the mechanism for creating, interpreting, and enforcing the laws in a specified jurisdiction.

The **legal system** specifies the rules that regulate behavior of individuals and companies, the processes by which the laws of a country are enforced, and the procedures used to resolve grievances. Legal systems differ across countries due to variations in tradition, precedent, usage, custom, or religious precepts. *Ceteris paribus,* legal systems aim to establish a comprehensive set of rules that support business formation, regulate transactions, and stabilize relationships. A functioning legal system ensures that a society can pursue economic development and, when disagreements arise, resolve them without resorting to lawlessness.

Modern legal systems share three components:

- A system of *constitutional law* translates the constitution of the country into an open and just legal system. Constitutional law sets the framework for the system of government and defines the authority and procedure of political bodies to establish laws and regulations.

- A system of *criminal law* safeguards society by specifying what conduct is criminal and prescribing punishment to those who breach these standards.

- A system of *civil and commercial laws* ensures fairness and efficiency in business transactions. It speaks to private rights and remedies in dealing with relations and conduct between individuals and/or organizations.

> Modern legal systems exhibit elements of constitutional law, criminal law, and civil and commercial laws.

Aspects of each component influence companies' actions in the host country. Consider, for instance, the legal concept of due diligence, which requires that the statements in a firm's security-registration forms be true and omit no material facts. Companies rely on due diligence to manage the risk of cross-border acquisitions; it enacts a legally binding process during which a potential buyer evaluates the assets and liabilities of a company. Hence, due diligence is often the difference between success and failure—provided the local legal codes permit the full examination of operations and management and the verification of material facts. However, in the European Union, data protection rules can interfere with assessing important elements of a potential acquisition, such as the physical condition or mental health of managers, patterns of trade union membership, and criminal histories.

Hence, prudent companies considering cross-border acquisitions pinpoint issues, the country or countries involved, and the citizenship and identity of people involved from the pre-due-diligence phase to the close of the deal. These decisions inevitably touch on aspects of constitutional law (i.e., what philosophies anchor ownership rights?), criminal law (i.e., what are the procedures and penalties for malfeasance?), and civil/commercial law (i.e., do regulations restrain disclosure and verification of information?). In summary, no matter the issue, a country's legal system influences managers' actions and companies' behavior.

Our opening case illustrates the importance of legal traditions and practices in a nation's ability to develop a legal system that attracts and retains foreign investment. Western investors are accustomed to clearly specified and fairly enforced bankruptcy laws that protect creditors. In China, however, this investment-oriented tradition has yet to take hold, and legal tradition protects debtors.

Case Review Note

TYPES OF LEGAL SYSTEMS

The type of legal system in a country determines the conduct of business transactions, who has what rights and obligations in the transaction, and the sorts of legal redress open to those who believe they've been wronged. Understanding the nuances of the legal system spurs managers to study several issues. Specifically, are laws based on abstractions or practicality? Do judges or juries pass judgment? Is justice the matter of man or the province of divinity? Peculiar as these questions sound, international business puts managers into situations where these issues anchor the legality of action.

Map 3.3 profiles the world in terms of the legal systems that prevail in countries and regions. Presently, managers face five types of legal systems: *common law, civil law, theocratic law, customary law,* or *mixed* legal systems.

> Presently managers face five types of legal systems
>
> - Common law
> - Civil law
> - Theocratic law
> - Customary law
> - Mixed

MAP 3.3   The Wide World of Legal Systems

The globalization of business practices has spurred the standardization of laws, regulations, and policies across countries. Still, enduring philosophical outlooks contribute to significant disparity in the types of legal systems worldwide.

Source: University of Ottawa, "World Legal Systems," at http://www.juriglobe.ca/eng/index.php (accessed June 2009).

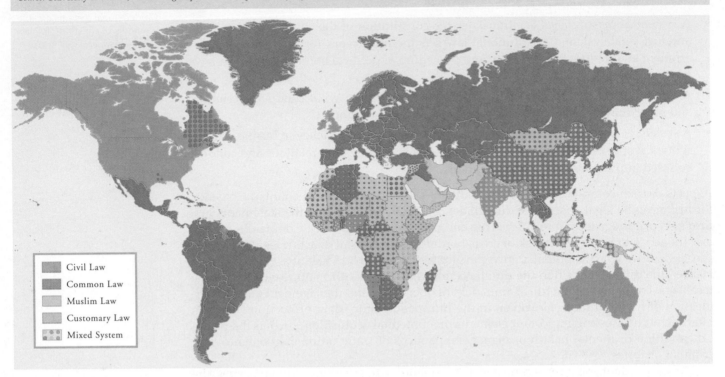

Civil Law
Common Law
Muslim Law
Customary Law
Mixed System

Common law is a legal system of jurisprudence based on judicial precedents.

Common Law   A common law system is based on tradition, judge-made precedent, and usage. It gives preeminece to existing case law in guiding dispute resolution. Judicial officials refer to statutory codes and legislation, but only after considering the rules of the court, custom, judicial reasoning, prior court decisions, and principles of equity. Indeed, the doctrine of *stare decisis* (or precedent) by courts is the major difference between a common law and a civil law system. The common law system has Anglo-American legacies; it prevails in countries such as Canada, the United States (excluding Louisiana), India, Hong Kong, England, New Zealand, and Australia.

Civil law is a legal system of jurisprudence based on statutory laws.

Civil Law   A civil law system is based on the systematic codification of laws and codes. Civil law systems charge political officials—not government-employed judges—with responsibility for specifying accessible, detailed, and written law that applies to all citizens. Rather than create law, as they do in the common law system, judges in the civil law system apply existing legal and procedural codes to resolve disputes. More than 70 countries, including Germany, France, Mexico, and Japan, have civil law systems.

Theocratic law is a legal system of jurisprudence based on religious teachings.

Theocratic Law   A theocratic law system relies on religious doctrine, precepts, and beliefs to define the legal environment. Ultimate legal authority is vested in religious leaders, who apply religious law to regulate business transactions and social relations. Unlike civil and common systems, theocratic laws see no separation of church and state. The theocracy regulates public and private matters and, as a result, government, law, and religion are one. The most prevalent theocratic system, Muslim or Islamic law (or *Shari'a*), is based on: the Koran—the sacred text of Islam; the *Sunnah*—decisions and sayings of the Prophet Muhammad; the writings of Islamic scholars, who derive rules by analogy from the principles established in the Koran and the Sunnah; and the consensus of legal communities in Muslim countries.[39] Muslim law prevails in the Middle East, notably in Saudi Arabia and Iran, and Northern Africa, notably Libya and Morocco.

Customary Law A customary law system is anchored in the wisdom of daily experience or, in more elegant terms, local spiritual legacies and philosophical traditions. Customary laws play important roles in many indigenous, local, and other traditional communities. These laws define the rights and responsibilities of community members in many matters. The legitimacy of customary law follows not from the power of a powerful individual or institution but from individuals recognizing the benefits of behaving in line with the expectation of fellow individuals. In customary law, offenses are treated as torts—private wrongs or injuries rather than crimes against the state or society. At the country level, few nations in the world today operate under a legal system that is wholly customary. Still, in many countries with mixed legal systems, customary law plays a significant role.[40] This type of legal system prevails in many developing countries, particularly those in Africa.

Customary law is based on norms of behavior practiced over a long period.

Mixed System A mixed legal system emerges when a nation uses two or more of the preceding legal systems. Map 3.3 shows that the majority of mixed legal systems are in Africa and Asia. For example, Nigeria has a mixed legal system comprised of common law, Islamic law, and customary law. Similarly, Pakistan has a common law system, a legacy of British colonial influence, and also incorporates theocratic law. Similarly, theocratic law influences the civil law system of Indonesia. Although the legal system of the United States is categorized as a common law system, technically it is a mixed system. Unlike the 49 states that practice common law, Louisiana has a civil law system.

TRENDS IN LEGAL SYSTEMS

Earlier sections highlighted the evolution of democracy around the world. Presently, the freedom stagnation threatens to devolve into a pushback against democracy. Managers struggle to pinpoint the implications of this trend to legal systems. We see agreement on several points.

First, the pushback against democracy powers a rise in totalitarianism. This poltical ideology emphasizes collective order at the expense of individual freedoms. Government in a totalitarian state uses the legal system to regulate business activity so that it supports the regime. There is no separation of law and state. Law is controlled, ruled, and regulated by the state, and the state controls all public and private matters. Bluntly put, justice is no longer blind but arbitary, oppressive, and state-serving. For example, recall earlier observations regarding justice in two totalitarian states. In Russia, doing business means you had better be "big enough to defend yourself against bureaucratic attacks [and] . . . ready to hold your nose when elections are rigged and political opposition is crushed."[41] In China, doing business means dealing with "a society that had no rules; or more accurately, plenty of rules, but they were seldom enforced. China appeared to be run by masterful showmen: appearances mattered more than substance, rules were there to be distorted." [42]

Second, the emergence of developing countries, like Brazil, India, and China, is resetting how managers interpret the legal environments of international business. Most notably, the scale and scope of the market performance of these emerging economies requires reassessing the philosophical basis of law. Emerging markets, once consigned to the periphery of the global economy, increasingly command center stage. The rise of these countries, along with their fundamentally different conception of legality, requires managers to ask: What is the *basis of rule* in a given country—is it the rule of man or the rule of law?

The Rule of Man The **rule of man** holds that ultimate power resides in a person. His word and whim, no matter how unfair or unjust, is law. The rule of man has prevailed for centuries in countries throughout the world. Indeed, for much of history, rulers and law

Concept Check

As we see in Chapter 1, every company's *competitive environment* varies by company, industry, and country. Granted, there are points of convergence in all three areas, but conducting **international business** means recognizing the existence of fundamental *differences* across countries. Here, we stress the importance of legal differences and the importance of complying with local laws.

Concept Check

As developed in the context of Chapter 2, the prevailing principles in a country's legal environment, including religious practices and other behavioral norms, are strongly influenced by its cultural orientation toward standards of accountability, equity, and fairness.

"*My goodness, if I'd known how badly you wanted democracy I'd have given it to you ages ago.*"

The rule of man The principle that every member of a society, except for the ruler, must follow a system of law that is arbitrarily specified and inconsistently enforced.

were synonymous—the law was the will of the ruler, whether called king, queen, emperor, empress, shogun, czar, raj, chief, or caliph. Today, these titles have given way to others like the party, chairman, generalissimo, dictator, supreme leader, or (in the case of North Korea) "Dear Leader." No matter the title, the rule of man defines a legal system in which the actions of the man, in whatever form and with whatever title, are not restricted by a constitution, regulated by laws, or open to opposition—as we see in the irony of Figure 3.4.

Totalitarian countries base their legal systems on the rule of man.

The rule of man is an instrumental device of totalitarianism. Organizing a legal system in terms of this doctrine frees the government to invoke the means necessary to suppress threats to, or reward support for, state authority. Constitutional issues are discretionary, criminal law is arbitrary, and commercial/civil matters are tainted by opportunism. The law is an apparatus of the state; rather than deficient, justice is absent.

The rule of law holds that no individual is above laws that are clearly specified, commonly understood, and fairly enforced.

The Rule of Law   The **rule of law** is a hallmark of a democracy; indeed, without it, democracy cannnot exist.[43] The rule of law institutes a just political and social environment, guarantees the enforceability of commercial contracts and business transactions, and safeguards personal property and individual freedom. Therefore, managers rely on the rule of law to validate laws, codes, and statutes.

The rule of law holds that governmental authority is legitimately exercised only in accordance with written, publicly disclosed laws that have been adopted and are enforced in accordance with established procedure. As such, no individual—public official or private citizen—stands above the law. Perhaps the primary purpose of the legal system is to regulate and restrain the behavior of the "man" as symbolized by government officials. Constitutional standards are absolute, criminal law is legitimate, and commercial/civil matters are anchored in princple. The law is independent of the state; rather than absent, justice is omnipresent.

IMPLICATIONS FOR MANAGERS

The concept of the rule of law originated in the West. Consequently, it has a negligible legacy in the legal traditions of many long-developing, now-emerging countries. A close look at Map 3.4 indicates that the rule of law flourishes in wealthier, westernized countries—namely, the United States, Canada, Japan, New Zealand, Australia, and most of Europe. In contrast, the countries that fall in the long crescent that begins in

MAP 3.4 The Rule of Law

The principle of the *rule of law* holds that government authority is legitimate only when it is exercised according to written laws and established enforcement procedures. The coding of the map here is based on selected dimensions of governmental practice; percentiles reflect scores falling below the rating of a given country. So, for example, the classification of the United States at the 90th percentile indicates widespread support for the rule of law. Conversely, North Korea's classification at below the 10th percentile indicates its widespread support for the rule of man.

Source: World Bank, *Governance Matters VI: Governance Indicators for 1996–2007*, at http://info.worldbank.org/governance/wgi/index.asp/ and http://info.worldbank.org/governance/wgi/worldmap.asp (accessed June 22, 2009).

Note: Given that this is a Mercator projection, the scale approximates east-west distance at the equator; however, the farther you move from the equator, the more the east-west distance is distorted.

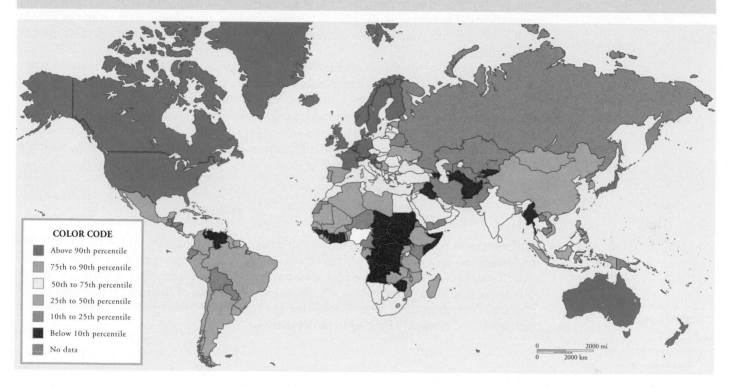

COLOR CODE

Above 90th percentile
75th to 90th percentile
50th to 75th percentile
25th to 50th percentile
10th to 25th percentile
Below 10th percentile
No data

extreme northern Russia, cuts southward through China toward the Middle East, and extends through Africa to South America show slight support for the rule of law. Conclusion? The rule of man prevails in the legal systems of the poorer, non-Western nations that we commonly call developing countries.

This situation is complicated by the acceptance of the rule of man in many developing countries, given that the political ideology in many of these nations is more totalitarian than not. Again, take a look at Map 3.4. Nearly every country that Freedom House rates as "Partly Free" or "Not Free" falls in the "rule of man crescent." Uncertainty about the nature of law and the goals of government in much of the world, consequently, creates a perplexing situation for managers. Whereas operating in Western economies permits them to rely on a consistent and systematic application of legal rules, operating in many developing countries offers few such safeguards.

So, for example, in the United States, action taken by foreign firms against local companies that counterfeit their products has proven remarkably forceful. In China, the same sorts of legal actions have proven nearly powerless. There, as in other rule-of-man systems, writs, injunctions, and lawsuits get trapped in the slow-grinding legal machine. Even when these procedures work, it is not unusual for the charges against the local violator to be dismissed by the court on the basis of dubious technical grounds.[44]

Perhaps a bit overoptimistically, some managers expect developing countries, especially those considered emerging economies, to follow the path of their developed counterparts and to recognize that the rule of law is the basis of a fair and just society. How long will they have to wait? In principle, legal theory holds that these countries

Uncertainty about the basis of law in a particular country creates challenging situations for managers.

will eventually come to adopt the rule of law. As Western economies moved from an agrarian to an industrial economy, society increasingly respected the sanctity of property rights. These concerns led to the development of a modern legal system that no longer appealed to the man in power but, instead, to the force of the written law. Therefore, extrapolating from Western history, managers presume that the shift from agrarianism to industrialism in developing countries will drive their adoption of the rule of law.

The more likely scenario is one where developing countries migrate from one basis of rule to another—that is, from the rule of man to "rule *by* law" and its implicit notion that even the ruler is subject to the law. The corresponding adoption of democratic principles will further fortify this transition, thereby laying the foundation for the society to then accept the rule *of* law.

As the global economic crisis highlights, trends detour and spiral in surprising ways. Hence, recent circumstances complicate the projected progression from the rule of man to the rule of law in developing countries. Most notably, the unfolding backlash against democracy has slowed, if not reversed, progression precisely because the rule of law is antithetical to totalitarianism. Therefore, managers monitor the third wave of democratization, seeing in its continuation the diffusion of the rule of law or, conversely, seeing in its reversal the endurance of the rule of man.

Legal Issues in International Business

Differences in political ideologies and the basis of rule are compounded by the fact that countries use any one of five types of legal systems. Moreover, new forms of business activity along with changing patterns of trade and investment often put firms in uncertain legal situations. Managers assess these issues in terms of their impact on operational concerns, which involve a business's day-to-day activity, and strategic concerns, which influences a company's long-term performance.

OPERATIONAL CONCERNS

Companies comply with local laws regarding starting, running, and closing a business. Activities such as employing workers, getting credit, protecting investors, paying taxes, trading across borders, and enforcing contracts comply with prevailing legal standards. In principle, business regulations should be efficiently designed, easily accessible, and straightforward in their implementation. In practice, business regulations differ from country to country.

One entrepreneur, for example, recalls his experience in starting up his first company in his home country, Brazil. He found that securing the necessary authorizations, licenses, and permits to start a new business—from seven different ministries no less—took about 150 days. When he started a U.S.-based business, however, "within a week I had formed an LLC [limited liability corporation], incorporated in Delaware, and set up bank accounts."[45]

The Rules of the Game   Table 3.3 shows how some countries regulate aspects of the day-to-day operations of businesses. Let's look at specifics.

Getting Started   Starting a business involves many legal activities: registering its name, choosing the appropriate tax structure, getting licenses and permits, arranging credit, and securing insurance. Some countries expedite this process, but others do not. For example, starting a business is a straightforward process in Australia, requiring one registration procedure that encompasses tax, labor, and administrative declarations. In the African nation of Chad, in contrast, one faces 19 procedural requirements, including

---

Operational concerns that face managers worldwide include

- Starting a business.
- Entering and enforcing contracts.
- Hiring and firing local workers.
- Closing down the business.

Concept Check

In Chapter 1, we assume that democratic political systems grant firms the freedom to engage in their preferred "modes of international business." Note, however, that the backlash against democracy that we have detailed in this chapter creates uncertainty about operating in particular countries. When it comes to dealing with certain modes of **international business,** some nations prohibit them, whereas others control them by applying—sometimes arbitrarily and unpredictably—technicalities buried in their legal codes.

TABLE 3.3   The Regulation of Day-to-Day Operations in Various Countries

Country	Legal Origin	Starting a Business			Enforcing Contracts			Closing a Business	
		Number of Procedures[1]	Time (Days)	Cost (% of Income per Capita)	Number of Procedures[2]	Time[3] (Days)	Cost[4] (% of Claim)	Time to Insolvency (Years)	Cost[5] (% of Estate)
Australia	Common (English)	2	2	0.8	28	395	20.7	1	8
Canada	Common (English)	1	5	0.5	36	570	22.3	0.8	4
Chad	Civil (French)	19	75	175.0	41	743	54.9	10	63
China	Civil (German)	14	40	8.4	34	406	11.1	1.7	22
France	Civil (French)	5	7	1.0	30	331	17.4	1.9	9
Germany	Civil (German)	9	18	5.6	30	394	14.4	1.2	8
Guatemala	Civil (French)	13	30	52.1	31	1459	26.5	3	15
India	Common (English)	13	30	70.1	46	1420	35.7	10	9
Japan	Civil (German)	8	23	7.5	30	316	22.7	0.6	4
Korea	Civil (German)	10	17	16.9	35	230	5.5	1.5	4
Russia	Socialist	8	29	2.6	37	2281	13.4	3.8	9
United Kingdom	Common (English)	6	13	0.8	30	4404	223.4	1	6
United States	Common (English)	6	6	0.7	332	300	79.4	1.5	7

Source: Compiled from "Doing Business 2009," The International Bank for Reconstruction and Development/The World Bank.

[1] Number of procedures that the entrepreneur must complete to start a business.

[2] Number of procedures mandated by law or court rules that demand interaction between the parties to the dispute or between them and the judge or court officer.

[3] The number of days from the moment the plaintiff files the lawsuit in court until the moment of settlement or actual payment.

[4] Cost incurred during dispute resolution, comprising court fees, attorney fees, and payments to other professionals.

[5] Cost of entire bankruptcy process, including court costs, insolvency practitioner costs, and the costs of independent assessors, lawyers, and accountants.

regulations pertaining to bank deposits, court registration, health benefits, and even company seal. The upshot: Whereas it takes about two days to start a business in Australia, you're looking at about 75 days in Chad.

Making and Enforcing Contracts   Once up and running, managers turn to entering and enforcing contracts with buyers and sellers. A contract is a binding legal agreement that formally exchanges promises, the breach of which triggers legal proceedings. The sanctity of contract is vital to business transactions. In general, the United Nations Convention on Contracts for the International Sale of Goods sets guidelines for formulating and enforcing contracts among businesses operating in signatory countries. Still, standards vary across types of legal systems. Countries with common law systems tend to encourage precise, detailed contracts. Countries with civil law systems encourage less specific contracts.

The same tendencies show up in contract-enforcement policies. Australia, Norway, and the United Kingdom impose the fewest number of enforcement procedures. Burundi, Angola, Bolivia, Cameroon, El Salvador, Mexico, and Panama require many procedures. Similarly, countries vary in the time span required to enforce a contract; the speediest enforcers, such as Russia, Korea, France, and the United Kingdom, need around 300 days. Elsewhere, say, in Italy, Poland, or Guatemala, the same activities stretch from 600 to nearly 1,500 days.

Hiring and Firing   No matter where you are operating, you will have to hire and, when necessary, fire workers. One would think that common sense would provide enough guidance to make legally appropriate decisions. However, legal issues around the world are rarely as straightforward as you may think. Singapore, New Zealand, and the United States are among the countries with the most flexible labor-regulation statutes. China has the most flexibility in hiring and firing plus the greatest discretion in setting employment conditions (work hours, minimum wages, and benefits). In contrast, Angola, Belarus, and Paraguay place rigid restrictions on firing: You have to provide documentation on the grounds for termination, establish detailed firing procedures, and furnish both generous prior notification and severance payments.

India's labor laws, little changed since they were enacted after independence in 1947, make it difficult to lay off employees even if a company's fortunes have hit hard times or the macro economy slows. Consequently, companies are reluctant to hire workers, given the risk of being unable to fire them if need be. Necessary terminations are extremely difficult to execute and often involve extensive negotiations and settlements. "[C]ompanies think twice, 10 times, before they hire new people," said the chair of the Hero Group, one of the world's largest manufacturers of inexpensive motorcycles.[46]

Getting Out or Going Under   Finally, some countries make the task of closing a business difficult. Under ordinary circumstances, there is far more involved in shutting operations than padlocking the doors. In the United States, for example, the Internal Revenue Service requires completing a series of forms that report, among many others points, changes in the business structure, the sale of assets, payments to subcontractors, and termination of retirement plans.

In extraordinary circumstances, companies declare bankruptcy and begin proceedings to liquidate the business. This process is anchored in the English bankruptcy law of 1732, the first modern law to address this issue, and its revision by the United States in 1800. France, Germany, and Spain adopted their bankruptcy laws in the early nineteenth century. Today, these legacies shape bankruptcy proceedings in their respective countries. Ireland, Japan, Canada, and Hong Kong make closing your doors both fast and cheap; procedures in India, the Philippines, Serbia, Chad, and Panama are among the slowest and most expensive.

Concept Check

In both Chapters 1 and 2, we discuss income and wealth as national resources; we also show how the availability of such resources impacts the actions that countries, both rich and poor, take to affect their business environments. We point out here that these factors also influence countries' approach to regulating the local operations of foreign firms.

General Relationships   Table 3.4 summarizes how countries' legal systems shape features of their business environments. You might have noticed in reading the preceding paragraphs an inverse relationship between a nation's general wealth and its tendencies in regulating business activity. Overall, richer countries regulate less and poorer countries regulate more. In high-income countries (e.g., the United States, Italy, Japan), the average number of procedures to start a new business is 7; it's 10 in upper-middle-income countries (Mexico, Poland, Malaysia), 12 in lower-middle-income countries (Brazil, Jamaica, China), and 11 in low-income countries (Angola, Ghana, Vietnam). In wealthier nations, furthermore, legal systems tend to regulate operational activities more consistently than do those in poorer countries—as one would expect, given the prevalence of the rule of law in the former and the rule of man in the latter.

Table 3.4 identifies the top-ranked and bottom-ranked 10 countries (out of a total set of 183 countries) that have developed a set of policies on the various dimensions that make for the most or least supportive business environments. In terms of the former, Singapore ranks the highest on one or two aspects, yet its government has developed a comprehensive legal code that fosters the most favorable business environment in the world. Likewise, the Central African Republic rates lowest on just a couple of dimensions, but its comprehensively poor performance combines to create the least favorable business environment in the world.

Looking over the list, based on our discussions thus far, confirms an important set of relationships. Specifically, the majority of the top-ranked countries in Table 3.4 have a democratic political system, a common or civil-law legal system, and a doctrine of the rule of law. In contrast, the majority of the bottom-ranked countries in Table 3.4 have a totalitarian political system, a mixed (largely civil, customary, and theocratic) legal system, and a doctrine of the rule of man.

> **Concept Check**
>
> A crucial theme of the text so far has been the notion of linkages and relationships among individuals, companies, countries, and institutions. Here, we emphasize the importance of linkages and relationships between ideas and ideals, namely the interplay among its type of political system, its organizing legal philosophy, and its prevailing doctrine of law. Making these connections helps put into perspective the systemic nature of the business environment in a country.

STRATEGIC CONCERNS

Operating concerns focus managers' attention on day-to-day operations. Strategic concerns shift managers' attention to long-term issues. In this realm, a country's legal

TABLE 3.4   The Ease of Doing Business: The Top and Bottom Ten Countries

The World Bank ranks the 183 economies of the world on ease of doing business—high scores signify favorable business environments, low scores unfavorable business environments. A high ranking on the summary measure of ease of doing business means a regulatory environment is conducive to the operation of business. A low ranking indicates the opposite. Technically, the ease-of-business index averages the country's percentile rankings on 10 aspects of the business environment: starting a business, dealing with construction permits, employing workers, registering property, getting credit, protecting investors, paying taxes, trading across borders, and enforcing contracts.

Country	Ranking	Country	Ranking
Singapore	1	Niger	174
New Zealand	2	Eritrea	175
Hong Kong, China	3	Burundi	177
United States	4	Venezuela	177
United Kingdom	5	Chad	178
Denmark	6	Republic of Congo	179
Ireland	7	São Tomé and Principe	180
Canada	8	Guinea-Bissau	181
Australia	9	Democratic Republic of Congo	182
Norway	10	Central African Republic	183

Source: Doing Business 2009. The World Bank. Rankings on the 183 countries are available at http://www.doingbusiness.org/EconomyRankings/

Strategic concerns that face managers worldwide include

- Product safety and liability.
- Marketplace behavior.
- Product origin and local content.
- Legal jurisdiction.
- Arbitration.

system shapes a company's strategic decisions on where to make a product, how to market it, and how to protect its unique features.

Marketplace Behavior   National laws determine permissible practices in all forms of business activities, including sourcing, distributing, advertising, and pricing products. Hence, countries permit and prohibit activities that then spur companies to adjust their manufacturing configuration, their supply chain coordination, and their marketing strategy. In France, for example, the legal system regulates when transport trucks can use motorways (not on Sundays) or when shops can hold sales (twice a year, on dates set by government officials).[47]

Far more dramatic cases show what happens to companies that disregard local regulations on marketplace behavior. The European Commission fined Intel, for example, a record U.S. $1.45 billion for abusing its dominance in the market for computer chips to exclude rival Advanced Micro Devices. Its marketplace behavior, by violating consumers' rights and undermining innovation, breached competition law in the European Union (EU). The EU Competition Commissioner explained that Intel used "illegal anticompetitive practices to exclude its only competitor and reduce consumers' choice—and the whole story is about consumers."[48] The fine imposed on Intel, after earlier decisions against General Electric and Microsoft, reminded the world of European regulators' role as leading enforcers of antitrust law. Some saw this situation spurring authorities worldwide to regulate the marketplace behavior of companies more aggressively.

In countries where the rule of man is the basis of law, acceptable marketplace behavior can be unpredictable. Companies operating in this legal gray zone complain of trumped-up charges, solicitation of bribes, and favoritism for local competitors. Especially controversial in legal systems where the rule of man prevails is the issue of the protection—or lack thereof—of intellectual property. Finally, the financial crisis has begun spurring governments to reshape their regulatory environments, effectively changing the rules of the game. These regulatory initiatives, by increasing the degree of systemic political risk, affect both domestic and foreign firms.

Country of Origin and Local Content   National laws affect the flow of products across borders. To determine charges for the right to import a product, host governments devise laws that consider the product's **country of origin,** namely the country of manufacture, production, or growth where a product comes from. Some countries apply this policy to product labels, under the title COOL (country-of-origin labeling), to better inform consumers as well as make it easier to support national producers. Currently, differing rules of origin fall under various national laws and international treaties.

Governments also pressure foreign producers to make a greater share of a given product in the local market. To spur reluctant investors, governments often resort to **local content** regulations. Governments impose these sorts of regulations in order to favor companies at the expense of their foreign competitors. For example, Nigeria required foreign oil companies to increase their level of activities done in country. At the time, only about 5 percent of their activities took place in Nigeria; the government aimed to boost this 40 percent with the expectation that doing so would spur the training of locals for engineering jobs as well as procure the latest technologies.

The global credit crisis and its implications to jobs have made issues of country of origin and local content regulation increasingly provocative themes of political debate.

Worries about declining economies due to the global economic crisis have boosted the popularity of country-of-origin and local-content regulations, as well as their populist cousin, buy-local campaigns.[49] The Indonesian government planned to penalize public officials if they did not buy locally produced food, drinks, shoes, clothes, music, and films. Consumers in Hangzhou, China, get a 13 percent subsidy if they buy Hangzhou-made refrigerators, televisions, mobile phones, and washing machines. The U.S. too is resetting the game. The U.S. House of Representatives has included "Buy American" provisions in stimulus-funded infrastructure projects that require purchase of iron and steel made in the United States. Similar policies called for mandating that the U.S. $20 billion allocated for computerizing medical records go exclusively to U.S. companies.[50] A deteriorating global economy will likely spur politicians to mandate buy-local programs and impose local-content regulations to appease voters, placate special interests, and preserve tax revenue. Consequently, escalating political risk in the local business environment may increasingly penalize international companies.

Product Safety and Liability International companies often customize products to comply with local standards. Often, these standards differ due to cultural values or social norms; companies then adapt the product to boost its appeal to local consumers. Similarly, countries often impose product-safety and liability laws that require a company to adapt a product or else forsake market access. By and large, wealthier countries impose stringent standards, whereas poorer countries, reflecting underdeveloped legal codes and rule-of-man legacies, apply inconsistent standards.

The European Union's product-liability directive is the most common influence on product-safety and liability laws.[51] This directive protects consumers' rights by outlining the legal responsibility of manufacturers for whatever products they produce. It also guides the process of product-liability compensation claims.

Legal Jurisdiction Countries stipulate laws that set the criteria for litigation when agents—whether legal residents of the same or of different countries—are unable to resolve a dispute. While court protocol differs depending on the type of legal system, in all cases the power of courts is indisputable. Usually, in the face of a cross-national dispute, each company petitions its home-country court to claim jurisdiction, in the belief that it is likely to receive more favorable treatment. This situation is especially pressing when a company from, say, the United States, a rule-of-law environment, has legal complications in China, a rule-of-man environment. Less so but still influential are differences posed by different legal systems; worry about legal proceedings in a customary legal system can spur companies to specify a common- or civil-law jurisdiction. Expectedly, a thoughtful contract between companies contains a choice-of-law clause that stipulates the country whose laws govern dispute resolution.

Arbitration Increasingly, companies choose to resolve disputes by means of arbitration, whereby both parties agree on an impartial third party to settle the matter. Most arbitration is governed by the worldwide standards set by the New York Convention. This convention, instituted in 1958, allows parties to choose their own mediators and resolve disputes on neutral ground. To render decisions more enforceable, the Convention limits appeal options to narrow circumstances. Complaints against governments are arbitrated by the International Centre for Settlement of Investment Disputes. This body is closely linked to the World Bank. Hence, the government that disregards the arbitration process risks financial penalties imposed by the World Bank.

Despite the best intentions, plans go awry due to the unpredictability of governments. For example, until early 2009, the Venezuelan government encouraged private investment in its national oil-services industry.[52] Literally overnight, Venezuelan President Chávez invoked the claim of national security and changed the law to make the industry a preserve of the state. So, in May 2009, the national guard took command of drilling rigs, docks, and boats operated by private contractors, both local and foreign, that had been hired by PDVSA, the state oil company. Officially, the Venezuelan constitution stipulates prior judicial review and "fair compensation" as conditions for the expropriation of assets. However, the reality of a rule-of-man legal system is such that the Venezuelan government plans to pay oil-service firms the official book value of their assets, as opposed to the much higher market value. To add insult to injury, the companies will be paid in Venezuelan government bonds, but only after the government deducts any labor or environmental liabilities it see fit to charge to the company. At this point, many of the afflicted companies point to their contract stipulation of the right to international arbitration in such matters; hence, hearings and lawsuits are soon to follow. Going forward, PDVSA demands that companies renounce arbitration rights as a precondition to doing business in Venezuela.

INTELLECTUAL PROPERTY RIGHTS

In Adam Smith's time, countries drew strength from their agricultural prowess. Later, smokestack industries defined a nation's prosperity and power. Now, countries look to their brainpower to create might, prestige, and wealth. We call the output of this brainpower **intellectual property**—the creative ideas, innovative expertise, or intangible insights that give an individual, company, or country a competitive advantage. The growing power of ideas in the global economy has made the protection of intellectual property a strategic challenge.

Here, in a nutshell, is the problem: Intellectual property, whether in the form of books, music, product designs, brand names, process innovations, software, film, and the like is tough to conceive but easy to copy. The range of products that get copied is mind boggling—books, music CDs, DVDs, aircraft parts, cigarettes, wristwatches, razor blades, batteries, medicine, motorcycles, automobiles, shampoo, pens, toys, wine, shoes, clothing, industrial equipment, luggage, foods, beer, perfume, and cleaning supplies; you name it, it is likely being copied somewhere and sold for a fraction of the price of the authentic version. Our closing case on software piracy further examines the problems resulting from the fact that "digital" products, in particular, are ridiculously easy to copy—the main reason why the global software industry is so vulnerable to widespread piracy and counterfeiting.

The costs of intellectual property theft—whether in terms of lost sales, ruined brand reputation, dangerous products, enforcement expenses, and legal costs—are stunning. The International Anti-Counterfeiting Coalition estimates that international trade in counterfeit products alone runs more than U.S. $600 billion a year—approximately 5 to 7 percent of world trade. Furthermore, piracy has grown over 10,000 percent in the past two decades, given its astounding profitability—gross margins of more than 1,000 percent have been reported for any number of counterfeited products.[53]

Another day at another stall in the infamous Silk Market of Beijing, China. Here, an accommodating vendor shows a selection of fake designer bags to one more of the millions of people who travel this market seeking cheap counterfeits. Behind her are products ready to go. The discerning shopper seeking a particular bag can put in a custom order for a surprisingly high-quality knockoff at a fraction of the price of the real thing. Special orders are oftentimes filled within an hour or two.
Source: PETER PARKS/AFP/Getty Images

International Property Rights (IPRs) Transnational institutions like the WTO and World Intellectual Property Organization (WIPO), along with many countries, push for better protection of intellectual property. The primary vehicle is **intellectual property rights (IPRs)** that grant the registered owners of inventions, literary and artistic works, and symbols, names, images, or designs the right to determine the use of their property. In other words, the registered owner of a copyright has the legal right to decide who may copy it or who may use it for another purpose.

Technically, an IPR constitutes a legally enforceable but limited monopoly granted by a country to the innovator. Because an IPR specifies a period during which other parties may not copy an idea, the innovator can then commercialize the idea in order to recoup initial expenses and capture potential profits. Companies exert great effort to safeguard proprietary knowledge by protecting intangible assets through enforceable patents, trademarks, and copyrights.

The pervasiveness of piracy worldwide shows just how hard it is to enforce IPRs. Poor compliance and enforcement in certain political systems, particularly those marked by rule-of-man bias and totalitarian political tendency, impose obstacles. Problems arise because not all countries formally support the various agreements that protect IPRs. The primary regulatory codes for intellectual property are the Paris Convention for the Protection of Industrial Property and the Berne Convention for the Protection of Literary and Artistic Works, both created in the 1880s and updated periodically. More recently, the Trade-Related Aspects of Intellectual Property Rights (TRIPS) code of the WTO has set stricter protection.

Matters of jurisdiction further complicate protection. An IPR protected by, say, a U.S. patent, trademark registration, copyright, or design registration extends only to the United States and its territories and possessions. It confers no protection in a foreign country. Furthermore, there's no shortcut to worldwide protection: Companies cannot register a "global" patent, trademark, or copyright (say, with TRIPS or WIPO). Moreover, countries interpret and enforce agreements more or less arbitrarily. Indian patent law regarding pharmaceuticals, for example, protects only the "processes" by which drugs are made, not the drugs themselves. This means that merely using a process that's different from the innovator's process lets Indian companies manufacture drugs patented in other countries. So, despite governments' claims to abide by these agreements and enforce IPRs, escalating piracy rates threaten popular or pricey products with a high content of imagination and ingenuity.

Legacies, Economics, and Orientations Many local issues pose reasonable challenges that can be met with improved international laws.[54] Unfortunately, we cannot say the same for intellectual property violation, given its roots in far more fundamental facets of life in many countries. Not only are some countries less inclined to protect intellectual property, but prevalent attitudes, anchored in legal legacies, economic conditions, and cultural orientations, encourage, if not legitimate, piracy.

Legal Legacies Most counterfeit goods are made in markets in which the rule of man is the basis of the legal system. A return trip to China, given its sluggishness in protecting intellectual property and tradition of the rule of man, highlights the scale and scope of the problem. Moreover, as China goes in protecting intellectual property, so too will most emerging markets.

Officially, China has a battery of laws that comply with international standards for market access, nondiscrimination, and transparency. The enduring legacy of the rule of man in China, however, means that neither the typical Chinese citizen nor the typical Chinese official sees as legitimate those laws passed by foreign governments and those that are inconsistently enforced in the local marketplace by national authorities. Explained one executive, noting the application of law in China, "I was dealing with a society that had no rules; or more accurately, plenty of rules, but they were seldom enforced. China appeared to be run by masterful showmen: appearances mattered more

Intellectual property rights refer to the right to control and derive the benefits from writing (copyright), inventions (patents), processes (trade secrets), and identifiers (trademarks).

Case Review Note

The predominant share of counterfeit products are made in countries in which the rule of man prevails.

than substance; rules were there to be distorted; and success came through outfacing an opponent."[55] This gap between domestic traditions and foreign standards appears in official proceedings. As explained by one Chinese judge, intellectual property laws "exist to protect Chinese intellectual property from foreign intellectual property."[56]

This situation is not unique to China. The Asian Development Bank evaluated the performance of Indonesia, Malaysia, the Philippines, South Korea, and Thailand, relative to the rest of the world, on measures of good governance—specifically, accountability, political stability, government effectiveness, regulatory quality, control of corruption, and the rule of law. Over the past decade, the performance of these East Asian countries had deteriorated on nearly every dimension.[57]

Calls for China (as well as Vietnam, Russia, Chad, India, Malaysia—to name just a few of the many who behave quite similarly) to protect intellectual property in the context of the rule of law may one day prove successful. Still, few managers anticipate quick progress. For China, the legal legacy of two millenniums of the rule of man—or, in this case, emperor—suggests that establishing the rule of law may be "one of the largest social infrastructure projects in the history of mankind."[58]

Wealth, Poverty, and Protection   The vigor of IPR protection often reflects a country's stage of economic development. Typically, poorer countries provide weaker legal protection than richer countries.[59] Why? Generally, developed countries contend that protecting ideas is the only way to energize the incentive to innovate. "If stuff you create can be misappropriated," reasoned an analyst, "your incentive for continuing to create valuable intellectual property diminishes significantly."[60] The perspective in poorer countries, and increasingly in wealthier countries, rejects this reasoning.

Disregarding the inflammatory charges of colonial oppression and economic imperialism, analysts offer several arguments against the protection of IP.[61] Specifically, they contend that intellectual property protection:

- Inhibits local development and lowers global welfare by constraining the use of existing knowledge.
- Creates intellectual monopolies that protect business interests, bestow monopoly profits, and lessen the efficiency gains of free trade.
- Inflates the prices that poor nations pay for products and processes that are available only from wealthy nations.
- Results in licensing fees and regulations burdens that increase the cost of idea creation and slow the rate of diffusion of new ideas.

Theory aside, the brutal economics in many communities is likely the key determinant of a country's unwillingness to protect IP. Besides sharing the doctrine of the rule of man, countries that don't rigorously protect IP often suffer pervasive poverty. People who have no wealth and little income have little money to spend on necessities, let alone for branded goods sold by corporations headquartered in distant wealthy countries. In the African nation of Kenya, for example, where the average annual income is about U.S. $1,500 and some people earn less than U.S. $300, it shouldn't come as a surprise that a lot of Kenyans "think you have to cheat to survive."[62] One means of survival, goes this scenario, is buying pirated copies of products that improve productivity (i.e., software), fight illness (medicines), or provide relief (consumer products).

Cultural Orientation   In addition, cultural orientation explains local differences in attitudes toward the protection of IP. Countries with an *individualist* orientation, such as the United States and Australia, tend to regard the concept of individual ownership of an idea as intrinsically legitimate; few dispute that if you create something, you should have the right to say who can copy it or use it for any given purpose.

In contrast, countries with a *collectivist* orientation, such as South Korea, Thailand, and China, extol the virtue of sharing over individual ownership; few dispute that if you create something, it should improve the welfare of society. For example, asked about software piracy in his country, a South Korean diplomat explained, "[H]istorically, Koreans have not viewed intellectual discoveries or scientific inventions as the private property of the discoverers or inventors. New ideas or technologies [are] 'public goods' for everybody to share freely. Cultural esteem rather than material gain [is] the incentive for creativity."[63] In many countries, cultural values anchored in a collectivist doctrine promote sharing knowledge without expecting personal reward. Knowledge under private control, goes this reasoning, does more social harm than economic good, given that it breaches the fundamental social contract among all to improve the welfare of society.

Presently, technology challenges the interplay of individualism and collectivism in the protection and violation of intellectual property. Among some demographics, no matter if they are in collectivist China or the individualistic United States, piracy is an increasingly mainstream behavior. On one hand, economics spurs piracy; many poor people seek affordable solutions—legality notwithstanding. Alternatively, others note that the prevalence of piracy among the teenagers and young adults in rich and poor countries reflects evolving attitudes and technological opportunism. Observed the general counsel for NBC Universal, "Young people, in particular, conclude that if it's so easy, it can't be wrong." Improving technology, ironically, accelerates violation of IPR. The proliferation of streaming sites, which allow one to start watching video immediately without transferring a full copy of the movie or show to their hard drive, makes piracy cheaper and easier.

The Driver of Change   Convincing countries to protect intellectual property confronts head-on a potent mix of legal legacies, economic conditions, and cultural orientations. On one level, institutional initiatives try to expedite productive change. The WTO, for example, gives wealthy countries a year to comply with its latest rules on intellectual property but grants the poorest countries a 5- to 10-year grace period. Longer grace periods, the thinking is, support gradual socialization of the benefits of protecting intellectual propery while recognizing economic conditions. Rising piracy rates suggest that these sorts of programs struggle to make a substantive difference.

Many pin hope on the future success of companies in those countries that presently do not rigorously protect intellectual property. When these companies, now idea consumers, become idea creators and begin to market products based on their own intellectual property, the benefits of protection will eclipse their gains from piracy. Generally, history shows that countries that create intellectual property—no matter the particular legal, economic, or cultural characteristics of those countries—enforce ownership rights.[64] Observers have noted, as a pointed example, that the United States was a notorious copyright and patent infringer when it was a developing country in the eighteenth century. As one analyst explained, "American political independence was founded on the notion of economic self-sufficiency. And technology piracy became the premier tool to industrial development."[65] Only upon inventing its own intellectual property did the U.S. then endorse the Paris and Berne Conventions, both of which originated in the 1880s.

Countries that generate intellectual property are strong advocates of protecting the ownership rights.

Trends in China show the start of this process in play. Long the factory floor of the world, China aims to be the new product lab. Presently, the Chinese patent office leads the world in patent applications; more than 800,000 were filed in 2008. Although many are for trivial improvements or minor modifications, a growing share are significant "invention" patents that grant the holder 20 years of protection, the same as in the West. Observers expect that Chinese companies will surpass their foreign counterparts in receiving invention patents in China in 2009. Abroad, Chinese firms are similarly ramping up, registering 1,225 patents in 2008 in the United States (up from 90 in 1999). Besides claiming new markets, the data suggest that Chinese firms plan to protect their intellectual property worldwide. Right now, the signals from Chinese officials and companies are confusing—increasing piracy yet increasing patent activity. The resolution of this conundrum will shape intellectual property protection practices throughout the world. [66]

Crime That Pays (and Pretty Well Too)

I head toward ground zero of counterfeiting—the notorious Silk Market in Beijing. I, as do some 10 million people a year, enter a 35,000-square-meter, seven-level piracy temple, packed with nearly 2,000 small stalls, staffed by enterprising vendors, many offering low-price knockoffs of the leading branded products in the world. Navigating a surreal bazaar gone wild, I sidle by stalls boldly displaying bogus Prada purses, Hugo Boss Shirts, and Hermes scarves; depending on how well you negotiate, each can be had for a ridiculous fraction of the real price. Moving on, stall after stall offers infamous "copy-watches," Nike gear, Gillette razors, Oakley sunglasses, Apple iPods, Zeiss binoculars, Nikon lenses, North Face jackets—one after another, in a seemingly endless procession of premier brand names. Despite spot-on quality, virtually all are counterfeit. Moving around, one comes to digital zones, finding copies of software, music, games, and movies. Rack upon rack displays products from some of the best and the brightest minds of the world, now selling for absurdly low prices—Microsoft Vista Ultimate for about a buck, Microsoft Office for $0.75, Photoshop for two bucks, AutoCAD for five dollars. Each stall is packed with an ever-changing collage of customers—Germans, Indians, Canadians, Brazilians, British, and Americans, and so on—each getting past the initial shock, and many buying multiple titles.

—DPS's stroll through the Silk Market, Beijing, Winter 2009.

Almost from its inception, software technology has been dogged by the problem of digital piracy—the illegal distribution and/or copying of software for personal or business use.[67] It's an explosive issue, and it cuts right to the perception and protection of intellectual property rights. Software pirates can be anyone from an individual making an unauthorized copy of a software product (for use, sale, or free distribution) to workers who mismanage a company's software licenses.

It's not that the rules against software piracy are ambiguous—quite the contrary. The United States, for example, stipulates that software is automatically protected by federal copyright law from the moment of its creation; relevant codes speak to any and all contingencies.[68] Nor is ignorance of the law any excuse for piracy. As far as the United States is concerned, violators are liable for copyright infringement whether or not they know that they're violating the law. This means that if you're a software user who's purchased a license from, say, Microsoft for its Windows 7 operating system, you've purchased the right to load the product onto *one* computer and the right to make another copy for "archival purposes only." In others cases, vendors permit installation of software such as virus protection programs on more than one machine, provided it is owned by and registered to you. In either event, an illegal copy can land you a six-figure fine and jail time. In contrast, the corresponding "threshold laws" in China "let you have as many as 499 pirated DVDs without a criminal penalty. And if you get caught with those you get the equivalent of a parking ticket."

For counterfeiters, piracy and software are a match seemingly made in heaven. The problem with software is that, like any "digital" product, it's extraordinarily easy to make copies that are as good as the original (Table 3.5). And that, in short, is why piracy continues to bedevil the global software industry.

Despite long-running efforts, global software piracy is rampant and shows little sign of slowing. By 2008, the worldwide PC software piracy rate rose for the second year in a row—from 38 to 41 percent. Put differently, of all the packaged software installed on PCs worldwide in 2005, 41 percent was obtained illegally, at a cost of U.S. $53 billion in foregone revenue to the software industry; that figure is up from losses of U.S. $34 billion in 2005 and U.S. $29 billion in 2003. For many nations, piracy rates topped 75 percent in 2008 (see Table 3.6). Regional data, while not as extreme, is discouraging. Some 66 percent of all software in use in Central/Eastern Europe in 2008 was pirated, 65 percent in Latin America, 59 percent in the Middle East and Africa, 61 percent in the Asia-Pacific region, and 21 percent in North America (see Table 3.7).

TABLE 3.5 How to Pirate Software

End-user piracy	If you're simply a user, feel free to copy software (whether for personal or business use) without appropriate licensing; don't bother monitoring the number of licenses that you install, and don't worry about acquiring enough licenses to cover your needs.
Preinstalled software	If you manufacture computers, make operations more efficient by installing one copy of licensed software on a whole batch of computers.
Internet piracy	If you want to capitalize on the ability of the Internet to facilitate transactions, use it to download unauthorized copies of software.
Counterfeiting	If you are, say, an unscrupulous entrepreneur, make illegal copies of software, being sure to reproduce the manufacturer's packaging as well as his product; remember too that it's not much more trouble to counterfeit registration cards (and don't forget unauthorized serial numbers).
Online auction piracy	If you want to get into the distribution end of the business, you have two options: (1) resell software that's not authorized for resale, or (2) use the Internet to auction off counterfeit or unlawfully obtained software as "liquidated inventory" or as merchandise acquired through "bankruptcy sales."

Source: Adapted from Microsoft Corporation, "Piracy Basics" (2008), at www.microsoft.com/canada/sam/piracy/default.mspx (accessed December 15, 2008). Used with permission from Microsoft.

TABLE 3.6 Software Piracy Rankings by Country

Scores refer to the percentage of installed software that was illegally acquired. In Georgia, for example, of all the packaged software installed on PCs in 2005, 95 percent was illegally obtained by users. In the United States, which has the lowest rate of illegal installations, one out of every five installations involved pirated software.

25 Countries with the Highest and Lowest Piracy Rates: 2008

Highest Piracy		Lowest Piracy	
Georgia	95%	United States	20%
Bangladesh	92%	Japan	21%
Armenia	92%	Luxembourg	21%
Zimbabwe	92%	New Zealand	22%
Sri Lanka	90%	Austria	24%
Azerbaijan	90%	Belgium	25%
Moldova	90%	Denmark	25%
Yemen	89%	Sweden	25%
Libya	87%	Switzerland	25%
Pakistan	86%	Australia	26%
Venezuela	86%	Finland	26%
Indonesia	85%	Germany	27%
Vietnam	85%	United Kingdom	27%
Iraq	85%	Netherlands	28%
Ukraine	84%	Norway	28%
Algeria	84%	Israel	32%
Montenegro	83%	Canada	32%
Paraguay	83%	Ireland	34%
Cameroon	83%	South Africa	35%
Nigeria	83%	Singapore	36%
Zambia	82%	UAE	36%
Bolivia	81%	Czech Republic	38%
Guatemala	81%	Taiwan	39%
China	80%	Reunion	40%
El Salvador	80%	France	41%

Source: Business Software Alliance, *Sixth Annual BSA-IDC Global Software Piracy Study* (2008) (accessed July 15, 2009).

TABLE 3.7   2008 Software Piracy Rankings by Region

No region is exempt; the only variation is the degree of piracy.	
Asia-Pacific	61%
Central/Eastern Europe	66%
Latin America	65%
Middle East/Africa	59%
North America	21%
Western Europe	33%
European Union	35%
WorldWide	41%

Source: Business Software Alliance, *Sixth Annual BSA-IDC Global Software Piracy Study* (2008) (accessed July 15, 2009).

Waging a Multifront War

Several parties, including software makers, industry associations, and governments, battle piracy. An early and enduring battlefront in the war against piracy has been waged by software makers. By and large, they have relied on technical and business measures as a counteroffensive. In the 1980s and 1990s, for example, many companies integrated anticopying mechanisms into products. Although effective, consumers complained that they made software unduly difficult to use. Companies turned to other devices, including distribution models (e.g., requiring site and shrink-wrap licenses) and technological protections (requiring passwords, registration numbers, and encryption codes). This time, customers, though mildly annoyed, grudgingly accepted them, and for a while it seemed that the new measures might control piracy.

At the same time, software companies lobbied governments to enact tougher IPR protection. The United States, for example, elevated software piracy from a misdemeanor to a felony (if 10 or more illegal copies were made within a six-month period and if those copies were worth more than U.S. $2,500). The United States also boosted enforcement efforts, threatening to sanction countries—such as China, Russia, Argentina, India, Thailand, Turkey, and the Ukraine—with records of "onerous and egregious" IPR violations. Politically, officials ramped up the rhetoric; the U.S. Trade Representative, for instance, declared that "we must defend ideas, inventions and creativity from rip-off artists and thieves."

Industry associations, notably the Business Software Alliance (BSA), the Software and Information Industry Association (SIIA), and the International Anti-Counterfeiting Coalition (IACC), have spearheaded efforts to spur governments to toughen laws. These organizations provided global services in public policy, business development, corporate education, and intellectual property protection.

Finally, software makers, governments, and associations have urged transnational institutions to police piracy. The World Intellectual Property Organization (WIPO), for example, pledged to developing IPR treaties. WIPO then lobbied members to ratify an array of antipiracy treaties—namely, the World Copyright Treaty (WCT) and the WIPO Performances and Phonograms Treaty (WPPT). Similarly, the World Trade Organization (WTO) enacted an agreement on Trade-Related Aspects of Intellectual Property Rights (TRIPS) to regulate enforcement of IPR violations. TRIPS requires all member nations to protect and enforce IPRs according to global, not local, standards.

Most believed that these tactics reflected a useful battle plan to conquer the pirates. The mix of technological barriers, consumer education, stronger intellectual property policies, effective law enforcement, and institutional support seemed to work. Concerted political and commercial action, supported by the growing global reach of software companies, high-profile legal proceedings, increased government cooperation, the criminalization of software piracy, and tougher trade agreements, led some to see an end to software piracy.

Piracy Persists

By 2009, the retreat of software piracy proved to be a dip in the long-running upward trend. Piracy is once again rising: the worldwide PC software piracy rate rose for the second year in a

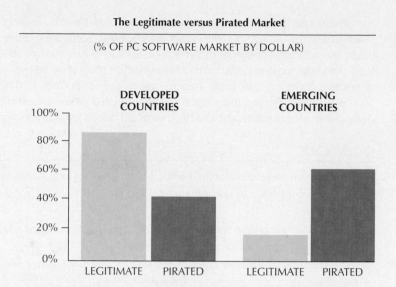

The Legitimate versus Pirated Market

(% OF PC SOFTWARE MARKET BY DOLLAR)

SOURCE: SIXTH ANNUAL BSA-IDC GLOBAL SOFTWARE PIRACY STUDY, MAY 2009

FIGURE 3.5 Software Piracy by Market Type: Developed versus Emerging Economies

Not surprisingly, developed countries constitute a more profitable market for pirated software than emerging countries. The latter group, however, includes many nations—some of them, like China, Russia, Vietnam, and India—in which growing waves of people look to integrate computers into their daily activities.

Source: Adapted from Business Software Alliance, *Sixth Annual BSA-IDC Global Software Piracy Study* (2008) (accessed July 15, 2009).

row, from 38 to 41 percent, with losses finally cracking the U.S. $50 billion threshold. Given recent successes, analysts were alarmed by the upturn in piracy rates.

Some observers now see the global cat-and-mouse game between software makers and pirates, far from winding toward a conclusion, possibly spiraling out of control. Growing piracy in big, fast-growing emerging markets like China and India spells big, fast-growing trouble. As more and more people in these countries enter the global software market—many of them eager to join the digital age despite income constraints—experts have warned that the worldwide quest for low prices will only fuel the growth of piracy. For example, whereas emerging economies account for 45 percent of the global PC hardware market, they account for less than 20 percent of the PC software market. Said one analyst, "If the piracy rate in emerging markets—where people are rapidly integrating computers into their lives and businesses—does not drop, the worldwide piracy rate will continue to increase." Data on piracy rates in developed versus emerging countries amplified this concern (see Figure 3.5).

"The Bandits Are Everywhere"

Compounding all the problems we've mentioned so far is the fact that pirates have found it easy to crack licensing codes, duplicate holograms, falsify e-mail headers, and set up anonymous post office boxes to perpetually stay one step ahead of the intellectual property police. "Like drug trafficking," notes one observer, "the counterfeiting problem is so massive [that] you don't know how to get a handle on it. The bandits are everywhere."

Worse still, counterfeiters are becoming sophisticated entrepreneurs. "When you are dealing with high-end counterfeits," explained a Microsoft attorney, "you are talking about organizations that have a full supply chain, a full distribution chain, full manufacturing tools all in place, and it is all based on profits." Ironically, piracy is getting a tremendous boost from the increasing availability of pirated software through Internet channels, such as P2P file-sharing sites and mail-order or auction sites.

Is Piracy Inevitable?

The pervasiveness and tenacity of software piracy poses profound questions for IPRs in general and the software industry in particular. Some worry that the different legal legacies and political ideologies among countries complicate even the most basic issues—such as the very legitimacy of piracy. TRIPS was supposed to settle such troublesome issues, but its most glaring shortcoming—its failure to deal with the impact of the Internet to ease the distribution of pirated software—made it, at least from the point of view of Microsoft, "woefully outdated."

Others fear that the antipiracy war may already be lost, fearing that consumers and businesses have few ethical qualms about using pirated software. Furthermore, the global economic crisis, by reducing consumer income, threatens to push more people to seek low-cost counterfeits. Similarly, some in collectivist cultures reason that software makers should honor the welfare of society, abandon their profit-maximizing business models, and shift their products to open-source software. Finally, there are those who regard piracy as simply the most effective way of dealing with monopolists who charge exorbitant prices for vital tools of economic development. ■

QUESTIONS

1. Collectivism and individualism, democracy and totalitarianism, rule of law and rule of man: What do these concepts say about the intellectual property rights of software and the legitimacy of its protection?
2. What is the relationship among governments, institutions, organizations, and companies in developing the legal means to fight software piracy?
3. Can the software industry control software piracy without government help? Why would the software industry dislike greater government regulation?
4. How do you think consumers in wealthier countries versus those in poorer countries justify software piracy?
5. Can you envision a scenario where companies and consumers reach a relationship that eliminates the profitability of piracy—whether it is for software, music, movies, and other digital products?

SUMMARY

- Political and legal systems converge and vary across countries in terms of guiding principles and practical routines.

- Two standards anchor assessment of a political system: the degree to which it emphasizes individualism as opposed to collectivism and the degree to which it is democratic as opposed to totalitarian.

- Individualism sees the primacy of individual freedoms in the political, economic, and cultural realms. This doctrine champions the interests of the individual over the interests of the state or social group.

- Collectivism holds that the needs of society take precedence over the needs of the individual. Collectivism encourages state intervention in society in the belief that government's role is to define and deliver the priorities of a country.

- Political officials and agencies have an extensive role in a collectivist society; they have a limited role in an individualistic society.

- Democracy champions the power of the many over the few. A democratic government protects personal and political rights, civil liberties, fair and free elections, and independent courts of law.

- Totalitarianism champions the power of the few over the many. The ruling political authority exercises control over aspects of life, the individual is subordinated to the state, and opposing political and cultural expression is suppressed.

- Political freedom measures the degree to which fair and competitive elections occur, the extent to which individual and group freedoms are guaranteed, the legitimacy ascribed to the rule of law, and the existence of freedom of the press.

- Recent data on the spread of democracy indicate a situation of freedom stagnation and possible resurgence of forms of totalitarianism.

- Political risk is the likelihood that political decisions, events, or conditions will affect a country's business environment in ways that will cost investors some or all of the value of their investments or force them to accept lower-than-projected rates of return.

- A legal system specifies the rules that regulate behavior, the processes that enforce the laws of a country, and the procedure used to resolve grievances.

- Modern legal systems share three components: a system of constitutional law that preserves an open and just political order, a system of criminal law that safeguards the social order, and a system of civil and commercial laws that promotes fairness and efficiency in business transactions.

- A common law system is based on tradition, precedent, custom, usage, and interpretation by the courts; a civil law system relies on a systematic collection of codes and statues that judges must follow; a theocratic legal system is based on religious precepts; a customary legal system follows the wisdom of daily experience; and a mixed legal system combines elements of the other systems.

- The rule of law endorses systematic and objective laws applied by public officials who are held accountable for their administration.

- The rule of man holds that legal rights derive from the will of the individual who commands the power to impose them.

- Primary legal issues in international business include product safety and liability, marketing practice, rule of origin, jurisdiction, and intellectual property protection.

- Intellectual property is the creative ideas, innovative expertise, or intangible insights that give an individual, company, or country a competitive advantage.

- Patents, trademarks, trade names, copyrights, and trade secrets are referred to as *intellectual property*.

- The protection of intellectual property rights within a country is moderated by its particular legal legacies, level of economic development, and cultural orientation.

KEY TERMS

collectivism (p. 137)
country of origin (p. 162)
democracy (p. 140)
freedom (p. 141)
individualism (p. 137)
intellectual property (p. 164)
intellectual property rights (IPR) (p. 165)

laissez-faire (p. 137)
legal system (p. 152)
local content (p. 162)
pluralism (p. 138)
political ideology (p. 138)
political risk (p. 149)
political spectrum (p. 139)

political system (p. 137)
rule of law (p. 156)
rule of man (p. 155)
third wave of democratization (p. 144)
totalitarian system (p. 143)

ENDNOTES

1 *Sources include the following:* Michael Sylvester, "Flaming Hoops," *Corporate Counsel: Market Report China* 11:10 (2004): 171; Mure Dickie, "A Call for More Chinese Walls: Foreign Companies Are Angered by Beijing's Inability to Tackle Piracy," *The Financial Times* (September 21, 2004): 9; Honglin Zhang, "What Attracts Foreign Multinational Corporations to China?" *Contemporary Economic Policy* (July 2001): 336; Jiang Xueqin, "Letter from China," *The Nation* (March 4, 2002): 23; "A Disorderly Heaven," *The Economist* (March 20, 2004): 12, US; "Bulls in a China Shop," *The Economist* (March 20, 2004): 10; "China Slams US Piracy Complaint," *BBC News* (April 10, 2007); *The Economist* Country Briefings: China, http://www.economist.com/countries/China/ (accessed September 26, 2009); U.S. Department of State, Background Note: China, http://www.state.gov/r/pa/ei/bgn/18902.htm (accessed June 29, 2009); Central Intelligence Agency, World Factbook http://www.cia.gov/library/publications/the-world-factbook/geos/ch.html (accessed June 28, 2009). The pace of change in China's business environment makes any discussion of it hazardous. Regard this case as a set of educated generalizations about the kinds of problems encountered by would-be foreign investors in China from the 1990s to date.

2 Chinese Negotiation: The Long Kiss Goodnight, http://www.chinesenegotiation.com/page/2/ (accessed May 14, 2009).

3 Steven Weisman, "Before Visit to China, a Rebuke," *New York Times* (December 12, 2006): A-1.

4 "The World's Greatest Fakes," *60 Minutes* (August 8, 2004), quote by Dan Chow, at www.cbsnews.com/stories/2004/01/26/60minutes/main595875.shtml (accessed June 15, 2006).

5 "The Sincerest Form of Flattery," *The Economist* (April 4, 2007): 67.

6 US move to file trade cases against China 'not wise', Consulate Gen. of the People's Republic of China. Retrieved from http://houston.china-consulate.org/eng/zt/zmgx/t324012.htm, September 21, 2009.

7 "Business in Russia: Dancing with the Bear," *The Economist* (February 1, 2007): 23.

8 "Business in Russia: Dancing with the Bear."

9 "Crocodile Tears," *The Economist* (April 28, 2007): 44.

10 Daniel Kaufmann, Aart Kraay, and Massimo Mastruzzi, "Governance Matters IV: Governance Indicators for 1996–2004," World Bank Policy Research Working Paper Series No. 3630 (May 2005).

11 Statement from the Declaration of Independence of the United States of America.

12 Extracted from Mission Statement, Freedom House, at http://www.freedomhouse.org/template.cfm?page=2 (accessed June 28, 2009).

13 Adrian Karatnycky, *Freedom in the World 2001–2002: The Democracy Gap* (New York, NY: Freedom House, 2002), at www.freedomhouse.org.

14 On December 10, 1948, the General Assembly of the United Nations adopted the Universal Declaration of Human Rights and has since called on all member countries to publicize the text and "to cause it to be disseminated, displayed, read and expounded principally in schools and other educational institutions, without distinction based on the political status of countries or territories." For the full text of the Declaration, go to www.un.org/Overview/rights.html.

15 In China, for example, the One Child Policy prohibits a family from having more than a single child; a couple that has a second child may be fined the equivalent of $1,300—a steep penalty in rural areas where most annual incomes are a fraction of that sum.

16 Anne-Marie Brady, *Marketing Dictatorship: Propaganda and Thought Work in Contemporary China* (Lanham, MD: Rowman & Littlefield, 2007).

17 Jaroslaw Piekalkiewicz and Alfred Wayne Penn, *Politics of Ideocracy* (Albany: State University of New York Press, 1995): 4.

18 Samuel P. Huntington, *The Third Wave: Democratization in the Late Twentieth Century* (Norman: University of Oklahoma Press, 1991).

19 Francis Fukuyama, *The End of History and the Last Man* (New York: Free Press, 1992).

20 Francis Fukuyama, *The End of History and the Last Man* (London: Penguin, 1992).

21 The Economist Intelligence Unit's Index of Democracy 2008, http://graphics.eiu.com/PDF/Democracy%20Index%202008.pdf (accessed June 24, 2009).

22 "Two Billion More Bourgeois," *The Economist* (February 14, 2009): 18.

23 "Politics Brief: Is There a Crisis?" *The Economist* (July 17, 1999): 49.

24 "The Global Crisis and the Poor: The toxins drift downward," *The Economist* (March 14, 2009): 62–64.

25 "Freedom in the World: The Annual Survey of Political Rights and Civil Liberties" (2006), at ww.freedomhouse.org/template.cfm?page=15 (accessed May 20, 2007).

26 "Freedom in the World 2009: Freedom Retreats for Third Year, Freedom in the World" (2009), The Freedom House, from http://www.freedomhouse.org/template.cfm?page=445 (accessed May 22, 2009).

27 "Freedom in the World 2009: Freedom Retreats for Third Year," at http://www.freedomhouse.org/template.cfm?page=70&release=756 (accessed June 29, 2009).

28 Laza Kekic, "A Pause in Democracy's March," *The Economist*, The World in 2007: 59–60. Annual Review, 2007

29 Laza Kekic, "A Pause in Democracy's March," xvi.

30 "Democracy? Hu Needs It," *The Economist* (June 28, 2007): 44. "A Warning for Reformers," *The Economist* (November 17, 2007): 67.

31 " 'I am a True Democrat': G-8 Interview with Vladimir Putin," *Spiegel Online* (June 4, 2007), at www.spiegel.de/international/world/0,1518,486345,00.html.

32 "Brazil's President Lula Says G7 Nations No Longer Speak for the World," *The Telegraph* (March 16, 2009): A-1.

33 "Freedom in the World: The Annual Survey of Political Rights and Civil Liberties," (2006), at www.freedomhouse.org/template.cfm?page=15 (accessed May 20, 2007).

34 Hassan Fattah, "Democracy in the Arab World, a U.S. Goal, Falters," *New York Times* (April 10, 2006): C-1.

35 Samuel Huntington, *The Clash of Civilizations and the Remaking of World Order* (New York: Simon & Schuster, 1996); Huntington, *Who Are We? The Challenges to America's National Identity* (New York: Simon & Schuster, 2004).

36 Jacob Talmon, *The Origins of Totalitarian Democracy* (London: Secker & Warburg, 1952).

37 Laza Kekic, "A Pause in Democracy's March," *The Economist*, The World in 2007.

38 "Venezuelan Bluster? Hugo Chávez Threatens to Seize Banks and a Steel-Maker," *The Economist Intelligence Unit* (May 8, 2007): 57.

39 Denis J. Wiechman, Jerry D. Kendall, and Mohammad K. Azarian, "Islamic Law: Myths and Realities," http://muslim-canada.org/Islam_myths.htm (accessed June 22, 2009).

40 Presently, the tiny nation of Andorra and the Guernsey and Jersey Islands, both of which belong to the United Kingdom, apply customary law only. The codification of civil law developed out of legal customs that evolved in particular communities and, over time, were collected and recorded by local jurists.

41 "Business in Russia: Dancing with the Bear."

42 "A Disorderly Heaven," *The Economist* (March 20, 2004): 75.

43 Paul Collier, *Wars, Guns, and Votes: Democracy in Dangerous Places* (New York: HarperCollins, 2009).

44 "The Sincerest Form of Flattery," *The Economist* (April 4, 2007).

45 Geoff Lewis, "Who in the World Is Entrepreneurial?" *Fortune: Small Business* (June 1, 2007): 24.

46 Keith Bradsher, "A Younger India Is Flexing Its Industrial Brawn," *New York Times* (September 1, 2006): A-1.

47 "Vive la difference! The French Model," *The Economist* (May 7, 2009): 31.

48 James Kanter, "Intel Fined Record $1.45 Billion in Antitrust Case," *New York Times* (May 13, 2009): A-1.

49 "Business in Asia: The Next Great Wall," *The Economist* (March 12, 2009): 67–68.

50 "Trade Policy: Buying American," *The Economist* (January 29, 2009): 40.

51 Duncan Fairgrieve and Geraint Howells, "Is Product Liability Still a Global Problem?," *Managerial Law* 49:1/2 (2007): 6–9.

52 "Venezuela's Oil Industry: Skint," *The Economist* (May 14, 2009): 52.

53 "Counterfeiting and Piracy: The New Face of Crime," at http://www.riponsociety.org/issues/2007_Policy_Issues/2007%20Policy%20Book%20China.pdf (accessed May 19, 2009).

54 "India: Cipla Launches 3-in-1 AIDS Pill," October 14, 2006, http://www.medindia.net/news/view_news_main.asp?x=15038 (accessed September 15, 2008).

55 "A Disorderly Heaven," *The Economist*, 1.

56 Veronica Weinstein and Dennis Fernandez, "Recent Developments in China's Intellectual Property Laws," *Chinese Journal of International Law* 3:1 (2004): 227.

57 "Gold from the Storm," *The Economist* (June 28, 2007): 65.

58 Zhenmin Wang, "The Developing Rule of Law in China," *Harvard Asia Quarterly* 4:4 (2000).

59 Robert L. Ostergard, Jr., "The Measurement of Intellectual Property Rights Protection," *Journal of International Business Studies* 31 (Summer 2000): 349.

60 Stephanie Sanborn, "Protecting Intellectual Property on the Web—The Internet Age Is Making Digital Rights Management Even More Important," *InfoWorld* (June 19, 2000): 40.

61 Economists Say Copyright and Patent Laws Are Killing Innovation; Hurting Economy, Washington University in St. Louis (March 6, 2009), http://www.newswise.com/articles/view/549822/?sc=dwhn (accessed May 10, 2009). See also Copyright and Wrongs, online debate of "This house believes that existing copyright laws do more harm than good" (May 11, 2009), http://economist.com/debate/debates/overview/144.

62 "Going Up or Down?" *The Economist* (June 7, 2007): 45.

63 "A High Cost to Developing Countries," *New York Times* (October 5, 1986): D2.

64 "A Gathering Storm," *The Economist* (June 7, 2007): 67.

65 Doron S. Ben-Atar, *Trade Secrets: Intellectual Piracy and the Origins of American Industrial Power* (New Haven, CT: Yale University Press, 2004).

66 "Battle of Ideas: Intellectual property in China," *The Economist* (April 25, 2009), http://www.economist.com/business/displaystory.cfm?story_id=13528318 (accessed May 8, 2009).

67 *Sources include the following:* Sixth Annual BSA-IDC Global Software Piracy Study (2009); Business Software Alliance (July 15, 2009), at http://bsa.org; International Anti-Counterfeiting Coalition Recording Industry (April 29, 2007), at www.iacc.org (accessed June 14, 2009); Recording Industry Association of America (April 29, 2007), at www.riaa.com; Motion Picture Association of America (April 29, 2007), at www.mpaa.org/home.htm (accessed June 29, 2009); Bryan W. Husted, "The Impact of National Culture on Software Piracy," *Journal of Business Ethics* 26 (August 2000): 197–211; Jennifer Lee, "Pirates on the Web, Spoils on the Street," *New York Times* (July 11, 2002): E1; Suzanne Wagner and G. Lawrence Sanders, "Considerations in Ethical Decision-Making and Software Piracy," *Journal of Business Ethics* 3 (January 2001): 161; Steve Lohr, "Software by Microsoft Is Nearly Free for the Needy," *New York Times* (April 19, 2007): C5; Brad Stone and Miguel Helft, "New Weapon in Web War over Piracy," *New York Times* (February 19, 2007): C1; "U.S. Puts 12 Nations on Copyright Piracy List," *The Associated Press* (April 30, 2007): 3; John Dvorak, "Inside Track," *PC Magazine* (July 17, 2007): 44.

68 Title 17 of the U.S. Copyright Act grants the copyright owner "the exclusive rights [to] reproduce the copyrighted work" and "to distribute copies" of it (Section 106). It also states that "anyone who violates any of the exclusive rights of the copyright owner . . . is an infringer of the copyright" (Section 501). The statute goes on to set forth specific penalties for violations. See http://www.copyright.gov/title17/92chap1.html

four
The Economic Environments Facing Businesses

Objectives

- To understand the importance of economic analysis
- To identify the major dimensions of international economic analysis
- To compare and contrast macroeconomic indicators
- To profile the characteristics of the types of economic systems
- To discuss the idea of economic freedom
- To profile the causes and consequences of economic change

A man is rich who owes nothing.

—French proverb

175

In the world of globalization, one often struggles to separate the hype from reality. Some view it in the extreme, as in the transformation of everything. Others see it as the latest stage in the evolution of the business environment. Some see it as the final phase before forces of deglobalization usher in the inevitable return to local enterprise. Despite far-ranging opinions, most agree that the integration of national economies into the global market has changed the business environment.

Discussions of the economic environment of globalization have taken a far more dramatic tone the past few years. Some commentators see trends that indicate a flattening of the world whereby advances in institutions, communications, and technology fundamentally change the economics of globalization. They speak of "distributed tools of innovation and connectivity empowering individuals from anywhere to compete, connect, and collaborate." Powered by a host of hardware and software innovations, companies can now do business anywhere, anytime—as long as they are plugged into the matrix.

Other analysts emphasize the entry of billions of people into the global marketplace. They reason that the world is in the "middle of a two-part revolution. Three billion new people—billion and a half Chinese, billion Indians, half a billion people from former Soviet bloc—have suddenly come into the global economy all at one time. Within these three billion people is a population as big as the United States, bigger than anybody in Europe or Japan, who are every bit as skilled and can do anything that could be done in the U.S. or Japan or any of the developed countries for ten cents on the dollar." The combination of low wages and billions of skilled workers changes how we interpret capital and labor in the production of goods and services.

MAP 4.1   Leading Emerging Markets, 2009

Source: Compiled from *The Economist* and the Morgan Stanley Emerging Markets Index.

Note: Given that this is a Mercator projection, the scale approximates east-west distance at the equator; however, the farther you move from the equator, the more the east-west distance is distorted.

Finally, the global economic meltdown has raised the specter of collapsing economic environments triggering waves of deglobalization. Rising trade barriers, risk-adverse companies, and nationalistic consumers slow the cross-national movement of information, people, products, capital, and jobs. Data paint a distressing picture: Countries' economies are shrinking and, by 2009, industrial production, exports, and equity valuations showed that globally were tracking or doing worse than during the Great Depression.[2] The global meltdown has spurred governments to constrain the animal spirits of capitalism, regulating what had become hazardously free markets. Economic freedom, as we saw with political freedom in Chapter 3, was under siege from surging government intervention.

Provocative in their own right, these interpretations suggest that, in the first decade of the twenty-first century, globalization has introduced developments and initiated trends that challenge economic orthodoxy. Combined, these developments and trends impact one's lifestyle, job, company, country, and future. The possibility that globalization has reached an inflection point—a time where old strategic patterns give way to the new—signals the need for managers to rethink their understanding of economic principles and practices.

The quest to understand where economic environments might be heading pushes executives to look at where the world is coming from. Initially, attention turned to how the world economy had changed between 1950 and 2000. During this time, the diffusion of democracy and free market principles powered growing trade among the richer, developed nations that also spilled over to many poorer, developing countries. Institutions like the IMF, WTO, and World Bank stabilized the playing field. Companies from the United States, Western Europe, and Japan—the so-called Triad—ruled international business.

The precedents from this era, however, fell increasingly short in helping managers interpret today's economic puzzles. Indeed, focusing on the tried-and-true indicators of the past gave a distorted picture of today's global economy. Unquestionably, measures of growth, inflation, unemployment, and productivity in developed countries still mattered greatly. But then again, they no longer mattered completely. Now, unfolding economic trends cast attention onto an alternative scenario, one that foreshadowed the epochal shift in the center of gravity of the global economy.

By 2050, four of the six largest economies in the world—Japan, China, India, and Russia—will be in greater Asia. Their growth will likely create a second tier of powerful economies among their Asian neighbors, such as South Korea, Indonesia, Taiwan, Vietnam, and Thailand. Countries in other parts of world, like Brazil in South America, South Africa in Africa, and Israel and Saudi Arabia in the Middle East, were developing economic environments in step with their Asian counterparts. All, although each at a different pace, were inexorably moving from the periphery to the center of the global economy.

Although 2050 seems far off, these countries had implemented economic policies that laid the foundation for future growth. Granted, extrapolation from 2010 out to 2050 is risky. Hard data, however, pointed to their growing success in transforming the global economy. For instance, the combined output of emerging economies reached a milestone in 2009: It accounted for more than half of total world GDP.[3] Similarly, emerging economies' share of world exports is nearly 50 percent (up from 20 percent in 1970), and their share of the world's foreign-exchange reserves is 70 percent (up from net deficits in the mid-1990s); China alone held more than 28 percent of total reserves in the world. Institutionally, the G7 expanded into the G20, thereby giving countries like China, India, Brazil, Mexico, and South Korea greater say in the world economy's main policy forum. Besides highlighting their performance, these achievements also signaled that the rich, powerful countries of the twentieth century would not dominate the global economy in the twenty-first century.

Analysis of the economic environment in emerging economies suggests that the revolution has only begun. Their ambition to improve infrastructure, increase productivity, create jobs, and alleviate poverty has put into motion what will likely be the biggest economic stimulus in history. The last transformation of similar magnitude—the Industrial Revolution—involved far fewer people in far fewer nations but still produced a century-and-a-half economic expansion that transformed lives everywhere. The revolution unfolding today covers nearly the entire globe and involves billions of people. As expected, analysts see emerging economies powering, if not steering, global growth. The transfer of the growth baton from rich countries to emerging markets shows increasing odds of resetting the nature, and our interpretation, of the economic environment of international business.

PRECEDENTS AND PREDICTIONS

The search for anchors to guide analysis leads some to seek precedent further back in history. Some say one need only review the past millennium to put the current economic drama into perspective. From roughly 1000 until the mid-1880s, China and India were the world's two biggest economies. Before the steam engine and the power loom drove the transfer of economic might from Asia to the West, today's emerging economies dominated world output. However, these countries "temporarily" lost their lead as internal failure, aggravated by colonial exploitation and unfair trade agreements, led them to retreat into isolationism. The technological revolution of the Industrial Revolution in Europe and America passed by these markets.

FIGURE 4.1   Emerging
Markets Make a Comeback

A millennium ago, today's emerging
economies, most notably China and
India, accounted for about 80 percent
of total global output. By the
twentieth century, today's developed
economies such as the United States
and France generated more than half
of total global output. Current market
trends suggest that by 2050, the
emerging economies will account for
more than 70 percent of total global
output.

*Source: The World Economy: A Millennial
Perspective*, by Angus Maddison (Paris:
OECD Development Centre Studies,
2001); IMF and the *The Economist*, Data
reported in Purchasing Power Parity.

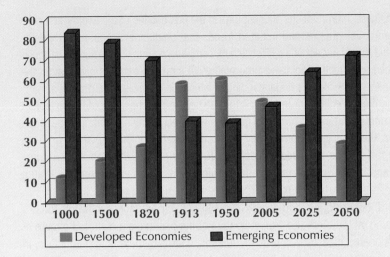

Developed Economies   Emerging Economies

Reports indicate that in the eight centuries leading up to 1820, today's emerging economies produced, on average, 70 to 80 percent of world output (see Figure 4.1). China alone generated one-third of the world's gross domestic product that year. By 1950, emerging economies' share of global output had fallen to 40 percent; China's share had fallen to 5 percent. The ambition of their current economic policies highlights their intention to return to their historic stature. Since 2001, annual growth in emerging markets has averaged nearly 7 percent, the fastest pace in recorded history; in contrast, the rich economies have growth rates just above 2 percent. In addition, while the global economic crisis has slammed the rich economies, pushing them to negative growth rates, the resiliency of many emerging economies sustained positive growth. The International Monetary Fund (IMF) forecast that over the next five years emerging economies will grow at an average rate of 6.8 percent a year, whereas the developed economies will be fortunate just to grow. If both groups continue in this way, in 20 years or so, today's emerging economies will complete their comeback and once again account for more than 70 percent of global output.

The shrinking role of today's leading rich economies, coupled with the accelerating scope of emerging economies, has triggered fundamental shifts in investment, trade, consumption, wealth, poverty, and fiscal and monetary policy. These shifts create opportunities and threats for international companies. Put differently, strategic inflection points do not necessarily lead to disaster, as cars did to buggy whips or the Internet to printed newspapers. Change in the way business is conducted creates prospects for players, whether newcomers or incumbents, who are adept at operating in the new economy, such as those who applied computer chips to cell phones or publishers that migrated to the Web.

Policymakers, executives, workers, and investors wrestle with making sense of the shift in the global economic environment. Against this backdrop, we turn to specifying the frameworks that will guide assessment. Certainly economic change, particularly the sort seen during the current global crisis, may seem inherently unpredictable. Nevertheless, as this chapter shows, there is rhyme and reason **CRN** that helps managers make sense of the economic environment.

Introduction

Earlier chapters looked at how cultural, political, and legal systems influence a company's decisions on where and how to do business internationally. This chapter completes this macro-profile by presenting the perspectives and tools that managers use to evaluate economic environments.[4]

The importance of this chapter follows from the fact that different countries have different levels of economic development, performance, and potential. For instance, in absolute terms, world economic output more than tripled between 1975 and 2008, approaching $50 trillion. In relative terms, many countries prospered, but some prospered more than others and, in a few cases, some not at all. Moreover, by mid 2009, it appears that many countries were joining the latter set; economic contraction in most of the industrial world and export declines in many economies (notably Japan and Germany) signaled the biggest global economic contraction since the Second World War. Japan saw its economy shrinking at an annualized 16 percent rate by summer 2009, its worst performance since the 1940s, whereas the U.K. economy suffered its biggest contraction since 1958. These were not isolated situations. By 2009, the year-over-year change in total exports from the 15 leading exporting countries—including Taiwan, France, Canada, Mexico, United States, and Australia—dropped nearly 30 percent.[5] This fall, the biggest in the post World War II era, signaled a dramatic economic slowdown in a host of nations. Thus, estimating the attractiveness of a country as a place to do business and then, once there, making prudent investment and operational decisions depends on how well managers understand, anticipate, and adapt to economic conditions.

When a company wants to do business in another country, it studies conventional wealth, income, employment, and policy standards. The dynamic nature of political and economic events requires that it also anticipate new situations. Besides assessing the foreign markets in which they operate, managers also need to monitor those in which they do not. Globalization connects countries in many ways; hence, economic change in one country likely has consequences in other countries. Companies also watch economic changes in those countries where they may not operate but where competitors do. Improving economic performance or revised economic policies in a particular country may strengthen their rivals.

Although the pace varies from country to country, national economic environments continually change. Since the 1980s, managers enjoyed economic opportunities as countries adopted the principles of capitalism and the practices of free markets. We have recently seen the credit crisis reset expectations. In the aftermath, there is growing government involvement in economic affairs. Changing economic policies reveal the ambitions of the government and the likely implications to economic freedoms. Managers aim to spot those changes, both big and small, that shape a country's economic environment.

Finally, economics is a vital topic to citizens, policymakers, and institutions. The apparent triumph of free markets over state-controlled economies had led countries to unleash ambitious programs. Economic development helped many countries improve their standard of living. Free market reforms spurred increasing investment, consumption, employment, and wealth. The global economic crisis has cast doubt on the sustainability of bold development programs. Free markets, we now realize, also spurred the misallocation of capital, excessive consumption, job displacement, high debt, and opportunism. Resetting the economic environment has prompted many governments to constrain the animal spirits of unbridled capitalism. Therefore, whether the catalyst is greater market liberalization or growing state intervention, the impact of resulting economic change has a variety of characteristics. Some shape patterns of trade and investment, while others influence companies and consumers. Some dramatically reconfigure the market, while others exert a subtle pressure on the economic environment. Hence, a fuller understanding of economic transitions and market evolution helps citizens, policymakers, and institutions make better decisions.

Managers study economic environments to estimate how market trends and government policy influence the performance of their companies.

Concept Check

In discussing "The Forces Driving Globalization" in Chapter 1, we explain how an economic environment responds to technology, trade, competition, consumer attitudes, and cross-border relationships. Here we point out that the scope of the connections among these conditions spurs companies to examine them as both discrete and interdependent factors.

A country's economic policies are a leading indicator of government's goals and its planned use of economic tools and market reforms.

Concept Check

A principle globalization is the broadening network of relationships among people, companies, countries, and institutions throughout the world. Philosophically, the same principle holds for our ideas about how economies emerge and evolve. Linkages and connections among economic ideas speak to questions about markets and performance.

INTERNATIONAL ECONOMIC ANALYSIS

The World Bank identifies 208 discrete economic environments in the world today—194 countries and 14 other economies with populations of more than 30,000.[6] Inevitably, managers ask which of those countries warrant investment. Resource constraints mean a firm cannot operate everywhere; it must prioritize its options and operate in those economies that offer the greatest return with the least risk. Unfortunately, there is no universal scheme to assess the performance and potential of a country. Granted, there are many useful approaches. Still, three conditions hamper specifying a universal method:

1. It is difficult to stipulate a definitive set of indicators that estimates the performance and predicts the potential of a country's economy. The complexity of even the simplest economic system defies straightforward classification.

2. The dynamism of the marketplace means that today's set of perfect measures may prove imperfect tomorrow. The global credit crisis has led to radical market changes. Indicators that worked in 2009 were flawed by 2010.

3. Just as no man is an island, no country is isolated. The consequence of connections is an integrated system of markets in which actions in one market influence outcomes in others. Interdependencies complicate interpreting the relationship among elements of the economic environment. Adjusting analysis for actions and reactions across a broad scope of markets is difficult.

Meaningful Dimensions and Systemic Relationships   Figure 4.3 identifies economic conditions that shape market, physical, and social factors in a country. While straightforward, their simplicity belies the difficulty of the challenge. Importantly, Figure 4.3 outlines a way to resolve this.

Research pinpoints key elements of an economic environment. These include, among many others, income, purchasing power, market size, market type, and economic freedom. Reducing the oft-overwhelming idea of an economic environment to its more easily understood elements, as this chapter shows, provides useful building blocks. Then, with that understanding in mind, we can analyze how they interact in building the economic environment.

Figure 4.3 also highlights the importance of applying a systems perspective—namely, that linkages among elements mean that change in one element in the economy affects other parts. For example, consider the consequences of a reduction in interest rates; a cut spurs more borrowing that fans greater demand that boosts inflation that erodes purchasing power that creates wage pressure that reduces profits and lowers savings and so on. Understanding how an economic environment works requires making sense of the interactions among its elements.

Therefore, the key takeaway from Figure 4.2 is that managers assess an economic environment by studying its key elements. Then, confident that these elements make

Key economic forces include

- Price stability.
- Capital markets.
- Factor endowments.
- Market size.
- Public policy.

FIGURE 4.2   Economic Factors Affecting International Business Operations

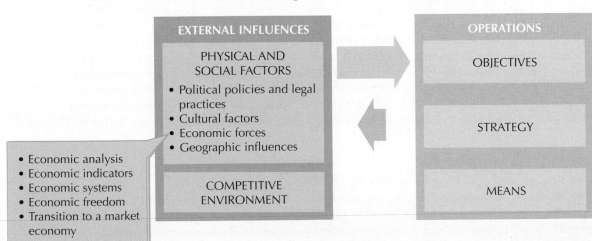

sense, managers assess their systemic relationship. Combined, this understanding supports managers' estimation of the likely development path and potential performance of the economy. This chapter follows this scheme. It starts by profiling features of an economic environment, moves on to types of economic systems, and closes with a look at processes of economic change.

Elements of the Economic Environment

Managers use different economic measures to assess a country's level of performance and potential. Some may be informal or idiosyncratic indicators—for example, the number of wireless phones, amount of electrical power generated, or newspaper circulation patterns. Typically, convention dominates practice. Managers usually begin their analyses by looking at the monetary value of the total flow of goods and services in the economy of a nation. They refine this analysis by considering issues like growth rates, income distribution, inflation, unemployment, productivity, debt, and the balance of payments. We now examine these factors.

GROSS NATIONAL INCOME

Gross national income (GNI) is the broadest measure of economic activity for a country. GNI measures the income generated by both total domestic production as well as the international production activities of national companies. GNI is the value of all production in the domestic economy plus the net flows of factor income (such as rents, profits, and labor income) from abroad during a one-year period.[7] Therefore, for example, the value of an Acer netbook that is built in Taiwan as well as the portion of the value of a Acer netbook made in Japan using Taiwanese capital and management is counted in the GNI of Taiwan. Similarly, the portion of the value of a Sony netbook built in Taiwan using Japanese capital and management counts in the GNI of Japan, not Taiwan. Table 4.1 identifies the 10 largest economies in the world in terms of GNI.

Gross national product (GNP) is the value of all final goods and services produced within a nation in a given year, plus the income earned by its citizens abroad, minus the

Concept Check

In discussing "Growing Consumer Pressures" among the drivers of **globalization**, Chapter 1 notes that worldwide consumption grew sixfold in the second half of the twentieth century. This trend, depending on the fallout of the global credit crisis, may accelerate. Here we stress the importance of such information to managers of global companies, who, in making investment decisions, must estimate how much income consumers in a given market have today and will likely have in the future.

TABLE 4.1   The Ten Largest Economies, 2008*

Rank	Country	GNI (U.S. $, millions)
1	United States	14,466,112
2	Japan	4,879,171
3	China	3,678,488
4	Germany	3,485,674
5	United Kingdom	2,787,159
6	France	2,702,180
7	Italy	2,109,075
8	Spain	1,456,488
9	Brazil	1,411,224
10	Canada	1,390,040

*Data calculated with the *Atlas method,* which smooths exchange rate fluctuations by using a three-year moving average, price-adjusted conversion factor.

Source: The World Bank, at www.worldbank.org. World Bank Development Indicators 2008. Copyright 2009 by the World Bank. Reproduced with permission of the World Bank. Accessed October 5, 2009.

GNI is the broadest measure of economic activity for a country.

GNP is the total value of all final goods and services produced within a nation in a particular year.

income earned by foreigners from domestic production. Conceptually, world GNP and world GNI are equal. However, GNP and GNI are often calculated differently, thereby resulting in a discrepancy at the country level. For example, Indonesia's GNP is larger than its GNI—the former was $432 billion, while the latter was $372 billion in 2007. The same situation exists for its neighbor, Thailand, with a GNI of $217 billion versus GNP of $246 billion in 2007. In contrast, the GNI of the United States was $13.88 trillion, while its GNP was $13.84 trillion in 2008. This discrepancy results from the fact that the net foreign factor income for Indonesia and Thailand is negative (i.e., a net outflow), whereas it is roughly balanced for the United States. Since GNI takes net flows into account, we have the resulting variance between GNI and GNP. As a rule, many developing countries produce more value than they receive as income, thereby leading to a higher GNP than GNI. Consequently, managers cross-check their analysis, paying particular attention to the assumptions underlying measurement and the characteristics of the country being examined.

GDP is the total market values of goods and services produced by workers and capital within a nation's borders during a given period—usually one year.

Gross Domestic Product   *Gross domestic product (GDP)* is the total value of all final goods and services produced within a nation in a particular year. Effectively, GDP is the total value of all goods and services produced within a nation's borders, no matter whether domestic or foreign-owned companies make the product.[8] As such, GDP is useful to assess countries in which the output of the multinational sector is a significant share of activity; for example, almost 90 percent of Irish exports are made by foreign-owned firms. Looking at GDP, not GNI, provides a far more accurate measure of the Irish economy.

Technically, GDP plus the income generated from exports, imports, and the international operations of a nation's companies equals GNI. So, both Acer and Sony netbooks made in Taiwan would contribute to Taiwan's GDP, but a netbook made in Japan by Acer would not. Lastly, the absolute size of GDP spotlights market opportunities in a country. For example, Bolivia and Brazil are neighbors in South America. Bolivia's GDP hit $18.94 billion in 2008, whereas Brazil clocked in at $1.66 trillion. Consequently, foreign companies often open operations in Brazil, given its greater market potential, and then export to Bolivia.

Managers improve the usefulness of GNI by adjusting it for
• Number of people in a country
• Growth rate of the economy
• Local cost of living
• Degree of economic sustainability.

Improving the Power of GNI   GNI is a robust estimator of an economy's absolute performance. However, GNI can mislead managers when they compare countries. For example, economic powers like the United States, Japan, and Germany consistently claim the top rankings of countries when sorted by GNI. Therefore, the data might give the misleading impression that these top-ranked countries are far wealthier, more productive, and faster growing than lower-ranked countries. Managers improve the usefulness of GNI by adjusting it for the number of people in a country, the growth rate of the economy, the local cost of living, and the degree of economic sustainability.

Per Capita Conversion   Managers transform GNI, as well as many other economic indicators, by the number of people who live in a country. This conversion is common sense given how unevenly the world's population of 6.81 billion, as of December 2009, is distributed across countries.[9] Therefore, adjusting GNI by population leads to a per capita estimator that measures a country's relative performance. Technically, we compute per capita GNI by taking the GNI of a country and converting it into a standard currency—say, the U.S. dollar at prevailing market rates—and then dividing this sum by its population.

This revised measure, along with other per capita indicators, explains an economy's performance in terms of the number of people who live in that country (see Map 4.2). For example, GNI may be low in absolute terms, such as is the case for Luxembourg, which ranks among the smaller economies of the world. However, Luxembourg ranks

MAP 4.2   GNI per Capita 2007

GNI is a raw number that refers to the market value of the final products produced by domestically owned factors of production. *GNI per capita* measures a country's performance in terms of its population. Thus, a nation might have a very high rank on the basis of GNI (e.g., Germany or France) but rank only in the middle on the basis of GNI per capita. In fact, China, which is the world's fifth largest economy according to GNI, ranks in the bottom tier of countries according to GNI per capita.

Source: World Bank: Measuring the Size of Economies (April 1, 2009). Accessed at http://web.worldbank.org/WBSITE/EXTERNAL/DATASTATISTICS/0,contentMDK: 20399244~menuPK:1504474~pagePK:64133150~piPK:64133175~theSitePK:239419,00.html

Note: Given that this is a Mercator projection, the scale approximates east-west distance at the equator; however, the farther you move from the equator, the more the east-west distance is distorted.

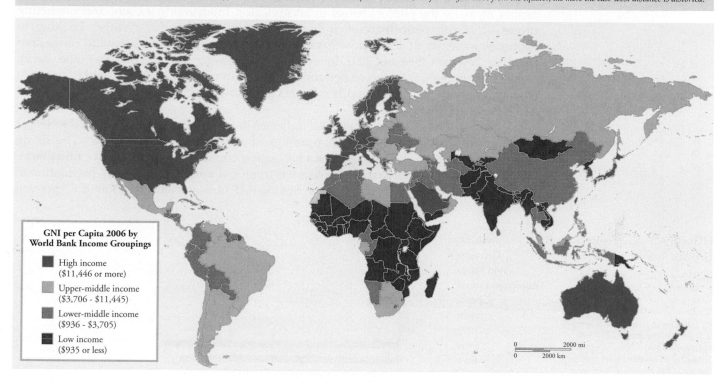

GNI per Capita 2006 by World Bank Income Groupings

- High income ($11,446 or more)
- Upper-middle income ($3,706 - $11,445)
- Lower-middle income ($936 - $3,705)
- Low income ($935 or less)

first in the world by GNI per capita in 2008, whereas the United States ranks 6th and Japan ranks 16th.

Officially, the World Bank reports that worldwide GNI per capita was $7,995 in 2007, up from $7,011 in 2005 and $5,500 in 2003.[10] Technically, the World Bank's classification scheme orders the countries of the world into one of four categories on the basis of their per capita GNI. The cutoffs for GNI per capita for the 52 low-income countries is $935 or less, $936 to $3,705 for the 54 lower-middle-income countries, $3,706 to $11,445 for the 41 upper-middle-income countries, and $11,446 or more for the 59 high-income countries.

A helpful point is in order here regarding the classification of countries. Most managers follow the World Bank's lead in labeling low- and middle-income countries as *developing countries*. These countries have low per capita income and most of their people have a low standard of living with limited access to few goods and services. Developing countries comprise the largest number of countries (151 or so according to the World Bank) and have the highest number of inhabitants (approximately 5.5 billion) in the world. The more prosperous developing countries such as China, Brazil, and India are often referred to as *emerging markets* or *emerging economies*. Currently, there are approximately 30 or so **emerging economies** in the world, as seen in Map 4.1. In contrast, developed countries have relatively high per capita income, and most people have a high standard of living with access to a variety of goods and services. Developed countries include Japan, Australia, New Zealand, Canada, the United States, and many in Western Europe. Less commonly, these countries are called high-income countries, advanced markets, or industrial countries.

The World Bank classifies countries as developing or developed on the basis of per capita income.

Case Review Note

Map 4.2 shows that high-income countries are clustered in a few regions of the world. High-income countries presently account for less than 15 percent of the world's population and over 75 percent of world GNI and report an average GNI per capita in the mid-tens of thousands. Lower-income countries are spread throughout the world. Although a large share of world population, these countries have a small share of the world's GNI and report GNI per capita figures from the mid-hundreds to low thousands.

Rate of Change   Gross figures are a snapshot of one year of activity. As such, they cannot measure the rate of change in an indicator. Interpreting present and predicting future economic performance requires pinpointing the rate of change. Looking at countries in terms of their growth rate for GNI per capita shows a wide range. For example, between 1998 and 2002, Ireland was the fastest growing economy in the world, expanding more than 8 percent per annum. Japan, in contrast, grew by only 0.2 percent over that period. Figure 4.3 reports the real GDP growth rates for a sample of developed and developing economies.

Generally, the GNI growth rate also indicates its economic potential—if GNI grows at a higher (or *lower*) rate than the population, standards of living are said to be rising (or *falling*). For example, Latin America has seen income per capita drop five times since the 1980s. The current global credit crisis has triggered a sixth occurrence—population in the region is growing 1.3 percent a year, but the IMF forecasts a contraction of 1.5 percent

FIGURE 4.3   GDP—Real Growth Rate

GDP increases from year to year partly because a country produces more goods and services and partly because prices go up. Measuring annual growth against price levels in a designated year, *real* GDP—as opposed to *nominal* GDP—keeps prices constant. What's left is annual growth in the actual production of goods and services. This conversion, by stripping out price effects, shows that many emerging economies are growing much faster than leading developed countries.

Source: Central Intelligence Agency, *The World Factbook,* at www.cia.gov (accessed June 1, 2009).

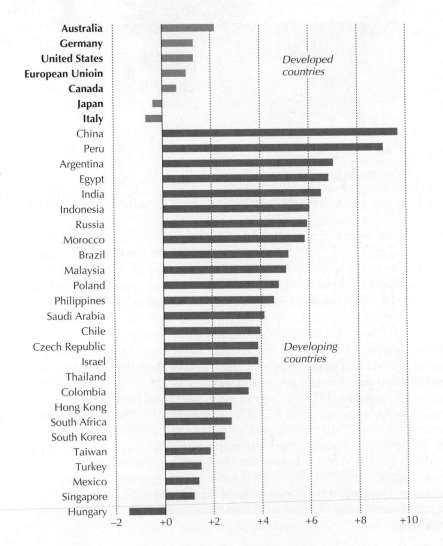

in GNI growth for 2009. Expectedly, consumer demand, public finances, financial reserves, and currency valuations—the lifeblood for many economies—will tumble in the region. This calamity is not unique to Latin America; the United Nations says that at least 60 developing markets will suffer falls in income per person in 2009, with especially hard times for Eastern Europe and sub-Saharan Africa.[11]

The GNI growth rate highlights likely business opportunities. For example, China has been one of the fastest-growing economies over the past 30 years, averaging high single-digit growth for the past several years. This growth, in turn, has resulted in the swiftest, most extensive rise out of poverty any nation has ever seen. Naturally, this rise has attracted foreign investment in anticipation of growing market opportunity powered by rising consumer demand. In addition, as we saw in our opening case, the so-called comeback of emerging economies foreshadows rising standards of living.

Managers, when comparing markets, often convert GNI in one nation in terms of the currency of their home market. Technically, comparing countries in terms of GNI per capita requires translating each currency into a common currency unit at the prevailing rate to trade one currency for another (the so-called exchange rate). So, converting Indian rupees to U.S. dollars at official exchange rates estimates Indian GNI per capita at just over $950 (versus $47,580 in the United States). This gap in per capita income suggests tremendous differences between the two countries. Some managers, in light of this gap, might wrongly decide to deemphasize the Indian market.

Purchasing Power Parity   Exchange rates tell us how many units of one currency it takes to buy one unit of another—for example, how many Indian rupees one needs to buy one U.S. dollar. The calculation of GNI per capita, however, does not account for differences in the cost of living from one country to another. Instead, it presumes that a dollar of income in Minneapolis has the same "purchasing power" of a dollar of income in Mumbai, even though the cost of living differs between the United States and India. Consequently, GNI per capita is unable to tell us much about how many goods and services someone can buy with a unit of income in one country relative to how much someone can buy with a unit of income in another country.

Managers adjust GNI per capita for a particular country in terms of its local **purchasing power parity (PPP),** a conversion that adjusts the exchange rate so that an identical good in two different countries has the same price when expressed in the same currency. For example, a loaf of bread that sells for 47 rupees in India should cost U.S. $1.00 in the United States when the exchange rate between India and the United States is 47 INR to U.S. $1. Technically, then, PPP is the number of units of a country's currency required to buy the same amounts of goods and services in the domestic market that one unit of income would buy in the other country.

One calculates PPP between countries by estimating the value of a universal "basket" of goods (like soap and bread) and services (like telephone and electricity) that can be purchased with one unit of a country's currency. The resulting estimate of the GNI per capita in terms of its local purchasing power in a country tells us what local consumers can buy with one unit of income. The most common PPP exchange rate comes from comparing a basket of goods and services in a country with an equivalent basket in the United States.

Table 4.2 shows the impact of adjusting a country's aggregate performance for local purchasing power. The rankings reported in Table 4.1 (the top 10 economies in terms of GNI) change after adjusting for PPP; China moves to second, India and Russia replace Canada and Spain, and Japan, the United Kingdom, France, and Italy drop. This effect is evident in country-to-country adjustment. Revisiting our comparison of the United States and India finds India's GNI per capita in 2007 is $950 but in terms of its local purchasing power, it is $2,740.[12] Effectively, then, GNI per capita expressed in terms of PPP is higher in India because it costs less to buy the same basket of goods in India than it does in the United States.

Case Review Note

PPP provides a method of measuring the relative purchasing power of different countries' currencies for the same basket of goods and services.

TABLE 4.2   Ten Largest Economies, 2008: GDP Adjusted for PPP

Rank	Country	GNP (U.S. $ billions)
1	United States	14,260
2	China	7,973
3	Japan	4,329
4	India	3,297
5	Germany	2,918
6	Russia	2,226
7	United Kingdom	2,226
8	France	2,128
9	Brazil	1,993
10	Italy	1,823

Source: GDP Source Country Comparisons—GDP (purchasing power parity), *CIA World Factbook*. Accessed October 5, 2009.

The opposite occurs in the case of countries with expensive standards of living, such as Switzerland. Specifically, given that the cost of living is higher in Switzerland than in the United States, Switzerland's GNI per capita falls from $60,820 to $44,410 when expressed in terms of PPP relative to the United States. On a broader scale, recall the gap in GNI per capita between low-income countries ($585) and high-income countries ($35,264). Adjusting these income levels for PPP increases low-income countries' performance to $2,470 and decreases high-income countries to $32,824. Map 4.3 profiles the countries of the world in terms of GNI adjusted for PPP.

Degree of Human Development   GNI, including its expression in terms of per capita, growth rate, and PPP, profiles growth and development in an economy. Some argue that these indicators, by measuring growth with purely monetary indicators, misrepresent the scale and scope of a country's level of development. Managers deal with these concerns by evaluating a country's degree of human development. Jointly considering the degree to which economic and social indicators support human development enables managers to measure market potential in terms of the capabilities and opportunities people enjoy.

Matters of human development do show up immediately in income or growth figures. Ultimately, the reasoning goes, they will.

> *The basic purpose of development is to enlarge people's choices. In principle, these choices can be infinite and can change over time. People often value achievements that do not show up at all, or not immediately, in income or growth figures: greater access to knowledge, better nutrition and health services, more secure livelihoods, security against crime and physical violence, satisfying leisure hours, political and cultural freedoms, and sense of participation in community activities. The objective of development is to create an enabling environment for people to enjoy long, healthy, and creative lives.*[13]

Economic indicators identify the potential for consumption and growth in a country. Still, their monetary basis risks missing the underlying effects of human development and capabilities that are, in due course, instrumental to GNI. To that end, managers complement monetary-based indicators by also analyzing the economic environment in terms of the overall quality of life in a country. This elaboration lets managers qualify a country's performance in developing favorable physical, intellectual, and social standards.

The U.N. Human Development Index   The United Nations translated this view into its Human Development Report and its principal indicator, the

MAP 4.3   GNI per Capita Adjusted for Purchasing Power Parity

Assume for a moment that income in every country has been converted to U.S. dollars. In countries like Canada and Australia, the average person has more than U.S. $30,000 with which to purchase goods and services over the course of a year. In countries like Bolivia, Sudan, and Pakistan, the average person would have only U.S. $1,000–3,000 to spend. Bear in mind that, because the *cost of living* is lower in the developing countries, each U.S. dollar will go a little further. The income disparity between nations, even after adjustment for PPP, remains glaring.

Source: World Bank: Measuring the Size of Economies (April 1, 2009). Accessed at http://web.worldbank.org/WBSITE/EXTERNAL/DATASTATISTICS/0,,contentMDK: 20399244~menuPK:1504474~pagePK:64133150~piPK:64133175~theSitePK:239419,00.html

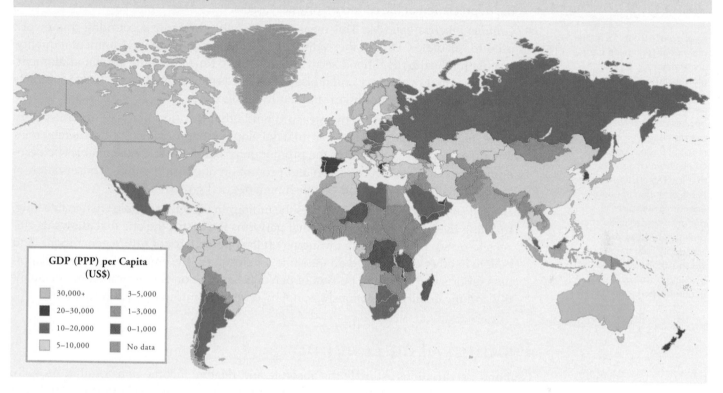

GDP (PPP) per Capita (US$)

- 30,000+
- 20–30,000
- 10–20,000
- 5–10,000
- 3–5,000
- 1–3,000
- 0–1,000
- No data

Human Development Index (HDI).[14] The HDI measures a country's achievements on three dimensions:

- *Longevity*, as measured by life expectancy at birth
- *Knowledge*, as measured by the adult literacy rate and the combined primary, secondary, and tertiary gross enrollment ratio
- *Standard of living*, as measured by GNI per capita expressed in PPP for U.S. dollars

The HDI aims to capture long-term progress in human development rather than short-term changes. While it does expand analysis, the HDI fails to include any ecological considerations, focusing exclusively on national performance and ranking. Moreover, it gives little attention to development from a global perspective.

> The Human Development Index combines indicators of real purchasing power, education, and health to more comprehensively measure economic development.

Green Measures   Concern for the ecological welfare of the world spurs calls for green measures of growth. **Green economics** holds that a country's economy is a component of, and dependent on, the natural world within which it resides. Consequently, GNI, GNP, and GDP measures of narrowly defined economic performance makes them misleading indicators of a country's long-term economic health and performance.

Measuring the quantity of market activity without accounting for the associated social and ecological costs mismeasures performance. Ensuring sustainable development requires managers to recognize economic activity must "meet the needs of the present without compromising the ability of future generations to meet their own needs."[15] Therefore, green economics calls for a wider view of what qualifies as economic growth—as seen in the Point-Counterpoint.

> Green measures of gross national production aim to gauge economic performance in terms of the effect of current choices on long-term sustainability.

Presently, there is no consensus on how to adjust GNI, GNP, or GDP for green concerns. Current candidates include the following:

- *Green Net National Product*: This view calls for measuring GNP to account for the corresponding depletion of natural resources and degradation of the environment (much the same way a company must depreciate both its tangible and intangible assets in making a product). The resulting indicator, net national product (NNP), adjusts for the depreciation of the country's physical assets.[16]

- *Genuine Progress Indicator:* This measure starts with the same accounting framework used to calculate GDP but then adjusts for values assigned to environmental quality, population health, livelihood security, equity, free time, and educational attainment. It values unpaid voluntary and household work as well as paid work. It also subtracts factors such as crime, pollution, and family breakdown.

- *Gross National Happiness:* This measure holds that development of human society takes place when material and spiritual development occur side by side, thereby reinforcing each other. It measures the promotion of equitable and sustainable socioeconomic development, preservation and promotion of cultural values, conservation of the natural environment, and establishment of good governance.

- *Happy Planet Index:* This idea captures the utilitarian view that people wish to live long, fulfilling lives. Hence, the country that performs the best is the one that allows its citizens to do so while avoiding infringing on the opportunity of future generations, and people in other countries, to do the same. Interestingly, the emerging science of happiness reports that nearly 70 percent of personal satisfaction is determined by the quantity and the quality of relationships, not by economic output or wealth creation.[17]

Features of an Economy

GNI and its variations estimate the absolute and relative income of a country. As such, these data create meaningful, first-order indicators of a country's performance and potential. Managers also study other features of an economy. As we now see, they anchor their analyses by considering inflation, unemployment, debt, income distribution, poverty, and the balance of payments.

INFLATION

In general, a sustained rise in prices measured against a standard level of purchasing power is called **inflation.** We measure inflation by comparing two sets of products at two points in time and computing the increase in cost that is not reflected by an increase in the quality. In mainstream economics, inflation results when aggregate demand grows faster than aggregate supply—essentially, too many people are trying to buy too few goods, thereby creating demand that pushes prices up faster than incomes grow. Other theories, notably the Austrian School of Economics, hold that inflation of overall prices is the consequence of an increase in the supply of money by central banking authorities.[25] Whatever the explanation, managers watch the rate of inflation, given its influence on many parts of the economic environment such as interest rates, exchange rates, living costs, general economic confidence, and political stability.[26]

Inflation and the Cost of Living   Consider the impact of inflation on the cost of living. Rising prices make it more difficult for consumers to buy products unless their incomes rise at the same or a faster pace. Sometimes this is practically impossible. For example, during periods of rapid inflation (or "hyperinflation")—for example, in

Inflation is a measure of the increase in the cost of living.

Point ▷◁ Counterpoint

Is Growth Good?

Point ▷ **Yes** Growth is not only good, it is the fundamental necessity of our existence. Growth is life, creating the basis for an individual, a community, an economy, an entity, an institution, and a society. Economic growth provides long-term benefits for the population of every country. It morally stabilizes society. It is the way to escape poverty. It reduces violent conflict. It raises living standards. It funds safety nets and government backstops. It creates material improvements that comfort life. It creates jobs, income, wealth, and prosperity for individuals and society. Let us turn to a closer look at the benefits of economic growth that endorse and elaborate these views.

Moral Stability Growth affects our social attitudes and our political institution, the keystones to the philosophical character and moral stability of society. As people experience rising incomes and economic improvement, they tend to be both tolerant of and benevolent toward each other. Hence, societies that grow economically develop the resources and resiliency to foster transparency of power, openness of opportunity, tolerance of diversity, pathways of social mobility, systems of fair and just laws, and virtues of democracy.

Poverty Reduction Notwithstanding the kindness of strangers, only growth powers the means to alleviate poverty for the billions struggling to sustain life. Growth in many impoverished countries has reduced the number of people living in abject poverty. In 1990, 34 percent of the global population survived on less than $1 a day. By 2008, freer markets had fueled economic growth, helping to reduce this number to 22 percent of the world. Without growth, we lose the war against poverty.

Business Dividend Growth stimulates higher employment, capital investment, profits, and business confidence. Rising asset valuations, stabilizing wealth effects, and resolute confidence in surviving tough times supports the prosperity of small and large businesses. Moreover, even amid the panic of the current global crisis, people find business growth appealing. A survey of Americans found that 76 percent agree that their country's strength is "mostly based on the success of American business" and that 90 percent admire people who "get rich by working hard."[18]

Fiscal Dividend Government finances are ultimately at the mercy of growth. A growing economy boosts tax revenues, thereby providing governments at local, state,

Counterpoint ◁ **No** We accept the premise that growth is life, fostering innumerable benefits in terms of morality, openness, tolerance, mobility, fairness, and democracy. However, the failure to understand the costs of these benefits—costs that seem to grow faster than growth itself—imperils civil society and, ultimately, the survival of humanity and the planet. Put bluntly, once you untangle the strands of half-truth, falsehood, and self-interest that lace the insidious appeal of pro-growth arguments, the promise of milk and honey for all devolves into a sad delusion. The problems of growth span the immediate and the future. Where one stops and the other starts is tough to pinpoint. Still, as this list shows, they all strike society hard.

Growth Is Inefficient The supreme benefit of growth is that "a rising tide lifts all boats." That is, as the economy grows, it generates higher wages, income, and wealth for all. In reality, the benefits of growth are unevenly distributed, creating extreme degrees of inequalities of income, wealth, and power. Therefore, we agree that over the long run, increasing economic growth has lifted the tide. However, a share of the global population have seen their dinghies capsize, many struggle to keep their leaky boats afloat, and a tiny number have upgraded to yachts.

Growth Is Misleading Growth does not deliver the benefits it promises. It rewards the financially strong but punishes the economically weak. It liberates people from old routines but enslaves them with new habits. It gives people free time to spend with family and community but then demands mobility and migration that breaks-up families. It promises new, improved products to enable self-fulfillment but then restarts a never-ending cycle of hope and deception. In a phrase, economic growth oversells and underdelivers, condemning people to "spiritual despair scarcely concealed by the frantic pace of life."[19] Increasingly, people seem to realize this: 37 percent of respondents in a recent survey believe that business strikes the right balance between profits and public interest, the lowest proportion since surveys began asking in 1987.[20]

Growth Threatens Life Polluted air, poisoned water, and toxic land—let alone global warming, biodiversity collapse, and resource depletion—are the byproducts of growth. Granted, some production and consumption is vital; however, overproduction and overconsumption destabilize the basis for life. Ironically, when we measure the value created by an economy, say in its GNI, none of these costs are tallied. Rather, they are mysteriously called province, regional, and national levels the monies to finance spending projects that support and sustain society. While theoretically appealing, history shows cheap government does not translate into good government.

Peace Dividend   Growth creates more opportunities for more people in more places. People who see the potential for prosperity behave peacefully. Moving poor people into the middle class, for example, enables them to think and behave differently. Free from the tyranny of continually seeking food and shelter, they become more open-minded, more concerned about their children's future, more influenced by abstract values than traditional norms, more inclined to settle conflicts peacefully, more supportive of free markets and democracy, and more likely to have faith in the future.

Environmental Benefits   Growth champions management innovations and better technologies, which together drive the effective allocation and efficient use of resources. The falling ratio of energy consumption per unit of GDP over the past 40 years, in the face of the growing abundance of goods and services, testifies to the virtuous benefits of growth.

Quest to Excel   Growth spurs people to bring to bear their ingenuity, their imagination, and their industriousness to find a better way, every day, to make a difference. Pushing back the frontier of human experience—whether it involves the trivial (such as forms of entertainment) or the substantive (such as finding alternative sources of energy)—only happens when there is a quest to grow.

Life   Economic growth supports longer lives. In 1900, life expectancy at birth was 47 years in the United States; by 2005, after a century of economic growth, it was 78 years. Moreover, people can now work almost half the time they once had to, relying on new tools to boost productivity, finding comfort in the rising quality-of-life standards, and taking solace in improving health care.

Unquestionably, as argued in the Counterpoint, growth imposes costs on individuals, society, and the planet. Moreover, we fully agree that these costs are striking. Still, our position is crystal clear: No matter the costs of growth, they pale in comparison to the unacceptable price of not growing. Put bluntly, when growth stops, decay starts. ▶

"externalities" and treated as costs that impact society but are conveniently excluded when we praise the amazing "benefits" of economic growth. Effectively, since nobody is responsible for the costs of externalities, nobody pays for them, and the growth engine chugs merrily along.

Growth Destroys Individuality   Growth's mandate to optimize efficiency requires massification—mass production, mass consumption, mass distribution, mass media, and onward. Massification does bring great benefits, but with high cost. Noted one observer, "a part of the price that people in the West pay for this unending procession of shiny assembly-line products is the concomitant loss of those now rarer things that once imparted zest and gratification—the loss of individuality, uniqueness and flavor; the loss of craftsmanship, local variety and richness; the loss of intimacy and atmosphere, of eccentricity and character."[21]

Current Growth Is Unsustainable   Humans are stripping nature at an unprecedented rate. Presently, human consumption is 30 percent larger than nature's capacity to regenerate. By 2050, at current trends, humanity will require five planets of natural resources.[22] "For more than 20 years we have exceeded the Earth's ability to support a consumptive lifestyle that is unsustainable and we cannot afford to continue down this path," said the Director-General of the Worldwatch Institute. Furthermore, he added, in light of consumer trends in emerging markets, "If everyone around the world lived as those in America, we would need five planets to support us."[23] Barring black-swan innovation in mining, agriculture, and manufacturing, Mother Earth is going to stop current growth patterns sooner than later.

In summary, our position is straightforward. The existence of epic poverty for billions of people, the slow-motion death spiral of the ecosystem, the false hope of actualization by consumption, the alienation of binge-buying, and the transformation of nominal democracies into functional oligarchies puts the world at the proverbial fork in the road. We can remain blissfully ignorant of the price of growth, continually surprised by its unintended side effects and underestimated externalities. Or we can face the issue full on and reset the equation so that economic growth "meets the needs of the present without compromising the ability of future generations to meet their own needs."[24] ◀

Hyperinflation is a rapidly accelerating rate of inflation that, if unchecked, leads to money losing value and markets moving to barter.

Brazil in the early 1990s or Turkmenistan in the mid-1990s—consumers spent their money as fast as they got it or else watched it quickly turn worthless.

More pointedly, in Zimbabwe over the past few years, prices have been rising one to 20 percent per day, and by mid-2009, the inflation rate hit an astounding 231 million percent.[27] Upon reflection, the chair of the Combined Harare Residents Association in

Zimbabwe noted, "There's a surrealism here that's hard to get across to people. If you need something and have cash, you buy it. If you have cash, you spend it today, because tomorrow it's going to be worth 5 percent less. Normal horizons don't exist here."[28] Adding to the surrealism, in early 2009, Zimbabwe's central bank introduced a 100 trillion note; at the time, it commanded the purchasing power of roughly U.S. $250 to $300.

Certainly, these are extreme cases. Still, history shows that chronic inflation—essentially annual inflation rates of 10 to 30 percent—erodes confidence in a country's currency and spurs people to search for better ways to store value.

Implications of Chronic Inflation   Chronic—or hyper—inflation has bleak implications for companies. Neither they nor their customers can effectively plan long-term investments, they have no incentive to save, and ordinary investment instruments like insurance policies, pensions, and long-term bonds become speculative. Inflation pressures governments to control it. Often, governments try to reduce inflation by raising interest rates, installing wage and price controls, or imposing protectionist trade policies and currency controls. Alone or together, these measures slow economic growth.

> Chronic inflation occurs when a country experiences high inflation for a prolonged period of time.

Price Indexes and Problems in Measuring Inflation   The measurement of inflation highlights a common difficulty—namely, what a country measures when calculating an economic variable. Specifically, price indexes are sensitive to decisions about their scope, the formulas by which they are calculated, and other factors decided by the agencies that disseminate them.

For instance, in the United States, the Consumer Price Index (CPI) is the official measure of inflation. In the European Union, it is the Harmonized Index of Consumer Prices (HICP). The CPI differs from the HICP in two major respects: First, the HICP includes the rural population in its scope and, second, the HICP excludes owner-occupied housing. Consequently, managers must be mindful of the process by which institutions report economic data.[29]

If Not Inflation, Then Deflation   A worrisome consequence of the global credit crisis has been the movement of deflation from theoretical discussion to practical concern. Presently, for the first time in generations, deflation, not inflation, posed the far-more-menacing risk. Summer 2009 saw the United States, for example, report its first year-over-year contraction in the CPI since 1951. Concurrently, Japan's consumer prices were falling at a record pace, adding to the risk that deflation will become entrenched and hamper a rebound from the nation's worst postwar recession. Overcapacity, shrinking credit, reduced corporate spending and falling consumer demand signaled deflationary dynamics in the global economy.

Deflation is the opposite of inflation (prices for products go down, not up); technically, deflation occurs when the annual inflation rate is less than zero. The global economic crisis highlights the dynamic of deflation, showing how a systematic and widespread reduction in the supply of money or credit triggers a contraction in personal and investment spending. Declining demand and growing supply triggers increasing quantity and a commensurate reduction in prices. Unchecked, economies can fall into deflationary spirals wherein companies find it increasingly difficult to sell products and, in recourse, increasingly discount prices to appeal to consumers increasingly prone to delay purchases. Explained a Japanese analyst, "Profits fall, then wages come down, then consumers stop shopping. And because people aren't shopping, companies lower prices. That's the process that we're starting to see. It isn't easy to break out of."[30]

> Deflation, a decrease in the general price level of goods and services, is often caused by a reduction in the supply of money or credit.

Acute deflation can prove complex—when prices fall quickly, consumers postpone buying, and the economy grinds to a halt. Deflation and unemployment are intricately linked: Lower demand lowers jobs, which then lowers demands, and so on. Presently, central banks and governments are relying on reflation—increasing the money supply and reducing taxes—to combat deflation. For example, the

Organization for Economic Cooperation and Development (OECD) has called upon the Bank of Japan to keep pumping cash into the economy "until underlying inflation is firmly positive."[31]

UNEMPLOYMENT

The *unemployment rate* is the number of unemployed workers who are seeking employment for pay divided by the total civilian labor force. Countries that are unable to create jobs for their citizens create a risky business environment. Generally, people out of work and unable to find jobs depress economic growth, create social pressures, and fan political instability. Furthermore, the proportion of unemployed workers in a country shows how well a country productively uses its human resources. People gainfully employed testify to the competency of policymakers to sustain a favorable business environment. Likewise, markets marked by persistent unemployment symbolize the ineptitude of the government in managing domestic affairs.

Some economists suggest that managers refine their assessment by estimating the *misery index*, which is the sum of a country's inflation and unemployment rates. The higher the sum, the greater the economic misery, and the more likely consumers and companies will curtail spending and investment. In addition, researchers have identified relationships between the misery index and various social cost indicators, such as increasing crime and growing despondency.[32]

Problems in Measuring Unemployment   Again, as with inflation, measuring the number of unemployed workers seeking work in various countries is difficult, given various assumptions and exclusions—as we see to confusing effect in Figure 4.4. In the United States, the unemployment rate may misestimate the impact of the economy on people. Technically, the unemployment figures indicate how many are not working for pay but seeking employment for pay; they do not count the number of people who are not working at all, are working without pay, have stopped looking for work, or are working illegally.

For example, the U.S. government reports unemployment statistics on a monthly basis using two key measures: "U3" and "U6." U3 is the "official unemployment rate," counting those who are not working but are willing and able to work for pay, currently

FIGURE 4.4   The Mysteries of Classification

While seemingly straightforward, calculating the unemployment rate has many assumptions and exceptions.

"The rise in unemployment, however, which was somewhat offset by an expanding job market, was countered by an upturn in part-time dropouts, which, in turn, was diminished by seasonal factors, the anticipated summer slump, and, over-all, a small but perceptible rise in actual employment."

available to work, and have actively searched for work. In late 2009, U3 was 10.2 percent. U6, on the other hand, is the broadest measure of unemployment; it includes "discouraged workers" (those who have stopped looking for work because current economic conditions make them believe that no work is available for them), other "marginally attached workers" (those who would like and are able to work but have not looked for work recently), and part-time workers (who want to work full time but cannot due to economic reasons). In late 2009, U6 was 17.5 percent.

Unemployment estimates throughout many poorer nations routinely underestimate the true degree of joblessness and, more significantly, the productivity of those who work. Many countries in Asia, Africa, and South America face difficult economic, political, and social problems because of widespread underemployment. That is, even though officially employed, people work only part time, thereby reducing productivity, lowering incomes, and decreasing social stability.

> Underemployment occurs when individuals working fewer hours a day than they would prefer or when individuals work below the level for which they have been trained.

Variation in Public Support   Besides measurement issues, the unemployment rate means different things in different countries due to different social policies.[33] Some countries, such as France and Germany, provide generous unemployment protection, whereas other countries, like China, Kenya, or Jordan, offer little to no support. Hence, managers judiciously evaluate the implications of reported unemployment, trying to parse the variability in measurement standards as well as the implication of different degrees and durations of unemployment support.

The Pension Problem   An unintended consequence of the global economic crisis has alerted managers' to a subtle feature of unemployment analysis. Specifically, growing unemployment is causing strains on public and private pension systems, threatening to turn the financial crisis into a perilous social crisis. Technically, a pension is an arrangement to provide people with an income when they are no longer earning a regular income from employment. Effectively, a pension is an investment fund accumulated during working life and then used to provide continuing income upon retirement.

Demographics indicate that the world's 65-and-older population will triple by mid-century to one in six people, leaving many countries, especially wealthier ones like the United States, Japan, and Germany, struggling to support the out-of-work in addition to the elderly. Falling returns on pension plan investments further complicate the issue—private pension plans across the world lost 23 percent of their net asset value in 2008. Hence, managers are resetting their analytics, moderating their assessment of unemployment given growing pension shortfalls, the inability of older employees to retire as scheduled, the economic problems for those that must, and the resulting burden placed on younger employees to defer careers or contribute additional funds.

DEBT

Debt, the sum total of a government's financial obligations, measures the state's borrowing from its population, from foreign organizations, from foreign governments, and from international institutions. The larger the total debt becomes, the more uncertain a country's economy becomes, in both the present, as interest expenses divert money from more productive uses, and the future, as people worry about the ability of future generations to pay back the debt.

The debt for many countries had been steadily, albeit slowly, increasing. This situation changed radically as governments responded to the global credit crisis. Funding company bailouts, unemployment benefits, and macro stimulus plans led to unprecedented debt creation. The IMF estimates, for example, that the debt of the leading 10 wealthiest countries will rise from 78 percent of their GDP in 2007 to nearly 115 percent by 2014; these governments, on average, will then owe approximately $50,000 for every one of their citizens.[34] Analysis shows that a percentage point increase in the projected deficit-to-GDP ratio raises the 10-year bond rate expected to prevail five years into the future by 25 basis points.[35] Hence, in the United States, long-term rates will likely climb 2 to 3 percentage points, with significant implications to consumers, companies, and investors.

Internal and External Debt   A country's debt has two parts: internal and external. **Internal debt** results when the government spends more than it collects in revenues. Internal deficits occur for any number of reasons, including when an imperfect tax system prevents the government from collecting revenue, when the costs of security and social programs exceed available tax revenues, when state-owned enterprises run deficits, or when governments borrow to finance economic rescues and stimulus. Consequently, every government struggles with setting spending priorities, better controlling expenses, improving budget management, and refining tax policy. Pressures to revise government policies to deal with growing internal debt create economic uncertainties for consumers, investors, and companies.

For consumers, growing public debt is usually an early indicator of future tax increases; for investors, growing public debt reduces economic growth; for companies, growing public debt encourages governments to promote inflation as a means to reduce the real cost of their liabilities. Complicating matters is the tendency for even the chance of such events occurring to damage consumer confidence, wealth effects, and capital investment programs. Furthermore, there's always the unexpected policy choice that governments may adopt to deal with their debt dilemma. For example, the global crisis prods countries to consider raising the retirement age as a means to boost tax revenues—given that people then must work longer—as well as provide an expedient way to reduce growing pension costs. In sum, stabilizing the system in the wake of the economic crisis has increased public debt worldwide. Managers' struggle to identify implications to operations, difficult in the best of circumstances, is much harder given related trends in deflation, unemployment, and growth.

External debt results when a government borrows money from lenders outside the country, such as private commercial banks, other governments, or international financial institutions (e.g., the IMF or World Bank). Interest on the debt, and eventually the debt itself, must be paid in the currency in which the loan was made. Hence, the borrowing country may have to export its goods to the lender's country to earn that currency or to convert its currency into that of its creditor. A debt crisis often occurs when a weak economy is unable to do this, or can do it only at high political, economic, and social cost. In this situation, the economy grinds to a halt before resetting to a more efficient, smaller-scale version.

INCOME DISTRIBUTION

GNI, even when weighted by the size of the population or purchasing power, can misestimate the relative wealth of a nation's citizens. That is, GNI per capita reports, on average, how much income the average person earns. But, because not everyone is average, it does not tell us what share of income goes to what segments of the population. For example, Brazil's GNI exceeds $2 trillion, a performance that ranks well in the world. Similarly, its GNI per capita is nearly $5,910.[36] However, Brazil's economic performance looks less impressive given that the richest fifth of Brazilians (about 35 million people) receive more than 60 percent of national wealth, while the poorest fifth of Brazilians receive about 3 percent.[37] Brazil is not the exception; dozens of countries show similar situations.

The Gini Coefficient   Managers control for **income distribution** in a particular country by examining its **Gini coefficient**. This measure assesses the degree of inequality in the distribution of family income in a country. A Gini index score of zero implies perfect equality (i.e., all households have equal share of resources), whereas a score of one implies perfect inequality (i.e. all resources belong to one household). Hence, the more nearly equal

Internal debt: Portion of the government debt that is denominated in the country's own currency and held by domestic residents.

External debt: Debt owed to foreign creditors and denominated in foreign currency.

Growing public debt is usually an early indicator of
- Tax increases.
- Reduced growth.
- Rising inflation.

Income distribution estimates the proportion of population that earns various levels of income.

The Gini coefficient measures the extent to which the distribution of resources deviates from a perfectly equal distribution.

The World at Night

In case you ever wondered, this is the Earth at night. The illumination of light highlights economic and social situations in interesting sorts of ways. Economically, the pattern of lights suggests that many large cities located near rivers or oceans to facilitate the exchange of goods. In addition, people followed, and heavily populated areas of the Earth's surface show people congregating near seaboards and waterways. Particularly dark areas include the central parts of South America, Africa, Asia, and Australia, show either the lack of power or people in these areas. By the way, this photo is actually a composite of hundreds of pictures made by DMSP satellites.

Source: NASA. Data courtesy Marc Imhoff of NASA GSFC and Christopher Elvidge of NOAA NGDC. Image by Craig Mayhew and Robert Simmon, NASA GSFC.

a country's income distribution, the lower its Gini coefficient (for example, Finland with an index of 26.9 or India at 36.8). The more unequal a country's income distribution, the higher its Gini coefficient (for example, Hong Kong with an index of 52 or Brazil at 56.7).

Uneven income distribution exists in virtually every country. In 1960, the wealthiest 20 percent of the world's population had 30 times the income of the poorest 20 percent. This grew to 32 times in 1970, 45 times in 1980, 60 times in 1990, and 75 times in 2000. In addition, the richest 1 percent of the population of the world claims as much income as the bottom 57 percent—in other words, the 50 million richest people received as much income as did the 3.8 billion poorest people. Widening inequality threatens stability and growth.

The United States has the largest inequality gap between rich and poor, compared to other industrialized nations. Puzzling is the fact that, in the United States, the top 1 percent receives more income than the bottom 40 percent; this gap is the widest it has been in 70 years. In the last 20 years, the share of income going to the top 1 percent in the United States has increased while at the same time decreasing for the poorest 40 percent. Presently, the top 1 percent of households in the United States owns 37 percent of all privately held stock, 65 percent of financial securities, and 62 percent of business equity. The top 10 percent of households in the United States own 85 to 90 percent of stocks, bonds, trust funds, and business equity, and over 75 percent of nonhome real estate. Collectively, as is the case in most countries, approximately 10 percent of U.S. citizens "own" the country.[38]

Urban versus Rural Income Distribution There is a strong relationship between skewed income distributions and the split between those who live in urban settings versus those who live in rural areas. For example, the booming urban centers of China— such as Beijing, Shanghai, Hong Kong, Shenzhen, and Guangzhou—saw their per capita income pass $1,900 in 2008, almost five times as much their rural counterparts.[39] Therefore, one sees Lexus, Porsche, and Mercedes-Benz dealerships in Beijing but many in rural China rely on bicycles and animals for transportation. Rising income disparities between the nation's booming cities and vast, impoverished countryside, if not resolved, threaten social stability and economic performance.[40]

As a rule, per capita income is higher in urban versus rural settings.

The Legacy of Income Inequality The historical record adds an important perspective to this discussion. Dramatic income equality is a recent phenomenon. In 2002, Jeffery Sachs of the Earth Institute observed:

> The world is more unequal than at any time in world history. There's a basic reason for that which is that 200 years ago everybody was poor. A relatively small part of the world

achieved what the economists call a modern economic growth. Those countries represent only about one-sixth of humanity, and five-sixths of humanity is what we call the developing world. It's the vast majority of the world. The gap can be 100 to 1, maybe a gap of $30,000 per person and $300 per person. And that's absolutely astounding to be on the same planet and to have that extreme variation in material well-being.[41]

Concept Check

As we suggest in Chapters 1 and 3, both income inequality and poverty should diminish as **international business** activity drives the more efficient use of resources. Here we reiterate the principle that more efficient trading relationships and more productive use of liberated capital help create job opportunities and foster income growth among more segments of the global population.

In summary, managers hone their sense of the economic potential of a country by adjusting their analyses to reflect its particular distribution of income. Moreover, managers realize that income inequality is not just bad for social justice; it is also bad for economic efficiency. Left to persist, it can fan crime, corruption, and risks that erode stability and limit growth.

POVERTY

The distribution of income is important to understand a market's performance and potential. Still, its reliance on central tendencies in income distribution presumes that there actually is a reasonable degree of income within a country. Hence, this statistic can misreads an economy if unchecked by an assessment of the scale and scope of poverty in a country. More precisely, India reports a Gini of 36.8 (the United States, Japan, Malaysia, and South Africa, respectively, are 46.3, 38.1, 40.3, and 57.8). India's laudable Gini score, however, is the outcome of its dire poverty: 80 percent of its population (more than 900 million of its 1.2 billion people) lives on less than $2 per day, and about 50 percent lives on less than $1 per day. India, while extreme, is not the exception. Despite long-running efforts by many groups, organizations, and institutions, poverty prevails in every part of the world. Therefore, managers fine-tune their study of income and wealth by considering the conditions and consequences of poverty.

What Is Poverty? Poverty has many dimensions. In general terms, it is a condition in which a person or community is deprived of, or lacks the essentials for, a minimum standard of well-being and life. These essentials can be life-sustaining material resources such as food, safe drinking water, and shelter; they may be social resources such as access to information, education, health care, and social status; they may be the opportunity to develop meaningful connections with other people. This text takes an income perspective in which a person is defined as being poor when his or her income is below the threshold considered the minimum to satisfy needs and wants.

> Poverty is the state of having little or no money and few or no material possessions.

Poverty According to the World Bank The World Bank reports that the world population is roughly 80 percent poor, 10 percent middle income, and 10 percent rich. Great attention is paid to more stark assessments of poverty. The World Bank defines *extreme poverty* as living on less than $1.25 per day (PPP) and *moderate poverty* as less than $2 per day (PPP). This standard shows that, in 2008, 1.4 billion lived on less than $1.25 a day.[42]

> There is a growing gap between the rich and poor in virtually every country in the world.

Poverty appears to be growing worldwide. Granted, estimates of the number of people in extreme poverty have fallen by approximately 200 million since 1990. However, this reduction has been concentrated in a few countries. Removing China from the tally reveals that the number of poor people in the developing world has remained almost the same, at about 1.2 billion between 1981 and 2005. The global credit crisis threatened many more; some saw it pushing another 200 million people in low-income countries deeper into poverty.[43]

Poverty and the Economic Environment Poverty of this scale and scope impacts economic environments. Throughout the world, people struggle for food, shelter, clothing, clean water, and health services, to say nothing of safety, security, and education. Failure to obtain such results in suffering, malnutrition, mental illness, death, epidemics, famine, and war. For example, 100 percent of Canadians have access to clean water, whereas 13 percent of the people in Afghanistan do; the per capita dietary protein supply in the United States is 121 grams, but 32 grams in Mozambique; the average life expectancy in Japan is 81 years, yet 34 years in Botswana.[44]

International companies facing such situations assess implications that impact virtually every feature of the economy. In extreme poverty, market systems may not exist, national infrastructures may not work, criminal behavior may be pervasive, and governments may be unable to regulate society consistently or adopt prudent economic policies. The growth of worldwide business activity and economic progress ultimately depends on alleviating poverty.

The Potential of the Poor   Despite the daunting gap between the rich and poor, managers monitor the potential of today's poor consumers. For example, in 2002, India had just fewer than 15 million mobile phone subscribers. By 2006, it had 136 million subscribers and was fast approaching 400 million by 2010. Powering the penetration of mobile phones is the fact that Indian companies offer the cheapest mobile services in the world yet still earn profits. India along with China account for no less than half the world's increase in wireless-technology subscriptions. Similar developments with computers (e.g., the XO-1 programs of low-cost laptops for children) and automobiles (the development of functional cars such as Tata's Nano, priced for U.S. $2,100) and housing (Tata's program to provide fully functional homes for U.S. $8,000–15,000) highlight the importance of finding opportunities in dire situations. More dramatically, one manager noted, "A billion customers in the world are waiting for a $2 pair of eyeglasses, a $10 solar lantern, and a $100 house."[45]

"Seeing" these opportunities, McKinsey & Company found calls for global market pioneers that have a particular mind-set. Specifically, they note that "When you look behind the success stories of leading globalizers, you find companies that have learned how to think differently from the herd. They seek out different information, process it in a different way, come to different conclusions, and make different decisions. Where others see threats and complexity, they see opportunity. Where others see a barren landscape, they see a cornucopia of choices."[46] Furthermore, the cornucopia of choices idea alert managers to the **Bottom of the Pyramid** phenomenon—the billions of people living on less than a few dollars per day who have been seen as inaccessible and unprofitable but may represent the next market frontier of the global economy.[47] The World Economic Forum estimates suggest that those people earning U.S. $8 per day or less had an aggregate income of more than U.S. $2.3 trillion in 2008. If growth rates remain steady, they could earn U.S. $4 trillion annually by 2015.

Success requires companies to develop affordable, easily used eco-sensitive products that work in harsh environments. For example, Nokia, Samsung, and Motorola have tailored cell phones to these markets, offering units with sealed faceplates (for water and dirt resistance), 400 hours of standby time on one battery charge, and larger screens that work in reflected light, use no internal lamp, and are specially enabled for text messaging. At the grassroots level, similar initiatives have built a refrigerator from clay (which uses no electricity yet can help keep vegetables fresh for several days) and a cheap crop duster in the form of a sprayer mounted on a motorcycle.[48] The Bottom of the Pyramid, in summary, sets a new standard: low-cost, high-powered, resource-minimizing, lifestyle-sensitive innovation.

> The Bottom of the Pyramid is the largest, but poorest socio-economic group in the world. Some see these 4-billion-plus people as the next market frontier.

LABOR COSTS

Companies scrutinize where it makes the most sense to locate activities. Changing economic conditions require companies look at cost structures in current terms as well as estimate likely wages 5 to 10 years out. North American footwear makers, like Nike for example, once made shoes in the United States but over a 30-year span moved production from subcontractors in Taiwan to the Philippines, Thailand, South Korea, Vietnam, and China in the quest for the lowest possible costs. Despite the growing uniformity of many markets, cost structures vary from country to country.

> Labor costs are dynamic, continually changing across countries.

Labor and Total Cost   For many goods and services, the cost of labor is a key element of total costs. Consequently, companies scan the world, looking for markets that offer lower-cost labor. For example, a factory worker in the United States typically costs between $15 and $30 per hour; factory wages in Mexico are about 11 percent of the U.S. level; in China, factory wages are 3 percent of the U.S. level.[49] For service employees, such as phone center workers, the cost differentials are also striking. The labor cost savings a company realizes by outsourcing a service job to India can be as much as 60 percent.

Consider the case of Wonder Auto of China. A maker of auto parts, it calculates that it cost U.S. $4 million to set up an assembly line employing 20 workers in Jinzhou, a city of 800,000 in northeastern China. The combined wages of these 20 workers are $40,000 a year—a sum that's roughly the annual base pay for one unionized auto-parts worker or two nonunion auto-parts workers in the United States.[50] A job at Wonder Auto and its top wage of $170 a month are a ticket to the middle class in China. In Jinzhou, a basic apartment without amenities like a refrigerator rents for about $40 a month, and a large meal at the restaurant of the city's best hotel costs less than $3. This being the case, jobs at Wonder Auto are much sought after, and turnover is almost zero. Said Sun Shaohua, 30, a factory line worker who strips copper wires for alternators, "Many people come, but nobody ever leaves."[51] Expectedly, companies in other countries see this situation, do their comparative cost calculations, and often opt to open operations in China.

PRODUCTIVITY

Productivity measures the efficiency with which products are produced.

Companies refine their interpretation of economic performance and potential costs by considering *productivity*—specifically, the amount of output created per unit input used. In terms of labor, productivity is the quantity produced per person per labor hour.[52] Productivity growth allows an economy to grow at high rates without causing wage or price inflation. Beginning in the late 1990s, the world, powered largely by developments in the emerging markets and developing countries, saw accelerating productivity growth (see Figure 4.5). World productivity growth slowed in 2008, however, and is set to decelerate further as the recession erodes production efficiency worldwide. Global productivity growth is likely to drop to 1.8 percent in 2009—less than half of the productivity growth rate in 2007. This strong decline reduces the potential to raise wages, drop prices, and support an increase in living standards. Going forward, China will record some growth in productivity, moving up to 9.1 percent in 2009, while the U.S. will decline 0.5 percent, Germany 1.5 percent, and Japan 0.5 percent.[53]

The strength of the rebound in productivity will likely respond to the conditions that powered its recent rise. Productivity worldwide has benefited from the combination of technological progress, an increasingly open trading system, rising cross-country capital flows, robust financial systems, and resilient macroeconomic policy frameworks. At this point, the global credit crisis is resetting these conditions.

BOP is a system of recording all of a country's economic transactions with the rest of the world over a period of one year.

THE BALANCE OF PAYMENTS

A country's **balance of payments (BOP),** officially known as the *Statement of International Transactions,* is the statement of the balance of a country's trade and financial transactions (as conducted by individuals, businesses, and government agencies located in that nation) with the rest of the world over a specific period (usually one year).

FIGURE 4.5   Global Productivity Performance*

Beginning in 1992, the productivity-growth rate of developing countries began accelerating. Then, in 1995–1997, it surpassed the advanced economies. The IMF estimates that a widening productivity gap between developing countries and advanced economies is largely due to the former's improving communications systems, transportation infrastructures, and management approaches.

*Rates indicate annual percentage increases as three-year moving average; output is measured as real GDP divided by working-age population.

Sources: World Bank, *World Development Indicators* (2006); IMF, *World Economic and Financial Surveys* (2007), at www.imf.org (accessed October 15, 2007).

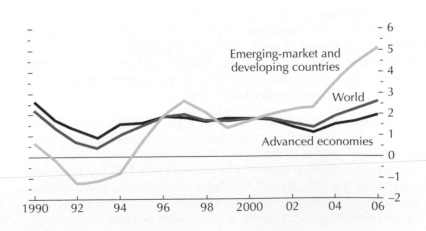

TABLE 4.3 Components of a Country's Balance of Payments

Current Account
- Value of exports and imports of physical goods, such as oil, grain, or computers (also referred to as *visible trade*)
- Receipts and payments for services, such as banking or advertising, and other intangible goods, such as copyrights and cross-border dividend and interest payments (also referred to as *invisible trade*)
- Private transfers, such as money sent home by expatriate workers
- Official transfers, such as international aid, on which the government expects no returns

Capital Account
- Long-term capital flows (i.e., money invested in foreign firms as well as profits made by selling those investments and returning the money home)
- Short-term capital flows (i.e., money invested in foreign currencies by international speculators as well as funds moved around the world for business purposes by companies with international operations)

Current and Capital Accounts The BOP has two main accounts:

- The **current account**, which tracks all trade activity in merchandise
- The **capital account**, which tracks both loans given to foreigners and loans received by citizens

Table 4.3 lists the components of each account. Mechanically, exports generate positive sales abroad while imports generate negative sales domestically. Positive net sales, accomplished simply by exporting more than importing, result in a current account surplus; conversely, importing more than exporting results in a current account deficit. Table 4.4 lists the five countries with the greatest current account surpluses and the five countries with the greatest current account deficits.[54]

The notion of *balance* means that all BOP transactions have an offsetting receipt. For instance, a country might have a surplus in merchandise trade (indicating that it is exporting more than it is importing) but may then report a deficit in another area, such as its investment income. In other words, because the current account and the capital account add up to the total account—which is necessarily balanced—a deficit in the current account is accompanied by an equal surplus in the capital account and vice versa. A deficit or surplus in the current account cannot be explained or evaluated without simultaneous explanation and evaluation of an equal surplus or deficit in the capital account.

BOP and Economic Stability Managers use the BOP to assess a country's economic stability. By measuring a country's transactions with those of the rest of the world, the BOP estimates a country's financial stability in the world market. For example, a deficit

TABLE 4.4 Current Account Balances: The Top Five and the Bottom Five

Top 5	Country	Current Account Balance (U.S. $, millions)
1	China	426,100
2	Germany	243,3100
3	Japan	156,600
4	Saudi Arabia	128,000
5	Russia	102,300
Bottom 5		
159	Greece	−51,530,
160	France	−52,910
161	Italy	−78,030
162	Spain	−131,800
163	United States	−673,300

Source: Central Intelligence Agency, "Country Comparison—Current Account Balance," *The World Factbook* (2009), at www.cia.gov (accessed October 2, 2009).

in merchandise trade means the supply of that country's currency is increasing throughout the world, given that its consumers are using it to buy the imports that then cause a trade deficit. Unless the government revises its economic policies, market forces will put downward pressure on the value of its currency.

BOP and Company Strategy   Monitoring trends in the BOP gives managers one more piece of data in deciding whether to do business in a country. BOP data help managers connect a company's strategy to macroeconomic activities and government policy. For example, some say the solution to the U.S. deficit is declining value of the U.S. dollar, slower growth in consumer spending, higher U.S. savings rate, and stronger growth in overseas markets. Each and all of these factors would reset the United States' economy as well as change economic policies in other countries.

Integrating Economic Analysis

The variability of economic development worldwide spotlights managers' dilemma. High-income countries are the logical place to do business because of the quality of resources and stability of political and legal environments. Moreover, the lion's share of global consumption takes place in high-income countries. Their collective 1 billion residents presently account for more than 80 percent of global consumption. The United States, for instance, represents about 4.5 percent of the world's population, yet it accounts for more than 30 percent of global consumption. For example, the average American consumes around 20 times more meat and fish, 60 times more paper, and 100 times more gasoline and diesel than the average Indian.[55]

Developing countries, especially emerging economies, however, exhibit accelerating growth and startling market potential. In sheer size, the developing countries are home to approximately 80 percent of the world's population. As to sheer needs, their 5.5 billion citizens aspire to live better lives. Moreover, consumption is increasing much faster in developing countries than in developed countries. Recall that Figure 4.4 profiled the real growth rate in GDP for various developed and developing countries. The data show the significantly faster growth rates in the latter. Faster growth rates translate into faster-growing demand. For instance, consumption trends in China outpace high- and low- income countries in many product groups; its motor fuel, paper, and meat consumption has more than doubled, and fish consumption has increased nearly fivefold since 1990.

The global credit crisis accelerates these differences. The economies of the bigger, least indebted developing countries like China, Brazil, and India are rebounding strongly while developed countries struggle with sluggish growth. The gap between growth in emerging Asian markets and the United States, Germany, and Japan has never been wider.[56] Retuning to discussion of the Bottom of the Pyramid, these trends signal the growing opportunity for fulfilling the needs and wants of the billions of low-income consumers worldwide.

Managers are mindful that presently the market at the Bottom of the Pyramid is too small to be sufficiently profitable for most MNEs. Profits are particularly constrained given the need to design and develop low-cost, reliable products. Such products require innovatively blending old and new technologies (recall earlier mention of extreme cell phones, clay refrigerators, and motorcycle-mounted crop dusters). Granted, fast-growing, poorer countries' current share of global consumption makes for a small base. Still, gambling that the Bottom of the Pyramid continues developing slowly is risky if competitors find fortune first.

Resolving the rich-country/poor-country dilemma ultimately rests on how accurately managers estimate a country's potential. Finite resources require that companies invest in markets with the greatest potential for profitable performance. Therefore, while it is attractive to hedge one's bets by investing in all markets, practicalities preclude doing so. Understanding the risk-return tension of worldwide investment options spurs managers to refine their analysis of economic environments. Managers shift analysis from individual elements to their collective interaction within the systemic context of a country's economic

Case Review Note

Companies monitor the balance of payments to watch for factors that could lead to currency instability or significant change in government policy.

Concept Check

Although the Bottom of the Pyramid is attractive in terms of economic potential, managers heed the discussions of Chapters 2 and 3 concerning the different cultural, political, and legal environments found in developing countries. Still, Chapter 1 notes the drivers of globalization steadily narrow the gap between the environments of developed and developing countries.

environment. Attention shifts, so to speak, from studying the characteristics of individual trees to understanding their configuration in terms of the overall forest.

Managers engage two perspectives to do so. The first evaluates the type of economic system in the country, emphasizing how current policies and practices shape activity. The second perspective investigates the dynamic of change, assessing the processes that move a country from one type of economic system to another. The insights on the current character of the market and the likely path of its evolution help managers pinpoint where investments should go and, more importantly, where they should not.

TYPES OF ECONOMIC SYSTEMS

An **economic system** is the set of structures and processes that guides the allocation of resources and shapes the conduct of business activities in a country. Spectrum analysis, as we applied in Chapter 3 with regard to political systems, gives a sense of the range of economic systems in the world today. One end of the spectrum of economic systems is anchored by the idea of capitalism, the other with that of communism. Differences between these ideas exist in terms of their implications for economic matters such as the ownership and control of factors of production and the freedom of price to balance supply and demand.

> An economic system is a mechanism that deals with the production, distribution, and consumption of goods and services.

Capitalism is a free market system built on a doctrine of private ownership and control. This philosophy holds that owners of capital have inalienable property rights that legitimate earning a profit in return for their effort, investment, and risk. The central axiom of capitalism is that the best allocation of resources follows from consumers exercising and producers responding accordingly in meeting aggregate demand. Implicit in this statement is the presumption of privacy: Whether in terms of private wealth, private investment, or private enterprise, capitalism holds that individuals' free choice powers a country's progress toward prosperity and peace.

> Capitalism is an economic system based on private ownership of capital.

Communism champions a centrally planned system built on state ownership of the factors of production and control of economic activity. Although nominally a socioeconomic structure and political ideology, communism calls for the establishment of an egalitarian, classless, and ultimately stateless society based on the government's full command and control of the economy. Only then, goes the theory, are the proletariat (the social class comprising those who do manual labor or work for wages) protected from exploitation by the bourgeois (the social class comprising the owners of the factors of production).

> Communism is an economic system and theory of government in which all factors of production are owned by a central government for the benefit of all citizens.

As is the case with any ideology defined in an idealized sense, that which is described rarely exists in practice. Hence, we see few instances of pure expression of capitalism or communism in the world today. Rather, managers use the endpoints set by these doctrines to analyze the types of economic systems that prevail across the world. These types predominantly include a market economy, a command economy, and a mixed economy.

Market Economy   A **market economy** is a system in which individuals, rather than government, make the majority of economic decisions. A market economy gives individuals the freedom to decide where to work, what to do and for how long, how to spend or save money, and whether to consume now or later. This view is anchored in the principle of **laissez-faire** and its notion that a market is best left to its own internal dynamics. Unfettered by government regulation, a free market efficiently determines the relationships among price, quantity, supply, and demand. This principle is credited to Adam Smith and his proposition that in a market economy, producers (spurred by the profit motive) efficiently make products that consumers (spurred by their need to maximize purchasing power) buy. Consequently, by virtue of what they do and do not buy, consumers ensure that producers put capital and labor to the best possible use.

> A market economy encourages open exchange of goods and services between producers and consumers.

> Laissez-faire refers to a policy of governmental noninterference in economic affairs.

Private Ownership of Resources   Because individuals make economic decisions, a market economy depends on individuals and companies, rather than the government, owning and controlling resources. Private ownership means that a market economy allocates factors of production as if, as Adam Smith wrote, an "invisible hand" were

Table 4.5   Dimensions of the Economic Freedom Index

Business Freedom	Trade Freedom
Monetary Freedom	Freedom from Government
Fiscal Freedom	Property Rights
Investment Freedom	Financial Freedom
Freedom from Corruption	Labor Freedom

Source: The Heritage Foundation and the *Wall Street Journal, The 2008 Index of Economic Freedom* (2007), at www.heritage.org (accessed June 4, 2009). Reprinted by permission of The Heritage Foundation.

income levels, growth rates, price stability, and employment. In addition, economic freedom is positively correlated with, life expectancy, literacy, human development, political openness, environmental sustainability, and less corruption. Collectively, these indicators show that countries free from high taxes, extensive regulations, and extreme government controls achieve the greatest economic growth and the highest standards of living.

Map 4.4 classifies 179 countries in terms of economic freedom. These data show that seven countries have free economies, 23 are rated mostly free, 53 are moderately free, 67 are mostly nonfree, and 29 are repressed. Regional data elaborate this situation. Figure 4.7 shows that economic freedom varies across regions, with people in North America and Europe enjoying greater economic freedom than those in other regions. Furthermore, the world's two freest regions—North America and Europe—have more than three times the per capita income found in the four less free regions.

THE EXPANDING ROLE OF THE STATE

For decades, economies steadily adopted the free market model.[64] The global credit crisis has interrupted this trend. By contesting the doctrine of laissez-faire, the crisis spurs a resurgence of state intervention. Dire circumstances inevitably fuel public clamor for government

FIGURE 4.6   Economic Freedom and the Standard of Living

The standard of living is a general measure of economic welfare, usually measured by per capita income, to reflect the availability of goods and services to satisfy wants rather than needs. In this profile, we see that increases in economic freedom and the standard of living have a strong, direct relationship.

Source: The Heritage Foundation and the *Wall Street Journal, The 2009 Index of Economic Freedom* (2009), at www.heritage.org (accessed June 6, 2009). Reprinted by permission of The Heritage Foundation.

Economic Freedom and Standard of Living

GDP per Capita, Measured by Purchasing Power Parity (PPP)

$40,253 Free
$33,428 Mostly Free
$15,541 Moderately Free
$4,359   Mostly Unfree
$3,926   Repressed

2009 Index of Economic Freedom Score

Source: *2009 Index of Economic Freedom* (Washington, D.C.: The Heritage Foundation and Dow Jones & Company, Inc., 2009), at *http://www.heritage.org/index*

Chart 1 ☎ heritage.org

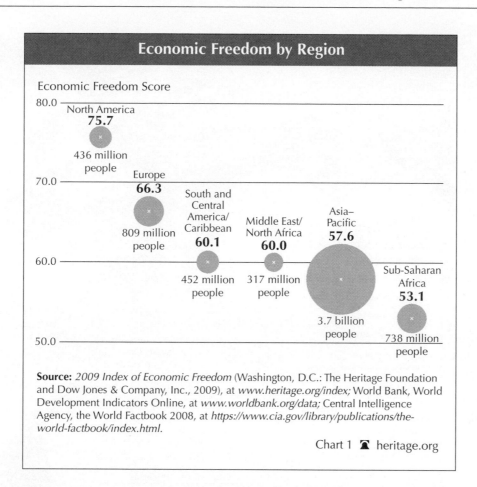

Economic Freedom by Region

Economic Freedom Score

- North America **75.7** — 436 million people
- Europe **66.3** — 809 million people
- South and Central America/Caribbean **60.1** — 452 million people
- Middle East/North Africa **60.0** — 317 million people
- Asia–Pacific **57.6** — 3.7 billion people
- Sub-Saharan Africa **53.1** — 738 million people

Source: *2009 Index of Economic Freedom* (Washington, D.C.: The Heritage Foundation and Dow Jones & Company, Inc., 2009), at *www.heritage.org/index;* World Bank, World Development Indicators Online, at *www.worldbank.org/data;* Central Intelligence Agency, the World Factbook 2008, at *https://www.cia.gov/library/publications/the-world-factbook/index.html.*

Chart 1 ☎ heritage.org

FIGURE 4.7   Economic Freedom by Region

The relationship between economic freedom and general measures of prosperity on a regional basis shows high degrees of freedom in Western countries and lower degrees of freedom in the rest of the world.

Source: The Heritage Foundation and the *Wall Street Journal, The 2009 Index of Economic Freedom* (2009), at www.heritage.org (accessed June 6, 2009). Reprinted by permission of The Heritage Foundation.

intervention, as citizens seeking stability call upon politicians to provide such. In 2008 and 2009, governments throughout the world aggressively intervened in the economy. In some situations, citizens urged state takeovers of markets, industries, and companies. In India, some asked, "Did the left save India?" associating the Communist party's opposition to free market reforms (effectively insulating India from the full impact of the global financial crisis) with the country's far less severe reaction than that suffered by others.[65]

◄ **Panic at a Job Fair**

Thousands of job seekers queue outside a talent exchange center holding a job fair in Zhengzhou, China. Anxieties run high, given that behind this throng are several more just as large and just as eager to interview for a job. The current global economic crisis has been reflected by the struggles of many Chinese college graduates, like their counterparts throughout the world, to find jobs.

Source: Bai Zhoufeng/Getty Images, Inc.

MAP 4.4 Global Distribution of Economic Freedom

The concept of *economic freedom* is based on the proposition that all citizens in every country have the right to work, produce, consume, and invest in the way that they prefer. At present, the Index of Economic Freedom classifies *economic freedom* into five categories: *free, mostly free, moderately free, mostly unfree,* and *repressed.* Classification criteria revolve around the degree to which governments influence people's economic choices.

Source: The 2008 Index of Economic Freedom (The Heritage Foundation and *Wall Street Journal*, 2009), http://www.heritage.org/Index/images/Index09_map.jpg.

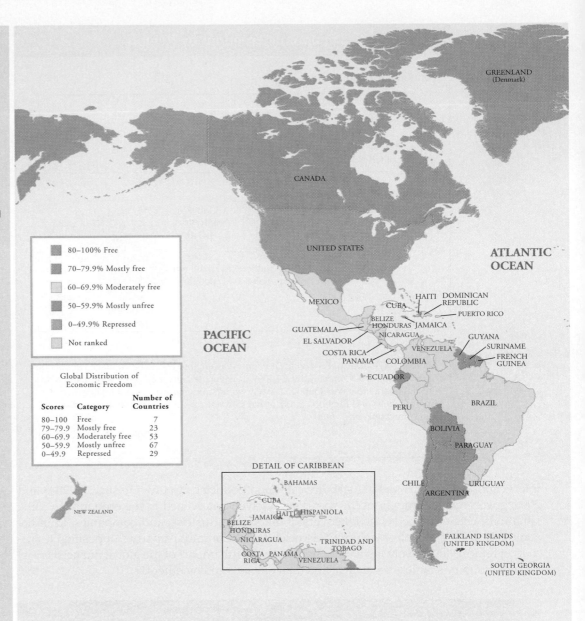

- 80–100% Free
- 70–79.9% Mostly free
- 60–69.9% Moderately free
- 50–59.9% Mostly unfree
- 0–49.9% Repressed
- Not ranked

Global Distribution of Economic Freedom

Scores	Category	Number of Countries
80–100	Free	7
79–79.9	Mostly free	23
60–69.9	Moderately free	53
50–59.9	Mostly unfree	67
0–49.9	Repressed	29

In the United States, President Obama and Congress have made the invisible hand increasingly visible, using government authority to fire the CEO of General Motors,[66] passing the most sweeping crackdown on the credit-card industry in decades, outlining compensation standards for executives of private companies, and proposing radical restructuring of the private health-care complex.[67] Other programs under the direction of the U.S. Treasury Department moved the government into areas of the financial world that had long run free of public oversight.

By mid-2009, the World Bank downgraded its forecast for global growth, saying the world economy would shrink 2.9 percent that year—worse than the 1.7 percent contraction it had predicted a few months earlier.[68] In late 2009 the IMF forecast no full recovery in developed countries until 2015; past experience, based on 88 banking crises over the past four decades, showed that economies take a significant number of years to regain momentum.[69] In addition, history suggests that if the economic crisis worsens, we are likely to see more people question the legitimacy of capitalism. Continuing erosion in the foundations for free markets, unless reversed soon, will fan belief that globalization is not

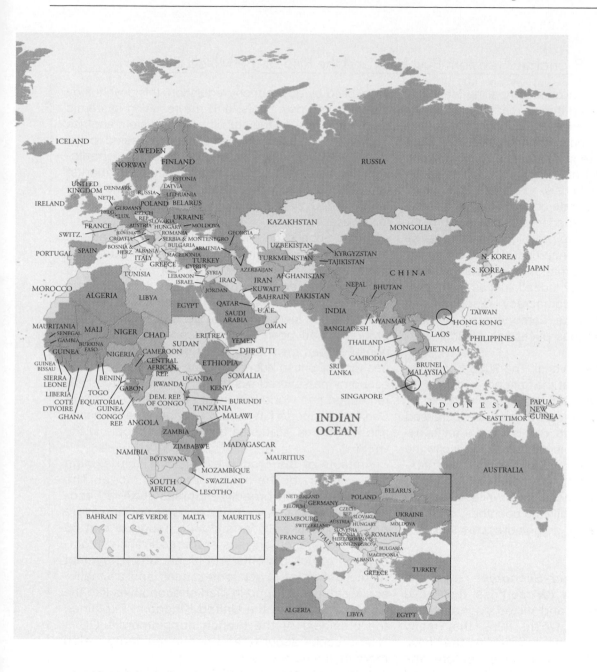

a historical inevitability. In this scenario, governments will rely upon the means of state capitalism and socialist policies to influence the structure and performance of local markets. National, not international, objectives will take precedence.

In principle, beliefs about the prevailing market type are often tied to how people feel about their own lives. Those whose lives are improving under capitalism are likely to support it; those whose lives are deteriorating are likely to call for state intervention. Notwithstanding support for free markets in many wealthy countries, the instability of the marketplace threatens the steadfastness of opinion. In developing countries, the fallout of the economic crisis has intensified the long-running debate over the merits of capitalism versus socialism. More pointedly, noted Joseph Stiglitz, "Every crisis comes to an end—and, bleak as things seem now, the current economic crisis too shall pass. But no crisis, especially one of this severity, recedes without leaving a legacy. And among this one's legacies will be a worldwide battle over ideas—over what kind of economic system is likely to deliver the greatest benefit to the most people."[70] Therefore, as we see in our "Looking to the Future" insert, market principles and economic freedom are in play.[71]

Looking to the Future

Economic Freedom Pushback and the Rise of the Mixed Economy

Although free markets provide a compelling ideal, the global economic crisis had thrown markets into disarray. Under the best of conditions, countries struggle to maintain political and macroeconomic stability, boost growth, improve legal regulations, and resolve social issues. Under the worst of conditions, such as those resulting from the global crisis, managers face growing demands for greater state control of the economy. Looking to the future, managers wonder what might transpire—will free markets prevail, protecting hard-won economic freedoms? Alternatively, have governments reclaimed the commanding heights in taking control of economic affairs? Indeed, just as the apparent pushback against democracy discussed in Chapter 3 provokes debate, some wonder whether there may be an analogous pushback against economic freedom.

So far, the data are equivocal: The 2008 Economic Freedom Index reported that the freedom scores of 83 countries increased from 2006 to 2007, while those for 65 fell. Certainly, the average freedom score increased from the previous year; however, it is down from its all-time high. More perplexing is the fact that despite the dividends of economic freedom, so few countries maximize it. Another look at Map 4.4 shows that just seven of 179 countries have free economies while another 23 are mostly free. Put differently, 30 countries, or about 17 percent of all countries, grant individuals substantial economic freedom.

The Return of the Mixed Economy Given the dramatic success stories of countries that have migrated from command and mixed economies to market economies, one would think that many countries would do the same. In actuality, they have not, thereby suggesting that, even before the economic crisis, individuals and officials questioned the ultimate benefit of a free market. Now, buffeted by the crisis, we see countries facing hardships that push them to ratchet down economic forecasts as well as deal with growing political and social unrest. Consequently, more people than perhaps at any point in the past generation question whether a market economy is the best approach for prosperity.

Critics of freer markets are quick to elaborate matters. They maintain that a free market cannot protect social values and skews income distribution. A free market encourages the accumulation of vast wealth and powerful self-interests that threaten social liberties and political rights. Allowed to run free, capitalism legitimates the psychology that greed is good. If unchecked by government regulation, this psychology devolves into psychosis, and the resulting systemic distortions threaten the stability of the system and risk the welfare of society—or, as Marx prophesied, capitalism eventually is destroyed by its own contradictions. Hence, they argue, the benefits of a market economy, when fully measured, fall short of the benefits provided by a strong government regulating a mixed economy.

As the global economic crisis wore on, advocates of a mixed economy pointed to continental Europe in general and France in specific as worthy models.[72] It appeared that countries that favored a larger state presence, higher taxes, heavier regulation, tougher job-protection laws, and more generous social safety programs had been better prepared for economic upheaval than their free market counterparts. As the free market British economy cratered, France's mixed economy persevered. As the economically free U.S. regrouped and wondered what next, the socialism of Denmark supported its steady economic performance and its citizens' status as the happiest people in the world.[73]

Aspects of the French experience help explain the resiliency of the mixed economic model. The French electorate broadly endorses state-led economic programs as well as extensive social welfare programs. One poll, for instance, reported that 66 percent of French citizens preferred France's combination of rich benefits and higher unemployment to the option of lower joblessness and a smaller social safety net found in market economies like the United States and the United Kingdom. Explained the president of the French conglomerate CGIP, "Here, social security and social solidarity weigh more than efficiency."[74]

Some raise the suggestion that a mixed economy does not necessarily condemn a country to poor economic performance that can then only be fixed by disengaging the state and dismantling social welfare programs. Rather, they advocate fine-tuning the government's economic role and modernizing social welfare institutions to meet the competitive standards of the global marketplace. Austria, Denmark, the Netherlands, and Sweden are taking this route. In the Netherlands, for example, labor unions and the government agreed on wage restraints, shorter working hours, budget discipline, and the trimming of social benefits. As a result, Dutch unemployment is about half that in neighboring countries, and the country enjoys macroeconomic stability.

The Free Market Strikes Back   Free market advocates are quick to point out that government-provided stability is not free. Relying on Big Brother to safeguard standards of living comes with a heavy price—namely, a sacrifice of freedom, a slowness to innovate, and the peril of slow growth. Certainly, history shows that government-directed economies can often perform well. Over time, however, the power of their typical advantages—cheap labor, large-scale production facilities, artificially cheap capital, low R&D investment—fade in the face of improving management systems and production processes in free markets.

More fundamentally, history also shows that government control decreases the risk-affinitive behavior of entrepreneurs and companies. Consequently, both are less likely to pursue innovations that power economic growth. Essentially, it boils down to a straightforward question: Why work hard and risk everything on a new idea if whatever you create is the property of a government that will then not reward you for your sacrifice?

The Battle Engaged   For decades, capitalist critiques had rung true. The reliance in mixed and command economies on expanding regulations had created sclerotic economies badly in need of free market reforms. However, the global economic crisis and its threat to systemic stability—precisely because of too little regulation, too little social concern, and too little government—have put free market advocates on the defensive. The capitalist ideology that drove the animal spirits of free and unfettered markets, some argue, is not an ideal to emulate but rather an evil to avoid. Dealing with the fallout of the economic meltdown and installing safeguards that prevent its recurrence, goes the reasoning, demands more government involvement in the economic affairs of the state, not less. Now, for the first time in years, some wonder whether economic success requires a regime where the roles of market and government are in balance, and where a strong state administers effective regulations that curb the power of special interests.[75]

Like a pendulum, it is quite likely that increasing zeal for the socialism of a mixed economy will swing to an extreme. It did, in a point of parallel, for free markets in the past—to such a degree that by 2006, few questioned Ronald Reagan's then-heretical declaration, made in his 1981 inaugural address, that "Government is not a solution to our problem. Government is the problem." Now, in 2009, many now seem increasingly mindful of the contention of Nicolas Sarkozy, president of France, that "The main feature of this crisis is the return of the state, the end of the ideology of public powerlessness."[76]

The aftermath of the meltdown saw leading companies reverse field, seeking solutions for their problems from their governments. Service companies like Citibank, Lloyds of London, American Express, Goldman Sachs, and Royal Bank of Scotland relied on rescue funds; manufacturers like Sony, Haier, Vale, Caterpillar, and Samsung pressed for more public stimulus. Whether this was a temporary anomaly or the start of a long-term trend is hotly debated. Whatever the outcome, standards of economic freedom, ideals of freer markets, and historical inevitability of globalization will change. ∎

THE MEANS OF ECONOMIC TRANSITION

Changing marketplace conditions and unfolding political trends signal uncertainty about the types of economic environments facing managers. No longer can managers safely presume, as they have for the past few decades, that markets will adopt reforms that increase economic freedom. Certainly, trends in many markets—most notably China, India, and Brazil—indicate movement toward freer markets. On the other hand, trends in many other markets—notably the United States, the United Kingdom, Japan, and Germany—indicate greater government involvement in economic affairs.

Earlier profiles of the market, mixed, and command types of economic environments give managers a framework to interpret change to marketplace philosophy. In addition, managers also monitor key indicators that provide an early-warning system on the direction and dynamic of transition from one type of economic environment to another. Most notably, these key indicators include a government's efforts to regulate the economy, its inclination to protect individual ownership and property rights, its ideas about fiscal and monetary policies, and its willingness to enforce antitrust regulation. We now profile each.

As we do so, please be mindful that the process of transition to different economic systems differs from country to country. The steps taken in Ireland, Thailand, Brazil, South Africa, and Mexico differ from those taken in China, Brazil, Estonia, Vietnam, or Ukraine. Nonetheless, the experiences of these and other countries confirm that

Transition to a market economy involves liberalizing economic activity, reforming business activity, and establishing legal and institutional frameworks that increase economic freedom.

governments adopt common principles and practices in powering the transition between market, mixed, or command economies.

Privatization   A necessary, but by no means sufficient, condition of creating a market economy is the state's transfers of its ownership and control of factors of production to private owners via **privatization** (the sale and legal transfer of government-owned resources to private interests). Privatization is an essential element of a market economy, not just for improving general efficiency but also because an unfettered private sector better regulates supply and demand, thereby leading to better production and consumption decisions. Hence, the ambition to move toward a market economy requires a government to disengage from the economy by privatizing state-owned enterprises.

In contrast, the government's acquisition of previously private assets is a strong signal of expanding involvement in economic affairs. For example, upon the bankruptcy of General Motors, the U.S. government exchanged its billions of dollars of support for a 60 percent equity position in the new company—which some suggested should now be called GM as in "Government Motors."

Regulation   The issue of regulation involves imposing restrictions on the free operation of markets and business practices. In principle, regulations prevent companies from maximizing efficiency, given that they sacrifice productivity in complying with regulations. Moreover, government regulations are regarded as the antithesis of economic freedom, given their systematic reduction of individual choice.

Regulations, however, can prove productive. The Office of Management and Budget of the United States, for example, estimated that federal regulations—namely the rules enforcing the laws passed by Congress—provide benefits from $135 billion to $218 billion annually, while costing taxpayers between $38 billion and $44 billion.[77] Regulations also police tendencies for the sorts of opportunism that led to poor decisions by many financial institutions in the global credit crisis.

Property Rights   Protection of property rights means that entrepreneurs who come up with an innovation can legally claim the rewards of their idea, effort, and risk. This protection supports a competitive economy by assuring investors and entrepreneurs that they, not the state, will prosper from their hard work. If lacking or arbitrarily applied, entrepreneurs and companies face a high risk of contract or property rights violations. For example, in its rush to save Detroit, some argue that the U.S. government violated creditors' property rights. Upon Chrysler's filing for bankruptcy, secured creditors—owed some $7 billion—recovered 28 cents per dollar. In contrast, an employee health-care trust (operated by the United Auto Workers union and ranking lower in the capital structure) received 43 cents on its $11 billion-odd of claims, as well as a majority stake in the restructured firm.[78]

Fiscal and Monetary Reform   Economic decision making by political officials often leads governments to adopt tax or spending policies that slow growth and increase interest rates, inflation, and unemployment. Mixed economies typically impose higher tax rates, spend more on social programs, and regulate executive compensation levels more aggressively than commonly seen in market economies.

One impediment to a free market economy is that capitalist principles require a government to rely on market-oriented instruments for macroeconomic stabilization, set strict budget limits, and use market-based policies to manage the money supply. These measures, by enforcing fiscal and monetary discipline, restrain governments' activities. If, on the other hand, a government disregards this discipline, it must then rely upon debt financing. For example, the U.S. government-sponsored rescue of financial institutions in the aftermath of the economic crisis had, by mid-2009, run to $12.3 trillion, nearly all financed by the sale of U.S. Treasury bills.

Antitrust Legislation   Markets can create situations in which a single seller or producer supplies a good or service. When one company is able to control a product's supply and, therefore, its price, it is considered a monopoly. The anticompetitive practices of monopolies

---

Privatization is the process of changing something from state to private ownership or control.

A property right is the exclusive authority to determine how a resource is used.

are antithetical to a free market. Consequently, liberalizing an economic system requires a government to legislate antitrust laws that encourage the development of industries with as many competing businesses as the market can sustain. In such industries, prices are kept low by the forces of competition. By enforcing antitrust laws, governments can prevent monopolies from exploiting consumers and restraining market growth.

> Antitrust legislation outlaws monopolies in order to promote free competition in the market place.

Meet the BRICs

The opening case for this chapter highlighted the accelerating success of emerging economies.[79] The focus of attention is now squarely on the vanguard of emerging economies, the so-called BRICs: Brazil, Russia, India, and China. The BRIC countries, although much larger in scale and scope than other emerging markets, represent trends that are developing throughout the world. Many presume that where the BRICs go, both good and bad, others will follow. As we look at the emergence of the BRICs, we discuss the implications for the economic environment as well as for company activity. Then, to close, we'll identify trends that threaten to crumble the BRICs and how their leadership is responding.

Changing of the Guard

First off, it's critical to remind oneself where the BRIC countries were just 30 or so years ago. Brazil was an economic basket case suffering hyperinflation, Russia was in lockdown behind the Iron Curtain, India was a socialist country that had kicked out IBM and Coca-Cola, and China was recovering from the bedlam of the Cultural Revolution. Presently, at current trends and with reasonable projections, over the next few decades Brazil, Russia, India, and China will become large, powerful players in the world economy. (See Figure 4.8.)

Originally, some thought it would take until 2050 before the BRICs bypassed today's rich countries. The global meltdown, however, fast-forwards the schedule; whereas China, India,

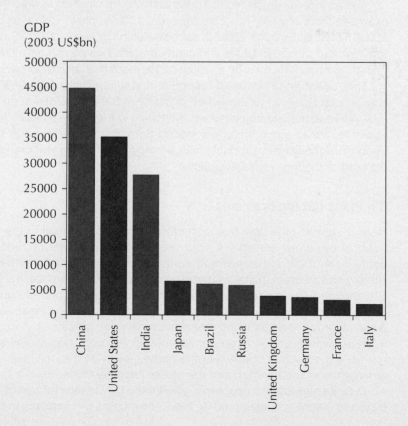

GDP
(2003 US$bn)

FIGURE 4.8   The Largest Economies in the World: 2050

Current projections see the economic order of the world changing dramatically over the next generation. By mid-century, China will likely claim the top rank, followed by the United States and India.

Source: Dominic Wilson and Roopa Purushothaman, "Global Economics Paper No. 99: Dreaming with BRICs: The Path to 2050" (Goldman Sachs, 2005), at www.gs.com (accessed October 15, 2007).

and Brazil (the so-called BIC set) are growing, the economies of Germany, Japan, the United Kingdom, and the United States are shrinking. Unquestionably, growth will resume for the latter. Still, it will likely fall short of that in the emerging markets, given their aging workforces and falling productivity. In the meantime, the speed of the BRICs' economic recovery has led some to see the global economic crisis as a pivotal milestone in the distribution of economic power.

So, again, thinking of where the BRIC countries were 30 or so years ago and then projecting the same trend line out 20 years from today makes for, depending upon your perspective, an astonishing or worrisome outcome. Certainly, the current economic crisis makes any time line for the changing of the guard speculative. It does, not, however change unfolding trends that will culminate in the BRICs housing more than 40 percent of the world's population, holding a combined PPP-adjusted GDP of nearly $18 trillion, and completing the comeback of the emerging economies. Moreover, the current crisis suggests that the most disruptive phase of the transition will take place over the next decade.

Changing Markets

The BRICs, like many Bottom of the Pyramid markets, are on the verge of rapid market growth. Historically, consumer demand takes off when GNI per capita income is between U.S. $3,000 and $10,000. The first economy to hit those levels was Russia; China, India, and Brazil are steadily heading there—and if adjusted for purchasing power, only India has yet to cross this threshold.

All of the BRICs, save Russia, have rapidly growing middle classes whose demand aspirations are changing quickly. Analysts predict that their middle class will expand from 50 million to 583 million people by 2025. More immediately, between 2005 and 2015, over 800 million people in the BRICs will cross the annual income threshold of U.S. $3,000. Entry into the middle class, besides permitting more consumption, often moves people from buying generic necessities to branded goods. By 2025, approximately 200 million people in the BRICs will have annual incomes above $15,000.

And as income grows, so too does demand for what once were inaccessible luxuries. For example, there are only two cars for every 100 people in China, as opposed to 50 cars per 100 Americans. By 2040, China's car ownership will likely rise to 29 cars per 100 people. The total number of cars in China and India combined could rise from around 40 million today to 750 million by 2040, thereby accounting for more than half of all cars on the world's roads.

The recent introduction of low-price autos like Tata's Nano—a small, affordable, rear-engined, four-passenger car aimed primarily at the Indian market and costing U.S. $2,100—may prove estimates conservative. Matching car ownership rates in the United States, for example, would move the upper bound from 750 million to north of a billion cars. Similar trends in virtually every product class, on the face of it, suggest market potentials last seen at the start of the Industrial Revolution.

Big Plans but Big Problems

Notwithstanding the spectacular performance and potential of the BRICs, many are skeptical. In principle, observers note the endemic problem of *recency bias,* which is the delusion that current trends will continue indefinitely and uninterrupted into the future. History shows great mistakes made by companies, executives, investors, and officials who extrapolated the present into the future. Inevitably, economic growth rates slow down, given an increasing base. Moreover, advantages such as cheap labor or low-cost capital wane as growing demand increases marginal price pressures. And always on the horizon is a black-swan event—a large-impact, hard-to-predict, and rare event beyond the realm of normal expectations that resets the game—such as the collapse of the Soviet Union, the emergence of the Internet, and the global financial crisis.

Despite high-octane economic growth, the BRICs face futures of widespread poverty and distorted income distributions. By 2025, the income per capita in today's richer countries will exceed U.S. $35,000 for more than a billion people. In contrast, perhaps 2 to 4 percent of the nearly 3 billion folks in the BRIC economies will hit that threshold. Longer term, income per capita in the United States is projected to reach $80,000 by 2050, while China will likely be just over $31,000, Brazil about $26,600, and India just $17,400. With the possible exception of Russia, hundreds of millions of people in the BRICs will be far poorer on average than individuals in Germany, France, Japan, Italy, Canada, and the United States. Consequently, for the first time in history, the largest economies in the world will no longer be the richest when measured by GNI per capita.

Each of the BRICs struggles with its particular problems. Today, Russia is probably the most vulnerable. Russia is dependent on various commodity exports, most notably oil, for revenue. Amid the global economic crisis, oil fell from U.S. $147 per barrel in July 2008 to below U.S. $40 in March 2009. This dropped Russia into a deep recession, with GDP shrinking almost 10 percent in the first half of 2009. Additionally, Russia is considered far riskier by foreign investors because of escalating tensions with the West and its failure to create a legal and political infrastructure that respects the rule of law. Long term, besides its aging and declining population, Russia's uncertain government, environmental degradation, and crumbling infrastructure confound growth projections. Some caution replacing the BRIC notion with that of the BICs.

Brazil's economic potential has been anticipated for decades, but it has struggled to achieve expectations due to problems in income equality, productivity, and education. India, in addition to other pressing economic and political challenges, has immense infrastructure shortfalls and hundreds of millions of extremely poor people. China's particular interpretation of the rule of law, rights of citizens, environmental sustainability, and principles of democracy poses problems. Too, China faces a steadily closing window of opportunity; by 2020, China will have the largest number of both old and very old people on earth.

Finally, so-called green constraints shadow the bright futures of all. The emergence of the BRICs sorely challenges the sustainability of the global environment. Global warming, diminishing raw materials, and escalating pollution suggest that there is a finite limit to how much the BRICs can develop before exceeding the capacity of the global economy to supply them and of the environment to support them. More worrisome, notes the Worldwatch Institute, is the fact that if China and India, to say nothing about Russia and Brazil, were to consume resources and produce pollution at the current U.S. per capita level, we would require two planet Earths just to sustain their two economies.

Mixing Mortar

Leaders of these countries have not been idly sitting by, watching these threats thwart their future. Overlapping ambitions and agendas have led the BRICs to develop bilateral and multilateral cooperation. India and China, the world's two most populous countries, formed a strategic partnership to end a border dispute and boost trade. The agreement eased decades of mutual distrust between the two as a result of a 1962 border war. "India and China can together reshape the world order," Indian Prime Minister Manmohan Singh proclaimed at a ceremony for his Chinese counterpart, Premier Wen Jiabao, at India's presidential palace.

Similarly, indications show strengthening ties between Russia and China. Bilateral China-Russia trade was $58 billion in 2008, up from $20 billion in 2005, and on its way to $70 billion in 2010. Both countries are leading members of the Shanghai Cooperation Council, one of the most influential economic centers in the world. In many people's eyes, Russia, by rolling back democracy and reviving its imperialist past, is now more politically aligned with the one-party state of China. Spearheading these efforts was Prime Minister Putin of Russia, with his goal to build "a new world economic architecture" that would reflect the rising power of emerging economies and the decline of the old heavyweights like the United States, Japan, and leading European countries.

The global credit crisis has accelerated these trends. Steadily, the BRIC leaders have been forming alliances that amplify their political, legal, economic, and strategic influence. They have increasingly tried to bypass the U.S. dollar as the means to settle international

Joining Forces

Here we see, moving left to right, Presidents Luiz Inacio Lula da Silva of Brazil, Dmitry Medvedev of Russia, Hu Jintao of China and Indian Prime Minister Manmohan Singh clasping hands during a group picture shoot in Yekaterinburg at the summer 2009 BRIC leaders summit. Leaders from the world's top emerging economic powers met for their first summit to plot a strategy to increase their clout amid the global crisis.

Source: Philippe Lopez/Getty Images, Inc.

transactions. The dollar, ever since the Bretton Woods Agreement of 1944, has functioned as the world's reserve currency; as such, it is widely held by governments and institutions around the world and is used to finance international transactions, including trade and the payment of debts.

Beginning in the spring of 2009, however, China and Brazil agreed to no longer use the U.S. dollar in doing business, instead adopting a yen-cruzeiro currency-swap agreement. China was involved in similar negotiations with Russia, again looking to eliminate the U.S. dollar as the basis for bilateral trade. To cap matters, the leaders of Brazil, Russia, India, and China met in Russia in June 2009 at the first ever BRIC Summit to discuss, among other issues, the role of the dollar in the global financial system and, some suspected, to champion a new supranational currency. In the backdrop was a sense, expressed by Prime Minister Putin, that "The world is changing before our very eyes. Countries that seemed hopelessly backward only yesterday are becoming the world's fastest-growing economies today." Emerging economies, led by the BRICs, no longer wanted simply to be part of the world's outdated architecture—instead, they wanted to go forward into a brave new world largely unencumbered by the past.

The Road Ahead

Inevitably, many speculate that the BRICs might turn into bricks in their march to miracle economies. Granted, their governments have developed economically sensible policies, opened trade and domestic markets, and begun building institutions that support economic freedom. Still, Russia's struggle shows how quickly conditions in one economy can fall out of sync. Would the same hold for the others, people wondered, as they struggled to transition from command-controlled economies to freer markets?

This chapter noted the importance of four preconditions of consistent growth—namely sound macroeconomic policies; political institutions committed to transparency, fairness, and the rule of law; openness to trade and capital; and strong education systems. By and large, the BRICs, along with other emerging markets, meet the general spirit of some of these standards. None, however, meets all. The fact that they continued to prosper as their rich-country counterparts struggle suggested that either conventional understanding of markets is flawed or the BRICs still face high hurdles in reforming their economies.

In summary, the emergence of the BRICs signals that the next generation of economic development of the global economy will be a thrilling ride. Even if the BRICs come close to reaching their apparent potential, their success will redefine the structure of economic environments, patterns of growth, and dynamics of economic activity. ∎

QUESTIONS

1. Map the likely evolution of the BRICs. What indicators might companies monitor to guide their investments and actions?

2. What are the implications of the emergence of the BRICs for careers and companies in your country?

3. Do you think recency bias has led to overestimating the potential of the BRICs? How would you, as a manager for a company assessing these markets, try to control this bias?

4. How might managers interpret the potential for their product in a market that is, in absolute economic terms, large but, on a per capita basis, characterized by a majority of poor to very poor consumers?

5. In the event that the BRICs fail to meet projected performance, what would be some of the implications for international business?

6. Compare and contrast the merits of GNI per capita versus the idea of purchasing power parity, human development, and green economics as indicators of economic potential in Brazil, Russia, China, and India.

SUMMARY

- The economic environment of a country shapes its attractiveness to foreign investors.

- Managers assess economic environments and forecast market trends to make better investment choices, operating decisions, and competitive strategies.

- Managers use several indicators to assess an economic environment; meaningful indicators include growth rates, income distribution, inflation, unemployment, wages, productivity, debt, and the balance of payments.

- Managers improve economic analysis by identifying meaningful indicators and then understanding how they interact with each other.

- The benefits of doing business in a country are directly influenced by the size of the market (GNI, GNP, GDP), the present income of consumers (GNI, GNP, or GDP per capita adjusted for purchasing power parity), and the likely future wealth of consumers (in terms of income distribution, human development, and sustainability).

- Green measures of economic performance take into consideration the ecological welfare of the world in the belief that sustainable development requires managers to heed the idea that economic activity must ultimately "meet the needs of the present without compromising the ability of future generations to meet their own needs."

- The Bottom of the Pyramid refers to the billions of people living on less than a few dollars per day yet whom some see as the next market frontier of the global economy.

- The type of economic system is a strong predictor of a country's present economic performance and future economic prospects.

- The economic system determines who owns and controls factors of production and, by extension, the price and quantity of goods and services.

- Economic freedom is the absence of government coercion or constraint on the production, distribution, or consumption of goods and services beyond the extent necessary for citizens to protect and maintain liberty itself.

- In a market economy, the goods and services that a country produces, and the quantity in which they are produced, are not planned. Rather, price and quantity, conveyed via the invisible hand, determine supply and demand.

- In a command economy, the government plans what goods and services a country produces, the quantity in which they are produced, and the price at which they are sold.

- A mixed economy includes some elements of market and command economies. Market forces as well as the government play a significant role in directing the investment activities of public and private enterprise and the consumption behavior of individuals.

- Economic freedom is the degree to which governments intervene in the economic environment. Free countries tend to have higher economic growth, higher standards of living, and more macroeconomic stability than do less-free or repressed countries.

- Transition to a market economy requires accepting the doctrine of capitalism, its principles of the invisible hand and laissez faire, and the goal of maximizing economic freedom.

- Transition to a mixed economy requires accepting the doctrine of state intervention, its principle of the visible hand of an activist government that commands and controls some factors of production, and the goal of constraining economic freedom.

- Transition to a command economy requires accepting the doctrine of communism, its principle of an activist government that commands and controls most if not all factors of production, and the goal of eliminating economic freedom.

- The recent legitimacy of free markets has been challenged by the global economic crisis. Governments in many countries have expanded their involvement in economic matters. Markets that have been free are now increasingly mixed.

- Managers watch key events to gauge the contest between the market, mixed, and command economies. These include how the government regulates the economy, protects individual ownership and property rights, sets fiscal and monetary policies, and enforces antitrust regulation.

KEY TERMS

balance of payments (BOP) (p. 198)
Bottom of the Pyramid (p. 197)
capitalism (p. 201)
command economy (p. 202)
communism (p. 201)
deflation (p. 191)
economic freedom (p. 205)
Economic Freedom Index (p. 205)

economic system (p. 201)
external debt (p. 194)
Gini coefficient (p. 194)
green economics (p. 187)
gross domestic product (GDP) (p. 182)
gross national product (GNP) (p. 181)
gross national income (GNI) (p. 181)
Human Development Index (HDI) (p. 187)

income distribution (p. 194)
inflation (p. 188)
internal debt (p. 194)
laissez-faire (p. 201)
market economy (p. 201)
mixed economy (p. 203)
privatization (p. 212)
purchasing power parity (PPP) (p. 185)

ENDNOTES

1 *Sources include the following:* Thomas Friedman, "The World Is Flat: A Brief History of the Twenty-first Century," Farrar, Straus, and Giroux, 2005; Clyde V. Prestowitz, *Three Billion New Capitalists: The Great Shift of Wealth and Power to the East* (New York: Basic Books, 2006); Clyde Prestowitz, "Three Billion New Capitalists," video transcript, *News Hour* (August 15, 2005), at www.pbs.org/newshour/bb/economy/july-dec05/prestowitz_8-15.html; Kenneth Rogoff, "Betting with the House's Money," *Project Syndicate,* at www.project-syndicate.org/commentary/rogoff27 (accessed May 7, 2007); Anne O. Krueger, "Stability, Growth, and Prosperity: The Global Economy and the IMF," at www.imf.org/external/np/speeches/2006/060706.htm (accessed June 7, 2006); Angus Maddison, *The World Economy, 1–2030 AD* (London: Oxford University Press, 2007); *The World Economy: Volume 1: A Millennial Perspective* (Paris: Development Centre, 2001); *Volume 2: Historical Statistics* (Paris: Development Centre, 2003); "BRICs, Emerging Markets and the World Economy: Not Just Straw Men," *The Economist* (June 18, 2009): 45; "Government v. Market in America: The Visible Hand," *The Economist* (May 28, 2009): 25–28, www.economist.com/displaystory.cfm?story_id=13743310 (accessed August 12, 2009); The Next Billions: Unleashing Business Potential in Untapped Markets, *World Economic Forum* (January 2009): 44.

2 A Tale of Two Depressions, Barry Eichengree and Kevin H. O'Rourke (June 4, 2009), at www.voxeu.org/index.php?q=node/3421 (accessed June 5, 2009).

3 As measured in terms of purchasing power parity.

4 Clyde Prestowitz, "Three Billion New Capitalists," video transcript, *News Hour* (August 15, 2005), at www.pbs.org/newshour/bb/economy/july-dec05/prestowitz_8-15.html (accessed July 18, 2007).

5 Specifically, data pertain to the February 2008 through February 2009 period. Countries included in the calculation are China,

Taiwan, Japan, France, Canada, Germany, Britain, Hong Kong, Mexico, Brazil, Argentina, the United States, India, South Korea, and Argentina. See "Global Systemic Crisis in Summer 2009: The Cumulative Impact of Three Rogue Waves," Global Europe Anticipation Bulletin (June 17, 2009).

6 The World Bank Group, at www.worldbank.org/data/databytopic/class.htm. See also "How Many Countries Are in the World?" at geography.about.com/cs/countries/a/numbercountries.htm (accessed July 24, 2009).

7 Andrew B. Abel and Ben S. Bernanke, *Macroeconomics* (Reading, MA: Addison-Wesley, 1992): 30.

8 Abel and Bernanke, *Macroeconomics*, 32–33. Historically, GNI was referred to as gross national product. The definition and measurement of GNI and GNP are analogous, but institutions such as the World Bank and International Monetary Fund now use the term GNI.

9 See U.S. and World Population Clocks—POPClocks, at www.census.gov/main/www/popclock.html, for current estimate (accessed December, 7, 2009).

10 For the record, the World Bank explains the Atlas method as follows: "In calculating gross national income (GNI—formerly referred to as GNP) and GNI per capita in U.S. dollars for certain operational purposes, the World Bank uses the Atlas conversion factor. The purpose of the Atlas conversion factor is to reduce the impact of exchange rate fluctuations in the cross-country comparison of national incomes. The Atlas conversion factor for any year is the average of a country's exchange rate (or alternative conversion factor) for that year and its exchange rates for the two preceding years, adjusted for the difference between the rate of inflation in the country, and through 2000, that in the G-5 countries (France, Germany, Japan, the United Kingdom, and the United States). For 2001 onwards, these countries include the Euro Zone, Japan, the United Kingdom, and the United States. A country's inflation rate is measured by the change in its GDP deflator."

www.worldbank.org/data/aboutdata/working-meth.html, (accessed July 2, 2009).

11 "BRICs, Emerging Markets and the World Economy: Not Just Straw Men," *The Economist* (June 18, 2009): 45.

12 World Bank, 2007 Survey (Atlas methodology for GNI per capita). Typically, the prices of many goods are considered and weighted according to their importance in the economy of the particular country.

13 Statement by Dr. Mahbub ul Haq, cofounder with A. Sen of the theory of HDI.

14 The index was developed in 1990 by Pakistani economist Mahbub ul Haq and has been used since 1993 by the United Nations Development Programme in its annual report. The HDI is comparable over time when it is calculated based on the same methodology and comparable trend data. HDR 2003 presents a time series in HDI for 1975, 1980, 1985, 1990, 1995, and 2001. This time series uses the latest HDI methodology and the most up-to-date trend data for each component of the index.

15 "Process of Preparation of the Environmental Perspective to the Year 2000 and Beyond," General Assembly Resolution 38/161 (December 19, 1983), at www.un.org/documents/ga/res/38/a38r161htm (accessed May 27, 2007).

16 Joseph Stiglitz, "Good Numbers Gone Bad: Why Relying on GDP as a Leading Economic Gauge Can Lead to Poor Decision-Making," *Fortune* (September 25, 2006).

17 Eric Weiner, "The Happiest Places in the World," *Forbes* (April 23, 2008). www.forbes.com/2008/04/23/happiest-places-world-oped-cx_ewe_0423happiest.html (accessed July 16, 2009).

18 "Government v. Market in America: The Visible Hand," *The Economist* (May 28, 2009): 25–28, www.economist.com/displaystory.cfm?story_id=13743310 (accessed August 12, 2009).

19 E. Mishan, *The Costs of Economic Growth* (New York: Praeger, 1967).

20 E. Mishan, "The Growth of Affluence and the Decline of Welfare", in H. Daly (ed.), *Economics, Ecology, and Ethics: Essays Toward a Steady-State Economy* (W. H. Freeman, San Francisco, 1980).

21 Ibid.

22 Jerome Glenn, Theodore Gordon, and Elizabeth Florescu, *2009 State of the Future, The Millennium Project*, www.millennium-project.org/millennium/sof2009.html

23 Humans will need two Earths, report claims: Global 'footprint' left by consumption is growing, conservationists argue (October 25, 2006).

24 *Process of Preparation of the Environmental Perspective to the Year 2000 and Beyond.* General Assembly Resolution 38/161 (December 19, 1983), at www.un.org/documents/ga/res/38/a38r161htm (accessed May 27, 2007).

25 Murray N. Rothbard, "Ludwig von Mises (1881–1973)," at www.mises.org/content/mises.asp (accessed May 27, 2009).

26 Economists use different types of indexes to measure inflation, but the one they use the most is the *Consumer Price Index (CPI)*. The CPI measures a fixed basket of goods and compares its price from one period to the next. A rise in the index indicates inflation.

27 "Zimbabwe to print first $100 trillion note," CNN.com (January 16, 2009), at www.cnn.com/2009/WORLD/africa/01/16/zimbawe.currency (accessed May 24, 2009).

28 Michael Wines, "How Bad Is Inflation in Zimbabwe?," *New York Times* (May 2, 2006).

29 For instance, as of 2003, only three countries had annual inflation rates in excess of 40 percent, the level above which it is generally considered to be acutely damaging to an economy. All major industrial countries had inflation under 3 percent (and in Japan, deflation persisted). Moreover, inflation in many middle- and lower-income countries, once stuck with extreme inflation pressure, had fallen well into single digits in the early twenty-first century. Many credited the fall in inflation to a combination of the price pressures of globalization along with more vigilant central bankers and economic policymakers. See Rogoff, "The IMF Strikes Back," *Foreign Policy* (January/February 2003): 39–48.

30 View of Junko Nishioka, chief Japan economist at RBS Securities Japan Ltd. in Tokyo. From "Japan Succumbs to Deflation as Consumer Prices Fall Record 1.1%," at Bloomberg.com (accessed June 29, 2009).

31 Junko Nishioka, "Japan Succumbs to Deflation as Consumer Prices Fall Record 1.1%."

32 The working-age population: Presently, the wealthier countries of the world are watching their working-age population shrink from approximately 740 to 690 million people between 2000 and 2025. However, over the same time, the working-age population will increase across poorer countries from about 3 to 4 billion people. In China alone, the population above the age of 16 will grow by 5.5 million annually on average in the next 20 years. The total population of working-age Chinese will reach 940 million by 2020. Presently, the youth of the world suffer the highest rates of unemployment in most countries, with rates twice that of adult (ages 25–65) unemployment. China, for example, sees the age structure of its population creating severe employment pressure within the next two decades.

33 See Constance Sorrentino, "International Unemployment Rates: How Comparable Are They?," *Monthly Labor Review* (June 2000): 3-20.

34 See U.S. National Debt Clock, at www.brillig.com/debt_clock (accessed October 1, 2009).

35 Thomas Laubach, "New Evidence on the Interest Rate Effects of Budget Deficits and Debt," *Board of Governors of the Federal Reserve System* (2003).

36 GNI data is adjusted by purchasing power parity (accessed July 14, 2009).

37 See "Gap between Rich and Poor: World Income Inequality," at www.infoplease.com/ipa/A0908770.html (accessed July 14, 2009).

38 William Domhoff, Wealth, Income, and Power (September 2005), at sociology.ucsc.edu/whorulesamerica/power/wealth.html (accessed May 5, 2009).

39 Chinese urban workers' per capita salary up 18 percent in H1, www.chinaview.cn 2008-07-28 11:41:09, news.xinhuanet.com/english/2008-07/28/content_8786414.htm (accessed June 19, 2009).

40 "Chinese Scholars Warn Growing Wealth Gap Likely to Trigger Social Instability," Sina, at english.sina.com/china/1/2005/0822/43237.html (accessed July 8, 2006).

41 "Transcript, Chapter 18, Episode Three: The New Rules of the Game," *Commanding Heights: The Battle for the World Economy*, at www.pbs.org/wgbh/commandingheights/lo/index.html (accessed June 28, 2007).

42 "Impossible Architecture," *Social Watch Report 2006*, at www.socialwatch.org/en/portada.htm (accessed May 27, 2007).

43 "Joseph Stiglitz, Wall Street's Toxic Message," *Vanity Fair* (July 2009), at www.vanityfair.com/politics/features/2009/07/third-world-debt200907 (accessed June 15, 2009); "The Poor and the Global Crisis: The Trail of Disaster," *The Economist* (June 18, 2009): 24.

44 The Food and Agriculture Organization (FAO) of the United Nations (UN) translates the food commodities available for human consumption in a country into their protein equivalent. This measure compensates for differences in protein supplied by different foods across countries. (Go to www.fao.org.)

45 Donald McNeil Jr., "Design That Solves Problems for the World's Poor," *New York Times* (May 29, 2007): B-2.

46 Jane Fraser and Jeremy Oppenheim, What's New about Globalization, *The McKinsey Quarterly* (May, 1997): 178.

47 The Next Billions: Unleashing Business Potential in Untapped Markets. *World Economic Forum* (January 2009), 44; C. K. Prahalad and S. L. Hart, "The Fortune at the Bottom of the Pyramid," *Strategy+Business,* (2002) 26: 54–67; C. K. Prahalad, "The Fortune at the Bottom of the Pyramid," Wharton School Publishing (2004).

48 See, for example, www.nextbillion.net.

49 Paul Krugman, "Divided over Trade," *New York Times* (May 14, 2007): A-15.

50 Calculated at the exchange rate of 7.65 yuan to the dollar, as of June 12, 2009.

51 Keith Bradsher, "Chinese Auto Parts Enter the Global Market," *New York Times* (June 7, 2007): B-8.

52 Productivity growth has two components: a long-term trend (set by the quality of the workforce, the pace of capital investment, and the speed of innovation) and more volatile short-term fluctuations driven by the business cycle. Early in an expansion, for instance, productivity takes off temporarily as firms squeeze their existing staff harder before hiring new workers. As an economy slows, it decelerates, given firms' reluctance to fire workers immediately.

53 Performance 2009: Productivity, Employment, and Growth in the World's Economies. The Conference Board at www.conference-board.org/utilities/pressDetail.cfm?press_id=3564 (accessed July 22, 2009).

54 See www.cia.gov/library/publications/the-world-factbook/rankorder/2187rank.html, (accessed October 2, 2009).

55 Ask EarthTrends: How much of the world's resource consumption occurs in rich countries?, www.earthtrends.wri.org/updates/node/236 (accessed July 2, 2009).

56 From Slump to Jump, *The Economist* (August 1, 2009): 36.

57 Companies in centrally planned economies exhibited a particular quirk. The absence of competition and bankruptcy in this sort of economic system meant that once an enterprise was up and running, it survived indefinitely, irrespective of performance.

58 Michael P. Todaro, *Economic Development*, 6th ed. (Reading, MA: Addison Wesley, 1996): 705.

59 Todaro, Government v market in America.

60 World Publics Welcome Global Trade—But Not Immigration: 47-Nation Pew Global Attitudes Survey (October 4, 2007), at pewglobal.org/reports/display.php?ReportID=258; The Chinese Celebrate Their Roaring Economy, As They Struggle With Its Costs at pewglobal.org/reports/display.php?ReportID=261 (accessed July 22, 2008).

61 "Emerging Markets and the Credit Crunch: Whom Can We Rely On?," *The Economist* (May 7, 2009): 61.

62 William W. Beach and Marc A. Miles, "Explaining the Factors of the Index of Economic Freedom," *2005 Index of Economic Freedom,* at www.heritage.org/research/features/index, p. 33 (accessed August 14, 2006).

63 The 2009 Index has expanded its coverage to include 21 countries not previously rated. For countries graded in both the 2008 and 2009 editions of the Index of Economic Freedom, average scores increased from 60.2 to 60.3. However, the average economic freedom score for all countries in the 2009 Index is only 59.5 because of the addition to the Index rankings of these 21 previously unrated economies, most of which score below the world average.

64 Some experts suggest characterizing the United States and a number of other similar countries as *established market economies (EMEs)*, the term referring both to their high levels of per capita income and to the well-developed and relatively stable nature of those institutions that support the efficient operation of sophisticated markets.

65 "Did the Left Save India," *Outlook* (November 10, 2008): 8.

66 In addition, upon the eventual bankruptcy of General Motors—an outcome largely initiated by the U.S. government—the charge of restructuring the company and tacitly rewriting the rules of capitalism fell upon a 31-year-old, newly appointed White House staff member, David Sanger. "The 31-Year-Old in Charge of Dismantling G.M.," *New York Times* (May 31, 2009):B-5, at http://www.nytimes.com/2009/06/01/business/01deese.html?_r=1&em.

67 S. Labaton, "White House Appoints Czar to Oversee Executive Pay" (June, 10, 2009): A-1, at www.nytimes.com/2009/06/11/business/11pay.html?_r=1&hp.

68 Economy to shrink 2.9% this year, World Bank says, CBCnews.ca, www.cbc.ca/money/story/2009/06/22/world-bank-forecast.html (accessed June 22, 2009).

69 No full recovery until 2015, says the IMF, *The Telegraph*, September 22, 2009. http://www.telegraph.co.uk/finance/financetopics/recession/6220089/No-full-recovery-until-2015-says-the-IMF.html (accessed September 22, 2009).

70 Joseph Stiglitz, Wall Street's Toxic Message.

71 Most worrisome to free market proponents is that, once a crisis passes, government control sometimes shrinks, but it never returns to its original size. Indeed, some argue that a mixed economy is essentially a move toward a socialist state.

72 The French model: Vive la différence! *The Economist* (May 7, 2009), at www.economist.com/world/europe/displaystory.cfm?story_id=13610197 (accessed June 21, 2009).

73 Denmark 'happiest place on earth,' *BBC News* (July 28, 2006), news.bbc.co.uk/2/hi/health/5224306.stm (accessed June 31, 2009). Russell Shorto, "Going Dutch: How I Learned to Love the Welfare State," *New York Times* (April 29, 2009), www.nytimes.com/2009/05/03/magazine/03european-t.html (accessed June 22, 2009).

74 Frank Vanden Broucke, "The EU and Social Protection: What Should the European Convention Propose?," The Foreign Policy Centre, at fpc.org.uk/articles/175 (accessed May 22, 2005).

75 Ibid. 42, Joseph Stiglitz, Wall Streets' Toxic Message, 2009.

76 "The State and the Economy: France. Back in the Driving Seat," *The Economist* (March 12, 2009): 23.

77 The report includes benefit-cost information by agency program as well as by agency. A copy of the report can be viewed at http://www.whitehouse.gov/omb/fedreg/2003draft_cost-benefit_rpt.pdf.

78 "An Offer You Can't Refuse," *The Economist* (May 9, 2009): 83.

79 ***Sources include the following:*** Dominic Wilson and Roopa Purushothaman, "Global Economics Paper No. 99: Dreaming with BRICs: The Path to 2050," Goldman Sachs, at www.gs.com/insight/research/reports/report6.html; "The BRICs Are Coming—Fast," *Business Week* (October 27, 2003): 33; Daniel Gross, "The U.S. Is Losing Market Share. So What?" *New York Times* (January 28, 2007): A-2; Nirmala George, "India, China to Form Strategic Partnership," *Associated Press* (April 11, 2004): 3; Andrew Kramer, "Putin Wants New Economic 'Architecture,' " *International Herald Tribune* (June 10, 2007): 1; "Chilling Time," *The Economist* (June 14, 2007): 24; Anand Giridharadas, "India's Edge Goes beyond Outsourcing," *New York Times* (April 4, 2007):1; Stephen Roach, "Unstable, Unbalanced, Uncoordinated, and Unsustainable," *Morgan Stanley Global Economic Forum* (March 19, 2007), www.morganstanley.com/views/gef/archive/2007/20070319-Mon.html (accessed June 30, 2007); State of the World 2006: China and India Hold World in Balance, Worldwatch Institute; see www.worldwatch.org; China-Russia trade faces challenges but bright prospects remain, China View, Viewed at news.xinhuanet.com/english/2009-03/19/content_11035553.htm (accessed June 23, 2009); N. Taleb, *The Black Swan: The Impact of the Highly Improbable* (New York: Random House, 2007); BRICs, "Emerging Markets and the World Economy: Not Just Straw Men," *The Economist* (June 18, 2009): 53.

five

Globalization and Society

Objectives

- To identify problems in evaluating the activities of multinational enterprises (MNEs)

- To evaluate the major economic effects of MNEs on home and host countries

- To understand the foundations of responsible corporate behavior in the international sphere

- To discuss some key issues in the social activities and consequences of globalized business

- To examine corporate responses to globalization

When the last tree has been cut down, the last river has been polluted and the last fish has been caught—only then do you realize that money can't buy everything.

—*Native American Proverb*

221

In February 2009, Justin Smith, manager of the *Good Business Journey* at Woolworths, a leading South African department store with an international footprint, was a worried man. Woolworths had launched its five-year sustainability strategy just under two years before. After undertaking an impact assessment, Smith was concerned that the original targets—which covered transformation, social development, the environment, and climate change—had been set without a clear understanding of exactly what it would take to achieve them. If the sustainability goals were not reached, Woolworths could lose credibility among its shareholders, staff, and consumers. What did Woolworths need to do to ensure that it achieved its sustainability goals, and had the company been too ambitious in the targets it had set initially? he wondered.

WOOLWORTHS' BACKGROUND

Woolworths was founded in 1931 with one store in Cape Town. By 2009, it had 408 retail stores, making it one of the largest retail chains in South Africa. In the 1990s, the company expanded into other regions of Africa and the Middle East. In addition, Woolworths owned a majority share in Australian retail chain Country Road. (It is worth noting that Woolworths is not affiliated with Woolworths in the United Kingdom or Woolworths Limited in Australia and New Zealand.)

Woolworths' main product assortments were food, clothing, and home goods, targeted predominantly at people in upper-middle to high income ranges. The company believed that the key to its success lay in providing customers high-quality fresh produce and convenience foods, as well as clothing that had a reputation for being a cut above everything else in value and quality. The company's core values were quality and style, value for money, service, innovation, integrity, energy, and sustainability. Critical to Woolworths' success was the drive to build lifetime relationships with its customers.

THE GOOD BUSINESS JOURNEY (GBJ)

After investigating what international retailers were doing in the area of sustainability, Woolworths stepped into the sustainable-development arena with the launch of the GBJ on April 19, 2007. "The ethos behind it was that we have a responsibility to our communities and the environment of the business."

The GBJ consisted of a comprehensive five-year plan (from 2007 to 2012) aimed at improving the company's sustainability performance, which included measuring and reducing the company's carbon footprint. This incorporated a range of targets centered on four key priorities that had been identified in accordance with the concept of the triple bottom line: transformation of the business according to employment equity and Black Economic Empowerment (BEE) requirements, social development, the environment, and climate change. (BEE was established by the government to undo the legacy of apartheid and redistribute assets to those who were previously disadvantaged.)

Transformation and Social Development

Large South African corporations were legally obliged to comply with BEE requirements. Transformation included employment equity and reworking the company's supplier base. This transformation involved three main areas: direct empowerment through ownership, employment equity, and indirect empowerment through preferential procurement and enterprise development. Over the five-year period, Woolworths intended to prioritize preferential BEE procurement and ensure that BEE supplier partners provided core products to Woolworths by 2012. Woolworths also pledged to advance skills development and equity ownership; one way it achieved this was by filling leadership positions with people from previously disadvantaged groups.

The Environment

Woolworths committed to increasing organic and free-range food sales fourfold by 2012. This would result in a reduction in the use of harmful pesticides and chemicals, which would ultimately benefit consumers and improve water quality. The company also committed to supporting free-range farming methods and animal welfare by encouraging consumers to purchase free-range chicken, beef, and lamb.

In addition, the company pledged to reduce and recycle product packaging; decrease plastic bag usage; increase the use of recycled plastic; and recycle all store equipment, including food trays, baskets, carts, and hangers.

Climate Change

Woolworths made a firm commitment to reducing the amount of carbon produced directly from the business by

Through the *Good Business Journey,* Woolworths has demonstrated its ongoing commitment to accelerating transformation, driving social development, protecting the environment, and addressing climate change.

Source: © capetowndailyphoto.com

30 percent. This would be achieved by means of reducing electricity usage by 30 percent, reducing product miles and relative transport emissions by 20 percent, and reinvesting the savings into exploring more sustainable forms of energy and more efficient ways of transporting goods. Woolworths pledged to source food regionally, wherever possible, to reduce reliance on long-distance road transport. Airfreight of food products would be restricted, and food imported by air would be clearly labeled to inform consumers.

IMPLEMENTATION

The GBJ was set up according to a self-funding model and was meant to be cost-neutral to the business. Woolworths managed the GBJ centrally, through the head of corporate governance and the corporate affairs office. The Woolworths sustainability committee was a formal subcommittee of the Woolworths Holdings board and operated at strategic level. The committee met quarterly to oversee the progress in achieving the targets of the GBJ.

In 2006, Woolworths created the Woolworths Sustainability Index through a series of workshops and one-on-one meetings with key stakeholders within the company. Based on the Global Reporting Initiative, the Woolworths Sustainability Index measured progress towards achieving the 2012 targets by means of a weighted measurement and tracking system of over 200 indicators. This provided a score for each business unit and for the organization as a whole, across each of the four key priorities.

After the announcement of the GBJ, feedback from stakeholders had been mixed. Those already involved in sustainability issues had been supportive, but some had cautioned that the targets were far reaching and would be a challenge for Woolworths to achieve. Gaining investor buy-in was a challenge, as many investors were only interested in immediate profit. There were "only a handful of socially responsible investors in South Africa who knew we were running a holistic programme—there was very little appetite from local analysts regarding sustainability."

In February 2009, Woolworths announced 10 key sustainability risk areas, grouped into four main categories, that might impact negatively on the company's ability to meet the 2012 targets: external trading conditions, transformation, the environment, and the role of suppliers. The company stated that the original targets had been based on an understanding of the international and local environments at that time, but that these environments had now changed, especially in view of the global economic downturn.

External Trading Conditions

The impact of the global economic downturn had been felt by retailers across the globe. In late February 2009, the South African economy contracted for the first time in a decade. In the group results released in February 2009, Woolworths said that there had been significant changes in spending patterns, with consumers shunning credit facilities, concerns about price, and a general reluctance to purchase nonessential items. It seemed that consumers were fast losing interest in sustainability issues and were looking instead for the cheapest price. However, Woolworths believed that their consumers were still concerned with social and environmental issues and that it was vital to deliver on consumer expectations.

Environmental Challenges

The management team had known that organic products would retail at higher prices than nonorganic products but had felt that Woolworths' customers would be "willing to pay a small premium for sustainable products." In 2008, organic clothing sales were 47 percent above target, and, because Woolworths began using organic cotton in 2004, it had become the world's third-largest consumer of organic cotton, behind American giants Wal-Mart and Nike.

In 2008, Woolworths headed the JSE's Top 100 carbon-disclosure leadership index in the low-carbon sector. Woolworths committed to reducing the relative amount of carbon produced directly by the business by 30 percent by 2012. It had opted to open two "green" stores that would trial between 15 and 20 environmentally friendly design elements—such as food-market under-floor heating supplemented by solar heating, variable-speed compressors for refrigeration, and the use of natural light and ventilation where possible. In addition, the company had begun rolling out similar initiatives across their stores.

Role of Suppliers

Woolworths was predominantly an own-brand business, selling products that had been specifically developed for the company under the Woolworths brand; this was the target of the GBJ. The GBJ could not be successful without the commitment of the company's suppliers, and this was one of the most difficult areas to control. Communication with suppliers took the form of supplier days, meetings with suppliers, performance reviews, trade shows, and exhibitions. All suppliers were bound by the Woolworths' Supplier Code of Business Principles. The code covered legal, ethical, and environmental requirements and helped to ensure that suppliers' employees were treated fairly. Each supplier was independently audited to ensure compliance with the code. The company believed that one of the company's greatest strengths was its "direct relationship with the supply chain, which means that our ability to influence is much stronger." Woolworths worked closely with its suppliers to ensure quality products and offered suppliers considerable business and technical assistance. Due to their relationship with Woolworths, many suppliers had grown from small operators to multimillion-rand companies on the "back of the Woolworths brand."

Woolworths had aimed to achieve 100 percent compliance to the code from its clothing suppliers by 2008 but had achieved only 73 percent compliance, due to difficulties in ensuring compliance from international suppliers. Smith stated that "internationally, we are a small player with less influence than locally. We sometimes battle to get cooperation with documents and audited certificates."

In 2006, Woolworths introduced the Eco-Efficiency Awards for suppliers and became the first retailer in the world to recognize its suppliers for their contributions to environmental protection. The company had also committed to promoting organic farming and persuading conventional farmers to use more environmentally friendly methods, including assisting farmers to reduce their water, chemical, and fertilizer usage by 25 percent.

CONCLUSION

The response of civil organizations to Woolworths' efforts thus far has been positive. Among the awards that it received was being named the 2008 International Responsible Retailer of the Year at the World Retail Awards. In winning this award, Woolworths had beaten both Sainsbury's and Tesco, two of the United Kingdom's largest grocery retailers, which were regarded as industry leaders with comprehensive corporate social responsibility and sustainability plans. The judges said, "By taking environmental concerns into the core of its business, the company captures the definition of this category, using innovative environmental strategies to improve business performance."

Smith knew that, for Woolworths to keep its public support, the company had to push the values of the GBJ hard and that now, more than ever, Woolworths could not be seen to be backing away from its stated sustainability targets or making too many adjustments to the original targets. With news on the economic front becoming increasingly gloomy and an escalating "price war" between the large retailers, how would Smith continue to ensure that the far-reaching sustainability goals of the GBJ were achieved in less than three years?[1]

Source: The case was written by John Luiz and is based upon a Wits Business School case of the same name that was originally prepared by Amanda Bowen and John Luiz.

Case Review Note

Introduction

As we learned in Chapter 1, there are three major criticisms of the globalization of business: threats to national sovereignty, growth and environmental stress, and growing income inequality and personal stress. There are many ways to engage in international business, but the greatest impact that MNEs have on host countries involves strategies of foreign direct investment (FDI). MNEs are constantly confronted with questions issuing from this set of criticisms and must answer for the effects of their activities, in both the home and the host country.

Government policies can either encourage or restrict FDI. In most respects, this ambiguity isn't hard to understand. Every country can use the money that comes with FDI, but many worry that the global orientation of the MNE may render it insensitive to local interests and concerns.

Likewise, although not all MNEs are huge, many of them are indeed immense, and sheer size bothers a lot of countries. Let's face it: If you're a country doing business with an MNE whose sales exceed your GDP, you have a right to worry about potential imbalance in the relationship. And make no mistake about it: Colossal MNEs wield considerable power in negotiating business arrangements with small governments; and in bargaining over the terms under which they'll operate in a foreign jurisdiction, top MNE executives often expect to deal directly with heads of state.

Not surprisingly, then, various groups in the host country (as well as in the home country) frequently pressure governments to adopt policies that regulate the activities of MNEs. Growth in worldwide FDI makes it likely that such groups will monitor MNEs even more closely in the future.

In this chapter, we analyze the impact of FDI on both home and host countries and then examine a series of issues pertaining to the social responsibilities of MNEs whose strategies include penetrating foreign markets or sourcing merchandise from abroad.

Concept Check

A definition refresher: In Chapter 1, we define a **multinational enterprise (MNE)** as a company with a worldwide approach to markets and production or one with operations in more than one country. In the same chapter, we define **foreign direct investment (FDI)** as a form of investment that gives the investor a controlling interest in a foreign company.

Concept Check

In Chapter 4, we observe that a country's economic policies are among the leading indicators of its government's goals, its planned use of economic tools, and any projected market reforms; we also point out that, because changes in policy can strengthen a rival's competitiveness, companies need to monitor policy changes in countries where industry rivals do business.

Evaluating the Impact of FDI

Foreign direct investment (FDI) was an important source of economic growth prior to the global economic crisis that began with the collapse of the housing market in the United States in 2007, gained speed with the downfall of banks and financial markets worldwide in 2008, and quickly spread to the broader global economy by the end of 2008 and into 2009. In fact, FDI flows rose steadily for over 30 years, with a few exceptions where flows slowed down. Prior to the current crisis, the most recent downturn occurred after the September 11, 2001, attack on the World Trade Center in New York City. During that period of steady growth, the stock of FDI rose tenfold to $12 trillion, three-fourths of which was hosted by the developed countries.[2] The United States was the largest host country of FDI, whereas the European Union was the largest host region. However, developing countries were already beginning to attract a larger percentage of FDI inflows as well as supplying FDI outflows. In particular, China rose in importance as a major exporter of capital as Chinese firms expanded abroad in acquiring natural resources, manufacturing sites, and services.

However, the global economic crisis resulted in a significant drop in FDI in 2008, extending into 2009. The drop in corporate profits, shortage of financial resources, instability in the global economy—including emerging markets—and drop in demand worldwide caused many traditional MNEs to stop and in some cases reverse their FDI decisions. Pressure groups pushed to restrict the activities of MNEs at home and abroad. Global FDI inflows were expected to fall from $1.7 trillion in 2008 to below $1.2 trillion in 2009 with a slow recovery in 2010.[3] The drop in FDI was initially more severe in the developed countries—25 percent compared to 2007—but FDI in the developing countries was expected to drop more significantly in 2009. An interesting note is that outward FDI from China continued to rise in 2008 and 2009.[4]

Although some countries respond with suspicion to FDI and any potential strings with which it may come attached, other countries, such as Vietnam, have eagerly replaced obstacles with incentives. One reason for Vietnam's continued success, even in the face of the global recession, is that its economy has been less reliant on exports compared with neighboring Thailand, so the collapse in export markets worldwide has allowed Vietnam to capitalize on its growing domestic market and therefore attract FDI to service the local economy. In addition, Chinese companies, which have seen their manufacturing costs rise, are now investing heavily in Vietnam to take advantage of lower wage rates and overall costs. The growing prevalence of FDI requires a better understanding of the views of home and host countries.

Prior to the global economic crisis, both developing and industrialized countries deregulated markets, privatized national enterprises, liberalized private ownership, and encouraged regional integration in an effort to create more favorable climates for foreign investment. However, the crisis caused major changes in government/business relationships, as illustrated by the rise in government ownership in autos and banking in the United States. The U.S. government even pushed aggressively for a partnership between Italian automaker Fiat and U.S.-based Chrysler in order to save Chrysler, thus actively encouraging FDI. The result, as you can see from Figure 5.1, is the emergence of FDI as a major contributor to global growth and development, spreading the benefits of capital, technology, management expertise, jobs, and wealth to just about every corner of the world. However, there is constant tension between the efforts of MNEs to demonstrate what they have to offer in order to reduce barriers to FDI and the efforts of home and host governments to restrict, control, and possibly attract FDI in order to achieve national objectives and priorities.

CONSIDERING THE LOGIC OF FDI

According to the eclectic paradigm of international production, there are three conditions that help explain the foreign production decision: ownership advantages of MNEs that

FIGURE 5.1 What MNEs Have to Offer

Their sheer size means that many MNEs have vast stores of resources in several areas that can be applied to the pursuit of a host country's economic and social objectives. Critics, however, wonder if these assets are always adequately applied to the economic and social tasks at hand.

Source: Adapted from *World Investment Report 1992: Transnational Corporations: Engines of Growth: An Executive Summary* by Transnational Corporations and Management Division © 1992. United Nations. Reprinted with permission of the publisher.

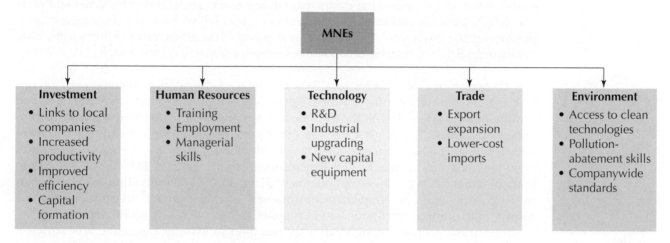

give them an advantage over companies in the host countries, location-specific advantages of the host country that make them attractive locations for FDI, and internalization advantages for the MNEs to utilize their specific ownership advantages rather than sell or license them for outsiders to exploit.[5] Figure 5.1 identifies some of the ownership-specific advantages of the MNE. In addition to the decision from the standpoint of the MNE, it is important to have an understanding of why, under varying circumstances, countries may react to FDI in a spirit of opposition, suspicion, or cooperation. This means that we must examine the relationship between two factors:

- The decisions of those who make foreign investments (typically, MNEs)
- Their possible effects on the countries on the receiving end of FDI

To get a better understanding of the various ways in which this relationship can affect FDI activities, we look at three areas in which we can see it at work and in which we can assess its effects: *stakeholder trade-offs, cause-and-effect relationships,* and *individual and aggregate effects.* As you'll see, in each of these areas we also encounter certain typical pitfalls in logic that we need to be aware of when we're trying to assess the outcomes of this relationship.

Stakeholder Trade-Offs To prosper (indeed, to survive), a company must satisfy different groups of **stakeholders** including shareholders, employees, customers, suppliers, and society at large. Obviously, this juggling act is often quite tricky. The stockholder–versus-stakeholder dilemma pits the demands of one stakeholder—the stockholder—against all the other stakeholders. The basic idea of focusing on stakeholders more broadly is that companies are able to take into consideration various socially important stakeholders as they make decisions.[6] In the short term, for example, group aims often conflict. *Stockholders* want additional sales and increased productivity (which result in higher profits and returns). *Employees* want safer workplaces and higher compensation. *Customers* want higher-quality products at lower prices. *Society* would like to see more jobs, increased corporate taxes, more corporate support for social services, and more trustworthy behavior on the part of corporate executives.

In the *long* term, all of these aims must be adequately met. If they aren't, there's a good chance that none of them will, especially if each stakeholder group is powerful enough to bring operations to a standstill. In addition, as we've already suggested, pressure

Companies must satisfy
- Shareholders.
- Employees.
- Customers.
- Society.

Case Review Note

groups—which may reflect the interests of any stakeholder group—lobby governments to regulate MNE activities both at home and abroad.

As we noted in our opening case, for example, the Woolworths *Good Business Journey* has generated pressure from various constituencies, including clients and shareholders concerned about profitability, governments concerned with drafting regulations; employees concerned about changes in the company's strategies and goals; and environmental lobbyists, NGOs (Non-Governmental Organizations), and fellow businesses concerned with preserving the environment. Each of these groups has a powerful influence on how Woolworths SA does business and on how successful it is in the marketplace.

The Question of Cause-and-Effect Relationships   Let's say that, when a decision has been made, two factors (for example, level of unemployment and level of FDI) are simultaneously affected, with the two effects reflecting an apparently predictable pattern (when one, for example, goes up, the other goes up). Can we conclude that they're interdependent? Not necessarily. A simultaneous rise in a nation's overall unemployment and a rise in FDI doesn't mean that increased FDI *caused* the rise in unemployment. Nevertheless, opponents of FDI persist in trying to link MNE activities to such problems in recipient countries as unemployment, inequitable income distribution, political corruption, environmental debasement, and social deprivation.[7]

| It is hard to determine whether the actions of MNEs cause societal conditions.

In contrast, proponents of MNE activities tend to assume a positive link between those activities and such effects in recipient countries as higher tax revenues, increased levels of employment and exports, and greater innovation. As a rule, both sides are more active during periods in which a local government is considering proposals either to restrict or to encourage FDI. In many cases, both groups present accurate and convincing data in support of their claims, but we're still faced with a problem: Our input is always incomplete because we can never know what would have happened had an MNE made a different decision—had located elsewhere, for instance, or instituted different practices.

Individual and Aggregate Effects   MNEs, according to one astute observer, are like animals in a zoo: "Multinationals (and their affiliates) come in various shapes and sizes, perform distinctive functions, behave differently, and make their individual impacts on the environment."[8] Obviously, then, it doesn't make much sense to fall back on generalizations about the investment activities of MNEs and their effects on the nations in which they choose to invest.

| The philosophy, actions, and goals of each MNE are unique.

Some countries evaluate MNEs and their activities on individual or case-by-case bases. Granted, this approach may foster greater fairness and tighter control, but it's time consuming and costly. Other nations, therefore, prefer to apply the same policies and control mechanisms to all MNEs, even though this approach risks missing some good opportunities while steering clear of dubious ones. Moreover, it's hard to choose between these two approaches because the governments that have applied one or the other have been far from perfect in predicting the future impact of FDI activities in their jurisdictions.

The Economic Impact of the MNE

MNEs may affect many facets of a country's economy. In this section, we will examine trade and capital flows that result from FDI, followed by a discussion of the growth and employment effects of FDI. Under different conditions, these effects may be positive or negative, for either the host country or the home country. In addition, the same can be said for the impact of foreign investment on MNEs themselves.

| The effect of an individual FDI may be positive or negative.

Although our discussion centers more on the impact of foreign direct investment (and of certain other entry modes) on home and host countries, it's important to realize that such activity is also strategically important to MNEs themselves. In addition, potential gains to host countries go up as local environments become more attractive for FDI.

BALANCE-OF-PAYMENTS EFFECTS

Why do countries want capital inflows? Because such inflows give them the foreign exchange they need to import goods and services and to pay off foreign debt. Remember, however, that FDI brings both capital inflows and capital outflows. Many countries, therefore, are concerned about the net **balance-of-payments effect** and about the possibility that, when the books are ultimately balanced, the effect of FDI on their net balance of payments may be negative.

Effect of Individual FDI   To better appreciate why countries must evaluate the effect of each investment on their balance of payments, we can examine two extreme hypothetical scenarios reflecting the effects of FDI on a nation's balance of payments.

- *Scenario 1:* Depositing funds in a Bermudan bank, a Mexican MNE makes an FDI when purchasing a Haitian-owned company. Because the MNE makes no changes in management, capitalization, or operations, profitability remains the same. Dividends, however, now go to the foreign owners rather than remaining in Haiti. There is thus a drain on Haiti's foreign exchange and a corresponding inflow to Mexico.

- *Scenario 2:* A Mexican MNE purchases idle resources (land, labor, materials, equipment) in Haiti and converts them to the production of formerly imported goods. Rising consumer demand leads the MNE to reinvest its profits in Haiti, where the import substitution increases the host country's foreign-exchange reserves.

Most FDI falls somewhere between these two extreme examples. That's why they're hard to evaluate, particularly when policymakers try to apply regulations to all in-bound investments. There is, however, a basic equation for analyzing the effect of FDI on a host country's balance of payments:

$$B = (m - m_1) + (x - x_1) + (c - c_1)$$

where

B = balance-of-payments effect

m = import displacement

m_1 = import stimulus

x = export stimulus

x_1 = export reduction

c = capital inflow for other than import and export payment

c_1 = capital outflow for other than import and export payment

Calculating Net Import Effect   Now, even though the equation itself is pretty straightforward, determining the *value for each variable* can be a challenge. Let's try our hand at it by evaluating the effect of the decision to locate a Toyota automobile plant in Brazil—an instance of FDI by a Japanese MNE. First, to calculate the *net import effect* $(m - m_1)$, we need to know *how much Brazil would import if the Toyota plant were not built.*

We must, of course, consider the amount that Toyota makes and sells in Brazil, but that would be only a rough indication of how much Brazil would import. Why? Because the selling price and product characteristics of the Brazilian-made cars may differ from those of the cars that Brazil would otherwise import from Japan. Moreover, sales of the Brazilian-made Toyota cars may come at the expense either of cars from other plants in Brazil or of imported foreign cars other than Toyotas. Note, too, that by definition, the value of m_1 should include the equipment, components, and materials brought by Toyota

Concept Check

Recall that in Chapter 4 we examine the ***balance-of-payments effect*** from the perspective of companies looking to invest in foreign countries. Ironically, because its own actions influence a host country's **balance of payments,** a firm doing business overseas is well advised to monitor that country's balance of payments, being particularly on the lookout for developments that could prompt a government to take actions intended to correct an imbalance.

The formula to determine the balance-of-payments effect is simple, but the data used must be estimated and are subject to assumptions.

On the import side, the balance-of-payments effect is positive if the FDI results in a substitution for imports and negative if it results in an increase in imports.

into Brazil. Remember, for example, that Toyota buys a lot of parts from suppliers that may import them from other countries.

Finally, the value of m_1 should also include estimates of the increase in Brazilian imports due to increases in national income caused by the capital inflow from Japan. Assume, for instance, that, because of the Toyota investment, Brazilian national income rises R$50 million (50 million reals). At this point, we have to consult the *marginal propensity to import principle,* which defines the fraction of a change in imports due to a change in income and states that the recipients of that income will spend some portion of it on imports. If we calculate this portion as 10 percent, imports should rise by R$5 million (that is, 10 percent of R$50 million).

On the export side, the balance-of-payments effect is positive if the FDI results in generating exports in the host country and negative if it produces only for the local market and stops exports.

The net export effect is the *export stimulus* minus the *export reduction* ($x - x_1$), but bear in mind that this figure is particularly controversial. Why? Because different evaluators, starting out with different assumptions, regularly arrive at widely varying conclusions. Let's go back to our Toyota example. In this case, we can make the assumption that the Brazilian plant merely substitutes for imports from and production in Japan. If in fact we proceed on this assumption, we get *no net export effect* for Brazil. For Japan, we arrive at a *negative net export effect* because of Toyota's export reduction (it's now selling cars made in Brazil to Brazilian consumers instead of exporting Japanese-made cars to Brazil). Toyota, however, might well defend itself on the grounds that its move abroad is (largely) defensive. How so? Under this assumption, Toyota can argue that it is capturing sales that would otherwise go to non-Japanese carmakers in Brazil. In that case, Toyota's export reduction from Japan amounts only to the *export replacement* (loss) resulting from the decision to build a production plant in Brazil.

In some cases, MNEs have argued that their overseas investments stimulate home-country exports of complementary products (say, in Toyota's case, auto parts) that they can sell in host countries through foreign-owned facilities.

The balance-of-payments effects of FDI are usually

- Positive for the host country initially and negative for the home country.
- Positive for the home country and negative to the host country later.

Calculating Net Capital Flow *Net capital flow* ($c - c_1$) is the easiest figure to calculate because of controls maintained by most central banks. There are, however, a few sticking points. Basing your evaluation on a given year for evaluation is problematic because there's a time lag between a company's outward flow of investment funds and the inward flow of remitted earnings. Because companies eventually plan to take out more capital than they originally put in, what appears at a given time to be a favorable (or unfavorable) capital flow may prove, over a longer period, to be the opposite. The time it takes Toyota to recoup its capital outflow to Brazil depends on such factors as the need to reinvest funds in Brazil, the ability to borrow locally (estimates of future exchange rates), and rules on the repatriation of capital.

As a rule, MNE investments are initially favorable to the host country and unfavorable to the home country. After some time, however, the situation usually reverses.[9] Why? Because nearly all foreign investors plan eventually to have their subsidiaries remit dividends back to the parent company in excess of the amount they sent abroad. If the net value of the FDI continues to grow through retained earnings, dividend payments for a given year may ultimately exceed the total amount of capital transfers comprising the initial investment.

GROWTH AND EMPLOYMENT EFFECTS

Growth and employment effects are not a zero-sum game because MNEs may use resources that were unemployed or underemployed.

In contrast to balance-of-payments effects, MNE effects on growth and employment don't necessarily amount to *zero-sum games* (games in which gains must equal losses) between home and host countries. Classical economists assumed that production factors were always at full employment; consequently, any movement of any of these factors from home to abroad would result in an increase in foreign output abroad and a decrease in domestic output. Even if this assumption were realistic, it's still possible that gains in the host country will be greater or less than the losses in the home country.

The argument that both home and host countries may gain from FDI rests on two assumptions:

1. Resources aren't necessarily being fully employed.
2. Capital and technology can't easily be transferred from one industry to another.

Let's say, for example, that a soft-drink maker is producing at maximum capacity for the domestic market but is limited (say, by high transportation costs) in generating export sales. In addition, moving into other product lines or using its financial resources to increase domestic productivity aren't viable options.

But what about setting up a foreign production facility? This move is appealing because it would allow the company to develop foreign sales without reducing resource employment in its home market. In fact, the company may wind up hiring additional domestic managers to oversee international operations; perhaps it will also end up earning dividends and royalties from the foreign use of its capital, brand, and technology.

Ultimately, the argument cuts two ways: Although stakeholders in both home and host countries may gain from FDI, some observers maintain that stakeholders in one country or the other are destined to end up with the short end of the economic stick. In the following sections, we look at some of the arguments advanced to support this position.

Home-Country Losses

In recent years, many U.S. and European garment manufacturers have moved production operations to low-wage countries to realize cost advantages.

In the process, they've shut down—or at least declined to expand—home-country operations. Thus overseas FDI in the garment-making industry has resulted in a loss of jobs in home countries while creating jobs abroad. The situation may be unfortunate, but the fact that it did come about may mean it was inevitable. In the absence of serious protection, argue some experts, home-country operations would have closed down because of competition from abroad, and jobs would have been lost anyway.

> Home-country labor claims that jobs are exported through FDI.

Host-Country Gains

Conversely, of course, host countries gain through the transfer of capital and technology. If that capital is used to acquire host-country operations that are going out of business, then the foreign investor may very well save host-country jobs and, through the import of technology and managerial ability, even create new jobs. In 2009, for example, Italian automaker Fiat purchased the bulk of the assets of U.S. automaker Chrysler, saving it from liquidation. The gain to the United States is the survival of Chrysler and the infusion of technology from Fiat.

In many cases, FDI provides foreign firms with increased capacity or enhanced capabilities. In China, for instance, foreign investors have done so much to improve the capabilities of Chinese automakers that China is now beginning to export cars. Sometimes, however, local politics can complicate FDI and compromise its potential advantages.

A case in point is the South American nation of Venezuela, which decided for such U.S. companies as ExxonMobil Corp. and Chevron Corp. as well as British-owned BP PLC to reduce the ownership of operations in Venezuela and give more control to the Venezuelan government as part of a program to assume more control over its valuable oil fields. In the process, Venezuelan officials exposed certain deficiencies in the capabilities of the domestic industry: They had sacrificed the expertise they needed to develop their own crude-oil resources. Ultimately, to retain access to needed management experience and process technologies, the Venezuelan government had to ask expelled foreign companies to maintain minority shares in local ventures.[10] Soon after that, many of the

> Host countries may gain from FDI through
>
> - More optimal use of production factors.
> - The use of unemployed resources.
> - The upgrading of resource quality.

foreign companies pulled out of the country completely. In the wake of plummeting oil prices in 2008, Venezuela recognized that it needed the money and expertise from these multinational companies.[11]

Host-Country Losses   Critics, however, contend that MNEs often make investments that domestic companies could otherwise make, thereby locking out local entrepreneurs. Likewise, they say, foreign investors often bid up prices when competing with local companies for labor and other resources.

Critics also claim that FDI destroys local entrepreneurship in ways that affect national development. Because entrepreneurs are inspired by the reasonable expectation of success, the collapse in several countries of small cottage industries, especially in the face of MNE efforts to consolidate local operations, may have played a role in undermining the competitive confidence of local businesspeople.

Not everyone, of course, accepts this claim.[12] The presence of MNEs, say pro-MNE analysts, may actually increase the number of local companies operating in host-country markets. How? By serving as role models for local talent to emulate. Avid entrepreneurs, they add, will regard MNEs not as obstacles but as challenges.

The Foundations of Ethical Behavior

In addition to worrying about balance of payments, growth, and employment, MNEs—regardless of how they enter a foreign business environment—must act *responsibly* wherever they go. In this section, we concentrate on the cultural and legal foundations of ethical behavior and then look at some specific examples of the sorts of ethical dilemmas faced by globalizing companies.

WHY DO COMPANIES CARE ABOUT ETHICAL BEHAVIOR?

First, however, let's take a brief look at a preliminary but fairly important question: Why should companies worry about ethical behavior at all? As we discuss later, there are cultural and legal reasons to behave ethically. Also, individuals may have high standards of ethical behavior that can be translated into company policy. Here's one way to look at this question. From a business standpoint, ethical behavior can be instrumental in achieving one or both of two possible objectives:

1. To develop competitive advantage
2. To avoid being perceived as irresponsible

As for the first objective, some analysts argue that responsible behavior contributes to strategic and financial success because it fosters trust, which, in turn, encourages commitment.[13] As we indicate in our opening case, for instance, Woolworths *Good Business Journey* reflects the belief of top managers that by proactively responding to social concerns about global warming, Woolworths can gain a strategic advantage over competitors; in particular, the company hopes to develop an edge in emerging markets facing severe environmental problems.

As for the second objective, companies are aware that more and more nongovernmental organizations are becoming active in monitoring—and publicizing—international corporate practices. The Interfaith Center on Corporate Responsibility (ICCR), for example, is an NGO that represents about 275 faith-based institutional investors, including national denominations, religious communities, pension funds, foundations, hospital corporations, economic development funds, asset management companies, colleges, and unions.[14] Initially organized to protest the policies of apartheid in South Africa, ICCR has gotten involved in a number of different projects. On its

Case Review Note

Web site, for example, it ranks companies in different industry sectors according to their carbon emissions. In 2009, it ranked Coca-Cola Enterprises Inc. as being below average in carbon emissions compared with other food and beverage companies while at the same time introducing a resolution at the annual shareholders' meeting to adopt principles for health-care reform.

THE CULTURAL FOUNDATIONS OF ETHICAL BEHAVIOR

During the early part of the twenty-first century, several U.S. companies faced severe financial problems and even dissolution because of their managers' unethical or illegal actions. Some of these companies hid their illicit actions for a number of years through their international operations. The upshot of these revelations included public outrage, investor anxiety, and, in general, a heightened interest in the activities of companies and the people who run them. (See Figure 5.2.)

> Values differ from country to country and sometimes between employees and companies.

Relativism versus Normativism Today, just about everyone agrees that the actions in question were wrong (although a couple of defendants still argue otherwise), and, indeed, there's almost universal agreement on what's right and wrong when it comes to ethical and socially responsible behavior in business.[15] In the real world, however, managers face many situations in which the difference between right and wrong is less than crystal clear. For one thing, people have different ideas about right and wrong. Beliefs about what's right and wrong are influenced by family and religious values, laws and social pressures, our own observations and experiences, and even our economic circumstances. Because ethical convictions tend to be deep seated, people tend to be avid in defending their views.

In addition, even within a given country there are starkly contrasting views on ethical matters; and to complicate things even more, our own personal values may differ from our employers' policies, from prevalent social norms, or both. Finally, everything that complicates dilemmas in the domestic business environment tends to complicate them even further in the international environment.

Relativism On the one hand, **relativism** holds that ethical truths depend on the values of a particular society and may vary from one society or country to another.[16] Relativism also implies that it would not be appropriate to inject or enforce one's ethical values on another. One thing to remember is the fact that the idea of accepting or adopting alien

> Relativism: Ethical truths depend on the groups holding them.

"Miss Dugan, will you send someone in here who can distinguish right from wrong?"

FIGURE 5.2 No Ethics for Old Men

Sometimes businesspeople face ethical dilemmas: They must consider cultural, moral, legal, and political factors in choosing between acceptable but opposing alternatives. On the other hand, of course, there are questions of right versus wrong—whether or not to do something that's unethical or downright illegal.

Source: The New Yorker, Dana Fradon, Cartoonbank.com (March 24, 1975).

cultural values is a uniquely Western notion—one that goes back at least as far as St. Ambrose's fourth-century suggestion that "When in Rome, do as the Romans do."

Normativism   **Normativism,** on the other hand, holds that there are indeed universal standards of behavior, which, although influenced differently by different cultural values, should be accepted by people everywhere. From this perspective, *nonintervention* is unethical. Not surprisingly, then, global firms are always struggling with the problem of how to implement their own ethical principles in foreign business environments: Should they consider their principles as reflections of universally valid "truths" (the normative approach), or should they be willing to adapt to local conditions on the assumption that every place has its own "truths" and needs to be treated differently (the relative approach)?

Walking the Fine Line between Relativism and Normativism   Often, a company faces certain pressures to opt for relativism—to comply with local norms. Such pressures may take the form of laws that permit—or even require—only certain practices that grant competitive advantages to firms accepting local norms or throw up roadblocks in front of companies that try to impose home-country practices in the local arena. Conversely, firms may face certain pressures *not* to comply. These pressures can come from the company's own internal values, from its home-country government, or even from constituencies that threaten retaliatory action if it buckles under to objectionable foreign practices.

Many individuals and organizations have laid out minimum levels of business practices that they say a company (domestic or foreign) must follow regardless of the legal requirements or ethical norms prevalent where it operates.[17]

One could consider this as behavior based on principles of honesty and fairness, or what can be called "ordinary decency."[18] Many argue that legal permission for some action may be given by uneducated or corrupt leaders who either do not understand or do not care about the consequences. They further argue that MNEs are obligated to set good examples that may become the standard for responsible behavior.

Negotiating between Evils   Another potential complication derives from the fact that both societies and companies must often choose between the lesser of two evils. Consider the following illustration. As most of us know by now, the pesticide DDT is dangerous to the environment (especially to birds), and high-income countries have banned its use. At the same time, companies headquartered in those countries have subsequently been chided for selling DDT to lower-income countries that need it to fight malaria, one of the world's worst diseases.[19]

THE LEGAL FOUNDATIONS OF ETHICAL BEHAVIOR

Dealing with *ethical dilemmas* is often a balancing act: a problem of balancing *means* (the actions we take and which may be right or wrong) and *ends* (the results of our actions, which may also be right or wrong). Ethics teaches that "people have a responsibility to do what is right and to avoid doing what is wrong."[20] Now, as we've already seen, proponents of cultural relativism suggest that there are no universally reliable standards for deciding whether any behavior is ever appropriate. In this book, however, we're going to take up the position that it is indeed possible to judge whether behavior is appropriate. For one thing, we must point out that individuals tend to seek justification for their behavior and, in so doing, raise issues concerning both cultural values (many of which are universal) and principles sanctioned by the legal system.

Legal Justification: Pro and Con   Indeed, some experts suggest that legal justification for ethical behavior is the only important standard. According to this theory, an individual or company can do anything that isn't illegal. Opponents respond that there are five good reasons why this is inadequate:

1. Because some things that are *unethical* are not *illegal,* the law is not an appropriate standard for regulating *all* business activity. Some forms of interpersonal behavior, for example, can clearly be wrong even if they're not against the law.

2. The law is slow to develop in emerging areas of concern. It takes time to legislate laws and test them in courts. Moreover, because laws are essentially responses to issues that have already surfaced, they can't always anticipate dilemmas that will arise in the future. Countries with well-developed systems of civil law rely on specificity in the law, and it isn't feasible to enact laws dealing with every possible ethical issue.

3. The law is often based on imprecisely defined moral concepts that can't be separated from the legal concepts they underpin. In other words, we must in any case consider moral concepts whenever we're considering legal ones.

4. The law often needs to undergo scrutiny by the courts. This is especially true of case law, in which the courts create law by establishing precedent.

5. The law simply isn't very efficient. "Efficiency" in this case implies achieving ethical behavior at a very low cost, and it would be impossible to solve every ethical behavioral problem with an applicable law.[21]

Unfortunately, things aren't that simple. Proponents of the legal-justification standard reply that there are also several good reasons for complying with it:

1. Because the law embodies many of a country's moral principles, it is in fact an adequate guide for proper conduct.

2. The law provides a clearly defined set of rules, and following it at least establishes a good precedent for acceptable behavior.

3. The law contains enforceable rules that apply to everyone.

4. Because the law represents a consensus derived from widely shared experience and deliberation, it reflects careful and wide-ranging discussions.[22]

Extraterritoriality When, however, you're trying to use the law to govern behavior in different countries, you'll soon run into a very basic problem—namely, the fact that laws vary from country to country. Recall, for instance, the challenges faced by Woolworths (described in the opening case), given its operations in several markets throughout Africa and the Middle East and having to deal with international variations in environmental laws. It may actually be in its interest to lobby governments in other countries to raise their environmental laws to a common international standard to ensure that it can develop a more uniform strategy and thereby lower transaction costs.

Interestingly, this brings us directly back to the relationship between ethics and moral concepts: Laws vary from country to country because moral values vary from country to country. In addition, strong home-country governments may adopt a practice known as **extraterritoriality:** That is, they may impose domestic legal and ethical practices on the foreign subsidiaries of companies headquartered in their jurisdictions. This has become very controversial and, as argued by some, inconsistent with increased globalization and the need to collaborate across national boundaries.[23]

Ethics and Corporate Bribery

Granted, we've gone from con to pro and back again in our introduction to the relationship between ethics and the law. Nevertheless, let's return once more to a pro-law argument. Why? Because despite all the problems that arise, considering the law is still a good place to

Concept Check

Note that in Chapter 3 we define a country's *legal system* as the fundamental institution that creates a comprehensive legal network to regulate social interaction; its purpose is to stabilize political and social environments as well as to ensure a fair, safe, and efficient business environment.

Concept Check

Recall our explanation in Chapter 3 of a *civil law system* as one based on a systematic and extensive codification of laws.

Legal justification for ethical behavior may not be sufficient because not everything that is unethical is illegal.

The law is a good basis for ethical behavior because it embodies local cultural values.

As countries tackle similar ethical issues, laws will become more similar.

Case Review Note

Concept Check

As we explain in Chapter 3, the continued democratization of countries has led to the diffusion of the rule of law in place of the rule of man, which is more symbolic of totalitarian regimes. However, the global economic crisis may have slowed that process for a while.

Corruption can have tragic consequences. Supporters of late former South Korean president Roh Moo-Hyun—who leapt off a cliff to his death while facing corruption allegations—hold a candlelight vigil during a demonstration in Seoul on May 30, 2009. The protestors staged the demonstration against the current conservative government, saying authorities incited state prosecutors to launch a probe against the ex-leader—a claim the government denies.
Source: PHILIPPE LOPEZ/AFP/ Getty Images

start when studying ethics. The reason shouldn't be surprising: As countries find themselves searching for common solutions to common problems (problems like the ones we discuss in the following sections), they find themselves taking common legal steps. In addition, in the effort to tackle important problems, they encounter certain **externalities** that must be solved in the public arena—certain by-products of activities that affect the well-being of people or the health of the environment even if those effects don't show up in market prices.

Now that we've discussed the cultural and legal foundations of ethical behavior—and have some tools for assessing worldwide corporate behavior—we should be prepared to examine some key ethical issues that companies must confront in doing business in foreign countries.

CORRUPTION AND BRIBERY

The first of these issues is *bribery*, which is actually one facet of the much bigger issue of *corruption*. The multifaceted determinants of corruption include cultural, legal, and political forces.[24] Corruption, as defined by Transparency International, is "the misuse of entrusted power for private gain."[25] There are some variations on this basic definition, but it is as good as any. In spite of the broader concept of corruption, we'll focus more on bribery in this chapter, because it is at the heart of corrupt behavior on the part of MNEs.

Congressional investigations of U.S. MNEs in the 1970s yielded anecdotal information indicating that questionable payments to foreign government officials by U.S. firms had long been business as usual in both industrial and developing countries. How much money was involved, both in payouts from U.S. MNEs and from those based in other countries? At that time, it was reported that 400 corporations had admitted making questionable or illegal payments in excess of $300 million.

Bribery of public officials takes place to obtain government contracts or to get officials to do what they should be doing anyway.

In comparison, the U.S. government reported that, between 1994 and 2001, it learned of cases in which foreign firms from more than 50 countries offered bribes to buyers in more than 100 countries; these cases involved more than 400 competitions for contracts valued at $200 billion.[26] It may be impossible to assess the true value of bribery, but it is huge.

Figure 5.3 also offers some interesting insight into the perceived levels of public-sector corruption, identifying how likely companies are to make bribes in the countries listed. Although it is true that no country is free of corruption, it is obvious that corruption is higher in countries that are also high in poverty. In addition, it is important to note that corruption requires someone to give a bribe in order for someone to take a bribe, and intermediaries, from bankers to accountants, are also necessary to facilitate the transactions. Thus

FIGURE 5.3   Where Bribes Are (and Are Not) Business as Usual

Transparency International asked country experts, nonresidents, and residents about the overall extent of corruption (frequency and/or size of bribes) in the public and private sectors. The scale runs from 0 to 10, with 10 least likely to pay a bribe. The figures include a sample of countries.

Source: Transparency International, "TI Corruption Perceptions Index" (2008), at http://transparency.org (accessed July 7, 2009).

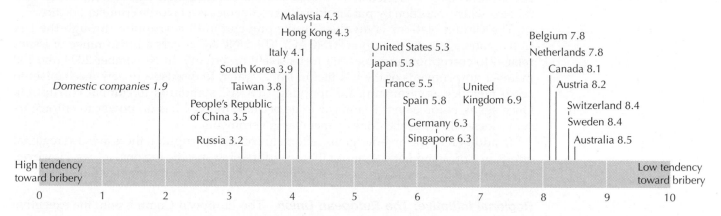

Transparency International not only publishes a Corruption Perceptions Index but also a Bribe Payers Index, which found in 2008 that individuals from Belgium and Canada were least likely to pay bribes; individuals from Russia, China, and Mexico were most likely to pay bribes; and the United States fit somewhere in between.[27]

The Consequences of Corruption   What's wrong with bribes? A number of things. First, bribery affects both the performance of companies and the economies of countries. Higher levels of corruption, for instance, correlate strongly with lower national growth rates and lower levels of per capita income.[28] Corruption can also erode the authority of governments that condone it. Over the years, bribery-based scandals have led to the downfall of numerous heads of state, many government officials have been jailed for accepting bribes, and numerous business executives and government officials have been forced to resign or have been fined or imprisoned. In an extreme case, China's former head of the State Food and Drug Administration—who was convicted of accepting bribes in return for approving certain medicines—was even executed.[29] Moreover, disclosures of corruption not only damage the reputations of companies and whole countries, but they also compromise the legitimacy of MNEs in the eyes of local and global communities.[30] Finally, corruption is expensive, inflating a company's costs and bloating its prices.

Bribes are payments or promises to pay cash or anything of value.

What's Being Done about Corruption?   Many efforts are currently under way to slow the pace of bribery as an international business practice at the global, regional, and national levels. Let's take a brief look at some of these accords. International multilateral accords for combating bribery at the global rather than regional level include those established by the OECD (Organization for Economic Cooperation and Development), the ICC (International Chamber of Commerce), and the United Nations through the UNCAC (United Nations Convention against Corruption).

   The OECD is comprised of 30 mostly high-income countries from around the world. The OECD Anti-Bribery Convention was signed in 1997 and went into effect in 1999. In addition to the 30 member countries, an additional eight countries had signed the Convention as of mid-2009. The convention establishes legally binding standards to criminalize bribery of foreign public officials in international business transactions and provides recommendations to the signatory countries. Of course, the member countries have to implement the recommendations into national law in order for them to have any weight. A study by Transparency International found that enforcement of the recommendations by member countries was uneven at best. In fact, they found that there was active enforcement by only four countries, with little or no enforcement by 21 countries.[31]

The ICC issued a code of rules against corrupt practices in 1999 and has since been active in supporting other multilateral approaches to combating bribery, including codes of conduct issued by the OECD and the United Nations (UN). Whereas the OECD Convention targets the supply side of companies bribing officials in the public sector, the ICC is particularly interested in the private sector and the demand side of cross-border economics, where extortion by public officials of companies is a favorite criminal practice.[32]

The United Nations is involved in the prevention of corruption through the UN Convention against Corruption (UNCAC). The UNCAC covers a broad range of issues related to corruption and does not focus solely on bribery. In November 2009, the 140 member governments of the UN met in Doha, Qatar, to discuss a review mechanism to see if member governments are applying UNCAC standards to combat corruption. Once again, enforcement is a major issue because the UN has no power to enforce its provisions—this must be done by member governments.

In addition to the broader global efforts to combat corruption, there are also regional efforts in Africa and Latin America that are addressing specific regional issues. However, the key is national legislation and enforcement. Changes in behavior take time.

Regional Initiative: The European Union   The European Commission, the executive branch of the EU, has an office of administrative affairs, audit, and antifraud that has ruled that companies found to have made bribes should not be allowed to bid for certain public contracts. However, there is not a uniformity and transparency of laws across the national members of the EU, and most antibribery provisions are left up to the member governments, who tend to be more strongly influenced by the OECD. Thus, regional approaches to antibribery are not considered very effective.

The Foreign Corrupt Practices Act is U.S. legislation that makes bribery illegal. It applies to domestic or foreign operations and to company employees as well as their agents overseas.

National Initiative: The U.S. Foreign Corrupt Practices Act   An example of a national approach is the **Foreign Corrupt Practices Act (FCPA)** in the United States. The FCPA outlaws bribery payments by U.S. firms to foreign officials, political parties, party officials, and political candidates. In 1998, FCPA coverage was extended to include bribery by foreign firms operating in U.S. territory. The FCPA applies not only to companies registered in the United States but also to any foreign company quoted on any stock exchange in the United States.

There's an apparent inconsistency in the provisions of the FCPA—namely the fact that although it's legal to make payments to officials to expedite otherwise legitimate transactions (officially called *facilitating payments* but sometimes referred to as *speed money* or *grease money*), they can't be made to officials who aren't directly responsible for the transactions in question. In 1988, an amendment to the FCPA actually excluded facilitating payments from the definition of *bribery*. Now, for example, payment to a customs official to clear legitimate merchandise is legal, whereas a payment to a government minister to influence a customs official is not. What's the difference? The FCPA allows payment in the former case because it recognizes that officials can delay legal transactions indefinitely or until they receive payments. However, sometimes behaviors that might be considered inappropriate by individuals in one country would be considered appropriate in another. In a survey of Chinese managers, it was found that gift giving is considered a normal part of the high-context Chinese culture and not a bribe, unless the gift is perceived as being so big that it results in contracts and favors in a business transaction.[33] The problem is in establishing the size of the gift. In 2007, the U.S. Justice Department levied a $2.5 million fine against U.S. telecommunications company Lucent Technologies Inc. for improperly recording millions of dollars in travel to Disney World and Las Vegas for about 1,000 Chinese employees of state-owned telecommunications companies.[34] Apparently, the Justice Department didn't consider the trips as mere gifts.

The U.S. government continues to step up anticorruption efforts both at home and abroad. In 2009, at least 120 companies were under investigation for violation of the FCPA as compared with only 100 at the end of 2008 and only 43 in 2007.[35] Additional legislation has been enacted since the FCPA that indirectly affects the crackdown on corporate bribery.

Most notable, perhaps, is the Sarbanes-Oxley Act (SOX). Passed in 2002, SOX was a response to an epidemic of well-known corporate scandals involving such companies as Enron and Tyco International. SOX toughened standards with regard to corporate governance, financial disclosure, and oversight of accounting and auditing practices. With the passage of SOX, the Justice Department began to use the FCPA more aggressively to combat bribery.

In addition to the U.S. government, other governments worldwide are starting to crack down harder on bribery. Although the European Union does not have an FCPA/SOX-type law against bribery, many European countries are starting to move more aggressively against bribery. Until recently, many European countries allowed companies to deduct commissions paid to win foreign contracts as tax-deductible expenses. However, France (in 2000) and Germany (in 2003) have now outlawed such practices, although Britain does not have a formal anticorruption law.[36]

> Sarbanes-Oxley legislation in the United States is helpful in combating corruption through more effective corporate governance, financial disclosure, and public accounting oversight.

Industry Initiatives Finally, various industries have recently stepped up their own efforts against bribery and corruption. In 2005, for example, in conjunction with the World Economic Forum, nearly 50 multinational construction and natural-resources companies, representing at least $300 billion in annual revenues, signed a "zero-tolerance" pact against extortion by bribery. By 2009, the number of signatory companies had risen to 140. This voluntary effort, called the Partnering Against Corruption Initiative (PACI), calls for member firms to set up "extensive internal programs to educate and oversee company officials and business partners and also [to] prohibit political contributions and charitable gifts designed to curry favor."[37] Although many firms still adhere to their own antibribery standards, participants hope that the PACI will encourage companies within the industry to monitor each other.

> A zero-tolerance pact against bribery was signed by companies at the 2005 World Economic Forum.

Relativism, the Rule of Law, and Responsibility Obviously, avoiding bribe payments when they're regarded as business as usual is a challenge, especially when business is being held up by foreign government officials. Although it might be easier to fall back on the standard of cultural *relativism* (and, say, simply pay bribes where they're accepted and/or expected), the international initiatives we've described in this section have made some headway in introducing the rule of law into more and more international business activity. Companies are now freer to establish policies and procedures that are consistent with both their own domestic laws and those of other countries. As the principles laid down by the OECD and the UN are incorporated into national statutes, companies are finding that laws and practices that once varied radically from country to country have become more uniform and easier to implement.

> **Concept Check**
>
> In Chapter 3, we explain how important it is for a nation's political process to generate rational laws that companies and individuals can follow. We also explain that, unfortunately, laws are based on cultural values that are bound to vary from country to country. Finally, we point out that laws, rational or otherwise, aren't necessarily enforced with the same rigor in every country.

Point ▷ Counterpoint

Are Top Managers Responsible When Corruption Is Afoot?

Point ▷ **Yes** Let's start by taking a trip back in time to the real world. In November 2006, German police raided the offices of the giant electrical engineering and electronics company Siemens AG. They netted nearly 36,000 documents to support allegations that Siemens regularly diverted funds filed under bogus consulting contracts into a network of "black accounts" for bribing officials in countries like Italy, Greece, Argentina, and Saudi Arabia where Siemens was seeking lucrative public-sector contracts. Following the raid, the company itself announced that it had uncovered over €420 million (U.S. $570 million) in suspicious payments going back as far as the early 1990s.

◁ **Counterpoint** **No** Granted, Siemens was up to its corporate neck in a culture of corruption. But is that fact supposed to excuse the actions of the individual grown-ups who were directly involved in the present case? Or, to put it in more legal-sounding, Latinate terms: Does it mitigate their culpability? At the end of the business day, the actions of individuals, more than the official codes and theoretical due diligence of top managers, actually shape a company's culture.

Even so, back when he was CEO, von Pierer not only authorized a strict company-wide code of conduct, but he also hired a few hundred compliance officers to enforce it.[44]

Several of the managers caught up in the probe insisted that corruption was endemic to the company's culture and that they had acted with the knowledge—and even the approval—of CEO Klaus Kleinfeld and board chief (and former CEO) Heinrich von Pierer.[38]

Now, nobody's going to deny that what Siemens employees did was misguided and wrongheaded, but let's be realistic: Step 1 in every textbook on foiling fraud is to *follow the money,* and in this case you can follow the money back to a culture that condones financial shenanigans. That means that the real blame for the company's current mess rests with top management.

Here's a little background on the business world in which Siemens is a leading corporate citizen. In comparison with some other countries (say, the United States), Germany was slow to enact laws prohibiting bribery. In fact, up until 1999, German law allowed you to write off overseas bribes as legitimate business expenses; and up until 2002, it was still legal to bribe employees of foreign companies if you were willing to absorb the cost without the tax break.[39] And even when the laws began to change, German businesses were slow to catch on. In 2005 alone, they racked up roughly 90,000 corporate crimes.[40]

The point? Like a lot of other companies in Germany, Siemens was hanging on to a corporate culture that was perfectly comfortable with bribery and other forms of corrupt behavior. One senior executive says that Siemens even had an encryption code for itemizing bribe payments. (If you're interested, it involved juggling letters standing for "make profit.") The same exec says that he himself got a call from a Saudi contractor demanding $910 million in commission payments or else he'd send a bunch of incriminating documents about Siemens's business practices to certain U.S. authorities. When he alerted his superiors—including Kleinfeld and von Pierer—they replied that $910 million was perhaps a little high but went on to suggest that a deal for $17 million in "past obligations" and $33 million in "hush money" wasn't beyond reason. According to this insider, most of his colleagues tossed off bribe payments as mere "peccadilloes" because, after all, "it was all for the good of the company."[41]

All of this transpired on the watches of von Pierer and Kleinfeld (who, by the way, was directly in charge of the telecommunications unit that handled most of the bribery). To say all of these goings-on completely escaped their notice is unrealistic. It's top management's responsibility to lay out the ethical boundaries at a company and to see that no one crosses them. Siemens management wasn't guarding its own ethical borders.

On top of everything else, Kleinfeld's "management style"—which boiled down to "fix, sell, or close"[42]—was hardly the right approach for a company that already had a dirty-tricks chapter in its playbook. Once he became CEO,

When his turn came, Kleinfeld instituted a "zero-tolerance" policy toward corruption.[45] But more importantly, in Siemens's case, in which you're talking about a far-flung, highly decentralized conglomeration with 11 business units run by separate boards as virtually independent operating entities, it's hardly reasonable to expect top executives back home in Munich to know everything that's going on from Siemens Turkey to Siemens Taiwan. Former CEO von Pierer is absolutely right in arguing that under such circumstances, "deducing a political responsibility" would be absurd. As most of us learned in business school, the job of senior executives is strategic planning; it doesn't involve auditing the books and double-checking every suspicious double entry.[46]

And while we're on the subject of top-level managers, it's true that a bunch of former employees who are in trouble with the law claim that top Siemens managers knew all about the bribery and other underhanded activities. So far, however, no one, including an independent law firm that's looking into the matter, has found any solid evidence that they're telling the truth. Plus, neither Kleinfeld nor von Pierer has been officially accused of any wrongdoing.

As for the question of whether dragging its governmental feet on antibribery legislation has anything to do with the resilience of corruption in Germany, there's little question that adapting to new laws may take some time (or that passing them may take a long time). But that doesn't justify breaking them until you're good and ready to obey them. Regardless of the *company's* approach to adapting to a new legal environment, those of its employees who perpetuated the practice of paying bribes fully understood what the law said and had to be fully aware that they were violating it. Besides, creating false consulting contracts and diverting company money into slush funds has come under the heading of legally dubious behavior for a long time and just about everywhere. Furthermore, no matter when a law goes into effect, it always comes with a pretty clear list of "do's and don'ts," and it's obvious that certain individuals at Siemens took it on themselves to ignore those guidelines.

Finally, what about the argument that employees had no choice but to violate the law because they had to protect their jobs? The fact that many of them now face criminal charges and jail time with no hope of continuing their careers at Siemens or anywhere else attests to the faulty logic of that claim. Meanwhile, their former employer, which is still responsible for nearly half a million paychecks worldwide, has already paid out €63 million ($85.7 million) to outside auditors and investigators and still faces a court-ordered fine of €38 million ($51.4 million) following the conviction of just one finance officer and one consultant.[47] By the end of 2008, U.S. and German authorities levied $1.6 billion in fines against Siemens. Why the United States? Because Siemens lists its stock in the United States

Kleinfeld immediately set high profit targets and started spinning off divisions that apparently weren't sufficiently inspired by the profit motive. His motto was "go for profit and growth," and when a team of managers failed to deliver, he just took an axe to the whole division. You did what you had to do to show a profit that satisfied Kleinfeld, or your whole division was out on the street.[43] Under top-down pressure like that, what other choice did anyone whose job depended on Kleinfeld really have? If the answer is "none," you have to admit that ultimate responsibility for company-wide behavior rests in the executive suite. ▶

and is therefore subject to the FCPA. Siemens also risks being banned from contract bidding in any one of the 190 countries where it does business and generates wealth. ◀

Ethics and the Environment

If for no other reason, environmental problems are important because they're a matter of life or death (either now or in the future). As we saw in our opening case, for example, Woolworths has come to see environmental responsibility as a matter of protecting not only the future of the environment but also the future of Woolworths itself. Like Woolworths, companies contribute to environmental damage in a variety of ways. Some, for example, endanger the environment by contaminating the air, soil, or water during manufacturing processes or by manufacturing products such as automobiles or electricity that release fossil-fuel contaminants into the environment.

In extracting natural resources, other companies also have a direct and unmistakable impact on the environment. But even in these cases, the issue isn't necessarily clear cut. Granted, although some resources (such as minerals and gas and oil) may not be renewable, others (such as timber) are, and some observers even suggest that resources can never really become scarce. Why? Because as they become less available, prices go up and technology or substitutes compensate for the scarcity.

Case Review Note

Companies that extract natural resources, generate air or water waste, or manufacture products such as autos that generate pollution need to be concerned with their environmental impact.

◀ Wind energy is truly a global business. Suzlon, headquartered in India and one of the world's leading suppliers of wind turbines, supplied these turbines to Wasatch Wind to construct a wind farm in Spanish Fork, Utah (USA). The farm harvests primarily the southeasterly nightly canyon wind resource considered to be one of the most reliable winds in the United States.

WHAT IS "SUSTAINABILITY"?

Sustainability involves meeting the needs of the present without compromising the ability of future generations to meet their own needs while taking into account what is best for the people and the environment.

Although there seems to be a lot of confusion and disagreement over the term, we will assume that **sustainability** means meeting the needs of the present without compromising the ability of future generations to meet their own needs. Proponents of the concept argue that sustainability considers what's best for both people and the environment. Nevertheless, it remains a controversial concept—one that's subject to different interpretations by environmentalists and businesspeople, neither of which groups can settle on their own definition of the term.[48] It is important, however, that, regardless of how they feel about the principle of sustainability, businesses that impact the environment establish policies for responsible behavior toward the environment—a responsibility that has both cultural and legal ramifications.

GLOBAL WARMING AND THE KYOTO PROTOCOL

Global warming results from the release of greenhouse gases that trap heat in the atmosphere rather than allowing it to escape.

To illustrate some of the challenges faced by these companies, we start by examining the issue of *global warming*, including the role of the *Kyoto Protocol* and its potential impact on corporate behavior.

The Kyoto Protocol was signed in 1997 to require countries to cut their greenhouse gas emissions to 5.2 percent below 1990 levels between 2008 and 2012. Some countries have adopted stricter requirements, and others, such as the United States, China, and India, have not ratified the Protocol.

The Kyoto Protocol   At the core of the international treaty called the Kyoto Protocol is the theory that global warming is a result of an increase in carbon dioxide and other gases that act like the roof of a greenhouse, trapping heat that would normally be radiated back into space and warming the planet. If carbon dioxide emissions aren't reduced and controlled, rising temperatures could have catastrophic consequences, including the melting of the polar ice cap, flooding in coastal regions, shifting storm patterns, reduced farm output, drought, and even plant and animal extinctions.[49] Even though most observers agree that the world is warming, however, there's no clear consensus on the cause or scope of the problem, much less the solution.[50]

It's clear that something can and must be done to reduce the carbon dioxide emissions from the burning of fossil fuels and methane, and that's why the Kyoto Protocol came about. Signed in 1997, the **Kyoto Protocol,** an extension of the UN Framework Convention on Climate Change of 1994, commits signatory countries to reducing greenhouse gas (GHG) emissions to 5.2 percent below 1990 levels between 2008 and 2012. The Convention encouraged countries to stabilize GHG emissions, whereas the Protocol commits the signatories to do so.

As of June 2009, 184 nations and regional economic organizations had ratified the Protocol.[51] The United States, which generates 25 percent of the world's greenhouse gases, initially signed the agreement in 1998 but withdrew in 2001, citing concerns about domestic economic growth and exemptions for rapidly expanding developing countries like China and India.[52] (Together, these two nations account for about 14 percent of the world's total emissions, but because they're regarded as developing countries, they aren't required to make reductions.) Why is the United States reluctant to get on board? Basically, it's banking on the development of low-carbon technologies to solve the problem and would prefer not to meet mandatory reductions for fear that reduced economic growth would create domestic employment problems. Although U.S. President Barack Obama is moving aggressively to implement new policies to reduce GHG emissions, he prefers to work on the new framework for climate control that will replace the existing Kyoto Protocol in 2012 rather than sign the existing Protocol. In addition, the G8 Summit that was held in July 2009 agreed to a broad mandate to reduce GHG emissions by 80 percent by 2050, but it failed to agree to set short-term, more concrete goals or to agree on the start date for the 80 percent cut. Germany and other European countries wanted emissions cut from 1990 levels, and President Obama wanted emissions cut from current levels—a significant difference. The resolution read that the reductions would be counted against 1990 levels "or later years" (a concession to the United States).[53]

One approach favored by many, including President Obama, is to invest more in renewable energy, such as wind and solar energy. When oil prices rose dramatically in 2007–2008, there was a lot of interest in renewable energy, but enthusiasm waned when energy prices fell. However, there is still a bright future in renewable energy, and suppliers are truly global. Germany, for example, produces more energy from wind than any other country, and German companies have a head start in penetrating global markets for wind energy. However, suppliers from India, Spain, and Denmark are also major suppliers of wind turbines and other parts.[54]

National and Regional Initiatives Meanwhile, companies operating in countries that have adopted the Protocol are under pressure to take one of two steps: reduce emissions or buy credits from companies that have reduced emissions below target levels. The choice isn't terribly attractive because they'll have to invest in new technologies, change the way they do business, or pay for others to clean up their acts. In addition, MNEs are now forced to reconsider their global strategies, particularly because firms with operations in countries that have adopted the Kyoto Protocol are required to adhere to the same standards as local companies. The European Union (EU) has set a target of an 8 percent reduction from 1990 levels—a figure that's more aggressive than Protocol target levels. The Germans went one step further, setting a target of 21 percent (based on the assumption that they'd be able to close down coal-fired power plants still operating in the former East Germany).[55]

Case Review Note

Company-Specific Initiatives As a result, of course, U.S. companies operating in Europe share the same stringent requirements with European-based firms. Not surprisingly, many U.S.-based MNEs, although not bound by Protocol targets at home, are preparing for what they believe is the inevitable. Between 2000 and 2005, for example, when GM took part in a voluntary emissions-reduction program, it achieved a 10 percent reduction in North American plant emissions. GM is now trying to determine what it needs to do to make its 11 European plants comply with EU standards.[56] DuPont has cut emissions by 65 percent since 1990,[57] and Alcoa has exceeded their goal of a 25 percent reduction of 1990 levels by 2010. They are currently at a 36 percent reduction.[58] Thus, companies are clearly changing the way they do business, whether or not they're bound by Protocol standards. Our opening case provides a good example: Recall that Woolworths committed to reducing the relative amount of carbon produced directly by the business by 30 percent by 2012.

Finally, bear in mind that many MNEs, based in the United States or elsewhere, also face the task of adapting to different standards in different countries. A European-based MNE with operations in, say, the United States, Germany, and China and a U.S.-based MNE with plants in the same countries are faced with a smorgasbord of regulatory environments. On the one hand, the *legal* approach to responsible corporate behavior says an MNE can settle for operating in accord with local laws. The *ethical* approach, on the other hand, urges companies to go beyond the law to do whatever is necessary and economically feasible to reduce greenhouse gas emissions, given that they still have multiple stakeholders to satisfy.

U.S.-based MNEs must comply with the Kyoto Protocol in compliance countries where they may have operations.

Case Review Note

Looking to the Future — How to See the Trees in the Rain Forest

When it comes to the emission of carbon dioxide (and other gases), the whole world is one big greenhouse. From Pago Pago to Peoria—it doesn't matter where you live—you're affected by greenhouse gas emissions. So what difference does it make if greenhouse gas emissions also affect, say, the city of Porto Velho in western Brazil? Porto Velho, situated on the Madeira River, a major tributary of the Amazon River, happens to be in the Amazon rain forest, which accounts for a third of the world's remaining tropical forest. Covering about

(continued)

60 percent of Brazil, the Amazon rain forest is home to no less than 30 percent of the world's animal and plant species. As forests go, it's quite large—roughly the size of Western Europe and just slightly smaller than the United States (including Alaska and Hawaii).

Rain forests may provide a key to solving the problem of global warming. The reason's simple: Trees absorb carbon dioxide. That's why one of the approaches to the reduction of greenhouse gas emissions proposed by the Kyoto Protocol involves reforestation. Given its size, the Amazon rain forest is obviously key to the success of any global reforestation project, but, unfortunately, it's currently under a twofold human-made assault: logging and burning. Logging is an important source of revenue for Brazil, which suffers from high rates of unemployment and underemployment. In addition, Brazilians are cutting down and burning large tracts of rain forest to make room for farming and cattle ranching. In some cases, ranchers turn around and sell their land to agricultural interests, clear additional land for pastures, and sell the lumber to the timber industry.

Not only does the burning of rain forest land add to the volume of carbon dioxide emissions, but also the destruction of the forests eliminates a vast carbon dioxide "sink" that could benefit the rest of the world by disposing of an immense amount of greenhouse gas emissions. Brazil, then, is a major front in the war against greenhouse gas pollution. Burning alone accounts for 75 percent of Brazil's greenhouse gas emissions (5.38 percent of the world's total), making Brazil one of the world's top 10 polluters. Moreover, the huge timber potential has already attracted heavy investment from many multinational logging firms that plan to harvest even more trees in the future. The Brazilian government has tried to bring order to chaos by issuing land titles in an area of the Amazon about the size of France. In doing so, Brazil hopes to reduce illegal land trade, make it easier to police the rain forest, and require the new land owners (which must be individuals, not companies) to pay taxes and follow environmental regulations.[59]

Climate control is a multifaceted issue. On one side, the world needs to engage in strong efforts to reduce GHG emissions as part of the effort to reduce global warming. On the other side, the world needs to work together to preserve regions like the Amazon rain forest that are so essential to absorbing GHG emissions. The challenge is to do what is right to protect the global environment while preserving Brazilian sovereignty over their own resources. And Brazil needs to balance its own development needs with its responsibility to the rest of the world. ■

Ethical Dilemmas and Other Business Practices

In addition to the ethical challenges resulting in bribery and reactions to global warming, let's examine two other examples of ethical dilemmas and socially responsible behavior. Sometimes the dilemmas are industry specific (e.g., pharmaceutical industry). Other times the dilemmas are not exactly industry specific but deal with issues that cross industries, such as bribery, global warming, and labor conditions in developing countries. We have chosen two examples—ethical dilemmas in the pharmaceutical industry and ethical dimensions of labor conditions—to demonstrate how companies have to examine their ethical conduct as they spread internationally. There are others we could have chosen, but we think these two, which are prominent in the news, will give you an idea of what you might face and how you can resolve the conflicts in a satisfactory way. We finish this section and the chapter by discussing the importance of corporate codes of conduct.

ETHICAL DILEMMAS IN THE PHARMACEUTICAL INDUSTRY

GlaxoSmithKline (GSK), one of the largest research-based pharmaceutical companies in the world, focuses on two lines of business: pharmaceuticals (prescription drugs and vaccines) and consumer health-care products. With revenues of $40.3 billion annually, the U.K.-based company operates in 114 countries and sells in more than 150. It employs about 100,000 people, with 35,000 working at 80 manufacturing sites in 37 countries, more than 15,000 of them in R&D.

To continue developing new products, GSK spends 15.1 percent of its revenues on R&D.[60] And, like most research-based pharmaceutical companies, it is involved in the R&D, manufacturing, and sales ends of the patented-pharmaceuticals industry. To fund their large R&D budgets and because so many of the drugs they try to develop never make it to market and because other drugs take so long to get to market, the companies sell their successful drugs at high prices as long as they are covered by patents.

After a patent expires, the drug becomes generic and is sold at a much lower price. Generic manufacturers specialize in selling drugs that are no longer patent protected. Although patent laws vary from country to country, branded pharmaceuticals are protected by U.S. patent for 17 years. Because generic drug manufacturers do not have to engage in R&D and are only selling proven products, their costs are much lower, and they are able to sell the drugs at lower prices.

Tiered Pricing and Other Price-Related Issues There are some exceptions to this pricing structure. Only 3 percent of GSK's revenues, for instance, come from the Middle East and Africa, where GSK offers preferential prices for vaccines. This practice is known as *tiered pricing,* in which consumers in industrialized countries pay higher prices and those in developing countries—especially low-income developing countries—pay lower, subsidized prices.

If a governmental buyer is still unsatisfied with the high cost of patented drugs, it may resort to substituting so-called generics (whose production is a major industry in countries such as India, Brazil, and China). Generics are legitimate *if* the countries in which they're produced extend patent protection to patent holders.

Here's an example of the kinds of problems that can arise when the cost of pharmaceuticals becomes a point of contention in the marketplace. AIDS is a major health problem in Brazil, where the government, at substantial cost, distributes AIDS drugs to anyone who needs them. In 2007, when drugmaker Merck offered to provide an AIDS drug at a 30 percent discount, the Brazilian government said thanks but no thanks and, instead, made it lawful for Brazilian firms to manufacture or buy generic versions of the drug while paying Merck only nominal royalty fees.[61]

Brazil has also resorted to the tactic of *reverse engineering* certain key drugs so they can be produced at lower prices. (One more point about generics: Often they're simply pirated versions of the real thing, and pirated versions—about 10 percent of medicines sold worldwide, according to the World Health Organization [WHO]—often lack key ingredients.[62])

Our closing case includes a similar illustration, which involves the efforts of GlaxoSmithKline to offer steep discounts on AIDS drugs to an MNE attempting to provide free treatment to workers in South Africa.

Taking TRIPS for What It's Worth The WTO Agreement on Trade-Related Aspects of Intellectual Property Rights (TRIPS) allows poor countries to counter the high cost of patented drugs by doing either of two things: (1) producing generic products *for local consumption* or (2) importing generic products from other countries *if they themselves don't have the capacity to produce generics.* In both cases, the developing nation is compelled to license patented drugs from legal patent holders, rather than buy the drug from pirated sources, so that the patent holders generate revenue on the drugs they developed. However, in claiming that health problems such as HIV/AIDS and heart disease are "national emergencies," Brazil and Thailand have permitted local companies to make *unlicensed* generics and thus take advantage of a TRIPS clause that allows them to avoid paying the royalties, even though some companies and countries dispute that decision.[63]

Not surprisingly, this tactic is a major concern for pharmaceutical companies. For one thing, they worry that these generic products will find their way back into the developed countries where they generate the majority of patent holders' revenues. They also worry about fakes for the same reason.

R&D and the Bottom Line Drugs are *very* expensive to develop. Moreover, developing them is a lot more expensive in developed countries than in developing countries. It's estimated, for example, that the price for developing a new drug is close to $1 billion in the United States but as little as $100 million in a country like India.

Case Review Note

As it happens, India, which is now home to a thriving industry in *unlicensed* generic drugs, once enjoyed hefty FDI in pharmaceuticals. But when it refused to secure patents on drugs made there by foreign companies, those companies chose to leave the country rather than give away all their secrets to local competitors. Today, however, a new patent-protection law has brought India into line with WTO guidelines and fostered a whole new environment for pharmaceuticals. Many Indian R&D facilities have sprung up to develop new drugs that can be legitimately produced and sold by Indian companies, and foreign pharmaceutical firms are now looking at different strategies for penetrating the Indian market—from FDI to licensing agreements with generic manufacturers.

In this arena, then, the issue of social responsibility comes down to developing ways in which drugmakers can generate enough revenues to create new products (which is, after all, their major source of competitive advantage) while at the same time responding to the needs of developing countries that are long on diseases and short on funds. Is finding solutions the responsibility of drugmakers or the responsibility of developing nations, perhaps in conjunction with industrialized countries in global forums such as the WHO? Should drugmakers encourage the development of generic products long before patents expire, or will they thereby run the risk of promoting a flood of cheaper products that will come back to haunt them in their home markets?

Countries with health crises, such as African countries with high rates of AIDS, are allowed by TRIPS to manufacture or import generic drugs.

India is a major manufacturer of generic drugs and is now moving to R&D of new drugs.

ETHICAL DIMENSIONS OF LABOR CONDITIONS

A major challenge facing MNEs today is the twofold problem of globalized supply chains and the working conditions of foreign workers. Labor issues—which involve companies, governments, trade unions, and nongovernmental organizations alike—include wages, child labor, working conditions, working hours, and freedom of association. They're especially critical in retail, clothing, footwear, and agriculture—industries in which MNEs typically outsource huge portions of production to independent companies abroad, usually located in the developing countries of Asia, Latin America, and Africa.

As an introduction to this section, look at Figure 5.4, which highlights the multiple pressures placed by external stakeholders on companies to adopt responsible employment practices in their overseas operations. A more specific listing of worker issues was developed by the Ethical Trading Initiative (ETI), a British-based organization that focuses on the ethical employment practices of MNEs. Its members include representatives from Gap Inc., Levi Strauss & Co., Marks & Spencer, The Body Shop International, and other companies, as well as from trade union organizations, NGOs, and governments.

The objective of ETI is to get companies to adopt ethical employment policies and then monitor compliance with their overseas suppliers. ETI's trading initiative base code identifies the following issues:

Major labor issues that MNEs get involved in through FDI or purchasing from independent manufacturers in developing countries are fair wages, child labor, working conditions, working hours, and freedom of association.

1. Employment is freely chosen.
2. Freedom of association and the right to collective bargaining are respected.
3. Working conditions are safe and hygienic.
4. Child labor shall not be used.
5. Living wages are paid.
6. Working hours are not excessive.
7. No discrimination is practiced.
8. Regular employment is provided.
9. No harsh or inhumane treatment is allowed.[64]

Although all issues identified by ETI are important, we focus on the one that, for a variety of good reasons, receives the most attention: *child labor.*

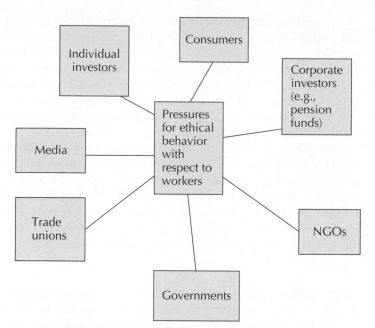

FIGURE 5.4 Sources of Worker-Related Pressures in the Global Supply Chain

The Problem of Child Labor Let's start by considering a couple of very brief cases:

- There are two arguments for the use of children in the Indian carpet industry: (1) They're better suited than adults to perform certain tasks, and (2) if they weren't employed, they'd be even worse off. In fact, children in India are often put to work because parents don't earn enough to support families, and if they don't make enough to pay off debts, children are often *indentured* to creditors.

- In the 1990s, the impoverished Asian nation of Bangladesh was pressured to stop employing thousands of child workers or face U.S. trade sanctions. In this case, the plight of the children did in fact go from bad to worse. Between 5,000 and 7,000 young girls, for example, went from factory work to prostitution.[65]

Child labor has often been used in industries such as carpet making, as illustrated in this picture of an eight-year-old boy working in Mirzapur, India for only a few rupees a day.
Source: Photo by Tom Stoddart/Getty Images

An estimated 250 million children between 5 and 17 years old are working, but only about 5 percent of child labor is involved in export industries.

Some companies avoid operating in countries where child labor is employed, whereas others try to establish responsible policies in those same countries.

MNEs may not be willing to hire local workers who want to work long hours, due to concerns about exploitation.

Concept Check

In discussing "Legal Issues in International Business" in Chapter 3, we enumerate certain "operational concerns" of which overseas managers should be conscious. In particular, they need to accept three facts: (1) They may need to jettison any plan to directly transfer principles and practices that work in the domestic business environment; (2) political and legal systems differ among countries; (3) these differences affect the ways in which firms can exploit opportunities and deflect threats.

According to the International Labor Organization (ILO), a UN institution, 250 million children between the ages of 5 and 17 are working worldwide. Of those, according to one report, 180 million are "young children or in work that endangers their health or well-being, involving hazards, sexual exploitation, trafficking, and debt bondage."[66] According to ILO guidelines, children who are at least 13 years old may be employed in "light" work that's not harmful to their health and doesn't interfere with school. All children under the age of 18 should be protected against the most abusive labor conditions.

For MNEs, the basic challenge is negotiating a global labyrinth of business environments with different cultural, legal, and political rules than those they're used to at home. In addition, they typically rely on local suppliers who are subject to specifically local pressures. Under these conditions, MNEs clearly can't solve all the problems revolving around child labor, especially given the fact that only about 5 percent of child labor worldwide occurs in industries supported by MNEs.[67] Most underage workers can be found in the informal sectors of an economy—especially agriculture—in which it's difficult to protect them.

What MNEs Can and Can't Do   This doesn't mean, however, that MNEs are powerless when it comes to labor-related matters in overseas facilities. The Swedish retailer IKEA, for example, ran into trouble in India because it was buying carpets from local companies that relied heavily on extensive child labor. Rather than trying to force suppliers to stop using child labor, IKEA identified and tackled two different problems. First, it helped working mothers increase family earning power so they could escape the clutches of the loan sharks to whom they were putting up their children as collateral. Second, IKEA set up "bridge schools" to enable working children to enter mainstream education channels within a year.[68]

Frequently, MNEs operating in countries where labor policies vary widely from those at home succumb to the pressure to simply leave the market. Usually, it turns out to be a shortsighted decision. Research shows, for instance, that companies like Nike have substantially improved the conditions of workers in overseas facilities. Granted, MNEs are in no position to revolutionize the employment practices of the countries in which they operate, but they can improve conditions at subcontract facilities and even influence the guidelines set by other foreign investors. In the case of IKEA, carpet sales make up a small percentage of sales, and it would have been easy to simply give up the product line and move out of India. But officials at IKEA felt a responsibility to the children and decided to do as much as possible to make a difference.

CORPORATE CODES OF ETHICS: HOW *SHOULD* A COMPANY BEHAVE?

So far, we've discussed numerous issues related to the impact of globalization on business, the role of businesses in the globalization process, and the impact of international businesses on society. But now we come to a qualitatively different question: *How* should *a company behave?* The United Nations Global Compact is a good start since it identifies ten broad principles in the areas of human rights, labor, environment and anti-corruption, all of which are issues we have described in this chapter.[69] The Global Compact is not legally binding, but it is a good guide for companies that are establishing a code of conduct. The initiative, which was launched in 2000, has more than 6,700 participants, of which over 5,200 are businesses from 130 countries. The UN Global Compact Web site allows you to search participating companies by country. It is interesting to note that on June 30, 2009, there were 446 French companies actively participating in the initiative, compared with 195 from the United States, 134 from the United Kingdom, and 101 from Germany. Brazil leads the BRIC countries with 185 active business participants, and both China and India have more than Germany.[70]

Motivations for Corporate Responsibility   Generally speaking, companies experience four strong motivations for acting responsibly:

1. Unethical and irresponsible behavior can result in *legal headaches,* especially in such areas as financial mismanagement, bribery, and product safety.

2. Such behavior could also result in *consumer action* such as boycotts.

3. Unethical behavior can affect *employee morale.* And, conversely, responsible behavior can have a positive influence on a workforce, both at corporate headquarters and at overseas facilities.

4. You never know when *bad publicity* is going to cost you sales. Perhaps this concern is one reason why Nike and other apparel and clothing companies responded so quickly to criticism about allegedly unfair employment practices in developing countries.

> Companies need to act responsibly because unethical and irresponsible behavior
> - Could result in legal sanctions.
> - Could result in consumer boycotts.
> - Could lower employee morale.
> - Could cost sales because of bad publicity.

Developing a Code of Conduct   A major component of most companies' strategies for ethical and socially responsible behavior is a **code of conduct.** In the context of international operations, we can take up two perspectives on codes of conduct: external and internal.

Bear in mind that external codes of conduct are useful only insofar as they give companies some general guidance on how to operate. The practical challenge for the company is familiarizing itself with the codes of many different organizations and, although codes will undoubtedly vary widely, use them to fashion its own *internal code of conduct.*

> A major component in a company's strategy for ethical and socially responsible behavior is a code of conduct.

What Makes a Good Internal Code of Conduct?   In this section, we focus on four criteria for an effective internal code of conduct:

1. *It sets global policies with which everyone working anywhere for the company must comply.* A good example is the code promulgated by the Finnish cell-phone company Nokia, which discusses how its code was set, who approved it, how it is communicated to its employees, and what its foundation values are.

2. *It communicates company policies not only to all employees but to all suppliers and subcontractors as well.* Gap, for example, maintains an education program to help subcontractors develop their own compliance programs that meet the objectives of Gap's code.[71]

3. *It ensures that the policies laid out in the code are carried out.* There are a variety of ways to approach this task:

   - GSK requires employees to confirm in writing that they've read and understand the company's code of conduct.. Then employees must sign off that they understand and will follow the policies.

   - Syngenta, an Anglo-Swiss agrochemicals group, found out through press reports that child labor was being used in its supply chain. To ensure that suppliers were adhering to its policies in the matter, the company arranged with the Fair Labor Association, a nonprofit NGO, to submit its operations to external monitoring.[72]

> Codes of conduct involve four dimensions:
> - Setting a global policy that must be complied with wherever the company operates.
> - Communicating the code to employees, suppliers, and subcontractors.
> - Ensuring that policies are carried out.
> - Reporting results to external stakeholders.

4. *It reports the results to external stakeholders.* This can be a complicated and sometimes tricky process. Up until a few years ago, for instance, Nike was willing to provide a lot of information about its labor practices. In 1998, however, when a lawsuit charged that the report constituted false advertising, Nike was forced to pay $1.5 million to the Fair Labor Association. Ever since the ruling came down in 2001, the giant shoe and apparel company has been less forthcoming about labor-related activities. Gap, however, has begun providing *more* information about its worldwide monitoring activities, including details about its code of conduct and practices; the Gap report also discusses its challenges—and failures—in getting subcontractors to act in accord with company policies.[73]

There's no reason to believe that in the future governments won't continue to compete for larger shares of the wealth and other benefits to be gained from the activities of MNEs. In the short term, most countries will probably work to create more favorable environments for foreign investors, and there are several good reasons why. On the one hand, investment inflows provide developing countries with ways to deal with debt burdens and capital-accounts problems. Meanwhile, industrial nations struggling with trade-deficit problems, like the United States, are more inclined to welcome FDI. The European Union, for example, will probably continue to welcome foreign investment as a means of fueling the growth that it hopes to attain through unification.

The long term, however, may tell a different story. Historically, attitudes toward FDI have tended to fluctuate, with governments tending to favor restrictions when economies are thriving and incentives when they're struggling. But according to some observers, if they don't experience the rate of rapid growth they're expecting from the substantial FDI that they've already attracted, developing countries may make the same about-face that such nations as Russia and Iran have already made—that is, place new restrictions on the flow of foreign investment.

Worse still, growing disappointment with the net results of foreign investment may lead some nations to attribute such problems as weakened sovereignty, increasing poverty, and cultural disintegration to overdependence on FDI. If this reaction to foreign investment is paired with growing criticism from NGOs and other external stakeholders, the ability of companies to operate globally will be further compromised.

Anglo American PLC in South Africa: What Do You Do When Costs Reach Epidemic Proportions?

By now it should be obvious that, regardless of where it chooses to do business, an MNE is going to face quite a variety of threats and disruptions—ranging from bureaucratic corruption and political instability to terrorism and even war—to its plans and operations. In 2007, Anglo American PLC, at that time one of the world's largest gold miners, found itself facing a threat that, although by no means new, defies most traditional categories of things that complicate business overseas—an HIV/AIDS epidemic in South Africa, the world's largest gold producer.[74]

In 2002, Anglo American made a landmark decision to provide free antiretroviral therapy (ART) to HIV-infected employees at its South African operations. Surprisingly, however, this commitment has met with mixed reactions from various stakeholders and achieved only controversial results, and the U.K.-based company is now asking itself, "Where do we go from here?"

AIDS in South Africa

How bad does a disease have to be to be accorded the status of an "epidemic"? Here's some background information. Sub-Saharan Africa, the portion of Africa lying south of the Sahara Desert, is home to just over 10 percent of the world's population and to 60 percent of all people infected with HIV, the virus that causes AIDS. Located at the southernmost tip of the African continent, the nation of South Africa has the highest number of people living with HIV/AIDS and suffers one of the world's highest rates of HIV infection—approximately 5.7 million cases (2007 estimate) in a population of 49 million (2009 estimate). Every day, almost 1,000 South Africans die from HIV/AIDS. Moreover, say the UN and the WHO, the epidemic has a long way to go before it reaches its peak.

Needless to say, the spread of the disease has, over the past decade, had a profound impact on both the people of South Africa and their economy. Life expectancy is 48.98 years compared to, say, 75.63 years in Poland, a country with a similar population size and GDP per capita.

AIDS has also had a devastating effect on the country's economy. Between 1992 and 2002, the South African economy lost $7 billion annually—around 2 percent of GDP—as a result of AIDS-related worker deaths. Experts predict that, as AIDS spreads throughout sub-Saharan Africa, it will continue to reduce per capita growth by 1 to 2 percent per year and, in the worst-affected countries, cut annual GDP growth by as much as 0.6 percent by 2010. The consequences include both diminishing populations and shrinking economies, with GDPs deflating anywhere from 20 to 40 percent of the sizes they would have reached in the absence of AIDS.

Anglo American Operations in South Africa

Anglo American PLC is a diversified mining conglomerate operating in 45 countries and employing 105,000 permanent employees to produce precious metals (platinum and diamonds), base metals (copper, nickel, zinc, and phosphates), and bulk metals (for ferrous metals and coal). Founded in 1917 as the Anglo American Corporation of South Africa, it was South Africa's first home-based public limited company. Anglo American is a multinational firm headquartered in London, with its primary listing in London and secondary listing in Johannesburg. Anglo American has a presence in Europe, Africa, Asia, North America, and South America. In spite of its global spread, the company dominates South Africa's domestic economy through direct employment, contractors, and its supply chain. Through majority-share ownership of subsidiaries and associate companies, Anglo American controls over 25 percent of all shares traded on the South African stock market. Anglo-American is huge: It is one of the world's largest mining companies, trailing such giants as BHP Billiton (dual-listed in Melbourne and London), Vale (Brazil), and Rio Tinto (Australia), and it is running the risk of being taken over by Australian-based Xstrata. With the rapid rise in commodity prices followed by their collapse during the global financial crisis in 2008, it has been an interesting period for the mining industry.

Anglo American and ART

With such a huge investment in South Africa, Anglo American has been hit hard by the HIV/AIDS epidemic that's descended on the country. Having recognized the threat as far back as the early 1990s, Anglo American was one of the first corporations to develop a comprehensive, proactive strategy to combat the ravages of the disease on its workforce and the repercussions for its operations.

Originally, the program consisted of prevention initiatives aimed at education and awareness, the distribution of condoms, financial and skill-related training to alleviate poverty, and a survey system to monitor the prevalence of the infection. Eventually, these policies were expanded to include voluntary counseling, testing, and care-and-wellness programs, and the services of all programs were extended to cover not only the families of employees but also the populations of surrounding communities. Anglo American also became a member of the Global Business Council on HIV/AIDS, an organization of multinational companies that focuses on alleviating the effects of AIDS throughout the world and on protecting the rights of infected workers.

By adopting these strategies so early, Anglo American became a de facto leader in the private-sector fight against HIV/AIDS in Africa. Many other MNEs—including Coca-Cola, Ford, Colgate-Palmolive, and Chevron Texaco—soon followed Anglo American's example and initiated prevention, education, and wellness programs of their own. Even then, however, the majority of companies operating in South Africa still hesitated, and that's why Anglo American's announcement that it would provide ART to its South African workforce (at company expense) was met with a good deal of excited approval from such interested parties as the WHO, the Global Business Council on HIV/AIDS, and a host of other NGOs.

The Costs of Operating in an Epidemic

The incentive for Anglo American's ART program largely came from the failure of its AIDS-prevention efforts to make much headway in stemming the spread of the disease. By 2001, according to Brian Brink, senior VP of the firm's medical division, the prevalence of HIV-positive workers had risen to an average of 21 percent across all operations—a figure that was climbing steadily at a rate of 2 percent annually. Bobby Godsell, CEO and chairman of the subsidiary AngloGold, reported that HIV/AIDS was adding as much as $5 to the cost of producing one ounce of gold, thereby tacking on $11 million a year to the company's production costs in addition to the $7 million it was spending annually to combat such AIDS-related illnesses as tuberculosis (which was five times as prevalent as it had been just a decade earlier).

Finally, in addition to losses in productivity, the company had to bear the costs entailed by high levels of absenteeism, the constant retraining of replacement workers, and burgeoning payouts in health, hospitalization, and death benefits. Studies conducted at the time indicated not only that the costs of AIDS could reach as much as 7.2 percent of the company's total wage bill but also that the costs of leaving employees untreated would be even higher than those of providing ART.

Seven years after it rolled out its ART program, Anglo American now finds itself struggling to please various stakeholders and to determine whether all of its efforts are making a difference in the underlying problem or merely masking its effects. By the end of 2008, for instance, although 3,080 employees—approximately 67 percent of those in need of treatment—were receiving ART, nearly 38 percent of those who had begun treatment had dropped out (for reasons such as death or termination of employment). By 2008, 18 percent of the company's South African workforce was infected with the deadly virus, which was actually an improvement compared with 1992.

On top of everything else, Anglo American also faces the problem of spiraling costs for the program itself. Even though the prices of most of the necessary drugs have been decreasing, the cost of distributing them remains high, and the treatment regime costs the company an estimated $4,000 per year per employee—quite expensive, especially when compared with the wages and benefits that Anglo American typically offers mineworkers. (Average monthly wages in the South African mining industry are about 5,100 rand, or U.S. $830.) Meanwhile, as Anglo American officials continue to remind investors that treating workers ultimately serves the bottom line, recent estimates project a total cost to the company of $1 billion or more over 10 years.

On the upside, cost per patient should decrease as the number of workers participating in the program increases. Unfortunately, one of the biggest challenges facing Anglo American is encouraging participation among a migrant and largely uneducated workforce laboring under harsh conditions in an unstable environment. In South Africa, HIV/AIDS still carries a severe stigma, and many South Africans refuse to be tested or to admit they've been infected for fear of discrimination by managers, fellow employees, and even society at large.

Moreover, many of those who had agreed to participate were confused by rumors and misinformation into assuming that they could stop using condoms once they were on the drugs—a situation, of course, that only exacerbated the prevalence of unsafe behavior. ART is in fact a lifelong regimen that can lead to various side effects and needs to be administered under strict supervision. Anglo American, however, continues to struggle with high levels of nonadherence. At one point, for example, supervisors were reporting that all workers undergoing treatment were taking medications as directed; urine tests, however, revealed that only 85 percent were actually doing so. By 2008, the company was forced to report that about 10 percent of participants had dropped out because of inability or unwillingness to adhere to the regimen. Now, physicians have to worry that extensive patterns of nonadherence pose a risk of fostering new drug-resistant strains of the virus.

In addition, harsh working conditions often make it hard for workers to take medications on time or to deal with certain side effects. Finally, migrant workers—about four-fifths of the total workforce—come from isolated villages located hundreds of miles away. They're 2.5 times more likely to contract the disease, which they take with them back to their villages.

Constituencies and Critics

Then there's the problem of pressure from various stakeholders. The National Union of Mineworkers has been hesitant to voice its support, citing the company's limitations on health-insurance benefits and lack of cooperation with national agencies. The union has also accused the company of helping to foster working conditions that exacerbate the problem. Even then-CEO Brian Gilbertson of BHP Billiton, another large mining concern operating in South Africa, charged Anglo American with merely trying to contain the problem instead of attacking its underlying causes: "You don't approach the problem by just throwing drugs at it," said Gilbertson.

Anglo American has countered many of these criticisms by insisting that it's beyond the resources and capacity of a single company to combat the overall problem and has called for more involvement on the part of the South African government. Instead of cooperation, however, the company has encountered outright opposition from political leaders. Indeed, the South African government has proved to be one of Africa's least committed to a program of effective intervention. Over the course of two years, the government diverted only 0.6 percent of the national budget to the HIV/AIDS crisis and has even resisted the wide distribution of antiretroviral drugs on the grounds that it's too expensive and too difficult to implement.

Matters weren't helped any when former President Thabo Mbeki publicly questioned the link between the HIV virus and the onset of AIDS. Then the country's health minister decried the Anglo American initiative as a "vigilante" move designed to place unreasonable burdens on the government, which would, after all, have to pick up the tab for treatments once workers had retired or left the company's employment.

In addition, dealing with pharmaceutical companies has proved a tricky proposition. On the one hand, Anglo American has a deal with GlaxoSmithKline allowing it to purchase antiretroviral drugs at a tenth of the market price in the industrialized world (the same that GSK charges not-for-profit organizations). At the same time, however, other drugmakers have been hesitant and unreliable at best, promising price cuts and then reneging over fears of violating intellectual property rights. As a matter of fact, several of these companies, complaining that cheap generic drugs made available in Africa will eventually be resold by profiteers on higher-priced Western markets, have put their energies into suing the South African government for what they claim to be generally poor enforcement of their patent rights.

Given the many challenges it's faced, not to mention the opposition from unexpected quarters, some observers have gone so far as to suggest that Anglo American would be better off by simply pulling back on its HIV/AIDS treatment program rather than pouring more resources into the effort to make it work. In the long run, however, the company must consider the continued pressure it will get from ethically minded shareholders as well as its own sense of moral responsibility.

There are also indications that the future may not be as bleak as it often appears. Of the workers who faithfully adhere to the drug regime, 95 percent have responded well to treatment and are working productively. The South African government may also be undergoing a gradual change of heart, having recently launched a National Strategic Plan for combating HIV/AIDS, which includes the aggressive goal of cutting the number of HIV infections in half by 2011. ■

QUESTIONS

1. Who are the various stakeholders that Anglo American needs to consider as it adopts an effective HIV/AIDS strategy?

2. What are the pros and cons of Anglo American's adoption of an aggressive strategy in combating HIV/AIDS among its South African workforce? What recommendations would you give the company concerning its HIV/AIDS policy?

3. Because such a large percentage of its workforce consists of migrant workers who are more likely to acquire and spread HIV/AIDS, should Anglo American adopt the policy of not hiring migrant workers? Should the South African government close the doors to migrant workers?

4. What role do pharmaceutical companies play in responding to the HIV/AIDS epidemic in South Africa? What policies or courses of action would you recommend to a company that produces HIV/AIDS drugs?

SUMMARY

- FDI is a major source of capital and expertise, but it is also the center of a controversy over the costs and benefits to home and host countries.

- MNEs must balance the interests of different constituencies that have different objectives.

- The economic and political effects of MNEs are difficult to evaluate because of conflicting influences on different countries' objectives, intervening variables that obscure cause-and-effect relationships, and differences among MNEs' practices.

- MNEs may affect countries' balance of payments, growth, and employment objectives. Under different conditions, these effects may be positive or negative for the host or home country.

- The balance-of-payments effects of FDI involve import stimulus versus import displacement, export stimulus versus export displacement, and capital inflows versus capital outflows. In the latter case, capital flows might be positive initially for the host country but negative later as the investor sends returns back to the home market.

- FDI creates jobs and economic growth in the host country. Given that resources are not fully employed, FDI may or may not have an adverse impact on jobs and economic growth in the home market.

- Relative behavior implies that we act according to the norms of the countries where we operate. Normative behavior implies that there are universal standards for ethical conduct that should be followed everywhere.

- The law is an important basis for ethical behavior, but not all unethical behavior is illegal. Thus ethical behavior must go beyond the law to include common decency.

- Bribery is a form of unethical behavior being addressed at the multilateral level, such as at the UN and the OECD, and at the national level, such as with the Foreign Corrupt Practices Act in the United States.

- Environmental concerns are raised with extractive industries and industries that generate air and water pollution or that produce products such as automobiles that use fossil fuels.

- The Kyoto Protocol, which requires the reduction of the emission of greenhouse gases, has not been adopted by all countries and is therefore still limited in its total global impact. However, companies must adapt to countries that have implemented the Kyoto Protocol.

- Pharmaceutical companies face challenges on how to make enough money to fund the R&D into new drugs and how to help provide critical drugs to developing countries at lower prices.

- A major challenge facing MNEs is the globalization of the supply chain and the impact on workers, especially in the areas of fair wages, child labor, working conditions, working hours, and freedom of association.

- Companies respond to the pressures for greater corporate social responsibility by establishing codes of conduct, distributing them to suppliers and subcontractors internationally, and ensuring compliance with the codes through effective training and auditing programs.

KEY TERMS

balance-of-payments effect (p. 229)
code of conduct (p. 249)
externality (p. 236)
extraterritoriality (p. 235)

Foreign Corrupt Practices Act
(FCPA) (p. 238)
Kyoto Protocol (p. 242)
normativism (p. 234)

relativism (p. 233)
stakeholder (p. 227)
sustainability (p. 242)

ENDNOTES

1 *Sources include the following:* "Ten + Ten: Successes and Failures," www.iisd.org, (April 1, 2009); "Sustainable Development June 1987," www.un-document.net, (April 1, 2009); P. Kotler and N. Lee, *Corporate Social Responsibility: Doing the Most Good for Your Company and Your Cause,* John Wiley & Sons, Inc, Hoboken, New Jersey, 2005, pp.10–11; "Corporate Social Responsibility," www.ethicsworld.org, (February 12, 2009); K. Naude, *Seeing Green,* www.fastmoving.co.za, (February 23, 2009); Email correspondence with Justin Smith, (March 4, June 15, 18, July 6, 2009); Woolworths Annual Reports 2004–2008, www.woolworthsholdings.co.za; C. Gilmour, "Woolworths Franchise Doing Trick Outside SA," *Financial Mail,* (April 1, 2005), www.saarf.co.za; www.woolworths.co.za; T. Dorfling and Professor G.J. Stockport, "Woolworths SA: Clothing Turnaround Strategy," case study, © 2006 Graduate School of Business Administration, University of the Witwatersrand; "Absa Gets Woolworths Financial

Services," www.fastmoving.co.za, (October 2, 2008); Michael Appel, *Inflation Targeting to Stay: Mboweni,* (August 6, 2008), www.southafrica.info; "Woolworths Lifts Diluted EPS by 11.5%," (February 19, 2009), www.moneyweb.co.za; Telephonic interview with Dorothy McClaren, June 24, 2008 and Justin Smith February 23, 2009; www.dti.gov.za; www.bbc.co.uk; Marian Isa, *Recession Stalks SA as Economy Shrinks 1.8%,* (February 25, 2009), www.businessday.co.za; www.shopriteholdings.co.za;G. Candy, *How Consumers are Dealing with a Downturn in SA,* (February 19, 2009), www.moneyweb.co.za;E. Swanepoel, *The Truth About Woolworths is in the Stores, Says Susman,* (March 4, 2009), www.busrep.co.za; A. Hattingh, *South Africa's Fabric Future,* www.ifashion.co.za (April 28, 2009); www.organicfacts.net; *The Woolworths Good Business Journey,* presentation at the ECR conference by Justin Smith, (October 29, 2008); C. Perkins, "The Dangers of CFLs," www.holistichelp.net (June

17, 2009); "How to Face the Challenge of Green," (June 17, 2009), www.supermarket.co.za; "Woolworths Recognises Suppliers for their Commitment to Protecting the Environment," (April 28, 2009), www.fastmoving.co.za; Michelle Nel, *Local Champ has Won Global Awards Too*, (June 6, 2008), www.mg.co.za; www.picknpay-ir.co.za; www.shoprite.co.za; www.spar.co.za; "Woolworths and ABSA Launch Financial Services Joint Venture," press release, (October 2, 2008); "Woolworths Announces the Good Business Journey," press release, (October 20, 2009); and "Organics, New Consumer Lifestyle Trend," press release, (November 11, 2004), accessed at www.woolworthsholdings.co.za.

2 *Development and Globalization: Facts and Figures* (United Nations Conference on Trade and Development, 2008): 28.

3 UNCTAD, *World Investment Report 2009: Transnational Corporations, Agricultural Production and Development* (United Nations, New York and Geneva), p. 8.

4 Ken Davies, "While Global FDI Falls, China's Outward FDI Doubles" (Columbia FDI Perspectives, Vale Columbia Center on Sustainable International Investment, No. 5, May 26, 2009).

5 John H. Dunning, "The Eclectic Paradigm of International Production: A Restatement and Some Possible Extensions," *Journal of International Business Studies* 19:1 (1988): 1–32.

6 Bradley R. Agle, Thomas Donaldson, R. Edward Freeman, Michael C. Jensen, Ronald K. Mitchell, and Donna J. Wood, "Dialogue toward Superior Stakeholder Theory," *Business Ethics Quarterly* 18:2 (2008): 153–90.

7 Mohsin Habib and Leon Zurawicki, "Corruption and Foreign Direct Investment," *Journal of International Business Studies* 33:2 (Summer 2002): 291–308.

8 John H. Dunning, "The Future of Multinational Enterprise," *Lloyds Bank Review* (July 1974): 16.

9 Ravi Ramamurti, "The Obsolescing 'Bargaining Model'? MNE-Host Developing Country Relations Revisited," *Journal of International Business Studies* 32 (Spring 2001): 23.

10 "Chavez Takes Over Foreign-Controlled Oil Projects in Venezuela" Simon Romero. *New York Times* (Late Edition (East Coast)). New York, N.Y.: May 2, 2007. pg. A.3

11 Rachel Jones, "Venezuela Seeks Aid from Oil Companies," *Spartanburg Herald-Journal* (January 26, 2009).

12 On the argument that MNEs contribute to host-country gains, see William Keng and Mun Lee, "Foreign Investment, Industrial Restructuring and Dependent Development in Singapore," *Journal of Contemporary Asia* 27 (March 1997): 58–71. On the opposite view, see Brian J. Aitken and Ann E. Harrison, "Do Domestic Firms Benefit from Direct Foreign Investment? Evidence from Venezuela," *American Economic Review* 89:3 (1995): 605.

13 David J. Vidal, *The Link between Corporate Citizenship and Financial Performance* (New York: Conference Board, 1999).

14 "Interfaith Center on Corporation Responsibility," http://www.iccr.org/ (accessed July 7, 2009).

15 Ronald Berenbeim, "The Search for Global Ethics," *Vital Speeches of the Day* 65:6 (1999): 177–78.

16 See John M. Kline, *Ethics for International Business: Decision Making in a Global Political Economy* (London and New York: Routledge, 2005).

17 S. Prakash Sethi, "Standards for Corporate Conduct in the International Arena: Challenges and Opportunities for Multinational Corporations," *Business and Society Review* (Spring 2002): 20–39.

18 "The Ethics of Business," in "A Survey of Corporate Social Responsibility," *The Economist* (January 22, 2005): 20.

19 See "Indonesia's Plague," *Far Eastern Economic Review* (July 12, 2001): 8; John Danley, "Balancing Risks: Mosquitos, Malaria, Morality, and DDT," *Business and Society Review* 107:1 (Spring 2002): 145–70.

20 Alfred Marcus, *Business & Society: Ethics, Government, and the World Economy* (Homewood, IL: Irwin, 1996).

21 John R. Boatright, *Ethics and the Conduct of Business* (Upper Saddle River, NJ: Prentice Hall, 1993): 13–16.

22 Boatright, *Ethics and the Conduct of Business*, 16–18.

23 Austebn L. Parrish, "The Effects Test: Extraterritoriality's Fifth Business," *Vanderbilt Law Review* 61:5 (October 2008): 1453+.

24 See A. M. Ali and I. H. Saiad, "Determinants of Economic Corruption," *Cato Journal* 22:3 (2003): 449–66; H. Park, "Determinants of Corruption: A Cross-National Analysis," *Multinational Business Review* 11:2 (2003): 29–48.

25 Transparency International, "How Do You Define Corruption? (in Frequently Asked Questions about Corruption), http://www.transparency.org/news_room/faq/corruption_faq (accessed July 7, 2009).

26 "The Short Arm of the Law—Bribery and Business," *The Economist* (March 2, 2002): 78.

27 Transparency International, "Bribe Payers Index 2008," http://www.transparency.org/news_room/in_focus/2008/bpi_2008 (accessed July 7, 2009).

28 See The World Bank, *World Development Report 2002: Building Institutions for Markets*; M. Habib and L. Zurawicki, "Country-Level Investments and the Effect of Corruption—Some Empirical Evidence," *International Business Review* 10:6 (2001): 687–700.

29 "China Execution Warning to Others," Aljazeera.net (July 11, 2007), at http://english.aljazeera.net (accessed August 20, 2007).

30 S. Ghoshal and P. Moran, "Towards a Good Theory of Management," in J. Birkinshaw and G. Piramal, eds., *Sumantra Ghoshal on Management: A Force for Good* (Upper Saddle River, NJ: Financial Times/Prentice Hall, 2005): 1–27.

31 Fritz Heimann and Gillian Dell, *Progress Report 2009: Enforcement of the OECD Convention on Combating Bribery of Foreign Public Officials in International Business Transactions* (Transparency International, June 23, 2009): 6.

32 International Chamber of Commerce, "Extortion and Bribery in International Business Transactions," (1999) revised version, at www.iccwbo.org/home/statements_rules/rules/1999/briberydoc99.asp (accessed April 23, 2005).

33 Qing Tian, "Perception of Business Bribery in China: The Impact of Moral Philosophy," *Journal of Business Ethics* 80 (2008): 437–45.

34 Dionne Searcey, "U.S. Cracks Down on Corporate Bribes," *Wall Street Journal* (May 26, 2009): 1, 4.

35 Dionne Searcey, "U.S. Cracks Down on Corporate Bribes."

36 Nicola Clark, "In Europe, Sharper Scrutiny of Ethical Standards," *New York Times* (May 7, 2008): C8.

37 Glenn R. Simpson. *Wall Street Journal (Eastern edition)*. New York, N.Y.: Jan 27, 2005. p. A.2

38 Colleen Taylor, "U.S., Japan Authorities Join in Siemens' 'Black Money' Probe," *Electronic News* (February 12, 2007): 7; David Crawford and Mike Esterl, "Room at the Top: German Giant Siemens Faces Leadership Crisis," *Wall Street Journal* (April 26, 2007); Crawford and Esterl, "Widening Scandal: At Siemens, Witnesses Cite Pattern of Bribery," *Wall Street Journal* (January 31, 2007): A.1.

39 "The Hollow Men," *The Economist* (March 17, 2007): 71.

40 Michael Connolly, "Germany Inc. under a Cloud," *Wall Street Journal* (November 24, 2006).

41 Crawford and Esterl, "Widening Scandal."

42 Konstantin Richter, "The House of Siemens," *Wall Street Journal* (April 27, 2007): 13.

43 Jack Ewing, "Siemens' Culture Clash: CEO Kleinfeld Is Making Changes, and Enemies," *Business Week* (January 29, 2007): 42–46.

44 Richter, "The House of Siemens," 13.

45 David Crawford and Mike Esterl, "Siemens to Decide if New Leader Is Needed amid Widening Probes," *Wall Street Journal* (April 25, 2007): A3.

46 Ewing, "Siemens' Culture Clash," 42–46; Richter, "The House of Siemens," 13.

47 G. Thomas Sims, "Siemens Struggles to Regain Equilibrium," *New York Times*, online edition (April 27, 2007); Sims, "Two Former Siemens Officials Convicted for Bribery," *New York Times*, online edition (May 15, 2007).

48 Josef Jabareen, "A New Conceptual Framework for Sustainable Development," *Environment, Development and Sustainability* 10:5 (April 2008): 29.

49 John Carey, "Global Warming," *Business Week* (August 16, 2004): 60–69.

50 "Hotting Up," *The Economist* (February 5, 2005): 73–74.

51 UNFCC home page, at http://unfccc.int/kyoto_protocol/status_of_ratification/items/2613.php (accessed June 19, 2009).

52 Alison Graab, "Greenhouse Gas Market to Slow Global Warming," CNN.com (accessed April 12, 2005).

53 Jonathan Weisman, "G-8 Climate-Change Agreement Falls Short,"*Wall Street Journal* (July 9, 2009), A.8

54 Jack Ewing, "The Wind at Germany's Back," *Business Week* (February 11, 2008): 68.

55 Mark Lander, "Mixed Feelings as Kyoto Pact Takes Effect," *New York Times* (February 16, 2005).

56 Lander, "Mixed Feelings as Kyoto Pact Takes Effect."

57 Carey, "Global Warming," 62.

58 "Alcoa Inc.; Alcoa Volunteers Set to Contribute to a More Sustainable Future," *Biotech Week* (May 13, 2009): 2792.

59 "Brazil Legalizes Rain-forest Ownership in France-Size Area," *Montreal Gazette* (June 27, 2009): A18.

60 *GlaxoSmithKline 2008 Annual Report*, various pages, at www.gsk.com/index.htm.

61 Miriam Jorda, "Brazil to Stir Up AIDS-Drug Battle," *Wall Street Journal* (September 5, 2003): A3; "Brazil to Break Merck AIDS Drug Patent," *Associated Press* story on MSNBC Web site (May 4, 2007).

62 Frederik Balfour, "Fakes!" *Business Week* (February 7, 2005): 56.

63 "A Gathering Storm: Pharmaceuticals," *The Economist* (June 9, 2007): 73.

64 Ethical Trading Initiative, at www.ethicaltrade.org (accessed August 20, 2007).

65 Ans Kolk and Rob van Tulder, "Child Labor and Multinational Conduct: A Comparison of International Business and Stakeholder Codes," *Journal of Business Ethics* (March 2002). Volume 36 Number 3 p. 291–301

66 Frances Williams, "Economic Case Made for Ending Child Labour," *Financial Times* (February 4, 2004): 5.

67 Kolk and van Tulder, "Child Labor and Multinational Conduct."

68 Edward Luce, "Ikea's Grown-Up Plan to Tackle Child Labour," *Financial Times* (September 15, 2004): 7.

69 United Nations, *United Nations Global Compact*, http://www.unglobalcompact.org/AboutTheGC/(accessed on October 1, 2009).

70 Ibid., Participants & Stakeholders, http://www.unglobalcompact.org/ParticipantsAndStakeholders/(accessed on October 1, 2009).

71 Amy Merrick, "Gap Offers Unusual Look at Factory Conditions," *Wall Street Journal* (May 12, 2004): A1.

72 "Syngenta Opens Up to Independent Scrutiny," *Financial Times* (May 12, 2004): 8.

73 Sarah Murray and Alison Matiland, "The Trouble with Transparent Clothing," *Financial Times* (May 12, 2004): 8.

74 *Sources include the following:* UNAIDS 2008 Report on the Global AIDS Epidemic; HIV and AIDS in South Africa, www.avert.org/aidssouthafrica.htm; A Global Business Fit for the Future: Annual Report 2008, Anglo American; Making a Difference Report to Society 2008, Anglo American; A Global Business Fit for the Future Annual Report 2008, Anglo American; "HIV/AIDS Co-Infection: Anglo American's Coal Division in South Africa Wins Global Business Coalition Award for Top International Workplace HIV and AIDS Programme, *Law & Health Weekly* (July 11, 2009): 849; Alec Russell, "Answers to an AIDS Epidemic: New Initiatives to Help Infected Workers Mark a Big Shift in Attitude and Approach at Some of South Africa's Largest Companies," *Financial Times* (October 4, 2007): 14; Mark Schoofs, "Anglo American Drops Noted Plan on AIDS Drugs," *Wall Street Journal* (April 16, 2002): A19; World Health Organization/AFRO, "Southern African Health Challenges Intensify," press release (September 13, 2004): 1–2; Mark Schoofs, "New Challenges in Fighting AIDS—Enlisting Multinationals in Battle," *Wall Street Journal* (November 30, 2001): B1; "AIDS in the Workplace," *Business Africa* (July 1, 2001): 1–2; "The Corporate Response," *Business Africa* (September 1, 2001): 4; Schoofs, "South Africa Reverses Course on AIDS Drugs," *Wall Street Journal* (November 20, 2003): B1; "Anglo American to Provide HIV/AIDS Help for Workers," *American Metal Market* (August 7, 2002): 4; Bruce Einhorn and Catherine Arnst, "Why Business Should Make AIDS Its Business—Multinationals Are Taking Baby Steps to Control the Disease in Their Workforce," *Business Week* (August 9, 2004): 83; "Digging Deep," *The Economist* (August 10, 2002): 55; James Lamont, "Anglo's Initiative," *Financial Times* (August 8, 2002): 10; "Anglo American to Give Mineworkers AIDS Drugs Free," *Wall Street Journal* (August 7, 2002): A13; Matthew Newmann, Scott Hensley, and Scott Miller, "U.S. Reaches Patent Compromise to Provide Drugs to Poor Nations," *Wall Street Journal* (August 28, 2003): A3; Statistics South Africa, "Labour Statistics Survey of Average Monthly Earnings," *Statistical Release P0272* (February 2002): 3; Central Intelligence Agency, *The World Factbook*, www.cia.gov/library/publications/the-world-factbook/index.html.

Theories and Institutions:
Trade and Investment

PART THREE

SIX

International Trade and Factor-Mobility Theory

Objectives

- To understand theories of international trade

- To explain how free trade improves global efficiency

- To identify factors affecting national trade patterns

- To explain why a country's export capabilities are dynamic

- To understand why production factors, especially labor and capital, move internationally

- To explain the relationship between foreign trade and international factor mobility

A market is not held for the sake of one person.

—African (Fulani) *proverb*

257

CASE Costa Rica: Using Foreign Trade to Trade Up Economically

Map 6.1 shows Costa Rica, a Central American country of about 4.5 million people, which borders the Pacific Ocean and the Caribbean arm of the Atlantic. Its name, "Rich Coast," refers to its fertile soil and bountiful biodiversity.[1] Costa Rica possesses some attributes we associate with developed countries and some that we associate with developing countries. With a per capita GDP of $11,600 (based on purchasing price parity in 2008), Costa Rica depends on agricultural commodities—primarily bananas, pineapples, and coffee—for about one-third of its merchandise export earnings. (Note the coffee farm in the opening photo.) However, its tourism earnings are higher than those from these top three agricultural exports combined. It has a fairly high level of external debt, a literacy rate of about 95 percent, a life expectancy at birth of 78 years, and a fairly even income distribution (the highest 10 percent of the population earns about 37 percent of its income). It has also enjoyed a long history of democracy and political stability.

MAP 6.1 Costa Rica

Although largely an agricultural country, the Central American nation of Costa Rica has succeeded in diversifying its economy. Tourism is strong, as is technology. Puerto Limón, for instance, is home to an oil refinery, and there's a petrochemical plant in nearby Moín. Intel operates a manufacturing facility and distribution center in Heredia, just east of the capital of San José.

Isla del Coco is not shown.

FOUR ERAS

Like all countries, Costa Rica relies on *international trade* and *factor-mobility policies*—strategies related to the movement of goods, services, and production factors across borders—to pursue its economic objectives. In any country, these two sets of policies change over time, as both domestic and foreign conditions evolve. They're also politically sensitive, especially when it comes to the economic priorities and judgments of the nation's leaders.

For Costa Rica, it's convenient to trace policy evolution through four historical periods, each characterized by particular strategies regarding international trade and factor mobility:

- *Late 1800s–1960: Liberal trade*—a policy calling for minimal government interference in trade and investment

- *1960–1982: Import substitution*—a policy calling for the local production of goods and services that would otherwise be imported

- *1983–early 1990s: Liberalization of imports,* export promotion, and incentives for most types of foreign investments

- *Early 1990s–present: Strategic trade policy* (also called an *industrial policy*) calling for the production of specific types of products—and openness to imports

LATE 1800s–1960

In the latter part of the 1800s, most nations permitted goods, capital, and people to move with relative freedom from one country to another. Governments tended to interfere only minimally, and the general result was an economic environment in which individual producers determined what to produce and where to produce it. Trade flourished and countries tended to specialize in selling what they could best produce.

Most Latin American countries, including Costa Rica until the early 1960s, specialized in either a single or a few commodities (raw materials or agricultural products), which they exported in exchange for other commodities and manufactured goods. Costa Rican farmers specialized first in coffee and later, after the development of refrigerated ships, in bananas as well. For most of the period, the country was well served by this policy, primarily because commodity prices, especially coffee prices, remained high.

Eventually, however, three factors convinced Costa Rican leaders to encourage more diversified production and economic self-sufficiency:

- Two world wars disrupted Costa Rica's ability to export its commodities and import products it did not produce.

- Coffee and banana prices dropped relative to the prices of manufactured products, particularly as new commodity producers (especially in Africa) entered world markets.

- Latin American countries with less-open international markets had insulated themselves more from adverse international conditions.

As a result of these developments, Costa Rica turned to policies centered on the idea of import substitution.

1960–1982

In the early 1960s, Costa Rican authorities reasoned that if they limited imports (say, by taxing them heavily), they'd provide both Costa Rican and foreign investors with an incentive to produce more things within Costa Rica to sell there. They also realized that, unfortunately, the Costa Rican market was too small to support investments requiring large-scale production.

To address this problem, Costa Rica joined with four other countries—El Salvador, Guatemala, Honduras, and Nicaragua—to form the Central American Common Market (CACM), which allowed goods produced in any member country to enter freely into the market of any other member. Thus, a company located in a member country could serve a five-country market rather than a one-country market.

Miscalculations and Mixed Results

The results were mixed. Costa Rica's economic dependence on agriculture was already declining before the import substitution policy, from 40.9 percent to 25.2 percent of GDP between 1950 and 1960. Thus, the decline to 18 percent by 1980 could not be attributed completely to the policy change.

Likewise, most new manufacturing foreign investment was earmarked for selling in Costa Rica and not the larger CACM market. For example, import substitution helped attract pharmaceutical investment, but the availability of a larger market was not the primary reason; in this case, the strategy worked basically because small-scale packaging and processing are efficient within this industry.

So why was the strategy of import substitution, even coupled with a complementary regional trade agreement, less successful than CACM leaders had hoped? Quite simply, neither local nor foreign investors were convinced that the CACM was destined to last, and as it turned out, they were right. By the late 1970s, civil wars in both El Salvador and Guatemala stifled those economies, and a new regime in Nicaragua was ideologically committed to complete governmental control of all aspects of the economy, including trade; El Salvador and Honduras even went to war with each other.

In some cases, import substitution did lead to increased exports, such as for Costa Rican processed coffee and cottonseeds. Many economists and prospective investors, however, began to worry that policies designed to protect local production—including price controls, import prohibitions, and subsidies—were channeling the country's resources away from areas of production in which Costa Rica had long been most efficient. For example, Costa Rica became nearly self-sufficient in rice production, but only because government policies kept lower-cost foreign-produced rice out of the market.

Moreover, the government managed to hold down consumer rice prices only by subsidizing domestic rice producers. And where did the money for these subsidies come from? They came in part from higher taxes on efficient industries—industries that, in turn, found it hard to expand because they were strapped for cash. Finally, some inefficient producers survived because they reaped the benefits of high consumer prices, leaving consumers with less disposable income to spend on any products, domestic or foreign.

At this point, Costa Rican policymakers concluded that the country must emphasize the production of goods that could compete in international markets. For one thing, they had the example of Asian countries that were achieving rapid growth by competing internationally. In 1983, therefore, Costa Rica shifted to a policy of promoting exports.

1983–EARLY 1990s

First, to help ensure that only internationally competitive companies and industries were likely to survive in the newly projected business environment, the government began removing import barriers. Rice imports, for example, rose substantially as the government removed the protective barriers it had erected around domestic production.

CINDE

Policymakers also decided to seek more outside capital and expertise to support economic reforms. Luckily, the United States launched its Caribbean Basin Initiative, which allowed products originating in the Caribbean region (including Costa Rica) to enter the United States at lower tariff (or import tax) rates than those originating elsewhere. To capitalize on this new opportunity, Costa Rica formed CINDE (Coalición Costarricense de Iniciativas de Desarrollo), a private organization funded by the government and grants from the U.S. government. The purpose of CINDE was to aid in economic development, and one of its top priorities was attracting foreign direct investment.

To augment CINDE's work, Costa Rica established an export processing zone (EPZ) that allowed companies exporting finished output to import all inputs and equipment tax free. They were also exempted from paying Costa Rican income tax for eight years and allowed to pay at a 50 percent discount for the next four years. By 1989, 35 companies—mainly textile and footwear producers seeking to take advantage of Costa Rica's pool of inexpensive labor—had located in the EPZ.

By this time, however, CINDE officials were beginning to worry about two potential problems facing its ambitious new initiatives:

1. That Costa Rica could not remain cost competitive in the type of products exported from the EPZ because other countries (mainly Mexico) were benefiting from even lower U.S. tariffs
2. That Costa Rica's highly skilled and educated workforce was being underutilized by the types of industries attracted to the EPZ

CINDE officials decided to work with the Costa Rican government to identify and attract investors who matched up better with Costa Rican resources.

EARLY 1990s–PRESENT

The Costa Rican government targeted industries for international competition that promised high growth potential and could pay higher wages and salaries than most of those that had already invested in the EPZ. The targeted industries included medical instruments and appliances, electronics, and software.

Costa Rican officials also took a close look at the characteristics of developing countries that were attracting significant amounts of foreign investment: a highly educated and largely English-speaking workforce (especially the availability of engineers and technical operators), political and social stability and relatively high levels of economic freedom, and a quality of life that would appeal to the managers and technical personnel that foreign investors would bring in to work in the facilities. The conclusion? In its targeted industries, Costa Rica should be able to compete on the international market.

WHAT CINDE RECOMMENDED

CINDE also hired the Foreign Investment Advisory Service (FIAS) of the International Finance Corporation (an arm of the World Bank) to study the feasibility of attracting companies in these industries and the best means of attracting them to Costa Rica. FIAS concluded that attracting the right number of the right companies was well within Costa Rica's reach.

It also suggested areas within this selection of targeted industries, such as power technologies, that best fit with Costa Rica's main advantage—a labor force that was well educated in relation to its cost—and recommended that officials target industries that supported the electronics and computer industries, such as plastics and metalworking. Finally, FIAS noted areas in which Costa Rica needed to improve, such as the protection of intellectual property rights and English proficiency among technicians and engineers. In response, Costa Rica put English language skills in a revised curriculum for training mid-level technicians and set up Spanish-language training for the personnel brought in by foreign investors.

Progress Report

Setting out to attract investments in electronics and software, Costa Rica landed such high-tech investors as Reliability, Protek, Colorplast, and Sensortronics. By far the largest investment, however, has been by Intel. What did CINDE officials do to make Costa Rica attractive to the computer-chip giant? By drawing up a list of all the questions and concerns that Intel might have, they were prepared to respond to them quickly and knowledgeably. They also involved top governmental and company leaders in meetings with Intel executives, who were even piloted by President José Figueres on a helicopter survey of plant sites.

Since then, Costa Rica has turned its attention to medical devices, an area in which it has attracted investments by such companies as Abbott Laboratories, Baxter, and Procter & Gamble. Although exports of coffee and bananas are still important to the nation's economy, about two-thirds of Costa Rica's merchandise exports are now manufactured goods, with high-tech products constituting the backbone **⊙RN** of the economy and export earnings.

Case Review Note

Introduction

The preceding case shows how Costa Rica has used trade and factor mobility (movement of capital, technology, and people) to help it achieve its economic objectives. Figure 6.1 shows that trade in goods and services and the movement of production factors are means by which countries are linked internationally. Like Costa Rica, other countries wrestle with the questions of what, how much, and with whom their country should trade. These questions are intertwined with considerations of what they can produce efficiently and if and how they can improve their competitiveness by increasing the quality and quantity of capital, technical competence, and worker skills.

Trade theory helps managers and government policymakers focus on these questions:

- What products should we import and export?
- How much should we trade?
- With whom should we trade?

Concept Check

Compare Figure 6.1 with Figure 1.1, which outlines certain conditions that may affect a firm's operations when it decides to do business on an international scale. Here the graphic focuses in on operational adjustments that a company faces when it takes specific strategic actions to go international—namely, to trade and transfer means of production.

LAISSEZ-FAIRE VERSUS INTERVENTIONIST APPROACHES TO EXPORTS AND IMPORTS

Once countries set economic and political objectives, officials enact policies—including trade policies—to achieve the desired results. These policies impact business because they affect which countries can produce given products more efficiently and whether countries will permit imports to compete against their own domestically produced goods and services. Some countries take a more *laissez-faire* approach, one that allows market forces to determine trading relations. *Free-trade theories* (absolute advantage and comparative advantage) take a complete laissez-faire approach because they prescribe that governments should not intervene directly to affect trade. At the other extreme are *mercantilism* and *neomercantilism,* which prescribe a great deal

FIGURE 6.1 International Operations and Economic Connections

To meet its international objectives, a company must gear its strategy to trading and transferring its means of operation across borders—say, from (Home) Country A to (Host) Country B. Once this process has taken place, the two countries are connected economically.

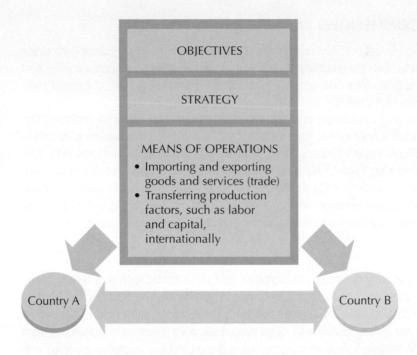

of government intervention in trade. Whether taking a laissez-faire or interventionist approach, countries rely on trade theories to guide policy development.

THEORIES OF TRADE PATTERNS

Some trade theories prescribe that governments should influence trade patterns; others propose a laissez-faire treatment of trade.

After a look at theories dealing with trade intervention or not, we examine those that help explain trade patterns (how much countries depend on trade, what products they trade, and with whom they primarily trade). These include theories of *country size, factor proportions*, and *country similarity*. Then we consider theories dealing with the dynamics of countries' trade competitiveness for particular products. These theories include the *product life cycle theory* and the *diamond of national advantage theory*.

TRADE THEORIES AND BUSINESS

Table 6.1 summarizes the major trade theories and their emphases. A check mark indicates that the theory deals with this question, and a dash indicates it does not. The yes and no apply only to the question "Should government control trade?" because the other theories don't deal with the question.

These different theories increase understanding about how government trade policies might affect companies' competitiveness. For instance, they provide insights about favorable locales and products for exports. Thus they help companies determine where to locate their production facilities when governments do or do not impose trade restrictions.

FACTOR MOBILITY THEORY

Because the stability and dynamics of countries' competitive positions depend largely on the quantity and quality of their production factors (land, labor, capital, technology), we conclude the chapter with a discussion of factor mobility.

TABLE 6.1 What Major Trade Theories Do and Don't Discuss: A Checklist

A check mark indicates that a theory of trade concerns itself with the question asked at the head of the column; if there's a dash, it doesn't. In columns 4-7, you can see how each theory responds to the specific question; again, a dash indicates that the theory does not address the question.

	Description of Natural Trade			Prescription of Trade Relationships			
Theory	How Much Is Traded	What Products Are Traded?	With Whom Does Trade Take Place?	Should Government Control Trade?	How Much Should Be Traded?	What Products Should Be Traded?	With Whom Should Trade Take Place?
Mercantilism	—	—	—	yes	✓	✓	✓
Neomercantilism	—	—	—	yes	✓	—	—
Absolute advantage	—	✓	—	no	—	✓	—
Comparative advantage	—	✓	—	no	—	✓	—
Country size	✓	✓	—	—	—	—	—
Factor proportion	—	✓	✓	—	—	—	—
Country similarity	—	✓	✓	—	—	—	—
Product life cycle (PLC)	—	✓	✓	—	—	—	—
Diamond of national advantage	—	✓	—	—	—	—	—

Interventionist Theories

We begin our discussion with mercantilism because it is the oldest trade theory, out of which neomercantilism has more recently emerged. Although these theories are based on some of the reasons for governmental intervention, there are other reasons as well. In fact, the subject is so large that it is the subject of the next chapter.

MERCANTILISM

Mercantilism is a trade theory holding that a country's wealth is measured by its holdings of "treasure," which usually means its gold. This theory formed the foundation of economic thought from about 1500 to 1800.[2] According to the theory, countries should export more than they import and, if successful, receive gold from countries that run deficits. Nation-states were emerging during the period, and gold empowered central governments to raise armies and invest in national institutions so as to solidify the people's primary allegiances to the new nations. One can see why mercantilism flourished.

According to mercantilism, countries should export more than they import.

Governmental Policies To export more than they imported, governments restricted imports and subsidized production that could otherwise not compete in domestic or export markets. Some countries used their colonies to support this trade objective by having them supply commodities that would otherwise have to be purchased from a nonassociated country and by running trade surpluses with them as an additional way of obtaining gold. They did this not only by monopolizing colonial trade but also by forcing the colonies to export less highly valued raw materials to them and import more highly valued manufactured products from them.

As the influence of the mercantilist philosophy weakened after 1800, the governments of colonial powers seldom aimed directly to limit the development of industrial capabilities within their colonies. However, their home-based companies had technological leadership, ownership of raw material production abroad, and usually some degree of protection from foreign competition. This combination continued to make colonies dependent on raw material production and to tie their trade to their industrialized mother countries. In fact, we still see vestiges of these relationships.

The Concept of *Balance of Trade*   Some terminology of the mercantilist era has endured. For example, a **favorable balance of trade** (also called a **trade surplus**) still indicates that a country is exporting more than it is importing. An **unfavorable balance of trade** (also known as a **trade deficit**) indicates the opposite. Many of these terms are misnomers. For example, the word *favorable* implies "benefit," and the word *unfavorable* suggests "disadvantage." In fact, it is not necessarily beneficial to run a trade surplus nor is it necessarily disadvantageous to run a trade deficit. A country that is running a surplus, or a favorable balance of trade, is, for the time being, importing goods and services of less value than those it is exporting.[3]

In the mercantilist period, the difference was made up by a transfer of gold, but today it is made up by holding the deficit country's currency or investments denominated in that currency. In effect, the surplus country is granting credit to the deficit country. If that credit cannot eventually buy sufficient goods and services, the so-called favorable trade balance actually may turn out to be disadvantageous for the country with the surplus.

Neomercantilism   Recently, the term **neomercantilism** has emerged to describe the approach of countries that try to run favorable balances of trade in an attempt to achieve some social or political objective. For instance, a country may try to achieve full employment by setting economic policies that encourage its companies to produce in excess of the demand at home and to send the surplus abroad. Or a country may attempt to maintain political influence in an area by sending more merchandise to the area than it receives from it, such as a government granting aid or loans to a foreign government to use for the purchase of the granting country's excess production.

Free Trade Theories

Thus far, we have intentionally ignored the question of why countries need to trade at all. Why can't Costa Rica (or any other country) be content with the goods and services produced within its own territory? In fact, many countries following mercantilist policy did try to become as self-sufficient as possible. In this section, we discuss two theories supporting *free trade: absolute advantage* and *comparative advantage*.

Both theories hold that nations should neither artificially limit imports nor promote exports.[4] The market will determine which producers survive as consumers buy those products that best serve their needs. Both free trade theories imply *specialization*. Just as individuals and families produce some things that they exchange for things that others produce, national specialization means producing some things for domestic consumption and export while using the export earnings to buy imports of products and services produced abroad.

THEORY OF ABSOLUTE ADVANTAGE

In 1776, Adam Smith questioned the mercantilists' assumptions by stating that the real wealth of a country consists of the goods and services available to its citizens rather than its holdings of gold. Smith's theory of **absolute advantage** holds that different countries produce some goods more efficiently than others and questions why the citizens of any country should have to buy domestically produced goods when they can buy them more cheaply from abroad.

Smith reasoned that if trade were unrestricted, each country would specialize in those products that gave it a competitive advantage. Each country's resources would shift to

---

Margin notes:

Running a favorable balance of trade is not necessarily beneficial.

A country that practices neomercantilism attempts to run an export surplus to achieve a social or political objective.

Concept Check

In Chapter 1, we observe that nations are currently in the mood to reduce barriers to the movement of trade, capital, technology, and people; we also explain that this policy reflects a couple of key facts—namely, that consumers want a greater variety of goods and services at lower prices and that competition spurs efficiency.

According to Adam Smith, a country's wealth is based on its available goods and services rather than on gold.

the efficient industries because the country could not compete in the inefficient ones. Through specialization, countries could increase their efficiency because of three reasons:

1. Labor could become more skilled by repeating the same tasks.

2. Labor would not lose time in switching from the production of one kind of product to another.

3. Long production runs would provide incentives for the development of more effective working methods.

A country could then use its excess specialized production to buy more imports than it could have otherwise produced. But in what products should a country specialize? Although Smith believed the marketplace would make the determination, he thought that a country's advantage would be either *natural* or *acquired*.

Natural Advantage   A country has a **natural advantage** in producing a product or service because of climatic conditions, access to certain natural resources, or availability of certain labor forces. As we saw in our opening case, Costa Rica's climate and soil support the production of bananas, pineapples, and coffee, while its biodiversity supports a thriving ecotourism industry. Costa Rica imports wheat. If it were to increase its production of wheat, for which its climate and terrain are less suited, it would have to use land now devoted to the cultivation of bananas, pineapples, and coffee or to convert some of its bio-diverse national park areas to agricultural production, thus reducing the earnings from these products or services.

Conversely, the United States could produce coffee (perhaps in climate-controlled buildings), but at the cost of diverting resources away from products such as wheat, for which its climate and terrain are naturally suited. Trading coffee for wheat and vice versa is a goal more easily achieved than if these two countries were to try to become self-sufficient in the production of both. The more the two countries' natural advantages differ, the more likely they will favor trade with one another.

Variations among countries in natural advantages also help explain in which countries certain manufactured or processed products might be best produced, particularly if by processing an agricultural commodity or natural resource prior to exporting companies can reduce transportation costs. Processing coffee beans into instant coffee reduces bulk and is likely to reduce transport costs on coffee exports. Producing canned latte could add weight, lessening the industry's internationally competitive edge.

Acquired Advantage   Most of the world's trade today is of manufactured goods rather than agricultural goods and natural resources. Countries that are competitive in manufactured goods have an **acquired advantage,** usually in either product or process technology. An advantage of *product technology* is that it enables a country to produce a unique product or one that is easily distinguished from those of competitors. For example, Denmark exports silver tableware, not because there are rich Danish silver mines but because Danish companies have developed distinctive products.

An advantage in process technology is a country's ability to efficiently produce a homogeneous product (one not easily distinguished from that of competitors). For example, Japan has exported steel despite having to import iron and coal—the two main ingredients for steel production—because its steel mills have encompassed new laborsaving and material-saving processes. Thus countries that develop distinctive or less expensive products have acquired advantages, at least until producers in another country emulate them successfully.

Acquired advantage through technology has created new products, displaced old ones, and altered trading-partner relationships. The most obvious examples of change are production and export of new products and services, such as computers and software. Products that existed in earlier periods have increased their share of world trade because of technological changes in the production process. For example, early hand-tooled automobiles reached only elite markets, but a succession of manufacturing

Case Review Note

Natural advantage considers climate, natural resources, and labor force availability.

Acquired advantage consists of either product or process technology.

innovations—from assembly lines to robotics—has enabled automobiles to reach an ever-widening mass market.

In other cases, companies have developed new uses for old products, such as aloe in sunscreen. Other products have been at least partially displaced by substitutes, such as natural fibers by artificial fibers. Finally, technology may be used to overcome natural advantages. Iceland now exports tomatoes grown near the Arctic Circle, and Brazil exports quality wine produced near the equator; in both cases, these were impossible until the development of fairly recent technology.[5]

Free trade will bring

- Specialization.
- Greater efficiency.
- Higher global output.

How Does Resource Efficiency Work?   We demonstrate absolute trade advantage here by examining two countries (Costa Rica and the United States) and two commodities (coffee and wheat). Because we are not yet considering the concepts of money and exchange rates, we define the cost of production in terms of the resources needed to produce either coffee or wheat. This example is realistic because real income depends on the output of goods and services compared to the resources used to produce them.

Start with the assumption that Costa Rica and the United States are the only countries and each has the same amount of resources (land, labor, and capital) to produce either coffee or wheat. Using Figure 6.2, let's say that 100 units of resources are available in each country. In Costa Rica, assume that it takes four units to produce a ton of coffee and 10 units per ton of wheat. This is shown with the red Costa Rican production possibility line, and we can see that Costa Rica can produce 25 tons of coffee and no wheat, 10 tons of wheat and no coffee, or some combination of the two.

In the United States, it takes 20 units per ton of coffee and five units per ton of wheat. This is shown in the blue U.S. production possibility line, which indicates that the United States can produce five tons of coffee and no wheat, 20 tons of wheat and no coffee, or some combination of the two. Costa Rica is more efficient (that is, takes fewer resources to produce a ton) than the United States in coffee production, and the United States is more efficient than Costa Rica in wheat production.

To demonstrate how production can be increased through specialization and trade, we need first to consider a situation in which the two countries have no foreign trade. We could start from any place on each production possibility line; for convenience, however, we assume that if Costa Rica and the United States each devotes half of its 100 resources, or 50, to producing coffee and half, or 50, to producing wheat, Costa Rica can produce

FIGURE 6.2 Production Possibilities under Conditions of Absolute Advantage

In short, specialization increases output.

ASSUMPTIONS
for Costa Rica

1. 100 units of resources available
2. 10 units to produce a ton of wheat
3. 4 units to produce a ton of coffee
4. Uses half of total resources per product when there is no foreign trade

ASSUMPTIONS
for United States

1. 100 units of resources available
2. 5 units to produce a ton of wheat
3. 20 units to produce a ton of coffee
4. Uses half of total resources per product when there is no foreign trade

PRODUCTION	Coffee (tons)	Wheat (tons)
Without Trade:		
Costa Rica (point A)	12½	5
United States (point B)	2½	10
Total	15	15
With Trade:		
Costa Rica (point C)	25	0
United States (point D)	0	20
Total	25	20

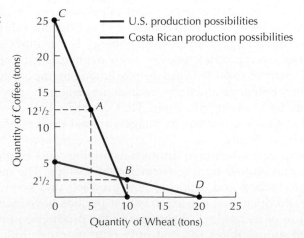

12.5 tons of coffee (divide 50 by 4) and five tons of wheat (divide 50 by 10). These values are shown as point A in Figure 6.2. The United States can produce 2.5 tons of coffee (divide 50 by 20) and 10 tons of wheat (divide 50 by 5). These are shown as point B in Figure 6.2.

Because each country has only 100 units of resources, neither one can increase wheat production without decreasing coffee production, or vice versa. Without trade, the combined production is 15 tons of coffee (12.5 + 2.5) and 15 tons of wheat (5 + 10). If each country specialized in the commodity for which it had an absolute advantage, Costa Rica then could produce 25 tons of coffee and the United States 20 tons of wheat (points C and D in the figure).

You can see that specialization increases the production of both products (from 15 to 25 tons of coffee and from 15 to 20 tons of wheat). By trading, global efficiency is optimized, and the two countries can have more coffee and more wheat than they would without trade.

THEORY OF COMPARATIVE ADVANTAGE

We have just described absolute advantage, which is often confused with and called *comparative advantage.* In 1817, David Ricardo examined the question "What happens when one country can produce all products at an absolute advantage?" and developed the theory of **comparative advantage.** This theory says that global efficiency gains may still result from trade if a country specializes in those products it can produce more efficiently than other products—regardless of whether other countries can produce those same products more efficiently or not.

> Gains from trade will occur even in a country that has absolute advantage in all products, because the country must give up less efficient output to produce more efficient output.

Comparative Advantage by Analogy Although this theory may seem initially incongruous, an analogy should clarify its logic. Imagine that the best physician in town also happens to be the best medical administrator. It would not make economic sense for the physician to handle all the administrative duties of the office, because the physician can earn more money by concentrating on medical duties, even though that means having to employ a less-skilled medical secretary to manage the office. In the same manner, a country gains if it concentrates its resources on the commodities it can produce most efficiently. It then trades some of those commodities for those commodities it has relinquished. The following discussion clarifies why this theory is true.

Production Possibility In this example, assume the United States is more efficient in producing coffee and wheat than Costa Rica is, thus having an absolute advantage in the production of both.[6] Take a look at Figure 6.3. As in our earlier example of absolute advantage, it assumes that there are only two countries, each with a total of 100 units of resources available, and half (50) of each country's resources used to produce each product. In this example, it takes Costa Rica 10 units of resources to produce either a ton of coffee or a ton of wheat, whereas it takes the United States only five units of resources to produce a ton of coffee and four units to produce a ton of wheat. Costa Rica can produce five tons of coffee and five tons of wheat (point A on the red line), and the United States can produce 10 tons of coffee and 12.5 tons of wheat (point B on the blue line). Without trade, neither country can increase its production of coffee without sacrificing some production of wheat, or vice versa.

Although the United States has an absolute advantage in the production of both coffee and wheat, it has a comparative advantage only in the production of wheat. This is because its advantage in wheat production is 2.5 times that of Costa Rica, but its advantage in coffee is only twice that of Costa Rica. Although Costa Rica has an absolute disadvantage in the production of both products, it has a comparative advantage (or less of a comparative disadvantage) in the production of coffee. Why? This is because Costa Rica is half as efficient as the United States in coffee production and only 40 percent as efficient in wheat production.

FIGURE 6.3 Production Possibilities under Conditions of Comparative Advantage

There are advantages to trade even if one country enjoys an absolute advantage in the production of all products.

ASSUMPTIONS
for Costa Rica
1. 100 units of resources available
2. 10 units to produce a ton of wheat
3. 10 units to produce a ton of coffee
4. Uses half of total resources per product when there is no foreign trade

ASSUMPTIONS
for United States
1. 100 units of resources available
2. 4 units to produce a ton of wheat
3. 5 units to produce a ton of coffee
4. Uses half of total resources per product when there is no foreign trade

PRODUCTION	Coffee (tons)	Wheat (tons)
Without Trade:		
Costa Rica (point A)	5	5
United States (point B)	10	12½
Total	15	17½
With Trade (increasing coffee production):		
Costa Rica (point C)	10	0
United States (point D)	6	17½
Total	16	17½
With Trade (increasing wheat production):		
Costa Rica (point C)	10	0
United States (point E)	5	18¾
Total	15	18¾

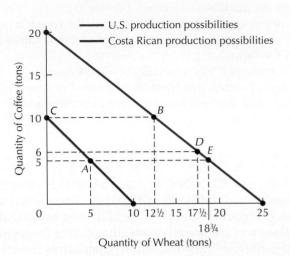

Without trade, the combined production is 15 tons of coffee (5 in Costa Rica plus 10 in the United States) and 17.5 tons of wheat (5 in Costa Rica plus 12.5 in the United States). Through trading, the combined production of coffee and wheat within the two countries can be increased. For example, if the combined production of wheat is unchanged from when there was no trade, the United States could produce all 17.5 tons of wheat by using 70 units of resources (17.5 tons times four units per ton). The remaining 30 U.S. resource units could be used for producing six tons of coffee (30 units divided by five units per ton). This production possibility is point D in Figure 6.3. Costa Rica would use all its resources to produce 10 tons of coffee (point C). The combined wheat production has stayed at 17.5 tons, but the coffee production has increased from 15 tons to 16 tons.

If the combined coffee production is unchanged from the time before trade, Costa Rica could use all its resources to produce coffee, yielding 10 tons (point C in Figure 6.3). The United States could produce the remaining five tons of coffee by using 25 units of resources. The remaining 75 U.S. units could be used to produce 18.75 tons of wheat (75 divided by 4). This production possibility is point E. Without sacrificing any of the coffee available before trade, wheat production has increased from 17.5 to 18.75 tons.

If the United States were to produce somewhere between points D and E, both coffee and wheat production would increase over what was possible before trade took place. Whether the production target is an increase of coffee or wheat or a combination of the two, both countries can gain by having Costa Rica trade some of its coffee production to the United States for some of that country's wheat output.

Don't Confuse Comparative and Absolute Advantage Most economists accept the comparative advantage theory, and it's influential in promoting policies for freer trade. Nevertheless, many government policymakers, journalists, managers, and workers confuse comparative advantage with absolute advantage and do not understand how a country can simultaneously have a comparative *advantage* and absolute *disadvantage* in the production of a given product.

THEORIES OF SPECIALIZATION: SOME ASSUMPTIONS AND LIMITATIONS

Both absolute and comparative advantage theories are based on specialization, which holds that it will increase output and be best for countries as they trade their output from specialization with each other. However, these theories make assumptions, some of which are not always valid.

Full Employment   The physician/secretary analogy we used earlier assumed that the physician could stay busy full time practicing medicine. If the physician is unable to stay busy full time with medical duties, he or she may perform administrative work while still maximizing earnings from serving as a physician. The theories of absolute and comparative advantage both assume that resources are fully employed. When countries have many unemployed or unused resources, they may seek to restrict imports to employ or use idle resources.

Full employment is not a valid assumption of absolute and comparative advantage.

Economic Efficiency   Our physician/administrator analogy also assumed that the physician who can do both medical and office work is interested primarily in maximization of profit, or maximum economic efficiency. Yet there are a number of reasons why physicians might choose not to work full time at medical tasks. They might find administrative work relaxing and self-fulfilling. They might fear that a hired secretary would be unreliable. They might wish to maintain secretarial skills in the somewhat unlikely event that administration, rather than medicine, commands higher wages in the future. Often, countries also pursue objectives other than output efficiency. They may avoid overspecialization because of the vulnerability created by changes in technology and by price fluctuations.

Countries' goals may not be limited to economic efficiency.

Division of Gains   Although specialization brings potential economic benefits to all countries that trade, the earlier discussion did not indicate how countries will divide increased output. In the case of our wheat and coffee example, if both the United States and Costa Rica receive some share of the increased output, both will be better off economically through specialization and trade. However, many people are concerned with relative and absolute economic growth. If they perceive that a trading partner is gaining too large a share of benefits, they may prefer to forgo absolute gains for themselves so as to prevent others from gaining a relative economic advantage.[7]

Two Countries, Two Commodities   As in our examples, both Smith and Ricardo assumed, for simplicity's sake, a simple world composed of only two countries and two commodities. Now, although this simplification is unrealistic, it does not diminish the usefulness of either theory. Economists have applied the same reasoning to demonstrate efficiency advantages in multiproduct and multicountry trade relationships.

Transport Costs   If it costs more to transport the goods than is saved through specialization, the advantages of trade are negated. In other words, in our examples of Costa Rica and the United States, some workers would need to forgo producing coffee or wheat in order to work in the shipment of coffee and wheat abroad. However, as long as the diversion reduces output by less than what the two countries gain from specialization, there are still gains from trade.

Statics and Dynamics   The theories of absolute and comparative advantage address countries' advantages statically—that is, by looking at them at one point in time. However, the relative conditions that give countries advantages or disadvantages in the production of given products are dynamic (constantly changing). For example, the resources needed to produce coffee or wheat in either Costa Rica or the United States

---

Concept Check

Recall from Chapter 2 our discussion of "Work Motivation," in which we explain that in **cultures** ranking high on so-called masculinity, people tend to value economic achievement over certain other values; we also observe, however, that in other cultures quality of life is valued over economic performance.

could change substantially because of advancements in and acceptance of genetically modified crops.[8] In fact, most trade today is due to acquired advantage; thus, changes in technological leadership may cause countries to gain or lose in both an absolute or relative sense.[9]

Case Review Note

In addition, as we show in our opening case, when Costa Rica focused on goods that could compete in international markets, it developed and enhanced a competitive advantage in some promising high-tech industries. Thus we should not assume that future absolute or comparative advantages will remain as they are today. We return to this theme later in the chapter as we examine theories to explain the dynamics of competitive production locations.

Services   The theories of absolute and comparative advantage deal with products rather than services. However, although a growing portion of world trade is in services, the theories apply because resources must also go into producing services. For instance, the United States sells an excess of such services as education to foreign countries (many foreign students attend U.S. universities), as well as credit card systems and collections. At the same time, it buys an excess of foreign shipping services. To become more self-sufficient in international shipping, the United States might have to divert resources from its more efficient use in higher education or in the production of competitive products.

Production Networks   Both theories deal with trading one product for another. Increasingly, however, a product may be partially made in different countries. For instance, a company may conduct R&D in Country A, secure components in Countries B and C, assemble final products in Country D, manage finances in Country E, and carry out call-center services in Country F. Although this type of development adds complexity to the analysis, it fits well with the concept of advantages through specialization. In other words, costs are saved by having activities take place in those countries where there is an absolute or comparative advantage for their production.

Mobility   The theories of absolute and comparative advantage assume that resources can move domestically from the production of one good to another—and at no cost. But this assumption is not completely valid. For example, a steelworker might not move easily into a software development job because of different skill needs. Even if able to move, the worker may be less productive than before.[10] The theories also assume that resources cannot move internationally. Increasingly, however, they do, and the movement affects countries' production capabilities. For instance, over 400,000 Nicaraguans are now living in Costa Rica.[11] Foreign companies have moved both personnel and capital to support their investments there, which has contributed to changing Costa Rican capabilities. Such movement is clearly an alternative to trade, a topic we discuss later in the chapter. However, it is safe to say that resources are more mobile domestically than they are internationally.

Case Review Note

Trade Pattern Theories

The free trade theories demonstrate how economic growth occurs through specialization and trade; however, they do not deal with trade patterns such as the amount, product composition, or partners a country will have if it follows a free trade policy. In this section, we discuss the theories that help explain these patterns.

HOW MUCH DOES A COUNTRY TRADE?

Free trade theories of specialization neither propose nor imply that only one country should or will produce a given product or service. There are **nontradable goods**—products and services that are seldom practical to export (such as haircuts and retail grocery distribution) primarily because of high transportation costs. Such goods and services are produced in every country. However, among tradable goods, some countries import and export more than others. We will now examine theories that help explain country differences.

Theory of Country Size   The **theory of country size** holds that large countries usually depend less on trade than small countries. Countries with large land areas are apt to have varied climates and an assortment of natural resources, making them more self-sufficient than smaller countries. Most large countries (such as Brazil, China, India, the United States, and Russia) import much less of their consumption needs and export much less of their production output than do small countries (such as Uruguay, the Netherlands, and Iceland).

Furthermore, distance to foreign markets affects large and small countries differently. Normally, the farther the distance, the higher the transport costs, the longer the inventory carrying time, and the greater the uncertainty and unreliability of timely product delivery. The following example illustrates why distance is more pronounced for a large country than for a small one.

Assume, for example, that the normal maximum distance for transporting a given product is 100 miles because prices increase too much at greater distances. Although almost any location in tiny Belgium is within 100 miles of a foreign country, the same isn't true for its two largest neighbors, France and Germany. Thus, Belgium's dependence on trade as a percentage of its production and consumption is greater than the comparable figures in either France or Germany, a fact that can be partially explained by the distance factor due to country size.

> Bigger countries differ in several ways from smaller countries. They
> - Tend to export a smaller portion of output and import a smaller part of consumption.
> - Have higher transport costs for foreign trade.

Size of the Economy   Although land area is the most obvious way of measuring a country's size, countries can also be compared on the basis of economic size. The world's top 10 exporters and importers are all developed countries except for China. China, although not a developed country, has a very large economy by virtue of its large population. The 10 countries account for over half the world's exports and imports.

Simply, developed countries produce so much that they have more to sell—both domestically and internationally. In addition, because these countries produce so much, incomes are high and people buy more from both domestic and foreign sources. At the same time, little of the trade of developing countries is with other developing countries.

WHAT TYPES OF PRODUCTS DOES A COUNTRY TRADE?

In our discussion of absolute advantage, we indicated that this advantage might be either natural or acquired. In this section, we discuss theories that help explain what types of products result from these natural and acquired advantages. We won't delve again into those factors we've already discussed (climate and natural resources) that give a country a natural advantage; however, we will examine the factor endowment theory of trade. For acquired advantage, we discuss the importance of production and product technology.

Factor-Proportions Theory   Eli Heckscher and Bertil Ohlin developed **factor-proportions theory,** which is based on countries' production factors—land, labor, and capital (funds for investment in plant and equipment). This theory said that differences in countries' endowments of labor compared to their endowments of land or capital explain differences in the cost of production factors. For instance, if labor were abundant in comparison to land and capital, labor costs would be low relative to land and capital costs. If labor were scarce, labor costs would be high in relation to land and capital costs. These relative factor costs would lead countries to excel in the production and export of products that used their abundant—and therefore cheaper—production factors.[12]

> According to the factor-proportions theory, factors in relative abundance are cheaper than factors in relative scarcity.

People and Land   Factor-proportions theory appears logical. In countries in which there are many people relative to the amount of land—for example, Hong Kong and the

Netherlands—land price is very high because it's in demand. Regardless of climate and soil conditions, neither Hong Kong nor the Netherlands excels in the production of goods requiring large amounts of land, such as wool or wheat. Businesses in countries such as Australia and Canada produce these goods because land is abundant compared to the number of people.

Manufacturing Locations   Casual observation of manufacturing locations also seems to substantiate the theory. For example, the most successful industries in Hong Kong are those in which technology permits the use of a minimum amount of land relative to the number of people employed: Clothing production occurs in multistory factories where workers share minimal space. Hong Kong does not compete in the production of automobiles, however, which requires much more space per worker.

| Production factors, especially labor, are not homogeneous.

Capital, Labor Rates, and Specialization   In countries where little capital is available for investment and the amount of investment per worker is low, managers might expect to find cheap labor rates and export competitiveness in products that need large amounts of labor relative to capital. An example would be agricultural products requiring a lot of labor for picking and packing, such as roses from Ecuador.

However, because the factor-proportions theory assumes production factors to be homogeneous, tests to substantiate the theory have been mixed.[13] Labor skills, in fact, vary within and among countries because people have different training and education. Training and education require capital expenditures that do not show up in traditional capital measurements, which include only plant and equipment values. When the factor-proportions theory accounts for different labor groups and the capital invested to train these groups, it seems to explain many trade patterns.[14] For example, because exports from developed countries embody a higher proportion of professionals such as scientists and engineers than do developing economies' exports, the former countries are using their abundant production factors to maintain their lead in exports. Exports of low-income economies, though, show a high intensity of less-skilled labor.[15]

This variation in labor skills among countries has led to more international specialization by task to produce a given product. For example, a company may locate its research activities and management functions primarily in countries with a highly educated population, while locating its production work in countries where it can employ less-educated and less-expensive workers.

| Companies may substitute capital for labor, depending on the cost of each.

Process Technology   Factor-proportions analysis becomes more complicated when the same product can be produced by different methods, such as with labor or capital. The photos show, for instance, that India uses lots of labor and few machines to harvest wheat, whereas Canada uses mechanized methods and few workers. In the final analysis, the optimum location of production depends on comparing the cost in each locale based on the type of production that minimizes costs there.

| Bigger countries depend more on products requiring longer production runs.

However, not all products lend themselves to such trade-offs in production methods. For some, the production technology requires huge amounts of fixed capital and long production runs to spread the fixed capital costs over more output units. The production of these products is most likely to develop in large countries with large markets.[16] However, companies may locate long production runs in small countries if they expect to be able to export from those countries.[17] In industries where long production runs reduce unit costs substantially, companies tend to locate their production in only a few countries, using these locations to export. Where long production runs are less important, we find a greater prevalence of multiple production units scattered around the world in different countries so as to minimize the cost of transportation through exporting.

In addition, high expenditures on research and development create high up-front fixed costs for companies. Therefore, the technologically intensive company from a small nation may need to sell more abroad than would a company with a large domestic market. This small-nation company may, in turn, pull resources from other industries and

In the top photo, wheat harvesting in India is labor intensive because of lower labor costs. The opposite is true for harvesting in Canada, which is shown in the bottom photo.

Source: Top: Mitchell Kanashkevich/ Getty Images-Creative Express; *Bottom:* Dave Reede/Getty Images-Creative Express.

companies within its domestic market, causing the small nation to have more national specialization than one finds in a larger nation.[18]

Product Technology Figure 6.4 shows the changing composition of world trade. Manufacturing is by far the largest sector, with commercial services the fastest-growing sector. Manufacturing competitiveness depends largely on technology to develop new products and processes. The technology depends, in turn, on a large number of highly educated people (especially scientists and engineers) and a large amount of capital to invest in research and development.

Because developed countries have an abundance of these features, they originate most new products and account for most manufacturing output and trade. Developing countries depend much more on the production of primary products; thus, they depend more on natural advantage.

Most new products originate in developed countries.

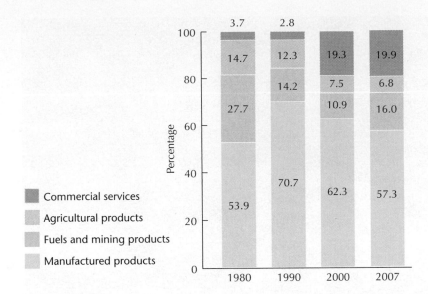

FIGURE 6.4   Worldwide
Trade by Major Sectors

As a percentage of total world trade,
manufactured products are more
important than products in any other
category. Services, however,
constitute the fastest-growing
category.

Source: From World Trade
Organization, *Annual Report* (Geneva,
various years).

WITH WHOM DO COUNTRIES TRADE?

We have already noted that developed countries account for the bulk of world trade. They also primarily trade with each other, whereas developing countries mainly export primary products and labor-intensive products to developed countries in exchange for new and technologically advanced products. Below, we discuss the roles that country similarity and distance play in determining trading partners.

Country-Similarity Theory   Thus far in this chapter, the theories explaining why trade takes place have focused on the differences among countries in terms of natural conditions and factor endowment proportions. We also showed that most trade takes place among developed countries, a pattern that can be further explained by **country-similarity theory.** This theory says that companies create new products in response to market conditions in their home market. They then turn to markets they see as most similar to those at home, because these markets are large and consumer economic levels are similar to what the companies are accustomed to.[19]

Developed countries primarily trade with each other because they

- Produce and consume more.
- Emphasize technical breakthroughs in different industrial sectors.
- Produce differentiated products and services.

Specialization and Acquired Advantage   However, in order to export, a company must provide consumers abroad with an advantage over what they could buy from their domestic producers. Trade occurs because *countries* specialize to gain acquired advantage—for example, by apportioning their research efforts more strongly to some sectors than to others. Germany is traditionally strong in machinery and equipment, Switzerland in pharmaceutical products, and Denmark in food products.[20] Even developing countries gain advantages through specialization in very narrow product segments. For instance, Bangladesh has been successful at exporting shirts, trousers, and hats but not bed linens or footballs, whereas Pakistan has been successful at exporting bed linens and footballs.[21]

Product Differentiation   Trade also occurs because *companies* differentiate products, thus creating two-way trade in what seem like similar products. For example, the United States is both a major exporter and a major importer of tourist services, vehicles, and passenger aircraft because different companies from different countries have developed product variations with different appeals. For instance, both Boeing from the United States and Airbus Industrie from Europe produce large jet passenger aircraft that will fly from point A to point B, but U.S. and European airlines buy both companies' aircraft because their models differ in such features as capacity, flying range, fuel consumption, and perceived reliability.[22] As a result, Boeing and Airbus Industrie sell them within their own and each other's home markets as well as within countries that produce no aircraft.

The Effects of Cultural Similarity   Importers and exporters find it easier to do business in countries they perceive as being culturally similar to their home countries, such as those that speak a common language. Likewise, historic colonial relationships explain much of the trade between specific developed and developing economies. For instance, France's colonial history in Africa has given Air France an edge in serving those former colonies' international air passenger markets.[23] Similarly, the lack of extensive trade among nations in the Southern Hemisphere is due partly to the absence of historic ties. Importers and exporters find it easier to continue business ties than to develop new distribution arrangements in countries where they are less experienced.

The Effects of Political Relationships and Economic Agreements   Political relationships and economic agreements among countries may discourage or encourage trade between them. For example, the political animosity between the United States and Cuba has diminished their mutual trade for about five decades. An example of trade encouragement is the agreement among many European countries to remove all trade barriers with each other, thereby causing a greater share of the countries' total trade to be conducted with each other.

The Effects of Distance   The theories regarding country differences and similarities help explain broad world trade patterns, such as those that link developed countries and developing countries, but they do not fully explain specific pairs of trading relationships. Although no single answer does, the geographic distance between two countries accounts for many of these world trade relationships.

In essence, greater distances usually mean higher transportation costs; that's why Intel's cost to ship semiconductors from Costa Rica to the United States is lower than if it had to bring them from, say, Argentina. Finland has an advantage in exporting to neighboring Russia because its transport costs are cheaper and faster than those of more distant countries. When Acer, a Taiwanese computer maker, built a plant in Finland to serve Russia, a major reason was that it realized savings by shipping from there rather than from Asia.[24]

Overcoming Distance   But transport cost is not the only factor in trade partner choice. For example, New Zealand competes with Chile, Argentina, and South Africa for out-of-season sales of apples to the Northern Hemisphere—but with a disadvantage in freight costs to the United States and Europe. It has countered this disadvantage by increasing yields, developing new premium varieties, bypassing intermediaries to sell directly to supermarkets abroad, and consolidating efforts through a national marketing board. However, such methods to overcome distance disadvantages are difficult to maintain. For example, both Chinese and Chilean orchardists have smuggled new strains of apple tree cuttings out of New Zealand.[25]

The Statics and Dynamics of Trade

Although we've alluded to the fact that trading patterns change, for example, because of political and economic relations among countries and the development of new product capabilities, we now discuss two theories—the product life cycle theory and the diamond of national advantage—that help explain how countries develop, maintain, and lose their competitive advantages.

Trading partners are affected by

- Cultural similarity.
- Political relations between countries.
- Distance.

Concept Check

In discussing "Cultural Distance" in Chapter 2, we show that "distance" is an index of similarities between countries based primarily on such shared cultural attributes as language, ethnicity, or values. We indicate that, by and large, a company from one country should expect fewer adjustments when moving to a country whose culture is close to that of its home base, but we also caution that, even in these cases, executives should be aware of subtle cultural differences.

Does Geography Matter? Variety Is the Spice of Life

As you study this chapter, you'll see that geography plays a role in many of the theories and questions concerning trade. We pull them together in this discussion.

Part of a country's trading advantage is explained by its natural advantage—climate, terrain, arable land, and natural resources. Thus Saudi Arabia trades oil, a natural resource, for U.S. rice, which needs huge wet areas for production. Remember, however, that technology may often negate natural advantage, as in the development of substitutes (synthetic nitrate for natural nitrate) and the development of different methods of production (Chile is not using traditional bogs for the successful growing of cranberries). Nevertheless, a country's geography—particularly ease of moving goods to markets in other countries—may give it an advantage or disadvantage. For instance, landlocked countries have a considerable transport cost disadvantage relative to countries with seacoasts.[26]

Factor-proportions theory helps explain where certain goods may be more efficiently produced, such as labor-intensive goods where labor is plentiful in relation to capital and land. Thus Bangladesh excels in the production of clothing requiring lots of labor in relation to either capital or land. However, these factors can change in both quantity and quality. Hong Kong has a very high population density, and it used to excel in the production of labor-intensive goods. But because Hong Kong has accumulated capital and upgraded the education of its workforce, its competitive production and exports now encompass more capital intensity and more skilled labor.

Usually, small countries need to trade more than large countries, primarily because they are apt to have less variety of natural advantages, but there are exceptions. Small countries that also have low incomes tend to depend little on trade because they produce and consume so little. Distance from foreign markets also plays a role. For instance, geographically isolated countries such as Fiji trade less than would be expected from their size because transportation costs increase the price of traded goods substantially.[27]

Conversely, Canada is a large developed country whose dependence on trade and trade per capita are not only among the world's highest but also much higher than we would expect from the theory of country size. This may be explained largely by Canada's population dispersion. Ninety percent of its population is within 100 miles of the U.S. border; thus shipping goods between, say, Vancouver and Seattle or Toronto and Cleveland is often more feasible than between Vancouver and Toronto.

Although distance helps us understand the importance of pairs of trading partners, political relationships and cultural similarity are important factors as well. For example, there is a large amount of trade within regional trading organizations and between former colonizers and their former colonies. Most important, though, is the preponderance of world trade among developed countries because they produce and consume more. Further, they engage in technological specialization and product differentiation to fit market niches.

However, this begs the question of why some countries are developed and others are not. This is a very complex issue that we cannot hope to answer. Nevertheless, some of the factors affecting income levels, and thus trade, are geographic. For instance, one study showed that 70 percent of the differences among countries in per capita income can be accounted for by four factors—malaria, hydrocarbon endowments, coastal access, and transportation costs—all of which relate to geography.[28] ●

PRODUCT LIFE CYCLE (PLC) THEORY

According to the PLC theory of trade, the production location for many products moves from one country to another depending on the stage in the product's life cycle.

The international **product life cycle (PLC) theory** of trade states that the location of production of certain manufactured products shifts as they go through their life cycle, which consists of four stages: *introduction, growth, maturity,* and *decline.*[29] Table 6.2 highlights these stages.

Changes over the Cycle   Companies develop new products primarily because they observe nearby needs for them. This means that a U.S. company is most apt to create a new product for the U.S. market, a French company for the French market, and so on. At the same time, almost all new technology that results in new products and production methods originates in developed countries.[30] They have most of the resources to develop new products and most of the income to buy them.

Table 6.2   Life Cycle of the International Product

During its life cycle, focus on a product's production and market locations often shifts from industrial to developing markets. The process is accompanied by changes in the competitive factors affecting both production and sales, as well as in the technology used to produce the product.

Life Cycle Stage

	1: Introduction	2: Growth	3: Maturity	4: Decline
Production location	• In innovating (usually industrial) country	• In innovating and other industrial countries	• Multiple countries	• Mainly in developing countries
Market location	• Mainly in innovating country, with some exports	• Mainly in industrial countries • Shift in export markets as foreign production replaces exports in some markets	• Growth in developing countries • Some decrease in industrial countries	• Mainly in developing countries • Some developing country exports
Competitive factors	• Near-monopoly position • Sales based on uniqueness rather than price • Evolving product characteristics	• Fast-growing demand • Number of competitors increases • Some competitors begin price cutting • Product becoming more standardized	• Overall stabilized demand • Number of competitors decreases • Price is very important, especially in developing countries	• Overall declining demand • Price is key weapon • Number of producers continues to decline
Production technology	• Short production runs • Evolving methods to coincide with product evolution • High labor input and labor skills relative to capital input	• Capital input increases • Methods more standardized	• Long production runs using high capital inputs • Highly standardized • Less labor skill needed	• Unskilled labor on mechanized long production runs

Introduction   Once a company has created a new product, theoretically it can manufacture that product anywhere in the world. In practice, however, the early-production stage, called the *introductory stage,* generally occurs in a domestic location so the company can obtain rapid market feedback and save on transport costs because most sales are domestic. The small export markets are mainly to other developed countries because more customers in those countries can afford the new products.

Production is apt to be more labor-intensive than in later stages because more labor-saving machinery may be introduced only when sales begin to expand rapidly and when the product becomes highly standardized. Although production is in developed countries with high labor rates, the education and skills usually make their labor efficient on nonstandardized production. Even if production costs are high because of expensive labor, companies can often pass costs on to consumers who are unwilling to wait for possible price reductions later.

The introduction stage is marked by

• Innovation in response to observed need.
• Exporting by the innovative country.
• Evolving product characteristics.

Growth   Sales growth attracts competitors to the market, particularly in other developed countries. Let's say that the innovator is in the United States and a competitor puts a manufacturing unit in Japan. The Japanese production is sold mainly in Japan for several reasons:

1. The growing demand in Japan does not allow for much attention to other markets.
2. Producers in Japan stay occupied in developing unique product variations for Japanese consumers.
3. Japanese costs may still be high because of production start-up problems.

Sales growth creates an incentive for companies to develop laborsaving process technology, but this incentive is partially countered because competitors are differentiating

Growth is characterized by

• Increases in exports by the innovating country.
• More competition.
• Increased capital intensity.
• Some foreign production.

their products, particularly to fit the needs of different countries. Thus the capital intensity, though growing, is less than will come later. The original producing country will increase its exports, especially to developing countries, but will lose certain key export markets in which local production commences.

Maturity   In the *maturity stage*, worldwide demand begins to level off, although it may be growing in some countries and declining in others. Typically, there is a shakeout of producers, more standardized production, and increased importance of price as a competitive weapon. Capital-intensive production reduces per-unit cost, thus creating even more demand in developing economies. Because markets and technologies are widespread, the innovating country no longer commands a production advantage. Producers have incentives to shift production to developing economies where they can employ less-skilled and less-expensive labor efficiently for standardized (capital-intensive) production. Exports decrease from the innovating country as foreign production displaces it.

Decline   As a product moves into the *decline stage,* those factors occurring during the mature stage continue to evolve. The markets in developed countries decline more rapidly than those in developing economies as affluent customers demand ever-newer products. By this time, market and cost factors have dictated that almost all production is in developing economies that export to the declining or small-niche markets in developed countries. In other words, the country in which the innovation first emerged—and exported from—then becomes the importer.

Verification and Limitations of PLC Theory   The PLC theory holds that the location of production facilities that serve world markets shifts as products move through their life cycle. Such products as ballpoint pens and hand calculators have followed this pattern. They were first produced in a single developed country and sold at a high price. Then production shifted to multiple developed country locations to serve those local markets. Finally, most production is located in developing countries, and prices have declined.

There are many types of products for which shifts in production location do not usually take place. In these cases, the innovating country may maintain its export ability throughout the product's life cycle. These exceptions include the following:

- Products with high transport costs may have to be produced close to the market, thus never becoming significant exports.

- Products that, because of very rapid innovation, have extremely short life cycles—a factor that makes it impossible to achieve cost reductions by moving production from one country to another. Some fashion items fit this category.

- Luxury products for which cost is of little concern to the consumer. In fact, production in a developing country may make the product seem less luxurious than it really is.

- Products for which a company can use a differentiation strategy, perhaps through advertising, to maintain consumer demand without competing on the basis of price.

- Products that require nearby specialized technical labor to evolve into their next generation. This seems to explain the long-term U.S. dominance of medical equipment production and German dominance in rotary printing presses.

Regardless of product, MNEs have increasingly tended to introduce new products at home and abroad almost simultaneously. In other words, instead of merely observing needs within their domestic markets, companies develop products and services for observable market segments that transcend national borders. In so doing, they eliminate delays as a product is diffused from one country to another, and they choose an initial production location that will minimize costs for serving markets in multiple countries. This production location may or may not be in the innovating company's home market.

<div class="margin-notes">

Maturity is characterized by
- A decline in exports from the innovating country.
- More product standardization.
- More capital intensity.
- Increased competitiveness of price.
- Production start-ups in emerging economies.

Decline is characterized by
- A concentration of production in developing countries.
- An innovating country becoming a net importer.

Not all products conform to the dynamics of the PLC.

</div>

THE DIAMOND OF NATIONAL ADVANTAGE

Why have countries developed and sustained different competitive advantages? For example, why do Italian companies have an advantage in the ceramic tile industry and Swiss companies in the watch industry? The **diamond of national advantage** is a theory showing four features as important for competitive superiority: demand conditions; factor conditions; related and supporting industries; and firm strategy, structure, and rivalry.[31] These are shown in Figure 6.5. We have largely discussed these conditions in the context of other trade theories, but how they combine affects the development and continued existence of competitive advantages.

The framework of the theory, therefore, is a useful tool for understanding how and where globally competitive companies develop and sustain themselves. Usually, but not always, all four conditions need to be favorable for an industry within a country to attain and maintain global supremacy.

Facets of the Diamond   Both PLC theory and country-similarity theory show that new products (or industries) usually arise from companies' observation of need or demand, which is usually in their home country.

Demand Conditions   *Demand conditions* are the first feature in the theory. Companies then start up production near the observed market. (Recall the premises of the country-similarity theory.) This was the case for the Italian ceramic tile industry after World War II: There was a postwar housing boom, and consumers wanted cool floors (which tile would provide) because of the hot Italian climate.

Factor Conditions   The second feature—*factor conditions* (recall natural advantage within absolute advantage theory and the factor-proportions theory)—influenced both the choice of tile to meet consumer demand and the choice of Italy as the production location. Wood was less available and more expensive than tile, and most production factors (labor with the needed skills, capital, technology, and equipment) were available within Italy on favorable terms.

Related and Supporting Industries   The third feature—the existence of nearby *related and supporting industries* (enamels and glazes)—was also favorable. Recall, for instance, our discussions of the importance of transport costs in the theory of country size, in assumptions of specialization, and in the limitation factors of PLC theory.

According to the diamond of national advantage theory, companies' development of internationally competitive products depends on their domestic

- Demand conditions.
- Factor conditions.
- Related and supporting industries.
- Firm strategy, structure, and rivalry.

Concept Check

In discussing the concept of the **market economy** in Chapter 4, we explain that such a system encourages an open exchange of goods and services among producers and consumers, both of which groups consist of "individuals" who make their own economic decisions; in this respect, then, the interaction among producers and consumers determines what products will be produced and in what quantities.

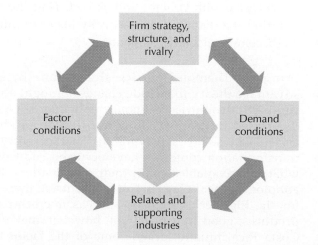

FIGURE 6.5   The Diamond of National Competitiveness

The diamond shows the interaction of four conditions that usually need to be favorable if an industry in a country is to gain and sustain a global competitive advantage.

Source: Adapted from Michael E. Porter, "The Competitive Advantage of Nations," Harvard Business Review, Vol. 68, No. 2, March-April 1990 and used with permission of the Harvard Business Review.

Firm Strategy, Structure, and Rivalry The combination of three features—demand, factor conditions, and related and supporting industries—influenced companies' decisions to initiate production of ceramic tiles in postwar Italy. The ability of these companies to develop and sustain a competitive advantage required favorable circumstances for the fourth feature: *firm strategy, structure, and rivalry.*

Barriers to market entry were low in the tile industry (some companies started up with as few as three employees), and hundreds of companies initiated production. Rivalry became intense as companies tried to serve increasingly sophisticated Italian consumers. These circumstances forced breakthroughs in both product and process technologies, which gave the Italian producers advantages over foreign producers and enabled them to gain the largest global share of tile exports.

Limitations of the Diamond of National Advantage Theory The existence of the four favorable conditions does not guarantee that an industry will develop in a given locale. Entrepreneurs may face favorable conditions for many different lines of business. In fact, comparative advantage theory holds that resource limitations may cause a country's companies to avoid competing in some industries even though they may have an absolute advantage. For example, conditions in Switzerland would seem to have favored success if companies in that country had become players in the personal computer industry. However, Swiss companies preferred to protect their global positions in such product lines as watches and scientific instruments rather than downsize those industries by moving their highly skilled people into a new industry.

A second limitation concerns the growth of globalization. The industries on which this theory is premised grew when companies' access to competitive capabilities was decidedly more domestically focused. We can see how globalization affects each of the four conditions:

1. Observations of foreign or foreign-plus-domestic, rather than just domestic, demand conditions have spurred much of the recent growth in Asian exports. In fact, such Japanese companies as Uniden and Fujitech target their sales almost entirely to foreign markets.[32]

2. Companies and countries are not dependent entirely on domestic factor conditions. For example, capital and managers are now internationally mobile.

3. If related and supporting industries are not available locally, materials and components are now more easily brought in from abroad because of advancements in transportation and the relaxation of import restrictions. In fact, many MNEs now assemble products with parts supplied from a variety of countries.

4. Companies react not only to domestic rivals but also to foreign-based rivals they compete with at home and abroad. Thus the absence of any of the four conditions from the diamond domestically may not inhibit companies and industries from becoming globally competitive.

Using the Diamond for Transformation By expanding the diamond of national advantage theory to include changes brought about by globalization, we can see the validity for countries' economic policies. As we saw in our opening case, Costa Rica diversified its economy from agricultural products to modern high-tech products, and it did so by satisfying the market entry conditions of the diamond. This transformation could not have occurred had Costa Rican authorities looked only at what was available within their own borders. It was possible because the country adopted a global view. In Costa Rica itself, there was (and still is) very little demand for the high-tech products, such as microchips and medical devices, that it now produces; good transportation, however, makes efficient export possible. Similarly, Costa Rica initially lacked some of the factor conditions necessary for producing

---

Domestic existence of all conditions

- Does not guarantee an industry will develop.
- Is not necessary with globalization.

Point ▶ Counterpoint

Should Nations Use Strategic Trade Policies?

Point ▶ **Yes** What's so important about acquiring advantage in world trade? For one thing, if you're a country that wants to compete in today's globalized business environment (and you have to), you obviously must develop and maintain some industries that will be internationally competitive. But there's more: Those industries must also grow and earn sufficient revenues to keep your domestic economy performing. What's the role of your government in the process of going global? It should be central to your whole effort; after all, we're talking about national economies here.

For one thing, a government's role is rarely neutral. A government may claim that its economic policies don't affect the performance of specific domestic industries on the world stage, but a lot of those policies are bound to have precisely that effect. For instance, who's going to argue that the U.S. government's efforts to "improve agricultural productivity" and "enhance defense capabilities" have nothing to do with the fact that the United States does a healthy business in the export of farm and aerospace products?

Moreover, just about every government policy designed to help one industry is going to have a negative effect on another one. European airlines, for example, complain (with some justification) that government support for high-speed rail traffic in Europe deprives them of the revenue they need to compete with U.S. overseas carriers, which don't have much to worry about from railroad passenger traffic at home. In other words, national policymakers everywhere are faced with trade-offs. Therefore, if every government policy is going to help one party while hurting another one anyway, why shouldn't a country's practices call for taking special care of the industries that will likely give the country its best competitive advantage?

In fact, executing such a plan can be pretty simple. First, target a growth industry and figure out what factors make it competitive (or potentially competitive). Next, identify your country's likely competitive advantages (and make sure you know why you have them). Finally, develop a little synergy between the strong points you've uncovered during both processes: Target the resources needed to support the industries that fit best with your country's advantages.

This program—which comes under the general heading of *strategic trade policy*—is particularly effective if you're a developing country. Why? Because you've probably already decided that (1) you need to integrate yourself into the global economy and that (2) you need to figure out the best way of getting into the international game. So far, so good, but you need to remember that simply opening up your borders to foreign competition doesn't necessarily mean that domestic producers are going to have an easier time competing either abroad or at home.

Counterpoint ◀ **No** Of course, countries should try to become most competitive in the industries that promise the best returns and have the most potential for going global. Obviously, they're the ones most likely to add value (in the form of high profits and good wages) to national production. However, strategic trade policy is not the best way to achieve the goals—about which just about everybody agrees.

I'll start by making a concession: There are limited circumstances under which a targeting program will work, particularly for small countries such as Costa Rica. Because Costa Rica's GDP amounts to less than 10 percent of the value of Wal-Mart's annual sales, it is manageable for parties involved to work together to reach mutually beneficial agreements with minimal frustration. But in a large economy? Impossible.

However, it's debatable just how much Costa Rica's economic success is due to strategic trade policy and how much goes back to conditions that existed before the government started the whole process of targeting industries. Costa Rica already had a well-educated workforce, a relatively high level of economic freedom, a large population of English-speaking workers, a quality of life that had some appeal to foreign personnel, and, last but not least, a high level of political stability. Yes, Costa Rica landed Intel, but it's only fair to point out that Intel had already decided to put a plant somewhere in Latin America. Costa Rica's job, then, was basically convincing Intel it was a better choice than certain countries, such as Brazil and Chile, which were at a distance disadvantage when it came to sending output to the United States.

An alternative is for a country to focus on conditions affecting its attractiveness to profitable companies in general instead of targeted industries in particular. In other words, a government can alter conditions affecting, say, factor proportions, efficiency, and innovation by upgrading production factors—such as by improving human skills, providing an adequate infrastructure, encouraging consumers to demand higher-quality products, and promoting an overall competitive environment—for any industry that's interested in doing business within its borders.

Let's turn to your comments about sub-Saharan Africa. I'll even make another concession: Institutional inertia is indeed a way of life in the area, and there's no reason to expect that it will go away any time soon.[37]

But what if we looked at things from another perspective? Wouldn't all of these bureaucratic agencies and ministries, rather than trying to focus on a specific industry in, say, the global high-tech universe, find it easier to review (and enforce) their own laws; take steps to stabilize their

When you throw open your borders, the first companies to take you up on the invitation will be foreign competitors with considerable advantages over the homegrown industries you're trying to develop. They've had a head start that's allowed them to develop not only certain internal efficiencies but cozy relations with everybody in the international distribution channel.

Moreover, no matter how promising your targeted industries may be, and no matter how carefully you've tried to match up your industries with your competitive advantages, as a developing country, you probably don't have the technology and marketing skills you'll need to compete with more experienced players.[33]

This brings us back to the reason why strategic trade policy (as opposed to adopting a policy of laissez-faire) is your optimal choice if you're a developing country: Your government must protect your local industries—say, by helping them get the skills and technology they're going to need. You could also focus your efforts to attract foreign investment on companies that have the marketing and technical skills you need; that's one good way of bringing in the kind of production you need. And it wouldn't hurt to extend incentives to the industries you're counting on.

If you're looking for some evidence that strategic trade policy is effective in helping developing nations go global, look at Singapore, which not only managed to attract companies with experience in consumer-electronics production but eventually emerged as a global competitor because it also had the competitive advantage of low wages.[34] By the same token, we have ample evidence that laissez-faire often doesn't work in developing countries. In sub-Saharan Africa, for example, government institutions are so deeply rooted that it's almost impossible for anyone—either individuals or multinational conglomerates—to make a move without getting entangled in the bureaucratic undergrowth.[35]

Moreover, because no single institution in developing countries has much in the way of resources, all of them are better off focusing their collective efforts on specific industries that have some potential for international competitiveness; otherwise, all you have is a bunch of underresourced agencies and ministries aiming at markets scattered all over the economic landscape.[36] ▶

populations and rectify their most glaring economic, social, and gender inequities; and support entrepreneurial activity in the informal sectors of their economies? Wouldn't they find it more productive to foster an environment of trust—one in which, say, the government helps cut transaction costs so local firms will be willing to work with other companies, domestic and foreign, to acquire a little of the knowledge and a few of the resources they need to be competitive?[38]

To repeat, instead of picking and haggling over special industries, wouldn't they be better advised to improve the investment environment in which, after all, everybody's ultimately going to have to operate anyway?

At this point, I might as well take the offensive in this debate. Strategic trade policies typically result in no more than small payoffs—primarily because most governments find it difficult to identify and target the right industries.[39] What if a country targets an industry in which global demand never quite lives up to expectations? That's what happened to the United Kingdom and France when they got together to underwrite supersonic passenger planes. Or what if the domestic companies in a targeted industry simply fall short of being competitive? That's what happened when Thailand decided to get into the steel business.[40]

What if too many nations target the same global industries, thereby committing themselves to excessive competition and inadequate returns?[41] What if two countries compete to support the same industry, as happened when both Brazil and Canada decided to produce regional jets in the same hemisphere?[42] Finally, what if a country successfully targets an industry only to have unexpected conditions arise? Should it stay the course even though it's probably reacting to various pressures, such as the pressure to support employment in a distressed industry?[43]

Finally, even if a government can identify a future growth industry in which a domestic firm is likely to succeed—a very big if—it doesn't follow that a company deserves public assistance. History recommends that nations permit their entrepreneurs to do what they do best: take risks that don't jeopardize whole sectors of the economy. The upshot will probably be the same as always: Some will fail, but the successful ones will survive and thrive competitively. ◀

high-tech products, especially trained personnel. Eventually, however, it altered its educational system to fit human resource development to production needs and allowed companies to bring in foreign managers and technicians to fill human resource gaps. Finally, it developed local factors, such as additional power and metalworking expertise, and it attracted enough high-tech companies to ensure a vibrant competitive environment. Thus, understanding and having the necessary conditions to be globally competitive is important, but these conditions are neither static nor purely domestic.

Factor-Mobility Theory

In the preceding discussions, we indicated that both the quantity and quality of countries' factor conditions change. As they do, countries' relative capabilities also change. The change may come about because of internal circumstances. For instance, if savings rates increase, countries have more capital relative to their factors of land and labor. If they spend relatively more on education, they improve the quality of the labor factor.

Currently, one of the biggest changes underway concerns relative population numbers. At present rates, 33 countries are projected to have smaller populations in 2050 than today, primarily because of low fertility rates—e.g., a projected decrease of 14 percent and 22 percent in Japan and Italy, respectively. The same countries with projected decreases or slow population growth are also encountering an aging population, leaving a smaller portion of the population to provide output. They will need large increases in immigration just to maintain the present ratios of employed people relative to retirees. Concomitantly, nine countries are expected to account for half of the world's population increase, with India, Pakistan, and Nigeria leading the pack.[44]

These changes, of course, are important in understanding and predicting changes in export production and import market locations. At the same time, the mobility of capital, technology, and people affect trade and relative competitive positions. In this section, we discuss the **factor-mobility theory** of trade patterns, which focuses on the reasons why production factors move, the effects that such movement has in transforming factor endowments, and the effect of international factor mobility (especially people) on world trade.

WHY PRODUCTION FACTORS MOVE

Capital   Capital, especially short-term capital, is the most internationally mobile production factor. Companies and private individuals primarily transfer capital because of differences in expected return (accounting for risk). They find information on interest-rate differences readily available, and they can transfer capital by wire instantaneously at a low cost. Short-term capital is more mobile than long-term capital such as direct investment because there is more likely to be an active market through which investors can quickly buy foreign holdings and sell them if they want to transfer capital back home or to another country.

Political and economic conditions affect investors' perceptions of risk and where they prefer to put their capital. At the same time, companies invest long term abroad to tap markets and lower operating costs. Figure 6.6 shows humorously companies' motive to lower costs. However, businesses do not make all the international capital movements. Governments give foreign aid and loans. Not-for-profit organizations donate money abroad to relieve worrisome economic and social conditions. Individuals remit funds to help their families and friends in foreign countries. Regardless of the donor or motive, the result affects factor endowments.

People   People are also internationally mobile, but less so than capital. Of course, some people travel to other countries as tourists, students, and retirees; however, this travel does not affect factor endowments because the travelers do not work in the destination countries. Unlike funds that can be cheaply transferred by wire, people must usually incur high transportation costs to work in another country. If they move legally, they must get immigration papers, and most countries give these documents sparingly. Finally, such people may have to learn another language and adjust to a different culture away from their families and friends who serve as their customary support groups. Despite the barriers, people endure hardships and risks to move to another country. The photo shows Central Americans stowing away on a train in southern Mexico en route to find jobs in the north, most likely in the United States.

During the latter part of the nineteenth and early part of the twentieth centuries, migration was the major engine of globalization, and at present it is important again. About

Concept Check

As we explain in Chapter 1, a foreign investment is an interest in a company or ownership of a loan made to another party; such a transaction can take place between countries, of course, and companies typically use some form of portfolio investment for short-term financial gain. We also point out that to earn higher yields on short-term investments, firms routinely move funds from country to country.

Capital and labor move internationally to

- Gain more income.
- Flee adverse political situations.

FIGURE 6.6   The Cosmoeconomic Question of the Day: Will Foreign Galaxies Prove to Be Sources of Less Expensive Labor?

Source: Joel Pett, Lexington-Herald Leader, 1997. Reprinted with permission. All rights reserved.

3 percent of the world's population (over 200 million people) has migrated to another country.[45] Because this 3 percent is spread unevenly, the percentage is much greater in some countries than in others, such as representing about 11 percent of the U.S. population.[46]

Of the people who go abroad to work, some move permanently and some move temporarily. For example, on the one hand, some people immigrate to another country, become citizens, and plan to reside there for the rest of their lives. On the other hand, MNEs assign people to work abroad for periods ranging from a few days to several years (usually to a place where they also transfer capital), and some countries allow workers to enter on temporary work permits, usually for short periods. For instance, about two-thirds of the population in the United Arab Emirates are temporary workers.[47] In

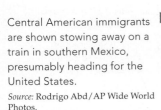

Central American immigrants are shown stowing away on a train in southern Mexico, presumably heading for the United States.

Source: Rodrigo Abd/AP Wide World Photos.

many cases, workers leave their families behind in the hopes of returning home after saving enough money while working in a foreign country. Some move legally, and others move illegally (that is to say, they are undocumented).

Economic Motives People, whether professionals or unskilled workers, largely work in another country for economic reasons. For example, Indonesian laborers work in Malaysia because they can make almost 10 times as much per day as they can at home.[48] State-enterprise hotels in China entice Western executives to work for them in China to improve the hotels' economic performance.[49] After the economic downturn of 2008, substantial numbers of immigrants worldwide returned to their native countries, such as an estimated 60,000 Indonesians who had been working in wealthier Asian nations.[50]

Political Motives People also move for political reasons—for example, because of persecution or war dangers, in which case they are known as refugees and usually become part of the labor pool where they live. Sometimes it is difficult to distinguish between economic and political motives for international mobility because poor economic conditions often parallel poor political conditions. For example, in the early twenty-first century, hundreds of thousands of Colombians left the country, fleeing both a civil war and unemployment. Map 6.2 highlights recent global immigration.

EFFECTS OF FACTOR MOVEMENTS

Neither international capital nor population mobility is a new occurrence. For example, had it not been for historical mass immigration, Australia, Canada, and the United States would have a greatly reduced population today. Further, many immigrants brought

| Factor movements alter factor endowments.

MAP 6.2   Global Immigration

Net gain and loss figures are in thousands and reflect annual average numbers of immigrants. Note that movement is primarily from developing to developed countries and that movement *into developing nations* consists largely of immigrants from neighboring countries. All in all, about 3 percent of the world's population—nearly 200 million people—live outside their nations of birth.

Source: Adapted from "Snapshots: Global Migration," *New York Times* (June 24, 2007): 8. Data from United Nations Population Division, The World Bank, and the International Monetary Fund.

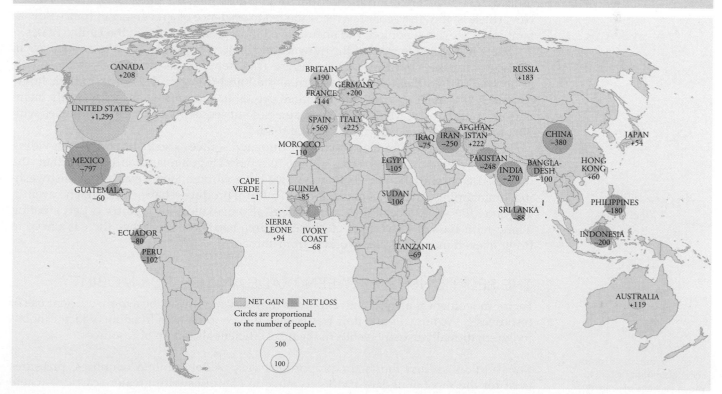

human capital with them, thus adding to the base of skills that enabled those countries to be newly competitive in an array of products they might otherwise have imported. Finally, these same countries received foreign capital to develop infrastructure and natural resources, which further altered their competitive structures and international trade.

What Happens When People Move?   Recent evidence is largely anecdotal. Nevertheless, factor movements are substantial for many countries and insignificant for others. For example, the foreign-born population as a percentage of total population is over 20 percent for Luxembourg, Australia, Switzerland, New Zealand, and Canada, but it is no more than 2 percent in South Korea, the Slovak Republic, Hungary, and Japan.[51]

The United States is currently an example of a country whose recent immigration is largely concentrated at the high and low ends of human skills. For instance, over a third of all people with doctoral degrees in the United States are foreign born. At the other extreme, although the United States classifies all people without a high school education as "low skilled," Mexican low-skilled workers in the United States average three years less formal education than their U.S. counterparts.[52] At both extremes, the United States—at least before the 2008 economic downturn—has had shortages of native-born workers, which has been partially alleviated through immigration.

Isolating a particular aspect of labor mobility is fraught with difficulty. Although labor and capital are different production factors, they are intertwined. For instance, Singapore has transformed itself from a labor-intensive and low-wage country to a capital-intensive and high-wage country largely because of capital accumulation that has come from abroad.[53] For example, much of Singapore's capital accumulation has been in human capital—that is, in the import of skilled foreigners and the education of its own workforce.

A controversial issue is the effect on countries of outward migration. On the one hand, countries lose potentially productive resources when educated people leave—a situation known as a *brain drain*. On the other hand, they may receive money from the people who leave. For example, Ecuador lost almost 5 percent of its population between 1999 and 2001, including 10,000 teachers and many other people with substantial work skills. However, many of these people are now sending remittances back to Ecuador. In fact, remittance flows to all countries for 2007 were estimated at U.S. $337 billion, and the inflows for several countries amounted to more than 15 percent of their GDP.[54] Nevertheless, the 2008 economic recession led to evidence of a reverse remittance flow as families in Mexico sent money to unemployed immigrant relatives in the United States.[55]

There is also evidence that the outward movement of people leads to an increase in start-up companies in their home countries. Their remittances increase capital available at home. Further, the immigrants learn abroad and transfer ideas back to their home countries. In some cases, they use remitted capital to start businesses with family members or on their own. Many of these businesses subsequently export to companies with which the immigrants had connections abroad.[56]

Finally, countries receiving productive human resources also incur costs by providing social services and acculturating people to a new language and culture. Further, the unskilled workers who take jobs that native-born workers don't want—like dishwashing, maintaining grounds, and picking agricultural produce—have children who eventually enter the workforce. If these children are also unskilled, the country is perpetuating a long-term class of "have-nots." If these children become skilled, then there is a need to bring in even more unskilled workers from abroad.

THE RELATIONSHIP BETWEEN TRADE AND FACTOR MOBILITY

Factor movement is an alternative to trade that may or may not be a more efficient use of resources.[57] We now discuss how free trade when coupled with freedom of factor mobility internationally usually results in the most efficient allocation of resources.

Substitution   When the factor proportions vary widely among countries, pressures exist for the most abundant factors to move to countries with greater scarcity—where

There are pressures for the most abundant factors to move to areas of scarcity.

they can command a better return. In countries where labor is abundant compared to capital, laborers tend to be unemployed or poorly paid. If permitted, many in the labor pool go to countries that have full employment and higher wages.

Similarly, capital tends to move away from countries in which it is abundant to those in which it is scarce. For example, Mexico gets capital from the United States, and the United States gets labor from Mexico.[58] If finished goods and production factors were both free to move internationally, the comparative costs of transferring goods and factors would determine the location of production.

However, as is true of trade, there are restrictions on factor movements that make them only partially mobile internationally—such as both U.S. immigration restrictions that limit the legal and illegal influx of Mexican workers and Mexican ownership restrictions in the petroleum industry that limit U.S. capital movements to invest in that industry.

A hypothetical example, shown in Figure 6.7, should illustrate the substitutability of trade and factor movements under different scenarios. Assume the following:

- The United States and Mexico have equally productive land available at the same cost for growing tomatoes.

- The cost of transporting tomatoes between the United States and Mexico is $0.75 per bushel.

- Workers from either country pick an average of two bushels per hour during a 30-day picking season.

The only differences in price between the two countries are due to variations in labor and capital cost. The labor rate is $20.00 per day, or $1.25 per bushel, in the United States

FIGURE 6.7 Unrestricted Trade, Factor Mobility, and the Cost of Tomatoes

Costs are lowest when trade is unrestricted and production factors are mobile.

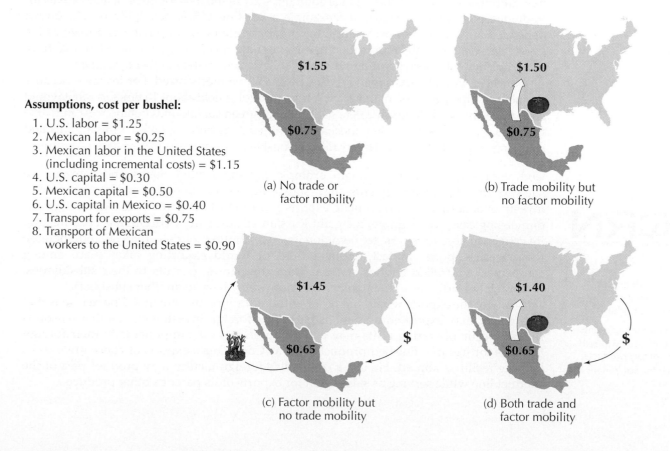

Assumptions, cost per bushel:

1. U.S. labor = $1.25
2. Mexican labor = $0.25
3. Mexican labor in the United States (including incremental costs) = $1.15
4. U.S. capital = $0.30
5. Mexican capital = $0.50
6. U.S. capital in Mexico = $0.40
7. Transport for exports = $0.75
8. Transport of Mexican workers to the United States = $0.90

$1.55

$0.75

(a) No trade or factor mobility

$1.50

$0.75

(b) Trade mobility but no factor mobility

$1.45

$0.65

(c) Factor mobility but no trade mobility

$1.40

$0.65

(d) Both trade and factor mobility

and $4.00 per day, or $0.25 per bushel, in Mexico. The capital needed to buy seeds, fertilizers, and equipment costs the equivalent of $0.30 per bushel in the United States and $0.50 per bushel in Mexico.

If neither tomatoes nor production factors can move between the two countries (see Figure 6.7[a]), the cost of tomatoes produced in Mexico for the Mexican market is $0.75 per bushel ($0.25 of labor plus $0.50 of capital), whereas those produced in the United States for the U.S. market cost $1.55 per bushel ($1.25 of labor plus $0.30 of capital). If the two countries eliminate trade restrictions on tomatoes between them (Figure 6.7[b]), the United States will import from Mexico because the Mexican cost of $0.75 per bushel plus $0.75 for transporting the tomatoes to the United States will be $0.05 less than the $1.55-per-bushel cost of growing them in the United States.

Consider another scenario in which neither country allows the importation of tomatoes but both allow certain movements of labor and capital (Figure 6.7[c]). Mexican workers can enter the United States on temporary work permits for an incremental travel and living expense of $14.40 per day per worker, or $0.90 per bushel. At the same time, U.S. companies will invest capital in Mexican tomato production, provided the capital earns more than it would earn in the United States—say, $0.40 per bushel, which is less than the Mexican going rate.

In this scenario, Mexican production costs per bushel will be $0.65 ($0.25 of Mexican labor plus $0.40 of U.S. capital), and U.S. production costs $1.45 ($0.25 of Mexican labor plus $0.90 of travel and incremental costs plus $0.30 of U.S. capital). Each country would reduce its production costs—from $0.75 to $0.65 in Mexico and from $1.55 to $1.45 in the United States—by bringing in abundant production factors from abroad.

> The lowest costs occur when trade and production factors are both mobile.

With free trade *and* the free movement of production factors (Figure 6.7[d]), Mexico will produce for both markets by importing capital from the United States. According to the three assumptions just stated, doing this will be cheaper than sending labor to the United States. In reality, because neither production factors nor the finished goods they produce are completely free to move internationally, slight changes in the extent of restrictions can greatly alter how and where goods may be produced most cheaply.

In some cases, however, the inability to gain sufficient access to foreign production factors may stimulate efficient methods of substitution, such as the development of alternatives for traditional production methods.[59] For example, at one time U.S. tomato growers in California depended almost entirely on Mexican temporary workers under what was known as the *bracero program*. Since the termination of this program, the California tomato harvests have quadrupled, while mechanization has replaced 72 percent of the number of workers.

However, not all harvesting jobs can reasonably be mechanized. For instance, because cantaloupes ripen at different times, pickers go through a field about 10 times. A robot would have to be able to distinguish colors so as to leave green cantaloupes behind.[60] At the same time, many other jobs that defy mechanization—such as bussing tables at restaurants and changing beds in hotels—are largely filled by unskilled immigrants in developed countries.

Complementarity   In our tomato example for the United States and Mexico, we showed that factor movements may substitute for or stimulate trade. Companies' investments abroad often stimulate exports from their home countries. As we show in our closing case, for example, the giant Russian oil company LUKOIL has been making investments abroad so as to own foreign distribution outlets that should increase Russian oil exports. In fact, about a third of world exporting takes place among companies' controlled entities, such as from companies' parents to their subsidiaries, from their subsidiaries to the parents, and from subsidiary to another subsidiary.

Many of the exports would not occur without foreign investments. One reason is that a company may export equipment as part of its foreign investment. Another reason is that domestic operating units may export materials and components to their foreign facilities for use in a finished product, such as Coca-Cola's exports of concentrate to its bottling facilities abroad. Finally, a company's foreign facility may produce part of the product line while serving as sales agent for exports of its parent's other products.

Case Review Note

> Factor mobility through foreign investment often stimulates trade because of
>
> • The need for components.
> • The parent's ability to sell complementary products.
> • The need for equipment for subsidiaries.

Looking to the Future

In What Direction Will Trade Winds Blow?

When countries have few restrictions on foreign trade and factor mobility, companies have greater latitude in reducing operating costs. For example, fewer trade restrictions give them opportunities to gain economies of scale by servicing markets in more than one country from a single base of production. Fewer restrictions on factor movements give them opportunities to combine factors for more efficient production. However, government trade and immigration restrictions vary from one country to another, from one point in time to another, and under different circumstances.

Nevertheless, it's probably safe to say that trade restrictions have been diminishing, primarily because of the economic gains that countries foresee through freer trade. Further, restrictions on the movement of capital and technology have become freer, but whether restrictions on the movement of people are freer is questionable.

However, there are uncertainties as to whether the trend toward the freer movement of trade and production factors will continue. Groups worldwide question whether the economic benefits of more open economies outweigh some of the costs, both economic and noneconomic. Although the next chapter discusses import restrictions (protectionism) in detail, it is useful at this point to understand the overall evolution of protectionist sentiment.

One key issue is the trade between developed and developing economies. At the same time that trade barriers are being lowered, some developing economies with very low wage rates are growing economically more rapidly than are developed countries. Concomitantly, as companies shift production to developing economies, they displace jobs within developed countries. As this occurs, displaced workers need to find new jobs. But there is uncertainty as to how fast new jobs will replace old ones and how much tolerance developed countries will have for employment displacement and job shifts. If they become very intolerant, they may enact protectionist measures that would stifle trade.

Another key issue is the future of factor endowments. If present trends continue, relationships among land, labor, and capital will continue to evolve. For example, the population growth rate is expected to be much higher in developing economies than in developed countries. This could result in continued shifts of labor-intensive production to developing economies and pressures on the developed countries to accept more immigrants.

Urbanization will likely grow faster in developing countries than in developed ones, which are already heavily urbanized. Considerable evidence indicates that productivity increases with urbanization because firms can more likely find people with the exact skills they need, because there are economies in moving supplies and finished products, and because knowledge flows more easily from one company and industry to another. Thus we might expect higher growth in some developing countries due to their pace of urbanization. Such growth should also lead these countries to account for a larger share of world trade.

At the same time, the finite supply of natural resources may lead to price increases for these resources, even though oversupplies have often depressed prices. The limited supply may work to the advantage of developing economies, because supplies in developed countries have been more fully exploited.

We will probably see the continued trend toward a more finely tuned specialization of production among countries to take advantage of specific country conditions. Although part of this will be due to wage and skill differences, other factors are important as well. For instance, country differences in protection of property rights may influence where technologically intensive companies choose to produce. For instance, they may locate more activities within countries that offer more protection. Or they may disperse production to different countries in order to hinder potential competitors from gaining the full picture needed to pirate their products and production processes.

Three factors are worth monitoring because they could cause product trade to become relatively less significant in the future:

1. As economies grow, efficiencies of multiple production locations also grow because they can all gain sufficient economies of scale. This may allow country-by-country production to replace trade in many cases. For example, most automobile producers have moved into China and Thailand—or plan to do so—as a result of China's and Thailand's growing market size.

(continued)

2. Flexible, small-scale production methods, especially those using robotics, may enable even small countries to produce many goods efficiently for their own consumption, thus eliminating the need to import those goods. For example, before the development of efficient minimills that can produce steel on a small scale, steel production used to take larger capital outlays that needed enormous markets.

3. Services are growing more rapidly than products as a portion of production and consumption within developed countries. Consequently, product trade may become a less important part of countries' total trade. Further, many of the rapid-growth service areas, such as retail gasoline distribution and dining out, are not easily traded, so trade in goods plus services could become a smaller part of total output and consumption. ∎

CASE

LUKOIL: Trade Strategy at a Privatized Exporter

In 2008, Russia's GDP grew by about 6 percent—its tenth straight year of significant growth.[61] That growth has been fueled by the oil and gas sector, which currently accounts for about 25 percent of GDP and 40 percent of all exports. Today, Russia consumes about 27 percent of its oil production and exports the other 73 percent; and so lucrative is its business in gas and oil that petroleum export taxes have allowed the government to pay off all foreign debt incurred by its Soviet predecessor. On the downside, of course, its dependence on petroleum exports makes Russia quite vulnerable to fluctuations in global petroleum markets. If the price per barrel of oil shifts by so much as $1, Russian revenues shift by about $1.4 billion in the same direction.

In recent years, so much oil has been discovered in Russia that the country now has one of the world's highest levels of proven reserves. In addition, as a result of diplomatic negotiations to enlist Russian support for the war against the Taliban and al Qaeda in Afghanistan, Russia also controls petroleum exports from the former Central Asian Soviet republics of Azerbaijan and Kazakhstan, both of which, like Russia itself, are oil rich. In fact, Russia's supplies are so plentiful that, according to one Moscow-based energy-intelligence expert, it's "choking on the crude it produces."

Because of fierce competition in the global oil industry, however, even control of such vast supplies is no guarantee Russia can sell its output at an acceptable margin. In addition, Russia depends on oil exports to pay for imports—primarily machinery needed to sustain the present pace of economic development—a top priority for the Russian government for two reasons:

1. At a purchasing price parity of $15,800 in 2008, Russian GDP per capita is still well below that of any other G8 country.

2. The oil sector—which is a capital- rather than labor-intensive industry—employs less than 1 percent of the country's population.

The Role of LUKOIL

As Russia's largest oil company, LUKOIL is the second-largest owner (and the largest private owner) of proven reserves in the world. (In some of the world's biggest oil-producing countries, such as Saudi Arabia and Venezuela, reserves are government owned.) Although it has gradually reduced its holdings in LUKOIL, the Russian government maintains close ties with LUKOIL. Controlling about 19 percent of all Russian production and refining, LUKOIL racked up sales of U.S. $108 billion in 2008; and in addition to huge investments in Russia itself, it has been busy investing some of its capital abroad (see Map 6.3, which locates and identifies the company's foreign operations). In the United States, for instance, it acquired Getty Petroleum in 2000 and, in 2004, a string of gasoline stations owned by ConocoPhillips—acquisitions whereby it now controls a U.S. retail network of nearly 2,000 outlets.

What's LUKOIL's Strategy?

As we've already seen, Russia has a lot of oil but desperately needs capital; we've also explained that both Russia and its premier oil company are highly dependent on export revenues. Given this situation, you might well ask why a Russian company sees any advantage in investing abroad. To answer this question, we first need to take a closer look at both LUKOIL's competitive situation and its strategy for dealing with it.

We know that LUKOIL has to sell in foreign markets, both to make adequate use of its capacity and to earn sufficient profits. We should also point out that, since the beginning of the twenty-first century, Russia's export position has been generally quite favorable. Between January 1999 and September 2000, for example, a combination of factors caused oil prices to triple—namely, bad weather, strong demand, and production cutbacks by the Organization of Petroleum Exporting Countries (OPEC), of which Russia is not a member. In the wake of economic uncertainty following 9/11, prices gave back about half this gain; but since then they fluctuated in an upward trend, again as a result of a combination of factors—political unrest in Venezuela and Nigeria, Chinese economic expansion, and further production curtailments by OPEC. Then they fell again as a result of the global recession.

As a general result, LUKOIL has been able to sell more oil, at higher prices, outside Russia than it could just a few years earlier. Thus favorable market conditions have for several years enabled LUKOIL to amass a substantial store of capital that could be channeled into foreign investment—if, of course, management concluded that such investment would enhance the firm's strategic position.

Why LUKOIL Went the Foreign Investment Route   In addition to its reliance on exporting as a means of using the firm's capacity, LUKOIL management has long wanted to use foreign expansion as a means both of earning bigger margins and of ensuring more reliable, full, on-time payment than it can get in Russia. The question, however, still remains: Why doesn't LUKOIL simply export rather than risk foreign investment? The answer lies in the following combination of factors.

Fluctuating Oil Prices   In spite of a general upward trend since the beginning of the century, oil prices—and with them the marketability of Russian oil abroad—have in the past been known to fluctuate widely. On more than one occasion, prices have surged over 100 percent and, in one year, plummeted to levels lower than those at which the boom began.

Thus, in the late 1990s, when a global oil glut and depressed prices combined to take a deep cut out of its profits, LUKOIL decided to emulate its larger Western competitors by venturing on a strategy of forward integration into the ownership of foreign distribution outlets. Its first foreign investments had been made no farther from home than the former Soviet satellite countries—and close longtime customers—Bulgaria and Romania, where it bought up some formerly state-owned production facilities. Since then, however, LUKOIL has ventured farther afield, almost exclusively by means of purchasing existing operations.

It's a sound strategy. Why? To put it simply, when oil producers invest in distribution, they strengthen their ties to markets in which they may be better able to sell crude oil in times of global oversupply. Moreover, integrating into distribution can potentially reduce operating costs, primarily because a producer doesn't have to rely on negotiating and enforcing a network of agreements by which it sells oil to intermediaries in other countries.

Political Uncertainty   Despite huge reserves at home and enviable success as an exporter abroad, LUKOIL was well aware of the fact that export sales are always subject to political disruptions. What if an importing country decides to reduce its purchases of Russian oil to protest some internal Russian political policy (or simply to diversify its own supply sources)?

Or consider another problem that's more or less unique to LUKOIL's situation. As it turns out, the Russian government owns the pipeline system through which virtually all Russian oil exports must pass, allocating access to the system by means of quotas among domestic oil companies. What if a competitor manages to gain sufficient influence with certain political decision makers to siphon off part of LUKOIL's quota?

MAP 6.3   LUKOIL: Expands Its Operations

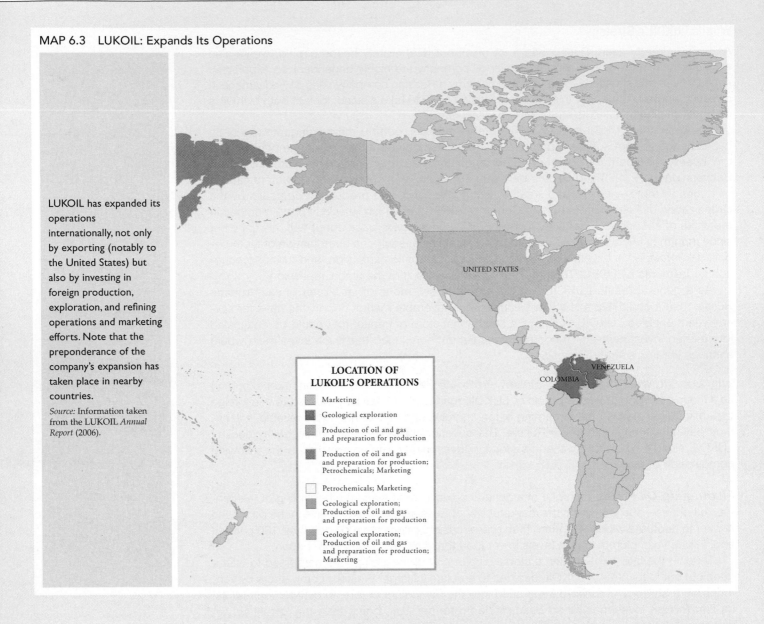

LUKOIL has expanded its operations internationally, not only by exporting (notably to the United States) but also by investing in foreign production, exploration, and refining operations and marketing efforts. Note that the preponderance of the company's expansion has taken place in nearby countries.

Source: Information taken from the LUKOIL *Annual Report* (2006).

LOCATION OF LUKOIL'S OPERATIONS

- Marketing
- Geological exploration
- Production of oil and gas and preparation for production
- Production of oil and gas and preparation for production; Petrochemicals; Marketing
- Petrochemicals; Marketing
- Geological exploration; Production of oil and gas and preparation for production
- Geological exploration; Production of oil and gas and preparation for production; Marketing

Finally, LUKOIL can never forget that, although it has itself been almost completely privatized, the Russian government still owns some of its domestic competitors and has often given its own firms preferential treatment in various matters. That's just one reason why LUKOIL is trying to increase foreign oil supplies to about 20 percent of its total.

Efficiency Imperatives   To be a major global competitor, LUKOIL must become as efficient as its major Western competitors. Toward that end, it must not only achieve operating efficiencies but also acquire state-of-the-industry technology and marketing skills.

In the past, LUKOIL's administrative expenses and cost of capital have been high compared with those of Western competitors. At home, such inefficiencies resulted in only minor problems because the competition consisted solely of other Russian oil companies hampered by the same operational inefficiencies inherited from the former state-owned oil monopoly.

Even in Russia, however, new competitive threats are starting to emerge (BP and TotalFinaElf, for instance, have bought interests in Russian oil companies). LUKOIL, however, sees foreign oil companies as something more than stiffer domestic competition: They're also potentially valuable sources of the technology and knowledge that it needs to compete not only at home but abroad as well.

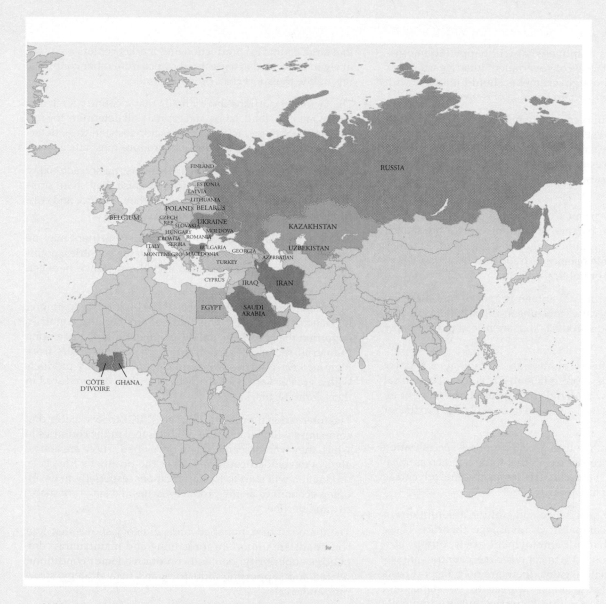

With this strategy in mind, it has placed independent directors from Western oil companies on its board. In addition, ConocoPhillips now owns 20 percent of LUKOIL, in part because LUKOIL is interested in tapping into the U.S. firm's management expertise. Meanwhile, foreign acquisitions, such as Getty in the United States, present another source of experienced personnel, technology, and competitive know-how. ■

QUESTIONS

1. What theories of trade help explain Russia's position as an oil exporter? Why? Which ones don't? Why not?

2. How do global political and economic conditions affect global oil markets and prices?

3. Discuss the following statement as it applies to Russia and LUKOIL:

Regardless of the advantages a country may gain by trading, international trade will begin only if companies within that country have competitive advantages that enable them to be viable traders—and they must foresee profits in exporting and importing.

4. In LUKOIL's situation, what is the relationship between factor mobility and exports?

5. Reviewing the opening case of this chapter, compare the role assumed by the Costa Rican government in using trade to meet national economic objectives with that of the Russian government.

SUMMARY

- Some trade theories examine what will happen to international trade in the absence of government interference. Other theories prescribe how governments should interfere with trade flows to achieve certain national objectives.

- Trade theory is useful because it helps explain what might be produced competitively in a given locale, where a company might go to produce a given product efficiently, and whether government practices might interfere with the free flow of trade among countries. Other theories address the explanation of trade patterns.

- Mercantilist theory proposed that a country should try to achieve a favorable balance of trade (export more than it imports) to receive an influx of gold. Neomercantilist policy also seeks a favorable balance of trade, but its purpose is to achieve some social or political objective.

- The theory of absolute advantage proposes specialization through free trade because consumers will be better off if they can buy foreign-made products that are priced more cheaply than domestic ones.

- According to the theory of absolute advantage, a country may produce goods more efficiently because of a natural advantage (e.g., raw materials or climate) or because of an acquired advantage (e.g., technology or skill for a product or process advantage).

- Comparative advantage theory also proposes specialization through free trade because it says that trade can increase total global output even if one country has an absolute advantage in the production of all products.

- Policymakers have questioned some of the assumptions of the absolute and comparative advantage theories. These assumptions are that full employment exists, output efficiency is always a country's major objective, countries are satisfied with their relative gains, there are no transport costs among countries, advantages appear to be static, and resources move freely within countries but are immobile internationally. Although the theories use a two-country analysis of products, the theories hold for multicountry trade and for services as well.

- The theory of country size holds that because countries with large land areas are apt to have varied climates and natural resources, they are generally more self-sufficient than smaller countries. A second reason for this greater self-sufficiency is

that large countries' production and market centers are more likely to be located at a greater distance from other countries, raising the transport costs of foreign trade.

- The factor-proportions theory holds that a country's relative endowments of land, labor, and capital will determine the relative costs of these factors. These factor costs, in turn, determine which goods the country can produce most efficiently.

- According to the country-similarity theory, most trade today occurs among developed countries because they share similar market characteristics and because they produce and consume so much more than developing economies.

- Much of the pattern of two-way trading partners may be explained by cultural similarity between the countries, political and economic agreements, and the distance between them.

- Manufactured products comprise the bulk of trade among high-income countries. This trade occurs because countries apportion their research and development differently among industrial sectors. It also occurs because consumers from high-income countries want and can afford to buy products with a greater variety of characteristics than are produced in their domestic markets.

- The international product life cycle (PLC) theory states that companies will manufacture products first in the countries in which they were researched and developed. These are almost always developed countries. Over the product's life cycle, production will shift to foreign locations, especially to developing economies as the product reaches the stages of maturity and decline.

- The diamond of national advantage theory shows that four conditions are important for gaining and maintaining competitive superiority: demand conditions; factor conditions; related and supporting industries; and firm strategy, structure, and rivalry.

- Production factors and finished goods are only partially mobile internationally. The cost and feasibility of transferring production factors rather than exporting finished goods internationally will determine which alternative is better.

- Although international mobility of production factors may be a substitute for trade, the mobility may stimulate trade through sales of components, equipment, and complementary products.

KEY TERMS

absolute advantage (p. 264)
acquired advantage (p. 265)
comparative advantage (p. 267)
country-similarity theory (p. 274)
diamond of national advantage
    theory (p. 279)

factor-mobility theory (p. 283)
factor-proportions theory (p. 271)
favorable balance of trade (p. 264)
mercantilism (p. 263)
natural advantage (p. 265)
neomercantilism (p. 264)

nontradable goods (p. 270)
product life cycle (PLC) theory (p. 276)
theory of country size (p. 271)
trade deficit (p. 264)
trade surplus (p. 264)
unfavorable balance of trade (p. 264)

ENDNOTES

1 *Sources include the following:* World Trade Organization, "Trade Profiles: Costa Rica," at http://stat.wto.org/CountryProfile/WSDBCountryPFView.aspx?Language=E&Country=CR (accessed July 16, 2007); Debora Spar, *Attracting High Technology Investment: Intel's Costa Rican Plant* (Washington, DC: The World Bank, Foreign Investment Advisory Service Occasional Paper No. 11, 1998); CIA Factbook, at http://CIA.GOV/CIA/publications/factbook/geos/cs.html (accessed July 7, 2009); Gail D. Triner, "Recent Latin American History and Its Historiography," *Latin American Research Review* 38:1 (2003): 219–38; John Weeks, "Trade Liberalisation, Market Deregulation and Agricultural Performance in Central America," *The Journal of Development Studies* 35:5 (June 1999): 48–76; Niels W. Ketelhöhn and Michael E. Porter, "Building a Cluster: Electronics and Information Technology in Costa Rica," *Harvard Business School Case 9703422* (November 7, 2002); John Schellhas, "Peasants against Globalization: Rural Social Movements in Costa Rica," *American Anthropologist* 103:3 (2001): 862–63; Jose Itzigsohn, *Developing Poverty: The State, Labor Market Deregulation, and the Informal Economy in Costa Rica and the Dominican Republic* (University Park, IL: Pennsylvania University Press, 2000); Roy Nelson, "Intel's Site Selection Decision in Latin America," *Thunderbird International Business Review* 42:2 (2001): 227-249; Andrés Rodríguez-Clare, "Costa Rica's Development Strategy Based on Human Capital and Technology: How It Got There, The Impact of Intel, and Lessons for Other Countries," *United Nations Human Development Report 2001* (New York: United Nations Development Programme, 2001).

2 For a good survey of mercantilism and the mercantilist era, see Gianni Vaggi, *A Concise History of Economic Thought: From Mercantilism to Monetarism* (New York: Palgrave Macmillan, 2002).

3 For reviews of the literature, see Jordan Shan and Fiona Sun, "On the Export-Led Growth Hypothesis for the Little Dragons: An Empirical Reinvestigation," *Atlantic Economic Review* 26:4 (1998): 353–71; George K. Zestos and Xiangnan Tao, "Trade and GDP Growth: Causal Relations in the United States and Canada," *Southern Economic Journal* 68:4 (2002): 859–74.

4 For a good discussion of the history of free trade thought, see Leonard Gomes, *The Economics and Ideology of Free Trade: A Historical Review* (Cheltenham, UK: Edward Elgar, 2003).

5 "Year Round Production of Tomatoes in Iceland," at www.freshplaza.com/news_detail.asp?id=3791 (accessed July 16, 2007); "The History of Wine Production in Brazil," at www.brazilian-wines.com/en/brazilie_histoire.asp (accessed July 16, 2007).

6 For simplicity's sake, both Smith and Ricardo originally assumed a simple world composed of only two countries and two commodities. Our example makes the same assumption. Now, although this simplification is unrealistic, it does not diminish the usefulness of either theory. Economists have applied the same reasoning to demonstrate efficiency advantages in multiproduct and multicountry trade relationships. Smith's seminal treatise remains abundantly in print; for a reliable recent edition, see *An Inquiry into the Nature and Causes of the Wealth of Nations* (Washington, DC: Regnery Publishing, 1998). Like Smith's *Wealth of Nations*, Ricardo's seminal work on comparative advantage, originally published in London in 1817, is continuously reprinted; see, for example, *On the Principles of Political Economy and Taxation* (Amherst, NY: Prometheus Books, 1996).

7 For a good discussion of this paradoxical thinking, see Paul R. Krugman, "What Do Undergraduates Need to Know about Trade?" *American Economic Review Papers and Proceedings* (May 1993): 23–26. For a discussion of some developing countries' views that monopolistic conditions keep them from gaining a fair share of gains from international trade, see A. P. Thirwell, *Growth and Development*, 6th ed. (London: Macmillan, 1999).

8 See Jennifer A. Thomson, *Seeds for the Future: The Impact of Genetically Modified Crops on the Environment* (Ithaca, NY: Cornell University Press, 2007; Hemel Hempstead, "Worldwide Project to Assess Safety of GM Crops," *Appropriate Technology* 29:1 (January–March 2002): 37–38.

9 Thomas I. Palley, "Institutionalism and New Trade Theory: Rethinking Comparative Advantage and Trade Theory," *Journal of Economic Issues* 42:1 (2008): 195–208.

10 Murray Kemp, "Non-Competing Factor Groups and the Normative Propositions of Trade Theory," *International Review of Economics and Finance* 17 (2008): 388–90.

11 Mike Lanchin, "Costa Rica Stands Apart," *BBC News* (July 27, 2004), n.p. at http://news.bbc.co.uk/2/hi/americas/3929177.stm (accessed October 2, 2009).

12 Eli J. Heckscher, *Heckscher-Ohlin Trade Theory* (Cambridge, MA: MIT Press, 1991).

13 For a discussion of ways in which the theory does not fit the reality of trade, see Antoni Estevadeordal and Alan M. Taylor, "A Century of Missing Trade?" *The American Economic Review* 92:1 (2002): 383–93. For a study supporting the theory, see Yong-Seok Choi and Pravin Krishna, "The Factor Content of Bilateral Trade: An Empirical Test," *The Journal of Political Economy* 112:4 (2004): 887–915.

14 See, for example, Donald R. Davis and David E. Weinstein, "An Account of Global Factor Trade," *The American Economic Review* 91:5 (2001): 1423–53; Oner Guncavdi and Suat Kucukcifi, "Foreign Trade and Factor Intensity in an Open Developing Country: An Input-Output Analysis for Turkey," *Russian & East European Finance and Trade* 37:1 (2001): 75–88.

15 See, for example, P. Krugman and A. J. Venables, "Globalization and the Inequality of Nations," *Quarterly Journal of Economics* 110 (1995): 857–80.

16 See Paul Krugman, "Scale Economies, Product Differentiation, and the Patterns of Trade," *The American Economic Review* 70 (1980): 950–59; James Harrigan, "Estimation of Cross-Country Differences in Industry Production Functions," *Journal of International Economics* 47:2 (1999): 267–93.

17 Drusilla K. Brown and Robert M. Stern, "Measurement and Modeling of the Economic Effect of Trade and Investment Barriers in Services," *Title Review of International Economics* 9:2 (2001): 262–86, discuss the role of economies of scale and trade barriers.

18 See Gianmarco I. P. Ottaviano and Diego Puga, "Agglomeration in the Global Economy: A Survey of the 'New Economic Geography,'" *The World Economy* 21:6 (1998): 707–31; Ottaviano, Takatoshi Tabuchi, and Jacques-François Thisse, "Agglomeration and Trade Revisited," *International Economic Review* 43:2 (2002): 409–35.

19 Stefan B. Linder, *An Essay on Trade Transformation* (New York: Wiley, 1961).

20 Dirk Pilat, "The Economic Impact of Technology," *The OECD Observer* 213 (August–September 1998): 5–8.

21 Anthony J. Venables, "Shifts in Economic Geography and Their Causes," *Economic Review—Federal Reserve Bank of Kansas City* 91:4 (2006): 61–85, referring to work by R. Hausmann and D. Rodrik, "Economic Development as Self Discovery" (2003), Harvard Kennedy School working paper.

22 Two discussions of intraindustry trade are: Don P. Clark, "Determinants of Intraindustry Trade between the United States and Industrial Nations," *The International Trade Journal* 12:3 (Fall 1998): 345–62; H. Peter Gray, "Free International Economic Policy in a World of Schumpeter Goods," *The International Trade Journal* 12:3 (Fall 1998): 323–44.

23 Daniel Michaels, "Landing Rights," *Wall Street Journal* (April 30, 2002): A1+.

24 "That's Snow-Biz," *The Economist* (April 13, 1996): 58.

25 Terry Hall, "NZ Finds Pirated Varieties in Chile," *Financial Times* (January 21, 1999): 24.

26 Anthony J. Venables, "Shifts in Economic Geography and Their Causes," *Economic Review—Federal Reserve Bank of Kansas City* 91:4 (2006): 61–85.

27 Jeffrey A. Frankel and David Romer, "Does Trade Cause Growth?" *The American Economic Review* 89:3 (June 1999): 379–99.

28 J. L. Gallup and J. Sachs, "Geography and Economic Development," in B. Pleskovic and J. E. Stiglitz, eds., *Annual World Bank Conference on Development Economics* (Washington, DC: The World Bank, 1998).

29 See Raymond Vernon, "International Investment and International Trade in the Product Life Cycle," *Quarterly Journal of Economics* 80 (May 1996): 190–207; David Dollar, "Technological Innovation, Capital Mobility, and the Product Cycle in North–South Trade," *American Economic Review* 76:1 (1986): 177–90.

30 This is true according to various indicators. See, for example, International Bank for Reconstruction and Development, "Science and Technology," *The World Development Indicators* (Washington, DC: International Bank for Reconstruction and Development, 2000): 300.

31 Michael E. Porter, "The Competitive Advantage of Nations," *Harvard Business Review* 68:4 (1990): 73–93.

32 Kiyohiko Ito and Vladimir Pucik, "R&D Spending, Domestic Competition, and Export Performance of Japanese Manufacturing Firms," *Strategic Management Journal* 14 (1993): 61–75.

33 Hubert Schmitz, "Reducing Complexity in the Industrial Policy Debate," *Development Policy Review* 25:4 (2007): 417–28.

34 James Kynge and Elisabeth Robinson, "Singapore to Revise Trade Priorities," *Financial Times* (January 21, 1997): 6.

35 Sonny Nwankwo and Darlington Richards, "Institutional Paradigm and the Management of Transitions: A Sub-Saharan African Perspective," *International Journal of Social Economics* 31:1/2 (2004): 111.

36 Jeffrey Sachs, "Institutions Matter, But Not Everything," *Finance and Development* (June 2003): 38–41.

37 Nwankwo and Richards, "Institutional Paradigm and the Management of Transitions," 111.

38 Andrés Rodríguez-Clare, "Clusters and Comparative Advantage: Implications for Industrial Policy," *Journal of Development Economics* 82 (2007): 43–57.

39 Paul Krugman and Alasdair M. Smith, eds., *Empirical Studies of Strategic Trade Policies* (Chicago: University of Chicago Press, 1993); Howard Pack and Kamal Saggi, "Is There a Case for Industrial Policy?" *The World Bank Research Observer* 21:2 (2006): 267.

40 Paul M. Sherer, "Thailand Trips in Reach for New Exports," *Wall Street Journal* (August 27, 1996): A8.

41 Richard Brahm, "National Targeting Policies, High-Technology Industries, and Excessive Competition," *Strategic Management Journal* 16 (1995): 71–91.

42 Andrea E. Goldstein and Steven M. McGuire, "The Political Economy of Strategic Trade Policy and the Brazil-Canada Export Subsidies Saga," *The World Economy* 27:4 (2004): 541.

43 Theresa M. Greaney, "Strategic Trade and Competition Policies to Assist Distressed Industries," *The Canadian Journal of Economics* 32:3 (1999): 767.

44 Department of Economic and Social Affairs, Population Division, *World Population Prospects: The 2008 Revision Highlights* (New York: United Nations, 2009): xi.

45 "Global Estimates and Trends," *World Migration 2008: Managing Labour Mobility in the Evolving Global Economy*, International Organization for Migration, www.iom.int/jahia/Jahia/about-migration/facts-and-figures/global estimates (accessed October 7, 2009).

46 Ron Hutcheson, "Defining 'American,' " *Miami Herald* (April 2, 2006): 16A.

47 Richard B. Freeman, "People Flows in Globalization," *Journal of Economic Perspectives* 20:2 (2006): 145–70.

48 John Salt, "The Future of International Labor Migration," *Migration Review* 26:4 (2002): 1077.

49 Ben Dolven, "China Recruits Foreign Talent," *Wall Street Journal* (April 15, 2004): A13.

50 Patrick Barta and Joel Millman, "The Great U-Turn," *Wall Street Journal* (June 6–7, 2009): A1.

51 *Trends in International Migration,* at oecd.org/dataoecd/7/49/24994376 (accessed March 18, 2005).

52 Freeman, "People Flows in Globalization."

53 See C. Chris Rodrigo, "East Asia's Growth: Technology or Accumulation?" *Contemporary Economic Policy* 18:2 (2000): 215–27; Paul Krugman, "The Myth of Asia's Miracle," *Foreign Affairs* 73:6 (1994): 62–78.

54 World Bank's Migration and Development Brief 5 (July 10, 2008).

55 Marc Lacey, "Mexicans Send Money to Aid Families in the U.S.," *Times Digest* [New York] (November 16, 2009): 2.

56 Paul M. Vaaler and R. Isil Yavuz, "Immigrant Remittances and the Venture Investment Environment in Developing Countries," paper presented at the Academy of International Business, San Diego, CA (June 27–30, 2009).

57 Keith Head and John Ries, "Exporting and FDI as Alternative Strategies," *Oxford Review of Economic Policy* 20:3 (2004): 409–29.

58 See Frank D. Bean et al., "Circular, Invisible, and Ambiguous Migrants: Components of Differences in Estimates of the Number of Unauthorized Mexican Migrants in the United States," *Demography* 38:3 (2001): 411–22; United Nations Conference on Trade and Development, *World Investment Report 2000: Cross-Border Mergers and Acquisitions and Development* (New York and Geneva: United Nations, 2000): 312.

59 Paul Windrum, Andreas Reinstaller, and Christopher Bull, "The Outsourcing Productivity Paradox: Total Outsourcing, Organisational Innovation, and Long Run Productivity Growth," *Journal of Evolutionary Economics* 19:2 (2009): 197–229.

60 June Kronholtz, "Immigrant Labor or Machines?" *Wall Street Journal* (December 19, 2006): A4.

61 *Sources include the following:* "Alliances, Acquisitions Key to LUKOIL Ambitions," *International Petroleum Finance* (June 8, 2007): 1; Sabrina Tavernise and Peter S. Green, "Oil Concerns in Russia Branch Out," *New York Times* (April 2, 2002): W1; Bhushan Bahree, "Western Oil Flirts with Russia Firms, Insider Says," *Wall Street Journal* (April 29, 2002): A13; Reuters, "Mobius and Chevron Exec Nominated for LUKOIL Board" (January 17, 2002), at http://biz.yahoo.com/rf/020117/117507998_1. html; Paul Starobin, "LUKOIL Is Lonesome," *Business Week Online* (April 24, 2000), at www.businessweek.com:2000/00_17/b3678229.htm?scriptFramed (accessed October 2, 2009); "LUKOIL Oil Company," at www.lukoil.com; Vidya Ram, "A More Refined Lukoil," *Forbers.com* at http://www.forbes.com/2008/06/24/erg-lukoil-refining-markets-equity-cx_vr_0624markets (accessed October 2, 2009); "Focus, the Russians Are Coming," *Petroleum Economist* (December 31, 2000); Andrew Jack and Arkady Ostrovsky, "LUKOIL in U.S. Petro Deal," *Financial Times* (November 4, 2000): 8; David Ignatius, "The Russians Are Pumping," *Pittsburgh Post-Gazette* (December 28, 2001): A-21; Tina Obut, "Perspective on Russia's Oil Sector," *Oil & Gas Journal* (February 1, 1999): 20; *LUKOIL Annual Report,* various years; "Event Brief of September 30: ConocoPhillips and LUKOil," *CCBN Wire Service* (September 30, 2004); "LUKOIL Leading Peers in Adding to Production outside Russia," *Platts Oilgram News* (April 13, 2004): 1; "World Oil Price Chronology" (March 2005), at www.eia.doe.gov/emeu/cabs/chron (accessed March 8, 2005); "Russia" www.cia.doe.gov/cabs/russia (accessed July 21, 2007).

seven
Governmental Influence on Trade

PROTON
PLATINUM

Objectives

- To explain the rationales for governmental policies that enhance and restrict trade

- To show the effects of pressure groups on trade policies

- To describe the potential and actual effects of governmental intervention on the free flow of trade

- To illustrate the major means by which trade is restricted and regulated

- To demonstrate the business uncertainties and business opportunities created by governmental trade policies

Charity begins at home.

—*English proverb*

CASE Protecting the Malaysian Automobile Industry

BACKGROUND INFORMATION

It is important to understand that Malaysia is a land of multiple ethnicities, languages and religions. In 2007, the population of 27 million people was comprised of Malays (55 percent of the population) who, together with the indigenous people (known also as *bumiputeras*) make up 61 percent. The rest of the population was made up of Chinese (25 percent) and Indian (7 percent) ethnic groups. Prior to 1970, Malaysia's development policy was primarily aimed at promoting growth with a strong emphasis on the export market. Although the economy grew very rapidly during this period at an annual average of six percent, the wealth was not distributed evenly, resulting in socio-economic imbalances among the ethnic groups with negative social consequences in the form of a racial riot in 1969. The New Economic Policy (NEP) was established in 1970 with the objectives of creating harmony and unity in a nation with many ethnic and religious groups.

Malaysia (see Map 7.1) is a country rich in natural resources such as tin, crude petroleum, natural gas, bauxite, palm oil, natural rubber, cocoa, pepper, and timber. About 60 percent of the agricultural workforce was in rubber and tin, the main exports. But volatile world prices for rubber and tin caused unstable unemployment and incomes, making it

MAP 7.1 Malaysia

Malaysia remains the only ASEAN country with a national car, despite the poor financial performance of both Proton and Perodua.

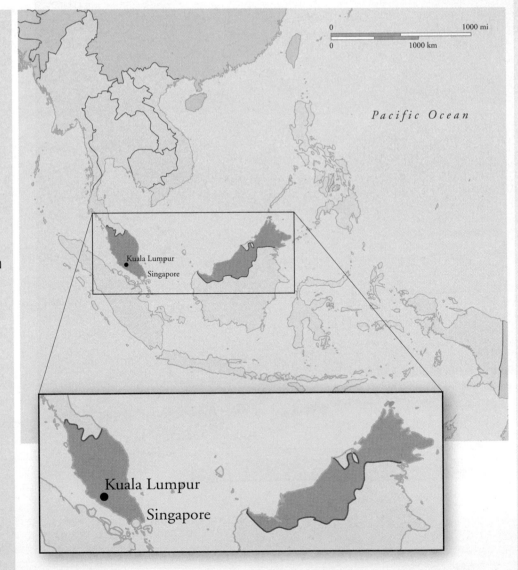

difficult to accommodate a young and expanding population. Malaysia then resorted to an import-substitution strategy. Previously imported consumer items such as textiles, leather and paper products, and various foods would be produced locally. Employment was promoted in numerous labor-intensive and light industries in processing, assembly, and packaging of raw materials. To acquire basic technologies, foreign direct investments were encouraged with fiscal measures such as the Pioneer Industries Ordinance 1958, which granted tax exemption of up to five years with assurances of repatriation of profits under the pioneer status. In 1968, the Investment Incentive Act extended the tax-relief period to stimulate more investments and jobs. Also, during the 1960s, the enactment of the Tariff Advisory Board and Federal Industrial Development Authority (FIDA) introduced import tariffs and quotas, thereby laying the foundation for "infant industries."

The Fourth Malaysia Plan (1981–1985) within the New Economic Policy, couched in a "look east" orientation, was an attempt to replicate the industrial successes of South Korea and Taiwan, and especially Japan—partly by acquiring technology and industrial skills from those countries for a more diversified and integrated economy with high-tech and heavy industries such as motorcycle-engine plants, steel mills, petrochemicals, cement plants, and automobile manufacturing. In 1982, the state-owned Heavy Industries Corporation of Malaysia (HICOM) was established to oversee the new projects, which would be protected with high import tariffs, import restrictions, and restrictive manufacturing licenses. (HICOM is the conduit for mobilizing Malays into employment, management, and capital of heavy industries.)

HISTORY OF PROTON

In 1982, the Malaysian cabinet approved a 1981 government plan for an automobile joint venture, thereby empowering HICOM in 1983 to formalize a pact with the Mitsubishi group to form the Perusahaan Otomobil Nasional—i.e., National Automobile Enterprise—to manufacture, assemble and market automobiles and related products such as accessories, spare parts, and various components. The name *Proton* is an acronym for the company name in Malay. In 1992, Proton was listed on Bursa Malaysia, formerly the Kuala Lumpur Stock Exchange. As of 2002, Khazanah Nasional Berhad owns 31.63 percent and Petroliam Nasional Berhad (Petronas) owns 11.57 percent, respectively, of Proton, making it a government-linked company.

The first Malaysian-manufactured car, the Proton Saga, modeled after the 1983 Mitsubishi Lancer Fiore, was launched in September 1985 by then–Prime Minister Dr. Mahatir Mohamad. Initially, automobile components were produced entirely by Mitsubishi, but they were gradually made locally as technologies and skills were acquired. Subsequent models included the 1993 Proton Wira, based on the Mitsubishi Lancer/Colt, and the 1995 Proton Perdana, based on the Mitsubishi Galant/Eterna. In 1996, Proton bought a controlling stake in Lotus Group International, a U.K.-based automotive engineering firm. The resulting access to more proprietary technologies enabled it to produce the first internally designed Malaysian car, the Proton Waja, in May 2000. Other Proton models include the Satria, Putra, Tiara, Juara, Arena, Gen-2, Savvy, Persona, and Exora.

Proton enjoyed various incentives, including exemptions from import tariffs on completely-knocked-down (CKD) units for assembly, while its competitors were levied import duties of 15 percent—later raised to 25 percent in 1983 and 40 percent in 1984. The excise duties, or within-border duties, were reduced by 50 percent, and with Malaysian civil servants eligible for low-interest loans to purchase the Proton Saga, the total concessions enabled prices to be 20 percent lower than the foreign competition.

In 1986, the first Proton Saga to be exported went to Bangladesh, an achievement that would eventually be capped to 50 countries, with the United Kingdom being its largest foreign customer. In 1987, the output had reached 50,000 cars, and the 100,000th Proton Saga was produced in January 1989. By 1993, manufacturing had reached 500,000 cars and its R&D facility was constructed. But that year also saw the establishment of a second national automobile company: Perodua.

HISTORY OF PERODUA

Perusahaan Otomobil Kedua Sdn Bhd—i.e., Second Automobile Manufacturer Limited Corporation in English—was established in 1993. The national agenda was for expansion in the range of automotive products and increase in manufacturing capability of components and parts. *Perodua* is an acronym of its Malay corporate name. It is a second automobile venture between Malaysian and Japanese partners, which is comprised of UMW Corporation Sdn Bhd (38 percent stake), Daihatsu Motor Co Ltd. of Japan (20 percent),

out among many people and throughout the year, consumers take little notice. For example, U.S. import restrictions on peanuts and sugar add to the price of peanut butter and confectionary products in the United States.[3] Even if consumers knew about this surcharge, they would likely not see enough incentive to band together and push their governmental leaders to rectify the situation.

Economic Rationales for Governmental Intervention

Governmental trade intervention may be classified as either economic or noneconomic, as shown in Table 7.1. Let's begin by analyzing some leading *economic rationales*.

FIGHTING UNEMPLOYMENT

There's probably no more effective pressure group than the unemployed; no other group has the time and incentive to protest publicly, contact governmental representatives, and confront trade-seeking organizations. Workers displaced because of imports are often the ones who are least able to find alternative work. When they have found alternative work, they have historically earned less in their new jobs than they did in their old jobs.[4] In addition, displaced workers often spend their unemployment benefits on living expenses rather than on retraining—in the hopes that they will be recalled to their old jobs. When they do seek retraining, many workers, especially older ones, lack the educational background necessary to gain required skills. Worse still, some train for jobs that do not materialize.

What's Wrong with Full Employment as an Economic Objective?
Although every country has full employment as an economic objective, using trade policy to achieve this is problematic. From a practical standpoint, gaining jobs by limiting imports may not fully work as expected. Even if successful, the costs may be high and need to be borne by someone.

The Prospect of Retaliation   One difficulty with restricting imports to create jobs is that other countries normally retaliate with their own restrictions. That is, trade restrictions designed to support domestic industries typically trigger a drop in production in some foreign countries, and they react.

However, large trading countries are more important in the retaliation process. For example, if the United States were to limit clothing imports in general, China would have more power to retaliate than Mauritius. Further, the United States is less apt to retaliate against Mauritian trade restrictions than against Chinese ones because the latter affect the U.S. economy more.

Even if no country retaliates, the restricting country may gain jobs in one sector only to lose jobs elsewhere. Why? There are three factors to consider:

1. Fewer imports of a product mean fewer import-handling jobs, such as those in the container-shipping industry.

2. Import restrictions may cause lower sales in other industries because they must incur higher costs for components. For example, U.S. import restrictions on steel raised

TABLE 7.1   Why Governments Intervene in Trade

Economic Rationales	Noneconomic Rationales
Fighting unemployment	Maintaining essential industries
Protecting infant industries	Dealing with unfriendly countries
Promoting industrialization	Maintaining or extending spheres of influence
Improving comparative position	Preserving national identity

Margin notes:

The unemployed can form an effective pressure group for import restrictions.

Import restrictions to create domestic employment

- May lead to retaliation by other countries.
- Are less likely retaliated against effectively by small economies.
- Are less likely to be met with retaliation if implemented by small economies.
- May decrease export jobs because of price increases for components.
- May decrease export jobs because of lower incomes abroad.

automobile manufacturing costs in the United States, and auto producers united to convince authorities to remove the restrictions.[5]

3. Imports stimulate exports, although less directly, by increasing foreign income and foreign-exchange earnings, which are then spent on new imports by foreign consumers. Thus, restricting earnings abroad will have some negative effect on domestic earnings and employment.

Analyzing Trade-Offs In deciding whether to restrict imports to create jobs, governments should compare the costs (in terms of prices or tax subsidies) of limiting imports with the costs of unemployment (in terms of unemployment benefits or retraining) from freer trade. These are challenging tasks that involve not only difficult economic but also social questions. For example, it is hard to put a price on the distress suffered by people who lose their jobs due to import competition. It is also difficult for working people to understand that they may be better off financially (because of lower prices) even if they must then pay higher taxes to support unemployment or welfare benefits for people who lose their jobs to rising imports.

In summary, persistent unemployment pushes many groups to call for protectionism. However, evidence suggests that efforts to reduce unemployment through import restrictions are usually ineffective.[6] Unemployment in and of itself is better dealt with through fiscal and monetary policies.

> Possible costs of import restrictions include higher prices and higher taxes. Such costs should be compared with those of unemployment.

PROTECTING "INFANT INDUSTRIES"

One of the oldest arguments for protectionism, the **infant-industry argument,** holds that a government should shield an emerging industry from foreign competition by guaranteeing it a large share of the domestic market until it is able to compete on its own. Many developing countries use this argument to justify their protectionist policies, especially if entry barriers are high and if foreign competition is formidable.

> The infant-industry argument says that production becomes more competitive over time because of
> • Increased economies of scale.
> • Greater worker efficiency.

Underlying Assumptions The infant-industry argument presumes that the initial output costs for an industry in a given country may be so high as to make its output noncompetitive in world markets. Eventual competitiveness is not the reward for endurance but the result of the efficiency gains that take time. Therefore, the industry's government needs to protect an infant industry long enough for its fledgling companies to gain economies of scale and their employees to translate experience into higher productivity. These achievements will enable a company to produce efficiently, thereby positioning it to compete internationally. At this point, the government can then recoup the costs of trade protection through benefits like higher domestic employment, lower social costs, and higher tax revenues.

Risks in Designating Industries Although it's reasonable to expect production costs to decrease over time, there is a risk that costs will never fall enough to create internationally competitive products. This risk poses two problems.

Determining Probability of Success First, governments must identify those industries that have a high probability of success. Some industries grow to be competitive because of governmental protection; automobile production in Brazil is a good example. However, as shown in the opening case with Malaysia's Proton, the protected industry remains inefficient even after 25 years of government aid.

If infant-industry protection fails to reduce costs enough to compete against imports, chances are its owners, workers, and suppliers will constitute a formidable pressure group that may prevent the importation of competing lower-priced products. Also, the security of government protection against import competition may deter managers from adopting the innovations needed to compete globally and to provide their own consumers with high-quality products at a low price.

Case Review Note

Who Should Bear the Cost?   Second, even if policymakers can determine those infant industries likely to succeed, it does not necessarily follow that companies in those industries should receive governmental assistance. Some segment of the economy must incur the higher cost when local production is still inefficient. These may be consumers who pay higher prices for the protected industries' products. Or they may be taxpayers who pay for subsidies. Further, when taxes go to pay subsidies, governments can spend less elsewhere, such as on education and infrastructure, to improve overall competitiveness. There are many examples of entrepreneurs who endured early losses to achieve future benefits, without any public help from consumers or taxpayers.

DEVELOPING AN INDUSTRIAL BASE

Countries with a large manufacturing base generally have higher per capita GDPs than those that do not. Moreover, a number of countries, such as the United States and Japan, developed an industrial base while largely restricting imports. Many developing countries try to emulate this strategy, using trade protection to spur local industrialization. Specifically, they operate under the following set of assumptions:

> Countries seek protection to promote industrialization because that type of production
>
> - Brings faster growth than agriculture.
> - Brings in investment funds.
> - Diversifies the economy.
> - Brings more income than primary products do.
> - Reduces imports and promotes exports.
> - Helps the nation-building process.

1. Surplus workers can more easily increase manufacturing output than agricultural output.
2. Inflows of foreign investment in the industrial sector promote sustainable growth.
3. Prices and sales of commodities (agricultural products and raw materials) fluctuate very much, which is a detriment to economies that depend on few of them.
4. Markets for industrial products grow faster than markets for commodities.
5. Industrial growth reduces imports and/or promotes exports.
6. Industrial activity helps the nation-building process.

In the sections that follow, we review each of these assumptions in some detail.

Surplus Workers   Disguised unemployment is high in rural areas of many developing countries where people are effectively contributing little, if anything, to the agricultural output. Consequently, many people can move into the industrial sector without significantly reducing agricultural output. Like the infant-industry argument, the **industrialization argument** presumes that the unregulated importation of lower-priced products prevents the development of a domestic industry. However, unlike the infant-industry argument, the industrialization rationale asserts that there will be economic growth even if domestic prices do not become globally competitive. In other words, growth occurs because underemployed resources become employed.[7]

Shifting people out of agriculture, however, can create at least two problems:

> When a country shifts from agriculture to industry,
>
> - Demands on social and political services in cities may increase.
> - Output increases if the marginal productivity of agricultural workers is very low.
> - Development possibilities in the agricultural sector may be overlooked.

1. In rural areas, the underemployed have a safety net through their extended families, which they may lose when they move. A major problem facing developing countries is the migration to urban areas of people with high expectations who then cannot find enough suitable jobs, housing, and social services. For example, millions of Chinese have moved to cities, where many have not prospered. Some estimate that China's urban unemployment rate runs three to five times the officially reported rate.[8]
2. Improved agriculture practices, not a drastic shift to industry, may be a better means of achieving economic success. Typically, few developing countries farm their land efficiently—doing so can create great benefits at low cost.[9] Many developed countries continue to profit from exports of agricultural products and maintain high per capita income with a mix of industry and efficient agricultural specialization.

> If import restrictions keep out foreign-made goods, foreign companies may invest to produce in the restricted area.

Investment Inflows   Import restrictions, applied to spur industrialization, also may increase foreign direct investment, which provides capital, technology, and jobs. Barred from an attractive foreign market by trade restrictions, foreign companies may transfer manufacturing to that country to avoid the loss of a lucrative or potential market. For example, Thailand's automobile import restrictions prompted foreign automakers to invest there.

Diversification Export prices of many primary products, such as oil and coffee, fluctuate markedly. Price variations due to uncontrollable factors—such as weather affecting supply or business cycles abroad affecting demand—can wreak havoc on economies that depend on the export of primary products. This is especially true for many developing countries that must rely on only a few commodities. Frequently, they are caught in a feast-or-famine cycle, as it were: able to afford foreign luxuries one year but unable to find the funds for replacement parts for essential equipment the next. Contrary to expectations, a greater dependence on manufacturing does not guarantee diversification of export earnings. The population of many developing economies is small; a move to manufacturing may shift dependence from one or two agricultural commodities to one or two manufactured products, which face competitive risks and potential obsolescence.

Growth in Manufactured Goods **Terms of trade** refers to the quantity of imports that a given quantity of a country's exports can buy—that is, how many bananas Country A must sell to Country B to purchase one refrigerator from Country B. Historically, the prices of raw materials and agricultural commodities have not risen as fast as the prices of finished products, although they have risen faster during short periods. Over time, therefore, it takes more low-priced primary products to buy the same amount of high-priced manufactured goods.

> Terms of trade for emerging economies may deteriorate because
> - Demand for primary products grows more slowly.
> - Production cost savings for primary products will be passed on to consumers.

In addition, the quantity of primary products demanded does not rise as rapidly as manufactured products and services. This is explained partly by the fact that people spend a lower percentage of income on food as their incomes rise and partly by raw-material-saving technologies. A further explanation is that because commodities are hard to differentiate, producers must compete on price. In contrast, the prices of manufactured products can stay high because competition is based more on differentiation.

Import Substitution and Export-Led Development Traditionally, developing countries promoted industrialization by restricting imports to boost local production for local consumption of products they would otherwise import. If the protected industries do not become efficient, an all-too-frequent outcome, local consumers may have to support them by paying higher prices or higher taxes. In contrast, some countries, such as Taiwan and South Korea, have achieved rapid economic growth by promoting the development of industries that export their output. This approach is known as **export-led development.** In reality, it's not easy to distinguish between import substitution and export-led development. Industrialization may result initially in import substitution, yet export development of the same products may be feasible later.

> **Concept Check**
>
> In the opening case of Chapter 6, we explain *import substitution* as a policy of calling for the local production of goods and services that would otherwise have to be imported. We also demonstrate why this policy failed to achieve certain goals of one country's long-term trade strategy.

Nation Building There is a strong relationship suggested between industrialization and aspects of the nation-building process. Industrialization helps countries build infrastructure, advance rural development, and boost the skills of the workforce. For example, Ecuador and Vietnam maintain that industrialization has helped them move from feudal economies suffering chronic food shortages to nations with improved food security and budding export competitiveness.[10]

> Industrialization emphasizes either
> - Products to sell domestically or
> - Products to export.

ECONOMIC RELATIONSHIPS WITH OTHER COUNTRIES

Every nation monitors its absolute economic welfare, compares its performance to that of other countries, and enacts practices aimed at improving its relative position.

Among the many practices, four stand out: making balance-of-trade adjustments, gaining comparable access to foreign markets, using restrictions as a bargaining tool, and controlling prices.

Balance-of-Trade Adjustments   A trade deficit creates problems for nations with low foreign exchange reserves—the funds that help a nation finance the purchase of priority foreign goods and maintain the trustworthiness of its currency. So, if balance-of-trade difficulties arise and persist, a government may take action to reduce imports or encourage exports to balance its trade account. Basically, it has two options that affect its competitive position broadly:

1. Depreciate or devalue its currency—an action that makes all of its products cheaper in relation to foreign products
2. Rely on fiscal and monetary policy to bring about lower price increases in general than those in other countries

Both of these options, however, take time. Furthermore, they aren't selective; for instance, they make both foreign essentials and foreign luxury products more expensive. Thus, a country may use protection more effectively so as to affect only certain products. Doing so is really a stopgap measure that gives the country time to address its fundamental economic situation—the perceived quality, characteristics, and prices of its products—that is causing its residents to buy more abroad than they are selling.

For example, since the 1970s the United States has run a trade deficit with Japan, largely because of automobile trade. The U.S. government has tried to correct the imbalance by limiting the number of Japanese vehicle imports, persuading Japanese auto companies to locate more production within the United States, and convincing Japan to ease the entry of U.S.-made cars. Nevertheless, the trade deficit continues.

Domestic producers may be disadvantaged if their access to foreign markets is less than foreign producers' access to their market.

Comparable Access or "Fairness"   Companies and industries often use the **comparable access argument,** which holds that they are entitled to the same access to foreign markets as foreign industries and companies have to their markets. Economic theory supports this idea for industries where there are substantial production cost decreases through economies of scale, such as semiconductors and chemicals. Companies that lack equal access to a competitor's market will struggle to gain enough sales to be cost competitive.[11]

The argument for comparable access is also presented as one of fairness. For example, the U.S. government permits foreign financial service companies to operate in the United States, but only if their home governments allow U.S. financial service companies equivalent market access. There are, however, at least two practical reasons for rejecting the idea of fairness:

1. Tit-for-tat market access can lead to restrictions that may deny one's own consumers lower prices.
2. Governments would find it impractical to negotiate and monitor separate agreements for each of the many thousands of different products and services that might be traded.

Countries levy trade restrictions to coerce other countries to change their policies.

Restrictions as a Bargaining Tool   The threat or imposition of import restrictions may be retaliatory measures for persuading other countries to lower their import barriers. The danger, however, is that each country escalates its restrictions, creating, in effect, a trade war that has a negative impact on all the countries' economies.

Nevertheless, to use restrictions successfully as a bargaining tool, you need to be very careful in targeting the products you threaten to restrict. In particular, you need to consider two criteria:

- *Believability:* Either you have access to alternative sources for the product or your consumers are willing to do without it. For instance, the EU successfully retaliated against U.S. import restrictions by threatening to impose trade restrictions on U.S.-grown soybeans when Brazil had surplus production.

- *Importance:* Exports of the product you're restricting are significant to certain parties in the producer country—parties who are sufficiently influential to prompt changes in their own country's trade policy. This consideration was emphasized after the United States had placed restrictions on the importation of steel. The EU threatened to place restrictions on the importation of apples from the state of Washington and oranges from Florida. Given the importance of these two states in a close presidential election, the decision to remove the steel import restrictions was hastened by this threat.

Price-Control Objectives Countries sometimes withhold goods from international markets in an effort to raise prices abroad. This action is most feasible when a few countries hold a monopoly or a near-monopoly control of certain resources. They can then limit supply so consumers must pay a higher price. However, this policy often encourages smuggling (for instance, of emeralds and diamonds), the development of technology (such as synthetic rubber in place of natural rubber), or different means to produce the same product (such as caviar from farm-grown rather than wild sturgeons).[12] Export controls are especially ineffective if a product can be digitized—such as music, video, and texts—because they are easily copied abroad. In addition, if prices are too high or supplies too limited, people will seek substitutes, such as ethanol for petroleum.

A country may also limit exports of a product that is in short supply worldwide to favor domestic consumers. Typically, greater supply drops local prices beneath those in the intentionally undersupplied world market. Egypt and India, for instance, have pursued this strategy by limiting exports of rice, and Canada has considered doing it with patented prescription drugs.[13] Favoring domestic consumers usually disfavors domestic producers, so they lack an incentive to maintain production when prices are low.

There is also fear that foreign producers will price their exports so artificially low that they will drive producers out of business in the importing country. If foreign producers are successful, there are two potential adverse consequences for the importing economy:

1. The foreign producers may be shifting their countries' unemployment abroad. However, the foreign taxpayers are subsidizing consumers abroad.
2. If there are high entry barriers, surviving foreign producers can charge exorbitant prices once their competitors go out of business. However, competition among producers from different countries usually limits anyone's ability to charge exorbitant prices. For example, low import prices have eliminated most U.S. production of consumer electronics. Still, the United States has some of the lowest prices in the world for consumer electronics because so many companies produce them in so many countries.

Dumping Companies sometimes export below cost or below their home-country price—a practice called **dumping.** Most countries prohibit imports of dumped products, but enforcement usually occurs only if the imported product disrupts domestic production. If there is no domestic production, then host-country consumers get the benefit of lower prices. Companies may dump products because they cannot otherwise build a market abroad—essentially, a low price encourages consumers to sample the foreign brand—after which they can charge a high enough price to make a profit.

Companies can afford to dump products if they can charge high prices in their home market or if their home-country government subsidizes them. Ironically, exporting-country consumers or taxpayers seldom realize that their payment of high prices or taxes results in lower prices for foreign consumers.

Margin notes:

Export restrictions may

- Keep up world prices.
- Require more controls to prevent smuggling.
- Lead to substitution.
- Keep domestic prices down by increasing domestic supply.
- Give producers less incentive to increase output.
- Shift foreign production and sales.

Import restrictions may

- Prevent dumping from being used to put domestic producers out of business.
- Get foreign producers to lower their prices.

An industry that believes it's competing against dumped products may appeal to its government to restrict the imports. U.S. companies in such industries as shrimp, candles, and furniture have done so in recent years.[14] However, determining a foreign company's cost or domestic price is difficult because of limited access to the foreign producers' accounting statements, fluctuations in exchange rates, and the passage of products through layers of distribution before reaching the end consumer. The result is that governments allegedly restrict imports arbitrarily through antidumping provisions of their trade legislation and are slow to dispose of the restrictions if pricing situations change. Companies caught by antidumping restrictions often lose the export market they labored to build.

Optimum-Tariff Theory   The **optimum-tariff theory** states that a foreign producer will lower its prices if the importing country places a tax on its products. If this occurs, benefits shift to the importing country because the foreign producer lowers its profits on the export sales.

Let's examine a hypothetical situation. Assume an exporter has costs of $500 per unit and is selling abroad for $700 per unit. With the imposition of a 10 percent tax on the imported price, the exporter may choose to lower its price to $636.36 per unit, which, with a 10 percent tax of $63.64, would keep the price at $700 in the foreign market. The exporter may feel that a price higher than $700 would result in lost sales and that a profit of $136.36 per unit instead of the previous $200 is better than no profit at all. Consequently, an amount of $63.64 per unit has thus shifted to the importing country.

As long as the foreign producer lowers its price by any amount, some shift in revenue goes to the importing country and the tariff is deemed an optimum one. There are many examples of products whose prices did not rise as much as the amount of the imposed tariff; however, it is difficult to predict when, where, and which exporters will voluntarily reduce their profit margins.

Noneconomic Rationales for Government Intervention

In protecting essential industries, countries must

- Determine which ones are essential.
- Consider costs and alternatives.
- Consider political consequences.

Economic rationales help explain many government actions on trade. However, governments sometimes use noneconomic rationales such as the following:

- Maintaining essential industries (especially defense)
- Preventing shipments to unfriendly countries
- Maintaining or extending spheres of influence
- Preserving national identity

Let's look at each rationale.

MAINTAINING ESSENTIAL INDUSTRIES

Governments apply trade restrictions to protect essential domestic industries during peacetime so a country is not dependent on foreign sources of supply during war. This is called the **essential-industry argument.** For example, the U.S. government subsidizes the domestic production of silicon so domestic computer-chip producers will not need to depend on foreign suppliers. Because of nationalism, this argument has much appeal in rallying support for import barriers. However, in times of real (or perceived) crisis or military emergency, almost any product could be deemed essential.

Because of the high cost of protecting an inefficient industry or a higher-cost domestic substitute, the essential-industry argument should not be (but frequently is) accepted without a careful evaluation of costs, real needs, and alternatives. It is difficult to remove protection, once given, because the protected companies and their employees support politicians who support their continued protection—even when the rationale for the subsidies has long ago disappeared. This is why the United States, for example, continued to subsidize its mohair producers more than 20 years after mohair was deemed no longer essential for military uniforms.[15]

PREVENTING SHIPMENTS TO "UNFRIENDLY" COUNTRIES

Groups concerned about security often use national defense arguments to prevent the export, even to friendly countries, of strategic goods that might fall into the hands of potential enemies. For example, the United States prevented exports of data-encryption technology (data-scrambling hardware and software) until a group of U.S. high-tech companies allied themselves with privacy advocacy groups to convince the U.S. government to relax the curbs by allowing them to export encryption products to members of the EU and other European and Pacific Rim allies.[16]

Export constraints may be valid if the exporting country assumes that there will be no retaliation that prevents it from securing even more essential goods from the potential importing country. Even then, the importing country may find alternative supply sources or develop a production capability of its own. In this situation, the country limiting exports is the economic loser. (Our ending case discusses U.S. barriers to trade with Cuba as a means of weakening the Communist nation's economy.)

Import trade controls also may be used as a weapon of foreign policy. For example, the United States found that nine Chinese companies and an Indian businessman had sold technology that Iran used for its chemical and conventional weapons programs. The United States imposed sanctions that barred these firms from doing business with the U.S. government and from exporting goods into the United States.[17]

Case Review Note

Point ▷ ◁ Counterpoint

Should Governments Impose Trade Sanctions?

Point **Yes** As I've said so many times before, let's face it: We're now living in a global society where actions in one country can spill over and affect people all over the world. For instance, the development of a nuclear arsenal in one country can escalate the damage that terrorists can do elsewhere. The failure of a country to protect endangered species can have long-term effects on the whole world's environment. We simply can't sit back and let things happen elsewhere that will come back to haunt us.

At the same time, some pretty dastardly things occur in some countries, and most of the world community would like to see them stopped. These include human rights violations in Myanmar, the use of child slaves to harvest cocoa in the Ivory Coast, and the use of diamond production in Sierra Leone to finance revolutions.

Even if we can't stop these occurrences, we have a moral responsibility not to participate even if it costs us. If I can draw an analogy, I may get some economic benefits by buying from a criminal, and I may not stop that criminal's

Counterpoint **No** Every time I turn around, I see my government imposing a new sanction. Although some don't affect my business, others do. When they do, I lose business that took me years to develop. For instance, a few years back, my company had worked hard to develop a market for office machinery in Iraq. Then, suddenly, we could not export to Iraq and were left holding inventory we had on the loading dock ready to ship. Thus the trade sanctions were aimed at hurting the government of Iraq, but we were the ones who were hurt even though we had never engaged in any objectionable behavior.

Besides, I really question whether these sanctions even work. For example, the United States maintained a 20-year trade embargo on Vietnam. Still, Vietnamese consumers were able to buy U.S. consumer products such as Coca-Cola, Kodak film, and Apple computers through other countries that did not enforce the sanctions.[20] The U.S. trade embargo with Panama only made Panama's Noriega government more adamant in its opposition to the United activity by withholding my business. However, I refuse to deal with the criminal because, in effect, that makes me a criminal's associate.

Although not all trade sanctions have been successful, many have at least been influential in achieving their objectives. These included UN sanctions against Rhodesia (now Zimbabwe), U.K. and U.S. sanctions against the Amin government of Uganda, and Indian sanctions against Nepal.[18] U.S. sanctions against Cuba may have slowed that country's ability to create revolutions elsewhere.

Finally, when a nation breaks international agreements or acts in unpopular ways, what courses of action can other nations take? Between 1827 and World War I, nations mounted 21 blockades, but these are now considered to be too dangerous. Military force has also been used, as for the overthrow of the Saddam regime in Iraq, but such measures have little global support. Thus, nations may take such punitive actions as withholding diplomatic recognition, boycotting athletic and cultural events, seizing the other country's foreign property, and eliminating foreign aid and loans. These may be ineffective in and of themselves without the addition of trade sanctions. In addition, countries may give incentives rather than taking punitive actions. This has occurred, for example, with North Korea to curb its nuclear program and has been suggested for Iran for the same purpose.[19] ▶

States, and it took a military invasion to depose him. Oil embargos against South Africa because of its racial policies merely spurred South African companies to become leaders in converting coal to oil.[21]

Furthermore, even if trade sanctions are successful at weakening the targeted countries' economy, who really suffers in that economy? You can bet that the political leaders still get whatever they need, so the costs of sanctions are borne by innocent people. This occurred in Iraq, where there were widespread reports of children's deaths because of inadequate supplies of food and medicine due to the sanctions. Moreover, the people adversely affected usually blame their suffering not on their internal regime but rather on the countries carrying on the sanctions. Despots are very good at manipulating public opinion.[22]

Finally, governments sometimes seem to impose trade sanctions based on one issue rather than on a country's overall record. For instance, some critics have suggested using trade policies to press Brazil to restrict the cutting of Amazon forests, even though its overall environmental record—particularly its limiting of adverse exhaust emissions by converting automobile engines to use methanol instead of gasoline—is quite good. ◀

MAINTAINING OR EXTENDING SPHERES OF INFLUENCE

There are many examples of governmental actions on trade designed to support their spheres of influence. Governments give aid and credits to, and encourage imports from, countries that join a political alliance or vote a preferred way within international bodies. The EU and the 77 members of the African, Caribbean, and Pacific Group of States signed the Cotonou Agreement to formalize preferential trade relationships that also strengthened political ties.[23] Venezuela has exported oil at low cost and with long-term financing to targeted Latin American countries to gain influence in the region.[24]

A country's trade restrictions may coerce governments to follow certain political actions or punish companies whose governments do not. For example, China delayed permission for Allianz, a German insurance group, to operate in China after Germany gave a reception for the Dalai Lama, the exiled Tibetan spiritual leader.[25]

PRESERVING NATIONAL IDENTITY

Countries are held together partially through a unifying sense of identity that sets their citizens apart from those in other nations. To sustain this collective identity, countries limit imports of certain foreign products and services. For many years, Japan, South Korea, and China maintained an almost total ban on rice imports, largely because rice farming has been a historically cohesive force in each nation.[26] Canada relies on a "cultural sovereignty" argument to prohibit foreign ownership or control

> **Concept Check**
>
> We observe in Chapter 2 that a primary function of **culture** is to support a nation's sense of its uniqueness and integrity. We also explain that— especially in developing countries—many people fear that the escalation and influence of global business interaction is a prelude to another era of **cultural imperialism** in which weaker nation-states will be weakened even further. Finally, we note that similar concerns are raised by the prospect of *cultural diffusion*—a process by which elements of a foreign culture may infiltrate themselves into a local culture.

FIGURE 7.2   Import-Fickle Consumers

Workers in industries favorably affected by trade policy are (relatively) easily motivated to support those policies—at least compared to *consumers*, who prefer the freedom to seek out the best products for the best prices.

Source: Mike Thompson, *Detroit Free Press.*

of publishing, cable TV, and bookselling.[27] South Korea requires theaters to show Korean films a certain number of days per year.[28] Despite these efforts, consumers generally seek out the best products and services they can buy for the least price, a situation characterized in Figure 7.2.

Instruments of Trade Control

Governments use many rationales and seek a range of outcomes when they try to influence exports or imports. We now review the instruments governments use to try to do so. The choice of trade-control instrument is crucial because each type may incite different responses from domestic and foreign groups. One way to understand trade-control instruments is by distinguishing between two types that differ in their effects:

- Those that indirectly affect the amount traded by directly influencing the *prices* of exports or imports
- Those that directly limit the *amount* of a good that can be traded

TARIFFS

Tariff barriers directly affect prices, and *nontariff barriers* may directly affect either price or quantity. A **tariff** (also called a **duty**) is the most common type of trade control and a tax that governments levy on a good shipped internationally. That is, governments charge a tariff on a good when it crosses an official boundary—whether it be that of a nation, say Mexico, or a group of nations, like the EU, that have agreed to impose a common tariff on goods entering their bloc.

Tariffs collected by the exporting country are called **export tariffs;** if they're collected by a country through which the goods pass, they're **transit tariffs;** if they're collected by importing countries, they are called **import tariffs.** Because import tariffs are by far the most common, we discuss them in some detail.

Import Tariffs   Unless they're *optimum tariffs* (which we discussed earlier in the chapter), import tariffs raise the price of imported goods by placing a tax on them that is

Tariffs may be levied

- On goods entering, leaving, or passing through a country.
- For protection or revenue.
- On a per unit or a value basis.

not placed on domestic goods, thereby giving domestically produced goods a relative price advantage. A tariff may be protective even though there is no domestic production in direct competition. For example, a country that wants its residents to spend less on foreign goods and services may raise the price of some foreign products, even though there is no domestic production, in order to curtail demand for imports.

Tariffs as Sources of Revenue   Tariffs also serve as a source of governmental revenue. Import tariffs are of little importance to developed countries, usually costing more to collect than they yield.[29] Tariffs are a major source of revenue in many developing countries, however. This is because government authorities in these countries may have more control over determining the amounts and types of goods crossing their borders and collecting a tax on them than they do over determining and collecting individual and corporate income taxes. Although revenue tariffs are most commonly collected on imports, some countries charge export tariffs on raw materials.[30] Transit tariffs were once a major source of countries' revenue, but governmental treaties have nearly abolished them.

Criteria for Assessing Tariffs   A government may assess a tariff on a per unit basis, in which case it is applying a **specific duty.** It may assess a tariff as a percentage of the value of the item, in which case it is an **ad valorem duty.** If it assesses both a specific duty and an ad valorem duty on the same product, the combination is a **compound duty.** A specific duty is more straightforward for customs officials to assess because they do not need to determine a good's value on which to calculate a percentage tax.

A tariff controversy concerns developed countries' treatment of manufactured exports from developing countries that seek to add manufactured value to their exports of raw materials (like instant coffee instead of coffee beans). Raw materials frequently enter developed countries free of duty (say, coffee beans); however, if processed, developed countries then assign an import tariff. Because an ad valorem tariff is based on the total value of the product (say, $5 for a jar of instant coffee), meaning the raw materials and the processing combined (say, $2.50 for the coffee beans and $2.50 for the processing), developing countries argue that the **effective tariff** on the manufactured portion turns out to be higher than the published tariff rate. In other words, a tariff rate of 10 percent is effectively 20 percent on the manufactured portion. This anomaly further challenges developing countries to find markets for their manufactured products. At the same time, the governments of developed countries cannot easily remove barriers to imports of developing countries' manufactured products, largely because these imports are more likely to displace workers who are least equipped to move to new jobs.

NONTARIFF BARRIERS: DIRECT PRICE INFLUENCES

Now that we've shown how tariffs raise prices and limit trade, let's turn to a discussion of other ways that governments alter product prices to limit their trade.

Governmental subsidies may help companies be competitive,

- Especially to overcome market imperfections because they are least controversial.
- But there is little agreement on what a subsidy is.
- But agricultural subsidies are difficult to dismantle.

Subsidies   **Subsidies** are direct assistance to companies, making them more competitive. (The photo shows a protest over the removal of an export subsidy, which previously enabled German milk producers to compete abroad.) Although this definition is straightforward, there are trade frictions because of disagreement on what constitutes a subsidy. In essence, not everyone agrees that companies are being subsidized just because they lose money, nor that all types of government loans or grants are subsidies. One long-running controversy involves commercial aircraft. Airbus Industrie and the EU claim that the U.S. government subsidizes Boeing through research and development contracts for military aircraft that also have commercial applications. Boeing and the U.S. government claim that the EU subsidizes Airbus Industrie through low-interest government loans.[31]

The photo in front of Germany's Department of Foreign Affairs shows a replica of the Agriculture and Consumer Protection Minister, Ilse Aigner, in front of an overturned milk can. The display was placed by farmers protesting the end of subsidies for exporting milk.

Source: Steffi Loos/Getty Images, Inc.

An area that may well raise future questions about subsidies is governmental support to shore up floundering companies and industries during the global recession. For instance, 12 countries have acted on behalf of their automobile industries, such as with generous loans and support for consumers to replace their old cars. Other countries have eliminated taxes on their companies' export earnings.[32]

Agricultural Subsidies   The one area in which everyone agrees that subsidies exist is agricultural products in developed countries. The official reason for granting subsidies to farmers is that food supplies are too critical to be left to chance. Although subsidies lead to surplus production, surpluses are preferable to the risk of food shortages.

Although this official reason seems compelling, there is an unofficial reason as well. Within the EU, Japan, and the United States, rural areas have a disproportionately high representation in government decision making. For instance, in the United States, there is one senator per 300,000 people in Vermont, a state with a 68 percent rural population, and one senator per 18 million in California, a state with a 93 percent urban population. The result is that internal politics effectively prevents the dismantling of such instruments as price supports for farmers, government agencies to improve agricultural productivity, and low-interest loans to farmers.

What is the effect? Developing countries are disadvantaged in serving the developed country markets with competitive agricultural products. Further, much of the surplus production from developed countries is exported at prices below those in the products' domestic markets, thus distorting trade and disadvantaging production from developing countries.[33]

Overcoming Market Imperfections   There is another subsidization area that is less contentious. Most countries offer potential exporters many business development services, such as market information, trade expositions, and foreign contacts. From the standpoint of market efficiency, these sorts of subsidies are more justifiable than tariffs because they seek to overcome, rather than create, market imperfections. There are also benefits to disseminating information widely because governments can spread the costs of collecting information among many users.

Aid and Loans　Governments also give aid and loans to other countries. If the recipient is required to spend the funds in the donor country, which is known as *tied aid* or *tied loans,* some products can compete abroad that might otherwise be noncompetitive. For instance, tied aid helps win large contracts for infrastructure, such as telecommunications, railways, and electric power projects.

However, there is growing skepticism about the value of tied aid, because it requires the recipient to use suppliers in the donor country who are shielded from competition and may not be the best. Tied aid can also slow the development of local suppliers in developing countries. These concerns led the members of the OECD to untie financial aid to developing countries, no longer obliging aid-recipient countries to purchase equipment from suppliers in the donor country.[34] However, China is using tied aid for nearly all its foreign projects.[35]

Because it is difficult for customs officials to determine the honesty of import invoices,

- They may arbitrarily increase value.
- Valuation procedures have been developed.
- They may question the origin of imports.

Customs Valuation　Tariffs for imported merchandise depend on the product, price, and origin. The temptation exists for exporters and importers to declare these wrongly on invoices to pay less duty. Generally, most countries have agreed to use the invoice information unless customs officers doubt its authenticity. Agents must then assess on the basis of the value of identical goods. If not possible, agents must assess on the basis of similar goods arriving in or about the same time.

For example, there is no sales invoice when imported goods enter for lease rather than purchase. Customs officials must then base the tariff on the value of identical or similar goods. If this basis cannot be used, officials may compute a value based on final sales value or on reasonable cost. Similarly, sometimes agents use their discretionary power to assess the value too high, thereby preventing the importation of foreign-made products.[36]

Valuation Problems　The fact that so many different products are traded creates valuation problems, especially since new products are coming on the market all the time and must be classified within existing tariff categories. It is easy (by accident or intention) to misclassify a product and its corresponding tariff. Administering more than 13,000 categories of products means a customs agent must use professional discretion to determine, say, if silicon chips should be considered "integrated circuits for computers" or "a form of chemical silicon." The differences among products in tariff schedules are also minute. For example, the United States has a different tariff on athletic footwear than on sports footwear. On each of these, there are different tariffs, depending on whether the sole overlaps the upper part of the shoe or not. Each type of accessory and reinforcement of the shoes' uppers have different tariffs.

Although classification differences may seem trivial, the disparity in duties may cost companies millions of dollars. Some contentious examples are whether the French company Agatec's laser leveling device would be used primarily indoors or both indoors and outdoors,[37] whether Marvel's X-Men Wolverines were toys or dolls, and whether sport utility vehicles—such as the Suzuki Samurai and the Land Rover—were cars or trucks.

Because countries treat products from different countries differently, customs must also determine products' origins. This is neither cheap nor easy. However, customs officials have uncovered many instances of transshipping products—such as shoes, cigarette lighters, garlic, and lightbulbs—from China through Cambodia to overcome quantity limitations and higher duties.[38]

Other Direct-Price Influences　Countries use other means to affect prices, including special fees (such as for consular and customs clearance and documentation), requirements that customs deposits be placed in advance of shipment, and minimum price levels at which goods can be sold after they have customs clearance.

NONTARIFF BARRIERS: QUANTITY CONTROLS

Governments use other nontariff regulations and practices to affect directly the quantity of imports and exports. Let's take a look at the various forms that such regulations and practices typically take.

Quotas The **quota** is the most common type of quantitative import or export restriction, limiting the quantity of a product that can be imported or exported in a given time frame, typically per year. *Import quotas* normally raise prices for two reasons: (1) They limit supply, and (2) they provide little incentive to use price competition to increase sales. A notable difference between tariffs and quotas is their effect on revenues. Tariffs generate revenue for the government. Quotas generate revenues only for those companies that are able to obtain and sell a portion of the intentionally limited supply of the product. (Sometimes governments allocate quotas among countries, based on political or market conditions.)

> A quota may
> - Set the total amount to be traded.
> - Allocate amounts by country.

To circumvent quotas, companies sometimes convert the product into one for which there is no quota. For instance, the United States maintains sugar import quotas that result in U.S. sugar prices averaging about double the world market price for sugar. As a result, many U.S. candy producers (e.g., Fannie May, Brach's, Mars, Tootsie Roll, Hershey) have moved plants to Mexico where they can buy lower-cost sugar and import the candy duty-free to the United States.[39]

Finally, import quotas are not necessarily imposed to protect domestic producers. Japan has maintained quotas on many agricultural products that are not produced within the country. It has then allocated import rights to competing suppliers as a means of bargaining for sales of Japanese exports as well as preventing excess dependence on any one country for essential foods in the event that adverse climatic or political conditions abruptly cut off supply.

Voluntary Export Restraint A variation of an import quota is the so-called **voluntary export restraint (VER).** Essentially, the government of Country A asks the government of Country B to reduce its companies' exports to Country A voluntarily. The term *voluntarily* is somewhat misleading; typically, either Country B volunteers to reduce its exports or else Country A may impose tougher trade regulations. Procedurally, VERs have unique advantages. A VER is much easier to switch off than an import quota. In addition, the appearance of a "voluntary" choice by a particular country to constrain its shipments to another country tends not to damage political relations between those countries as much as an import quota does.

A country may establish *export quotas* to assure domestic consumers of a sufficient supply of goods at a low price, to prevent depletion of natural resources, or to attempt to raise export prices by restricting supply in foreign markets. To restrict supply, some countries band together in various commodity agreements, such as OPEC for petroleum, which then restrict and regulate exports from the member countries.

Embargoes A specific type of quota that prohibits all trade is an **embargo.** As with quotas, countries—or groups of countries—may place embargoes on either imports or exports, on whole categories of products regardless of origin or destination, on specific products with specific countries, or on all products with given countries. Governments impose embargoes in an effort to use economic means to achieve political goals. As we explain in our closing case, for instance, the U.S.-imposed embargo on Cuba was conceived to weaken the Cuban economy and thus induce a demoralized populace to overthrow the Communist regime.

Case Review Note

"Buy Local" Legislation Another form of quantitative trade control is so-called *buy local legislation.* Government purchases are a large part of total expenditures in many countries; typically, governments favor domestic producers. Sometimes governments specify a domestic content restriction—that is, a certain percentage of the product must

Through "buy local" laws

- Government purchases give preference to domestically made goods.
- Governments sometimes legislate a percentage of domestic content.

Other types of trade barriers include

- Arbitrary standards.
- Licensing arrangements.
- Administrative delays.
- Reciprocal requirements.
- Service restrictions.

be of local origin. For example, the United States economic stimulus package of 2009 to counter the economic recession requires any funded project to use only U.S.-made steel, iron, and manufactured goods.[40] Sometimes governments favor domestic producers through price mechanisms, such as permitting a government agency to buy a foreign-made product only if the price is at some predetermined margin below that of a domestic competitor.

Standards and Labels Countries can devise classification, labeling, and testing standards to allow the sale of domestic products but obstruct foreign-made ones. Take product labels, for instance. The requirement that companies indicate on a product where it is made provides information to consumers who may prefer to buy products from certain nations. In addition, countries may dictate content information on packaging that is not required elsewhere. These technicalities add to a firm's production costs, particularly if the labels must be translated for different export markets.

In addition, raw materials, components, design, and labor increasingly come from many countries, so most products today are of such mixed origin that they are difficult to sort out. For example, the United States stipulated that any cloth "substantially altered" (woven, for instance) in another country must have the country identified on its label. Consequently, designers like Ferragamo, Gucci, and Versace must declare "Made in China" on the labels of garments that contain Chinese silk.[41]

The professed purpose of standards is to protect the safety or health of the domestic population. However, some companies argue that standards are just another means to protect domestic producers. For example, some U.S. and Canadian producers have contended that EU regulations and labeling requirements on genetically engineered corn and canola oil are merely means to keep out the products until their own technology catches up.[42]

In another case, following publicity about contaminated foods from China in the United States, China upped its rejection of foodstuffs from the United States—citing contamination with drugs and salmonella.[43] In reality, there's no way of knowing to what extent products are kept out of countries for legitimate safety and health reasons versus arbitrarily to protect domestic production. Nevertheless, the U.S. FDA publishes a monthly summary of rejected food import shipments by country, and this list is substantial. For example, for May 2009, it rejected 1,233 shipments from 67 different countries. The highest rejections, in order, were from China, Mexico, India, and Germany.[44]

Specific Permission Requirements Some countries require that potential importers or exporters secure permission from governmental authorities before conducting trade transactions. This requirement is known as an **import or export license.** A company may have to submit samples to government authorities to obtain an import license. This procedure can restrict imports or exports directly by denying permission or indirectly because of the cost, time, and uncertainty involved in the process.

A **foreign-exchange control** is a similar type of control. It requires an importer of a given product to apply to a governmental agency to secure the foreign currency to pay for the product. As with an import license, failure to grant the exchange, not to mention the time and expense of completing forms and awaiting replies, obstructs foreign trade.

Administrative Delays Closely akin to specific permission requirements are intentional administrative delays, which create uncertainty and raise the cost of carrying inventory. For example, United Parcel Service provisionally suspended its ground service between the United States and Mexico because of burdensome Mexican customs delays. Competitive pressure, however, moves countries to improve their administrative systems. Chinese trade authorities, for example, cut the time taken for goods manufactured by Hong Kong firms in Guangdong to pass through internal customs checks from one week to one day. Improved processes, such as electronic submission of cargo manifests, affected 68,000 nonmainland firms and reduced administrative costs more than U.S. $70 million.[45]

Reciprocal Requirements Exporters, because of government regulations in the importing countries, sometimes must take merchandise or buy services in lieu of receiving cash payment. This requirement is common in the aerospace and defense industries—sometimes because the importer does not have enough foreign currency. For instance, Indonesia bought Russian jets in exchange for commodities such as rubber.[46]

Countertrade **Countertrade** or **offsets** are government requirements in the importing country whereby the exporter must provide additional economic benefits such as jobs or technology as part of the transaction.[47] For example, McDonnell Douglas sold helicopters to the British government but had to equip them with Rolls-Royce engines (made in the United Kingdom) as well as transfer much of the technology and production work to the United Kingdom.[48]

Reciprocal requirements often mean that exporters must find markets for goods outside their lines of expertise or engage in complicated organizational arrangements that require them to relinquish some operating control. All things being equal, companies avoid these transactions.[49] However, some companies have developed competencies in these types of arrangements in order to gain competitive advantages.

Restrictions on Services Services are the fastest-growing sector in international trade. In deciding whether to restrict trade in services, countries typically consider three factors: *essentiality, standards,* and *immigration.*

Essentiality Countries judge certain service industries to be essential because they serve strategic purposes or because they provide social assistance to their citizens. They sometimes prohibit private companies, foreign or domestic, in some sectors because they feel the services should not be sold for profit. In other cases, they set price controls or subsidize government-owned service organizations that create disincentives for foreign private participation.

Not-for-Profit Services Mail, education, and hospital health services are often not-for-profit sectors in which few foreign firms compete. When a government privatizes these industries, it customarily prefers local ownership and control. Some essential services in which foreign firms are sometimes excluded are media, communications, banking, utilities, and domestic transport.

Standards Governments limit entry into many service professions to ensure practice by qualified personnel. The licensing standards of these personnel vary by country and include such professionals as accountants, actuaries, architects, electricians, engineers, gemologists, hairstylists, lawyers, physicians, real estate brokers, and teachers.

At present, there is little reciprocal recognition in licensing from one country to another because occupational standards and requirements differ substantially. This means, for example, that an accounting or legal firm from one country faces obstacles in another country, even to service its domestic clients' needs. The company must hire professionals within each foreign country or else try to earn certification abroad. The latter option can be difficult because the professionals may have to take examinations in a foreign language and study materials different from those in their home country. Further, there may be lengthy prerequisites for taking an examination, such as internships, time in residency, and course work at a local university.

Concept Check

In Chapter 1, we define **service exports** and **imports** and discuss the significance of services for some companies and countries. We also divide them into three categories: tourism and transportation, service performance, and asset use.

Three main reasons for restricting trade in services are

- Essentiality.
- Standards.
- Immigration.

Immigration   Satisfying the standards of a particular country is no guarantee that a foreigner can then work there. In addition, governmental regulations often require that an organization—domestic or foreign—search extensively for qualified personnel locally before it can even apply for work permits for personnel it would like to bring in from abroad.[50]

Dealing with Governmental Trade Influences

Government intervention in trade affects the flow of imports and exports of goods and services between countries. When companies face possible losses because of import competition, they have several options to deal with this situation, four of which stand out:

When facing import competition, companies can

- Move abroad.
- Seek other market niches.
- Make domestic output competitive.
- Try to get protection.

1. Move operations to another country.
2. Concentrate on market niches that attract less international competition.
3. Adopt internal innovations, namely greater efficiency or superior products.
4. Try to get governmental protection.

There are costs and risks with each option. Nevertheless, the record of many companies shows that they undertake different options. For example, competition from Japanese imports spurred the U.S. automobile industry to move some production abroad (such as to subcontract with foreign companies to supply cheaper parts), develop niche markets through the sale of minivan and sport utility vehicles (SUVs) that initially had less international competition, and adopt innovations such as lean production techniques to improve efficiency and product quality. Finally, General Motors and Chrysler have received substantial government funding to survive.

TACTICS FOR DEALING WITH IMPORT COMPETITION

Granted, these methods are not realistic for every industry or every company. Companies may lack the managerial, capital, or technological resources to shift production abroad. They may not be able to identify more profitable product niches. In addition, even if they manage to develop product niches or improve efficiency, foreign competitors may quickly copy their innovation. In such situations, companies often ask their governments to restrict imports or open export markets.

Convincing Decision Makers   Governments cannot try to help every company that faces tough international competition. Likewise, helping one industry may hurt another. Thus, as a manager, you may propose or oppose a particular protectionist measure. Inevitably, the burden falls on you and your company to convince governmental officials that your situation warrants particular governmental policies. You must identify the key decision makers and convince them by using the economic and noneconomic arguments presented in this chapter. In any situation, companies must convey to public officials that voters and stakeholders support their position.[51]

Involving the Industry and Stakeholders   Companies improve the odds of success if they can ally most, if not all, domestic companies in their industry. Otherwise, officials may feel that a particular company's problems are due to its specific inefficiencies rather than the general challenge of imports or difficulty in gaining export sales. Similarly, it helps to involve other stakeholders, such as the taxpayers and merchants in the communities where they operate. Finally, companies can lobby decision makers and endorse the political candidates who are sympathetic to their situation.

Preparing for Changes in the Competitive Environment Companies can take different approaches to deal with changes in the international competitive environment. Frequently, companies' attitudes toward protectionism are a function of the investments they have made to implement their international strategy. Companies that depend on freer trade and those that have integrated their production and supply chains among countries tend to oppose protectionism. In contrast, companies with single or multidomestic production facilities, such as a plant in Japan to serve the Japanese market and a plant in Taiwan to serve the Taiwanese market, tend to support protectionism.

Companies also differ in their self-perception of being able to compete against imports. In nearly half the cases over a 60-year period in which U.S. firms proposed protecting a U.S. industry, one or more companies in that industry opposed it. The latter typically commanded competitive advantages in terms of scale economies, supplier relationships, or differentiated products. Thus they reasoned that not only could they successfully battle international rivals, but they also stood to gain even more as their weaker domestic competitors failed to do so.[52]

Concept Check

As we point out in Chapter 3, although representative democracies tend to share many features, the process whereby citizens select representatives to make decisions on their behalf varies from country to country, especially when it comes to the *centralization* or *decentralization* of authority. Among other things, the task of locating decision makers for business purposes thus differs from one country to another.

Looking to the Future Dynamics and Complexity

When trade restrictions change, there are winners and losers among countries and among companies and workers within them. Thus it's probably safe to say that we'll see mixtures of pushes for freer trade and greater protection.

In addition, gains to consumers from freer trade may be at the expense of some companies and workers—people who see themselves as big losers. They are not apt to lose without a struggle; they'll garner as much support for protection as they can, and they may win. This support may well come from alliances that cross national borders, such as the alliances among clothing companies in various developing nations that are uniting to push governments to enact quota agreements to protect their markets in developed countries against Chinese and Indian competition. Thus, if you are a manager in an industry that may be affected by changes in governmental protection, you must watch closely to predict how the politics may affect your own economic situation.

Finally, the international regulatory situation is becoming more, rather than less, complex—a situation that challenges companies to find the best locations in which to produce. New products are coming onto the market regularly, thus making the task of tariff classification more complex. Services available over the Internet, such as international online gambling, challenge governments to find means of regulation and collection of taxes. Heightened concerns about terrorism and product safety compound considerations of what should or should not be traded and with whom.

In Chapter 8, we discuss the trade agreements that countries are reaching; nevertheless, it's useful at this point to say a word or two about the impact these have on decision making. Every time countries negotiate a trading agreement (and these agreements are proliferating), there is the possibility that a new optimum production location emerges. For instance, the United States and Mexico negotiated a free trade pact, which caused some U.S. imports to shift from Taiwan to Mexico. However, with an additional free trade agreement between the United States and Central America, some of the production that developed in Mexico might now shift to a Central American country. Another free trade agreement might cause another shift in the future. All of this creates uncertainties and dynamics for companies' operations. ∎

U.S.–Cuban Trade: When Does a Cold War Strategy Become a Cold War Relic?

The U.S. embargo of Cuba has been a resilient foreign policy, able to weather a variety of political leaders, economic events, and historical eras.[53] (Some major events are shown in Figure 7.3.) In 2008, Fidel Castro ceded Cuban leadership to his younger brother Raúl (age 76), which led to speculation about Fidel's future behind-the-scenes influence and whether Raúl would make economic and political reforms.

Shortly before this, the United States tightened economic relations with Cuba by requiring any export sales to Cuba to be paid in cash in advance of shipment, reducing the maximum remittances that people in the United States could send to family in Cuba and restricting visits to Cuba by Cuban Americans to once in three years instead of once a year. The reasoning was straightforward and similar to one that had prevailed over nearly five decades: The Cuban economy was so weak that a demoralized population would overthrow Castro if economic conditions deteriorated just a little more. However, shortly after taking office in 2009, the Obama administration lifted the visit and remittance restrictions for people with family in Cuba along with the requirement of advance cash payments for U.S. exports. These moves led to speculation that commercial relations would grow between the two countries. Many observers want more relations and many do not, but let's first look at the history of the situation.

After the Revolution

In the 1950s, more than two-thirds of Cuban foreign trade took place with the United States. After Castro overthrew the Batista government in 1959, he threatened to incite revolutions elsewhere in Latin America. The United States countered by canceling its agreements to buy Cuban sugar, and Cuba retaliated by seizing U.S. oil refineries. The oil companies refused to supply Cuba with crude oil. Cuba then turned to the Soviet Union for replacement supplies.

The Cold War Sets In

This conflict occurred at the height of the Cold War tension between the United States and the Soviet Union. In 1962, the United States severed diplomatic relations and initiated the full trade embargo of Cuba. In 1963, the Treasury Department set forth regulations that prohibited all unlicensed financial transactions, forbade direct or indirect imports from Cuba, and imposed a total freeze on Cuban government assets held in the United States. Trade between the United States and Cuba stopped.

The incidents that strained relations during the next decades are too numerous to detail. Some threatened peace; others bordered on the absurd. They included the U.S. sponsorship

FIGURE 7.3   The Saga of U.S.-Cuba Relations

Relations between the United States and the island nation of Cuba have been embroiled in the vicissitudes of international politics for more than a century—and especially since Fidel Castro took power in 1959.

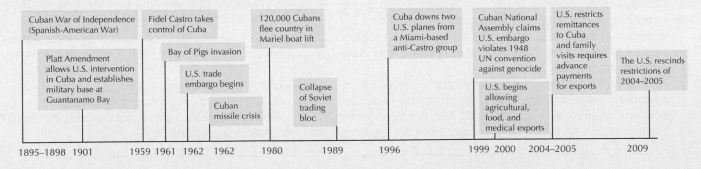

of an invasion by Cuban exiles at the Bay of Pigs, the placement and removal of Soviet missiles in Cuba, the deployment of Cuban forces to overthrow regimes the United States supported (such as in Nicaragua and Angola), and exposés claiming the CIA had tried to airlift someone to assassinate Castro and had tried to develop a powder to make his beard fall out. Figure 7.3 gives a time line of major events in U.S.-Cuban relations.

Enacting the Embargo

During this period, the U.S. trade embargo endured as originally set. Despite the collapse of communism in most of the world in the early 1990s, the U.S. Congress passed the Cuban Democracy Act in 1992. This policy codified the ban on American travel to Cuba and extended the embargo to the foreign subsidiaries of U.S. companies operating abroad—there would be no trade, direct or otherwise, between the United States and Cuba. The act also required Cuba to hold democratic elections before the U.S. executive branch could repeal the embargo.

Shifting Sympathies

Over time, the U.S. role in the Cuban drama has played to a less sympathetic audience worldwide. Initially, many countries supported the U.S. embargo. All members of the Organization of American States (OAS) except Mexico agreed in 1964 to endorse it. Gradually, countries began trading with Cuba anyway. In 2008, the United Nations voted 185 to 3 against the U.S. embargo. Only Israel and Palau voted with the United States. In 2009, the OAS lifted a 47-year suspension of Cuba as a member, basically by redefining democracy to include Marxist-Leninist ideology and not requiring property rights, transparent elections, and free speech as part of the definition.

The Cold War Thaws

Events increasingly created questions about the rationale for continuing the embargo. The fall of the Berlin Wall and the end of the Cold War in the early 1990s triggered many changes. The attendant collapse of the Soviet Union deprived Cuba of annual subsidies that sustained its feeble economy. Before long, the export of revolution from Cuba seemed less of a threat.

In fact, Cuba's staggering economy seemed on the brink of collapse. On the one hand, in 2000, U.S. Secretary of State Colin Powell ruled out the possibility of completely lifting the Cuban embargo until Castro departed. On the other hand, in the same year, congressional legislation allowed certain exports of U.S. agricultural, food, and medical products. After the passage of this act, the United States has become the fifth largest exporter to Cuba after Venezuela, China, Spain, and Canada.

The Argument for Policy Change

The U.S. public has been increasingly divided on the usefulness of the embargo on Cuba. Those in favor of establishing diplomatic relations with Cuba argue that hard-liner policies have failed for more than 50 years to dislodge Castro from power while causing adversity for over 11 million Cubans. They further contend that tighter restrictions would not weaken Castro's political power. In fact, they point to the Cuban government's past actions against the Cuban people in retaliation for new, stringent U.S. economic policies. These have included the raising of prices in Cuba for foreign-produced goods and the elimination of the U.S. dollar as an official currency.

Moreover, they warn that Cuban economic problems merely aggravate U.S. immigration tensions with Cuba. A growing number of leaders in the United States (including heads of major firms, Democratic and Republican members of Congress, and labor leaders) have publicly favored normalization of U.S.-Cuban trade. In essence, they believe that increasing exposure to the United States, not the embargo, would be a more promising force of change.

Are There U.S. Business Advantages in Cuba?   Repealing the embargo might help many U.S. industries and companies inasmuch as companies from other countries have already found advantages in tapping Cuba's highly qualified workforce, near-perfect literacy rate, and demand for foreign products and services. Groups in the United States have noted the market potential of Cuba for U.S. industries such as tourism and transportation. Further, there are bright spots for the Cuban economy. Venezuela has been supplying Cuba with about 98,000 barrels per day of petroleum products at preferential terms, and prices have generally been high for its nickel and cobalt exports. In addition, Cuba receives substantial remittances from its citizens working abroad, such as from its many doctors working in Venezuela.

At the same time, many argue that the potential for business with Cuba is highly limited. Cuba's per capita GDP is low, which when coupled with its small population (a little over 11 million) does not amount to much purchasing power. This is evident by the prevalence of 1950s cars in Cuba even though European and Japanese auto companies face no embargos on their sales.

In addition, Cuba has to export enough to pay for imports. Cuba depends heavily on commodity exports—sugar, nickel, tobacco, citrus, coffee—for which the United States has ample alternative supplies. In fact, the U.S. sugar quota system with a number of countries would surely cause a political backlash in those countries if part of their sugar quotas were given to Cuba. Certainly, there is the possibility of tourism, but there is disagreement about the unused capacity of its hotels. Further, there has been concern in some countries, such as the Bahamas and the Dominican Republic, that tourist growth in Cuba would be at their expense.

Is the Embargo a Cold War Relic?   Finally, there has been debate over the basis for the pro-embargo position. Some argued that, in an age when China is a member of the WTO and nations like Vietnam are trading with the United States, the Cuban embargo looked like a Cold War relic. Moreover, besides being far tougher than the U.S. economic sanctions against Iran and North Korea, the Cuban embargo is the longest and harshest embargo by one state against another in modern history.

However, a change in U.S. commercial policy toward Cuba does not necessarily mean that Cuba would welcome or accept it. For example, former U.S. secretary of state Lawrence Eagleburger reasoned that U.S. trade actions have given the Cuban government something other than inept policies to blame for economic blunders. "The worst thing that could happen [to Castro]," said Eagleburger, "would be for the U.S. to open the gates of trade and travel." Cuban leadership may think the same way. For instance, when the OAS allowed Cuba's reentry, Cuba rejected the overture by calling the OAS "totally anachronistic." Fidel Castro has said that the OAS will end up "in the garbage dump of history." Further, Raúl Castro purged Cuba's political leadership in 2009 by referring to former aides as foreign lackeys and indicating that he would not allow any cozying up to foreigners. ■

QUESTIONS

1. Should the United States seek to tighten the economic grip on Cuba? If so, why?
2. Should the United States normalize business relations with Cuba? If so, should the United States stipulate any conditions?
3. Assume you are Cuba's leader. What kind of trade relationship with the United States would be in your best interest? What type would you be willing to accept?
4. How does the structure and relationships of the U.S. political system influence the existence and specification of the trade embargo?

SUMMARY

- Despite the documented benefits of free trade, no country permits an unregulated flow of goods and services across its borders.

- It is difficult to determine the effect on employment from protecting an industry due to the likelihood of retaliation and the fact that imports as well as exports create jobs.

- Policymakers continue to struggle with the problem of income redistribution due to changes in trade policy.

- The infant-industry argument for protection holds that governmental prevention of import competition is necessary to help certain industries evolve from high-cost to low-cost production.

- Governmental interference is often argued to be beneficial if it promotes industrialization, given the positive relationship between industrial activity and certain economic objectives.

- Trade controls to improve economic relations with other countries include objectives of improving the balance of payments, raising prices to foreign consumers, gaining fair access to foreign markets, preventing foreign monopoly

prices, assuring that domestic consumers get low prices, and shifting revenue from foreign producers to domestic tax receipts.

- Considerable governmental interference in international trade is motivated by political rather than economic concerns, including maintaining domestic supplies of essential goods and preventing potential enemies from gaining goods that would help them achieve their objectives.

- Trade controls that directly affect price and indirectly affect quantity include tariffs, subsidies, arbitrary customs valuation methods, and special fees.

- Trade controls that directly affect quantity and indirectly affect price include quotas, VERs, "buy local" legislation, arbitrary standards, licensing arrangements, foreign-exchange controls, administrative delays, and reciprocal requirements.

- A company's development of an international strategy will greatly determine whether it will benefit more from protectionism or from some other means for countering international competition.

KEY TERMS

ad valorem duty (p. 312)
comparable-access argument (p. 306)
compound duty (p. 312)
countertrade (p. 317)
dumping (p. 307)
duty (p. 311)
effective tariff (p. 312)
embargo (p. 315)
essential-industry argument (p. 308)

export-led development (p. 305)
export tariffs (p. 311)
foreign-exchange control (p. 316)
import (or export) license (p. 316)
import tariff (p. 311)
industrialization argument (p. 304)
infant-industry argument (p. 303)
offsets (p. 317)
optimum-tariff theory (p. 308)

protectionism (p. 301)
quota (p. 315)
specific duty (p. 312)
subsidy (p. 312)
tariff (or duty) (p. 311)
terms of trade (p. 305)
transit tariff (p. 311)
voluntary export restraint (VER) (p. 315)

ENDNOTES

1 Cheng Ming-yu, May 2008, *Malaysia: Moving towards vision 2020*, ACI Working Paper Series, Lee Kuan Yew School of Public Policy, National University of Singapore; Akifumi Kuchik, September 2007, *A Flowchart Approach to Malaysia's Automobile Industry Cluster Policy*, IDE Discussion Paper No. 120, http://ir.ide.go.jp/dspace/bitstream /2344/630/1/ARRIDE_Discussion_No.120_kuchiki.pdf; Barbara Watson Andaya and Leonard Y. Andaya, *A History of Malaysia*, 2nd ed. (London: Palgrave, 2001); Faezahwaty Abdul Mohamed Ibnu and Jane Ramli, *The recent changes to the National Automotive Policy* (December 2009), accessed at http://naqiz.com; www.bernama.com (various online issues); Malaysian Economic Planning Unit: http://www.epu.gov.my/historyeconomic; KretaDotInfo corporate website: http://kereta.info/(various online issues); Proton corporate website: www.proton.com.my; Perodua corporate website: http: //www.perodua.com.my/; AFP, "Malaysia liberalizes struggling auto industry" (October 28, 2009), reproduced in Google-hosted news: http://www.google.com/hostednews/afp/article/ALeqM5iO8UhV-RmV3iv0r74YymGI6O3hl9g.

2 The opinion is by Scott Miller in John McCary and Andrew Batson, "Politics & Economics," *Wall Street Journal* (June 23, 2007): A4.

3 Hans S. Nichols, "Taking the Fix out of Farm Subsidies," *Insight on the News* (August 13, 2001): 20.

4 Lori Kletzer, *Job Loss from Imports: Measuring the Costs* (Washington, DC: Institute for International Economics, 2001); Alan M. Field,

"WTO Approves Sanctions against U.S." *Journal of Commerce–Online* (August 31, 2004): WP.

5 Greg Hitt, Paul Glader, and Mike Spector, "Trade Ruling on Steel May Boost Auto Industry," *Wall Street Journal* (December 15, 2006): A3.

6 Fuat Sener, "Schumpeterian Unemployment, Trade and Wages," *Journal of International Economics* 54 (2001): 119.

7 This argument is most associated with the writings of Raul Prebisch, Hans Singer, and Gunnar Myrdal in the 1950s and 1960s. For a recent discussion, see John Toye and Richard Toye, "The Origins and Interpretation of the Prebisch-Singer Thesis," *History of Political Economy* 35:3 (2003): 437–57.

8 Jiang Xueqin, "Letter from China," *The Nation* (March 4, 2002): n.p.

9 Steve Padgittm, Peggy Petrzelka, Wendy Wintersteen, and Eric Imerman, "Integrated Crop Management: The Other Precision Agriculture," *American Journal of Alternative Agriculture* 16 (January 2001): 16.

10 Hou Hexiang, "Vietnam to Accelerate Industrialization and Modernization of Rural Areas," *Xinhua News Agency* [China] (June 2, 2002): 1008; "Pushing Ecuador into the 21st Century," *Latin Finance* (March 2002: 30), at http://web.lexis-nexis.com/universe (accessed July 17, 2002); "Is Inequality Decreasing? Debating the Wealth and Poverty of Nations," *Foreign Affairs* (August 2002): 178.

11 Gerald K. Helleiner, "Markets, Politics, and Globalization: Can the Global Economy Be Civilized?" *Global Governance* (July–September

2001): 243; Marina Murphy, "EU Chemicals Need Flexibility: A Level Playing Field Should Be Established between the EU and U.S. Chemicals Industries," *Chemistry and Industry* (July 1, 2002): 9; Lisa Schmidt, "How U.S. Sees Trade Rows," *Calgary Herald* [Canada] (June 25, 2002): A2.

12 Annie Gowen, "U.S. Caviar with a Russian Accent," *Washington Post* (December 31, 2004): Metro, B1.

13 Alan Beattie and Javier Blas, "Precious Grains," *Financial Times* (April 14, 2008): 9; Randall Palmer, "Canada Mulls Nonprescription-Drug Tactic," *Seattle Times* (February 19, 2005): A13.

14 Edward Alden and Raphael Minder, "EU and Canada Impose Retaliatory Duties on U.S. Imports," *Financial Times* (April 1, 2005): 6.

15 Stephen Moore, "Tax Cut and Spend: The Profligate Ways of Congressional Republicans," *National Review* (October 1, 2001): 19.

16 George Leopold, "U.S. Eases Regulations on Cryptography Exports," *Electronic Engineering Times* (July 24, 2000): 43.

17 James Dao, "U.S. to Punish 10 Businesses for Iran Sales," *New York Times* (July 20, 2002): D1.

18 Lance Davis and Stanley Engerman, "Sanctions: neither War nor Peace," *Journal of Economic Perspectives* 17:2 (Spring 2003): 187–97.

19 "Leaders: A Grand Bargain with the Great Satan? Testing Iran's Nuclear Intentions," *The Economist* (March 12, 2005): 10.

20 Philip Shenon, "In Hanoi, U.S. Goods Sold but Not by U.S.," *New York Times* (October 3, 1993): A1.

21 Patrick Barta, "Black Gold," *Wall Street Journal* (August 16, 2006): A1+.

22 Jacob Weisberg, "Sanctions Help to Sustain Rogue States," *Financial Times* (August 3, 2006): 11.

23 "EU/Latin America/Caribbean: Leaders Aim to Revive Ties," *European Report* (May 15, 2002): 501.

24 Vanessa Bauza, "In Struggle for Influence, It's Better to Give," *Knight Ridder Tribune Business News* (March 24, 2007): 1.

25 Tony Walker, "China Warns Australia over Dalai Lama Visit," *Financial Times* (September 18, 1996): 1; Ying Ma, "China's America Problem," *Policy Review* (February 2002): 43–57.

26 Gail L. Cramer, James M. Hansen, and Eric J. Wailes, "Impact of Rice Tariffication on Japan and the World Rice Market," *American Journal of Agricultural Economics* 81 (1999): 1149.

27 Matthew Fraser, "Foreign Ownership Rules Indefensible: And There Appears to Be Appetite for Change," *Financial Post* (May 28, 2001): C2.

28 John Larkin, "Now Playing: Korea's Movie Industry Prevents Invest-ment Pact with the U.S.," *Wall Street Journal* (March 20, 2002): A19.

29 "Futile Fortress," *Financial Times* (August 26, 2003): 16.

30 Bernard Hoekman and Kym Anderson, "Developing-Country Agriculture and the New Trade Agenda," *Economic Development & Cultural Change* 49 (October 2000): 171.

31 Neil King, Jr., Scott Miller, Daniel Michaels, and J. Lynn Lunsford, "U.S., Europe Sue Each Other at WTO over Aircraft Subsidies," *Wall Street Journal* (October 7, 2004): A2+.

32 John W. Miller, "WTO Warns Members Not to Undermine Trade," *Wall Street Journal* (March 27, 2009): A8.

33 G. Chandrashekhar, "Should India Demand Farm Subsidy Cuts by Developed Nations?" *Businessline* (January 4, 2006): 1.

34 Chi-Chur Chao and Eden S. H. Yu, "Import Quotas, Tied Aid, Capital Accumulation, and Welfare," *Canadian Journal of Economics* 34 (2001): 661; Mark Rice, "Australia Must Join Other Countries in Untying Overseas Aid," *Australian Financial Review* (April 4, 2002): 59.

35 Jamil Anderlini, "China 'Ties' 5 B[illio]n Aid to Africa," *Financial Times* (June 26, 2007): 8.

36 Mohsin Habib and Leon Zurawicki, "Corruption and Foreign Direct Investment," *Journal of International Business Studies* 33 (2002): 291–308.

37 "National Import Specialist Addresses Outreach to the Public," *U.S. Customs Border Protection Today* (October–November 2006), at www.customs.ustreas.gov/xp?CustomsToday/2006/october_

november/import_article (accessed July 13, 2007); *Customs Bulletin and Decision* (June 27, 2007): 58.

38 John W. Miller, "Why Some China Exports Are Taking Illegal Detours," *Wall Street Journal* (May 25, 2007): B1+.

39 Jeremy Grant, "Signs of Decay as Companies Desert the U.S. Candy Capital," *Financial Times* (January 21, 2004): 14; Christopher Swann, "Shielding Sugar Industry 'Costs Thousands of Jobs,' " *Financial Times* (February 15, 2006): 6.

40 Sarah O'Connor, "Tug of War over Buy American," *Financial Times* (June 24, 2009): 4.

41 Blaise J. Bergiel and Erich B. Bergiel, "Country-of-Origin as a Surrogate Indicator: Implications/Strategies," *Global Competitiveness* 7 (1999): 187.

42 Jeremy Grant and Ralph Minder, "Comment & Analysis: Agribusiness," *Financial Times* (February 1, 2006): 11.

43 Anita Chang, "Food Safety," *Miami Herald* (July 15, 2007): 18A.

44 "Import Refusal Report: May 2009," http://www.accessdata.fda .gov/scripts/ImportRefusals/ir_byCountry (accessed July 15, 2009).

45 Peggy Sito, "Guangdong to Slash Internal Customs Delays," *South China Morning Post* (May 16, 2002): 1.

46 Devi Asmarani, "MPs Criticise Jakarta for Buying Pricey Russian Jets," *Singapore Straits Time* (June 19, 2003).

47 Chong Ju Choi, Soo Hee Lee, and Jai Boem Kim, "A Note on Countertrade: Contractual Uncertainty and Transaction Governance in Emerging Economies," *Journal of International Business Studies* 30 (Spring 1999): 189.

48 "McDonnell and Partner Win $4 Billion British Copter Deal," *New York Times* (July 14, 1995): C5.

49 Choi et al., "A Note on Countertrade," 189.

50 Sara Robinson, "Workers Are Trapped in Limbo by I.N.S.," *New York Times* (February 29, 2000): A12.

51 Ralph G. Carter and Lorraine Eden, "Who Makes U.S. Trade Policy?" *International Trade Journal* 13:1 (1999): 53–100.

52 Eugene Salorio, "Trade Barriers and Corporate Strategies: Why Some Firms Oppose Import Protection for Their Own Industry," unpublished DBA dissertation, Harvard University, 1991.

53 *Sources include the following:* Patricia Treble, " 'Putrid' OAS Attacked for Cuba Invite," *Maclean's* 122:23 (June 22, 2009): 33; Mary Anastasia O'Grady, "Latin America's Brave New World," *Wall Street Journal* (June 8, 2009): A15; Marc Franc, "Raúl Castro Uses Film to Lay Down the Law and Cast Off Fidel's Legacy," *Financial Times* (July 15, 2009): 1; Will Weissert, "Can Cuba Cope with an Onslaught of Americans?" *Yahoo News* (April 13, 2009), at http://news.yahoo .com/s/ap_travel_brief_cuba_american_tourism (accessed July 15, 2009); Lesley Clark and Frances Robles, "Showdown on Cuba Policy Not Over Yet," *Miami Herald* (March 11, 2009): A1; Joel Millman, "Cuba Receives More Cash from Workers Abroad," *Wall Street Journal* (March 5, 2009): A12; Laura Meckler and Amy Schatz, "U.S. Eases Firms' Access to Cuba," *Wall Street Journal* (April 14, 2009): A#; Anne Gearan, "U.S. Public's Feelings Mixed on Castro," *Miami Herald* (February 8, 2007): 12A; "CIA World Factbook—Cuba," at www.cia.gov/library/publications/the-world-factbook/geos/ cu.html (accessed July 15, 2009); Pascal Fletcher, "U.S. Anti-Cuba Law Feeds Businessmen's Paranoia," *Financial Times* (July 2, 1996): 5; William M. Leo Grande, "From Havana to Miami: U.S. Cuba Policy as a Two-Level Game," *Journal of Interamerican Studies and World Affairs* 40:1 (1998): 67–86; Albert R. Hunt, "End the Anachronistic Embargo against Cuba," *Wall Street Journal* (April 22, 1999): A23; Daniel P. Erikson, "The New Cuba Divide," *The National Interest* (Spring 2002); Kathleen Parker, "Exposure, Not Embargoes, Will Free Fidel's Cuba," *Seattle Times* (March 14, 2001): B6; Timothy Ashby, "Who's Really Being Hurt?" *Journal of Commerce* (January 31, 2005): 1; "The Web Site of Cuban Industry," at www.cubaindustria.cu/English (accessed October 5, 2009); Theresa Borden, "Cubans Feel Pinch from Dollar Ban," *Atlanta Journal-Constitution* (November 10, 2004): 6F.

eight
Cross-National Cooperation and Agreements

Objectives

- To identify the major characteristics and challenges of the World Trade Organization

- To discuss the pros and cons of global, bilateral, and regional integration

- To describe the static and dynamic impact of trade agreements on trade and investment flows

- To define different forms of regional economic integration

- To compare and contrast different regional trading groups, including but not exclusively the European Union (EU), the North American Free Trade Agreement (NAFTA), the Southern Common Market (MERCOSUR), and the Association of Southeast Asian Nations (ASEAN)

- To describe other forms of global cooperation such as the United Nations and the Organization of the Petroleum Exporting Countries (OPEC)

Marrying is easy, but housekeeping is hard.

—German proverb

325

Anna Kessler put the key into the ignition of her brand-new Toyota Yaris, started the engine, and began to navigate her way home from work through the crowded streets of Berlin, Germany.[1] Having owned the car for just over a week, she was already satisfied with her decision. She liked the car's distinctive European look, the generous warranty it had come with, and its low fuel consumption.

Her decision the previous week marked the first time Anna had ever owned a vehicle manufactured by an Asian company; in fact, it was the first time she had considered one. When she had made her last car purchase, the thought of buying a car from Toyota—then known for its lackluster designs, limited options, and seven-month-long waiting lists—had not even entered her mind. However, as she was researching different vehicles, she found that Toyota had ranked the highest in several categories in a recent quality survey and that the Yaris had achieved an outstanding four-star Euro NCAP safety rating, which led her to investigate the car more thoroughly.

With her purchase, Anna became another one of the millions of Toyota vehicle owners located around the globe, contributing to the Japanese automaker's rapid growth over the past decade. In 1990, the company possessed 20 production facilities in 14 countries; now it has 53 overseas manufacturing facilities in 27 countries, including eight located in Western and Eastern Europe.

Known for its low-cost, efficient production operations, Toyota finally surpassed General Motors as the largest car manufacturer in the world in 2008, and also as the most profitable—at least until FY 2009 (the year ending March 31, 2009) when the full impact of the global financial crisis was felt. Although Toyota is only number seven in market share in Europe behind Volkswagen and other European companies as well as Ford and GM, Toyota and other major Asian automakers have been experiencing marked success compared with their European counterparts. Toyota and Honda are the only two Asian companies in Europe's top 10, but they are followed by Nissan, Hyundai, Suzuki, Kia, and Mazda in the top 15.

Given Toyota's steady increase in market share, it is hard to believe that before 2002, Toyota had not posted a profit for its European operations for three decades and had suffered from consistently low market share and growth in the region. So why has it taken Toyota so long to crack into the competitive European market, and why are European companies only now beginning to feel the pressure from Asian manufacturers? Many analysts have pointed to an agreement between the Japanese government and the European Community (EC)—predecessor to the European Union (EU)—in which the two negotiated a quota each year for the number of Japanese cars imported into Europe. The quota amounts agreed upon each year depended on such factors as the level of consumer demand and sales growth in the region and were fixed at 11 percent of the European market.

The arrangement was set up to allow European carmakers to become more competitive as the EC made the transition to a common market; previously, several independent European nations possessed their own import and registration restrictions on Japanese cars. Italy, for example, limited the number of imported Japanese vehicles to 3,000, while France kept them at a 3 percent share of its market. Britain, Spain, and Portugal imposed similar restrictions. This policy goes back to the end of World War II when the Japanese government asked the European automakers to curtail exports to Japan to help Japan rebuild its industry. The Europeans reciprocated by limiting the access of Japanese autos to their market. At the time, that wasn't a problem. However, when the Japanese auto companies became export conscious, they wanted access to the European markets. The quota system helped protect the domestic industry.

Under the new system, these countries had to abandon their individual policies, but French carmakers fought to include an 80 percent local-content rule and an allowance to export 500,000 cars a year to Japan, five times the then-current level. In the end, the EC disregarded these additional requests, and in the first year of the agreement, 1.089 million Japanese cars were allowed to be imported.

The quota, however, also fixed separate caps for each participating country and then divided this amount among the Japanese automakers according to their historic market shares. The caps essentially prevented the Japanese from being able to transfer their excess imports from countries where their quotas weren't being met to ones where they were unable to meet demand due to having already reached the maximum limits. It was primarily for this reason that they never actually met their quota for the EC; during the seven years the quota system was in effect, Toyota was held to a 2 to 3 percent market share in most EU countries.

Although the system seemed to be having the desired effect, even some French auto officials admitted that the eventual opening of the market was inevitable. One noted, "Can we put off change for years? Officially, yes. But honestly, I don't think so." That statement proved prophetic when the EU lifted the import quota in 1999 and additionally made it easier for the Japanese auto manufacturers to expand distribution and to sign up dealers. Although this move did not necessarily cause the Japanese to flood the European market with their products, it did open the way for them to invest more heavily in design and manufacturing facilities in the EU, to broaden the range of products they marketed there, and to customize their offerings to better appeal to European tastes.

Toyota responded to the drop in barriers by introducing a new strategy of designing vehicles targeted specifically at European customers. The new strategy involved setting up a European Design and Development center in southern France and allowing design teams across the globe to compete for projects. The Yaris, Toyota's best-selling vehicle in the EU, was designed by a Greek and was the first to be developed within the region. It subsequently was named Car of the Year 2000 in both Europe and Japan. In addition, it received five stars in the Euro NCAP (New Car Assessment Programme) tests for adult occupant protection in 2008.

As another key element of its European strategy, Toyota has also set up additional production centers in the region and now manufactures all of its best European-selling vehicles in Europe. The new-generation Toyota Corolla, voted 2002 European Car of the Year, and the Avensis, the first Toyota vehicle to be exported from Europe to Japan, were both designed and built in Europe. In December 2006, Toyota celebrated its one millionth made-in-Europe Yaris at its Valenciennes plant in France.

Manufacturing facilities in Eastern Europe allow the Japanese automaker to lower production costs due to lower wages. For example, workers in Toyota's plant in Turkey earn only $3.60 an hour, giving Toyota a distinct cost advantage over European competitors such as Volkswagen, which pays as much as $40.68 per hour to the workers in its plants in Germany.

The difference in wages, in addition to its efficient operations, has allowed Toyota to remain profitable while others are undergoing layoffs and industry-wide restructuring. Volkswagen cut nearly 20,000 jobs and introduced longer shifts in its German factories. GM's European unit cut 13,000 jobs to help it reduce costs and restore profitability after seven consecutive years of losses in the region. Additionally, Ford, Fiat SpA, and Volkswagen have undergone substantial management changes as they've sought to rein in operations to keep costs from running over in the new competitive market in which they are slowly losing market share.

The situation seems even bleaker as Japanese competitors continue to open up facilities in the Eastern bloc countries recently admitted to the EU as well as in other low-wage areas such as China. Toyota has already set up state-of-the-art production plants in the Czech Republic and Poland—the one in the Czech Republic being established in cooperation with France's PSA Peugeot Citroën to develop good relationships with PSA's local suppliers. Because of the elimination of internal tariffs in the EU, Toyota can manufacture automobiles anywhere within the EU and ship them to all markets duty-free. Before the reduction in tariff barriers, this would not have been possible.

◀ Toyota established a manufacturing presence in Europe through a joint venture in Kolin, Czech Republic, with French PSA Peugeot Citroën. The factory produces 300,000 Toyota Aygo, Peugeot 107 (shown here), and Citroën C1 cars per year—1,050 cars per day. A new car leaves the factory every 56 seconds.
Source: Hana Kalvachova/Getty Images, Inc.

Other recent trends in the EU have also favored Toyota since the quotas were eliminated. In light of a sluggish European economy facing high unemployment and low growth, Europeans are becoming less loyal to European brands in their search for more economical, higher-quality vehicles. In recent J.D. Power customer surveys in the United Kingdom and Germany, Toyota ranked first overall and scored the highest in three of seven categories; Ford, Renault, and Volkswagen all ranked below average. In addition, Toyota's environmentally friendly hybrid vehicle, the Prius, was voted the 2005 European Car of the Year. In light of its growing presence in Europe, the company's application to become a full member of the European Automobile Manufacturers' Association has been accepted.

Riding on its success in Europe and its growth internationally, Toyota has ambitious goals for the future. However, the global financial crisis put a crimp in those plans. Although Toyota overtook GM for global leadership of sales in 2008, worldwide sales dropped nearly 22 percent in FY 2009 compared with FY 2008, and Toyota posted a ¥436.9 billion loss in FY 2009 compared with net income of ¥1,717.8 billion in FY 2008. Toyota has had to lay off people worldwide but has so far resisted the move to shut down plants. At least it has survived, which is in stark contrast to GM and Chrysler, who have gone through government bailouts, bankruptcy, and restructuring. Toyota was smart to manufacture in the Czech Republic with cheap wages and to partner with PSA Peugeot Citroën. Given the state of the market and uncertainty ahead, you have to wonder if Anna Kessler is still driving her Yaris, or if she has traded it in for another Yaris or something else.

CRN
Case Review Note

Introduction

Approaches to economic integration—political and economic agreements among countries in which preference is given to member countries—may be

- Bilateral.
- Regional.
- Global.

In some respects, the United States is the perfect example of economic integration—the largest economy in the world composed of 50 states in the continental United States, Alaska, and Hawaii, a common currency, and labor and capital mobility. However, it is just one country. What about the rest of the world? **Economic integration** is the political and economic agreements among countries in which preference is given to member countries. There are three ways to approach economic integration:

- **Bilateral integration,** where two countries decide to cooperate more closely together, usually in the form of tariff reductions.
- **Regional integration,** where a group of countries located in the same geographic proximity decide to cooperate, as is the case with the European Union.
- **Global integration**, where countries from all over the world decide to cooperate through the WTO.

In the mid- to late 1940s, countries decided that if they were going to emerge from the wreckage of World War II and promote economic growth and stability within their borders, they would have to assist—and get assistance from—nearby countries. This chapter discusses some of the important forms of economic cooperation.

Why do you need to understand the nature of these agreements? Trading groups, whether bilateral, regional, or global, are an important influence on the strategies of MNEs. Such groups can define the size of the regional market and the rules under which companies must operate. In fact, an increase in market size is the single most important reason for trading groups.[2] Companies in the initial stages of foreign expansion must be aware of the regional economic groups that encompass countries with good manufacturing locations or market opportunities. As companies expand internationally, they must change their organizational structure and operating strategies to take advantage of regional trading groups. As we noted in our opening case, Toyota has been able to find success in Europe by taking advantage of changes in EU policy that allow it to adjust its design and production strategies to meet the unique needs of European consumers.

MNEs are interested in regional trade groups because the MNEs themselves tend to be regional as well. Although we often think of MNEs as companies that do business in all of the **triad** regions of the world—Europe, North America, and Asia—current research demonstrates that most MNEs generate a majority of their revenues in their home regions. Using a sample of the top 500 companies in the world that tend to generate most of the world's trade and foreign direct investment, it was found that 320 MNEs generate at least 50 percent of their revenues from their home region, 25 MNEs are biregional (at least 20 percent of their revenues from two regions but less than 50 percent from any single region), 11 MNEs are host-region oriented (more than 50 percent of their revenues from a region outside of their home region), and only nine MNEs are truly global (at least 20 percent of their revenues from each of the three triad regions and with less than 50 percent of their sales from one region).[3]

However, that does not minimize the importance of different regions for MNEs. For example, RC Willey—the regional furniture, electronics, and appliances store in the United States owned by Berkshire Hathaway—does not generate any foreign sales. However, it imports products from all over the world. Managers of the company are very interested in trade agreements because such agreements could have an impact on where they source their purchases to reduce costs and improve quality.

The World Trade Organization (WTO)

Governments often actively cooperate with each other to remove trade barriers. The following discussion looks at the **World Trade Organization (WTO),** the successor to the General Agreement on Tariffs and Trade and the major multilateral forum through which governments can come to agreements and can settle disputes regarding trade.

GATT: PREDECESSOR TO THE WTO

In 1947, 23 countries formed the **General Agreement on Tariffs and Trade (GATT)** under the auspices of the United Nations to abolish quotas and reduce tariffs. By the time the WTO replaced GATT in 1995, 125 nations were members. Many believe that GATT's contribution to trade liberalization made possible the expansion of world trade in the second half of the twentieth century.

Trade without Discrimination   The fundamental principle of GATT was that each member nation must open its markets equally to every other member nation; any sort of discrimination was prohibited. The principle of "trade without discrimination" was embodied in GATT's **most-favored-nation (MFN) clause**—once a country and its trading partners had agreed to reduce a tariff, that tariff cut was automatically extended to every other member country, irrespective of whether they were a signatory to the agreement.

Over time, GATT grappled with the issue of nontariff barriers in terms of industrial standards, government procurement, subsidies and countervailing duties (duties in response to another country's protectionist measures), licensing, and customs valuation. In each area, GATT members agreed to apply the same product standards for imports as for domestically produced goods, treat bids by foreign companies on a nondiscriminatory basis for most large contracts, prohibit export subsidies except on agricultural products, simplify licensing procedures that permit the importation of foreign-made goods, and use a uniform procedure to value imports when assessing duties on them.

Case Review Note

Concept Check

In Chapter 7, we explain that, in principle, no country allows an unregulated flow of goods and services across its borders; rather, governments routinely influence the flow of imports and exports. We also observe that governments directly or indirectly *subsidize* domestic industries to help them compete with foreign producers, whether at home or abroad. (In Chapter 1, we list the motivations for governments to engage in cross-national agreements— indeed, to cooperate at all.)

Concept Check

In Chapter 7, we define a **tariff** as the most common type of trade control and describe it as a "tax" that governments levy on goods shipped internationally. Here we emphasize the fact that tariff barriers affect the prices of goods that cross national borders.

Concept Check

In discussing "Nontariff Barriers" as instruments of *trade control* in Chapter 7, we include **subsidies,** which we describe as direct government payments made to domestic companies, either to compensate them for losses incurred from selling abroad or to make it more profitable for them to sell overseas.

GATT slowly ran into problems. Its success led some governments to devise craftier methods of trade protection. World trade grew more complex, and trade in services—not covered by GATT rules—grew more important. Procedurally, GATT's institutional structure and its dispute-settlement system seemed increasingly overextended. In addition, GATT could not enforce compliance with agreements. These market trends and organizational challenges made trade agreements harder to work out. Restoring an effective means for trade liberalization led officials to create the WTO in 1995.

WHAT DOES THE WTO DO?

The World Trade Organization is the major body for

- Reciprocal trade negotiations.
- Enforcement of trade agreements.

The WTO adopted the principles and trade agreements reached under the auspices of GATT but expanded its mission to include trade in services, investment, intellectual property, sanitary measures, plant health, agriculture, and textiles, as well as technical barriers to trade. Currently, the WTO has 153 members, including the BRIC countries of Brazil, India, and China, but not Russia. The members collectively account for more than 97 percent of world trade. The entire membership makes significant decisions by consensus. However, there are provisions for a majority vote in the event of a nondecision by member countries. Agreements then must be ratified by the governments of the member nations.

The highest-level decision-making body in the WTO's structure is the Ministerial Conference; it meets at least once every two years. The next level is the General Council (usually ambassadors and the director of a country delegation) that meets several times a year. The General Council also meets as the Trade Policy Review Body and the Dispute Settlement Body.

At the next level are the Council for Trade in Goods, the Council for Trade in Services, and the Council for Trade-Related Aspects of Intellectual Property Rights (TRIPS). Specialized committees, working groups, and working parties deal with the individual agreements and other areas, such as the environment, development, membership applications, and regional trade agreements. WTO members deal with these areas separately and on an ongoing basis.

Concept Check

We explain *TRIPS* in Chapter 5 as an agreement that allows poor countries to either produce generic products for local consumption or import them from countries other than patent holders' home countries.

Most Favored Nation   The WTO continued the MFN clause of GATT, which implies that member countries should trade without discrimination, basically giving foreign products "national treatment." Although the WTO restricts this privilege to official members, members are allowed some exceptions, as follows:

1. Developing countries' manufactured products have been given preferential treatment over those from industrial countries.
2. Concessions granted to members within a regional trading alliance, such as the EU, have not been extended to countries outside the alliance. (Recall from our opening case, for instance, that although EU members can export and import cars from other EU nations without limitations, Japanese carmakers must comply with strict import tariffs.)
3. Countries can raise barriers against member countries who they feel are trading unfairly.

Exceptions are made in times of war or international tension.

Dispute Settlement   Countries may bring charges of unfair trade practices to a WTO panel, and accused countries may appeal. There are time limits on all stages of deliberations, and the WTO's rulings are binding. If an offending country fails to comply with the panel's judgment, its trading partners have the right to compensation. If this penalty is ineffective, then the offending country's trading partners have the right to impose countervailing sanctions.

Concept Check

In Chapter 7, we show how the imposition of import restrictions can be used as a means of persuading other countries to lower import barriers. Here we point out that the same practice can also be used to punish nations whose policies fail to comply with provisions of the WTO or other agreements.

Doha Round   Most of the agenda of the WTO was established by negotiations (also known as rounds) held by GATT, especially the Uruguay Round which took place from 1986 to 1994 and led up to the creation of the WTO. Perhaps the most complex set of issues the WTO is currently faced with, however, is those it is trying to address through the Doha Round, which commenced in Doha, Qatar, in 2001 and is focused on giving a boost to developing countries on the world scene. The largest of the disputes has essentially resulted in a split between developed members, such as the United States, Japan, and the EU, and developing nations, led by Brazil and India, over the large agricultural subsidies maintained by the richer nations and the industrial subsidies enforced by developing nations.

As we see later in the chapter, the challenges facing a resolution at Doha go beyond the typical developed/developing country differences and include differences between different groups of developing countries. Despite continued trade talks, the parties have remained deadlocked on the issue, with Brazil and India—representing their alliance of developing nations known as the "Group of 22"—walking out of negotiations in frustration on several occasions.

The initial deadline for completing the Doha agenda was January 1, 2005, but the deadline came and went as countries could not agree on key issues. The next deadline was the end of 2006, but that was missed as well, as did negotiations in July 2008 and 2009. By the third quarter of 2009, attempts to solve the problem of lowering tariffs on industrial goods (a demand by the United States and the EU) in return for a reduction of agricultural barriers (a demand of many developing countries) were not successful. In an interesting twist, Brazil sided with the United States and the EU, while India and China rejected the proposals because of their fear that imports would devastate their local economies, in terms of both industrial and agricultural goods.[4] The sense of urgency seemed to stall as global trade increased by 70 percent to $14 trillion and FDI flows were up 25 percent to $1.5 trillion, even in the absence of the Doha Round.[5]

Then the global financial crisis got everyone's attention. Initially it put the Doha agenda temporarily on hold as governments struggled to bring their economies back to life and reignite global trade, which collapsed in 2008. The World Bank estimated that the global economy would shrink by 2.5 percent in 2009 and trade would fall by 6.1 percent, the first such negative growth since the early 1980s.[6] (The WTO predicted a 9 percent or more drop in world trade in 2009.)[7] However, the Doha Round is not dead, and there is still hope that countries will be able to get together to resolve their differences and continue to reduce trade barriers and increase world trade. One of the key concerns is the rise in protectionism as countries try to get their own economies going without losing market share to imports.[8]

The WTO is not without its critics. The critics of globalization feel that the efforts of the WTO are undermining the uniqueness of countries and benefitting the rich at the expense of the poor. This has become such a big issue in recent years that the WTO published two brochures on its Web site called "10 Benefits of the WTO Trading System" and "10 Common Misunderstandings about the WTO."[9]

◄ Protesters shout slogans during an anti–World Trade Organization (WTO) protest in front of the trade ministry in Jakarta on June 8, 2009. U.S. trade representative Ron Kirk met WTO director general Pascal Lamy in Indonesia during talks on farm exports concerning the global trade crisis, which is hampering global efforts to reduce barriers to trade.

Source: Bay Ismoyo/Getty Images, Inc.

The Rise of Bilateral Agreements

Bilateral agreements can be between two individual countries or may involve one country dealing with a group of other countries.

As the negotiations over the Doha Round broke down, Brazil and the EU announced a proposed strategic alliance between them. The agreement would give Brazil the same trading status that China and Russia have with the EU and would initiate discussions in other areas, such as energy, climate change, and human rights. In a similar fashion, South Korea signed a free trade pact with the United States, and India began negotiating a deal with the EU.[10] These examples highlight the increasing willingness of individual countries to circumvent the multilateral system and engage in bilateral agreements—also known as *preferential trade agreements* (PTAs) or *free trade agreements* (FTAs)—with each other to meet their global trade objectives.

The term *bilateral* is a little misleading. In most cases, the treaties involve two countries, such as a treaty between the United States and Australia. In other cases, the bilateral treaties involve one country with several other countries linked together in a free trade agreement. Because the EU negotiates trade as one trading bloc, its agreements with other countries, such as between the EU and Brazil, are technically bilateral agreements.

Another example of a bilateral agreement is the agreement between the United States and the Central American Free Trade Agreement–Dominican Republic (CAFTA-DR), even though the agreement really involves seven countries.

Regional Economic Integration

Regional trade agreements— integration confined to a region and involving more than two countries.

Geographic proximity is an important reason for economic integration.

Going beyond the bilateral approach is the regional approach, called *regional trade agreements*, or RTAs. Not all are in force, but as of December 2008, 230 of the 324 RTAs notified by the WTO were in force. Taking into account RTAs that are enforced but have not been notified, those signed but not enforced, those currently being negotiated, and those in the proposal stage, the WTO has identified nearly 400 RTAs.[11] These statistics count bilateral as well as regional agreements. For example, 11 RTAs are listed for the United States, and nine of them involve the U.S. and one other country. These agreements, whether bilateral or regional, are also called *preferential trade agreements* or *PTAs*. The rationale for the term *PTA* is that signatory countries give preferential treatment to those in the group.

It's logical that most trade groups contain countries in the same area of the world. Neighboring countries tend to ally for several reasons:

Concept Check

In discussing *geographic distance* in Chapter 6, we observe that because greater distances ordinarily mean higher transportation costs, geographic proximity usually encourages trade cooperation. In the same chapter, we explain **country-similarity theory** by showing that once a company has developed a new product in response to conditions in its home market, it will probably try to export it to those markets that it regards as most similar to its own.

- The distances that goods need to travel between such countries are short.
- Consumers' tastes are likely to be similar, and distribution channels can easily be established in adjacent countries.
- Neighboring countries may have common histories and interests, and they may be more willing to coordinate their policies than nonneighboring nations.[12]

As also noted earlier, the major reason to establish a regional trade group is to increase market size. There are two basic types of regional economic integration from the standpoint of tariff policies:

Major types of economic integration:

- Free trade area—no internal tariffs.
- Customs union—no internal tariffs plus common external tariffs.
- Common market—customs union plus factor mobility.

- *Free Trade Agreement (FTA)* The goal of an FTA is to abolish all tariffs between member countries. Free trade agreements usually begin modestly by eliminating tariffs on goods that already have low tariffs, and there is usually an implementation period during which all tariffs are eliminated on all products. In addition, each member country maintains its own external tariffs against non-FTA countries. About 90 percent of the RTAs identified by the WTO are free trade agreements.

- *Customs Union* In addition to eliminating internal tariffs, member countries levy a common external tariff on goods being imported from nonmembers. For example, the EU established a common external tariff in 1967. It had begun to remove internal tariffs in 1959, and that process was completed in 1967, at the same time the common external tariff was established. Now the EU negotiates as one region in the WTO rather than as separate countries.

(Thus, as we observed in our opening case, when it came to import quotas on cars shipped to EU members, Japan had to negotiate with the EU as a whole, rather than with individual countries.) However, most trade gains come from membership in a free trade agreement, not a customs union, which is driven more by political than economic reasons.[13] Customs unions account for less than 10 percent of the RTAs identified by the WTO.

Case Review Note

Common Market (or Economic Integration Agreement) Beyond the reduction of tariffs and nontariff barriers, countries can enhance their cooperation in a variety of other ways. The EU, for example, also allows free mobility of production factors such as labor and capital. This means that labor, for example, is free to work in any country in the common market without restriction. This type of cooperation where free mobility of factors of production is added to a customs union results in a **common market.** In the absence of the common market arrangement, a worker from a member country would have to apply for an immigration visa, and that might be difficult to come by.

In addition, the EU has harmonized its monetary policies through the creation of a common currency, complete with a central bank. This level of cooperation creates a degree of political integration among member countries, which means they lose a bit of their sovereignty. The EU is formally listed by the WTO as a customs union and economic integration agreement.

THE EFFECTS OF INTEGRATION

Regional economic integration can affect member countries in social, cultural, political, and economic ways. Initially, however, our focus is on the economic rationale for regional integration. As we noted in Chapter 7, the imposition of tariff and nontariff barriers disrupts the free flow of goods, affecting resource allocation.

Regional integration has social, cultural, political, and economic effects.

Static and Dynamic Effects Regional economic integration reduces or eliminates those barriers for member countries. It produces both *static effects* and *dynamic effects.* **Static effects** are the shifting of resources from inefficient to efficient companies as trade barriers fall.

Static effects of integration— the shifting of resources from inefficient to efficient companies as trade barriers fall.

Dynamic effects are the overall growth in the market and the impact on a company caused by expanding production and by the company's ability to achieve greater economies of scale. As shown in Figure 8.1, free trade agreements result in static and dynamic effects on trade and investment flows.

Static effects may develop when either of two conditions occurs:

Dynamic effects of integration—the overall growth in the market and the impact on a company caused by expanding production and by the company's ability to achieve greater economies of scale.

1. *Trade Creation:* Production shifts to more efficient producers for reasons of comparative advantage, allowing consumers access to more goods at a lower price than would have been possible without integration. Companies protected in their domestic markets face real problems when the barriers are eliminated and they attempt to compete with more efficient producers.

   Trade creation—production shifts to more efficient producers for reasons of comparative advantage.

   The strategic implication is that companies that might not have been able to export to another country—even though they might be more efficient than producers in that country—are now able to export when the barriers come down. Thus there will be more demand for their products, and the demand for the protected, less efficient products will fall. Also, it is possible that investment might shift to countries that are more efficient or that have a comparative advantage in one or more of the factors of production.

2. *Trade Diversion:* Trade shifts to countries in the group at the expense of trade with countries not in the group, even though the nonmember companies might be more efficient in the absence of trade barriers.

   Trade diversion—trade shifts to countries in the group at the expense of trade with countries not in the group.

For example, assume that U.S. companies are importing the same product from Mexico and Taiwan. If the United States enters into an FTA with Mexico but not with

FIGURE 8.1   Impact of Free Trade Agreements

When economic integration reduces or eliminates trade barriers, the effects on the nations involved may be either *static* or *dynamic*. *Static effects* apply primarily to trade barriers themselves—for member countries they go down, and for nonmembers they go up. *Dynamic effects*, on the other hand, apply to economic changes affecting the newly structured market—not only does the market expand, but so do local companies, which take advantage of the larger market.

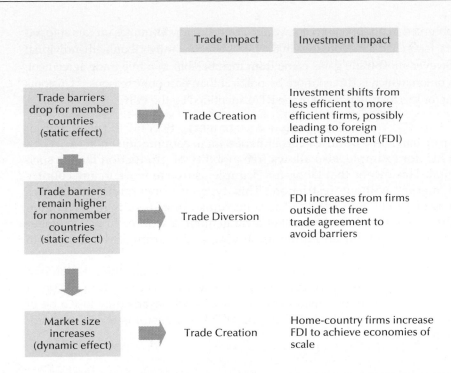

In Chapter 6, we define **comparative advantage** as the theory that global efficiency gains may result from trade *if* a country specializes in those products it can produce more efficiently than other products (regardless of whether other countries can produce the same products even more efficiently).

Economies of scale—the average cost per unit falls as the number of units produced rises; occurs in regional integration because of the growth in the market size.

European Union:

- Changed from the European Economic Community to the European Community to the European Union.
- The largest and most successful regional trade group.
- Free trade of goods, services, capital, and people.
- Common external tariff.
- Common currency.

Taiwan, these companies might be more likely to import goods from Mexico than from Taiwan due to lower tariffs. Also, MNEs from countries outside the FTA might consider investing in the FTA countries to service the market more effectively. Trade diversion is a major criticism of RTAs, because the agreements result in greater trade among a few members but not among all members of the WTO. This undermines the multilateral process of the WTO.

Economies of Scale   Dynamic effects of integration occur when trade barriers come down and the size of the market increases. Because of the larger size of the market, companies can increase their production, which will result in lower costs per unit, a phenomenon we call **economies of scale.** Companies can produce more cheaply, which is good because they must become more efficient to survive. This could result in more trade between the member countries (trade creation) or an increase in FDI as the market increases and it becomes feasible for MNEs to invest in the larger market.

Increased Competition   Another important effect of the FTA is the increase in efficiency due to increased competition. Many MNEs in Europe have attempted to grow through mergers and acquisitions to achieve the size necessary to compete in the larger market. Companies in Mexico were forced to become more competitive with the passage of NAFTA due to competition from Canadian and U.S. companies. This could result in investment shifting from less efficient to more efficient companies, or it could result in existing companies becoming more efficient.

Major Regional Trading Groups

The two ways to look at different trading groups are by location and by type. Major trading groups exist in every region of the world. It is impossible to cover every group in every region, so we discuss a few of the major groups. As noted above, most regional groups are free trade agreements, although a small percentage are also customs unions. Some, such as the EU, are common markets that are organized for political as well as economic reasons.

Companies are interested in regional trading groups for their markets, sources of raw materials, and production locations. The larger and richer the new market, the more likely it is to attract the attention of the major investor countries and companies.

THE EUROPEAN UNION

The largest and most comprehensive regional economic group is the **European Union (EU).** It began as a free trade agreement with the goal of becoming a customs union and to integrate in other ways. The formation of the European Parliament and the establishment of a common currency, the euro, make the EU the most ambitious of all the regional trade groups.[14] Table 8.1 summarizes the key milestones for

TABLE 8.1   European Union Milestones

From its inception in 1957, the EU has been moving toward complete economic integration. However, it is doubtful that its initial adherents ever dreamed that European cooperation would have achieved such integration as to move to a common currency.

1948	The Organization for European Economic Cooperation (OEEC) is created to coordinate the Marshall Plan.
1951	The Six (Belgium, France, Germany, Italy, Luxembourg, the Netherlands) sign the Treaty of Paris establishing the European Coal and Steel Community (ECSC), to begin in 1952.
1957	The Six sign the Treaties of Rome, establishing the European Economic Community (EEC) and the European Atomic Energy Community (Euratom or EAEC). These become effective on January 1, 1958.
1959	The first steps are taken in the progressive abolition of customs duties and quotas within the EEC.
1960	The Stockholm Convention establishes the European Free Trade Association (EFTA) among seven European countries (Austria, Denmark, Norway, Portugal, Sweden, Switzerland, the United Kingdom). The OEEC becomes the Organization for Economic Cooperation and Development (OECD).
1961	The first regulation on free movement of workers within the EEC comes into force.
1962	The Common Agricultural Policy is adopted.
1965	A treaty merging the ECSC, EEC, and Euratom is signed. The treaty enters into force on July 1, 1967.
1966	Agreement is reached on a value-added tax (VAT) system; a treaty merging the Executives of the European Communities comes into force; and the EEC changes its name to European Community (EC).
1967	All remaining internal tariffs are eliminated, and a common external tariff is imposed.
1972	The currency "snake" is established in which the Six agree to limit currency fluctuations between their currencies to 2.25 percent.
1973	Denmark, Ireland, and the United Kingdom become members of the EC.
1979	European Monetary System comes into effect; European Parliament is elected by universal suffrage for the first time.
1980	Greece becomes the 10th member of the EC.
1986	Spain and Portugal become the 11th and 12th members of the EC. Single European Act (SEA) is signed, improving decision-making procedures and increasing the role of the European Parliament; comes into effect on July 1, 1987.
1989	Collapse of the Berlin Wall; German Democratic Republic opens its borders.
1990	The first phase of European Monetary Union (EMU) comes into effect. Unification of Germany.
1992	European Union signed in Maastricht; adopted by member countries on November 1, 1993.
1993	The Single European Market comes into force (January 1, 1993). Council concludes agreement creating European Economic Area, effective January 1, 1994.
1995	Austria, Finland, and Sweden become the 13th, 14th, and 15th members of the EU.
1996	An EU summit names the 11 countries that will join the European single currency with all EU countries joining except Britain, Sweden, Denmark (by their choice), and Greece (not ready).
1999	The euro, the single European currency, comes into effect (January 1, 1999).
2001	Greece becomes the 12th country to adopt the euro (January 1, 2001).
2002	The euro coins and notes enter circulation (January 1, 2002). All 15 member states ratify the Kyoto Protocol.
2004	Admission of Cyprus, the Czech Republic, Estonia, Hungary, Latvia, Lithuania, Malta, Poland, Slovakia, and Slovenia, bringing number of member states to 25.
2007	Bulgaria and Romania join, bringing number of member states to 27. Candidate countries are Croatia, Former Yugoslav Republic of Macedonia, and Turkey.
2009	Iceland clears the first hurdle to join the EU. The Treat of Lisbon is ratified by member countries and went into effect on December 1, 2009.

Source: Europa, "The History of the European Union," at http://europa.eu/abc/history (accessed July 2009). © European Communities, 1995–2009. Reprinted with permission.

European Free Trade Association—FTA involving Iceland, Liechtenstein, Norway, and Switzerland, with close ties to the EU.

the EU, and Map 8.1 identifies the members of the EU and other key European groups.

Predecessors   Because of the economic and human destruction left by World War II, European political leaders realized that greater cooperation among their countries would help speed up recovery. Many organizations were formed, including the European Economic Community (EEC), which eventually emerged as the organization that would bring together the countries of Europe into the most powerful trading bloc in the world. Several other countries, including the United Kingdom, formed the European Free Trade Association (EFTA) with the limited goal of eliminating internal tariffs, but most of those countries eventually became part of the EU, and those that have decided not to leave EFTA (Iceland, Liechtenstein, Norway, and Switzerland) are linked together with the EU as a customs union.

The EEC, later called the European Community (EC) and finally the European Union (EU), set about to abolish internal tariffs to integrate European markets more closely and ideally allow economic cooperation to help avoid further political conflict.

Organizational Structure   The EU encompasses many governing bodies, among which are the European Commission, Council of the European Union, European Parliament,

MAP 8.1   European Trade and Economic Integration

Although the 27-member EU is easily the dominant trading bloc in Europe, it's not the only one. Founded in 1960, the four-member European Free Trade Association (EFTA) also maintains joint free trade agreements with several other countries. The European Economic Area (EEA) includes three members of the EFTA and all members of the EU. The Central European Free Trade Agreement (CEFTA) was originally formed to integrate Western practices into the economies of former Soviet bloc nations, two of whom have already been admitted into the EU.

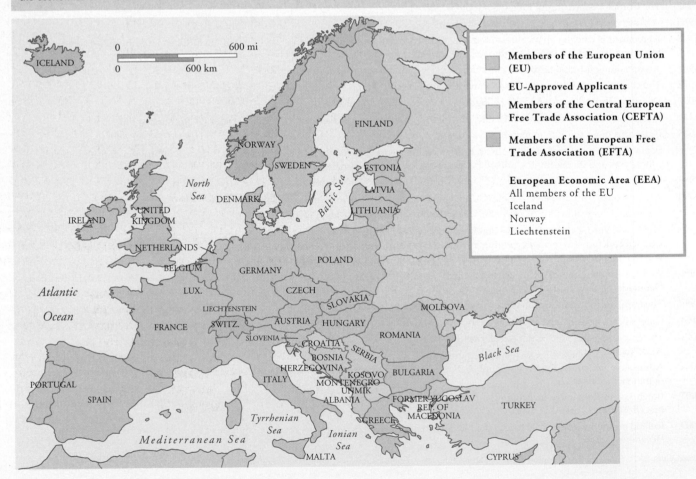

European Court of Justice, and European Central Bank. Details about all of the governing bodies can be found on the official EU Web site at http://europa.eu, so we focus briefly on only the key bodies just mentioned. The European Central Bank, an important institution governing certain financial activities in the EU, is discussed in Chapter 10.

In Chapter 3, we note how important it is for MNE management to understand the political environment of every country where it operates. The same is true for the EU. To be successful in Europe, MNEs need to understand the governance of the EU, just as they need to understand the governance process of each of the individual European countries in which they are investing or doing business. These institutions set parameters within which companies must operate, so management needs to understand the institutions and how they make decisions that could affect corporate strategy. Recall from our opening case, for example, how EU policies shaped Toyota's corporate strategy in the region, inducing it to shift from limited exporting to the establishment of full design and manufacturing facilities.

Case Review Note

Key Governing Bodies   The European Commission provides the EU's political leadership and direction. It is composed of commissioners nominated by each member government and approved by the European Parliament for a five-year term of office. The president of the commission is nominated by the member governments and approved by the European Parliament. The commissioners run the different programs of the EU on a day-to-day basis rather than serve as representatives of their respective governments. The commission drafts laws that it submits to the European Parliament and the Council of the European Union.

> The European Commission provides political leadership, drafts laws, and runs the various daily programs of the EU.

An important activity of the commission deals with competition and antitrust regulation. In 2009, Microsoft bowed to pressure from European antitrust regulators, agreeing to let European users of its Windows software have the option to choose which Web browsers they would like to use and be able to turn off Internet Explorer. If this is accepted by the commission, Microsoft may be able to avoid paying fines; it has already paid over $2 billion in fines due to antitrust violations in Europe.[15] U.S. chip maker Intel appealed an antitrust judgment in 2009 based on human rights violations. The EU's antitrust commissioner has the power to supervise investigations, decide guilt or innocence, and establish penalties. Intel, and even European companies like Saint-Gobain Glass France SA and Schindler Holding Ltd., are arguing that their human rights are being violated because they are being denied a court trial to defend themselves.[16]

The Council of the European Union is composed of representatives of each member country and represents the interests of the countries. The council is responsible, along with the European Parliament, for passing laws and making and enacting major policies, including those in the areas of security and foreign policy. The respective ministers of each country meet periodically to discuss the issues facing those ministries. For example, the ministers of agriculture meet to discuss issues facing agriculture. The presidents and/or prime ministers meet up to four times a year to set broad policy.

> The Council of the European Union, or European Summit, is composed of the heads of state of each member country.

The Parliament is composed of 736 members from all 27 member nations, who are elected every five years, and its membership is based on country population. The three major responsibilities of the Parliament are legislative power, control over the budget, and supervision of executive decisions. The commission presents community legislation to the Parliament; Parliament must approve the legislation before submitting it to the council for adoption.[17]

> The three major responsibilities of the European Parliament are legislative power, control over the budget, and supervision of executive decisions.

The Court of Justice ensures consistent interpretation and application of EU treaties. Member states, EC institutions, and individuals and companies may bring cases to the Court. The Court of Justice is an appeals court for individuals, firms, and organizations fined by the commission for infringing treaty law.[18]

> The European Court of Justice ensures consistent interpretation and application of EU treaties.

The Single European Act   The passage of the Single European Act of 1987 was designed to eliminate the remaining barriers to a free market, such as customs posts and different certification procedures, rates of value-added tax, and excise duties. In addition, the Single European Act resulted in closer cooperation in trade (the EU has one negotiator for the WTO who negotiates for all members of the EU), foreign policy, and the environment.

> The Single European Act was designed to eliminate the remaining nontariff barriers to trade in Europe.

Monetary Union: The Euro   In 1992, the members of the EU signed the Treaty of Maastricht in part to establish a monetary union. The decision to move to a common currency, the **euro,** in Europe has eliminated currency as a barrier to trade for member countries that have adopted it. As of December 31, 2009, 16 of the members of the EU had adopted the euro, and other members are preparing to adopt the currency. Only Denmark, Sweden, and the United Kingdom have opted out of the euro. Other European countries also use the euro, even though they are not members of the EU. We'll discuss the euro in more detail in Chapter 10.

Expansion   One of the EU's major challenges is that of expansion. The May 2004 expansion has been its largest and included Cyprus, the Czech Republic, Estonia, Hungary, Latvia, Lithuania, Malta, Poland, the Slovak Republic, and Slovenia. Bulgaria and Romania were admitted at the beginning of 2007, and candidates for future membership currently include Turkey, the former Yugoslav Republic of Macedonia, and Croatia. However, Turkey has been put on hold while it continues to improve its human rights record. In July 2009, Iceland was put on a fast track to membership; it is leapfrogging several countries that are in the queue to join. In spite of the collapse of Iceland's currency and economy, the country is better poised to join the EU than some aspiring countries from Eastern Europe. Some of the challenges of expansion are "cooling public opinion toward expansion, the economic crisis and the difficulty the bloc is experiencing in integrating Bulgaria and Romania."[19]

Old and New Members   The acquisition of the 12 new countries increased the EU's population and added economic output, but the expansion added countries that are poor, have fledgling democracies, and depend greatly on agriculture—as much as 10 percent of GDP, compared with only 2.6 percent on average in the EU. They will thus strain the EU's financial resources. The new member states are coming in with lower wages and lower taxes, but also with two to four times the growth rates of the original 15 members. Although the global financial crisis that began in 2007 exposed problems in all of the EU member countries, the poorer countries of Eastern Europe really suffered. When exports fell and capital inflows dried up, their currencies fell as well. The new members are becoming quite a challenge for the stability of the EU, despite the hope they initially brought as new, dynamic economies.

In spite of the growth rates, many people from the new countries are trying to immigrate to the higher-income countries, creating some real challenges. Citizens of new member countries are denied unlimited freedom to work anywhere they want in the EU until 2010, giving the older member countries time to gear up for the rise in immigration. The United Kingdom, Ireland, and Sweden are the only EU countries that have given guest workers from the 12 new countries permission to work inside their national boundaries. For the United Kingdom alone, this has resulted in an influx of nearly 638,000 immigrants from the 12 recently added members.[20]

Table 8.2 illustrates the differences in the old and new members of the EU in terms of population and per capita GNI. The four most powerful members of the EU—France, Germany, Italy, and the United Kingdom—have 54.1 percent of the population and generate 62.2 percent of the GDP. However, the new countries already rely heavily on the EU for trade. For example, 85.0 percent of the Czech Republic's exports and 78.8 percent of Poland's exports go to EU countries. This compares with 64.7 percent for Germany, 57.5 percent for the United Kingdom, 65.5 percent for France, and 75.3 percent for the Netherlands.

Again, this points out how important regional trade groups are to the member countries and how much that affects trade and investment decisions of MNEs and other companies doing business in the EU. As noted in Table 8.2, the continued expansion of the EU has increased its size and importance relative to NAFTA, which is dominated economically by the United States.

Bilateral Agreements   In addition to the reduction of trade barriers for member countries, the EU has signed numerous bilateral free trade agreements with other

TABLE 8.2   Comparative Statistics by Trade Group

EU Member Countries	Population in Millions (2005)	GNI Billions of $ (2005)	Per Capita GNI in $ (2005)
Austria	8	303.6	36,980
Belgium	10	373.8	35,700
Denmark	5	256.8	47,390
Finland	5	196.5	37,460
France	61	2,177.7	34,810
Germany	82	2,852.3	34,580
Greece	11	218.1	19,670
Ireland	4	166.6	40,150
Italy	57	1,724.9	30,010
Luxembourg	0.5	35.1	76,040
Netherlands	16	598.0	36,620
Portugal	11	170.0	16,170
Spain	43	1,100.1	25,360
Sweden	9	370.5	41,060
United Kingdom	60	2,263.7	37,600
Cyprus	1	13.6	18,430
Czech Republic	10	109.2	10,710
Estonia	1	12.2	9,100
Hungary	10	101.2	10,030
Latvia	2	15.1	6,760
Lithuania	3	24.1	7,050
Malta	0.4	5.5	13,610
Poland	38	271.4	7,110
Slovakia	5	42.8	7,950
Slovenia	2	34.7	17,350
Bulgaria	8	26.7	3,450
Romania	22	82.9	3,830
Turkey	73	342.2	4,710
Macedonia FYR	2	5.8	2,830
Croatia	4	35.8	8,060
E-15	382.5	12,807.7	36,640
E-10 2004 Admits	72.4	629.8	10,810
E-2 2007 Admits	30	109.6	3,640
E-27 (E-15, E-2, E-10)	484.9	13,547.1	17,030
E-30	563.9	13,930.9	8,158
NAFTA Member Countries			
Canada	32	1,051.9	32,600
Mexico	103	753.4	7,310
United States	296	12,969.6	43,740
Total	431	14,774.9	27,883
MERCOSUR Member Countries			
Argentina	39	173.0	4,470
Brazil	186	644.1	3,460
Paraguay	6	7.9	1,280
Uruguay	3	15.1	4,360
Total	234	840.1	3,590

Source: Emmanual Y. Jimenez, *World Bank Development Report.* © The International Bank for Reconstruction and Development/The World Bank, 2006. Reproduced with permission of The World Bank in the format textbook via Copyright Clearance Center.

Implications of the EU for corporate strategy:

* Companies need to determine where to produce products.
* Companies need to determine what their entry strategy will be.
* Companies need to balance the commonness of the EU with national differences.

Case Review Note

Case Review Note

Case Review Note

countries outside of the European region. Of the 26 bilateral agreements signed by the EU, one includes Mexico, which is a member of NAFTA. However, the EU has not signed bilateral agreements with Canada and the United States, two other members of NAFTA.

Closer to home, the EU entered into an agreement with the members of the European Free Trade Association, with the exception of Switzerland, to form the European Economic Area (EEA). The three EFTA countries participate in the basic four freedoms with the EU: freedom of movement of goods (excluding agriculture and fisheries, which are included in the agreement only to a very limited extent), persons, services, and capital. The difference between the EEA and the expansion of the EU is that the members of EFTA are not interested in complete membership in the EU but just want to take advantage of the free flow of food, labor, services, and capital. However, Iceland has now applied to join the EU, so EFTA will drop back to three countries, and it will be interesting to see what happens to them in the future.

How to Do Business with the EU: Implications for Corporate Strategy   The EU is a tremendous market in terms of both population and income, and so it is one that companies cannot ignore. In addition, the EU is a good example of how geographic proximity and the removal of trade barriers can influence trade. As noted earlier, more than half of the merchandise exports and imports of EU countries are considered to be intrazonal trade.

Doing business in the EU can influence corporate strategy, especially for non-EU MNEs, in these three ways:

1. *Determining where to produce products.* One strategy is to produce products in a central location in Europe to minimize transportation costs and the time it takes to move products from one country to another. However, the highest costs are in central Europe. As we saw in our opening case, for instance, manufacturing wages in the German auto industry top $40 per hour, compared with much lower wages in Eastern European members of the EU. That's why Toyota opted to set up operations in lower-wage countries such as the Czech Republic and Poland.

2. *Determining whether to grow through new investments, through expanding existing investments, or through joint ventures and mergers.* As we've seen, Toyota, in order to take advantage of the European carmaker's supplier network, has entered into a joint venture with PSA Peugeot-Citroën to build a new factory in the Czech Republic. Mergers and acquisitions have really picked up in Europe. The market in Europe is still considered fragmented and inefficient compared with the United States, so most experts feel that mergers, takeovers, and spinoffs will continue in Europe for years to come. U.S. companies are buying European companies to gain a market presence and to get rid of competition.

3. *Balancing "common" denominators with national differences.* To quote the phrase "distance matters,"[21] there are wider national differences in the EU than in the different states in the United States, mostly due to language and history. But there are also widely different growth rates in the EU. Many smaller nations, such as Ireland and Belgium, are experiencing unprecedented growth because their membership in the EU has increased their attractiveness for FDI, helped them develop global perspectives, and sheltered them from economic risks.

Meanwhile, Germany, Europe's biggest economy and historically the engine for economic growth in Europe, and France have been faced with stagnant growth and high unemployment.[22] And what about Toyota? In terms of products, Toyota is busy designing a European car, but for which Europe? Tastes and preferences—not to mention climate—vary greatly between northern and southern Europe. Toyota, however, is attempting to use production location and design to facilitate a pan-European strategy.

Companies will always struggle with the degree to which they develop a European strategy versus different national strategies inside Europe. In spite of the challenges, there are many opportunities for companies to expand their markets and sources of supply as the EU grows and encompasses more of Europe.

THE NORTH AMERICAN FREE TRADE AGREEMENT (NAFTA)

The **North American Free Trade Agreement (NAFTA),** which includes Canada, Mexico, and the United States, went into effect in 1994. The United States and Canada historically have had various forms of mutual economic cooperation. They signed the Canada-U.S. Free Trade Agreement effective January 1, 1989, which eliminated all tariffs on bilateral trade by January 1, 1998. In February 1991, Mexico approached the United States to establish a free trade agreement. The formal negotiations that began in June 1991 included Canada. The resulting North American Free Trade Agreement became effective on January 1, 1994.

Why NAFTA? NAFTA has a logical rationale in terms of both geographic location and trading importance. Although Canadian-Mexican trade was not significant when the agreement was signed, U.S.-Mexican trade and U.S.-Canadian trade were. The two-way trading relationship between the United States and Canada is the largest in the world. As we indicate in Table 8.2, NAFTA is a powerful trading bloc with a combined population greater than the 15-member EU and GDP greater than the 27-member EU. What is significant, especially when compared with the EU, is the tremendous size of the U.S. economy in comparison with those of Canada and Mexico. In addition, Canada has a much richer economy than that of Mexico, even though its population is about a third that of Mexico.

Even though NAFTA is a free trade agreement in both goods and services instead of a customs union or a common market, its cooperation extends far beyond reductions in tariff and nontariff barriers to include provisions for services, investment, and intellectual property. In addition, the agreement establishes a new dispute resolution process.

Mexico made significant strides in tariff reduction after joining GATT in 1986. At that time, its tariffs averaged 100 percent. Since then, it has reduced tariffs dramatically. As a result of NAFTA, most tariffs on originating goods traded between Mexico and Canada were eliminated immediately or phased in over a 10-year period that ended on December 31, 2003. In a few exceptions, the phaseout period was completed by the end of 2008. Tariffs between the United States and Mexico were, in general, either eliminated immediately or phased out over a 5- or 10-year period that ended on December 31, 2003. In the first five years after passage of the agreement, Mexico trimmed its average tariff on U.S. goods from 10 to 2 percent, and U.S. tariffs on Mexican products dropped to less than 1 percent.[23]

Static and Dynamic Effects NAFTA provides the static and dynamic effects of economic integration discussed earlier in this chapter. For example, Canadian and U.S. consumers benefit from lower-cost agricultural products from Mexico, a static effect of economic liberalization. U.S. producers also benefit from the large and growing Mexican market, which has a huge appetite for U.S. products—a dynamic effect.

Trade Diversion In addition, NAFTA is a good example of trade diversion. Prior to NAFTA, many U.S. and Canadian companies had established manufacturing facilities in Asia to take advantage of cheap labor. After NAFTA, Mexico became a good option

---

The North American Free Trade Agreement

- Includes Canada, the United States, and Mexico.
- Went into effect on January 1, 1994.
- Involves free trade in goods, services, and investment.
- Is a large trading bloc but includes countries of different sizes and wealth.

NAFTA rationale:

- U.S.-Canadian trade is the largest bilateral trade in the world.
- The United States is Mexico's and Canada's largest trading partner.

NAFTA calls for the elimination of tariff and nontariff barriers, the harmonization of trade rules, the liberalization of restrictions on services and foreign investment, the enforcement of intellectual property rights, and a dispute settlement process.

NAFTA is a good example of trade diversion; some U.S. trade with and investment in Asia have been diverted to Mexico.

for U.S. and Canadian companies to establish manufacturing facilities. For example, IBM is making computer parts in Mexico that were formerly made in Singapore. In five years, IBM boosted exports from Mexico to the United States from $350 million to $2 billion. Had the subassemblies not been made in and exported from Mexico, they would have been made in Singapore and other Asian locations and exported to the United States.

Non-NAFTA companies are also investing in Mexico to take advantage of the FTA with Canada and the United States. Sony has huge manufacturing facilities in Mexico, especially in Tijuana, just over the border from Southern California. In 2009, Sony closed five factories worldwide—one in Pittsburgh, Pennsylvania, and another in Mexicali, Mexico, which was manufacturing LCD televisions. However, Sony expanded its work-force in Tijuana to take up the slack by adding 1,500 new jobs.[24] Sony is able to take advantage of NAFTA free trade provisions to ship product to the United States and save on time and transportation costs.

Rules of Origin and Regional Content An important component of NAFTA is the concept of rules of origin and regional content. Because NAFTA is a free trade agreement and not a customs union, each country sets its own tariffs to the rest of the world. That's why a product entering the United States from Canada must have a commercial or customs invoice that identifies the product's ultimate origin. Otherwise, an exporter from a third country could always ship the product to the NAFTA country with the lowest tariff and then reexport it to the other two countries duty-free. A major criticism of RTAs like NAFTA is that the rules of origin are complex and detract from the spirit of multilateral tariff reductions in the WTO.

| Rules of origin—goods and services must originate in North America to get access to lower tariffs.

Rules of Origin "Rules of origin" ensure that only goods that have been the subject of substantial economic activity within the free trade area are eligible for the more liberal tariff conditions created by NAFTA. This is a major contrast with the European Union, which is a customs union rather than just a free trade agreement. When a product enters France, for example, it can be shipped anywhere in the EU without worrying about rules of origin, because tariffs are the same for all EU member countries. If NAFTA were a customs union instead of a free trade agreement, a product entering Mexico from Japan, for example, and shipped to the United States would enter duty-free into the United States because the United States and Mexico would have the same duty on imports.[25]

| Regional content:
| • The percentage of value that must be from North America for the product to be considered North American in terms of country of origin.
| • 50 percent for most products; 62.5 percent for autos.

Rules of Regional Content According to regional content rules, at least 50 percent of the net cost of most products must come from the NAFTA region. The exceptions are 55 percent for footwear, 62.5 percent for passenger automobiles and light trucks and the engines and transmissions for such vehicles, and 60 percent for other vehicles and automotive parts.[26] For example, a Ford car assembled in Mexico could use parts from Canada, the United States, and Mexico, as well as labor and other factors from Mexico. For the car to enter Canada and the United States according to the preferential NAFTA duty, at least 62.5 percent of its value must come from North America.

Special Provisions Most free trade agreements in the world are based solely on one goal: to reduce tariffs. However, NAFTA is a very different free trade agreement. Because labor unions and environmentalists strongly objected to the agreement, two auxiliary agreements covering their concerns were included in NAFTA. When first debating NAFTA, opponents worried about the potential loss of jobs in Canada and the United States to Mexico as a result of Mexico's cheaper wages, poor working conditions, and lax environmental enforcement.

NAFTA opponents, particularly U.S. union organizers, thought companies would close down factories in the north and set them up in Mexico. As a result, the labor lobby in the United States forced the inclusion of labor standards such as the right to unionize, and the environmental lobby pushed for an upgrade of environmental standards in Mexico and the strengthening of compliance. This is a challenge internationally because not all countries care about labor and environmental standards. The United States often uses trade agreements to advance political and moral objectives. When China enters into a preferential trade agreement with other countries, it does not include labor, environmental, or moral objectives in the agreements, so it is easier for countries to enter into trade agreements with China than with the United States.

The Impact of NAFTA   There are pros and cons to any trade agreement, and NAFTA is no exception. It is obvious that trade and investment in NAFTA have increased significantly since the agreement was signed in 1994. The trading relationship between the United States and Canada is the largest bilateral flow between two countries of goods, services, and income in the world, reaching nearly $550 billion. Canada is the largest export market for U.S. goods, and Mexico is number three after the EU. The EU, China, Canada, and Mexico are the four largest exporters to the U.S. market in terms of merchandise exports.

It's important to note the importance of the United States to both Canada and Mexico. Canada exports 79 percent of its merchandise to and imports 54.2 percent of its imports from the United States. Mexico exports 82.2 percent of its merchandise to and imports 49.6 percent of its imports from the United States. Although trade between Canada and Mexico has increased since the implementation of NAFTA, the U.S. market still remains the most significant market for Canadian and Mexican firms because of its size.

Wages, Investment, and Labor   The United States is more diversified in terms of its trade relationships, but it still relies on its NAFTA partners for 33.1 percent of its merchandise exports and 26.3 percent of its merchandise imports.[27] As noted earlier in the chapter, this is in contrast with the EU, where intrazonal trade is above 50 percent for all countries.

Because of low wages in Mexico, U.S. companies invested significantly in Mexico. It is complicated to determine wage rates, however, due to factors such as exchange rates and trying to identify comparable wage rates. The Bureau of Labor Statistics reported that the hourly compensation costs in U.S. dollars for production workers in manufacturing in 2007 was $2.92 for Mexican workers, compared with $24.59 for U.S. workers and $28.91 for Canadian workers.[28] Based on this information, it is easy to see the magnitude of the difference, and it is interesting to note that wages are higher in Canada than the United States. As MNEs assess where to locate production facilities, they can't ignore the wage differences.

Additional NAFTA provisions:

- Workers' rights.
- The environment.
- Dispute resolution mechanism.

FDI from the United States to Mexico has averaged around $12 billion per year since the passage of NAFTA, and the United States has accounted for about 62 percent of all FDI into Mexico during that period.[29] In 2008, FDI into emerging markets slowed down worldwide, but the United States invested $8.9 billion of the $18.6 billion in FDI. In that year, the U.S. provided only 41 percent of all FDI in Mexico.[30] Not only has that resulted in the inflow of capital, but it has also brought with it technology, management skill, and access to international markets. The rise of FDI and the increase in Mexican exports has helped raise Mexico's per capita income as well. Mexico's per capita income rose to an estimated $14,200 in 2008 on a PPP basis, compared with only $6,000 in China, and was higher than in any other country in Latin America, including Brazil.[31]

The investment and employment pictures are complicated. One concern for U.S. workers when the agreement was being debated was that investment would move to Mexico because of that country's lower wages and lax environmental standards. When NAFTA was signed, companies like IBM and Canon began investing in Mexico instead of Asia for certain types of manufacturing. They could enjoy many tax and tariff exemptions, labor was plentiful and cheap, and high U.S. demand was just miles away. Foreign investment in Mexico rose from $4 billion per year in 1993 to $11.8 billion per year in 1999.[32]

In 2001, however, when NAFTA required Mexico to strip the *maquiladoras* (companies on the Mexican border) of their duty-free status, foreign companies started looking elsewhere. This was also compounded by the weakening U.S. economy and the stronger peso. Companies like Sanyo, Canon, and French battery producer Saft left Mexico and relocated to China, Vietnam, and Guatemala, where labor is cheaper.[33] In addition, now that China has opened up its market to more foreign investment as it becomes a part of the WTO, Mexicans are concerned that foreign investment is being diverted to China to take advantage of even lower manufacturing wages and generous incentives.

Even though employment in the *maquiladora* factories has dropped by more than 20 percent since 2000, Mexico is still an attractive market for investment, and the border areas are still important for U.S. firms. The U.S. government reported that in 2008, 58 percent of all U.S. manufacturing investment in Mexico went to the six border states where the majority of the maquiladora operations are housed. As you'll see in the case at the end of the chapter, prior to China's entry into the WTO in 2001, China worked collaboratively with the United States and the European Union to negotiate the foreign investment entry schedules in China's core telecommunications sector.

Case Review Note

| A major challenge to NAFTA is illegal immigration.

Immigration   A major challenge to NAFTA is immigration. As trade in agriculture increased with the advent of NAFTA, it is estimated that 1.3 million farm jobs disappeared in Mexico due to competition from the United States. Many of these farmers ended up as illegal immigrants in the United States working in the agricultural and other sectors, sending home more money in wire transfers (see the opening case in Chapter 9) than Mexico receives in FDI. This has become a major political issue in both the United States and Mexico, especially as the United States tries to figure out how to stop the flow of illegal immigration and what to do with illegal immigrants already in the United States.

How to Do Business with NAFTA: Implications for Corporate Strategy   Although NAFTA has not expanded beyond the original three countries due to political obstacles, each member of NAFTA has entered into bilateral agreements with other countries.

Predictions and Outcomes   Several predictions were made when NAFTA was signed. One prediction was that companies would look at NAFTA as one big regional market, allowing companies to rationalize production, products, financing, and the like. That has largely happened in a number of industries—especially in automotive products and in electronics (e.g., in computers). Each country in NAFTA ships more automotive products, based on specialized production, to the other two countries than any other manufactured goods. Employment has increased in the auto industry in the United States since NAFTA was established, even as it has declined in Mexico because of productivity.[34]

Rationalization of automotive production has taken place for years in the United States and Canada, but Mexico is a recent entrant. Auto manufacturing has moved into Mexico from all over the world. Over 500,000 Mexicans make parts and assemble vehicles for all of the world's major auto producers. NAFTA's rules of origin requiring 62.5 percent regional content have forced European and Asian automakers to bring in parts suppliers and set up assembly operations in Mexico.

In one case, a Canadian entrepreneur established a metal-stamping plant in Puebla, Mexico, to supply Volkswagen, the German auto manufacturer. The VW plant assembles the revitalized Beetle that is being supplied to the U.S. market.[35] DaimlerChrysler is producing 45,000 cars and 200,000 trucks in Mexico; between 80 and 90 percent of them are being exported to the United States and Canada. DaimlerChrysler began producing the PT Cruiser in Toluca, Mexico, for export to Canada, the United States, and Europe. It is using that one plant to manufacture one model for the entire world.

The story of DaimlerChrysler's production in the United States is similar. In 1993, Chrysler exported only 5,300 vehicles to Mexico. The following year, after the signing of NAFTA, it exported 17,500, and in 2000 it exported 60,000.[36] The examples indicate how production is intertwined among the member countries. However, some companies are simply leaving the United States and Canada and moving to Mexico. This is happening in the apparel and furniture industries. Initially, NAFTA rules on apparel caused the Mexican textile industry to bring jobs back from Asia, and U.S. textile companies set up operations in Mexico to supply both the Mexican and U.S. apparel markets.

A second prediction was that sophisticated U.S. companies would run Canadian and Mexican companies out of business once the markets opened up. That has not happened. In fact, U.S. companies along the border of Canada are finding that Canadian companies are generating more competition for them than low-wage Mexican companies. Also, many Mexican companies have restructured to compete with U.S. and Canadian companies. The lack of protection has resulted in much more competitive Mexican firms. However, as was discussed in the context of agriculture, some industries have been hard hit by U.S. competitors. As we show in the case at the end of the chapter, Vodafone faced huge difficulties in raising its stake in China Mobile (Hong Kong) because of the government's protectionist policies.

Case Review Note

A final prediction had to do with looking at Mexico as a consumer market rather than just a production location. Initially, the excitement over Mexico for U.S. and Canadian companies was the low-wage environment. However, as Mexican income continues to rise—which it must do as more investment enters Mexico and more Mexican companies export production—demand is rising for foreign products.

REGIONAL ECONOMIC INTEGRATION IN THE AMERICAS

If you look at Map 8.2 and Map 8.3, you'll see that there are six major regional economic groups in the Americas. They can be divided into Central American and South American. In Central America (not including NAFTA member Mexico) are the Caribbean Community (CARICOM), the Central American Common Market (CACM), and the Central American Free Trade Agreement (CAFTA-DR)—which includes the members of CACM but also Honduras and the Dominican Republic, along with the United States. The two major groups in South America are the Andean Community (CAN) and the Southern Common Market (MERCOSUR). The Andean Community is a customs union, whereas MERCOSUR is set up to be a common market. In addition, there's the proposed Union of South American Nations, although that has not been officially recognized by the WTO as a regional trade agreement. It is very much in the infancy stage.

The major reason for these different groups in Central and South America entering into collaboration was market size. The post–World War II strategy of import substitution to resolve balance-of-payments problems in many of the markets in Latin America was doomed because of Latin America's small national markets. Therefore, some form of economic cooperation was needed to enlarge the potential market size so Latin American companies could achieve economies of scale and be more competitive worldwide.

CARICOM: Benchmarking the EU Model   The **Caribbean Community (CARICOM)** is working hard to establish an EU-style form of collaboration, complete with full

MAP 8.2   Economic Integration in Central America and the Caribbean

Throughout Central America and the Caribbean, the focus on economic integration has shifted from the concept of the *free trade agreement* (whose goal is the abolition of trade barriers among members) to that of the *common market* (which calls for internal factor mobility as well as the abolition of internal trade barriers). The proposed structure of the Caribbean Community and Common Market (CARICOM) is modeled on that of the EU.

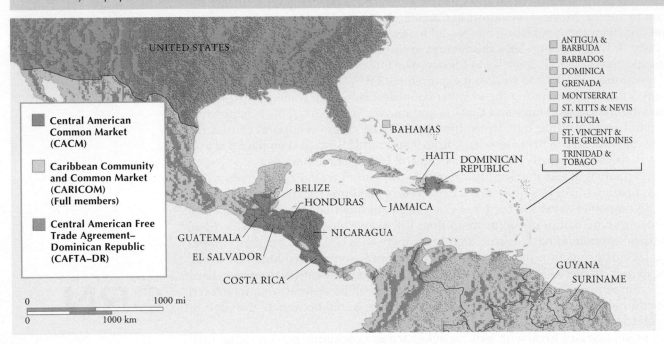

- **Central American Common Market (CACM)**
- **Caribbean Community and Common Market (CARICOM) (Full members)**
- **Central American Free Trade Agreement–Dominican Republic (CAFTA–DR)**

UNITED STATES

BAHAMAS
HAITI   DOMINICAN REPUBLIC
BELIZE
HONDURAS
JAMAICA
GUATEMALA
NICARAGUA
EL SALVADOR
COSTA RICA
GUYANA
SURINAME

- ANTIGUA & BARBUDA
- BARBADOS
- DOMINICA
- GRENADA
- MONTSERRAT
- ST. KITTS & NEVIS
- ST. LUCIA
- ST. VINCENT & THE GRENADINES
- TRINIDAD & TOBAGO

0   1000 mi
0   1000 km

MAP 8.3   Latin American Economic Integration

There are only two key RTAs in South America: the Andean Group and MERCOSUR. The Latin American Integration Association, which was established in 1980, has failed to establish a free trade agreement or a dispute resolution mechanism.

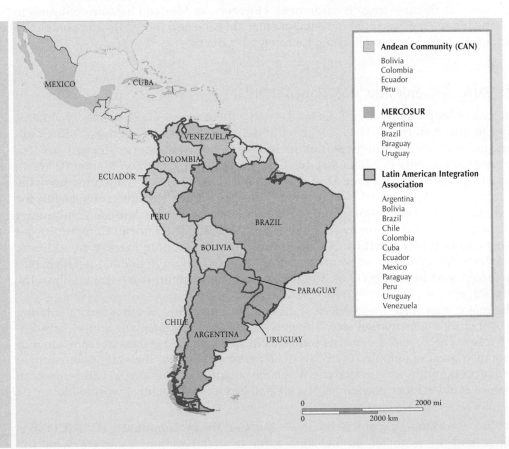

MEXICO   CUBA
VENEZUELA
COLOMBIA
ECUADOR
PERU
BRAZIL
BOLIVIA
PARAGUAY
CHILE
ARGENTINA   URUGUAY

- **Andean Community (CAN)**
  Bolivia
  Colombia
  Ecuador
  Peru

- **MERCOSUR**
  Argentina
  Brazil
  Paraguay
  Uruguay

- **Latin American Integration Association**
  Argentina
  Bolivia
  Brazil
  Chile
  Colombia
  Cuba
  Ecuador
  Mexico
  Paraguay
  Peru
  Uruguay
  Venezuela

0   2000 mi
0   2000 km

movement of goods and services, the right of establishment, a common external tariff, free movement of capital, a common trade policy, free movement of labor, and so on. It is officially classified by the WTO as an Economic Integration Agreement. Many of these initiatives have come about through an initiative called the CARICOM Single Market and Economy (CSME).

In some ways, the changes in the Caribbean Community mirror what has happened in the EU, although on a smaller scale. The entire population of the Caribbean Community is only 6.5 million people, and 60 percent of them live in only two countries: Jamaica and Trinidad and Tobago. That would put the entire Caribbean Community on the level of EU-member Bulgaria in terms of population. However, it is important for the Caribbean Community to succeed in order to expand market size and attract more investment and jobs.

The Challenge of Export Reliance The problem is that countries in Latin America and the Caribbean rely heavily on countries outside of the region for trade. For example, Jamaica, a member of the Caribbean Community, relies on the United States as a destination for 37.2 percent of its merchandise exports and the EU for 26.8 percent of its exports. Although Trinidad and Tobago is the second major exporter of merchandise to Jamaica, no other member of the Caribbean Community is significant to Jamaica as either a destination or a source for its exports.

The same could be said for most of Latin America. The United States and EU represent significant markets for most countries in Latin America.

MERCOSUR   The major trade group in South America is **MERCOSUR,** which was established in 1991 by Brazil, Argentina, Paraguay, and Uruguay. Its major goal is to become a customs union with free trade within the bloc and a common external tariff. MERCOSUR is classified as a customs union by the WTO for trade in goods, whereas it is an economic integration agreement for trade in services.

Size MERCOSUR is significant because of its size: It has a population of 249 million people and a GDP of $2.05 trillion and generates 75 percent of South America's GDP. That makes MERCOSUR the fourth largest trading bloc in the world after the EU, NAFTA, and the Association of Southeast Asian Nations (ASEAN). Progress has been slow in implementing the programs of MERCOSUR. It has neither eliminated internal barriers to trade nor completed the implementation of a common external tariff.

MERCOSUR has not made much progress for several reasons, but a large part is the role of Brazil. Since Brazil represents 70 percent of the GDP of the bloc, it is enormously influential. Trade disputes with Argentina have become more serious with the global economic crisis, and Brazil's leading role in multilateral trade talks has sapped much of the energy of MERCOSUR.[37] It remains to be seen if it will be influential in the same way as the other major regional trade groups.

Andean Community (CAN)   Although the **Andean Community (CAN)** is not as significant economically as MERCOSUR, it is the second most important regional group in South America. CAN has been around since 1969. However, its focus has shifted from one of isolationism and statism (placing economic control in the hands of the state—the central government) to being open to foreign trade and investment.

Latin American Integration Association (LAIA)   The LAIA includes members of MERCOSUR and CAN, as well as Chile, Cuba, and Mexico. The predecessor of the LAIA was the Latin American Free Trade Association, which was signed in 1060. However, the LAIA was signed into effect in 1980 with the hope of going beyond a FTA to becoming a common market.

Concept Check

In Chapter 6, we observe that little of the trade of low-income countries is conducted with other low-income countries. By and large, emerging economies rely heavily on trade with high-income countries, typically exporting primary and labor-intensive products in exchange for new and technologically advanced products.

MERCOSUR is a customs union among Argentina, Brazil, Paraguay, and Uruguay.

The Andean Community is one of the original regional economic groups but has not been successful in achieving its original goals.

Point ▶ Counterpoint

Is CAFTA-DR a Good Idea?

Point ▶ **Yes** CAFTA-DR is a *great* idea. The Central American Free Trade Agreement and Dominican Republic will link the United States together with six other countries in a free trade agreement: five countries in Central America plus the Dominican Republic in the Caribbean. CAFTA-DR is an agreement that holds enormous benefits for both the United States and the nations that have signed it.

It will open the door for increased trade between the United States and the region and will stimulate economic growth in the region by encouraging foreign direct investment and by offering shorter international supply chains in which CAFTA-DR companies will be able to more easily participate. Furthermore, it will encourage not only economic reform but also political reform in an area historically plagued by Marxism, dictatorships, and civil wars.

One of the biggest benefits the United States has to gain is reciprocal tariff treatment from the participating nations. Due to temporary trade-preference programs and other regional agreements that are currently in place, 80 percent of the products from at least five Central American nations already enter the United States duty-free. U.S. manufactured exports are subject to tariffs that average 30 to 100 percent higher than the tariffs Central American exports face when entering the United States.[38]

CAFTA-DR will allow the Central American nations to maintain these favorable gains, but it will also level the playing field for the United States to benefit in a similar way by reducing restrictions on 80 percent of U.S. industrial exports and on more than 50 percent of its agricultural exports to the region. CAFTA-DR is now the third largest export market in Latin America for U.S. goods after Mexico and Brazil and the 14th largest U.S. export market in the world (or 10th largest if the EU is considered a single destination).[39]

There's fear that the freer inflow of Central American agricultural products will undercut U.S. agricultural prices. However, as mentioned before, the United States is already largely open to these products, and although the heavily subsidized U.S. sugar industry adamantly opposed CAFTA-DR, the sugar deal will set a quota that will amount to only 1.7 percent of U.S. production in 15 years.

Many critics argue that the benefits certain CAFTA-DR countries gain will come at the expense of other participating countries, but in truth the gains will be mutual. For example, the growth that CAFTA-DR will foster in Central American industries, particularly its apparel industry, will also benefit exporters in the United States whose products are used in their manufacturing processes.

Fifty-six percent of the apparel exports from the Central American region are produced from textiles exported from

Counterpoint ▶ **No** CAFTA-DR is *not* a good idea at all—not for the United States or for the impoverished nations it is allegedly supposed to help. Recently, much has been said about how the accord will boost trade between the two regions, support constructive economic and political reforms in Central America, create thousands of jobs, and demonstrate the benefits of free trade and open competition. However, there is neither the evidence to bear out these claims nor consideration for the consequences of the results. Besides, CAFTA-DR undermines the efforts of the WTO to liberalize trade worldwide rather than region by region.

The agreement will open the participating Central American countries to more duty-free exportation on behalf of U.S. manufacturers and farmers, but will this really translate into benefits for either side? The U.S. agricultural industry already can sell pretty much all the products it wants on the worldwide market; what it really needs is an increase in the worldwide market prices, but Central America's economies are too small to even affect world prices. Plus, the increased flow of U.S. corn and rice into Central America will devastate the region's own farm economies.

The idea that it will benefit the region by allowing increased imports to the United States is also faulty. Due to its giant deficit, the United States really cannot afford to tolerate many more imports, and the value of these imports to the United States is also expected to decrease in value, which means Central America will gain little economic advantage from them anyhow, especially given the concessions it must make in return.

In addition, CAFTA-DR will actually be increasing some barriers to free trade. For example, the accord may make it harder for countries such as Guatemala to obtain access to affordable lifesaving medicines because of stringent intellectual property clauses included in the agreement.

CAFTA-DR is also a bad move for labor and workers' rights. It will most likely trigger the loss of manufacturing jobs in the United States and agricultural jobs in Central America. Although proponents of the deal assert that it will stem illegal immigration from these poorer nations, the shift in jobs will most likely increase immigration, as it did with NAFTA.

Furthermore, it will trigger a "race to the bottom" when it comes to wages. The accord will open up U.S. labor markets to competition against a low-wage area, which will drive down the current wage level. NAFTA and other trade agreements currently in place have already stymied wage growth, which has grown a meager 9 percent over the last 30 years compared to an increase of 80 percent in worker productivity. And this depression of wages and shift of jobs the United States; 40 percent of yarn exports and about 25 percent of fabric exports from the United States are purchased by these nations. By working together through CAFTA-DR, the United States and Central America will prevent the loss of Central American apparel jobs to China, whose products contain little or no input from the United States. The National Council of Textile Organizations, which represents more than 75 textile companies, strongly supports CAFTA-DR.

Another argument that critics make is that CAFTA-DR will create shifts in the job market that will lead to thousands of job losses in the manufacturing and agricultural sectors. However, predictions from the U.S. Chamber of Commerce don't bear out this claim. For example, it predicts that in North Carolina alone, CAFTA-DR will increase industrial output by $3.9 billion and create 28,913 jobs over nine years. Other sources have stated that 250,000 jobs in Central America depend on CAFTA-DR being approved. And although labor organizations have decried the lack of worker-protection clauses in the agreement, a report from the International Labor Organization actually praises Central American labor laws and standards.[40]

If the United States had decided to opt out of CAFTA-DR, it would have seriously hurt its position as the leading champion of global free trade and open competition, possibly damaging its position in the WTO and its relationships with other nations with which it wishes to establish bilateral agreements. ▶

created by current agreements has done little to improve the economic conditions of the developing Central American nations, where wages have grown only 12 percent since 1980, compared with 80 percent during the period between 1960 and 1979. Furthermore, no clauses in the agreement address the protection of workers or the banning of child labor.[41]

Because the accord involves developing countries with vastly different interests than the United States, it will be hard to please all parties. Costa Rica had a hard time ratifying the agreement and only came on board on January 1, 2009, long after the final agreement went into force in 2007 in the Dominican Republic. Costa Rica faced opposition from trade unions, farm groups, and even businesses, as well as fears about the accord's stringent intellectual-property clauses and the chance that it might force the country to privatize its free universal health-care system. Costa Rica's hesitancy undermines the argument posed by Washington that CAFTA-DR is something earnestly sought after by struggling Central American countries, even though Costa Rica eventually came on board.[42] ◀

REGIONAL ECONOMIC INTEGRATION IN ASIA

The WTO recognizes several different RTAs in Asia, but the most important is the Association of Southeast Asian Nations and the ASEAN Free Trade Area. As is the case in Latin America, regional integration in Asia has not been as successful as the EU or NAFTA because most of the countries in the region have relied on U.S. and EU markets for as much as 20 to 30 percent of their exports, which is not as extensive as in Latin America but still significant.

Association of Southeast Asian Nations (ASEAN) The **Association of Southeast Asian Nations (ASEAN),** organized in 1967, is a preferential trade agreement that comprises Brunei Darussalam, Cambodia, China, Indonesia, Laos, Malaysia, Myanmar, the Philippines, Singapore, Thailand, and Vietnam (see Map 8.4). It possesses a combined GDP of over $1.5 trillion, total trade of $1.698 trillion, and a population of 583.7 million people.[43]

ASEAN promotes cooperation in many areas, including industry and trade. Because of its large size, ASEAN is the third largest free trade agreement in the world after the EU and NAFTA and above MERCOSUR. Member countries are protected in terms of tariff and nontariff barriers, yet they hold promise for market and investment opportunities because of their large market size.

ASEAN Free Trade Area On January 1, 1993, ASEAN officially formed the ASEAN Free Trade Area (AFTA). AFTA's goal was to cut tariffs on all intrazonal trade to a maximum of 5 percent by January 1, 2008. The weaker ASEAN countries would be

The ASEAN Free Trade Area is a successful trade agreement among countries in Southeast Asia.

MAP 8.4   The Association of Southeast Asian Nations

Although the total population of ASEAN countries (as of 2004) is larger than that of either the EU or NAFTA, per capita GDP is considerably lower. Economic growth rates among ASEAN members, however, are among the highest in the world.

allowed to phase in their tariff reductions over a longer period. By 2005, most products traded among the AFTA countries were subject to duties from 0 to 5 percent, so AFTA has been successful in its free trade objectives. Trade is crucial to the member countries because their ratio of exports to GDP is almost 70 percent. The best achievement of AFTA is that is has reduced tariffs, attracted FDI, and turned the region into a huge network of production, leading to what some call "factory Asia."[44]

CALLS FOR CLOSER COOPERATION

In spite of some of the challenges of operating in the AFTA countries, many companies have been able to take advantage of AFTA. Dell Computer, for example, established computer assembly operations in Malaysia to take advantage of Malaysia's location-specific advantages, such as the Multimedia Supercorridor, which is like a little Silicon Valley and links Dell with its suppliers, offers favorable tax rates, and provides a good workforce. In addition, Malaysia's membership in AFTA gives Dell duty-free access to the other ASEAN countries.

APEC is composed of 21 countries that border the Pacific Rim; progress toward free trade is hampered by size and geographic distance between member countries and the lack of a treaty.

Asia Pacific Economic Cooperation (APEC) **APEC,** the **Asia Pacific Economic Cooperation,** was formed in November 1989 to promote multilateral economic cooperation in trade and investment in the Pacific Rim.[45] It's composed of 21 countries that border the Pacific Rim—in both Asia and the Americas; however, it is not an RTA as defined by the WTO and does not show up on their list of RTAs. To accomplish its objectives, APEC leaders committed themselves to achieving free and open trade in the region by 2010 for the industrial nations (which generate 85 percent of the regional trade) and by 2020 for the rest of the members.[46] One could argue, of course, that APEC's success at reducing barriers is really the success of the WTO, of which APEC is not a member.

Challenges to Solidity   The difference between APEC and other regional trade groups is that there are no binding treaties. Although the group is huge, accounting for approximately 41 percent of the world's population (2.6 billion people), 56 percent of world GDP (U.S. $19,254 billion), and about 49 percent of world trade, it operates by consensus and does not have the same teeth as the RTAs recognized by the WTO. It also includes countries that border the Pacific, such as NAFTA countries, Chile, Russia, China, Hong Kong, Taiwan, many members of AFTA, and Australia and New Zealand. It is more than an Asian trade bloc, but it is not a very solid bloc.

The Goal of "Open Regionalism" APEC has the potential to become a significant economic bloc, especially because it generates such a large percentage of the world's output and merchandise trade. APEC is trying to establish "open regionalism," whereby individual member countries can determine whether to apply trade liberalization to non-APEC countries on an unconditional, MFN basis or on a reciprocal, free trade agreement basis. The United States prefers the latter approach. The key will be whether or not the liberalization process continues at a good pace.[47]

REGIONAL ECONOMIC INTEGRATION IN AFRICA

Africa is complicated because of the large number of countries on the continent and the fact that there are three regional monetary unions and five existing regional trade associations. On Map 8.5, we have selected only three of the RTAs. The problem is that African

> There are several African trade groups, but they rely more on their former colonial powers and other developed markets for trade than they do on each other.

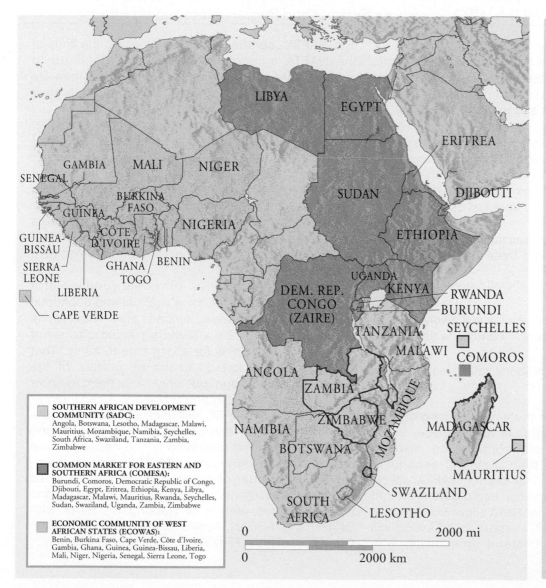

MAP 8.5 Regional Integration in Africa

Although African nations have joined to form several groups for the purpose of economic integration, total amount of trade among members remains relatively small. African nations tend to rely heavily on trading relationships with countries elsewhere in the world—notably with industrialized nations.

SOUTHERN AFRICAN DEVELOPMENT COMMUNITY (SADC):
Angola, Botswana, Lesotho, Madagascar, Malawi, Mauritius, Mozambique, Namibia, Seychelles, South Africa, Swaziland, Tanzania, Zambia, Zimbabwe

COMMON MARKET FOR EASTERN AND SOUTHERN AFRICA (COMESA):
Burundi, Comoros, Democratic Republic of Congo, Djibouti, Egypt, Eritrea, Ethiopia, Kenya, Libya, Madagascar, Malawi, Mauritius, Rwanda, Seychelles, Sudan, Swaziland, Uganda, Zambia, Zimbabwe

ECONOMIC COMMUNITY OF WEST AFRICAN STATES (ECOWAS):
Benin, Burkina Faso, Cape Verde, Côte d'Ivoire, Gambia, Ghana, Guinea, Guinea-Bissau, Liberia, Mali, Niger, Nigeria, Senegal, Sierra Leone, Togo

0   2000 mi

0   2000 km

countries have been struggling to establish a political identity, and the different trade groups have political as well as economic underpinnings.

The African Union One group not shown on Map 8.5 is the African Union, created by 53 African countries in 2002 to take the place of the Organization of African Unity (OAU). The OAU was established in 1963 to focus on political issues in Africa, notably colonialism and racism. However, the new AU is modeled loosely on the EU, although that type of integration will be extremely difficult in Africa. Civil war, corruption, diseases such as AIDS, and poor government infrastructures have hampered African countries and their ability to progress economically.

Because most African countries rely more on trade links with former colonial powers than with each other, intrazonal trade is not significant. African markets, with the notable exception of South Africa, are relatively small and undeveloped, making trade liberalization a relatively minor contributor to economic growth in the region. However, any type of market expansion through regional integration will help these small countries.

Looking to the
Future   Will the WTO Overcome Bilateral and Regional Integration Efforts?

Will regional integration be the wave of the future, or will the WTO become the focus of global economic integration? The WTO's objective is to reduce barriers to trade in goods, services, and investment. Regional groups attempt to do that and more. Although the EU has introduced a common currency and is increasing the degree of cooperation in areas such as security and foreign policy, the WTO will likely never engage in those issues. Regional integration deals with the specific problems facing member countries, whereas the WTO needs to be concerned about all countries in the world.

However, regional integration might actually help the WTO achieve its objectives in three major ways:

1. Regionalism can lead to liberalization of issues not covered by the WTO.
2. Regionalism, given that it typically involves fewer countries with more similar conditions and objectives, is more flexible.
3. Regional deals lock in liberalization, especially in developing countries.

NAFTA and the EU are the key regional groups in which significant integration is taking place. In the future, these groups will continue to develop stronger linkages, and then they will expand to include other countries. The key for NAFTA will be whether the U.S. Congress can avoid getting caught up in protectionist sentiment and allow expansion to take place. If it does not, Canada and Mexico will continue to engage in bilateral agreements with non-NAFTA countries in the region along the lines of the NAFTA agreement. The EU will continue to expand east until it meets Russia, and then its expansion will either stop or take on a whole new character.

In addition, the EU faces a real dilemma as it tries to figure out what to do with Turkey, which has applied for entrance into the EU. However, Turkey has a larger population than every country in the EU except for Germany and would be the only country in the EU with a predominantly Muslim population. Given the concerns with radical Islam and the fact that EU members have a common passport and full mobility of labor, it has to be a security nightmare for the other members of the EU.

Regional integration in Africa will continue at a slow pace due to the existing political and economic problems there. However, Africa is flush with natural resources and will be a favorite trading partner of resource-hungry China for a long time to come. That will help fill the foreign exchange coffers of the African countries and possibly help them resolve some of their long-standing problems. Asian integration, primarily in AFTA, will pick up steam as the economies of East and Southeast Asia recover and open up. Since the beginning of the decade, Asian countries have signed over 70 FTAs among themselves. In a matter of months, Japan alone ratified free trade agreements with Singapore, Malaysia, and the Philippines, and it is working on RTAs with Switzerland, ASEAN, Australia, the Gulf Cooperation Council, India, the Republic of Korea, and Vietnam.[48]

However, the key to their growth may be China and its rapidly growing influence in Asia and the rest of the world.

The challenges to the WTO come not only from the growing strength of regional groups but also from the strong divisions between developed and developing countries within the WTO. As we noted earlier in the chapter, the Doha agreement has been a disaster so far. After several rounds of negotiations, member countries cannot agree on how to solve the substantive issues surrounding agriculture and manufactured products. Initially, it appeared that the problem was the resistance of rich countries such as the United States and members of the EU to reduce farm subsidies and the hesitancy of developing countries to reduce tariffs on manufactured goods. However, it now appears that there are problems within the developing countries as some countries, like Brazil and India, favor reducing

tariffs on manufactured goods to 25 to 30 percent because of their fear of being swamped by imports from China.

Other developing countries would prefer a lower level of tariffs on manufactured goods and are irritated that larger developing countries like Brazil and India are speaking on their behalf. The poorest African nations feel like they have no voice at all.[49] Will the developing countries develop a common voice in current and future trade negotiations, or will the dialogue involve the developed countries (with the United States and the EU not always agreeing on issues), the rapidly growing and large developing countries, China, and the less-developed countries? If the current trend continues, it will become increasingly difficult for countries to agree on multilateral trade agreements, pushing more of the substantive effort to bilateral and regional talks. ■

OTHER FORMS OF INTERNATIONAL COOPERATION

Up to this point, the chapter has focused on treaties between nations designed to reduce trade and investment barriers and increase trade and investment among member nations. We moved from the global—the WTO—to the bilateral and the regional. However, there are other forms of cooperation worth mentioning that could have an influence on the strategies of MNEs.

The United Nations   The first form of cooperation worth exploring is the United Nations. The UN was established in 1945 in response to the devastation of World War II to promote international peace and security and to help solve global problems in such diverse areas as economic development, antiterrorism, and humanitarian actions. If the UN performs its responsibilities, it should improve the environment in which MNEs operate around the world, reducing risk and providing greater opportunities.

Organization and Membership   The UN family of organizations is too large to list, but it includes organizations such as the World Trade Organization (discussed earlier in the chapter) and the International Monetary Fund and the World Bank, which are discussed in subsequent chapters. These organizations are all part of the UN Economic and Social Council, one of six principal organs of the UN System, which also includes the General Assembly, the Security Council, and the International Court of Justice.

There are 192 member states in the UN represented in the General Assembly, including 15 member states that comprise the Security Council. There are five permanent members of the Security Council—China, France, the Russian Federation, the United Kingdom, and the United States—and 10 other members elected by the General Assembly to serve two-year terms.[50]

Focus on Developing Nations: UNCTAD   As noted, the UN is involved in a variety of social, political, and economic activities. In addition, the UN tends to focus on the problems of the developing countries in an attempt to resolve major issues facing them. One of the most important organizations in the UN that affects MNEs is the UN Conference on Trade and Development, or UNCTAD, a program authorized by the

> The UN was established in 1945 following World War II to promote international peace and security. It deals with economic development, antiterrorism, and humanitarian movements.

> UNCTAD was established to help developing countries participate in international trade.

General Assembly and established in the 1960s to tackle the problems of the developing countries in international trade.

UNCTAD is involved in a variety of different activities, such as trade and commodities; investment, technology, and enterprise development; and macroeconomic policies and debt and development financing. Obviously, these are just a few activities of UNCTAD. It has also been active in conducting the so-called North-South dialogue (between the developed and the developing countries), formulating international commodities agreements, developing codes of conduct, working to resolve the debt crisis, and a variety of other projects.

NGOs: Private nonprofit institutions that are independent of the government.

Nongovernmental Organizations (NGOs)   Nongovernmental, nonprofit voluntary organizations are all lumped under the category of *NGOs*. This refers to private institutions that are independent of the government. Some NGOs operate only within the confines of a specific country, whereas other NGOs are international in scope. The International Red Cross is an example of an international NGO. It is concerned with humanitarian issues around the world, not just in one country.

Many NGOs, such as Doctors without Borders, are like the Red Cross in that they are concerned about humanitarian issues. Other NGOs came about as a response to what is perceived as the negative side of globalization. Many of these NGOs were discussed in Chapter 5 with respect to the environment and labor issues. For example, in that chapter we discussed the U.K.-based Ethical Trading Initiative, or ETI.

Several NGOs concerned about workers' rights, such as Africa Now, Anti-Slavery International, Quaker Peace and Social Witness, Save the Children, and Working Women Worldwide, are members of ETI. NGOs perform an important role in bringing potential abuses to light and tend to be very narrowly focused, usually on a specific issue. There is a Committee on Non-Governmental Organizations that is a part of the Economic and Social Council (ECOSOC) of the UN that meets to discuss issues of importance to general and specific NGOs.

Global Compact   As noted in Chapter 5, the United Nations Global Compact is a strategic policy initiative for businesses in the areas of human rights, labor, environment, and anticorruption. Although all of these areas are important, the issues of sustainability and anticorruption seem to be of great significance to the business community, especially in light of our discussions in Chapter 5 on global social responsibility. The Global Compact identifies 10 key principles that should govern the behavior of companies.[51] The Global Compact board members include high-profile members of the business community (such as the president and CEO of Petrobras, Brazil), international labor and business organizations (such as the general secretary of the International Trade Union Confederation and the secretary-general of the International Chamber of Commerce), and civil society (such as the Chair of Transparency International). The issues being discussed in the Global Compact and the commitment of the broad community in these efforts is quite remarkable and important.

Commodity Agreements

Commodities refer to raw materials or primary products that enter into trade, such as metals or agricultural products. Primary commodity exports—such as crude petroleum, natural gas, copper, tobacco, coffee, cocoa, tea, and sugar—are still important to the developing countries. "[O]ut of 141 developing countries," notes a UN report, "95 are more than 50 percent dependent on commodity exports. In sub-Saharan Africa, the figure is 80 percent."[52]

COMMODITIES AND THE WORLD ECONOMY

Both long-term trends and short-term fluctuations in commodity prices have important consequences for the world economy. On the demand side, commodity markets play an important role in industrial countries, transmitting business cycle disturbances to the rest of the economy and affecting the rate of growth of prices. On the supply side, as noted above, primary products account for a significant portion of the GDP and exports of many commodity-producing countries.

CONSUMERS AND PRODUCERS

For many years, countries tried to band together as producer alliances or joint producer/consumer alliances to try to stabilize commodity prices. However, these efforts—with the exception of OPEC, which we discuss later—have not been very successful. UNCTAD established a Commodities Branch to attempt to deal with the issues facing developing countries because of high dependence on commodities, especially agricultural commodities, for export revenues.

The most important international commodity organizations and bodies, such as the International Cocoa Organization, the International Coffee Organization, and the International Copper Study Group, take part in UN-led discussions to help commodity-dependent countries establish effective policies and strategies. However, each organization, such as the International Coffee Organization (ICO), has its own organizational structure independent of the UN. For example, the ICO is composed of 45 exporting countries and 32 importing countries. All of the exporting countries are developing countries, and most of the importing countries are developed countries.

Whereas many of the original commodity agreements were designed to influence price through a variety of market-interfering mechanisms, most of the existing commodity agreements are established to discuss issues, disseminate information, improve product safety, and so on. Very little can be done outside of market forces to influence price.

Finally, because commodities are the raw materials used in the production process, it is important for managers of companies that use commodities to understand the factors that influence their prices. Investment and pricing decisions must be based on the cost of inputs, and it is difficult to forecast those costs when the commodities markets are highly volatile.

For many years, commodity prices fluctuated but did not increase dramatically. In the decade of the 2000s, however, global economic growth pulled up the price of commodities. China, in particular, was growing so fast that it was pulling up the prices of most commodities. This led to trade agreements between China and many commodity-producing countries, as well as significant foreign investment. The global economic crisis, however, caused a significant contraction in commodity prices, which had a very negative impact on the economies of the commodity-producing countries. Most experts feel that the drop is temporary and that commodity prices will come roaring back when the global economy recovers.

THE ORGANIZATION OF THE PETROLEUM EXPORTING COUNTRIES (OPEC)

The **Organization of the Petroleum Exporting Countries (OPEC)** is an example of a producer cartel that relies on quotas to influence prices. It is a group of commodity-producing countries that have significant control over supply and band together to control output and price. OPEC is part of a larger category of energy commodities, which also includes coal and natural gas. OPEC is not confined to the Middle East. The members are Algeria, Angola, Ecuador, Iran, Iraq, Kuwait, Libya, Nigeria, Qatar, Saudi Arabia, the United Arab Emirates, and Venezuela. Indonesia suspended its membership in January 2009.

Price Controls and Politics   OPEC controls prices by establishing production quotas on member countries. Saudi Arabia has historically performed the role of the dominant supplier in OPEC that can influence supply and price. Periodically—at least annually— OPEC oil ministers gather together to determine the quota for each country based on estimates of supply and demand.

Politics are also an important dimension to OPEC deliberations. OPEC member countries with large populations need large oil revenues to fund government programs. As a result, they are tempted to exceed their export quotas to generate more revenues.

Output and Exports   OPEC member countries produce about 46 percent of the world's crude oil and 18 percent of its natural gas. However, OPEC's oil exports represent about 60 percent of the oil traded internationally.[53] Therefore, OPEC can have a strong influence on the oil market, especially if it decides to reduce or increase its level of production.

Sometimes OPEC policies work; sometimes they don't. In addition, events beyond OPEC's control can influence prices. The rapidly escalating price of crude oil in recent years is a mixture of rising demand worldwide (especially in China), a shortage of refining capacity and environmental rules in some countries that preclude the building of new refineries, and political instability in the Middle East. At the height of the growth in the global economy and strong demand for all commodities, including oil, oil prices spiked to $145 a barrel in July 2008 and then dropped to $33 a barrel in December 2008, before rising again to about $68 a barrel in July 2009. Strong debates were taking place over whether the price rise was due to supply and demand, speculators, or a combination of the two.[54]

The Downside of High Prices   Keeping oil prices high has some downside for OPEC. Competition from non-OPEC countries increases because the revenues accruing to the competitors are higher. Because some OPEC countries are putting up

The downside of high oil prices for OPEC:

- Producers investing in countries outside of OPEC.
- Depression of worldwide growth and demand.
- Lack of competitive pressures to improve industries.
- Complication of balancing social, political, and economic objectives.

FIGURE 8.2

Got Oil? Given the spike in oil prices in 2008, everyone is looking for more oil to satisfy the demands of consumer countries, especially China.

Source: The New Yorker.

GREGORY

"This galaxy he's from—ask him if it's got oil."

roadblocks to production, major producers like BP, ExxonMobil, and Shell are investing heavily in areas like the Caspian Basin, the Gulf of Mexico, and Angola and are trying to enter areas like the Russian Federation. Production in these areas is expected to grow significantly.

Another problem is that higher oil prices could depress growth worldwide and thus lower demand for oil. Also, because of OPEC's power, for the most part its countries have been able to avoid competitive pressures to improve their industries—and some are, therefore, decades out of date.[55]

Political and social forces are also affecting oil prices. High oil prices have permitted President Hugo Chávez of Venezuela to spend millions on domestic poverty programs and foreign aid while underinvesting in Venezuela's oil infrastructure. As long as prices are high, he has no incentive to balance his priorities between spending and investment. When prices fell, however, he began to face the twin problems of deteriorating production and social unrest.

Vodafone Turns East

CASE

China Unicom, one of the largest mobile operators in China, was forced to make strategic moves to tackle fresh competition within the mobile telecommunications market. Since Vodafone's entry into the Chinese market by forming an equity alliance with China Mobile (Hong Kong) Limited (CMHK), China Unicom has seen increasing competition from both foreign and domestic companies. Vodafone's strong international footprint and technological expertise have brought strengths and new opportunities to CMHK. Now management must decide if China Unicom's recent alliance with South Korea (SK) Telecom will be sufficient to compete against Vodafone and CMHK.

With competition from global giants such as Vodafone, what is the future for China Unicom? China's mobile telecommunications sector has undergone major reconstruction because of the increasing trade liberalization promoted by the government. After a long period of protectionism, China joined the WTO in 2001 to help boost its international trade. Under the WTO treaties, Hong Kong, the former British colony before 1997, became a member of the WTO in its own right, despite technically being a Special Administrative Region (SAR) of China. Coinciding with China's entry into the WTO in 2001, Sir Christopher Gent, the-then CEO of Vodafone, attended a ceremony held at the China World Tower to announce the opening of new offices in Beijing and Hong Kong, confirming Vodafone's plans to expand into the Chinese market.

In late 2000, Vodafone made an initial investment worth U.S. $2.5 billion to purchase a 2.19 percent stake from CMHK. The stake was increased to 3.2 percent in 2002 with Vodafone's further purchase of U.S. $750 million shares. The partnership between Vodafone and CMHK was strengthened by increasing cooperation in many business areas, such as new product development and customer services. Although Vodafone's stake in CMHK might be small compared to its other global holdings, the potential market growth level and the possibility of a bigger ownership presence was still promising. With the steady growth in the Chinese market, Vodafone also set it sights on Hong Kong. In 2004, the U.K. mobile operator formed a partnership with SmarTone, Hong Kong's leading mobile operator in multimedia services. SmarTone re-branded its business to SmarTone-Vodafone, allowing Vodafone to build its presence in Hong Kong. Under the partnership agreement, both companies collaborated in developing and delivering products and services to international travelers and domestic customers.

Prior to 2001, Vodafone was already one of the world's largest mobile telecommunication companies. With 110 million mobile service subscribers in 2001 and a significant-number increase to over 515 million in 2007, the lucrative Chinese telecommunications market now attracts investment attention from the likes of Vodafone and other foreign companies. There is also steady growth in the Hong Kong telecommunications market, with 11.758 million subscribers in 2009. By forming partnerships with CMHK and SmarTone, Vodafone can gain access to 477 million and 1.139 million subscribers, respectively, in China and Hong Kong. By 2009, Vodafone had significantly increased its global presence, with equity interests in over 30 countries and over 40 partner networks worldwide.

To what extent can Vodafone's success be attributed to China's entry into the WTO? What part can be attributed to Vodafone's international strategies and internal policies?

Vodafone's Competitive Advantage

Much of Vodafone's global triumph stems from the managing processes upon which the U.K. division bases its success. These managing processes lie in the key areas of technology and resources, as well as customer services. Vodafone holds key technologies and resources, which include the telecommunications licenses and the related network infrastructure. It also has mobile licenses in all of the countries in which it operates, as well as fixed licenses in a number of markets. Vodafone operates 2G networks in all of its mobile operating subsidiaries, as well as an increasing number of 3G networks, offering customers an enhanced data experience. R&D work is at the core of Vodafone's technology and resources development, which helps its innovation and product development.

A key factor to Vodafone's success is its ability to build long and lasting relationships with its customers. With over 300 million proportionate mobile customers across the world, Vodafone seeks to identify and deliver solutions that meet their customers' ever-changing needs whether it be at home or in the workplace. Customer segments are targeted through a wide range of tariffs and propositions and Vodafone is good at localizing the customer's preferences and needs in the globally diversified market. This has been achieved through a customer measurement system called "customer delight," to identify and drive customer satisfaction in its global market. This system is diagnostic in nature, with the focus on tracking customer-satisfaction levels across all points of interaction with Vodafone and identifying what drives customer delight and its possible impact. Vodafone uses this information to track any areas for further improvement and focus.

China's Entry into the WTO

Before China's entry into the WTO in 2001, the mobile telecommunications market was largely dominated by two major domestic state-owned enterprises: CMHK and China Unicom. The fixed-line telecommunication market was dominated by China Telecom and China Tietong. The market was also protected by the government from foreign competitors. In negotiations for China's WTO membership, the opening of the telecommunications sector was one of the biggest stumbling blocks. Subsequently, China agreed to open up the basic telecommunications to foreign companies for cross-border trading and also agreed to the establishment of joint ventures (JVs). These market access schedules were based on the bilateral agreement that China negotiated with the United States and the European Union in 1999 and 2000, respectively.

Under the WTO agreements, foreign companies would be able to establish JVs to deliver domestic telecommunications services, with maximum 25 percent foreign stakes, within 3 years of China's accession. No restrictions were imposed on the number of these JVs. Initially, they were to be limited to telecommunications within and between the cities of Beijing, Shanghai and Guangzhou. Within 5 years of accession, there would be two further extensions of foreign investments in the Chinese domestic telecommunications sector. First, foreign stakes in these JVs were to be increased to 35 percent. Second, the number of cities opened to these JVs would increase from 3 to 17. The JVs would be able to provide services within and between these cities. In the final stage of market opening that would happen within 6 years of accession, the JVs will be able to lift foreign stakes to 49 percent.

In order to meet the accession commitments, China's telecommunications sector has been undergoing major reconstruction. CMHK would acquire fixed-line operator China Tietong; dominant fixed-line player China Telecom would absorb mobile provider China Unicom's network; China Netcom, the country's smaller fixed-line player, would merge with China Unicom. The reconstruction would leave China with three key telecommunication players, each able to offer fixed and mobile services.

With the reshuffling of China's telecommunications sector, there is one big question looming for the global telecommunications players: Will China's telecommunications market finally open to global companies like Vodafone, which has been constrained to a minority stake of less than 4 percent among Chinese telecommunications operators? The answer seems less than likely, because there is no guarantee it will actually happen. For the past couple of years, China's telecommunications operators have suspended their investment plans while government officials have debated over the reconstruction agenda. In 2000, Vodafone's then-CEO Sir Christopher Gent said he wished to raise the British telecommunications giant's stake in CMHK to 20 percent in four or five years' time. Today, Vodafone's stake in China Mobile is still a minority 3.2 percent.

That is largely because China has been particularly reluctant to loosen its control on what it considers its strategic telecommunications industry. When China joined the WTO, it promised to allow up to 49 percent foreign investment in the telecommunications industry by 2007. But as of today, no foreign strategic investor is anywhere near that ceiling. In order to expand business in the Chinese telecommunications market, foreign investors have to wait for the government to open policies further.

Formation of China Unicom-SK Telecom Equity Alliance

Under the reconstruction, CMHK still retains its prime position in the domestic telecommunications market. Its partnership with Vodafone has allowed CMHK to make advancements in product and research development. The Joint Innovation Lab (JIL) was established by CMHK, Vodafone, and SOFTBANK (a giant Japanese telecommunications player) to help accelerate the uptake of innovative mobile technologies in the global market. In 2009, Verizon Wireless—a JV of U.S. Verizon Communications and Vodafone—joined the JIL.

This CMHK-Vodafone partnership imposed a huge threat to China Unicom. China Unicom has always played the role of industry precursor in the domestic market. It was established in 1994 with a mission to "break up monopolies and bring on competition." However, China Unicom is faced with the dilemma of technological advancement, an area that CMHK has improved significantly after the partnership with Vodafone. Looking for a way out of its technological constraints compelled China Unicom to look for foreign partners. In 2006, China Unicom and SK Telecom signed a strategic alliance agreement under which SK Telecom became China Unicom's sole partner in several fields of its core business. With almost 7 percent of China Unicom's stakes in exchange for U.S. $1 billion, SK Telecom can finally dive into the Chinese telecommunications market. For China Unicom, in addition to the considerable capital it gains, it also gets a precious opportunity to optimize its technological networks. In SK Telecom's ambitious overseas expansion plan, China will be the most important target market. After trying to improve its technological networks, China Unicom is hoping that SK Telecom's expertise will help it seize a more favorable position in future research and technology development.

There is no doubt that the China Unicom-SK Telecom partnership is a substantial force for competing against the CMHK-Vodafone collaboration. With the reshuffling of the telecommunications sector, other domestic players like China Telecom and China Netcom also want to increase their market share. In 2005, Telefonica, one of the largest telecommunications operators in Spain, bought a 3 percent stake in China Netcom for U.S. $ 290 million. China Telecom is seeking synergy with a foreign strategic partner to enhance its operation and management, although there has been no substantive discussion on this issue.

When the Chinese telecommunications companies sold minority stakes to foreign investors in the past, not surprisingly, they were aiming to get something in return. CMHK wanted to learn how mobile-phone standards were regulated worldwide so it collaborated with Vodafone and joined in the international standards committees to learn the rules of international trade. China Unicom teamed up with SK Telecom to strengthen technological development. The move to allow foreign investment is not purely driven by capital, but more for technological know-how. Despite the uncertainties in the reconstruction of China's telecommunications sector, there is one thing for certain: China Telecom will not stand still while watching the burgeoning foreign partnerships formed by its domestic peers.[56] ∎

QUESTIONS

1. How has China's entry into the WTO affected Vodafone's development in China and Hong Kong? How has it affected foreign telecommunications investment in general?

2. Why has Vodafone still held a minority stake in CMHK? What factors do you think have inhibited Vodafone's investment in the Chinese telecommunications market?

3. What has China Unicom done in its attempt to remain competitive? What are the advantages and challenges of such a strategy, and how effective do you think it will be?

4. What actions do you think China Telecom should take, given the competitive position of the CMHK-Vodafone and China Unicom-SK Telecom partnerships?

SUMMARY

- The General Agreement on Tariffs and Trade (GATT), begun in 1947, created a continuing means for countries to negotiate the reduction and elimination of trade barriers and to agree on simplified mechanisms for the conduct of international trade.

- The World Trade Organization (WTO) replaced GATT in 1995 as a continuing means of trade negotiations that aspires to foster the principle of trade without discrimination and to provide a better means of mediating trade disputes and of enforcing agreements.

- Efforts at regional economic integration began to emerge after World War II as countries saw benefits of cooperation and larger market sizes. The major types of economic integration are the free trade area and the customs union, followed by broader economic and political integration in the common market.

- Free trade agreements result in trade creation and trade diversion as barriers drop for member countries but remain higher for nonmember countries. There are static effects of the reduction of trade barriers. The static effects of economic integration improve the efficiency of resource allocation and affect both production and consumption. The dynamic effects are internal and external efficiencies that arise because of changes in market size.

- Once protection is eliminated among member countries, trade creation allows MNEs to specialize and trade based on comparative advantage.

- Trade diversion occurs when the supply of products shifts from countries that are not members of an economic bloc to those that are.

- Regional, as opposed to global, economic integration occurs because of the greater ease of promoting cooperation on a smaller scale.

- The European Union (EU) is an effective common market that has abolished most restrictions on factor mobility and is harmonizing national political, economic, and social policies. It is composed of 27 countries, including 12 countries from mostly Central and Eastern Europe that joined since 2004. The EU has abolished trade barriers on intrazonal trade, instituted a common external tariff, and created a common currency, the euro.

- The North American Free Trade Agreement (NAFTA) is designed to eliminate tariff barriers and liberalize investment opportunities and trade in services. Key provisions in NAFTA are labor and environmental agreements.

- There are key trade groups in other parts of the world, including Latin America, Asia, and Africa.

- The United Nations is composed of representatives of most of the countries in the world and influences international trade and development in a number of significant ways.

- Many developing countries rely on commodity exports to supply the hard currency they need for economic development. Instability in commodity prices has resulted in fluctuations in export earnings. OPEC is an effective commodity agreement in terms of attempting to stabilize supply and price.

KEY TERMS

Andean Community (CAN) (p. 347)
Asia Pacific Economic Cooperation
   (APEC) (p. 350)
Association of Southeast Asian
   Nations (ASEAN) (p. 349)
bilateral integration (p. 328)
Caribbean Community (CARICOM)
   (p. 345)
common market (p. 333)
dynamic effect (p. 333)

economic integration (p. 328)
economies of scale (p. 334)
euro (p. 338)
European Union (EU) (p. 335)
General Agreement on Tariffs and
   Trade (GATT) (p. 329)
global integration (p. 328)
MERCOSUR (p. 347)
most-favored-nation (MFN) clause
   (p. 329)

North American Free Trade Agreement
   (NAFTA) (p. 341)
Organization of the Petroleum Exporting
   Countries (OPEC) (p. 355)
regional integration (p. 328)
static effect (p. 333)
triad (p. 329)
World Trade Organization (WTO)
   (p. 329)

ENDNOTES

1 *Sources include the following:* Stephen Power, "EU Auto Industry
   Faces Overhaul as Japanese Gain in Market Share," *Wall Street
   Journal* (October 14, 2004): A1; Jathon Sapsford, "Toyota Aims to
   Rival GM Production," *Wall Street Journal* (November 2, 2004): A3;
   Mari Koseki, "Quota on Auto Exports to EC Curbed at 1.089
   Million in '93," *Japan Times* (April 12–18, 1993): 14; Nick Maling,
   "Japan Poised for EU Lift of Export Ceiling," *Marketing Week* (May
   6, 1999): 26; Todd Zaun and Beth Demain, "Leading the News:
   Ambitious Toyota, Buoyed by Europe, Sets Global Goals," *Wall
   Street Journal* (October 22, 2002): A3; Mark M. Nelson, Thomas F.
   O'Boyle, and E. S. Browning, "International—The Road to
   European Unity—1992: EC's Auto Plan Would Keep Japan at
   Bay—1992 Unification Effort Smacks of Protectionism," *Wall Street
   Journal* (October 27, 1988): A1; Sapsford, "Toyota Posts 3.5% Profit
   Rise, Boosts Sales Forecast for Year," *Wall Street Journal* (February
   4, 2005): A3; Gail Edmondson and Chester Dawson, "Revved Up
   for Battle," *Business Week* (January 10, 2005): 30; Joe Guy Collier,
   "Toyota Posts Record $14-Billion Profit," *Knight Ridder Tribune
   Business News* (May 9, 2007): 1; "ACEA Board of Directors
   Recommends Accepting Toyota Motor Europe Membership
   Application," *PR Newswire Europe Including UK Disclose* (May 4,
   2007); Toyota home page, "Toyota—Joining Europe," at
   www.toyota-europe.com/experience/the_ company/toyota-in-
   europe.aspx (accessed May 10, 2007); Toyota home page, "Toyota:
   Company Company Profile," at www.toyota.co.jp/en/about_
   toyota/outline/index.html (accessed May 10, 2007); Christoph
   Rauwald, "Leading the News: Toyota Sales in Europe Jump as
   Market Stalls," *Wall Street Journal* (March 16, 2007): 2; "World
   Business Briefing Europe: Germany: Sale of Unit Helps VW," *New
   York Times* (February 21, 2007): C10; Mark Milner, "Financial: Car
   Boss Calls on EU to Tackle Yen," *UK Guardian* (March 30, 2007): 32.

2 Peter J. Buckley, Jeremy Clagg, Nicolas Forsans, and Kevin T.
   Reilly, "Increasing the Size of the 'Country': Regional Economic
   Integration and Foreign Direct Investment in a Globalised
   World Economy," *Management International Review* 41:3 (2001):
   251–75.

3 Alan M. Rugman and Alain Verbeke, "A Perspective on Regional
   and Global Strategies of Multinational Enterprises," *Journal of
   International Business Studies* 35 (2004): 7.

4 John W. Miller, "Global Trade Talks Fail as New Giants Flex
   Muscle," *Wall Street Journal* (July 30, 2008): A1.

5 Daniel Ikenson, "Greasing the World Economy without Doha,"
   Wall Street Journal (July 30, 2008): A15.

6 Marcus Walker, Joellen Perry, and Kelly Evans, "Global Slump
   Seen Deepening," *Wall Street Journal* (April 1, 2009): A1.

7 John W. Miller, "WTO Predicts Global Trade Will Slide 9% This
   Year," *Wall Street Journal* (March 24, 2009): A8.

8 John Lyons, "Brazil's da Silva Warns against Protectionism," *Wall
   Street Journal* (March 11, 2009): A8. See also "World Trade: Barriers
   to Entry," *The Economist* (December 20, 2008): 121.

9 http://www.wto.org/english/thewto_e/whatis_e/10ben_e/
   10b00_e.htm and http://www.wto.org/english/thewto_e/
   whatis_e/10mis_e/10m00_e.htm (accessed October 1, 2009).

10 John W. Miller, "Brazil and Others Push outside Doha for Trade
   Pacts," *Wall Street Journal* (July 5, 2007): A6; "EU Proposes
   'Strategic Partner' Status for Brazil," CNN.com (accessed July 6,
   2007).

11 "Regional Trade Agreements," World Trade Organization,
   http://www.wto.org/english/tratop_e/region_e/region_e.htm
   (accessed July 29, 2009).

12 Bela Balassa, *The Theory of Economic Integration* (Homewood, IL:
   Richard D. Irwin, 1961): 40; Panjak Ghemawat, "Distance Still
   Matters: The Hard Reality of Global Expansion," *Harvard Business
   Review* (September 2001): 3–11.

13 Buckley et al., "Increasing the Size of the 'Country.' "

14 For more information on the EU, check out its Web site at
   http://europa.eu.int/index_en.htm (accessed October 1, 2009).

15 Charles Forelle, "Microsoft Yields to EU on Browsers," *Wall Street
   Journal* (July 25/26, 2009): B1.

16 Charles Forelle, "Intel Cites Human Rights in EU Fight on
   Antitrust," *Wall Street Journal* (July 23, 2009): B1.

17 "The European Parliament" (2005), at http://europa.eu.int/
   institutions/parliament/index_en.htm (accessed October 1, 2009).

18 "The European Court of Justice" (2002), at http://europa.eu.int/
   inst/en/cj.htm (accessed October 1, 2009).

19 Stephen Castle, "European Union Puts Out the Welcome Mat for
   Once-Aloof Iceland," *The New York Times* (July 28, 2009): B4.

20 Damien Henderson, "8000 New Workers Arrive after EU
   Expansion," *Miami Herald* (May 23, 2007): 2.

21 Pankaj Ghemawat, "Distance Still Matters: The Hard Reality of
   Global Expansion," *Harvard Business Review* 79:8 (September 2001):
   137.

22 Tom Hundley, "How Uniting Europe Helped Small Nations,"
   Seattle Times (March 24, 2007): 7.

23 Richard Lawrence, "NAFTA at 5: Happy Birthday?" *Journal of
   Commerce* (February 1, 1999), 4A.

24 Sandra Dibble, "Sony Will Increase Work Force in Tijuana," *The
   San Diego Union-Tribune* (June 26, 2009), E1.

25 Text of the North American Free Trade Agreement, "Chapter 4:
   Rules of Origin," at www.sice.oas.org/Trade/NAFTA/
   naftatce.asp (accessed October 2, 2009).

26 "Text of the North American Free Trade Agreement, Chapter 4:
   Rules of Origin/Regional Content."

27 Data from the WTO Web site, at www.wto.org (accessed October 2, 2009). Updated information can be found by searching the WTO Statistics Database for each member country.

28 Bureau of Labor Statistics, "International Comparisons of Hourly Compensation Costs in Manufacturing, 2007," Table B, at www.bls.gov/news.release/ichcc.nr0.htm (accessed July 29, 2009).

29 Jesus Cañas, Roberto Coronado, and Robert W. Gilmer, "U.S.-Mexico Deepen Economic Ties," *Southwest Economy* (January/February 2006), Federal Reserve Bank of Dallas, at www.dallasfed.org/research/swe/2006/swe0601c.html (accessed July 21, 2007).

30 "U.S.–Mexico at a Glance: Foreign Direct Investment," U.S. Embassy (June 2009), http://www.usembassy-mexico.gov/eng/eataglance_trade_FDI.pdf (accessed October 1, 2009).

31 Central Intelligence Agency, "CIA World Factbook" (July 2009).

32 Geri Smith and Elisabeth Malkin, "Mexican Makeover: NAFTA Creates the World's Newest Industrial Power," *Business* Week, December 21, 1998, 51.

33 "The Decline of the Maquiladora," *Business Week* (April 29, 2002): 59.

34 Sydney Weintraub, "A Politically Unpopular Success Story," *Los Angeles Times* (February 7, 1999): 2.

35 Smith and Malkin, "Mexican Makeover," 51.

36 Robert B. Zoellick, "Speech on NAFTA before the Foreign Trade Council," *USTR* (July 26, 2001): http://www.ustr.gov/speech-test/zoellick/zoellick_7.pdf.

37 Mario Osava, "South America: Brazil Outshines Regional Bloc," *Global Information Network* (July 27, 2009). http://www.proquest.com (accessed October 2, 2009).

38 Alan M. Field, "Showdown for CAFTA-DR," *Journal of Commerce* (April 11, 2005): 1.

39 Harold McGraw and Mark Weisbrot, "Is CAFTA-DR a Good Thing?" *Miami Herald* (April 16, 2005): 25A; new data from "U.S.—CAFTA-DR Free Trade Agreement: How U.S. Companies Can Benefit," www.export.gov/FTA/cafta-dr/index.asp (accessed July 29, 2009).

40 Field, "Showdown for CAFTA-DR," 1.

41 McGraw and Weisbrot, "Is CAFTA-DR a Good Thing?" 25A.

42 John Lyons, "Costa Rica Balks at Free-Trade Pact," *Wall Street Journal* (May 3, 2005): A2.

43 ASEAN, "Selected Basic ASEAN Indicators" (June 9, 2009), at www.aseansec.org/19226.htm (accessed July 2009).

44 "AFTA Doha," *The Economist* (September 6, 2008): 85.

45 Asia-Pac Paul Cashin, Hong Liang, and C. John McDermott, "Do Commodity Price Shocks Last Too Long for Stabilization Schemes to Work?" *Finance & Development* 36:3 (Summer 1999); Asia-Pacific Economic Cooperation, "About APEC," at www.apecsec.org.sg (accessed October 1, 2009).

46 Go to www.apecsec.org.sg/apec/about_apec.html (accessed May 23, 2005).

47 Go to www.apecsec.org.sg/apec/about_apec.html (accessed May 23, 2005).

48 "Asia: The Japan Syndrome; Free-Trade Agreements," *The Economist* (May 12, 2007): 65; "Regional Trade Agreements Information System," World Trade Organization.

49 Steven R. Weisman, "After Six Years, the Global Trade Talks Are Just That: Talk," *New York Times*, online edition (July 21, 2007) C1.

50 The United Nations, at www.un.org. Go to "Main Bodies" for more information about the principal organs of the UN and the different organizations that make up the UN system (accessed October 1, 2009).

51 United Nations, "United Nations Global Compact," http://www.unglobalcompact.org/AboutTheGC/TheTenPrinciples/index.html (accessed October 1, 2009).

52 Nations Conference on Trade and Development, "Commodity Information," in International Trade and Commodities/Highlights/Commodity Information, http://www.unctad.org (accessed October 1, 2009).

53 OPEC, "Does OPEC Control the Oil Market?," at www.opec.org/library/FAQs/aboutOPEC/q13.htm (accessed July 2009).

54 Ianthe Jeanne Dugan and Alistair MacDonald, "Traders Blamed for Oil Spike," *Wall Street Journal* (July 28, 2009): A1.

55 "Does OPEC Have Sand in Its Eyes?" *Business Week* (July 1, 2002): 60.

56 *Sources include the following:* Jessica Ramakrishnan, "Vodafone Acquires more of CMHK," WMRC *Daily Analysis* (May 2002), at http://global.factiva.com/sb/default.aspx?NAPC=S; Access Asia Ltd., "WTO Impact on the Telecommunications Industry in China: A Strategic Analysis" (August 2001), at http://www.globalbusinessinsights.com/content/rbaa0091t.pdf; Business Monitor International Ltd., "Hong Kong Telecommunications Report" (September 2009 Quarterly), at http://www.businessmonitor.com/telecommunications/hongkong.html; Wu Ying, "Foreign Investment Debuts in Chinese Telecoms," *China Business Feature* (November 7, 2006), at http://www.cbfeature.com/multinational/news/foreign_investment_debuts_in_chinese_telecoms; Lex Column, "Chinese Telecoms," *Financial Times* (May 2008), at http://global.factiva.com/ha/default.aspx; Vodafone Group Press, "Vodafone Adds Hong Kong's SmarTone to Partner Network Community" (December 2004), at http://www.vodafone.com/start/media_relations/news/group_press_releases/2004/press_release15_12.html; PR Newswire, "Vodafone Opens Offices in Beijing and Hong Kong" (November 2001), at http://proquest.umi.com/pqdweb?did=88950819&sid=4&Fmt=3&clientId=46002&RQT=309&VName=PQD; Matt Ottinger, "China Mobile Buys Phone Networks From Parent," *Wall Street Journal (Eastern Edition)* (May 2002), at http://proquest.umi.com/pqdweb?did=120057062&sid=1&Fmt=3&clientId=46002&RQT=309&VName=PQD; China Daily Information Company, "Joining WTO Boosts Technology Sector," China Daily (December 2006), at http://www.chinadaily.com.cn/chinagate/imindu.html; "Verizon Wireless to Join China Mobile, SOFTBANK and Vodafone in Creating the Largest Global Platform for Mobile Developers," *ACN Newswire – Asia Corporate News* (April 2009), at http://proquest.umi.com/pqdweb?did=1768154321&sid=2&Fmt=3&clientId=46002&RQT=309&VName=PQD; Chi-Chu Tschang, "Chinese Telecom: Who Wins, Who Loses? A Restructuring Will Shift Power Among Chinese Operators, but Will Foreign Players Become Full Participants in the World's Largest Market?" *Business Week Online* (July 2008), at http://www.businessweek.com/globalbiz/content/jul2008/gb2008079_485740.htm.

World Financial
Environment

nine

Global Foreign-
Exchange Markets

PART FOUR

Objectives

- To learn the fundamentals of foreign exchange

- To identify the major characteristics of the foreign-exchange market and how governments control the flow of currencies across national borders

- To describe how the foreign-exchange market works

- To examine the different institutions that deal in foreign exchange

- To understand why companies deal in foreign exchange

*Another man's trade
costs money.*

—*Portuguese
Proverb*

363

CASE Going down to the Wire in the Money-Transfer Market

Long known as "the fastest way to send money," U.S.-based Western Union controls nearly 80 percent of the money-transfer market and is widely acknowledged as the world leader in *wire transfers*—electronic transfers of funds from one financial institution to another.[1] In this case, it's a transfer from one Western Union office to another. However, Western Union is now facing stiff competition from banks threatening to encroach on its market share of the electronic money-transfer business.

Western Union was started in 1851 when a group of businessmen in Rochester, New York, formed a printing telegraph company. The company changed its name to Western Union in 1861 when it completed the first transcontinental telegraph line. Western Union introduced its money-transfer service in 1871 and started offering this service outside North America in 1989. Today, over 375,000 Western Union agent locations are found in over 200 countries and territories around the

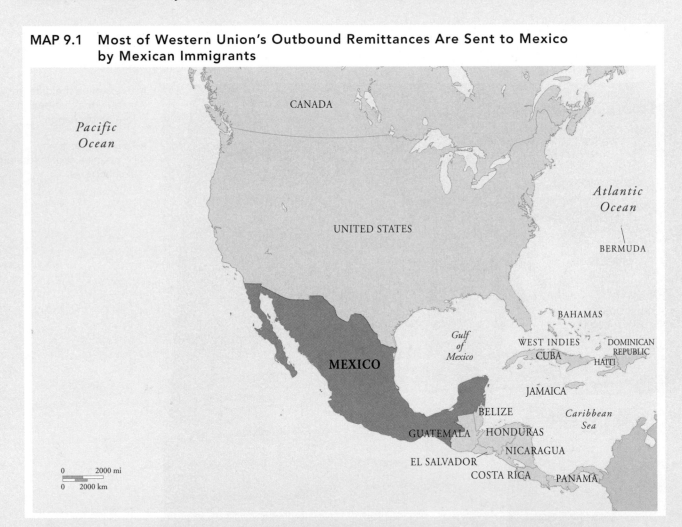

MAP 9.1 Most of Western Union's Outbound Remittances Are Sent to Mexico by Mexican Immigrants

world. Money transfers account for 85 percent of Western Union's revenues, and about $50 billion is transferred annually through Western Union.

Customers have many different options when sending money through Western Union. Money can be sent in person at an agent location, over the phone, or online, and senders may use cash, debit cards, or credit cards. For example, to send

money to Ukraine using a Western Union agent location, the customer must fill out a "Send Money" form. He or she then receives a receipt, which includes a Money Transfer Control number. This number must be given to the person receiving the funds. The receiver fills out a "Receive Money" form and presents the Money Transfer Control number along with valid identification at a Western Union agent location in Ukraine to receive the money.

CONVERTING CURRENCY

The funds are converted into the foreign currency using an exchange rate set by Western Union. The transfer fees for sending money are determined based on how much money is sent, in what form it is sent (cash or debit/credit card), and where it is going. For example, sending $500 to Mexico from Utah costs $15; sending $500 to the Philippines from Utah costs $12. Part of Western Union's attractiveness is its speed and anonymity. Western Union can move cash from one location of the world to another in just minutes. Money can be sent through an agent by cash, debit card, credit card, or a Western Union Gold Card. People sending money are required to fill out a form and show a proper ID.

The Mexican Connection (I)

The United States is home to about 50 million immigrant workers, the most of any country in the world. Most of these workers come from Latin America and the Caribbean, which received $69.2 billion in remittances in 2008. Most of Western Union's wire transfer business in the United States comes from Mexican immigrants who send part of their paychecks home to support their families (Map 9.1). In 2009, Mexico received at least $25 billion in remittances, making it the largest host country in Latin America for remittances, followed by Brazil. However, due to the economic crisis, the Inter-American Development Bank estimated that remittances to Latin America and the Caribbean could fall significantly from $69.2 billion in 2008, after a decade of continual growth. Remittances already exceed foreign direct investment and overseas aid as sources of foreign exchange. Annual remittance income has passed tourism to become the second-largest source of foreign-exchange income in Mexico after oil revenues.

EXCHANGE RATES AND COMPETITION

A class-action lawsuit was filed against Western Union in 1997, charging that Western Union offered its customers lower exchange rates than the market exchange rates without informing them of the difference. The lawsuit was settled in 2000, and Western Union is now required to state on its receipts and advertisements that it uses its own exchange rate on transactions and that any difference between the company rate and the market rate is kept by the company. For example, the market exchange rate on July 6, 2009, for Mexican pesos was 13.2770 pesos/U.S. $ (U.S. $500 = 6,638.50 pesos); Western Union's offered exchange rate was 13 pesos/U.S. $ (U.S. $500 = 6,500 pesos).

Financial institutions such as banks have pressured Western Union to use better exchange rates. Profit margins in the money-transfer business can reach 30 percent, and many banks have started to offer their own money-transfer services in an attempt to take advantage of the continued expected growth of the foreign money-transfer industry. For example, in 2001, Wells Fargo agreed to accept consular identification cards from Mexican immigrants who want to open bank accounts but lack U.S. driver's licenses. These cards verify Mexicans' identities without revealing their immigration status. After Wells Fargo began accepting the consular identification card, the number of bank accounts opened with the consular ID jumped by over 500 percent within three years.

The Mexican Connection (II)

Wells Fargo and other U.S. banks, including Citi and Bank of America, have established alliances with Mexican banks to offer remittance accounts to the immigrant workers in the United States. Workers can now open U.S. bank accounts with their consular IDs and each ask for two ATM cards. They can then deposit remittance money in the U.S. account, and their family members at home can withdraw the money from the associated Mexican bank.

In 2005, the Federal Reserve teamed up with Mexico's central bank to create a new program that facilitates remittances made from the United States to Mexico. This program allows U.S. commercial banks to make money transfers for Mexican workers through the Federal Reserve's own automated clearinghouse, which is linked to Banco de México, the Mexican central bank.

Even the wire transfer fees at banks are cheaper than Western Union's. For example, Wells Fargo charges a $5 fee to send $500 to Mexico, compared with Western Union's $15 fee for the same transaction. Many banks are moving toward eliminating exchange-rate spreads (the difference between the market rate and the rate they use for the wire transfer) and transfer fees to Mexico to provide more attractive alternatives to immigrant workers.

This new onslaught of competition by banks has forced Western Union to cut its fees and offer new services, including a home-delivery service, where money is delivered directly to the recipient's door. Western Union is also moving into countries such as China and India to increase its market share. The increased competition has driven down remittance fees around the world. In Ukraine, for example, Western Union was forced to drop its fee from $43 to $20.

The Mexican Connection (III)

Immigrant workers complain about the high transfer fees and exchange-rate spread associated with Western Union, but many continue to use this service instead of the lower-cost method of remitting money through banks. Mexico has a history of unstable currencies and widespread inflation, resulting in a traditional mistrust of banks. Other immigrants base their choice on word of mouth or convenience and location. Many are simply unaware of the variety of choices available for sending money and do not know how to get the best deal.

Another reason why many continue to use Western Union is its worldwide availability. For thousands of tiny villages, Western Union is the main link to the outside world. For example, Coatetelco is a small Mexican village south of Mexico City with no bank. A few people grow maize, chilies, and fruit, but remittances—mostly from agricultural or construction workers in Georgia and the Carolinas—account for 90 percent of the villagers' incomes. Patricio, 49, says that at the end of each month, he gets a call from his two sons, who are working illegally in Georgia. They give him a code number, and he drives or rides his horse 4 miles to the nearest Western Union office, located in a government telegraph office, to pick up the $600 they spent $40 to wire to him. Less expensive remittance services are available at the nearby Banamex bank in Mazatepec, but so far, Patricio and his neighbors are not willing to travel the 8 miles to get there. Besides, he says, "we do not trust the banks, and they make everything **€RN** more difficult."

Introduction

When we introduced the idea of a **multinational enterprise (MNE)** in Chapter 1, we emphasized that MNEs are firms that take a global approach to production and markets. Here we add that the need to deal with **foreign exchange** is one of the important factors in the environment in which MNEs must conduct business.

Changing money from one currency to another and moving it around to different parts of the world is serious business, on both a personal and a company level. To survive, both MNEs and small import and export companies must understand foreign exchange and exchange rates. In a business setting, there is a fundamental difference between making a payment in the domestic market and making a payment abroad. In a domestic transaction, companies use only one currency. In a foreign transaction, companies can use two or more currencies. For example, a U.S. company that exports skis to a French distributor may ask the French store that buys skis to remit payment in dollars, unless the U.S. company has some specific use for euros (the currency France uses), such as paying a French supplier.

Assume you're a U.S. importer who has agreed to purchase a certain quantity of French perfume and to pay the French exporter €4,000 for it. Assuming you had the money, how would you go about paying? First, you would go to the international department of your local bank to buy €4,000 at the going market rate. Let's assume the euro/dollar exchange rate is €0.7071 per dollar. Your bank would then charge your account $5,657 ($4,000/€0.7071) plus the transaction costs and give you a special check payable in euros made out to the exporter.

The exporter would deposit it in a French bank, which would then credit the exporter's account with €4,000. Then the foreign-exchange transaction would be complete.

Foreign exchange—money denominated in the currency of another nation or group of nations.

WHAT IS *FOREIGN EXCHANGE*?

Foreign exchange is money denominated in the currency of another nation or group of nations.[2] The market in which these transactions take place is the **foreign-exchange market.** Foreign exchange can be in the form of cash, funds available on credit and debit cards, traveler's checks, bank deposits, or other short-term claims.[3] As our opening case illustrates, for example, Mexican immigrant workers in the United States often use Western Union to convert dollars to pesos and then wire the pesos to offices in Mexico where relatives can retrieve the cash.

An **exchange rate** is the price of a currency. It is the number of units of one currency that buys one unit of another currency, and this number can change daily. For example, on July 1, 2009, €1 could purchase U.S. $1.4142. Exchange rates make international price and cost comparisons possible.

Exchange rate—the price of a currency.

Case Review Note

PLAYERS ON THE FOREIGN-EXCHANGE MARKET

The foreign-exchange market is made up of many different players. The **Bank for International Settlements (BIS),** a central banking institution in Basel, Switzerland, owned and controlled by 55 member central banks, divides the market into three major categories: *reporting dealers,* other *financial institutions,* and *nonfinancial institutions.*

Who Are the Players?   *Reporting dealers,* also known as *money center banks,* are widely assumed to include the 10 largest banks in terms of overall market share in foreign-exchange trading: Deutsche Bank, UBS, Barclays Capital, RBS, Citi, JP Morgan, HSBC, Goldman Sachs, Credit Suisse, and Bank of America. (In our closing case, we show how a dominant bank—in this case Kaupthing—can change the course of an entire country.) Because of the volume of transactions that the money center banks engage in, they are influential in setting prices and are the market makers. The other financial institutions include commercial banks other than the money center banks (local and regional banks), hedge funds, pension funds, money market funds, currency funds, mutual funds, specialized foreign-exchange trading companies, and so forth. Western Union, whose current activities are detailed in our opening case, is a good example of a nonbanking financial institution that deals in foreign exchange.

The Bank for International Settlements divides the foreign-exchange market into reporting dealers (also known as dealer banks or money center banks), other financial institutions, and nonfinancial institutions.

Case Review Note

Case Review Note

Whom Do the Players Serve?   Nonfinancial customers include governments and companies (MNEs as well as small- and medium-size corporations and companies). The BIS reported in its triennial survey of reporting dealers that 43 percent of their counterparties were other reporting dealers, 40 percent were other financial institutions, and 17 percent were nonfinancial institutions.[4]

What Do Players Do?   Dealers, at whatever level, can operate on a proprietary basis where they trade currencies to generate profit from those transactions, or they can provide a wide range of foreign-exchange services for their customers. In the interbank market, or the market between dealer banks, banks either deal directly with each other or operate through foreign-exchange brokers. The trades can be conducted by voice or electronically; however, the trend is clearly moving to and dominated by electronic trades.

Electronic Services   Dealers, whether in the money center banks or other financial institutions, use one or a combination of electronic services to trade currencies. Three of the most widely used are Reuters, EBS (bought by U.K.-based ICAP in 2006), and Bloomberg. Reuters is also a U.K.-based firm, whereas Bloomberg is a U.S.-based firm. A bank or other customer gets access to the automated system by purchasing the service from one of the providers and paying a monthly fee to receive a link through telephone lines to the bank's computers. Then the bank can use the automated system to trade currency. The automated system is efficient because it lists bid and sell quotes, allowing the

Concept Check

In discussing "The Political Environment" in Chapter 3, we observe that the relationships comprising a country's political system—relationships among its institutions, organizations, and interest groups—depend on the "political norms and rules" over which its government exercises control. As we'll see in Chapter 10, these strictures include rules for trading currency; moreover, governments are active traders of foreign currency through money center banks.

Dealers can trade foreign exchange

- Directly with other dealers.
- Through voice brokers.
- Through electronic brokerage systems.

An employee watches trading on several computer screens at the Standard Chartered Bank's new trading room at the Dubai International Financial Center (DIFC). At the time, this was the largest trading room in the Middle East with over 200 trading seats and providing services in Risk Management Advisory, Structuring, Interest Rates Derivatives, Foreign Exchange, E-commerce, Credit Trading and Capital Markets capabilities.

Source: Marwan Naamani/Getty Images, Inc.

Reuters, EBS, and Bloomberg facilitate foreign-exchange trades on automated trading systems.

bank to trade immediately. Bloomberg has invested heavily in the services it provides customers and provides excellent analytics, charts, and reports for customers—more so than Reuters, although both systems are widely used.

Also, the services provide a great deal of market data, news, quotes, and statistics about different markets around the world. It is not uncommon for a trading room to have more than one electronic service and for traders to have different preferences within the same office. For example, one trader may prefer Reuters, whereas another may provide Bloomberg, even though both work in the same trading room. Bloomberg and Reuters provide market quotes from a large number of banks, so their quotes are close to the market consensus. EBS provides live trades through their system. Deutsche Bank, UBS, and Barclays Capital are moving to dominate e-trading of foreign exchange on their proprietary platforms. If you are accepted to trade on their platforms, you have to trade at the rates they quote. However, a quick check of the market consensus on Bloomberg or Reuters will let you know how good those quotes are.

SOME ASPECTS OF THE FOREIGN-EXCHANGE MARKET

Foreign-exchange market:

- Over-the-counter (OTC) commercial and investment banks.
- Securities exchanges.

The foreign-exchange market has two major segments: the over-the-counter market (OTC) and the exchange-traded market. The OTC market is composed of commercial banks as just described, investment banks, and other financial institutions. The exchange-traded market is composed of securities exchanges, such as the CME Group (Chicago Mercantile Exchange), NASDAQ OMX, and NYSE Liffe, where certain types of foreign-exchange instruments, such as exchange-traded futures and options, are traded.

Traditional foreign-exchange instruments:

- Spot.
- Outright forward.
- FX swap.

Some Traditional Foreign-Exchange Instruments   Several different types of foreign-exchange instruments are traded in these markets, but the traditional foreign-exchange instruments that compose the bulk of foreign-exchange trading are *spot transactions, outright forwards,* and *FX swaps:*

The spot rate is the exchange rate quoted for transactions that require delivery within two days.

- **Spot transactions** involve the immediate exchange of currency, which is generally made on the second business day after the date on which the two foreign-exchange dealers agree to the transaction. The rate at which the transaction is settled is the **spot rate.** (Our opening case, which discusses Western Union's policies on currency conversion, gives a good idea of how individuals can trade foreign exchange on the spot market.)

- **Outright forward transactions** involve the exchange of currency on a future date. It is the single purchase or sale of a currency for future delivery. The rate at which the transaction is settled is the forward rate and is a contract rate between the two parties. The forward transaction will be settled at the forward rate no matter what the actual spot rate is at the time of settlement.

- In an **FX swap,** one currency is swapped for another on one date and then swapped back on a future date. Most often, the first leg of an FX swap is a spot transaction, with the second leg of the swap a forward transaction. For example, assume that IBM receives a dividend in British pounds from its subsidiary in the United Kingdom but has no use for British pounds until it has to pay a British supplier in pounds in 30 days. It would rather have dollars now than hold on to the pounds for 30 days. IBM could enter into an FX swap in which it sells the pounds for dollars to a dealer in the spot market at the spot rate and agrees to buy pounds for dollars from the dealer in 30 days at the forward rate. Although an FX swap is both a spot and a forward transaction, it is accounted for as a single transaction.

Derivatives In reality, outright forward transactions and foreign-exchange swaps are **derivatives.** Other derivatives are currency swaps, options, and futures.[5] Spot transactions, outright forward transactions, FX swaps, and currency swaps are OTC instruments; options are traded both OTC and on exchanges, and futures are exchange-traded instruments.

- **Currency swaps** deal more with interest-bearing financial instruments (such as a bond), and they involve the exchange of principal and interest payments. As we observe in our closing case, Kaupthing is involved in a variety of foreign-currency transactions, including a range of OTC products. Western Union, the subject of our opening case, is more directly involved in spot transactions and in transferring funds from one country to another.

- **Options** are the right, but not the obligation, to trade foreign currency in the future.

- A **futures contract** is an agreement between two parties to buy or sell a particular currency at a particular price on a particular future date, as specified in a standardized contract to all participants in that currency futures exchange.

Size, Composition, and Location of the Foreign-Exchange Market Before we examine the market instruments in more detail, let's look at the size, composition, and geographic location of the market. Every three years, the BIS conducts a survey of foreign-exchange activity in the world. In the 2007 survey, it estimated that $3.2 trillion in foreign exchange is traded every day.[6] Although the next survey won't be done until 2010, it is safe to assume that the daily trading volume in foreign exchange will hit at least $5 trillion by the next survey.

Foreign-exchange activity increased substantially in 2007 by 71 percent compared with the 2004 survey. This increase more than reversed the fall in global foreign-exchange activity from 1998 to 2001. Some of the reasons for the increase are the growing importance of foreign exchange as an alternative asset and a larger emphasis on **hedge funds**—funds typically used by wealthy individuals and institutions that are

Outright forwards involve the exchange of currency beyond three days at a fixed exchange rate, known as the forward rate.

An FX swap is a simultaneous spot and forward transaction.

Three other important foreign-exchange instruments:
- Currency swaps.
- Options.
- Futures.

Size of the foreign-exchange market—$3.2 trillion daily.

allowed to use aggressive strategies unavailable to mutual funds. Even with the collapse in the global economy in 2007–2009, there is every indication that foreign-exchange activity continued to grow. However, it is hard to tell if the growth was as large as it was from 2004–2007.

Figure 9.1 illustrates the trends in foreign-exchange trading beginning with the 1989 survey. The $3.2 trillion daily turnover includes traditional foreign-exchange market activity only—spots, outright forwards, and FX swaps. In the OTC derivatives market (but not including derivatives traded on exchanges), daily activity increased by 74 percent to $4.2 trillion. This is also a significant escalation in activity compared with the period of 1998–2001, when activity increased by 10 percent.

Using the U.S. Dollar on the Foreign-Exchange Market

The U.S. dollar is the most important currency on the foreign-exchange market; in 2007, it comprised one side (buy or sell) of 86.3 percent of all foreign currency transactions worldwide, as Table 9.1 illustrates. This means that almost every foreign-exchange transaction conducted on a daily basis has the dollar as one leg of the transaction. Numbers in the table are percentages and add up to 200 percent because there are two sides to each transaction.

There are five major reasons why the dollar is so widely traded:[7]

1. It's an investment currency in many capital markets.
2. It's a reserve currency held by many central banks.
3. It's a transaction currency in many international commodity markets.
4. It's an invoice currency in many contracts.
5. It's an intervention currency employed by monetary authorities in market operations to influence their own exchange rates.

Because of the ready availability of U.S. dollars worldwide, this currency is important as a vehicle for foreign-exchange transactions between two countries other than the United States. An example of how the dollar can be used as a vehicle currency for two

Concept Check

It's interesting (though not necessarily surprising) to note that the most widely traded currencies in the world are those issued by countries that enjoy high levels of political freedom (see Chapter 3) and economic freedom (see Chapter 4).

The dollar is the most widely traded currency in the world:

- An investment currency in many capital markets.
- A reserve currency held by many central banks.
- A transaction currency in many international commodity markets.
- An invoice currency in many contracts.
- An intervention currency employed by monetary authorities in market operations to influence their own exchange rates.

FIGURE 9.1 Foreign-Exchange Markets: Average Daily Volume, 1992–2007

The data compiled by the BIS include traditional foreign-exchange activity (such as spots, outright forwards, and FX swaps), as well as the volume of derivatives (such as hedge funds) traded in the OTC. In fact, the growth in hedge fund trading is one factor in the significant increase in activity between 2001 and 2007.

Source: Bank for International Settlements, *Central Bank Survey of Foreign Exchange and Derivatives Market Activity,* 2007 (Basel, Switzerland: BIS, December 2007): 2. Reprinted by permission of the Bank for International Settlements.

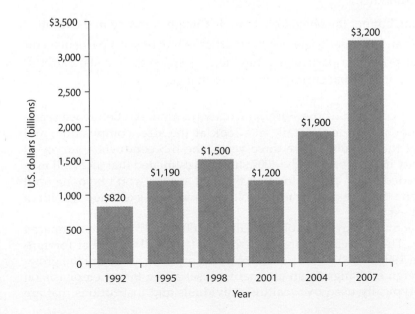

TABLE 9.1 Global Foreign Exchange: Currency Distribution

The U.S. dollar is involved in a whopping 86.3 percent of all worldwide foreign-exchange transactions. Because it's so readily available, it's a popular choice for exchanges between two countries other than the United States, and it's involved in four of the seven most frequently traded currency pairs (the $/€ is number one, the $/¥ number two).

Currency	April 1992	April 1995	April 1998	April 1998	April 2001	April 2007
U.S. dollar	82.0%	83.3%	87.3%	90.3%	88.7%	86.3%
Euro	—	—	—	37.6	37.2	37.0
Japanese yen	23.4	24.1	20.2	22.7	20.3	16.5
Pound sterling	13.6	9.4	11.0	**13.2**	16.9	15.0
Swiss franc	8.4	7.3	7.1	**6.1**	6.1	6.8
All others	72.6	75.9	74.4	30.1	30.8	38.4

Source: Bank for International Settlements, *Central Bank Survey of Foreign Exchange and Derivatives Market Activity, 2007* (Basel, Switzerland: BIS, December 2007): 11. Reprinted by permission of the Bank for International Settlements.

other countries is when a Mexican company importing products from a Japanese exporter converts Mexican pesos into dollars and sends them to the Japanese exporter, who converts the dollars into yen. Thus, the U.S. dollar has one leg on both sides of the transaction—in Mexico and in Japan.

There may be a couple of reasons to go through dollars instead of directly from pesos to yen. The first is that the Japanese exporter might not have any need for pesos, whereas it can use dollars for a variety of reasons. The second is that the Mexican importer might have trouble getting yen at a good exchange rate if the Mexican banks are not carrying yen balances. However, the banks undoubtedly carry dollar balances, so the importer might have easy access to the dollars. Thus, the dollar has become an important vehicle for international transactions, and it greatly simplifies life for a foreign bank because the bank will not have to carry balances in many different currencies.

> The dollar is part of four of the top seven currency pairs traded:
>
> • The dollar/euro is number one.
> • The dollar/yen is number two.

Frequently Traded Currency Pairs   Another way to consider foreign currency trades is to look at the most frequently traded currency pairs. The top seven currency pairs in the 2007 BIS Survey involve the U.S. dollar, with the top two pairs being the euro/dollar (EUR/USD)—27 percent of total—and the dollar/yen (USD/JPY).[8] Because of the importance of the U.S. dollar as the currency through which most foreign exchange trades take place, the exchange rate between two currencies other than the U.S. dollar is known as a **cross rate.**

The trade between the dollar and yen is very sensitive politically, because the exchange rate is often a function of trade negotiations between Japan and the United States.[9] The Japanese yen is an important currency in Asia because its value reflects the competitive positions of other countries in the region and because it is freely traded, unlike the Chinese yuan, which is more tightly controlled by the government but, as will be discussed in Chapter 10, is moving to become more of a regional and eventually a global currency.

The Euro   The euro is also in four of the top 10 currency pairs. Although the dollar is still more popular in most emerging markets, the euro is gaining ground, particularly in Eastern European countries like the Czech Republic and Hungary. Prior to the introduction of the euro, the German mark, or Deutsche mark, was one of the most important

> The biggest market for foreign exchange is London, followed by New York, Tokyo, and Singapore.

FIGURE 9.2 Foreign-Exchange Markets: Geographical Distribution, April 2007

The United Kingdom handles a little over 34 percent of all world foreign-exchange activity (compared to just over 16.6 percent by the United States). Location is a big factor in the United Kingdom's popularity: London is close to all the capital markets of Europe, and its time zone makes it convenient for making trades in both the U.S. and Asian markets.

Source: Bank for International Settlements, *Central Bank Survey of Foreign Exchange and Derivatives Market Activity, 2007* (Basel, Switzerland: BIS, December 2007): 11. Reprinted by permission of the Bank for International Settlements.

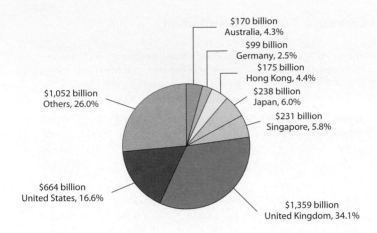

$170 billion
Australia, 4.3%
$99 billion
Germany, 2.5%
$175 billion
Hong Kong, 4.4%
$238 billion
Japan, 6.0%
$231 billion
Singapore, 5.8%
$1,052 billion
Others, 26.0%
$664 billion
United States, 16.6%
$1,359 billion
United Kingdom, 34.1%

trading currencies in the world. In the 1998 BIS survey, the Deutsche mark represented 30.1 percent of the average daily turnover in foreign exchange (down from a high of 39.6 percent in the 1992 survey), but as noted in Table 9.1, the euro represented only 37.0 percent of the average daily turnover in the 2007 survey. That shows how important the Deutsche mark was and how influential Germany is as a member of the European Monetary System.

Given that the dollar is clearly the most widely traded currency in the world, you'd expect the biggest market for foreign-exchange trading would be in the United States. As Figure 9.2 illustrates, however, the biggest market by far is in the United Kingdom.

The four largest centers for foreign-exchange trading (the United Kingdom, the United States, Japan, and Singapore) account for 62.5 percent of the total average daily turnover. The U.K. market is so dominant that more dollars are traded in London than in New York.[10]

Does Ge🌐graphy Matter? Foreign-Exchange Trades

Given that the U.S. dollar is the most widely traded currency in the world, why is London so important as a trading center? There are two major reasons for London's prominence. First, London, which is close to the major capital markets in Europe, is a strong international financial center where a large number of domestic and foreign financial institutions have operations. Thus, London's geographic location relative to significant global economic activity is key.

Second, London is positioned in a unique way because of the time zone where it is located. In Map 9.1, note that at noon in London, it is seven in the morning in New York and evening in Asia. The London market opens toward the end of the trading day in Asia and is going strong as the New York foreign-exchange market opens up. London thus straddles both of the other major markets in the world.

Another way to illustrate the importance of geography is to note the daily volume of market activity that takes place in different markets around the world, especially in North America and Europe. Figure 9.3 illustrates the average number of electronic conversations per hour as monitored by Reuters.

It illustrates how market activity is concentrated on the time period when Asia and Europe are open or when Europe and the United States are open, even though the market is really open 24 hours a day. Because the U.S. dollar is the most widely traded currency in the world and London is the major market center for dollars traded outside the United States, it makes sense that most market activity would take place during the hours that the U.S. and London markets are open. A better price for currencies can be had when the markets are active and liquid. ●

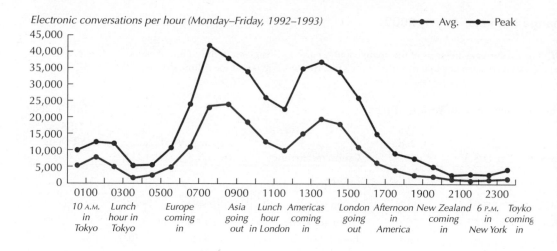

Electronic conversations per hour (Monday–Friday, 1992–1993)

● Avg. ● Peak

0100	0300	0500	0700	0900	1100	1300

10 A.M. in Tokyo — Lunch hour in Tokyo — Europe coming in — Asia going out in London — Lunch hour in London — Americas coming in — London going out — Afternoon in America — New Zealand coming in — 6 P.M. in New York — Toyko coming in

FIGURE 9.3   The Circadian Rhythms of the Foreign-Exchange Market

Peak periods for foreign-exchange activity occur between about 0600 and 1200 hours (when both European and U.S. markets are open for business) and 1200 and 1800 hours (when both U.S. and Asian markets are active). Time (0100– 2400) is Greenwich Mean Time.

Source: Zaheer, Srilata, "Circadian Rhythms: The Effects of Global Market Integration in the Currency Trading Industry, " Journal of International Business Studies, 1995, Vol. 26, Issue 4, pp. 699–728, Figure 1.

Major Foreign-Exchange Markets

THE SPOT MARKET

Foreign-exchange dealers are the ones who quote the rates. The dealers always quote a *bid (buy)* and *offer (sell) rate.* The **bid** is the price at which the dealer is willing to buy foreign currency; the **offer** is the price at which the dealer is willing to sell foreign currency. In the spot market, the **spread** is the difference between the bid and offer rates, and it is the dealer's profit margin. In our opening case, we explain how Western Union quotes exchange rates for the purpose of trading dollars for pesos. Its rates are often different from those quoted by commercial banks, but some people prefer to use Western Union, pay higher fees, and get lower exchange rates. Why? In part, because of a lack of trust in the banking system.

Case Review Note

Direct and Indirect Quotes   Let's look at an example of how a bid and offer rate might work. The rate a dealer quotes for the British pound might be $1.6469/71 (assume the dealer is U.S. based). This means the dealer is willing to buy pounds at $1.6469 each and sell them for $1.6471 each. Obviously, a dealer wants to buy low and sell high. In this example, the dealer quotes the foreign currency as the number of U.S. dollars for one unit of that currency. This method of quoting exchange rates is called the **direct quote,** also known in the foreign-exchange industry as **American terms.** It represents a quote from the point of view of someone in the United States.

The other convention for quoting foreign exchange is known as **European terms,** which is the direct quote for someone located in Europe. Using the example of the British pound and U.S. dollar, that means the direct quote in Europe would be the number of British pounds per dollar. This is also sometimes called the **indirect quote** in the United States. In Table 9.2, the direct quote for the U.K. pound is $1.6469, and the indirect quote is £0.6072.

Base and Term Currencies   When dealers quote currencies to their customers, they always quote the **base currency** (the denominator) first, followed by the **terms currency** (the numerator). A quote for USD/JPY (also shown as USDJPY = X) means the dollar is the base currency and the yen is the terms currency. If you know the dollar/yen quote, you can divide that rate into 1 to get the yen/dollar quote. In other words, the exchange rate in American terms is the reciprocal or inverse of the exchange rate in European terms. For example, using the rates in Table 9.2 for the Japanese yen, $1/.010348 = ¥96.64$.

In a dollar/yen quote, the dollar is the denominator and the yen is the numerator. By tracking changes in the exchange rate, managers can determine whether the base

Key foreign-exchange terms:

- Bid—the rate at which traders buy foreign exchange.
- Offer—the rate at which traders sell foreign exchange.
- Spread—the difference between bid and offer rates.
- American terms, or direct quote—the number of dollars per unit of foreign currency.
- European terms, or indirect quote—the number of units of foreign currency per dollar.

TABLE 9.2   Foreign-Exchange Markets, July 1, 2009

The *direct* quote—the price of the foreign currency in terms of the home-country currency—is given in the column headed "In U.S. $"; the *indirect* quote—the price of the home-country currency in terms of the foreign currency—is given in the column headed "Per U.S. $."

Currencies

U.S. dollar foreign-exchange rates in late New York trading   July 1, 2009

Country/currency	Wed In U.S.$	Wed Per U.S.$	US$vs, YTDchg (%)	Country/currency	Wed In U.S.$	Wed Per U.S.$	US$vs, YTDchg (%)
Americas				**Europe**			
Argentina peso*	0.2633	3.7979	10.0	**Czech Rep.** koruna**	0.05494	18.202	−5.3
Brazil real	0.5174	1.9327	−16.5	**Denmark** krone	0.1900	5.2632	−1.2
Canada dollar	0.8701	1.1493	−5.5	**Euro area** euro	1.4142	0.7071	−1.2
1 mo forward	0.8702	1.1492	−5.6	**Hungary** forint	0.005256	190.26	0.1
3 mos forward	0.8706	1.1486	−5.6	**Norway** krone	0.1578	6.3371	−8.9
6 mos forward	0.8710	1.1481	−5.5	**Poland** zloty	0.3251	3.0760	3.6
Chile peso	0.001859	537.92	−15.7	**Russia** ruble†	0.03233	30.931	1.3
Colombia peso	0.0004794	2,085.94	−7.2	**Sweden** krona	0.1319	7.5815	−3.1
Ecuador US dollar	1	1	unch	**Switzerland** franc	0.9303	1.0749	0.7
Mexico peso*	0.0763	13.1148	−4.4	1 mo forward	0.9307	1.0745	0.7
Peru new sol	0.3314	3.018	−3.7	3 mos forward	0.9315	1.0735	0.7
Uruguay peso†	0.04320	23.15	−5.1	6 mos forward	0.9329	1.0719	0.9
Venezuela b. fuerte	0.465701	2.1473	unch	**Turkey** lira**	0.6558	1.5249	−1.0
				UK pound	1.6469	0.6072	−11.4
Asia-Pacific				1 mo forward	1.6469	0.6072	−11.5
Australia dollar	0.8072	1.23892	−11.9	3 mos forward	1.6467	0.6073	−11.5
China yuan	0.1463	6.8341	−0.2	6 mos forward	1.6463	0.6074	−11.5
Hong Kong dollar	0.1290	7.7498	unch				
India rupee	0.02093	47.778	−1.7	**Middle East/Africa**			
Indonesia rupiah	0.0000981	10194	−6.5	**Bahrain** dinar	2.6526	0.3770	unch
Japan yen	0.010348	96.64	6.5	**Egypt** pound*	0.1788	5.5935	1.7
1 mo forward	0.010352	96.60	6.5	**Israel** shekel	0.2593	3.8565	2.0
3 mos forward	0.010359	96.53	6.6	**Jordan** dinar	1.4138	0.7073	−0.2
6 mos forward	0.010374	96.39	6.7	**Kuwait** dinar	3.4763	0.2877	4.1
Malaysia ringgit	0.2842	3.5186	1.9	**Lebanon** pound	0.0006634	1,507.39	unch
New Zealand dollar	0.6390	1.5649	−8.2	**Saudi Arabia** riyal	0.2667	3.7495	−0.1
Pakistan rupee	0.01240	80.645	1.9	**South Africa** rand	0.1292	7.7399	−17.6
Philippines peso	0.0209	47.962	1.1	**UAE** dirham	0.2723	3.6724	unch
Singapore dollar	0.6925	1.4440	0.8				
South Korea won	0.0007942	1,259.13	−0.3				
Taiwan dollar	0.03057	32.712	−0.2				
Thailand baht	0.02937	34.048	−2.1				
Vietnam dong	0.00005618	17,801	1.8	SDR††	1.5468	.6465	-0.4

*Floating rate
†Financial
§Government rate
†Russian Central Bank rate
**Rebased as of Jan 1, 2005
††Special Drawing Right (SDR); from the International Monetary Fund; based on exchange rates for U.S. dollar, British pound, euro, and Japanese yen.
Note: Based on trading among banks of $1 million and more, as quoted at 4 p.m. ET by Reuters.

MAP 9.2   International Time Zones and the Single World Market

The world's communication networks are now so good that we can talk of a single world market. It starts in a small way in New Zealand at around 9:00 a.m. (local time), just in time to catch the tail end of the previous night's market in New York (where it's about 4:00 p.m. local time). Two or three hours later, Tokyo opens, followed an hour later by Hong Kong and Manila, and then half an hour later by Singapore. By now, with the Far East market in full swing, the focus moves to the Near and Middle East. Mumbai (formerly Bombay) opens two hours after Singapore, followed after an hour and a half by Abu Dhabi and Athens. At this stage, trading in the Far and Middle East is usually thin as dealers wait to see how Europe will trade. Paris and Frankfurt open an hour ahead of London, and by this time Tokyo is starting to close down, so the European market can judge the Japanese market. By lunchtime in London, New York is starting to open up, and as Europe closes down, positions can be passed westward. Midday in New York, trading tends to be quiet because there is nowhere to pass a position to. The San Francisco market, three hours behind New York, is effectively a satellite of the New York market, although very small positions can be passed on to New Zealand banks. (Note that in the former Soviet Union, standard time zones are advanced an hour. Also note that some countries and territories have adopted half-hour time zones, as shown by hatched lines.)

Source: Adapted from Julian Walmsley, *The Foreign Exchange Handbook* (New York: John Wiley, 1983): 7–8. Reprinted by permission of John Wiley & Sons, Inc. Some information taken from *The Cambridge Factfinders,* 3rd ed., David Crystal (ed.) (New York: Cambridge University Press, 1998): 440.

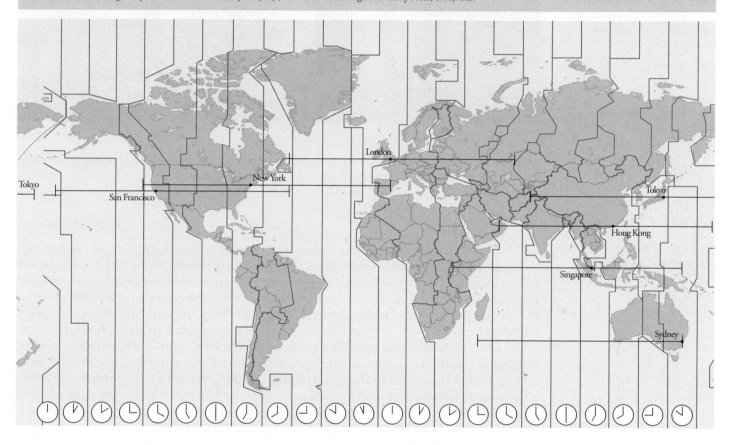

currency is strengthening or weakening. For example, on June 1, 2009, the dollar/yen rate was ¥95.37210/$1.00, and on July 15, 2009, the rate was ¥93.11880/$1.00. As the numerator falls, the base currency—the dollar—is weakening or getting less expensive. Conversely, the terms currency—or the yen in this case—is strengthening or getting more expensive from a dollar perspective.

There are many ways to get exchange rate quotes, including online as well as in print media. Because most currencies constantly fluctuate in value, many managers check the values daily. For example, the *Wall Street Journal* provides quotes in American terms (U.S. $ equivalent) and European terms (currency per U.S. $), as shown in Table 9.2. All quotes, except those noted as one-month, three-month, and six-month forward, are spot quotes.

Interbank Transactions   The spot rates provided by the WSJ are the selling rates for interbank transactions of $1 million and more. **Interbank transactions** are transactions between banks. Retail transactions, those between banks and companies or individuals, provide fewer foreign currency units per dollar than interbank transactions. Similar

Tourists in Istanbul, Turkey, get cash from one of four automatic teller machines (ATMs)–Garanti, HSBC, AKBANK, TÜERKIYE BANKASI. ATMs usually offer better exchange rates than tourists can get by exchanging cash with a foreign-exchange trader. HSBC is the only non-Turkish bank, but all four normally honor debit cards from other countries.
Source: Getty Images, Inc.

quotes can be found in other business publications and online. However, these are only approximations, and exact quotes are available through the dealers.

THE FORWARD MARKET

> The forward rate is the rate quoted for transactions that call for delivery after two business days.

As noted earlier, the spot market is for foreign-exchange transactions that occur within two business days, but in some transactions, a seller extends credit to the buyer for a period longer than two days. For example, a Japanese exporter of consumer electronics might sell television sets to a U.S. importer with immediate delivery but payment due in 30 days. The U.S. importer is obligated to pay in yen in 30 days and may enter into a contract with a currency dealer to deliver the yen at a forward rate—the rate quoted today for future delivery.

In addition to the spot rates for each currency, Table 9.2 shows the forward rates for the British pound, Canadian dollar, Japanese yen, and Swiss franc. These are the most widely traded currencies in the forward market. However, forward contracts are available from dealers in many other currencies as well. The more exotic the currency, the more difficult it is to get a forward quote out too far in the future, and the greater the difference is likely to be between the forward rate and the spot rate.

> A forward discount exists when the forward rate is less than the spot rate.

Forward Discounts and Premiums   Building on what we said earlier, we now can say that the difference between the spot and forward rates is either the **forward discount** or the **forward premium.** An easy way to understand the difference between the forward rate and the spot rate for U.S. companies is to use currency quotes in American terms. If the forward rate for a foreign currency is less than the spot rate, then the foreign currency is selling at a forward discount. If the forward rate is greater than the spot rate, the foreign currency is selling at a forward premium. Using the direct quotes in Table 9.2 for the Swiss franc for a six-month forward contract, the premium or discount would be computed as follows:

$$\frac{0.9329 - 0.9303}{0.9303} \times \frac{12}{6} = 0.0055894 \text{ or } 0.56\%$$

> A premium exists when the forward rate is greater than the spot rate.

The premium percentage is annualized by multiplying the difference between the spot and forward rates by 12 months divided by the number of months forward—or six months in this example. Because the forward rate is greater than the spot rate, the Swiss franc is selling at a premium in the forward market by only 0.56 percent over the spot market.

OPTIONS

An *option* is the *right*, but not the *obligation*, to buy or sell a foreign currency within a certain time period or on a specific date at a specific exchange rate. An option can be purchased OTC from a commercial or investment bank, or it can be purchased on an exchange. For example, assume a U.S. company purchases an OTC option from a commercial or investment bank to buy 1,000,000 Japanese yen at ¥118.76 per U.S. $ ($0.008420 per yen)—or $8,420. The writer of the option will charge the company a fee for writing the option. The more likely the option is to benefit the company, the higher the fee. The rate of ¥118.76 is called the *strike price* for the option. The fee or cost of the option is called the *premium*.

On the date when the option is set to expire, the company can look at the spot rate and compare it with the strike price to see what the better exchange rate is. If the spot rate were ¥125 per U.S. $ ($0.00800 per yen)—or $8,000—it would not exercise the option because buying yen at the spot rate would cost less than buying them at the option rate. However, if the spot rate at that time were ¥96 per U.S. $ ($0.01042 per yen)—or $10,417— the company would exercise the option because buying at the option rate would cost less than buying at the spot rate.

The option provides the company flexibility because it can walk away from the option if the strike price is not a good price. In the case of a forward contract, the cost is usually cheaper than the cost for an option, but the company cannot walk away from the contract. So a forward contract is cheaper but less flexible than an option.

The above example is for a simple, or *vanilla*, option. However, exotic or structured options are used more widely to hedge exposure, especially by European companies. The idea behind a structured option is to provide an option product for a company that meets the company's risk profile and tolerance and results in a premium that is as close to zero as possible. The writer of the option can still make money on the structured option, but if the option is set up effectively, the company buying the option won't have to write out a big check for the premium. Exchange-traded options are more of the vanilla variety, whereas nonexchange traders have more flexibility to sell structured options.

> An option is the right, but not the obligation, to trade a foreign currency at a specific exchange rate.

FUTURES

A foreign currency futures contract resembles a forward contract insofar as it specifies an exchange rate some time in advance of the actual exchange of currency. However, a future is traded on an exchange, not OTC. Instead of working with a banker, companies work with exchange brokers when purchasing futures contracts. A forward contract is tailored to the amount and time frame the company needs, whereas a futures contract is for a specific amount and specific maturity date.

The futures contract is less valuable to a company than a forward contract. However, it may be useful to speculators and small companies that cannot enter into a forward contract.

> A futures contract specifies an exchange rate in advance of the actual exchange of currency, but it is not as flexible as a forward contract.

The Foreign-Exchange Trading Process

When a company sells goods or services to a foreign customer and receives foreign currency, it needs to convert the foreign currency into the domestic currency. When importing, the company needs to convert domestic to foreign currency to pay the foreign supplier. This conversion usually takes place between the company and its bank.

Originally, the commercial banks provided foreign-exchange services for their customers. Eventually, some of these commercial banks in New York and other U.S. money centers, such as Chicago and San Francisco, began to look at foreign-exchange trading as a major business activity instead of just a service. They became intermediaries for smaller banks by establishing correspondent relationships with them. They also became major dealers in foreign exchange.

The left side of Figure 9.4 shows what happens when U.S. Company A needs to sell euros for dollars. This situation could arise when U.S. Company A receives payment in

> Large MNEs go through their money center banks to settle foreign-exchange balances, but other firms use local banks or other financial institutions.

euros from a German importer. The right side of the figure shows what happens when U.S. Company A needs to buy euros with dollars. This situation could arise when a company has to pay euros to a German supplier.

In either case, the U.S. company would contact its bank for help in converting the currency. If the company is a large MNE, such as a Fortune 500 company in the United States or a Global Fortune 500 company, it will probably deal directly with a money center bank like HSBC (as shown on the top arrow in Figure 9.4) and not worry about another financial institution. Generally, because the MNE already has a strong banking relationship with its money center bank (or several different money center banks), the bank trades foreign exchange for the client as one of the services it offers. Companies below the Fortune 500 level operate through other financial institutions, such as local or regional banks or other banking institutions that can facilitate foreign-exchange trades. In that case, Financial Institution A and Financial Institution B still operate through a money center bank to make the trade, because those institutions are too small to trade on their own. They typically have correspondent relationships with money center banks to allow them to make the trades.

Assume that U.S. Company B is going to receive euros in the future. Because it cannot convert in the spot market until it receives the euros, it can consider a forward, swap, options, or futures contract to protect itself until the currency is finally delivered. Financial Institution B can do a forward, swap (or options) contract for Company B. However, Company B can also consider an options or futures contract on one of the exchanges, such as the CME Group. The same is true for Company A, which will need euros in the future.

BANKS AND EXCHANGES

At one time, only the big money center banks could deal directly in foreign exchange. Regional banks had to rely on the money center banks to execute trades on behalf of

FIGURE 9.4   The Foreign-Exchange Trading Process

Let's say that you're U.S. Company A, that you've received euros in payment for goods, and that you want to sell your euros in return for dollars. To make the exchange, you may contact your local bank or go directly to a money center bank.

On the other hand, perhaps you're U.S. Company B and you expect to receive euros as a future payment. To protect yourself against fluctuations in the exchange rate, you want to buy euros that you can subsequently trade back for dollars. You could choose, say, a forward or a swap, and your path would be essentially a mirror image of Company A's.

Finally, either Company A or Company B could choose to convert by such means as an option or a futures contract—in which case the trade could be made by an options and/or futures exchange, either directly or through a broker.

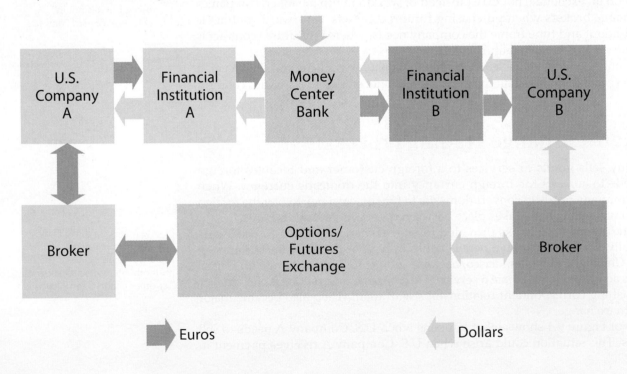

their clients. The emergence of electronic trading has changed that, however. Now even the regional banks can hook up to Bloomberg, Reuters, or EBS and deal directly in the interbank market or through brokers. Despite this, the greatest volume of foreign-exchange activity takes place with the big money center banks. Because of their reach and volume, they are the ones that set the prices in global trading of foreign exchange.

Top Foreign-Exchange Dealers   There is more to servicing customers in the foreign-exchange market than size alone. Each year, *Euromoney* magazine surveys treasurers, traders, and investors worldwide to identify their favorite banks and the leading dealers in the interbank market. In addition to examining transaction volumes and quality of services, the criteria for selecting the top foreign-exchange dealers include the following:

- Ranking of banks by corporations and other banks in specific locations, such as London, Singapore, and New York
- Capability to handle major currencies, such as the U.S. dollar and the euro
- Capability to handle major cross-trades—for example, those between the euro and pound or the euro and yen
- Capability to handle specific currencies
- Capability to handle derivatives (forwards, swaps, futures, and options)
- Capability to engage in research and analytics.[11]

Given the differing capabilities of banks, large companies may use several banks to deal in foreign exchange, selecting those that specialize in specific geographic areas, instruments, or currencies. In the past, for example, AT&T used Citibank for its broad geographic spread and wide coverage of different currencies, but it also used Deutsche Bank for euros, Swiss Bank Corporation for Swiss francs, NatWest Bank for British pounds, and Goldman Sachs for derivatives.

Table 9.3 identifies the top banks in the world in terms of foreign-exchange trading. They are the key players in the OTC market and include both commercial banks (such as Deutsche Bank and Citi) and investment banks (such as UBS—the London-based investment banking division of Union Bank of Switzerland and Swiss Bank Corporation). Whether one is looking at overall market share of foreign-exchange trading or the best banks in the trading of specific currency pairs, these top-10 banks are usually at or near the top in every category.

TABLE 9.3   Foreign-Exchange Trades: Top Commercial and Investment Banks, 2009 as Ranked by Overall Market Share

Trading Bank	Estimated Market Share %	Best in Euro/$	Best in $/Pound	Best in Euro/Pound	Best in $/Yen
1. Deutsche Bank	20.96%	1	1	1	1
2. UBS	14.58%	3	4	3	3
3. Barclays Capital	10.45%	5	2	2	5
4. RBS	8.19%				
5. Citi	7.32%	2	5	5	2
6. JP Morgan	5.43%				
7. HSBC	4.09%	4	3	4	4
8. Goldman Sachs	3.35%				
9. Credit Suisse	3.05%				
10. BNP Paridas	2.26%				

*Estimated Market Share source: "FX Poll 2009: Overall Market Share," Euromoney (May 2009) and Best in Currency source: "FX Poll 2008: Best for Currencies," Euromoney (May 2008)

The top banks in the interbank market in foreign exchange are so ranked because of their ability to

- Trade in specific market locations.
- Engage in major currencies and cross-trades.
- Deal in specific currencies.
- Handle derivatives (forwards, options, futures, swaps).
- Conduct key market research.

Concept Check

In Chapter 11, we explain why companies work so hard to establish and maintain effective value chains—frameworks for dividing value-creating activities into separate processes. For one thing, a reliable value chain permits a firm to focus on its core competencies—the unique skills or knowledge that make it better at something than its competitors. Because managing currencies and cross-trades is typically not among a firm's core competencies, its bankers are key components of its value chain.

TOP EXCHANGES FOR TRADING FOREIGN EXCHANGE

In addition to the OTC market, foreign-exchange instruments, mostly options and futures, are traded on commodities exchanges. Three of the best-known exchanges are the **Chicago Mercantile Exchange (CME) Group,** NASDAQ OMX, and NYSE Euronext.

Firms can also use securities exchanges for derivatives trade in foreign exchange.

CME Group   The CME Group was formed on July 9, 2007, as a merger between the CME (Chicago Mercantile Exchange) and the Chicago Board of Trade. The CME operates according to so-called open outcry: Traders stand in a pit and call out prices and quantities. The platform is also linked to an electronic trading platform, which is increasing in popularity. The CME Group trades many different commodities. In terms of foreign exchange, it trades a variety of futures and options contracts in numerous currencies against the dollar as well as in cross rates—such as the euro against the Australian dollar.

In 2005, CME entered into an agreement with Reuters to have its futures contracts quoted, which should increase the access of trades to futures contracts.[12] In March 2007, CME and Reuters teamed up again to launch the world's first centrally cleared global foreign-exchange platform called *FXMarketSpace.* The basic idea behind the model is to establish a centrally cleared global platform that allows customers to buy and sell currencies anonymously. The new venture is targeting hedge funds that are using computer-driven trading models to trade foreign exchange.[13]

Major exchanges that deal in foreign currency derivatives are the CME Group, NASDAQ OMX, and NYSE Liffe.

NASDAQ OMX   Prior to 2008, the Philadelphia Stock Exchange was one of the pioneers in trading currency options. In July 2008, PHLX merged with NASDAQ OMX. With this merger, they created the third-largest options market in the United States. They also formed a new hybrid of trading, which involves traditional floor trading and online trading as well. Options were being offered by PHLX in the Australian dollar, the British pound, the Canadian dollar, the euro, the Japanese yen, and the Swiss franc. Futures were offered in British pounds and the euro.[14] These activities have now been absorbed by NASDAQ OMX.

NYSE Liffe   The London International Financial Futures and Options Exchange (LIFFE) was founded in 1992 to trade a variety of futures contracts and options. It was subsequently bought in 2002 by Euronext, then a European stock exchange based in Paris but with subsidiaries in other European countries. Beginning in 2003, the electronic platform where its derivatives products traded on member exchanges was known as LIFFE CONNECT. In 2007, Euronext merged with the New York Stock Exchange to create NYSE Euronext. The international derivatives business of NYSE Euronext is now handled by NYSE Liffe, using the LIFFE CONNECT platform developed before the merger between NYSE and Euronext. According to their corporate Web site, NYSE Liffe is the world's second-largest derivatives exchange by value of transacted business.

Looking to the Future   Where Are Foreign-Exchange Markets Headed?

Significant strides have been made and will continue to be made in the development of foreign-exchange markets. The speed at which transactions are processed and information is transmitted globally will certainly lead to greater efficiencies and more opportunities for foreign-exchange trading. The impact on companies is that costs of trading foreign exchange should come down, and companies should have faster access to more currencies.

In addition, exchange restrictions that hamper the free flow of goods and services should diminish as governments gain greater control over their economies and as they liberalize currency markets. Capital controls still impact foreign investment, but they will continue to become less of a factor for trade in goods and services. The introduction of the euro has allowed cross-border transactions in Europe to progress more smoothly. As the euro solidifies its position in Europe, it will reduce exchange-rate volatility and should lead to the euro taking some of the pressure off the dollar, so that it is no longer the only major vehicle currency in the world. In addition, the yuan, the Chinese currency, is attempting to become more of an international currency, as will be discussed in Chapter 10.

Technological Developments

Technological developments may not cause the foreign-exchange broker to disappear entirely, but they will certainly cause foreign-exchange trades to be executed more quickly and cheaply. The advent of technology clearly has caused the market to shift from phone trades to electronic trades.[15]

It is hard to know how extensive online trading will become. Numerous companies now advertise online trading for investors, but that is not where most of the trades take place. The growth of Internet trades in

currency will take away some of the market share of dealers and allow more entrants into the foreign-exchange market. Internet trade will also increase currency price transparency and increase the ease of trading, thus allowing more investors into the market. It is interesting to note that Barclays Capital, the third-largest bank in foreign-exchange trades, is trying to build its online trading portal by offering automated exchange tools to financial and nonfinancial clients. One idea is to offer the system to their correspondent banks, who can then offer the system to their corporate clients. This is a response to the fact that foreign-exchange trading is shifting from telephone trades to online trades.[16] This will force the banks to offer more services to clients. In addition, Deutsche Bank and UBS, the top two foreign-exchange traders, are expected to expand their proprietary platforms for e-trading. ∎

How Companies Use Foreign Exchange

Companies enter the foreign-exchange market to facilitate their regular business transactions and/or to speculate. The treasury department of a company is responsible for establishing policies for trading currency and for managing banking relationships to make the trades. From a business standpoint, companies first of all trade foreign exchange for exports or imports and the buying or selling of goods and services.

For example, when Boeing sells the new 787 Dreamliner commercial airplane to LAN, the largest airline in South America, it has to be concerned about the currency in which it will be paid and how it will receive payment. In this case, the sale is probably denominated in dollars, so Boeing will not have to worry about the foreign-exchange market (nor, in theory, will its employees—see the cartoon in Figure 9.5). However, LAN will have to worry about the market. Where will it come up with the dollars, and how will it pay Boeing?

Concept Check

In Chapter 19, we discuss the functions of a company's CFO, not only in managing its cash flows, but in managing its *foreign-exchange exposure*— the extent to which fluctuations in currencies can affect the costs of its international transactions.

FIGURE 9.5 The Working Man's Foreign-Exchange Dilemma

Source: Copyright John Morris, Cartoonstock.com.

"Last week I had pesetas in my wage packet, this week it's escudos - that's the trouble with working for a multi-national company."

BUSINESS PURPOSES (I): CASH FLOW ASPECTS OF IMPORTS AND EXPORTS

When a company must move money to pay for purchases or receives money from sales, it has options as to the documents it can use, the currency of denomination, and the degree of protection it can ask for. Obviously, if Boeing wanted the greatest security possible, it could ask LAN to pay for the Dreamliner before LAN takes title to the aircraft. That is not very practical in this case, but sometimes it happens when the seller has all of the control in the transaction. More common is the use of commercial bills of exchange and letters of credit.

Commercial Bills of Exchange   When an individual or a company pays a bill in a domestic setting, they can pay cash, but they typically use checks—often electronically transmitted. The check is also known as a **draft** or a **commercial bill of exchange.** A draft is an instrument in which one party (the *drawer*) directs another party (the *drawee*) to make a payment. The drawee can be either a company, like the importer, or a bank. In the latter case, the draft would be considered a bank draft.

Documentary drafts and documentary letters of credit are often used to protect both the buyer and the seller. They require that payment be made based on the presentation of documents conveying the title, and they leave an audit trail identifying the parties to the transactions. If the exporter requests payment to be made immediately, the draft is called a **sight draft.** If the payment is to be made later—for example, 30 days after delivery—the instrument is called a **time draft.**

Letters of Credit   With a bill of exchange, it is always possible that the importer will not be able to make payment to the exporter at the agreed-on time. A **letter of credit (L/C),** however, obligates the buyer's bank in the importing country to honor a draft presented to it, provided the draft is accompanied by the prescribed documents. Of course, the exporter still needs to be sure the bank's credit is valid as well. The letter of credit could be a forgery issued by a "nonexistent bank." The exporter, even with the added security of the bank, still needs to rely on the importer's credit because of possible discrepancies that could arise in the transaction. The L/C could be denominated in the currency of the exporter or of the importer. If it is denominated in the currency of the importer, the exporter will still have to convert the foreign exchange into their currency through their commercial bank.

Although a letter of credit is more secure than a documentary draft without an L/C, there are still risks. For the L/C to be valid, all of the conditions described in the documents must be adhered to. For example, if the L/C states that the goods will be shipped in five packages, it will not be valid if they are shipped in four or six packages. It is important to understand the conditions of the documents. In addition, there is also counterparty risk, as mentioned above. Although a forged L/C is an obvious risk, the global financial crisis in 2008 exposed counterparty risk when banks did not have sufficient capital to stand behind their L/Cs. Prior to this, counterparty risk was not such a big thing, but businesses were hesitant to trust their banks in the fall of 2008 because they didn't know if the banks would be able to deliver on an L/C. In addition, letters of credit are irrevocable, which means that they cannot be canceled or changed in any way without the consent of all parties to the transaction.

A key issue related to this chapter is that the L/C needs to specify the currency of the contract. If the L/C is not in the exporter's currency, the exporter will have to convert the foreign exchange into their currency as soon as it is received.

Confirmed Letter of Credit   A letter of credit transaction may include a confirming bank in addition to the parties mentioned previously. With a **confirmed letter of credit,** the exporter has the guarantee of an additional bank—sometimes in the exporter's home country, sometimes in a third country. It rarely happens that the exporter establishes the confirming relationship. Usually, the opening bank seeks the confirmation of the L/C

With a draft or commercial bill of exchange, one party directs another party to make payment.

A sight draft requires payment to be made when it is presented. A time draft permits payment to be made after the date when it is presented.

A letter of credit obligates the buyer's bank to honor a draft presented to it and assume payment; a credit relationship exists between the importer and the importer's bank.

with a bank with which it already has a credit relationship. For an irrevocable letter of credit, none of the conditions can be changed unless all four parties to the L/C agree in advance.[17]

BUSINESS PURPOSES (II): OTHER FINANCIAL FLOWS

Companies may have to deal in foreign exchange for other reasons. For example, if a U.S. company has a subsidiary in the United Kingdom and the subsidiary sends a dividend to the parent company in British pounds, the parent company has to enter into the foreign-exchange market to convert pounds to dollars. If the parent company lends dollars to the British subsidiary, the British subsidiary has to convert the dollars into pounds. When they pay principal and interest back to the parent company, they have to convert pounds into dollars.

> Companies also deal in foreign exchange for other transactions, such as the receipt or payment of dividends or the receipt or payment of loans and interest.

Speculation   Sometimes companies deal in foreign exchange for profit. That is especially true for some banks, traders, and investors, but sometimes corporate treasury departments look at their foreign-exchange operations as profit centers and also buy and sell foreign exchange with the objective of earning profits.

Speculators take positions in foreign-exchange markets and other capital markets to earn a profit.

Investors can use foreign-exchange transactions to speculate for profit or to protect against risk. **Speculation** is the buying or selling of a commodity, in this case foreign currency, that has both an element of risk and the chance of great profit. For example, an investor could buy euros in anticipation that the euro will strengthen against other currencies. If it strengthens, the investor earns a profit; if it weakens, the investor incurs a loss. Speculators are important in the foreign-exchange market because they spot trends and try to take advantage of them. They can create demand for a currency by purchasing it in the market, or they can create a supply of the currency by selling it in the market. However, speculation is also a very risky business. In recent years, the advent of e-trading has attracted a lot of day traders in foreign exchange. The problem is that day traders rarely make money speculating in exchange rates. As we will show in Chapter 10, forecasting currency movements is indeed a risky business.

Arbitrage   One type of profit-seeking activity is **arbitrage,** which is the purchase of foreign currency on one market for immediate resale on another market (in a different country) to profit from a price discrepancy. For example, a dealer might sell U.S. dollars for Swiss francs in the United States, then Swiss francs for British pounds in Switzerland, and then the British pounds for U.S. dollars back in the United States, with the goal of ending up with more dollars.

> Arbitrage is the buying and selling of foreign currencies at a profit due to price discrepancies.

Here's how the process might work. Assume the dealer converts 100 dollars into 150 Swiss francs when the exchange rate is 1.5 francs per dollar. The dealer then converts the 150 francs into 70 British pounds at an exchange rate of 0.467 pounds per franc and finally converts the pounds into 125 dollars at an exchange rate of 0.56 pounds per dollar. In this case, arbitrage yields $125 from the initial sale of $100. Given the transparency of exchange rate quotes globally, it is difficult to make a lot of money on arbitrage, but it is possible for an investor who has a lot of money and can move quickly.

Interest arbitrage is the investing in debt instruments, such as bonds, in different countries. For example, a dealer might invest $1,000 in the United States for 90 days; or the dealer could convert $1,000 into British pounds, invest the money in the United Kingdom for 90 days, and then convert the pounds back into dollars. The investor would try to pick the alternative that would yield the highest return at the end of 90 days.

> Interest arbitrage involves investing in interest-bearing instruments in foreign exchange in an effort to earn a profit due to interest rate differentials.

Point **Yes** People trade in foreign exchange for a number of reasons, and one of them is speculation, which is not illegal or necessarily bad. Just as stockbrokers invest people's money to try to earn a return that is higher than the market average, foreign currency traders invest people's money in foreign exchange to make a profit for the investor. Or individuals can become day traders and try to make a profit trading online on their own. Speculation is merely taking a position on a currency in order to profit from market trends.

The electronic trading of foreign exchange has made it easier for a variety of different kinds of investors to speculate in foreign exchange. Hedge funds are an important source of foreign-exchange speculation. There is no one specific strategy that hedge fund managers follow to speculate in foreign exchange. However, the transparency in trading has driven the smaller players out of the market and allowed the large institutions and traders to earn profits on small margins that require large volumes of transactions. Hedge funds generally deal in minimum investments that are quite large, so the hedge fund managers that trade in foreign exchange trade in very large volumes. They might make long-term bets on a currency based on macroeconomic conditions, or they might try to balance off buy and sell strategies in currencies so that one side offers protection against the other side. In either case, the hedge fund manager is betting on the future position of a currency to earn money for the investors in the fund.

However, speculation is not for the faint of heart. Political and economic conditions outside the control of the speculators can quickly turn profits to losses, and probably quicker than is the case in the stock market. Currencies are inherently unstable. Consider the problems of the U.S. dollar in 2007 and 2008, when the dollar was quite weak against the euro and Japanese yen. What should hedge fund managers do? Their expectation of the future might be that the dollar will continue to weaken. But what if it strengthens? Conversely, they might think the dollar has reached its floor and is ready for a rise. That would argue that the managers should buy dollars. But when will the dollar rise and by how much? By mid-March 2008, the dollar had declined by 15 percent in the prior 12 months, but by May 2008, many experts felt that the dollar had reached a low point and was expected to rise. This was based on the market expectations that interest cuts by the Fed were expected to stop and that the credit crisis was beginning to soften. Now the speculators have to decide what to do with those expectations.

Sometimes speculators can buy a currency on the basis of good economic fundamentals, or they can buy or sell currency

Counterpoint **No** There are plenty of opportunities for a trader, whether in foreign exchange or securities, to make money illegally or contrary to company policy. The culture of individual traders trying to make money off trading foreign exchange or other securities, combined with lax controls in financial institutions, contributes greatly to these scandals.

One of the most publicized events in the derivatives markets in recent years involved 28-year-old Nicholas Leeson and the 233-year-old British bank Barings PLC. Leeson, a dealer for Barings PLC, went to Singapore in the early 1990s to help resolve some of the bank's problems. Within a year, he was promoted to chief dealer. The problem was that he was responsible for trading securities and booking the settlements. This meant that there were no checks and balances on his trading actions, thus opening the door to possible fraud.

When two different people are assigned to trade securities and book settlements, the person booking the settlements can confirm independently whether the trades were accurate and legitimate. In 1994, Leeson bought stock index futures on the Singapore International Monetary Exchange, or SIMEX, on the assumption that the Tokyo stock market would rise. Most dealers watching Leeson's feverish trading activity assumed Barings had a large client that Leeson was trading for, but it turns out he was using the bank's money to speculate. Because the Japanese economy was recovering, it made sense to assume the market would continue to rise, thus generating more profits for Leeson and Barings. Unfortunately, something happened that nobody could predict—the January 17, 1995, earthquake that hit the port city of Kobe.

As a result of the devastation and uncertainty, the market fell, and Leeson had to come up with cash to cover the margin call on the futures contract. A *margin* is a deposit made as security for a financial transaction that is otherwise financed on credit. When the price of an instrument changes and the margin rises, the exchange "calls" the increased margin from the other party—in this case, Leeson.[18]

However, Leeson soon ran out of cash from Barings, so he had to come up with more cash. One approach he used was to write options contracts and use the premium he collected on the contracts to cover his margin call. Unfortunately, he was using Barings' funds to cover positions he was taking for himself, not for clients, and he also forged documents to cover his transactions.

As the Tokyo stock market continued to plunge, Leeson fell further and further behind and eventually fled the country, later to be caught and returned to Singapore for trial and eventually prison. Barings estimated that Leeson generated because they feel that governments are following poor economic policies. When speculators looked at the economic fundamentals behind the economy of Thailand in 1997, they felt that the government was making poor choices and that the Thai baht could not continue to trade at its existing level. So they sold Thai baht on the assumption that the currency would have to fall. Is there anything wrong with that? Was the subsequent fall in the Thai baht because of evil speculators, or was it because the speculators profited on the inevitable? As long as markets are free and information is available, traders ought to be able to make some money on their predictions of the future.

The key is that currency speculation is a different way to invest money and allows investors to diversify their portfolios from traditional stocks and bonds. Just as foreign exchange can be traded for speculative purposes, trading in shares is also speculation. Even though we call such trades "investments," they are just another form of speculation hoping to gain a return that is higher than the market average and certainly higher than what a CD can yield. ▶

losses in excess of $1 billion, and the bank eventually was purchased by Dutch bank ING.[19]

Since the collapse of Barings, measures have been put into place in banks to prohibit such consequences, yet negative outcomes of rogue trading continue to happen. Leeson's record losses were surpassed in 2008 by Jérôme Kerviel of French bank Société Générale. Kerviel, a one time employee in the back office of Sociéte Générale (the part of the bank that processes transactions), became a trader in 2005 in the relatively unimportant Delta One trading unit. In his new position, he began trading futures on the bank's own account. His role was to take opposite positions on the direction of the market in order to earn money on the spread. However, he began to take one-way positions to earn even more money for the bank and hopefully earn a bigger bonus. The problem is that he bet that the European markets would rise, but instead they fell rather sharply in early 2008. Through a variety of actions that went against the internal controls of the banks as well as outright lies about what he was doing, he was able to fool bank insiders while he was hoping to cover his positions. However, the bank eventually found out what he was doing, and they discovered that Kerviel had exposed the bank to a €50 billion risk. By the time they had unwound all of their trading positions, the bank had lost €1.5 billion or $2.22 billion. Unlike Leeson, Kerviel was not using the bank's money to trade on his own account, but like Leeson, he created serious problems for his bank, which lost a lot of money.[20] ◀

The Global Economic Crisis: Icelandic Saga

CASE

In 2007, Iceland was named by the UN as one of the most successful economies in the West, ousting its Scandinavian neighbor Norway from the head of the league table of 177 countries that compared per capita on income, education, health care, and life expectancy. This was nothing short of a modern-day economic miracle for a country with a population of just 313,000, which, until just a few years earlier, had largely derived its meager income from the fishing industry. After turning its attention to finance, Iceland had presided over the fastest expansion of a banking system anywhere in the world.

In the thick of the action was Kaupthing. Founded in 1982 as a small financial advisory agency and securities brokerage, it went on to become Iceland's largest and most successful bank, doubling in size year after year in its heyday. As well as hoovering up Icelandic banks, it also became a key player in the economies of many other European countries.

Then, in October 2008, against the backdrop of the collapse in the global economy that created stresses in the entire banking industry, Iceland's success story began to spectacularly unravel. The bankruptcy of Lehman Brothers in the U.S. on September 15, 2008, had already sent a shock wave throughout the banking industry worldwide, resulting in mergers, more bankruptcies, and the unprecedented bailout of troubled banks and intervention by the U.S. and other governments. On October 8th, after the U.K. government mooted using antiterrorism legislation to freeze Kaupthing's U.K.-based assets, the Icelandic government stepped in to take control, and the once mighty financial giant was forced into administration.

A Little Background on Kaupthing

Kaupthing's humble early beginnings gave little indication of its later capacity to dominate financial markets. For the first decade, with less than 30 employees, senior staff was required to man the switchboard of the struggling brokerage during the receptionist's lunch break.

Its big break came in the mid-1990's, along with the liberalization of Iceland's economy and financial markets. The government was determined that its country would no longer be forced to rely on fishing as its principle source of wealth. The free market reforms fueled a credit boom, sent the stock market soaring, and created a wave of companies with overseas ambitions.

Acquisitions and Diversification

Kaupthing's initial foray abroad, made after establishing Iceland's first global mutual fund at home, was launching a company in Luxembourg. Growth then continued at a pace. Kaupthing launched on the Icelandic Stock Exchange in October 2000 and continued to plough resources into increasing its international operations. Between 2002 and 2005, Kaupthing negotiated nine deals in Switzerland, Sweden, and Norway, agreed to a $720 million (£446 million) merger with rival Bunadarbanki, and bought Danish bank FIH.

Kaupthing also became a key player in the British economy. In just five years, it underwrote more than £3 billion of debt to finance British deals and had taken stakes in major U.K. businesses, such as supermarket group J Sainsbury and leisure group Mitchells & Butler. It also snapped up U.K. merchant bank Singer & Friedlander for $884 million (£547 million) in 2005 and became a big investor in the London property market.

Iceland's Story

To understand some of the problems that later emerged, it is useful to look at Iceland's history too. The cicilized history of the volcanic and geologically active island began in the ninth century with the arrival of the first permanent settlers from Norway. After being ruled by Norway and then Denmark, it did not gain full independence until 1944.

As late as 1973, Iceland was classified as a developing country by the World Bank because of its poverty and excessive dependence on the fishing industry. Price setting was centralized on the isolated island, and taxes and trade tariffs were high, while imports and exports were highly regulated.

The financial system and political power of the island were intrinsically linked, until David Oddson, the prime minister between 1991 and 2004, led the movement to deregulate the capital markets and privatize state-owned companies—most significantly the banking sector.

Paying the Bill

Iceland's finance minister, Steingrimur Sigusson, a left-wing politician who had spent many years warning of the need to rein in the banks, summed up Iceland's position following the global credit crisis by saying that at the end of every good party, there is a bill that has to be paid. In Iceland's case, it was a very large bill indeed. In 2008, by the time the government stepped in to renationalize the banks, including Kaupthing, Iceland's banking assets amounted to around nine times its gross domestic product. The nation's currency, the krona, had lost more than half its value against the euro, inflation was running at 14 percent, and interest rates had been raised to 15.5 percent to deal with the crisis. At the center of the crisis were Iceland's banks, which, since being deregulated, had borrowed billions from international wholesale money markets with virtually no regulation.

Yet everyone became part of the boom, which took off in earnest at the turn of the millennium. For decades one of the poorest countries in Europe, Iceland could suddenly celebrate as the average family's wealth grew by 45 percent over five years. That wealth was invested in property, and easy access to 100 percent mortgages in foreign currencies was seen as a welcome change to the traditional pattern of young Icelanders living with their relatives until their mid-20s. It quickly became the norm to take a 100 percent loan (again, in a foreign currency) to furnish a house and buy a car. People rushed to put their savings and investments into stock-market-linked funds at the big Icelandic banks, with Kaupthing leading the way.

Many older people too became carried away by the new regime and were persuaded by the banks to invest their savings in high-yielding money-market accounts. Reykjavik, the nation's capital and home to Iceland's booming stock market, quickly adapted to the new era, transforming from a provincial fishing port to a glitzy hub. *Sed og*—Iceland's equivalent of "Hello!"—Magazine spoke gushingly of private jets, extravagant private parties, lavish second homes in St. Moritz, and yachts in St. Tropez. The banks, meanwhile, financed major construction projects, such as the National Concert Hall. It was a big change in culture for the country. Icelanders are, by nature, frugal people. Iceland was, for example, one of the few countries in the world that could meet the needs of its aging population with a fully funded pension system.

The Icelanders were not the only people to get carried away with the boom. Some 160,000 Britons deposited $4 billion (£2.5 billion) with Kaupthing Edge. And another account, 'Icesave' from rival Landsbanki, snapped up millions of investors with its aggressive saving rates of above 7 percent. More than 100 public bodies—including universities, charities, and local authorities—also ploughed more than $1.6 billion (£1 billion) of savings into Icelandic banks. Kaupthing, which was at the forefront of this newfound prosperity, was dubbed "the Goldman Sachs of the Arctic."

Early Warnings

There were many early warnings that all was not well. In a mere seven years since bank deregulation and privatization, Iceland's financial institutions had managed to rack up $75 billion of foreign debt. Or, to put it in context, Iceland's banks had borrowed more than $250,000 for every man, woman, and child in the country. Looming large in the background was an impossible burden on the modest reserves of the central bank in the event of default.

As far back as 2005, commentators said that the Icelandic economy was overheating. The krona was overvalued, and a current account deficit of 16.5 percent was a record high. Inflation was 8 percent—against the central bank's inflation target of 2.5 percent—fueled by a rapid rise in house prices, which topped 40 percent that year.

Although the government's policy of tax cuts took a share of the blame, the decision to let banks enter the state-controlled housing-loan market was seen as a major factor. To calm the problem, the central bank increased interest rates on 14 occasions, to the high of 15.5 percent. The move only attracted short-term investors, lured by the prospect of high-yielding Icelandic bonds after borrowing in low-interest environments elsewhere.

With alarm bells ringing, Fitch, the credit-rating agency, downgraded its outlook for Iceland, blaming imbalances in the economy. This prompted a similar action from Standard & Poor's, and a number of international investment banks began to speak publicly of their concerns. A spiral effect had begun.

In 2006, U.S. lenders refused to roll over $600 million in loans to Kaupthing, citing concerns over the domestic economy. The bank found alternative financing in Japan and Canada, but, alarmed by the change in attitude, it began to retrench. It sold assets, slowed lending growth, reduced costs, and even backed away from what would have been the biggest acquisition in its history: a buyout of NIBC, the Dutch merchant bank.

However, the more the krona weakened in response to international concerns, the louder the criticism emerged over Iceland's overheated economy. The more people talked of the potential crisis, the more investments flowed away from Iceland. Alarmed by their change in fortunes, the Icelandic government and business community set off on a series of international road shows to try to set the record straight. Their argument was that two thirds of the earnings of the country's main businesses were derived from abroad; therefore, they were less vulnerable to a downturn. In its favor was Iceland's well-stocked pension funds, which were funded at 120 percent of GDP, as well as a wave of foreign investment in its burgeoning aluminum and power industries.

It was not enough. In the autumn of 2008, as conditions tightened in the global credit market, it was quickly apparent that Icelandic banks were unable to refinance their loans. The krona was in free fall on the capital markets and was attracting some unwelcome comparisons to the catastrophic failure of the Zimbabwean currency. Foreign currency, the lifeblood of the Icelandic boom, was running out as international banks refused all pleas to lend money. The effects were felt all the way down the line, with ordinary householders waking up to find their foreign-currency home loans virtually doubling in size compared to the dwindling value of their incomes.

The Depths of the Crisis

On September 29th, the Icelandic government took a 75 percent stake in the country's third largest bank, Glitnir, to stem its short-term funding problems. One week later, with international markets becoming increasingly alarmed at the situation in Iceland and real fears that it could end in national bankruptcy, trading in Iceland's six-biggest financial shares (including Kaupthing) was suspended on the OMX Nordic Exchange Iceland. The government offered an unlimited guarantee for all savers, and Iceland's parliament, the Althing, swiftly passed emergency legislation enabling the government to intervene extensively in Iceland's financial system. Kaupthing's chairman, Sigurdur Einarsson, urged people not to be alarmist, saying that his was a strong and well-diversified bank with a good asset quality and a highly diversified loan portfolio. By this time, the writing was on the wall for all the major Icelandic banks, and pressure was mounting from the international community. In the U.K., for example, billions of dollars of taxpayer money was tied up with Iceland; its government, which was facing a credit crisis among its own domestic banks, was not in a forgiving mood. On October 7th, Iceland's government took control of the second- and third-largest banks, Landsbanki and Glitnir.

The repercussions were huge. More than $27 billion of depositors' money across Europe was in jeopardy. Kaupthing rushed to sell assets and loans around the world, in a desperate bid to stay in business—a move that had serious knock-on effects on creditors. It was, however, too late. On October 8th, the U.K.'s Financial Services Authority moved to stem a panic run on online deposit accounts at Kaupthing's U.K. subsidiary Kaupthing Singer Friedlander. The British regulator summarily sold deposit operations to its Dutch rival ING Direct, placing the remainder of Kaupthing's U.K. operations into administration. The British government then threatened to invoke antiterror legislation to freeze Kaupthing's assets, leaving Iceland with little choice than to seize control of its biggest bank and suspend trading on the stock exchange. On October 9th, Kaupthing was placed into receivership, following the resignation of the entire board of directors. In the following days, governments in Finland and Norway took control of operations on their home soil to prevent money from being sent back to Iceland.

Iceland's Prime Minister Geir Haarde was highly critical of his U.K. counterpart Gordon Brown, saying that he would be preparing legal action against the United Kingdom because the move to freeze its assets was partly responsible for Kaupthing's demise.

However, a more pressing concern was the desperate state of the economy. The mood of crisis was heightened further when the government suspended all public-service broadcasting, a measure usually reserved for volcano warnings. Haarde appeared on television to say the government was passing emergency legislation to save the economy from total collapse. At the same time as formally establishing new Glitnir, Landsbanki, and Kaupthing banks, the government cut interest rates by 3.5 percent from their record high of 15.5 percent, and the central bank raised its key interest rate to 18 percent from 12 percent.

In November 2008, the International Monetary Fund orchestrated a $2.1 billion package of bailout loans for Iceland, making it the first Western European nation to get an IMF loan since the United Kingdom in 1976. Sadly for the proud nation, the loan comes with stringent conditions that impose external financial controls and impinge heavily on Iceland's hard-won sovereign independence. It was a situation that Haarde could not recover from; in the face of widespread public protest, the Prime Minister called an election for May 9th the following year. He, in fact, only survived until January, when, having failed to form a coalition with the Social Democratic Alliance party, he announced the immediate resignation of parliament.

Johanna Sigurdardottir, the leader of the Social Democratic Alliance party that took over in February 2009, made it a priority to replace the central bank board, which had failed to prevent the collapse of the banking system, and to apply for full membership of the European Union, which the government has been reluctant to do for years. The path has also been set for the eventual abandonment of the krona in favor of the euro.

After much wrangling, Iceland has now embarked on the process of becoming an EU member. It has agreed to pay the British and Dutch governments more than $5.7 billion over the next few years to compensate them for the cost of bailing out savers who lost money to Icelandic banks. Icelanders now have to cope with the cuts in services and standard of living that will inevitably follow. Iceland's domestic production is expected to shrink by 9 percent in 2009 and a further 1 or 2 percent in 2010. It is estimated that 65 percent of Icelandic businesses are on the brink of bankruptcy, and unemployment has grown to 1 in 10 of the workforce. Inflation is at 12 percent, and house prices have plunged.

One survey found that a disturbing 50 percent of 18- to 20-year-olds were considering emigration, so the country now faces the prospect of its brightest talent being lured overseas.

It is a sorry finale to an economic transformation that turned a poor, isolated community into a powerhouse of banks and entrepreneurs, with global investments ranging from fund management to retailing.

Where Does Kaupthing Go from Here?

In November 2009, what was left of Kaupthing changed its name to Arion banki as part of the government's aim of total withdrawal from the banking industry following the crash. The move was billed as a signal of a new direction and new values, and the operation bears no resemblance to the previous financial powerhouse.

Meanwhile, regulators and prosecuting authorities are still looking forensically into the background of the collapse of the Icelandic banks. Under scrutiny are the many complex relationships Kaupthing forged with its major clients, as well as controversial transactions entered into during its last months of existence before it was taken into administration. Analysis of the company shows that its highest loans, totaling $9.6 billion, were given to companies connected to just six clients, four of whom were major shareholders in the company.

Legal experts and social commentators are expected to spend many years raking over Kaupthing's failure and the role of the various people involved in the bank. Although the first prosecutions are unlikely to take place before the end of 2010, it is likely that repercussions of the story have many years to run.[21] ■

QUESTIONS

1. What are the major factors that caused the krona to initially fall in value against other world currencies? What did the government of Iceland do to reverse the decline in the economy?

2. How has the fall in the value of the krona affected business opportunities for companies doing business in Iceland and in exporting and importing? Should the government replace the currency with the euro in order to stimulate the recovery? Why or why not?

3. What do you think the future of Arion should be in Iceland?

SUMMARY

- Foreign exchange is money denominated in the currency of another nation or group of nations. The exchange rate is the price of a currency.

- The foreign-exchange market is dominated by the money center banks, but other financial institutions (such as local and regional banks) and nonfinancial institutions (such as corporations and governments) are also players in the foreign-exchange market.

- Dealers can trade currency by telephone or electronically, especially through Reuters, EBS, or Bloomberg.

- The foreign-exchange market is divided into the over-the-counter (OTC) market and the exchange-traded market.

- The traditional foreign-exchange market is composed of the spot, forward, and foreign-exchange swap markets. Other key foreign-exchange instruments are currency swaps, options, and futures.

- Spot transactions involve the exchange of currency on the second day after the date on which the two dealers agree to the transaction.

- Outright forward transactions involve the exchange of currency three or more days after the date on which the dealers agree to the transaction. A foreign-exchange swap is a simultaneous spot and forward transaction.

- Approximately $3.2 trillion in foreign exchange is traded every day. The dollar is the most widely traded currency in the world (on one side of 86.3 percent of all transactions), and London is the main foreign-exchange market in the world.

- Foreign-exchange dealers quote bid (buy) and offer (sell) rates on foreign exchange. If the quote is in American terms, the dealer quotes the foreign currency as the number of dollars and cents per unit of the foreign currency. If the quote is in European terms, the dealer quotes the number of units of the foreign currency per dollar. The numerator is called the *terms currency* and the denominator the *base currency*.

- If the foreign currency in a forward contract is expected to strengthen in the future (the dollar equivalent of the foreign currency is higher in the forward market than in the spot market), the currency is selling at a premium. If the opposite is true, it is selling at a discount.

- An option is the right, but not the obligation, to trade foreign currency in the future. Options can be traded OTC or on an exchange.

- A foreign currency future is an exchange-traded instrument that guarantees a future price for the trading of foreign exchange, but the contracts are for a specific amount and specific maturity date.

- Companies work with foreign-exchange dealers to trade currency. Dealers also work with each other and can trade currency through voice brokers, electronic brokerage services, or directly with other bank dealers. Internet trades of foreign exchange are becoming more significant.

- The major institutions that trade foreign exchange are the large commercial and investment banks and securities exchanges. Commercial and investment banks deal in a variety of different currencies all over the world. The CME Group and the Philadelphia Stock Exchange trade currency futures and options.

- Companies use foreign exchange to settle transactions involving the imports and exports of goods and services, for foreign investments, and to earn money through *arbitrage* or *speculation*.

KEY TERMS

American terms (p. 373)
arbitrage (p. 383)
Bank for International Settlements (BIS) (p. 367)
base currency (p. 373)
bid (p. 373)
Chicago Mercantile Exchange (CME) Group (p. 380)
confirmed letter of credit (p. 382)
cross rate (p. 371)
currency swap (p. 369)
derivative (p. 369)
direct quote (p. 373)

draft (or commercial bill of exchange) (p. 382)
European terms (p. 373)
exchange rate (p. 367)
foreign exchange (p. 367)
foreign-exchange market (p. 367)
forward discount (p. 376)
forward premium (p. 376)
futures contract (p. 367)
FX swap (p. 369)
hedge fund (p. 369)
indirect quote (p. 373)
interbank transaction (p. 375)

interest arbitrage (p. 383)
letter of credit (L/C) (p. 382)
offer (p. 373)
option (p. 369)
outright forward transactions (p. 369)
sight draft (p. 382)
speculation (p. 383)
spot rate (p. 369)
spot transaction (p. 368)
spread (p. 373)
terms currency (p. 373)
time draft (p. 382)

ENDNOTES

1 *Sources include the following:* "Immigrants Sent 3.7 Billion Euros from Spain to Latin America in 2006, Says IDB Fund," press release, Inter-American Development Bank (June 5, 2007); "Remittances to Latin America and the Caribbean to Top $100 Billion a Year by 2010, IDB Fund Says," press release, Inter-American Development Bank (March 18, 2007); Marla Dickerson, "Cash Going to Mexico Likely to Start at a Bank," *Los Angeles Times*, (February 14, 2007): 21; Miriam Jordan, "U.S. Banks Woo Migrants, Legal or Otherwise," *Wall Street Journal* (Eastern Edition) (October 11, 2006): B1; Ioan Grillo, "Wired Cash," *Business Mexico* 12:12/13:1 (2003): 44; Julie Rawe, "The Fastest Way to Make Money," *Time* (June 23, 2003): A6; Rosa Salter Rodriguez, "Money Transfers to Mexico Peak as Mother's Day Nears," *Fort Wayne* (IN) *Journal Gazette* (May 1, 2005): 1D; Deborah Kong, "Mexicans Win Back Fee on Money They Wired," *Grand Rapids* (MI) *Press* (December 19, 2002): A9; Karen Krebsbach, "Following the Money," *USBanker* (September 2002): 62; Tyche Hendricks, "Wiring Cash Costly for Immigrants," *San Francisco Chronicle* (March 24, 2002): A23; Nancy Cleeland, "Firms Are Wired into Profits," *Los Angeles Times* (November 7, 1997): 1; David Fairlamb, Geri Smith, and Frederik Blafour, "Can Western Union Keep On Delivering?" *Business Week* (December 29, 2003): 57; Heather Timmons, "Western Union: Where the Money Is—In Small Bills," *Business Week* (November 26, 2001): 40.

2 Sam Y. Cross, *All about the Foreign Exchange Market in the United States* (New York: Federal Reserve Bank of New York, 1998): 9.

3 Cross, *All about the Foreign Exchange Market*, 9.

4 Bank for International Settlements, "Central Bank Survey of Foreign Exchange and Derivatives Market Activity in 2007" (Basel: BIS, December 2007): 5–8. The BIS Survey is done only once every three years, and the next survey will be completed in 2010.

5 Cross, *All about the Foreign Exchange Market*, 31.

6 Bank for International Settlements, "Central Bank Survey," 1.

7 Cross, *All about the Foreign Exchange Market*, 19.

8 Bank for International Settlements, "Central Bank Survey," 10.

9 Brian Dolan, "Tailoring Your Technical Approach to Currency Personalities," www.forex.com/currency_pairs.html (accessed October 8, 2009).

10 Cross, *All about the Foreign Exchange Market*, 12.

11 See "Foreign Exchange Poll 2009: Methodology," *Euromoney* (May 2009), 76.

12 Deborah Kimbell, "E-FX Takes Another Step Forward," *Euromoney* (February 2005): 1.

13 Peter Garnham, "Reuters Reveals Ambitions on Launch of FXMarketSpace," *Financial Times* (March 26, 2007): 21.

14 PHLX News Release, "The Philadelphia Stock Exchange and the Philadelphia Board of Trade to Expand World Currency Product Line with Launch of Options and Futures on Major Currencies," http://phlx.com/news/pr2007/07pr042707.htm (accessed April 27, 2007).

15 Steve Bills, "State St.'s Forex Deal a Lure for Hedge Funds," *American Banker* (January 23, 2007): 10.

16 Steve Bills, "Barclays Seeking Forex Boost via Online Offerings," *American Banker* (October 10, 2006): 17.

17 A confirmed letter of credit adds the obligation of the exporter's bank to pay the exporter.

18 More specifically, Leeson did not actually buy the contracts outright but rather paid a certain percentage of the value of the contract, known as the *margin*. When the stock market fell, the index futures contract became riskier, and the broker who sold the contract required Leeson to increase the amount of the margin.

19 "The Collapse of Barings: A Fallen Star," *The Economist* (March 4, 1995): 19–21; Glen Whitney, "ING Puts Itself on the Map by Acquiring Barings," *Wall Street Journal* (March 8, 1995): B4; John S. Bowdidge and Kurt E. Chaloupecky, "Nicholas Leeson and Barings Bank Have Vividly Taught Some Internal Control Issues," *American Business Review* (January 1997): 71–77; "Trader in Barings Scandal Is Released from Prison," *Wall Street Journal* (July 6, 1999): A12; Ben Dolven, "Bearing Up," *Far Eastern Economic Review* (July 15, 1999): 47; "Nick Leeson and Barings Bank," *bbc.co.uk*, at www.bbc.co.uk/crime/caseclosed/nickleeson.shtml (accessed May 19, 2005); Nick Leeson and Edward Whitley, *Rogue Trader* (London: Little, Brown, 1996): 272.

20 David Gauthier-Villars and Carrick Mollenkamp, "Société Générale Blew Chances to Nab Trader," *Wall Street Journal* (January 29, 2008): 1; Gauthier-Villars, Mollenkamp, and Alistair MacDonald, "French Bank Rocked by Rogue Trader," *Wall Street Journal* (January 25, 2008): A1; Gauthier-Villars and Mollenkamp, "Portrait Emerges of Rogue Trader at French Bank," *Wall Street Journal* (February 2, 2008), A1.

21 "An Unhappy Chain of Events but Nothing Is Broken," *Financial Times* (July 20, 2006); "The New Viking Invasion," *Times* (June 17, 2007); "A Cruel Wind," *Financial Times* (October 10, 2008); "Iceland Struggles for Control As It Nationalizes Kaupthing," *Times* (October 10, 2008; "UK Companies Locked Out of Landsbanki Accounts," *Times* (October 11, 2008); "The Big Chill," *Financial Times* (November 15, 2008); "Timeline: Iceland Economic Crisis," *BBC News* (February 2, 2009); "Kaupthing Leak Exposes Loans," Telegraph (August 4, 2009); "Iceland After a Year of Financial Crisis," *Financial Times* (October 9, 2009); "Iceland Pins Hopes on Financial Outsider," *Financial Times* (October 28, 2009); "Author of an Icelandic Saga That Went from Rock Stars to Ruin," *Guardian* (November 5, 2009); "Kaupthing Investment Deadline Looms," *Ice News* (November 30, 2009).

ten

The Determination of Exchange Rates

Objectives

- To describe the International Monetary Fund and its role in the determination of exchange rates

- To discuss the major exchange-rate arrangements that countries use

- To explain how the European Monetary System works and how the euro became the currency of the euro zone

- To identify the major determinants of exchange rates

- To show how managers try to forecast exchange-rate movements

- To explain how exchange-rate movements influence business decisions

He that has no money has no friends.

—*Arabian proverb*

its debt payments to the IMF and the World Bank. However, they finally worked out a concession while Argentina continued to work with its private creditors. As all of this was going on, the IMF issued a report criticizing some of Argentina's decisions that helped lead to the crisis. As it defended Argentina's dollarization of the peso, the government was forced to pile up a lot of debt to support the currency. Eventually, this debt was not sustainable, and the crisis ensued.[7]

The SDR is
- **An international reserve asset given to each country to help increase its reserves.**
- **The unit of account in which the IMF keeps its financial records.**

Special Drawing Rights (SDRs) To help increase international reserves, the IMF created the **special drawing right (SDR)** in 1969. Basically, the IMF printed money—the SDR—to support the fixed exchange-rate system that existed at that time. For a country to support its currency in foreign-exchange markets, it could use only U.S. dollars or gold to buy currency. However, there was not enough gold and dollars to do that, so the IMF created the SDR to give member countries instant reserve assets to supplement dollars and gold, thus expanding global liquidity.[8]

Therefore the SDR is an international reserve asset created to supplement members' existing reserve assets (official holdings of gold, foreign exchange, and reserve positions in the IMF). SDRs serve as the IMF's unit of account and are used for IMF transactions and operations. By *unit of account*, we mean the unit in which the IMF keeps its records. So instead of the IMF keeping its records in U.S. dollars or another currency, it keeps its records in terms of SDRs.

Currencies making up the SDR basket are the U.S. dollar, the euro, the Japanese yen, and the British pound.

For example, we noted earlier that the total quota the IMF holds is SDR 325 billion, which at current exchange rates (i.e., in the third quarter of 2009) was about $503 billion. The value of the SDR is based on the weighted average of four currencies. On January 1, 1981, the IMF began to use a simplified basket of four currencies for determining valuation. In 2009, the U.S. dollar made up 44 percent of the value of the SDR, the euro 34 percent, the Japanese yen 11 percent, and the British pound 11 percent.[9] These weights were chosen because they broadly reflect the importance of each particular currency in international trade and payments.

Unless the executive board decides otherwise, the weights of each currency in the valuation basket change every five years. The board determined this rule in 1980. A new value was established in 2000 for the period 2001–2005, and then again in 2005 for the period 2006–2010.

THE GLOBAL FINANCIAL CRISIS AND THE SDR

One of the fallouts of the global financial crisis in 2007–2009 was the concern over global liquidity, especially in the emerging markets. The G8 countries injected hundreds of billions of dollars into their financial systems and implemented large stimulus packages to get their economies moving. In addition, they injected huge amounts of cash into the IMF. In April 2009, the G20 (the G8 expanded to include the central bank governors of 19 countries and the EU) voted to give approval to the IMF to raise $250 billion by issuing SDRs and to put another $500 billion into the IMF for them to use in case of a systemic crisis. This increase of $750 billion will bring the IMF's available resources to $1 trillion, a significant amount of money.

Because of the global financial crisis, the G20 voted to significantly increase reserves available to the IMF to help countries in distress.

In addition, the Chinese and Russians are arguing for an expanded role of the SDR in the global economy, hopefully to offset the influence of the U.S. dollar as the world's main reserve asset. This is largely due to the fact that the dollar index fell 16 percent in the 2000s, hurting the dollar investments of the Chinese. The SDR is more stable than any single currency because it is valued by currencies that don't necessarily move in the same direction and magnitude. There is less variability in the value of the SDR than in the dollar. The Chinese would also like to see other currencies, such as the Chinese yuan (also known as the *renminbi*), be part of the basket of currencies that determines the value of the SDR.[10]

EVOLUTION TO FLOATING EXCHANGE RATES

The IMF's system was initially one of fixed exchange rates. Because the U.S. dollar was the cornerstone of the international monetary system, its value remained constant with respect to the value of gold. Other countries could change the value of their currency against gold and the dollar, but the value of the dollar remained fixed.

On August 15, 1971, as the U.S. balance-of-trade deficit continued to worsen, U.S. president Richard Nixon announced that the United States would no longer trade dollars for gold unless other industrial countries agreed to support a restructuring of the international monetary system. He was afraid that the United States would lose its large gold reserves if countries, worried about holding so many dollars resulting from the large U.S. trade deficit, turned in their dollars to the U.S. government and demanded gold in return.

The Smithsonian Agreement   The resulting **Smithsonian Agreement** of December 1971 had several important aspects:

- An 8 percent devaluation of the dollar (an official drop in the value of the dollar against gold)

- A revaluation of some other currencies (an official increase in the value of each currency against gold)

- A widening of exchange-rate flexibility (from 1 to 2.25 percent on either side of par value)

> Exchange-rate flexibility was widened in 1971 from 1 percent to 2.25 percent from par value.

This effort did not last, however. World currency markets remained unsteady during 1972, and the dollar was devalued again by 10 percent in early 1973 (the year of the Arab oil embargo and the start of fast-rising oil prices and global inflation). Major currencies began to float (i.e., each one relied on the market to determine its value) against each other instead of relying on the Smithsonian Agreement.

The Jamaica Agreement   Because the Bretton Woods Agreement was based on a system of fixed exchange rates and par values, the IMF had to change its rules to accommodate floating exchange rates. The **Jamaica Agreement** of 1976 amended the original rules to eliminate the concept of par values and permit greater exchange-rate flexibility. The move toward greater flexibility can occur on an individual country basis as well as on an overall system basis. Let's see how this works.

> The Jamaica Agreement of 1976 resulted in greater exchange-rate flexibility and eliminated the use of par values.

Exchange-Rate Arrangements

The Jamaica Agreement formalized the break from fixed exchange rates. As part of this move, the IMF began to permit countries to select and maintain an exchange-rate arrangement of their choice, provided they communicate their decision to the IMF. However, the IMF surveillance program determines the *de facto* exchange-rate system that a country uses. Then it classifies member countries according to the exchange-rate regime and monetary policy framework it actually uses.

The IMF also consults annually with countries to see if they are acting openly and responsibly in their exchange-rate policies. Each year, the countries notify the IMF of the exchange-rate arrangement they will use, and then the IMF uses the information provided by the country and evidence of how the country acts in the market to place each country in a specific category. Table 10.1 identifies the different exchange-rate arrangements and the countries that have each one. The arrangements described in the table are ranked primarily on their degree of flexibility, from

> The IMF surveillance and consultation programs are designed to monitor exchange-rate policies of countries and to see if they are acting openly and responsibly in exchange-rate policies.

TABLE 10.1   Exchange-Rate Arrangements and Anchors

Exchange rate arrangement	Exchange rate anchor				Monetary Policy Framework			
	US dollar	Euro	Composite	Other	Monetary aggregate target	Inflation-targeting	Other	Total
Exchange rate arrangement with no separate legal tender	7	2		1				10
Currency board arrangement	8	4		1				13
Other conventional fixed-peg arrangement	36	20	7	5	4			72
Pegged exchange rate within horizontal bands		1	2					3
Crawling peg	6		2					8
Crawling band	1		1					2
Managed floating with no pre-determined path for the exchange rate	8		3		17	10	6	44
Independently floating					1	34	5	40
Total	66	27	15	7	22	44	11	192

Source: Adapted from the International Monetary Fund, "De Facto Classification of Exchange Rate Regimes and Monetary Policy Frameworks," http://www.imf.org/external/np/mfd/er/2008/eng/0408.htm (April 30, 2008).

least to most flexible. It is also important to note that the classifications are based on each country.

The IMF classifies the currency regimes of countries according to the degree of flexibility—or lack thereof.

In addition, the IMF requires countries to identify their specific monetary policy framework. Some countries use an exchange rate such as the U.S. dollar as their anchor. Others use either monetary aggregate targets (such as M1 money supply) or inflation targets. Table 10.1 identifies the most recent exchange-rate arrangements and the monetary-policy framework used by each. The actual countries that fit in each cell can be found on the IMF Web site, as cited at the bottom of the table and in Map 10.1.

FIXED VERSUS FLEXIBLE CURRENCIES

The IMF classifies currencies into one of eight different categories, moving from the least to the most flexible. In reality, you could say that currencies are either *fixed* or *flexible*. If they are fixed, they lock their value onto something and don't change. If they are flexible, they move up and down in value against market forces. Their value is based on supply and demand.

Exchange Arrangements with No Separate Legal Tender

But what does that actually mean? At one end of the spectrum is the El Salvador colón, which has an exchange arrangement with no separate legal tender. That means that it uses another currency as an anchor. Note that seven out of 10 currencies in that category use the dollar as their anchor. A few other European countries use the euro as their separate legal tender.

Dollarization   Using the dollar as an exchange arrangement with no separate legal tender is also called *dollarization* of the currency, as illustrated in the opening case. The idea would be for a country to take all of its currency out of circulation and replace it with dollars. Basically, the U.S. Federal Reserve Bank (the Fed) would have greater control over monetary decisions instead of the governments of the local countries so dollarizing. Prices and wages would be established in dollars instead of in the local currency, which would disappear.

> Countries can adopt another currency in place of their own, as is the case with El Salvador.

The concern is that this would result in a loss of sovereignty and could lead to severe economic problems if the United States decided to tighten monetary policy at the same time those countries needed to loosen policy to stimulate growth. Unfortunately, this is exactly what happened in Argentina in 2002. Although Argentina's exchange-rate regime did not go to the extreme of dollarization, its currency board regime was just a step away. The currency board tied the peso closely enough to the dollar and to the decisions made by the U.S. Fed that the government's ability to use monetary policy to strengthen its stalling economy was limited. As a result of the experiences in Argentina and the low popularity of the U.S. government, most countries in Latin America have decided not to go the route of dollarization.[11]

CURRENCY BOARD ARRANGEMENTS

The second category of fixed exchange rates is *currency board arrangements*, which is what Argentina used to have. Now, however, only eight countries have currency boards. A currency board is an organization generally separate from a country's central bank. Its responsibility is to issue domestic currency that is typically anchored to a foreign currency. If it does not have deposits on hand in the foreign currency, it cannot issue more domestic currency.

> Other forms of fixed-exchange-rate regimes are currency boards, conventional fixed-peg systems, and pegged exchange rates within crawling horizontal bands.

The Hong Kong (HK) currency board uses the U.S. dollar as its anchor currency. Even though the HK dollar is locked onto the U.S. dollar, it moves up and down against other currencies as the dollar changes in value. Thus the HK dollar is both

◄ A bank employee loads an automatic teller machine with dollars in San Salvador, El Salvador. The U.S. dollar became the legal currency in El Salvador on January 1, 2001, replacing the currency of El Salvador, the colón.
Source: Getty Images, Inc.

MAP 10.1 Exchange-Rate Arrangements, 2008

About half of the nations in the world have opted for floating exchange rates; the rest have some sort of fixed rates. The U.S. dollar is the single most important currency anchor. Inflation targeting is popular for countries with floating exchange rates.

Source: Data is from "De Facto Classification of Exchange Rate Regimes and Monetary Policy Frameworks" (April 30, 2008), International Monetary Fund, http://www.imf.org/external/np/mfd/er/2008/eng/0408.htm.

Note: Given that this is a Mercator projection, the scale approximates east-west distance at the equator; however, the farther you move from the equator, the more the east-west distance is distorted.

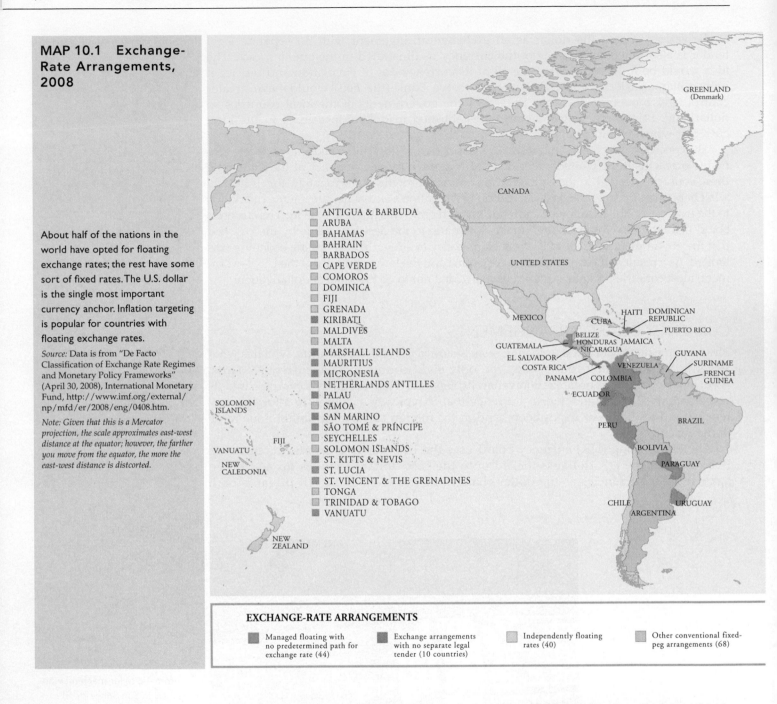

EXCHANGE-RATE ARRANGEMENTS

Managed floating with no predetermined path for exchange rate (44)

Exchange arrangements with no separate legal tender (10 countries)

Independently floating rates (40)

Other conventional fixed-peg arrangements (68)

fixed (against the U.S. dollar) and flexible (because the U.S. dollar is an independently floating currency).

PEGGED ARRANGEMENTS

In a *conventional fixed-peg arrangement*, a country pegs its currency to another currency or basket of currencies and allows the exchange rate to vary plus or minus 1 percent from that value. It is more similar to the original fixed exchange-rate system used by the IMF.

This is the largest category of all, with 72 countries, or 37.5 percent of the total. 56 of the 72 countries in this category use either the dollar or the euro as the anchor. A few countries peg their currencies within horizontal bands, which simply means that the degree of flexibility is just a little more than in a conventional fixed peg but not freely floating.

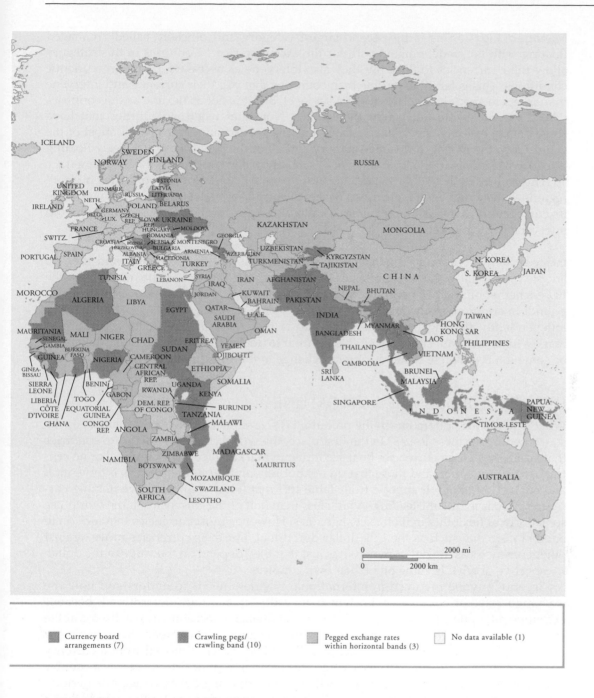

Currency board arrangements (7)

Crawling pegs/ crawling band (10)

Pegged exchange rates within horizontal bands (3)

No data available (1)

MORE FLEXIBLE ARRANGEMENTS

The last four categories have a much wider degree of flexibility.

Crawling Pegs   In the case of a *crawling peg* and a *crawling band*, the country maintains the value of the currency within a very tight margin (or slightly looser in the case of a crawling band), but it changes the value of the currency as needed. Thus it tries to maintain the value of the currency but does not hold rigidly to that value as economic conditions change. China is an example of a country that uses a crawling-peg exchange-rate arrangement. Even though it officially says that it uses a basket of currencies as its monetary policy framework, the IMF identifies the U.S. dollar as its *de facto* monetary policy framework. We note in our opening case that, whereas El Salvador has adopted the dollar as its currency, Costa Rica and Nicaragua, two of the countries with which it competes in CAFTA-DR, have adopted crawling pegs or crawling bands.

Flexible exchange-rate regimes include crawling pegs, exchange rates within crawling bands, managed floating rates, and independently floating rates.

Case Review Note

Managed Float   This is the second-largest category and officially called "managed floating with no predetermined path for the exchange rate." Countries in this category allow their currencies to float, but they also intervene as necessary, based on economic conditions. This is far more flexible than countries that peg their currency and intervene in markets to keep their currencies at a set level, but it is not as flexible as the countries whose currencies are independently floating. Note that whereas countries that have some degree of fixed or pegged exchange rate use an exchange-rate anchor, most of the countries in the managed floating category and all of the countries in the freely floating category use monetary policy frameworks such as money supply and inflation targets.

The countries that fit in this category are primarily developing countries from all regions of the world. Singapore uses a basket of currencies to determine how it will allow its currency to change value, whereas Thailand targets inflation to determine when to intervene in the markets.

Independently Floating   "Independently floating" is the final category and the one adopted for some of the key currencies in the world: the U.S. dollar, the members of the EU—whether or not they use the euro—the Swiss franc, the Japanese yen, and the British pound. In addition, many developing countries, such as Brazil, Mexico, and Chile, have independently floating currencies. This means that the currency floats according to market forces without central bank intervention to determine a rate, although there may be some intervention to moderate rates of change in the value of the currency.

EXCHANGE RATES: THE BOTTOM LINE

What is really the bottom line in the preceding discussion, and why should managers be concerned about these issues? In the first place, the world can be divided into countries that basically let their currencies float according to market forces with minimal or no central bank intervention and those that do not but rely on heavy central bank intervention and control. Although it appears from Table 10.1 that fewer countries have floating currencies, that is a little misleading. A little less than half of the currencies in the world use some form of flexibility in their exchange rates. However, most currencies that lock on to another currency such as the U.S. dollar don't float, but their currencies move against other currencies as the dollar moves. It is just that they depend on the value of the dollar, irrespective of what is going on in their own countries.

> Countries may change the exchange-rate regime they use, so managers need to monitor country policies carefully.

Second, anyone involved in international business needs to understand how the exchange rates of countries with which they do business are determined, because exchange rates affect marketing, production, and financial decisions, as we discuss at the end of the chapter. Note that sometimes countries change their approach to managing or not managing their currency, as Argentina did in 2002 when it moved from a currency board to managed floating currency. Chile was listed in a prior IMF survey as a country that kept its exchange rate within a crawling band, adjusting the exchange rate periodically according to inflation. But in late 1999, Chile suspended the trading bands that it had established around the peso and moved to a floating-rate regime in an effort to stimulate export-led economic growth—and it is still in that category. Likewise, in 2001, Iceland moved from a pegged regime, within a horizontal band, to a free-floating regime. Brazil did the same thing in early 1999; so did Turkey in 2001.[12]

Map 10.1 identifies the countries that fit into each category summarized in Table 10.1. Because a country's classification is constantly subject to change, managers should consult the IMF frequently for updates. In addition, it is necessary to supplement the IMF information with current events, as illustrated in the earlier examples of currency regime changes in Chile and Iceland.

It is important for MNEs to understand the exchange-rate arrangements for the currencies of countries where they are doing business so they can forecast trends more accurately. It is much easier to forecast a future exchange rate for a relatively stable currency pegged to the U.S. dollar, such as the Hong Kong dollar, than for a currency that is freely floating, such as the Japanese yen.

THE EURO

One of the most ambitious examples of an exchange arrangement with no separate legal tender is the creation of the euro. Not content with the economic integration envisaged in the Single European Act, the EU nations signed the Treaty of Maastricht in 1992, which set steps to accomplish two goals: political union and monetary union. The decision to move to a common currency in Europe has eliminated currency as a barrier to trade. To replace each national currency with a single European currency called the euro, the countries had to converge their economic policies first. It is not possible to have different monetary policies in each member country and one currency.

The European Monetary System and the European Monetary Union European monetary union did not occur overnight. The roots of the system began in 1979, when the **European Monetary System (EMS)** was put into place. The EMS was set up as a means of creating exchange-rate stability within the European Community (EC) at the time. A series of exchange-rate relationships linked the currencies of most members through a parity grid. As the countries narrowed the fluctuations in their exchange rates, the stage was set for the replacement of the EMS with the Exchange Rate Mechanism (ERM) and full monetary union.

According to the Treaty of Maastricht, countries had to meet certain criteria to comply with the ERM and be part of the **European Monetary Union (EMU).** Termed the Stability and Growth Pact, the criteria outlined in the treaty—which continue for euro applicants today—are the following:

Concept Check

Each of these commitments to greater economic cooperation represents a step in the direction of **regional integration,** a form of **economic integration** that we defined in Chapter 8 as the elimination of economic discrimination among geographically related nations. Here we emphasize that the **EU** has introduced a common currency to its already-existing internal free trade agreement and common external tariff policy.

The criteria that are part of the Growth and Stability Pact include measures of deficits, debt, inflation, and interest rates.

- Annual government deficit must not exceed 3 percent of GDP.
- Total outstanding government debt must not exceed 60 percent of GDP.
- Rate of inflation must remain within 1.5 percent of the three best-performing EU countries.
- Average nominal long-term interest rate must be within 2 percent of the average rate in the three countries with the lowest inflation rates.
- Exchange-rate stability must be maintained, meaning that for at least two years the country concerned has kept within the "normal" fluctuation margins of the European Exchange Rate Mechanism.[13]

After a great deal of effort, 11 of the 15 countries in the EU joined the EMU on January 1, 1999, and Greece joined on January 1, 2001. Those of the original 15 countries not yet participating in the euro are the United Kingdom (see the cartoon in Figure 10.1), Sweden, and Denmark (by their choice). Sweden announced in July 2002 that it had met all the criteria for joining the EMU,[14] but voters' rejection of the euro in 2003 has placed its entry on hold for the time being.[15] Denmark's currency is pegged to the euro, whereas the currencies of the United Kingdom and Sweden are free floating. With the exception of those three countries, the other members of the EU that do not use the euro as their currency are new member states. New member states that had adopted the euro as of 2009 are Cyprus, Malta, Slovenia, and Slovakia, so 16 of the 27 countries in the EU have now adopted the euro. In Table 10.1, 27 countries are identified as using the euro as their exchange-rate anchor. Five of those countries are members of the EU that have not yet adopted the euro, and most of the rest are countries in Africa or Eastern Europe. Most of the remaining EU countries that have not adopted the euro have independently floating currencies, and they use inflation as the framework to target the value of their currencies. This is consistent with the role of the European Central Bank in closely monitoring inflation as a means of setting interest-rate policy.

The euro is being administered by the **European Central Bank (ECB),** which was established on July 1, 1998. The ECB has been responsible for setting monetary policy and for managing the exchange-rate system for all of Europe since January 1, 1999. The ERM is important in converging the economies of the EU. Because the ECB is an

The United Kingdom, Sweden, and Denmark are the only members of the original 15 EU countries that opted not to adopt the euro.

The European Central Bank sets monetary policy for the adopters of the euro.

independent organization like the U.S. Federal Reserve Board, it can focus on its mandate of controlling inflation. Of course, different economies are growing at different rates in Europe, and it is difficult to have one monetary policy that fits all. Countries might be tempted to use an expansion fiscal policy to stimulate economic growth, but the deficit requirements of the ERM keep countries from stimulating too much.

PLUSES AND MINUSES OF THE CONVERSION TO THE EURO

The move to the euro has been smoother than predicted. It is affecting companies in a variety of ways. Banks had to update their electronic networks to handle all aspects of money exchange, such as systems that trade global currencies, buy and sell stocks, transfer money between banks, manage customer accounts, or print out bank statements. Deutsche Bank estimated that the conversion process cost several hundred million dollars.[16]

However, many companies also believe the euro will increase price transparency (the ability to compare prices in different countries) and eliminate foreign-exchange costs and risks. Foreign-exchange costs are narrowing as companies operate in only one currency in Europe, and foreign-exchange risks between member states are also disappearing, although there are still foreign-exchange risks between the euro and nonmember currencies—such as the U.S. dollar, British pound, Swiss franc, and so on.

The Euro and the Global Financial Crisis   After the initial introduction of the euro, the currency has steadily increased in strength and importance. In mid-2008, the euro was trading at around $1.59 per euro. But after Lehman Brothers filed for bankruptcy on September 15, 2008, the Dow Jones Industrial Average (DJIA) dropped over 500 points, followed by an even bigger loss on September 29, 2008. (The DJIA is a price-weighted average of 30 actively traded blue-chip stocks that is the most widely used indicator of the overall condition of the stock market in the United States.) An interesting thing happened in the exchange-rate relationship between the dollar and the euro. As can be seen in Figure 10.2, the collapse of the U.S. stock market at the end of September 2008 resulted in a drop in the value of the euro against the dollar. Two things emerged from these events. The first is that the initial reaction by global investors when the economic collapse hit was to put money into U.S. dollars—the flight to safety. Funds were pulled

During the global financial crisis, investors fled to dollars as a safe-haven currency and returned to euros when their appetite for risk increased.

FIGURE 10.2 The Euro vs. the Dollar

In the last quarter of 2008 when the global financial crisis hit, the euro fell against the dollar due to the safe-haven status of the dollar. As the U.S. economy began to recover and the stock market went up, investors fled dollars in search of higher returns, boosting the value of the euro.

Source: Data from "FXHistory®:Historical Currency Exchange Rates," *Oanda.com: The Currency Site,* at www.Oanda.com.

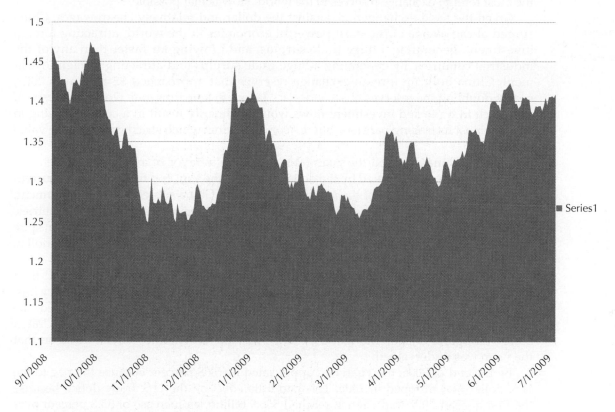

out of emerging markets and put into dollars as a safe-haven currency. This also pushed down the value of the euro. The second thing is that the value of the euro began to track with the fortunes of the U.S. stock market. As the market collapsed, so did the euro. When the stock market began to recover somewhat, so did the value of the euro. That is because the market sentiment shifted from safety to risk. The risk appetite meant that investors were pulling money out of dollars and investing them in emerging markets and equities. Then the euro became more attractive than the dollar as a place to invest money. As can be seen in Figure 10.2, the relationship between the euro and the dollar has been very volatile, with lots of peaks and valleys.

The role of the European Central Bank is to protect the euro against the ravages of inflation. Thus interests in Europe on average are likely to be higher than they are in the United States, especially during the crisis when the U.S. was keeping interest rates low to stimulate economic growth. Therefore, the spread in interest rates between the euro and dollar widened, favoring the euro as a place to invest funds.

The Chinese Yuan

Unlike the euro, the Chinese yuan (CNY)—also known as the renminbi (RMB)—is not an independently floating currency, but rather has a pegged exchange rate. Given the importance of China in the global economy, it is amazing that it does not have a floating exchange rate like the other major economies in the world. Going back to 1994, the Chinese government decided to fix the value of the yuan to the U.S. dollar at ¥8.690 (the symbol for the yuan is the same as the symbol for the Japanese yen). Now fast-forward to 2009, and the exchange rate is about ¥6.83, which is only 21 percent higher than it was 15 years earlier. However, China—one of the BRIC economies—is the third-largest country in the world, one of the largest trading countries, and the most populous nation on earth, and clearly has the most foreign-exchange reserves in the world. How is that possible?

Given the fixed exchange rate against the dollar and relatively cheap wages, China surged ahead as one of the most powerful economies in the world, attracting foreign investment, generating a huge trade surplus, and growing far faster than any of the industrial countries. By generating a huge trade surplus and attracting foreign investment, China built up foreign-exchange reserves that approached $2 trillion in 2009, nearly doubling the reserves of second-place Japan. In a floating-rate world, that type of mismatch in trade and investment flows would ordinarily result in a currency rising in value against its trading partners, but not so with China, which strictly controls the value of the CNY.

In 2005, China delinked the yuan from the dollar in favor of a currency basket. The basket is largely denominated by the dollar, the euro, the yen, and the won. These currencies were selected because of the impact they have on China's foreign trade, investment, and foreign debt. The yuan is also influenced by the currencies of several other countries, including Singapore, Britain, Malaysia, Russia, Australia, Thailand, and Canada. In spite of the basket, the IMF classifies China as using a de facto anchor against the U.S. dollar, not a currency composition as stated by China.

The central bank of China in Beijing decides a central parity rate daily and then allows a trading band on either side of the decided point. The move to the currency basket increased the yuan-to-dollar rate by 2.1 percent. Before the peg was delinked, the yuan was kept around $8.28; immediately following, it traded around $8.11. The United States, Europe, and Japan thought the change was too small and continued to assert that the yuan was undervalued.

By the end of 2006, the yuan had appreciated by 5.68 percent because the peg to the U.S. dollar was dropped in 2005. This had little effect on the U.S. trade deficit because the first quarter 2007 trade deficit reached $56.9 billion, an increase of 35.8 percent over the $41.9 billion deficit in the first quarter of 2005. Pressures from the international community, including the European Union, continued to be heaped on China. The central bank of China responded to the pressures by slightly widening the trading band of the yuan on May 18, 2007.

Some experts believe that China is gradually moving in the right direction; others believe they made an insignificant adjustment to gain goodwill in the international community before their trading partners made changes that would negatively affect them. Despite the widening of the trading band, pressure continues to mount on China to revalue its currency. Even the Big Mac Index discussed below identifies the CNY as being 48 percent overvalued.

PLAYING IT SAFE

Until the yuan began its ascent against the dollar, it was very easy to deal in foreign exchange in China because the rate was fixed against the U.S. dollar. It doesn't take a lot of judgment for a trader to operate in a fixed-rate world. In June 2005, the State Administration of Foreign Exchange (SAFE) in China decided to allow banks in Shanghai to trade and quote prices in eight currency pairs, including the dollar-sterling and euro-yen. Prior to that, licensed banks were only allowed to trade the yuan against four currencies—the U.S. dollar, the Hong Kong dollar, the euro, and the yen.

However, all the trades were at fixed rates, and they did not involve trades in non-yuan currency pairs. SAFE also decided to open up trading to seven international banks (HSBC, Citigroup, Deutsche Bank, ABN AMRO, ING, Royal Bank of Scotland, and Bank of Montreal) and two domestic banks (Bank of China and CITIC Industrial Bank).

Some argue that the steps being taken by SAFE are designed to build institutions and regulatory sectors as well as capability in trading before opening up the yuan to greater flexibility. SAFE is responsible for establishing the new foreign-exchange trading guidelines as well as for managing China's foreign-exchange reserves.

THE GLOBAL FINANCIAL CRISIS AND THE FUTURE OF THE CNY

The global financial crisis has pushed China closer to liberalizing its currency. One fear of the Chinese is that their massive dollar holdings might lose value if the U.S. economic stimulus results in future inflation. It has been lobbying for something else to replace the dollar as the major reserve currency in the world. Given that China would overtake Japan as the second-largest economy in the world by 2010 and Germany as the second-largest trading country in the world by the end of 2009, it is clear that they have to do something. Short of letting its currency float, China is working with the central banks of several countries to allow a bilateral swap in currencies so that they don't have to settle their transactions in dollars first. If their liberalization works, they hope to be able to directly settle on a bilateral basis of nearly half of their trade flows with emerging markets by 2012, making the CNY one of the top three currencies used in global trade.[17]

In addition, two non-Chinese banks, HSBC and Hong Kong–based Bank of East Asia, have been given permission to issue yuan-denominated bonds in Hong Kong.[18] Clearly, China is moving to put its currency on the world stage as an important currency, but until it allows the CNY to become independently floating, it will lack the status and liquidity of the other major currencies in the world.

China is trying to increase the importance of the yuan in the global economy and reduce the importance of and reliance on the U.S. dollar.

Point ▷ ◁ Counterpoint

Should Africa Develop a Common Currency?

Point ▷ **Yes** The success of the euro and the deep economic and political problems in Africa have caused many experts to wonder if African nations should attempt to develop one common currency in Africa with a central bank to set monetary policy.[19] In 2003, the Association of African Central Bank Governors of the African Union (AU) announced it would work to create a common currency by 2021. The 53-member AU was created as a successor to the African Economic Community and the Organization of African Unity.

The development of a common currency would be great for Africa because it would hasten economic integration in a continent that desperately needs to increase market size to achieve more trade and greater economies of scale. A common currency would lower transaction costs and make it easier to engage in trade among countries.

There are several degrees of economic cooperation in Africa already, including three forms of currency cooperation. These three regional monetary unions are the Common Monetary Area (CMA), including Lesotho, South Africa, and Swaziland, based on the South African rand; the Economic and Monetary Community for Central Africa (CAEMC), including Cameroon, Central African Republic, Chad, Republic of Congo, Equatorial Guinea, and Gabon; and the West African

◁ **Counterpoint** **No** There is no way that the countries of Africa will ever establish a common currency, even though the African Union hopes to do so by 2021. The institutional framework in the individual African nations is not ready for a common currency. Few of the individual central banks are independent of the political process, so they often have to stimulate the economy to respond to political pressures. If the process is not managed properly and the currency is subject to frequent devaluation, there will be no pride in the region or clout on the international stage.

Further, each country will have to give up monetary sovereignty and will have to rely on other measures, such as labor mobility, wage and price flexibility, and fiscal transfers, to weather the shocks. Even though there is good labor mobility in Africa, it is difficult to imagine that the African countries will be able to transfer tax revenues from country to country to help stimulate growth. In addition, it is difficult to transfer goods among the different countries in Africa because of transportation problems that are not an issue in the EU.

The establishment of the euro in the EU was a monumental task that took years to establish, following a successful customs union and a gradual tightening of the ERM in

Economic and Monetary Union (WAEMU), including Benin, Burkina Faso, Côte d'Ivoire, Guinea-Bissau, Mali, Niger, Senegal, and Togo. The CMA countries are fixed to the South African rand, which is an independently floating currency. The linkage with the rand helps stabilize trading relations among the member countries.[20] The latter two monetary unions are part of the CFA franc zone, designated by the IMF as "other conventional fixed-peg arrangements" pegged to the euro. Although initially pegged to the French franc, the peg shifted to the euro in 1999 when France adopted the euro as its currency. All of the countries in the CFA franc zone are former colonies of France and maintain French as the official language, except for Guinea-Bissau and Equatorial Guinea, which were ruled by Portugal and Spain, respectively. The two groups of countries in the CFA franc zone each have central banks that monitor the value of the CFA franc.

The CFA franc zone has been successful in delivering low inflation, but it has not necessarily delivered high growth. The CMA is controlled by South Africa because of the size of its economy and the fact that the currency of the CMA is the South African rand. The members of the CMA are classified as "other conventional fixed-peg arrangements," with the exception of South Africa, which has an independently floating currency.

In addition to the three regional monetary unions, there are five existing regional economic communities: Arab Monetary Union, Common Market for Eastern and Southern Africa, Economic Community of Central African States, Economic Community of West African States, and Southern African Development Community. These groups are working hard to reduce trade barriers and increase trade among member countries, so all these groups would have to do is combine into one large African economic union, form a central bank, and establish a common monetary policy like the EU has.

A major advantage of establishing a central bank and common currency is that institutions in each African nation will have to improve, and the central bank may be able to insulate the monetary policy from political pressures, which often create inflationary pressures and subsequent devaluations. ▶

Europe. For Africa to establish a common currency, there needs to be closer economic integration first, so it is important to be patient and give Africa a chance to move forward. Maybe one way to move to a common currency is to strengthen the existing regional monetary unions and then gradually open up the unions to neighboring countries until there are three huge monetary unions. Then the three unions can discuss ways to link together into a common currency in Africa. ◀

Determining Exchange Rates

There are a lot of different factors that cause exchange rates to change. The exchange-rate regimes described earlier in the chapter are either fixed or floating, with fixed rates varying in terms of how fixed they are and floating rates varying in terms of how much they actually float. However, currencies change in different ways depending on whether they are in floating-rate or fixed-rate regimes. First we examine how supply and demand determines currency values in a floating world in the absence of government intervention. Then we show how governments can intervene in markets to help control the value of a currency.

NONINTERVENTION: CURRENCY IN A FLOATING-RATE WORLD

Currencies that float freely respond to supply and demand conditions free from government intervention. This concept can be illustrated using a two-country model involving

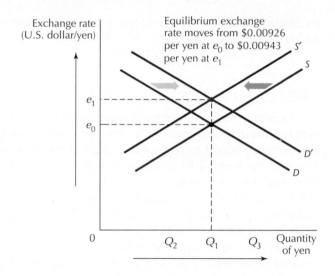

Exchange rate (U.S. dollar/yen)

Equilibrium exchange rate moves from $0.00926 per yen at e_0 to $0.00943 per yen at e_1

FIGURE 10.3   The Equilibrium Exchange Rate and How It Moves

Let's say that inflation in the United States is comparatively higher than in Japan. In that case (and assuming that Japanese consumers are buying U.S. goods and services), the *demand* for the Japanese yen will go up, but the *supply* will go down. What if Japan wants to keep the dollar-to-yen exchange rate at e_0? It can increase the supply of yen in the market—and therefore lower the exchange rate—by selling yen for dollars.

the United States and Japan. Figure 10.3 shows the equilibrium exchange rate in the market and then a movement to a new equilibrium level as the market changes. The demand for yen in this example is a function of U.S. demand for Japanese goods and services, such as automobiles, and yen-denominated financial assets, such as securities.

The supply of yen in this example is a function of Japanese demand for U.S. goods and services and dollar-denominated financial assets. Initially, the supply of and demand for yen in Figure 10.3 meet at the equilibrium exchange rate e_0 (for example, 0.00926 dollar per yen, or 108 yen per dollar) and the quantity of yen Q_1.

Assume demand for U.S. goods and services by Japanese consumers drops because of, say, high U.S. inflation. This lessening demand would result in a reduced supply of yen in the foreign-exchange market, causing the supply curve to shift to S'. Simultaneously, the increasing prices of U.S. goods might lead to an increase in demand for Japanese goods and services by U.S. consumers. This, in turn, would lead to an increase in demand for yen in the market, causing the demand curve to shift to D' and finally lead to an increase in the quantity of yen and an increase in the exchange rate.

The new equilibrium exchange rate would be at e_1 (for example, 0.00943 dollar per yen, or 106 yen per dollar). From a dollar standpoint, the increased demand for Japanese goods would lead to an increase in supply of dollars as more consumers tried to trade their dollars for yen, and the reduced demand for U.S. goods would result in a drop in demand for dollars. This would cause a reduction in the dollar's value against the yen.

> Demand for a country's currency is a function of the demand for that country's goods and services and financial assets.

INTERVENTION: CURRENCY IN A FIXED-RATE OR MANAGED-FLOATING-RATE WORLD

In the preceding example, Japanese and U.S. authorities allowed supply and demand to determine the values of the yen and dollar. That does not occur for currencies that fix their exchange rates and do not allow them to move according to market forces. There can be times when one or both countries might not want exchange rates to change.

Assume, for example, that the United States and Japan decide to manage their exchange rates. Although both currencies are independently floating currencies, their respective governments could intervene in the market. The U.S. government might not want its currency to weaken, because its companies and consumers would have to pay more for Japanese products, which would lead to more inflationary pressure in the United States. Or the Japanese government might not want the yen to strengthen, because it would mean unemployment in its export industries.

But how can the governments keep the values from changing when the United States is earning too few yen? Somehow the difference between yen supply and demand must be neutralized. To understand this process, let's first examine the role of central banks in foreign-exchange markets.

THE ROLE OF CENTRAL BANKS

Central banks control policies that affect the value of currencies; the Federal Reserve Bank of New York is the central bank in the United States.

Each country has a central bank responsible for the policies affecting the value of its currency, although countries with currency boards independent from the central bank use the currency board to control the value of the currency. The central bank in the United States is the Federal Reserve System (the Fed), a system of 12 regional banks. The New York Fed, in close coordination with and representing the Federal Reserve System and the U.S. Treasury, is responsible for intervening in foreign-exchange markets to achieve dollar exchange-rate policy objectives and to counter disorderly conditions in foreign-exchange markets. The U.S. Treasury is responsible for setting exchange-rate policy, whereas the Fed is responsible for executing foreign-exchange intervention. Further, the Federal Reserve Bank of New York serves as a fiscal agent in the United States for foreign central banks and official international financial organizations.[21]

In the European Union, the European Central Bank coordinates the activities of each member country's central bank to establish a common monetary policy in Europe, much as the Federal Reserve Bank does in the United States.

Central bank reserve assets are kept in three major forms: gold, foreign-exchange reserves, and IMF-related assets. Foreign exchange is 98 percent of reserve assets worldwide.

Central Bank Reserve Assets   Central bank reserve assets are kept in three major forms: foreign-exchange reserves, IMF-related assets (including SDRs), and gold. Foreign exchange comprises over 90 percent of total reserves worldwide. In the second quarter of 2009, the Composition of Official Foreign Exchange Reserves (COFER) reported that U.S. dollars represented about 62.8 percent of the total allocated foreign-exchange reserves (which includes only those reserves for which the currency is known), followed by the euro at about 27.5 percent of the total. Other currencies, such as the Japanese yen, British pound, and Swiss franc, are also reserve assets but at relatively small percentages. Clearly, the U.S. dollar and the euro are the two main reserve asset currencies. Their percentage of the total varies from year to year depending on their relative strengths, and their relative position for different countries also varies.[22]

Having strong central bank reserve assets is essential to the financial strength of a country. When the financial crises in Asia, Russia, and South America hit in the late 1990s, very few countries had strong central bank reserve assets. As a result, they had to borrow a lot of U.S. dollars, which turned out to be devastating when they finally had to devalue their currencies. Since 2000, however, the picture has changed. Due to strong commodity prices, expanding exports, and restraint in incurring dollar debt, many of those same countries have strengthened their financial position by increasing their reserves.

Take Brazil, for example. Its foreign-exchange reserves were $192.9 billion at the end of 2008, leading the way for the rest of Latin America, where reserves have increased fourfold since 2000.[23] However, this is relatively small compared with China, which had nearly $2 trillion in reserves. The ranking of the top countries in the world in terms of total reserves is China, Japan, Russia, Taiwan, India, South Korea, Hong Kong, and Brazil.

Central banks intervene in currency markets by buying and selling currency to affect its price.

How Central Banks Intervene in the Market   A central bank can intervene in currency markets in several ways. The U.S. Fed, for example, usually uses foreign currencies to buy dollars when the dollar is weak or sells dollars for foreign currency when the dollar is strong. Depending on the market conditions, a central bank may do any of the following:

- Coordinate its action with other central banks or go it alone
- Enter the market aggressively to change attitudes about its views and policies
- Call for reassuring action to calm markets
- Intervene to reverse, resist, or support a market trend

- Announce or not announce its operations—be very visible or very discreet
- Operate openly or indirectly through brokers[24]

Case: The U.S. Dollar and the Japanese Yen   Although the U.S. dollar is an independently floating currency, let's continue with the example illustrated in Figure 10.2 (p. 407) and show how a central bank could intervene. In a managed fixed-exchange-rate system, the New York Federal Reserve Bank would hold foreign-exchange reserves, which it would have built up through the years for this type of contingency. It could sell enough of its yen reserves (make up the difference between Q_1 and Q_3 in Figure 10.3) at the fixed exchange rate to maintain that rate. Or the Japanese central bank might be willing to accept dollars so that U.S. consumers can continue to buy Japanese goods. These dollars would then become part of Japan's foreign-exchange reserves. Although this is a two-country example, sometimes several central banks coordinate their intervention to support a currency rather than just have two countries involved.

The fixed rate could continue as long as the United States had reserves or as long as the Japanese were willing to add dollars to their holdings. Sometimes governments use monetary policy such as raising interest rates to create a demand for their currency and to keep the value from falling. However, interest rate policy is usually a function of inflationary expectations and/or concerns about economic growth rather than just to influence exchange rates. Unless something changed the basic imbalance in the currency supply and demand, the New York Federal Reserve Bank would run out of yen and the Japanese central bank would stop accepting dollars because it would fear amassing too many, similar to what happened to South Korea in early 2005 and Thailand in 2007. At this point, it would be necessary to change the exchange rate to lessen the demand for yen.

If a country determines that intervention will not work, it must adjust its currency's value. If the currency is freely floating, the exchange rate will seek the correct level according to the laws of supply and demand. However, a currency pegged to another currency or to a basket of currencies usually is changed on a formal basis—in other words, through a devaluation (a weakening of the currency) or revaluation (a strengthening of the currency), depending on the direction of the change.

Different Attitudes toward Intervention   Government policies change over time, depending on economic conditions and the attitude of the prevailing administration in power, irrespective of whether the currency is considered to be freely floating.

Previously, however, the attitude toward intervention was a little different. The George H. W. Bush administration, in 1989 alone, bought and sold dollars on 97 days and sold $19.5 billion. In the first two and a half years of the first Clinton administration, the Fed intervened in the market by buying dollars on only 18 days, spending about $12.5 billion in the process.[25] But the U.S. government is hesitant to directly intervene in the foreign-exchange market, preferring to allow the market to determine the correct value. According to the New York Fed, the United States intervened in foreign-exchange markets on eight different days in 1995, but only twice from August 1995 through December 2006.[26] Due to the large U.S. trade deficit, the administration of President George W. Bush preferred to let the market determine the value of the U.S. dollar, hoping a weakening of the dollar would lead to an expansion of exports and reduction of imports, thus improving the trade balance.

Governments vary in their intervention policies by country and by administration.

The global financial crisis has roiled foreign-exchange markets and forced many central banks to intervene to support their currencies. Let's take Hungary, for example. Hungary is a member of the European Union, but it has not adopted the euro yet. However, the EU is Hungary's most important market, with 79.2 percent of its exports going to other EU members and 69.9 percent of its imports coming from EU members. The rising value of the euro against the U.S. dollar, as shown in Figure 10.2, created serious economic problems for Hungary. The Hungarian forint fell 22 percent against the euro in the first few months of 2009, forcing the Hungarian central bank to intervene in foreign-exchange markets to support the forint.[27]

The Russian ruble is another currency affected by the global financial crisis. The ruble is a pegged currency that uses a composite of currencies as its benchmark for determining the value of its currency. During the September–December 2008 time period in the global economic crisis, the Russian government was supporting the value of the ruble despite the fall in oil prices (its major source of foreign-exchange earnings) and capital flight from Russia by foreign investors who were taking their money from emerging markets and putting it into dollars. In order to keep the ruble from crashing in value, the government loosened the trading band for ruble trades and allowed the currency to weaken in a more orderly manner rather than exhibit the large swings that we saw in the dollar/euro exchange rate in Figure 10.2.

The global financial crisis basically destroyed the economy and currency of Iceland, which does not use the euro. In October 2008, the government raised interest rates to 18 percent in order to try to save the currency. At the same time, Hungary—which we discussed above—agreed to a massive infusion of cash orchestrated by the IMF in order to support the forint.[28]

However, the intervention by the government of Iceland did not work. Everyone from banks to individuals incurred huge foreign debts because foreign interest rates were so much lower than interest rates in Iceland. When the crisis hit, the currency fell in value and nobody could pay their debts. In July 2009, as the crisis escalated for Iceland, Parliament narrowly voted to join the EU and eventually adopt the euro.[29]

The central bank of South Korea has intervened aggressively in the foreign-exchange markets on many different occasions to manage the value of their currency, the won. Although the currency is classified as independently floating, it is subject to central bank intervention if it rises too much, threatening Korea's export industries. In 2005, the central bank intervened in currency markets to try to slow down the rise in the won against the dollar by selling won and buying dollars. From 2002 to 2005, the won appreciated 30 percent against the dollar, 17 percent of which occurred in 2004. However, the cost of intervention was high, and South Korea decided to stop when its foreign-exchange reserves reached $206 billion, the fourth highest in the world at that time.[30] In September 2008, the won was trading at about 1107 USD/SKW (or 1107 won per dollar). However, the won quickly lost value before recovering at the end of 2008, and then it dropped again until March 2009, when it quickly rose in value. By the end of April 2009, South Korea had dropped to sixth in the world in terms of foreign-exchange reserves behind China, Japan, Russia, Taiwan, and India. However, its rising balance-of-trade surplus and large reserves gave it quite a war chest to intervene in markets if necessary. One reason why South Korea's foreign-exchange reserves had risen was that it had sold a lot of its foreign currency reserves to strengthen the won during the crisis of 2008, and now it was buying back won to replenish the reserves. Some were suggesting that if the won continued to strengthen in the latter part of 2009, the central bank would again intervene in the markets to push down the value of the won.[31]

Besides the illustrations above, other countries were forced to intervene in the foreign-exchange markets to support their currencies during the global financial crisis. It was estimated that Brazil, Mexico, Russia, and India collectively drew down their foreign-exchange reserves by more than $75 billion between the end of September 2008 and the end of October 2008 in an effort to protect their currencies, which had dropped dramatically against the dollar.[32] It seems to be a never-ending battle for balance in the foreign-exchange markets.

CHALLENGES WITH INTERVENTION As noted above, the United States disapproves of foreign-currency intervention. The reason is that it is very difficult, if not impossible, for intervention to have a lasting impact on the value of a currency. Given the daily volume of foreign-exchange transactions, no one government can move the market unless its movements can change the psychology of the market. Intervention may temporarily halt a slide, but it cannot force the market to move in a direction it doesn't want to go, at least for the long run. For that reason, it is important for countries to focus on correcting economic fundamentals instead of spending a lot of time and money on intervention. However, countries still intervene, and the above examples illustrate different approaches to intervention, from raising interest rates to using foreign-exchange reserves to buy and sell currencies. When daily foreign-exchange trades are about $4 trillion, it is hard to intervene enough to move the markets very much. Any intervention can be construed as a central bank signal, but the long-term policies are what will eventually make the big difference.

REVISITING THE BIS   Coordination of central bank intervention can take place bilaterally or multilaterally. The Bank for International Settlements (BIS) in Basel, Switzerland, links together the central banks of the world. As we noted in Chapter 9, the BIS was founded in 1930 and is owned and controlled by the major central banks of the world. The major objective of the BIS is to promote the cooperation of central banks to facilitate international financial stability. Although only 55 central banks or monetary authorities are shareholders in the BIS—11 of which are the founding banks and are from the major industrial countries—the BIS has dealings with some 140 central banks and other international financial institutions worldwide.[33]

The BIS acts as a central banker's bank. It gets involved in swaps and other currency transactions between the central banks in other countries. It is also a gathering place where central bankers can discuss monetary cooperation and is increasingly getting involved with other multilateral agencies, such as the IMF, in providing support during international financial crises. In addition, the BIS conducts the triennial central bank survey of foreign-exchange and derivatives market activity that is the basis for much of the trading data provided in Chapter 9.

BLACK MARKETS

In many of the countries that do not allow their currencies to float according to market forces, a black market could parallel the official market and be aligned more closely with the forces of supply and demand than is the official market. The less flexible a country's exchange-rate arrangement, the more likely there will be a thriving black (or parallel) market. A **black market** exists when people are willing to pay more for dollars than the official rate. In order for the black market to work, the government must control access to foreign exchange so it can control its price.

One example of black market transactions occurred in Shenzhen, China, in 2009 when people who were worried about the future value of the Chinese yuan bought Hong Kong dollars on the black market. Some people even figured out that the demand for Hong Kong dollars was so high that they could buy HK dollars at state banks and make a tidy profit by selling them to others who could not get access to HK dollars at the state banks.[34]

Zimbabwe has terrible financial problems, and they are manifest in the currency markets. Zimbabwe's official currency regime is a fixed-peg arrangement and is pegged to the U.S. dollar. However, that doesn't seem to have helped much. In 2007, with inflation hitting around 4,500 percent—the highest in the world—the currency was dropping like a rock. A loaf of bread in 2007 cost 44,000 Zimbabwean dollars, which was only 18 cents at black-market rates or $176 at the official exchange rate.[35] By early 2009, the economy was still a disaster and there was a cholera epidemic and political turmoil. Hyperinflation was so bad that the central bank issued a $100 trillion banknote that was worth about U.S. $33 on the black market. Prices were doubling every day, and food and fuel were in short supply. In spite of an official exchange rate, most people were trading currency at the black-market rate.[36]

Even oil-rich Venezuela has problems with the black market. Sometimes black markets are illegal, and sometimes they are an essential part of the economy. When Rosemont Finance Corp., a small Florida financial firm, was shut down due to money-laundering

Concept Check

In Chapter 9, we discuss the importance of the **BIS** in collecting information about the massive volume of activity on the global **foreign-exchange market.** Here we add that the BIS may also help coordinate the policies of central banks in matters of foreign-exchange intervention.

The Bank for International Settlements in Basel, Switzerland, is owned by and promotes cooperation among a group of central banks.

A black market closely approximates a price based on supply and demand for a currency instead of a government-controlled price.

charges against its owner, key black-market foreign-exchange transactions ground to a halt. Although Venezuela has an official ban against private firms buying and selling currency at black market rates, it relies on black-market trading houses to keep currency in the market. When oil prices fell in the latter part of 2008, a liquidity crisis hit Venezuela, and the Venezuelan finance ministry and state-owned oil company began selling dollars on the black market at three times the official rate, thus allowing them to continue operations.[37] The shutdown of Rosemont really hurt the ability of Venezuelan companies to get access to foreign exchange.

FOREIGN-EXCHANGE CONVERTIBILITY AND CONTROLS

Some countries with fixed exchange rates control access to their currencies. *Fully convertible currencies* are those that the government allows both residents and nonresidents to purchase in unlimited amounts.

Hard and Soft Currencies   Hard currencies—such as the U.S. dollar, euro, British pound, and Japanese yen—are currencies that are fully convertible. They also are relatively stable in value over a short period of time and are highly liquid. In addition, they are generally accepted worldwide as payment for goods and services. In addition, they are desirable assets. Currencies that are not fully convertible are often called **soft currencies.** They have just the opposite characteristics of hard currency: they are very unstable in value, not very liquid, and not widely accepted as payment for goods and services. They tend to be the currencies of developing countries. A major reason why countries restrict convertibility of their currencies is that they are short on foreign-exchange reserves and try to use the reserves for essential transactions. That's why soft currencies tend to be from developing countries where foreign-exchange reserves are low. The higher the reserves, the less a country has to resort to restricting convertibility. However, it is interesting to note that the developing countries dominate the list of the countries with the highest foreign-exchange reserves. In spite of that, their currencies are not very liquid and are not widely accepted as payment for exports and imports. They need to go through hard currencies such as the dollar, euro, and yen.

A hard currency is a currency that is usually fully convertible and strong or relatively stable in value in comparison with other currencies.

A soft currency is one that is usually not fully convertible and is also called a weak currency.

Most countries today have *nonresident* (or *external*) *convertibility,* meaning that foreigners can convert their currency into the local currency and can convert back into their currency as well. Tourists generally have no problems converting their currencies into local currencies and back again, although sometimes countries put restrictions or conditions on trade from the local currency back to the hard currency when tourists leave the country.

Controlling Convertibility   To conserve scarce foreign exchange, some governments impose exchange restrictions on companies or individuals who want to exchange money. The devices they use include *import licensing, multiple exchange rates, import deposit requirements,* and *quantity controls.*

In 2007, for instance, the Thai baht was rising in value, approaching a 10-year high against the U.S. dollar. The baht is a managed floating currency that targets inflation in determining the value of the currency. Given that the Thai government had limited the convertibility of the baht in some areas, they decided it might be best to loosen controls and encourage an outflow of currency to try to reduce the value of the baht. On June 25, 2007, the government announced several measures to reduce controls: "Among the measures, effective immediately, was approval for Thai-listed companies to purchase foreign exchange of up to $100 million a year for foreign investment. Institutional investors no longer need central bank approval to invest in deposits with foreign institutions, and individuals may now send up to $1 million a year overseas as transfers to expatriate relatives, as donations or to buy real estate."[38] The quote serves to illustrate ways in which governments institute foreign-exchange controls to preserve a currency's value.

Licenses Government licenses fix the exchange rate by requiring all recipients, exporters, and others who receive foreign currency to sell it to its central bank at the official buying rate. Then the central bank rations the foreign currency it acquires by selling it at fixed rates to those needing to make payment abroad for essential goods. An importer may purchase foreign exchange only if that importer has obtained an import license for the goods in question.

> Licensing occurs when a government requires that all foreign-exchange transactions be regulated and controlled by it.

Multiple Exchange Rates Another way that governments control foreign-exchange convertibility is by establishing more than one exchange rate. This restrictive measure is called a **multiple exchange-rate system.** The government determines which kinds of transactions are to be conducted at which exchange rates. Countries with multiple exchange rates often have a floating exchange rate for luxury goods and financial flows, such as dividends. Then they have a fixed, usually lower, exchange rate for other trade transactions such as imports of essential commodities and semimanufactured goods.

> In a multiple exchange-rate system, a government sets different exchange rates for different types of transactions.

Import Deposits Another form of foreign-exchange convertibility control is the **advance import deposit.** In this case, the government tightens the issue of import licenses and requires importers to make a deposit with the central bank—often for as long as one year and interest free—covering the full price of manufactured goods they would purchase from abroad.

> Advance import deposit—a government requires deposit of money prior to the release of foreign exchange to pay for imports; varies to as long as a year in advance.

Quantity Controls Governments may also limit the amount of exchange through quantity controls, which often apply to tourism. A quantity control limits the amount of currency that a local resident can purchase from the bank for foreign travel. The government sets a policy on how much money a tourist is allowed to take overseas, and the individual is allowed to convert only that amount of money.

> Quantity controls—the government limits the amount of foreign currency that can be used in a specific transaction.

In the past, currency controls have significantly added to the cost of doing business internationally, and they have resulted in the overall reduction of trade. However, the liberalization of trade in recent years has eliminated a lot of these controls to the point that they are found to be a minor impediment to trade.[39] In addition, the move from fixed to flexible exchange rates has also eliminated the need for controls in many countries.

EXCHANGE RATES AND PURCHASING POWER PARITY

The next three sections of the chapter will examine three interrelated issues: the relationship between inflation and exchange rates, the relationship between interest rates and exchange rates, and the factors you can use to forecast (or at least attempt to forecast) future exchange rates. Purchasing power parity, from the standpoint of exchange rates, seeks to define the relationships between currencies based on relative inflation.

Purchasing power parity (PPP) is a well-known theory that seeks to define relationships between currencies. In essence, it claims that a change in relative inflation (meaning a comparison of the countries' rates of inflation) between two countries must cause a change in exchange rates to keep the prices of goods in two countries fairly similar. According to the PPP theory, if, for example, Japanese inflation were 2 percent and U.S. inflation were 3.5 percent, the dollar would be expected to fall by the difference in inflation rates. Then the dollar would be worth fewer yen than before the adjustment, and the yen would be worth more dollars than before the adjustment.

The "Big Mac Index" An interesting illustration of the PPP theory for estimating exchange rates is the "Big Mac index" of currencies used by *The Economist* each year. Since 1986, the British periodical *The Economist* has used the price of a Big Mac to estimate the exchange rate between the dollar and another currency (see Table 10.2). Because the Big Mac is sold in more than 31,000 restaurants serving more than 58 million people in 118 countries every day, it is easy to use it to compare prices. PPP would suggest that the exchange rate should leave hamburgers costing the same in the United

services. Long term, the expectation is that the currency of that country will strengthen vis-à-vis its trading partners. Conversely, a current account deficit means that a country imports more than it exports and is building up debt abroad as it struggles to find the foreign exchange to pay for its imports. In that case, the long-term expectation is that the currency will weaken vis-à-vis its trading partners.

Business Implications of Exchange-Rate Changes

Why do we need to bother with predicting exchange-rate changes? As we will see in the closing case, exchange-rate changes can dramatically affect operating strategies as well as translated overseas profits. We now look briefly at how exchange-rate changes can affect companies' marketing, production, and financial decisions.

MARKETING DECISIONS

> **Strengthening of a country's currency value could create problems for exporters.**

Marketing managers watch exchange rates because they can affect demand for a company's products at home and abroad. In early 2008 when the euro was surging against the U.S. dollar, Italian companies struggled to export their products abroad. Conversely, U.S. companies were benefitting from a weak U.S. dollar. Task Force Tips, an Indiana-based company that makes fire-hose nozzles, doubled its exports in the three years prior to 2008, and exports represented one-third of its sales.[50] As long as the dollar was falling, U.S. companies were looking closely at export markets as a place to offset the slowdown in the domestic market. However, once the dollar began to rise in the fourth quarter of 2008, the situation reversed. Currency changes can create opportunities, and they can pull them back as well.

PRODUCTION DECISIONS

> **Companies might locate production in a weak-currency country because**
> - **Initial investment there is relatively cheap.**
> - **Such a country is a good base for inexpensive exportation.**

Exchange-rate changes can also affect production decisions. A manufacturer in a country where wages and operating expenses are high might be tempted to relocate production to a country with a currency that is rapidly losing value. The company's currency would buy lots of the weak currency, making the company's initial investment cheap.

Further, goods manufactured in that country would be relatively cheap in world markets. For example, BMW made the decision to invest in production facilities in South Carolina because of the unfavorable exchange rate between the Deutsche mark (now the euro) and the dollar. However, the company announced plans to use the facilities not only to serve the U.S. market but also to export to Europe and other markets.[51] The issue worsened in 2004 when the euro rose significantly against the dollar. The devaluation of the Mexican peso came shortly after the introduction of NAFTA. Although companies had already begun to establish operations in Mexico to service North America, the cheaper peso certainly helped their manufacturing strategies.

FINANCIAL DECISIONS

> **Exchange rates can influence the sourcing of financial resources, the cross-border remittance of funds, and the reporting of financial results.**

Finally, exchange rates can affect financial decisions primarily in the areas of sourcing of financial resources, the remittance of funds across national borders, and the reporting of financial results. In the first area, a company might be tempted to borrow money in places where interest rates are lowest. However, recall that interest-rate differentials often are compensated for in money markets through exchange-rate changes.

In deciding about cross-border financial flows, a company would want to convert local currency into its own home-country currency when exchange rates are most favorable so it can maximize its return. However, countries with weak currencies often have currency controls, making it difficult for MNEs to do so.

Finally, exchange-rate changes can influence the reporting of financial results. A simple example illustrates the impact that exchange rates can have on income. If a U.S. company's Mexican subsidiary earns 2 million pesos when the exchange rate is 9.5 pesos per dollar, the dollar equivalent of its income is $210,526. If the peso depreciates to 10.2 pesos per dollar, the dollar equivalent of that income falls to $196,078. The opposite will occur if the local currency appreciates against that of the company's home country. United Technologies, a U.S.-based manufacturer of elevators, aerospace equipment, and other products, reported that for every penny the euro increases against the dollar, UT records an additional $10 million in extra profits.[52] It is important to learn about exchange rates and the forces that affect their change. Several years ago, a large U.S.-based telephone company was preparing a bid for a major telecommunications project in Turkey. The manager preparing the bid knew nothing about the Turkish lira, and he prepared his bid without consulting with the company's foreign-exchange specialists. He figured out the bid in dollars, then turned to the foreign-exchange table in the *Wall Street Journal* to see what rate he should use to convert the bid into lira. What he didn't realize was that the lira at that time was weakening against the dollar. By the time he awarded the project, he had lost all of his profit to the change in the value of the lira against the dollar, and by the time he had finished the project, he had lost a lot of money. If he had talked to someone who knew anything about the lira, he could have forecast the future value (or at least tried to forecast the value) and maybe entered into a hedging strategy to protect his receivables in lira. If managers don't understand how currency values are determined, they can make serious, costly mistakes.

Concept Check

In Chapter 18, we'll explain how companies factor in foreign exchange in preparing financial statements. In Chapter 19, we'll show how exchange rates influence financial flows and describe some of the strategies that companies enlist to protect themselves against exchange-rate risk.

Looking to the Future Changes in the Relative Strength of the U.S. Dollar, the Euro, the Yen, and the Yuan

The international monetary system has undergone considerable change since the early 1970s when the dollar was devalued the first time. New countries have been born with the breakup of the Soviet empire, and with them have come new currencies. As those countries have gone through transition to a market economy, the currencies have adjusted as well. The countries will continue to change over to a floating-rate system as they get their economies under control.

It will be interesting to see what will happen to the currencies of Latin America. Since the collapse of the Argentine peso, economists across all ideologies have stepped up to the plate to predict what will happen with Argentina's exchange-rate regime. After the first election of President da Silva in Brazil, the real steadily strengthened against the dollar. Until the global financial crisis hit, the real was on an upward trajectory. In the latter part of 2008, however, the real plummeted as investors pulled money out of Brazil and other emerging markets. The real has since recovered, but there has been significant intervention by the Brazilian central bank. The future of the real depends in large part on what happens to its export markets and whether investors continue to have faith in the Brazilian

economy. Similar statements could be made about Mexico as well, the other major economy in Latin America.

Another thing is clear at this point: South American currencies strengthened with the rise in commodity prices. As commodity prices dropped in the wake of the global economic crisis, so did the value of their currencies. As commodity prices recover, so too should the value of the emerging market currencies.

The euro will continue to succeed as a currency and will eventually take away market share from the dollar as a prime reserve asset. In addition, its influence will spread throughout Europe as non–euro-zone countries adopt the euro or at least come into harmony with it. The countries that joined the EU since 2004 have been pushing the EMU to allow them to switch to the euro. Slovenia was recently allowed to adopt the euro as its currency. The EU will allow other countries to adopt the euro as the countries come into convergence with the ERM. Increasing trade links throughout Europe with non–euro-zone countries will dictate closer alliance with the euro.

For Asia, no Asian currency can compare with the dollar in the Americas and the euro in Europe. The yen

(continued)

is too specific to Japan, and the inability of the Japanese economy to reform and open up will keep the yen from wielding the same kind of influence as the dollar and the euro, even though the yen is one of the most widely traded currencies in the world. In fact, it is far more likely that the dollar will continue to be the benchmark in Asia insofar as Asian economies rely heavily on the U.S. market for a lot of their exports.

However, the real wild card in Asia is the Chinese yuan. The Chinese decided to delink the yuan-to-dollar peg in 2005 and widened the trading band in 2007. These adjustments have had very little impact, and many countries insist that China is still practicing currency manipulation. Further changes will probably have to be made to the currency to avoid a major trade war with Europe and the United States. But clearly China is moving forward in its efforts to establish the CNY as one of the major currencies in the world. The trend will continue to lead to greater flexibility in exchange-rate regimes, whether as managed floats or as freely floating currencies. Even countries that lock on to the dollar will float against every other currency in the world as the dollar floats. Capital controls will continue to fall, and currencies will move more freely from country to country. If the federal stimulus packages in the United States ignite long-term budget deficits and higher inflation, the dollar will come under even greater pressure in the global economy, and it could fall in value significantly. If it does, this could give impetus for a greater role of the Chinese yuan in the global economy and a diminishing importance of the U.S. dollar. ∎

CASE

Welcome to the World of Sony—Unless the Yen Keeps Rising[53]

2008 was a pretty tough year for Sony, and 2009 didn't seem to be getting much better. The global economic crisis not only resulted in a huge drop in demand worldwide, it also roiled the foreign currency markets. By mid-2009 and the release of Sony's first-quarter 2009 financial results (Sony, like most Japanese companies, has a fiscal year that ends on March 31), the yen was trading at ¥94.7 per dollar, an increase in value against the dollar which was trading at ¥90.9 at the beginning of 2009, and ¥110.5583 on August 15, 2008, shortly before the crash of the global economy. The crazy currency swings had a devastating impact on Sony and all other major MNCs in Japan. What will the future bring?

The Past

Before attacking the future, let's look at the past—especially from the perspective of the Japanese yen. In the post–World War II years, the yen was extremely weak against the dollar, trading at ¥357.65 in 1970. That hardly seems possible with today's high rates (remember that the lower the USD/JPY exchange rate, the higher the value of the yen against the dollar). Sony, founded in 1946 as Tokyo Tsushin Kogyo Corporation, officially became known as Sony Corporation in 1958, the year its stock was first listed on the Tokyo Stock Exchange. It also became the first Japanese company to list American Depositary Receipts (ADRs) on the New York Stock Exchange in 1961 and finally listed its own shares on the NYSE in September 1970.

In those early years of operation, Sony had the luxury of operating in a currency that was not only weak against the dollar, but also highly controlled by the government. Japanese foreign-exchange policies favored companies and industries that the government wanted to succeed, especially in export markets. With a cheap yen, it was easy for companies to expand exports rapidly.

The First Endaka

From its 1970 high, the yen steadily strengthened until 1985, when it *really* shot up in value. Due to economic problems in the United States, the dollar began to fall during the latter part of

1985, and the yen ended at ¥200 per dollar by the end of 1985. By the latter part of 1986, the yen was trading at ¥150, a steep rise from its historical highs. The Japanese called this strengthening of the yen *endaka,* which literally translates "high yen." *Endaka* resulted in serious problems for Japanese exporters and potential pain for the entire Japanese economy, which was very dependent on international trade. However, one upside to *endaka* was that imports were cheaper, and Japan relied heavily on imports of virtually all commodities. Thus its input costs fell, even as it found its export prices rising.

The strong yen was due primarily to a strong Japanese economy, large trade surpluses, and the largest foreign-exchange reserves in the world. In addition, Japan had low unemployment, low interest rates, and low inflation. But cracks began to show in the Japanese economy. A combination of a drop in the stock market, a rise in inflation, and a real estate bubble hurt the Japanese economy and confidence in the yen. The governor of the Bank of Japan raised interest rates in December 1989, but the resulting furor forced him to stop raising rates. Since the interest rates in the United States were higher, investors pulled money out of Japan and put it into U.S. dollars to take advantage of higher returns. This drop in demand for yen and rise in demand for dollars pushed up the value of the dollar against the yen, and the yen closed out 1989 at ¥143.45, whereas it was ¥125.85 only a year earlier.

Both the United States and Japan were worried about inflation in the early 1990s, and they tried to coordinate exchange-rate policies, but the United States didn't want to push down the value of the dollar too much and lose its own fight against inflation. The United States and Japan tried to get the central banks of Germany, the United Kingdom, and other countries to intervene in the markets and sell their currencies for yen in order to strengthen the yen. But there wasn't much they could do to move the market given that interest rates were driving market psychology.

In the ensuing years, many factors influenced the yen/dollar exchange rate, including a weak U.S. economy (favoring a drop in interest rates), the Persian Gulf War (which favored the dollar as a safe-haven currency), a rise in Japanese interest rates relative to U.S. interest rates, and a lack of agreement among G8 countries in 1993 about whether the yen was too weak or about right.

A Second *Endaka*

As if one *endaka* were not enough, a second one hit in 1995, when the yen rose to ¥80.63 per dollar. Toyota announced that a one-point increase in the yen eliminated $111 million in dollar-denominated profits from their U.S. operations, and exporters were having a difficult time figuring out how to remain competitive in export markets. As they did with the first *endaka,* Japanese companies looked for ways to cut costs and remain competitive. During that period, the Japanese economy was in a recession, so the Bank of Japan dropped interest rates to stimulate demand, and the yen fell against the dollar, favoring exporters once again.

Competitive Pressures

During these decades of currency swings, Sony kept moving along as one of the premier companies in the world in consumer electronics, games, music, and movies. The wide array of product innovations earned Sony a premium in the market. However, competition began to step in. Korean companies, like Samsung and LG, began to produce cheaper products that rose in quality as each year went by. Samsung began to develop a reputation for innovation in electronics, which threatened Sony. In addition, Samsung and other competitors to Sony began setting up plants offshore, especially in China, to improve their cost advantage even more. Some of Sony's Japanese competitors, including Toshiba and Panasonic, responded by reducing their exposure to a strong yen by moving plants overseas, such as to Indonesia and the Philippines, and increasing the dollar-based imports of parts. By 2003, Toshiba was manufacturing 30 percent of its products outside Japan, compared with only 17 percent in 1995.

From the beginning of 2003 until the end of 2004, the dollar continued to weaken against both the euro and the yen. In an attempt to strengthen the dollar, the Japanese central bank spent a record 20 trillion yen in 2003 and 10 trillion yen in the first two months of 2004. Despite the efforts of the Japanese authorities, the yen rose 11 percent against the dollar in 2003 and continued to strengthen through 2004. The Japanese finance ministry stopped its foreign-exchange intervention in March 2004, but the dollar's continued weakening against both the euro and the yen at the end of 2004 sparked new threats of intervention by the Japanese and Europeans. A senior Japanese finance ministry official said, "It is natural for Japan and Europe to act when the dollar alone is falling. If the (dollar's) movement affects the European economy and the Japanese economy, we should defend ourselves."

Fast-Forward to 2008

The collapse in the housing market in the United States and the ensuing credit crisis that hit in 2007, followed by the bankruptcy of Lehman Brothers and the U.S. government takeover of global insurer AIG in September 2008, had a devastating impact on the global economy. The U.S. stock market crashed, followed by similar crashes around the world, and investors pulled funds out of risky emerging markets and placed them in safe-haven assets. Who were the major beneficiaries? The U.S. dollar and the Japanese yen! The euro dropped against both the dollar and the yen, and the Chinese yuan wasn't a factor because its currency is fixed against the dollar rather than flexible and subject to normal market forces. Although China is a good bet for foreign investment, the yuan is not an investment currency like the dollar and yen due to currency controls and lack of liquidity.

Why did this happen? In the case of the U.S. dollar, the market reaction was a standard flight to safety, which often happens when global events get scary, even when the U.S. markets started the collapse. The size of the U.S. economy and political stability, even in the face of a presidential election in November 2008, tend to make the United States an attractive place for investment. Thus the fear factor seemed to be a critical vote for the dollar during the crisis. This is a short-term phenomenon, however, and will eventually be replaced by economic fundamentals. With the slowdown in the U.S. economy, export-dominated countries, especially emerging markets, were expected to suffer. Also, the credit crisis that the United States was going through was expected to expand to other countries. The euro is obviously a strong and important currency, but it lacks a strong central government that can coordinate a response to economic crisis. The European Central Bank can influence interest rates, but that's about all. Another thing that came out of the crisis is that the euro tends to be very sensitive to the U.S. stock market. When the market was falling, so was the euro. When the market began to recover, so did the euro. Thus the dollar has been up and down depending on what news was most important. When the crisis was the news, the dollar was strong. When the news favored a recovery of the U.S. economy, money flowed into equity markets, both in the United States and abroad, seeking for higher returns and causing the dollar to drop in value.

What about the yen? Interestingly enough, the yen also became a safe-haven currency during the crisis, along with the dollar. Obviously, the yen is the most important currency in Asia, because Japan has the second-highest foreign-exchange reserves in the region and the world, just after China, but it is a freely convertible currency with high market liquidity and is also an important trading currency. Also, with Japanese interest rates so low, many investors were borrowing in yen and investing their proceeds abroad to get access to higher returns. When the crisis hit, the money quickly left the emerging markets and returned to Japan, a practice called *carry trade.* Whenever volatility in currency markets goes up, investors unwind (reverse) their trades, which gave strength to the yen.

The markets also demonstrated that the yen and U.S. stock market were inversely related. When markets are less risk-averse, stocks gain in value and the yen drops in value. When markets are more risk-averse, stock prices fall, and the yen trades higher. To illustrate that point, in July 2009 when the stock market started to climb, the yen fell against the dollar, although the fall was not dramatic or large.

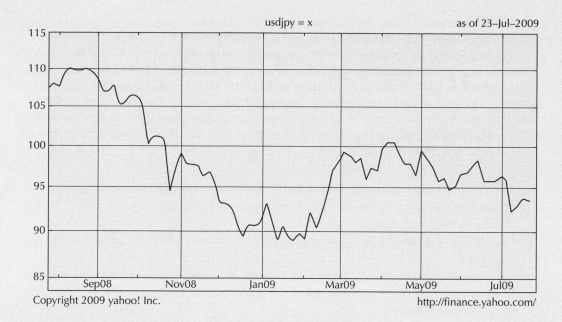

usdjpy = x   as of 23–Jul–2009

Copyright 2009 yahoo! Inc.   http://finance.yahoo.com/

FIGURE 10.4 USD/JPY (number of yen per dollar), year ended July 23, 2009

This illustrates how the yen steadily strengthened against the dollar during the initial phases of the global financial crisis, the only major currency in the world to do so. However, it briefly weakened early in 2009 and then floated back and forth, creating problems for Sony and other large Japanese MNCs.

What Does All This Mean to Sony?

In 2008, Sony generated 23.2 percent of its sales in Japan, 25.1 percent in the United States, 26.2 percent in Europe, and 25.5 percent elsewhere. Thus Sony was well diversified geographically, operating in some countries where the local currency was weaker and others where the local currency was stronger than the yen. Sony was also targeting the BRIC countries for future growth.

According to Sony's 2008 annual report, in addition to targeting global markets for sales, Sony was taking advantage of production outside of Japan. In the electronics division, about 50 percent of its FY production was in Japan, and the rest was spread out elsewhere. About 60 percent of its Japanese production was destined for other regions. China accounted for about 15 percent of total annual production, of which 70 percent was for export markets. The rest of Asia accounted for 10 percent of total annual production, with approximately 60 percent destined for Japan, the United States and Europe. The Americas and Europe accounted for the balance of about 25 percent of total production, most of which was for local markets.

One major effect of the strong yen and the global slowdown was the sharp drop in exports from Japan. In January 2009, for example, exports dropped 49 percent compared with January 2008. As exporters found their sales falling, they cut orders from their suppliers, so there was a ripple effect in the Japanese economy, affecting both production and employment. These events caused a sharp contraction in the Japanese economy as GDP fell 12.1 percent in the fourth quarter of 2008 compared with the fourth quarter of 2007, and many experts felt that Japan was going through its worst recession since World War II. Deflation was also affecting the Japanese economy again, and consumers were delaying purchases hoping that prices would continue to fall, and companies were hesitant to invest more.

The strong yen was also hurting Sony's financial statements. As Sony translates U.S. dollar or euro financial statements into yen, net assets and earnings will be worth less in yen, dragging down Sony's consolidated results. The only way to offset this drop is to sell more and improve profit margins, both of which are hard to do in a slow global economy. From a cash-flow point of view, Sony's operations abroad are remitting dividends back to Japan, but they are worth less yen as the dollar and euro weaken against the yen. One silver lining is that the purchasing power of the yen rises as it strengthens compared with other currencies, so everything it imports into Japan for its manufacturing is cheaper. The same would be true for anything manufactured outside of Japan, thus reducing costs and hopefully increasing margins. As long as Sony is invoicing its exports in dollars to customers worldwide, it needs to match the dollar revenues with dollar expenses through investing more in the United States or in other countries in Asia, like Taiwan, where components such as flat panel displays are cheaper and where Sony can invoice its purchases in dollars.

One big challenge Sony faces is its competition from other Asian companies such as Samsung. Sony has to carefully watch the value of the yen against the Korean won to see what its competitive position is. If the yen rises against the won and other Asian currencies, Sony risks losing market share to other Asian companies because it will not be price competitive. This is forcing Sony to move offshore faster and localize production in other markets it hopes to penetrate. Sony has a lot of strengths, but it also has a lot of challenges that it will have to resolve in the future. ■

QUESTIONS

1. Why did the contraction of the U.S. and Japanese economies and the rise in the value of the yen hurt Sony's exports from Japan?
2. In what other ways has the strong yen affected Sony's bottom line? What would be the effect of a weak yen?
3. Given the instability in the currency markets, why do you think it is important for Sony to manufacture more products in the United States and Europe and to also buy more from suppliers in other countries in Asia?
4. What are the major forces that affected the Japanese yen prior to the global financial crisis in the fourth quarter of 2008? What has had the greatest impact on the yen since then, and where do you forecast the future value of the yen?

SUMMARY

- The International Monetary Fund (IMF) was organized in 1945 to promote international monetary cooperation, to facilitate the expansion and balanced growth of international trade, to promote exchange-rate stability, to establish a multilateral system of payments, and to make its resources available to its members who are experiencing balance-of-payments difficulties.

- The special drawing right (SDR) is a special asset the IMF created to increase international reserves.

- The IMF started out with fixed exchange rates but now allows countries to choose how fixed or flexible they want their exchange rates to be.

- The euro is a common currency in Europe that has been adopted by 12 of the first 15 members of the EU, and was adopted by 16 total countries by the end of 2009, with other new EU members working to meet the convergence criteria.

- The Chinese yuan is poised to be one of the most influential currencies in the world as it strengthens its institutions and the regulatory structure and trading capacity of its banks and other financial institutions.

- African countries are committed to establishing a common currency by 2021, but many obstacles may prevent them from accomplishing this objective.

- Currencies that float freely respond to supply and demand conditions free from government intervention. The demand for a country's currency is a function of the demand for its goods and services and the demand for financial assets denominated in its currency.

- Fixed exchange rates do not automatically change in value due to supply and demand conditions but are regulated by their central banks.

- Central banks are the key institutions in countries that intervene in foreign-exchange markets to influence currency values.

- The Bank for International Settlements (BIS) in Switzerland acts as a central banker's bank. It facilitates communication and transactions among the world's central banks.

- A central bank intervenes in money markets by increasing a supply of its country's currency when it wants to push down the value of the currency and by stimulating demand for the currency when it wants the currency's value to rise.

- Many countries that strictly control and regulate the convertibility of their currencies have a black market that maintains an exchange rate more indicative of supply and demand than the official rate.

- Fully convertible currencies, often called *hard currencies,* are those that the government allows both residents and nonresidents to purchase in unlimited amounts.

- Currencies that are not fully convertible are often called *soft currencies* or *weak currencies.* They tend to be the currencies of developing countries.

- To conserve scarce foreign exchange, some governments impose exchange restrictions—such as import licensing, multiple exchange rates, import deposit requirements, and quantity controls—on companies or individuals who want to exchange money.

- Some factors that determine exchange rates are purchasing power parity (relative rates of inflation), differences in real interest rates (nominal interest rates reduced by the amount of inflation), confidence in the government's ability to manage the political and economic environment, and certain technical factors that result from trading.

- Major factors that managers should monitor when trying to predict the timing, magnitude, and direction of an exchange-rate change include the institutional setting (what kind of exchange-rate system the country uses), fundamental analysis (what is going on in terms of the trade balance, foreign-exchange reserves, inflation, etc.), confidence factors (especially political factors), events (like meetings of the G8 group of countries to discuss exchange rates), and technical analysis (trends in exchange-rate values).

- Exchange rates can affect business decisions in three major areas: marketing, production, and finance.

KEY TERMS

advance import deposit (p. 417)
black market (p. 415)
Bretton Woods Agreement (p. 397)
European Central Bank (ECB) (p. 405)
European Monetary System (EMS) (p. 405)
European Monetary Union (EMU) (p. 405)

Fisher Effect (p. 420)
fundamental forecasting (p. 422)
hard currency (p. 416)
International Fisher Effect (IFE) (p. 420)
International Monetary Fund (IMF) (p. 396)
Jamaica Agreement (p. 399)
multiple exchange-rate system (p. 417)

par value (p. 397)
purchasing power parity (PPP) (p. 417)
quota (p. 397)
Smithsonian Agreement (p. 399)
soft (or weak) currency (p. 416)
special drawing right (SDR) (p. 398)
technical forecasting (p. 422)

ENDNOTES

1 *Sources include the following:* "El Salvador Learns to Love the Greenback," *The Economist* (September 26, 2002), p. 62; John Lyons, "Squeezed by Dollarization," *Wall Street Journal* (March 8, 2005): A18; Bureau of Economic and Business Affairs, U.S. Department of State, "2001 Country Reports on Economic Policy and Trade Practices" (February 2002), at www.state.gov/documents/organization/8202.pdf (accessed May 30, 2005); U.S. Department of State, "Background Note—El Salvador," at www.state.gov/r/pa/ei/bgn/2033.htm (accessed May 30, 2005); U.S. Department of State, "Background Note—Ecuador," www.state.gov/r/pa/ei/bgn/35761.htm (accessed May 30, 2005); Juan Forero, "Ecuador's President Vows to Ride Out Crisis over Judges," *New York Times* (April 18, 2005), A12.

2 International Monetary Fund, "IMF Chronology," at http://imf.org/external/np/exr/chron/chron.asp (accessed August 22, 2007).

3 IMF, "The IMF at a Glance," *International Monetary Fund,* http://imf.org/external/np/exr/facts/glance.htm (accessed June, 2009).

4 IMF, "About IMF," at http://imf.org/external/about/overview.htm (accessed July 23, 2009).

5 IMF, "The IMF at a Glance."

6 IMF, "Organization," at http://imf.org/external/np/obp/orgcht.htm (accessed July 23, 2009).

7 Todd Benson, "Report Looks Harshly at IMF's Role in Argentine Debt Crisis," *New York Times* (July 30, 2004): W1.

8 IMF, "Special Drawing Rights (SDRs): A Factsheet," at http://imf.org/external/np/exr/facts/sdr.htm (accessed August 21, 2007).

9 IMF, "Special Drawing Rights (SDRs)."

10 Kim Kyoungwha and David Yong, "Dollar's Role Is Safe as IMF Expands Own Currency," Bloomberg.com (accessed on April 3, 2009); "Presto: Another $750 Billion," *Wall Street Journal* (April 14, 2009): A14; Joana Slater, "Emerging Markets Go on a Tear," *Wall Street Journal* (April 13, 2009): c1.

11 See Guillermo A. Calvo and Carmen M. Reinhart, "Capital Flow Reversals, the Exchange Rate Debate, and Dollarization," *Finance & Development* 36:3 (1999), p. 13 ; "No More Peso?" *The Economist* (January 23, 1999): 69; Steve H. Hanke, "How to Make the Dollar Argentina's Currency," *Wall Street Journal* (February 19, 1999): A19; Michael M. Phillips, "U.S. Officials Urge Cautious Approach to Dollarization by Foreign Countries," *Wall Street Journal* (April 23, 1999): A4; "A Decline without Parallel," *The Economist* (February 28, 2002), www.economist.com.

12 Craig Torres, "Chile Suspends Trading Band on Its Peso," *Wall Street Journal* (September 7, 1999): A21; "IMF Welcomes Flotation of Iceland's Krona," *IMF News Brief* (accessed March 28, 2001), www.imf.org/external/np/sec/nb/2001/nb0129.htm.

13 "Convergence Criteria for European Monetary Union," *Bloomberg News* (accessed August 9, 2002), www.bloomberg.com.

14 "Prime Minister Says Sweden Fulfills Criteria to Adopt Euro," *Dow Jones Newswires* (August 19, 2002), www.wsj.com (accessed August 19, 2002).

15 Christopher Rhoads and G. Thomas Sims, "Rising Deficits in Europe Give Euro Its Toughest Challenge Yet," *Wall Street Journal* (September 15, 2003): A1.

16 Edmund L. Andrews, "On Euro Weekend, Financial Institutions in Vast Reprogramming," *New York Times* (January 2, 1999), www.nytimes.com (accessed October 12, 2009).

17 Peter Garnham, "China Plans Global Role for Renminbi," *Financial Times* (July 14, 2009) 23.

18 Jeremiah Marquez, "China Allows HSBC and Bank of East Asia to Sell Chinese Currency Bonds in Hong Kong," *Associated Press Newswires* (accessed May 19, 2009).

19 Paul Masson and Catherine Patillo, "A Single Currency for Africa?" *Finance & Development* (December 2004): 9–15; "History of the CFA Franc," at www.bceao.int/internet/bcweb.nsf/pages/umuse1 (accessed May 30, 2005); IMF, "The Fabric of Reform—An IMF Video," at www.imf.org/external/pubs/ft/fabric/backgrnd.htm (accessed May 30, 2005).

20 Lambertus van Zyl, "South Africa's Experience of Regional Currency Areas and the Use of Foreign Currencies," in *Regional Currency Areas and the Use of Foreign Currencies*, BIS Papers # 17 (May 2003): 134.

21 "U.S. Foreign Exchange Intervention," at http://www.ny.frb.org/aboutthefed/fedpoint/fed44.html (accessed July 24, 2009).

22 International Monetary Fund, "Currency Composition of Official Foreign Exchange Reserves (COFER)," http://www.imf.org/external/np/sta/cofer/eng/index.htm (last updated September 30, 2009 and accessed October 8, 2009).

23 Joanna Slater and John Lyons, "Emerging Markets Lose a Little of Their Resilience—Now Face Stress Test," *Wall Street Journal* (July 17, 2007): C1.

24 Sam Y. Cross, *All about the Foreign Exchange Market in the United States* (New York: Federal Bank of New York, 2002): 92–93.

25 David Wessel, "Intervention in Currency Shrinks under Clinton," *Wall Street Journal* (September 14, 1995): C1.

26 Federal Reserve Bank of New York, "U.S. Foreign Exchange Intervention," http://www.ny.frb.org/aboutthefed/fedpoint/fed44.html (accessed July 25, 2009).

27 Paul Evans, "Dollar Climbs Back on Rivals," *Wall Street Journal* (March 11, 2009): C14.

28 Charles Forelle and Bob Davis, "Iceland Raises Key Rate to 18% to Defend Currency," *Wall Street Journal* (October 29, 2008): A10.

29 Charles Forelle, "Iceland Votes to Try Joining EU," *Wall Street Journal* (July 17, 2009): A7.

30 "South Korea to Stop Currency Intervention: Report," *Yahoo! News* (May 18, 2005), at http://news.yahoo.com/s/afp/20050518/bs_afp/forexusskorea_050518191953 (accessed May 30, 2005).

31 Evan Ramstad, "Trade Surplus Lifts Prospect of Won's Rise," *Wall Street Journal* (May 4. 2009): A10; In-Soo Nam, "Foreign Exchange Reserves Rise Sharply in South Korea," *Wall Street Journal* (June 3, 2009): 9.

32 Joanna Slater and Jon Hilsenrath, "Currency-Price Swings Disrupt Global Markets," *Wall Street Journal* (October 25–26, 2008): A10.

33 Bank for International Settlements, "About BIS: Organisation and Governance," at www.bis.org/about/orggov.htm (accessed July 24, 2009).

34 He Huifeng, "Shenzhen Traders Profit from Currency Uncertainty: Black Market Demand for HK Dollar Offers Opportunity," *South China Morning Post* (March 31, 2009): 4.

35 Sheridan Prasso, "Zimbabwe's Disposable Currency," *Fortune* (August 6, 2007), CNNMoney.com (accessed August 25, 2007).

36 "Zimbabwe Unveils $1090-Trillion Banknote as Nation Battles Inflation," *National Post* (January 17, 2009): A11.

37 John Lyons and José Córdoba, "U.S. Seizure Slams Market for Dollars in Venezuela," *Wall Street Journal* (March 28–29, 2009): A1.

38 Phisanu Phromchanya, "Thai Currency Controls Eased in Bid to Cool Baht," *Wall Street Journal* (July 25, 2007): 2.

39 Natalia T. Tamirisa, "Exchange and Capital Controls as Barriers to Trade," *IMF Staff Papers* 46:1 (1999): 69.

40 "The Big Mac Index," *The Economist* (January 24, 2009), p. 106.

41 "The Big Mac Index: Food for Thought," *The Economist* (May 27, 2004), p. 75; quoting Michael Pakko and Patricia Polland, "For Here or to Go? Purchasing Power Parity and the Big Mac" (St. Louis, MO: Federal Reserve Bank of St. Louis, January 1996).

42 Evan Ramstad, "Blogger Arrested in Korea for Post that Led to Won's Decline," *Wall Street Journal* (January 13, 2009): A11.

43 Michael Phillips, "Geithner's Gaffe Briefly Hits Dollar," *Wall Street Journal* (March 26, 2009): A6.

44 "Forecasting Currencies: Technical or Fundamental?," *Business International Money Report* (October 15, 1990): 401–02.

45 See Ian H. Giddy and Gunter Dufey, "The Random Behavior of Flexible Exchange Rates: Implications for Forecasting," *Journal of International Business Studies* 6:1 (1975): 1–32; Christopher J. Neely and Lucio Sarno, "How Well Do Monetary Fundamentals Forecast Exchange Rates?" St. Louis Fed (September/October 2002), 51–74. https://www.research.stlouisfed.org/publications/review/02/09/51-74Neely.pdf. (accessed October 8, 2009).

46 Andrew C. Pollock and Mary E. Wilkie, "Briefing," *Euromoney* (June 1991): 123–24.

47 Dominic Lau, "Market Jitters Making HK Currency Peg Debate Taboo," *Reuters News Service,* http://asia.news.yahoo.com (accessed September 24, 2002).

48 David A. Moss, *A Concise Guide to Macro Economics* (Boston: Harvard Business School Press, 2007): 131.

49 Cross, *All about the Foreign Exchange Market*, 114.

50 Timothy Aeppel and Joanna Slater, "Surging Exports Lighten the Gloom," *Wall Street Journal* (March 24, 2008): A2.

51 Oscar Suris, "BMW Expects U.S.-Made Cars to Have 80% Level of North American Content," *Wall Street Journal* (August 5, 1993): A2.

52 Suris, "BMW Expects U.S.-Made Cars to Have 80% Level of North American Content."

53 Jamie McGeever, "Dollar Gets Battered across the Board," *Wall Street Journal* (December 9, 2003): C17; Sebastian Moffett, "Japan's Yen Strategy Offers Economic Relief," *Wall Street Journal* (January 12, 2004): A2; Miyako Takebe, "Japan Plans to Keep Intervening in Markets to Hold Down the Yen," *Wall Street Journal* (March 17, 2004): B4E; Alan Beattie, "Japan and ECB Consider Joint Currency Move as Dollar Falls," *Financial Times* (December 2, 2004): 11; Sony 2008 Annual Report; Robert Flint, "Yen Gains on Dollar, Europe in Flight from Risk," *Wall Street Journal* (January 13, 2009): C2; Joanna Slater, Yuka Hayashi, and Peter Stein, "Move to Stem Yen's Rise Is Likely," *Wall Street Journal* (October 28, 2008): C1; Stanley Reed, "What's Driving Up the Dollar," *Business Week* (December 8, 2008): 38; John Murphy and Hiroko Tabuchi, "Japan's Companies, Consumers, React to New Reality," *Wall Street Journal* (October 29, 2008), A13; John Murphy, "Toyota's Global Woes Start to Hit Home in Japan," *Wall Street Journal* (November 4, 2008): A10; Yumiko Ono and Andrew Monahan, "Japan Exports Fall 49% as U.S. Trade Plunges," *Wall Street Journal* (March 26, 2009): A7; John Murphy, Peter Stein, and Neil Shah, "Dollar Vexes Asian Central Banks," *Wall Street Journal* (May 26, 2009): C1.

Global Strategy, Structure, and Implementation

eleven

The Strategy of International Business

Objectives

- To identify how managers develop strategy

- To examine industry structure, firm strategy, and value creation

- To profile the features and functions of the value-chain framework

- To assess how managers configure and coordinate a value chain

- To explain global integration and local responsiveness

- To profile the types of strategies firms use in international business

Vision without action is a daydream. Action without vision is a nightmare.

—*Japanese proverb*

CASE Value Creation in the Global Apparel Industry

Strategy in the global apparel industry is a combination of design, production, buying, and distribution conditions.[1] Historically, national retailers outsourced apparel production, via global brokers, to thousands of small apparel makers. The typical apparel manufacturer, usually located in a low-wage country, is a small-scale operation that employs a few to a few dozen workers. In a labor-intensive process, workers make specific pieces of clothing, often in a narrow range of sizes and colors. These pieces are then integrated with the output of hundreds of other such companies spread across dozens of countries. As more countries make more specialized products—for example, one factory makes zippers, one makes linings, one makes buttons—multinational trading companies perform as cross-border intermediaries and supervise the assembly of component pieces into finished goods.

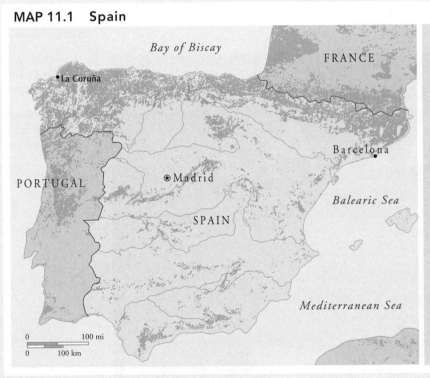

MAP 11.1   Spain

Bay of Biscay

FRANCE

La Coruña

PORTUGAL

⊗ Madrid

Barcelona

Balearic Sea

SPAIN

Mediterranean Sea

0   100 mi
0   100 km

Zara is headquartered in La Coruña, in the extreme northwest corner of the country. Contemporary Spain increasingly looks to its growing textile and apparel industry, which has made the country an international center for the fashion business.

Once assembled, finished goods are shipped to apparel retailers. Increased speed and flexibility in responding to market shifts was a constant concern for apparel retailers. Therefore, they pushed multinational trading companies to improve coordination between themselves and overseas factories. Planning collections closer to the selling season, testing the market, placing smaller initial orders, and reordering more frequently let retailers reduce forecasting errors and inventory risks.

The final links in this chain are markets and customers. Although there is overlap among countries, local customers' preferences had traditionally varied. For example, the British seek stores based on social sensitivities, Germans are value conscious, and shoppers in the United States look for a mix of variety, quality, and price. Collectively, these conditions create a buyer-driven chain in the global apparel industry that links fragmented factories, global brokers, dispersed retailers, and local customers.

Globalization is changing these relationships. Traditionally, industry wisdom spurred firms to choose a "sliver" of a particular activity—to make zippers, manage logistics, focus on store design, or cater to customer segments—instead of trying to create value across several different activities. The standard of "do what you do best and outsource the rest" prevailed throughout the global apparel industry.

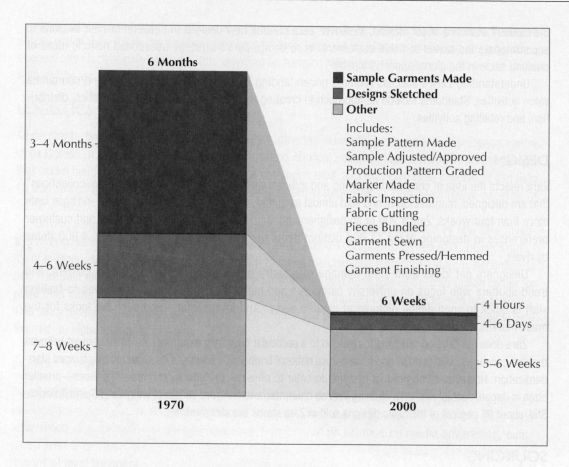

FIGURE 11.1 Cycle Time in the Global Apparel Industry

In the apparel industry, as in many other industries, globalization has brought changes that open options for players in the market. For example, innovations in technology, sourcing, and production let apparel makers steadily compress by the *cycle time* required for value activities. Contracting the time that elapses from the beginning to the end of a process improves effiencies and boosts profits.

Source: Adapted from Zara company documents.

Today, reductions in tariff barriers, integration of markets, and improving communications create new industry standards and strategic choices. A compelling example is the compression of cycle times in the apparel-buyer chain (see Figure 11.1). In the 1970s, getting a garment from the factory to the customer took six months. In 2009, it takes, on average, anywhere from nine months down to about six weeks to run this cycle. However, for one firm, Zara, it takes less than two weeks. By rejecting conventional standards, Zara has redefined the relationship among industry structure, company strategy, and firm performance.

Who is Zara? First, some demographics on Zara. In addition to Zara, Inditex, the parent corporation, also ran seven other retail chains, such as Bershka and Massimo Dutti, from its headquarters in Artexio, near La Coruña, a midsize city in northwest Spain (see Map 11.1). The Inditex Group employs about 90,000 people, half of them in Spain and the rest in the various countries where it operates. The company workforce is young (the average age is 26) and female (besides representing almost 83 percent of employees, women hold more than half of the executive, technical, and managerial positions). Inditex's revenue was $14.1 billion for 2008, just behind the worldwide leader Gap's $14.5 billion. International sales accounted for 66 percent of total sales, and 85 percent of its total retail surface area of its 4,264 storesfronts worldwide was outside of Spain; it planned to open about 450 new stores worldwide in 2009. The market acknowledged the company's performance. From June 2004 through March 2009, Inditex's stock price appreciated more than 60 percent while that of Gap fell 35 percent. In 2007, Inditex was named Global Retailer of the Year by the World Retail Congress.

Zara was the flagship of the Inditex Group. The first Zara shop opened its doors in 1975 in La Coruña. Zara now has a network of 1,292 stores spread across 72 countries. Zara uses an innovative strategy to power its global performance, integrating infotech, fashion, and e-business to make and move sophisticated clothing at appealing prices—as one analyst noted, "Armani at moderate prices." Zara translates the latest fashion trend from a catwalk in Paris to its store shelves in Shanghai in as little as two weeks versus

FIRM INFRASTRUCTURE

The infrastructure that Zara has built to coordinate these value activities is a key competency. There are many, but two stand out: managers' sense of customers and markets and their ability to coordinate activity worldwide.

Managers believe the allure of Zara is the freshness of its offerings, the creation of a sense of exclusiveness, an attractive in-store ambience, and positive word of mouth. These ideas drive rapid product turnover, with new designs arriving in twice-weekly shipments. Zara's fans learn which days of the week goods are delivered and shop accordingly. About three-quarters of the merchandise on display changes every three to four weeks. This corresponds to the average time between visits, given estimates that the average Zara shopper visits the chain 17 times a year—versus three to four visits per year for competitors.

Attractive stores, both inside and out, are an asset. As Luis Blanc, a director at Inditex, explains, "We invest in prime locations. We place great care in the presentation of our storefronts. That is how we project our image. We want our clients to enter a beautiful store where they are offered the latest fashions. But most important, we want our customers to understand that if they like something, they must buy it now, because it won't be in the shops the following week. It is all about creating a climate of scarcity and opportunity."

Rapid turnover fans a sense of "buy now because you won't see it later." Zara reinforces scarcity with small shipments, sparsely stocked shelves, and a display limit of one month. Rapid turnover means that consumers visit Zara three or four times a season rather than just once. These policies also keep Zara's shops looking fresh and reduce markdowns; the number of items that it puts on clearance sale is about half the industry average.

Managers' adept coordination of the overlapping activities among its designers, workers, salespeople, and plants testifies to the power of its strategy. No other company can ship new fashion designs to stores as speedily as Zara. Still, besides growing faster, Zara hits the same profit margins with higher sales per square foot than do its rivals. Zara's strategy and business design leave rivals with less time to figure out how to better configure and coordinate operations. Some believe that firms have little option but to follow Zara's strategic lead. If they don't, warns a leading retail analyst, they "won't be in business in 10 years."

CRN
Case Review Note

Introduction

The first half of our text explains that international companies operate in an environment shaped by cultural, political, legal, economic, trade, monetary, governmental, and institutional forces. These forces comprise the environment of international business that sets the context for managers' actions (see Figure 11.2). It is this latter perspective—what managers do, given conditions and trends in the environment, to make their companies competitive—that anchors this chapter and the remainder of the text.

This chapter looks at how managers devise strategies to engage international markets that boost current performance and sustain long-term growth. Although commonalities that integrate countries create opportunities for companies, differences endure that constrain their actions. This chapter accepts this understanding and identifies factors that then influence managers' strategic analyses. Among them are the managers' evaluation of the idea of strategy, the tools that support their choices, and the processes that convert their vision into action.

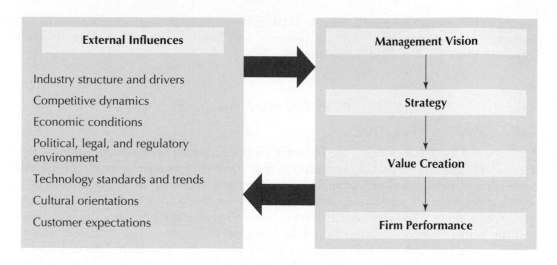

External Influences

Industry structure and drivers

Competitive dynamics

Economic conditions

Political, legal, and regulatory environment

Technology standards and trends

Cultural orientations

Customer expectations

Management Vision

Strategy

Value Creation

Firm Performance

FIGURE 11.2 The Role of Strategy in International Business

In Chapter 1, we introduce the idea of the operating environment to encompass the physical/social and competitive factors that influence the external environment in which an international business conducts its operations. Among these operations, we include *strategy*: the means by which managers establish and sustain the company's competitive position within its industry. Beginning with the current chapter, we focus on the way in which a firm's strategy responds to as well as shapes the physical/social and competitive factors in its external environment.

The remaining chapters of our text elaborate the framework we build in Chapter 11. That is, our understanding of strategy guides the analysis of subsequent issues, including how firms enter foreign markets, make investments, form alliances, and organize activities. In the final section of the text, ideas from Chapter 11 anchor discussions of how MNEs design and implement their marketing, manufacturing, supply, accounting, finance, and human resource strategies.

> Strategy is the framework that managers apply to determine the competitive moves and business approaches that run the company.

Revisiting Zara   Our opening profile of Zara previews many of these issues. When Zara began its global expansion, for instance, strategy in the apparel business was dictated by the structure of the industry—a structure that was inefficient (it took too much time to design and deliver clothing) and ineffective (apparel makers and sellers were plagued by forecasting and inventory problems). Figure 11.1 (p. 435) shows that Zara rejected the conventions dictated by this structure and, over the next decade, developed an innovative strategy to reset the standards of operational efficiency and market effectiveness.

Zara's strategy changed the apparel industry in ways that redefine ideas of global integration (standardizing worldwide activities to maximize efficiency) and national responsiveness (adapting local activities to maximize effectiveness). More specifically, Zara changed how a company in the apparel industry creates value in design, manufacturing, logistics, and marketing. In addition, it reset standards regarding how a company coordinates the business functions that support value creation. Finally, Zara's long-running series of choices highlight the value of strategy for the international company—managing the tension between global integration and local responsiveness in converting strategy into superior value.

Concept Check

Recall that in Chapter 3 we rely on the dichotomy between **democracy** and **totalitarianism** and the idea of political freedom as a framework for integrating information about international business. In Chapter 4, we use the differences among **market, mixed,** and **command economies** and the notion of economic freedom to build a similar framework. A key framework in this chapter is the different ways managers study **strategy** within the context of industry structure and the configuration and coordination of value activities.

Industry, Strategy, and Firm Performance

Before profiling strategy in the MNE, we review fundamental features of strategic management. In specific, we look at the ideas of and relationships among industry, strategy, and firm performance. We begin by looking at the idea of an industry because it influences the profitability of the typical company. The forces in the MNE's environment that routinely have the greatest impact on its strategy are in its immediate industry environment. For example, BMW worries how trends in interest rates, changes in political leadership, and innovations in technologies affect the potential for

> Strategy expresses management's idea on how to best
> - Attract customers.
> - Operate efficiently.
> - Compete effectively.
> - Create value.

An industry is composed of the companies engaged in a particular kind of commercial enterprise.

profits in the auto industry. However, BMW is far more sensitive to the actions of fellow industry members like Toyota, Goodyear, and Bosch because they directly affect its competitive position and performance.

INDUSTRY ORGANIZATION PARADIGM LEADING STRATEGY PERSPECTIVES

A prominent model of strategy, the **Industry Organization (IO) paradigm,** captures this thesis. To begin, the IO paradigm presumes that markets demonstrate **perfect competition**—that is, there are many firms with small market shares, all firms are price takers, identical products are sold by all firms, companies can freely enter and exit the industry, and there is perfect knowledge (i..e, buyers know the features of the product being sold and the prices charged by other firms). In this idealized market, risk-adjusted rates of return should be constant across firms and industries—over time, no one firm or industry should consistently outperform others.[2] In cases where industries generate high profits, new companies enter, thereby creating competition that then lowers prices and profits.

Perfect competition presumes

- Many buyers and sellers such that no individual affects price or quantity.
- Perfect information for both producers and consumers.
- Few, if any, barriers to market entry and exit.
- Full mobility of resources.
- Perfect knowledge among firms and buyers.

Firm conduct refers to the strategic and tactical choices a company makes regarding research and innovation, product strategy, plant investment, pricing behavior, and the like that influence its profitability.

The IO paradigm assumes that firm performance is a function of its conduct, which is ultimately determined by industry factors that shape the corresponding pattern of competition. For example, an industry with few barriers to entry, lots of accessible buyers, and an expanding supply of low-cost, powerful technologies—as seen in e-commerce—tends to have many firms competing for profits. Therefore, this industry's stucture shapes firm conduct, namely its strategic and tactical choices regarding research and innovation, product strategy, plant investment, pricing behavior, and the like that determine its profitability. Research supports this view, finding that industry effects explain 75 percent of the difference in average returns for companies in an industry.[3]

THE EXCEPTIONS OF IMPERFECT COMPETITION

The fact that many industries are imperfectly competitive constrains the power of the IO paradigm.[4] Recurringly, different companies in different industries sustain different levels of profitability in ways that are shaped, but not determined, by industry structure. Specifically, many industries exhibit situations where entry barriers deterred potential rivals, there was the presence of a few, large sellers who behaved like oligarchs, or there was a market of many buyers (whether intermediate or end consumers) who were passive price takers. These sorts of "imperfect" industries included firms that were outstanding performers, consistently earning above-average, risk-adjusted returns. Examples include Microsoft in software, Huawei in networking equipment, Johnson & Johnson in health care, Li & Fung in logistics, Google in Internet search, Goldman Sachs in capital markets, and Nestlé in food services.

These two anomalies—markets are not always perfectly competitive and some firms consistently outperform industry averages—suggest that industry structure is not entirely deterministic of firm performance. Instead, firm performance is influenced by the presence of bright, motivated managers and their keen sense of innovative products or processes. Essentially, industry context matters, but so too does the quality of managers.[5] Bright managers find innovative ways to create value that are not easily matched or cheaply copied by rivals. This realization qualifies the IO paradigm for the potential for bright managers who develop better strategies and build better companies to outperform their counterparts. In other words, innovative strategic thinking lets managers achieve and sustain competitive advantages in spite of the prevailing structure of the industry.

As we saw in our opening case, for example, Zara's strategy of making and moving sophisticated, moderately priced fashions demanded adept integration of design talent, customer responsiveness, and information technology. At the time, market conditions and industry structure posed barriers to this strategy. Zara's managers developed a repertory of competencies spanning design, production, logistics, and retailing that converted their strategy into action. The company's standout performance, while other industry rivals struggle, highlights the payoff of bright ideas.

In summary, strategic management research emphasizes two relationships:

1. Industry structure influences a company's profitability, especially so in situations of perfect competition, less so in situations of imperfect competition.
2. Bright managers convert innovative strategies into above-average, risk-adjusted profitability, especially so in situations of imperfect competition, less so in situations of perfect competition.

Therefore, powerful relationships among industry structure and profitability require that managers understand strategy, the tools used to design it, and the performance implication of competing choices. The next parts of this chapter develop these ideas, profiling how managers interpret industry structure and then use this knowledge to craft their strategy.

ASSESSING INDUSTRY STRUCTURE

Interpreting **industry structure** relies on the concepts and tools developed in the IO paradigm.[6] Managers apply the elements shown in Table 11.1 but often rely on the **five-forces model** to integrate analysis. This model, shown in Figure 11.3, helps managers determine an industry's attractiveness, interpreting the implications of the various features of the industry to potential profitability. The five-forces model identifies how industry forces

The idea of industry structure helps explain the functions, form, and interrelationships among

- Suppliers of inputs.
- Buyers of outputs.
- Substitute products.
- Potential new entrants.
- Rivalry among competing sellers.

TABLE 11.1 The Industrial Organization Paradigm: Key Categories and Elements

Making sense of an industry is difficult. Analysts focus on features that evidence shows significantly influence structure in diverse industries. Below, we see key categories and their corresponding elements that help frame analysis

Basic Conditions	Industry Structure	Firm Conduct	Firm Performance	Government Policy
• Globalization	• Concentration	• Research & development	• Price	• Protectionism
• Consumer demand	• Number of buyers and sellers	• Advertising	• Production efficiency	• Strategic trade policy
• Foreign trade	• Barriers to entry of new firms	• Price behavior	• Allocative efficiency	• Regulation
• Production	• Product differentiation	• Segmentation	• Brand equity	• Antitrust
• Elasticity of demand	• Vertical integration	• Plant investment	• Product quality	• Barriers to entry
• Technology	• Diversification	• Legal programs	• Technical standards	• Subsidies
• Substitutes		• Product differentiation	• Leverage	• Quotas
• Raw materials		• Collusion	• Profits	• Investment incentives
• Seasonality		• Mergers and acquisitions		• Employment programs
• Unionization		• Niche segmentation		• Fiscal policies
• Rate of growth		• Process skills		• Macroeconomic policies
• Location effects		• Learning-curve advantages		
• Scale economies		• Product functionality		
• Scope economies				
• Learning effects				

FIGURE 11.3 The Five-Forces Model of Industry Structure

From the strategists' perspective, analysis of these five forces—and of the ways in which they interact—is important because it spurs them to engage vital questions. For example: Which forces are driving industry change? Which forces are likely to determine the strategic moves of competitors? Which forces will shape the potential for profitability? Which forces will be particularly important in the future? Managers' insights on these and similar issue translates into better understanding of the potential for profitablity.

Source: Adapted from Michael E. Porter, "How Competitive Forces Shape Strategy," *Harvard Business Review* 57:2 (March–April 1979): 137–45. Reprinted by permission of *Harvard Business Review,* "Industry Structure" from "How Competitive Forces Shape Strategy" by Michael E. Porter (March/April 1979). Copyright © 1979 by the Harvard Business School Publishing Corporation; all rights reserved.

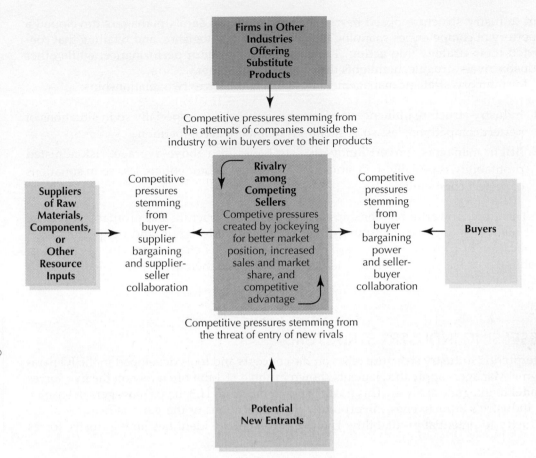

shape strategic conduct, supplies, buyers, rivals' likely moves, and drivers of sustainable competitiveness. The interaction among these forces helps managers estimate the likely profitability within an industry. As a rule of thumb, an unattractive industry is one where perfect competion drives down overall profitability, whereas an attractive industry is one where far-from-perfect competition holds the potential for above-average profitability.

The value of any framework lies in its specification of a basic conceptual structure that guides the assessment of a complex issue. Figure 11.3 serves this purpose well. It provides managers the perspective to better integrate the elements of Table 11.1 into a stucture of five fundamental forces that collectively represent competitive intensity in the industry.

INDUSTRY CHANGE

The structure of industries is dynamic. New products, new firms, new markets, and new managers trigger new developments in rivalry, pricing, substitutes, buyers, and suppliers. These developments often change a minor feature of the industry, such as the expansion of an existing distribution channel. Minor changes leave industry members the discretion of operational tweaks or patient adjustments.

Occasionally, an extraordinary change redefines one or more of the five forces in an industry. Often, big changes follow big mergers, like that of Wyeth and Pfizer in pharmaceuticals, or game-changing acquisition, such as Aluminum Corp of China buying Rio Tinto. More commonly, industry change follows disruptive market trends. For example, out of nowhere, netbooks—small, cheap, and light computers optimized for basic tasks such as Web browsing and e-mail—began reshaping the PC industry in 2009. Traditional personal computers and the many companies that make their components, like Samsung, Intel, and Microsoft, faced the biggest upheaval in industry conditions since the rise of the

A global industry is one in which a firm's competitive position in one country is significantly affected by its position in other countries.

laptop. Forecasted one analyst, "A broad shift in the consumer market toward low-cost PCs would clearly put pressure on the revenues of nearly every player in the value chain, from component suppliers to retailers."[7] Significant change, whatever the catalyst, demands immediate study of the impact on industry structure and firm profitability.

More recently, changes due to the global economic crisis are resetting the structure of most, if not all, industries. Abrupt dislocations in financial markets have altered credit terms and financing options, thereby resetting the cost of capital and investment thresholds. Consequential falls in consumer and industrial demand have reset the power of suppliers and buyers as well as intensifying competitive rivalry. Finally, the pushback against economic freedom and the growing state intervention into the economy resets free markets. The potential for profitability in all sorts of industries—from banks to automobiles to minerals to health care—is in flux.

Forces That Change Industry Structure   Certain forces affect firm conduct in some industries more than others do. The ball bearings industry, for instance, is more likely to change due to rapid escalation of pricing pressures, whereas the insurance business is more likely to change to reflect the emergence of international and online rivals. Although many forces of change play in any given industry, generally no more than a few command the power to reset the five forces.

Forces that transform an industry's structure include the following:

- Changes in the long-term industry growth rate
- New technologies, like containerization and wireless communications
- New consumer buying and usage patterns, such as buying music online or renting, receiving, and returning DVDs via the mail
- Manufacturing innovations that revise cost and efficiency frontiers, like *Six Sigma* programs
- The diffusion of business, executive, and technical expertise across countries, such as the transfer of the Western management approach to emerging Asian companies
- Change in government regulation, such as the privatization of state assets or escalating government involvement in capital markets
- The entry or exit of firms, such as the emergence of large-scale foreign companies
- Black swan events that are highly improbable (and unforeseen and therefore omitted from models) that nonetheless occur and have significant impacts—such as the Internet or the global economic crisis

> Industry structure changes because of events like
>
> - Competitors' moves.
> - Government policies.
> - Changes in economics.
> - Shifting buyer preferences.
> - Technological developments.
> - Rate of market growth.

STRATEGY AND VALUE

Earlier, we profiled the view that great managers make great strategies that make great companies that outperform their industry rivals. Much has been done to distill the principles and practices of these relationships. The most formidable task has been specifying the standards of a great strategy. A quick look through any library finds thousands of views of the standards of a great strategy. All are informative and insightful. Paradoxically, that is precisely the predicament—the fact that all are informative and insightful means that identifying the best is often more speculation than selection.

Still, there are universal hallmarks. Strategy defines the perspectives and tools managers use to appraise the company's present situation, it identifies the direction the company should go to optimize performance, and it outlines how the company will get there. These issues challenge any firm. They are especially tough for the international company because, besides dealing with the issues that face the domestic company, it faces the different consumers, industries, institutions, and environments that represent international business.

These issues often prove overwhelming. Managerial practices, however, indicate a way to deal with them. Taking a step back, they advise, reveals that the foundation principle and organizing practice of strategy is to create value. The idea of value can be defined in a variety of ways, including economic value, market value, pro forma value, social value, book value, insurance value, use value, par value, and replacement value. Value can also be defined from different perspectives, such as those of customers, employees, stakeholders, or shareholders.

Like companies worldwide, we define **value** as the measure of a firm's capability to sell what it makes for more than the costs incurred to make it. Therefore, **strategy** is the effort of managers to build and sustain the company's competitive position within its industry to create value. Put simply, strategy helps managers design and deliver activities that create value.

CREATING VALUE

Creating value spurs the firm to develop a compelling value proposition (why a consumer should buy its goods or use its services) that specifies its targeted customer markets (those consumers for whom a firm creates goods or services). This analysis, whether done on a nation-by-nation or worldwide basis, requires the firm identify how to make and sell products that exceed customers' expectations. The more successfully the company does so, the more powerful its strategy and the greater its profits.

The issues of value propositions and target markets, particularly when adjusted for international business, can make for unduly abstract interpretations. Companies translate these ideas into operational standards that put it at the proverbial fork in the strategy road: either create value by making products for a lower cost than competitors make them (the strategy of cost leadership) or by making products for which consumers willingly pay a premium price (the strategy of differentiation). We now discuss each.

Cost Leadership   Firms that choose this strategy strive to be the low-cost producer in an industry for a given level of quality. This strategy requires that a firm sell its products at the average industry price to earn a profit higher than that of rivals or below the average industry prices to capture market share. Even when making the same product, say a commodity like memory chips or gasoline, companies incur different costs. Variance follows from differences in such matters as raw materials costs, wage rates, productivity of employees, scale of production, and promotion and distribution expenses.

A cost-leadership strategy is a vital advantage in highly competitive industries, such as the airline, mortgage, ball bearing, package delivery, network router, pension administration, and memory-chip markets. Competing in this situation engages rivals who must exploit the cost-saving economies of large-scale standardization to offset high capital requirements. Presently, many Chinese companies use the cost leadership strategy. They have combined efficient manufacturing operations, inexpensive labor, and global distribution to undercut rivals on price.[8] Notably, companies like Southwest Airlines, UPS, Haier, Tata, and Virgin Mobile apply cost leadership strategies.

In the brutal game of low-cost competition, increasing volume puts great pressure on less efficient and smaller-scale companies to compete and, ultimately, survive. In the event of a price war, for example, the low-cost leader can cut prices, thereby imposing losses on competitors, yet still earn some profits. Even without a price war, as the industry matures and prices decline, the firm that makes products more cheaply will earn profits longer than its rivals. No matter the scenario, managers interpret industry structure to estimate the attractiveness of the cost leadership strategy.

Differentiation   Industries marked by a continuous stream of branded product innovations—as in the digital camera, Internet search, cell phone, wealth management, or fashion markets—have imperatives other than minimizing costs. Now, creating value depends on how well a company generates customer insights, translates those ideas into innovations, designs high-profile marketing programs, and gets its products to market quickly. Think for a moment of our opening profile of Zara, particularly the comment by an executive that "The key driver in our stores is the right fashion. Price is important, but it comes second."

Similar differentiation dynamics play in other markets. For example, Sony began selling its first netbook computer in the fall of 2009, finally entering the only sector of the PC market showing significant growth.[9] Sony's netbook uses the same processor found in competing products and, like other netbooks, Sony's machine has a 10-inch screen. However, at the time the Sony display has a resolution of 1,366 by 768 pixels rather than the more common 1,024 by 600 pixels; that means more of a Web site can be fitted onto the screen and the user will have to scroll less to see more. In addition, when one must scroll, Sony's machine provides a touch panel that is about the same size as that found on conventional laptops. Hence, Sony is using the higher resolution and larger touch pad as key differentiators between its product and competing netbooks.

As we see, then, the differentiation strategy fixates on product innovation, not relentless cost leadership, as the basis for sustainable value creation. Adjusting the color spectrum for a summer blouse line, enlarging mouse pads, or improving screen resolution are not earth-shattering revolutions in product design. However, they do create the basis for a company to claim its products are different, and therefore better, than those offered by competitors. Notably, companies like Apple, BMW, Cisco, Intel, Toyota, and LVMH apply differentiation strategies.

A differentiation strategy requires that products offer unique attributes that are valued by customers and that customers perceive them as superior to or different from alternatives available from rivals. The unique value customers see in the product, in turn, supports charging a premium price. In addition, the differentiation strategy requires a company to develop unique competencies that rivals find hard, if not impossible, to match or copy. The coolness of an iPod, the quality of a Lexus sedan, the superior service at a Ritz-Carlton, the fashion of a Zara suit, or the one-of-a-kind search system of Google, besides generating profits for the company, makes it hard for rivals to copy or challenge.

> Unique product attributes that are valued by customers is the basis of the differentiation strategy.

The presence of bright competitors throughout the world, in both advanced and emerging economies (as we see in our closing case), makes the task of identifying the basis of differentiation an ongoing critical challenge. Innovations conceived in Germany quickly diffuse throughout the world to competitors in Brazil, the United States, or China. Hence, companies battling on the basis of a superior product feature must, as the CEO of IBM notes, tirelessly determine "what will cause work to move to me? On what basis will I differentiate and compete?"[10]

The Firm as Value Chain

In principle, a firm can opt for cost leadership or differentiation (the asymmetric demands of each make it impractical to pursue both simultaneously). Whatever its choice, the potential profitability of a firm's strategy is a function of the value that customers see in its product relative to its corresponding costs. A firm earns higher profits than its rivals when it creates more value for its customers and, in turn, earns higher margins. Understanding this relationship and developing bright ideas to implement it are hallmarks of superior strategy.[11]

At some point, managers move from theorizing about the decision of a cost leadership or a differentiation strategy to the task of translating ambitions into reality. Quickly, countless questions arise. For example, as seen in our opening case, Zara offers "Armani at moderate prices." Implementing this differentiation strategy triggers many decisions: Where do we find design ideas? Where should we make products? How do we distribute worldwide? What are the most effective marketing tools? What kind of people should we hire to staff retail outlets? What should be headquarters' role in decision making?

Common to these questions are fundamental concerns about creating value: how the company will design, make, move, and sell products; how it will find efficiencies in doing so; and how it will coordinate the decisions in one part of the business with those made in other parts.[12] In isolation, these questions are tough. Global trends and conditions further complicate matters. Still, there are tried and true solutions. Specifically, thinking of the many activities the firm engages as elements of a value chain helps managers make productive decisions.

WHAT IS THE VALUE CHAIN?

The **value chain** takes its conceptual cue from the principle that "every firm is a collection of discrete activities performed to do business that occur within the scope of the firm."[13] In practice, the value chain is a straightforward framework that lets managers deconstruct the general idea of "create value" into a step-by-step system. Upon specifying the features of their company's value chain, managers can then target their insights and investments to activities that create value.

Moving from the general idea of value creation to modeling the step-by-step sequence of a value chain requires a series of analytical steps. In short order, companies configure business functions and coordinate management processes that move a product from its conception in research and development through sourcing raw materials and intermediate inputs, distribution to target markets, designing marketing programs to engage customers, and set-up of service options. Figure 11.4 maps this flow, identifying the steps and sequence of functions, often called *primary activities*, that define the value chain of a company.

Primary activities define the core business functions of a company, dealing with the development of the product, moving on to the operations built to produce a product, and, from there, to its marketing, distribution, and servicing (see Table 11.2). Primary activities reflect classical business functions and managerial orientations; hence, they carry functional labels such as product design, operations, marketing, and so on.

Performing primary activities calls upon secondary processes and programs, often called *support activities* (see Table 11.3). Support activities comprise the general infrastructure of the firm that anchor the day-to-day execution of the primary activities. Functions like systems and solution development and human resource management are instrumental aspects of the company. As we see in Figure 11.5, support activities apply to each primary activity; human resources, for example, are needed at each step of the value chain, from supervising the arrival of raw materials, to running production processes, to shipping products and filling orders, to selling and serving customers.

| Product Design | Operations | Outbound Logistics | Marketing | Service |

MANAGING THE VALUE CHAIN

Operating internationally requires companies determine how to spread value activities across different countries and at the same time determine how to link those activities. Dispersing value activities where and in how many places in the world is the issue of **configuration.** Integrating these globally distributed activities is the issue of **coordination.** Configuration and coordination are intrinsically related, but each has unique features. We now profile each.

CONFIGURATION

The option to go anywhere in the world to do any activity gives MNEs tremendous choice in where to locate value activities. No matter how big or small, every MNE looks to put elements of its value chain in the highest productivity spot in the world. In theory, configuration ranges from concentrated (the company performs all value-chain activities in one location) to dispersed (the company performs various value activities in different

---

The value chain is the set of linked value-creating activities the company performs to design, produce, market, distribute, and support a product.

Value-chain analysis helps managers understand the behavior of costs and existing and potential sources of differentiation.

A value chain disaggregates a firm into

- **Primary activities that create and deliver the product.**
- **Support activities that aid the individuals and groups engaged in primary activities.**

FIGURE 11.4   The Value-Chain Framework

Creating value is a powerful idea in the business world. Managers use the value-chain framework to understand the system of activities they configure and coordinate to create value. We see here a high-level model of the mechanics of value creation, beginning with the development of powerful ideas, then organizing production, and, finally, adding value through marketing and service activities.

Value chains identify the format and interactions between different activities of the company.

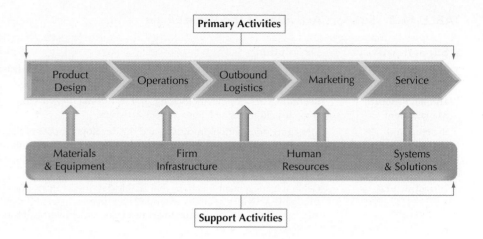

FIGURE 11.5   Primary and Support Activities

Value chains are made up of primary that reflect classical business functions and managerial orientations. Value chains also rely on support activities that help carry out the day-to-day execution of the primary activities. Each support activity is relevant to all primary activities and runs along the entire value chain.

countries). The tension between concentration and dispersion follows from the implication of costs to conducting a value chain. Recall that value creation is a function of a firm's capability to sell what it makes for more than the costs incurred to make it. Hence, MNEs configure value activities to exploit **location economies**—namely, the economies that arise from performing a value activity in the most productive location given prevailing economic, political, legal, and cultural conditions.

The decision to concentrate or disperse value activities follows the interaction between location and economics as they impact the cost of creating value. For example, if a single market, such as the United States or China, provides the most productive environment for all activities, then a company could concentrate its value chain in that locale. The company would then serve its global market through exports. Conversely, dispersed value chains make sense when costs vary across countries. Thus, if the best industrial designers are in Sweden, the MNE can base design operations there. If the most productive labor force for assembly operations is in China, that's where it builds assembly operations. If the most creative advertising minds are in South Africa, then the firm can create its advertising campaign there. Given that few MNEs can rely on a single location to concentrate their value chain, dispersing value activities among different countries to exploit cross-national cost differentials is an enduring source of competitive advantage.

Although this scenario depicts a simplified situation, in actuality there are several complications. Despite managers' preference to emphasize the efficiencies of decision making, location decisions are subject to the unpredictability of the "given prevailing economic, legal, political, and cultural conditions." This constraint frustrates configuration processes, given that abrupt change can turn a favorable location prohibitively expensive. At one

Configuration is the way in which managers arrange the activities of the value chain.

Concept Check

In discussing "Elements of the Economic Environment" in Chapter 4, we describe information on such factors as labor costs, wage rates, and productivity as key elements of a company's strategy for operating in foreign countries. In Chapter 6, we discuss methods of interpreting the relative economic performance of different countries. Here we underscore the importance of these processes in helping managers determine optimal locations for international operations.

TABLE 11.2   Primary Activities of the Value Chain

Primary Activity	Description
Product Design	The basis of the firm's advantage that sets the functions, characteristics, and aesthetics of the product or process.
Operations	Activities that transform inputs into finished product; issues of concern include raw materials procurement, sourcing components, supply chains, plant location, manufacturing process, parts production, and assembly.
Marketing	Informing buyers and consumers about products and services. Encouraging consumption by applying the marketing mix, developing a sales force, devising packaging schemes, defining the brand, and advertising.
Outbound Logistics	The task of moving the finished product from operations to wholesalers, retailers, or the final consumer. Issues of concern include demand chains, channels, inventory, warehousing, and transportation.
Service	Customer support in terms of installation, after-sales service, complaints handling, and training. Key activities include warranty, captive or independent service networks, market coverage, and speed of response.

TABLE 11.3   Support Activities of the Value Chain

Support Activity	Description
Materials and Equipment	Management of the procurement, transportation, storage, and distribution of materials and equipment necessary to conduct primary activities.
Human Resource Management	Recruiting, developing, motivating, and rewarding the workforce of the company. Supervising labor-relations activities.
Systems and Solutions	Managing information processing and the development of specialized knowledge of primary activities. Issues involve management information systems and process automation, along with the integration of relevant technologies such as telecom, wireless, and cloud systems.
Infrastructure	General management functions that enable day-to-day operations in the company. Activities include accounting and finance, legal and regulatory affairs, safety and security, quality control, and other overhead functions.

point, following the latest gyration in the business environment, Jack Welch, former chair and CEO of General Electric, thought the best location for GE factories was a mobile platform, explaining, "Ideally, you'd have every plant you own on a barge, to move with currencies and changes in the economy."[14]

The impracticality of an armada of barges requires managers to monitor cost factors closely in estimating both current and long-term location economics to value-chain

MAP 11.2   International Labor Costs

The map summarizes the officially mandated weekly compensation in various countries. Labor costs differ significantly between so-called *high-cost countries*, such as Denmark, Canada, Australia, Switzerland, and the United States, versus *low-cost countries*, such as Uganda, Tanzania, Vietnam, Nigeria, Morocco, and Nepal. Cross-national compensation differences will likely persist for years, thereby accelerating the ongoing migration of sourcing and manufacturing operations to low-cost locations.

Source: http://en.wikipedia.org/wiki/list_of_minimum_wages_by_country. Notes: (1) minimum wages given refer to a gross amount, i.e. before deduction of taxes and social security contributions, which vary from one country to another; (2) figures expressed in international dollar, a hypothetical unit of currency that has the same purchasing power that the U.S. dollar had in the United States at a given point in time.

Note: Given that this is a Mercator projection, the scale approximates east-west distance at the equator; however, the farther you move from the equator, the more the east-west distance is distorted.

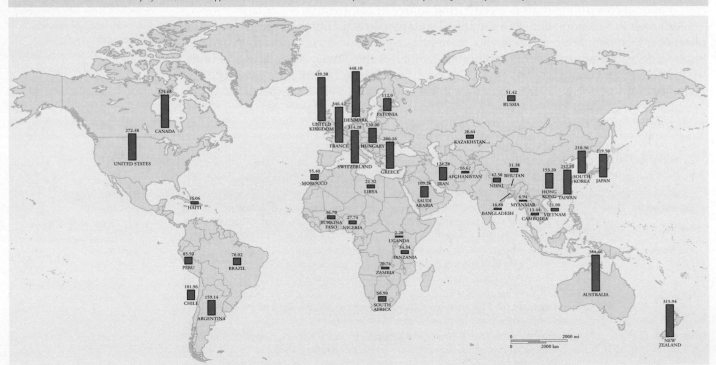

configuration. The dynamism of prevailing economic, legal, political, and cultural conditions spurs managers to consider the cost implication of broader features of the environment. Effectively, managers organize their configuration of value activities in terms of *macro cost factors* as well as the moderating influence of *cluster effects, logistics, digitization, economies of scale, and business environments.* We now profile each.

Factors that influence value-chain configuration include

- *Cluster effects.*
- *Logistics.*
- *Digitalization.*
- *Economies of scale.*
- *Business environments.*

Macro Cost Factors   Differences in wage rates, worker productivity, inflation rates, and government regulations—among the host of factors that shape macroeconomics—mean costs of conducting activities vary from country to country. And, with regards to value-chain configuration, cost differentials spur dispersing value activities. Consider, for example, the matter of labor costs. In 2003, the average hourly compensation (including benefits) for production workers in China was $0.80 versus $25.34 in the United States.[15] By 2007, wages in Mexico were about 11 percent of the U.S. level; in China, wages were 3 percent of the U.S. level.[16] In 2009, weekly labor rates varied from country to country. Map 11.2, for example, shows an astonishing range in the average weekly wage rates. At the high end, we have Denmark mandating $448 per week while at the low end, Uganda requires about $2.20 per week. The variation between these endpoints for the countries reported in Map 11.2 is similarly startling. The mean weekly wage is $136, but the standard deviation is $133.[17] Furthermore, relative productivity performances cannot neutralize many of these differences—effectively, a worker in Uganda would need to be approximately 200 times more productive than a worker in Denmark to equalize the per unit labor rate.

Consequently, wage differences, both present and projected, drive value-chain configuration for many MNEs. For instance, the quest for productive, low-cost labor has led tens of thousands of MNEs to open operations in China—with the resulting view that China has become the factory floor for the world. Furthermore, wage data indicate accelerating migration of manufacturing operations from high-cost to rapidly developing low-cost countries in Southeast Asia, Central and Eastern Europe, and South America.

Manufacturing costs vary from country to country because of wage rates, worker productivity, resource availability, and fiscal and monetary policies.

Table 11.4 gives a sense of the likely direction of migration. It ranks countries with the largest labor forces, thereby providing a first-order sign of where companies will seek labor with the assumption that high supply results in low wages. Notably, two countries—China and India—presently account for 41 percent of total labor in the world.

TABLE 11.4   Global Distribution of Labor: Top 10 Countries

From the standpoint of primary cost factors, China and India are attractive sources for firms seeking abundant, productive, and low-cost labor. As such, China and India demonstrate the idea of location economies—specifically, those economies that companies select to perform value-chain activities where prevailing economic, political, and cultural conditions create productive operating locations.

Rank	Country	Labor Force	Share of Total World Labor Pool[1]
1	China	807,300,000	24.9%
2	India	523,500,000	16.1
3	European Union	224,400,000	6.9
4	United States	154,300,000	4.7
5	Indonesia	112,000,000	3.4
6	Brazil	93,650,000	2.9
7	Russia	75,700,000	2.3
8	Bangladesh	70,860,000	2.2
9	Japan	66,500,000	2.0
10	Nigeria	51,040,000	1.6

[1]The total labor count for the world is approximately 3,232,000,000 workers.

Source: Excerpted from Central Intelligence Agency, "Country Comparisons: Labor Force," *The World Factbook 2008,* at www.cia.gov (accessed December 30, 2009).

MAP 11.3 Economic Clusters around the World

Economic clusters exist in virtually every industry in every part of the world—one authoritative source identifies more than 800 specific economic clusters. Here we see a sampling of clusters in various industries across various countries.

Source: Various sources contribute to this representation—most notably, the Cluster Profiles Project of the Institute for Strategy and Competitiveness at Harvard Business School.

Note: Given that this is a Mercator projection, the scale approximates east-west distance at the equator; however, the farther you move from the equator, the more the east-west distance is distorted.

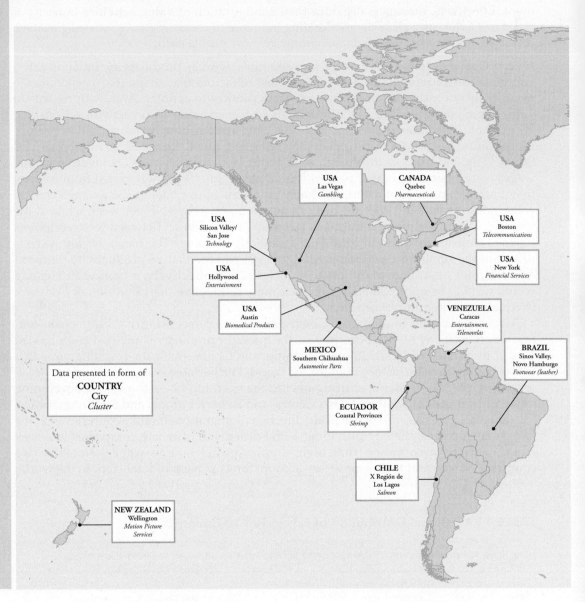

USA
Las Vegas
Gambling

CANADA
Quebec
Pharmaceuticals

USA
Silicon Valley/
San Jose
Technology

USA
Boston
Telecommunications

USA
Hollywood
Entertainment

USA
New York
Financial Services

USA
Austin
Biomedical Products

VENEZUELA
Caracas
*Entertainment,
Telenovelas*

MEXICO
Southern Chihuahua
Automotive Parts

BRAZIL
Sinos Valley,
Novo Hamburgo
Footwear (leather)

Data presented in form of
COUNTRY
City
Cluster

ECUADOR
Coastal Provinces
Shrimp

CHILE
X Región de
Los Lagos
Salmon

NEW ZEALAND
Wellington
*Motion Picture
Services*

In the longer term, many companies will look past China to India for investment opportunities. Between 2004 and 2050, India's population will increase by more than 500 million, whereas China's will rise about 79 million; the United States, in comparison, will grow by about 98 million.

Auguste Comte, a nineteenth-century social scientist, reasoned, "demography is destiny." So it is too, in large degree, with the configuration of value chains with regards to labor. The demography of labor spurs companies whose activities are sensitive to labor cost differentials—such as those companies implementing a cost leadership strategy—to anchor their configuration decisions in the data shown in Map 11.2 and Table 11.4. Doing so leads to value chains that configure operations to maximize value creation by operating in low-cost, productive countries. Outcomes in the marketplace exemplify this situation. IBM, for example, has increased its labor force in India from just a few hundred in 1999 to nearly 100,000 in 2009. Cisco and GE, among a host of others, have similarly reconfigured their value chains.

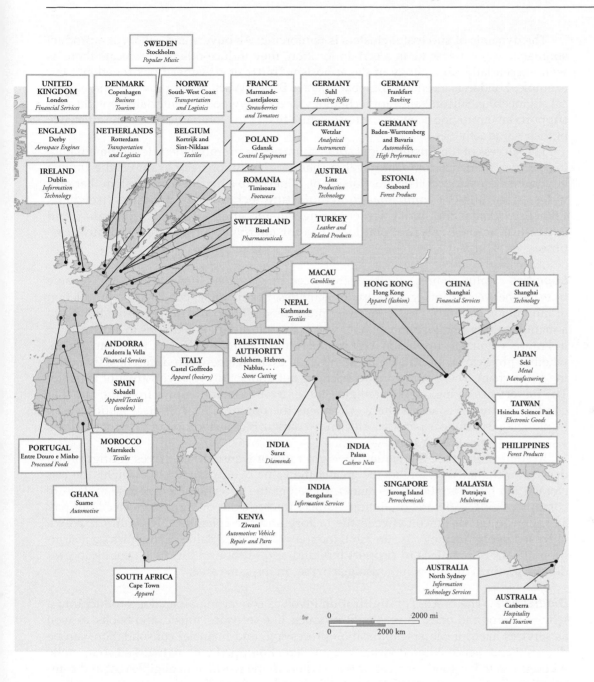

Cluster Effects A peculiarity of value creation is the so-called cluster effect, in which a particular industry gradually clusters more and more related value creation activities in a specific location.[18] Effectively, industry clusters are geographic concentrations of competing, complementary, or interdependent firms and industries that do business with each other and share overlapping needs for talent, technology, and infrastructure.[19] Map 11.3 identifies a few of the 800-plus clusters around the world. The firms that comprise a cluster may be direct competitors or aligned in cooperative alliances. Typically they purchase inputs from and rely on services provided by other cluster members. Clustering related businesses and organizations in common locations creates systems of interdependent microeconomic capabilities that support collaboration as well as intensify competition. In addition, clustering companies create unique location advantages that offer firms access to specialized resources that, in turn, support optimizing value-chain configurations. Collectively, economics principles suggest that the market-driven, collaborative, and interactive features of clusters spark more insights and innovations.

An industry cluster is a system of businesses and institutions engaged with one another at various levels.

The dynamic of successful clusters is reinforcing: As buyers and sellers of a product spontaneously congregate in a certain location, they induce others to relocate there as well—essentially, an analogy of the aphorism "birds of a feather flock together." For example, London is a center for global finance, Baden-Württemberg for cars and electrical engineering, Silicon Valley for technology, and Hollywood for entertainment. Success supports an improving economic infrastructure that helps companies boost the efficiency of their value activities.

The success of the cluster model spurs countries to promote their development and, in so doing, influence companies' value-chain configurations. For example, the Taiwan government developed Hsinchu, outside of Taipei, into a high-tech ecosystem that provides a full range of companies to manufacture technologies designed elsewhere. Likewise, China and India are engaging cluster effects to make Shanghai and Bengaluru, respectively, optimal locations for microchip production and business-process outsourcing.

Logistics entails how companies obtain, produce, and exchange material and services in the proper place and in proper quantities for the proper value activity.

Logistics   Value chains, whether centralized or dispersed, are marked by extensive transfers between primary and support activities. For example, consider the production of lithium ion batteries. First, companies must mine lithium and move it from Bolivia to a manufacturing plant in Guangzhou, which ships lithium ion batteries to a distributor in France, who then supplies market channels in the European Union. Each transaction, whether physical or informational, involves an exchange between different activities of the value chain. These exchange transactions fall under the broad construct of logistics. The importance of logistics to configuration of a value chain follows from the fact that conducting business across the world opens the potential for high transaction costs. Minimizing exchange expense by efficiently configuring the location of value activities is a source of competitive advantage.

In some situations, the value-to-weight ratio of transactions drives configuration decision making. For example, the greater the value of a product to its weight, the less storage and transportation costs matter. Therefore, the decision of where to manufacture computer chips, software, or aircraft—unlike tractor axles or carpeting—need not pay attention to the distance between the factory and the consumer. In addition, as we observed in our opening case on Zara, the company whose value chain relies on just-in-time inventory practices to support inbound and outbound logistics usually locates design, production, and warehousing activities in the same area.

Case Review Note

Digitization is the conversion of analog information into digital information.

Digitization   The process of **digitization** involves converting an analog product into a string of zeros and ones. Increasingly, products like software, music, and books, as well as services like call centers, application processing, and financial consolidation, can be digitized and, hence, located virtually anywhere. Equipped with networked computers, workers can move goods and services anywhere in the world at negligible cost and complication. Consequently, the potential for digitization of goods or services influences how a company configures its value chain.

For example, many activities that could be done only in a few specialized places, such as due diligence processes in mergers and acquisitions that once took place largely in New York City, London, or Tokyo, are now offshored to firms in Bengaluru.[20] Again, for companies like IBM, the fact that much of its work can be digitized supports its migration of activity and employment from Western countries to India. Going forward, the narrowing digital divide—the gap between those with regular, effective access to digital and information technology and those without this access—plugs more companies into the matrix, thereby expanding configuration options. In addition, as we see in the photo of young children experimenting with the low-priced laptops provided by the One Laptop per Child program, fewer and fewer spots of the world remain disconnected from the network. As these children here, and their counterparts throughout the world, become increasingly fluent and familiar with information technologies, companies can rethink the configuration value activities to tap emerging sources of competencies. Going

Future competitors, collaborators, and customers: schoolchildren sit with their newly arrived laptops at their rural school in Rincon de Vignoli some 80 km north of Montevideo, Uruguay. The government of Uruguay is providing a laptop to every schoolchild with the goal of equipping the next generation of value creators with the tools to join globalization. Similar programs are unfolding in countries throughout the world. The implications of this program to the division of labor, the trade of products, and the performance of markets will shape strategy fundamentally.

Source: Miguel Rojo/Getty Images, Inc. AFP. Courtesy of Infosys Technologies Limited.

forward, the construction of Internet bases with wireless transmissions in remote villages increasingly supports "new business models to connect the poorest two billion people to the evolving nervous system of civilization."[21]

Economies of Scale   The concept of **economies of scale** refers to a situation wherein a firm doubles its cumulative output yet total cost less than doubles due to efficiency gains. Effectively, reductions in the unit cost of a product result from the increasing efficiency that comes with larger operations. The source of efficiency gains are varied, including material acquisition (i.e., bulk buying of materials through long-term contracts), production (distributed fixed costs across a large number of units), financial (access to to a greater range of financial instruments in a greater range of countries), and advertising (spreading the cost of a promotion concept over more markets). The power of these relationships, in the context of economies of scale, explains many patterns of value-chain configurations.

> Scale economies refer to the decrease in the unit cost of production associated with the increase in total output.

For example, an efficient, minimum-size factory to manufacture flat-panel displays costs roughly US $5 billion.[22] Steep up-front capital costs create high potential for scale economies; long production runs lower per unit costs as the plant's marginal cost of production decreases as the plant's operation increases. Companies facing steep scale economies, particularly those following the cost leadership strategy, configure sourcing and manufacturing to exploit the scale potentials of a few, large centralized plants. Certainly, companies can opt to operate several smaller plants dispersed worldwide. The reduced efficiency of a distributed value chain, however, erodes its competitiveness.

Business Environment   Recall from earlier discussion that Jack Welch thought that the best location for GE factories was a mobile platform, explaining, "Ideally, you'd have every plant you own on a barge, to move with currencies and changes in the economy."[23] The impracticality of this option pushes companies to configure value chains to access or avoid a particular country based on its business environment. Often, opportunistic governments recruit foreign investment. As part of the promotion of their country, they commonly promise business-friendly markets that offer tax holidays, reduced long-term tax rates, low-cost capital agreements, flexible operating requirements, and responsive public policies. Companies sift through various opportunities looking to streamline

> **Concept Check**
>
> A consistent theme of our text thus far is the intrinsic differentiation of business environments from country to country. Chapters 1 through 10 highlight the range of factors that vary, spanning the dimensions of people, product, process, and perspectives, that moderate a country's business environment.

value activities and improve cost competitiveness. In 2009, Denmark, followed by the United States, Canada, Singapore, and New Zealand, were widely regarded as the best countries for business.

In contrast, governments can create risky environments that escalate costs for current producers as well as deter potential investments. For example, governments that support the rule of man versus the rule of law deter firms fearful of intellectual property theft. In 2009, Zimbabwe, Chad, Kyrgyzstan, Cambodia, and Venezuela were regarded as the least favorable business environments in the world.[24]

Chapter 3 discussed the growing importance of intellectual property to companies' long-term competitiveness. Today, no matter where in the world one operates, policy-making and senior executives emphasize innovation. Moreover, a key engine of innovation—technology—is accelerating. Advocates of the "singularity" principle hold that "in the first 20 years of the twentieth century, we saw more advancement than in all of the nineteenth century. And we won't experience 100 years of progress in the twenty-first century—it will be more like 20,000 years of progress at the current rate."[25] Hence, managers configure value chains with an eye toward locating activities in knowledge-intensive, technology-enabled business environments.

Table 11.5 ranks the most innovative countries in the world—as determined by their performance in promoting leading-edge technologies, expanded human capacities, better organizational and operational capability, and improved institutional performance.[26] The United States tops the rankings, reflecting its superior environment for leveraging knowledge into market-changing innovations. European nations claim five of the top 10

Concept Check

In citing some of the notable features of emerging markets in Chapter 4—the appearance of new companies looking to expand internationally, the influence of millions of consumers who are experiencing rising incomes, and the emergence of the Bottom of the Pyramid—we focus on the fact that customer needs are changing rapidly. Here we emphasize the role of these developments in spurring firms to rethink the implication of innovation to the configuration of value chains.

TABLE 11.5   Global Innovation Index, 2007

The vitality of innovation spurs efforts to estimate the degree to which countries develop business environments that support knowledge creation, increased competitiveness, and greater wealth generation. The following index values measure the relative performance of various countries in generating ideas and developing them into innovative products.

Rank	Country	Index Value[1]
1	United States	5.80
2	Germany	4.89
3	United Kingdom	4.81
4	Japan	4.48
5	France	4.32
6	Switzerland	4.16
7	Singapore	4.10
8	Canada	4.06
9	Netherlands	3.99
10	Hong Kong	3.97
11	Denmark	3.95
12	Sweden	3.90
13	Finland	3.85
14	United Arab Emirates	3.81
15	Belgium	3.77
16	Luxembourg	3.72
17	Australia	3.71
18	Israel	3.68
19	South Korea	3.67
20	Iceland	3.66

[1]An index value ranges from one to seven; a higher index value indicates better performance.

Source: Based on Soumitra Dutta and Simon Caulki, "The World's Top Innovators," *The World Business/INSEAD Global Innovation Index 2007* (January 2007), at www.worldbusinesslive.com (accessed June 18, 2007).

spots—the United Kingdom, France, Switzerland, and the Netherlands, alongside Germany—and 11 in the top 20. The data suggest rising innovation in Asia; Japan, Singapore, Hong Kong, and South Korea ranked high. In addition, India and China are rising in the ranks. Collectively, Asia appears to be moving from practices that optimized efficiency and quality to policies that improve the environment for innovation.[27]

COORDINATION

UPS and Federal Express are expanding their operations worldwide, most recently reinforcing their beachheads in China with the expansion of local hubs in Shanghai. Similarly, General Electric, Microsoft, and Accenture have opened research and development facilities in India, reasoning that the productivity of the local scientific community offers new points of value creation. As companies globally configure value activities, they must develop coordination tools. Coordinated well, MNEs can leverage their core competencies, using them to serve customers, boost sales, and improve profits. For example, breakthroughs at GE's Technology Center in Bengaluru spread to sister operations in Hungary, Brazil, China, the United States, and onward. Coordinated poorly, MNEs fail to leverage their core competencies from country to country—e.g., GE's breakthroughs in Bengaluru never make it out of India.

> Coordination is the way that managers connect the activities of the value chain.

Concept Check

In discussing the worldwide "Increase and Expansion of Technology" in Chapter 1, we note the role of technology in fostering new ways of communicating information among worldwide operations. What we want to underscore here is the impact of new technologies on the ability of companies to experiment with options—many of them unprecedented—for coordinating the geographically dispersed parts of their value chains.

Against this backdrop, then, we define coordination as the means by which management applies the systems that link a company's value activities—whether performed in one or in many countries. One way to think of this situation is to conceptualize the configuration process as placing pieces atop the global game board; coordination in this context is the specification of how the pieces move about the global game board. In theory, movement can range from not at all (in which case each piece has full autonomy) to highly coordinated (in which case each piece is tightly linked to the others). As discussed above, contemporary business practices far more often result in the latter scenario. Coordinating dispersed value activities hinges on the adept management of the movement of ideas, materials, people, and capital. Done well, the MNE achieves superior performance; done poorly, the MNE struggles.

For example, Zara's strategy of rapid response to fashion trends demands extensive coordination among activities that define its value chain. First, headquarters-based managers coordinate salespeople who act as wired grassroots market researchers that interpret buying trends, relay customer comments, and process orders. Real-time data on customer preferences is uploaded to headquarters, which then processes it so that it informs product designers, materials managers, production supervisors, and logistics controllers. The task for managers can be brutal: They must coordinate idea flows from a thousand-plus storefronts spanning the globe, oversee its translation into innovative product, organize material flows from suppliers, forward working orders to factories, and orchestrate delivery back to the thousand-plus storefronts—all within two weeks. Furthermore, adding another level of complexity is the fact that linkages exist as well between primary and support activities; for example, ensuring the availability of human resources to staff operations or updating technologies to expedite transactions. Combined, the coordination demands posed by primary and support activities are challenging. But when managed well, the resulting integration of value activities fortfiies the company's competitiveness.

Case Review Note

Intensifying the importance of skillfully coordinating activities is the growing appreciation for leveraging core competencies throughout the value chain.[28] Like beauty, the issue of a core competency defies precise specification—it is an almost ethereal concept that many see as the basis for a company's distinctive pattern of success. Generally, a **core competency** is a special outlook, skill, capability, or technology that runs through the firm's operations, weaving together disparate value activities into an integrated value chain.[29] A core competency, so to speak, gives everyone in the MNE, not just a few executives at headquarters, a principle that helps them coordinate transactions between

> A company's core competency is
> - The unique skills and/or knowledge that it does better than its competitors.
> - Essential to its competitiveness and profitability.

value activities. Understanding the exchanges among value activities and linking them to the firm's core competency spurs managers to see particular activities not as ends unto themselves but as parts of the larger, integrated scheme of creating value.

Popular examples of core competencies include Apple's eye for product design, Wal-Mart's sophisticated information-management and product-distribution systems, Tata's legacy of product innovation, Honda's insight into engine technology, Nestlé's marketing skills, or Google's ability to organize the world's information. In the case of the latter, for example, Google has set its value chain to build operations that makes information universally accessible and useful; coordinating these activities takes its cue from Google's core competency in organizing the world's information. Put differently, Google's capability to associate its various activities, assets, costs, and revenues with its core competency improves the coordination of its value chain.

Coordination Concerns　Managers configure value chains with an eye to how they will then coordinate the various activities. Several factors moderate managers' analyses of coordination. We profile the implications of *national cultures, learning effects, operational obstacles,* and *subsidiary networks.*

National Cultures　The globalization of a company's value chain, such as design done in Finland, inputs sourced from Brazil, production done in China, distribution organized in the United States, and service done in Mexico, presses managers to understand how foreign cultures influence coordination. For example, the performance of even the simplest value chain depends on each link meeting a precise timetable. Companies in Western countries generally see deadlines as firm promises of delivery. Some cultures, however, see deadlines as loose guidelines. Neglected, these sorts of gaps undermine coordination.

National cultures also impose hurdles in coordinating a transaction from one stage of the value chain to another. Units anchored in individual versus collectivist cultures may disagree over information sharing or collaboration responsibilities; conflicts complicate coordination. Hence, features of national culture require managers to understand their implications to the collaborative relationship that shape the cooordination of value actvities.

Learning Curve　The notion that "practice makes perfect" underlies the learning curve. Essentially, as managers use and improve coordination practices, their increasing proficiency improves the performance of the value chain. Managers, for example, learn by recurring experiences how to transfer best practices from country to country, thereby gaining insights of the value chain as a whole instead of a collection of parts. This sort of information helps managers plan, execute, evaluate, and leverage performance. For instance, successfully transferred coordination methods enable the MNE following a cost leadership strategy to convert higher productivity into lower costs, or, for the MNE implementing a differentiation strategy, to translate higher customer satisfaction into higher margins.

The matter of learning shapes how manufacturing and service MNEs coordinate value chains. In the case of the former, MNEs often adapt production activities for different attitudes and approaches to manufacturing. For example, an MNE may have factories in different countries, such as Japan and Mexico, which manufacture the same product but apply different production philosophies. The Mexican factory may use a traditional assembly-line operation given the local conditions of inexpensive labor, patchy transportation infrastructure, and marginal cost of high technology. The Japanese factory, in contrast, may use a *lean production system* given local labor competency, manufacturing expertise, and efficient logistics. The different manufacturing approaches complicate how managers coordinate activities between factories. Planning to learn how to coordinate these links in the value-chain positions the MNE to gain production efficiencies that lead to lower costs, higher quality, satisfied customers, and new sales.

A core competency can emerge from various sources, including

- Product development.
- Employee productivity.
- Manufacturing expertise.
- Marketing imagination.
- Executive leadership.

Several factors influence value-chain coordination:

- National cultures.
- Learning effects.
- Operational obstacles.
- Subsidiary networks.

Concept Check

In Chapters 2, 3, and 4, we show how different national cultures influence the social, workplace, political, legal, and economic contexts of markets around the world. It is important to remember that differences in cultural conditions also influence a company's strategic options, shaping such choices as where to locate an operation, how to staff it, and what role it plays in the value chain.

A learning curve is the commonsense principle that the more one does something, the better one gets at it. Companies configure value-chain activities to exploit the learning curve.

Service industries run into similar challenges in coordinating the sharing of specialized knowledge. Unlike manufacturing systems, the key factor of production for service companies is people. Therefore, coordinating activities ultimately rests on "synchronizing" people across countries and cultures. Management consulting firms like McKinsey & Company, Boston Consulting Group, and Bain & Company exemplify a successful approach. Their strategic asset is the consistent performance of their talented employees. These companies rely on extensive socialization processes to instill their preferred principles. They reinforce these programs by promoting seamless integration among offices, largely done by rotating personnel through various offices, as well as requiring sharing of information and encouraging flexibility. Hence, experience indicates that coordinating attitudes among the people links in the service value chain supports coordinating value activities.

Operational Obstacles   MNEs run into problems getting the various links of their global value chain to engage. Granted, an immense range of technology offers several means to work with one another; from proprietary company systems to public channels, all turbocharged by faster and cheaper voice, video, and data transfer options. Still, operating internationally inevitably runs into communication challenges because of time zones, differing languages, and ambiguous meanings. Picture for a moment a company whose value chain spans the globe. Parts and products flow from Kenya and Chile to their ultimate destination in Vietnam. Each transfer, from mines to plants to shipping to warehouses to storefronts, creates links that require coordination. Toss into the mix multiple time zones and multiple languages and the potential for multiple meanings is clear.

Increasingly, companies rely on browser-based communications methods to coordinate the handoffs from link to link. The thinking goes that electronically linked producers and retailers can lower coordination costs throughout the value chain. In addition, standardizing the format for data input helps standardize the format for interpretation. Electronic transactions boost efficiency by reducing intermediary transactions and the associated unneeded coordination (streamlining the distributor link in the value chain by eliminating an intermediary, for example). In larger markets, this interface is largely limited to manufacturers and their first-tier suppliers, such as the relationship between Carrefour and Procter & Gamble. Other groups champion the open-source language protocol of the World Wide Web, specifically hypertext markup language (HTML) or XML, as a global standard. So far, though, there is no consensus on interface standards, as evidenced in the proliferation of complements such as ebXML Business Process Specification Schema, Web Services Business Process Execution Language, Business Transaction Protocol, Web Service Choreography Interface, Web Services Flow Language, and so on. Still, the promise of this format for diminishing operational obstacles to coordination suggests that progress on many fronts is an inexorable game changer.

Subsidiary Networks   A network is an interconnected system of elements, such as people, associations, or business units. With that in mind, the number of MNEs has grown from 30,000 in 1990 to nearly 70,000 operating through approximately 850,000 subsidiaries today. Hence, the average MNE has a subsidary network of about 12 units, with a range of a few to a few hundred.[30] Given that globalization and technology trends have built a world marked by real-time connectivity with anyone, anywhere, subsidiary networks are marked by extensive relationships. The trend toward growing connectivity among growing numbers of MNEs with expanding subsidiary networks influences the goals and practices of coordination.

Managers coordinate the value chain so that it enables efficient transactions and ideally fortifies core competencies throughout the global network. The advent of social networks, such as those exemplified by LinkedIn, Orkut, Facebook, or MySpace, signal significant change in how managers achieve these goals. Study of the successful practices of social networks directs managers to shape how subsidiaries interact with each other, paying heed to the informal connections that link executives together as well as

Concept Check

As we explained in the closing case in Chapter 4, the emergence of the so-called *BRIC markets*—Brazil, Russia, India, and China—has spurred fundamental shifts in global investment and company strategy. Here we observe that one of these shifts moves companies to explore strategies for operating in different environments with a keen eye toward leveraging innovations across subsidiaries.

The growing prevalence of social networks provides perspectives for managers to better understand the dynamics of their subsidiary networks.

associations and connections between individual employees across countries. Rather than exchange predicated upon traditional business directives, social network analysis indicates that information flows more efficiently in a collaborative and peer-to-peer manner. Hence, network dynamics show that workers are more inclined to communicate and collaborate while simultaneously contributing and participating in coordinating the value chain. Preference among users to search, choose, modify, and consume relevant content shifts coordination emphasis within subsidiary networks to the users of information.

For example, managers from Canada GE identified a New Zealand appliance maker, Fisher & Paykel, producing a broad range of products very efficiently in its small, low-volume plant. When the Canadians used the flexible job-shop techniques to increase productivity in their high-volume factory, the U.S. appliance business became interested. Workers from GE's Louisville plant went to Montreal to study the accomplishments. Convinced of its potential, they systematized the program and transferred it to their operation. They soon reported that they had cut their production cycle in half and reduced inventory costs by 20 percent. GE's Appliance Park in Louisville soon became a "must see" destination for other GE units, and within a year, others used this knowledge to improve value chains in the locomotive and jet engine businesses.

CHANGE AND THE VALUE CHAIN

Once configured, managers cannot see the firm's value chain as set in stone. The features and functions of products that consumers want change over time—as we see in personal computers, financial services, clothing, entertainment, cell phones, and so on. Hence, the basis of value creation in an industry evolves. Moreover, as the global economic crisis shows, marketplace change can be abrupt and fundamentally disruptive. Consider that two of the five top-rated business environments in the summer of 2008—namely Ireland and the United Kingdom—saw crushed financial markets, spiraling unemployment, collapsing currencies, and shaken consumer confidence by winter 2008.[31] Similar, albeit less drastic, trends were evident in the United States, Taiwan, Japan, Spain, France, Germany, and Australia, to name just a few, by mid-2009.

Certainly, some firms, like Zara and Google, appear distinctively able to anticipate market situations and then smartly configure and adeptly coordinate their value chains. Explanations for such sorts of prescient management tend toward retrospective sense making. The distillation of their practices into anecdotal prescription typically has limited transitivity to other companies in dissimilar industries and countries. Consequently, far more common are situations wherein firms must rethink, if not reject, their value chains in the face of adverse market trends and unstable industry situations.

The configuration and coordination of value chains respond to changes in customers, competitors, industries, and environments.

A Case in Point   In 1997, Sony Corporation, Japan's premier electronics company, took little notice of the Samsung Electronics Company, a South Korean television maker then snared in a life-or-death struggle to endure the Asian currency crisis. A decade later, Samsung had nearly twice the market capitalization of Sony and commanded the role once claimed by Sony—the competitor with a portfolio of cool products and the appeal of a premium brand.

Samsung powered its rise by radically reconfiguring its value chain. In 1997, Samsung was a back-of-the-store brand with bulky, low-quality televisions. Since then, Samsung upgraded its product lines and corporate image to compete with Sony for the premium market. In terms of R&D, Samsung has been one of the world's "top 10" in U.S. patents for several years, relying on more than 13,000 researchers to invent tomorrow's products. In addition, Samsung's quest to become "world's best" drives one of the biggest capital-spending programs in the world. Samsung has turned this investment into plants that manufacture components for its many products, like memory chips and display panels, at some of the lowest production costs in the world. Similarly, Samsung has annually invested billions of dollars in advertising. By 2005, the change was complete: For the first time, Samsung's $14.6 billion brand value exceeded Sony's value of $10.7 billion, a lead it has maintained since then.[32] As one observer noted, "Samsung is like the old Sony. . . . [I]t has much of the spirit of Sony 10 years ago."

Concurrently, Sony invested billions to improve its value chain but to little gain in market share and profits. Sony's growing anxiety about its fading competitiveness led to shock therapy—it took the unprecedented step, for a major Japanese MNE, of naming an American as its chairperson in mid-2004.[33] Changes have fallen short of ambition. By 2009, Sony faced a situation where virtually every product line was unprofitable. The company reported a loss of nearly $3 billion for 2008, its first loss in 14 years. And while the global crisis hit Samsung too, it reported growing market share and continuing profitability.[34]

Caveat: The Risk of Strategy Interesting in its own right, the Sony-Samsung contest spotlights a fundamental limitation of strategy. The strategy literature holds that a decisive sense of purpose anchors short-term competitiveness and long-term sustainability. However, this outlook can also stifle creativity and erode the effectiveness of decision making, setting the stage for the fall of the mighty.[35] Again, think back to Sony's experiences. As Samsung steadily encroached on its territory, Sony's management worked feverishly to improve its products, serve its customers, and anticipate new markets. Also, it appointed a non-Japanese CEO, reorganized product and market divisions, and invested in promising ventures to reconfigure its value chain. Ultimately, though, these efforts fell short of management's vision and Sony struggles.

The upshot is that no matter how sensitive the company's strategic compass, executives' cognitive limitations, along with marketplace uncertainty, can turn prized core competencies and superbly configured and well-coordinated value chains into liabilities. Faced with such adversity, managers often return to basics, retry tired methods, and delude themselves that their strategy will prevail. Compounding these limitations is large-scale change in the environment, whether owing to severe market disruptions—as seen in the ongoing global financial crisis—or to struggles to adjust the value creation tools of the twentieth century with the opportunities and challenges of the twenty-first century. Our look at the contest between real versus virtual value chains highlights the latter situation.

> Designing and delivering a strategy is an ongoing struggle for companies. While some succeed, many fall short of their objectives.

Point > Counterpoint

Value Chains: Real or Virtual?

Point **Yes** The reality of the value chain has a strong applied legacy. Analysts conceived it in the 1960s and 1970s as a means to chart a step-by-step development strategy for mineral-exporting economies in developing countries—essentially, the value chain meant to map a system of production where none existed.[36] It was then adopted in French planning literature as a *filière* (literally, a "thread") to describe the need for French industrial capability to span the complete thread of a value chain in order to build a competitive economic infrastructure.[37] According to French planning reasoning, the idea of *filière*, or what we now loosely call core competency, suggests that the full chain of activities that goes into a product should take place within national boundaries.

Therefore, a country intent on developing leading capabilities in TVs would set industry policies that create an

Counterpoint **No** Implicit in the profile of the value chain is a beguiling yet flawed assumption. Ultimately, management is not a science with immutable laws that predictably govern the configuration and coordination of activities. The presumption that one can do so, which is implicit in the profile of the value chain, is precisely its critical shortcoming in times of change—both evolutionary and disruptive. That is, the conventional specification of the value chain presumes that the static, sequential depiction of classic business functions transcends time and place. In this context, companies struggling to sustain competitive advantage need only to reapply with greater vigor the precise analytics of the value chain. Clarification of why costs are escalating or links are breaking then prepares management to reset the cofiguration schema and coordination discipline.

economic infrastructure commanding expertise in display technology, support circuit board design and manufacturing, and enable design and production of integrated circuits, liquid crystal, and other electronic components, as well as metal- and plastic-forming technologies. Specifying the optimal *filière,* the thinking was, gave governments and companies a holistic view of corresponding configuration and coordination requirements.

Since French adaptation, value-chain analysis has become a widespread management tool. Today, the value chain helps managers do a number of things. It frames the evaluation of the company's strengths and weaknesses. It interprets the determinants of the internal cost structure, the basis of core competencies, and relationships with customers. The value-chain model helpfully defines a firm's core competency, emphasizing activities that support a cost leadership or differentiation strategy. In the case of cost leadership, the value chain spurs management to understand costs and the potential for their reduction in different value activities. In the case of differentiation, the value chain focuses management's attention on those activities that support outperforming competitors on features for which customers willingly pay a premium. Finally, the value chain links the internal features and functions of a rival's competencies to its marketplace strategy and guides interpreting industry structure. Value-chain analysis, in summary, enables managers to leverage core competencies, set configuration and coordination strategies, and then stress test the strategic choices against industry scenarios.

The discipline of the value chain boosts the performance effectiveness of strategic analysis in international companies. Standardizing the interpretation of market opportunities and constraints is difficult in any context, but particularly so in the face of the extenuating variability brought about by multinational operations. The value chain, however, brings to bear analytical precision, intellectual impact, and policy relevance that guides managers' interpretation of a variety of market environments that overlap on some characteristics but diverge of others. Furthermore, its industry-centric view of globalization highlights the linkages between competitors and collaborators across the broad geographic space of international business.

The value chain, however, does impose analytical restrictions. Value-chain analysis spurs managers to follow the model's template in data collection and interpretation. This template is defined by the real activities, functions, and business processes the firm performs in moving a product through its various stages of design, production, marketing, and distribution to the end consumer. In theory, anchoring analysis and making decisions based on the orderly progression of value-chain activities allows managers to formulate optimal strategies. Still, as is the case with any systematic model, value-chain templates can reject data that

In contrast, the dynamicism of the marketplace signals the necessity of a flexible framework that guides managers' adaptation of strategy to changing trends and events, no matter how trivial, no matter how disruptive. Again, one needs only see the number of companies that struggle to restore competitiveness and the number who ultimately fail to understand the intrinsic limitations of conventional notions of the value chain. More pointedly, as reality gives ways to virtuality, courtesy of the Internet, traditional principles of the value chain give way to emergent practices.[38]

Already, companies in agrochemical, biotech, and furniture industries see the intersection of Internet technologies and management practices heralding the advent of the virtual value chain.[39] From the ordinary to the extraordinary, products and processes once locked into conventional formats now evolve into unprecedented forms. Moreover, the global economic crisis ratchets up the pressure on firms to accept this inevitability. Tough times require rethinking the panacea of traditional cost cutting. For many, rebooting their company requires taking a hard look at the economics of their businesses, a requirement that calls for abandoning reality for virtuality.

Principles of virtuality tap into the Internet's capacity to support new business architectures that challenge the industrial-age view of the value chain as a series of sequential steps organized by classic business functions. Virtuality calls for managers to rethink their traditional focus on static, internally focused "chains" and consider the potential of configuring activities as dynamic "webs." These sorts of virtual value networks, as seen at companies like Alibaba, Li & Fung, eBay, Facebook, Cisco, and Google, form open, interconnected systems that support dynamic configurations of activities. By trumping the rigidities of conventional value chains, dynamic configurations support adept coordination of the company's core competency.

Collecting and coordinating information flows among the members of an organization is the heart of virtuality. Leveraging ideas and insights lets companies generate new products to serve new markets, much in the way Google has evolved from a single-product search engine to a diversified information-management and media company prepared to liberate information in whatever form it takes. In addition, virtuality pioneers paths for value creation, allowing managers to capture lower search, coordination, contracting, and collaboration costs among agents. Streamlining information flows supports new methods of coordinating value activities, a competency that then supports new methods of configuring value activities.

Virtuality has provocative implications to how managers decide what to do and where to do it. For example, Nike has limited production facilities and Reebok owns no plants. Both companies outsource production to manufacturers in fits poorly, distort the interpretation of disruptive change, and misdirect strategic responses—as seen in several company struggles over the past few years, such as those of Sony, Dell, General Motors, Porsche, and Burger King, to name just a few.

Furthermore, dealing with the "hard realities" of international operations, whether by expanding into familiar markets or heading to distant and different territories, is best done within the context of the "real" value chain. Granted, the idea of virtual companies operating in cyberspace, free of physical constraints, may come to pass. And we agree that the corresponding counterpoint does offer interesting points. However, falling prey to the sort of ideas that float around cyberspace and invoke notions of the matrix risks mismapping global operations—as always, one must be cautious not to confuse analysis with speculation. Indeed, the dazzle of virtuality may lead companies to lose sight of the intrinsic difficulties of configuring and coordinating value chains.

Bluntly put, international business takes place within a world marked by geographic borders, regulated by national governments, and populated by companies running real value chains. And given that the world operates in real terms, real value chains have a tried-and-true record of well equipping an MNE to engage the reality of the global market. ▶

China, Vietnam, and other low-cost labor countries. Although nominally independent but in actuality extensively integrated through coordination systems, these subcontractors create virtual production capabilities for Nike and Reebok. The subcontractors prosper by translating tighter relationships with large-volume buyers into improved competencies. Likewise, Nike and Reebok prosper by leveraging their core competencies in design and marketing, all the while confident in suppliers' expertise to adapt product mixes as consumer preferences evolve. Similar situations take place at Acer, Apple, Dell, Corning, and Li & Fung.

Ultimately, it is tempting to oversell the virtues of virtuality. Prudent management realizes that the relative importance of a real versus virtual value chain depends on the characteristics of a company's products, the imperatives imposed by industry structure, and the prevailing context of the market environment. As such, the potential of virtuality has transformational implications for Google's global expansion of its geography-free network but middling implications for companies like Nestlé that deal with physical situations in different geographies. Therefore, notions of virtuality may be far-fetched for some companies, but likely define the future for others. In any case, however, just asking the question "real or virtual?" sparks useful debate on improving the configuration and coordination of value activities. ◀

Global Integration versus Local Responsiveness

Companies that operate internationally face asymmetric forces: pressures for **global integration** and pressures for **local responsiveness.** This asymmetry puts contradictory demands on how the firm configures and coordinates its value chain. Quite simply, should a firm standardize value activities to maximize economies of scale or should it customize activities to the particular circumstances of each country? Research suggests straightforward relationships: The higher the pressure for global integration, the greater the need to maximize efficiency; and, conversely, the higher the pressure for local responsiveness, the greater the need to adapt to local conditions. Few companies, however, operate in an industry that tolerates sensitivity to just one perspective. Rather, the commonplace scenario is an industry dynamically balancing the competing imperatives of global integration and local responsiveness. Reconciling this tension influences how managers configure and coordinate value activities. We now profile the ideas and drivers of each pressure point.

Global integration is the process of combining differentiated parts into a standardized whole. Local responsiveness is the process of disaggregating a standardized whole into differentiated parts.

PRESSURES FOR GLOBAL INTEGRATION

A theme of this text is the pervasive globalization of business. Presently, global markets produce and consume more than 20 percent of world output and are projected to multiply twelvefold, to more than 80 percent of world output, by 2025. Similarly, more cross-national economic integration will take place in the next 30 years than occurred in the previous 10,000. Again, think of the agents promoting globalization: From 30,000 in 1990, the number of MNEs has grown to nearly 70,000, operating through approximately 850,000 subsidiaries spread across the world.

The convergence of national markets, standardization of business processes, and the drive to maximize production efficiency push for the integration of value activities.

Managers, companies, and industries react accordingly, as seen in the ongoing formation of global markets in chemicals, credit cards, financial services, accounting, food, health care, mass media, forest products, information technology, automobiles, telecommunications, and so on. Earlier chapters identified many contributing factors. We highlight here two drivers of global integration: the *globalization of markets* and the *efficiency gains of standardization*.

Globalization of Markets   A provocative thesis, increasingly supported by global buying patterns and companies' strategies, suggests that consumers worldwide seek global products—whether they are Apple iPods, Samsung plasma screens, Facebook connections, Starbucks espressos, Google searches, or Zara blouses.[40] Two conditions—one demand-pull, the other supply-push—influence this trend. Powering demand-pull conditions are the intrinsic functions of money. No matter the society, money exhibits inalienable features: it is hard to acquire (one typically must work for it), difficult to save (on average, people spend more than they make), and always in scarce supply (no matter the amount one has, it often seems never enough). Economic theory reasons that these functions push consumers worldwide to maximize their purchasing power by buying the highest-quality product for the lowest-possible price. Ultimately, the theory goes, consumers do not care who provides the product, as long as it delivers superior value.

Assorted technologies strengthen these relationships, installing infrastructures that converge consumer preferences. First, improving communication and transportation logistics promotes and distributes standardized products worldwide. Shrinking the digital divide gives more people access to common media. Similarly, the logistics network of globalization, designed by institutions, sanctioned by governments, and executed by companies, makes products available everywhere. The quest to maximize individual purchasing power coupled with the growing exposure and access to higher-quality goods at lower prices compels the globalization of markets. In response, many companies configure value chains to maximize standardization in the pursuit of global integration.

Our opening case chronicles one company's response to these imperatives. Zara realized that by offering standardized fashion styles at reasonable prices, it could leverage fixed design, manufacturing, and retail costs. Largely standardized products that offered superior value neutralized stubborn local preferences, Zara found. The compelling value proposition of high quality and fashionable design, coupled with relatively inexpensive prices, spoke to the needs of a global market segment. Zara's global retail network, supported by state-of-the-art logistics, gave customers worldwide, real-time access to the latest, greatest fashion trends. Similar circumstances in high-tech and high-touch products—seen most dramatically in not nation-by-nation but worldwide releases of new goods and services—highlight the connection of global integration and value creation.

Efficiency Gains of Standardization   Earlier discussion of the idea of economies of scale in terms of moderating value-chain configuration foreshadows the influence of standardization. Standardization is the handmaiden of globalization, encouraging supply conditions that produce volumes of low-cost, high-quality products. That is, standardization is the push dynamic that drives supply, whereas the globalization of markets represents the pull dynamic that converges consumer preferences.

The logic of standardization is straightforward. Repeatedly doing the same task the same way improves the efficiency of effort. Improving efficiency in the value chain, in turn, supports aggressive product development, lower-cost production processes, and lower prices (see Table 11.6). For example, the MNE that standardizes machinery in the production stage of its value chain often negotiates quantity discounts on material purchases, streamlines materials management, and accelerates distribution logistics. The MNE also realizes efficiencies in value activities such as R&D (leveraging a common design platform) and advertising (communicating a universal message). Therefore, standardization, by pushing a company to mass-produce at optimal locations in the world, lets it offer higher-quality, lower-cost products. Inevitably, this accelerates globalization.

TABLE 11.6   The Benefits of Standardization to the Value Chain

Standardization involves specifying a consistent set of procedures that make for efficient design, administration, and integration.

Configuration Advantages	**Coordination Advantages**
• Minimizes differences in operating procedures among value activities	• Optimizes routine coordination procedures
• Provides standards to improve quality and reliability of value-chain performance	• Improves communication by lowering the transaction costs of information gathering, negotiating, and market planning
• Drives down the production costs of higher-quality products	• Promotes systematic dissemination of ideas and highlights opportunities for collaboration
• Increases competition among suppliers in providing inputs or support services	• Facilitates cooperation among dispersed units by setting standards of credible knowledge
• Simplifies agreements with joint-venture partners and alliance members	

Trends boost the potential for standardization. Virtually every country in the world is a member of, or waiting to join, the WTO; membership requires replacing differentiated national codes with international standards. Standardizing the rules of the globalization game, so to speak, supports standardizing the methods of play. The liberalization of trade spurs standardizing value activities in optimal locations without forsaking access to markets worldwide. For example, business-process outsourcing firms in India, steel producers in China, and chip designers in Taiwan can design value chains to leverage location-specific advantages without sacrificing access to consumers in other countries.

> Standardization is a powerful means to improve the efficiency of operations.

PRESSURES FOR LOCAL RESPONSIVENESS

Companies prefer a seamless operating environment that permits the straightforward transfer of standardized practices and processes. As such, globalization makes for a cooperative marketplace. Still, earlier chapters discuss the influence of the external environment, state intervention in economic affairs, and government influence on trade and investment programs. Later chapters profile the effects of cross-national differences in product standards, financial regulations, distribution channels, and human resources. At this point, the key idea to engage is that a diversity of agents, regulations, and attitudes pressure international companies to tailor their operations to particular conditions in particular countries. Prominent pressures for local responsiveness are *consumer divergence* and *host-government policies*.

Consumer Divergence   Contrary to the globalization-of-markets thesis, others argue that divergences in consumer preferences across countries necessitate locally responsive value chains. Certainly, money, media, and technology standardize consumption, encouraging buying behavior that emphasizes purchasing power over distinctive preferences or national allegiance. Nevertheless, differences in local consumers' preferences endure due to cultural predisposition, historical legacy, and endemic nationalism (i.e., buy-local campaigns).[41] Regardless of the cause, consumers often prefer goods that are sensitive to the particular idiosyncrasies of their daily life. Consequently, cross-national divergence presses MNEs to adapt value activities to the demands of local markets.

Local responsiveness takes many forms. Prominent examples include designing and making a product that local customers prefer (e.g., large cars in the United States, smaller cars in Europe, still smaller cars in emerging markets), tailoring channel structures to buyer preferences (e.g., Web-based and 3G-driven content in the United States, print and media promotion in France, personal selling in Brazil), and adapting marketing practices

Concept Check

In Chapter 1, we discuss opposition to globalization from critics who argue that it creates high costs, which are, in turn, passed on as economic penalties to local consumers. **Globalization,** we observe, though a powerful force, is not an inevitable outcome of current business trends. Chapters 3 and 4 elaborate this thesis by noting that democratic systems and freer markets are not inevitable outcomes of current trends. Here we add that, for similar sorts of reasons, both consumer needs and host-government pressures prompt companies to adapt value-chain conditions.

to consumption patterns (e.g., large package sizes in Australia, smaller sizes in Japan, single-unit sizes in poorer countries). Adapting to these sorts of local preferences spurs companies to sacrifice degrees of global standardization, a response that requires fine-tuning, if not resetting, the configuration of value activities.

In some industries, local responsiveness is not an option but simply good business sense. For example, food processors like Nestlé have slight incentive to integrate many value activities across countries. Food inputs are generally commodities, production has limited potential for scale economies, widespread distribution faces high costs given the low product value-to-weight ratio, and marketing is best done locally given differentiated tastes, competitors, and retail channels. In these sorts of situations, managers can standardize some value activities such as brand names, as we see in the examples of Nestea or Perrier. Ultimately, many activities of the Nestlé value chain are intrinsically unsuitable for global standardization.

Host-Government Policies   A theme of our text is the variability of political, legal, cultural, and economic environments around the world. The source of many variations is the policies, or the lack thereof, mandated by host-country governments. Earlier chapters show that movement toward privatization, economic freedom, legal uniformity, and deregulation had reduced cross-national variability. This situation, which had dominated market ideology since the 1980s, is changing as governments worldwide deal with the global economic crisis. Capturing the emerging zeitgeist, Nicolas Sarkozy, president of France, observed that the "main features of this crisis is the return of the state, the end of the ideology of public powerlessness." Like-minded leaders from around the world echoed this sentiment in justifying state intervention in the marketplace.

Granted, prior to the economic crisis, companies confronted policy differences as they moved from country to country. However, these differences had been narrowing as capitalism and economic freedom shaped policy in a growing number of countries. Now, in the early phases of the crisis, governments' distrust of market mechanisms spurs revising the rules of the market. Moreover, despite calls for coordinated policy initiatives, different countries have taken different paths to reset fiscal, monetary, and business policies. Collectively, these trends required companies to rethink their value chains. Constrained options for standardization and wavering momentum of globalization spotlight the sustainability of value chains biased toward local responsiveness.

A Case in Point   The pharmaceutical industry likely foreshadows how this situation will play out. The competitiveness of pharmaceutical companies hinges on achieving cost advantages of global integration where and when possible. For example, many pharmaceutical companies sell undifferentiated, low-margin products (such as aspirin or acetaminophen) that make the efficient scale of production vital to profitability. Alternatively, for companies offering branded, proprietary products, such as Lipitor or Advair, high research and development costs demand the returns that are available only from a global market. Complicating both scenarios is rare is the country that lacks an administrative system to regulate the development and delivery of health care.

Consequently, pharmaceutical firms usually manufacture their products in several locations in several countries, despite the fact that dispersal is far less efficient than concentrated production. Moreover, cost concerns do not determine the configuration of manufacturing sites. Rather, configuration choices comply with the clinical testing, registration procedures, pricing restrictions, and marketing regulations mandated by a particular government. In sum, global integration calls for economics to drive the configuration and coordination of value activities. In contrast, the imperative of local responsiveness rejects this orientation, requiring the company to trade off economic efficiency for political expediency in order to preserve market access.

In theory, a pharmaceutical company could reject industry practices, as Zara did in apparel, and maximize the efficiency of its value chain. The extensive regulation of health care industry nullifies this option. In the least, government authorities approve each product in each country; antagonizing political officials by deemphasizing local responsiveness is hazardous. Furthermore, most governments fund significant shares of the national health care budget. Qualifying companies often must demonstrate sensitivity to the structure of the national health care system, standards of care for citizens, and the many national stakeholders in the public health debate.

A few years ago, few industries fell into this sort of situation; the global economic crisis suggests that in a few years many industries will. Banks, hedge funds, capital agents, insurance providers, health care management, carmakers, and airlines, to name the most obvious, may fall under the policy purview of national governments. Meeting growing demands for transparency will push companies to make value chains locally responsive. Those that protest will likely face stern rebuke. Host governments have forceful tools to ensure that MNEs respond to their concerns. These tools can be broad policy directives calling for economic nationalism, trade protectionism to encourage local production, local content rules that require making a portion of products locally, regulations that constrain market moves, product standards that can be met only by local operations, or directives to depart the country.

WHEN PRESSURES INTERACT

Managers map the interaction of global integration and local responsiveness using the **integration-responsiveness (IR) grid.** The IR grid expresses how a company's strategy is a function of the relationship between its value chain and the prevailing pressures for global integration or local responsiveness in its industry.[42] Figure 11.6 illustrates this interaction by placing particular industries in the quadrants that best correspond to their market position.

In practical terms, the IR grid identifies the generic classes of industry settings in terms of the relative trade-off of integration and responsiveness pressures. For example, strong pressures for local responsiveness but low pressures to integrate globally, the IR grid indicates, encouage adapting value activites to country conditions. So, in this

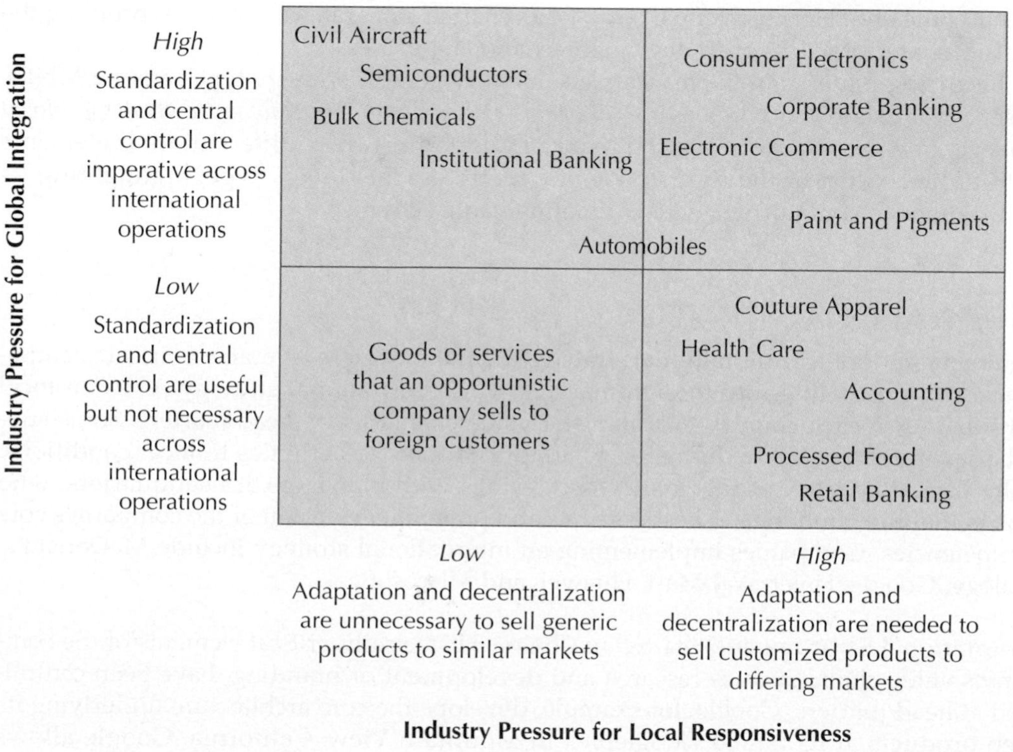

> The Integration-Responsiveness grid helps managers measure the global and local pressures that influence the configuration and coordination of their value chains.

Industry Pressure for Global Integration

High — Standardization and central control are imperative across international operations	Civil Aircraft / Semiconductors / Bulk Chemicals / Institutional Banking	Consumer Electronics / Corporate Banking / Electronic Commerce / Paint and Pigments
	Automobiles	
Low — Standardization and central control are useful but not necessary across international operations	Goods or services that an opportunistic company sells to foreign customers	Couture Apparel / Health Care / Accounting / Processed Food / Retail Banking

Low	High
Adaptation and decentralization are unnecessary to sell generic products to similar markets	Adaptation and decentralization are needed to sell customized products to differing markets

Industry Pressure for Local Responsiveness

FIGURE 11.6 Integration-Responsiveness (IR) Grid: Industry Types

Every company's strategy embodies its concept of *value creation.* To what extent do its strategic decisions reflect its response to asymmetric pressure toward global integration versus local responsiveness? Resolving this dilemma invariably entails *trade-offs* between the competing calls for standardization and adaptation.

scenario, companies like Nestlé see scant benefits from global integration but high returns from responding to the intricacies and expectations of local markets. Alternatively, high pressure to integrate globally along with slight pressure for local responsiveness endorses value chains that champion global standardization. So, for example, firms like Intel in processor technologies, Huawei in network solutions, or ArcelorMittal in metals and mining face cost and competitive calls for standardized products in a global market. There is little need or reward in responding to local market conditions with, respectively, customized computer chips, ethernet switches, or stainless steel.

Finally, a third class of industries, such as telecommunications, information technology, pharmaceuticals, and, increasingly, capital institutions, fall in the center space of the IR grid. These industries face pressures pushing for integration on a global basis yet at the same time strong demands for local responsiveness. Configuring and coordinating value activities to resolve this dilemma poses enduring challenges. Efforts at companies in this dilemma, such as Procter & Gamble and Infosys, require more complex configuration structures and coordination systems that command the flexibility to accommodate both types of pressures. The IR grid helps managers pinpoint the trade-off they face by plotting the company's strategy in terms of the intensity of pressures for global integration and those for local responsiveness.

Concept Check

When managers design a **strategy** for a foreign environment, they consider numerous factors, ranging from local culture to global trade theory. The perspectives that managers themselves introduce into the equation can ultimately be characterized as versions of what, in Chapter 2, we explain as *ethnocentrism, polycentrism,* or *geocentrism.*

Types of Strategy

Chapter 1 introduced a continuing theme, namely that companies look to international markets for growth opportunities, cost reductions, and risk diversification. This chapter elaborates the same, with the message that companies achieve these objectives by anchoring their plans in terms of the configuration and coordination of value activities given prevailing pressures for global integration and local responsiveness in their particular industry.[43] At this point, managers face a final task, relating the specifics of these objectives to a broader-level conception of their company's strategy. That is to say, the value chain defines the means, industry structure sets the context, and company strategy specifies the end. Hence, the final part of this chapter integrates these ideas, profiling the principles and practices of strategy in international business.

Recurring patterns in the marketplace identify generic strategy types among MNEs. Research labels these types as the *international strategy, multidomestic strategy, global strategy,* or *transnational strategy.* Figure 11.7 identifies their differentiating elements within the context of the IR grid. We now define each strategy type, highlighting its implications to configuring and coordinating value activities.

INTERNATIONAL STRATEGY

The international strategy leverages a company's core competencies in foreign markets. It allows limited local customization.

Companies adopt an **international strategy** when they aim to leverage their core competencies by expanding into foreign markets. The international strategy relies on local subsidiaries in each country to administer value chains set by headquarters. Some subsidiaries may have some discretion to adapt products or activities to local conditions. Still, ultimate control of the value chain resides with managers at headquarters, who reason that they understand best the basis and potential extension of the company's core competencies. Companies implementing an international strategy include McDonald's, Kellogg, Google, Haier, Wal-Mart, Huawei, and Microsoft.

International Strategy and the Value Chain   Historically, critical elements of the company's value chain, such as research and development or branding, have been centralized at headquarters. Google, for example, develops the core architecture underlying its Web products at its famed Googleplex in Mountain View, California. Google allows

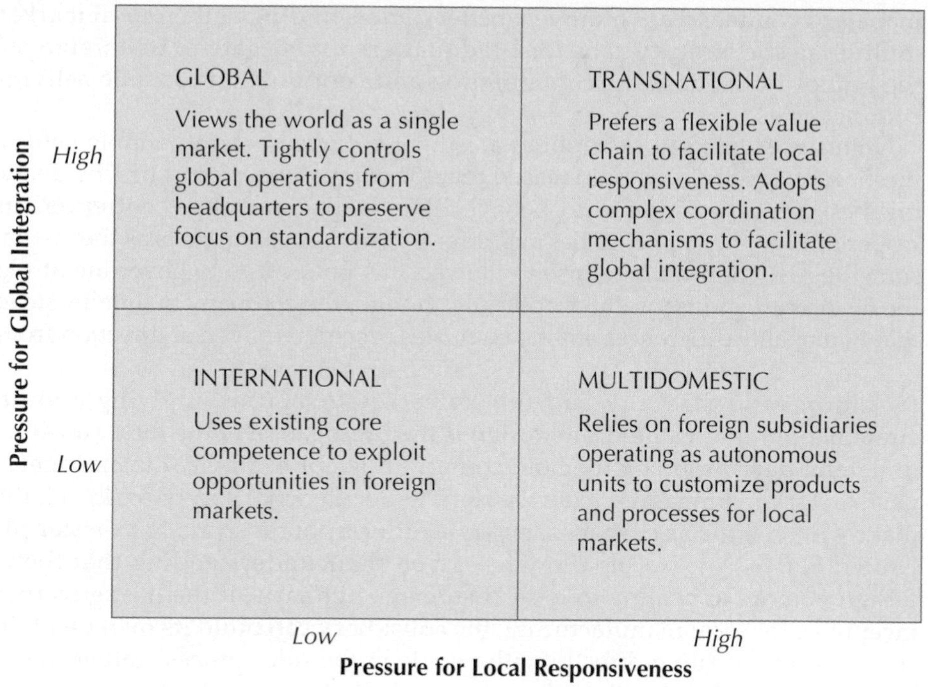

FIGURE 11.7   Integration-Responsiveness (IR) Grid: Strategy Types

What factors enter into a firm's strategic decisions about dealing with the competing pressures toward integration and localization? Again, it is a matter of trade-offs between competing imperatives of globalization and localization. Managers' interpretation of these trade-offs, in turn, determines the most appropriate type of strategy for their company.

national subsidiaries to customize minor aspects of its Web pages to deal with local differences in language and alphabet. Ultimately, though, the Googleplex is the source of new products and processes for overseas operations.

Benefits of International Strategy   An international strategy creates value by transferring core competencies and unique products to foreign markets where rivals are unable to compete. The international strategy, therefore, facilitates the transfer of skills and ideas from the parent company to subsidiaries. Headquarters translates their expertise in and control over value activities into direct command of foreign operations.

An international strategy works well when (1) a firm has a core competence that foreign competitors lack and (2) industry conditions do not demand high degrees of global integration or local responsiveness. In such circumstances, an international strategy incurs moderate operational costs (the expenses of product extension and administrative oversight) yet earns high profits (the yield of international leverage).

> An international strategy works well when a firm has a core competence that foreign rivals lack and industry conditions do not demand high degrees of global integration or local responsiveness.

Limitations of International Strategy   Earlier chapters discussed the situation wherein headquarters' ethnocentric orientation—a one-way view from the home office to the rest of the world—can misread foreign-market opportunities and threats. Similar dynamics constrain the international strategy. Leveraging the firm's core competency, as best understood by home-office executives, downplays adapting value activities for local conditions. The testing ground of new ideas, goes this thinking, is the home market, not foreign countries. This orientation proves successful as long as local rivals scramble futilely. Still, the odds are that one day, one will find a way to compete. Unless aware, the company implementing the international strategy can be blindsided by an unexpectedly innovative rival. Google, for example, faces increasingly adept local rivals in South Korea, specifically Naver, and China, specifically Baidu, whose native sensitivities to local search tendencies pose threats.

MULTIDOMESTIC STRATEGY

The **multidomestic strategy** holds that unique physical and metaphysical features differentiate national markets. These boundaries prevent the home office from effectively supervising foreign operations. Instead, the company concedes that local

> The multidomestic strategy adjusts products, services, and business practices to meet the needs of local markets.

managers command an intuitively better understanding of their local market. Thus the multidomestic strategy calls for headquarters to delegate to its foreign subsidiaries the authority to adapt the configuration and coordination of value activities to local contingencies.

Johnson & Johnson exemplifies a company that successfully implements a multidomestic strategy. Its leadership reason that the company performs best by allowing its 250 business units worldwide to behave like small, innovative, entrepreneurial firms, responding to the opportunities and threats in their local markets as they believe best. To some degree, Johnson & Johnson followed this policy due to government regulation of the health care industry. Philosophically, though, the company maintains steadfast belief that inalienable differences among countries preclude universal direction from one.

Multidomestic Strategy and the Value Chain   Firms applying a multidomestic strategy hold that value-chain design is the prerogative of the local subsidiary, not the unilateral declaration by the home office. Thus, for example, the managers of a backpack factory in Singapore have the right to decide what sort of backpack they want to make—even if the size, shape, and style differ from those made by sister plants in the United States, Mexico, or Ukraine—given their understanding that their preferred design is more appealing to local customers. Similarly, if the host government offers incentives for local manufacturing, the subsidiary can build its own plant; if local consumers prefer dealing directly with people in the sales process rather than relying on mass media for information, the subsidiary can build a sales force; if the country has an unfavorable work environment, the subsidiary can import products made elsewhere. Hence, the key principle of the multidomestic strategy is that local operations have the authority to adapt value activities to prevailing economic, political, legal, and cultural conditions.

Management that chooses the multidomestic strategy believes in customizing value activities to the unique conditions that prevail in different markets.

Benefits of Multidomestic Strategy   A multidomestic strategy makes sense when the company faces a high need for local responsiveness and low need to reduce costs via global integration (the lower right-hand space of the IR grid). It has other benefits as well, such as minimizing political risk given the local standing of the company, lower exchange-rate risk given reduced need to repatriate funds to the home office, greater prestige given its national prominence, higher potential for innovative products from local R&D, and higher growth potential due to entrepreneurial zeal. For example, Procter & Gamble follows a multidomestic strategy. The R&D unit at its Japanese subsidiary, responding to the low storage space in the typical Japanese home, invented technology that reduced the thickness of an infant's diaper without reducing absorbency. This innovation created value for Procter & Gamble in Japan and, eventually, for Procter & Gamble worldwide.

Limitations of Multidomestic Strategy   The multidomestic strategy leads to widespread replication of management, design, production, and marketing activities—the outcome of building "mini-me" units around the world. Customizing products and processes to local markets inevitably increases costs. Different product designs require different materials, production runs become shorter, marketing programs are adapted, distribution requires new channels, and different transactions require different coordination methods. Hence, the multidomestic strategy is impractical in cost-sensitive situations. Carrefour, for instance, ran into problems in the United States when, to deal better with local tastes and preferences, it shifted from its international strategy to a multidomestic approach. Costly problems ultimately pushed Carrefour to close its failing U.S. operations.

Companies that adapt value activities often suffer coordination complications. Unlike the international strategy, in which headquarters directs the value chain, the multidomestic strategy decentralizes control to local managers. Local adaptation can create different management styles and value-chain designs. Usually, headquarters resorts to persuasion in lieu of command to coordinate value chains. Ensuing power struggles can collapse the business, as in the case of Carrefour, or blunt the company's competitiveness, as was the case for Johnson & Johnson. Regarding the latter, Johnson & Johnson launched Tylenol in 1960 as an over-the-counter pain reliever in the United States. The product was available to worldwide units shortly thereafter. The Japanese unit, even under duress from headquarters, opted to begin selling it in 2000.

GLOBAL STRATEGY

The **global strategy** emphasizes improving worldwide performance through the sales and marketing of common goods and services with minimum product variation. Companies translate the global strategy into competitive advantage by basing operations in the superior location. The global strategy directs managers' attention to two absolute production and marketing standards. In terms of production, the global strategy spurs exploiting available location economies and achieving the efficiency potentials of lean operations. Hence, the company looks to perform value activities in the optimal location and organize production under the assumption that the expenditure of resources for any goal other than the creation of low-cost, high-quality products for the customer is wasteful. In terms of marketing, the global strategy spurs developing standardized products requiring little adaptation. In both cases, the competitive necessity of global integration trumps calls for local responsiveness.

> A global strategy champions worldwide consistency and standardization.

For some products, notably **commodities,** the global strategy is essentially the only option. Commodities serve a universal need (think of gasoline, steel, memory chips, sugar, or wheat). The preferences of consumers in different countries, if not identical, are highly similar. The fact that consumers choose between essentially identical products (i.e., Company X gasoline versus Company Y gasoline) makes price a key point of differentiation. Hence, the global strategy leverages the efficiency gains that result from the standardization of value-chain activities.

The global strategy is not restricted to commodity markets. The globalization of markets encourages companies, such as Zara in apparel or LVMH in luxury goods, to standardize historically differentiated products for a world market, manufacture them on a global scale in a few, efficient plants, and market them through a few focused distribution channels. Unquestionably, cross-national differences in consumer preferences exist. The global strategy, however, presumes that local consumers will, if given the opportunity, buy a high-quality, low-priced product no matter its country of origin. Moreover, if the product offers comparatively higher quality at a lower price than the locally made substitute, consumers intent on maximizing their purchasing power will discount nationalism. Therefore, if the company can configure and coordinate its value chain to meet the demanding standards of cost leadership, it then has a fighting chance to capture a global market.

Global Strategy and the Value Chain   Global firms strive to make, market, and service a standardized product worldwide that lets them convert global efficiency into price competitiveness. The efficiency goals of the global strategy have stark implications for configuring a value chain: the company must either be the low-cost player, or at least be competitive with that company, in its industry. Low-cost leadership entails building global-scale production facilities in low-cost locations that create the platforms for efficient operations—whether it is a shoe factory in Vietnam, an auto-parts maker in China, or a service call center in India. Expanding this logic to other value activities results in a fundamental prescription: Optimize the value chain by locating activities in the most favorable locations. Once configured, headquarters coordinates dispersed activities by standardizing practices and processes. Little, if any, strategic authority goes to the local level.

> Firms that choose the global strategy face strong pressure for cost reductions but weak pressure for local responsiveness.

Benefits of Global Strategy   Generally, the global strategy is suited to industries that emphasize efficient operations and where local responsiveness needs either are nonexistent or can be neutralized by offering a higher-quality product for a lower price than the local substitute (essentially, the upper left-hand corner of the IR grid). Increasingly, these conditions prevail in many manufacturing and service-sector industries. The wireless industry, for example, endorses global standards that fuel demand for standardized products worldwide.[44] Similarly, the credit card industry has specified a range of standards for electronic payment protocols that supports customers using and merchants accepting this form of payment around the world. In both cases, firms act accordingly; Nokia in wireless and American Express in credit cards pursue a global strategy.

Limitations of Global Strategy   As noted earlier, countries whose markets demand local responsiveness reduce the attractiveness of the global strategy. More fundamentally, the strength of the global strategy, ironically, is its weakness. The cost sensitivity and standardization bias of a global strategy gives MNEs little latitude to adapt value activities to local conditions. Moreover, disruptive market changes or product breakthroughs can turn a fine-tuned value chain into a misfiring machine. Notable examples in the fallout of the global economic crises were money center banks like Citibank, Royal Bank of Scotland, ING, or Fortis. Global leaders in capital markets, the disruptive change of the crisis turned many of their strengths into liabilities.

TRANSNATIONAL STRATEGY

The **transnational strategy** holds that today's environment of interconnected consumers, industries, and markets requires an MNE to configure a value chain that can exploit location economies as well as coordinate value activities to leverage core competencies while simultaneously responding to local pressures. Admittedly a lot to process, think of the transnational strategy as a compromise between global integration and local responsiveness within a strategic mindset of capitalizing on the specialized knowledge the firm commands. In practical terms, the transnational strategy spurs an MNE to differentiate its capabilities from country to country according to prevailing economic, political, legal, and cultural conditions. But in a critical break from the multidomestic strategy, the transnational strategy calls upon managers to perfect methods that can take the insights gained from unique experiences in local markets and diffuse them throughout global operations. Diffusing cool ideas leverages newfound proprietary knowledge, thereby boosting competitiveness.

A transnational strategy simultaneously engages pressures for global integration and local responsiveness in ways that leverage insight to improve the firm's core competency.

Transnational Strategy and "Global Learning"   The transnational concept of strategy endorses a sophisticated framework of integration, differentiation, and learning. The first-order condition of the transnational strategy combines the market sensitivity of local responsiveness with the competitive efficiency of global integration. However, a unique aspect of the transnational strategy champions interactive "global learning," by which the MNE learns new ways to leverage its core competencies and then distributes these innovations throughout its global organization.

A transnational strategy makes the exchange of ideas across value activities a key element of competitive advantage.

The transnational strategy aggressively communicates the specialized knowledge that permeates the value chain throughout the units of the company. So, rather than the top-down (headquarters to foreign subsidiary) or bottom-up (foreign subsidiary to headquarters) flow of information, the transnational strategy promotes knowledge flows from the idea generator to idea adopters, no matter where one or the other resides in the company. Rather, as we have discussed earlier regarding social networks, the transnational strategy sees its subsidiary network as a point of competitive advantage, provided it can find ways to encourage workers to communicate and collaborate in the process of coordinating the value chain. Successfully done, the transnational company fortifies its value chain by diffusing the lessons it has learned and knowledge it has earned throughout its worldwide operations.

The company implementing a transnational strategy aims not to work harder or work smarter than competitors but rather work differently based on diffusing the lessons it has learned and the knowledge it has earned throughout its worldwide operations.

Transnational Strategy: A Case in Point Can a firm effectively pursue a transnational strategy? Although difficult, the General Electric Company (GE) was able to do so. In the 1980s, growing threats from emergent low-cost competitors in Asia pushed GE to look to global markets to sell products, reasoning that expanding sales volumes would lead to greater scale economies. At the time, Jack Welch declared, "the idea of a company being global is nonsense. Businesses are global, not companies."

In 1987, GE redefined its outlook toward globalization, elevating it to a dominant strategic theme. Since 1981, the performance standard for each business had been to "be either number 1 or 2" in its domestic industry or else face divestment. In 1987, Jack Welch raised the standard to the business's position in its global industry. Soon thereafter, GE's sense of globalization moved from finding new markets to finding new worldwide sources that supplied higher-quality resources at lower cost.

Around this time, Jack Welch articulated his vision of the *boundaryless company,* a term suggestive of the transnational organization. Welch reasoned that a boundaryless company was an "open, antiparochial environment, friendly toward the seeking and sharing of new ideas, regardless of their origins." More specifically, Welch explained that the "boundaryless company we envision will remove the barriers among engineering, manufacturing, marketing, sales, and customer service; it will recognize no distinctions between domestic and foreign operations—we'll be as comfortable doing business in Budapest and Seoul as we are in Louisville and Schenectady."

Success stories emerged from GE's value chain: increased efficiency in its appliance business, productivity solutions in lighting, transaction effectiveness in GE capital, cost-reduction techniques in aircraft engines, and global account management in plastics. Lessons learned spread to other business units. Indeed, careers ended if managers refused to share ideas with others. Welch explained, "We take people who aren't boundaryless out of jobs. If you're turf-oriented, self-centered, don't share with people, and aren't searching for ideas, you don't belong here."

Soon thereafter, GE moved to phase three of its globalization evolution. Besides emphasizing global markets and global sources, Welch now called on his managers to "globalize the intellect of the company," seeking the best practices and compelling ideas from anyone, anywhere and then diffusing them throughout GE's global operations.

By 1999, at the end of Welch's tenure, GE was again named the most respected company in the world by the *Financial Times,* and Jack Welch was judged the CEO of the twentieth century. His successor, Jeffrey Immelt, has continued these efforts, explaining that success in international business is "truly about people, not about where the buildings are. You've got to develop people so they are prepared for leadership jobs and then promote them. That's the most effective way to become more global."[45]

GE's performance speaks to principles of the transnational strategy. GE made ideas—constantly renewed, enhanced, and exchanged across units spanning the world—the basis of configuring and coordinating its value chain. In this way, as managers translated ideas into better production methods, designs, and programs, the more they made profitable decisions around the world. As ideas flowed from one unit in one part of the value chain to counterparts in far-flung parts of the company, integration happened more efficiently, responsiveness happened more effectively, and innovations emerged more regularly.

> Ideas are the primary source of competitiveness for companies implementing a transnational strategy.

Benefits of Transnational Strategy The learning orientation of the transnational strategy drives many benefits—most visibly its fine-tuned balancing of global integration and local responsiveness. The vitality of learning in the transnational strategy pushes managers to respond to changing environments, configuring resources and coordinating processes without imposing more bureaucracy. Ultimately, these capabilities permit standardizing some links of the value chain to generate the efficiencies warranted by global integration pressures, while also adapting other links to meet pressures for local responsiveness—but without sacrificing the benefits of one for the other.

With that said, which sorts of firms, then, aspire to a transnational strategy? Generally, firms facing pressures for global integration and for local responsiveness yet seeing opportunities to leverage the unique knowledge that permeates the value chain find the transnational option appealing. In the 1990s, this option attracted few companies. The impracticality of prevailing communications systems prevented efficiently distributing information throughout a subsidiary network. Moreover, national differences had yet to begin the convergence powered by large-scale globalization. The turn of the century saw industry conditions (i.e., increasing numbers of competitive MNEs emerged around the world) and environmental trends (i.e., the Internet and ancillary telecommunication systems, along with growing globalization) that supported translating the transnational strategy from theory to actions.

Presently, resurgent calls for restoring MNEs' local responsiveness may accelerate the trend toward transnational strategies. Governments' growing mistrust of the global agendas and agency conflicts of MNEs prompts aggressive local regulation. Preserving competitiveness in the face of host-country intervention requires MNEs to devise sophisticated value chains that develop the learning capacity to leverage efficiencies of global integration without ignoring rising calls for local responsiveness.

Transnational strategy, admittedly difficult to even specify in theory, is even more difficult to implement in practice. Limitations arise from complicated agendas, high costs, and cognitive limits.

Limitations of Transnational Strategy   The transnational strategy is difficult to configure, tough to coordinate, and prone to performance shortfalls. The difficulty of reconciling integration and responsiveness pressures, further complicated by the need to adeptly manage knowledge worldwide, can overwhelm the best-intentioned managers. Indeed, for every GE, there are Philipses, Panasonics, and Acers that struggled to engage a transnational strategy. Furthermore, developing a network mindset among employees, installing the requisite information systems, and navigating the ambiguity of multicriteria decision making is expensive. These sorts of costs may prove difficult to justify as the current global crisis spurs companies to economize. Finally, as we see in our "Looking to the Future" insert, the emergence of other strategy types may offer more powerful value-creation platforms.

Looking to the Future   What's New in the World of Strategy Types?

The strategy gamut of "international-multidomestic-global-transnational" has prevailed for several years in international business theory. Unfolding trends of slowing globalization and growing host-nation intervention pose a provocative issue: *What types of strategies might MNEs follow in the future?*

Evolution of the Multinational Corporation

Some see an evolutionary dynamic playing out. In this scenario, MNEs respond to the cues of the globalization game. The person with perhaps the best view regarding this state of affairs is Sam Palmisano, the CEO of IBM. Reflecting on the evolution of IBM, he contends that the company has passed through three strategic phases on its path to a global powerhouse.

- First there was the nineteenth-century "international model, whereby the company was headquartered both physically and mentally in its home country; it sold goods, when it was so inclined, through a scattering of overseas sales offices." Although one could consider this international, the company focused on its business dealings in its home country. Headquarters configured and coordinated the value chain with no input from overseas units.

- Phase two of the evolution ushered in the classic, multinational firm of the late twentieth century. This model saw the parent company creating smaller versions of itself in foreign markets. These smaller satellite companies were run by home-nation executives sent from headquarters, who typically had great technical expertise but little cultural fluency and minimal foreign-language competency. Therefore, in a sense, the only thing multinational about these executives was their particular (and temporary) overseas location. Steadily, the changing context of global competition eroded the economics of the "mini-me" option. Extensive redundancy—each country essentially ran its own value chain—grew unacceptably costly.

- The third phase, the "globally integrated enterprise," is one that builds a company-wide value chain that put people, jobs, and investments anywhere in the world "based on the right cost, the right skills and the right business environment. . . . now work flows to the places where it will be done best, that is, most efficiently and to the highest quality."[46] Previously, configuration and coordination barriers blocked the effective flow of knowledge and efficiency of production and distribution. Now, like the Internet, the globally integrated enterprise designs its strategy, configures its activities, and coordinates its processes to connect everything, everywhere, 24/7.

Visions of the Future

Others trumpet a world where a dynamic ecology of locations and firms pushes business beyond the historic division of local firms versus global companies.[47] This view provides for different types of companies following different types of strategies. In a sense, these companies create a natural ecology that reacts to, and interacts with, their different environments. The diversity of these strategies and companies in this global ecology creates a business world populated by a variety of local firms, regional firms, firms that operate in a few countries or many countries, centralized firms, and networks of firms. Against this backdrop, questions about the collocation of different places with different types of firms mean strategy emerges from the interplay among firms and places. Ultimately, companies will more or less remain the same, although the context with which they create value changes.

The "Metanational" Company

Others see the emergence of a new type of global corporation, the so-called metanational company, which thrives on seeking unique ideas, activities, and insights that complement its existing operations as well as creating leverage points. The metanational company "builds a new kind of competitive advantage by discovering, accessing, mobilizing, and leveraging knowledge from many locations around the world."[48] The metanational companies, goes the theory, will conquer international markets

by developing value chains with three core competencies:

- The ability to prospect for and access untapped pockets of technology and emerging consumer trends from around the world.
- The ability to leverage knowledge scattered throughout its local subsidiaries.
- The ability to mobilize fragmented knowledge to generate innovations that produce, market, and deliver value on a global scale.

Some see MNEs like Shiseido and PolyGram as emergent metanationals, showcasing the capacity to mobilize scattered knowledge into global-dominant innovations.

"Micro-Multinationals"

Others argue that the evolutionary frontier for MNEs is a matter of size. We have long assumed that MNEs must be colossi that straddle the globe. And although the number of MNEs grows worldwide, their average size is falling—most of the 70,000 or so firms that operate internationally employ less than 250 people. This anomaly signals the era of so-called micro-multinationals: clever, small companies that are born global and operate worldwide from day one.[49] Unlike their bigger counterparts that expanded internationally by gradually entering new markets, micro-multinationals go global immediately, entering countries with plentiful customers, productive labor, and powerful markets. The proliferation of micro-multinationals suggests they may represent a new form of value creation in international business.

The "Cybercorp"

Finally, there is the idea of the *cybercorp,* a form of company that was unimaginable a generation ago but plausible today.[50] To this type of MNE, national boundaries no longer organize consumers, markets, or industries. Instead, the cyberspace created by evolving Internet technologies—not the physical geography of lines on a map—defines markets. The cybercorp develops competencies that let it react in real time to changes in its customers, competition, industry, and environment. The cybercorp, therefore, engages perspectives and strategies that bias its value chain toward virtuality in order to dynamically link competencies with ever-changing networks of allies. Some believe the cybercorp, built for speed and able to engage strategies

(continued)

that learn, evolve, and transform, will define the standards of the competitive international company.

No Matter Which Type...

All things considered, the next global strategy type is more speculation than stipulation. No matter what types emerge, we expect each to exemplify the historic markers of great strategy: superior value creation, superb core competencies, and bright people who can articulate clear visions and practical goals while developing the organizational capability to redefine the play of ideas—within either real or virtual boundaries. ■

CASE

Value Chains: Where, When, and Why[51]

The diffusion of work, technology, and companies outward from the United States and fellow rich countries into emerging markets changes the game of globalization. Companies throughout advanced and emerging markets respond in kind, rethinking their strategies and resetting their value chains to compete in the brave new world. On both sides of the market equation, the improving sophistication of information technology and supply-chain logistics enables reorganizing of production across borders. New frontiers have opened for products (solar cell panels made in Shanghai but sold in Stockholm) as well as previously nontradable services (X-rays taken in Boston but read in Bangkok). The changing standards of configuring and coordinating value activities, by both companies in the wealthier markets and their counterparts in emerging economies, spur companies to question the way they think of strategy and the way they set their value chains.

Advanced Economies: Realization and Adaptation

First consider the activities of companies from advanced economies. While some have been paralyzed by the global meltdown, other scramble to reorient their operations to the still-thriving markets of developing countries. Whereas richer countries face low growth prospects, their counterparts in the emerging-market bloc are growing; China, for example, is growing 10 percent, while India and Brazil are running nearly 5 percent. Moreover, long-term trends signal the likelihood of progressively slower growth in advanced markets, even upon recovery, whereas recovery will likely turbocharge growth in developing countries. For many companies, just being in leading emerging economies, no matter the shape or form of investment, takes precedence over carefully serving specific product markets. Others are further along in their reorientation, some motivated by the opportunity, many motivated by the realization that "companies that don't take a vigorous approach to China and India will face threats to their very existence in as little as 10 years' time."[52]

For example, GM is going great guns in China, even though it struggles in the United States. Its China sales jumped 50 percent—to 151,084 units year-on-year in April 2009—even as it encountered a 50 percent slump in the first quarter in the United States. Shanghai GM, which makes the Buick and Cadillac models, increased its local sales by 34 percent; sales of SAIC-GM-Wuling, GM's mini commercial-vehicle joint venture that makes Chevrolet cars, saw sales rocket 60 percent over the same time. Consequently, as GM streamlines its value-chain setup in the United States, it expands its scale and scope of activities throughout Asia.

Likewise, Russia is McDonald's fastest growing market; it had 240 outlets in 2009, up from 128 in 2005. And while the global meltdown has reduced sales, the company plans to add hundreds more in the next few years, given the belief that "Russia remains the most dynamic, fastest-growing and profitable market for our system."[53] Similarly, Wal-Mart and Bharti Enterprises (a leading Indian cell phone operator) steadily unfold their pan-India strategy of wholesale warehouses. But, in reflection on life at the Bottom of the Pyramid, the stores, under the brand name BestPrice Modern Wholesale, will be cash-and-carry only.

Other tales amplify the strategic significance of emerging economies. In 2005, Cisco combined all its emerging-markets activities into a single unit. In 2007, Cisco decided that 20 percent of its top talent should be in India within five years and, to spearhead the change, it moved one of its highest-ranking executives to Bengaluru with the title of chief globalization officer. Since then, the share of its revenues coming from emerging markets has risen from 8 to 15 percent, accounting for 30 percent of its total revenue growth. "We identify the country's most important industries and go to them with a blueprint for a strategy to improve them using our technology to beat global benchmarks; this is about revolutionary, not incremental change," explained the director of Cisco's emerging-markets business.

More dramatically, IBM is slowly making India the company's center of gravity. From a local labor force of a few hundred in 1999 to 9,000 in 2003, IBM now employs about 100,000 in India—meaning that almost one in four IBM workers call India home. Symbolizing the growing primacy of its Indian operations is IBM's historic decision to hold its annual Investors Day in 2007 on the grounds of the Bangalore Palace; this event had never before been held outside of the United States. But the change made perfect sense given that "India is at the epicenter of the flat world," explained Michael J. Cannon-Brookes, vice president for business development in India and China at IBM.

As IBM resets its axis of value creation, it accelerates century-long trends in the company's evolution of its value chain. Recall from our earlier discussion of "What's New in the World of Strategy Types" that the CEO of IBM describes a three-phase change. The current stage sees IBM revolutionizing its value chain to support a "globally integrated enterprise" that can put people, jobs, and investments anywhere in the world "based on the right cost, the right skills and the right business environment." Strategically, this means IBM's quest to find new ways to grow foreshadows radical new value-chain designs that move operations toward uncharted forms of virtuality. Operationally, IBM is doing cutting-edge research and development, as well as writing next-generation software in India, to say nothing of running low-cost call centers in locations that just a decade earlier were far removed from the global economy. Together, these trends mean that IBM now has more employees in India than in any other country except America. And simple projection of current trends shows that IBM will employ more in India than America within the next decade. Not surprisingly, some propose renaming IBM—officially International Business Machines—to "India-Beijing Machines."

Emerging Economies: Opportunity and Adventure

Certainly, it is tempting to presume that large, established MNEs—such as McDonald's, Cisco, and IBM—go where they wish, follow their own rules, and inevitably triumph. Increasingly, though, Western companies face enterprising local rivals whose value-chain configurations and coordination choices have positioned them to prosper in the face of the current global crisis.

Strong already, the global economic crisis has fortified the relative position of emerging market firms. First, while growth in developing countries has slowed, it has not vanished as it has in many advanced markets; hence, while foreign rivals regroup in their faltering home markets, emerging giants power forth on the strength of their domestic markets. For example, car sales and car companies have collapsed in the rich world but are growing in many developing countries—some forecast double-digit growth in China and India in 2010.

Second, as competitors and consumers around the world economize, they cut down costs and trade. The emerging giants' low-cost production models—configured on the basis of cheap but productive local labor and coordinated through increasingly efficient information technologies—gives them an even greater competitive advantage. Furthermore, long-standing bias toward frugal engineering in developing countries spurs designing value-chain activities that fit the economic profile of the immense Bottom of the Pyramid market. In addition, the fact that many of these companies have only recently begun operations liberates them from the legacy mindset and costs that hamper the flexibility of established MNEs.

Like their Western counterparts who reset their value chain, companies from the emerging markets are also rethinking the way they configure and coordinate value activities. For example, AirTel, the Indian market leader in mobile telephony, and Safaricom, the market leader in Kenya, charge some of the the lowest prices in the world for nationwide calls yet generate growing profits. Increasing success spurs these and other companies to leverage their innovation globally—albeit the one they believe they know best. Indeed, a host of emerging markets companies are taking their business models to other emerging markets, betting that they will transfer more effectively between developing economies than in a jump from developing to developed ones.

Specifically, Desarrolladora Homex is a Mexican builder of low-cost housing. It has begun configuring its value chain, explained its CEO, to serve communities "in highly populated and underserved areas where we believe our replicable business model will most effective."[54] The company has launched a joint venture in India and has an alliance with an Egyptian company to build 50,000 low-cost new homes in Cairo. Then again, there are those with even grander ambitions. Tata, maker of the Nano, the new "people's car" that will sell for around $2,000 or so, did not merely leverage "cheap Indian engineers" or accept lower standards on safety or environmental emissions. Rather, Tata rethought the basic functionality of the car, applied state-of-the-art virtual design technology, and made ingenious design breakthroughs. So while obscure names to many companies—such as Haier, a Chinese white-goods firm; Asus, a Taiwanese computer manufacturer; CVRD, a Brazilian miner; MISC, a Malaysian shipping company; Sasol, a South African energy producer; Tenaris, an Argentine steel maker; Cemex, a Mexican cement company; Embraer, a Brazilian aircraft maker; Infosys, an Indian software giant; and Ranbaxy, an Indian drug company—will progressively move from local prominence to global distinction.

Going Forward

Unquestionably, as the current global economic crisis shows, circumstances can change far more dramatically than even the most optimistic or dire forecasts. Therefore, situations and trends will likely look different in five years' time. Still, market circumstances in place today compel companies from around the world to reset the configuration and coordination of their value chains. As the CEO of IBM notes, the forces powering this trend "are irresistable. . . . The genie's out of the bottle and there's no stopping it."[55] Configuration standards and coordination protocols, always dynamic, only become more so going forward. ■

QUESTIONS

1. What sorts of conditions and motivations best explain how companies see themselves developing strategies that create sustainable value?

2. Dynamism creates opportunity as well as constraints. Identify the most promising opportunities facing companies from advanced markets. Then do the same for firms from developing markets. How are they similar? How are they different?

3. If given the option to work for a company in a particular market, would you choose to work for a Western MNE such as IBM, moving into a developing country such as India or would you choose to work for a company from an emerging economy, such as Safaricom, moving into a Western market such as France? Why?

4. Looking out over the next decade, estimate the likely standards of value creation. How would you advise a company like IBM or Cisco to configure and coordinate its value chain to prosper in this environment? Would you give the same advice to a company like Tata or AirTel?

5. What sorts of management skills and executive perspectives do you believe would make you an attractive candidate for a Western company expanding into emerging economies? Would they differ, and if so how, for a company expanding from its home base in an emerging economy into a Western economy?

SUMMARY

- Managers devise strategies to engage international markets in ways that sustain the company's growth and boost its profitability.

- Industry structure influences a company's profitability, especially so in situations of perfect competition, less so in situations of imperfect competition.

- Bright managers convert innovative strategies into above-average, risk-adjusted profitability, especially so in situations of imperfect competition, less so in situations of perfect competition.

- Value can be defined in many ways; for our purposes, it measures a firm's ability to sell what it makes for more than the cost it incurred to make it.

- Managers typically anchor analysis of industry structure in the context of the five-forces model—specifically, the interaction among competitive rivalry, threat of new entrants, substitutes, supplier power, and buyer power.

- Competitive rivalry refers to the moves of rivals battling for market share. Threat of new entrants refers to entry of new rivals seeking market share. Substitutes refers to substitute products that increase the odds that customers will respond to growing price differences by switching to the less expensive alternative. Supplier power refers to the push by input suppliers to charge more for their inputs. Buyer power is the push by output buyers to pay less for products.

- Firms create value through a cost leadership strategy or a differentiation strategy. The former drives a firm to reduce its economic costs below its competitors' while the latter drives firms to increase the perceived value of its products relative to the perceived value of rivals' products.

- Interpreting the firm within the context of the value chain improves the accuracy of strategic analyses and decisions.

- The value chain lets managers deconstruct the general idea of "create value" into a series of discrete activities.

- Managers configure value activities to take into account cross-national cost factors, cluster effects, logistics, degree of digitization, economies of scale, and business environments.

- Managers coordinate value activities to take into account national cultures, learning effects, operational obstacles, and subsidiary networks.

- A core competency is the special outlook, skill, capability, or technology that runs through the firm's value activities, integrating disparate dimensions into competitive advantage.

- Companies that operate internationally face the asymmetric pressures of global integration versus local responsiveness.

- Drivers of globalization are the integration of national markets and efficiency gains of standardization. Drivers of local-responsiveness are crossnational consumer divergences and host-country intervention.

- The firm entering and competing in foreign markets can adopt an international, multidomestic, global, or transnational strategy.

- An international strategy creates value by transferring core competencies to foreign markets where local rivals lack those competencies.

- A multidomestic strategy emphasizes responsiveness to the unique circumstances that prevail in a country's market.

- A global strategy emphasizes improving worldwide performance through the production of standardized products that are marketing with minimum adaptation to local market conditions.

- A transnational strategy aspires simultaneously to leverage core competencies worldwide, reduce costs by exploiting experience-based cost and location economies, and responding to local market conditions.

KEY TERMS

commodity (p. 469)
configuration (p. 446)
coordination (p. 446)
core competency (p. 455)
digitization (p. 452)
economies of scale (p. 453)
five-forces model (p. 441)
global integration (p. 461)

global strategy (p. 469)
industry organization (IO) paradigm (p. 440)
industry structure (p. 441)
integration-responsiveness (IR) grid (p. 465)
international strategy (p. 466)
local responsiveness (p. 461)

location economies (p. 447)
multidomestic strategy (p. 467)
perfect competition (p. 440)
strategy (p. 444)
transnational strategy (p. 470)
value (p. 444)
value chain (p. 446)

ENDNOTES

1   **Sources include the following:** A. R. Bonnin, "The Fashion Industry in Galicia: Understanding the 'Zara' Phenomenon," *European Planning Studies* 10 (2002): 519; "The Stars of Europe—Armancio Ortega, Chairman, Inditex," *Business Week* (June 11, 2001): 65;

"Rapid Response Retail," *Marketing* (April 3, 2003): 43; Richard Heller, "Galician Beauty," *Forbes* (May 28, 2001): 28; Patrick Byrne, "Closing the Gap between Strategy and Results," *Logistics Management* (March 2004): 13; Rachel Tiplady, "Zara: Taking the

Lead in Fast-Fashion," *Business Week* (June 4, 2006): 19; "Shining Examples," *The Economist* (June 15, 2006): 54; "Zara Grows as Retail Rivals Struggle," *Wall Street Journal* (March 26, 2009): C-1.

2 In general, the higher the risk, the higher the return. Therefore, riskier projects and investments must be evaluated differently from their riskless counterparts. By discounting risky cash flows against less-risky cash flows, risk-adjusted rates account for changes in the profile of the investment.

3 Jens Boyd, "Intra-Industry Structure and Performance: Strategic Groups and Strategic Blocks in the Worldwide Airline Industry," *European Management Review* 1 (2004): 132–45; Schmalensee (1985) tested for evidence of business-specific differences through a single, exogenous measure of market share. His analysis also included corporate-parent effects, which he called "firm effects." Industry effects accounted for about 20 percent of variance, market-share effects accounted for less than 1 percent of variance, and corporate-parent effects did not significantly contribute to variance. Managerial influences were not important compared to differences in industry structure; R. Schmalensee, "Do Markets Differ Much?" *American Economic Review* 75:3 (1985): 341–51.

4 See B. Wernerfelt, "A Resource-Based View of the Firm," *Strategic Management Journal* 5 (1984): 171–80; In addition, Rumelt (1991) found that corporate-parent effects contributed to the variance in firm performance (Richard Rumelt, "How Much Does Industry Matter?" *Strategic Management Journal* 6 [1985]: 167–86); McGahan and Porter (2002) found similar evidence of corporate-parent effects: see "What Do We Know about Variance in Accounting Profitability?" *Management Science* 48 (2002): 834–51.

5 See Wyn Jenkins, "Competing in Times of Evolution and Revolution: An Essay on Long-Term Firm Survival," *Management Decisions* 43 (January 1, 2005): 26; Belen Villalonga, "Intangible Resources, Tobin's Q, and Sustainability of Performance Differences," *Journal of Economic Behavior & Organization* 54 (June 2004): 205. Determining whether a money manager outperforms a market index relies on separating the returns available from market movements (*beta* in the jargon) and managerial skill (*alpha*). Like great product managers, great money managers find innovative ways to earn in excess of what would be predicted by an equilibrium model like the *capital asset pricing model* (CAPM). More specifically, we can compare the performance of investment managers by allowing for portfolio risk with the so-called Jensen index, also called Alpha. This measure uses the CAPM as its basis for determining whether a money manager outperformed a market index. The sum of the outperformance is known as alpha.

6 Michael Porter, *Competitive Advantage* (New York: Free Press, 1985).

7 Ashlee Vance and Matt Richtel, "Light and Cheap, Netbooks Are Poised to Reshape PC Industry," *New York Times* (April 1, 2009): C-1.

8 "Special Report: The China Price," *Business Week* (December 6, 2004), www.businessweek.com/magazine/content/04_49/b3911401.htm (accessed June 25, 2005).

9 "Update 1-Sony to Enter Netbook PC Market with New VAIO," *Reuters* (July 7, 2009): 3.

10 "Hungry Tiger, Dancing Elephant: How India Is Changing IBM's World," *The Economist* (April 4, 2007): 58–61.

11 Michael E. Porter, "What Is Strategy?" *Harvard Business Review* (November–December 1996): 61–79.

12 Managers may make decisions that they strongly reason support the firm's strategy but, in actuality, more often do not. Challenges emerge because often few managers understand the full demands of the company's strategy and its implications for international operations. More worrisome, managers are far more likely to make the wrong than right decision. See Dan Lovallo and Daniel Kahneman, "Delusions of Success: How Optimism Undermines Executives' Decisions," *Harvard Business Review* (July 2003): 56.

13 M. E. Porter, "Competition in Global Industries: A Conceptual Framework," in M. Porter (ed.), *Competition in Global Industries* (Boston: Harvard Business School Press, 1986).

14 Janet C. Lowe, *Welch: An American Icon* (New York: Wiley and Sons, 2002).

15 See Arindam Bhattacharya et al., "Capturing Global Advantage: How Leading Industrial Companies Are Transforming Their Industries by Sourcing and Selling in China, India, and Other Low-Cost Countries," Boston Consulting Group Publications (April 9, 2004), esp. Exhibit 7.

16 Paul Krugman, "Divided over Trade," *New York Times* (May 14, 2007):A-18.

17 The mean is the statistical norm or average value, the standard deviation is the measure of the dispersion of a collection of values, and a high standard deviation indicates that the data are spread out over a large range of values.

18 George Norman and Lynne Pepall, "Knowledge Spillovers, Mergers and Public Policy in Economic Clusters," *Review of Industrial Organization* 25 (September 2004): 155–75.

19 Industry Cluster Overview, Economic Development Administration, U.S. Department of Commerce, at www.eda.gov/Research/ClusterBased.xml (accessed June 21, 2009).

20 "Offshoring has created a truly global operating model for financial services, unleashing a new and potent competitive dynamic that is changing the rules of the game for the entire industry.... There has never been an economic discontinuity of this magnitude in the history of the world," said Bain's Mark Gottfredson. "These powerful forces are allowing companies to rethink their sourcing strategies across the entire value chain." Financial firms are expanding into other areas like insurance claims processing, mortgage applications, equity research, diligence, valuation, and accounting. Deloitte forecasts that by 2010 the 100 largest global financial institutions will move $400 billion of their work offshore for $150 billion in annual savings. Quotes reported in "Financial Firms Hasten Their Move to Outsourcing," *New York Times* (August 18, 2004): C-1.

21 2009 State of the Future, The Millennium Project, (2009): 22.

22 "A Grim Picture," *The Economist* (November 2, 2006): 34.

23 Lowe, *Welch: An American Icon*.

24 Jack Gage, "The Best Countries for Business," *Forbes* (March 3, 2009), at www.forbes.com/2009/03/18/best-countries-for-business-bizcountries09-business-washington-best-countries.html (accessed April 15, 2009).

25 2009 State of the Future, The Millennium Project, (2009): 22, defines singularity as the "time in which technological change is so fast and significant that we today are incapable of conceiving what life might be like beyond the year 2025." Quote reported in text sourced from Ray Kurzweil, "The Law of Accelerating Returns," at www.kurzweilai.net/articles/art0134.html?printable=1 (accessed June 18, 2007).

26 Soumitra Dutta and Simon Caulki, "The World's Top Innovators," *The World Business/INSEAD Global Innovation Index* (2007), at www.worldbusinesslive.com/article/625441/the-worlds-top-innovators (accessed June 18, 2007).

27 Dutta and Caulki, "The World's Top Innovators."

28 *Synergy* is defined as the combination of parts of a business, such that the sum is worth more than the individual parts. It is often expressed in the equation $2 + 2 = 5$, with the additional unit of value the result of synergy. Research reports a relationship between a firm's performance and a manager's sophistication in diffusing core competencies throughout the value chain. See David Collis and Cynthia Montgomery, "Competing on Resources: Strategy in the 1990s," *Harvard Business Review* (July–August 1995): 118–28.

29 Technically, a core competence satisfies three conditions: It provides consumer benefits, it is difficult for competitors to imitate, and it is leveraged to different products and markets. The fact that rivals cannot easily match or replicate a firm's core competency serves as a powerful competitive advantage

30 Medard Gabel and Henry Bruner, *An Atlas of the Multinational Corporation Globalinc* (New York: The New Press, 2003).

31 Jack Gage, "The Best Countries for Business," *Forbes* (June 26, 2008): 55.

32 "Top 100 Global Brands Scoreboard," *Business Week*, 208, at bwnt .businessweek.com/brand/2005/ and bwnt.businessweek.com/ brand/2006 (accessed May 19, 2007); The Best Global Brands, www.interbrand.com/best_global_brands.aspx (accessed April 8, 2009).

33 James Brooke and Saul Hansel, "Samsung Is Now What Sony Once Was," *New York Times* (March 9, 2004): A-1.

34 "Samsung Profit Beats Forecast, Cautious on Recovery," *Reuters*, www.reuters.com/article/businessNews/idUSTRE53N09S200904 24 (accessed April 24, 2009).

35 Dan Lovallo and Daniel Kahneman, "Delusions of Success: How Optimism Undermines Executives' Decisions," *Harvard Business Review* (July 2003): 56.

36 N. Girvan, "Transnational Corporations and Non-Fuel Primary Commodities in Developing Countries," *World Development* 15 (1987): 713–40.

37 Raphael Kaplinsky and Mike Morris, "A Handbook for Value Chain Research," at www.seepnetwork.org/files/2303_file_ Handbook_for_Value_Chain_Research.pdf (accessed May 14, 2009.

38 Richard Pascale, "Surfing the Edge of Chaos," *Sloan Management Review* (Spring 1999): 83; Eric Beinhocker, "Strategy at the Edge of Chaos," *McKinsey Quarterly* 1 (1997): 25; Mary J. Cronin, *Unchained Value: The New Logic of Digital Business* (Boston: Harvard Business School Press, 2001).

39 See Andreas Hinterhuber, "Value Chain Orchestration in Action and the Case of the Global Agrochemical Industry," *Long Range Planning* 35 (2002): 615; G. D. Bhatt and A. F. Emdad, "An Analysis of the Virtual Value Chain in Electronic Commerce," *Logistics Information Management* 45 (January 17, 2001): 78; S. Winter, John McIntosh, and David May, "Survival in the Korean Furniture Industry: Value-Chain Networking," *Journal of Managerial Issues* 15 (2003): 450.

40 Theodore Levitt, "The Globalization of Markets," *Harvard Business Review* 61 (1983): 92–102.

41 Regarding cultural predisposition, Japanese doctors disfavor the American-style, high-pressure sales force. Pharmaceutical sales representatives, therefore, adapt their marketing practices in that country. Regarding historical legacy, people drive on the left side of the road in England, thereby creating demand for right-hand-drive cars, whereas people in Italy drive on the right side of the road, thereby creating demand for left-hand-drive cars. Similarly, consumer electrical systems are based on 110 volts in the United States, whereas many European countries use a 240-volt standard.

42 C. Prahalad and Y. Doz, *The Multinational Mission: Balancing Local Demands and Global Vision* (New York: Free Press, 1987).

43 The term *multinational corporation* (MNC) is also commonly used in the international business arena and often is a synonym for MNE. We prefer the *MNE* designation because there are many internationally involved companies, such as accounting partnerships, which are not organized as corporations.

44 "A World of Connections," *The Economist* (April 26, 2007): 65.

45 Direct quotes from the following: Jack Welch and John A. Byrne, *Jack: Straight from the Gut* (New York: Warner Business Books, 2001); Chris Bartlett and Meg Wozny, "GE's Two-Decade Transformation: Jack Welch's Leadership," *Harvard Business School Case 399150* (1999); Lowe, *Welch: An American Icon.*

46 "Hungry Tiger, Dancing Elephant: How India Is Changing IBM's World," *The Economist* (April 4, 2007): 58–61.

47 Joan Ricart, Michael J. Enright, Pankaj Ghemawat, Stuart L. Hart, and Tarun Khanna, "New Frontiers in International Strategy," *Journal of International Business Studies* 35 (May 2004): 175.

48 Yves Doz, Jose Santos, and Peter Williamson, *Global to Metanational: How Companies Win in the Knowledge Economy* (Cambridge, MA: Harvard Business School Press, 2001).

49 Michael V. Copeland, "How Startups Go Global," *Business 2.0* (July 28, 2006): 424; Jim Hopkins, "The Rise of the Micro-Multinationals," *USA Today* (February 11, 2005): B-1.

50 Marc Singer, "Beyond the Unbundled Corporation," *The McKinsey Quarterly*, www.mckinseyquarterly.com/Beyond_the_ unbundled_corporation_1085 (accessed July 12, 2009); Remo Hacki and Julian Lighton, "The Future of the Networked Company," *McKinsey Quarterly*, www.mckinseyquarterly.com/The_future_ of_the_networked_company_1091 (accessed July 12, 2009); James Martin, "Only the Cyber-Fit Will Survive," *Datamation* (November 1996): 60.

51 "The New Champions," *The Economist* (September 18, 2008); Thomas Friedman, "The World Is Flat: A Brief History of the Twenty-First Century" (New York: Farrar, Straus and Giroux, 2005); Clyde V. Prestowitz, *Three Billion New Capitalists. The Great Shift of Wealth and Power to the East* (New York: Basic Books, 2006); "The Next Billions: Unleashing Business Potential in Untapped Markets," *World Economic Forum* (January 2009); 44; C. K. Prahalad and S. L. Hart, "The Fortune at the Bottom of the Pyramid," *Strategy+Business* 26 (2002): 54–67; C. K. Prahalad, *The Fortune at the Bottom of the Pyramid* (Philadelphia: Wharton School Publishing, 2004); Antoine van Agtmael, *The Emerging Markets Century: How a New Breed of World-Class Companies Is Overtaking the World* (Minneapolis, MN: Free Press, 2007).

52 Anil K. Gupta and Haiyan Wang, "How to Get China and India Right," *Wall Street Journal* (April 23, 2007).

53 "McDonald's Eyes Russia Growth with 40 New Stores," *Reuters*, uk.reuters.com/article/idUKLQ86281720090226 (accessed February 26, 2009).

54 Reported in "The New Champions," www.financialexpress.com/ printer/news/365882/ (accessed October 4, 2009).

55 "Hungry Tiger, Dancing Elephant: How India Is Changing IBM's World," *The Economist* (April 4, 2007): 58–61.

twelve
Country Evaluation and Selection

Objectives

- To grasp company strategies for sequencing the penetration of countries

- To see how scanning techniques can help managers both limit geographic alternatives and consider otherwise overlooked areas

- To discern the major opportunity and risk variables a company should consider when deciding whether and where to expand abroad

- To know the methods and problems of collecting and comparing international information

- To understand some simplifying tools for helping decide where to operate

- To consider how companies allocate emphasis among the countries where they operate

- To comprehend why location decisions do not necessarily compare different countries' possibilities

The place to get top speed out of a horse is not the place where you can get top speed out of a canoe.

—*African (Hausa) proverb*

481

Carrefour, which opened its first store in 1960, is now the largest retailer in Europe and Latin America and the second largest worldwide.[1] By 2009, it had more than 15,000 stores and about 495,000 employees, selling a combination of food and nonfood items. In 2008, Carrefour derived 54 percent of its sales and 58 percent of its profits outside its home country of France. The Institute of Grocery Distribution ranks Carrefour as the world's most global retailer, based on foreign sales, number of countries with operations, and ratio of foreign sales to total sales. As of 2009, it had a presence in 33 countries.

Carrefour must continue to decide which countries to emphasize in its expansion and where in each country to locate the new stores. In 2009, Carrefour announced its future priorities in choice of country. Its first priority is leadership in France. The second is to maintain growth or improve performance in three other European countries—Belgium, Italy, and Spain. And its third priority is to establish operations in countries with strong growth potential—mainly BRIC countries (Brazil, Russia, India, and China). Of these four, Carrefour entered Russia in 2009 and plans to begin operating in India by the end of 2010. Finally, the lowest priority is made up of other countries. Map 12.1 shows those countries.

Concomitantly, Carrefour must decide what to do with underperforming stores and countries. It sells stores and moves from countries that offer less potential profits than if capital is placed elsewhere. For instance, in 2006, it sold its operations in South Korea and Slovakia while expanding heavily in Poland.

Carrefour sells in five types of stores: hypermarkets, supermarkets, hard discount stores, cash-and-carry stores, and convenience stores. Its hypermarkets account for the largest portion of its sales, retail space, and number of countries with retail operations. Carrefour invented and opened the first hypermarket—an enormous store combining a department store and a supermarket. Whereas a typical supermarket might have 40,000 square feet, a hypermarket might have 330,000.

MAP 12.1   Carrefour's Priority among Countries

In 2009, Carrefour published its priority among countries. Note that defense of present positions is most important; large growth markets are next in importance.

Source: The order of countries was taken from "Strategic Orientations March 2009," http//www.carrefour.com/cdc/group/our-strategy (accessed July 20, 2009).

First priority (France)

Second priority (Belgium, Italy, Spain)

Third priority (Brazil, China, India, Russia)

Rest of world

As a rule of thumb, a hypermarket requires 500,000 households within a 20-minute drive to derive sufficient business. Carrefour's supermarkets carry less variety than its hypermarkets, and its hard discount stores and cash-and-carry stores carry even less. The cash-and-carry stores cater strictly to the trade, such as to restaurant owners and hoteliers. Its convenience stores (more than 95 percent are franchise operations) are still smaller and carry fewer items. One of Carrefour's key contributions to franchisees is helping to select locations for their stores.

Carrefour's French hypermarket operation was a success from the beginning, due largely to the timing for introducing the concept. French supermarket operations were not yet well developed; consumers generally shopped for foods in different outlets—such as bread, meat, fish, cheese, and fresh vegetables in different specialty stores or markets. Moreover, few retailers had convenient or free parking, so customers had to make frequent and time-consuming trips to numerous stores. Carrefour came along when more French families had cars, refrigerators large enough to store a week's supply of fresh products, and higher disposable incomes to spend on nonfood items. Further, more women were working, and they wanted one-stop shopping. Thus French consumers flocked to Carrefour's suburban hypermarkets, which offered free parking and discounted prices on a very wide selection of merchandise.

However, French government authorities at times have restricted new hypermarket permits to safeguard town centers, protect small businesses, and prevent visual despoliation of the countryside. As a consequence, Carrefour decided to expand internationally. Figure 12.1 provides a chronology of Carrefour's expansion into foreign markets via company-owned outlets. Its first foreign entry was a partnership in Belgium, and its first wholly owned foreign store was in Spain. Both are in neighboring countries, both entries were with hypermarkets, and both countries had consumers who were going through lifestyle changes similar to those we described for France.

Carrefour easily managed these ventures because its French suppliers provided much of the stores' stock and because its French managers could easily travel to oversee the operations. Since then, a guiding principle for Carrefour's international expansion has been countries' economic evolution. Its former CEO, Daniel Bernard, said, "We can start with a developing country at the bottom of the economic curve and grow within the country to the top of the curve." When Carrefour has deviated from this principle, it has failed. It expanded unsuccessfully into the United States and the United Kingdom after both countries had gone through economic transitions and other distributors had satisfied the changed consumer needs. It also entered the Mexican, Japanese, Korean, and Chilean markets late and sold their operations there. Bernard said later, "To go global, you need to be early enough. Generally, in new countries you need to be the first in for the first win. When you arrive as number three or four, it is too late."

Some additional factors caused problems for Carrefour in markets it has abandoned. In the United States, customers simply have not wanted to spend the time shopping in a hypermarket where they had to walk long distances before reaching even the first aisle. In the United Kingdom, Carrefour did well on food

FIGURE 12.1   Carrefour's Major Locations and Entry Dates

Data refer to company-owned outlets and do not include franchises. Carrefour also entered and exited some foreign markets, including the United Kingdom, the United States, and Japan.

Source: Based on data from Groupe Carrefour, "The Carrefour Group's Store Locations," at www.carrefour.com (accessed June 11, 2007) and updated via a variety of sources.

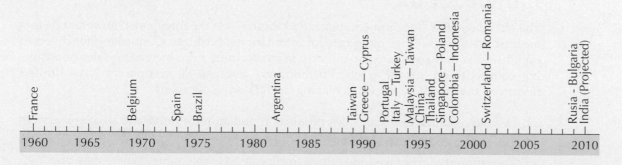

sales, but consumers preferred to shop for durables in city centers where they could compare the products offered by different distributors. In Mexico, Carrefour was up against an established Wal-Mart, which could integrate buying and distribution with its successful U.S. operations. In Japan, consumers were disappointed not to find a French shopping experience. In both Hong Kong and Chile, Carrefour was unable to build enough stores to gain the needed economies of distribution.

Another factor influencing Carrefour's choice of country has been the ability to find a viable partner familiar with local operating needs. It has found these with the Maus group in Switzerland, President Enterprise in Taiwan, the Sabanci group in Turkey, and Harbor Power Equipment in China. However, Carrefour entered Mexico well after Wal-Mart, which had teamed with the best local partner, Cifra. It entered Japan without a partner because management believed its traditional operating costs, which were lower than those of Japanese rivals, would enable it to compete. At the time, a retail analyst prophetically noted, "Their [Carrefour's] chances of success are zero." Carrefour lasted only four years before selling out.

Why would another company want to partner with Carrefour? Aside from financial resources, Carrefour brings to a partnership expertise on store layout, clout in dealing with global suppliers (for example, it runs a global sales campaign, "Most Awaited Month," in which the largest manufacturers of global consumer goods provide its stores worldwide with lower prices for a one-month sale), direct e-mail links with suppliers that substantially reduce inventories and the need for Carrefour's buyers to visit suppliers, and the ability to export unique bargain items from one country to another.

Carrefour also considers whether a location can justify sufficient additional store expansion to gain economies of scale in buying and distribution. To help gain these economies, Carrefour and some of its competitors have recently been expanding via acquisition. However, some analysts have felt that Carrefour may be expanding retail operations to too many countries and will not be able to build sufficient presence in each to gain necessary economies of scale. In contrast, the British retailer Tesco is expanding to fewer countries but is building a large presence in each one.

Carrefour depends on locally produced goods for about 90 percent of its sales, using manufacturers' trademarks or no trademarks at all. This strategy contrasts with such retailers as Tesco, which depends heavily on own-label products. Thus consumers can easily compare prices of most Carrefour products with those of competitors because few of its products have unique labels.

Nevertheless, Carrefour has recently been pushing global purchasing. For example, when stores in one country find an exceptional supplier, the management passes on the information to Carrefour's merchandising group in Brussels, which then seeks markets within Carrefour stores in other countries. The Malaysian operation, for example, found a good local supplier of disposable gloves, and Carrefour now sells them in its stores worldwide.

Despite Carrefour's success in many markets, analysts feel that it will never become the world's largest retailer without a significant presence in the United States and the United Kingdom. Its only **⊕RN** presence in either is a minority interest in Costco in the United States.

Introduction

The old adage that "location, location, and location" are the three most important factors for business success rings quite true for international business. Countries offer different opportunities and risks as companies try to create value from increasing sales or acquiring competitively useful assets. Furthermore, because all companies have limited resources, they must be careful in making the following decisions:

1. In which countries to locate sales, production, and administrative and auxiliary services
2. The sequence for entering different countries
3. The amount of resources and efforts to allocate to each country where they operate

Committing human, technical, and financial resources to one locale may mean forgoing or delaying projects elsewhere. In our opening case, for instance, we saw that Carrefour, although the world's second largest retailer, has taken over 40 years to move into roughly only 15 percent of the world's countries, and its presence in some of those countries is still quite small. So to become a significant player in more than a few countries, managers usually need to take time. Even after companies are well established in most countries, they still need to allocate resources by emphasizing some countries more than others. Thus picking the right locations affects companies' ability to gain and sustain competitive advantage.[2]

Figure 12.2 highlights the importance of companies' location decisions. By examining the external environment and comparing this environment with the company's objectives and capabilities, managers might ask: Where can we best leverage our existing competencies? and Where can we go to best sustain, improve, or extend our competencies?

To answer those questions, managers need to answer two more: Which markets should we serve? and Where should we place production to serve those markets? On the one hand, the answers to these questions can be one and the same, particularly if transport costs or government regulations mean that companies must produce in the countries where they sell. Many service industries, such as hotels, construction, and retailing (such as Carrefour), must locate facilities near their foreign customers.

On the other hand, companies' large-scale production technology may favor producing in only a few countries and exporting to others, such as occurs for companies in the capital-intensive automobile and steel industries. Finally, companies' location decisions may be more complex, such as using multiple countries for sourcing raw materials and components that go into one finished product. Or they may divide operating functions, such as having headquarters in the United States, a call center for handling service in India, and an R&D facility in Switzerland.

Companies need to
- Determine the order of country entry.
- Set the rates of resource allocation among countries.

In choosing geographic sites, a company must decide
- Where to sell.
- Where to produce.

FIGURE 12.2 Location Decisions Affecting International Operations

In choosing locations for international operations, a company should begin by analyzing three factors: its *objectives*, its *competencies*, and its comparative *environmental fit* with conditions in *the countries under consideration*.

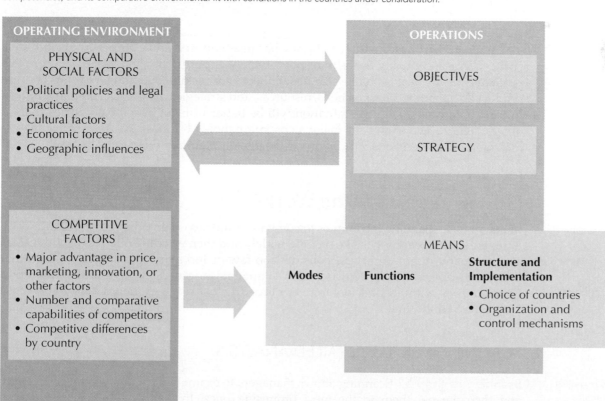

FIGURE 12.3   The Location-Decision Process

Location, location, location: Committing resources to an overseas location may entail a risky trade-off—say, delaying or abandoning projects elsewhere. The decision-making process is essentially twofold: examining the external environments of proposed locations and comparing each of them with the company's objectives and capabilities.

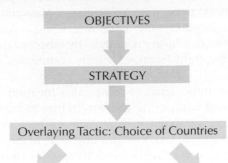

OBJECTIVES

STRATEGY

Overlaying Tactic: Choice of Countries

Choosing new locations
- Scan for alternatives
- Choose and weight variables
- Collect and analyze data for variables
- Use tools to compare variables and narrow alternatives

Allocating among locations
- Analyze effects of reinvestment versus harvesting in existing operating locations
- Appraise interdependence of locations on performance
- Examine needs for diversification versus concentration of foreign operations

Making final decisions
- Conduct detailed feasibility study for new locations
- Estimate expected outcome for reinvestments
- Make location and allocation decisions based on company's financial decision-making tools

Flexibility in locations is important because country and competitive conditions change. Thus a company needs to respond to new opportunities and withdraw from less profitable ones. There is no one-size-fits-all theory for picking operating locations because product lines, competitive positions, resources, and strategies make each company unique. In turn, a company's unique situation will be better utilized in some countries than in others.[3] Figure 12.3 shows the major steps international business managers must take in making location decisions. The following discussion examines these steps in depth.

How Does Scanning Work?

Without scanning, a company may
- Overlook opportunities and risks.
- Examine too many or too few possibilities.

Managers use scanning techniques to compare countries on broad indicators of opportunities and risks. Scanning is like seeding widely and then weeding out: It is useful insofar as a company might otherwise consider too few or too many possibilities. Given that there are approximately 200 countries, managers might easily overlook some good opportunities without first looking very broadly. Instead, they might zero in on those that come to mind first.

SCANNING VERSUS DETAILED ANALYSIS

On-site visits follow scanning and are part of the final location decision process.

Scanning as Step 1   Scanning allows managers to examine most or all countries broadly and then narrow them to the most promising ones. In scanning, managers compare country information that is readily available, inexpensive, and fairly comparable—usually without having to incur the expense of visiting foreign countries. Instead they analyze publicly available information, such as from the Internet, and they communicate with experienced people. They compare countries on a few conditions that could significantly affect the success or failure of their business and that fit with the company's resources and objectives. Because of using fairly easy-to-find information, managers may consider a large group of countries at this point, such as all the countries within a global region.

Detailed Analysis as Step 2   Once managers narrow their consideration to the most promising countries, they need to compare the feasibility and desirability of each. At this point, unless they are satisfied enough to outsource all their production and sales, they almost always need to go on location to analyze and collect more specific information.

    Take a situation in which managers need to decide where to place their sales efforts. They will likely need to visit the countries shortlisted through scanning, to conduct, for example, market research and visit with distributors before making a final decision. Or take a situation in which managers need to decide where to locate production of a finished product or component. If they plan to outsource this production, they may want to inspect potential contractors' facilities. If they plan to own facilities themselves, they will need to collect such specific on-site information as availability of land and suppliers before committing significant resources.

    Intel's manufacturing expansion into Latin America offers an illustrative example. Intel used scanning techniques to limit visits to a few Latin American countries. The follow-up visits sought much more detailed information—even the availability of suitable housing, medical services, and food products for the personnel it would need to transfer. The visits also allowed the visiting team to gain qualitative information, such as their impressions of the welcome they might get from local government officials and business leaders.

    The more time and money companies invest in examining an alternative, the more likely they are to accept it, regardless of its merits—a situation known as an **escalation of commitment.** A feasibility study should have clear-cut decision points, which are points where managers can cut the commitment before they invest too much time and money.

What Information Is Important in Scanning?

Managers should consider country conditions that could significantly affect success or failure. These conditions should reveal both opportunities and risks, which we discuss in the coming section.

OPPORTUNITIES

We divide the section on opportunities into sales expansion and resource acquisition, although some conditions affect both, given the relationship between decisions of where to sell and where to produce.

Sales Expansion   Expansion of sales is probably the most important factor motivating companies to engage in international business, because they assume that more sales will lead to more profits. Thus it is vital for them to decide where best to make those sales.

    Of course, managers would like to have sales figures for the type of product they want to sell, but such information may not be available, especially if the product is a new one. In such instances, one way to make rough estimates of sales potential is to base projections on what has happened to sales for a similar or complementary product. For instance, they might project the potential sales of flat-screen televisions based on figures for DVD equipment sales.

Concept Check

In Chapter 11, we focus on the importance of **value**—the measure of a company's ability to sell products for more than it costs to make them—in a firm's **strategy,** adding that "creating value" is primarily a matter of meeting (indeed, exceeding) customer expectations. Here we point out the importance of both factors—cost and customer needs—in taking advantage of overseas opportunities.

FIGURE 12.4   Aluminum Consumption vs. GDP per Capita

By plotting a line based on GDP per capita, you can get a fairly good estimate of demand per capita for aluminum.

Source: From a presentation by Paul Thomas, North American Fabricated Products of Alcoa (April 20, 2004); "Globalization and the Aluminum Market—Opportunities and Challenges," The Aluminum Association Inc. (2004), at www. aluminum.org (accessed October 29, 2007).

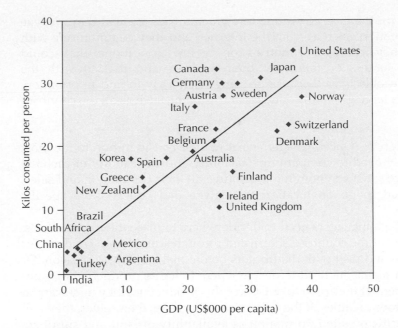

| Expectation of a large market and sales growth is probably a potential location's major attraction.

However, such complementary figures may not be available either. So what can they do? They can use economic and demographic data as sales potential—particularly historical data on other countries. For instance, Figure 12.4 shows an example of aluminum per capita consumption among a sample of countries. Management may make a rough estimate that aluminum demand for all countries will increase along the trend line as GDP per capita increases.

Of course, you should examine indicators related directly to the products you wish to sell. For example, if you're trying to sell luxury products, GDP per capita may tell you very little. Instead, you need to know how many people have income above a certain level. For instance, India's GDP per capita is low, but it has enough millionaires to support the sale of high-end products by companies like LMVH that sell Tag Heuer watches.

Furthermore, although your product or service may not appeal to the average customer, you may seek out niches within that market. Pollo Campero, a Guatemalan-based fast-food chain, and Gigante, a Mexican supermarket chain, have both successfully entered the United States by going to cities with large Central American and Mexican populations.[4]

| Companies must consider variables other than income and population when estimating potential demand for their products in different countries.

Examining Economic and Demographic Variables   Here are some of the main things to consider when examining economic and demographic variables:

- *Obsolescence and leapfrogging of products.*   Consumers in developing economies do not necessarily follow the same patterns as those in higher-income countries. In China, for example, consumers have leapfrogged the use of landline telephones by jumping from having no telephones to using cellular phones almost exclusively.[5]

- *Prices.*   If prices of essential products are high, consumers may spend more on these products than what one would expect based on per capita GDP, thus having less to spend on discretionary purchases. The expenditures on food in Japan, for instance, are higher than would be predicted by either population or income level because food is expensive and work habits promote eating out.

- *Income elasticity.*   A common tool for predicting total market potential is to divide the percentage of change in product demand by the percentage of change in income in a given country. The more that demand changes in relation to income changes, the more elastic is the demand. Demand for necessities such as food is usually less elastic than is demand for discretionary products such as flat-screen TVs.

- *Substitution.* Consumers in a given country may more conveniently substitute certain products or services than consumers in some other countries. For example, there are fewer automobiles in Hong Kong than one would expect based on income and population, because the crowded conditions make the efficient mass transit system a desirable substitute for automobiles.

- *Income inequality.* Where income inequality is high, the per capita GDP figures are less meaningful, because many people have little to spend and many others have substantial income to spend, as in our example of luxury product sales in India.

- *Cultural factors and taste.* Countries with similar per capita GDPs may have different preferences for products and services because of values or tastes. For example, the large Hindu population in India reduces per capita meat consumption there. However, there is a large niche market of Indians who are neither Hindu nor vegetarian.

- *Existence of trading blocs.* Although a country may have a small population and GDP, its presence in a regional trading bloc gives its output access to a much larger market. For instance, Uruguay has a small domestic market, but its production has duty-free access to three other countries in the Southern Common Market (MERCOSUR).[6]

Given all of the factors just cited, managers cannot project potential demand perfectly. However, by considering factors that may influence the sale of their products, they can make workable estimates that help them narrow detailed studies to a reasonable number.

Resource Acquisition Companies undertake international business to secure resources that are either not sufficiently available or too expensive in their home countries. They may purchase these resources from another organization, or they may establish foreign investments to exploit them. In either case, they must prioritize where they can best secure what they want.

If they want to acquire a scarce resource, they are obviously limited to those locales that have it, such as securing petroleum only in those countries that have reserves. However, even when the resource is limited to a few countries, there are better opportunities in some countries than in others. In the case of petroleum reserves, for example, there are cost differences in extraction, transportation, and taxes. When considering cost differences, a particular resource may be overriding for specific industries or companies, such as sugar for candy companies or low-cost water power for aluminum companies.

Cost Considerations However, a company's total cost is made up of numerous subcosts. Many of these are industry- or company-specific. Nevertheless, there are several—*labor, infrastructure, ease of transportation and communications,* and *government incentives*—that apply to a large cross section of companies. We discuss these next.

LABOR Although capital intensity is growing in most industries, labor compensation remains an important cost for most companies. In the scanning process, you can examine such factors as labor market size, labor compensation, minimum wages, customary and required fringe benefits, education levels, and unemployment rates to compare labor cost, skills, and availability.

Labor, however, is not homogeneous. Neither are companies' labor needs. For example, the desire to establish a low-cost call center has led many U.S. companies to locate in the Philippines, where there are many English speakers, but not in Senegal, where many French companies locate call centers to serve French-language markets. Or you may wish to establish an R&D facility where figures on the number of science and engineering graduates give you a rough idea that needed skills are available. In fact, many companies have recently set up R&D facilities in China, Hungary, India, and Israel because of the availability of technical talent at low cost.[7]

If a country's labor force lacks the specific skill levels required, a company might have to train, redesign production, or add supervision—all of which are expensive.

Concept Check
Recall our discussion of "Regional Economic Integration" in Chapter 8, where we explain the **dynamic effects** of integration. As we point out, when trade barriers come down within a regional bloc, the size of the market available to small member nations typically increases quite dramatically.

Costs—especially labor costs—are an important factor in companies' production-location decisions.

Keep in mind also that there may be sector and geographic differences in wage rates within countries. For example, Mexican tire wages are much higher than the average Mexican industrial wage, and wages in the capital and other large cities are higher than elsewhere.[8]

In addition, you should look for conditions that can cause changes in labor availability and cost. For example, the HIV rate is very high in southern African countries, a problem that may drastically reduce their labor forces over the next 10 to 15 years.

When companies move into developing countries because of labor-cost differences, their advantages may be short-lived for one or more of three reasons:

- Competitors follow leaders into low-wage areas.
- There is little first-mover advantage for this type of production migration.
- The costs rise quickly as a result of pressure on wage or exchange rates.

Infrastructure problems add to operating costs.

INFRASTRUCTURE   Poor internal infrastructure may easily negate cost differences in labor rates. In many developing countries, infrastructure is both poor and unreliable, which adds to companies' costs of operating.

Take the case of Cadbury Schweppes in Nigeria. Its workers spend extra hours getting to and from work on congested roads, which makes them less productive. The company, like many others in Nigeria, uses its own power generators at two and a half times the cost of the unreliable publicly provided power. Otherwise, assembly lines could stop and the food products it makes could spoil. Because phone lines are often unavailable for days at a time, Cadbury Schweppes must send people out to visit customers and suppliers. When goods are ready for delivery, they must again face the slow roads and congestion.[9]

The need to coordinate product, process, production, and sales influences on location decisions.

EASE OF TRANSPORTATION AND COMMUNICATIONS   Related to infrastructure is the advantage of locating near customers and suppliers. For example, companies with rapidly evolving technologies need to tightly coordinate product, process, and production technologies to speed new products to market and diminish competitors' opportunity to copy them.[10] This tends to push more production for this type of company into developed countries, where they conduct most of their R&D.

Two other factors affect location when companies need to have tight connections among transportation and communications functions. First, there is distance, which roughly correlates with time and cost of shipments; thus a geographically isolated country, such as New Zealand, does not fit as easily into a company's global integration strategy, because supplies to and production from such locations may be untimely and costly.[11] Second, there are advantages to locating in countries with few trade restrictions in order to reduce tariff costs and better assure a continuous flow of components where they are needed.[12]

Companies may also find advantages in being near specialized private and public institutions such as banks, financing firms, insurance groups, public accountants, freight forwarders, customs brokers, and consular offices, all of which handle international functions. In this respect, some companies have moved their headquarters to another country to be nearer to their markets and centers of finance.[13]

For instance, Halliburton relocated its CEO and corporate headquarters from the United States to Dubai to be closer to its customers and employees. If a company is looking for a production location that will serve sales in more than one country, the ease of moving goods into and out of the country is very important; thus it is useful to consider the efficiency of port facilities along with the country's trade liberalization agreements.[14]

Government practices may increase or decrease companies' costs.

GOVERNMENTAL INCENTIVES AND DISINCENTIVES   Most countries at this writing seek foreign investment because of the jobs it will create, the competitiveness it will enhance, and the impact it will have on their trade balance. Thus, it is common to see ads in business newspapers to entice foreign companies to consider a particular country as an investment location.[15]

Because countries compete to attract investors, many offer incentives, through regulations or negotiations, that lower companies' costs of operating. These incentives include such things as lower taxes, training of employees, loan guarantees, low-interest loans, exemption of import duties, and subsidized energy and transportation. Differences in tax rates are particularly important when deciding where to produce within a regional trading bloc, inasmuch as companies can serve the entire region from any country within the bloc.

At the same time, companies may begin operating more quickly and with fewer steps in some countries than in others. World Bank studies show that countries differ in terms of the ease or difficulty of starting a business, entering and enforcing contracts, hiring and firing workers, getting credit, and closing a business.[16] Governmental actions may delay or prevent companies from bringing in expatriate personnel and from timely clearing of needed imports through customs.

In addition, countries differ in both legal transparency and corruption. A disincentive occurs when companies must spend excessive time in satisfying government agencies on such matters as taxes, labor conditions, and environmental compliance when they are unsure of the legal consequences of their actions and when they may be required to pay bribes to be competitive.[17]

A CAVEAT The continuous development of new production technologies makes cost comparisons among countries more difficult. As the number of ways to make the same product increases, a company might have to compare the cost of labor-intensive production in a low-wage country with that of capital-intensive production in a high-wage country. For example, Volkswagen moved some production from Germany to Slovakia and switched from a highly automated, capital-intensive assembly line to a labor-intensive plant because the low Slovakian wages and high productivity cut costs from those in Germany.[18] A company should also compare the cost from large-scale production that reduces fixed costs per unit by serving multicountry markets with the cost from multiple smaller-scale production units that reduce transport and inventory costs.

Concept Check

We show in Chapter 6 that, in applying **factor-proportions theory** to determine the best place to locate a manufacturing facility, a company may compare the amount (and cost) of machinery that it will need in one place to the number (and cost) of people that it will need in another.

RISKS

Any company decision involves weighing opportunity against risk. For example, a sales-seeking company may not necessarily go to the country showing the highest sales potential. Nor will an asset-seeking company necessarily go where the assets are cheapest. In both cases, this is because decision makers may perceive that the risks in those locales are too high.

Factors to Consider in Analyzing Risk Keep in mind several factors as we discuss specific types of risk:

1. *Companies and their managers differ in their perceptions of what is risky,* how tolerant they are of taking risk, what they expect returns should be for the risk they take, and the portion of their assets they are willing to put at risk.[19]

2. *One company's risk may be another's opportunity.* For example, companies offering security solutions (e.g., alarm systems, guard services, insurance, weapons) may find their biggest sales opportunities where other companies find only operating risks.

3. *There are means by which companies may reduce their risks other than avoiding locations,* such as by insuring, but all these options incur costs that decision makers should take into account.

4. *There are trade-offs among risks.* For instance, avoidance of a country where political risk is high may leave a company more vulnerable to competitive risk if another company earns good profits there. Finally, returns are usually higher where risk is higher.

Bolivia has been a risky environment for foreign investors because of expropriation, demonstrations, and violence. The photo shows an evacuation of a building in La Paz (2009) because of a bomb threat. The building housed such international companies as Sinchi Wayra (subsidiary of Switzerland's Glencore International) and Associated Press (United States).
Source: AP Wide World Photos

Companies should
- Examine views of government decision makers.
- Get a cross section of opinions.
- Use expert analysts.

Although the preceding discussion emphasizes the individual nature of risk assessment, there are a number of factors that large numbers of companies consider important. We have grouped these into three categories—political, monetary, and competitive—which we'll now discuss.

Political Risk   Political risk may occur because of changes in political leaders' opinions and policies, civil disorder, and animosity between the host and other countries, particularly with the company's home country. It may be expensive to companies because of the loss or damage of property, disrupted operations, and the need to adjust to changes in the rules governing business. The photo shows temporarily disrupted operations in Bolivia because of a bomb scare.

Recently, for example, Unilever has encountered difficulty in attracting foreign executives to work in Pakistan because of security concerns; Chiquita Brands paid money to terrorists in Colombia to protect its employees there; oil companies such as Total had their investments expropriated in Venezuela; Marriott had a hotel bombed in Indonesia; and Coca-Cola has had interrupted services (police protection of its trucks and telephone connections) in Angola.[20]

Managers use three approaches to predict political risk: *analyzing past patterns, analyzing opinions,* and *examining the social and economic conditions that might lead to such risk.*

Analyzing Past Patterns   Predicting foreign companies' risk on the basis of past political occurrences is problematic because situations may change for better or worse. Further, examining a country's overall situation masks political risk differences within countries and among companies. For example, unrest that leads to property damage and disruption of supplies or sales may be limited geographically. During the civil war that led to the breakup of Yugoslavia, companies in Slovenia escaped the damage that companies incurred in other parts of the country. Moreover, with few exceptions, government takeovers of companies have been highly selective, primarily affecting operations that have a visible widespread effect on the country because of their size or monopoly position.

When a company does incur property damage or asset takeover, it does not necessarily mean a full loss to investors. First, property damage may be covered by insurance. Second, governments have preceded most takeovers with formal declarations of intent and have followed with legal processes to determine the foreign investor's compensation.

In addition to the investment's book value, other factors may determine the adequacy (or not) of compensation. On the one hand, the compensation may earn a lower return elsewhere. On the other hand, other agreements (such as purchase and management contracts) may create additional benefits for the former investor. In analyzing political risk, managers should predict the likely loss if political problems occur, and past settlements may serve as indicators.

Analyzing Opinions   Because influential people may sway future political events affecting business, managers should access statements by political leaders both in and out of office to determine their philosophies toward private business, foreign business relations, the means of effecting economic changes, and their feelings toward given foreign countries. They should also access polls showing different leaders' likelihood of gaining political office. Modern technology has improved access to global newspapers and television so that managers can retrieve reports quickly.

Managers should eventually visit the short-listed countries to listen to a cross section of opinions, such as from embassy officials, foreign and local businesspeople, journalists, academicians, middle-level local government authorities, and labor leaders. These people usually reveal their own attitudes, which often reflect political conditions that may change and affect the business sector.

A company also may rely on commercial risk-assessment services, of which there are many. In fact, companies have been relying more on these services rather than generating their own risk analyses because the services offer concise reports that management decision makers view as credible. Nevertheless, it is useful to determine what type of information goes into these reports, how it is collected, and what the track record has been for their predictions.[21]

Examining Social and Economic Conditions   Countries' social and economic conditions may lead to unrest if population segments have unmet aspirations. Frustrated groups may disrupt business by calling general strikes and destroying property and supply lines. For example, this has been the recent experience in the Niger Delta region of Nigeria, where groups have attacked foreign oil companies' property and kidnapped their employees.[22] Frustrated groups might also replace government leaders.

Moreover, political leaders might harness their support by blaming problems on foreigners and foreign companies. This may lead to boycotts or rule changes for foreign companies or even expropriation of their properties. However, there is no general consensus as to what constitutes dangerous conditions or how such instability can be predicted. The lack of consensus is illustrated by the diverse reactions of companies to the same political situations.

Rather than political stability itself, the direction of change in government seems to be very important. But even if a company accurately predicts the direction of change in government that will affect business, it will still be uncertain as to how long the government will take to enact new practices.

Monetary Risk   Companies may be affected by either changes in exchange rates or the ability to move funds out of a country. We now examine these two types of risks.

Exchange-Rate Changes   The change in value of a foreign currency is a two-edged sword, depending on whether you are going abroad to seek sales or resources. Let's say you are a U.S. company doing business in India. If you are seeking export sales, then a deterioration in the value of the Indian rupee will make you less competitive because it will cost more rupees to buy the U.S. products or services. If the U.S. company produces within India to serve the Indian market, its competitiveness in India will not change, but its rupee profits from India will buy fewer U.S. dollars when they are brought back to the United States. If, however, the U.S. company is seeking assets from India, say Indian personnel to staff a call center, a fall in the rupee value lowers the U.S.-dollar cost of the personnel.

Concept Check

As we explain in Chapter 9, an **exchange rate** is the price of a currency; in Chapter 10, we discuss some of the causes of exchange-rate changes (including *floating rate* regimes and interest rates) and explain various methods of forecasting exchange-rate movements (such as focusing on trends in economic variables or trends in the rates themselves).

Companies may accept a lower return in order to move their financial resources more easily.

Mobility of Funds   If a company is to invest abroad, then the ability to get funds out of the country is a factor when comparing countries. A theory that helps to explain this is **liquidity preference,** which is much like option theory in that it states that investors usually want some of their holdings to be in highly liquid assets on which they are willing to take a lower return. They need liquidity in part to make near-term payments, such as paying out dividends; in part to cover unexpected contingencies, such as stockpiling materials if a strike threatens supply; and in part to be able to shift funds to even more profitable opportunities, such as purchasing materials at a discount during a temporary price depression.[23]

The comparative liquidity among countries varies because of the activity of capital markets and because of governmental exchange control. An active capital market, particularly a stock market, helps a company sell its assets, especially if it wishes to sell shares on a local exchange or sell the entire operation. Thus, when comparing countries, you may wish to include the existence of an active stock market as a favorable variable.

If the government restricts the conversion of funds (at this writing, for example, such countries as China, India, Thailand, and Venezuela have various degrees of exchange control), the foreign investor will be forced to spend some profits or proceeds from share sale in the host country. Thus it's not surprising that, if other things are equal, investors prefer projects in strong-currency countries where there is little likelihood of exchange controls.

Does Ge⊕graphy Matter? Don't Fool with Mother Nature

In 2009 major earthquakes hit southern Asia and a swine flu pandemic spread from Mexico. These events publicized global vulnerability to natural disasters and communicable diseases. Each year, about 130 million people are exposed to earthquake risk, 119 million to tropical cyclone hazards, 196 million to catastrophic flooding, and 220 million to drought. On average, there are 184 deaths per day from natural disasters. In addition, they cause physical damage to industrial plants, crops, inventories, and infrastructure, affecting business negatively.

These natural disasters are spread unevenly around the world. For instance, Iran, Afghanistan, and India are heavily exposed to earthquakes, and some African states have the highest vulnerability to drought. The United Nations Development Programme has published a disaster risk index (DRI) that shows the relative level of physical exposure to natural disaster hazards by country.[24]

Although only 11 percent of the people exposed to these disasters live in the world's poorest countries, these countries account for 55 percent of the deaths because so much of their population is in poor housing and lacks adequate medical assistance. Likewise, the rural-to-urban migration areas in developing countries are largely to dangerous mountainsides, ravines, and low-elevation areas that are ill equipped to deal with earthquakes and cyclones. For instance, when Hurricane Mitch hit Honduras in 1998, it left 10,000 dead, 20,000 missing, and 2.5 million needing emergency aid.[25]

What does this have to do with companies' international locations? Catastrophic events upset markets, infrastructure, and production while damaging companies' property and injuring their personnel. Although they are most devastating in the world's poorer areas, events in high-income areas can play havoc with global supplies as well. For instance, the Kobe earthquake in Japan upset the world computer industry's production because it created semiconductor shortages.[26]

Thus natural events create additional operating risks and additional costs to insure against them. In turn, insurance companies are challenged to estimate the likelihood and cost of these events.

The World Health Organization has developed global atlases of infectious diseases.[27] Many of these diseases are where medical facilities are weakest because of the diseases' association with poverty. They are also associated with natural disaster, such as cholera and malaria outbreaks after flooding. Thus they tend to follow geographic patterns. For example, malaria kills about 2 million people a year, mainly in Africa.

The debilitating effects of disease impact labor force participation and life expectancy. In turn, they are costly to companies. For instance, Sasol Petroleum had to set up a clinic in Mozambique to treat its workers for malaria.[28] Companies also hesitate to send their personnel to epidemic areas. For example, during the Asian severe acute respiratory syndrome (SARS) outbreak, a number of companies (such as Wal-Mart, Gap, Liz Claiborne, and Kenneth Cole) banned employee travel to affected countries, thus hindering their buying and quality-assurance programs.[29] ●

Competitive Risk   The comparison of likely success among countries is largely contingent on competitors' actions. We now examine four competitive factors you should consider when comparing countries: *making operations compatible, spreading risk, following competitors or customers,* and *heading off competitors.*

Making Operations Compatible   Because companies operating abroad encounter less familiar environments, they encounter operating risks relative to local companies. Thus companies initially prefer to operate where they perceive conditions to be more similar to their home countries, provided, of course, that the countries additionally offer sufficient opportunities in terms of sales or resource acquisition.[30] (The major types of attributes of similarity versus dissimilarity are shown in Table 12.1.) As companies gain experience, they improve their assessments of consumer, competitor, and government actions, thereby reducing their uncertainty. In fact, foreign companies have a lower survival rate than local companies for many years after they begin operations—a situation known as the **liability of foreignness.** However, those foreign companies that learn about their new environments and manage to overcome their early problems have survival rates comparable to those of local companies in later years.[31]

This concept helps explain why, for instance, U.S. companies put earlier and greater emphasis on Canada and the United Kingdom than would be indicated by the opportunity and risk variables we've discussed thus far. In short, managers feel more comfortable doing business in a similar language, culture, and legal system.[32] These similarities may also keep operating costs and risks low because of easier communications. The ending case shows that Burger King has had a strong emphasis on Latin America and the Caribbean, largely because of distance and communications between that area and the headquarters in Miami.

Finally, economic similarity is important. Both Canada and the United Kingdom have high per capita GDPs, similar to those in the United States, which indicate a likely demand for products first created for the U.S. market. Thus, in comparing countries, you might consider their similarity to your country in terms of culture and economic level.

Managers should also try to ensure that countries' policies and norms are compatible with their companies' competitive advantages. For example, Blockbuster failed in Germany because it could not duplicate its successful formula of depending on evening, Sunday, and holiday movie rentals when people make last-minute rental decisions. Laws in Germany prevented Blockbuster from operating at these times. Further, Blockbuster creates a store environment to attract the whole family. However, consumers in Germany preferred to see family entertainment in a movie house and sought pornographic films from video stores.[33]

Concept Check

In discussing "Cultural Distance" in Chapter 2, we observe that when two countries are culturally close, a company usually expects fewer differences—and must make fewer adjustments— when moving operations from one to the other. Here we point out that economic similarity often fosters the same conditions of compatibility.

Case Review Note

TABLE 12.1   Distance Framework

The distance framework helps managers identify and assess the impact of distance of different types.

Cultural Distance	Administrative Distance	Geographic Distance	Economic Distance
	Attributes creating distance		
Different languages	Absence of colonial ties	Physical remoteness	Difference consumer incomes
Different ethnicities; lack of connective ethnic or social networks	Absence of shared monetary or political association	Lack of a common border Lack of sea or river access	Different costs and quality of:
		Size of country	• natural resources
Different religions	Political hostility	Weak transportation or communication links	• financial resources
Different social norms	Government policies		• human resources
	Institutional weakness	Different in climates	• infrastructure
			• intermediate inputs
			• information or knowledge

Source: Pankaj Ghemawat, "Distance Still Matters," *Harvard Business Review,* 79:8 (September 2001): 140.

Companies may also give preference to locales that will permit them to operate with product types, plant sizes, and operating practices familiar to their managers. When examining locales, teams that include personnel with backgrounds in each functional area—marketing, finance, personnel, engineering, and production—will more likely uncover the best fits with their companies' resources and objectives.

Companies also consider local availability of resources in relation to their needs. Many foreign operations require local resources, a requirement that may severely restrict the feasibility of given locales. For example, the company may need to find local personnel or a viable local partner who understands its type of business and technology. Or it may need to add local capital to what it is willing to bring in.

Spreading Risk   By operating in diverse countries, companies may be able to smooth their sales and profits, which may give them a competitive advantage in raising funds.[34] They may further guard against the effects of currency value changes by locating in countries whose exchange rates are not closely correlated with each other.[35] Such a strategy is in many ways opposite to what we just discussed about preferring countries similar to the home country. This is because the best smoothing of sales and profits will likely occur from operating in economies that are the least correlated.

Following Competitors or Customers   Managers may purposely crowd a market to prevent competitors from gaining advantages therein that they can use to improve their competitive positions elsewhere—a situation known as **oligopolistic reaction.**[36] For example, oligopolistic reaction helps explain why China now has more automobile producers than any other country, far more than automobile market analysts believe the market can sustain.[37]

At the same time, companies may gain advantages by locating where competitors are. To begin with, the competitors may have performed the costly task of evaluating locations and building market acceptance for a particular type of product, so followers may get a so-called free ride. Moreover, there are clusters of competitors (sometimes called **agglomeration**) in various locations—think of all the computer firms in California's Silicon Valley and in Dubai.[38]

These clusters attract multiple suppliers and personnel with specialized skills. They also attract buyers who want to compare potential suppliers but don't want to travel great distances between them. Companies operating in the cluster area may also gain better access to information about new developments, because they frequently come in contact with personnel from the other companies.[39]

There are also advantages of following customers into a market. For example, Bridgestone Tires was a major supplier to Japanese auto companies in Japan, and it followed them when they established U.S. manufacturing facilities. First, Bridgestone's track record with Japanese auto companies, such as Toyota, gave it an advantage over other tire manufacturers in the United States. Second, if another tire manufacturer were to develop a strong relationship with Toyota in the United States, it might use this experience as a successful springboard to undermine Bridgestone's position elsewhere.

Heading Off Competition   A company may try to reduce competitive risk by getting a strong foothold in markets before competitors do, by avoiding strong competitors altogether, or, when its innovative advantage may be short lived, by moving quickly into markets before competitors can copy the innovation.

In our opening case, we showed how Carrefour tries to enter growth markets before its major competitors. The reasons, as we saw, are fairly obvious: By being the first major competitor in a market, Carrefour can more easily gain the best partners, best locations, and best suppliers—a strategy to gain **first-mover advantage.** Another advantage of being first into a market is the potential of gaining strong relations with the government, such as Volkswagen in China and Lockheed with Russia.[40]

FIGURE 12.5 Where No Competitor Has Gone Before

Source: Copyright Martha Murphy, CartoonResource.com.

"Maybe there's a good reason why
no one else has broken into this market."

Companies may also develop strategies to avoid significant competition, rather than going where the competition is located. For example, PriceSmart, a discount operator, has all its warehouse stores outside its home country (the United States), and it has been successful by targeting locations in Central America, the Caribbean, and Asia that are considered too small to attract warehouse stores from competitors like Wal-Mart and Carrefour.[41] As Figure 12.5 suggests, however, competitors tend to note whether locations are good or not.

One strategy for exploiting temporary innovative advantages is known as the **imitation lag,** whereby a company moves first to those countries where local competitors are most likely to catch up to the innovative advantage.[42] Those countries apt to catch up more rapidly are the ones whose companies invest a great deal in technology.

Collecting and Analyzing Data

Companies undertake business research to reduce outcome uncertainties from their decisions and to assess their operating performance. The research includes finding answers to questions like these: Can we hire qualified personnel? Will the economic and political climate allow us to reasonably foresee our future? Are our distributors servicing sufficient accounts? and What is our market share?

Clearly, information helps managers improve their companies' performance. However, they can seldom get all the information they want, due to time and cost constraints. Thus managers should compare the estimated costs of information with the probable payoff the information will generate in revenue gains or cost savings.

Information is needed at all levels of control.

• Companies should compare the cost of information with its value.

SOME PROBLEMS WITH RESEARCH RESULTS AND DATA

The lack, obsolescence, and inaccuracy of data on many countries make much research difficult and expensive to undertake. Although there are problems everywhere, the problems are most acute in developing countries. We now discuss the two basic problems: inaccurate information and noncomparability in information from different countries.

Inaccurate Information   For the most part, there are five basic reasons why reported information may be inaccurate:

1. Governmental resources may limit accurate data collection.
2. Governments may purposely publish misleading information.
3. Respondents may give false information to data collectors.
4. Official data may include only legal and reported market activities.
5. Poor methodology may be used.

Limited Resources   Countries may have such limited resources that other projects necessarily receive priority in the national budget, such as spending to improve the literacy rate rather than spending to measure it. Even if they place an emphasis on data collection, funds may be short for buying the latest computer equipment and training the people to use it. The result is that there may be gaps in reliable and timely information.

False or Misleading Data   Of equal concern to the researcher is the publication of false or purposely misleading information designed to mislead government superiors, the country's rank and file, or companies and institutions abroad. For example, an in-house investigation in China's National Bureau of Statistics found over 60,000 cases of statistical misrepresentations that distorted such important figures as GDP, economic growth, and energy use.[43]

Mistrust of how the data will be used may lead respondents to answer questions incorrectly, particularly if they probe financial details or anything else that respondents may consider private. For example, many government figures are collected through questionnaires, such as those in the United States to estimate international travel and tourism expenditures. People may misstate their actual expenditures, particularly if they had not reported the true value of foreign purchases on incoming customs forms.

Reliance on Legally Reported Market Activities   Further distortions may occur because nationally reported income figures include only legal and reported market activities. Thus illegal income from such activities as the drug trade, theft, bribery, and prostitution is not included in national income figures, or it appears in other economic sectors because of money laundering. Contraband figures do not appear in official trade statistics and may be substantial. For instance, it is estimated that about $3 billion of Nigerian oil per year is stolen and shipped abroad. Finally, many economic activities, such as payments in cash to avoid tax payments on income, may also be substantial.[44]

Poor Research Methodology   Finally, many inaccuracies are due to poor collection and analysis by researchers both within and outside the government. Too often, broad generalizations are drawn from too few observations on nonrepresentative samples and on poorly designed questionnaires.

Noncomparable Information   Countries do not necessarily publish reports such as censuses, output figures, and trade statistics for the same time periods or at the same time as each other. So companies need to extrapolate in order to estimate how countries compare. In addition, countries differ in how they define items and what takes place in the market economy. Finally, there are also numerous definitional differences among countries, such as family income, literacy, and foreign direct investment. Activities taking place outside the market economy—for example, within the home—do not show up in income figures. Thus, the different extent among countries in terms of people producing for their own consumption (for example, growing vegetables, preparing meals at home, sewing clothes, or cutting hair) distorts country comparisons.

Accounting rules such as depreciation also differ, resulting in noncomparable net national product figures. Another comparability problem concerns exchange rates, which must be used to convert countries' financial data to some common currency. For instance, a 10 percent appreciation of the Japanese yen in relation to the U.S. dollar will result in a 10 percent increase in the per capita GDP of Japanese residents when figures are reported in dollars. Does this mean the Japanese are suddenly 10 percent richer? Obviously not, because they use about 85 percent of their yen income to make purchases in yen in the Japanese economy; thus they have no additional purchasing power for 85 percent of what they buy.

EXTERNAL SOURCES OF INFORMATION

Although information is needed for making good location decisions, there are simply too many sources for us to include a comprehensive list. Chances are, at least for scanning purposes, that you will use the Internet to collect most of your information. Some searches will lead you to free information, and others will lead you to services for which you must pay. The following discussion highlights the major types of information sources in terms of their completeness, reliability, and cost.

Individualized Reports   Market research and business consulting companies conduct studies for a fee. They generally are the most costly information source because the individualized nature restricts prorating among a number of companies. However, the fact that a company can specify what information it wants often makes the expense worthwhile.

Specialized Studies   Research organizations prepare and sell fairly specific studies at costs much lower than those for individualized studies. These specialized studies are sometimes directories of companies that operate in a given locale, perhaps containing financial or other information about the companies. They may also be about business in certain locales, forms of business, or specific products.

Service Companies   Most companies providing services to international clients—for example, banks, transportation agencies, and accounting firms—publish reports. These reports are usually geared toward either the conduct of business in a given area or some specific subject of general interest, such as tax or trademark legislation. Because the service firms intend to reach a wide market of companies, their reports tend to be fairly general. Some service firms also offer informal opinions about such things as the reputations of possible business associates and the names of people to contact in a company.

Government Agencies   When a government wants to stimulate foreign business activity, the amount and type of information it makes available may be substantial. For example, the U.S. Department of Commerce compiles news about and regulations in individual foreign countries. It disseminates specific information on product sales location in the National Trade Data Bank, and its representatives also help set up appointments with businesspeople abroad.

International Organizations and Agencies   Numerous organizations and agencies are supported by more than one country. These include the United Nations (UN), the World Trade Organization (WTO), the International Monetary Fund (IMF), the Organisation for Economic Co-operation and Development (OECD), and the European Union (EU). All of these organizations have large research staffs that compile basic statistics as well as prepare reports and recommendations concerning common trends and problems. Many of the international development banks even help finance investment-feasibility studies.

Trade Associations   Trade associations connected to various product lines collect, evaluate, and disseminate a wide variety of data dealing with technical and competitive factors in their industries. Many of these data are available in the trade journals published by such associations; others may or may not be available to nonmembers.

INTERNALLY GENERATED DATA

MNEs may have to collect much information themselves. Sometimes this may consist of no more than observing keenly and asking many questions. Investigators can see what kind of merchandise is available, see who is buying and where, and uncover the hidden distribution points and competition. Hidden competition for ready-made clothing may be seamstresses working in private homes; for vacuum cleaners, it may be servants who clean with mops. Surreptitiously sold contraband may compete with locally produced goods. Traditional analysis methods would not reveal such facts.

Point ▶ Counterpoint

Should Companies Operate in Violent Areas?

Point ▷   **Yes** Where there's risk, there are usually rewards. Companies should not shun areas with violence. Companies have always taken risks, and employees have always gone to risky areas. As far back as the seventeenth century, immigrants to what are now the United States, India, and Australia encountered disease and hostile native populations. Had companies and immigrants not taken chances, the world would be far less developed today.

You can't look at the risk from violence in isolation from other risks. Although we don't have historical data, risks are probably lower today. Disease is still a bigger risk than violence, but medical advances against a number of historical killers (such as polio, measles, smallpox, and tuberculosis) have lessened the risk from disease. Further, evacuation in case of a *real* emergency situation is much faster.

But let's assume for a moment that we decide that we should avoid countries with the potential for violence against our facilities and employees. Is there any such place? The opinions we get from so-called risk experts are certainly conflicting. One said, "It's an even playing field around the world. You can go to London, Caracas, Madrid, or New York, and from a terrorism standpoint, the risk is the same."[45] Another intelligence provider placed the United States as riskier for terrorism than Iraq and placed Britain as riskier than Nepal.[46]

Although these analyses seem intuitively wrong, bombings in London and Oklahoma City, along with school and university shootings in the United States, certainly make me wonder. The deputy assistant director of the FBI said, "We

◀ **Counterpoint**   **No** I say they shouldn't. We're no longer concerned simply about being caught in the crossfire between opposing military groups. Antiglobalization groups want to harm our personnel and facilities so that we leave or that they gain international publicity. Groups see us as easy marks for extortion by threatening harm or kidnapping our personnel. Still others are against foreigners, regardless of their aims. For instance, such a group in Afghanistan killed five staff members from Médecins sans Frontières who were there to treat sick and injured people.

At the same time, getting caught in the crossfire has become a bigger risk. Arms trafficking has increased and has lowered prices not only to revolutionaries but also to drug and alien smugglers and money launderers.[49] As MNEs, we can't help being visible, and this visibility makes us vulnerable.

In essence, if we operate where risk of violence is great, we put our personnel at risk. Although local personnel may be at a lesser risk of say, kidnapping, experience shows that they are not immune either. Furthermore, we have to send foreign personnel there. Some go as managers or technicians on long assignments; others must go on business trips, such as to audit books, ensure quality control, and offer staff advice that must involve on-site visits. The dangers are not inconsequential. There are about 8,000 reported kidnappings per year, many targeting foreign workers and their families. For instance, there were more than 200 reported Nigerian kidnappings of foreign workers in 2006 and the first half of 2007.[50]

are dealing every single day with a variety of domestic terrorism threats that are alive and well and in this country [United States]."[47] About the only places that everyone agrees are low-risk are Greenland and Iceland.

In addition, some industries don't have the luxury of avoiding violent countries. Take the petroleum industry. The companies have to go where there is a high likelihood of finding petroleum. Although it would be great to find all the petroleum in places like Iceland and Switzerland, this is not the reality. Most of the realistic alternatives are in areas that have had recent bombings, kidnappings, or organized crime—the Middle East, West Africa, the Central Asian former Soviet republics, Ecuador, and Venezuela.[48] If they didn't go to these places, they'd be out of business.

In effect, we'll keep operating anywhere that there are opportunities. If a place seems physically risky, we'll take whatever precautions we can. We'll share intelligence reports, put people through safety training courses (there are plenty of these available now), and take security actions abroad. And perhaps we won't transfer spouses and children to risky areas so we do not have to be on top of what is happening with as many people. ▶

It's simply unethical to put our employees in such situations. Of course, we don't force people to go to dangerous places, and we can get enough people to work in these areas, especially during a global recession. However, our experience is that there are three types of people who want or are willing to work in these areas, and none of these types are ideal. First, there are people, some of whom are experienced in military or undercover activities, who simply want the high compensation and big insurance policies. They tend to be highly independent and hard to control. Second, there are the naïve, who don't understand the danger and are difficult to safeguard through training and security activities. Third, there are the thrill seekers, who find that adrenaline is like an addictive drug. These are most at risk because of the thrill of danger and the reluctance to leave when situations worsen.[51]

High risk to individuals is indicative of a political situation out of control. Thus it is a harbinger of additional risks that may occur through governmental changes, falls in consumer confidence, and a general malaise that negatively affects revenues and operating regulations. This is not the kind of country in which to conduct operations. ◀

Country Comparison Tools

Once companies collect information on possible locations through scanning, they need to analyze the information. Two common tools for analysis are *grids* and *matrices*. In preparing either, it is useful to use a team made up of people from different functions so that production, marketing, finance, human resource, and legal factors are all considered. However, once companies commit to locations, they need continuous updates. We now discuss grids and matrices.

GRIDS

A company may use a grid to compare countries on whatever factors it deems important. Table 12.2 is an example of a grid with information placed into three categories. The company may immediately eliminate certain countries from consideration because of characteristics it finds unacceptable (companies vary in what they consider unacceptable). These factors are in the first category of variables, by which Country I is eliminated. The company assigns values and weights to other variables so that it ranks each country according to the relative importance of attributes to the company. In this hypothetical example, we've attached more weight to the size of investment needed than to the tax rate. For example, the table graphically pinpoints Country II as high return–low risk, Country III as low return–low risk, Country IV as high return–high risk, and Country V as low return–high risk.

Both the variables and the weights differ by product and company depending on the company's internal situation and its objectives. For instance, managers in a company selling a low-priced consumer product might heavily weigh population size as an indicator of market opportunity, whereas those in a company selling tire retreading services might heavily weigh the number of vehicles registered. The grid technique is useful even when a company does not compare countries, because it can set the minimum score needed for either investing additional resources or committing further funds to a more

Grids are tools that

- May depict acceptable or unacceptable conditions.
- Rank countries by important variables.

TABLE 12.2 Simplified Market-Penetration Grid

This table is simply an example: In the real world, a company chooses the variables that it regards as most important and may weight some as more important than others. Here managers rate Country II the most attractive because it's regarded as high return–low risk. Country IV also promises a high return and Country III low risk. Note that Country I is eliminated immediately because the company will only go where 100 percent ownership is permitted.

		Country				
Variable	**Weight**	**I**	**II**	**III**	**IV**	**V**
1. Acceptable (A), Unacceptable (U) factors						
a. Allows 100 percent ownership	—	U	A	A	A	A
b. Allows licensing to majority-owned subsidiary	—	A	A	A	A	A
2. Return (higher number = preferred rating)						
a. Size of investment needed	0–5	—	4	3	3	3
b. Direct costs	0–3	—	3	1	2	2
c. Tax rate	0–2	—	2	1	2	2
d. Market size, present	0–4	—	3	2	4	1
e. Market size, 3–10 years	0–3	—	2	1	3	1
f. Market share, immediate potential, 0–2 years	0–2	—	2	1	2	1
g. Market share, 3–10 years	0–2	—	2	1	2	0
Total			18	10	18	10
3. Risk (lower number = preferred rating)						
a. Market loss, 3–10 years (if no present penetration)	0–4	—	2	1	3	2
b. Exchange problems	0–3	—	0	0	3	3
c. Political-unrest potential	0–3	—	0	1	2	3
d. Business laws, present	0–4	—	1	0	4	3
e. Business laws, 3–10 years	0–2	—	0	1	2	2
Total			3	3	14	13

detailed feasibility study. Grids do tend to get cumbersome, however, as the number of variables increases. Although they are useful in ranking countries, they often obscure interrelationships among countries.

MATRICES

With an opportunity-risk matrix, a company can

- Decide on indicators and weight them.
- Evaluate each country on the weighted indicators.

To more clearly show the opportunity and risk relationship, managers can plot values on a matrix such as the one shown in Figure 12.6. In this particular example, Countries E and F are high-opportunity and low-risk countries in comparison with Countries A, B, C, and D. Thus Countries E and F are better candidates for detailed analysis than the other countries.

In reality, however, managers may sometimes have to choose between two countries, one with a high risk and high opportunity and another with a low risk and low opportunity. They are apt to make their decision based on their tolerance for risk and on the portfolio of countries where the company is already operating. Further, although A, B, C, and D are less appealing than E and F, the company may nevertheless find opportunities in A, B, C, and D without necessarily making a large commitment. For example, these countries may be ideal candidates for licensing or shared-ownership arrangements.

But how can managers plot values on such a matrix? They must determine which factors are good indicators of their companies' risk and opportunity and weight them to reflect their importance. For instance, on the risk axis they might give 20 percent (0.2) of the weight to expropriation risk, 25 percent (0.25) to foreign-exchange controls,

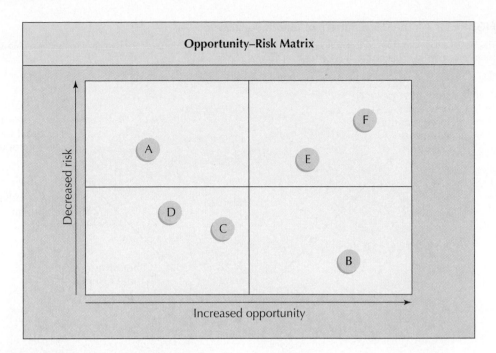

20 percent (0.2) to civil disturbances and terrorism, 20 percent (0.2) to natural disasters, and 15 percent (0.15) to exchange-rate change, for a total allocation of 100 percent.

They would then rate each country on a scale, such as from 1 to 10 for each variable (with 10 indicating the best score and 1 the worst), and multiply each variable by the weight they allocate to it. For instance, if they give Country A a rating of 8 on the expropriation-risk variable, the 8 would be multiplied by 0.2 (the weight they assign to expropriation) for a score of 1.6. They would then sum all of Country A's risk-variable scores to place it on the risk axis. They would similarly plot the location of Country A on the opportunity axis.

A key element of this kind of matrix, and one that managers do not always include in practice, is the projection of where countries will be in the future, or at least the direction in which they *should* move. Such a projection is obviously useful, but the farther one forecasts into the future, the less certain is the projection.

Allocating among Locations

The scanning tools we have just discussed are useful for narrowing country alternatives and allocating operational emphasis among countries. We now discuss three complementary strategies for international expansion: alternative gradual commitments, geographic diversification versus concentration, and reinvestment versus harvesting.

ALTERNATIVE GRADUAL COMMITMENTS

We have discussed that because of liability of foreignness, companies favor operations in countries similar to their home countries. Nevertheless there are alternative means of risk-minimization expansion patterns they can undertake. We show these in Figure 12.7, and as you examine this figure, note that the farther a company moves from the center on any axis, the deeper its international commitment becomes.

However, a company does not necessarily move at the same speed along each axis. In fact, it may jump over some of the steps on an axis. A slow movement along one axis may free up resources that allow faster expansion along another. For example, a company may find the best growth opportunities in countries that are dissimilar to those in its

Companies may reduce risks from the liability of foreignness by

- Going first to countries with characteristics similar to those of their home countries.
- Having experienced intermediaries handle operations for them.
- Operating in formats requiring commitment of fewer resources abroad.
- Moving initially to one or a few, rather than many, foreign countries.

FIGURE 12.7   The Usual Pattern of Internationalization

The farther a company moves outward along any of the axes (A, B, C, D), the deeper its international commitment. Most companies move at different speeds along different axes.

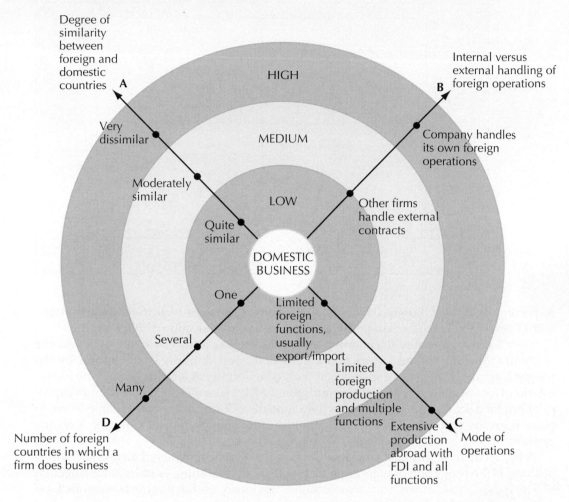

home country, so it may go first to those countries but limit the resources it puts at risk. Let's now examine Figure 12.7 more closely.

Axis A shows that companies generally move gradually from a purely domestic focus to one that eventually encompasses operations in multiple countries, some of which are quite dissimilar from one's own country. However, an alternative when moving quickly along the A axis is to move slowly along the B axis, especially for dissimilar countries. The B axis shows that a company may use intermediaries to handle foreign operations during early stages of international expansion, because this minimizes the resources it puts at risk and its liability of foreignness.

Thus a company can then commit fewer resources to both international endeavors, instead relying on intermediaries that already know how to operate in the foreign market. But if the business grows successfully, the company may want to handle the operations with its own staff. This is because it has learned more about foreign operations, and the countries where the intermediaries have secured business considers them less risky than at the onset, and it realizes that the volume of business may justify the development of internal capabilities such as hiring trained personnel to maintain a department for foreign sales or purchases.

Axis C shows that importing or exporting is usually the first international mode a company undertakes. At an early stage of international involvement, importing and exporting require the least placement of a company's resources abroad. In fact, it may involve the least need to invest more resources if the company can use excess production capacity to produce more goods, which it would then export. Thus moving along the C axis is a means to minimize the risk of the liability of foreignness because of forgoing such functions as managing a foreign workforce for production.

Later, the company might, in addition to exporting, make an even higher commitment through foreign direct investments to produce abroad. Its infusion of capital, personnel, and technology is highest for these operations. Axis D shows that companies can move internationally one country at a time, thus not having to become overwhelmed by learning about many countries at the same time. However, as we discuss in the next section, there may be a competitive impulse to move to a number of countries almost simultaneously.

GEOGRAPHIC DIVERSIFICATION VERSUS CONCENTRATION

Ultimately, a company may gain a sizable presence and commitment in most countries; however, there are different paths to that position. Although any move abroad means some geographic diversification, the term **diversification strategy** when used for location decisions describes a company's rapid movement into many foreign markets, gradually increasing its commitments within each one. A company can do this, for example, through a liberal licensing policy to ensure sufficient resources for the initial widespread expansion. The company will eventually increase its involvement by taking on activities that it first contracted to other companies.

At the other extreme, with a **concentration strategy,** the company will move to only one or a few foreign countries until it develops a very strong involvement and competitive position there. There are, of course, hybrids of the two strategies—for example, moving rapidly to most markets but increasing the commitment in only a few. Table 12.3 sums up the major variables that a company should consider when deciding which strategy to use.[52] We discuss each of these variables in the following sections.

> Strategies for ultimately reaching a high level of commitment in many countries are
>
> - Diversification—go to many fast and then build up slowly in each.
> - Concentration—go to one or a few and build up fast before going to others.
> - A hybrid of the two.

Growth Rate in Each Market   When the growth rate in each market is high or needs to be high, a company should usually concentrate on a few markets, because it will cost a great deal to expand output sufficiently in each one. In our opening case, for instance, we point out that to be cost effective in an overseas market, Carrefour focuses on building a sufficient distribution presence in target countries. However, slower growth or the need for growth in each market may result in the company's having enough resources to build and maintain a market share in several different countries.[53]

Case Review Note

TABLE 12.3   To Diversify or to Concentrate: The Role of Product and Market Factors

If a company determines that "Product or Market Factors" satisfy the conditions in the column headed "Prefer Diversification," it may benefit from moving quickly into several markets simultaneously. If the same factors satisfy the conditions under "Prefer Concentration," it may decide to enter and work initially to develop a substantial presence in just one or a few markets.

Product or Market Factor	Prefer Diversification If:	Prefer Concentration If:
1. Growth rate of each market	Low	High
2. Sales stability in each market	Low	High
3. Competitive lead time	Short	Long
4. Spillover effects	High	Low
5. Need for product, communication, and distribution adaptation	Low	High
6. Program control requirements	Low	High

Source: "Marketing Expansion Strategies in Multinational Marketing," *Journal of Marketing* 43 (Spring 1979): 89.
Reprinted by permission of the American Marketing Association © 1979.

Sales Stability in Each Market   As we have discussed, a company may smooth its earnings and sales because of operations in various parts of the world. The more stable sales and profits are within each market, the less advantage there is from a diversification strategy. Similarly, the more correlated markets are, the less smoothing is achieved by selling in each.

Competitive Lead Time   We have discussed why Carrefour has wanted to gain first-mover advantages. If a company determines that it has a long lead time before competitors are likely to be able to copy or supersede its advantages, then it may be able to follow a concentration strategy and still beat competitors into other markets. Otherwise, it may need to either cede leadership in some countries to competitors or follow a diversification strategy.

Spillover Effects   **Spillover effects** are situations in which the marketing program in one country results in awareness of the product in other countries. These effects are advantageous because additional customers may be reached with little additional cost. This can happen if the product is advertised through media sent cross-nationally, such as U.S. television ads that reach Canadians. When marketing programs reach many countries, such as by satellite television or the Internet, a diversification strategy has advantages.

Need for Product, Communication, and Distribution Adaptation   Companies may have to alter products and their marketing to sell abroad, a process that, because of cost, favors a concentration strategy. The adaptation cost may limit the resources the company has for expanding in many different markets. Further, if the adaptations are unique to each country, the company cannot easily spread adaptation costs over sales in more than one country to reduce total unit costs.

Program Control Requirements   The more a company needs to control its operations in a foreign country, the more favorable a concentration strategy is. This is because the company will need to use more of its resources to maintain that control, such as by taking a larger percentage of ownership in the operation. Its need for more control could result from various reasons, including the fear that collaboration with a partner will create a competitor.

REINVESTMENT AND HARVESTING

So far, we've discussed the sequencing of countries to enter. In addition, once a company is operating abroad, it must evaluate how much effort to allocate to each location.

With foreign direct investments, the company transfers financial capital and also has physical and human capital in place abroad. If the investment is successful, the company will earn money that it may remit back to headquarters or reinvest to increase the value of the investment. Over time, most of the value of a company's foreign investment, if successful, comes from reinvestment. If the investment is unsuccessful or if its outlook is less favorable than possible investments in other countries, the company may consider using the capital elsewhere or even discontinuing the investment.

A company may have to make new commitments to maintain competitiveness abroad.

Reinvestment Decisions   Companies treat decisions to replace depreciated assets or to add to the existing stock of capital from retained earnings in a foreign country somewhat differently from original investment decisions. Once committed to a given locale, a company may find that it doesn't have the option of moving a substantial portion of the earnings elsewhere; to do so would endanger the continued successful operation of the given foreign facility. The failure to expand might result in a falling market share and a higher unit cost than that of competitors.

Aside from competitive factors, a company may need several years of almost total reinvestment and allocation of new funds in one area to meet its objectives, such as to meet target sales and production. Another reason a company treats reinvestment decisions differently is that once it has experienced personnel within a given country, it may believe that those workers are the best judges of what is needed for that country, so headquarters managers may delegate certain investment decisions to them.

Harvesting Companies commonly reduce commitments in some countries because those countries have poorer performance prospects than do others—a process known as **harvesting (or divesting).** Carrefour, for example, sold off underperforming operations in Korea and Slovakia to have funds for more promising ventures into the Chinese, Indian, and Russian markets. There are other reasons as well. For instance, J. Sainsbury withdrew from the Egyptian market because its management did not expect a turnaround in its poorly performing operation there.[54] Dana sold its U.K. facility to use funds to concentrate on developing different automotive technologies.[55] Goodyear sold its Indonesian rubber plantation because of its decision to no longer produce rubber itself.[56]

Some indications suggest that companies might benefit by planning divestments better and by developing divestment specialists. Companies have tended to wait too long before divesting, trying instead expensive means of improving performance, such as those proposed by local managers, who fear losing their positions if the company abandons the operation.

Ideas for investment projects typically originate with middle managers or with managers in foreign subsidiaries who are enthusiastic about collecting information to accompany a proposal as it moves upward in the organization. After all, the evaluation and employment of these people depend on growth. They have no such incentive to propose divestments. These proposals typically originate at the top of the organization after upper management has tried most remedies for improving operational performance.[57]

Companies may divest by selling or closing facilities. They usually prefer selling because they receive some compensation. A company that considers divesting because of a country's political or economic situation may find few potential buyers except at very low prices. In such situations, the company may try to delay divestment, hoping that the situation will improve. If it does, the firm that waits out the situation generally is in a better position to regain markets and profits than one that forsakes its operation.

A company cannot always simply abandon an investment either. Governments frequently require performance contracts, such as substantial severance packages to employees, that make a loss from divestment greater than the direct investment's net value. Further, the length of time to go through insolvency (up to 10 years in some countries) alters the percentage of value recovered from a divestment. For example, in Japan, Singapore, and Finland, investors recover an average of over 90 percent of the value, whereas in Brazil, Cambodia, and Madagascar, they typically recover nothing.[58] Finally, many MNEs fear adverse international publicity and difficulty in reentering a market if they do not sever relations with a foreign government on amicable terms.

> Companies must decide how to get out of operations if
> - They no longer fit the overall strategy.
> - There are better alternative opportunities.

Noncomparative Decision Making

Because companies have limited resources at their disposal, it might seem that they maintain a storehouse of foreign operating proposals that they can rank by some predetermined criteria. If this were so, managers could simply start allocating resources to the top-ranked proposal and continue down the list until they could make no further commitments. This is often not the case, however. They make **go-no-go decisions** by examining one opportunity at a time and pursuing it if it meets some threshold criteria.

To begin with, companies sometimes need to respond quickly to prospects they had not anticipated. For example, many companies need to respond to unsolicited proposals

> Most companies examine proposals one at a time and accept them if they meet minimum-threshold criteria.

to sell abroad or sign joint venture or licensing contracts. For example, many companies initiate export activity passively; that is, foreign companies or export intermediaries approach them to be suppliers. Similarly, undertakings may be onetime possibilities because a government or another company solicits requests, such as the government of India's announcement that foreign companies could invest in Indian newspapers, but would have to apply quickly.[59]

Or there may be a chance to buy properties that another company divests. For instance, when Enron faced bankruptcy, it needed to sell many of its foreign facilities; thus companies such as Tractebel from Belgium and Royal Dutch/Shell bid on its Korean facilities.[60] Further, we have discussed the competitive advantages of following customers' and competitors' moves into foreign markets, and we know that we cannot always foresee when the customers and competitors will move.

Another factor inhibiting the comparison of country operations is that they may be so interdependent that one cannot meaningfully evaluate country operations separately. Profit figures from individual operations may obscure the real impact those operations have on overall company profits. For example, if a U.S. company were to establish an assembly operation in Australia, the operation could either increase or reduce exports from the United States, thus affecting U.S. profit figures. In addition, headquarters may have to incur additional costs to oversee the Australian operation and to coordinate the movement of components into Australia. These costs are difficult to estimate and will likely not show up in the Australian income figures.

Or perhaps by building a plant in Brazil to supply components to Volkswagen of Brazil, the company may increase the possibility of selling to Volkswagen in other countries. As a result of the Australian or Brazilian projects, management would have to make assumptions about the changed profits for the company's global operations as a whole. Finally, interdependence occurs because much of the sales and purchases of foreign subsidiaries are among units of the same parent company. The prices the company charges on these transactions will affect the relative profitability of one unit compared to another.

Clearly, some companies cannot afford to conduct very many feasibility studies simultaneously. Even if they can, the studies are apt to be in various stages of completion at any given time. For example, suppose a company completes its study for an Australian project while continuing studies on New Zealand, Japan, and Indonesia. Can the company afford to hold off on making a decision about Australia? Probably not. Waiting would likely invalidate much of the Australian study, thus necessitating added expense and further delays to update it. In sum, three factors inhibit companies from comparing investment opportunities: cost, time, and the interrelation of operations on global performance.

Looking to the Future   Will Prime Locations Change?

We discussed in the "Factor Mobility Theory" section of Chapter 6 that demographers expect a slowing in the growth of global population through 2050, with some countries experiencing declining populations. At the same time, population growth should remain robust in many developing economies, particularly those in sub-Saharan Africa. The projection is that the percentage of people living in currently developed countries is expected to fall to 13.7 percent from a 2000 figure of 19.7 percent. The least developed countries will have the biggest population increase.

Further, because the world's population will continue to age, the share of what we now consider the working-age population should fall for developed countries and increase in many developing countries. Because there is a positive relationship between the proportional size of the working-age population and per capita GDP, the growth in per capita GDP should be higher in today's developing economies than in today's developed countries.[61] These demographic changes, if they materialize, will have implications for both the location of markets and the location of labor forces.

An intriguing possibility is the near-officeless headquarters for international companies. Technology may permit more people to work from anywhere as they e-mail and teleconference with their colleagues, customers, and suppliers elsewhere. Thus they can live anywhere in the world and work from their homes, as is already occurring within some professions.[62]

However, if people can work from their homes, they may move their homes where they want to live rather than living where their employers are now located. Because we're talking here about highly creative and highly innovative self-motivated people, they can usually get permission to live in almost any country of the world.

A leading researcher on urbanization and planning has shown that beginning at least as early as the Roman Empire, these types of people have been drawn to certain cities that were the centers of innovation. He says that this attraction is due to people's improvement through interchange with others like themselves—like "a very bright class in a school or a college. They all try to score off each other and do better." Thus, if he's correct, the brightest minds may work more at home but still need the face-to-face interaction with their colleagues.[63]

His arguments are provocative, particularly because we now have technology to allow people to communicate without traveling as much, yet the continued increase in business travel shows that people need face-to-face interaction. He further suggests that these people will be drawn to the same places that attract people to visit as tourists.

Concomitantly, another view is that in leading Western societies, the elite made up of intellectuals and highly educated people is increasingly using its capability to delay and block new technologies. If successful, their efforts will result in the emergence of different countries at the forefront of technological development and acceptance.[64] ■

Burger King Beefs Up Global Operations

CASE

Burger King is the world's largest flame-broiled fast food restaurant chain.[65] As of mid-2009, it operated about 12,000 restaurants in all 50 states and in 74 countries and U.S. territories worldwide through a combination of company-owned and franchised operations, which together employed nearly 400,000 people worldwide. Only Yum Brands (A&W, KFC, Long John Silver, Pizza Hut, and Taco Bell), McDonald's, and Subway, with 36,000, 32,000, and 28,000 restaurants, respectively, were larger. Given that Yum Brands has no hamburger units, Burger King is second in the fast food hamburger restaurant segment/market. Burger King plans to increase the number of net operating units by 3 to 4 percent per year in the near future, with most of that increase coming in international operations.

Two major ways in which Burger King differentiates itself from competitors are the way it cooks hamburgers—by its flame-broiled method as opposed to grills that fry—and the options it offers customers as to how they want their burgers. This latter distinction has been popularized with the "have it your way" theme. About two-thirds of Burger King's restaurants are in the United States, and its U.S. and Canadian operations accounted for 69 percent of its $2.54 billion revenue in fiscal 2009. The geographic distribution of Burger King's restaurants is shown on Map 12.2. Although the company began in 1954 by offering just burgers, fries, milk shakes, and sodas, the menu has expanded to include breakfast as well as various chicken, fish, and salad offerings. Nevertheless, burgers remain the mainstay of the company, and 2007 marked the 50th anniversary of the Whopper sandwich, which is considered Burger King's signature product.

Burger King has also differentiated itself with some innovative advertising campaigns through the years, such as its use of a figure of a man who is the Burger "King." Recently, the company ran a "Whopper Virgins" campaign in which it assembled people who had never tasted a burger—such as from remote parts of Greenland, Thailand, and Transylvania—to participate in a comparative taste test between Whopper sandwiches and Big Macs. The Burger King logo has changed slightly through the years; for example, going from two buns separating a burger to two buns separating the company's name.

MAP 12.2   Burger King's Operations by Country

As of March 31, 2009, Burger King operated in 74 countries. The number of countries by geographic area was: Americas (2), Latin America & Caribbean (27), Europe (24), Middle East (8), and Asia Pacific (13).

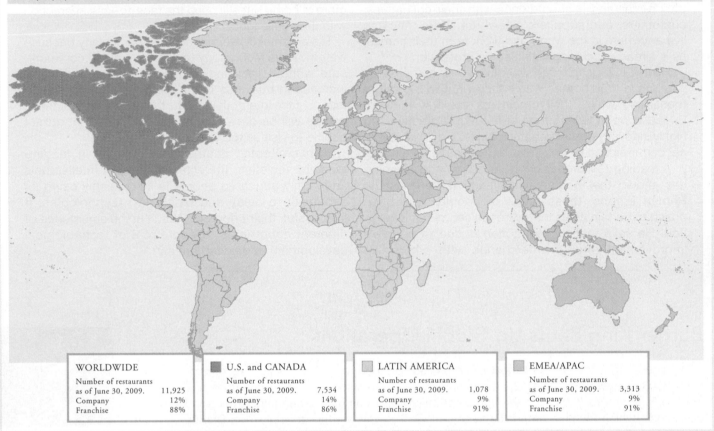

WORLDWIDE		U.S. and CANADA		LATIN AMERICA		EMEA/APAC	
Number of restaurants as of June 30, 2009.	11,925	Number of restaurants as of June 30, 2009.	7,534	Number of restaurants as of June 30, 2009.	1,078	Number of restaurants as of June 30, 2009.	3,313
Company	12%	Company	14%	Company	9%	Company	9%
Franchise	88%	Franchise	86%	Franchise	91%	Franchise	91%

Yet it has always been displayed and recognizable globally, as illustrated in the photo of a restaurant in Taiwan with Mandarin lettering.

A Bit of History

Burger King can trace its roots to 1954, when it started as InstaBurger King. In 2006, the company went public, and since then the company has operated independently.

During its first five years, the private company grew to five restaurants, all in the Miami, Florida, area. In 1959, the name was changed to Burger King, and it began domestic franchising. In 1967, Pillsbury, which had several other retail food groups—such as Bennigan's, Steak and Ale, and Godfather's Pizza—bought Burger King, which by then had 274 restaurants. During the first few years of Pillsbury's ownership, franchising increased substantially. Then in 1989 Pillsbury got out of the restaurant business and sold Burger King to the British company Grand Metropolitan, which then converted most of its Wimpy restaurants in the United Kingdom to Burger King restaurants. Grand Metropolitan merged with Guinness in 1997 to form Diageo, and Diageo divested itself of restaurant operations in 2002 when it sold Burger King to a consortium of private equity firms controlled by TPG Capital, Bain Capital Partners, and the Goldman Sachs Funds. In May 2006, Burger King consummated its initial public offering, becoming a publicly traded company listed on the New York Stock Exchange. The years of transformed ownership took a toll on Burger King as emphases changed and the company's interests were sometimes made secondary to those of its parent company. For instance, in the period leading into the twenty-first century, some of Burger King's franchisees experienced financial problems.

Burger King uses a common logo wherever it operates but puts information into the local language. The photo shows a restaurant in Taiwan with writing in Mandarin.

Source: The BURGER KING® trademarks and images are used with permission from Burger King Corporation.

Despite Burger King's evolving ownership, the company did expand internationally. In the early 1960s, it entered the Bahamas and Puerto Rico. In the 1970s, it entered markets in Europe, Asia, and Latin America. While some of these moves turned out to be highly successful, a few were not. It entered and then retreated from operations in such countries as Colombia, France, Japan, and Oman. (We will see in later discussion that Burger King has re-entered some of these markets.) Much of Burger King's early international forays came about either because someone in another country approached Burger King or because someone in the company was familiar with a particular country and thought it would offer opportunities. Two reasons have been prevalent in the decision to leave a market: (1) the franchisee does not perform adequately, such as not investing sufficiently in the business or not making royalty payments; and (2) the market turned out to be too small to support the necessary infrastructure, such as being too small to develop slaughterhouse and beef grinding facilities.

Over time, especially since the company went public, Burger King has taken a more systematic approach toward restaurant expansion. While it still sees substantial growth opportunities within the United States, it sees the United States as a mature market for fast food, especially for hamburgers, in comparison with many foreign countries. In looking for new countries to enter, Burger King looks most favorably at those with large populations (especially of young people), high consumption of beef, availability of capital to franchisees for growth, a safe pro-business environment, growth in shopping centers, and availability of a potential franchisee with experience and resources.

Overall, Burger King has expanded internationally later than its primary rival competitor, McDonald's. This has resulted in both advantages and disadvantages. On the one hand, later entry is a disadvantage in very small markets because there may be few adequate suppliers. For instance, there may be only one slaughterhouse, and the owners may be unwilling to work with more than one customer. On the other hand, in larger markets, such as in the BRICs, being a later entrant may be advantageous because the earlier entrants have built demand for fast food and have created a supply infrastructure. In some later-entry markets, Burger King has been able to concentrate almost entirely on emphasizing its product (have it your way, good taste of flame-broiled burgers), without incurring the early developmental costs. For instance, in Latin America and the Caribbean, McDonald's and Burger King compete in 27 country markets, with Burger King currently leading McDonald's in the number of restaurants in 15 of those markets.

However, keep in mind that local companies also learn from the successes of foreign fast food companies, and they sometimes alter their menus and flavorings to appeal to local tastes. Some notable examples are Bembos in Peru, Mr. Bigg's in Nigeria, Pollo Campero in Guatemala, and Quick in France.

Outside of Burger King's Americas group (United States and Canada), 37.0 percent of the countries and 24.6 percent of the restaurants are in the Latin American and Caribbean group, yet these countries accounted for only 13.5 percent of the non-Americas group revenue in fiscal 2009. This is largely because many of these countries have very small populations, such as the Cayman Islands, Aruba, and Saint Lucia. So why did Burger King develop a presence in these markets, even though at this writing it is not in countries with much bigger populations, such as India, Pakistan, Nigeria, Russia, and South Africa? The answer is largely due to a location factor. Burger King remains headquartered in Miami, which is often called the capital of Latin America. Because so many people from Latin America and the Caribbean come to or through Miami, Burger King's reputation spilled over to that area early on. This simplified gaining brand recognition and acceptance. Further, the nearness of the Latin American and Caribbean countries to Miami enhances the ability of Burger King's management to visit these countries and for franchisees to visit Burger King's headquarters. In 2008, Burger King opened its thousandth restaurant in the Latin American and Caribbean region.

Although Burger King prefers to operate in markets through franchising, doing so is sometimes initially difficult because suppliers and prospective franchisees do not know the company well enough. If such a market looks sufficiently attractive, Burger King will enter with its owned operations. (Overall, Burger King owns 12 percent of its restaurants and franchises the rest.) By owning, Burger King demonstrates market commitment. For instance, there may only be one meat-processing plant, and the owners may otherwise be reluctant to invest in added capacity or the processing of ground beef. Further, if the country turns out to be as attractive as anticipated, then the owned operations may be more profitable for Burger King than royalties received from franchisees.

Throughout its long history, the company has consistently focused on expanding its global portfolio into new and existing markets. Since becoming a publicly traded company, it has entered a number of markets for the first time, including Indonesia, Egypt, Hong Kong, Suriname, and the Czech Republic. It has also re-entered several markets that it had earlier abandoned, including Japan, Curacao, Uruguay, and Colombia. Let's take a look at the decision to re-enter Colombia.

Re-Entering Colombia

Burger King entered the Colombian market in the early 1980s but pulled out after several years of operating in the market because it was not allowed to expatriate royalty payments. In addition to the problem of expatriation of royalty payments, Colombia was going through a prolonged period of economic and political turmoil. Also, at the turn of the century, the beef industry suffered from foot-and-mouth disease outbreaks and cattle rustling by guerilla groups. These conditions combined to make Colombia a less attractive market for fast food restaurants.

Burger King re-entered Colombia in 2008. By this time, Colombian cities were considered safe for people to go out to eat. The beef health and rustling problems were largely under control. (Currently, Colombia accounts for about 2 percent of global beef production.) With about 44 million people, Colombia is the third most populated country in Latin America, after Brazil and Mexico. The Colombian peso was strong and, when coupled with a rise in two-income families, there was more disposable income to spend on eating out. In 2005, about 77 percent of the population was classified as urban, and Colombia boasted some large cities such as Barranquilla, Bogotá, Cali, and Medellin—all with large and recently built shopping centers. About 31 percent of the population was under 15 years of age. Although incomes were very unevenly distributed, the richest 20 percent of the population (almost 9 million people) had a per capita expenditure in 2007 of over U.S. $17,000.

While all the above factors were favorable, there were some negative things to consider. From a political standpoint, there were potential problems with leftist-leaning governments in the neighboring countries of Ecuador and Venezuela, which could support a resurgence of political unrest. Economic problems in the United States from the global recession and in Venezuela from fluctuating oil prices could cause Colombia to lose sales because those two countries comprise half of the country's export earnings. Further, about 2 percent of Colombian GDP in 2007 came from remittances of Colombians working abroad, mainly in Spain. These were at risk because Spain was hard hit by the global recession. In effect, economic downturns could hit sales of fast foods. Burger King learned this lesson in Mexico and Germany, which in response caused the company to tactically develop a more relevant value proposition, including value meals.

Overall, though, the Colombian situation looked bright. Burger King signed an agreement with KINCO for franchise rights to Medellin, Cali, and northern Colombia. KINCO is a well-established Colombian company with restaurant experience. Burger King signed a second franchise agreement with Alsea, a Mexican company, for rights to Bogotá. Alsea owns 75 percent of the Colombian operation of Domino's Pizza and operates Burger King restaurants in Mexico. Thus both of these companies seem very compatible with Burger King's criteria for selecting franchise operators with capital and restaurant experience. Although Burger King's operations in Colombia are still in the early stages of development at the time of this writing, Burger King's management is optimistic about the future of Colombia and its own future therein.

Brazil as Model for Entry into Russia

In our "Meet the BRICs" case in Chapter 4, we explored why so many companies have been putting emphasis on Brazil, Russia, India, and China. Burger King is no exception. The possibilities in these four countries are simply too great to ignore.

Burger King opened its first restaurants in two of the BRICs, Brazil and China, almost simultaneously, in November and June 2004 respectively. By then, many foreign fast food franchisors had entered the markets, many without success. For the most part, failure occurred because of underestimating what it would take to succeed in such a large country. However, Burger King's success in Brazil has led it to use the Brazilian experience as a model for entry into Russia, which is expected in the near future.

On the one hand, Burger King had a recognition advantage in Brazil because thousands of Brazilians fly into Florida, where Burger King restaurants abound. In addition there are about 300,000 Brazilians living in the South Florida area, most of whom have relatives back in Brazil. On the other hand, the failure of many prior fast food entrants into Brazil made potential suppliers apprehensive.

By observing the mistakes of other fast food chains, Burger King forged a strategy that has proved successful. In fact, for the last few years, Brazil has been one of Burger King's fastest growing markets. By mid-2009, it had 68 restaurants in Brazil. This strategy can be summarized in five parts: (1) develop an infrastructure before putting in restaurants, (2) develop a local management team, (3) focus development on major cities and adjacent geographies with established shopping mall location, prevalent in Brazil's largest cities, instead of the whole country, (4) establish a local office, and (5) support continuous development and the use of local suppliers that meet Burger King's global specifications.

For smaller markets or those where all the restaurants are franchised, Burger King does not set up a regional restaurant support center or local headquarters. However, management deemed a Brazilian office necessary because of Brazil's size (in both area and population), its language barrier (Portuguese), and the magnitude of investment that suppliers and franchisees would eventually need to make. At first, the office served to demonstrate the company's market commitment and to handle early supply-chain procurement and management. The result was that Burger King was able to initially secure about 80 percent of its supplies within Brazil and has since upped that figure to over 90 percent. By focusing initially on São Paulo, Brazil's largest city, Burger King was able to develop economies in its marketing and distribution. Its subsequent expansion has focused on cities and states near São Paulo. Finally, by building a staff of Portuguese-speaking Brazilians, the company showed its commitment to the country and developed a competency to deal with external stakeholders.

Burger King's success in Brazil has led its management to follow the same strategy for expansion into Russia. It has offices in Moscow, where initial penetration is planned. In fact, duplication of the successful Brazilian strategy may be even more important for Russia because Burger King lacks the same pre-entry brand recognition that it had in Brazil.

The Future

At this point, Burger King has many opportunities for expansion, such as moving into new countries and growing operations within markets where it is already operating. Despite its international growth, it is still in less than 40 percent of the world's countries. Thus, it faces the challenge of deciding where the best locations are for placing its future emphasis. ■

QUESTIONS

1. By mid-2009, Burger King was not in any of the following five countries: France, India, Nigeria, Pakistan, and South Africa. Compare these countries as possible future locations for Burger King.
2. When entering another country, discuss the advantages and disadvantages that an international restaurant company, specifically Burger King, would have in comparison with a local company in that market.
3. About two-thirds of Burger King's restaurants and revenues are in its Americas region (United States and Canada) and one-third elsewhere. Should this relationship change? If so, why and how?
4. The case mentions that Burger King prefers to enter countries with large numbers of youth and shopping centers. Why do you think these conditions would be advantageous?
5. How has Burger King's headquarters location influenced its international expansion? Has this location strengthened or weakened its global competitive position?
6. Evaluate Burger King's strategy of using the Brazilian experience to guide its entries into Russia.

SUMMARY

- Because companies seldom have sufficient resources to exploit all opportunities, two major considerations facing managers are which markets to serve and where to locate the production to serve those markets.

- Companies' decisions on market and production location are highly interdependent, because companies often need to serve markets from local production and because they want to use existing production capacity.

- Scanning techniques aid managers in considering alternatives that might otherwise be overlooked. They also help limit the final, detailed feasibility studies to a manageable number of those that appear most promising.

- Because each company has unique competitive capabilities and objectives, the factors affecting the choice of operating location will be different for each. Nevertheless, a large number of companies consider similar-country comparative indicators when seeking advantages from foreign sales or foreign assets.

- Four broad categories of risk that companies may consider are political, monetary, natural disaster, and competitive.

- The amount, accuracy, and timeliness of published data vary substantially among countries. Managers should be particularly aware of different definitions of terms, different collection methods, and different base years for reports, as well as misleading responses.

- Companies frequently use several tools to compare opportunities and risk in various countries, such as grids that rate country projects according to the number of separate dimensions and matrices—for example, a matrix on which companies plot opportunity on one axis and risk on another.

- When allocating resources among countries, companies need to consider how to treat reinvestments and divestments, the interdependence of operations in different countries, and whether they should follow diversification versus concentration strategies.

- Companies may reduce the risk of liability of foreignness by moving first to countries more similar to their home countries. Alternatively, they may contract with experienced companies to handle operations for them, limit the resources they commit to foreign operations, and delay entry to many countries until they are operating successfully in one or a few.

- Companies must develop location strategies for new investments and devise means of deemphasizing certain areas and divesting if necessary.

- Companies often evaluate entry to a country without comparing that country with other countries. This is because they may need to react quickly to proposals or respond to competitive threats, and because multiple feasibility studies seldom are finished simultaneously.

KEY TERMS

agglomeration (p. 496)
concentration strategy (p. 505)
diversification strategy (p. 505)
escalation of commitment (p. 487)

first-mover advantage (p. 496)
go-no-go decision (p. 507)
harvesting (or divesting) (p. 507)
imitation lag (p. 497)

liability of foreignness (p. 495)
liquidity preference (p. 494)
oligopolistic reaction (p. 496)
spillover effect (p. 506)

ENDNOTES

1 *Sources include the following:* Carrefour, at www.carrefour.com (accessed July 20, 2009); "Business Crossroads: Carrefour," *The Economist* (March 17, 2007): 87; Elena Berton, "Carrefour Unveils Three-Year Growth Plan," *WWD* 198:1 (July 1, 2009): 7; "Carrefour Firms Up Plans for India Operations," (April 16, 2009): n.p.; Eirmalas are Bani, "Carrefour Gives Priority to Locally-Made Products," *Business Times* [Malaysia] (November 9, 1998): 3; *Business & Company News*, n.p.; Michiyo Nakamoto, "Carrefour Sounds Alarm for Japan's Ailing Retail Market," *Financial Times* (December 8, 2000): 36; Rosabeth Moss Kanter, "Global Competitiveness Revisited," *Washington Quarterly* (Spring 1999): 39–58; "Global Strategy—Why Tesco Will Beat Carrefour," *JRetail Week* (April 6, 2001): 14; "Carrefour Closes Hong Kong Chain after Site Pitfalls," *JRetail Week* (September 1, 2000): 3; "Carrefour Beats Wal-Mart to Global Crown," *JRetail Week* (December 15, 2000): 5; "Carrefour Aims to Win Global Retail Battle," *MMR* (June 26, 2000): 60; "Hypermarkets for Britain," *The Economist* (July 3, 1976): 77; "French Retailer Abandons 'Hypermarkets' in U.S.," *New York Times* (September 8, 1993): D4; "Strategies for Retail Globalisation," *Financial Times* (March 13, 1998): 4; Robert Guy Matthews, "Problems in Carrefour's Home Market Sank CEO," *Wall Street Journal* (February 4, 2005): A1+; Dexter Roberts, Wendy Zellner, and Carol Matlack, "Let China's Retail Wars Begin," *Business Week Online* (January 17, 2005), http://www.businessweek.com/magazine/content/05_03/b3916063_014.htm (accessed October 5, 2009); Luc Vandevelde, "Carrefour n'a besoin de personne pour se développer," *Les Echos* [France] (March 1, 2005): 32.

2 Shige Makino, Takehiko Isobe, and Christine M. Chan, "Does Country Matter?" *Strategic Management Journal* 25 (2004): 1027–43.

3 Tony W. Tong, Todd M. Alessandri, Jeffrey J. Reuer, and Asda Chintakananda, "How Much Does Country Matter? An Analysis of Firms' Growth Options," *Journal of International Business Studies* 39:3 (2008): 387–405.

4 David Gonzalez, "Fried Chicken Takes Flight, Happily Nesting in U.S.," *New York Times* (September 20, 2002): A4; Joel Millman, "California City Fends Off Arrival of Mexican Supermarket," *Wall Street Journal* (August 7, 2002): B1+.

5 Don E. Schultz, "China May Leapfrog the West in Marketing," *Marketing News* (August 19, 2002): 8–9.

6 Makino, Isobe, and Chan, "Does Country Matter?"

7 Anil Khurana, "Strategies for Global R&D," *Research Technology Management* (March/April 2006): 48–59.

8 David Luchnow, "Missing Piece of the Mexican Success Story," *Wall Street Journal* (March 4, 2002): A11+.

9 Michael Peel, "Bitter-Sweet Confections of Business in Nigeria," *Financial Times* (November 20, 2002): 10.

10 Andrew Bartmess and Keith Cerny, "Building Competitive Advantage through a Global Network of Capabilities," *California Management Review* 35:2 (Winter 1993): 78–103.

11 G. Bruce Knecht, "Going the Wrong Way down a One-Way Street," *Wall Street Journal* (March 18, 2002): A1.

12 Alfredo J. Mauri and Arvind V. Phatak, "Global Integration as Inter-Area Product Flows: The Internationalization of Ownership and Location Factors Influencing Product Flows across MNC Units," *Management International Review* 41 (2001): 233–49.

13 Julian Birkinshaw, Pontus Braunerhjelm, and Ulf Holm, "Why Do Some Multinational Corporations Relocate Their Headquarters Overseas?" *Strategic Management Journal* 27 (2006): 681–700.

14 Nagesh Kumar, "Multinational Enterprises, Regional Economic Integration, and Export-Platform Production in the Host Countries: An Empirical Analysis for the U.S. and Japanese Corporations," *Weltwirtschaftliches Archive* 134:3 (1998): 450–83.

15 Anthony Rowley, "Investing in Japan," *Wall Street Journal* (June 7, 2007): A8; "Doors and Opportunities Open in Japan," *Financial Times* (June 7, 2007): 7.

16 World Bank, International Finance Corporation, *Doing Business in 2005* (Washington, DC: The International Bank for Reconstruction and Development, 2005).

17 Hoon Park, "Determinants of Corruption: A Cross-National Analysis," *Multinational Business Review* 11:2 (2003): 29–48.

18 "Volkswagen Switches Work to Low-Cost Unit in Slovakia," *Financial Times* (December 19, 1995): 4.

19 John D. Daniels and James A. Schweikart, "Political Risk, Assessment and Management of," in Rosalie L. Tung (ed.), *IEBM Handbook of International Business* (London: International Thomson Business Press, 1999): 502–14.

20 See Luciano Gremone and Ben Tsocanos, "Ongoing Political Risk in Venezuela Still Poses Challenges for Foreign Oil and Gas Companies," *Business News Americas* (February 14, 2007): 1; Farhan Bokhari, "Western Expatriates Give Way to Local Heroes," *Financial Times* (August 30, 2002): 8; Joseph T. Hallinan and Janet Adamy, "Chiquita Says It Paid Terrorists to Protect Workers in Colombia," *Wall Street Journal* (May 11, 2004): B10; Henri E. Cauvin, "Braving War and Graft, Coke Goes Back to Angola," *New York Times* (April 22, 2001): Sec. 3, 1+.

21 Marvin Zonis and Sam Wilkin, "Driving Defensively through a Minefield of Political Risk," *Financial Times* (May 30, 2000): Mastering Risk, 8–10.

22 Chip Cummins, "Dirty Work," *Wall Street Journal* (June 7, 2007): 1+.

23 Much like options theory, theory of liquidity preference is associated with the work of Robert C. Merton, Myron S. Scholes, and Fisher Black. For good, succinct coverage, see John Krainer, "The 1997 Nobel Prize in Economics," FRBSF Economic Letter No. 98–05 (February 13, 1998).

24 United Nations Development Programme, *Reducing Disaster Risk: A Challenge for Development* (New York: United Nations, 2004).

25 Paul L. Knox and Sallie A. Marston, *Places and Regions in Global Context*, 3rd ed. (Upper Saddle River, NJ: Pearson Education, 2004): 120.

26 Robert A. Manning, "The 21st Century Will Be Asia's Century," *Pittsburgh Post-Gazette* (January 2, 2000): E1.

27 WHO, Public Health Mapping and GIS, Map Library, at http://gamapserver.who.int/mapLibrary/default.aspx (accessed June 11, 2007).

28 "A Threat Deadlier than a Landmine," *Financial Times* (December 2, 2002): 10.

29 Amy Merrick and Ann Zimmerman, "Wal-Mart Bans Some Work Travel Due to SARS," *Wall Street Journal* (April 10, 2003): 36.

30 Paul D. Ellis, "Does Psychic Distance Moderate the Market Size-Entry Sequence Relationship?" *Journal of International Business Studies* 39:3 (2008): 351–69.

31 See Srilata Zaheer and Elaine Mosakowski, "The Dynamics of the Liability of Foreignness: A Global Study of Survival in Financial Services," *Strategic Management Journal* 18 (1997): 439–64; Stewart R. Miller and Arvind Parkhe, "Is There a Liability of Foreignness in Global Banking? An Empirical Test of Banks' X-Efficiency," *Strategic Management Journal* 23 (2002): 55–75.

32 Mikhail V. Gratchev, "Making the Most of Cultural Differences," *Harvard Business Review* (October 2001): 28–30.

33 Khanh T. L. Tran, "Blockbuster Finds Success in Japan," *Wall Street Journal* (August 19, 1998): A14; Cecile Rohwedder, "Blockbuster Hits Eject Button as Stores in Germany See Video-Rental Sales Sag," *Wall Street Journal* (January 16, 1998): B9A.

34 Jon A. Doukas and Ozgur B. Kan, "Does Global Diversification Destroy Firm Values?" *Journal of International Business Studies* 37 (2006): 352–71.

35 B. Kazaz, M. Dada, and H. Moskowitz, "Global Production Planning under Exchange-Rate Uncertainty," *Management Science* 51 (2005): 1101–09.

36 Edward B. Flowers, "Oligopolistic Reactions in European and Canadian Direct Investment in the United States," *Journal of International Business Studies* 7:2 (Fall–Winter 1976): 43–55; Frederick Knickerbocker, *Oligopolistic Reaction and Multinational Enterprise* (Cambridge, MA: Harvard University, Graduate School of Business, Division of Research, 1973).

37 David Murphy and David Lague, "As China's Car Market Takes Off, the Party Grows a Bit Crowded," *Wall Street Journal* (July 3, 2002): A8; James Mackintosh and Richard McGregor, "Auto Industry," *Financial Times* (August 25, 2003): 13.

38 Hugh Pope, "Q: Why Are the World's IBMs Putting Down Roots in the Desert? A: Dubai," *Wall Street Journal* (January 23, 2001): A18; Lynn K. Mytelka and Lou Anne Barclay, "Using Foreign Investment Strategically for Innovation," paper presented at the Conference on Understanding FDI-Assisted Economic Development, University of Oslo, Norway (May 22–25, 2003).

39 See J. Myles Shaver and Fredrick Flyer, "Agglomeration Economies, Firm Heterogeneity, and Foreign Direct Investment in the United States," *Strategic Management Journal* 21 (2000): 1175–93; Philippe Martin and Gianmarco I. P. Ottaviano, "Growth and Agglomeration," *International Economic Review* 42 (2001): 947–68; Edward E. Leamer and Michael Storper, "The Economic Geography of the Internet Age," *Journal of International Business Studies* 32 (2001): 641–65.

40 Jedrzej George Frynas, Kamel Mellah, and Geoffrey Allen Pigman, "First Mover Advantages in International Business and Firm-Specific Political Resources," *Strategic Management Journal* 27 (2006): 321–45; Makino, Isobe, and Chan, "Does Country Matter?"

41 Joel Millman, "PriceSmart to Restate Results Due to an Accounting Error," *Wall Street Journal* (November 11, 2003): B9.

42 Philip Parker, "Choosing Where to Go Global: How to Prioritise Markets," *Financial Times* (November 16, 1998): Mastering Marketing, 7–8.

43 James Kynge, "Pyramid of Power behind Numbers Game," *Financial Times* (February 28, 2002): 6.

44 Chip Cumins, "Crude Theft," *Wall Street Journal* (April 13, 2005): A1+.

45 Mary Kissel, "U.S. Expats Deal with Terror Threat," *Wall Street Journal* (May 12, 2004): B4a, quoting Frank Holder, of Kroll, Inc.

46 "Global Terrorism Index," *The Economist* (August 30, 2003): 74, using data from the World Markets Research Centre.

47 Andrew Ward, "Terror Threat from Within Keeps America on High Alert," *Financial Times* (April 19, 2005): 3, quoting John Lewis.

48 Harry Hurt III, "Making the World Safer, One Client at a Time," *New York Times* (May 11, 2004): C12.

49 Moisés Naím, "The Five Wars of Globalization," *Foreign Policy* (January–February 2003): 29–36.

50 "You're in Good Hands," at www.comebackalive.com/df/kidnapp/goodhand.htm (accessed June 12, 2007); "Five Britons Set Free by Nigerian Kidnapping Gang" (June 12, 2007), at http://news.scotsman.com/international.cfm?id=917782007 (accessed June 12, 2007).

51 "Doing Business in Dangerous Places," *The Economist* (August 14, 2004): 11.

52 Igal Ayal and Jehiel Zif, "Marketing Expansion Strategies in Multinational Marketing," *Journal of Marketing* (Spring 1979): 84–94.

53 Makino, Isobe, and Chan, "Does Country Matter?"

54 Susanna Voyle and James Drummond, "J. Sainsbury to Withdraw from Egypt," *Financial Times* (April 10, 2001): 23.

55 Nikki Tait, "Dana Set to Sell UK-Based Components Arm," *Financial Times* (November 29, 2000): 22.

56 Makino, Isobe, and Chan, " Does Country Matter?"; Bernard Simon, "Goodyear Sells Its Last Plantation," *Financial Times* (December 1, 2004): 18.

57 See Jean J. Boddewyn, "Foreign and Domestic Divestment and Investment Decisions: Like or Unlike?" *Journal of International Business Studies* 14: 3 (Winter 1983): 28; Michelle Haynes, Steve Thompson, and Mike Wright, "The Determinants of Corporate Divestment in the U.K.," *Journal of Industrial Organization* 18 (2000): 1201–22; Jose Mata and Pedro Portugal, "Closure and Divestiture by Foreign Entrants: The Impact of Entry and Post-Entry Strategies," *Strategic Management Journal* 21 (2000): 549–62.

58 World Bank and International Finance Corporation, *Doing Business in 2005* (Washington, DC: The International Bank for Reconstruction and Development, 2005): 69.

59 Edna Fernandes, "India to Let Foreigners Invest in Newspapers," *Financial Times* (June 26, 2002): 6.

60 "Enron Assets Outside U.S. Go Up for Sale; Activity Seen in South Korea and India," *Wall Street Journal* (January 22, 2002): A6.

61 International Monetary Fund, *World Economic Outlook, September 2004* (Washington, DC: International Monetary Fund, 2004): 143–49.

62 Deborah Hargreaves, " 'Virtual' Staff Make Themselves at Home in Offices of the Future," *Financial Times* (May 14, 1999): 8.

63 Peter Hall, *Cities in Civilization: Culture, Technology, and Urban Order* (London: Weidenfeld & Nicholson, 1998).

64 David Aviel, "The Causes and Consequences of Public Attitudes to Technology: A United States Analysis," *International Journal of Management* 18 (2001): 166.

65 *Sources include the following:* We'd like to acknowledge the invaluable assistance of Julio A. Ramirez, Executive Vice President Global Operations, Burger King Corporation, and Ana Miranda, Senior Manager Investor Relations, Burger King Corporation. Additional information came from "Burger King," Wikipedia, http://en.wikipedia.org/wiki/Burger_King (accessed April 14, 2009); John Owen, "Burger King 'Whopper Virgins' Sets an Example to Brands Everywhere," *Revolution* (June 2009): 1; Business Monitor International, *Colombia Food & Drink Report Q1 2009*, (London: Business Monitor International, 2009); Elaine Walker, "Despite Spike in Profits, Burger King Lowers Annual Expectations," *McClatchy—Tribune Business News* (April 30, 2009): n.p.; Gemma Charles, "Burger King Adds First 'Value Meal' to Menu," *Marketing* (February 11, 2009): 3; "Burger King Corp. Opens Its 1,000th Restaurant in the Latin America & Caribbean Region," *Business Wire* (August 14, 2008): n.p.; "The Burger King's Brand Enters Colombia," *Business Wire* (December 13, 2007): n.p.

thirteen
Export and Import Strategies

Objectives

- To introduce the ideas of export and import

- To identify the elements of export and exporting strategies

- To compare direct and indirect selling of exports

- To identify the elements of import and importing strategies

- To discuss the types and roles of third-party intermediaries

- To profile the role of countertrade

When one is prepared, difficulties do not come.

—Ethiopian proverb

517

The biggest exporters, such as Boeing, Caterpillar, and General Electric, generate about a third of merchandise exports from the United States.[1] Their smaller shipments are usually much larger than the largest shipments of smaller companies. Still, small and medium-size enterprises (SME), namely companies with fewer than 500 workers, account for 97 percent of all U.S. exporters. In addition, SMEs account for more than 98 percent of the growth in the exporter population. Moreover, in terms of volume, SMEs are responsible for at least half of all U.S. exports to 85 countries. One such SME is Grieve of Round Lake, Illinois.

Grieve manufactures laboratory and industrial ovens, furnaces, and heat-processing systems. Grieve-built equipment is found in many product markets, including commercial heat treating, drug discovery, and integrated circuits. The company began operations in 1949 with "one goal in mind . . . to create a line of industrial heat-processing equipment our customers could believe in." The company has always taken pride in offering complete custom-engineering design and manufacturing services. To this day, it believes it builds "ovens and furnaces for which there simply are no equals."[2]

Since 1949, Grieve's primary business has been to design and manufacture laboratory and industrial ovens and furnaces for industries worldwide. Over time, Grieve has built core competencies in meeting customers' particular requirements, officially aiming to be "more than manufacturers but, rather, problem solving professionals who take the time to understand your needs."

Grieve operates out of its 100,000-square-foot facility in Round Lake, Illinois, which houses its corporate headquarters, sales, engineering, research, and manufacturing divisions. The company applies its knowledge and experience to build industrial ovens and furnaces ranging from routine heating applications to state-of-the-art systems that meet the clean-room specifications of semiconductor and pharmaceutical environments. The customized design and construction of each product goes hand-in-hand with rigorous testing. Then, before crating a unit for shipment, management quality-checks more than 100 features.

Improving customer responsiveness led Grieve to expand its Web site. The site showcases the company's proficiency in the design, manufacture, and delivery of standard, as well as custom, heat-processing equipment and systems. The site details over 400 standard ovens and furnaces; it displays the range of product customization through hundreds of examples, each with a photograph and a description of the unit and its application. The Web site allows one to index equipment photographs by feature or style. Customers can submit online their particular heat-processing requirements and receive a price quote from Grieve. Because Grieve sells its equipment worldwide through a network of manufacturers' representatives, its Web site allows a customer to enter a zip code into the "rep locator" area to get contact information. As a rule, Grieve representatives are experienced engineers.

The Changing Game Over time, Grieve has run into problems when some of its customers moved their manufacturing overseas. Initially, Grieve supplied those customers via exporting. However, customers' purchases often faded as they began sourcing from less-expensive local providers. Despite more than a few lost sales, three reasons had dissuaded Grieve from aggressively exporting:

1. *The nature of its product.* Industrial ovens and furnaces, besides being relatively expensive, are large and bulky. Management assumed that the product's size and resulting high shipping costs would prove prohibitive. For example, shipping a fully automated furnace system from the factory in Round Lake to a customer in the Philippines cost more than $40,000

2. *Doubts about chances of success abroad.* Management also assumed that Grieve, as a SME, lacked the resources needed to support a successful export program. Serving customers in the domestic market kept the company quite busy. They struggled to see how they could stretch their already-thin management structure to develop and direct export activity.

3. *General concern about competition.* Grieve battled seasoned exporters from Germany, Japan, and the United Kingdom. These companies were fierce rivals that made good products for a good price. Even within the United States, Grieve ran into strong competition from rival's local operations.

Eventually, Grieve confronted the issue of expanding overseas. Not only was the company losing customers to local suppliers, but it was also facing growing competition from foreign competitors in the U.S. market. Management realized that it needed to respond or risk its market position. In addition, Grieve regularly shipped its products to both California and Connecticut. Both have strong local competition and high transportation costs. Management reasoned experiences here prepared the company to expand overseas.

Mindful of these issues, Patrick Calabrese, Grieve's president, attended a trade seminar that featured market analysis and trade reports on countries in the Association of South East Asian Nations (ASEAN—specifically, as seen in Map 13.1, Brunei, Cambodia, Indonesia, Laos, Malaysia, Myanmar, the Philippines, Singapore, Thailand, and Vietnam). Since exports promote economic growth, policymakers and government agencies offer extensive assistance, such as these sorts of market seminars. Listening to the opening presentations, Mr. Calabrese again wondered whether it made sense to build an export strategy to serve Asia.

By the time the final presenter spoke, Calabrese believed there might be opportunities for his firm in one of the world's fastest-growing regions. However, his unfamiliarity with the ASEAN region compounded the complication of his company's lack of local sales representatives. He was also concerned about how Grieve would engage British, German, and Japanese rivals who commanded strong positions in those markets.

To test the waters, Grieve decided to sample potential interest by advertising in industry reports and trade publications that circulated in Southeast Asia; ads were run in the *Asian Industrial Reporter, Asian Literature Showcase,* and *World Industrial Reporter.* To learn more about the market, Calabrese worked with a representative from the International Trade Administration of the Chicago Export Assistance Center. This center, like others in major metropolitan areas in the United States, is a one-stop shop ready

MAP 13.1   The Association of South East Asian Nations (ASEAN)

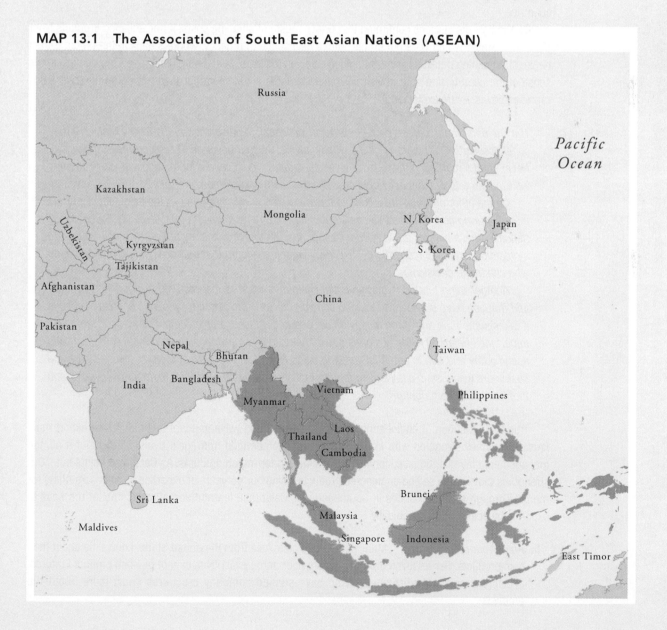

to provide SMEs—which, unlike large firms, depend on government export-promotion programs—with export assistance. Officially, this center houses representatives of the U.S. Small Business Administration, the U.S. Department of Commerce, the U.S. Export-Import Bank, and similar organizations. Representatives of the Chicago Export Assistance Center helped Calabrese plan his trip to Asia by arranging for interpreters at each stop on his itinerary and by coordinating meetings at U.S. embassies in ASEAN markets.

The goals of Calabrese's trip were to assess market potential and begin recruiting sales representatives. He had received inquiries from distributors familiar with Grieve's product line, but disinterest in export at the time had led Grieve not to respond. However, Calabrese's staff had begun filing correspondence and sales contacts by country, rather than using their earlier system of sorting them according to company name. This game him a start on locating potential customers. Calabrese also tapped the Department of Commerce's Agent/Distributor Search to get leads on possible distributors. This service helps SME exporters enlist commercial specialists at U.S. embassies and consulates to search the market for qualified agents, distributors, and representatives.

Armed and ready, Calabrese departed for Asia. During his monthlong odyssey he interviewed 28 potential agents. The trip was successful: Calabrese signed exclusive trade representatives in several countries.

Calabrese's discussions confirmed that Grieve must cut shipping costs. If not, shipping products from the United States would wipe out profits. With a new sense of urgency, workers back in the United States began streamlining packaging and rethinking shipping logistics. In addition, Calabrese's trip confirmed his sense of the need to find time to visit customers in Asia personally rather than relying on the local sales representatives. As he explained:

> The one thing that I found is that almost to an individual, [Asian customers] are very keen on a personal association. If I were to give anybody advice, I would never send a second-level individual. Never send a marketing manager or sales manager; I would send a top manager. If your company isn't too large to prohibit it, I would send the president or chairman.
>
> On the other end, you are talking to the owner of a small distributor or the president of a small manufacturing company, and you've got to meet [that person] on an equal level. My limited experience is [these people] are very cognizant of this; in other words, they are pretty much attuned to a president talking to a president. They also like to feel secure that they are dealing with someone who can make decisions.
>
> Another thing I found is that potential customers want to feel that you are financially secure and that you have sufficient funding to continue to work with them for a period of years, because it takes some time and some money on our end to get these people going. Follow-up is incredibly important. I heard all kinds of stories about American [businesspeople] who would come over and spend a day and talk to potential customers and leave [catalogs]. Then the first time the potential customers would send a fax asking for information, they didn't hear from them for two weeks, and that just turns them right off.

True to its tradition of engineering solutions, Grieve found ways to adapt its products for export markets. Still, Grieve struggled with transport costs and competition from local rivals. Throughout it all, top management stayed optimistic, confident that they had top-notch products. As Calabrese points out, "Our strength is that we are selling engineered products, using our 45 years of expertise to build something for them." Through his experiences in Southeast Asia, Calabrese learned some lessons about the keys to exporting successfully—specifically:

1. *Know your products well.* Many people who go to Asia from the United States know little about their own products. Far removed from the factory floor, some executives cannot pinpoint product features. In some cases, potential agents who have studied company brochures know more about the products.

2. *Learn about the competition in the foreign market and the potential sales for your products.* Keep an open mind: You may have to adjust your selling strategy—or often your product—to appeal to customers.

3. *Jump-start your brand image.* A plan to build acceptance slowly can lead to getting lost in fast-changing markets full of hard-charging rivals.

4. *Work hard.* Many executives, when scouting foreign markets, play golf or see sights. Demonstrate your work ethic, showing locals that time zones, jet lags, and general fatigue will not slow you down.

5. *Build a strong response base back home.* Many foreign customers complain about poor factory backup, lengthy delays in getting correspondence answered, and delays in getting quotations. Set up the systems to reply quickly, precisely, and authoritatively.

6. *Arrange for your own transportation, and do not rely on the potential representative to solve your problems for you.* Get ready to plug through the trenches. Communicate your commitment to make things happen.

7. *Make someone at the home office the principal contact for the representative.* People need someone who will answer questions and provide assistance. Give local customers a person's name, not a title or a department, to contact.

8. *Learn the customs and business etiquette of the countries you visit.* Once again, the U.S. Department of Commerce, among other government agencies, offers assistance. Qualified officials are there, courtesy of your tax dollars, to help you—provided you ask.

9. *Have the authority to make decisions and commit the company.* If you are going to meet with the top person as a potential customer, have the authority to make the same sorts of decisions as she would. Otherwise, you are wasting her and your time.

10. *Be prepared.* Before hopping on a plane, determine the right market for your company and think about how you will service overseas customers. Map it out before you depart, revise as you go along, and plan to learn.

Calabrese's initial foray overseas led to a new appreciation of the rewards and pitfalls of exporting. On balance, though, he realized that export was no longer an option: Exporting had to become part of Grieve's strategy.

Gradually, as Grieve gained experience in Asian markets, it expanded export activity to other countries. By 2007, Grieve listed Latin America/Caribbean, South America, Western Europe, Africa, Middle East, Europe, Canada, and Mexico as export markets. Although exporting has created challenges, it helped Grieve gain greater success. **CRN** Case Review Note

Introduction

Our look at Grieve highlights that exporting is loaded with opportunities and challenges. Once a company identifies the product it wants to sell abroad, it must assess the many market options in the world. Table 13.1, in listing the top exporting and importing countries, gives a first cut of the markets that managers study. Next, the company determines how to prepare the product for the market, optimize transporting logistics, promote and sell it, receive payment, and respond to service calls and warranty claims. Complicating matters is that the company will need to manage these activities while at the same time dealing with different political conditions, cultural norms, economic forces, financial systems, and legal requirements that are endemic to doing business in foreign markets.

Granted, a firm could try to go it alone. However, the planning required at each step persuades many companies—especially so-called **small and medium-sized enterprises (SMEs)** that employ fewer than 500 employees and that typically do not have export

Concept Check

In explaining "Why Companies Engage in International Business" in Chapter 1, we focus on three major operating objectives: expanding sales, acquiring resources, and minimizing risk. We then explain that, in order to achieve one or more of these objectives, companies choose from among various "Modes of Operations in International Business" and point out that, among these modes, **exporting** and **importing** are the most prevalent, especially among smaller and medium-sized firms.

TABLE 13.1   The World's Top Trading Countries (in billions U.S. $)

	Exports*			Imports**	
*	World	$15,970	*	World	$15,800
1	European Union	$1,952	1	United States	$2,112
2	Germany	$1,498	2	European Union	$1,690
3	China	$1,435	3	Germany	$1,232
4	United States	$1,291	4	China	$1,074
5	Japan	$746	5	Japan	$708
6	France	$601	6	France	$692
7	Italy	$546	7	United Kingdom	$636
8	Netherlands	$533	8	Italy	$547
9	Russia	$471	9	Netherlands	$475
10	United Kingdom	$465	10	South Korea	$427

Source: CIA World Factbook (accessed October 13, 2009).　　　　*Source: CIA World Factbook* (accessed October 15, 2009).

*The total U.S. dollar amount of merchandise imports on a CIF (cost, insurance, and freight) or FOB (free on board) basis. Figures are calculated on an exchange-rate basis.　　　**The total U.S. dollar amount of merchandise exports on an FOB (free on board) basis. Figures are calculated on an exchange-rate basis.

managers—to seek assistance. Some, confident in their competencies, go it alone. Others rely on shippers to move products from one country to another, agents or distributors to sell the products banks to process payment, and public agents to lend wisdom.

EXPORTING AND IMPORTING

Companies respond to many motivations when entering foreign markets. In this chapter, we start by looking at the idea of an export strategy (see Figure 13.1). Before beginning, we define two fundamental terms. **Exporting** refers to the sale of goods or services produced by a company based in one country to customers that reside in a different country. **Importing** is the converse: the purchase of products by a company based in one

FIGURE 13.1   Environmental Factors Influencing Export and Import Operations

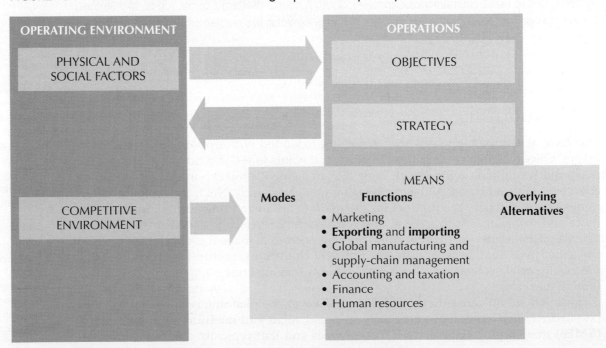

The intrinsic symmetry of international trade is illustrated here—one country's imports, the ship heading in to port, is another country's exports, the ship heading out to sea. These two ships, both post-Panamax class, carry more than 10,000 TEUs (the 20-foot container unit commonly seen on transport trucks or railcars). These ships, too large to navigate the Panama Canal, are seen near the Port of San Francisco, in transit to and from Asia.

Source: Courtesy of National Oceanic and Atmospheric Administration/Seattle.

country from sellers that reside in another. The idea of exporting manufactured goods presents a clear situation, as in the case of a German company manufacturing physical goods that are then shipped to customers in India, Brazil, or Russia.

Aspects of services, such as hotels, consulting, or banking, make it a bit tougher to define exporting and importing.[3] Engineering contractors, such as Bechtel, Skanska AB, or Kajima, export services when they construct buildings, roads, utilities, airports, seaports, or other forms of infrastructure in a foreign country. Management consultants such as McKinsey & Company export when they perform services for foreign clients. Investment banks such as Goldman Sachs export when they help a foreign company arrange financing from global sources or offer advice on capital markets. With all that said, however, the opening of a Sofitel, Starbucks, or Zara in a foreign market is not considered exporting but rather a foreign direct investment. The remainder of the chapter elaborates these ideas, examining export and import strategies, the features of indirect versus direct selling in international markets, aspects of public and private support, and the characteristics of countertrade.

Export Strategy

In Chapter 12, we showed that a company's choice of entry mode into a foreign market depends on different factors, such as the ownership advantages of the company, the location advantages of the market, and the internalization advantages that result from integrating transactions within the company's value chain.[4] In the following sections, we look at these factors as they pertain to export strategies.

ADVANTAGES TO CONSIDER

Ownership advantages are the firm's specific assets, international experience, and the ability to develop either low-cost or differentiated products within a value chain. For instance, Grieve capitalizes on its ownership advantage through the development of sophisticated ovens and furnaces; doing the same is difficult for a new entrant to a market.

Concept Check

In Chapter 12, we discuss some of the reasons why companies in a variety of industries find *exporting* the most attractive way to increase sales or acquire useful assets in foreign markets. We showed in our opening case how one medium-size manufacturer used export operations to fortify its approach to creating *value*, especially in product design and sales diversification. Similarly, the opening case in Chapter 11 shows how a large apparel maker shaped its **strategy** for maximizing export potentials in configuring its **value chain**.

The *location advantages* of a particular market are a combination of sales opportunity and investment risk. High-potential markets provide optimal targets for aspiring and experienced traders. Grieve, for example, saw events and trends in the ASEAN bloc providing favorable locations. *Internalization advantages* are the benefits of retaining a core competency within the company and threading it through the value chain rather than opting to license, outsource, or sell it. Again, Grieve could have opted to license its oven and furnace technology to local manufacturers in Asia. Instead, management preferred to control its core competencies and serve Asia through exports from its U.S. plant.

In general, companies that have low levels of ownership advantages do not enter foreign markets or, if they do, they enter through low-risk modes such as exporting. Exporting requires significantly less expertise, time, and capital than other modes of international expansion, such as FDI. Exporting allows managers to exercise operational control but less marketing control. An exporter usually resides far from the end consumer and often enlists various intermediaries to manage marketing and service activities.[5] Expectedly, the lower risk of export results in lower profits than often achieved by other modes of international business. In other words, the return on export sales may not be tremendous, but neither is the risk.

QUESTIONS TO ASK

The choice of exporting as an entry mode is not just a function of ownership, location, and internalization advantages; it also must fit the company's strategy. Companies typically consider the following questions in evaluating the export option:

- What do we want to gain from exporting?
- Is exporting consistent with our goals?
- Will exporting put undue demands on our resources—management and personnel, production capacity, and financing? If so, how will we meet them?
- Does exporting leverage our core competency?
- Does exporting fit the current configuration of our value chain?
- Do our coordination systems support the needs posed by exporting?
- Are the projected benefits of exporting worth the costs?
- Would our resources be better used to develop new domestic business?[6]

If uncertain where to start, managers often study industry and competitive conditions. For example, many industries have only a few major players, and a company's strategy for penetrating a particular market depends on its competitive position. If rivals are servicing markets by exporting, the company might also do so. However, if rivals have found ways to create superior value by servicing a foreign market through local production, relying on exports will likely limit profitability.[7]

STRATEGIC ADVANTAGES OF EXPORTING

Companies export for several reasons. Companies that are capital and research intensive, like pharmaceutical or cell phone companies, export to achieve economies of scale; generating sales over several markets amortizes the costs of new product development and capital-intensive production. Service companies, such as advertisers, lawyers, and consultants, export their services to meet the needs of overseas clients. Some companies export rather than invest abroad given the higher risk of international operations. Serving foreign markets from the home office negates many operational and personnel requirements.

Concept Check

Chapter 11 profiled the five-forces model of industry analysis, anchored within the Industrial Organizations paradigm, and its implication to a company's choice regarding the cost leadership or differentiation strategy. These perspectives and principles influence managers' assessment of the fit of export with their larger strategy.

Exporting helps companies

- Expand sales.
- Achieve scale economies.
- Diversify Sales.

Companies that are not leaders in their domestic markets may export to counter the volume advantage commanded by the national market leader. In Japan, Panasonic and Toyota are market leaders in consumer electronics and motor vehicles, respectively. Electronic manufacturers Sony and Sanyo, as well as automakers Nissan and Honda, lag behind. Consequently, the latter companies approach exports more aggressively in order to generate sales.

Diversification   Exporting enables companies to diversify their activities, thereby fortifying their adaptability to changes in the home market. As we saw in our opening case, for example, Grieve developed markets in Asia to expand its sales base as well as to reduce its worrisome overreliance on the U.S. market. Because economic growth rates differ from market to market, diversification via exporting allows a company to use strong growth in one country to offset weak growth in another. Similarly, the company that develops more customers in different markets reduces its vulnerability to the loss of particular customers. Client diversification also improves its bargaining power with existing clients.

Case Review Note

The Role of Serendipity   It is appealing to depict the export process as a proactive strategy that management meticulously designs, such as portrayed in the case of Grieve. However, research tells of accidental exporters who, responding to happenstance or odd circumstances, successfully enter overseas markets. In other words, **serendipity** is a catalyst for companies to begin exporting.

Edward Cutler is such a case. He is the owner and founder of Pennsylvania-based Squigle, a toothpaste for those who cannot tolerate the abrasives, flavors, tartar-control agents, and bleaches found in mass-produced toothpastes. Upon launching his toothpaste in 1998, Cutler focused on the U.S. market. News of the product's performance spread over the Internet, and Squigle began getting inquiries from Taiwan, Turkey, and elsewhere. One customer, a canker-sore sufferer in Britain, was so enthusiastic about the toothpaste that he began importing Squigle to England for sale there. That was good news for Cutler because it let him expand abroad at little cost and low risk. Now he is eager to start exporting more products, explaining, "We're looking to sell overseas for the same reason the big companies do: Most of the world's population lies outside the United States."[8] Indeed, 95 percent of the world's consumers live outside of the United States. Hence, the U.S. business that sells domestically only reaches a small share of total potential customers.

Profit Potential   A strategic advantage of exporting is the potential of greater profitability. For several reasons, companies can sell their products at a greater profit abroad than at home. This often happens because the competitive environment in the foreign market is different. The product may have no substitute or be in a different stage of its life cycle in foreign markets. A mature product at home often triggers extreme price competition, whereas a growth stage in foreign markets allows for premium prices. Similarly, greater profitability may result because of different government actions at home and abroad, such as differences in the taxation of earnings or the regulation of prices.

Concept Check

We explain in Chapter 1 that the attractiveness of *trade* as a means of entering international business has been enhanced by several developments that boost the efficiency of import and export. We cite, for instance, the liberalization of the cross-border movement of resources and the development of services that support trade. Here we observe that many of these developments have made importing and exporting more attractive to a broader range of companies.

CHARACTERISTICS OF EXPORTERS

No matter company size, companies can grow in the domestic market without having to export. Eventually, companies aiming to increase sales look to export.[9] And, yes, the largest companies, such as Sony, Boeing, and Nokia, are routinely the biggest exporters in their countries. Still, SMEs are steadily expanding their export capabilities. More than two-thirds of exporters have fewer than 20 employees. Furthermore, SMEs make up about 88 percent of U.S. exporters but account for a fifth of the value of exports from the United States.[10]

Although the largest companies are the biggest exporters, small companies are also expanding their export capability.

This relationship prevails worldwide. More than 98 percent of total enterprises in the Asia-Pacific region are SMEs. In China, for example, there are around 42 million SMEs—defined by Chinese officials as enterprises with annual revenues less than $250 million. Chinese SMEs account for about 99 percent of all companies and contribute approximately 60 percent of GDP, 50 percent of overall tax collection, over 70 percent of China's employment, and more than 80 percent of exports in 2008.[11]

Grieve, the subject of our opening case, is a good example. Although it is a small company in terms of total sales, Grieve's growing export revenues enhance its competitiveness and performance, and its export activity fortifies its competitive position in the United States. Research reports similar effects: A study of Canadian companies found that the size of the firm was not the most important factor in determining a company's propensity to export, the number of countries it exported to, or its degree of involvement in export. Similarly, a study of Swedish companies suggests that efficiency, not firm size, predicts export activity; specifically, firms with higher ex ante productivity tend to self-select into export markets, while those with lower productivity focus on the domestic market.[12] Likewise, a study of exporters in 158 manufacturing industries in China found the low labor costs, low R&D demands, and less state participation better predicted the degree of **export intensity** (the share of the firm's total output that is exported).[13] Finally, a study of British exporters reports that managers' commitment to overseas activities, not the particular strategy or size of the company, is the far stronger influence on exporting activity.[14]

Company practices around the world suggest that the probability of being an exporter increases with firm size; growing resouces support expanding into foreign markets. Nevertheless, a firm's export intensity is strongly influenced by other factors—i.e, management interest, production skills, foreign market awareness—that are not a function of company size. Hence, the key takeaway here is that the export intensity of a firm is related to and often determined by firm-specific features that are independent of its size.

TWO VIEWS OF EXPORT DEVELOPMENT

Two perspectives guide interpretation of the process that moderates firms' decision to export.[15] The first perspective sees exporting as the initial step of an incremental, sequential process that leads a company to expand from its home market to the most proximate countries (geographically and socially). **Incremental internationalization** holds that as a company gains experience, resources, and confidence, it progressively exports to increasingly distant and dissimilar countries. So, in one scenario, companies in the United States first export to Canada and then, in sequence, move on to Mexico and England, until ultimately exporting to countries in Africa, Asia, and the Middle East. Squigle Toothpaste, for example, illustrates a popular variation of this sequence: following its initial success in England, it has since expanded to Australia and New Zealand.

Shaping the evolution of the firm's incremental export expansion is a learning process, in which managers' growing experience with and knowledge of foreign markets creates the confidence to export to incresingly more diverse countries. Figure 13.2 identifies the three phases of the sequential view of export development. These phases, by the way, are tied not to company size but rather to the degree of export development; big and small companies can be at any particular stage, depending on the characteristics of their export activity.[16]

The second perspective, derived from the international enterpreneurship literature, holds that a firm can be **born-global.** Looking around, one sees newly formed companies begin exporting sooner in their life cycles than ever before. Rather than slowly learning about foreign markets, born-global companies step straight onto the world stage, exporting from day one of operations. Essentially, a new generation of entrepreneurs and managers, adopting a global focus from the outset, launch companies that are born global and are involved in export from that moment.

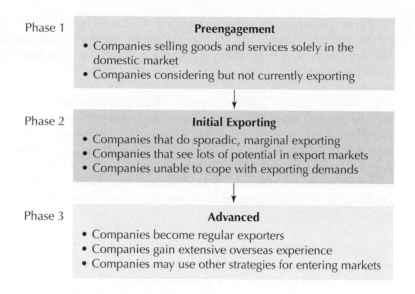

Phase 1

Preengagement
- Companies selling goods and services solely in the domestic market
- Companies considering but not currently exporting

Phase 2

Initial Exporting
- Companies that do sporadic, marginal exporting
- Companies that see lots of potential in export markets
- Companies unable to cope with exporting demands

Phase 3

Advanced
- Companies become regular exporters
- Companies gain extensive overseas experience
- Companies may use other strategies for entering markets

FIGURE 13.2 Phases of Export Development

As exporters gain greater experience and expertise, they often diversify into increasingly dissimilar foreign markets, expanding operations to include countries that are farther away from home or countries whose business environments differ more significantly from that of the home country.

Ismail Karaoglu, for example, founded a new venture in Istanbul, Turkey, with a straightforward idea: source fine leather and high-quality accessories like zippers and clasps in Italy; manufacture wallets, mobile-phone cases, and other leather fashion goods in Istanbul; and sell them in Russia and the former Soviet republics. A few years after start-up, his firm sells several million dollars' worth of leather goods, but without selling a single bag or wallet in his home market. While perhaps extreme, we see other firms, such as Calzeus of Portugal, Technico of Australia, or Biohit of Finland, that started with a global perspective, quickly using exports to penetrate foreign markets, and ultimately relies on their home market for small share of total revenue.

We see born-global companies in many countries, including the United States, Australia, Norway, France, Denmark, China, India, and Canada. Common explanations for the emergence of born globals include the increasing globalization of markets, falling trade barriers, growing demand for specialized products, improving communication and information technology, and the growing number of people with international experience who launch start-ups.[17]

These two perspectives—incremental internationalization versus born globals—shape how one interprets a company's export activity. Researchers have studied the issues of managerial attitudes, product features, organizational resources, firm strategy, and public policy, as they influence a company's export activity. Reports have covered a lot of territory with some consensus but also divergence. Indeed, as far back as 1991, research identified over 700 explanatory variables as plausible determinants of a company's export activity.[18] Today, the key to making sense of these reports is to specify the perspective—whether the incremental internationalization or born-global view—that anchors analysis.

PITFALLS OF EXPORTING

Companies often see exporting as different—and far more difficult—from selling in their home market. Most companies, particularly SMEs, concentrate on domestic rather than foreign markets, as seen in the fact that even though SMEs comprise 97 percent of all exporters in the United States, less than 1 percent of all SMEs export. Furthermore, of SMEs that export, nearly two-thirds of them export to just one foreign market. Asked why, managers often cite a company's native familiarity with its home market along with reluctance to adjust procedures for the different market, cultural, and financial practices of foreign markets.

An enduring barrier to exporting is misunderstanding the difficulty of profitably serving consumers in foreign markets.

First-time exporters often become discouraged or frustrated with the exporting process, given the inevitably of external barriers and internal shortfalls.

Export veterans explain that selling abroad is fraught with difficulties. Exporting strains resources, staff, and attention, thereby putting tough demands on management. War stories as well as systematic analysis indicate that the following pitfalls commonly complicate export:

Adjusting Financial Management   The currency and credit processes of export require adept financial management. Companies often struggle with the fact that completing an export sale requires them to help foreign customers obtain credit.[19] If exporters fail to help foreign customers secure financing—whether in the form of trade credits, government-financed support, or bank guarantees—they risk losing the sale. Companies used to offering financing in terms of the traditional 30- or 60-day trade-credit cycle in their home market are fearful of the greater risk involved in financing export sales.

Adjusting Customer Management   Worldwide, customers demand a greater range of services from their vendors. The fact that most products are available from many vendors boosts the buyer's negotiating power. "The new notch in the bar for us is the requests from our customers for additional services beyond the port of delivery," said the materials manager of Seco/Warwick Corp., a manufacturer of heat-treating furnaces. "In previous years, I would be responsible for cost, insurance, and freight (CIF) to the port of import, but now I'm often tasked with all aspects of the delivery to the customer's plant location. Now we're often involved in the installation and startup of the equipment, so we have service engineers and cranes waiting for the on-time delivery."[20]

Adjusting for Information Technology   Although information technologies reduce the cost of communications, they often increase customer expectations. Historically, exports were arm's-length, ship-it-and-forget-it transactions. Contact with customers relied on hard-copy documents either faxed or posted overnight. This situation created useful time lags with which to deal with customers' concerns. Now, the ease of contacting vendors via e-mail or inexpensive voice-over-Internet-protocol (VoIP) gives customers real-time access, thereby increasing demands on the exporter. Historically, an appealing aspect of export was its limited range of demands, a situation that fit the lower margins of exports versus other modes of international business. Now, customers' escalating expectations, coupled with the same or shrinking margins, can reduce the export's appeal.

A Catalog of Additional Stumbling Blocks   New exporters typically stumble once or twice before hitting their stride. Then, once up and running, just as rare is the exporter who has too much time or too many resources. Therefore, we get a better sense of the challenge of developing an export strategy by identifying pitfalls that exporters face.[21]

- Insufficient commitment by top management to overcome the inevitable difficulties of export
- Underestimating the usefulness of public and private export expertise
- Misestimating the costs of shipping and the complexity of customs regulations and procedures
- Poor selection of local agents to represent the company abroad
- Reacting to orders from around the world instead of designing a purposeful sales strategy
- Neglecting export markets when the domestic market booms
- Misclassifying products in terms of the destination country's tariff schedule, thereby incurring a higher tax or slowing delivery
- Failure to treat international distributors on an equal basis with those in the home market

Concept Check

As straightforward as the concept of **exporting** may seem on the surface, we hasten to reinforce a theme that we have touched upon throughout the book—namely, that whether you are a born-global entrepreneur or an established global, you will run into problems. In Chapter 2, we high-light *behavioral barriers* to the smooth flow of international operations. In Chapter 3, for example, we discuss difficulties posed by various political regulations as well as complying with different *legal systems*, and Chapter 5 explores the pitfalls inherent in any effort to heed the imperatives of social *responsibility*. In Chapter 7, we describe the difficulties that arise in trying to capitalize on *government incentives*, and in Chapter 9, we explain some of the problems that arise in dealing with *foreign-exchange instruments*.

- Unwillingness to modify products to meet other countries' regulations or cultural preferences
- Failure to print service, sales, and warranty messages in local languages
- Bypassing public export assistance when the company lacks qualified personnel
- Failure to prepare for disputes with customers

DESIGNING AN EXPORT STRATEGY

Some companies begin exporting by serendipity rather than by design. An unsolicited order arrives in the mail, a new hire has connections to a foreign market, a contact is made at an industry conference, personal travel abroad alerts a manager to new options,

In designing an export strategy, managers

- Assess their firm's export potential.
- Target appropriate markets.
- Adapt the configuration of value activities.
- Install coordination systems to implement their plans.

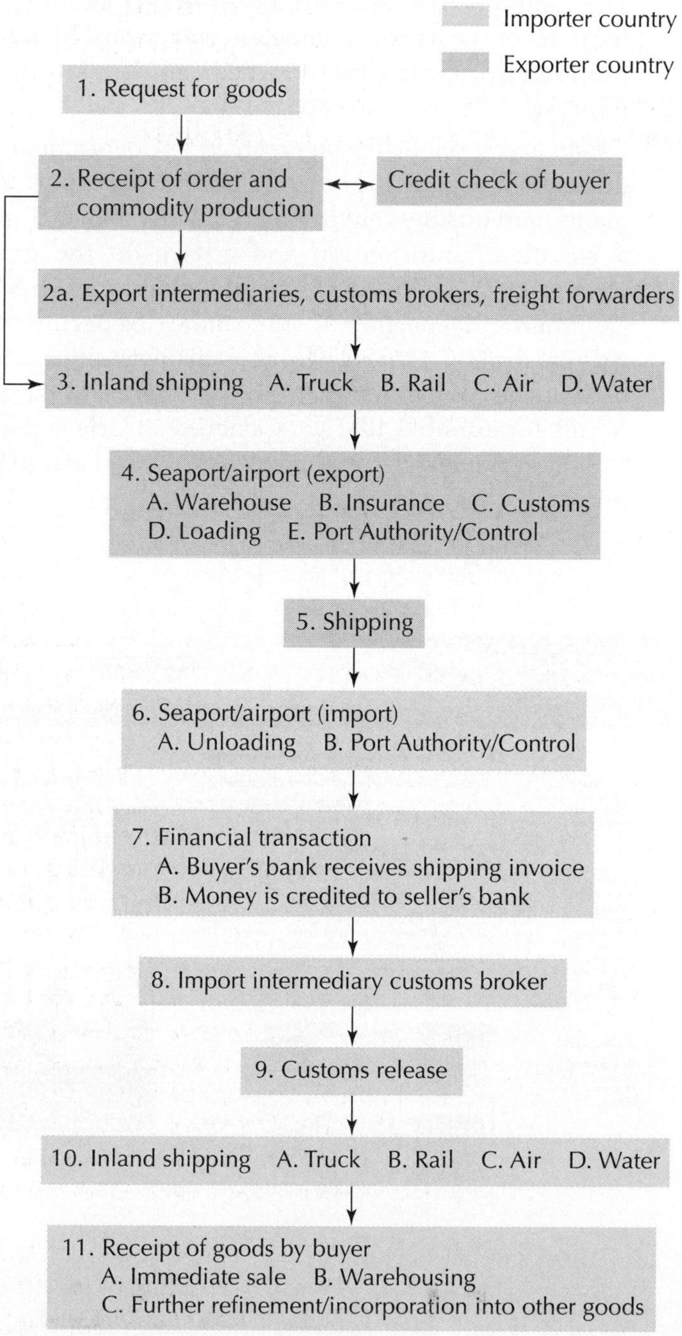

□ Importer country
□ Exporter country

1. Request for goods

2. Receipt of order and commodity production ←→ Credit check of buyer

2a. Export intermediaries, customs brokers, freight forwarders

3. Inland shipping   A. Truck   B. Rail   C. Air   D. Water

4. Seaport/airport (export)
   A. Warehouse   B. Insurance   C. Customs
   D. Loading   E. Port Authority/Control

5. Shipping

6. Seaport/airport (import)
   A. Unloading   B. Port Authority/Control

7. Financial transaction
   A. Buyer's bank receives shipping invoice
   B. Money is credited to seller's bank

8. Import intermediary customs broker

9. Customs release

10. Inland shipping   A. Truck   B. Rail   C. Air   D. Water

11. Receipt of goods by buyer
    A. Immediate sale   B. Warehousing
    C. Further refinement/incorporation into other goods

FIGURE 13.3   The International Transaction Chain

Between the point at which they negotiate an international sale and the point at which products have been delivered both the exporter and the importer manage a complex array of financial and distribution tasks. Each of these tasks defines a link in the *transaction chain* forged by each firm's respective strategy. Note, by the way, that financial transactions run along the chain.

Source: Export America 1 (November 1999): 17. Magazine published by the International Trade Administration of the U.S. Dept. of Commerce.

and so on. The often-unplanned export trigger, if not dealt with systematically, can prove costly. Therefore, achieving the strategic advantages of exports depends on developing a sound, insightful export strategy. No matter whether a company is born global or is an incremental exporter, designing an **export strategy** helps managers capture opportunities and avoid pitfalls.

Figure 13.3 shows an international business transaction chain. These are the sorts of activities companies heed when selling or buying a product across national borders. At times, some activities are more pressing than others. Still, over time, all come into play. Therefore, a successful export (and, as we will see, import) strategy evaluates the elements of this transaction chain. Successful exporting requires that management apply the following steps:

1. *Assess the company's export potential by examining its opportunities and resources.* The company determines if there is a market for its product. It identifies whether it can leverage its core competency overseas. Managers confirm there is sufficient production capacity, or that they can develop it, if success comes sooner than forecast.

2. *Obtain expert counseling on exporting.*   Governments provide export assistance for domestic companies, given the benefits of export to job creation, balance of payments, and business environment quality. The U.S. government, for example, offers a wealth of information and advice on the practical points of exporting—www.export.gov is the official gateway to trade support provided by the Commerce Department, the State Department, and the Small Business Administration. Finally, help is available at the many export assistance centers run by branches of the Commerce Department and the Small Business Administration. Recall, for example, that Mr. Calabrese of Grieve used information provided by the U.S. government to learn about Asian markets, plan business trips, and identify potential sales agents.

Case Review Note

Export.gov is the gateway to a range of resources for international traders. Here, both the aspiring and experienced exporter can find information, opportunities, and solutions for many aspects of international trade.

In addition, exporters also evaluate:

- *Specialized Financial Assistance.* As a company's export strategy expands, it can seek specialized assistance from banks, lawyers, freight forwarders, export management companies, export trading companies, and others. Companies help foreign customers obtain the necessary cash or credit; often specialized financial assistance is necessary. One method has the buyer secure irrevocable letters of credit (covered in Chapter 19), which are guaranteed by a local bank. Another option is to secure government payment guarantees from organizations, such as the Export-Import Bank of the United States (Ex-Im Bank), or purchase government-backed insurance, such as from the Federal Credit Insurance Association.

- *Agents.* Hiring an agent, such as freight forwarders or master shippers, helps simplify exporting. Instead of dealing with individual orders and making sure the product and paperwork line up, the exporter hires a distributor to do so. Explained Edward Cutler, maker of Squigle toothpaste, "It is just easier to deal with distributors. We prefer to deal in master shippers of 144 tubes. We don't have to do anything then but slap a label on it."[22]

3. *Select a market or markets.* The facet of export strategy that trips up many companies, particularly SMEs, is selecting the "right" market. SMEs are often discouraged when their initial overseas forays fail. Instead of applying the standards of sound strategy that made their companies successful in the first place, many follow hunches about foreign markets. Entrepreneurs often overestimate the need for their product. It is tough to try to conquer customers from Bonn to Beijing to Benares in a day. Advised one analyst, "Look at a few markets where you'll have success rather than trying to sell throughout Europe."[23]

    Many companies approach export passively. The company learns of markets by responding to unsolicited requests from abroad. Then, encouraged by the potential demand, the company begins to investigate its export options. Recall from our opening case, for instance, that requests for product information fanned Grieve's interest in Southeast Asia.

    The incremental internationalization view of exporting holds that companies target countries that are similar to their home market. To this end, the U.S. Census Bureau publishes extensive statistics on foreign trade activities and patterns. Exporters analyze this data to identify similar high-potential markets. The National Trade Data Bank provides, on a monthly basis, industry reports for different countries. Companies scan this data to estimate consumption trends in foreign markets, identifying income, social, or infrastructure similarities that indicate demand for their product.

4. *Formulate and implement an export strategy.* An export plan is an essential element of an effective export strategy. Export ambitions ultimately must translate into precise objectives, planned tactics, hard time lines, and resource allocations that deliver products to foreign buyers. Table 13.2 profiles how many companies develop an export plan. The development of the plan depends on the company, its outlook toward export markets, and its core competency. In SMEs, given resource constraints, senior managers develop the plan. Large companies often establish a stand-alone export manager or group. No matter the size of the company, top managers' commitment is a key predictor of a firm's export success.[24]

Case Review Note

Concept Check
In detailing the concept of "The Firm as Value Chain" in Chapter 11, we define a **core competency** as a special outlook, skill, capability, or technology that creates unique **value** for a firm. Here we observe the need for would-be **exporters,** especially SMEs, to explore the opportunities for leveraging core competencies when they are designing export strategies.

TABLE 13.2   An Export Business Plan

In deciding if an export strategy is right for your business, you need to estimate its risks and benefits. Successful exporters show that converting your assessment into an export business plan is a critical step. Typically, your plan evaluates several interrelated issues. The following list identifies, by key category, issues that warrant your attention.

1. Executive Summary
- Key elements of the export plan
- Description of business and target markets
- Specification of management team
- Summary of projections

2. Company Description
- History
- Goals and objectives
- Core competency
- Management
- The export team
- Company finances

3. Product/Service Description
- Export opportunity
- Fit of company's products in export market
- Growth potential
- Product strategy

4. Foreign Marketplace Analysis
- Rationale for exporting
- Rationale for targeted foreign market
- Country profile
- Industry profile
- Competitor analysis
- Specification of key assumptions

5. Market Entry Strategies
- Form of operation
- Indirect/direct exporting
- E-commerce options
- Target customer profile
- Pricing strategies
- Sales and promotion strategies
- Logistics and transportation

6. International Law
- Dispute resolution
- Language consideration
- Contract terms and conditions

- Product liability considerations
- Intellectual property protection
- Sales agent and/or distributor agreements
- Export/import regulations

7. Financial Analysis
- Facility and equipment requirements
- Sales forecast
- Cost of goods sold
- Projected international income statement
- Projected international cash flow
- Breakdown analysis
- Financing requirements
- Current financing sources
- Tax consequences

8. Risk Management
- Country risk
- Commercial risk
- Credit risk
- Currency risk
- Market risk
- Political risk

9. External Assistance
- Export America
- U.S. Commerce Department
- Census Bureau
- Customs and Border Protection
- www.export.gov
- International Trade Administration
- U.S. Export-Import Bank
- National, regional, and local organizations
- Cross-border trade consultancies

10. Implementation Schedule
- Operational time line
- Performance milestones
- Contingency plans

Import Strategy

Thus far, we have talked mostly about exporting. The flip side of exporting is *importing*. Theoretically, importing is the process of moving products from country X into country Y for sale or trade. The import of goods is straightforward. Toyota's shipment of an automobile from Japan to Nigeria registers as an import. Service imports, given their intangibility, take a variety of forms. The German software company SAP is a service provider even though software often comes in a physical package; nonetheless, we classify software sales as a service transaction. Customers who receive financial services from foreign banks, such as a French citizen using HSBC, generate service imports. Similarly, when Lloyds of London writes an insurance policy for a client in Brazil, trade authorities in Brazil record an import transaction.

In the normal course of international business, there are many borderline cases between the import of a good versus a service—e.g., the installation of industrial equipment in country X when a project is of limited duration by its nature, even though it is a hard good, qualifies as a service import. The standards to keep in mind is that an import of services consists of all services that do not result in ownership and that are rendered by nonresidents to the local residents in a country.

TYPES OF IMPORTERS

Our discussion of exports indentified its strategic and environmental motivations. Similar observations pertain to import. The study of **import strategy** identifies three types of importers:

- Importers that look opportunistically for any product around the world that they can deliver to local citizens for a profit. These companies see a gap in the local marketplace, whether real (customers cannot find what they want) or perceived (the presumption that products from some countries are intrinsically superior to local substitutes) that can be better filled by a product available from a foreign source.

- Importers that look to foreign sourcing to get the highest-quality products at the lowest possible price. This motivation is timeless—an agent profitably arbitrages cost or quality differences between countries. For instance, a small Utah-based company called ForEveryBody began selling bath and body products. It then diversified into home decorations based on low-cost products available from Chinese manufacturers. In this way, it evolved into an importer.

- Importers that use foreign sourcing to optimize their supply chains. Companies search the globe for the best possible inputs, then direct them to various processing points dispersed among various countries, which assemble the inputs into finished goods that are then imported by markets worldwide. The flow of inputs and finished goods from country to country, besides representing exports, also qualifies as imports. Chapter 16 profiles the idea and mechanics of supply chains.

> There are three types of importers:
> - Those looking for any product around the world to import and sell.
> - Those looking for foreign sourcing to get products at the cheapest price.
> - Those using foreign sourcing as part of their global supply chain.

STRATEGIC ADVANTAGES OF IMPORTS

Like any smart shopper, an importer scans world markets, seeking lower-priced, better-quality, or locally unavailable products. This simple supposition begs the question: Why do these market anomalies exist? Absent these gaps, there is little need for import and, for that matter, export to take place. Other parts of the text—particularly Chapters 6, 7, 11, and 12—speak to this issue. For our purposes, it is useful to note the following triggers for import and export.

> A service import refers to all services that do not result in ownership and that are rendered by nonresidents to the local residents in a country.

Specialization of Labor The specialization of labor makes export to and import from countries around the world more efficient than manufacturing every product in every country. For instance, Nike buys shoes manufactured by companies located in several Asian countries, including Korea, Taiwan, China, Thailand, Indonesia, and Vietnam, because of their ability to make higher-quality shoes for lower cost. Nike finds it impossible to manufacture the same products in countries with high production costs, sell them at a reasonable price, and still make a profit. Hence, it relies on imports and exports.

Global Rivalry Industries with a high degree of global competitive rivalry, such as telecommunications, automobiles, and business services, pose relentless pressures.

> **Concept Check**
> Our coverage of the "Theory of Comparative Advantage" in Chapter 6 notes that specialization results in greater overall efficiency. Different relative cost structures, say for labor or capital, create value for both parties even when one can produce all goods with fewer resources than the other; hence the basis for exporting and importing goods.

These pressures often spur a company to combat import competition by switching to foreign suppliers whose components enable it to lower the cost or boost the quality of its finished products.

Local Unavailability   Companies import products that are, due to geographic, policy, or developmental reasons, locally unavailable. For example, Canada imports bananas from tropical climates because of its unsuitable climate; absent imports, Canadians would not enjoy fresh bananas. Other scenarios of unavailability exist for products from medical devices to computer chips. Similarly, a potential importer may seek new foreign products that complement its existing product lines, thereby giving it more ways to create value.

Diversification of Operating Risks   An importer, like an exporter, diversifies its operating risks by tapping international markets. In many industry settings, developing alternative suppliers makes a company less vulnerable to fortunes of a single supplier. For example, customers of U.S. steelmakers have diversified their steel purchases to include European, Chinese, Indian, and South Korean suppliers. This strategy reduces the risk of supply shortages or unexpected price hikes by U.S. steelmakers.

The Import Process

Like yin and yang, the import process and export process are complementary opposites within the greater whole called *international trade*. Many of the strategic and practical issues of the import process mirror those of the export process. Managers typically adapt the export business plan in Table 13.2 (p. 532) to serve as the framework for an import business plan. That is, as in the export process, managers start the import process by studying potential markets, looking to pinpoint possible suppliers, market asymmetries, and consumer tendencies. They then determine the legal aspects of importing a product, in terms of both the product and the countries from which they originate. Then, like export managers who need to move product from their home to foreign markets, import managers evaluate third-party intermediaries

Here we have a bird's-eye view of containers stacked high and deep at Busan Port, located in the southeast of the Korean peninsula. Busan Port, like seaports along the coastline of Asia, is a gateway connecting thousands of nearby factories with billions of customers around the world. Around 130 container ships daily, or nearly 50,000 annually, power through Busan Port. This performance presently ranks Busan fifth in the world—behind the seaports of Singapore, China/Shanghai, Hong Kong, and China/Shenzhen.

Source: Chung Sung-Jun/Getty Images, Inc.

such as freight forwarders and customs agents. Throughout it all, importers consult with financial intermediaries and government agencies to clarify contingencies. We now turn to a closer look at these issues and their implications to designing an import strategy.

IMPORT BROKERS

Importing requires expertise with institutions, such as customs agencies and trade regulators, and documentation, such as shipping manifests or security authorizations. Not every company commands these proficiencies. Consequently, some opt to hire an **import broker,** also known as a **customs broker.** An import broker provides access to several suppliers or producers as well as helps companies during price negotiation, arranging transportation and insurance, overseeing logistics, and dealing with damaged and rejected goods. Some import brokers have foreign offices that are familiar with local cultures and business practices, including services to help importers locate suppliers.

An import broker is an intermediary, who helps importers navigate trade regulations.

Key Broker Functions   Import brokers provide many services. Companies commonly look to import brokers for the following:

- *Valuing products in such a way that they qualify for more favorable duty treatment.* Different product categories have different duties, or assessed taxes, when crossing borders. For example, finished goods typically have a higher duty than do parts and components. The task, clearly, is to determine the classification that results in the lowest tariff. Brokers' expertise help do.

- *Qualifying for duty refunds through drawback provisions.*   Some exporters use imported parts and components, on which they paid a duty, in their manufacturing process. In the United States, so-called drawback provisions allow domestic exporters to apply for a 99 percent refund of the duty paid on the imported goods, as long as those goods become inputs into the exporter's product.

- *Deferring duties by using bonded warehouses and foreign trade zones.*   Companies need not pay duties on imports stored in bonded warehouses and foreign trade zones until the goods are removed for sale or used in a manufacturing process. A broker ensures compliance with the provisions of the foreign trade zone.

- *Document and paper-flow management.*   A large volume of paperwork goes hand in hand with international trades, particularly for those that fall under the broad label of homeland security. A broker obtains various government permissions and other clearances before forwarding the requisite paperwork to the carrier that is scheduled to deliver the goods to the importer. Import brokers in the United States must be certified by the U.S. Bureau of Customs and Border Protection to oversee product shipments into the United States.

- *Limiting liability by properly marking an import's country of origin.*   Because governments assess duties on imports based in part on the country of origin, a mistake in marking the country of origin may increase the import duty. For example, in the United States, if a product or its container is improperly marked when it enters the country, the product may be assigned a marking duty equal to 10 percent of the declared customs value. This charge is in addition to the normal tariff.[25]

CUSTOMS AGENCIES

Bringing goods into any country requires that a company understand the customs operations of the importing country. Revenue, security, and trade regulations specify that once cargo reaches its port of entry, say going from Singapore to Seattle, U.S. customs

TABLE 13.3 Where the Trading Is Easy—and Where It Is Not

Free trade agreements, particularly the European Union, facilitate export and import. The persistence of convoluted customs regulations, notably in Africa, makes trade more difficult. These data reflect the average of a country's rankings in terms of the (1) number of documents and (2) length of time and overall cost required to complete an import or export transaction.

Easiest	Rank	Hardest	Rank
Singapore	1	Niger	174
New Zealand	2	Eritrea	175
Hong Kong, China	3	Burundi	176
United States	4	Venezuela	177
United Kingdom	5	Chad	178
Denmark	6	Republic of Congo	179
Ireland	7	São Tomé and Principe	180
Canada	8	Guinea-Bissau	181
Australia	9	Democratic Republic of Congo	182
Norway	10	Central Africa Republic	183

Source: The International Bank for Reconstruction and Development/The World Bank, "Doing Business" (accessed October 13, 2009).

officials take nominal control of the product. (In this context, "customs" are the country's import and export procedures and restrictions, not its cultural aspects.) Customs officials release the product when procedures and paperwork satisfy regulations.

Countries vary in the degree to which their **customs agencies** help international traders (see Table 13.3). For example, trading across Europe is becoming seamless, owing to the European Union and related free trade agreements. Thus, Table 13.3 shows that several of the top 10 countries on the ease-of-trading list are European. Free trade pacts in other parts of the world achieve similar effects. In contrast, inconsistent customs practices in African and South Asian markets hamper exports and imports. Moving from port to port in these markets finds a hodgepodge of vague regulations.

In the case of the United States, the Bureau of Customs and Border Protection (CBP, formerly the U.S. Customs Service) of the Department of Homeland Security monitors imports and exports. This agency assesses and collects duties, taxes, and fees on imported merchandise, enforces customs and related laws, and administers certain navigation laws and treaties. It polices smuggling operations and is charged with protecting the United States from threatening imports.[26]

Procedural Assistance   Successful importing hinges on knowing how to clear goods through customs, assigning optimal customs duties, and complying with regulations. In terms of procedures, when merchandise reaches the port of entry, the importer must file documents with customs officials. These agents then assign a provisional value and tariff classification to the merchandise. The United States has nearly 10,000 classifications in its Harmonized Tariff Schedule. Approximately 60 percent of them are subject to interpretation—that is, a particular product could fit more than one classification. It is a near art form to determine the tariff classification that results in the lowest assessment.

Tariff classification depends on various factors, which vary according to the type of product involved. The CBP advises traders, or their agents, to provide a complete description of the good in its imported condition, including component materials; the good's principal use in the United States; the commercial, common, or technical designation; illustrative literature, sketches, digital photographs, or flow charts; and any special invoicing requirements. Experienced traders follow the CBP's recommendation to consult the Harmonized Tariff Schedule in proposing the applicable classification. Those who don't do so face the prospect that when the cargo arrives at the border or port, customs officials will closely examine it to determine whether there are any restrictions on their importation. If so, the goods may be rejected and prohibited from entering the country. If allowed to enter, the importer then pays the duty in order to release the goods. The amount of the duty depends on the product's country of origin, the type of product, and other factors.

Efficiency Improvement   Customs agents, well aware that time is money, steadily improve the efficiency of processing exports and imports. Long delays, too many documents, and high administrative fees boost costs that increase prices. For those reasons, customs agents continually test technologies and management systems.[27] For example, improving risk management techniques such as pre- and post-clearance audits allow countries to target higher-risk cargo for expedited customs inspections. Pre- and post-clearance audits verify the accuracy and authenticity of declarations based on traders' commercial data, business systems, and records books. Once certified, a trader's cargo qualifies for immediate release or reduced release times from customs inspection.

In Tanzania, for example, more than 90 percent of international cargo is now risk-assessed before it arrives at Dar es Salaam. New risk-management tools used in Nicaragua have reduced physical inspections to less than 10 percent of international trade shipments. Post-clearance audits in Egypt, Jordan, and Romania allow customs agents to release cargo to importers quickly, with the contents of a shipping container verified after it reaches the warehouse. These innovations, by instituting similar initiatives such as uniform customs forms and electronic filing, reduce trade barriers. Steady progress on these fronts, as we see in our "Looking to the Future" insert, opens markets.

Looking to the Future

Future   The Technology of Trade

Advances in transportation and communications systems, by making it easier and cheaper for companies to export and import, accelerate growth in trade. The growing availability of electronic filing of cargo documents has reduced delays in many ports. Software that works in Hamburg or Sydney is used in Hong Kong and San Diego, further powered by simpler customs and transit forms that are increasingly standardized across countries. Consequently, the speed of trading is now greater than ever: Between January 2005 and April 2006, the time needed to comply with export-related requirements fell by nearly 1.5 days worldwide.

The Internet helps individuals throughout the world engage each other easily and quickly. This, in turn, reduces many historically high transaction costs of international trade. The flexibility and cost efficiencies of generating international sales via the Internet make online companies, as well as their more conventional counterparts, increasingly engage export.

Companies can connect the flow of goods, funds, and information within an integrated system of different technologies. The real-time synchronization of import and export activities redefines the way companies, both big and small, connect with their foreign suppliers and customers. Historically, big MNEs reaped the biggest rewards. Their superior resources positioned them to capture the advances in information flows. The technology of trade now seems to offer bigger benefits to smaller companies. Technology makes it harder to tell the difference between an SME exporter and a larger MNE. Historically, the latter had access to more capital, diverse markets, better systems, and economies of scale. Small exporters had to make do with shoestring budgets. Now, technologies create solutions and platforms that blur the distinction between the big, global giant and the small, neighborhood start-up.

On one front, software helps SME exporters do things that were impossible just a few years ago. Said one executive, "There's been an explosion of collaborative business software in the past few years. It's created a total revolution in what small businesses are able to accomplish overseas."[28] Collaborative software lets the entrepreneurial exporter or importer with single-digit head counts establish close relationships with and keep close track on foreign vendors without traveling the world.

(continued)

For example, Edgar Blazona used to log 100,000 miles of air travel annually, visiting factories in the Far East. Now, Blazona uses two factories—one in Thailand and one in India—to make his products that he then imports into the United States. He uses a meeting and document-sharing program to work in real-time tandem with his overseas factories. Costing about $50 per month, this software cuts down on confusion, costly mistakes, and the need to ship designs overnight across the globe.

Similarly, Evertek Computer Corporation, a small U.S. company, capitalized on software innovations to change its market frontier. Evertek began in 1990 selling new and refurbished computers and parts. By 2008, it had become the world's largest excess computer distributor, closeout computer wholesaler, clearance computer supplier, and closeout electronics wholesaler. Evertek purchased an Internet-based program from the U.S. Commerce Department called BuyUSA.com, which helps it find buyers around the world. Within a year of using BuyUSA.com, Evertek began selling in 10 new countries, with single purchases reaching up to $75,000. In 2009, Evertek exported to customers in over 100 countries.

Other companies use similarly innovative programs to manage networks of overseas factories that once only big MNEs could finance. China Manufacturing Network, for instance, relies on its 10-person staff in California to coordinate production of laboratory and industrial-device lasers among more than 90 independent factories in China, Malaysia, and Singapore. China Manufacturing uses an on-demand, scalable enterprise software product to track activity in each factory, thereby determining where to place orders, monitor build rates, and manage inventory.

On another front, improvements in overnight shipping provide a flexible and powerful platform to manage imports and exports. Growing availability of low-cost overnight shipping has robbed big firms of a long-running competitive advantage; SMEs also have the affordable option to ship products quickly across the globe. Now, the no-name, one-person exporter down the street from you, because of his big-name shipping partners who span the globe, has many of the same logistics capabilities commanded by a large MNE.

Moreover, SMEs increasingly have as much shipping flexibility as big companies, if not a bit more. The diffusion of supply chains throughout the world often runs into logistics bottlenecks. Whether it's lost shipments, customs tie-ups, or out-of-sync links in the supply chain, the resulting holdups create delays that cost money. Unlike big companies that rely on their in-house systems, SMEs can tap a range of sophisticated solution providers. Help is available from traditional intermediaries, like export management companies, and emerging forms (so-called **third-party logistics,** or "3PLs"), like FedEx and UPS. These companies have developed state-of-the-art technology that helps traders understand their current trade practices, identify opportunities and risks, and shepherd exports and imports from buyers to sellers.

These logistics intermediaries, notably the 3PLs, command system capabilities that enable international traders to do their jobs more efficiently. The 3PLs offer integration mechanisms, like online shipping and tracking information, thereby helping the company and customer know when the shipments enter customs. They also consolidate billing inclusive of all transportation, customs brokerage, duties, taxes, and package delivery services. Finally, they have the capability to handle product returns, warranty claims, parts exchanges, and reverse logistics.

A small international trader can hire any of these sorts of firms to warehouse, truck, sail, fly, and deliver goods from factories in Asia to customers in Europe—all the while avoiding any sort of physical proximity to the goods. For example, South West Trading in Arizona, a family-owned start-up that markets yarns made from bamboo, corn, and soy fibers by fabric plants in China, had a long history of supply-chain problems. UPS, through its Supply Chain Solutions program, enabled South West Trading to use the UPS facility in Shanghai to consolidate orders from various factories into one shipping container, manage customs paperwork, and truck the goods to the company's warehouse in Phoenix. The benefit to South West Trading's bottom line was immediate. The company once paid $9,400 to run four China-to-Arizona shipments per month; now its monthly UPS shipment costs about $3,600 and reliably takes 21 days to travel.

Big or small, companies respond to these innovations, confident that technology will create tools to let them jump the hurdles and capture the opportunities of international trade. SMEs in particular see the chance to prosper from the improving technology of trade. By decoupling the issues of firm size and performance, technology resets the trade game. Observed the CEO of China Manufacturing, "Our customers can't really tell how big we are. In a way, it's irrelevant. What matters is that we can get the job done."[29] ∎

IMPORT DOCUMENTATION

Import transactions trigger paperwork. The arrival of a shipment at a port requires the importer to file several documents with various officials and agents to take title. For instance, importers typically receive products without purchasing them—that is, they take the title of ownership but without laying out any money. This arrangement requires two types of documents:

- Those that determine whether customs will release the shipment.
- Those that contain information, as noted above, for duty assessment and statistical purposes.

The specific documents that customs requires vary by country but usually include an entry manifest, a commercial invoice, and a packing list. For example, the exporter's commercial invoice contains information such as the country of origin, the port of entry to which the merchandise is destined, information on the importer and exporter, a detailed description of the merchandise including its purchase price, and the currency used for the sale.

Bureaucratic Impediments An irony of growing globalization is import inefficiencies due to delays, documention, and administrative fees. Notwithstanding the success of the WTO, many rules and regulations hinder trade. For example, a Zambian trader noted, "My cargo of copper wire was held up in Durban, South Africa, for a week. The port authorities required proof that the wooden pallets on which the wire was loaded were free of pests. After some days the Ministry of Agriculture's inspector checked that the wood was fumigated, for a $100 fee."[30] More generally, government agencies sometimes must clear the priority ratings for various markets; refusals come easily to officials worried about product shortages at home or political tension abroad.

These hindrances are unlikely to disappear soon, given the heightened importance of national economic agendas and security concerns. Consequently, international traders navigate complex national, regional, and global trade agreements, all the while minding their compliance with pertinent regulations.

In the United States, homeland security issues have begun to match tariffs as areas of concern for importers. The logistics manager at Schott North America points out, "The real danger to your supply chain these days isn't tariffs. . . . [I]t's that your containers are stuck down at the terminal in New York [harbor] waiting for inspection" by radiation detection instruments before receiving customs authorization to enter the United States.[31] Importers turn to software programs' frequent updates of the latest regulations that affect international trade, including regulations issued by the Department of Homeland Security.

The Export Process

Exports take one of two formats. **Direct exports** are products sold to an independent intermediary outside of the exporter's home country, which then sells the product in the export market to the final consumer. **Indirect exports** are sold to an independent intermediary in the domestic market, which then sells the product in the export market to the final consumer. Services are more likely sold in a direct fashion, whereas companies export goods directly and indirectly. We now examine each.

INDIRECT SELLING

An exporter using **indirect selling** sells goods to or through an independent domestic intermediary in its home country. The intermediary then exports the products to customers in foreign markets. Indirect selling permits the exporter to use the same customer

Concept Check

In reviewing "Legal Issues in International Business" in Chapter 3, we discuss various ways in which a country's legal system can affect the operating decisions of any firm involved in international business, including importers. In Chapter 7, we make a related point about trade policies and the arsenals of trade-control instruments with which governments influence import flows. Here we add policies on revenue collection, product safety, competitive fairness, and homeland security to the list of moderators that regulate import activities.

The efficiency of importing is challenged by delays, documentation, and fees.

Principal types of exporting:

- Direct—products sold to an independent party outside of the exporter's home country.
- Indirect exports—products sold to an intermediary in the domestic market, which then sells the goods in the export market.

solicitation methods, terms and conditions of sale, packaging, shipping logistics, and credit and collection procedures for all customers, no matter whether they are down the street or around the world. The company transfers the responsibility of dealing with the complications created by export sales to the export intermediary.

Export Intermediaries   Figure 13.3 shows that exporters and importers use a variety of third-party intermediaries—companies that facilitate the trade of goods but are not related to the exporter or the importer. **Export intermediaries** range in size from small, specialized one-person operations to international trading companies with a globally dispersed staff. A company that exports or is planning to export decides whether its internal staff will handle activities or if it will contract with independent agents. Successful exporting requires that agents, either internal to the company or external intermediaries, perform the following:

Concept Check

In Chapter 1, we suggest that **international business** is challenging for people who like to do everything themselves. For example, collecting information about foreign markets and cultures can get tough quickly. Consequently, some companies prefer help in finding information about the key factors in a country's *external environment*. Third-party intermediaries can be valuable sources of *knowledge* about such policies (e.g., trade laws, regulations, taxes).

- Direct market research, generate sales, and obtain orders
- Make credit investigations and perform payment-collection activities
- Handle foreign traffic and shipping
- Support the company's sales, distribution, and advertising

A company's experience in export and import, along with the sophistication of its financial and management resources, influences its inclination for indirect selling. The challenge of preparing export and customs documents along with identifying the best means of transportation overwhelms many companies. Companies often turn to intermediary brokers when they begin exporting. These brokers are familiar with trade laws, regulations, taxes, duties, insurance, and transportation. In addition, technicalities in the law or glitches in the system often create problems at the entry port. Brokers expedite resolution or, as need be, represent their clients in matters of disputes. Companies, particularly those launching export strategies, find that intermediaries offer an operationally easier and relatively risk-free approach.[32]

Exporters see trade intermediaries as useful means to navigate complex homeland security concerns. Increasing government regulation, in the interest of national security, regarding what can be shipped where and to whom has led to lengthy border delays and unexpected holdups.[33] Companies enlist brokers to keep pace with ever-changing homeland security regulations. Trade intermediaries, with the help of advanced software applications, improve their expertise in customs compliance strategies, regulatory requirements, licensing requirements, and goods valuation and classification practices.

Intermediaries charge exporters for their expertise and services. Commonly, brokers operate on (1) a commission rate that often ranges from 10 percent for consumer goods to 15 percent or more for industrial products; (2) a buy-sell basis that asks for your best home-country discount plus an extra discount for a product that will be marked up when sold abroad; and/or (3) a "special event" contribution such as a 50/50 sharing of costs to exhibit products in a foreign trade show or an advance payment for advertising and promotion.

Hiring an intermediary requires that an exporter forsake control over important aspects of its international sales. Companies that enlist a trade intermediary sometimes have little control over whom it sells to, the selling price it charges, the quality of promotional campaigns, its stated delivery schedules, or the quality of customer service. Some companies have discovered that if an agent does not actively promote their products, then they may be unable to do much to generate export sales. Hence, some companies fear that using a trade intermediary will lead them to relinquish far too much control of foreign sales. Companies intent on retaining control employ export intermediaries in less comprehensive ways, including providing short-term financing and dealing with border-protection agencies. Companies trade off their preference for control with the cost of directly managing export operations.[34]

EMCs and ETCs   The major types of indirect intermediaries are the **export management company (EMC),** the **export trading company (ETC),** and export agents, merchants, or remarketers. *EMC* and *ETC* are often used interchangeably, especially for smaller intermediaries. Larger intermediaries, however, are usually referred to as ETCs because they deal with both exports and imports.

EXPORT MANAGEMENT COMPANIES   An EMC usually acts as the export arm of a manufacturer—although it can also deal in imports—and often uses the manufacturer's own letterhead in communicating with foreign sales representatives and distributors. The EMC's task is generating orders for its clients' products through the selection of appropriate markets, distribution channels, and promotional campaigns. Additionally, it collects, analyzes, and furnishes credit information and advice regarding foreign accounts and payment terms. The EMC may also oversee trade documents, arrange transportation (including the consolidation of shipments among multiple clients to reduce costs), direct patent protection, and establish alternative business modes, such as licensing.[35]

EMCs operate on a contractual basis, often as the agent for an exporter, and they provide exclusive representation in a foreign market. Their contract with the company specifies pricing, credit and financial policies, promotional services, and method of payment. An EMC might operate on a commission basis (unless it takes title to the merchandise) and charge a retainer for other services. EMCs usually concentrate on complementary and noncompetitive products from various companies so that they can present a more complete product line to a limited number of foreign importers.

> EMCs operate on a contractual basis—usually as an agent of the exporter.

In the United States, most EMCs are entrepreneurial companies that specialize by product, function, or market area. Some EMCs are large concerns, handling lines from different manufacturers, cutting across a wide range of industries, and exporting to many countries. Other EMCs are smaller and work with a few carefully selected clients. Some EMCs specialize in certain products and/or focus on selected countries or regions, while other EMCs are generalists. Some EMCs may be involved in other export-related activities such as procurement on behalf of foreign clients. The Federation of International Trade Associations (FITA) estimates that nearly 1,000 EMCs operate in the United States and that each represents, on average, about 10 suppliers. This means that few U.S. companies use EMCs, although FITA believes that thousands more would benefit from doing so.[36]

EMCs, while versatile, are not a universal solution. EMCs, for the most part, are small, stand-alone companies with limited financial resources. Some may not be able to warehouse a company's product or offer extended in-house financing to foreign customers. EMCs focus their efforts on those products that bring them the most profits. They avoid new lines, or those with questionable potential, until market conditions call for reconsideration.

> EMCs are not a universal solution. Often they have few resources, devote too little attention, and assume too much control.

EXPORT TRADING COMPANIES   In 1982, the U.S. enacted the Export Trading Company Act, which removed some of the antitrust obstacles to the creation of ETCs. This legislation allowed the formation of ETCs by groups of competitors to market products jointly, without fear of antitrust action, as Dutch, Japanese, and British competitors have done for decades. By using ETCs without the legal barriers that constrained companies' export mobility, U.S. companies boosted their international competitiveness.

The legislation permitted banks to make equity investments in commercial ventures that qualified as ETCs—something that had been prohibited. Policymakers reasoned that permitting banks to engage in commercial nonbanking transactions in the context of an ETC would encourage more international trade transactions, thereby removing additional barriers that had diminished the export activity of U.S. companies.

Operationally, the Federal Reserve Board approves these applications before the bank can start export operations. Many banks concentrate on customers in their geographic market and in parts of the world in which they have a network in place. Banks look to ETCs to boost their performance by providing a means to extend their support beyond financing.

> ETCs are like EMCs, but they tend to operate based on demand rather than supply. They identify suppliers who can fill orders in overseas markets.

A distinction between ETCs and EMCs is that ETCs operate more on the basis of demand than supply. ETCs are like independent distributors that match buyers with sellers and, as such, see their value creation as a function of determining what foreign customers want and then identifying domestic suppliers. Therefore, rather than representing a single manufacturer, an ETC works with many manufacturers. Effectively, ETCs operate as commissioned agents, charging the seller or the buyer a percentage of the value of the export while generally avoiding carrying inventory in their own name or performing post-sale service.

Foreign Trading Companies   The only similarity between foreign trading companies and U.S. export trading companies is the designation "trading company." Exporters from Japan, Great Britain, the Netherlands, and several other trading nations found long ago that wide-reaching trading companies could market and distribute products more efficiently than a single producer. This, as noted earlier, was the basis for the legislation that permitted ETCs to operate in the United States. More recently, exporting companies from nontraditional trading countries, like Brazil, have applied this lesson to their own export promotion policies.[37]

DIRECT SELLING

Competitive pressures to improve the performance of value chains push exporters to determine the best go-to market mode. For most exporters, this quandary reduces to either (1) assembling a network of independent distributors and sales representatives stationed in key markets worldwide, such as EMCs, that manages indirect selling to local buyers, retailers, and end-users or (2) developing their own international marketing capability, charging in-house personnel to manage **direct selling** through foreign distributors.

Direct Selling through Distributors   A distributor in a foreign country is a merchant who purchases the products from the manufacturer and, based on their understanding of the local market, profitably sells them. Enlisting a sale agent usually requires that the company transfer exclusive sales rights in a particular geographic area. Some exporters prefer to have various distributors compete with other representatives who also represent the firm; this option usually dissuades potential agents. Hence, sales representatives commonly have exclusive rights to a territory. For example, Grieve's sales representatives operate exclusively in their respective markets.

Case Review Note

Evaluating Distributors   Distributors usually carry a stock of inventory as well as handle service calls. Moving product from manufacturer to customer means they must deal with larger buyers, retailers, and small end users in the market. Hence, companies identify credible distributors based on:

- Size and capabilities of its sales force
- Sales record in various product areas
- Analysis of its coverage of the targeted market territory
- Current mix of companies it represents and product it sells
- State of its warehouse facilities and logistics systems
- Record of marketing versatility and promotion successes

Direct Selling to Foreign Retailers and End Users   Increasingly, exporters opt to bypass distributors and sell directly to foreign retailers, given that it translates into greater control and higher margins. Direct selling of this sort has recently become economical due to the intersection of retail and globalization trends. The growth of global retail chains, such as Wal-Mart, Carrefour, and Ahold, facilitates the movement of products from the exporter to storefronts around the world. This option gives active exporters greater market coverage. In particular, it supports the ambitions of many born-global companies, notably those in China and other emerging markets, by providing immediate access at low cost to the worldwide market.[38]

An example of a company that sells directly to buyers is Cooley Distillery, the sole Irish-owned distiller of Irish whiskey. Cooley exports more than 80 percent of its production, up from about 25 percent in 1990. Cooley has a powerful customer list and sells in over 40 countries, including the top 25 retailers in Europe. Despite this, Cooley elected to sell the distillery, requiring that customers take title and handle shipments. Cooley maintains a small, bonded warehouse in the United Kingdom to supply just-in-time shipments to supermarket chains that order small quantities. Generally, it prefers that buyers handle shipping and storage in foreign markets.[39]

Direct Selling over the Internet E-commerce is an important means by which companies, both big and small, trade internationally. Studies show that e-commerce is easy to engage, provides faster and cheaper delivery of information, generates quick feedback on new products, improves customer service, accesses a global audience, levels the field of competition, and supports electronic data interchange (EDI) with both suppliers and customers.[40] E-commerce is especially vital to SMEs that cannot afford to establish a sales network internationally.

E-commerce is a driver of the born-global phenomenon. Going global a generation ago involved many decisions in a climate of slow-acting trade officials directing slow-moving data in tough-to-assess export markets; hence, incremental internationalization was the practical choice. Now, e-commerce, as we saw in our profile in the "Looking to the Future" insert, gives a start-up immediate global reach; hence, born global is now a practical choice.

Internet marketing is growing among export companies in emerging countries, creating virtual export channels that overcome capital and infrastructure limitations.[41] For example, exporters in Chile use extranets to communicate with importers around the world. Similarly, exporters in Costa Rica found online shops to be a good way of increasing product turnover with higher margins.[42] Finally, companies can expand their international trading by posting their home pages in different languages to target different audiences; they can install software to track site hits and then have web bots or sales representatives contact potential customers.

Concept Check

In Chapter 2, we discuss ways in which the Internet has influenced political change in potential overseas markets; in Chapter 9, we explain the impact of electronic communications on the operations of **foreign-exchange markets;** and in Chapter 11, we emphasize the importance of e-commerce in configuring and coordinating both real and virtual **value chains.** Here we report on evidence that the Internet is reshaping export and import activity by opening new markets, supporting new types of firms, and providing new sorts of tools.

The cost, flexibility, and competitive consequences of e-commerce drive the born-global phenomenon.

Internet marketing allows companies—large and small, born global or incrementally international—to engage efficiently in direct-marketing processes.

Point ▶ Counterpoint

A Dirty Dilemma: Exporting Hazardous Waste

Point ▶ **Yes** Many people see export as a positive sum process: The more companies and countries that export, the more they improve their performance, and consumers and companies worldwide get what they want—a seemingly win-win situation for everyone. However, a dark side of exporting is emerging, namely the trade of hazardous waste in the form of obsolete computer equipment. E-waste—trash composed of electronic equipment such as computers, monitors, cell phones, MP3 players, game consoles, printers, and so on—is rising. The General Accounting Office of the United States estimated that in 2006, nearly 66 million used electronic components, up from 63 million in 2005, were collected for reuse or recycling, and most were exported.[43] As shown in the major e-waste shipping routes (see Map 13.2), most is generated by developed countries and exported to developing countries.

Low labor costs, weak environmental regulations, and growing processing capacity have made Asia and Africa a

◀ Counterpoint **No** Many observers and institutions contend that growth in hazardous waste exports has created dangerous recycling industries in many countries. Electronic waste is a mixture of more than a thousand chemicals, including toxic metals (e.g., lead, barium, and mercury), acids, plastics, and chlorinated and brominated compounds. For example, an average computer monitor can contain as much as eight pounds of lead, along with plastics laden with flame retardants and cadmium. Burning electronic parts to separate copper, solder, or other metals from plastic coatings releases dioxins and other hazardous chemicals.

Most developing countries lack the regulatory codes or disposal infrastructure to safeguard people and the environment from the dangers of electronics recycling. For example, processing wastes from recycling commonly run off into municipal drains or simply drift outside the perimeter of the reclamation facility. Local air quality suffers as, for example, "circuit boards dumping ground for everything from simple computer chips to elaborate circuit boards.[44] In addition, tons of obsolete information technology ends up in shipping containers bound for China, Mali, India, and Bangladesh, among other countries. For example, some 500 containers of used electronic equipment enters Nigeria monthly, each one carrying about 800 computers, for a total of nearly 400,000 used computers. In these countries, rudimentary industries have sprung up to dismantle old computers, monitors, circuit boards, scanners, printers, routers, cell phones, and network cards for recycling.

Countries and companies find this process has several benefits. It gives them a way to meet growing social pressure to retain responsibility for the products they sell. More and more companies, such as Samsung, Mitsubishi, and Nokia, support corporate cradle-to-grave responsibility for obsolete cell phones. Today, honoring this obligation is nearly effortless, as they export the products to other, particularly poorer, countries that have an interest in and an infrastructure for recycling. Laggards, spurred by state regulation, also must accept the virtue of green recycling. Since 2004, 18 states in the United States have approved laws that make manufacturers responsible for recycling electronics; similar laws are on deck in 13 other states. Consequently, companies increasingly must take responsibility for recycling the growing torrent of toxic and outdated electronic equipment.

Disposal costs for hazardous waste in developing countries are a fraction of the cost of those in wealthier countries. As far back as 1988, disposal costs in these countries ranged from $2.50 to $50 per ton, compared with costs of $100 to $2,000 per ton in the United States, Japan, and the United Kingdom.[45] Although costs have increased in poorer countries, they have increased much faster in wealthier countries. By 2010, electronics manufacturers in the United States say a reasonable rate for collection and processing of waste is 25 to 30 cents a pound, or about $5,000 to $6,000 per ton.[46] Lower disposal costs in developing countries exist because of low or nonexistent environmental standards, less stringent laws, and absence of public opposition. Given these considerations, the economics of exporting hazardous waste from wealthy to poor countries is indisputable.

There are other benefits. Entrepreneurs in emerging markets create value for themselves and their countries by recovering, recycling, and reusing scarce resources. Copper, an increasingly valuable commodity, can represent nearly 20 percent of a mobile phone's total weight. Says Atul Maheshwar, owner of a mud-brick recycling depot in India, speaking of U.S. exports: "If your country keeps sending us the material, our business will be good."[47]

Much of the equipment shipped to Asia and Africa is from recyclers in the United States who send it abroad for repair,

are burned after acid washing, spewing deadly smoke and exposing workers and people living around these facilities."[48] Extracting the precious metals found in e-waste, such as gold and silver, often leads cash-strapped, loosely regulated reclyers to use unsafe, antiquated open-air incineration methods. Topping this witches' brew, once local scrap shops finish disassembling equipment, their trash typically goes into public landfills, their acid runoff flows into the groundwater, and the noxious fumes follow air currents. All in all, a flood of toxins that mercilessly contaminates the environment.

Though severe, agrees Madhumita Dutta of Toxics-Link Delhi, a nongovernmental organization, these problems are far less disturbing than the problems created by the "appalling" working conditions in the typical recycling facility: "Everything from dismantling the computer to pulling out . . . parts of the circuit boards to acid washing boards to recover copper is done with bare hands without any protective gear or face protection." Rare is the work site that uses safe disposal practices, thereby placing workers and society at risk as well as undermining environmental sustainablity.

What, then, of the premise of charity—that is, sending computer equipment from countries where it has little use to countries where it has tremendous use? Critics quickly shred this straw man, asserting that U.S. businesses donate obsolete equipment to emerging markets to dodge high recycling expenses. The Basel Action Network's report, "The Digital Dump: Exporting Reuse and Abuse to Africa," concludes that "too often, justifications of 'building bridges over the digital divide' are used as excuses to obscure and ignore the fact that these bridges double as toxic waste pipelines." The fact that many counties and municipalities in the United States ban outright dumping of those items in local landfills drastically boosts recycling costs.

The majority of the equipment arriving in Lagos, the study reports, is unusable and neither economically repairable nor resalable. "Nigerians are telling us they are getting as much as 75 percent junk that is not repairable . . . [and] as a result, developing nations are carrying a disproportionate burden of the world's toxic waste from technology products."[49] Other data suggest this is a pervasive problem. Inspections of 18 European seaports in 2005 found that as much as 47 percent of waste destined for export, including e-waste, was illegal.[50]

Growing fear among developing countries has prompted them to address the ceaseless waves of electronic waste shipped to their countries. The Asia-Pacific Regional Scoping Workshop on the Environmentally Sound Management of Electronic Wastes proposes that manufacturers of electronic wastes should be responsible for hazardous materials at the end of the products' lives.[51] Companies have moved in this direction, sponsoring green campaigns to recycle old technologies. Substantive progress has been slow in coming. Environmentalists recommend tougher standards to monitor, control, and certify cross-border shipments of electronic waste.

sale, or dismantling. Graham Wollaston of Scrap Computers, a recycler in Phoenix, claims there is a reuse for virtually every component of old electronic devices. For example, old televisions turn into fish tanks in Malaysia, and a silicon glass shortage has created demand for old monitors, which evolve into new ones. "There's no such thing as a third-world landfill," Mr. Wollaston explains. "If you were to put an old computer on the street, it would be taken apart for the parts." Similarly, Luc Lateille of the Canadian firm BMP Recycling says, "we don't send junk—we only send the materials that they are looking for."

Certainly, some recyclers dump useless equipment around the world that then moves into landfills. In addition, agree some, freedom from certifying the condition or destination of all the equipment creates the basis for opportunism. Still, proponents of exporting hazardous waste maintain that the system works—especially given the alternative. Regarding the latter, the U.S. Environmental Protection Agency (EPA) admits that "inappropriate practices" have occurred in the recycling industry but argues that stopping exports, besides possibly creating other problems, is not an option. ▶

Then again, presumed solutions can lead to unintended problems. The fact that many states in the United States require that companies take responsibility for recycling electronic equipment has curtailed the export of electronic waste to developing countries—but only of the more valuable components. Recycling programs cherry-pick the parts of the machines that can be refurbished for new use; if not, machines are disassembled, and their glass and precious metals are recycled. The remaining trash, typically in the form of plastics, has no reuse market and is shipped to developing countries for disposal.[52]

Others endorse worldwide compliance with the rule of the Basel Convention on the Transboundary Movement of Hazardous Wastes and Their Disposal, a UN treaty regulating the generation, management, transboundary movements, and disposal of hazardous waste. Commissioned in 1992, this treaty pushes for aggressive measures, including an international ban on the export of all hazardous wastes, no matter whether for recovery, recycling, reuse, or final disposal. As of mid-2009, 172 countries had ratified the Basel Convention. The United States, which generates approximately 60 percent of the world's hazardous waste, while endorsing the Basel Convention, has yet to ratify it.[53] ◀

MAP 13.2   Where E-Waste Gets Shipped (or Dumped)

When computers, cell phones, MP3 players, and other electronic equipment become obsolete, they are unwanted trash in developed countries. They do, however, retain some value in developing countries, and that is exactly where, as exports, they usually end up. Critics of the practice charge that most e-waste is hazardous waste and that exporters are exploiting low labor costs and lax environmental protections in destination countries.

Source: Basel Action Network; Silicon Valley Toxics Coalition.

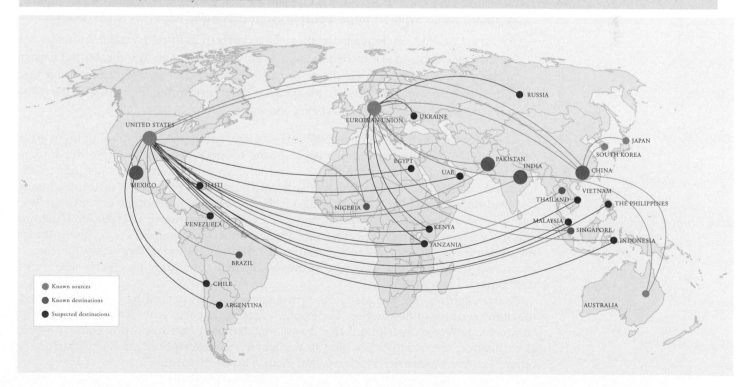

EXPORT DOCUMENTATION

Direct selling requires that the exporter comply with documents that regulate international trade. Although overlapping, duty rates, customs clearances, and entry processes differ for each country. Different tariff classifications, value declaration, and duty management increase costs. Customs and security initiatives impose new regulations on international traders. Getting past these obstacles spurs the exporter to keep track of the paper trail that documents, certifies, and legalizes export transactions. Following is a list of key documents.

- A *pro forma invoice* is a formal document from the exporter to the importer that outlines the selling terms, price, and delivery if the goods are actually shipped. If the importer likes the terms and conditions, it will send a purchase order and arrange for payment. At that point, the exporter can issue a commercial invoice.

- A *shipper's export declaration,* the most common of all export documents, is used by the exporter's government to monitor exports and to compile trade statistics.

- A *bill of lading* is a receipt for goods delivered to the common carrier for transportation, a contract for the services rendered by the carrier, and a document of title. The customer usually needs an original as proof of ownership to take possession of the goods.

- A *consular invoice* is sometimes required by countries as a means of monitoring imports. Governments can use the consular invoice to monitor prices of imports and to generate revenue for the embassies that issue this document.

- A *certificate of origin* indicates where products originate and is usually validated by an external source, such as the chamber of commerce. It helps countries determine the specific tariff schedule for imports.

- A *commercial invoice* is a bill for the goods from the seller to the buyer. It lists a description of the goods, address of buyer and seller, and delivery and payment terms. Governments commonly use this form to determine the true value of goods when assessing customs duties. Figure 13.4 shows a sample of this form, identifying the various data an exporter must report in order to comply with U.S. trade policy.

- An *export packing list* itemizes the material in each individual package, indicates the type of package, and is attached to the outside of the package. It indicates the type of package, such as a box, crate, drum, or carton. The shipper or freight forwarder, and sometimes customs officials, use the packing list to determine the nature of the cargo and whether the correct cargo is being shipped.

These forms aim to be comprehensive. For many companies, completing them accurately is time consuming and a process prone to error. Again, take another look at Figure 13.4 to get a sense of this task—and keep in mind that this is just one of the many forms required. Mistakes can arise at any number of points. For example, "many loss-and-damage challenges stem in part from the sizeable percentage of exporters that use incorrect Incoterms," reports the FedEx Trade Network's Trade & Customs Advisory Services (*Incoterms* is short for International Commercial Terms, the rules for the division of cost and risk in international sales transactions). Reporting the correct Incoterms helps exporters avoid disputes with their customers by clearly specifying each party's responsibilities.

Many exporters fail to classify their products accurately according to the tariff schedule of the country of destination. For example, goods that arrive overseas with imprecise commercial invoice descriptions that do not match those of the importing country's tariff classification are usually classified under a catchall description, such as "machinery, other." A more precise description might incur a lower duty rate.

FIGURE 13.4 Sample Commercial Invoice

Here we see a sample of the sorts of forms the United States requires exporters to complete. In this case, the sample commercial invoice, essentially a bill for the goods from the buyer to the seller, requires the exporter to provide information on the company, the goods being shipped, the addresses of active parties, and delivery and payment terms. Completing this form correctly makes for efficient transfers; completing it incorrectly results in costly delays and oftentimes higher duty charges.

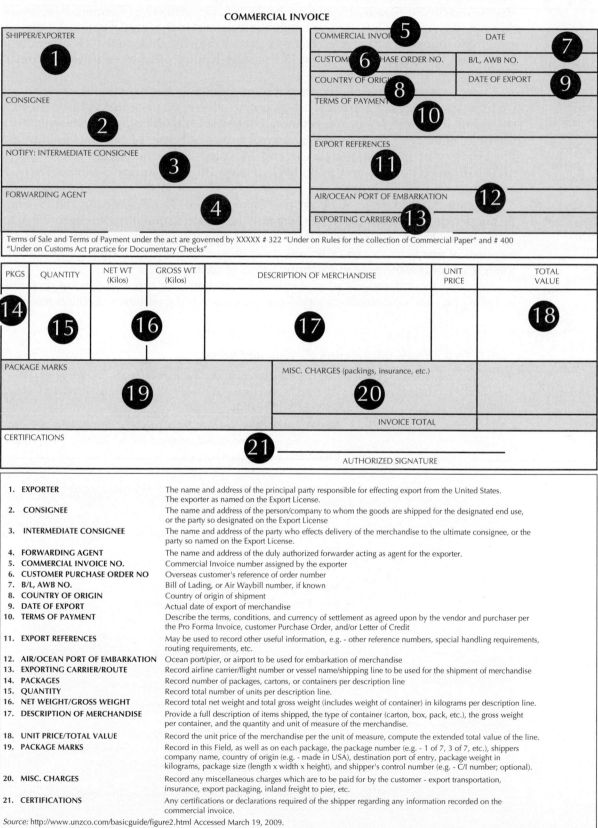

COMMERCIAL INVOICE

SHIPPER/EXPORTER ①	COMMERCIAL INVOI ⑤	DATE ⑦
	CUSTOME HASE ORDER NO. ⑥	B/L, AWB NO.
	COUNTRY OF ORIGI ⑧	DATE OF EXPORT ⑨
CONSIGNEE ②	TERMS OF PAYMEN ⑩	
NOTIFY: INTERMEDIATE CONSIGNEE ③	EXPORT REFERENCES ⑪	
FORWARDING AGENT ④	AIR/OCEAN PORT OF EMBARKATION ⑫	
	EXPORTING CARRIER/R ⑬	

Terms of Sale and Terms of Payment under the act are governed by XXXXX # 322 "Under on Rules for the collection of Commercial Paper" and # 400 "Under on Customs Act practice for Documentary Checks"

PKGS ⑭	QUANTITY ⑮	NET WT (Kilos) ⑯	GROSS WT (Kilos)	DESCRIPTION OF MERCHANDISE ⑰	UNIT PRICE	TOTAL VALUE ⑱

| PACKAGE MARKS ⑲ | MISC. CHARGES (packings, insurance, etc.) ⑳ | |
| | INVOICE TOTAL | |

CERTIFICATIONS ㉑

AUTHORIZED SIGNATURE

1. **EXPORTER** — The name and address of the principal party responsible for effecting export from the United States. The exporter as named on the Export License.
2. **CONSIGNEE** — The name and address of the person/company to whom the goods are shipped for the designated end use, or the party so designated on the Export License
3. **INTERMEDIATE CONSIGNEE** — The name and address of the party who effects delivery of the merchandise to the ultimate consignee, or the party so named on the Export License.
4. **FORWARDING AGENT** — The name and address of the duly authorized forwarder acting as agent for the exporter.
5. **COMMERCIAL INVOICE NO.** — Commercial Invoice number assigned by the exporter
6. **CUSTOMER PURCHASE ORDER NO** — Overseas customer's reference of order number
7. **B/L, AWB NO.** — Bill of Lading, or Air Waybill number, if known
8. **COUNTRY OF ORIGIN** — Country of origin of shipment
9. **DATE OF EXPORT** — Actual date of export of merchandise
10. **TERMS OF PAYMENT** — Describe the terms, conditions, and currency of settlement as agreed upon by the vendor and purchaser per the Pro Forma Invoice, customer Purchase Order, and/or Letter of Credit
11. **EXPORT REFERENCES** — May be used to record other useful information, e.g. - other reference numbers, special handling requirements, routing requirements, etc.
12. **AIR/OCEAN PORT OF EMBARKATION** — Ocean port/pier, or airport to be used for embarkation of merchandise
13. **EXPORTING CARRIER/ROUTE** — Record airline carrier/flight number or vessel name/shipping line to be used for the shipment of merchandise
14. **PACKAGES** — Record number of packages, cartons, or containers per description line
15. **QUANTITY** — Record total number of units per description line.
16. **NET WEIGHT/GROSS WEIGHT** — Record total net weight and total gross weight (includes weight of container) in kilograms per description line.
17. **DESCRIPTION OF MERCHANDISE** — Provide a full description of items shipped, the type of container (carton, box, pack, etc.), the gross weight per container, and the quantity and unit of measure of the merchandise.
18. **UNIT PRICE/TOTAL VALUE** — Record the unit price of the merchandise per the unit of measure, compute the extended total value of the line.
19. **PACKAGE MARKS** — Record in this Field, as well as on each package, the package number (e.g. - 1 of 7, 3 of 7, etc.), shippers company name, country of origin (e.g. - made in USA), destination port of entry, package weight in kilograms, package size (length x width x height), and shipper's control number (e.g. - C/I number; optional).
20. **MISC. CHARGES** — Record any miscellaneous charges which are to be paid for by the customer - export transportation, insurance, export packaging, inland freight to pier, etc.
21. **CERTIFICATIONS** — Any certifications or declarations required of the shipper regarding any information recorded on the commercial invoice.

Source: http://www.unzco.com/basicguide/figure2.html Accessed March 19, 2009.

Case Review Note

Concept Check

In Parts I and II (especially Chapters 1, 3, and 4), we underscore the fact that **international business** creates jobs, generates income, and expands national wealth. We pursue this theme in moving from Part II to Part III (Chapters 6–8) by showing how government actions shape economic environments by adopting pro-trade policies. Here we observe that governments often go to great lengths to boost the ease and efficiency of **exporting** and **importing.**

In the United States, a number of institutions, most notably the Department of Commerce and its affiliates, help firms identify and realize export and import opportunities.

SOURCES OF REGULATORY ASSISTANCE

Companies choose resources from the private and public sectors to help them navigate the trade regulations. Our look at Grieve highlighted the assistance provided by the International Trade Administration of the Chicago Export Assistance Center and the Agent/Distributor Search program run by the U.S. Department of Commerce (accessible through www.export.gov). Traders tap public resources in the form of national, state, and local trade offices, in addition to resources provided by freight forwarders, international banks, and trade consultants. Table 13.4 profiles leading sources and their customary services.

Federal, state, and local governments, recognizing the benefits of international trade, aid potential and active exporters and, to a lesser degree, protect the interests of struggling importers. Japan, for instance, relies on several offices, such as the Small and Medium Enterprise Agency, the Agency of Industrial Science and Technology, and the Ministry of International Trade and Industry. The latter, often referred to as *MITI*, develops policies and provides assistance to help Japanese companies trade internationally.

Programs in the United States provide financial help. The Ex-Im Bank and the Small Business Administration (SBA), for instance, help international traders secure private sector loans. These and related federal agencies help arrange financing for manufacturing costs of goods for export or the purchase of goods or services. They also assist with foreign accounts receivable and standby letters of credit.

Similarly, most states and several cities fund and operate export financing programs, including pre- and post-shipment working-capital loans and guarantees, accounts receivable

TABLE 13.4   Trade Information by Type and Source

If your company is thinking about getting into export, various organizations and agencies offer assistance.

Source	Types of Assistance
Government Agencies	• Market demographics, product demand, and competition • Complying with domestic and foreign trade regulations • Customs, regulatory, and tax issues • Sales financing, credit, and insurance • Guidance for developing your strategy and marketing plan from trade specialists and commercial officers • Trade events, partners, and trade leads • Shipping documentation and requirements • Pricing, quotes, and negotiations • Step-by-step guides to exporting and importing
Trade Associations	• Market demographics, product demand, and competition • Export training seminars online and on-site • Advertising and sales promotion alternatives • Profile distribution channels and logistics networks • Customs regulations and tax issues; compliance with global trade laws • Navigating homeland security programs • Standardizing and streamlining trade processes
Trade Intermediaries	• Customs management system, trade compliance, tariff classification and rulings • Legal, accounting, security, and tax compliance • Software solutions; secure electronic procurement, transport, and logistics management; automated supply chain process • Trade finance, credit scoring, and insurance • Infrastructure for global business-to-business procurement of goods

financing, and export insurance. The limited reserves of some states and cities force them to make their assistance contingent on the exporter's proof that they do not risk losing much if the deal fails. An exporter need only provide proof of a letter of credit or sufficient credit insurance to satisfy this requirement (Chapter 19 examines export financing). In some situations, states and cities require the exporter to transact part of the export deal within the jurisdiction of the funding authority. Often, meeting this call for local content can be done by using local transportation facilities, such as an airport or seaport.

Freight Forwarders

Companies that sell directly to foreign customers but are reluctant to supervise the transport of goods often hire a freight forwarder. Popularly known as the "travel agents of cargo," freight forwarders help traders move shipments to and from foreign suppliers. A **freight forwarder** is an agent for the exporter who takes responsibility for moving cargo to an overseas destination.[54] The freight forwarder is used for both imports and exports, given that one company's exports are another company's imports.

Forwarder Functions Freight forwarders make up the largest export intermediary in terms of the value and weight of products shipped internationally. Generally, the services they offer are more limited than those of an EMC. Typically, upon finalizing a foreign sale, an exporter hires a freight forwarder to arrange the fastest, cheapest transportation method. The freight forwarder, balancing the constraints of space availability, speed, and cost, identifies the optimal path to move products from the manufacturing facility to the truck, rail, air or ocean terminal, through customs, and onto the foreign buyer.

In the same process, the freight forwarder secures space on trucks, planes, railcars, or ships, and in storage prior to shipment, reviews the letter of credit, obtains export licenses, pays consular fees, secures special documentation, and prepares required shipping documents. It also may advise on packing and labeling, purchase of transportation insurance, repacking of shipments damaged en route, and warehousing products. However, a freight forwarder does not take ownership title to the goods or act as a sales representative in a foreign market—that falls in the realm of the EMC or ETC.

TRANSPORTATION OPTIONS Freight forwarders, especially smaller ones, sometimes specialize in a transportation mode—surface freight, ocean freight, or airfreight—along with a primary geographical area—e.g., Asia or Europe. Increasingly, the efficiencies of the Internet and telecommunications enable freight forwarders to manage a variety of transportation modes traveling to and from any port in the world.[55]

The movement of goods across different modes, from origin to destination, is known as **intermodal transportation.** Ocean freight is the cheapest way to move merchandise. Although the slowest, ocean freight predominates due to containerization. This particular transport mode is built on the platform of standard ISO containers that can be loaded and sealed intact onto container ships, railroad cars, planes, and trucks. Freight forwarders commonly refer to these containers in terms of 20-foot equivalent units (TEU)—a 20 × 8 × 8-foot box—the number of which define a ship's cargo carrying capacity or a shipping terminal's cargo handling capacity. Containerization has revolutionized cargo shipping, powering tremendous efficiencies in loading, cargo volume, and unloading. Today, approximately 90 percent of nonbulk cargo worldwide moves by TEU containers.

Basic supply and demand for container space, in terms of the ports and the direction the goods travel, determine shipping costs. For example, different rates apply to shipments from the United States to China and to shipments from China to the United States. Shipping one container of furniture (total volume weight 30,000 pounds or 13,607.91 kilos) from Philadelphia to Shanghai costs U.S. $2,019. The shipping charge for the same cargo, but from Shanghai to Philadelphia, is $3,555.[56] The comparative volume of exports from China to the United States, and the corresponding higher demand for

A foreign freight forwarder is an export or import specialist dealing in the movement of goods from producer to consumer.

Primary transportation modes include

- Surface freight (truck and rail), ocean freight, and airfreight.
- Intermodal transportation—the movement across different modes from origin to destination.

container space, drives the different charges. One way to keep track of prevailing shipping rates is to monitor the **Baltic Dry Freight Index.** Issued daily by the London-based Baltic Exchange, this index provides an assessment of the price of moving major raw materials— such oil, coal, iron ore, and grain—by sea, as determined by shipping rates charged on 26 major sea routes.

Despite the cost advantage of containerization, the airfreight business thrives, given the needs for frequent, lighter-weight, and higher-value shipments. The trends toward global manufacturing and integrated global supply chains spur airfreight traffic. Because of these trends, airfreight is sometimes more effective than ocean freight.

Freight Forwarder Fees   The freight forwarder usually charges the exporter a percentage of the shipment value, plus a minimum charge depending on the number of services provided. The forwarder also receives a brokerage fee from the carrier. Most companies, especially SMEs, find it costly to dedicate a department to deal with freight-forwarding issues. In addition, forwarders' expertise enables them to secure shipping space at better rates as well the flexibility to consolidate shipments for less than TEU-sized orders. Consequently, it is usually less expensive for an exporter, particularly SMEs, to outsource shipment supervision to a freight forwarder.

Freight Forwarders and 3PLs   Earlier, we profiled the growing role of 3PLs— **third-party logistics** companies—in the movement of goods across borders. Recall that successful 3PLs work in partnership with manufacturers, shippers, and retailers to relieve them of distribution headaches. The value proposition of a 3PL is not simply that it commands a fleet of trucks and planes or that it operates that fleet more efficiently. Rather, a 3PL offers logistics expertise that drives greater efficiencies throughout the client's distribution systems.

Expanding globalization and trade liberalization accelerates the outsourcing of logistics operations to 3PLs. The global Fortune 500 third-party logistics market grew to $200 billion in 2008.[57] Nearly 80 percent of domestic Fortune 500 companies use 3PL providers for logistics and supply-chain functions; Procter & Gamble, Wal-Mart, PepsiCo, and Ford, for example, each use the services of 30 or more 3PLs. Manufacturers and retailers agree that 3PLs are winning their business at the expense of traditional freight forwarders. In response, traditional freight-forwarding companies are expanding beyond their historic role as "travel agents of cargo" to offer "third-party" support for multiple phases of the distribution process and, ultimately, a company's logistics function.

Countertrade

Currency is the preferred payment medium for any export or import transaction—it is easy, fast, and straightforward. Sometimes, though, companies face buyers that cannot pay in cash, either because their home country's currency is nonconvertible or because the country does not have enough cash or credit. In addition, other situations such as resolving bad debts, repatriating blocked funds, or building customer relationships push companies to accept alternative forms of payment.

Companies and countries sometimes cannot generate the foreign exchange to pay for imports. The collapse in bank lending in 2009 meant many countries struggled to secure credit. Failure pushed them to resort to countertrade deals to buy all sorts of products. For example, Malaysia announced that it had signed a deal swapping palm oil for fertilizer and machinery with North Korea. Russia was negotiating with Morocco, Jordan, Syria, and Iran about similar deals. Thailand, the world's largest exporter of rice, negotiated barter deals with Middle Eastern countries, whereas the Philippines, the world's largest importer of rice, secured rice supplies through an agreement with Vietnam.[58] Finally, on a more exotic note, Pepsi-Cola, which has the marketing rights for all Stolichnaya Vodka in the United States, delivers syrup that is

TABLE 13.5 Common Types of Countertrade

While one would think it rather straightforward to exchange produces that are paid for, in whole or part, with other products, there are actually several options. The list below identifies the most common mechanisms.

Barter	Transaction in which products are exchanged directly for products of equal value without the use of money as a means of purchase or payment.
Buyback	Transaction in which a supplier of capital or equipment agrees to accept future output generated by the investment as payment. For example: The exporter of equipment to a chemical plant may be repaid with output from the factory to whose owner it "sold" the equipment.
Offset	Transaction in which an exporter sells products for cash and then helps the importer find opportunities to earn hard currency for payment. For example: Offsets are most common when big-ticket products (e.g., military equipment) are involved.
Switch Trading	Transaction (also known as a *swap* deal) in which one company sells to another its obligation to purchase something in a foreign country; so called because the arrangement often involves switching the documentation and destination of merchandise while it's in transit.
Counter Purchase	Transaction in which a company that sells products to a foreign country promises to make a future purchase of a specific product made in that country; in short, a supplier agrees to purchase products from a foreign buyer as a condition of getting the buyer's order.

paid for with Stolichnaya Vodka. In addition, early on, Pepsi took delivery of 17 submarines, a cruiser, a frigate, and a destroyer from the Russian government in payment for Pepsi products. In turn, Pepsi then sold its "fleet" of 20 naval vessels for scrap steel.[59]

These sorts of trades fall under the umbrella term **countertrade,** which refers to any one of several different arrangements that parties use to trade products with limited or no use of currency. We partition countertrade into two classes: barter, based on clearing arrangements used to avoid money-based exchange, and buybacks, offsets, and counter purchases, which are used to impose reciprocal commitments between the various parties.[60] Table 13.5 profiles common types of countertrade.

Inconsistent disclosure makes it tough to gauge the volume of countertrade. Secretive government-to-government deals and disguised transactions are not unusual. The WTO estimates that countertrade accounts for around 5 percent of world trade, whereas the British Department of Trade and Industry has suggested as much as 15 percent. The general consensus is that countertrade is somewhere between 10 and 20 percent of all world trade.[61] No matter the absolute size, the fact that countertrade generally increases in economies that are experiencing economic problems makes it an enduring feature of international trade.

Countertrade has unique costs and benefits. Specifically:

Inefficient Companies prefer the efficiency of cash or credit. In the case of countertrade, rather than simply consulting current foreign-exchange rates to set the terms of the deal, buyers and sellers negotiate a fair value on the exchange—how many tons of rice for how many farm tractors, for example. In some situations, the goods sent as payment may be of poor quality, packaged unattractively, or difficult to sell and service. In addition, there is a lot of room for price and financial distortion in countertrade deals, given that nonmarket forces set the prices of these goods. Ultimately, countertrade and its variations threaten free markets with protectionism and price-fixing.

Flexibility Countertrade is often unavoidable for companies that want to do business in markets that have limited or no access to cash or credit. Some companies and countries prefer countertrade to preserve their limited monetary assets, generate foreign exchange,

Countertrade is an umbrella term for several sorts of trade, such as barter or offset, in which the seller accepts goods or services, rather than currency or credit, in payment for its products.

Concept Check

Recall our discussions of poverty in Chapters 4 and 5. Here we point out that shortages of resources impoverish nations as well as individuals. Some countries, for example, struggle to acquire the foreign reserves they need to purchase goods from other nations. When they are unsuccessful in this effort, they often turn to such methods that qualify as **countertrade.** In Chapter 9, we show how and why companies conducting international business must deal with the implications of such economic conditions (e.g., exchange rate and capital fluctuations) in foreign markets.

Alibaba offers new channels to trade services. For example, the classic home inventor in, say, Caracas or Chicago now has the option to design a product and then use Alibaba to find Chinese factories to manufacture and ship to customers worldwide.

Operationally, buyers around the world use Alibaba to find potential suppliers that often have some of the lowest costs in the world. This feature then eliminates the need to hire a representative in China to buy directly from the manufacturers on their behalf. So, for example, an enterprising company in Argentina looking to buy 500 DVD players can visit Alibaba.com, search among the dozens of potential suppliers, learn their terms of trade, contact the preferred vendor, and set the deal in motion. Said the cofounder of www.meetchina.com, a similar e-commerce site, "We want to make buying 1,000 bicycles from China as easy as buying a book from Amazon.com."

Historically, an importer often worried about being defrauded by an unknown supplier—that is, how does an importer from Buenos Aires find a trustworthy supplier in Guangzhou? Increasingly, as sites like Alibaba inject more transparency into trade, buyers worry less about fraud. Users of Alibaba, like those on similar e-commerce sites, post information about their companies on the site and access information about the reliability of other users.

Buyers can access Alibaba's basic screening and background checks on its registered users. Too, buyers can access the seller's posted references, like one from the seller's bank, to verify the seller's status. Collectively, these data let the importer in Argentina cross-check potential trade partners in China, quickly getting a sense of their credibility.

This system of checks and balances is how Alibaba makes money. It offers a basic service of listing a company and its products on its Web site free of charge. It then generates revenue from the 85,000 members who pay $300 to $10,000 a year for services such as personalized Web pages, high-quality online introduction, and priority listing of products.

The global financial crisis, Jack Ma reasoned, created an opportunity to transform Alibaba.com from a China-focused e-commerce provider into a global Web marketplace. "Before this financial crisis, we were helping China's products abroad. Now we are thinking about helping small and medium-sized enterprises in other parts of the world," said Mr. Ma. Too, he saw the chance to expand the historic outward flow of China products to the world to include flows throughout the world. "We want to help them sell across the nations, help them sell to China," Mr. Ma explained. "I believe in the next three years, China will be one of the world's largest buying markets. China needs to buy these things."

Technology creates many opportunities for international traders. In the past, globalization gave a disproportionate amount of power and benefits to large companies. Large companies relied on their well-equipped international divisions to supervise imports and exports. Today, the Internet diffuses opportunities throughout the world in ways that give the smallest trader easy, cheap, and direct access to the biggest markets. ■

QUESTIONS

1. Visit www.alibaba.com, go to the "Advanced Search" box, and enter the product you seek. Select required criteria and click on "Search." Review the list of companies that qualify and find a suitable one. Analyze this process for ease, usefulness, and potential value.

2. List, in separate columns, the benefits and costs of using sites like Alibaba to trade internationally. What does your analysis say to companies like Grieve (our opening case) as they think about their export strategy?

3. Visit www.alibaba.com, www.trade-india.com, and www.tradekey.com. Compare and contrast their features.

4. Is it reasonable to speculate that eventually most trade between companies might take place in the context of sites like Alibaba.com?

5. How transparent do sites like Alibaba.com make the import-export transaction? Would you still worry about fraud?

6. How might the global financial crisis create opportunities and threats for Alibaba.com?

SUMMARY

- Exporting refers to the sale of goods or services produced by a company based in one country to customers that reside in a different country. Importing is purchase of products by a company based in one country from sellers that reside in another.

- Export intensity—the share of output that a firm exports is (1) related to but not determined by its size and (2) related to and often determined by a range of firm-specific features like management interest, production efficiency, low labor costs, and low R&D demands.

- The incremental internationalization view holds that exporting begins as a sequential process that leads a company to expand from its home market to the most proximate (geographically and socially) and then progressively to increasingly distant and dissimilar countries.

- The born-global perspective on export development holds that companies step straight onto the world stage, exporting from day one of operations.

- The idea of serendipity refers to so-called accidental exporters who, responding to happenstance or odd circumstances, enter overseas markets by chance.

- Born-globals and incremental exporters design export strategies to leverage assets and avoid pitfalls.

- As a company builds its export business plan, it assesses export potential, obtains expert counseling, selects a country or countries where it will focus its exports, formulates its strategy, and determines how to get its goods to market.

- Importers improve the odds of success by studying strategic issues (importing vs. buying domestically) and procedural issues (the steps needed to get goods into the country).

- Customs agencies assess and collect duties as well as ensure compliance with import regulations.

- An import broker helps by valuing products to qualify for more favorable duty treatment, qualifying products for duty refunds through drawback provisions, deferring duties by using bonded warehouses and foreign trade zones, and limiting liability by properly marking an import's country of origin.

- Exporters may deal directly with agents or distributors in a foreign country or indirectly through third-party intermediaries such as export management companies or other types of trading companies.

- Internet marketing is a form of direct exporting that allows companies to access export markets at low cost but with high impact.

- Trading companies perform many of the functions for which manufacturers lack expertise. In addition, exporters use the services of other specialists, such as freight forwarders, to facilitate exporting. These specialists help an exporter with the documentation that accompanies exports.

- All services that do not result in ownership and that are rendered by nonresidents to the local residents in a country qualify as service imports.

- Government agencies in some countries provide assistance in terms of direct loans to importers, bank guarantees to fund an exporter's working capital needs, and insurance against commercial and political risk.

- Freight forwarders, the "travel agents of cargo," act as agents for international traders in supervising the movement of cargo to overseas destinations.

- Third-party logistics (or 3PLs) develop state-of-the-art technology to help companies understand trade practices, identify opportunities, manage risks, and shepherd exports and imports from buyers to sellers.

- Countertrade is any one of several different arrangements by which products are traded, either bilaterally or multilaterally, in transactions that do not involve cash or credit.

- Barter means trading products for goods or services. Offsets are agreements by which the exporter helps the importer earn foreign exchange or the transfer of technology or production to the importing country.

KEY TERMS

Baltic Dry Freight Index
   (p. 550)
born global (p. 526)
countertrade (p. 551)
customs agencies (p. 536)
direct exports (p. 539)
direct selling (p. 542)
export intensity (p. 526)
export intermediaries (p. 540)

export management company
   (EMC) (p. 541)
export strategy (p. 530)
export trading company (ETC) (p. 541)
exporting (p. 522)
freight forwarder (p. 549)
import broker (customs broker)
   (p. 535)
import strategy (p. 533)

importing (p. 522)
incremental internationalization (p. 526)
indirect exports (p. 539)
indirect selling (p. 539)
intermodal transportation (p. 549)
serendipity (p. 525)
small and medium-sized enterprise
   (SME) (p. 521)
third-party logistics (p. 538)

ENDNOTES

1 *Sources include the following:* Grieve Corp., at www.grievecorp.com (accessed June 2005, March 2007, April 2009); U.S. Census Bureau, *Profile of U.S. Exporting Companies* (2002–2003), at www.census.gov/foreign-trade/aip/edbrel-0203.pdf; *Small & Medium-Sized Exporting Companies: Statistical Overview* (2003), at www.ita.doc.gov/TD/Industry/OTEA/sme_handbook/SME_index.htm.

2 Comments extracted from company materials posted at www.grievecorp.com (accessed July 14, 2007).

3 D. D. Chadee and J. Mattsson, "Do Service and Merchandise Exporters Behave and Perform Differently? A New Zealand Investigation," *European Journal of Marketing* 32 (1998): 830.

4 John H. Dunning, "The Eclectic Paradigm of International Production: Some Empirical Tests," *Journal of International Business Studies* 12 (Spring 1988): 1–31.

5 S. Agarwal and S. Ramaswami, "Choice of Foreign Market Entry Mode: Impact of Ownership, Location and Internalization Factors," *Journal of International Business Studies* 23:1 (1992): 2–5.

6 U.S. Department of Commerce, *Guide to Exporting, 1998* (Washington, DC: U.S. Department of Commerce and Unz & Co. Inc., November 1997): 3.

7 W. Chan Kim and Peter Hwang, "Global Strategy and Multinationals' Entry Mode Choice," *Journal of International Business Studies* 23:1 (1992): 32–35.

8 Mark Stein, "Export Opportunities Aren't Just for the Big Guys," *New York Times* (March 24, 2005):A-15.

9 A. Bonaccorsi, "On the Relationship between Firm Size and Export Intensity," *Journal of International Business Studies* 23:4 (1992): 606.

10 Paul Magnusson, "The Split-Up That's Slanting the Trade Deficit," *Business Week* (June 7, 1999): 38.

11 Hernan G. Roxas, Vai Lindsay, Nicholas Ashill, and Antong Victorio, "Institutional Analysis of Strategic Choice of Micro, Small, and Medium Enterprises: Development of a Conceptual Framework," *Singapore Management Review* 30.2 (July–December 2008): 47; Nancy Ku, "SMEs Look to Non-Traditional Lenders," *China Brief*, American Chamber of Commerce in China (March 2009).

12 David Greenway, Joakim Gullstrand, and Richard Kneller, "Exporting May Not Always Boost Firm Productivity," *Review of World Economics* 4 (December 1, 2005): 561–582.

13 L. Yun, "Determinants of Export Intensity and FDI Presence: Case of Manufacturing Industries of Guangdong Province, the People's Republic of China," *International Journal of Logistics Systems and Management* 2:3 (2006): 230–54.

14 D. Crick, "U.K. SMEs' Motives for Internationalizing: Differences between Firms Employing Particular Overseas Market Servicing Strategies," *Journal of International Entrepreneurship* 5:1–2 (2007): 11–23.

15 Julia Armario, David M. Ruiz, and Enrique M. Armario, "Market Orientation and Internationalization in Small and Medium-Sized Enterprises," *Journal of Small Business Management* 46 (October 2008): 485.

16 Paul Westhead, Mike Wright, and Deniz Ucbasaran, "International Market Selection Strategies Selected by 'Micro' and 'Small' Firms," *Omega* 30 (February 2002): 51.

17 Oystein Moen, Roger Sorbeim, and Truls Erikson, "Born Global Firms and Informal Investors: Examining Investor Characteristics," *Journal of Small Business Management* 46 (October 2008): 536.

18 Hans-Georg Gemunden, "Success Factors of Export Marketing: A Meta-Analytic Critique of the Empirical Studies," in *New Perspectives on International Marketing*, S. Paliwoda (ed.) (London: Routledge, 1991): 33–62.

19 "Congress Pushes More Export Financing for Small Business," *Business Week* (September 5, 2006) www.businessweek.com/smallbiz/running_small_business/archives/2009/10/government_push.html (accessed March 4, 2007).

20 John Kerr, "Exporters Need to Connect with Customers," *Logistics Management* (March 1, 2006): 41.

21 "Most Common Mistakes of New-to-Export Ventures," *Business America* (April 16, 1984): 9.

22 Stein, "Export Opportunities Aren't Just for the Big Guys."

23 Benson Smith and Tony Rutigliano, *Discover Your Sales Strengths* (New York: Warner Business Books, 2003).

24 Paul Beamish et al., "The Relationship between Organizational Structure and Export Performance," *Management International Review* 39:1 (1999): 51.

25 U.S. Department of the Treasury, U.S. Customs Service, *Importing into the United States* (Washington, DC: U.S. Government Printing Office, September 1991).

26 Because a practical discussion of importing procedures in every trading country of the world is impossible within this chapter, we focus on the matter of importing to the United States. We note that although U.S. import requirements and procedures provide a sufficient base for judging situations in other countries, a company must assess the importing regulations applicable to those countries in which it plans to engage. For an organizational chart of the U.S. Customs Bureau, including a roster of specific responsibilities, go to the home page of the U.S. Bureau of Customs and Border Protection, at www.customs.ustreas.gov.

27 The International Bank for Reconstruction and Development/The World Bank, "Doing Business."

28 Julie Sloane, Justin Martin, and Alessandra Bianchi, "Small Companies That Play Big," *FSB Magazine* (November 1, 2006): 34, quoting Ram Iyer.

29 Sloane, Martin, and Bianchi, "Small Companies That Play Big," quoting Everette Phillips.

30 International Bank/World Bank, "Doing Business in 2007," 43.

31 Kerr, "Exporters Need to Connect with Customers."

32 Lee Li, "Joint Effects of Factors Affecting Exchanges between Exporters and Their Foreign Intermediaries: An Exploratory Study," *Journal of Business & Industrial Marketing* 18 (February–March 2003): 162–78.

33 Kerr, "Exporters Need to Connect with Customers."

34 "Basic Question: To Export Yourself or to Hire Someone to Do It for You?" *Business America* (April 27, 1987): 14–17.

35 See U.S. Department of Commerce, *Guide to Exporting* (1998): 20; Philip MacDonald, *Practical Exporting and Importing*, 2nd ed. (New York: Ronald Press, 1959): 30–40 (accessed October, 23, 2004).

36 Courtney Fingar, "ABCs of EMCs," The Federation of International Trade Associations (July 2001), at http://fita.org/emc.html; Nelson T. Joyner, "How to Find and Use an Export Management Company" (April 1999), at www.fita.org/aotm/0499.html.

37 One anomaly to note are Japanese trading companies such as Mitsubishi, Mitsui, and Itochu, which are huge conglomerates with marketing, financial, and distribution arms with truly global reach. In 1995, these three Japanese companies were the top three companies on *Fortune* magazine's list of the 500 largest global companies. By 2004, though, none of these three remained anywhere near the top, and all trading companies from Japan, Korea, Germany, etc. have tumbled as a result of new accounting rules that significantly lowered their revenues. Previously, foreign trading companies booked the gross value of their trades as revenue, but now they comply with U.S. Generally Accepted Accounting Principles and report transactions on a net basis.

38 Jiang Jingjing, "Wal-Mart's China Inventory to Hit U.S. $18B This Year," *China Business Weekly* (November 29, 2004), at www .chinadaily.com.cn/english/doc/2004–11/29/content_395728.htm (accessed July 13, 2006).

39 John Daniels' interview with John Teeling, executive chairman of Cooley Distillery (2002).

40 A. J. Campbell, "Ten Reasons Why Your Business Should Use Electronic Commerce," *Business America* (May 1998): 12–14.

41 Anna Morgan-Thomas and Susan Bridgewater, "Internet and Exporting: Determinants of Success in Virtual Export Channels," *International Marketing Review* 21:4 (2004): 393.

42 Merlin Bettina, "Internet Marketing in Exports—A Useful Tool for Small Businesses," *Small Enterprise Development*, 15 (December 2004): 38.

43 J. Laurie Flynn, "Poor Nations Are Littered with Old PC's, Report Says," *New York Times* (October 24, 2005): A-1.

44 Helen Baulch, "Error: Dumping Does Not Compute," *Alternatives Journal* (Summer 2002): 2.

45 Zada Lipman, "A Dirty Dilemma: The Hazardous Waste Trade," *Harvard International Review* 23 (2002): 67.

46 Leslie Kaufman, "A Green Way to Dump Low-Tech Electronics," *New York Times* (June 30, 2009).

47 Reported by Karl Schoenberger, "E-Waste Ignored in India," *Mercury News*, at www.ban.org/ban_news/ ewaste_ignored_031228.html (accessed July 21, 2007).

48 Baulch, "Error: Dumping Does Not Compute."

49 Basel Action Network, at www.ban.org/index.html (May 5, 2007); Flynn, "Poor Nations Are Littered with Old PC's" (accessed July 21, 2007).

50 "Where Does E-Waste End Up?" at www.greenpeace.org/ international/campaigns/toxics/electronics/where-does-e-waste- end-up (accessed July 21, 2007).

51 "E-Waste Importers," *Hazardous Waste Superfund Week* (December 23, 2002): 5.

52 L. Kaufman, "A Green Way to Dump Low-Tech Electronics."

53 See "Secretariat of the Basel Convention, Competent Authorities," Membership List at www.basel.int (accessed March 26, 2009). By definition, a "Competent Authority" means one governmental authority designated by a party to be responsible within such geographic areas as the party may think fit, for receiving the notifi- cation of a transboundary movement of hazardous wastes or other wastes, and any information related to it, and for responding to such a notification.

54 U.S. Department of Commerce, *Guide to Exporting* (1998): 63.

55 Helen Richardson, "Freight Forwarder Basics: Contract Negotiation," *Transportation & Distribution* (May 1996), available in Lexis/Nexis News: CURNWS (accessed June 3, 2005).

56 Estimates calculated on May 15, 2007, at www.freight- calculator.com/apxocean.asp.

57 "Global 3PLs Grew 6.5 Percent," (January 29, 2009), at http://www.joc.com/ (accessed March 24, 2009).

58 Javier Blas, "Nations Turn to Barter Deals to Secure Food," *Financial Times* (January 26, 2009), at http://www.ft.com/ cms/s/0/3e5c633c-ebdc-11dd-8838-0000779fd2ac.html (accessed March 11, 2009).

59 Dan West, "Countertrade—An Innovative Approach to Marketing," at www.barternews.com/approach_marketing.htm (accessed May 15, 2007).

60 J. F. Hennart, "Some Empirical Dimensions of Countertrade," *Journal of International Business Studies* 21 (1990): 243–70.

61 West, "Countertrade—An Innovative Approach to Marketing."

62 *Sources include the following:* Various sources at www.Alibaba.com; Forbes Global (April 25, 2005): 30; Trade Stats Express, at http://tse.export.gov (accessed July 1, 2009); John Heilemann, "Jack Ma Aims to Unlock the Middle Kingdom," *Business 2.0 Magazine* (July 31, 2006): 22; Jack Ma, "China Discovers Its Future," *International Herald Tribune* (December 17, 2008); "Alibaba Prepares for Global Expansion," *Financial Times* (January 19, 2009).

63 For example, the U.S. Small Business Administration estimates that the number of small businesses exporting products tripled from 1994 through 2004. In terms of monetary flows, the value of exports from the United States grew from $731 billion in 2001 to $1.03 trillion in 2006, and imports grew from $1.14 to $1.9 trillion over the same period.

There are also financial considerations. A company depending substantially on local financing rather than on transferring capital may find local capital suppliers more willing to put money into a known ongoing operation than to invest with a foreign enterprise that they know less well. In addition, a foreign company may merge with an existing company through an exchange of stock.

In other ways, acquisitions may reduce costs and risks—and save time. A company may be able to buy facilities, particularly those of a poorly performing operation, for less than the cost of new construction. If an investor fears that a market does not justify added capacity, acquisition enables it to avoid the risk of depressed prices through overcapacity. Finally, by buying a company, an investor avoids inefficiencies during the start-up period and gets an immediate cash flow rather than tying up funds during construction.

Making Greenfield Investments   Although acquisitions offer advantages, companies frequently invest in sectors where there are few, if any, companies operating, so finding a company to buy may be difficult. In addition, local governments may prevent acquisitions because they want more competitors in the market and fear market dominance by a single foreign enterprise.

Even if acquisitions are available, they often don't succeed.[23] First, turning around a poorly performing operation is difficult because it may have personnel and labor relations problems, ill will toward its products and brands, and inefficient or poorly located facilities. Second, managers in the acquiring and acquired companies may not work well together because of different management styles and organizational cultures or because of conflicts over decision-making authority.[24] In this respect, intuition tells us that acquisitions in more culturally distant countries would perform less well than those in more culturally similar countries; however, evidence shows the contrary. This disparity is likely due to a combination of factors, such as organizational gains from added diversity, greater care in selection in culturally dissimilar countries (particularly to get a better match between organizational cultures), and less attempt to integrate these operations into the corporate culture.[25] Finally, a foreign company may find local financing easier to obtain from development banks if it builds facilities because of being able to show that it is creating employment.

Companies may choose to build if

- No desired company is available for acquisition.
- Acquisition will lead to carryover problems.
- Acquisition is harder to finance.

Why Companies Collaborate

Companies collaborate abroad for much the same reasons as they do domestically. In our opening case, for example, we saw that Coca-Cola franchises most of its bottling operations in both the United States and foreign countries. However, companies also collaborate abroad for some additional reasons. For example, one of the reasons that Coca-Cola established a joint venture in India was because Indian law prohibited its gaining 100 percent ownership.

Figure 14.3 shows both the general and internationally specific reasons for collaborative arrangements.

ALLIANCE TYPES

Some different terms are used to describe alliances based on their objectives and where they fit in a firm's value chain. In terms of objectives, *scale alliances* aim at providing efficiency through the pooling of similar assets so that partners can carry out business activities in which they already have experience. For example, Coca-Cola and Procter & Gamble allied to gain distribution economies by combining grocery sales of Coca-Cola's juices and Procter & Gamble's snacks.

FIGURE 14.3 Collaborative Arrangements and International Objectives

A company may enter into a collaborative arrangement for the same *general* reason that it may enter into a domestic arrangement (e.g., to spread costs). In other cases, it may enter into a collaborative arrangement to meet objectives that are *specific* to its foreign-expansion strategies (e.g., to diversify geographically).

OBJECTIVES OF INTERNATIONAL BUSINESS
- Sales expansion
- Resource acquisition
- Risk minimization

MOTIVES FOR COLLABORATIVE ARRANGEMENTS
General
- Spread and reduce costs
- Specialize in competencies
- Avoid or counter competition
- Secure vertical and horizontal links
- Learn from other companies

MOTIVES FOR COLLABORATIVE ARRANGEMENTS
Specific to International Business
- Gain location-specific assets
- Overcome legal constraints
- Diversify geographically
- Minimize exposure in risky environments

Link alliances use complementary resources so that participating companies can expand into new business areas.[26] For example, GM entered a joint venture with Russian AvtoVAZ. GM gained production of AvtoVAZ's low-priced vehicle to sell in developing countries, and AvtoVAZ gained GM's financial and technical resources to make sport utility vehicles in Russia.

While we're on the subject, it's probably worthwhile to take a quick look back at our opening case. In terms of its value chain, Coke's typical franchising arrangement with bottlers calls for a type of *vertical alliance*, because each partner functions on a different level of the value chain. Its partnership with Inca Kola, in contrast, calls for a *horizontal alliance*, because it extends Coca-Cola's operations on the same level of the value chain.

Case Review Note

GENERAL MOTIVES FOR COLLABORATIVE ARRANGEMENTS

In this section, we explain the reasons that companies collaborate with other companies in either domestic or foreign operations: to spread and reduce costs, to allow them to specialize in their competencies, to avoid competition, to secure vertical and horizontal links, and to gain knowledge.

To Spread and Reduce Costs To produce or sell abroad, a company must incur certain fixed costs. At a small volume of business, it may be cheaper for it to contract the work to a specialist rather than handle it internally. A specialist can spread the fixed costs to more than one company. If business increases enough, the contracting company may then be able to handle the business more cheaply itself.

If a company has excess production or sales capacity, it can use that excess to handle the activities for a client company. This may lower its average costs by covering its fixed costs more fully, and it will prevent the client from having to incur fixed costs and longer delays for start-up and receipt of cash flows.

In addition, individual companies may lack the resources to "go it alone"—especially small and young companies.[27] By pooling their efforts, they may be able to undertake activities that otherwise would be beyond their means. But large companies may also benefit when the cost of development and/or investment is very high. For example, the

Concept Check

We introduce the idea of the **value chain** in Chapter 11, where we explain how a company configures its global value chain by organizing a series of both primary and secondary activities—activities that naturally include the operations of its overseas partners. Needless to say, its global alliances must accommodate the structure of each firm's value chain.

Sometimes it's cheaper to get another company to handle work, especially
- At small volume.
- When the other company has excess capacity.

States is primarily concerned about security; thus the president can halt any foreign investment that endangers national security.

The United States also prohibits foreign control of television and radio stations, because they could be used as foreign propaganda instruments. It protects domestic transportation, a vital sector for national security, by prohibiting foreign control of domestic airlines and by preventing foreign airlines and ships from transporting passengers and cargo from one U.S. city to another.

The rationale for protecting key industries is supported by history, which shows that home governments have used powerful foreign companies to influence policies in the countries where they operate. During colonial periods, firms such as Levant and the British East India Company often acted as the political arm of their home governments.

More recently, home governments, especially the United States, have pressured their companies to leave certain areas (e.g., Libya, Nicaragua), not to pay taxes to a regime (e.g., Angola, Panama), and to prohibit their subsidiaries from doing business with certain countries (e.g., Cuba, North Korea), even though the prohibition is counter to the interests of the countries where the subsidiaries were located.

At the same time, some companies are so powerful that they can influence their home-country governments to intercede on their behalf. Probably the most notorious example was United Fruit Company (UFC) in so-called banana republics, which persuaded the United States to overthrow governments to protect its investments. Miguel Angel Asturias, a Nobel laureate in literature, referred to UFC's head as the "Green Pope" who "lifts a finger and a ship starts or stops. He says a word and a republic is bought. He sneezes and a president . . . falls. . . . He rubs his behind on a chair and a revolution breaks out."[45]

Whenever a company is controlled from abroad, that company's decisions can be made abroad. Such control means that corporate management abroad can make decisions about personnel staffing, export prices, and the retention and payout of profits. These decisions might cause different rates of expansion in different countries and possible plant closings with subsequent employment disruption in some of them.

Further, by withholding resources or allowing strikes, MNEs may affect other local industries adversely. In essence, the MNE looks after its global interests, which may not coincide with what is best for an operation in a given country. ▶

based on some home-country or local socioeconomic agenda. At the same time, their decisions have to adhere to local laws and consider the views of their local stakeholders. Of course, MNEs sometimes make locally unpopular decisions, but so do local companies. In the meantime, governments can and do enact laws that apply to both local and international companies, and these laws can ensure that companies act in the so-called local interest.

Although preventing foreign control of key industries may be well intentioned, the resultant local control may lead to the protection of inefficient performance. Further, the key-industry argument appeals to emotions rather than reason. That's why the arguments in the United States for security make little sense on close examination. Although foreign propaganda through foreign ownership of radio and television stations is the rationale for ownership restrictions, there are no such restrictions on foreign ownership of U.S. newspapers. (Is this because people who read the news are presumed to be less swayed by propaganda?) In fact, Murdoch (Australian) and Thompson (Canadian) own many U.S. newspapers.

The protection of U.S. domestic transportation for security reasons is a sham, just to protect the U.S. shipbuilding industry and U.S. maritime employees. For instance, U.S. merchant flagships must employ only U.S. citizens as crews because of the vulnerability to bombs on ships in U.S. waters, but foreign flag carriers regularly use U.S. ports and foreigners can join the U.S. Navy.

The banana-republic arguments are outdated and go back to *dependencia theory,* which holds that emerging economies have practically no power in their dealings with MNEs.[46] More recent *bargaining school theory* states that the terms of a foreign investor's operations depend on how much the investor and host country need each other.[47] In effect, companies need countries because of their markets and resources. Countries need international companies because of their technology, capital, access to foreign markets, and expertise. Through a bargaining process, they come to an agreement or contract that stipulates what the MNE can and cannot do.

I completely disagree that either countries or companies can necessarily gain the same through collaborative agreements as through foreign direct investment. Although collaborative agreements are often preferable, there are company and country advantages from foreign-controlled operations. For example, with wholly owned operations, companies are less concerned about developing competitors and are more willing to transfer essential and valuable technology abroad. ◀

Prior Expansion of the Company   When a company already has operations (especially wholly owned ones) in place in a foreign country, some of the advantages of collaboration are no longer as important. The company knows how to operate within the foreign country and may have excess plant or human resource capacity it can use for new production or sales.

However, much depends on the compatibility between the existing foreign operations and the new ones the company is planning abroad. If there is similarity, as with production of a new type of office equipment when the company already produces office equipment in that country, the new production will likely be handled internally. If there is dissimilarity by product, function, or location, it may be more advantageous to collaborate with an experienced company.

LICENSING

Under a licensing agreement, a company (the licensor) grants intangible property rights to another company (the licensee) to use in a specified geographic area for a specified period. In exchange, the licensee ordinarily pays a royalty to the licensor. The rights may be for an *exclusive license* (the licensor can give rights to no other company for the specified geographic area for a specified period of time) or nonexclusive (it can give away rights).

The U.S. Internal Revenue Service classifies intangible property into these five categories:

1. Patents, inventions, formulas, processes, designs, patterns
2. Copyrights for literary, musical, or artistic compositions
3. Trademarks, trade names, brand names
4. Franchises, licenses, contracts
5. Methods, programs, procedures, systems

Usually, the licensor is obliged to furnish sufficient information and assistance, and the licensee is obliged to exploit the rights effectively and to pay compensation to the licensor.

Licensing agreements may be
- *Exclusive or nonexclusive.*
- *Used for patents, copyrights, trademarks, and other intangible property.*

Major Motives for Licensing   Frequently, a new product or process may affect only part of a company's total output and then only for a limited time. In such a situation, the company may foresee insufficient sales volume to warrant establishing its own foreign manufacturing and sales facilities. Meanwhile, it may find a licensee that can produce and sell at a low cost and within a short start-up time. In turn, the licensee's cost may be less than if it developed the new product or process on its own.

For industries in which technological changes are frequent and affect many products, companies in various countries often exchange technology or other intangible property rather than compete with each other on every product in every market. Such an arrangement is known as **cross-licensing.** For example, Microsoft (U.S.) and LGE (South Korea) entered a technology-sharing, cross-licensing agreement for complementary computer technology.[48]

Licensing often has an economic motive, such as the desire for faster start-up, lower costs, or access to additional resources.

Payment Considerations   The amount and type of payment for licensing arrangements vary, as each contract is negotiated on its own merits. For example, the value to the licensee will be greater if potential sales are high. Potential sales depend, in turn, on such factors as the geographic scope of the sales territory, the length of time the asset will have market value, and the market experience of using the asset elsewhere.

Putting a Price on Technology and Knowledge   Companies commonly negotiate a "front-end" payment to cover technology transfer costs. Licensors of technology do this because usually more is involved than simply transferring *explicit* knowledge, such as through publications and reports. The move requires the transfer of *tacit* knowledge, such as through engineering, consultation, and adaptation, and these face-to-face interactions incur costs. The licensee usually bears the transfer costs so that the licensor is motivated to ensure a smooth adaptation. Of course, the license of some assets, such as copyrights or brand names, has much lower transfer costs.

Technology may be old or new, obsolete, or still in use at home when a company licenses it. Many companies transfer technology at an early or even a developmental stage so products hit different markets simultaneously. This simultaneous market entry is important when selling to the same industrial customers in different countries and when global advertising campaigns can be effective. On the one hand, a licensee may be willing to pay more for a new technology because it may have a longer useful life. On the other hand, a licensee may be willing to pay less for a newer technology, particularly one in the development phase, because of its uncertain market value.

Selling to Controlled Entities   Although we think of licensing agreements as collaborative arrangements among unassociated companies, licensing is also common between parents and their wholly and partially owned operations abroad. One reason is that operations in a foreign country, even if 100 percent owned by the parent, are usually subsidiaries, which are legally separate companies. When a company owns less than 100 percent, a separate licensing arrangement may be a means of compensating the licensor for contributions beyond the mere investment in capital and managerial resources. (We noted in our opening case, for example, that Danone licensed its brand names to the joint venture that it established with Coca-Cola.)

Case Review Note

FRANCHISING

Franchising includes providing an intangible asset (usually a trademark) and continually infusing necessary assets.

Franchising is a specialized form of licensing in which the franchisor not only grants a franchisee the use of the intangible property (usually a trademark), but also operationally assists the business on a continuing basis, such as through sales promotion and training. In many cases, the franchisor provides supplies, such as the concentrate Coca-Cola sells to its bottlers. In a sense, a franchisor and a franchisee act almost like a vertically integrated company, because the parties are interdependent and each produces part of the product or service that ultimately reaches the consumer.

Today, franchising is most associated with U.S. fast-food operations, although many international franchisors are from other countries and in many other sectors. A Danish company, Cryos International, even franchises sperm banks in about 40 countries and supplies the frozen sperm from donors in Denmark.[49]

Many types of products and many countries participate in franchising.

Franchisors once depended on trade shows a few times a year and costly visits to foreign countries to promote their expansion. However, because of the Internet, they can now additionally receive e-mailed requests for information around the clock, seven days a week.

Franchise Organization   A franchisor may penetrate a foreign country by dealing directly with individual franchisees or by setting up a *master franchise* and giving that organization the rights to open outlets on its own or develop subfranchisees in the country or region. In the latter case, subfranchisees pay royalties to the master franchisee, which then remits some predetermined percentage to the franchisor. Coca-Cola handles most of its bottling franchising this way. Companies are most apt to use a master franchise system when they are not confident about evaluating potential individual franchisees and when overseeing and controlling them directly would be expensive.[50]

If the franchisor is not well known to many local people, or if local people are unsure about the franchisor's market commitment, it may be difficult to convince them to make investments. In effect, people are usually willing to invest only in known franchises, because the name is a guarantee of quality that can attract customers. Therefore, lesser-known franchisors commonly enter foreign markets with some company-owned outlets that serve as a showcase to attract franchisees.

Operational Modifications   Finding suppliers can add difficulties and expense for food franchisors. For example, McDonald's had to build a plant to make hamburger buns in the United Kingdom, and it had to help farmers develop potato production in Thailand.[51]

Franchisors' success generally depends on three factors: product and service standardization, high identification through promotion, and effective cost controls. A dilemma when operating abroad is that the first of these may be difficult to transfer. For example, standardization is important for food franchising so that consumers know what to expect. But when a company enters a foreign country, the taste preferences may be different. In fact, even regionally within large countries tastes may differ. In response to regional differences in China, Yum! Brands is offering regionally different food in its KFC and Pizza Hut outlets.[52]

At the same time, the more adjustments made for the host consumers' different tastes, the less a franchisor has to offer a potential franchisee. U.S. food franchisors' success in Japan is mostly due to that country's enthusiastic assimilation of Western products. Even so, food franchisors have had to make adjustments there. Wendy's sells a teriyaki burger, and Little Caesars has asparagus, potatoes, squid, and seaweed as pizza toppings.[53]

Franchisors face a dilemma:
- *The more standardization, the less acceptance in the foreign country.*
- *The more adjustment to the foreign country, the less the franchisor is needed.*

MANAGEMENT CONTRACTS

In a foreign management contract, a company transfers management personnel and administrative know-how abroad to assist a company for a fee. Contracts usually cover three to five years, and fixed fees or fees based on volume rather than profits are most common.

An organization may pay for managerial assistance when it believes another company can manage its operation more efficiently than it can. The ability to manage more efficiently is most apt to occur because of industry-specific capabilities. For example, the British Airport Authority (BAA) has contracts to manage airports in Indianapolis (U.S.), Naples (Italy), and Melbourne (Australia) because it has developed successful airport management skills.[54]

With management contracts, the owners and host country get the assistance they want without foreign companies' control of the operations. In turn, the management company receives income without having to make a capital outlay. This pattern has been important in hotel operations where some governments restrict foreign ownership and where some hotel owners know more about real estate than about managing a hotel. Further, evidence indicates that hotel chains favor management contracts over franchising when they have insignificant brand reputation in a market. Yet they can offer quality and organizational competence through their management, which are important to the hotels' competitive success.[55]

Foreign management contracts are used primarily when the foreign company can manage better than the owners.

TURNKEY OPERATIONS

Turnkey operations are a type of collaborative arrangement in which one company contracts with another to build complete, ready-to-operate facilities. Turnkey operators are most frequently industrial-equipment manufacturers, construction companies, and consulting firms. In addition, manufacturers sometimes decide to construct facilities for others if they believe an investment on their own behalf is infeasible. The customer for a turnkey operation is often a governmental agency. Recently, most large projects have been in those developing countries that are moving rapidly toward infrastructure development and industrialization.

Turnkey operations are
- *Most commonly performed by industrial-equipment, construction, and consulting companies.*
- *Often performed for a governmental agency.*

Contracting to Scale   One characteristic that sets the turnkey business apart from most other international business operations is the size of many of the contracts, frequently for hundreds of millions of dollars and into the billions. This means that a few very large companies—such as Bechtel (U.S.), Fluor (U.S.), Skanska (Sweden), and Hochtief (Germany)—account for a significant share of the international market. For example, Bechtel built a semiconductor plant for Motorola in China and a pipeline for BP in

Algeria, and it is now contracted for Egypt's first nuclear power plant.[56, 57] Smaller firms often either serve as subcontractors for primary turnkey suppliers or specialize in a particular sector, such as the handling of hazardous waste.

Making Contacts   The nature of these contracts places importance on hiring executives with top-level contacts abroad, as well as on ceremony and building goodwill, such as opening a facility on a country's independence day or getting a head of state to inaugurate a facility. Although public relations is important to gaining turnkey contracts, other factors—such as price, export financing, managerial and technological quality, experience, and reputation—are necessary to sell contracts of such magnitude.

Marshaling Resources   Many turnkey contracts are for construction in remote areas, necessitating massive housing construction and importation of personnel. Projects may involve building an entire infrastructure under the most adverse conditions, such as Bechtel's complex for Minera Escondida, which is high in the Andes. So turnkey operators must have expertise in hiring workers willing to work in remote areas for extended periods and in transporting and using supplies under very adverse conditions. One such area with adverse conditions has been Iraq, where large turnkey operations are being used for reconstruction.[58]

If a company holds a monopoly on certain assets or resources, such as the latest refining technology, other companies will find it difficult to compete to secure a turnkey contract. As the production process becomes known, however, the number of competitors for such contracts increases. Companies from developed countries have moved largely toward projects involving high technology, whereas companies from such countries as China, India, Korea, and Turkey can compete better for conventional projects for which low labor costs are important. For example, the Chinese companies China State Construction Engineering and Shanghai Construction Group have worked on a subway system in Iran, a railway line in Nigeria, an oil pipeline in Sudan, and office buildings in the United States.[59]

Arranging Payment   Payment for a turnkey operation usually occurs in stages as a project develops. Commonly, 10 to 25 percent comprises the down payment, with another 50 to 65 percent paid as the contract progresses, and the remainder paid once the facility is operating in accordance with the contract. Because currency fluctuations can occur during the long time frame between conception and completion, contracts commonly include price escalation clauses or cost-plus pricing.

Because the final payment is usually made only if the facility is operating satisfactorily, there are sometimes disagreements on what constitutes "satisfactorily." For this reason, many turnkey operators insist on performing a feasibility study as part of the contract so they don't build something that, although desired by a local government, may be too large or inefficient.

JOINT VENTURES

Joint ventures may have various combinations of ownership.

Case Review Note

A type of ownership sharing popular among international companies is the joint venture, in which more than one organization owns a company. Although companies usually form a joint venture to achieve particular objectives, it may continue to operate indefinitely as the objective is redefined. Joint ventures are sometimes thought of as 50/50 companies, but they may involve more than two companies, and one company may own more than 50 percent. The joint venture described in the ending case, if approved, will have three partners. When more than two organizations participate, the joint venture is sometimes called a **consortium.**

Possible Combinations   Almost every conceivable combination of partners may exist in an international joint venture as long as at least one of the partners is foreign. These include the following:

- Two companies from the same country joining together in a foreign market, such as NEC and Mitsubishi (Japan) in the United Kingdom

- A foreign company joining with a local company, such as Great Lakes Chemical (U.S.) and A. H. Al Zamil in Saudi Arabia

- Companies from two or more countries establishing a joint venture in a third country, such as that of Tata Motors (India) and Fiat (Italy) in Argentina

- A private company and a local government forming a joint venture (sometimes called a *mixed venture*), such as that of Petrobras (Brazil) with the Venezuelan government-owned company PDVSA

- A private company joining a government-owned company in a third country, such as BP Amoco (private British-U.S.) and Eni (government-owned Italian) in Egypt

The more companies in the joint venture, the more complex its management becomes. For example, development of the Boeing 787 (the Dreamliner) is a joint effort among numerous companies from eight countries. At this writing, the project is over two years behind schedule.[60] In essence, the project is hard to control, and a delay by any one of the participating companies delays the other participating companies. Figure 14.4 shows that as a company increases the number of partners and decreases the amount of equity it owns in a foreign operation, its ability to control that operation decreases.

Certain types of companies favor joint ventures more than do others. Companies that like joint ventures are usually new at foreign operations or have decentralized domestic decision making. Because these companies are used to extending control downward in their organizations, it is easier for them to do the same thing in a joint venture.

EQUITY ALLIANCES

An **equity alliance** is a collaborative arrangement in which at least one of the collaborating companies takes an ownership position (almost always minority) in the other(s). You'll recall from our opening case, for instance, that Coke maintains significant ownership positions in the master franchise bottlers that account for a significant part of its overseas sales. In some

Case Review Note

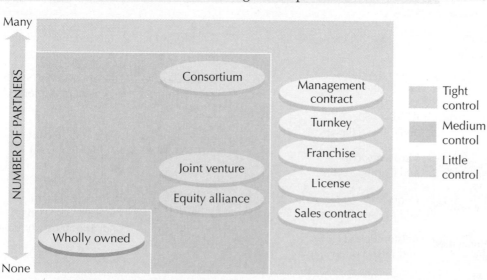

FIGURE 14.4   Collaborative Strategy and Complexity of Control

The more equity a firm puts into a collaborative arrangement, coupled with the fewer partners it takes on, the more control it will have over the foreign operations conducted under the arrangement. Note that nonequity arrangements typically entail at least one and often several partners.

Source: Adapted from Shaker Zahra and Galal Elhagrasey, "Strategic Management of International Joint Ventures," *European Management Journal* 12:1 (March 1994): 83–93. Reprinted with permission of Elsevier.

cases, each party takes an ownership, such as by buying part of each other's shares or by swapping some shares with each other. For instance, Panama-based Copa and Colombia-based AeroRepublic (airlines) took equity in each other.[61]

The purpose of the equity ownership is to solidify a collaborating contract, such as a supplier-buyer contract, so that it is more difficult to break—particularly if the ownership is large enough to secure a board membership for the investing company.

Problems with Collaborative Arrangements

Keep in mind that all parties to a collaborative arrangement must be satisfied with performance. Otherwise, the arrangement may break down. Many collaborative arrangements develop problems that lead partners to renegotiate their relationships in terms of responsibilities, ownership, or management structure. In spite of new relationships, many agreements break down or are not renewed at the end of an initial contract period. For example, in the case of joint ventures, about half break up because at least one partner becomes dissatisfied with the venture. Often, one partner buys out the other's interest, and the operation continues as a wholly owned foreign subsidiary. In other breakups, companies agree to dissolve the arrangement or they restructure their alliance.

Figure 14.5 shows that joint venture divorce (and divorce from other collaborative arrangements) can be planned or unplanned, friendly or unfriendly, mutual or nonmutual. The major strains on collaborative arrangements are due to five factors:

- Relative importance to partners
- Divergent objectives
- Control problems
- Comparative contributions and appropriations
- Differences in culture[62]

FIGURE 14.5 How to Dissolve a Joint Venture

There's more than one way to dissolve a joint venture—and to influence the future of its erstwhile operations.

Source: Adapted from Manuel G. Serapio Jr. and Wayne F. Cascio, "End Games in International Alliances," *Academy of Management Executive* (May 1996): 67.

DIVORCE SCENARIOS	EXAMPLES	OUTCOMES	EXAMPLES
Planned	General Motors (U.S.) and Toyota (Japan)	Termination by acquisition	Daewoo Motors (South Korea) and General Motors (U.S.)
vs.			
Unplanned	AT&T (U.S.) and Olivetti (Italy)	Termination by dissolution	Meiji Milk (Japan) and Borden (U.S.)
Friendly	Vitro (Mexico) and Corning (U.S.)		
vs.		Termination by reorganization/ restructuring of the alliance	Matsushita Electric Industries Co. (Japan) and Solbourne Computer (U.S.)
Unfriendly	Coors Brewing Co. (U.S.) and Molson Breweries (Canada)		
Mutually agreed upon	Ralston Purina (U.S.) and Taiyo Fishery (Japan)		
vs.			
Disputed	Sover S.P.A. (Italy) and Suzhou Spectacles No. 1 Factory (China)		

In spite of our focus on these problems, we do not mean to imply that there are no success stories. There are. For example, the joint venture between Xerox (U.S.) and Rank (U.K.) has performed well for a long period of time, and it even has a joint venture itself in Japan with Fuji Photo, which has also performed well.

RELATIVE IMPORTANCE

One partner may give more management attention to a collaborative arrangement than the other does. If things go wrong, the active partner blames the less active partner for its lack of attention, and the less active partner blames the more active partner for making poor decisions. The difference in attention may be due to the different sizes of partners. For example, if the joint venture is between a large and a small company, the venture comprises a larger portion of operations for the small company than for the large one, so the small company may take more interest in the venture.

In addition, if disagreements need to be settled legally, the smaller firm may be disadvantaged because it lacks the resources to fight the larger company. For example, Igen, a small U.S. firm, licensed its technology to Boehringer Mannheim of Germany, a company whose sales are more than 100 times those of Igen. When the two companies disagreed over royalty payments, Igen fought for four years and spent $40 million in legal fees (about the amount of one year of its sales) to win a settlement of over a half billion dollars.[63] However, this example is unusual, because most small companies cannot or will not fight a larger company so effectively.

DIVERGENT OBJECTIVES

Although companies enter into collaborative arrangements because they have complementary capabilities, their objectives may evolve differently over time. For instance, one partner may want to reinvest earnings for growth and the other may want to receive dividends. One partner may want to expand the product line and sales territory, and the other may see this as competition with its wholly owned operations. (For instance, the latter point has been a disagreement between BP and its Russian partner, TNK.)[64] A partner may wish to sell or buy from the venture, and the other partner may disagree with the prices.

Finally, there may be different views about performance standards. For example, GM has a joint venture in Thailand with Fuji Heavy Industries to make and export vehicles. Because of disagreements over quality, both companies perform inspections, which is time consuming and expensive. They have even argued over standards for paint jobs.[65]

QUESTIONS OF CONTROL

Sharing assets with another company may generate confusion over control. For example, the Israeli company Remedia, partly owned by the U.S. company H. J. Heinz, partnered with the German company Humana Milchunion to make baby formula. But Humana Milchunion removed vitamin B_1 from the formula concentrate without notifying its partners, and its failure to add the vitamin led to the deaths of three infants.[66]

When companies license their logos and trademarks for use on products they themselves do not produce, they may lack the ability to discern and control quality. Yet poor quality may affect sales of all products using the brand name and logo. For example, Pierre Cardin licensed its label for hundreds of products, from clothing to clocks to deodorants. But poor-quality Pierre Cardin–labeled products hurt the image of the high-quality ones. Pierre Cardin had to restructure its agreements and advertise heavily to reestablish the cachet of its name.[67] In today's world, problems in one country are quickly communicated to consumers in other countries.

In collaborative arrangements, even though control is ceded to one of the partners, both may be held responsible for problems. For example, in KFC's joint venture in China, the financial reporting to Chinese authorities was the Chinese partner's responsibility. However, the authorities held both partners liable for tax evasion as a result of underreporting income.[68] Moreover, in joint ventures and management contracts, there are gray areas as to who controls employees. Further, employees may have anxieties about who is in charge. For example, in a proposed joint venture between Merrill Lynch, from the United States, and UFJ, from Japan, a Japanese senior manager queried, "Who is going to be in charge—a Japanese or an American, or both?"[69]

When no single company has control of a collaborative arrangement, the operation may lack direction. At the same time, if one partner dominates, it must still consider the other company's interests.

COMPARATIVE CONTRIBUTIONS AND APPROPRIATIONS

Partners' relative capabilities of contributing technology, capital, or some other asset may change over time. For example, in P&G's joint venture with Phuong Dong Soap & Detergent in Vietnam, P&G wanted to expand, but Phuong had neither the funds to expand nor the willingness to allow P&G to gain a larger ownership.[70] (Figure 14.6 offers a humorous view of how a poorly performing company may wish to ally with a well-performing one.) Relative contributions may also change because partners may alter their strategy. For instance, a joint venture between Coca-Cola and P&G broke down because P&G shifted its product emphasis away from the food items assigned to the joint-venture agreement.

In addition, one partner may suspect that the other is taking more from the operation (particularly knowledge-based assets) than it is, which would enable it to become a competitor. In the face of such suspicions, information may be withheld, which, in time, weakens the operation. In fact, there are many examples of companies "going it alone" after they no longer needed their partner—particularly if the purpose of the collaboration was to gain knowledge.

CULTURE CLASHES

Differences in Country Cultures   Managers and the companies for which they work are affected by their national cultures, such as in how they evaluate the success of their operations. For example, U.S. companies tend to evaluate performance on the basis of

FIGURE 14.6   Why Some Companies Don't Play Hard to Get

Source: © Copyright Chris Wildt, Cartoonstock.com.

"How does this sound:'Single, nearly solvent company seeks relationship with like-minded, prosperous multinational.' "

profit, market share, and specific financial benefits. Japanese companies tend to evaluate primarily on how operations help build their strategic positions, particularly by improving their skills. European companies rely more on a balance between profitability and achieving social objectives.[71] Within China, government-owned companies often put employment maximization ahead of efficiencies and profits.[72] These differences can mean that one partner is satisfied while the other is not. Anheuser-Busch (now owned by Inbev of Belgium) attributed its joint venture breakup with Modelo (Mexican) to the fact that Modelo was run like a family business and was reluctant to share control.[73]

Finally, some companies don't like to collaborate with companies of very different cultures. Despite these potential problems, joint ventures from culturally distant countries can survive, because partners learn to deal with each other's differences.[74]

Differences in Corporate Cultures In addition to national culture, differences in corporate cultures may create problems within joint ventures. For example, one company may be accustomed to promoting managers from within the organization, whereas the other opens its searches to outsiders. One may use a participatory management style and the other an authoritarian style. One may be entrepreneurial and the other risk averse. Thus, many companies develop joint ventures only after they have had long-term positive experiences with the other company, such as through distributorship or licensing arrangements. However, as is the case with marriage, a positive prior relationship between two companies does not guarantee that partners will be well matched in a joint venture.[75]

Managing International Collaborations

If collaboration can achieve the company's strategic objectives better than "going it alone," the company should give little consideration to taking on duties itself. However, as the arrangement evolves, partners will need to reassess certain decisions. For example, a company's resource base may change compared to that of other companies, making collaboration either more or less advantageous.

In addition, the external environment changes. Perhaps a certain location becomes economically risky or its host government forbids or eases foreign ownership in areas where the arrangement would like to do future business. Because of these changes, a company needs to continually reexamine the fit between collaboration and its strategy. Thus a company is likely to use various modes of operations simultaneously because of its own capabilities (including experience), the specific products involved, and the characteristics of each foreign market.

We now discuss how companies change their operating forms, how they may find potential partners and negotiate with them, and how they need to assess the performance of collaborative arrangements.

The evolution to a different operating mode may

- Be the result of experience.
- Necessitate costly termination fees.
- Create organizational tensions.

DYNAMICS OF COLLABORATIVE ARRANGEMENTS

Companies' capabilities may change over time and influence the form of operations undertaken. For example, collaboration provides a company the opportunity to learn from its partner, enabling it to make a deeper commitment confidently. However, the cost of switching from one form to another—for example, from licensing to wholly owned facilities—may be high because of possibly having to pay contractual termination fees to another company.

Country Attractiveness and Operational Options Figure 14.7 illustrates a type of matrix that relates country attractiveness with operating forms. The company should ordinarily make a higher level of commitment, such as wholly owned operations, in the

FIGURE 14.7   Country
Attractiveness/Company
Strength Matrix

In a given scenario, a country in the
upper left-hand corner may be the
most attractive place for a company
to locate operations. Why? Because
its market is well suited to the
company's greatest competitive
strength and thus to its highest level
of commitment (e.g., establishing a
wholly owned subsidiary). A country
in the upper right-hand corner also
boasts an attractive market but
poses a problem for a company
whose competitive strengths don't
quite match the opportunity
(perhaps it has no experience in this
particular market). It needn't forgo
the opportunity, but it will probably
prefer a joint venture or some other
form of collaborative operation.
Finally, note that because everything
is subject to change—both a
company's capabilities and the
features of a country's market—firms
try to be dynamic in their approach
to potential operating modes.

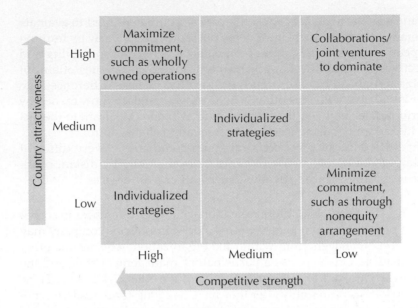

countries that appear in the top left corner of the matrix, because those countries not only are very attractive but also fit best with the company's capabilities.

In the top right corner, the country attractiveness is also high, but the company has a weak competitive strength for those markets, perhaps because it lacks knowledge of how to operate therein. If the cost is not too high, the company might attempt to gain greater domination in those markets by partnering with another company whose assets are complementary.

A company might divest in countries in the bottom right corner or "harvest" by pulling out all possible cash it can generate while at the same time not replacing depreciated facilities. It could also engage in nonequity arrangements, thereby generating some income without the need to make investment outlays. In other areas, the company must analyze situations individually to decide which approach to take. These are marginal areas that do not fit as neatly in the analysis.

Although this type of matrix may serve to guide decision making, managers must use it with caution. First, it is often difficult to separate the attractiveness of a country from a company's position. In other words, the country may seem attractive because of the company's fit with it. Second, some of the recommended actions take a defeatist attitude to a company's competitive position. There are many examples of companies that built competitive strength in markets that competitors had previously dominated or that built profitable positions without being the competitive leader.

Changing Conditions   Tension may develop internally as a company's form of international operations changes, because individuals may gain or lose responsibilities. For example, moving from exporting to foreign production may reduce the size of domestic marketing and manufacturing divisions. The people who then end up with less responsibility may be disadvantaged if bonuses and promotions are based largely on the size of their sales or profits. Given that their lower performance is due to decisions outside their control, companies should evaluate largely on those things that are controllable by personnel in different divisions.

Some evidence indicates that as companies enter more collaborative arrangements, they get better performance from them.[76] However, better performance is most associated with the use of similar types of collaborations, such as joint ventures, from one place to another.[77] In essence, companies may choose partners better and learn how to get better synergies between their partners and themselves. At the same time, the ways of effectively managing alliances has been undergoing significant changes; thus, companies cannot necessarily replicate what has succeeded for them in the past.[78]

FINDING COMPATIBLE PARTNERS

A company can seek out a partner for its foreign operations or it can react to a collaboration proposal from another company. In either case, it is necessary to evaluate the potential partner not only for the resources it can supply but also for its motivation and compatibility.

A company can identify potential partners by monitoring journals, attending technical conferences, and developing links with academic institutions. It can even find partners through social situations as acquaintances offer introductions to managers in other firms.[79] A company can increase its own visibility by participating in trade fairs, distributing brochures, and nurturing contacts in the locale of potential collaboration—increasing the probability that other companies will consider it as a partner.

The proven ability to handle similar types of collaboration is a key professional qualification. Because of a good track record, a partner may be able to depend more on trust rather than expensive control mechanisms to ensure that its interests are carried out. Once into a collaboration, partners may also be able to build partner trust with each other through their actions.[80] But every company has to start somewhere. Without a proven track record, a company may have to negotiate harder with and make more concessions to a partner.

NEGOTIATING THE ARRANGEMENT

The value of many technologies would diminish if they were widely used or understood. Contracts historically have included provisions that the recipient will not divulge this information. In addition, some sellers have held on to the ownership and production of specific components so recipients will not have the full knowledge of the product or the capability to produce an exact copy of it.

Many times, a company wants to sell techniques it has not yet used commercially. A buyer is reluctant to buy what it has not seen, but a seller that shows the work in process to the potential buyer risks divulging the technology. Thus, it is common to set up pre-agreements that protect all parties.

A controversial negotiation area is the secrecy surrounding the financial terms of arrangements. In some countries, for example, governmental agencies must approve licensing contracts. Sometimes these authorities consult their counterparts in other countries regarding similar agreements to improve their negotiating position with MNEs. Many MNEs object to this procedure, because they believe that contract terms between two companies are proprietary information with competitive importance, and market conditions usually dictate the need for very different terms in different countries.

In technology agreements,
- A seller does not want to give information without assurance of payment.
- A buyer does not want to pay without evaluating information.

DRAWING UP THE CONTRACT

Contracts with other companies cause some loss of control over the asset or intangible property that is transferred. A host of potential problems attend this lack of control and should be settled as much as possible in the original agreement. Mutual goals should be set so all parties understand what is expected, and the expectations should be spelled out in the contract. At the same time, not everything can be included in a contract. You need to develop sufficient rapport with partners so that common sense, along with the contract, plays a part in running the collaboration.[81] Thus, it helps to know a potential partner well before entering into a formal agreement. Frank communications may help determine potential partners' underlying expectations, which may otherwise come as a surprise. For example, one study of local partners in China and Russia discovered that

Concept Check

In discussing "Behavioral Factors" with regard to international business in Chapter 2, we observe that there are substantial differences in the degrees of *trust* that people in different **cultures** extend to others. We go on to explain that when trust is high, managers tend to spend more time focusing on operational issues and less fussing over every little detail. Not surprisingly, the cost of doing business tends to be lower in this scenario.

they had expected their foreign partners to deal much more with the Chinese and Russian governments (such as to alleviate bribery payments) than the foreign partners actually did.[82]

A Few Specific Issues   Although contracts have limits, their provisions should at least address the following issues:

- Will the agreement be terminated if the parties don't adhere to the directives?
- What methods will be used to test for quality?
- What geographic limitations should be placed on an asset's use?
- Which company will manage which parts of the operation outlined in the agreement?
- What will be each company's future commitments?
- How will each company buy from, sell to, or otherwise use intangible assets that result from the collaborative arrangement?

In addition to contract terms, how much you trust the management of another company is an important consideration in choosing a partner. At the same time, trust is affected by national culture and, in turn, influences how much a partner wants to cover within a contract. Thus, if parties from cultures with similar levels of trust come together, they are more likely able to agree on what must be incorporated in detailed contractual arrangements and what must be left to trust.[83]

IMPROVING PERFORMANCE

When collaborating with another company, managers must

- Continue to monitor performance.
- Assess whether to change the form of operations.
- Develop competency in managing a portfolio of arrangements

Contracting a compatible partner is necessary but insufficient to ensure success of a collaborative arrangement. Once an agreement is operational, it must be managed effectively. Management should estimate potential sales and costs, determine whether the arrangement is meeting quality standards, and assess servicing requirements to check whether the collaborative arrangement is meeting its goals and whether each partner is doing an adequate job.

In addition to the continual assessment of the partner's performance in collaborative arrangements, a company also needs to assess periodically whether the type of collaboration should change, such as replacing a licensing agreement with a joint venture. At the same time, as a company's number of collaborations grows, it should consider developing competency in managing the portfolio of arrangements so that it applies what it learns in one situation to other situations as well.[84]

Looking to the Future   Why Innovation Breeds Collaboration

A half century ago, John Kenneth Galbraith wrote that the era of cheap invention was over and "because development is costly, it follows that it can be carried out only by a firm that has the resources associated with considerable size."[85] The statement seems prophetic in terms of the estimated billions of investment dollars needed to bring a new commercial aircraft to market, eliminate death from diseases, develop defenses against unfriendly countries and terrorists, guard against cyberspace intrusions, and commercialize energy substitutes for petroleum. However, the statement overlooks the ability of companies to pool resources through collaboration, and such collaboration will likely continue to grow.

Moreover, markets must be truly global if high development costs are to be recouped. The sums companies need for developing and marketing these new inventions are out of reach of most companies acting alone, even if they become ever larger through internal growth or through mergers and acquisition. Although we have seen some examples of such growth, governments have nevertheless placed limits because of antitrust concerns.

Furthermore, companies realize the cost of integrating a merged or acquired company can be very high. Therefore, collaborative arrangements will likely become even more important in the future. They are likely to involve both horizontal and vertical linkages among companies from many industries in many countries. However, some evidence indicates that collaborative arrangements slow the speed of innovation because of the internalization and appropriation factors we have discussed.[86] Thus large companies that have resources to go it alone may have advantages over small companies that do not.

Although some product development requires huge sums, most is much more modest. Nevertheless, companies lack all the product- and market-specific resources to go it alone everywhere in the world, especially if national differences dictate operating changes on a country-to-country basis. These situations present opportunities for alliances that employ complementary resources from different companies.

Collaborative arrangements will bring both opportunities and problems as companies move simultaneously to new countries and to contractual arrangements with new companies. For example, collaborations must overcome differences in a number of areas:

- Country cultures that may cause partners to obtain and evaluate information differently
- National differences in governmental policies, institutions, and industry structures that constrain companies from operating as they would prefer
- Corporate cultures that influence ideologies and values underlying company practices that strain relationships among companies
- Different strategic directions resulting from partners' interests that cause companies to disagree on objectives and contributions
- Different management styles and organizational structures that cause partners to interact ineffectively[87]

The more partners in an alliance, the more cumbersome the decision-making and control processes. ■

Will the Transatlantic Joint Ventue of British Airways and American Airlines Fly?

CASE

OneWorld Alliance, launched in London in September 1998 by British Airways and American Airlines, is one of the best-known airline alliances. It has 11 full members and 19 affiliates who between them offer services to 720 destinations in 140 countries, operating fleets of more than 2,200 aircraft and carrying more than 330 million passengers a year. To date, the alliance is restricted to sharing frequent-flyer schemes, airport lounges, and some marketing, but it has nevertheless been successful. When carriers in the OneWorld alliance joined BA in the brand new, state-of-the-art T5 at London's Heathrow, making it their European hub, it was the envy of all their competitors. However, regulators have been unwilling to let them make the next step of selling seats on each other's flights and coordinating schedules and prices.

In 2008, BA and AA got together with another OneWorld member, Spanish airline Iberia, to seek approval for a nonequity joint venture covering routes that connect North America (the United States, Canada, and Mexico) and 27 European countries (the European Union plus Norway and Switzerland). Their operating routes are shown on Maps 14.2(a), (b), and (c). This joint venture, if approved, will allow representatives from each airline to jointly manage capacity and decide on prices and means of allocating revenues and expenses. The major impetus for this venture is to cut operating costs by better controlling capacity, avoiding disruptive price competition among them, and scheduling so as to gain better gate utilization.

This proposal is merely an extension to an historical series of alliances linking international airlines. In fact, the airline industry is unique in that its need to form collaborative arrangements has been important almost from the start of international air travel because of

MAP 14.2 (a), (b), (c)   North Atlantic Operations of Three Proposed Partners

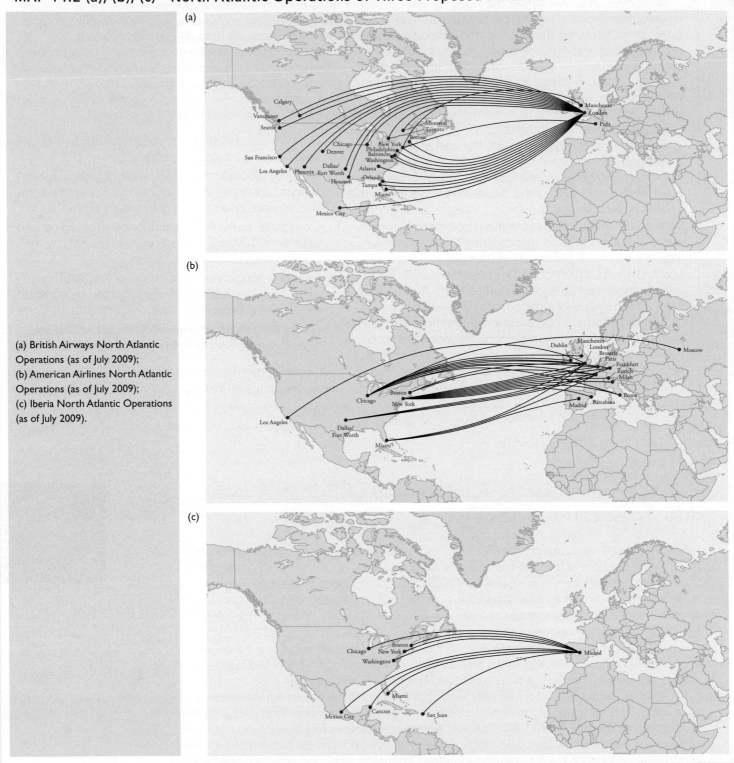

(a) British Airways North Atlantic Operations (as of July 2009);
(b) American Airlines North Atlantic Operations (as of July 2009);
(c) Iberia North Atlantic Operations (as of July 2009).

regulatory, cost, and competitive factors. In recent years, this need has accelerated because of airlines' poor profit performance.

In effect, the airlines have been squeezed. Costs have been rising, particularly because of oil prices and the requirement for greater security since 9/11. For instance, crude oil prices reached an all-time high in mid-2008. While predeparture airport passenger security checks are well publicized, some other costly airline security processes are not. These include, for example, providing governmental agencies with advance passenger information and working with freight forwarders and supply-chain operators to assure the safety of cargo shipments carried on passenger aircraft. There has also been a long-term trend toward greater price competition, which hinders airlines' ability to pass on increased costs to passengers. This situation has been exacerbated by customers' ability to search the Internet for lower fares and the emergence of discount airlines. From a shorter-term perspective, the global recession has reduced passenger demand substantially.

Although international passenger jet travel has been a major factor spurring globalization, no airline has sufficient finances or aircraft to serve the whole world. Yet passengers are traveling the whole world and perceive advantage in dealing with seamless airline connections that will both minimize distances and connecting times at airports and offer them reasonable assurance of reaching their destinations with their checked bags more or less on schedule. Thus, airlines have increasingly worked together to provide more seamless experiences for passengers and to cut costs.

The above discussion should not imply that all cost cuts necessitate collaboration. For example, in recent years, airlines have implemented a number of changes that cover the gamut from ticket purchase to arrival at destination. Online purchases of electronic tickets have largely replaced airlines' need to pay hefty commissions to travel agencies and to issue and maintain costly inventories of paper tickets. Self-service check-in at airports reduces the need for agents. On board, especially on short flights, less is included in the price of the ticket, such as snacks, pillows, and headphones. BA, for example, has abolished free meals on short flights and now charges passengers who wish to choose their seats when they book.

A Bit of History: Changing Government Regulation

Historically, governments played a major role in airline ownership. Many government-owned airlines were monopolies within their domestic markets, were money losers, and were recipients of government subsidies. However, there has been a subsequent move toward privatization.

What Governments Can Regulate

Despite the move toward privatization, governments still regulate airlines and agree on restrictions and rights largely through reciprocal agreements. Specifically, they designate:

- Which foreign carriers have landing rights
- Which airports and aircraft the carriers can use
- The frequency of flights
- Whether foreign carriers can fly beyond the country—for instance, whether Iberia, after flying from Spain to the United States, can then fly from the United States to Panama.
- Overflight privileges
- Fares they can charge

There have been several notable regulatory changes in recent years. Firstly, there have been several open-skies agreements that permit any airline from the agreement countries to fly from any city in one signatory area to any city in the other signatory area. Further, these flights have no restrictions on capacity, frequency, or type of aircraft. For instance, the European Union (plus Switzerland and Norway) has open-skies agreements with both the United States and Canada. These permit AA, for example, to fly directly to 12 European cities from 6 different U.S. cities. (Most of Asia remains without open-skies agreements.) Second, most European countries have enacted open-skies agreements with each other. These allow BA to serve a route between Paris and New York, rather than serving the United States only from points in the United Kingdom. Third, the same European countries have also deregulated, which contributed to the demise of certain European airlines, such as Sabena from Belgium. It has permitted cross-national acquisitions, such as those of KLM by Air France and

Swissair by Lufthansa. Finally, the U.S. domestic market has also been deregulated, which means that any approved U.S. carrier can fly any U.S. domestic route in any frequency while charging what the market will bear. Once deregulation was instituted, many U.S. airlines (such as Braniff, Eastern, and TWA) were forced competitively to go out of business.

Why Governments Protect Airlines

Four factors influence governments' protection of their airlines:

1. Countries believe they can save money by maintaining small air forces and relying on domestic airlines in times of unusual air transport needs. For example, the U.K. government put out to tender the task of flying troops from Iraq and awarded the contract to a small Slovakian airline.

2. Public opinion favors spending "at home," especially for government-paid travel. The public sees the maintenance of national airlines and the requirement that government employees fly on those airlines as foreign-exchange savings.

3. Airlines are a source of national pride, and aircraft (sporting their national flags) symbolize a country's sovereignty and technical competence. BA's 1997 decision to replace the Union Jack design on its plane tailfins with abstract designs was greeted with nationwide protests and had to be withdrawn.

4. Countries have worried about protecting their airspace for security reasons. This is less of a concern today because foreign carriers routinely overfly a country's territory to reach inland gateways, such as BA's flights between London and Denver. Further, overflight treaties are quite common, even among unfriendly nations. For example, Cubana overflies the United States en route to Canada, and AA overflies Cuba en route to South America.

Regulatory Obstacles to Expansion

Even if airlines had the financial capacity to expand everywhere in the world, national regulations would limit this expansion. With few exceptions, airlines cannot fly on lucrative domestic routes in foreign countries. For example, BA cannot compete on the New York to Los Angeles route because the U.S. government allows only U.S. airlines on that route, and it limits foreign ownership in a U.S. airline to 25 percent of voting stock.

Thus, airlines cannot easily control a flight network abroad that will feed passengers into their international flights. For example, BA has no U.S. domestic flights to feed passengers into Chicago for connections to London, but AA has scores of such flights. However, BA has an advantage within Europe, where AA cannot originate passengers to connect in London to Miami.

In addition to direct regulation against foreign control of airlines, there are sometimes governmental pressures to prevent foreign takeovers. For example, BA owns 9.9 percent of Iberia, and the airlines have now reached a preliminary agreement for a merger, which, if it is approved by the European Commission, will go ahead in late 2010. However, Spain had initially resisted the deal because it wanted to further develop the Madrid airport (Barajas) as a hub and feared that traffic would shift to London with BA's ownership.

Finally, airlines usually cannot service pairs of foreign countries. AA cannot fly between Brazil and South Africa, because the Brazilian and South African governments give landing rights on these routes only to Brazilian and South African airlines. To avoid these restrictions, airlines must ally themselves with carriers from other countries.

Collaboration Examples Related to Motives

Cost Factors

Certain airlines have always dominated certain international airports. They have amassed critical capabilities in those airports, such as baggage handlers and baggage-handling equipment. Sharing these capabilities with other airlines may spread costs. For example, BA has long handled passenger check-in, baggage loading, and maintenance for a number of other airlines in London's Heathrow Airport.

The high cost of maintenance and reservations systems has led to joint ventures involving multiple airlines from multiple countries, such as ownership in the Apollo and Galileo reservation systems. Actually, the reservations systems are motivated by more than cost savings inasmuch as the pooling of resources allows customers to get better service.

Connecting Flights

Given that governments restrict domestic or regional routes to their own carriers, airlines have long had agreements whereby passengers can transfer from one airline to another with a through ticket. A problem with these agreements is that the connections from one airline to another often appear in flight information after those connections that involve only one airline. There is a tendency for people to select from among the first routings that show up on a computer screen. Further, when passengers see that they must change airlines, they worry about making those connections across great distances within ever-larger airline terminals. To avoid these problems, airlines have agreed to code sharing, a procedure whereby the same flight may have a designation for more than one carrier. For instance, BA flight 6122 from Miami to London is also listed as American flight 6213. This enables both airlines to show a same-airline connection, thus helping to pacify passengers who worry about connecting from one airline to another.

The Proposed Joint Venture

The Participants

As members of the OneWorld Alliance, the three airlines—BA, AA, and Iberia—cooperate on various programs, such as allowing passengers to earn credits for free or upgraded travel on any one of the alliance members. The three airlines, which are among the world's largest, have a combined network of over 400 destinations in over 100 countries and account for more than 6,000 daily departures. Furthermore, their routes have synergy. AA is one of the largest carriers within the United States in terms of passenger-kilometers flown. BA's main hub is London Heathrow, which is the world's busiest international airport. Iberia is the largest carrier between Europe and Latin America.

Collectively, the three airlines fly 48 different routes between Europe and North America, which include 22 North American and 13 European cities. Of these 48 routes, they compete directly on only nine.

Why Not Just Continue the Present Alliances?

The three airlines already have extensive cooperative agreements, so what would be gained through the proposed joint venture? The present agreements are limited in that antitrust provisions prevent their discussing and coordinating schedules, fares, and the division of routes. If given antitrust immunity—which is necessary for the joint venture to be approved—they can plan schedules so that feeder routes will connect smoothly with the transatlantic routes. If more than one of the joint venture partners flies the same route, they can schedule departures that are less competitive timewise. This can improve schedules for passengers, make OneWorld members more competitive, improve their capacity utilization, and decrease passenger costs. Through the joint venture, the participants can also schedule flight arrivals and departures so that gates are used efficiently.

Finally, the OneWorld Alliance is presently disadvantaged across the Atlantic because Star Alliance and Sky Team have already received antitrust immunity for their transatlantic flights. The Star Alliance includes, for example, Continental, Lufthansa, and United. Sky Team includes Air France/KLM and Delta.

Why Not a Merger or an Acquisition?

To begin with, governmental regulations, such as the ownership requirements we have discussed, would prevent a merger or acquisition. However, even if they did not, there would be daunting problems in fusing any combination of the three companies together. For example, the respective pilots' unions are strong and operate under different operating and compensation systems. The proposed joint venture, however, allows each company to keep its own identity and to operate independently.

The Opposition

The most forceful critic of the plan has been Sir Richard Branson, founder of Virgin Atlantic in the United Kingdom, whose airline is now owned 49 percent by Singapore Airlines. (His criticism of OneWorld goes back several decades.) He has vowed to do everything possible to prevent a "monster monopoly," even though the three airlines in the proposed joint venture carry less than half the passengers between the United States and the United Kingdom. He has also announced plans to paint Virgin Atlantic's fleet with the slogan "No way BA-AA."

The appropriate departments of the carriers' home governments also need to approve the joint venture. In the case of the United States, it is the Department of Transportation (DOT); for BA and Iberia, it is the European Commission. European regulators have already expressed concern that the agreement is likely to result in "appreciable competitive harm" on seven European/U.S. routes and that the alliance may be forced to give up valuable take-off and landing slots if the tie-up is to go ahead.

Congressman Oberstar (United States) has introduced a congressional bill that would require the DOT to reassess any antitrust immunity grants to airline alliances every three years. His concern is that the number of airlines competing on North Atlantic routes has declined and that the members of the three large alliances (Star, SkyTeam, and OneWorld) control over 87 percent of the traffic between the United States and Europe. One may argue, however, that by combining the transatlantic operations of AA, BA, and Iberia, they might be able to generate sufficient traffic to justify flights on routes that none are now serving across the Atlantic.[88] ∎

QUESTIONS

1. Should the proposed joint venture among British Airways, American Airlines, and Iberia be approved? What are the implications, if approved, for these airlines' solvency and for customers?

2. Some airlines, such as Southwest, have survived as niche players without extensive international connections. Can they continue this strategy?

3. Why should an airline not be able to establish service anywhere in the world simply by demonstrating that it can and will comply with the local labor and business laws of the host country?

4. The U.S. law limiting foreign ownership of U.S. airlines to no more than 25 percent of voting shares was enacted in 1938. Is this law an anachronism, or are there valid reasons for having it today?

5. What will be the consequences if a few large airlines or networks dominate global air service?

6. Many airlines have recently been no more than marginally profitable. Is this such a vital industry that governments should intervene to guarantee their survival? If so, how?

7. What methods could the three joint-venture partners use to divide revenue and expenses on the North Atlantic routes?

SUMMARY

- Selling abroad by exporting home-country production may not be advantageous because of lower production costs abroad, high transport costs, the need to alter products substantially, protectionist barriers, lack of domestic capacity, and consumer preferences to buy from specific countries.

- Companies often prefer to operate with foreign direct investment, especially wholly owned, because such operations may lower their costs, lessen the possibility of developing competitors, and free them to follow global strategies.

- Some advantages of collaborative arrangements, whether a company is operating domestically or internationally, are to

spread and reduce costs, allow a company to specialize in its primary competencies, avoid certain competition, secure vertical and horizontal links, and learn from other companies.

- Some motivations for collaborative arrangements that are specific to international operations are to gain location-specific assets, overcome legal constraints, diversify among countries, and minimize exposure in risky environments.

- The forms of foreign operations differ in how many resources a company commits and the proportion of resources committed at home rather than abroad. Collaborative arrangements reduce a company's commitment.

- Although the type of collaborative arrangement a company chooses should match its strategic objectives, the choice often means a trade-off among objectives.

- Licensing is granting another company the use of some rights—such as patents, copyrights, or trademarks—usually for a fee. It is a means of establishing foreign production and reaching foreign markets that may minimize the licensor's capital outlays, prevent the free use of assets by other companies, allow the receipt of assets from other companies in return, and allow for income in some markets in which exportation or investment is not feasible.

- Franchising differs from licensing in that granting the use of intangible property (usually a trademark) requires the franchisor to assist in the operation of the business on a continuing basis.

- Management contracts are a means for a company to secure income by managing a foreign operation while providing little of the capital outlay.

- Turnkey projects are contracts for construction of another company's operating facilities. These projects have historically been large and diverse, necessitating specialized skills and abilities to deal with top-level government authorities.

- Joint ventures are a special type of collaborative arrangement in which two or more organizations have equity in a venture.

- There are various combinations of owners, including governments and private companies and two or more owners from the same or different countries.

- Equity alliances occur when a company takes an equity position in the company with which it has a collaborative arrangement so as to solidify the collaborating contract.

- A common motive for jointly owned operations is to take advantage of different companies' complementary resources.

- Problems occur in collaborative arrangements when partners place different levels of importance on and have different objectives for them, find a shared ownership arrangement difficult to control, worry that their partner is putting in too little or taking out too much from the operation, and misunderstand each other as a result of their different country or company cultures.

- Contracting performance by another company does not negate management's responsibility to assess the other company's work.

- Companies may use different types of collaborative arrangements for their foreign operations in different countries or for different products. As diversity increases, coordinating and managing the foreign operations becomes more complex.

KEY TERMS

appropriability theory (p. 567)
consortium (p. 578)
cross-licensing (p. 575)

equity alliance (p. 579)
internalization (p. 566)

resource-based view (of the firm) (p. 570)

ENDNOTES

1   *Sources include the following:* The Coca-Cola Company, "Around the World" (2007), at www.thecoca-colacompany.com/ourcompany/aroundworld.html (accessed July 3, 2007); Valerie Bauerlein, "Coca-Cola CEO Defends Bottling System," *Wall Street Journal* (April 22, 2009): B3; Bernardette S. Santo Domingo, "Coca-Cola Pledges $1-B Investment to Expand RP Operations," *Business World* (August 3, 2009), at http://iiiprxy.library.miami.edu:3122/us/Inacademic/frame.do?reloadEntirePage=true&ran (accessed October 9, 2009); Andrew Martin, "Does Coke Need a Refill?," *New York Times* (May 27, 2007): Sec. 3, 1+; Leo Paul Dana, "Turkish Coca-Cola," *British Food Journal* 101:5/6 (1999): 468; "Coca-Cola Dome-Sasol Management Contract Renewed," at www.thebeexhibitions.co.za/press5.htm (accessed July 3, 2007); Sara Yin, "Coca-Cola Opens Concept Store," *Media* (December 1, 2006): 2; "Coca-Cola, Danone Create Joint Venture to Sell Bottled Water," *Wall Street Journal* (June 18, 2002): C18; "Coca-Cola, Nestlé Narrow Joint Venture," *Beverage Industry* 98:4 (2007): 6; Drake Weisert, "Coca-Cola in China: Quenching the Thirst of a Billion," *China Business Review* 28: 4(July–August 2001): 52-55; Kevin Parker, "ERP and SOA at the Coca-Cola Company," *Manufacturing Business Technology* 25:5 (2007): 2; Betsy McKay, "Smaller Brands Hitch Brands with Coke Distributors," *Wall Street Journal* (January 29,

2007): B1; Betsy McKay, "More Fizz," *Wall Street Journal* (June 1, 2007): A1+; *Coca-Cola 2008 Annual Report.*

2   Hugh Pope, "Ford Forges Ahead with Turkey Plans," *Wall Street Journal* (July 24, 2000): A17+.

3   John Griffiths, "VW May Build Beetle in Europe to Meet Demand," *Financial Times* (November 11, 1998): 17.

4   Peter Marsh, "The World's Wash Day," *Financial Times* (April 29, 2002): 6.

5   "Skoda Brings New Luxury Car, Octavia," *The Statesman* [India] (November 17, 2001): FT Asia Africa Intelligence Wire.

6   Aluf Benn, "Why Peace Doesn't Pay," *Foreign Policy* 124 (May–June 2001): 64–65.

7   Jill Gabrielle Klein, "Us versus Them, or Us versus Everyone? Delineating Consumer Aversion to Foreign Goods," *Journal of International Business Studies* 33:2 (2002): 345–63.

8   "Yes, You Can Help Our Balance of Payments," *The Daily Telegraph* (Sydney) (June 4, 2005): 5.

9   Lynda V. Mapes, "Food Fight Ensues over Labeling," *Seattle Times* (April 25, 2002): A1; Ken Leiser, "Toyota's Inroads with State Bypass 'Buy American' Law" (March 6, 2002): A1.

10 John S. Hulland, "The Effects of Country-of-Brand and Brand Name on Product Evaluation and Consideration: A Cross-Country Comparison," *Journal of International Consumer Marketing* 11 (1999): 23–39.

11 *Internalization theory,* or holding a monopoly control over certain information or other proprietary assets, builds on earlier market-imperfections work by Ronald H. Coase, "The Nature of the Firm," *Economica* 4 (1937): 386–405. It has been noted by such writers as M. Casson, "The Theory of Foreign Direct Investment," Discussion Paper No. 50 (Reading, UK: University of Reading International Investment and Business Studies, November 1980); Alan M. Rugman, *Inside the Multinationals: The Economics of Internal Markets* (New York: Columbia University Press, 1981); David J. Teece, "Transactions Cost Economics and the Multinational Enterprise," Berkeley Business School International Business Working Paper Series No. IB-3 (1985); B. Kogut and U. Zander, "Knowledge of the Firm and the Evolutionary Theory of the Multinational Corporation," *Journal of International Business Studies* 24:4 (1993): 625–45; and Peter W. Liesch and Gary A. Knight, "Information Internalization and Hurdle Rates in Small and Medium Enterprise Internationalization," *Journal of International Business Studies* 30:2 (1999): 383–96.

12 Eric M. Johnson, "Harnessing the Power of Partnerships," *Financial Times* (October 8, 2004): Mastering Innovation, 4.

13 Paul Marer and Vincent Mabert, "GE Acquires and Restructures Tungsram: The First Six Years (1990–1995)," *OECD, Trends and Policies in Privatization* III:1 (Paris: OECD, 1996): 149–85; and their unpublished 1999 revision, "GE's Acquisition of Hungary's Tungsram."

14 James Mackintosh and Arkady Ostrovsky, "Partners Settle Lada Parts Dispute," *Financial Times* (February 21, 2006): 16.

15 Gary Gentile, "Hair Products," *Miami Herald* (September 3, 2004): 4C.

16 Stephen Magee, "Information and the MNC: An Appropriability Theory of Direct Foreign Investment," in Jagdish N. Bhagwati (ed.), *The New International Economic Order* (Cambridge, MA: MIT Press, 1977): 317–40; C. W. Hill, L. P. Hwang, and W. C. Kim, "An Eclectic Theory of the Choice on International Entry Mode," *Strategic Management Journal* 11 (1990): 117–18; Ashish Arora and Andrea Fosfuri, "Wholly Owned Subsidiary versus Technology Licensing in the Worldwide Chemical Industry," *Journal of International Business Studies* 31:4 (2000): 555–72.

17 Peter Wonacott, "Global Aims of China's Car Makers Put Existing Ties at Risk," *Wall Street Journal* (August 24, 2004): B1+; Norihiko Shirouzu and Peter Wonacott, "People's Republic of Autos," *Wall Street Journal* (April 18, 2005): B1+.

18 Jean-Paul Roy and Christine Oliver, "International Joint Venture Partner Selection: The Role of the Host-Country Legal Environment," *Journal of International Business Studies* 40:5 (2009): 779–801.

19 Andrew Taylor, "Overseas Groups Get on the UK Utility Map," *Financial Times* (June 17, 2002): 4.

20 Anne-Wil Harzing, "Acquisitions versus Greenfield Investments: International Strategy and Management of Entry Modes," *Strategic Management Journal* 23:3 (2002): 211–27.

21 Jaideep Anand and Andrew Delios, "Absolute and Relative Resources as Determinants of International Acquisitions," *Strategic Management Journal* 23:2 (2002): 119–34.

22 Geoff Dyer, Francesco Guerrera, and Alexandra Harney, "Chinese Companies Make Plans to Join the Multinational Club," *Financial Times* (June 23, 2005): 19.

23 One such indication is from a study by Alan Gregory, which is cited in Kate Burgess, "Acquisitions in U.S. 'Disastrous' for British Companies," *Financial Times* (October 11, 2004): 18.

24 John Child, David Faulkner, and Robert Pitethly, *The Management of International Acquisitions* (Oxford: Oxford University Press, 2001); Peter Martin, "A Clash of Corporate Cultures," *Financial Times* (June 2–3, 2001): Weekend section, xxiv.

25 Rajesh Chakrabarti, Swasti Gupta-Mukherjee, and Narayanan Jayaraman, "Mars-Venus Marriages: Culture and Cross-Border M&A," *Journal of International Business Studies* 40:2 (2009): 216–36; See also Mary Yoki Brannen and Mark F. Peterson, "Merging Without Alienating: Interventions Promoting Cross-Cultural Organization and Their Limitations," *Journal of International Business Studies* 40:3 (2009): 468–89.

26 Pierre Dussauge, Bernard Garrette, and Will Mitchell, "Asymmetric Performance: The Market Share Impact of Scale and Link Alliances in the Global Auto Industry," *Strategic Management Journal* 25 (2004): 701–11.

27 A. L. Zacharakis, "Entrepreneurial Entry into Foreign Markets: A Transaction Cost Perspective," *Entrepreneurship Theory & Practice* 22:2 (1998): 23–39; Rodney C. Shrader, "Collaboration and Performance in Foreign Markets: The Case of Young High-Technology Manufacturing Firms," *Academy of Management Journal* 44:1 (2001): 45–60.

28 Rahul Jacob, "Hong Kong Banks on New Disney Park for Boost," *Financial Times* (August 31, 2001): 6.

29 Doug Cameron, "Manufacturing Enters a New Era," *Financial Times* (June 18, 2007): 6.

30 "New World Ready to Build Caribbean Fiber System," *Fiber-Optics News* (June 26, 2000): 1.

31 Betsy McKay and Robert Frank, "Coke, Danone Discuss Joint Venture," *Wall Street Journal* (June 17, 2002): B5.

32 John M. Connor, "Global Antitrust Prosecutions of Modern International Cartels," *Journal of Industry, Competition and Trade* 4:3 (2004): 239.

33 Luiz F. Mesquita and Sergio G. Lazzarini, "Horizontal and Vertical Relationships in Developing Economies: Implications for SMEs' Access to Global Markets," *Academy of Management Journal* 51:2 (2008): 359–80.

34 Peter Marsh, "Profile Duracell," *Financial Times* (May 10, 1999): 27.

35 Destan Kandemir and G. Tomas Hult, "A Conceptualization of an Organizational Learning Culture in International Joint Ventures," *Industrial Marketing Management* 34:5 (2005): 440.

36 Robert F. Howe, "The Fall of the House of Mondavi," *Business 2.0* 6:3 (2005): 98.

37 Yumiko Ono and Ann Zimmerman, "Wal-Mart Enters Japan with Seiyu Stake," *Wall Street Journal* (March 15, 2002): B5.

38 "Merck and Chugai Form OTC Venture," *Financial Times* (September 19, 1996): 17; Michiyo Nakamoto, "Global Reach through Tie-Ups," *Financial Times* (April 30, 2002): Health-Care section, 3.

39 Peter Wonacott and Eric Bellman, "Foreign Firms Find Rough Passage to India," *Wall Street Journal* (February 1, 2007): A6; Neil Buckly, "Russia Sets New Rules for Investors in Key Sectors," *Financial Times* (May 6, 2009): 3; Amy Kazmin, "Ikea Ditches Plans for India after New Delhi Refuses to Change Law," *Financial Times* (June 12, 2009): 13.

40 "Northrop Grumman, Rolls-Royce Awarded Type 45 Destroyer Engine Contract," *Defense Daily International* (March 16, 2001): 1.

41 Julie Bennett, "Road to Foreign Franchises Is Paved with New Problems," *Wall Street Journal* (May 14, 2001): B10.

42 "H&M Wins Back Name in Russia," *Managing Intellectual Property* (April 2007): 1.

43 Peter J. Lane, Jane E. Salk, and Marjorie A. Lyles, "Absorptive Capacity, Learning, and Performance in International Joint Ventures," *Strategic Management Journal* 22 (2001): 1139–61.

44 Steven White and Steven Siu-Yun Lui, "Distinguishing Costs of Cooperation and Control in Alliances," *Strategic Management Journal* 26 (2005): 913–32.

45 Miguel Angel Asturias, *Strong Wind,* trans. Gregory Rabassa (New York: Delacorte Press, 1968): 112.

46 For an extensive treatise on the theory, see Robert A. Packenham, *The Dependency Movement: Scholarship and Politics in Development Studies* (Cambridge, MA: Harvard University Press, 1992). For some different national views of its validity, see Ndiva Kofele-Kale, "The Political Economy of Foreign Direct Investment: A Framework for Analyzing Investment Laws and Regulations in Developing Countries," *Law & Policy in International Business* 23:2/3 (1992): 619–71; and Stanley K. Sheinbaum, "Very Recent History Has Absolved Socialism," *New Perspectives Quarterly* 13:1 (1996).

47 Ravi Ramamurti, "The Obsolescing 'Bargaining Model'? MNC-Host Developing Country Relations Revisited," *Journal of International Business Studies* 32 (2001): 23; Yadong Luo, "Toward a Cooperative View of MNC-Host Government Relations: Building Blocks and Performance Implication," *Journal of International Business Studies* 32 (2001): 401.

48 "Microsoft and LG Ink Broad Patent-Licensing Pact," *Wireless News* (June 10, 2007): 1.

49 Lizette Alvarez, "Spreading Scandinavian Genes, without Viking Boats," *New York Times* (September 30, 2004): A4.

50 Fred Burton, Adam R. Cross, and Mark Rhodes, "Foreign Market Servicing Strategies of UK Franchisors: An Empirical Enquiry from a Transactions Cost Perspective," *Management International Review* 40:4 (2000): 373–400.

51 John K. Ryans, Jr., Sherry Lotz, and Robert Krampf, "Do Master Franchisors Drive Global Franchising?" *Marketing Management* 8:2 (1999): 33–38.

52 Janet Adamy, "Chinese Food the KFC Way," *Wall Street Journal Asian Edition* (October 20–22, 2006): 14–15.

53 Julie Bennett, "Product Pitfalls Proliferate in a Global Cultural Maze," *Wall Street Journal* (May 14, 2001): B11; Jane Wooldridge, "Fast Food Universe," *Miami Herald* (November 28, 2004): J1.

54 British Airport Authority, "International Airports" (2007), at http://www.baa.com/portal/page/Corporate%5EAbout+BAA%5EWho+does+what%5EInternational+airports/b0ccadc5c5c72010VgnVCM100000147e120a__/448c6a4c7f1b0010VgnVCM200000357e120a__/ (accessed July 6, 2007).

55 Chekitan S. Dev, M. Krishna Erramilli, and Sanjeev Agarwal, "Brands across Borders," *Cornell Hotel and Restaurant Administration Quarterly* 43:6 (2002): 91–104.

56 "Contract Will Be Signed in April with Bechtel to Carry Out First Nuclear Plant," *Info–Prod Research* (Middle East) (March 30, 2009): n.p.

57 Bechtel Corporation, "Projects" (2007), at http://www.bechtel.com/default_projects.htm (accessed October 30, 2007).

58 Glenn R. Simpson and Chip Cummins, "Fuel for the Fire," *Wall Street Journal* (April 14, 2004): A1+; Sheila McNulty, "Haliburton Boosted by Iraq Work," (April 23–24, 2005): 8.

59 David Murphy, "Chinese Construction Companies Go Global," *Wall Street Journal* (May 12, 2004): B10.

60 Peter Sanders, Daniel Michaels, and August Cole, "Boeing Delays New Jet Again," *Wall Street Journal* (June 24, 2009): A1+; Peter Sanders, "Boeing Settles In for a Bumpy Ride," *Wall Street Journal* (October 7, 2009): B1+.

61 Luis Zalamea, "AeroRepublica, Copa Offer Details of New Alliance," *Aviation Daily* (March 11, 2005): 5.

62 There are many different ways of classifying the problems. Two useful ways are found in Manuel G. Serapio Jr. and Wayne F. Cascio, "End Games in International Alliances," *Academy of Management Executive* 10:1 (1996): 62–73; and Joel Bleeke and David

Ernst, "Is Your Strategic Alliance Really a Sale?" *Harvard Business Review* (January–February 1995): 97–105.

63 Terrence Chea, "No Perfect Partnership," *Washington Post* (June 3, 2002): E1.

64 Mikhail Fridman, "BP Has Been Treating Russians as Subjects," *Financial Times* (July 7, 2008): 9.

65 Gregory L. White, "In Asia, GM Pins Hope on a Delicate Web of Alliances," *Wall Street Journal* (October 23, 2002): A23.

66 Ramit Plushnick-Masti, "German Firm Faulted for Taking Vitamin out of Baby Formula," *Miami Herald* (November 12, 2003): 19A.

67 William H. Meyers, "Maxim's Name Is the Game," *New York Times Magazine* (May 3, 1987): 33–35; Keith W. Strandberg, "EganaGoldpfeil Group Moves Forward with Pierre Cardin Watches," *National Jeweler* (October 1, 2002): 36.

68 Marcus W. Brauchli, "PepsiCo's KFC Venture in China Is Fined for Allegedly False Financial Reporting," *Wall Street Journal* (July 27, 1994): A10.

69 David Ibison, "Culture Clashes Prove Biggest Hurdle to International Links," *Financial Times* (January 24, 2002): 17.

70 Samantha Marshall, "P&G Squabbles with Vietnamese Partner," *Wall Street Journal* (February 27, 1998): A14.

71 Joel Bleeke and David Ernst, "The Way to Win in Cross-Border Alliances," *Harvard Business Review* (November–December 1991): 127–35.

72 James T. Areddy, "Danone Pulls Out of Disputed China Venture," *Wall Street Journal* (October 1, 2009): B1.

73 Leslie Crawford, "Anheuser's Cross-Border Marriage on the Rocks," *Financial Times* (March 18, 1998): 16.

74 Seung Ho Park and Gerardo R. Ungson, "The Effect of National Culture, Organizational Complementarity, and Economic Motivation on Joint Venture Dissolution," *Academy of Management Journal* 40:2 (April 1997): 279–307; Harry G. Barkema, Oded Shenkar, Freek Vermeulen, and John H. J. Bell, "Working Abroad, Working with Others: How Firms Learn to Operate International Joint Ventures," *Academy of Management Journal* 40:2 (April 1997): 426–42, found survival differences only for differences in uncertainty avoidance.

75 Mike W. Peng and Oded Shenkar, "Joint Venture Dissolution as Corporate Divorce," *Academy of Management Executive* 16:2 (May 2002): 92–105.

76 Bharat Anand and Tarun Khanna, "Do Firms Learn to Create Value? The Case of Alliances," *Strategic Management Journal* 21:3 (March 2000): 295–315.

77 Anthony Goerzen and Paul W. Beamish, "The Effect of Alliance Network Diversity on Multinational Enterprise Performance," *Strategic Management Journal* 26 (2005): 333–54.

78 Rachelle C. Sampson, "Experience Effects and Collaborative Returns in R&D Alliances," *Strategic Management Journal* 26 (2005): 1009–31.

79 Anne Smith and Marie-Claude Reney, "The Mating Dance: A Case Study of Local Partnering Processes in Developing Countries," *European Management Journal* 15:2 (1997): 174–82.

80 Sanjiv Kumar and Anju Seth, "The Design of Coordination and Control Mechanisms for Managing Joint Venture–Parent Relationships," *Strategic Management Journal* 19:6 (June 1998): 579–99; T. K. Das and Bing-Sheng Teng, "Between Trust and Control: Developing Confidence in Partner Cooperation in Alliances," *Academy of Management Journal* 23:3 (July 1998): 491–512; Arvind Parkhe, "Building Trust in International Alliances," *Journal of World Business* 33:4 (1998): 417–37; Prashant Kale, Harbir Singh, and Howard Perlmutter, "Learning and Protection of Proprietary Assets in Strategic Alliances: Building Relational Capital," *Strategic Management Journal* 21:3 (March 2000): 217–37.

81 Africa Ariño and Jeffrey J. Reuer, "Designing and Renegotiating Strategic Alliance Contracts," *Academy of Management Executive* 18:3 (2004): 37–48.

82 Gary D. Burton, David Ahlstrom, Michael N. Young, and Yuri Rubanik, "In Emerging Markets, Know What Your Partners Expect," *Wall Street Journal* (December 15, 2008): R5.

83 Srilata Zaheer and Akbar Zaheer, "Trust across Borders," *Journal of International Business Studies* 37:1 (2006): 21.

84 Prashant Kale and Harbir Singh, "Managing Strategic Alliances: What Do We Know Now and Where Do We Go from Here?" *Academy of Management Perspectives* 23:3 (August 2009): 45–62.

85 John Kenneth Galbraith, *American Capitalism* (Boston: Houghton Mifflin, 1952): 91–92.

86 Eric H. Kessler, Paul E. Bierly, and Shanthi Gopalakrishnan, "Internal vs. External Learning in New Product Development: Effects of Speed, Costs and Competitive Advantage," *R & D Management* 30:3 (2000): 213–23.

87 These are adapted from Arvind Parkhe, "Interfirm Diversity, Organizational Learning, and Longevity in Global Strategic Alliances," *Journal of International Business Studies* 22:4 (1991): 579–601.

88 We wish to acknowledge the assistance of several American Airlines executives, who, although wishing to remain anonymous, supplied useful information for and feedback on this case. Additional information came from "Europe: Trans-Atlantic Alliances Are Set to Tighten," *Oxford Analytica Daily Brief Service* (January 3, 2008): 1; Douglas Hanks, "Proposed Deal Could Boost MIA," *McClatchy–Tribune Business News* (August 15, 2008): n.p.; James L. Oberstar, "A Bill to Ensure Adequate Airline Competition Between United States and Europe," *Congressional Record—Extensions*, 11th Congress, 1st Session 155 Cong Rec E 190 (February 3, 2009); Sarah Arnott, "BA Seeks Clearance for Transatlantic Alliance," *Business* (August 15, 2008): 44; Alfred Kahn and Dorothy Robyn, "The Sky Must Be No Limit to Global Competition," *Financial Times* (February 15, 2006); "Canada, Europe Reach 'Open Skies' Airline Deal," *Wall Street Journal* (May 7, 2009); Terry Maxon, "Lufthansa's Americas Chief Sees Little Threat If American Airlines Alliance Gets Antitrust Immunity," *McClatchy–Tribune Business News* (June 8, 2009): n.p.; Bruce Bernard, "American Airlines Seeks OK for Trans-Atlantic Tie-up," *Journal of Commerce Online* (August 15, 2008); International Air Transport Association, *Annual Report 2008*; "Virgin Atlantic Set to Ramp Up Anti-BA/AA Campaign," *Marketing Week* (December 4, 2008): 9.

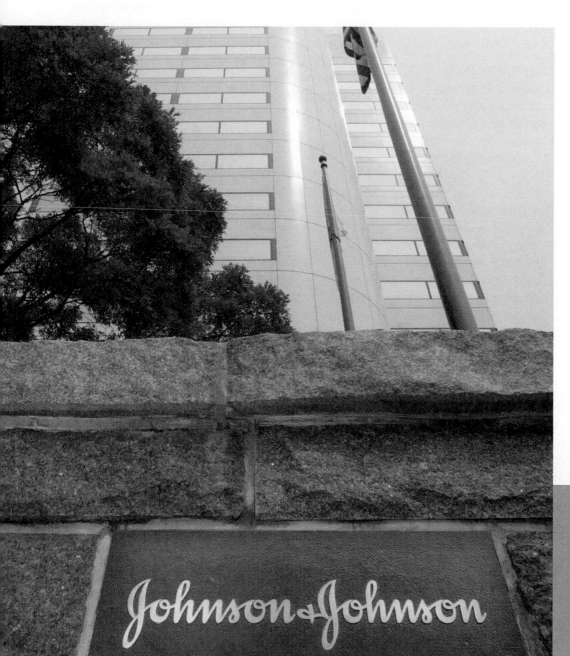

fifteen

The Organization of International Business

Objectives

- Profile the evolving understanding of organizing a company for international business

- Describe the antecedents and features of traditional structures

- Describe the antecedents and features of contemporary structures

- Study the systems used to coordinate and control international activities

- Profile the role and characteristics of organization culture

- Link the ideas of strategy and organization in the international company

Johnson & Johnson

Laws control the lesser man. Right conduct controls the greater one.

—Chinese proverb

The typical pharmaceutical company relies on global integration due to steep product development costs and potential scale economies.[1] Meanwhile, it must respond to local market conditions, obtaining government approval for each product in each country, and establishing local sales and distribution systems. This task requires configuring locally responsive value chains that are then coordinated through sophisticated collaboration between headquarters and subsidiaries. Building an organization that can meet this mission is tough. One standout company that does so is Johnson & Johnson (J&J).

A LITTLE BACKGROUND

How J&J Grew

Since the start of its U.S. operations in 1886, J&J has evolved into the most broadly based health-care company in the world. International activity began in 1919 with J&J Canada. J&J, headquartered in New Brunswick, New Jersey, now lists more than 250 operating companies across the world and sells products in more than 175 countries. It employs about 119,000 people worldwide, with nearly 70,000 working in 57 countries outside the United States. Its steady success is renowned. It holds nearly 54,000 U.S. and foreign patents and is the world's leader in a several medical segments, such as adhesive bandages, contact lenses, prescription pharmaceuticals, and medical devices. Through 2007, J&J's annual sales had grown for 75 consecutive years, reaching $61 billion by 2009. It has maintained profitability since going public in 1944, with 45 consecutive years of dividend increases. Surveys rank J&J as the most admired pharmaceutical company in the world.

What J&J Sells

J&J develops, manufactures, and markets products to consumers and health-care professionals worldwide. It aims for industry leadership in pharmaceuticals, medical devices and diagnostics, and consumer products. The pharmaceutical segment includes products in areas like anti-infective, cardiovascular, dermatology, immunology, and oncology. These products are distributed to retailers, wholesalers, and health-care professionals for prescription use by the public. The medical devices and diagnostics segment includes products distributed to wholesalers, hospitals, and retailers and used in professional fields by physicians, nurses, therapists, hospitals, diagnostic laboratories, and clinics. The consumer segment makes and markets products used in the baby and childcare, skin care, oral and wound care, and women's health-care fields, as well as nutritional and over-the-counter pharmaceuticals. These products, available without prescription, are marketed to the public and sold to wholesalers and to retailers throughout the world.

How J&J Is Run

J&J's nine-member Executive Committee is the principal management group responsible for operations and allocation of the resources worldwide; it oversees and coordinates the activities of the business segments. Executive committee members also chair worldwide Group Operating Committees (GOCs), composed of managers who represent operations within the group as well as management expertise in other specialized functions. The GOCs coordinate the activities of domestic and international units that fall in the pharmaceutical, medical device and diagnostics, and consumer segments.

DECENTRALIZED DECISION MAKING

Decentralization is the heart of J&J's organization—it allows managers who are closest to customers and competitors to make decisions. As the company says, it aims to be big and small all at once, building a global profile based on the conglomeration of many small units. By design, each unit operates with substantial autonomy, commanding the freedom to act as it sees best given local market conditions. Each operating company acts as its own small business, entrepreneurial in character and aware that success depends on anticipating customers' needs and delivering meaningful solutions. Decentralization, explains Ralph Larsen, CEO from 1989 to 2002, "gives people a sense of ownership and control—and the freedom to act more rapidly." His successor, William Weldon, concurs, adding, "The magic around J&J is decentralization." He expanded on these ideas, explaining:

The decentralized manner in which we operate our businesses marries the best qualities of smaller companies with entrepreneurial drive for growth and close proximity to customers with the resources, know how, and investment capital of a Fortune 500 company. This strategic approach gives us many advantages over a centralized operation. One is a strong sense of ownership, entrepreneurship, agility and accountability seldom seen in large multinational corporations. The leadership and employees of our

250 operating companies around the world are intensely competitive. We look to the leaders of our decentralized businesses to grow their businesses faster than their competitors. They are driven to innovate . . . [and] to bring greater value to the marketplace through internal discoveries, application of new science, technology, in-licensing and acquisition. We believe our decentralized approach to running the business yields better decisions—in the long run—for patients, health professionals and other customers, because the decision makers are close to the customers and are in a better position to understand their needs. Finally, our decentralized approach to managing the business is a tremendous magnet for talent, because it gives people room to grow and room to explore new ideas, thus developing their own skills and careers.

This philosophy enables J&J to behave like 250 small, innovative, entrepreneurial firms, responding to the unique opportunities and threats in their local markets. Yet at the same time, each unit can tap the know-how and resources of a large, successful MNE, thereby giving it access to deep pools of products, processes, and people.

Supporting Subsidiaries

J&J entered new markets by adding subsidiaries through investment, alliance, or acquisition of companies. Upon startup, J&J did not dispatch armies of home-office managers directed by headquarters-based generals. Rather, J&J provides the subsidiary the resources that local managers believe support achieving superior results. Its philosophy is that people who understand how the company creates value, have familiarity with the company's core competencies, and are culturally familiar and physically close to the market ought to be running the local business. Thus, for example, baby oil managers in Italy decided how big a bottle to use, even if that bottle differed from the one sold in Germany, Japan, or Mexico.

The heads of J&J's foreign subsidiaries once commanded so much autonomy that they were seen as "kings of their own countries." Headquarters would install some systems to coordinate activities among countries, often negotiating financial targets with the heads of the separate business units. It would then leave them to figure, given local market conditions, how to achieve those targets. With few exceptions, each international subsidiary is run by citizens of the country where it is located.

Growing pressures for global integration tested J&J's commitment to decentralization. Senior management conceded that decentralization resulted in inconsistent market development and duplication of efforts. For example, J&J launched Tylenol in 1960 as an over-the-counter pain reliever in the United States. Although it was available to local operating units shortly thereafter, the Japanese unit did not begin local sales until 2000. Therefore, although decentralization enabled J&J to respond to local needs, it slowed the global diffusion of products and programs.

Decentralization also created agency dilemmas for local management, creating questions regarding their primary allegiance: should they improve local performance at the expense of global corporate objectives? The risk came into play in 2007 when J&J revealed that some of its foreign units made improper payments related to the sale of medical devices in two "small-market countries." Management did not disclose details of the payments but said they were "contrary to the company's policies" and "may fall within the jurisdiction of the Foreign Corrupt Practices Act." Simultaneously, the company announced the early retirement of the executive responsible for the units, the then worldwide chair of medical devices and diagnostics.

Streamlining Coordination and Control

Senior management has since streamlined the way country managers coordinate value activities, recentralizing certain activities from the 250 subsidiaries to headquarters. The GOCs now deal with issues common to operating units, such as human resources, finance, science and technology, and government affairs. Managing certain activities at headquarters frees the units to concentrate on day-to-day performance. It also improves headquarters' coordination of production and marketing around the world. Input from local managers is still sought in formulating a unified marketing strategy; for example, they may debate whether cleanliness or beauty is the better promotion theme. Ultimately, though, when J&J rolls out a product, country managers no longer have the option to reject it.

Coordination has proven beneficial. For example, implementing an updated version of Windows across all operating units at the same time saved J&J an estimated $80 million. Still, years after starting to integrate information technologies, benign changes still meet resistance. Some business units, for instance, argue that they cannot adopt corporate technology standards or bear their share of the cost for infrastructure upgrades. For example, when she first started to integrate information technology, the then–chief information officer had difficulty getting answers on what type of systems were in operation. Similar sorts of problems have led to selective use of market control systems to benchmark the performance of operating units against competitors and each other.

The value of leveraging knowledge and expertise across the company shapes J&J's structure. J&J aimed to improve the global perspective of local decision making. Channels of communication and forums for discussion cut across the organization, encouraging and enabling far-flung units to share their ideas. Self-directed councils—for research, engineering, and operations, among others—meet to swap ideas. Successful employees rotate among operating units, sharing their expertise with their new work groups.

PEOPLE, CULTURE, AND THE CREDO

Management maintains that people and values are J&J's greatest assets. As they often note, every invention, every product, and every breakthrough the company has brought to human health and well-being has been powered by people. The bedrock of the organization was J&J's organization culture—what former CEO Ralph Larsen referred to as the "glue that binds this company together." The basis of this "glue" is a one-page ethical code of conduct, "Our Credo," that guides how J&J fulfills its business responsibilities (see Figure 15.1). Crafted in 1943 by Robert Wood Johnson, company chair from 1932 to 1963 and a member of the company's founding family, the Credo defined J&J's vision of organization.

The Credo tells J&J managers worldwide who and what to care about and in what specific order. J&J's "first responsibility is to the doctors, nurses, patients, mothers and fathers who use our products and services." It addresses the communities where J&J operates and the roles and duties of J&J employees.

FIGURE 15.1 The J&J Credo

Originally spelled out in 1943, the J&J Credo has been updated over the years to reflect the changing market and circumstances of J&J.

Source: Johnson & Johnson, "Our Company: Our Credo" (November 14, 2005), at www.jnj.com.

Notably, shareholders come last. The Credo declares that shareholders receive fair returns only upon tending to the other constituents; essentially, the company holds that the business will be well served by putting the customer first. As declared on the title sheet of the 2006 annual report, the "Credo underscores J&J's personal responsibility to put the needs . . . of the people we serve first. It liberates our passion and deepens our commitment to delivering meaningful health innovations." The company maintains that the Credo is more than just a moral compass. Rather, J&J believes it is the basis of success and finds proof in the fact that it is one of a handful of companies that have flourished through more than a century of change.

Translating the Credo

The Credo is available in 36 languages across Africa, Asia-Pacific, Eastern Europe, Latin America, the Middle East, and North America. Executives worried that the language and attitude differences might distort the clear, shared understanding of the company's mission among its global workforce. Consequently, the company periodically surveys employees on how well J&J meets the call of its Credo. These assessments are returned to senior management and, where there are shortcomings, the company takes action. J&J continues to update some of the language of the Credo as the world evolves; adaptations include the environment and the balance between work and family. Despite revisions, management believes the founding spirit of the Credo endures.

No matter the details of its particular structure, systems, and culture, J&J's leaders believe that the basis of the company's continued success is building an organization that is flexible enough to leverage the knowledge held by employees. Indeed, given the choice between staffing international operations with folks who implement top management's orders or hiring local people who are entrepreneurial innovators, J&J opts for the latter. Management reasoned that the benefits of front-line managers capitalizing on their initiative, developing their capabilities, and broadening their perspectives exceeded the risk of poor decisions. Decentralization has been, is, and will be the foundation of J&J's continued success. More pointedly, explained the CEO, "I am here to passionately protect the values of J&J. Our Credo is value-based. It comes down to people, values, and environment." **CRN** Case Review Note

Introduction

Artfully engineering an organization that coordinates global activities to meet the mandates of multinational operations is the frontier of international business. Competitive advantage follows from devising an organization that directs value creation in the face of pressures for worldwide integration versus local differentiation.[2] Therefore, this chapter examines how managers build an organization to implement their strategies.

> Organizing is the process of creating the structure, systems, and culture needed to implement the company's strategy.

Strategy as a Process We begin with the premise that an insightful strategy is a necessary, although insufficient, condition for long-term success. An MNE must implement its strategy, putting into practice what it has planned. The task turns managers' attention to how they should organize international operations. J&J exemplifies this situation, (1) showing the power of building an organization that integrates a network of decentralized national units, (2) tailoring technology, human resources, reward systems, and information systems to coordinate and control value activities, and (3) relying on its Credo to sustain a meaningful organization culture.

Case Review Note

Throughout these tasks, managers articulate what must be done to sustain the company's competitive advantage. They focus on how employees do their jobs, how the company coordinates interdependencies among value activities, the means taken to control situations that go awry, and the values that define its culture. In this way, J&J gives a sense of the efforts managers make to build the organization that implements their strategy.

FIGURE 15.2 Factors Affecting Organizing Operations

Organization refers to the activities through which a company builds the structures, systems, and culture that create a dynamic work environment. A company organizes operations to turn its ideas into actions.

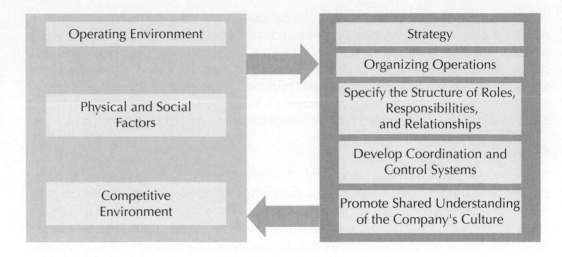

Operating Environment	
Physical and Social Factors	→
Competitive Environment	←

| Strategy |
| Organizing Operations |
| Specify the Structure of Roles, Responsibilities, and Relationships |
| Develop Coordination and Control Systems |
| Promote Shared Understanding of the Company's Culture |

Implementing strategy requires managers to build the necessary organization.

J&J highlights the variety of organizational activities performed by managers at headquarters and subsidiaries. Complicating their tasks are the numerous ways to administer activities. Many activities must be launched and supervised across units across countries. While many workers will heed calls to collaborate, some may resist change. Consequently, building the requisite organization, as we see in Figure 15.2, means managers must integrate the efforts of people, teams, units, and divisions into a smoothly functioning whole. Although difficult, an innovative organization design has powerful benefits.[3]

Change: The Critical Factor

How an MNE organizes is a key issue. Our ideas of the organization of international business are undergoing changes that demand reinterpreting fundamental principles.

Historic notions of the formal structure of a company emphasized arranging constraints and contracts to ensure workers' compliance.

A Brief History of Approaches to Organizational Change For generations, managers building an organization focused on the system of lines and boxes that depicted its formal structure. Managers specified the formal arrangement of work within the company by specifying who did what job, who worked in which unit, who reported to whom, and who could make which decisions. The output of this effort was the company's formal structure. The formal structure instituted a control system that specified constraints and contracts to ensure workers' compliance.

Beginning with General Motors and DuPont in the early twentieth century, this model worked for many MNEs. However, environmental trends, industry conditions, and market opportunities—to say nothing of the current global economic crisis—spur MNEs to configure novel value chains. Think, for example, of the implication of the Bottom of the Pyramid market—the largest, but poorest socio-economic consumer segment in the world—to traditional notions of strategy. Accessing the Bottom of the Pyramid will require "new business models to connect the poorest two billion people to the evolving nervous system of civilization."[4] New configurations of value activities create coordination and control challenges that can overwhelm the precise functionality outlined in a formal structure.

Some reason that asking how an organization should be formally structured is anachronistic, given awareness that "reconfiguring the formal structure is a blunt and sometimes brutal instrument of change. A new structure creates useful managerial ties, but those can take months and often years to evolve into effective knowledge-generating and decision-making relationships."[5] In times of dramatic change, such as the current global credit crunch, few MNEs have the luxury to await the emergence of "knowledge-generating and decision-making relationships."

The situation at Sony is a case in point. We noted in Chapter 11 that Sony faces a situation where virtually every product line was unprofitable. As such, Sony reported its first loss in 14 years in 2008. The global crisis exposed weaknesses in the Sony system, explained its CEO, Sir Howard Stringer, that "we didn't want really to admit." Fighting to reorient the company, the CEO had to jump-start the development of new relationships. Hence, Sir Howard reset the organization of the company in 2009. He began by replacing senior executives opposed to restructuring efforts with four young, loyal lieutenants—whom Sir Howard dubbed "the Four Musketeers"—to lead Sony's reorganized business units. Ironically, explained Sir Howard, "When this crisis came along, for me it was a godsend, because I could reorganize the company without having to battle the forces of the status quo."[6]

Contemporary Approaches to Organizational Change   The past few years have pushed MNEs to rethink, as Sony is doing, how they organize their workplaces. Calls for radical change, often in terms of downsizing, delayering, restructuring, reengineering, and reinventing the organization are widespread. Today, managers elaborate their traditional ideas of structure as the specification of boxes and lines with complementary systems and a cohesive culture that supports the company's strategy. Several trends spur managers to engage this perspective.

Changes in the market environment and nature of work push managers to rethink how they organize their workplace.

- *Expansion of International Business* The growth of international business has changed the opportunity set and efficiency frontier. MNEs respond in kind, engaging unprecedented strategies that demand more sophisticated organizations—think of, for example, the cases of Zara or Alibaba.

- *Importance of Knowledge as a Competitive Advantage* The second trend is a bit more subtle, involving the growing importance of knowledge as an engine of sustainable competitive advantage. More MNEs see the necessity of an organization that accelerates the development of ideas.

- *Power of the Internet as a Design Standard* The performance of the Internet as an organization metaphor pushes managers to rethink their assumptions of how they get people to do their jobs. The Internet is an efficient and effective global organization of knowledge, resources, and people. In the height of irony, however, the Internet has no formal organization, no board of directors, and no central administrator. The self-organizing and self-regulating capabilities of the Internet prompt questioning how to do the same in a company.

- *Workplace Adjustments* Workplace trends reset organization standards for many companies. The evolving nature of work changes the conduct and context of employees' jobs, whether it takes place in the biggest headquarters or the smallest subsidiary. Employees working with computers create value of astonishing variability, problem solving, and intellectual content. In earlier times, management could standardize the operating script for various jobs. Now, brighter workers along with technological flexibilities means senior managers can standardize fewer jobs.

Strategies that are more sophisticated involve activities that require organizational innovations.

- *Managerial Adjustments* Change in the nature of work has changed the nature of management. Besides being difficult, it is often counterproductive to supervise workers charged with reasoning or problem-solving tasks—generally, the bright people who staff such slots prefer less direct supervision. Moreover, the higher the level of manager in the hierarchy, historically, the more he or she knew about the various jobs in the company; that is no longer the case. Similarly, front-line employees at the subsidiary level once knew little more than their immediate responsibilities in the local marketplace;

network matter more in contempory organizations. Leading types of contemporary structures include the network and virtual organization. We now profile each.

Network Structure   The **network structure** is a core organization that outsources value activities in which it does not command as core competencies to those that do—or, as the saying goes, "Do what you do best and outsource the rest." For example, MNEs like Nike and Cisco Systems emphasize their design skills and hire companies, like Yue Yuen Industrial or Flextronics, to make their products. Similarly, financial institutions, hotel chains, and credit card companies find they can create more value by offshoring call-center functions to those companies that command a core competency in that activity.

MNEs adopt a network structure to coordinate outsourced activities while maintaining a unifying sense of organization. That is, the relationship between the MNE and the companies in its network is not predicated on the efficiency of transactions. Rather, the network structure promotes a web of relationships between different companies in ways that let managers coordinate the workflow even though other companies are doing it (see Figure 15.5). Essentially, an MNE collaborates with select suppliers and then develops specialized decision-making relationships that let the collectivity of companies jointly coordinate value activities.[23] In doing so, managers replace the visible hand of the command and control structure with the invisible hand of self-interest in the network.

Though a novel format for many MNEs today, the network structure is not unprecedented. Japanese companies have long used the *keiretsu* structure, an integrated collectivity of nominally independent companies in which each company owns a small percentage of others in the network. Keiretsus rely on long-term personal relationships among executives in the different companies. The same directors often serve on more than one board. Sometimes keiretsus are vertical, where managers connect the factors of production of a certain product—for example, the network between Toyota and its parts suppliers. Other times keiretsus are horizontal and connections link companies across industries, typically centered on a trading company (a so-called *sogo shosha*) or financial institution. The Mitsubishi keiretsu exemplifies this form.

Worldwide, companies manifesting hallmarks of the network structure include the the Virgin Group, Tata Group, and Cisco Systems. Many German companies are similarly

Concept Check

Chapter 4 discusses the notion of the invisible hand, courtesy of Adam Smith, that guides the efficient actions of self-interested individuals. In its absence, the visible hand of the state supervises transactions and relationships. In strict economics, the invisible hand offers a superior solution, able to optimize the allocation of resources and improve the potential return of effort. Similar dynamics are at play in the network structure, with its reliance essentially on the invisible hand to regulate the transactions and relationships among its members.

FIGURE 15.5   A Simplified Network Structure

A network is an interconnected system of people, products, and processes. At the center of the network structure is a core unit. Its function is to outsource value-adding activities for which it does not possess *core competencies*. The network itself consists of partner organizations that focus on areas in which they can deliver maximum value. Finally, there are the channels through which units communicate with other units. To manage the network, the core unit uses these channels to coordinate and integrate activities carried on throughout the system.

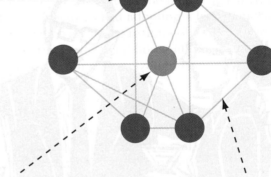

Differentiated units to which headquarters delegates decision-making authority. These units, whether they are local marketing subsidiaries, international production centers, or cross-functional teams, are the front line of the network with responsibility for sensing, processing, and acting upon specialized and generalized information in an entrepreneurial fashion.

The formal center of the network that coordinates strategic objectives and operational policies across the differentiated units. This unit ensures the efficient flow of resources, supplies, components, and funds throughout the network. It aims to, and effectively collects, sorts, and distributes the organization's accumulated wisdom, knowledge, and experiences.

The channels of exchange that manage and fine-tune the volume, content, and flow of hard and soft information. These linkages animate the network by setting paths of interaction, coordination, and integration between differentiated yet interdependent functional, area, and product units.

intertwined as keiretsus, but there is no formal term to describe them.[24] Like their Japanese counterparts, these groups are marked by extensive cross-company connections that sustain the network. Unlike their Japanese countreparts, the German format uses more centralization.

Virtual Organization   A **virtual organization** is the antithesis of a vertical hierarchy. Rather than seeking to control value-chain activities through direct ownership of activities, virtual organizations acquire strategic capabilities by creating a temporary network among independent companies, suppliers, customers, and even rivals. The ensuing virtual organization relies on information technology to create the links that coordinate skills, costs, and access to various markets.[25]

The precedent for this structure hails from the film industry. Making movies involves organizing people who, as "free agents," move from project to project, applying their skills—acting, directing, costuming, makeup, set design—as needed. The typically short span of virtual organizations means that free agents organize and reorganize in response to opportunities.[26] Collegiality and contracts, rather than authority and hierarchy, hold the virtual organization together. Well-performing companies return; poor performers depart.

A virtual organization consists of a core of full-time employees that coordinates free agents as opportunities arise. One example is StrawberryFrog, an international advertising agency. A rare amphibian with a red body and blue legs inspired the peculiar name of this company. Its CEO explains that the nimble strawberry frog is the opposite of the existing "dinosaur agencies, established in the industrial age as monoliths, which have the greatest difficulty in adapting to the new era."[27] Competing with companies employing thousands, StrawberryFrog has a small staff, known as "frogs," in New York, São Paulo, and London. It bulks up as needed by enlisting freelancers from around the world.[28] Free from the overhead, constraints, and complexity of hierarchies, StrawberryFrog offers clients agility and cost effectiveness. The company has leveraged its network to do work in Europe, Asia, and the United States for Mitsubishi, Sony Ericsson, Pfizer, Sprint, IKEA, MTV, and Research in Motion.

Pitfalls of Contemporary Structures   As we have already seen, hierarchies suffer from endemic limitations. So too do contemporary structures. First is the difficulty of coordinating something that by definition is ever changing. The dynamism of networks makes adaptive reconfiguration and responsive coordination an ongoing job.[29] In the best of circumstances, managers struggle to adapt the network by adjusting supporting infrastructures. As such, coordinating a structure that some argue should require little coordinating complicates building contemporary structures. Leaders may champion decentralization yet when push comes to shove, often intrude in decision making. Frequent intervention erodes the credibility of the promised independence.

Moreover, hidden hierarchies lying latent in contemporary structures endure. As one observer notes, "I've been inside a lot of companies that espouse flat organizational structures and self-management. But when you really start looking at how things actually work, you find that there is in fact a hierarchy—just one that is not explicit."[30] Workers are prone to organize around the rules, rewards, and punishments in the company, creating a subtle, unspoken hierarchy even if officially there is none. These difficulties make the idea of a contemporary organization less appealing. Hence, contemporary organizations of various sorts have given way to more traditional structures.[31]

Few dispute the potential for innovative coordination in a structure that encourages sharing information and eliminating boundaries that slow decision making. Unleashing the power of their value chain to capture the opportunities of today's economy urges companies to rethink traditional structures. Managers facing the dilemma of a traditional or contemporary structure—or, as we see in our Point-Counterpoint, hierarchy or hyperarchy—face rethinking the integration of individual behavior, structure, and culture.

Companies evaluate results in comparison to budgets but often find it hard to compare countries using standard operating ratios.

Cost and Accounting Comparisons   Different costs due to location effects among subsidiaries complicate comparing performance. For example, the ratio of labor to sales for a subsidiary in one country may be much higher than that for a subsidiary in another country, even though unit production costs may not differ. Making sure apples line up with apples and oranges with oranges requires evaluation processes that take into account cross-national cost-differential indicators.

Different financial practices and disclosure standards create reporting and accountability contingencies. Most MNEs keep one set of books that comply with home-country principles and another to comply with market requirements. Besides recognizing the intricacies of tax treatments, headquarters adjusts accounting metrics to qualify for exceptions in local subsidiaries' performance.

Evaluation Metrics   Headquarters evaluates subsidiaries and their managers on many measures. Financial metrics dominate evaluation, particularly when an MNE relies on coordination by plan and control by bureaucracy. Important performance metrics are "budget compared with profit" and "budget compared with sales value." These metrics affect consolidated corporate figures, so headquarters monitors them. Many nonfinancial criteria are also important, such as market-share increase, quality control, turnover ratios, and managers' relationship with stakeholders.

A system that relies on a combination of measurements is more reliable than one that does not.

MNEs adjust evaluation metrics to avoid penalizing or rewarding managers for conditions beyond their control. For example, headquarters may decide to reduce operations in a country given its slow growth and risky environment. Punishing managers for the country's adverse situation, independent of their performance, is demotivating. Rather, the task is qualifying evaluation for local conditions given global trends.

Information Systems   Information technologies provide powerful control tools. Most MNEs use enterprise resource planning (ERP) to monitor value activities, such as product planning, parts purchasing, maintaining inventories, customer service, and order fulfillment. The Japanese retailer Ito-Yokado, which operates the 7-Eleven franchise in Japan, has linked each store's cash registers into an ERP system that records sales, monitors inventory, and schedules tasks for store managers. The ERP system also tracks how often managers use the built-in analytical tools. Managers who have not checked in often enough are told to do so.[45]

MNEs face constraints in acquiring information: the cost of information compared to its value, identifying redundant information, and excluding irrelevant information. Much of the information useful to a subsidiary—such as which government official clears items through customs—need not be reported to headquarters. Companies reevaluate information sources to cope with the information deluge. They anchor their expectation in their choices regarding centralization, coordination, and control.

Organization Culture

Organization culture is the shared meaning and beliefs that shape how employees interpret information, make decisions, and implement actions.

So far, we have looked at the roles that structure and systems play in organizing a company. We now turn to the final element: the culture of the organization. One can consider organization culture in an applied fashion, specifying it as the way things are done in a company. Alternatively, we can follow the suggestion in Chapter 2 and adopt a philosophical view. This view defines organization culture as an embedded set of shared normative principles that guide action and serve as the standard to evaluate workers' behaviors.

We integrate these perspectives, defining **organization culture** as the coherent set of assumptions about the organization and its goals and practices that members of the company share. So specified, organization culture is a system of shared values about what is important and beliefs about how the world works that shapes how decisions are made and actions are taken.

THE IMPORTANCE OF CULTURE

Companies have been sensitive to the idea that culture plays a role in how they design their organizations. Research identifies a significant link between organization culture and the financial performance of a firm. Facets of organization culture, such as the values and principles of management, the nature of the work climate and atmosphere, and traditions and ethical standards, influence a company's financial performance.[46] Hence, managers now take an expansive view of organization culture, seeing it as a powerful tool that can support the goals and behaviors that help the company implement its strategy.

Others report that culture is a critical component of a company's transition from "good" to "great" status. Technology, product development, and financial stewardship play key roles in this transition. Still, managers link the goal of becoming a great company to developing an organization culture that champions unwavering faith and passion, rigorous discipline and focus, plainly communicated values, strong work ethics, and promoting people with the preferred outlook.[47] In summary, great companies develop organization cultures, much as J&J does with its Credo, which give employees a consistent way to relate to their jobs, to each other, to customers, to shareholders, and to business partners.

The importance of organization culture will increase in coming years. Earlier chapters highlight growing pressures on companies to improve their global competitiveness. Later chapters detail the approaches that companies use to do so—for instance, reconfiguring their value chains to streamline manufacturing processes or maximizing supply-chain efficiencies with better coordination mechanisms. These objectives have scant chance of success without a complementary organization culture. Indeed, it is wise for a company to undertake strategic moves that fit the values shared by managers and employees. In the absence of fit, companies then must rely on constraints, controls, and contracts to compel employees.

Culture and Values   Successful companies develop an organization culture that instills in their employees enthusiasm beyond that justified by economic rewards. "Objectives don't get you there. Values do," said Jack Welch of GE. A strategy-supportive culture spurs people to engage the company's vision, to do their jobs well, and to collaborate with others. In addition, a powerful organization culture lessens the need to regulate employees' behaviors with elaborate structures and systems. Therefore, a culture's capacity to power high performance puts the onus on managers to build a company that commands this resource. Great companies build an organization that people do not just want to work for but also want to belong to.

MNEs and the verse use activities to promote shared values. Toyota relies upon its famed Technical Skills Academy to meet several objectives. Sessions teach auto maintenance techniques as well as broad management skills. These classes are a part of senior managers' goal to inculcate the principles of the "Toyota Way" in the next generation of company leaders. Socializing employees to engage the Toyota Way, managers believe, enables everyone in the company to base decisions on a "philosophical sense of purpose, to think long term, to have a process for solving problems, to add value to the organization by developing its people, and to recognize that solving root problems drives organizational learning."

The shared values that enact organization culture influence what employees perceive, how they interpret, and what they do to respond to their world. As does Toyota with its Toyota Way, J&J anchors its ideas of value creation and strategic purpose in the principles of its Credo. Recall from our opening case that this manifesto champions values that embody the company's responsibilities to its stakeholders worldwide. J&J's Credo ensures that, when confronted with opportunities or threats anywhere in the world, employees define, analyze, and resolve issues in ways that respect and reinforce the culture of the company.

Key features of a company's organization culture include

- Values and principles of management.
- Work climate and atmosphere.
- Patterns of "how we do things around here."
- Traditions.
- Ethical standards.

Case Review Note

An organization's culture shapes its strategic choices.

Case Review Note

Culture and the Value Chain Sophisticated value-chain configurations increase coordination and control demands. Improving coordination and maintaining control requires managers to consult colleagues more often. Managers develop cross-cultural teams to tackle issues common to foreign operations. Many teams are composed of people chosen because of their expertise, not because of their positions, and they behave as equals, not superiors and subordinates. Often, the team's ability to reach consensus depends on members' adoption of common values, rather than dutiful compliance with coordination codes or control routines.

CHALLENGES AND PITFALLS

Few companies permit an organization culture to emerge naturally. As they do with structure and systems, companies socially engineer organization culture. Managers often struggle to shape their organization's culture. Typically, managers from different countries have values that differ from those endorsed by the company. Complicating matters are situations where workers have slight exposure to the values endorsed by senior managers.

The difficulty of this task is proportional to the importance of knowledge-generating and decision-making relationships to the MNE's competitiveness.[48] That is, convergent values ease the exchange of ideas between people from different countries. In contrast, different values create boundaries. Similar conflicts prevent cross-national teams from working. For instance, at one company, the U.S. managers complained that the U.K. managers were too bureaucratic, and the U.K. managers complained that the U.S. managers made decisions without thorough analysis.[49]

Companies promote closer contact among managers from different countries to overcome these challenges. A popular objective is fostering shared understandings of global goals and norms, along with improving the transfer of ideas and best practices from one country to another.[50] Some take a direct approach, posting people from the home office throughout global units. For example, Wipro, an Indian technology company, employs 54,000 people in 35 countries. More than 11,000 of these people work for units outside of India, of which more than 90 percent are Indian. Explained Sanjay Joshi, chief executive of global programs, "We sprinkle Indians in new markets to help seed and set up the culture and intensity."[51] Some take a less direct approach. For example, GE's Leadership Development Center runs programs that share knowledge and communicate best practices. Classes pull managers from different businesses and different parts of the world. Besides spreading best practices throughout the organization, this sort of knowledge sharing improves understanding of the company's culture.[52] Explained Jeffrey Immelt, chair and CEO of General Electric, the company tries "very hard to provide a company, a set of values, and a culture that employees can be proud of, whether it be in Pittsfield, Paris, Shanghai, or London."[53]

Lastly, Mattel, the toy maker, has 25,000 employees in 36 countries and sells its products in 150 nations. Although you would think that selling the fun of toys would converge cultural ideals, transcending different values has proven problematic. Facing dissension throughout its global operations, the company launched leadership programs at its Conference Leadership Center. The programs extend to facilities throughout the world through an e-learning system. Twice a year, the company runs a weeklong leadership program on global business growth for 35 directors and officers drawn from around the world.

Dealing with critical issues facing Mattel has increased the knowledge of management worldwide, and now "global management is more closely aligned with the corporate strategies and goals," says the vice president of leadership development. "This, in turn, produces innovative and creative products, reduces costs, and improves employee satisfaction." Now employees are becoming "one Mattel company," rather than workers of various companies operating separately.[54]

Against this backdrop, one must heed nagging questions about the performance impact of organization culture. Thus far, few organizations have been able to parlay a robust organization culture into consistently high performance. A survey of 1,200 international executives, for example, found that "fewer than 10 percent of companies currently succeed at building high-performance cultures." This shortfall stands in sharp contrast to the fact that 9 in 10 CEOs acknowledge that "corporate culture is as important as a strategy for business success."[55]

ORGANIZATION CULTURE AND STRATEGY

The principles and practices of organization culture vary with the requirements of the company's strategy (see Figure 15.6). For example, the company implementing a global strategy aims to develop a robust culture that helps everyone around the world unquestioningly accept common goals and practices. Standardizing value activities requires standardizing employees' views about purposes and practices. Therefore, companies implementing this strategy tend to adopt functional or product structure along with coordinating through standardization and controlling through bureaucracy.

Alternatively, companies following a multidomestic strategy encourage greater variety in the local interpretation of corporate goals. This, in turn, means that people across the differentiated units of the organization share fewer common values. Adapting value activities for local markets requires accepting more local autonomy, a requirement that rests on sensitivity to local outlooks and norms. Therefore, multidomestic companies tend to adopt a traditional area structure, decentralizing authority to local markets, along with opting for systems of coordination by planning and control according to market standards.

Concept Check

In Chapter 2, we classify "Company and Management Orientations" as *ethnocentric*, *polycentric*, and *geocentric*. In Chapter 11, we suggest various ways in which these perspectives affect a company's implementation of its strategy for conducting worldwide operations, whether *international*, *multidomestic*, *global*, or *transnational*. Here, in putting these pieces together, we suggest that when they are organizing operations, managers heed the company's global "orientation" and its fit with environments.

Over time, organization culture varies with the type of strategy the company pursues; often, like human nature, culture is slow to change no matter the situation.

GLOBAL
Strategic objectives: Productivity and efficiency

Strategic emphasis: Integration, competitive advantage

Dominant attribute: Standardized goal achievement, global competitiveness

Leadership style: Production and achievement-oriented, decisive control orientation

Bonding: Goal orientation, production, competition

TRANSNATIONAL
Strategic objectives: Integration, responsiveness, learning

Strategic emphasis: Innovation, ideas, and growth

Dominant attribute: Innovation, creativity, dynamism, flexibility

Leadership style: Innovator, risk affinitive, congruence between individual values and company goals

Bonding: Flexibility, risk, entrepreneurship

INTERNATIONAL
Strategic objectives: Leverage core competencies

Strategic emphasis: Control, stability, predictability

Dominant attribute: Formal order, rules and regulations, uniformity

Leadership style: Director, administrator, enforcer

Bonding: Rules, policies and procedures, clear expectations

MULTIDOMESTIC
Strategic objectives: Local responsiveness

Strategic emphasis: Esprit de corps, commitment, consensus

Dominant attributes: Cohesiveness, trust, affiliation

Leadership style: Mentor, facilitator, coach, adaptability

Bonding: Loyalty and tradition

Pressure for Global Integration — High / Low

Pressure for Local Responsiveness — Low / High

FIGURE 15.6 Strategy and Organizational Culture in International Business

The four strategies charted here correspond to the four types of MNE strategies covered in Chapter 11. Each sheet type specific indications for the features in forms of the company's organization. A company opting for a *global strategy*, for example, markets a standardized product for a specific global segment. Logically, it will socially engineer its *corporate culture* to help employees around the world accept and adopt a standardized set of goals.

Despite practical differences from company to company and strategy to strategy, organization culture shares philosophical features. First, no matter the company's strategy, employees perceive an organization culture based on what they see, hear, or experience within the company. Thus, senior managers exemplify the set of assumptions about the company and the shared values and ideals. Top management's commitment to "walking the talk" legitimizes an MNE's culture.

Second, even though individuals have different backgrounds, work at different organizational levels, or champion different ambitions, they tend to describe the company's culture in similar terms. That is, workers in Beijing, Bonn, Benares, and Boston vary on a variety of demographic and social criteria. However, working for IBM, for example, leads all of them to describe the company's culture with similar metaphors, analogies, and principles. Socializing people to share common values has dramatic implications to productivity and profitability. Increasingly, MNEs forsake manipulating employees through traditional approaches of reward and punishment and adopt culturally sensitive methods that motivate them to accept "how things are done around here." Executives work to develop, communicate, and practice the values that encourage individual involvement in the collective enterprise. A useful tool, as our "Looking to the Future" insert shows, are the cultural overtones of executive education.

Looking to the Future   The Role and Rise of Corporate Universities

Many managers believe that instead of letting the organization's culture emerge naturally, companies must purposefully develop shared values. This has led to a variety of approaches to socialize employees to accept the normative code of the company's culture. One intriguing development is the boom in corporate universities—physical and virtual institutions that lead training efforts, facilitate learning, and help upgrade competencies—all within a context of advocating the philosophical ideals of the company's culture.

The past few years has seen exponential growth in corporate universities. Worldwide, more than a thousand new corporate universities have begun operations. By region, corporate universities are growing by leaps and bounds in the United States, thriving in Europe, and making serious inroads in Asia. In the United States, for example, the number of corporate universities grew from around 400 in 1988 to more than 20,000 in 2007 and includes nearly half of the Fortune 500.[56]

Some universities are housed at headquarters, while others are sprinkled among offices at remote sites. Unisys, for example, has campuses in each of the five geographic areas where it has a large presence: North America, Europe, the United Kingdom, Latin America, and Asia and the South Pacific. Some have opted to break free from the constraints of geography, opening virtual online universities where employees learn via the Internet and interactive videoconferencing. They utilize e-learning tactics like live Webcasts, online chat and discussion groups, and teleconferences. At the

current growth rate, the number of corporate universities will exceed the number of traditional universities by 2010. In a nutshell, the boom in corporate universities symbolizes the growing appreciation among managers of the importance of managing the emergence and evolution of the company's culture.

Corporate universities were originally created to teach employees practical skills and workplace systems. For example, McDonald's Hamburger University in Illinois opened in the 1950s with the objective of preparing people to run the day-to-day operations of a franchise. Today, "Training isn't just a nice thing to do anymore," reported the American Society for Training and Development. "Companies are now thinking of training as a strategic imperative."[57] Our upcoming profile of Infosys highlights a company that relies upon its famed corporate university to embed new hires with an understanding of its value activities, which is explicitly anchored in its organization culture.

Others amplify this theme, explaining that their corporate university aims to "inculcate everyone, from the clerical assistant to the top executive, in the culture and values that make the organization unique and special and to define behaviors that enable employees to 'live the values.'"[58] The goal of coupling executive learning to the company's strategy drives the recent and projected growth of the corporate-university model. For example, the CEO of Unipart, a British auto-parts maker, notes that his company's university "is at the very heart of the business" and a "key enabler for future growth of the business."[59] Like many other CEOs, he runs his own course on the philosophy and principles of his company's business approach.

Senior executives that take on the hat of teacher generate benefits. The director of LVMH's university believes that putting top people into the teaching pit "gives them access to people they would never get access to. It is the role of our top senior executives to get a feel for what is going on."[60] Managers at LVMH gain similar benefits. Typically, they go through two-and-a-half-day forums that create networking opportunities. Then, when they return to their unit, if they run into a problem, they can more comfortably call someone for help. In addition, they pick up new management tools, often reporting that they return to their divisions with several ideas. Finally, they return with a much better sense of how their professional development compares to counterparts.

A growing mandate for corporate universities is integrating diverse workforces. Hiring engineers in Mumbai or Sophia to help people in Redmond makes economic sense. Preempting a tower of Babel requires that companies help people learn to work in proliferating global work groups. Again, hiring people from around the world, coupled with the presumption that teams outperform individuals, leads to the inevitability of a growing number of teams composed of an expanding mix of nationalities and ethnicities. Tempting as it is to rely upon happenstance to coordinate the process, cultural discussions highlight the risk of benign neglect. Corporate universities provide a robust platform to coordinate the process in a controlled, purposeful setting. Done well, explains the vice president of Unisys University, corporate universities provide continual learning for employees in ways that align employees' learning with the strategy of the business and culture of the organization.[61]

A recent change in the corporate-university model is finding new ways to prepare future leaders. The search for global leaders drives performance and future growth. Corporate universities design executive programs that engage high-potential executives on topics that influence the company and industry. The scripted structure of a corporate university pushes executives to develop the insights and cultivate the relationships they might need to reshape their company. Monique Elliott of GE Capital Solutions, after a class at GE's corporate university, believes that, given that her fellow students are all GE employees, the experience is more rewarding because "[w]e all speak the same language, and we are comfortable in the GE culture."[62]

The unfolding global economic crisis boosts the role of corporate universities—but for less charitable reasons. Analysts and educators debate whether the way business students have been taught within traditional university settings may have contributed to the depth and despair of the global economic crisis.[63] A common criticism holds that orthodox MBA programs grew too scientific, too detached from real-world issues, and too isolated from the moral implications of choice and action. Others contend that traditional MBA programs give students a limited and distorted view of the ethical and social considerations of business leadership. Hence, goes this reasoning, MBA programs' moral, ethical, and sociological shortcomings ill-prepare business-school graduates to do the right thing for their companies and for society. As employers question the value of an MBA, a growing number are setting up or expanding existing corporate universities to help executives develop skills as well as social responsibilities. ∎

Infosys: The Search for the Best and the Brightest

CASE

India produces about 300,000 engineering graduates each year, offering a fresh pool of talented, hard-working, and ambitious candidates eager to work at a fraction of the cost of their counterparts in the West.[64] This advantage has helped catapult India from a slow-moving economy to the forefront of the global offshore market. India's offshoring sector, the world's largest and fastest growing, is dominated by its information technology (IT) services. By 2007, that sector employed about 1.5 million people and accounted for 7 percent of India's GDP. Growth is expected to accelerate; India's software services exports exceeded $31 billion in 2007 and are targeted to reach $60 billion by 2010. Leading the charge is Infosys Technologies Limited (Infosys).

Infosys: An Introduction

Infosys, founded in Pune, India, in 1981, is headquartered in Bangalura, ground zero of the Indian offshoring industry. Infosys is a global technology-services firm that defines, designs, and delivers IT-enabled, end-to-end business solutions that leverage technology for its clients in financial services, manufacturing, telecommunications, retail, utilities, logistics, and other industries. Infosys's offerings span business and technology consulting; application services; systems integration; product engineering; custom software development, maintenance, reengineering, independent testing, and validation services; IT infrastructure services; and business process outsourcing. To do this, Infosys has opened more than 50 offices and development centers in India, China, Australia, the Czech Republic, Poland, the United Kingdom, Canada, and Japan. In 2009, Infosys had more than 103,000 employees.

Historically, Indian software companies executed most of their software projects end-to-end at overseas locations. That is, Indian software engineers were sent to work at clients' facilities in foreign countries where they completed the job. Infosys turned this concept upside down, presuming that it could perform this function much more cost efficiently if it could tap the talent-rich Indian market to do the job from India-based offices. The economics of this simple yet compelling innovation were indisputable—application-development costs in India are a fifth that of U.S. levels. This innovation laid out a clear-cut challenge: Management had to build an organization that could coordinate a value-chain configuration that relied upon local Indian workers to service clients who spanned the globe. Explained Narayana Murthy, the company's founder, top management saw the absolute need to develop an organization—complete with structure, systems, and culture—that could "source capital from where it is cheapest, produce where it is most cost-effective, and sell where it is most profitable, all without being constrained by national boundaries."

The Global Delivery Model

Infosys translated this ambition into its pioneering Global Delivery Model (GDM). The GDM moves Indian engineers abroad to the location where the best talent is available, where it made the best economic sense to do the job, and which posed the least amount of risk. In other words, Infosys would accept a software design job, break it down into its logical components, and then distribute these components to the optimal locations in the Infosys world. Originally, the Infosys world was bounded by its talent in India. Over time, given growing success and the enabling technology of improving telecommunications systems, Infosys built additional capabilities to reinforce this model. Today, Infosys runs a global network of managers, software designers, and engineers.

Two Decades of Growth

Infosys began in 1981 with a capitalization of US $250. The company grew modestly during its first decade, finishing 1991 with revenues of $3.89 million. The liberalization of the Indian economy in 1991, fueled by the growing adoption of free market principles, accelerated growth. Executives began to focus on global markets, supported by sophisticated and inexpensive communication technologies. Infosys's revenues increased to $121 million by 1999. By 2009, the company's revenues approached $5 billion, with net income nearing $1.5 billion. Along the way, the employee head count grew from the original "founding seven" to more than 103,000 worldwide.

Stating (and Restating) a Mission   Although a global juggernaut today, the company's humble beginnings carry great weight. Murthy, along with six friends, began the idea of Infosys with a meeting in the bedroom of his small apartment, where they debated the mission of the company. After hours of discussion, they resolved that their mission was not, he says, "to be the best, the biggest or the most profitable company, but to earn the respect of all our stakeholders. . . . My view was if we sought respect, we'd automatically do the right thing by each of them. We'd satisfy our customers, be fair to our employees, and follow the finest principles with respect to investors . . . we would not violate laws, and, finally, we'd make a difference to society. . . . [A]utomatically, you'll get revenues and profits and all that."

He went on to add that "We started out as seven people in 1981, with $250. We had just one customer. . . . We never imagined we would come this far." And although many successful companies share this characteristic, the founding vision of Infosys is a legacy that the company fervently works to imbue throughout the company. Indeed, the founding vision still infuses the company's current mission statement: "To achieve our objectives in an environment of fairness, honesty, and courtesy towards our clients, employees, vendors and society at large."

Senior managers translated these ideals into the philosophical pillars of the company's culture. More poetically, the company noted, "We believe that the softest pillow is a clear conscience. The values that drive us underscore our commitment to:

- **Customer Delight** To surpass customer expectations consistently
- **Leadership by Example** To set standards in our business and transactions and be an exemplar for the industry and ourselves
- **Integrity and Transparency** To be ethical, sincere and open in all our transactions
- **Fairness** To be objective and transaction-oriented, and thereby earn trust and respect
- **Pursuit of Excellence** To strive relentlessly, constantly improve ourselves, our teams, our services and products to become the best"

Being Smart as a Core Competency

At Infosys, senior executives develop knowledge through a process of observation, data collection, analysis, and conclusion. A company ably managed, they reasoned, enables translating newfound knowledge into pioneering software solutions. Nevertheless, as the saying goes, even the grandest vision depends on the success of the smallest details. The evolution and success of Infosys—it took the company 23 years to become a $1 billion company but only 23 months to double that—depends on the smallest components of the company.

Infosys holds firm that this knowledge cannot be archived in a static database. Rather, its knowledge is encapsulated in the people Infosys hires. Explained Murthy, "Our respect for our professionals can be summed up by our belief that the market capitalization of Infosys becomes zero after working hours end at 5 p.m., no matter what it was during the day. . . . It's our belief that the first duty of a corporation is to uphold respect and dignity for the individual."

Recruiting: Looking for "Learnability"

Fast-growing companies often struggle to communicate this vision to employees. Infosys was no exception. However, Infosys's approach to socializing employees to its philosophy and practices took new paths. In 2007, the company staffed about 25,000 slots. Although entry-level jobs carried annual salaries of about $5,000, more than 1.4 million people applied for these slots. Each applicant was required to pass a rigorous examination composed of math equations and logic puzzles designed to assess their aptitude for "learnability" (Infosys-speak for being a quick study). Few survive this screening. Ultimately, Infosys hired less than 1 percent of the 1.4 million applicants.

Infosys new hires shared similar characteristics. First, they were smart. They had shown the ability to learn quickly—a critical competency, given the dynamic nature of the company and its markets. Indeed, learnability was an important criterion in selection, promotion, and retention decisions because the rapid evolution of information technology demanded workers who could learn as technology advanced, customers and clients emerged, and market circumstances changed. Lastly, Infosys screened people for their overall attitude, looking for those individuals with positive outlooks on life.

Transferring an understanding of the company to new employees requires more than escorting new hires to their workstations. Rather, the importance of values to performance put a premium on transferring the corporation's culture. Infosys CEO Nandan Nilekani summed it up this way: "There aren't many companies growing like this. . . . Companies haven't been investing enough in people. Rather than train them, they let them go. Our people are our capital. The more we invest in them, the more they can be effective." To that end, Infosys invests $65 of every $1,000 in revenue in training programs and educational initiatives. No competitor matches this sum.

Training: Preaching "Technical Evangelism"

Training and development begin right off the bat. Even though the applicants selected have excelled academically, all go through a 14-week brain-busting boot camp. Each new hire attends a rigorous training program, taking classes from more than 150 instructors—or, in the world of Infosys, so-called "technical evangelists." Courses include analytical-thinking and problem-solving skills as well as principles of operating database-management systems and information networks. Infosys's move from India into overseas markets has expanded the curriculum to include social-networking perspectives and instruction in team building, customer facing, business etiquette, and negotiation skills.

Throughout this program, the company goes to great lengths to communicate its values, systems, and processes. The training program addresses an intriguing aspect of the Indian psyche. Explained Murthy, "We have realized that our challenge is to take the reactive mind-set of Indian youngsters and change them into proactive problem-solving ones. By and large, because of our culture, family background, etc., we are reactive. To change that, we have to understand problem-solving as a science and an art. We have to understand algorithmic thinking."

For the average hardworking, stressed-out student, surviving the training program is no guarantee that he or she will "graduate." Completing the 14-week program earns the student a slot to take two three-hour comprehensive exams. Successful students move from the status of "freshers" to "Infoscions."

Tapping a Global Labor Pool

The geographic distribution of Infosys's clients—18 countries account for 98 percent of the company's business—pushed it to diversify its labor pool to optimize customer service. Karthik Sarman, vice president of human resources, reasoned, "a Japanese worker will tend to do better in Japan. It is a matter of being able to connect with clients on more than just the technical level." Hence, Infosys launched its Global Talent Program to recruit job candidates from around the world with the goal of hiring individuals who shared cultural nuances and languages with its clients.

Caution about hiring people unfamiliar with its approaches spurred Infosys to bring employees hired in countries other than India to Bangalura for technical education and

An auditorium on the Bangaluru campus of Infosys. Blazoned on the screen is the message, *powered by intellect, driven by values,* that encapsulates the company's philosophy and purpose.
Source: Courtesy of Infosys Technologies, Ltd.

executive socialization. New recruits visit India for a six-month training and orientation program, and then return to their home countries as local agents. The first cohorts of this program included 96 "Infoscions" from China and 78 from Mauritius. Infosys also included 300 college graduates from the United States. The pursuit of talent beyond its home country's borders has proven successful—Infosys's employees represent 75 nationalities, who speak among them more than 40 languages. Nevertheless, Sarman notes, "[t]he need for qualified talent will become more pressing as we continue to mature."

Looking to the Future

Thus far, maturity from a small start-up to a global juggernaut has gone well. Performance suggests that Infosys commands a keen sense of how a company builds an organization to succeed in global markets. Infosys is well aware that its accomplishments do not guarantee future success. Growing threats are evident in the evolution of offshoring, where companies no longer rely on the combination of low-cost labor and brute code-writing skills to beat the competition.

On the people side, the goal was direct—to be among the top companies in the world that "inspire, nurture and empower a new generation of global leaders." Management believed that achieving this goal began far earlier than when people joined the company. About half of the people in the IT sector in India hailed from small towns, and most were children of low-skilled workers. However, through brute force of intellect and persistence, parents in innumerable small villages—many without access to classrooms, libraries, or technology—found the means to educate their children. The son or daughter who joined Infosys meant, for the parents, great pride, and for themselves, perseverance, accomplishment, and great potential.

On the business side of the equation, Infosys, along with its rivals, aimed to move to more sophisticated, higher-margin value activities. The company had to integrate low-cost, high-quality software-development services with its competency of managing large-scale projects in distributed locations. Results were promising: Airbus, for instance, had hired Infosys to design part of the intricate wing structure of the superjumbo A380 aircraft.

Success has generated threats. Infosys's profitability attracted rivals from around the world, while also motivating domestic competitors. Fast-moving global competitors—including IBM, Wipro, Tata Consultancy Services, Accenture, Cisco, and Cognizant—were expanding operations to offer higher-end offshoring solutions.

Three Critical Challenges

These changes, although part of the ongoing evolution of Infosys, pose challenges. Asked his views, Murthy identified three critical challenges:

> Our biggest challenge is to become proactive problem-definers rather than be reactive problem-solvers. Right now, we solve problems our customers define. We need to be able to go to customers and say, "These are the problems we believe you will face, and here are some solutions." Our focus is on providing solutions leveraging IT. We need to help shape the design of the technology solutions and then implement those solutions. This is the biggest challenge we face—there's no doubt about that.
>
> The second challenge is to become more and more and more multicultural. We have efforts under way to integrate people across various cultures. For instance, on large deals we make sure that people from different parts of the world contribute, on a collaborative basis, to prepare a proposal, to defend the proposal, and to execute the proposal. We also lay great emphasis on integrating leadership. We rotate selected managers from our operations everywhere in the world through our Infosys Leadership Institute. But there is much more that we need to do. For instance, it has not been easy for us to transfer somebody from the United States to India. We are able to transfer people from the United States to Europe and from one function to another—from software development to sales and marketing, for instance. But transferring an employee from the United States to India is not easy.
>
> Finally, the third challenge is to continue to retain the soul of a small organization in the body of a large organization. It will be tricky to balance the tension between scaling the

organization as quickly as we have been doing against the need to maintain disciplined processes as well as an integrated multicultural organization.

Undoubtedly, a full set of challenges for any company. Infosys, ever humble but sincerely confident, believes it has built an organization that can meet these challenges head-on, as its CEO declares, to "win in a flat world." ∎

QUESTIONS

1. Consider the options presented in the chapter regarding structural design, coordination and control, and corporate culture. Map the interplay among these dimensions with respect to Infosys.
2. What do you think was the key event in the organizational evolution of Infosys? What do you think the Infosys organization will look like in 2015?
3. Can Infosys continue its historic growth in sales and employees and still retain its founding values? What approaches and tools would you recommend to do so?
4. What organizational problems do you think prove troublesome to executives at Infosys?
5. Given what you have read, do you think you would like to work for Infosys? Why or why not?

SUMMARY

- The organization of international business is challenging due to adjustment for geographic and cultural circumstances.

- Organization in an MNE is a function of how the company defines the structure that specifies the framework for work, develops the systems that coordinate and control what gets done, and cultivates shared values among employees.

- Environmental and workplace trends, along with the fallout of the global economic crisis, push managers to refine their customary approaches to organizing their companies.

- Organization structure is the formal arrangement of roles, responsibilities, and relationships within a company.

- Vertical differentiation is the matter of how the company balances the centralization versus the decentralization of decision making.

- Horizontal differentiation is the matter of how the company opts to divide itself into specific units to do specific jobs.

- The degree of centralization in a company is influenced by the pressures for global integration versus local responsiveness, the competence of headquarters versus subsidiary personnel, and the importance, expediency, and quality expectations of the decision.

- Traditional structures, like the functional, divisional, and matrix formats, rely on hierarchical formats to specify the arrangement of roles, responsibilities, and relationships among employees.

- Contemporary structures arrange work roles, responsibilities, and relationships in ways that eliminate the horizontal, vertical, or external boundaries that block the development of knowledge-generating and decision-making relationships.

- Firms engaging different strategies build different organizations. Firms engaging international, multidomestic, global, or transnational strategies tailor their structures, systems, and cultures to the demands of the chosen strategy.

- MNE use coordination systems to ensure the synchronization and integration of value activities and work responsibilities, to help the company use its resources efficiently and make decisions effectively.

- Coordination takes place via standardization, plans, and mutual adjustment. Standardization relies on specifying standard operating procedures; planning relies on general goals and detailed objectives; and mutual adjustment relies on frequent interaction among related parties.

- Managers use control systems to compare performance to plans, identify differences, and, where found, assess the basis for the gap and implement corrective action.

- Companies exercise control through market, bureaucratic, and clan mechanisms. Market control relies on external market mechanisms, bureaucratic control relies on extensive rules and procedures, and clan control relies on shared values among all employees.

- Organization culture refers to the set of values and norms that is shared among employees.

- Values and norms express themselves as the behavior patterns or style of an organization that fellow employees encourage new employees to follow.

- MNEs opt to develop and manage their shared values, just as they do with regard to their structures and systems.

KEY TERMS

boundaries (p. 613)
boundarylessness (p. 613)
centralization (p. 605)

contemporary structure (p. 612)
control systems (p. 620)
coordination (p. 617)

coordination by mutual adjustment (p. 619)
coordination by plan (p. 618)

coordination by standardization (p. 617)
decentralization (p. 605)
divisional structure (p. 609)
functional structure (p. 607)
horizontal differentiation (p. 607)

matrix structure (p. 610)
mixed structure (p. 611)
network structure (p. 614)
organization (p. 604)
organization culture (p. 622)

organization structure (p. 605)
unity-of-command principle
  (p. 611)
vertical differentiation (p. 605)
virtual organization (p. 615)

ENDNOTES

1 *Sources include the following:* J&J 2009 Annual Report, www.jnj.com (accessed July/August 2009); "Profit up at Johnson & Johnson," *New York Times* (January 24, 2007): A-1; Katharine Seelye, "J. & J. Says Improper Payments Were Made," *New York Times* (February 13, 2007): C-4.

2 "The Organization Man, Dead at 76," *Journal of Business Strategy* 18:6 (1997): 55.

3 Lowell Bryan and Claudia Joyce, "Better Strategy through Organizational Design," *McKinsey Quarterly* (May 2007).

4 2009 State of the Future, The Millennium Project, (2009):22.

5 Chris Bartlett and Sumantra Ghoshal, "Matrix Management: Not a Structure, a Frame of Mind," *Harvard Business Review* 68 (July–August 1990): 138–45.

6 "Game On: Sir Howard Stringer Believes He Is Finally in a Position to Fix Sony," *The Economist* (March 5, 2009): 73.

7 Karina Frayter, "IBM to Laid-Off: Want a Job in India?," *CNN Money* (February 5, 2009), http://money.cnn.com/2009/02/05/news/companies/ibm_jobs/index.htm (accessed September 14, 2009).

8 "The World according to Chambers," *The Economist* (August 29, 2009): 59–62.

9 Micheline Maynard, "Toyota Said to Weigh Reorganizing U.S. Operations," *New York Times* (April 9, 2009), http://www.nytimes.com/2009/04/10/business/global/10toyota.html (accessed October 16, 2009).

10 Tao offers insight on this standard. The second principle of Taoism is that of dynamic balance. There are always two basic distinctions in nature, symbolized by the yin and yang (sun and moon, heaven and earth, dark and light, chaos and order, etc.), but Taoism sees balance as the basic characteristic underlying these distinctions.

11 Harold Sirkin, James Hemerling, and Arindam Bhattacharya, "Globality: Competing with Everyone from Everywhere for Everything," Boston: *Business Plus* (2008): 3.

12 Julian Birkinshaw, "The Structures behind Global Companies," *Financial Times* (December 4, 2000): Mastering Management section, 2–4.

13 Andria Cheng, "Nike Reorganizes into Six Geographic Regions: Faster-Growing China, Eastern Europe Regions to be Managed Separately," *Market Watch* (March 20, 2009), http://www.marketwatch.com/story/nike-reorganizes-six-geographic-regions-as (accessed June 28, 2009).

14 "Nestlé Is Starting to Slim Down at Last," *Business Week* (October 27, 2003): 56–58; "Daring, Defying, to Grow," *The Economist* (August 7, 2004): 55–57.

15 John W. Hunt, "Is Matrix Management a Recipe for Chaos?," *Financial Times* (January 12, 1998): 10.

16 Richard Hodgetts, "Dow Chemical CEO William Stavropoulos on Structure," *Academy of Management Executive* (May 30, 1999): 30.

17 John Gapper and Nicholas Denton, "The Barings Report," *Financial Times* (October 18, 1995): 8.

18 "Axe to Fall Heavily at IBM, Unions Fear," *New York Times* (May 6, 2005): C-1.

19 The *strategy-structure-systems model* was first adopted by General Motors, DuPont, Sears, and Standard Oil in the 1920s. Not until the post–World War II era did many companies began to develop divisional structures that then led to the rapid adoption of

diversification strategies. Some reason that the network structure and its variants will follow the same pattern, moving from the few in the early 2000s to the many over the ensuing decades.

20 "Hungry Tiger, Dancing Elephant: How India Is Changing IBM's World," *The Economist* (April 4, 2007): 58–61.

21 Others pointed to W. L. Gore and its egalitarian workforce philosophy (no titles, workers collaborating in small teams, and no hierarchy fuels creativity and innovation): "We work hard at maximizing individual potential, maintaining an emphasis on product integrity and cultivating an environment where creativity can flourish," says CEO Terri Kelly. "A fundamental belief in our people and their abilities continues to be the key to our success, even as we expand globally." "It isn't a company for everyone," Brinton says. "It takes a special kind of person to be effective here—someone who is really passionate about sharing information, as opposed to controlling it."

22 Statement from Jack Welch's Letter to Shareholders, "Boundaryless Company in a Decade of Change," reported in GE's 1990 *Annual Report.*

23 Cisco, for instance, is essentially a research and development company that uses many outside suppliers and independent manufacturers to assemble the products it designs. Capitalizing on its core competency in design but still retaining its outsourced production led Cisco to build a global network. Operationally, Cisco has entered into joint-ownership arrangements with other companies to share production, distribution, and technology-development facilities. It contracts with other companies to share technology and relies on other companies to produce and distribute goods and components. Cisco organizes its many alliances with the communication technology that made Cisco successful. The company uses the Internet, e-mail, file sharing, and conferencing to link partners across corporate and national boundaries. More formally, the company designed the Cisco Connection and Cisco Internet Business Roadmap in order to give its partners easier communication and flexible relationships.

24 "A Tangled Web," *Financial Times* (June 12, 2001): Germany section, 7.

25 Sonny Ariss, Nick Nykodym, and Aimee Cole-Laramore, "Trust and Technology in the Virtual Organization," *SAM Advanced Management Journal* 67 (Autumn 2002): 22–26; William M. Fitzpatrick and Donald R. Burke, "Competitive Intelligence, Corporate Security and the Virtual Organization," *Advances in Competitiveness Research* 11 (2003): 20–46.

26 Alf Crossman and Liz Lee-Kelley, "Trust, Commitment and Team Working: The Paradox of Virtual Organizations," *Global Networks: A Journal of Transnational Affairs* 4 (October 2004): 375–91; Philip J. Holt and James E. Lodge, "Merging Collaboration and Technology: The Virtual Research Organization," *Applied Clinical Trials* 12 (October 2003): 38–42.

27 Scott Goodson, StrawberryFrog, "Special Report: Global Players," *Advertising Age* (January 26, 2004): S4; Juliana Koranteng, "Virtual Agency Goes Global via the Web," *Ad Age Global* 1 (2000): 46.

28 Theresa Howard, "Strawberry Frog Hops to a Different Drummer," *USA Today* (October 10, 2005): C-1.

29 Dmitry Ivanov, Boris Sokolov, and Joachim Kaeschel, "Structure Dynamics Control-Based Framework for Adaptive Reconfiguration of Collaborative Enterprise Networks," *International Journal of Manufacturing Technology and Management* 17 (2009): 23.

30 Nicolai J. Foss, "Selective Intervention and Internal Hybrids: Interpreting and Learning from the Rise and Decline of the Oticon Spaghetti Organization," *Organization Science* 14 (May–June 2003): 331–50.

31 Patrick Kiger, "Hidden Hierarchies," *Workforce Management* (February 27, 2006): 24.

32 Karen Beaman, "An Interview with Christopher Bartlett," *Boundaryless HR: Human Capital Management in the Global Economy* (Austin, TX: IHRIM Press, June 2002).

33 Darrell Rigby, "Bain & Company's 2005 Management Tools & Trends," at www.bain.com/management_tools (accessed August 2, 2005).

34 Steve Lohr, "How Crisis Shapes the Corporate Model," *New York Times* (March 28, 2009): A-1.

35 Lowell Bryan and Claudia Joyce, "The 21st-Century Organization," *McKinsey Quarterly* 3 (2005): 24–33.

36 Loren Cary, "The Rise of Hyperarchies," *Harvard Business Review* (March 1, 2004). Prod. #: U04030-HCC-ENG.

37 The Boston Consulting Group, "Reorganized Information Processing Vital to Improving U.S. Intelligence Capabilities," *BCG Media Releases*, at www.bcg.com/news_media/news_media_releases .jsp?id=928 (accessed May 6, 2007).

38 Adam Lashinsky, "Chaos by Design," *Fortune* (October 2, 2006), http://money.cnn.com/magazines/fortune/fortune_archive/2006/1 0/02/8387489/index.htm (accessed October 27, 2006); Geoffrey Colvin, "Managing in Chaos," *Fortune* (October 2, 2006), http://money.cnn.com/ magazines/fortune/fortune_archive/2006/ 10/02/8387417/index.htm (accessed October 27, 2006).

39 More specifically, Grove reasoned: "Let chaos reign, then rein in chaos. Does that mean that you shouldn't plan? Not at all. You need to plan the way a fire department plans. It cannot anticipate fires, so it has to shape a flexible organization that is capable of responding to unpredictable events." Michael E. Rock, "Case Example: Intel's Andy Grove," *Canada One* (2006), at www.canadaone.com/ magazine/mr2060198.html (accessed October 31, 2007).

40 Daniel Erasmus, "A Common Language for Strategy," *Financial Times* (April 5, 1999): Mastering Information Management section, 7–8.

41 Sumantra Ghoshal and Christopher Bartlett, "Changing the Role of Top Management: Beyond Structure to Process," *Harvard Business Review* 73 (January–February 1995): 93–94.

42 Jennifer Spencer, "Firms' Knowledge-Sharing Strategies in the Global Innovation System: Empirical Evidence from the Flat Panel Display Industry," *Strategic Management Journal* 23 (March 2003): 217–33.

43 "The World according to Chambers," *The Economist* (August 29, 2009): 59–62.

44 From a philosophical view, clan control represents humanist values that contrast with the scientific norms of bureaucratic control.

45 N. Shirouzu and J. Bigness, "7-Eleven Operators Resist System to Monitor Managers," *Wall Street Journal* (June 16, 1997): B1.

46 Eric Flamholtz and Rangapriya Kannan-Narasimhan, "Differential Impact of Cultural Elements in Financial Performance," *European Management Journal* 23 (February 2005): 50–65; Ursula Fairbairn, "HR as a Strategic Partner: Culture Change as an American Express Case Study," *Human Resource Management* 44 (Spring 2005): 79–84.

47 Jim Collins, *Good to Great: Why Some Companies Make the Leap . . . and Others Don't* (New York: HarperCollins, 2001); for example, on the importance of technology, Collins reports that "80 percent of the good-to-great executives—from more than 1400 companies over a 15-year span—we interviewed didn't even mention technology as one of the top five factors in the transition."

48 Tatiana Kostova, "Transnational Transfer of Strategic Organizational Practices: A Contextual Perspective," *Academy of Management Review* 24 (1999): 308–24; Nitin Nohria and Sumantra Ghoshal, "Differentiated Fit and Shared Values: Alternatives for Managing Headquarters-Subsidiary Relations," *Strategic Management Journal* 15 (July 1994): 491–502. For a discussion of how capabilities improve with experience, see Andrew Delios and Paul Beamish, "Survival and Profitability: The Roles of Experience and Intangible Assets in Foreign Subsidiary Performance," *Academy of Management Journal* 44 (2001): 1028–38.

49 Alison Maitland, "Bridging the Culture Gap," *Financial Times* (January 28, 2002): 8.

50 Dinker Raval and Bala Subramanianm, "Effective Transfer of Best Practices across Cultures," *Competitiveness Review* (Summer–Fall 2000): 183.

51 "Staffing Globalisation: Travelling More Lightly," *The Economist* (June 23, 2006): 44.

52 John A. Byrne, "How Jack Welch Runs GE," *Business Week* (June 8, 1998): 90; Miriam Leuchter, "Management Farm Teams," *Journal of Business Strategy* (May 1998): 29–32; "The House That Jack Built," *The Economist* (September 18, 1999): 65.

53 "In Search of Global Leaders: View of Jeffery Immelt, Chairman and CEO, General Electric," *Harvard Business Review* (August 1, 2003): 6.

54 Leslie Gross Klaff, "Many People, One Mattel," *Workforce Management* (March 2004): 42–44.

55 Bain & Company, "Executives Are Taking a Hard Look at Soft Issues" (March 27, 2007), at www.bain.com/bainweb/publications/ printer_ready.asp?id=25728 (accessed October 31, 2007).

56 Rebecca Knight, "Corporate Universities: Move to a Collaborative Effort," *Financial Times* (March 19, 2007): 3.

57 Donna Fenn, "Corporate Universities for Small Companies," Inc.com (February 1999), at www.inc.com/magazine/19990201/ 730.html (accessed May 6, 2007).

58 Jeanne C. Meister, *Corporate Universities: Lessons in Building a World-Class Work Force* (New York: McGraw-Hill, 1998).

59 John Griffiths, "Unipart University," *Financial Times* (March 21, 2002), http://specials.ft.com/businesseducation/ (accessed May 2005).

60 Della Bradshaw, "LVMH," *Financial Times* (March 21, 2002), http://www.ft.com/businesseducation (accessed May 5, 2005).

61 Steve Trehern, "More Than Just Learning Process," *Financial Times* (March 21, 2002): 22.

62 Knight, "Corporate Universities."

63 Kelley Holland, "Is It Time to Retrain B-Schools?," *New York Times* (March 14, 2009), http://www.nytimes.com/2009/03/15/ business/15school.html?ref=business (accessed March 22, 2009).

64 *Sources include the following:* Edward Luce, *In Spite of the Gods: The Strange Rise of Modern India* (New York: Doubleday, 2007); Julie Schlosser, "Harder Than Harvard," *Fortune* (March 17, 2006); "Virtual Champions, Survey: Business in India," *The Economist* (June 1, 2006); Anand Giridharadas, "India's Edge Goes beyond Outsourcing," *New York Times* (April 4, 2007); Steve Hamm, "Passing the Baton at Infosys," *Business Week* (June 16, 2006); "Infosys' Murthy: Sharing a 'Simple yet Powerful Vision,'" *Knowledge@Wharton* (May 23, 2001); Gautam Kumra and Jayant Sinha, "The Next Hurdle for Indian IT," *McKinsey Quarterly* (2003), Special Edition: Global Directions; Subir Roy, "Infosys Builds a Realistic Terrain," Rediff.com (2005), at www.rediff.com/money/ 2005/jun/16spec.htm (accessed October 31, 2007); Gina Ruiz, "Infosys Technologies: Optimas Award Winner for Global Outlook," *Workforce Management* (March 26, 2007): 27; "Life Lessons from Narayana Murthy, Rediff" (June 16, 2009), at http://www.rediff .com/money/2007/may/28bspec.htm (accessed October 14, 2009); "The Amazing Infosys Story, Rediff," at http://specials.rediff.com/money/2006/jul/11sld1.htm (June 16, 2009).

Managing International
Operations

sixteen
Marketing Globally

PART SIX

Objectives

- To understand a variety of international product policies and their appropriate circumstances

- To be aware of product alterations when deciding between standardized and differentiated marketing programs among countries

- To appreciate the pricing complexities when selling in foreign markets

- To be familiar with country differences that may necessitate alterations in promotional practices

- To comprehend the different branding strategies companies may employ internationally

- To discern effective practices and complications of international distribution

- To perceive why and how emphasis within the marketing mix may vary among countries

Markets have customs and communes have traditions.

—*Vietnamese proverb*

CASE Tommy Hilfiger: Clothes Make the Man and Vice Versa

Chances are that when you think of Tommy Hilfiger, the first image that comes to your mind is a piece of clothing with a little red, white, and blue logo visibly displayed.[1] This logo has been a hallmark of Hilfiger's success since its beginning, and marketing has been the company's forte. Hilfiger has added such lines as fragrances, bedding, and bath products. It also acquired the Karl Lagerfeld label, but our discussion centers on the clothing brands using the Hilfiger name. Before we examine its international marketing practices, let's look for a moment at the company's description and history.

A BRIEF HISTORY

The early success of the Hilfiger brand was largely due to two men: U.S. designer Tommy Hilfiger and Indian textile magnate Mohan Murjani. Hilfiger designed blue jeans for Jordache, but in 1984 when he was 33, Murjani sought him out to be a designer for Murjani International. As one of the instrumental people in bringing about the designer blue-jeans craze of the 1970s, Murjani wanted to resurrect the jeans craze and develop a new brand of clothing by offering a line of slightly less preppy and less expensive clothes than those offered by Ralph Lauren that he thought would appeal to a young mass-appeal audience.

Sales success came quickly for the Hilfiger brand, but Murjani International faced financial problems. Murjani also had licenses to sell other clothing brands, such as Gloria Vanderbilt and Coca-Cola. In effect, it had difficulty separating its attention among its different brands, which it needed to sell to the same department stores. Hilfiger, Murjani, and two other investors bought out Murjani International in 1988 and changed the name to Tommy Hilfiger.

Hilfiger began with only a men's line, but its men's and women's clothing each account for about half of its sales. The company also had a line of children's wear that it discontinued in 2006 because of poor performance. Hilfiger began pushing internationally, and sales outside the United States now account for more than half of total sales. Europe alone accounts for 45 percent of sales.

PROMOTION AND BRANDING

Hilfiger's promotion and branding have been so intertwined that it is almost impossible to separate them. At the beginning, Murjani saw two primary needs: to convince stores to stock a new brand and to convince customers to want it. His approach turned out to be pure genius. Although his ad budget for the first year (1985) was U.S. $1.4 million—quite small for selling in a mass consumer market, especially for an unknown brand—the ads were aimed strictly at getting Tommy Hilfiger's name known. He placed two-page ads in leading magazines and newspapers, along with a billboard in New York's Times Square *without* showing any clothes or any models. The ads included Hilfiger's face, the logo for the clothes, and words describing him as being on a par with such well-known designers as Ralph Lauren, Perry Ellis, and Calvin Klein.

The ads were so unusual that the brand received free publicity through write-ups in newspapers. Even Johnny Carson quipped about Hilfiger on his popular evening TV show. Within a short time, surveys in New York revealed that people thought of Hilfiger as one of the four or five most important U.S. designers. Department and specialty stores were willing to sell the clothes, and the logo-loving public was rushing to buy them. There was also some fortunate timing involved. Not only was the public in love with the label, but also many young managers were eager to be seen in upscale sportswear during the newly popular "casual Friday" workdays.

Early on, Hilfiger received much publicity in newspaper and magazine columns globally that mentioned or showed celebrities wearing its clothes. These celebrities were certainly an eclectic group and included Bill Clinton, the Prince of Wales, Michael Jackson, Elton John, and Snoop Dogg. This fed into the image that Hilfiger clothes had cachet; thus the company's image was fairly well established internationally before the company expanded internationally. Hilfiger himself has always sought out entertainers and points out that he dressed Bruce Springsteen before anyone knew who he was.

Hilfiger has used celebrity advertising— including the French soccer star Thierry Henry and the husband-wife team of entertainer David Bowie and supermodel Iman—to help sell in Europe. However, aside from celebrities, Hilfiger learned that the type of models it uses to sell its merchandise successfully in the United States does not work well in Europe. For example, its models for men's underwear in Europe, including those on point-of-purchase package displays, must be thinner and less muscular than those it uses in the United States. But it augments these thinner models by adding scantily clad, seductive-looking women who stand behind the male models in the photos. Hilfiger also found that its average consumer in Germany was older than its average consumer in the United States, so it has dropped the Tommy Jeans name because it sounded too much like a teenage name.

PRODUCT AND PRICE

Although early promotion with the brand name has been instrumental in Hilfiger's success, logo and image are not enough. From the start, Hilfiger clothes have been casual and of good quality. They are distinctive enough in color and shape so the public can usually distinguish a Hilfiger from clothing made by competitors. Nevertheless, this is an industry in which product lines must evolve. Hilfiger said, "Fashion brands have to reinvent themselves, just like Madonna does." Hilfiger has gone from preppy to urban and back again.

Hilfiger has encountered some negative reactions abroad to its image of being a U.S. brand. Although some U.S. clothing products have been well received abroad (such as jeans), most U.S. clothing brands—for example, Nautica, Gap, and North Face—have encountered problems in Europe, because Europeans tend to see France and Italy as the centers of upscale fashions. Thus, clothing brands from other countries find this opinion difficult to overcome. However, the perception that the brand and price are a step below the pure luxury brands actually helped Hilfiger's European sales during the global recession starting in 2008. But let's go back to the image of being a U.S. brand. This may have dampened sales during much of the aught decade because of anti-Americanism in Europe, but Hilfiger hopes to ride the wave of Barack Obama's popularity there.

In addition, Hilfiger has encountered some differing national preferences. For example, in Germany, Hilfiger's largest European market, men don't mind paying $50 more than the highest-priced Hilfiger shirts in the United States, but they want them in a higher-quality cotton. Hilfiger has found throughout Europe that there is hardly any demand for the cotton sweaters so popular in the United States, so it has switched to wool sweaters. Hilfiger has adjusted to the European preference for slimmer-looking jeans and smaller logos on shirts. It has also created a line of added-luxury items, such as leather jackets and cashmere sweaters for the Italian market.

To make these changes, Hilfiger set up a design staff in Amsterdam that includes almost 30 different nationalities. It has adapted the Hilfiger look to the European demands. Its CEO announced his plan to harmonize the products offered in the United States and Europe by moving upmarket in the United States and depending more on the European design team.

These product changes for Europe have increased production costs. Further, European operational costs are about three times those in the United States because of its more fragmented retail and wholesale system. On top of that, the margins at the final consumer level in Europe run from 50 to 100 percent higher than in the United States. The result is that prices for Hilfiger merchandise are much higher in Europe than in the United States.

DISTRIBUTION

In the United States, Hilfiger traditionally relied mainly on wholesaling to about 1,800 department stores, of which many had stand-alone Hilfiger departments within. It has stayed away from chains that are viewed as more lower end, such as JCPenney and Sears, but it does sell its outdated stock to discount chains T.J. Maxx and Marshalls. However, in 2007, Hilfiger gave Macy's exclusive rights to sell its sportswear lines. Although Macy's has about 800 stores, the move required Hilfiger to pull sales from other department stores, such as Dillard's.

Distribution is perhaps the biggest difference that Hilfiger found when entering Europe. Because the company succeeded in the United States by first going into department stores, it put an early European emphasis on department stores as well. This led to its entry into such leading chains as Galeries Lafayette in France and El Corte Inglés in Spain. Hilfiger's CEO has described the U.S. market as one of concentration (sending a lot to department stores) and the European market as one of fragmentation (sending small amounts to small stores that carry select pieces).

Hilfiger now has about 5,000 wholesale accounts in Europe—much more than in the United States. Further, it has decentralized its showrooms by opening 21 of them so that small retailers can visit them more easily. Finally, finding good, competitive locations for its company-owned stores is **CRN** problematic, because space in prime locations opens infrequently.

Introduction

The Hilfiger case points out that similar marketing principles are at work in domestic and foreign markets. In other words, regardless of where a company operates, it must have desirable products and services, inform people of their availability, and offer them at acceptable prices and accessible locations that consumers favor. However, as we noted in the opening case, environmental differences may cause companies to apply these principles differently abroad, such as by offering product variations to correspond with local preferences, as Hilfiger has done by offering higher-quality cotton for shirts in Germany. Hilfiger's experience also emphasizes the need to find the right balance between the benefits of local responsiveness and the efficiency gains of standardization.

Keep in mind that whatever marketing approach a company takes abroad should be compatible with its overall aims and strategies. However, this does not imply that it must follow the same strategy for every one of its products or for every country. For example, cost leadership or differentiation may be more important for a product in some markets than in others. If it does choose to follow the same tactics globally, such as offering the same product to all countries, this may lead it to a mass-market orientation in one country and a focused strategy in another. Finally, the degree of global standardization versus national responsiveness may vary within elements of the marketing mix, such as seeking maximum product standardization while promoting the product differently among countries.

Figure 16.1 shows the place of marketing in international business. We first discuss the application of different marketing strategies to international operations. Then we examine the elements within the marketing mix—product, pricing, promotion, branding, and distribution—and explain the major factors that managers need to consider for each of these when operating internationally. Finally, we discuss how emphasis within the marketing mix may need to vary to fit the conditions of each country where the company is selling.

Concept Check

Recall that we devote an entire section of Chapter 11 to the issue of "Global Integration versus Local Responsiveness." As we point out, when expanding into foreign markets, a company can save money by standardizing many of its policies and practices and— particularly if it's pursuing a global strategy of expansion— its products. Here we observe that a strategy of marketing *standardized products*— marketing the same or similar versions to specific global segments—falls at one end of the *global integration/local responsiveness* spectrum.

FIGURE 16.1   Marketing as a Means of Pursuing an International Strategy

Recall that we used Figure 14.1 to introduce the various *means* by which a company can pursue its international objectives and strategy. Among those *means* we included *functions*, and here we focus on one of the most important of those *functions: marketing.*

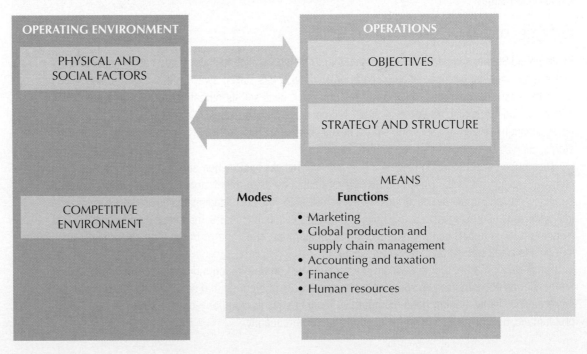

Marketing Strategies

We begin this section with a discussion of the international application of the marketing orientations commonly found in marketing texts. We conclude with a discussion of market segmentation and targeting and how they relate both to the orientations and to the elements of the marketing mix.

MARKETING ORIENTATIONS

This section highlights the international application of five common marketing orientations: *production, sales, customer, strategic marketing,* and *social marketing.*

Production Orientation With production orientation, companies focus primarily on production—either efficiency or high quality—with little emphasis on marketing. There is little analysis of consumer needs; rather, companies assume that customers want lower prices or higher quality. Although this approach has largely gone out of vogue, it is used internationally for certain cases:

- *Commodity sales,* especially those for which there is little need or possibility of product differentiation

- *Passive exports,* particularly those that serve to reduce surpluses within the domestic market

- *Foreign-market segments or niches* that may happen to resemble segments to which the product is aimed at home

Commodity Sales Companies sell many undifferentiated raw materials and agricultural commodities (such as grapes and tin) primarily on the basis of price, because there is universal demand. However, even for commodities, companies have sometimes had positive international sales results through differentiation, such as with the Chiquita brand on bananas.

In addition, oil producers, such as PDVSA, LUKoil, and Aramco, have bought branded gasoline-distribution operations abroad to help them sell an otherwise undifferentiated product. Commodity producers also put efforts into business-to-business marketing by providing innovative financing and ensuring timely, high-quality supplies.

Passive Exports Many companies begin exporting very passively by filling unsolicited requests from abroad. At this point, they adapt their products very little, if at all, to foreign consumers' preferences. This practice suffices for many companies that view foreign sales only as a means to dispose of excess inventory they can't reasonably sell domestically. In fact, if fixed costs are covered from domestic sales, they can quote lower export prices to liquidate inventories without disrupting their domestic markets.

Foreign Niches A company may aim a product at a large share of its domestic market and then find that there are a few consumers abroad who are also willing to buy that product. For instance, Inca Kola, the largest-selling soft drink in Peru, has only small niche markets abroad, primarily among people who were consumers in Peru. However, keep in mind that a niche market abroad may become a mass market, as is the case with Mexico's Corona beer.

A company may also use a production orientation when selling in countries with only a small market potential, particularly in small developing countries. In effect, the market size does not justify the alteration expense—for instance, not even changing electrical plugs to fit local sockets, which local purchasers must convert themselves.

Sales Orientation Internationally, sales orientation means a company tries to sell abroad what it can sell domestically, and in the same manner, on the assumption that consumers are sufficiently similar globally. For example, Whirlpool successfully launched its high-capacity front-loading washing machines almost simultaneously in multiple countries.[2] Of course, companies constantly introduce new products or variations of old ones. Once they are operating within a country, a strong information exchange between the foreign subsidiary and headquarters can facilitate the development of products that can be sufficiently standardized and still fit the needs of consumers in different countries.[3]

This orientation differs from the production orientation because of its active rather than passive approach to promoting sales. However, there is much anecdotal evidence of foreign-marketing failures because companies merely assume without sufficient research that product acceptance will be the same as at home or that heavy sales efforts abroad can overcome negative foreign attitudes toward the product, its price, or method of distribution. Even so, there are successful examples of marketing abroad with little or no research on what foreign consumers want. Figure 16.2 offers a humorous twist on this point.

Of course, there are products other than commodities that need no adaptation on a country basis, such as razor blades, aircraft, cat food, and cameras. For other products, however, a company may succeed best with a sales orientation by selling to countries where culture and customer characteristics are similar to those at home and where there is also a great deal of spillover in product information, such as between the United States and Canada.[4]

| A customer orientation takes geographic areas as given.

Customer Orientation   In a company that operates according to the sales orientation we just discussed, management is usually guided by answers to questions such as these: Should the company send some exports abroad? Where can the company sell more of product X? That is, the product is held constant and the sales location is varied.

In contrast, a customer orientation asks: What and how can the company sell in country A? In this case, the country is held constant and the product and method of marketing it are varied. A company may most likely take this approach because it finds the country's size and growth potential attractive. In the extreme of this approach, a company would move to completely different products—an uncommon strategy that some companies nonetheless have adopted. For example, Compañía Chilena de Fósforos, a Chilean match producer, wanted to tap the Japanese market because of its growth and size. However, because the company's matches were not price competitive in Japan, it successfully entered the Japanese market by making chopsticks, a product that would use its poplar forest resources and wood-processing capabilities.[5]

Business-to-business suppliers may be primarily concerned with promoting their production capabilities, prices, and delivery reliability rather than determining what will sell in foreign markets. Instead, they depend on other companies' purchasing agents to give them product specifications. For example, the Hong Kong company Yue Yuen Industrial is the world's largest branded-footwear manufacturer, making athletic shoes to the specifications of companies such as Nike, New Balance, and Adidas.[6]

| The most common strategy is product changes as adaptations, done by degree.

Strategic Marketing Orientation   Most companies committed to continual rather than sporadic foreign sales adopt a strategy that combines production, sales, and customer orientations. Companies that don't make changes to accommodate the needs of foreign

FIGURE 16.2   **The Functionally Flexible Call Center**

Sometimes you can sell products when and where conditions aren't particularly promising. For the most part, however, you need a well-conceived and well-implemented marketing program to facilitate the sale of just about any product.

Source: DILBERT © Scott Adams/Dist. by United Features Syndicate Inc.

customers may lose too many sales, especially if aggressive competitors are willing to make desired adaptations. At the same time, they must consider their competencies, lest they deviate too much from what they can do well. Thus, they tend to make marketing variations abroad without deviating very far from experience. For example, breweries such as Heineken, Stroh, Bass, and Lion, when faced with restrictions against alcoholic beverages in Saudi Arabia, have turned to sales of nonalcoholic beer (marketed as malt rather than beer), which is closely related to their managers' areas of expertise. The U.S. home builder Pulte Homes, in entering the Argentine market, kept the same floor plans and exterior look of its U.S. homes to gain economies of standardization, but it added bidets in the bathrooms and large rear patios to fit Argentine preferences.[7]

Social Marketing Orientation Companies with social marketing orientations realize that successful international marketing requires serious consideration of potential environmental, health, social, and work-related problems that may arise when selling or making their products abroad. Such groups as consumer associations, political parties, and labor unions are becoming more globally aware—and vocal. They can quell demand when they feel a product in some way violates their concept of social responsibility.

> Companies consider the effects on all stakeholders when selling or making their products.

Companies must increasingly consider not only how a product is purchased but also how it is made and disposed of and how it might be changed to be more socially desirable. Such considerations have led Coca-Cola to develop a vitamin-enriched beverage for Botswana and returnable glass containers for Argentina and Brazil.[8]

SEGMENTING AND TARGETING MARKETS

Although population and income may give a rough estimate of market size, there are few products that virtually the entire population can be convinced to consume with the same marketing mix. Thus, based on the orientations we have just discussed, companies must segment markets for their products and services and then decide which segment(s) to target and how.

> Companies must decide on their target markets, which may include segments that exist in more than one country.

The most common way of segmenting markets is through demographics, such as by income, age, gender, ethnicity, and religion. Of course, these may be combined, by identifying, for example, a segment that consists of women age 20 to 30 with incomes between $20,000 and $30,000 per year. Companies may further refine these segments by adding psychographics (attitudes, values, and lifestyles).

Three Approaches to Segmentation Internationally, there are three basic approaches to segmentation.[9]

By Country A company may decide, for example, to go for the time being only to the Japanese market because of its population size and purchasing power. It will then need to segment the Japanese market and decide whether to target a single segment or multiple segments within Japan, whether to use the same marketing mix to sell to all segments, whether to tailor the products separately to each segment, and whether to vary the promotion and distribution separately for the different segments.

Although this approach may lead to success within Japan, it overlooks the possible similarities of various Japanese market segments with those in other countries. Thus there may be little opportunity of gaining economies through standardization to serve market segments that cut across countries.

By Global Segment A company may identify some segments globally, such as segments based primarily on income. Thus each country may have some people within this same segment, but the proportional size of each segment will vary by country. Although this may bring about economies of standardization, a company may still need to prioritize by country of entry, may have to delay tapping bigger markets in some countries, and may face high entry costs in other countries where the targeted segment is small.

> **Concept Check**
>
> In Chapter 12, we describe the importance of economic *demographic* variables in the process whereby companies evaluate and select countries as locations for international operations. Many of the demographic data considered in international marketing decisions are the same. In addressing the question "Will Prime Locations Change?" for example, we point out that while populations in such high-income countries as Japan are declining, those in many developing countries are growing.

By Multiple Criteria Finally, a company can combine these by looking first at countries as segments, second by identifying segments within each country, and third by comparing these within-country segments with those in other countries. Once a company makes this determination, it can determine similarities for targeting the most promising cross-country segments, gain efficiencies through standardization, and still tailor other aspects of its marketing mix—product offerings, promotion, branding, and distribution—so they are compatible with the needs of each country's market.

In effect, a company may hold one or more elements of these marketing functions constant while altering the others. For instance, Chanel aims its cosmetics sales to a segment that transcends national boundaries. It uses branding, promotion, pricing, and distribution globally, but it adapts the cosmetics to local ethnic and climatic norms.[10]

Mass Markets versus Niche Markets At the same time, most companies have multiple products and product variations that appeal to different segments; thus they must decide which to introduce abroad and whether to target them to mass markets versus niche segments. Sales to a mass market may be necessary if a company is to gain sufficient economies in production and distribution. For example, some foreign beer companies entered China with a focus strategy by concentrating on the premium sector. Although the Chinese premium beer market is large, it is so dispersed that high distribution costs made it unprofitable.[11] In contrast, General Motors (GM) entered the Chinese market only with its Buick models aimed at a high-income segment. GM found a large enough market to gain production and distribution economies, because distributing cars nationally is very different from distributing beer nationally.

Because the percentage of people who fall into any segment may vary substantially among countries, a niche market in one country may be a mass market in another. A company may be content to accept a combination of mass and niche markets; however, if it wishes to appeal to mass markets everywhere, it may need to change elements in its marketing program. For instance, U.S.-based Bell South managed successfully to reach a larger and more mass Venezuelan market by selling fewer minutes on phone cards. It added $4 phone cards to the $10 and $20 cards it customarily sold.[12]

Product Policies

Cost is a compelling reason for standardizing marketing as much as possible globally. When companies change any part of their marketing mix (product, price, promotion, brand, and distribution) to serve foreign markets, they incur additional costs to develop a change. Then they have the costs of coordinating and controlling added diversity. Within the marketing mix, MNEs attempt to standardize products, because their changes generally incur the most expense.[13] Nevertheless, product adaptations are common. We now consider the reasons for making product alterations for foreign markets, the costs of product alterations, the extent and mix of product lines, and product life-cycle considerations.

WHY FIRMS ALTER PRODUCTS

We now examine the legal, cultural, and economic reasons for companies to alter their products to fit the needs of customers in different countries.

Legal factors are usually related to safety or health protection.

Legal Considerations Explicit legal requirements, usually meant to protect consumers, are the most obvious reason for altering products for foreign markets. If you don't comply with the law, you won't be allowed to sell.[14] Pharmaceuticals and foods are particularly subject to regulations concerning purity, testing, and labeling. Automobiles must conform to diverse safety, pollution, and fuel-economy standards.[15]

When standards, such as for safety, differ among countries, companies may either conform to the minimum standards of each country or make and sell products fabricated to the highest global standard everywhere. The company must consider cost along with any ill will that may result by having lower standards in some countries. Critics have complained, for example, about companies' sales abroad—especially in developing countries—of such products as toys, automobiles, contraceptives, and pharmaceuticals that did not meet safety or quality standards elsewhere.

Packaging Requirements   One of the more cumbersome product alterations for companies concerns laws on packaging, such as the placement of warning labels. For example, the EU and the U.S. have different labeling requirements for bioengineered foods.[16] This difference has caused Unilever to use different types of oil (soy oil in the United States and vegetable oil in Europe) in its Hellmann's mayonnaise so as to avoid warning labels in Europe.[17]

Environmental-Protection Regulations   Another problem concerns laws that protect the environment, such as Denmark's ban on aluminum cans. Other countries restrict the volume of packaging materials to save resources and decrease trash. There are also differences in national requirements as to whether containers must be reusable and whether companies use packaging materials that must be recycled, incinerated, or composted.

Point ▸ Counterpoint

Should Home Governments Regulate Their Companies' Marketing in Developing Countries?

Point ▸   Yes International companies advertise, promote, and sell products in developing countries that their home countries ban. If we have made a domestic decision not to sell these products because of their dangers, we have a moral obligation to prevent the same dangers abroad.

I know that my statement smacks of extraterritoriality. But let's face it: Too many consumers in developing countries lack sufficient education and access to reliable information to make intelligent decisions. Further, they often have corrupt political leaders who do not look after their interests. Finally, we have some moral obligation to ensure that these consumers spend on needs rather than on wants that our MNEs have created through clever promotion programs. If developed countries don't regulate to protect consumers in developing countries, no one will.

Companies also export products that don't meet quality standards at home. There are also examples of exporting dangerous products. For example, DDT is so dangerous to the environment that all developed countries have banned its use—but not its production. Developed countries have pretty much abandoned the battery recycling business because of strict antipollution requirements to prevent lead poisoning, which shows up only after slow, cumulative ingestion through the years. Thus companies export the batteries to developing countries that have either weak or weakly enforced pollution laws.[18]

◂ Counterpoint   No The answer is education rather than limiting people's choices by regulating international companies. In fact, there are many examples of behavior change, by both consumers and governments in developing countries, when they learn the facts. For instance, Thailand has restricted tobacco smoking in response to statistics linking smoking with death.[24]

Your argument that products banned at home should not be sold abroad assumes that the home government knows best, which may reflect a difference in morals rather than a problem of creating physical danger. For instance, some countries have banned the sale of the morning-after pill RU-486 on moral grounds. To ban sales in other countries that accept a different morality would seem to be cultural imperialism.

In addition, the conditions between rich and poor countries are sometimes so different that they need different regulations. Let's take your example of DDT exports. Developing countries are aware of DDT's adverse long-term effect on the environment, but in the short term, many of these countries face a crisis from malaria. South Africa was persuaded to ban the use of DDT and turned instead to using a different pesticide. The number of new malaria cases tripled in four years, when South Africa renewed DDT spraying and brought the number of new cases down again.[25] Until there is some better solution for malaria, DDT bans will do more harm than good. Certainly, if one

Developed countries have attempted to limit tobacco use through warning labels, restrictions on sales to minors, and prohibitions on smoking in certain public areas. The World Health Organization (WHO) estimates that tobacco is the leading cause of preventable death in the world, killing about 100 million people in the twentieth century and a possibility of 1 billion during the twenty-first. Just 5 percent of the global population is protected by programs—such as bans on promotion, national smoke-free laws, warning labels, and help measures for people who want to quit—and these are centered almost entirely in developed countries.[19] As developed countries have taken more actions against tobacco, tobacco companies from developed countries have increased their promotions in developing countries.

There are also examples of products that are suitable for most customers in developed countries but not for those in developing countries. The most famous case involved infant-formula sales in developing countries, where infant mortality rates increased when bottle-feeding supplanted breast-feeding. Because of low incomes and poor education, mothers frequently overdiluted formula and gave it to their babies in unhygienic conditions. The governments of developing countries did little to stop the sales.

Global publicity about the situation led WHO to pass a voluntary code to restrict formula promotion, but not sales, in developing countries. Critics hit Nestlé hardest, because it had the largest share of infant-formula sales in developing countries and because its name-identified products facilitated the organization of a boycott. The company ceased advertising that could discourage breast-feeding, limited free formula supplies at hospitals, and banned personal gifts to health officials.[20]

MNEs also pay too little attention to the needs of consumers in developing countries. Instead, they primarily develop products suitable to the needs of consumers in developed countries who can afford them. In some cases, these are superfluous products for low-income consumers, but MNEs introduce and promote them heavily there. Thus poor consumers end up buying them instead of spending their money on nutritional and health needs.

Take bottled water, sold mainly in plastic bottles by such companies as Nestlé, Danone, Coca-Cola, and PepsiCo. It is often no better than tap water (in fact it often *is* tap water), but it sells for 10,000 times more. The bottles are thrown out and take 1,000 years to biodegrade. The crude oil used to make bottles just for the United States could fuel 100,000 cars per year.[21]

Furthermore, MNEs spend little to develop products to fit the needs of developing countries. Take pharmaceutical research. Only 10 percent of the global health research budget is spent on diseases that account for 90 percent of the global disease burden—mainly diseases that largely bypass developed countries.[22] Instead of spending heavily

government has found a product dangerous, it should pass on this information to other governments; in terms of DDT and toxic materials exports, this is already being done.

It's true that tobacco companies are now promoting more heavily in developing countries. Keep in mind, though, that a good part of that promotion is for smokeless tobacco products (snuff), which are safer than cigarettes and can help smokers stop.[26] However, if developed countries' governments were to limit their companies' sales or promotion of tobacco to those countries, their citizens would still be able to buy tobacco. Many developing countries have indigenous tobacco companies, of which some are even government-owned, such as the China National Tobacco Company.

I'm glad you brought up the infant formula situation, because it shows the complexity of the issue we're discussing. Factors other than instant formula also influenced the increase in bottle-feeding—specifically, more working mothers and fewer products and services originating in the home. Together, these factors led people to feed babies "home brews," but they were also often unsanitary. Promotion of infant formula may simply have persuaded them to give up the home brews in favor of the most nutritious breast-milk substitute available. Nevertheless, well-intentioned antiformula groups succeeded in reversing bottle-feeding with breast-feeding. However, the HIV virus is transmitted through breast milk, which is a particular problem in southern Africa where many women are infected with HIV/AIDS.[27] Now there are campaigns to get mothers not to breast-feed. This simply shows the futility of trying to legislate what is good for people.

In fact, how far can we go to try to protect people? In developed countries, obesity is a growing health problem. We're attacking it through education—the same way I said we should attack problems in developing countries. I can't imagine us rationing or banning sugars, fats, and carbohydrates. Certainly, products such as soft drinks seem superfluous when people are ill nourished and in poor health. But there is no clear-cut means of drawing a line between people who can afford and people who can't afford these products. Furthermore, companies such as Coca-Cola have experimented with adding nutrition to products, but consumers have not been very receptive.

Companies *do* alter products to fit the needs of low-income people—everything from smaller packages to less-sleek electrical appliances. Although you criticized pharmaceutical companies for not attacking low-income health needs, these same companies spend heavily to find solutions to health problems that attack both rich and poor people, such as cancer and diabetes. In fact, drug companies have seen, and expect to see, huge prescription drug growth in emerging markets.[28]

on life-threatening diseases like malaria, Chagas disease, and sleeping sickness, they spend on lifestyle treatments, such as for penile erectile dysfunction and baldness. The U.S. Food and Drug Administration (FDA) did institute an incentive in 2008 (faster approval of potential "blockbuster drugs") for drug companies that research previously neglected diseases. However, there is skepticism about whether the FDA can really comply with faster approvals.[23] Surely we can find the regulatory means to force companies to meet the real needs of developing countries rather than concentrating on selling dangerous and superfluous products there. ▶

However, pharmaceutical companies must recoup their expenses if they are to survive; thus they must concentrate on drugs for which they can be paid. Governmental research centers and nonprofit foundations are better candidates for solving the developing countries' health problems. In fact, some of these are working jointly with pharmaceutical companies to find solutions, and the National Institutes of Health (NIH) of the United States has instituted a program to find treatments for some of the 6,800 diseases for which there is likely insufficient revenue to recoup research expenditures.[29] ◀

Indirect Legal Considerations   Indirect legal requirements also affect product content or demand. In some countries, companies cannot easily import certain raw materials or components, forcing them to construct an end product with local substitutes that may alter the final result substantially. Legal requirements such as high taxes on heavy automobiles also shift companies' sales to smaller models, thus indirectly altering demand for tire sizes and grades of gasoline.

Issues of Standardization   A recurring issue is the need to arrive at international product standards and eliminate some of the wasteful product requirements for alterations among countries. Although countries have reached agreements on some products (sprocket dimensions on movie film, technical standards on mobile phones, bar codes to identify products), other products (railroad gauges, power supplies, and electrical-socket shapes) continue to vary. A global standard has usually resulted from companies wanting to emulate a dominant producer, such as making personal computers that are IBM (PC) compatible.

Although some standardization of products would eliminate wasteful alterations, there is resistance because
- A changeover would be costly.
- People are familiar with the "old."

In reality, there is both consumer and economic resistance to standardization—such as U.S. consumers' reluctance to adapt to the metric system. Economically, a complete changeover would be more costly than simply educating people and relabeling. Containers would have to be redesigned and production retooled so that sizes would be in even numbers. (Would U.S. football have a first down with 9.144 meters to go?) Even for new products or those still under development, companies and countries are slow to reach agreement, because they want to protect the investments they've already made. At best, international standards will come very slowly.

Cultural Considerations   Religious differences obviously limit the standardization of product offerings globally; thus food franchise companies limit sales of pork products in Islamic countries and meat of any kind in India. However, cultural differences affecting product demand are often not so easily discerned. For example, Toyota initially failed to sell enough pickup trucks in the United States until it redesigned the interior with enough headroom for drivers to wear 10-gallon cowboy hats.[30] Volkswagen and Audi have extended the wheelbase for China to accommodate more passengers for weekend outings.[31] International food marketers alter ingredients (especially fat, sodium, and sugar) substantially to fit local tastes and requirements. For instance, a Kellogg's All-Bran bar has three times as much salt in the United States as in Mexico.

Examination of cultural differences may pinpoint possible problem areas.

Economic Considerations

Income   If a country's average consumers have low incomes, too few of them may be able to buy a product the MNE sells domestically. But this creates an opportunity to design a cheaper alternative, like some companies are doing with very inexpensive

Personal incomes and infrastructures affect product demand.

cars.[32] In some cases, consumers have so little extra cash that they buy personal items such as razor blades in small quantities as they use them. In another example, Kraft initially introduced packages of 14 Oreo cookies unsuccessfully in China, but then had success by reducing the number of cookies and the package price by more than half.[33]

Infrastructure   Poor infrastructure may also require product alterations, such as building products that will withstand rough terrain and utility outages. For instance, Whirlpool sells washing machine models in remote areas of India that have rat guards to protect hoses, extra-strong parts to survive transportation on potholed roads, and heavy-duty wiring to cope with electrical ebbs and surges.[34] Although Japan has an excellent infrastructure, it is characterized by crowded conditions and high land prices. Some large foreign automobile models are too wide to fit into elevators that carry cars to upper floors to be parked, and they cannot make narrow turns on back streets.

Income Distribution   Finally, very uneven income distribution may create demand for labor, such as household servants, at the expense of laborsaving products. Whirlpool discovered this when trying to sell automatic washing machines in some markets. It bought "obsolete" technology from Korea so as to sell less-automated two-tub machines in those markets.[35]

ALTERATION COSTS

Companies can usually reduce production and inventory costs substantially through product standardization. Nevertheless, as we have just demonstrated, there sometimes are compelling reasons to alter products for different national markets. Some product alterations, such as package labeling, are cheaper to make than others, such as the design of a different car model. However, even packaging changes may necessitate costly research if the aim is to convey a particular product perception to a target market with different characteristics than those at home. For example, there is evidence that consumers are partially swayed in buying decisions by packaging and that the needed image to sway them may differ by target market.[36] Thus, companies should always compare the cost of an alteration with the likely cost of lost sales from no alterations.

Companies can compromise between uniformity and diversity by standardizing products a great deal while altering some components. For instance, Whirlpool puts the same basic compressor, casing, evaporator, and sealant system in its refrigerators for all countries, but it changes such features as doors and shelves for different countries.[37]

THE PRODUCT LINE: EXTENT AND MIX

It is doubtful that all of a company's multiple products could generate sufficient sales to justify the cost of penetrating each market with each product. Even if they could, a company might offer only a portion of its product line, perhaps as an entry strategy.

Sales and Cost Considerations   In reaching product-line decisions, a company should consider the possible effects on sales and the cost of having a large versus small family of products. Sometimes a company finds that it must produce and sell a wide variety of products if it is to gain distribution with large retailers. In contrast, if the foreign sales per customer are small, selling costs per unit may be high because of the fixed costs associated with selling. In such a case, the company can broaden the product line it handles, either by introducing a larger family of products or by grouping sales of several manufacturers.

Product Life-Cycle Considerations   Countries may differ in either the shape or the length of a product's life cycle. Thus a product facing declining sales in one country may have growing or sustained sales in another. For example, cars are a mature product in Western Europe, the United States, and Japan. They're in the late growth stage in South

---

Concept Check

In Chapter 12, we list the factors that companies consider when "scanning" potential overseas locations to determine what conditions in the host country's environment are likely to affect the success of international operations. Under "Cost Considerations," we point out that poor internal *infrastructure* inflates operating costs and can in fact negate cost savings afforded by low labor rates.

Some alterations cost less than others.

Broadening the product line may gain distribution economies.

Korea and in the early growth stage in India. At the mature stage, automobile companies must emphasize characteristics that encourage people to replace their still-functional cars, such as by emphasizing lifestyle, speed, and accessories. In the early growth stage, they need to appeal to first-time buyers who worry about cost; thus they emphasize fuel consumption and price.[38]

Pricing Strategies

Within the marketing mix, a price must be low enough to gain sales but high enough to guarantee the flow of funds required to cover such expenses as R&D, production, and distribution. The company's strategy on how to compete, such as through cost leadership versus product differentiation, also affects pricing decisions. The proper price will not only ensure short-term profits but also give the company the resources necessary to achieve long-term competitive viability.

POTENTIAL OBSTACLES IN INTERNATIONAL PRICING

Pricing is more complex internationally than domestically because of the following factors:

- Government intervention
- Market diversity
- Export price escalation
- Fluctuations in currency value
- Fixed versus variable pricing
- Relations with suppliers

Let's examine each of these factors.

Government Intervention   Every country has laws that affect the prices of goods, such as price controls that set either minimum or maximum prices. Minimum prices are usually set to prevent companies from eliminating competitors to gain monopoly positions. Maximum prices are usually set so that poor consumers can buy products and services.

The WTO, under its antidumping regulations, permits countries to establish restrictions against any import entering at a price below cost. However, why would a company wish to sell below its cost? First, it may wish to induce customers to try a product, such as by offering a low price or even free samples. Second, it may sell below cost to test the market. Let's look at a test market example. Nestlé exported Lean Cuisine products from Canada to the United Kingdom at a price below the cost. Why? Nestlé wanted to test the market by selling temporarily at the consumer price that it would charge if it produced the frozen foods in the United Kingdom. The loss was small compared to the value of the information gained and the amount of Nestlé's eventual commitment. However, antidumping regulations may prevent companies from fully utilizing the advantages from selling temporarily below their costs.

Governmental price controls may

- Set minimum or maximum prices.
- Prohibit certain competitive pricing practices.

Market Diversity   Although a company can segment the domestic market and charge different prices in each segment in numerous ways, country-to-country variations create even more natural segments. For example, companies can sell few sea urchins or tuna eyeballs in the United States at any price, but they can export them to Japan, where they are delicacies. By way of another example, Levi's jeans often cost twice as much in the United Kingdom as in the United States.[39]

Consumers in some countries simply like certain products more and are willing to pay more for them.

Pricing Tactics   In some countries, a company may have many competitors and thus little discretion in setting its prices. In other countries, it may have a near monopoly

Push is more likely when

• Self-service is not predominant.
• Advertising is restricted.
• Product price is a high portion of income.

Factors in Push-Pull Decisions   Several factors help determine the mix of push and pull among countries:

• Type of distribution system
• Cost and availability of media to reach target markets
• Consumer attitudes toward sources of information
• Price of the product compared to incomes

Generally, the more tightly controlled the distribution system, the more likely a company is to emphasize a push strategy to distributors, because it requires a greater effort to get them to handle a product. This is true, for example, in Belgium, where most distributors are small and highly fragmented, forcing companies to concentrate on making their goods available.

Also affecting the push-pull mix is the amount of contact between salespeople and consumers. In a self-service situation in which there are no salespeople to whom customers can turn for opinions on products, it is more important for the company to use a pull strategy by advertising through mass media or at the point of purchase.

SOME PROBLEMS IN INTERNATIONAL PROMOTION

Because of diverse national environments, promotional problems are extremely varied. For example, about 70 percent of India's population is rural, and many in rural areas are illiterate, poor, and without access to televisions and radios. Some mass consumer merchandisers such as Colgate-Palmolive, Unilever, Coca-Cola, and Pepsi are providing samples at religious pilgrimages that millions attend, in the expectation that their subsequent word-of-mouth promotions will yield sales.[47]

In many countries, government regulations pose an even greater barrier. For example, Scandinavian television has long refused to accept commercials. Other countries may put legal constraints on what a company says. For example, in the United States, pharmaceutical companies have been using more pull promotions than previously for prescription drugs, talking about physical symptoms in television ads and telling viewers to ask their physicians about a particular brand. European countries are more restrictive about mentioning the name of a drug; thus, Pfizer's European ads tell TV viewers to talk with their physicians about erectile dysfunction, but they never mention the drug Viagra.[48]

Finally, when a product's price compared to consumer income is high, consumers will usually want more time and information before making a decision. Information is best conveyed in a personal selling situation that fosters two-way communication. In developing economies, MNEs usually have to use push strategies for more products, because more incomes are low compared to price.

Advantages of standardized advertising include

• Some cost savings.
• Better quality at local level.
• Rapid entry into different countries.

Standardization: Pro and Con   The savings from using the same advertising programs as much as possible, such as on a global basis or among countries with shared consumer attributes, are significant, though not as great as those from product standardization.

In addition to reducing costs, advertising standardization may improve the quality of advertising at the local level (because local agencies may lack expertise), prevent internationally mobile consumers from being confused by different images, and speed the entry of products into different countries.

However, globally standardized advertising usually means a program that is *similar* from market to market rather than one that is *identical* in each. For example, Apple used the same theme in its "Mac versus PC" ad series in the United States and in the United Kingdom, but it used U.S. TV personalities for the U.S. version and U.K. TV personalities for the U.K. version.[49]

Standardization usually implies using the same advertising agency globally. However, companies may differentiate campaigns among countries even if they use the same agency everywhere. By using the same agency, companies such as IBM, Colgate, and Tambrands have found that they can take good ideas from one market and quickly introduce them into other markets, because they need not worry about legal and ethical problems from having one agency copy what another has done. However, some companies, such as Procter & Gamble, prefer to use more than one agency to keep the agencies in a state of perpetual competition and to cover one agency's weak spots by drawing on the ideas of another.

A Few Related Issues Finally, the issue of standardization in advertising raises problems in a few other areas—namely, *translation, legality,* and *message needs.*

TRANSLATION When media reach audiences in multiple countries—such as MTV programs aired throughout most of Europe or satellite TV services throughout Latin America—ads in those media cannot be translated, because viewers watch the same transmission. A problem of using multicountry media, however, is that the product may not be available everywhere it is advertised.

When, however, a company is going to sell in a country with a different language, translation is usually necessary unless the advertiser is trying to communicate an aura of foreignness. The most audible problem in commercial translation is dubbing, because words on an added sound track never quite correspond to lip movements. Companies can avoid dubbing problems by creating commercials in which actors do not speak, along with a voice or print overlay in the appropriate language.

A growing type of dubbing in advertising involves product placement in movies and television shows. Because these shows are widely distributed internationally, a wide audience sees the placement. However, the product may not be available everywhere. Technology now permits the products to be removed and replaced for given markets. *Spider-Man 2* had Cadbury Schweppes's Dr Pepper logo on a refrigerator for U.S. screenings, but in Europe it had PepsiCo's Mirinda logo.[50]

On the surface, translating a message would seem to be easy. However, some messages, particularly plays on words, simply don't translate—even between countries that have the same language. The number of ludicrous but costly mistakes companies have made attest to translation difficulties. Sometimes what is an acceptable word or direct translation in one place is obscene, misleading, or meaningless in another. For example, the Milk Board's ad "Got milk?" comes out as "Are you lactating?" in Spanish.[51] In the same Apple commercial to which we referred earlier, the U.S. version used the word "doozy" and the U.K. version used the word "humdinger." Another problem is in choosing the language when a country has more than one. For example, in Haiti, a company might use Creole to reach the general population but French to reach the upper class.

LEGALITY What is legal advertising in one country may be illegal elsewhere. The differences result mainly from varying national views on consumer protection, competitive protection, promotion of civil rights, standards of morality and behavior, and nationalism. For instance, China bans ads for feminine hygiene pads, hemorrhoid medications, and athlete's foot ointment during mealtimes.[52] It also bans the use of pigs in ads, because the use might offend its Muslim population.[53]

In terms of consumer protection, policies differ on the amount of deception permitted and what can be advertised to children. The United Kingdom and the United States allow direct comparisons with competitive brands (such as Pepsi versus Coca-Cola); the Philippines prohibits them. Only a few countries regulate sexism in advertising.

Some governments restrict the advertising of some products (such as contraceptives), because they feel they are in bad taste. Elsewhere, governments restrict ads that might prompt children to misbehave or people to break laws (such as advertising automobile speeds that exceed the speed limit) and those that show barely clad women. New Zealand banned a Nike ad in which a rugby team tackles the coach, as well as a Chanel ad in which the model said to her male lover before kissing him, "I hate you. I hate you so much I think I'm going to die from it, darling." In both cases, the ads were deemed to threaten violence.[54]

Concept Check

In Chapter 2, we emphasize that although language practice *within* a culture serves as a "cultural stabilizer," the effort to apply language practices *across* cultures can have an entirely different effect. In discussing "Spoken and Written Language," we identify several reasons why internationally minded companies should be careful in translating a message conceived in one language into a message to be delivered in another. As for advertising in visual media, we also discuss a variety of potential pitfalls in "Silent Language"—nonverbal communication ranging from body language to the use of colors.

a national brand, because stretching the promotional budget over so many brands means that promotions are not as effective as they might be, given that less is spent on any one brand to build significant positive recognition.[64] Overall the proportion of local brands to international brands is decreasing; however, there are many examples of strong local brands that companies cannot easily displace.[65]

Images of products are affected by where they are made.

Country-of-Origin Image Companies should consider whether to create a local or a foreign image for their products because of quality perceptions.[66] For example, many Japanese believe that clothing made abroad is superior to that made in Japan. Thus Burberry has created separate labels for its products made in Japan and those made in the United Kingdom (Burberry London brand). The British have a positive image of Australian wine; thus a young Australian winery sought a very Australian name, Barramundi, for its wine exports to the United Kingdom.[67]

Keep in mind, though, that both the country of origin and the brand have positive and negative images, which interact. Evidence suggests that a positive brand image can overcome negative perceptions of the country where the product is made.[68]

- The brand image may overcome the country image.
- Images can change.

But images can change. Consider that for many years various Korean companies sold abroad under private labels or under contract with well-known companies. Some of these Korean companies, such as Samsung, now emphasize their own trade names and the quality of Korean products. At the same time, the Korean LG Group, best known for its Gold Star brand, has introduced a line of high-end appliances with a European-sounding name, LG Tromm.[69] Nevertheless, there is evidence that consumers have limited knowledge of the country of origin of most brands.[70]

One ongoing international legal debate concerns product names associated with location. The EU protects the names of many EU products based on location names, such as Roquefort and Gorgonzola cheeses, Parma ham, and Chianti wine. More recently, the EU has pushed for protection against foreign use of terms such as *clos, chateau, tawny, noble, ruby,* and *vintage*, because they are regulated names within Europe.[71]

If a brand name is used for a class of product, the company may lose the trademark.

Generic and Near-Generic Names Companies want their product names to become household words, but not so much that competitors can use trademarked brand names to describe their similar products. In the United States, the brand names Xerox and Kleenex are nearly synonymous with copiers and facial tissue, but they have nevertheless remained proprietary brands. Some other names that were once proprietary, such as cellophane, linoleum, and Cornish hens, have become **generic**—available for anyone to use.

In this context, companies sometimes face substantial differences among countries that may either stimulate or frustrate their sales. For example, *aspirin* and *Swiss Army knives* are proprietary names in Europe but generic in the United States, a situation that impairs European export sales of those products to the United States, because U.S. companies can produce aspirin and Swiss Army knives.

Distribution Strategies

A company may accurately assess market potential, design goods or services for that market, price them appropriately, and promote them to probable consumers. However, it will have little likelihood of reaching its sales potential if it doesn't make the goods or services conveniently available to customers. Companies need to place their goods where people want to buy them. At the same time, a company's system of distribution may give it strategic advantages not easily copied by competitors, such as Avon's strategy of selling directly through independent reps and Amazon.com's Internet sales.

Distribution is the course—physical path or legal title—that goods take between production and consumption. In international marketing, a company must decide on the method of distribution among countries as well as the method within the country where final sale occurs.

Companies may limit early distribution in given foreign countries by attempting to sell regionally before moving nationally. Many products and markets lend themselves to this sort of gradual development. In many cases, geographic barriers and poor internal transportation systems divide countries into very distinct markets. In other countries, very little wealth or few potential sales may lie outside the large metropolitan areas. In still others, advertising and distribution may be handled effectively on a regional basis.

> A company may enter a market gradually by limiting geographic coverage.

We've already discussed operating forms for foreign-market penetration. In Chapter 13, we discuss distribution channels to move goods among countries and how the title to goods gets transferred. This section does not review these aspects of distribution; it discusses distributional differences and conditions within foreign countries that an international marketer should understand.

DECIDING WHETHER TO STANDARDIZE

Within the marketing mix, MNEs find distribution one of the most difficult functions to standardize internationally for several reasons. Each country has its own distribution system, which an MNE finds difficult to modify because it is entwined with the country's cultural, economic, and legal environments. Nevertheless, many retailers are successfully moving internationally.

> Distribution reflects different country environments:
> - It may vary substantially among countries.
> - It is difficult to change.

Some of the factors that influence how goods will be distributed in a given country are citizens' attitudes toward owning their own store, the cost of paying retail workers,

Does Geography Matter? Is Necessity the Mother of Invention?

You've probably heard the saying that it is as "difficult as selling a refrigerator to Eskimos." Climate is a great influence on the demand for many products—clothes, sporting equipment, snow tires, air conditioners, and sunscreen, to name a few—and is a variable when identifying market segments. Furthermore, seasonal changes that occur at opposite times in the Northern and Southern Hemispheres allow you to spread your sales more evenly throughout the year, such as by focusing ski sales in Switzerland from December through March and in Chile from June through September. This hemispheric difference may also cause you to make adjustments. Films aimed at young audiences sometimes debut months apart between the Northern and Southern Hemispheres so as to be viewed during school vacation periods that correspond to the hot months.

Natural conditions—such as mountains, waterways, and deserts—create both barriers and expediencies to distribution. For example, countries can more easily build infrastructure where there are flat areas without obstructions; thus, other things being equal, these areas provide better internal distribution possibilities.

Immigration is largely clustered, because people move where others of their ethnic group have gone before, thus forming subcultures. Understanding where these groups exist can help identify potential markets.[72] For instance, Guatemala's Pollo Campero, when entering the U.S. market, went first to Los Angeles, where there are more than a million Central Americans.

Because transportation cost roughly correlates with distance, there is usually a higher cost when the distance between production and market is greater. This extra cost must be either passed on to consumers or absorbed by the selling company. In addition, if markets are close to each other, it is more difficult to maintain different price schedules between them, because promotion likely reaches both markets. In turn, consumers will buy from the less expensive location. In fact, the closeness of most Canadians to the U.S. border has influenced Canadian stores to stay open longer and operate on more days, lest Canadians cross the border to buy in the United States.

Although geography does play a role in product demand, higher disposable income and technology help overcome many geographic constraints. Thus people in hot climates do buy winter clothes and skis, because they travel to snowy areas for recreation, and people in Dubai enjoy an indoor ski resort complex. And there's even a market for refrigerators among the Eskimos. ●

legislation differentially affecting chain stores and individually owned stores, legislation restricting the operating hours and size of stores, the trust that owners have in their employees, the efficacy of the postal system, the quality of the infrastructure system, and the financial ability to carry large inventories.

For example, Hong Kong supermarkets, compared with those in the United States, carry a higher proportion of fresh goods, are smaller, sell smaller quantities per customer, and are located more closely to each other. This means that companies selling canned, boxed, or frozen foods encounter less demand per store in Hong Kong than in the United States. They would also have to make smaller deliveries because of store sizes and would have a harder time fighting for shelf space.

A few other examples should illustrate how distribution norms differ. Finland has few stores per capita because general-line retailers predominate there, whereas Italian distribution has a fragmented retail and wholesale structure. In the Netherlands, buyers' cooperatives deal directly with manufacturers. Japan has cash-and-carry wholesalers for retailers that do not need financing or delivery services. In Germany, mail-order sales are very important; not so in many developing countries that have less-reliable delivery systems.

How do these differences affect companies' marketing activities? One soft-drink company, for example, has targeted most of its European sales through grocery stores. However, the method for getting its soft drinks to those stores varies. In the United Kingdom, one national distributor has been able to gain sufficient coverage and shelf space so that the soft-drink company can concentrate on other aspects of its marketing mix. In France, a single distributor has been able to get good coverage in the larger supermarkets but not in the smaller ones; consequently, the soft-drink company has been exploring how to get secondary distribution without upsetting its relationship with the primary distributor. In Norway, regional distributors predominate, so the soft drink company has found it difficult to effect national promotion campaigns. In Belgium, the company could find no acceptable distributor, so it has had to assume that function itself.

CHOOSING DISTRIBUTORS AND CHANNELS

We now compare why companies handle their own distribution or contract other companies to do it for them and discuss how they should choose outside distributors.

Is Internal Handling Feasible?   When sales volume is low, it is usually more economical for a company to rely on external distributors. As sales grow, it may handle distribution itself to gain more control. However, such self-handling may still be difficult for small companies that lack necessary resources.[73]

Circumstances conducive to the internal handling of distribution include not only high sales volume but also the following factors:

- When a product has the characteristic of high price, high technology, or the need for complex after-sales servicing (such as aircraft), the producer probably will have to deal directly with the buyer. The producer may simultaneously use a distributor within the foreign country that will serve to identify sales leads.

- When the company deals with global customers, especially in business-to-business sales—such as an auto-parts manufacturer that sells original equipment to the same automakers in multiple countries—such sales may go directly from the producer to the global customer.

- When the company views its main competitive advantage to be its distribution methods, it may control this distribution abroad. The ending case demonstrates how Avon has successfully transferred its U.S. direct-selling distribution by independent representatives to its operations abroad. Dell Computer has successfully handled its own mail-order sales in Europe. In addition, food franchisors typically maintain some restaurants of their own to serve as "flagships."

> Distribution may be handled internally
>
> - When volume is high.
> - When companies have sufficient resources.
> - When there is a need to deal directly with the customer because of the nature of the product.
> - When the customer is global.
> - When the distribution form is a competitive advantage.

Which Distributors Are Qualified?   A company can usually choose from a number of potential foreign distributors. These are some common criteria for selecting a distributor:

- The company's financial strength
- Its good connections
- Extent of its other business commitments
- Current status of its personnel, facilities, and equipment
- Its reliability as an honest performer
- Its image in relation to the product or service being sold

The distributor's financial strength is important because of the potential long-term relationship between producer and distributor and because of the assurance that money will be available for such things as maintaining sufficient inventory. Good connections are particularly important if sales must be directed to certain types of buyers, such as governmental procurement agencies. They are also important in societies, such as China, where connections and mutual loyalty are often more important than product and price for making sales.[74]

The amount of other business commitments can indicate whether the distributor has time for the company's product and whether it currently handles competitive or complementary products. The current status of the distributor's personnel, facilities, and equipment indicates not only its ability to deal with the product but also how quickly start-up can occur and how likely the distributorship will stay in business. A distributor's history and image as a responsible business entity help create trust as a means of enforcing performance.[75] This is especially important in some parts of the Middle East and Latin America where manufacturers cannot easily terminate agreements simply because distributors have performed poorly.

How Reliable Is After-Sales Service?   Consumers are reluctant to buy products that may require spare parts and service in the future unless they feel assured that these will be readily available in good quality and at reasonable prices. The more complex and expensive the product, the more important is after-sales servicing. When after-sales servicing is important, companies may need to invest in service centers for groups of distributors that serve as intermediaries between producers and consumers. Earnings from sales of parts and after-sales service may sometimes exceed that of the original product.

THE CHALLENGE OF GETTING DISTRIBUTION

Companies must evaluate potential distributors, but distributors must choose which companies and products to represent and emphasize. Both wholesalers and retailers have limited storage facilities, display space, money to pay for inventories, and transportation and personnel to move and sell merchandise, so they try to carry only those products that have the greatest profit potential.

In many cases, distributors are tied into exclusive arrangements with manufacturers that impede new competitive entries. For example, for many years, breweries in the United Kingdom owned the pubs, where they sold only their own beer. This forced Anheuser-Busch to enter the market strictly with supermarket sales. Currently, Japan is a country in which many manufacturers, such as Shiseido, Toshiba, and Hitachi, have arrangements with thousands of distributors to sell only their products.

In addition, any company that is new to a country and wants to introduce products that some competitors are already selling may meet difficulty in finding distributors to handle its brands. Even established companies sometimes find distribution difficult for their new products, although they have the dual advantage of being known and of being able to offer existing profitable lines only if distributors accept the new unproven products.

Some evaluation criteria for distributors include their

- *Financial capability.*
- *Connections with customers.*
- *Fit with a company's product.*
- *Other resources.*
- *Trustworthiness.*
- *Compatibility with product image.*

Spare parts and service are important for sales.

Distributors choose which companies and products to handle. Companies

- *May need to give incentives.*
- *May use successful products as bait for new ones.*
- *Must convince distributors that product and company are viable.*

A company wanting to use existing distribution channels may need to analyze competitive conditions carefully to offer effective incentives for the distributors to handle the product. It may need to identify distributors' problems so as to gain their loyalty by offering assistance. Companies alternatively may offer other incentives such as higher profit margins, after-sales servicing, and promotional support. In the final analysis, however, incentives will be of little help unless the distributors believe that a company's products are viable. The company must sell the distributors on its products as well as on itself as a reliable company.

Of course, a company may use a combination of self-distribution and independent distributors. For instance, Kodak has done this very successfully in Russia. It handles some direct sales to big customers, such as LUKoil, which it convinced to give cameras as gifts to employees rather than giving them books or bottles of vodka. Otherwise, it handles retail operations through distributors that it supports with extensive advertising, store decorations, rebate programs, and market research.[76]

HIDDEN COSTS AND GAINS IN DISTRIBUTION

When companies consider launching products in foreign markets, they must determine what final consumer prices will be to estimate sales potential. Five factors that often contribute to cost differences among countries in distribution are *infrastructure conditions, the number of levels in the distribution system, retail inefficiencies, size and operating-hour restrictions,* and *inventory stock-outs.*

In many countries, the roads and warehousing facilities are so poor that getting goods to consumers quickly, at a low cost, and with minimum damage or loss en route is problematic. For example, in China, despite its market potential, companies find difficulty in transporting their products nationally because of poor roads and theft en route to and from warehouses.[77]

Many countries have multitiered wholesalers that sell to each other before the product reaches the retail level. For example, national wholesalers sell to regional ones, who sell to local ones, and so on. Japan, although changing rapidly, has had many more levels of distribution than such countries as France and the United States. Because each intermediary adds a markup, they drive prices up.

In some countries, particularly developing countries, low labor costs and owners' basic distrust of non-family members result in many retailers engaging in practices that result in lower labor productivity to serve customers. This distrust is evident in retailers' preference for counter service rather than self-service. A customer who decides to purchase something gets an invoice to take to a cashier's line to pay. Once the invoice is stamped as paid, the customer must go to another line to pick up the merchandise after presenting the stamped invoice. In some countries, counter service is common for purchases as small as a pencil. On the one hand, the additional personnel add to retailing costs, and the added time people must be in the store means fewer people can be served in the given space. On the other hand, because the retailers tend to be small and highly dispersed, they reduce the time, cost, and effort for customers to shop.[78] In contrast, most retailers in some (mainly economically developed) countries have equipment that improves the efficiency of handling customers and reports, such as electronic scanners, cash registers linked to inventory-control records, and machines connecting purchases to credit-card companies.

Many countries, such as France, Germany, and Japan, have laws to protect small retailers. These effectively limit the number of large retail establishments and the efficiencies they bring to sales. Most countries have historic and present patchwork systems that limit days or hours of operations for religious purposes or to protect employees from having to work late at night or on weekends.[79] At the same time, the limits keep retailers from covering the fixed cost of their space over more hours, so these costs are passed on to consumers.

Where most retail establishments are small, particularly in developing countries, there is little space to store inventory. Wholesalers must incur the cost of making small deliveries to many more establishments, and sometimes they may have to visit each retailer more frequently because of stock outages. However, these latter costs may be overcome because of labor and transport cost savings resulting from low-paid delivery personnel who may carry small quantities of merchandise on bicycles. Further, the retailers themselves incur lower costs because their inventory-carrying costs are low compared with their sales.[80]

E-COMMERCE AND THE INTERNET

Estimates vary widely on the current and future number of worldwide online households and the electronic commerce generated through online sales. Nevertheless, they all indicate substantial growth. As electronic commerce increases, customers worldwide can quickly compare prices from different distributors, which should drive prices down. There is evidence that online shoppers universally have some similar characteristics: They want convenience, are heavy users of e-mail and the Internet, and have favorable attitudes toward direct marketing and advertising.[81]

Opportunities   Electronic commerce offers companies an opportunity to promote their products globally. However, it does not relieve them of the need to develop the marketing tools we have discussed throughout the chapter. For some products and services, such as airline tickets and hotel space, the Internet has largely replaced traditional sales methods. But even here, companies may need to adapt to country differences, such as providing access through different languages.[82] There are certainly many success stories. For example, the New Zealand company Tristyle International sells prefabricated housing. About 95 percent of its sales are export and 40 percent of its sales are through the Internet.[83]

The Internet also permits suppliers to deal more quickly with their customers. For example, Lee Hung Fat Garment Factory of Hong Kong supplies apparel to about 60 companies in Europe and now flashes pictures of merchandise samples to them over the Web. Customers such as Kingfisher of the United Kingdom can tinker with the samples and transmit new versions back to Hong Kong so that Lee Hung Fat produces exactly what the distributors want.[84]

> The growth in online households creates new distributional opportunities and challenges in selling globally over the Internet.

Problems   Global Internet sales are not without problems. Many households, especially in developing countries, lack access to Internet connections. Therefore, if a company wants to reach mass global markets, it will need to supplement its Internet sales with other means of promotion and distribution. This can be very expensive. Further, a switch to Internet sales may upset existing distribution and, if unsuccessful, make future sales more difficult.[85]

A company cannot easily differentiate its marketing program for each country where it operates. The same Web advertisements and prices reach customers everywhere, even though different appeals and prices for different countries might yield more sales and profits. If the company makes international sales over the Internet, it must expeditiously deliver what it sells. This may necessitate having warehouses and service facilities abroad.

Finally, the company's Internet ads and prices must comply with the laws of each country where the company makes sales. This is a challenge, because a company's Web page reaches Internet users everywhere. Clearly, although the Internet creates opportunities for companies to sell internationally, it also creates challenges for them.

Managing the Marketing Mix

Although every element in the marketing mix—product, price, promotion, brand, and distribution—is important, the relative importance of one versus another may vary from place to place and over time. Thus management must monitor and adjust its marketing programs accordingly.

GAP ANALYSIS

Once a company is operating in a country and estimates that country's market potential, it must calculate how well it is doing there. A useful tool in this respect is **gap analysis,** a method for estimating a company's potential sales by identifying potential customers it is not serving adequately.[86] When sales are lower than the estimated market potential for a given type of product, the company has potential for increased sales.

The difference between total market potential and a company's sales is due to gaps:

- Usage—less product sold by all competitors than potential.
- Product line—company lacks some product variations.
- Distribution—company misses geographic or intensity coverage.
- Competitive—competitors' sales not explained by product line and distribution gaps.

Figure 16.4 is a bar showing four types of gaps: *usage, competitive, product line,* and *distribution.* To construct such a bar, a company first needs to estimate the potential demand for all competitors in the country for a relevant period, say for the next year or the next five years. This figure gives the height of the bar. Second, a company needs to estimate current sales by all competitors, which is point A. The space between point A and the top of the bar is a *usage gap,* meaning that this is the growth potential for all competitors in the market for the relevant period. Third, a company needs to plot its own current sales of the product, point B.

Types of Gaps   Finally, the company divides the difference between point A and point B into types of gaps based on its estimate of sales lost to competitors. The *distribution gap* represents sales lost to competitors who distribute where the company does not, such as to additional geographic areas or types of outlets. The *product line gap* represents sales lost to competitors who have product variations the company does not have. The *competitive gap* is the remaining unexplained sales lost to competitors who may have a better image or lower prices.

Usage Gaps   Companies may have different-sized gaps in different markets. The large chocolate companies have altered their marketing programs among countries because of their different gaps.[87] In some markets, they have found substantial usage gaps; that is, less chocolate is being consumed than would be expected on the basis of population and income levels. Industry specialists estimate that in many countries, much of the population

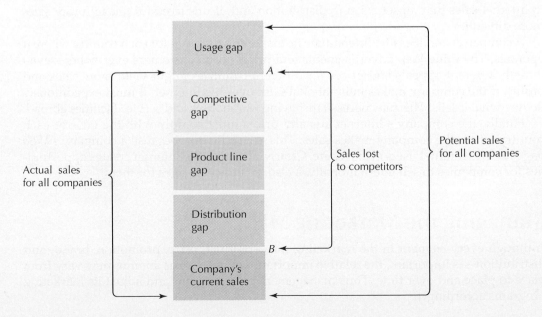

FIGURE 16.4   Gap Analysis

Why aren't sales as much as they could be? That's the question asked by a company's managers when they undertake *gap analysis.* The arrow at the top represents *total sales potential* for all competitors during a given period. The arrow at A indicates *actual sales.* Notice that there's a gap between the product's potential and actual sales—the so-called *usage gap.* But there are other gaps as well. The arrow bracketing points A and B, for example, designates all sales lost by the company to its competitors— the *gap,* that is, between what the company did sell and what it could have sold if, for a variety of reasons, it hadn't lost so many sales to competitors. Finally, remember that in the real world, gap sizes will fluctuate.

has never tasted chocolate. This has led companies to promote sales in those areas for chocolate in general.

The U.S. market shows another type of usage gap. Nearly everyone in this market has tried most chocolate products, but per capita consumption has fallen because of growing concern about weight. To increase chocolate consumption in general, Nestlé for a short time promoted chocolate as an energy source for the sports minded. Note, however, that building general consumption is most useful to the market leader. Nestlé, with U.S. chocolate sales below those of Mars and Hershey, actually benefited its competitors during the short-lived campaign.

Product Line and Distribution Gaps   Chocolate companies have also found that they have product-line gaps. For example, some lack sugar-free chocolate products, which boosts competitors' sales. Or their products may be sold in too few places. Ferrero Rocher has recently emphasized product placement in more mainstream outlets.

Competitive Gaps   Finally, there are competitive gaps—sales by competitors that cannot be explained by differences between a company's own product line and distribution and those of the competitors. That is, competitors are making additional sales because of their prices, advertising campaigns, goodwill, or any of a host of other factors. In markets where per capita chocolate consumption is high, companies exert most of their efforts in gaining sales at the expense of competitors. For instance, Switzerland has the world's highest per capita chocolate consumption. In that market, such competitors as Migros, Lindt, and Nestlé's Cailler go head to head in creating images of better quality.[88]

Although gap analysis is primarily a means of prioritizing elements in the marketing mix within given countries, it is also possible to use the tool by aggregating needs among countries. For example, let's say that the product-line gap is too small in a single country to justify the expense of developing a specific new product, such as a heat-resistant chocolate bar. Nevertheless, the combined market potential among several countries for this product may justify the product- and promotional-development costs. Thus gap analysis may help managers improve country-level performance along with enhancing synergies among the countries where they operate.

Looking to the Future    Evolving Challenges to Segment Markets

Recall the discussion earlier in the chapter on three approaches to segmentation. While all of these involve the geographic unit of the nation as one of the key components, such segmentation also involves both demographics and psychographics. How both of these will unfold in future years will likely affect international marketing. The following discussion highlights a key area of both.

Income Demographics

Most projections are that disparities between the "haves" and "have-nots" will grow in the foreseeable future, both within and among countries. Furthermore, because haves will be more educated and more connected to the Internet, they will be better able to search globally for lower prices for what they buy. Therefore, globally, the affluent segment will have even more purchasing power than their incomes indicate.

As these people's discretionary income increases, some luxury products will become more commonplace (partly because it will take fewer hours of work to purchase them), and seemingly dissimilar products and services (such as cars, travel, jewelry, and furniture) will compete with each other for the same discretionary spending. For example, Japan was the premier importer of luxury goods, such as Louis Vuitton bags and Hermes scarves, during the 1980s and early

(continued)

1990s, but competition from an array of other luxury products and services, such as spas and expensive restaurants, have eroded those imports.[89] Because of better communications and rising educational levels of the haves, they will want more choices. However, market segments may not fall primarily along national lines. Rather, companies will identify consumer niches that cut across country lines.

At the other extreme, because of growing numbers of poor people with little disposable income, companies will have opportunities to develop low-cost standardized products to fit the needs of the have-nots. In reality, low-income households collectively have considerable purchasing power, and it is a segment that MNEs have largely ignored. For instance, 680 million households have incomes of less than $6,000 per year in the 18 largest developing and transitional economies. They have roughly $1.7 trillion to spend—mainly on housing, food, health care, education, communications, finance charges, and consumer goods.[90] Thus companies will have conflicting opportunities: to develop luxury to serve the haves and to cut costs to serve the have-nots.

Despite the growing proportions of haves and have-nots, demographers project that the actual numbers of people moving out of poverty levels and into middle-income levels will increase. This is largely because of population and income growth in some low-income countries, especially in Asia. Such a shift will likely mean that companies' sales growth in low-income countries will mainly be for products that are mature in industrial countries, such as many consumer electronics and household appliances.

Will National Markets Become Passé?

In addition to demographic differences, especially those concerning incomes, attitudinal differences affect demand in general as well as demand for particular types of products and services. Although global communications are reaching far-flung populations, different people react differently to them. At least three types of personality traits interact and affect how potential consumers react.[91] These are not mutually exclusive traits. They exist in all countries (thus creating a segment that cuts across countries), but the portion of people who are strongly influenced by one versus the other presently varies by country. How these factors evolve in the future will likely have a profound influence on the future of international marketing.

The first of the traits is *materialism,* which refers to the importance of acquiring possessions as a means of self-satisfaction and happiness, as well as for the appearance of success. There is evidence of a growing and spreading global materialistic culture. However, there is also some evidence that people who have always been affluent may exhibit lower materialistic behaviors than those who have recently become affluent. The second of these traits is *cosmopolitanism,* which refers to openness to the world. While there is debate on whether this is a learned or an in-born trait, some of the characteristics include comparing oneself with the world rather than with the local situation. Cosmopolitanists may actually seek out foreign products and services. The third of these traits is *consumer ethnocentrism,* which refers to preference of local to global, such as seeking out local alternatives when buying products and services. ◼

Avon Calls on Foreign Markets

Avon, founded in 1886, is one of the world's oldest and largest manufacturers and marketers of beauty and related products.[92] Many are most familiar with Avon through its long-standing ad, "Ding dong, Avon calling," but the company has recently switched to "Hello Tomorrow" to change its image and better reflect the company's new marketing approaches.

Where Opportunity Currently Knocks

Avon is headquartered in the United States, but over three-quarters of its sales and employees are outside its North American division. It seems to be selling everywhere—moisturizer to Inuits above the Arctic Circle and makeup delivered by canoe to residents of Brazil's Amazon region. It has its own sales operations in 66 countries and territories, and it distributes to another 44. Altogether, there are about 5.8 million independent representatives selling Avon products.

However, Avon was 28 years old (an adult by human standards) before it ever ventured abroad, and then only to nearby Canada. Forty years later, a geriatric in human terms, it moved into its second foreign market, Venezuela. Map 16.1 shows how Avon now divides the world regionally and the portion of its business in each region.

Why Avon Went Global

So why has Avon put so much emphasis on international expansion in recent years? First, Avon forecast a slow growth potential in the U.S. market, because there is virtually no remaining untapped market for cosmetics, fragrances, and toiletries. To grow rapidly in the United States would mean taking sales from competitors, and the U.S. beauty market is *very* competitive. If you doubt this, just try weaving through a large U.S. department store without being accosted and sprayed on.

Avon has preferred to put emphasis on less-competitive markets, and its latest annual report even states that it expects U.S. "growth to be in line with that of the overall beauty market"—which means its domestic sales will depend primarily on the population growth of women in the cosmetics-using age group. Even if there were a considerable untapped U.S. market, less than 5 percent of the world's population lives in the United States.

Second, you need to understand Avon's distribution system to appreciate why Avon worried about U.S. sales in the latter part of the twentieth century. Avon has always depended on direct selling by contracted independent salespersons (almost always women working part time and known as "Avon ladies" or "Avon representatives"), who sell to households by demonstrating products and giving beauty advice. These reps place sales orders with Avon and deliver orders to the customers once they receive them.

Historically, these direct sales have been the backbone of Avon's success. To begin with, direct selling offers Avon a cost-savings advantage by enabling the company to maintain a

MAP 16.1   Where Avon Sells (and How Much)

Avon sells on every continent (except Antarctica) and derives most of its sales outside its home country. The labeled countries are where Avon has operations.

Source: Lists of countries and geographic segments of operations are taken from Avon Products Inc., *Avon 2006–2008 Annual Reports.*

Note: Given that this is a Mercator projection, the scale approximates east-west distance at the equator; however, the farther you move from the equator, the more the east-west distance is distorted.

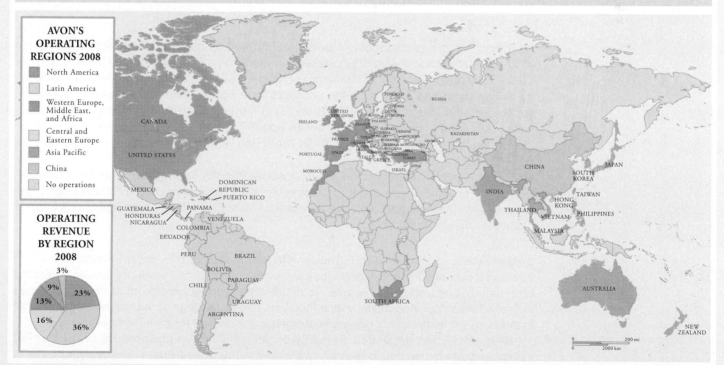

smaller number of employees, keep its advertising budget low (the Avon ladies do much of the promotion), and avoid having to pay for shelf space in stores. The lower costs have facilitated Avon's maintenance of generally lower prices than those that competitors charge in department stores. Thus Avon has consistently maintained an image of good value for the money.

Direct selling also offers additional marketing advantages, because word-of-mouth customers tend to be quite loyal to the Avon ladies they befriend. However, in the late twentieth century, the outlook for U.S. direct sales of any kind of product looked bleak. Droves of U.S. women were entering the workforce full time, which made them less receptive to door-to-door salespersons and less willing to spend time on makeup demonstrations and the arrangements for a later receipt of their purchases. Because of working full time, the pool of women seeking part-time employment also seemed to be drying up.

Meanwhile, Back in the Home Market   In an effort to combat the problem of house-to-house sales, Avon has allowed reps to open retail outlets, which are usually small kiosks in shopping malls. Further, Avon ladies have pretty much given up their old "ding dong" routines by selling instead to friends and family, to colleagues at work, and through ads on their own Web sites. In the meantime, the prediction that the pool of part-time job seekers would dry up proved wrong. Between 1996 and 2007, the number of direct sellers in the United States for all companies increased from 8.5 million to 15 million, and sales value has increased proportionately. The global recession has since increased the availability of people to sell independently.

When the U.S. outlook looked gloomy, the outlook in foreign markets looked bright. For example, the lack of developed infrastructure in the rural areas of such countries as Brazil and the Philippines deters women from leaving their homes to shop for cosmetics. But in these countries, Avon ladies reach consumers in some of the most remote areas, because there are ample numbers of potential Avon ladies.

For instance, Avon has 800,000 representatives in Brazil alone. In transitional economies, Avon's market entry coincided with pent-up demand from the period of centrally planned economic policies. In rapid-growth economies, such as Chile and Malaysia, Avon taps a growing middle-class market that can afford its products.

The International Strategy

Global Products

As Avon moved internationally, it pretty much allowed its country managers to decide what products would sell in their markets. Either Avon's R&D unit in the United States or a local R&D unit would then develop them. These were largely produced within the country selling them and included such products as a combination skin cream (moisturizer, sunscreen, and insect repellent) in Brazil, skin-lightening creams in parts of Asia, long-lasting citrus fragrances in Mediterranean countries, technology-driven skin products in Japan, health and wellness products in Argentina, and bigger bottles of personal-care products in Spain.

Once products are developed, Avon disseminates the information to its facilities elsewhere. For example, Avon-Japan developed emulsion technologies to produce lotions and creams with lighter textures and higher hydration levels, and many Avon operations in other countries now use the process.

Some Pitfalls of Product Proliferation   On the one hand, this decentralization to fit the wants of local consumers has undoubtedly given consumers the products they want. On the other hand, it has come with costs. To begin with, the resultant product proliferation has increased manufacturing costs, which threatens Avon's strategy of maintaining a good profit margin while simultaneously offering customers a good value for their money.

Next, Avon has depended primarily on its catalogs to promote its products. For instance, it distributes catalogs every two weeks in the United States and every four weeks abroad. Its circulation dwarfs that of any other commercial publication. However, as its product line grew—13,000 products for the Mexican market alone—the catalogs became too bulky, and the Avon ladies could not possibly know enough about the line to sell effectively. In 2006, Avon cut its product line by 25 percent, and it plans to cut the line even more. It is also moving toward more large-scale centralized production to save on manufacturing costs.

Although Avon is paring its product line, this does not imply a cutback in new products, which are important in the industry. In fact, Avon has signed exclusive agreements with several universities worldwide (such as in Australia, China, Japan, and Thailand) to help develop new products. For example, Asia has long been a leader in herbal and therapeutic treatments. Avon's venture with Chiang Mai University in Thailand has produced one of Avon's latest products using this Asian expertise, Anew Alternative, which is purported to diminish fine lines and wrinkles.

Global Branding

Avon now emphasizes global brands that include Anew, Rare Gold, beComing, and Far Away fragrances. Through standardized branding, Avon creates a uniform global quality image while saving costs by using uniform ingredients and packaging. Global branding also helps inform consumers that the company is international. This helps sales in countries such as Thailand, where consumers prefer to buy beauty products made by foreign companies.

Although Avon prominently displays its name on most of its products worldwide, some of its brand names differ among countries. For instance, when Avon has made foreign acquisitions, it has sometimes kept the successful brand name and goodwill it has acquired. For example, when Avon acquired Justine in South Africa, it kept the Justine name.

The company prints instructions in local languages but may or may not put the brand names in that language. It sometimes uses English or French brand names, because consumers consider the United States and France high-quality suppliers for beauty products. For example, Avon sells skin-care products called Rosa Mosqueta (in Spanish), Revival (in English), and Renaissage (in French) in Chile, Argentina, and Japan, respectively. In each case, the Avon logo appears prominently on the products' containers as well.

Global Pricing

Each country operation sets its own prices to reflect local market conditions and strategic objectives. However, at times the price difference between neighboring countries has created demand for contraband shipments from the country with lower prices—such as has recently occurred between Colombia and Venezuela. The prices are subject to change for each sales campaign. Avon runs a new campaign with different special offers every two weeks in the United States and every four weeks abroad. The shortness of campaigns is helpful for adjusting prices in highly inflationary economies. Avon also has a strategy of introducing two-tiered products that sell at different prices. The aim is to capture more upmarket sales while maintaining the existing clientele. For instance, it has contracted with Christian Lacroix to develop fragrances that will sell at a higher price than Avon's traditional ones.

Global Promotion

Although Avon's promotion is primarily through its brochures and catalogs, it also advertises. It uses such media as broadcasts and billboards and has four primary objectives:

- To sell newly launched products
- To accelerate sales in some of its fastest-growing markets, such as Russia
- To recruit reps in places like China
- To use a campaign called "Hello Tomorrow" to change the public perception of its products as unfashionable and outdated to stylish and modern

"Hello Tomorrow"   This campaign is Avon's first global ad campaign aimed at the image of its overarching Avon brand. Its prior global campaigns aimed at selling specific products. Despite the global campaign, some of Avon's ads vary by country. For instance, it sponsors a British TV drama about footballers' wives and one in Russia that includes a character who sells Avon products. Avon is also using celebrities to help sell its products. The Mexican film star Salma Hayek is the face of Avon. Academy Award–winning actress Jennifer Hudson is the spokesperson for Imari fragrance. Baseball player Derek Jeter (yes, Avon does have *some* products for men too) has his name on a collection of skin-care products.

Meeting the Needs of Women Worldwide   Perhaps Avon's most important campaign is to develop a global image as a company that supports women and their needs, a campaign that has generated favorable publicity in media reports. Building on this theme, Avon cohosted a Global Summit for a Better Tomorrow at the United Nations during International Women's Day, and it gives annual Women of Enterprise Awards to leading women entrepreneurs. It also publicizes how being an Avon lady heightens the role of women, which has been particularly successful at attracting new reps in developing countries such as Malaysia and the Philippines.

Undoubtedly, Avon's biggest social-responsibility projects are its work internationally in fighting breast cancer and domestic violence. Avon ladies disseminate information about breast cancer along with their promotion brochures and sell items to raise money for local needs. Avon is the largest corporate donor to breast cancer research. The fight against domestic violence is a newer Avon program. It is working through local organizations to prevent violence through education and to treat women who have been victims.

Global Distribution

Avon basically duplicates its distribution method in foreign countries, which means that it sells to independent representatives who have taken orders from customers they have either communicated with or visited. However, there are some variations. We have already discussed some of the changes in the United States. In Japan, there is a substantial mail-order business. In Argentina, Avon has beauty centers.

Probably the biggest deviation from direct selling occurred in China, the only single-country division in Avon's global network. In response to a 1998 Chinese law prohibiting house-to-house sales, Avon quickly opened about 6,000 beauty boutiques, lined up 9,000 independent stores to carry Avon, and opened 1,000 beauty counters. Thus Avon made its products available in virtually every corner of the country. In 2005, the Chinese government loosened its house-to-house sales regulations but with many restrictions, such as capping the commission for salespeople and preventing them from recruiting others to work on a shared-commission plan.

Avon seeks to transfer successful practices in one country to other countries. To encourage the transfer of know-how, Avon brings marketing personnel from different countries together to share what it calls "best practices," and it passes on information from country to country. It also promotes competition among countries, such as awards for country-level initiatives to improve sales, quality, and efficiency.

Looking toward the Future

Avon has several challenges for the future. Although its direct-sales method has been important in Avon's success, there are drawbacks to it. For one, customers cannot obtain a product whenever they want it. For another, reps report many returns because customers cannot always discern exact colors from catalogs. For another, it may be difficult for Avon to capture clientele in a higher-price category while maintaining the value-for-money clientele.

Avon anticipates that international operations will account for the bulk of its growth in the foreseeable future. Its products are still not available to a large portion of the world's women. It is already operating in all four BRIC countries, however, and is the market leader in two of them (Brazil and Russia). ∎

QUESTIONS

1. The chapter describes different marketing orientations. Discuss the applicability of each to Avon's international operations.

2. Why is Avon so much more dependent on its foreign operations than on its home (U.S.) operations?

3. Discuss socioeconomic and demographic changes that could affect Avon.

4. How might a global recession, such as the one that began in 2008, impact Avon's operations?

5. What are the major competitive advantages that Avon has? How easily might other companies duplicate these advantages?

6. Avon does not sell within the United States in retail establishments (with the exception of kiosks handled by some of its reps). What are the pros and cons of distributing that way?

SUMMARY

- Although the principles for selling abroad are the same as those for selling domestically, the international businessperson must deal with a less familiar environment.

- International marketing strategies depend on companies' orientations, which include production, sales, customer, strategic, and social.

- Companies need to decide which market segments to target. These segments may include different or similar groups from different countries. Once they make this determination, their product, branding, promotion, pricing, and distribution decisions should be compatible with the needs of their target markets.

- A standardized approach to marketing means maximum uniformity in products and programs among the countries in which sales occur. Although this approach minimizes expenses, most companies make changes to fit country needs to increase sales volume.

- A variety of legal, cultural, and economic conditions may call for altering products to capture foreign demand, but the cost of alteration relative to additional sales potential should be considered. In addition to determining when to alter products, companies also must decide how many and which products to sell abroad.

- Government regulations may directly or indirectly affect the prices that companies charge. International pricing is further complicated because of fluctuations in currency values, differences in product preferences, price escalation in exporting, and variations in fixed versus variable pricing practices.

- For each product in each country, a company must determine not only its promotional budget but also the mix between push and pull strategies and promotions. The relationship between push and pull should depend on the distribution system, the cost and availability of media, consumer attitudes, and the product's price compared with incomes.

- Major problems for standardizing advertising among countries are translation, legality, and message needs.

- Global branding is hampered by language differences, expansion by acquisition, nationality images, and laws concerning generic names. Nevertheless, global brands help develop a global image.

- Distribution channels vary substantially among countries. The differences may affect not only the relative costs of operating but also the ease of making initial sales.

- Companies need to choose distributors carefully, both on the basis of their abilities and on their trustworthiness. At the same time, companies have to sell themselves to get distributors to handle their products and services.

- Although the Internet offers opportunities to sell internationally, using the Internet does not negate companies' needs to develop sound programs within their marketing mix.

- Gap analysis is a tool that helps companies determine why they have not met their market potentials for given countries and decide what part of the marketing mix to emphasize.

KEY TERMS

cost-plus strategy (p. 648)
distribution (p. 656)
gap analysis (p. 662)
generic (p. 656)

gray market (p. 649)
penetration strategy (p. 648)
product diversion (p. 649)

pull (p. 651)
push (p. 651)
skimming strategy (p. 648)

ENDNOTES

1 *Sources include the following:* Elizabeth Rigby, "Hilfiger Plans U.S. Push with 10 Stores a Year," *Financial Times* (April 28, 2008): 23; Ian King, "Cool American Chic, Tommy Bets on Obama Effect," *The Times* (June 8, 2009): 39; Michael Barbaro, "Macy's and Hilfiger Strike Exclusive Deal," *New York Times* (October 27, 2007): 1; Cathy Horyn, "Still Tommy after All These Years," *New York Times* (December 7, 2008): Section M3, 182; *Holiday Magazine*, 182; "Top Notch," *Canberra Times* [Australia] (May 28, 2008): 4; "Tommy Hilfiger: 2006 Company Profile Edition," *Just-Style* (August 2006); "Business & Company Resource Center: Tommy Hilfiger," at http://iiiprxy.library.miami.edu:2309/servlet/BCRC?locID = Miami_richter&srchtp = cmp&c (accessed June 24, 2007); Teri Agins, "Costume Change," *Wall Street Journal* (February 2, 2007): A1+; Samantha Conti, "Hilfiger Signs French Soccer Star," *DNR* (December 11, 2006): 12; Miles Socha, "Tommy Takes Paris," *DNR* (October 23, 2006): 26; Socha, "Tommy's Latest Take," *WWD* (October 20, 2006): 1; Julie Naughton, "Hilfiger and Lauder Aim for Perfect 10," *WWD* (June 23, 2006): 4; Lisa Lockwood, "CEO Says Tommy to Now Trade Up," *WWD* (May 11, 2006): 3; *Tommy Hilfiger 2004 Annual Report*; Krysten Crawford, "The Big Opportunity," *Business 2.0* 7:2 (2006): 94.

2 "The World's Wash Day," *Financial Times* (April 29, 2002): 6.

3 Ruby P. Lee, Qimei Chen, Daekwan Kim, and Jean L. Johnson, "Knowledge Transfer between Multinational Corporations' Headquarters and Their Subsidiaries: Influences on and Implications for New Product Outcomes," *Journal of International Marketing* 16:2 (2008): 1–31.

4 Constantine S. Katsikeas, Saeed Damiee, and Marios Theodosiou, "Strategy Fit and Performance Consequences of International Marketing Standardization," *Strategic Management Journal* 27 (2006): 867–90.

5 Matt Moffett, "Learning to Adapt to a Tough Market, Chilean Firms Pry Open Door to Japan," *Wall Street Journal* (June 7, 1994): A10.

6 Yue Yen Industrial (Holdings) Limited, "Welcome to Yue Yuen," at www.yueyuen.com (accessed June 22, 2007).

7 Evan Pérez, "A Bit of America Rises near Old-World Buenos Aires," *Wall Street Journal* (January 16, 2002): B1.

8 Betsy McKay, "Drinks for Developing Countries," *Wall Street Journal* (November 27, 2001): B1+; McKay, "Coke's Heyer Finds Test in Latin America," *Wall Street Journal* (October 15, 2002): B4.

9 Manoj K. Agarwal, "Developing Global Segments and Forecasting Market Shares: A Simultaneous Approach Using Survey Data," *Journal of International Marketing* 11:4 (2003): 56.

10 Rebecca Rose, "Global Diversity Gets All Cosmetic," *Financial Times* (April 10–11, 2004): W11.

11 Leslie T. Chang, "Nestlé Stumbles in China's Evolving Market," *Wall Street Journal* (December 8, 2004): A10.

12 Allen L. Hammond and C. K. Prahalad, "Selling to the Poor," *Foreign Policy* (May–June 2004): 30–37.

13 Katsikeas et al., "Strategy Fit."

14 "Music for the Masses," *Financial Times* (December 14, 2004): 9.

15 Milo Geyelin and Jeffrey Ball, "How Rugged Is Your Car's Roof?" *Wall Street Journal* (March 4, 2000): B1.

16 Scott Miller, "EU's New Rules Will Shake Up Market for Bioengineered Food," *Wall Street Journal* (April 16, 2004): A1.

17 Deborah Ball, Sarah Ellison, Janet Adamy, and Geoffrey A. Fowler, "Recipes without Borders?" *Wall Street Journal* (August 18, 2004): B1+.

18 Bernardo V. Lopez, "Upshot," *Business World* (September 18, 2003): 1.

19 Andrew Jack, "WHO Says Smoking Fight Is Being Lost," *Financial Times* (February 8, 2008): 5.

20 "Cause for Concern with Nestlé in the Spotlight Again over Its Advertising Tactics," *Marketing Week* (February 11, 1999): 28–31.

21 Andrew Ward, "Global Thirst for Bottled Water Attacked," *Financial Times* (February 13, 2006): 3, referring to data from the Earth Policy Institute.

22 Sarah Houlton, "Drugs for Neglected Diseases," *Pharmaceutical Executive* 23:8 (2003): 28.

23 Andrew Jack, "FDA to Stimulate Tropical Disease Research," *Financial Times* (May 1, 2008): 6.

24 Garrett Mehl, Heather Wipfli, and Peter Winch, "Controlling Tobacco," *Harvard International Review* 27:1 (Spring 2005): 54–58.

25 Michael Finkel, "Bedlam in the Blood: Malaria," *National Geographic* (July 2007): 63.

26 Kevin Helliker, "Smokeless Tobacco to Get Push by Venture Overseas," *Wall Street Journal* (February 4, 2009): B1+.

27 Michael Waldholz, "Sparks Fly at AIDS Meeting over Breast-Feeding," *Wall Street Journal* (July 12, 2000): B2; Jolene Skordis and Nicoli Nattrass, "Paying to Waste Lives: The Affordability of Reducing Mother-to-Child Transmission of HIV in South Africa," *Journal of Health Economics* 21:3 (May 2002): 405.

28 Avery Johnson, "Drug Firms See Poorer Nations as Sales Cure," *Wall Street Journal* (July 7, 2009): A1+.

29 Andrew Jack, "Anti-Malaria Drug to Sell at Cost Price," *Financial Times* (March 2, 2007): 3; Jennifer Corbett Dooren, "Research to Target Neglected Diseases," *Wall Street Journal* (May 21, 2009): 16.

30 Norihiko Shirouzu, "Tailoring World's Cars to U.S. Taste," *Wall Street Journal* (January 15, 2001): B1.

31 Norihiko Shirouzu and Peter Wonacott, "People's Republic of Autos," *Wall Street Journal* (April 18, 2005): B1+.

32 John Reed, Amy Yee, and Joe Leahy, "India's Tata to Overtake Suzuki in Race for World's Cheapest Car," *Financial Times* (June 4, 2007): 13.

33 Julie Jargon, "Kraft Reformulates Oreo, Scores in China," *Wall Street Journal* (May 1, 2008): B1+.

34 Keith Bradsher, "India Gains on China among Multinationals," *International Herald Tribune* (June 12–13, 2004): 13.

35 Niraj Dawar and Amitava Chattopadhyay, "The New Language of Emerging Markets," *Financial Times* (November 11, 2000): Mastering Management section, 6.

36 Yonca Limon, Lynn R. Kahle, and Ulrich R. Orth, "Package Design as a Communications Vehicle in Cross-Cultural Values Shopping," *Journal of International Marketing* 17:1 (2009): 30–57.

37 "The World's Wash Day," *Financial Times*, 6.

38 Arvind Sahay, "Finding the Right International Mix," *Financial Times* (November 16, 1998): Mastering Marketing section, 2–3.

39 Brandon Mitchener, "Inexpensive Levi's May Soon Be Easier to Find in Britain," *Wall Street Journal* (April 6, 2001): A13.

40 Matthew B. Myers, "The Pricing of Export Products: Why Aren't Managers Satisfied with the Results?" *Journal of World Business* 32:3 (1997): 277–89.

41 Peter Rosenwald, "Surveying the Latin American Landscape," *Catalog Age* 18:2 (February 2001): 67–69.

42 Jenny Wiggins and Chris Flood, "Coke to Shrink Size of Cans in Hong Kong," *Financial Times* (July 25, 2008): 18.

43 Carol Wolf, "Losing $63 Billion in Diverted U.S. Goods Is Sleuth Obsession," Bloomberg.com (accessed April 9, 2009), referring to a study by Deloitte & Touche.

44 Ana Campoy, "Think Locally," *Wall Street Journal* (September 27, 2004): R8.

45 C. Gopinath, "Fixed Price and Bargaining," *Business Line* (July 15, 2002): 1.

46 Claude Cellich, "FAQ . . . about Business Negotiations on the Internet," *International Trade Forum* 1 (2001): 10–11.

47 Rasul Bailay, "A Hindu Festival Attracts the Faithful and U.S. Marketers," *Wall Street Journal* (February 12, 2001): A18.

48 David Pilling, "Direct Promotion of Brands Gives Power to the Patients," *Financial Times* (April 30, 2001): iii; Sarah Ellison, "Viagra Europe Ads to Focus on Symptoms," *Financial Times* (March 22, 2000): B10.

49 Miho Inada, "Mac and PC's Overseas Adventures," *Wall Street Journal* (March 1, 2007): B1.

50 Charles Goldsmith, "Dubbing in Product Plugs," *Wall Street Journal* (December 6, 2004): B1+.

51 Rick Wartzman, "Read Their Lips," *Wall Street Journal* (June 3, 1999): A1.

52 Geoffrey A. Fowler, "China Cracks Down on Commercials," *Wall Street Journal* (February 19, 2004): B7A.

53 Gordon Fairclough and Geoffrey A. Fowler, "Pigs Get Ax in China TV Ads, in Nod to Muslims," *Wall Street Journal* (January 25, 2007): A1+.

54 Sally D. Goll, "New Zealand Bans Reebok, Other Ads It Deems Politically Incorrect for TV," *Wall Street Journal* (July 25, 1995): A12.

55 Deborah Ball, "Women in Italy Like to Clean but Shun the Quick and Easy," *Wall Street Journal* (April 25, 2006): A1+.

56 Andrew Ward, "Home Improvements Abroad," *Financial Times* (April 6, 2006): 8.

57 Sarah Ellison, "Sex-Themed Ads Often Don't Travel Well," *Wall Street Journal* (March 31, 2000): B7.

58 Tulin Erdem, Joffre Swait, and Ana Valenzuela, "Brands as Signals: A Cross-Country Validation Study," *Journal of Marketing* 70:1 (2006): 34; Desmond Lam, "Cultural Influence on Proneness to Brand Loyalty," *Journal of International Consumer Marketing* 19:3 (2006): 7.

59 Mei Fong, "Chinese Refrigerator Maker Finds U.S. Chilly," *Wall Street Journal* (March 18, 2008): B1+.

60 "Top 100 Brands Scoreboard 2006," *Business Week Online* (2000–2007), at http://bwnt.businessweek. com/brand/2006 (accessed November 2, 2007).

61 Laura Bogomolny, "The Name Game," *Canadian Business* 78:18 (September 25, 2005): 134–135.

62 Mure Dickie, "Google Becomes Gu Ge in China," *Financial Times* (April 13, 2006): 19.

63 Lee Simmons and Robert M. Schindler, "Cultural Superstitions and the Price Endings Used in Chinese Advertising," *Journal of International Marketing* 11:2 (2003): 101.

64 Miriam Jordan, "Sara Lee Wants to Percolate through All of Brazil," *Wall Street Journal* (May 8, 2002): A14+.

65 Isabelle Schuiling and Jean-Noël Kapferer, "Executive Insights: Real Differences between Local and International Brands: Strategic Implications for International Marketers," *Journal of International Marketing* 12:4 (2004): 197.

66 Philip Kotler and David Gertner, "Country as Brand, Product, and Beyond: Place Marketing and Brand Management," *Journal of Brand Management* 9:4/5 (2002): 249–61; Keith Dinnie, "National Image and Competitive Advantage: The Theory and Practice of Country-of-Origin Effect," *Journal of Brand Management* 9:4/5 (2002): 396–98.

67 Gideon Rachman, "Christmas Survey: The Brand's the Thing," *The Economist* (December 18, 1999): 97–99.

68 Daniel Laufer, Kate Gillespie, and David H. Silvera, "The Role of Country of Manufacture in Consumers' Attributions of Blame in an Ambiguous Product-Harm Crisis," *Journal of International Consumer Marketing* 21 (2009): 189–201.

69 Seah Park, "LG's Kitchen Makeover," *Wall Street Journal* (September 22, 2004): A19.

70 Saeed Samiee, Terrence A. Shimp, and Subash Sharma, "Brand Origin Recognition Accuracy: Its Antecedents and Consumers' Cognitive Limitations," *Journal of International Business Studies* 36 (2005): 379–97.

71 Kevin McCallum, "Grape Debate," *Miami Herald* (March 27, 2009): 1C+.

72 "Opportunities in Sub-Culture," *Business Line* (February 12, 2004): 1.

73 Oliver Burgel and Gordon C. Murray, "The International Market Entry Choices of Start-Up Companies in High-Technology Industries," *Journal of International Marketing* 8:2 (2000): 33–62.

74 Gary F. Keller and Creig R. Kronstedt, "Connecting Confucianism, Communism, and the Chinese Culture of Commerce," *Journal of Language for International Business* 16:1 (2005): 60–75.

75 S. Tamer Cavusgil, Seyda Deligonul, and Chun Zhang, "Curbing Foreign Distributor Opportunism: An Examination of Trust, Contracts, and the Legal Environment in International Channel Relationships," *Journal of International Marketing* 12:2 (2004).

76 Gary C. Anders and Danila A. Usachev, "Strategic Elements of Eastman Kodak's Successful Market Entry in Russia," *Thunderbird International Business Review* 45:2 (2003): 171.

77 James T. Areddy, "Solving China's Logistics Riddle," *Wall Street Journal* (October 15, 2003): A18+.

78 Tomasz Lenartowicz and Sridhar Balasubramanian, "Practices and Performance of Small Retail Stores in Developing Economies," *Journal of International Marketing* 17:1 (2009): 58–90.

79 Marko Grunhagen, Stephen J. Grove, and James W. Gentry, "The Dynamics of Store Hour Changes and Consumption Behavior: Results of a Longitudinal Study of Consumer Attitudes toward Saturday Shopping in Germany," *European Journal of Marketing* 37:11/12 (2003): 1801–19.

80 Lenartowicz and Balasubramanian, "Practices and Performance of Small Retail Stores in Developing Economies."

81 Thomas G. Brashear, Vishal Kashyap, Michael D. Musante, and Naveen Donthu, "A Profile of the Internet Shopper: Evidence from Six Countries," *Journal of Marketing Theory and Practice* 17:3 (Summer 2009): 267–81.

82 Rita Marcella and Sylvie Davies, "The Use of Customer Language in International Marketing Communication in the Scottish Food and Drink Industry," *European Journal of Marketing* 38:11/12 (2004): 1382.

83 *New Zealand Business* 18:11 (2004): 21–27.

84 Anil K. Gupta and Vijay Govindarajan, "The Rising Cost of Waiting," *CIO* 13:19 (2000): 54.

85 Moen Øystein, Iver Endresen, and Morten Gavlen, "Executive Insights: Use of the Internet in International Marketing: A Case Study of Small Computer Software Firms," *Journal of International Marketing* 11:4 (2003): 129–144.

86 J. A. Weber, "Comparing Growth Opportunities in the International Marketplace," *Management International Review* 1 (1979): 47–54; Van R. Wood, John R. Darling, and Mark Siders, "Consumer Desire to Buy and Use Products in International Markets: How to Capture It, How to Sustain It," *International Marketing Review* 16:3 (1999): 231–42.

87 "Chocolate Makers in Switzerland Try to Melt Resistance," *Wall Street Journal* (January 5, 1981): 14; William Hall, "Swiss Chocolate Groups Aim to Keep Outlook Sweet," *Financial Times* (April 11–12, 1998): 23; William Hall, "Wraps Come Off Chocolate's Best-Kept

Secret," *Financial Times* (June 5, 1998): 20; Stephanie Thompson, "Chocolate Gets Boost," *Advertising Age* (July 29, 2002): 12.

88 Haig Simonian, "Nestlé Enriches Its Choc Value," *Financial Times* (March 24, 2006): 9.

89 Michiyo Nakamoto, "Japanese Fall out of Love with Luxury," *Financial Times* (June 3, 2009): 15.

90 Allen L. Hammond and C. K. Prahalad, "Selling to the Poor," *Foreign Policy* (May/June 2004): 30–37.

91 For an excellent discussion of these traits and their interactions, see Mark Cleveland, Michel Laroche, and Nicolas Papadopoulos, "Cosmopolitanism, Consumer Ethnocentrism, and Materialism: An Eight-Country Study of Antecedents and Outcomes," *Journal of International Marketing* 17:1 (2009): 116–46.

92 *Sources include the following:* Information came from "Business: Ding Dong! Empowerment Calling; Face Value," *The Economist* 391 (May 30, 2009): 70; Nanette Byrnes, "Avon: More than

Cosmetic Changes," *Business Week* (March 12, 2007): 62; Jennie Rodriguez, "Direct Sales on the Rise," *Knight Ridder Tribune Business News* (February 25, 2007): 1; Barney Stokes, "Benchmark—Avon," *Marketing Week* (April 6, 2006): 33; Jessica Kiddle, "Cosmetic Enhancement," *The Scotsman* (March 22, 2007): 22; "Avon Launches First Global Ad Campaign," *Marketing Week* (March 8, 2007): 10; Mei Fong, "Avon Calling, but China Opens Door Only a Crack," *Wall Street Journal* (February 26, 2007): B1; "Avon Celebrates New Breed of Sales Leaders," *Manila Times* (May 13, 2007): n.p.; Mitchell Edgar, "Avon Celebrates Women's Day at U.N. Summit," *Women's Wear Daily* (March 9, 2007): 8; Umesh Pandey, "Avon Looks to Asia for Inspiration," *Knight Ridder Tribune Business News* (June 9, 2007): 1; Avon *Annual Reports* from 1995 through 2008; *Outlook* (Avon's monthly in-house magazine) from 1995 through 2002; AVP–Q4 2004, Avon Products, Earning Conference Call (February 1, 2005).

seventeen

Global Manufacturing and Supply-Chain Management

Objectives

- To describe the different dimensions of a global manufacturing strategy

- To examine the elements of global supply-chain management

- To show how quality affects the global supply chain

- To illustrate how supplier networks function

- To explain how inventory management is a key dimension of the global supply chain

- To present different alternatives for transporting products along the supply chain from suppliers to customers

A cheap thing doesn't lack defect, nor an expensive thing quality.

—*Afghan proverb*

CASE Samsonite's Global Supply Chain

THE SAMSONITE STORY

Samsonite, the world's biggest luggage maker, is a U.S.-based company that manufactures and distributes luggage all over the world.[1] The company was founded in 1910 in Denver, Colorado, and it took many years for it to become a global company. In 1963, Samsonite set up its first European operation in the Netherlands and later, in 1965, began production in Belgium. Shortly thereafter, it erected a joint-venture plant in Mexico to service the growing but highly protected Mexican market. By the end of the 1960s, Samsonite was manufacturing luggage in Spain and Japan as well. In addition to its manufacturing operations, Samsonite was selling luggage worldwide through a variety of distributors.

In the 1970s, business began to take off in Europe. In 1974, Samsonite developed its first real European product, called the Prestige Attaché, and business began to expand in Italy, causing the country to rival Germany as Samsonite's biggest market in Europe. Although the U.S. market began to turn to soft-side luggage in the 1980s, the European market still demanded hard-side luggage, so Samsonite developed a new hard-side suitcase for Europe called the Oyster case. At that point, soft-side luggage began to increase in importance, although Europe was still considered a hard-side market. In the 1980s, Samsonite opened a new plant in France to manufacture the Prestige Attaché and other key products.

With the fall of the Iron Curtain in the early 1990s, Samsonite purchased a Hungarian luggage manufacturer and began to expand throughout Eastern Europe. During this same time period, Samsonite established several joint-venture companies throughout Asia, including China, to extend its reach there.

STRATEGIES FOR THE 1990s

The Quality Initiative

To establish products of high quality, Samsonite embarked on two different programs. The first was an internal program in which Samsonite conducted drop, tumble, wheel, and handle tests to determine if its products were strong enough and of sufficient quality for customers. The second was composed of two different, independent quality-assurance tests:

- The European-based ISO 9002 certification
- The GS Mark, which is the number-one government-regulated third-party product test mark (similar to brand) of Germany

MAP 17.1 Where Samsonite Operates in Europe

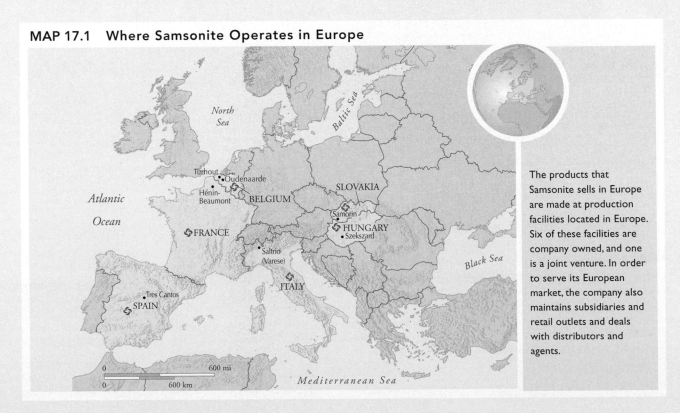

The products that Samsonite sells in Europe are made at production facilities located in Europe. Six of these facilities are company owned, and one is a joint venture. In order to serve its European market, the company also maintains subsidiaries and retail outlets and deals with distributors and agents.

The GS Mark, *Gepruefte Sicherheit* (translated "Tested for Safety"), is designed to help companies comply with European product liability laws as well as other areas of quality and safety. To enhance quality, Samsonite introduced state-of-the-art CAD-CAM machinery in its plants. Samsonite also introduced a manufacturing technique in which autonomous cells of about a dozen employees assembled a product from start to finish.

As you can see in Map 17.1, Samsonite has three company-owned production facilities and two headquarters offices in Europe. In addition, it has subsidiaries, joint ventures, retail franchises, distributors, and agents set up to service the European market. Although Samsonite initially serviced the European markets through exports, the transportation costs were high, and the demand for luggage soared in Europe, so Samsonite decided to begin production in Belgium in 1965.

SUPPLY-CHAIN DECENTRALIZATION

In the early years, Samsonite had a decentralized supply chain, as illustrated in Figure 17.1, whereby it operated through different wholesale layers before it finally got the product to the retailers.

As Samsonite's business grew, management decided to centralize its supply chain so that products were manufactured and shipped to a central European warehouse, which then directly supplied retailers upon request (see Figure 17.2). This centralized structure was put into place to eliminate the need to rely on wholesalers.

Samsonite had to worry about transporting manufactured products to the warehouse, storing them, and transporting them to the retailers in the different European markets. The company invested heavily in information technology to link the retailers to the warehouse and thereby manage its European distribution system more effectively. Retailers would place an order with a salesperson or the local Samsonite office in their area, and the order would be transmitted to the warehouse and shipping company by modem.

The retail market in Europe began shifting at the turn of the new century, so Samsonite responded by opening franchised retail outlets in October 2002, beginning in Antwerp and spreading to other areas. As the vice president of marketing and sales put it, "We are anticipating a shift in the market, in which the traditional luggage channel will no longer be at the forefront and a wide new retail opportunity will emerge."

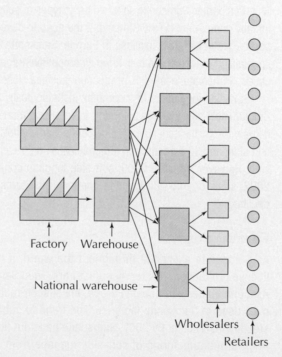

Factory Warehouse

National warehouse →

Wholesalers ↑

Retailers

FIGURE 17.1 The Samsonite European Supply Chain (I): Decentralized, 1965–1974

For about a decade after it had first penetrated the European market, Samsonite shipped products from *factories* to *factory warehouses* and then to *national warehouses*. From there, products went to *wholesalers* and, at long last, to *retailers*. Needless to say, the system was cumbersome, lengthening the factory-to-retailer process and bumping up costs at every step of the way.

Source: F. De Beule and D. Van Den Bulcke, "The International Supply Chain Management of Samsonite Europe," Discussion Paper No. 1998/E/34 (Centre for International Management and Development, University of Antwerp, 1998): 13.

FIGURE 17.2   **The Samsonite European Supply Chain (II): Centralized, 1975–Mid-1980s**

In the mid-1970s, Samsonite decided to streamline the cumbersome supply chain illustrated in Figure 17.1. For the next decade or so, the company shipped products from *factories* to a *central European warehouse*, which then shipped them, upon request, to *retailers* located across the continent.

Source: F. De Beule and D. Van Den Bulcke, "The International Supply Chain Management of Samsonite Europe." Discussion Paper No. 1998/E/34 (Centre for International Management and Development, University of Antwerp, 1998): 14.

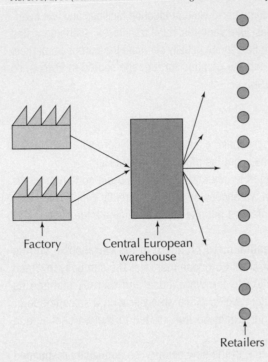

Factory   Central European
warehouse

Retailers

R&D and Product Innovation

As noted earlier, Samsonite sold two basic types of suitcases: hard side and soft side. Most of the R&D was initially done in the United States, but the need to develop products for the European market led the company to establish R&D facilities in Europe. Samsonite invested heavily in R&D and in the manufacture of specialized machinery to help keep a competitive edge. To facilitate the transportation and storage of suitcases, Samsonite located its production facilities close to the centralized warehouse.

Soft-side luggage is less complex technologically than hard side, and Samsonite purchased Oda, the Belgium soft-side luggage company, to enter that market. Then it licensed its technology to other European companies. By the mid-1990s, 48 percent of Samsonite's sales came from hard-side luggage, 22 percent from soft side, and 30 percent from attaché cases and travel bags, some of which were hard side and some soft side. However, by fiscal 2000, soft-side luggage comprised 51 percent of European sales. In 2001 and 2002, sales of soft-side luggage continued to increase as a percentage, and hard-side luggage sales declined.

Outsourcing

As Samsonite expanded throughout the world, it continued to manufacture its own products and license production to other manufacturers. Then Samsonite entered into subcontract arrangements in Asia and Eastern Europe. In Europe, the subcontractors provide final goods as well as the subassemblies used in Samsonite factories. The trend to outsource more and more of its production has been steadily increasing. By 2007, Samsonite had shut down several of its plants in Europe and decreased internal manufacturing of soft-side luggage from 23 percent in 2004 to just 10 percent in 2007. Although it still produces the majority of its hard-side luggage internally, the company now sources

FIGURE 17.3 The Samsonite European Supply Chain (III): Globalized, 1996–Present

As it expanded production throughout Europe, Samsonite was soon obliged to establish arrangements with subcontractors (who provided both final products and subassemblies). Because the company now had to coordinate outsourced goods and parts in addition to production from its own factories, it reconfigured its supply chain once again: Today, all products and parts, whether company produced or outsourced, go to a central European warehouse and, from there, straight to retailers.

Source: F. De Beule and D. Van Den Bulcke. "The International Supply Chain Management of Samsonite Europe," Discussion Paper No. 1998/E/34 (Centre for International Management and Development, University of Antwerp, 1998): 21.

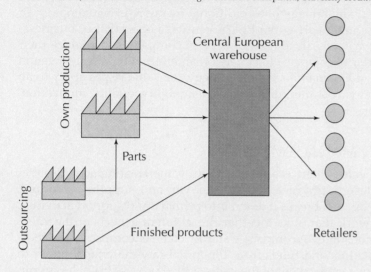

90 percent of its soft-side luggage from third-party manufacturers to consolidate its manufacturing capacities and to achieve cost savings. Figure 17.3 illustrates Samsonite's coordination of outsourced parts and finished goods, along with its own production.

The Future of Samsonite

The slowdown in international travel and consumer spending in 2008 to 2009 nearly drove Samsonite under. It is owned by private equity firm CVC, and a deal between CVC and Royal Bank of Scotland injected enough cash in the business to save the company. CVC's goal is to push Samsonite more aggressively into Asia, where a growing middle class loves to travel. More than half of Samsonite's sales are generated outside the United States, and the emerging markets appear to be the wave of the future. One approach Samsonite is taking is to enter into strategic joint ventures to distribute its products internationally. The company signed an agreement with Turkish firm Desa and Philippine company Rustan Group to penetrate those markets. In addition, it has other joint-venture arrangements in Thailand, Australia, and Chile that will help with its expansion in those countries. Of course, Samsonite will have to figure out how to organize its supply chain, as it did in Europe, but in a larger, more complex international environment. However, the **CRN** experience in Europe should help the company as it establishes its supply chain worldwide.

Introduction

Our opening case illustrates a number of dimensions of the supply-chain networks that link suppliers with manufacturers and customers. This chapter examines these different networks and how a company can manage the links most effectively to reach customers. Global manufacturing and supply-chain management are important in companies' international business strategies. Most companies agree that effective supply-chain management is one of their most important tools in reducing costs and increasing revenue.[2]

As we discuss global supply-chain management, we cover the following major issues: an *effective global manufacturing strategy*, the *role of information technology in global supply-chain management*, *quality*, *supplier networks*, and *inventory management*, including the importance of effective transportation networks.

It's important to note that effective supply-chain management is important for services as well as manufacturing. Our opening case about luggage maker Samsonite traces developments in the supply-chain strategy of a traditional manufacturing company. In our closing case, however, which deals with ePLDT Ventus, a specialist in business-process outsourcing, we show how critical it is for service companies to analyze their supply-chain strategies in order to compete effectively on an international scale. Even in the section of the chapter on global manufacturing strategy, the same issues apply to an effective global *services* strategy: cost minimization, dependability, quality, innovation, flexibility, and service locations.

WHAT IS SUPPLY-CHAIN MANAGEMENT?

In Chapter 11, we define the value chain as a set of linked, value-creating activities that the company performs to design, produce, market, deliver, and support a product. Figure 11.5 takes the value chain and breaks it down into primary and support activities. The **supply chain** is the network that links together the different aspects of the value chain all the way to the final consumer. A company's supply chain encompasses the coordination of materials, information, and funds from the initial raw-material supplier to the ultimate customer.[3] It is the management of the value-added process from the suppliers' supplier to the customers' customer.[4] In this chapter, we use supply-chain management in its broadest definition, encompassing everything from supplier relationships to getting the product to the final consumer, with logistics as an important aspect of supply-chain management.

Suppliers can be part of the manufacturer's organizational structure, as would be the case in a vertically integrated company, or they can be independent of the company. Direct suppliers also have their networks. In a global context, suppliers can be located in the country where the manufacturing or assembly takes place, or they can be located in one country and ship materials to the country of manufacture or assembly. The output of the suppliers can be shipped directly to the factory or to an intermediate storage point. The output of the manufacturing process can be shipped directly to the customers or to a warehouse network, as was the case with Samsonite. The output can be sold directly to the end consumer or to a distributor, wholesaler, or retailer, who then sells the output to the final consumer. As is the case in the supplier network, the output can be sold domestically or internationally.

An important dimension of the supply chain is **logistics**, also sometimes called **materials management**. Materials management is inbound logistics, or the movement and management of materials and products from purchasing through production to meet the demands of the consumer.[5] The difference between supply-chain management and logistics is one of degree. Logistics focuses much more on the transportation and storage of materials and final goods, whereas supply-chain management extends beyond that to include the management of supplier and customer relations. However, firms often have their own interpretation of what is supply-chain management and what is logistics.

The MNEs that have excelled in their ability to manage their supply-chain networks come from all over the world, including Apple in the United States, Tesco in the United Kingdom, Samsung in Korea, Nokia in Finland, Toyota in Japan, and AstraZeneca in Sweden.[6] The companies we study in this chapter are considered part of a global network that links together designers, suppliers, subcontractors, manufacturers, and customers. The supply-chain network is quite broad, and the coordination of the network takes place through interactions between firms in the network.[7]

Supply chain—the coordination of materials, information, and funds from the initial raw-material supplier to the ultimate customer.

Logistics (also called materials management)—that part of the supply-chain process that plans, implements, and controls the efficient, effective flow and storage of goods, services, and related information from the point of origin to the point of consumption in order to meet customers' requirements.

Global Manufacturing Strategies

Case Review Note

Recall from our opening case that Samsonite initially exported to Europe but eventually set up manufacturing facilities in several European countries. We point out that Samsonite invested in Europe because of *location-specific advantages* (notably, hefty demand) and chose to enter the market through foreign direct investment in order to take advantage of its own *firm-specific assets* (especially an excellent product line and a solid manufacturing process). Finally, we emphasize Samsonite's strategic decision to internalize those advantages rather than sell them to an outside manufacturer.[8] Thus, although Samsonite entered into some licensing agreements and subcontracted some manufacturing, it initially kept most of its production—especially in high-end hard-side luggage—under its own control.

Although Samsonite engaged in its own manufacturing for the most part, it eventually subcontracted, or outsourced, manufacturing to other firms. Nike, as another example, does not own any manufacturing facilities, but it subcontracts manufacturing to other companies. So Nike is basically a design and marketing company. Mattel does not own manufacturing facilities in China to manufacture Barbie dolls, but it subcontracts the manufacturing to a Hong Kong–based company that has investments in China. Some of the toys in McDonald's Happy Meals or Burger King's meals are also subcontracted to a Hong Kong–based manufacturer that produces the toys in China.

FOUR KEY FACTORS IN MANUFACTURING STRATEGY

The success of a global manufacturing strategy depends on four key factors: *compatibility, configuration, coordination,* and *control.*[9]

Compatibility Compatibility in this context is the degree of consistency between the foreign investment decision and the company's competitive strategy. Direct manufacturing, for instance, made sense in Samsonite's case but not in Nike's. Here are some company strategies that managers must consider:

- *Efficiency/cost*—reduction of manufacturing costs
- *Dependability*—degree of trust in a company's products, its delivery, and its price promises
- *Quality*—performance reliability, service quality, speed of delivery, and maintenance quality of the product(s)
- *Innovation*—ability to develop new products and ideas
- *Flexibility*—ability of the production process to make different kinds of products and to adjust the volume of output[10]

Efficiency/Cost Strategies *Cost-minimization strategies* and the drive for global efficiencies force MNEs to establish economies of scale in manufacturing, often by producing in areas with low-cost labor. This is one of the major reasons why many MNEs have established manufacturing facilities in Asia, Mexico, and Eastern Europe. This type of foreign direct investment is known as **offshore manufacturing**.

OFFSHORE MANUFACTURING Offshore manufacturing escalated sharply in the 1960s and 1970s in the electronics industry as one company after another set up production facilities in the Far East, mostly in Taiwan and Singapore. Those locations were attractive because of low labor costs, the availability of cheap materials and components, and the proximity to markets. Even the athletic-shoe market left the United States for Taiwan and Korea.

As wages rose in Korea, however, manufacturing began to shift to other low-cost countries—China, Indonesia, Malaysia, Thailand, and Vietnam. China, particularly, has

Compatibility—the degree of consistency between FDI decisions and a company's competitive strategy.

Concept Check

In Chapter 11, we explain **value** as the underlying principle of *strategy*, defining it as "the measure of a firm's capability to sell what it makes for more than the costs incurred to make it." Here, while further refining our discussion of strategy to enumerate factors contributing to a successful strategy, we hasten to repeat our definition of **strategy** as the effort of managers to build and sustain the company's competitive position within its industry to create value.

Concept Check

In discussing the process of "Creating Value" in Chapter 11, we explain that a firm that aspires to a position of "Cost Leadership" strives to be the low-cost producer in an industry *for a given level of quality*. This **strategy,** we observe, means that the firm adopts one of two tactics, both of which must be *compatible* with the structure of its **value chain:** (1) earning a profit higher than industry rivals by selling products at average industry prices or (2) capturing *market share* by selling products at prices *below* the industry average.

Workers put the finishing touches to new Piaggios inside the Binh Xuyen industrial park in Vinh Phuc province, Vietnam, on June 24, 2009. Italian group Piaggio inaugurated its first Vespa factory in Vietnam, an investment of more than $30 million, with a capacity of 100,000 units. Two-wheelers are highly popular in Vietnam, where almost 23 million motorbikes and motorcycles had been registered with authorities at the end of 2008.
Source: Aude Genet/Getty Images, Inc.

Offshore manufacturing—any investment that takes place in a country other than the home country.

Case Review Note

become the hot spot for manufacturing and has even been termed by the *Wall Street Journal* as "the world's factory floor." Companies manufacture abroad to be closer to markets and to take advantage of cheaper labor costs. Piaggio could have manufactured Vespa motorbikes in Italy and exported them to Vietnam, but it made more sense to manufacture them in Vietnam, where costs are cheaper, there are no problems with transportation and tariffs, and there is a good market for the product.

China's output is so large and wide ranging that it exerts deflationary pressure around the world on products such as textiles, TVs, furniture, auto parts, and mobile phones. It is now the world's fourth-largest industrial base behind the United States, Japan, and Germany. Many MNEs set up operations in China in the 1980s to capitalize on China's huge population and growing demand.

As we indicate in our opening case, Samsonite is among the companies that have found it more cost effective to manufacture products in China—and not just for the Chinese market, but for export to the rest of the world as well. Meanwhile, Dutch company Philips Electronics produces some of its products solely in China and plans to make China its global supply base, from which it will export its products around the world.[11] Still other companies, such as U.S.-based Hewlett-Packard, Microsoft, and Motorola, have looked beyond simply outsourcing manufacturing to China and have established R&D centers within the country. IBM and General Motors are even using China as a global center for their companies' procurement operations.[12]

However, when employing a cost-minimization strategy, many companies overlook important elements—such as shipping distances, extra inventory, political and security risks, and the availability of skilled and educated workers—which causes them to underestimate the costs of outsourcing to low-wage countries. In other words, when making decisions to source abroad, companies should consider the total cost of facilitating the strategy, as opposed to merely the acquisition cost.

Total cost analysis—an in-depth assessment of the complete cost of a transaction that takes into account acquisition, ownership, and disposal costs.

TOTAL COST ANALYSIS   A *total cost analysis* takes into account the costs of ownership, such as storing and transporting inventory as well as disposal. In some instances, labor is such a small percentage of overall costs that employing cheap labor abroad does not effectively save the company money. For example, Nike decided to employ a small contractor in San Francisco to produce some of its made-to-order goods, in spite of its $15-per-hour rates that are 20 times those of the contractors in China. Nike determined that labor costs were a small portion of the total cost and that overhead costs, such as management of the flow of goods from halfway around the world and the risk of stockouts and high inventories, were much more important considerations.[13]

In our closing case, however, we explain why companies like Ventus, a business-process provider whose costs are due almost entirely to labor, is likely to be a very attractive option for many companies. Remember, however, that high turnover rates and expensive training costs often plague operations in low-wage areas and can in fact negate any potential cost savings.[14]

Dependability Strategies   Many other factors besides cost must also be taken into consideration. The growing customer demand for *dependability* and prompt deliveries has caused companies such as Dell to locate plants closer to customers rather than in low-wage areas. As the supply chain lengthens, there are risks of not being able to get components or finished goods to market on time. Thus, shortening the distance in the supply chain can improve dependability.

Innovation and Quality Strategies   Many companies are also responding to the importance of *innovation* and *quality*. When companies invest abroad to take advantage of low-cost labor, they are not as concerned about innovation. But as more and more companies establish R&D facilities abroad, they will be able to move beyond low-end manufacturing.

Quality is a major issue, though—one we discuss in more detail later in the chapter. If foreign operations can ensure high quality and contribute to innovation, companies will continue to set up operations abroad. However, after a decade-long trend of sourcing in low-cost countries like China, Japanese companies (such as Honda, Canon, and Sharp) are now relocating production back in their home country.

In 2006, Japanese companies registered to build 1,782 factories in Japan and only 182 abroad, compared to 2003 when 844 and 434, respectively, were built. These Japanese companies have been responding to the need for access to Japan's pool of skilled workers, as well as its proximity to engineers, parts suppliers, and decision makers. They believe that to ensure innovation and quality, close communication between product development and manufacturing is essential.[15] However, the strong yen has forced many Japanese companies to rethink their investment strategies and invest more offshore to take advantage of weaker-currency countries in the Asia region.

Flexibility Strategies   The need for responsiveness or *flexibility* because of differences in national markets may result in regional manufacturing to service local markets. It may not be possible to produce all products in one location and ship them around the world. Wall's Unilever, for example, produces ice cream in China, and because of its local operations, it is able to develop products that are unique to the Chinese market as well as produce its global brands, such as the Magnum Bar and the Cornetto.

However, Unilever has found that it can produce some of its global brands during the winter when demand is down and ship them to South Africa and Australia during their summer. This flexibility has enabled the company to utilize excess production facilities and reduce costs to markets outside China.[16] However, differences in measurement systems, time zones, and problem-solving approaches can also add unnecessary complexity to the supply chain.

Changes in Strategy   As a company's competitive strategies change, so too do its manufacturing strategies. In addition, MNEs may adopt different strategies for different product lines, depending on the competitive priorities of those products. For example, to reduce the cost and complexity of its products, Finnish mobile-phone maker Nokia designs phones that contain fewer parts and bases its different models on the same basic components. This manufacturing strategy has allowed Nokia to maintain 16.8 percent profit margins on its low-end phones and 18.8 percent on its higher-end models, which are substantial in the highly competitive market for cellular phones.[17]

Toyota has always prided itself on high quality and has traditionally relied on manufacturing in Toyota City, Japan, where it is close to suppliers and can ensure high quality

CRN
Case Review Note

Concept Check

In Chapter 11, in discussing "Configuration" as a factor in creating a **value chain,** we explain the importance of identifying the best **location economies**—those in which operations can be most effective given prevailing economic, political, and cultural conditions. We also analyze several factors that may influence a company's decisions in configuring its value chain (e.g., cost, logistics, **economies of scale,** buyers' needs).

Concept Check

Recall from Chapter 11 our extended discussion of "Global Integration versus Local Responsiveness" as an issue in *configuring* and *coordinating* a firm's **value chain.** We then proceed to explain how efforts to resolve this issue may contribute to the formulation of a **global strategy** or a **multidomestic strategy** for international operations. Here we analyze ways in which this same issue can put pressure on specific strategic decisions about the configuration of manufacturing facilities.

and adherence to its manufacturing strategy. However, Toyota has developed a family of vehicles based on a single low-cost platform that is targeted to emerging markets. To keep the prices of these vehicles low enough to compete in the developing world, Toyota has abandoned its traditional practice of sourcing key components from its Japanese plants. Instead, it is locating factories for these parts in low-wage areas such as South America, Africa, and Southeast Asia, which has allowed the company to reduce the costs by 20 to 25 percent (although managers are concerned that they may lose control over quality).[18] And, as illustrated in the opening case in Chapter 10, Toyota is manufacturing the Yaris in the low-cost Czech Republic to sell in Europe.

Manufacturing Configuration   Next, the company's managers need to determine the configuration of manufacturing facilities. The three basic configurations that MNEs consider as they establish a global manufacturing strategy are *centralized, regional,* and *multidomestic.*

Manufacturing configuration:

- Centralized manufacturing in one country.
- Manufacturing facilities in specific regions to service those regions.
- Multidomestic facilities in each country

Centralized Manufacturing Strategy   The first configuration is to have *centralized manufacturing* that offers a selection of standard, lower-priced products to different markets. That is basically a manufacture-and-export strategy. It is common for new-to-export companies to use this strategy, typically through their home-country manufacturing facilities. This is also important for expensive items where economies of scale in manufacturing are important and there is little need to localize the product for consumption in different markets, such as aircraft.

Regional Manufacturing Strategy   The second configuration is the use of *regional manufacturing* facilities to serve customers within a specific region. That is what Samsonite initially did in Europe with its production facilities in Belgium and what Toyota is doing in its markets in developing countries.

Case Review Note

Multidomestic Manufacturing Strategy   Third, market expansion in individual countries, especially when the demand in those countries becomes significant, might argue for a *multidomestic approach* in which companies manufacture products close to their customers, using country-specific manufacturing facilities to meet local needs.[19] As we saw in our opening case, for example, Samsonite chose not to manufacture in every European country in which it marketed its products, but rather it segmented the broad European market into smaller areas supplied by seven well-placed manufacturing facilities. Unless the company has manufacturing facilities in every country where it is doing business, it must combine exporting with manufacturing. In reality, MNEs choose a combination of these approaches depending on their product strategies.

Countries often also specialize in the production of parts or final goods—a process known as *rationalization.* A good example can be borrowed from our opening case. In the 1980s, Samsonite opened a new factory in Hénin-Beaumont, France, specifically to manufacture Prestige Attaché and a few other products. In so doing, it was able to remove production of those products from its facility in Oudenaarde, Belgium, where it was then able to focus on its new Oyster product line. This strategy of specializing the manufacture of certain products in certain plants eventually made it feasible to export all production to a centralized European warehouse, from which Samsonite could then distribute its whole product line to retailers all over Europe.

Case Review Note

Coordination is linking or integrating activities into a unified system.

Coordination and Control   Coordination and control fit well together. *Coordinating* is the linking or integrating of activities into a unified system.[20] The activities include everything along the global supply chain from purchasing to warehousing to shipment.

It is hard to coordinate supplier relations and logistics activities if those issues are not considered when the manufacturing configuration is set up.

Once the company determines the manufacturing configuration it will use, it must adopt a control system to ensure that company strategies are carried out. *Control* can be the measuring of performance so companies can respond appropriately to changing conditions. Another aspect of control structure is the organizational structure, as discussed in more detail in Chapter 15. Recall from our opening case, for example, that Samsonite established a European headquarters in Belgium (in Oudenaarde) for the basic purpose of controlling all of its European activities—a strategy also designed to maximize the company's ability to respond to local and/or regional differences in a very large market.

Information Technology and Global Supply-Chain Management

A comprehensive supply-chain strategy is most effective with a strong commitment to information technology.

With competitive demands to produce high-quality products quickly and efficiently, manage inventory levels proficiently, communicate effectively with suppliers, and meet customer demand adequately, companies are coming to rely more and more on information technology (IT) to meet their needs.

Electronic Data Interchange (EDI) The key to making a global information system work is getting the relevant information in a timely manner. As we note in our opening case, for example, Samsonite invested heavily in IT designed to speed up delivery time to retailers. In particular, the new technology made it possible for retailers or salespeople to trigger orders directly by contacting a central warehouse. Many companies use **electronic data interchange (EDI)** to link suppliers, manufacturers, customers, and intermediaries, especially in the food-manufacturing and car-making industries, in which suppliers replenish in high volumes.

In a global context, EDI has been used to link exporters with customs to facilitate the quick processing of customs forms, thus speeding up the delivery of products across borders. Wal-Mart is known for its revolutionary use of EDI to connect its suppliers to its inventory ordering system.[21] Wal-Mart depends on over 61,000 suppliers located in 70 countries.[22] Wal-Mart's information system was one of its competitive advantages in lowering costs and capturing market share in Mexico.

However, EDI has some drawbacks. It is relatively limited and inflexible. It provides basic information but does not adapt easily to rapidly changing market conditions—a necessary condition in the global marketplace. It is relatively expensive to implement, so many small- and medium-size companies find it difficult to afford. Also, it is based on proprietary rather than on widely accepted standards, so systems tend to only be able to link together suppliers and their customers. In addition, it focuses more on the business-to-business value chain and does not deal effectively with end-use customers.[23]

Enterprise Resource Planning/Material Requirements Planning The next wave of technology affecting the global supply chain was the implementation of information technology packages known as **enterprise resource planning (ERP)**. Companies such as German software giant SAP, Oracle, Baan, and PeopleSoft introduced software to integrate everything in the back office of the firm—the part of the business that dealt with the firm itself but not with the customer (that part known as the *front office*). ERP is essential for bringing together the information inside the firm and from different

Case Review Note

Control systems, such as organizational structure and performance measurement systems, ensure that managers implement company strategies.

A key to making the global supply chain work is a good information system.

Case Review Note

EDI (electronic data interchange)—the electronic linkage of suppliers, customers, and third-party intermediaries to expedite documents and financial flows.

ERP (enterprise resource planning)—software that can link information flows from different parts of a business and from different geographic areas.

geographic areas, but its inability to tie in to the customer and take advantage of e-commerce has been a problem.

Material requirements planning (MRP)—computerized information system that addresses complex inventory situations and calculates the demand for parts from the production schedules of the companies that use the parts.

An extension of ERP is *material requirements planning* (MRP), a computerized information system that addresses complex inventory situations and calculates the demand for parts from the production schedules of the companies that use the parts. DENSO, the Japanese manufacturer of auto parts that is a major supplier to Toyota, uses MRP extensively, because it manufactures parts not only for Toyota but for other auto companies as well. It uses MRP to calculate the demand for parts from the production schedules of the non-Toyota companies that it supplies.

Radio Frequency ID (RFID)

Radio frequency ID (RFID)—a system that labels products with an electronic tag, which stores and transmits information regarding the product's origin, destination, and quantity.

A newer wave has recently been sweeping the technology scene in the form of *radio frequency ID (RFID)*, a system that labels a product with an electronic tag, which stores and transmits information regarding the product's origin, destination, and quantity. When electronic readers scan the tags, by means of radio waves, the data on the tags can be rewritten or captured and sent to a computer-network database. The database collects, organizes, stores, and moves the data and is often used in conjunction with an ERP system.

This real-time information allows manufacturers, suppliers, and distributors to keep track of products and components throughout their manufacturing processes and transportation networks, resulting in increased efficiencies and more visibility along the supply chain. In June 2003, Wal-Mart mandated that its top suppliers use RFID tags at the pallet level. It decided to use RFID instead of bar codes in order to save money, predicting that it could save billions of dollars for the entire retail industry through supply-chain efficiencies.[24] The use of RFID in the Las Vegas airport to track luggage has resulted in more accurate sorting, better tracking, and fewer lost bags—a great boon to international travelers who frequent Las Vegas.[25]

E-Commerce

E-commerce—the use of the Internet to join together suppliers with companies and companies with customers.

The next technological wave linking together the parts of the global supply chain is **e-commerce**. As an example, Dell Computer Corporation has a factory in Ireland that supplies custom-built PCs all over Europe. Customers can transmit orders to Dell via call centers or Dell's Web site. The company relays the demand for components to its suppliers. Trucks deliver the components to the factory and haul off the completed computers within a few hours.

A sales clerk demonstrates a virtual makeup system, which enables her to display a before- and after-makeup face reading radio frequency identification (RFID) tags with Japanese cosmetics giant Shiseido's products during a demonstration of the "future-store project" at Tokyo's Mitsukoshi department store. Mitsukoshi, Shiseido, and Japan's electronics giant Fujitsu started operation of customer service and stock control using RFID tags and information devices.
Source: Yoshikazu Tsuno/Getty Images, Inc.

All of this activity, of course, is made possible by the Internet. Wal-Mart, for example, moved its EDI-based infrastructure from traditional but expensive value-added networks (VANs) to the Internet. This has been good news for many of its 61,000 worldwide vendors. All of their transactions with Wal-Mart are now on the Web—a substantial cost savings over VANs for Wal-Mart and its vendors.[26]

Most experts agree that the Internet will revolutionize communications across all levels of the global supply chain, but it will occur at different speeds in different areas. The number of worldwide Internet users is rising—increasing from 420 million in 2000 to surpassing the one-billion mark in 2005. It is predicted that the number of users will reach 2 billion by 2011.[27]

Extranets and Intranets Dell has established an **extranet** for its suppliers—a linkage to Dell's information system via the Internet—so suppliers can organize production and delivery of parts to Dell when the company needs more parts. Dell uses the Internet to plug its suppliers into its customer database so they can keep track of changes in demand. It also uses the Internet to plug customers into the ordering process and allows them to track the progress of their orders from the factory to their doorsteps.[28]

The real attraction of the Internet in global supply-chain management is that it not only helps to automate and speed up internal processes in a company through its **intranet**, but also spreads efficiency gains to the business systems of its customers and suppliers.[29] The new technology wave using the Internet is that of **private technology exchange (PTX)**, an online collaboration model that brings manufacturers, distributors, value-added resellers, and customers together to execute trading transactions and to share information about demand, production, availability, and more.

"The Digital Divide" The challenge in global supply-chain management is that some networks can be managed through the Internet, but others—particularly in emerging markets—cannot because of the lack of technology, especially high-speed access to the Internet. The use of the Internet varies by location and by industry. North America is at least five years ahead of some countries in Europe, especially Eastern Europe, but it is behind Asia, especially in some key infrastructures. Industries such as computing and electronics, aerospace and defense, and motor vehicles are blasting ahead; industrial equipment, food and agriculture, heavy industries, and consumer goods are lagging behind.

This so-called digital divide has created difficulties for companies such as U.S.-based Newmont Mining Corporation. Newmont has struggled to implement its ordering and inventory management information system with its suppliers in Indonesia, who have to rent computers in different towns to even access the Internet and whose managers are typically former farmers who have often never even used e-mail.[30] It is no coincidence that the leaders in e-commerce are those who have invested significant amounts of money over the years in IT—notably in the defense and motor-vehicles industries.

It's clear from the preceding discussion that IT can help companies manage their global supply chains, but it has to be carefully integrated into the company's overall strategy. Because IT is highly technical as well as a support to the lines of business of a company, it is often difficult to align IT with the strategy of the firm. This is especially true in the international area where personnel in different countries may be used to their own IT systems and may have difficulty adopting a global IT format that will allow the firm to achieve some economies of scale as well as fully integrate IT in the firm's overall strategy.

Quality

An important aspect of all levels of the global supply chain is quality management, which is true for service as well as manufacturing companies. **Quality** is defined as meeting or exceeding the expectations of the customer. More specifically, it is the conformance to specifications, value, fitness for use, support (provided by the company), and psychological impressions (image).[31]

Private technology exchange (PTX)—an online collaboration model that brings manufacturers, distributors, value-added resellers, and customers together to execute trading transactions.

Concept Check

In discussing "Contemporary Approaches to Organizational Change" in Chapter 15, we observe that the Internet, which accelerates the spread of ideas throughout an organization, has become a "metaphor" for organization structure. In other words, as a supremely efficient and effective means of organizing global knowledge, resources, and people, the Internet has inspired many people to imagine new ways of effectively organizing a company's resources (especially its people). We also point out the ironic attractiveness of a self-regulating organizational model that features no formal organizational hierarchy.

Quality—meeting or exceeding the expectations of a customer.

For example, no one wants to buy computer software that has a lot of bugs. However, the need to get software to market quickly may mean getting the product to market as soon as possible and correcting errors later. In the airline industry, service is key. Some airlines, such as Singapore Air, have developed a worldwide reputation for excellence in service. That is a distinct competitive advantage, especially when trying to attract the business traveler.

Case: Car Quality   Quality—or lack thereof—can have serious ramifications for a company. Ford Motor Company lost around $1 billion in 2001 because of faulty Firestone tires placed on its Ford Explorers. Because of this and other quality problems, Ford, General Motors, and DaimlerChrysler are taking a hard look at the way Japanese carmakers manufacture their cars with higher efficiency and fewer defects. As DaimlerChrysler puts it, we're "raiding Toyota Motor Corporation for quality expertise."

The American car companies, which have typically lagged behind the Japanese in quality, are learning to root out problems before assembly and bring each supplier into the design process earlier, hoping to spot component problems early. They are finding some success, particularly in their international plants. Ford's Brazil plant produces some of the best-quality results of any of its factories.[32]

Each year, J.D. Power and Associates releases two different quality rankings on automobiles: the Initial Quality Study (IQS) and the Vehicle Dependability Study (VDS), which measures quality after three years of ownership. In the 2009 J.D. Power and Associates Dependability Ratings, Toyota won nine awards across the different categories, although Ford/Lincoln/Mercury was in second place. As a whole, Japanese companies walked away with 13 awards compared with six for U.S. companies. Although the Japanese automakers have long dominated the rankings, the 2009 results exhibited marked improvements for American carmakers.[33]

ZERO DEFECTS VERSUS ACCEPTABLE QUALITY LEVEL

| Zero defects—the refusal to tolerate defects of any kind.

| Acceptable quality level (AQL)—a tolerable level of defects that can be corrected through repair and service warranties.

Quality can mean **zero defects**, an idea perfected by Japanese manufacturers who refuse to tolerate defects of any kind. Before the strong emphasis on zero defects, many companies operated according to the premise of **acceptable quality level (AQL)**. This premise allowed an acceptable level of poor quality. It held that unacceptable products would be dealt with through repair facilities and service warranties. This type of manufacturing/operating environment required buffer inventories, rework stations, and expediting. The goal was to push through products as fast as possible and then deal with the mistakes later. However, it is increasingly evident that AQL is inferior to zero defects and that global companies that take quality more seriously will beat the competition.[34]

THE DEMING APPROACH TO QUALITY MANAGEMENT

In the late 1970s, when Japanese companies began to seriously outpace American companies in their achievement of high-quality products and processes, a new emphasis was placed on actively managing the operations that affect quality. One of the contributors to this focus on *quality management,* and one of the people who trained the Japanese in quality, was W. Edwards Deming.

| Deming's 14 Points encompass the idea that the responsibility for quality resides within the policies and practices of managers.

Deming's 14 Points   To espouse the idea that the responsibility for quality resides within the policies and practices of managers, Deming developed several suggestions, which have come to be known as *Deming's 14 Points:*

1. Create constancy of purpose.

2. Adopt a new philosophy.

3. Cease mass inspection.

4. End awarding business on the basis of price tag.

5. Constantly improve the system.

6. Institute training on the job.

7. Improve leadership.

8. Drive out fear.

9. Break down barriers between departments.

10. Eliminate slogans.

11. Eliminate work standards.

12. Remove barriers to pride.

13. Institute education and self-improvement.

14. Put everybody to work.[35]

The emphasis on quality management has continued to provide a major source of competitive advantage and to play a major role for companies across the globe. However, just as different countries possess varying cultures, product preferences, and business practices, different regions of the world have approached the concept of quality management in different ways. The Japanese have long focused on lean production processes that eliminate waste and increase visibility, whereas the American approach has historically been more statistically based. The Europeans have opted to concentrate more on standards of quality.[36] These varying attitudes toward quality create a high level of complexity for multinational enterprises with global operations. As we will see, however, many of the best practices concerning quality have been perfected in Japan and are being used worldwide.

TOTAL QUALITY MANAGEMENT (TQM)

The Japanese approach to quality is **total quality management (TQM)**, a process that stresses three principles: *customer satisfaction, continuous improvement,* and *employee involvement*.[37] The goal of TQM is to eliminate all defects. TQM often focuses on benchmarking world-class standards, product and service design, process design, and purchasing.[38]

The center of the entire process, however, is customer satisfaction, the achievement of which may raise production costs. The difference between AQL and TQM centers on the attitude toward quality. In AQL, quality is a characteristic of a product that meets or exceeds engineering standards. In TQM, quality means that a product is so good that the customer wouldn't think of buying from anyone else.

TQM is a process of continuous improvement at every level of the organization—from the mailroom to the boardroom. It implies that the company is doing everything it can to achieve quality at all stages of the process, from customer demands to product design to engineering. For example, if management accounting systems are focused strictly on cost, they will preclude measures that could lead to higher quality. The key is to understand the company's overall strategy.

TQM does not use any specific production philosophy or require the use of other techniques, such as a just-in-time system for inventory delivery. TQM is a proactive strategy. Although benchmarking—determining the best processes used by the best companies—is an important part of TQM, using the best practices of other companies is not intended to be a goal. TQM means that a company will try to be better than the best.

Executives who have adopted the zero-defects philosophy of TQM claim that long-run production costs decline as defects decline. The continuous improvement process is also known as *kaizen*, which means identifying problems and enlisting employees at all levels of the organization to help eliminate problems. The key is to make continuous improvement a part of the daily work of every employee.

TQM in a global setting is challenging because of cultural and environmental differences. In 1987, for instance, Samsonite entered into an agreement with a Hungarian manufacturer to supply low-end soft-side luggage. Unfortunately, a lack of advanced technology prevented the Hungarian firm from delivering products that satisfied

Concept Check

Compare the concept of *employee involvement* as it's characterized here with the idea of *coordination by mutual adjustment*, which we discuss in Chapter 15. Both approaches to coordination signal a willingness to coordinate value activities through a range of *informal* mechanisms, including means by which employees are encouraged to engage one another in decisions about matters of mutual importance.

Total quality management (TQM)—a process that stresses customer satisfaction, employee involvement, and continuous improvement of quality. Its goal is to eliminate all defects.

Samsonite's world-class quality standards. As a result, Samsonite was forced to invest heavily in its Hungarian partner in order to get a supply of products that would satisfy even the low end of its European market.

SIX SIGMA

Six Sigma—a quality control system aimed at eliminating defects, slashing product cycle times, and cutting costs across the board.

Six Sigma is a statistical approach to quality management that has been very effective and is popular in the United States. It is a highly focused system of quality control that scrutinizes a company's entire production system. It aims to eliminate defects, slash product cycle times, and cut costs across the board. The Six Sigma process uses data and rigorous statistical analysis to identify "defects" in a process or product, reduce variability, and achieve as close to zero defects as possible. It involves driving toward six standard deviations between the mean and the nearest specification limit in any process—from manufacturing to transactional and from product to service.[39]

Motorola introduced Six Sigma in the 1980s, and it's been adopted by many MNEs, including General Electric, GlaxoSmithKline, and Lockheed Martin. Although some have accused the Six Sigma program of diverting attention away from customers and of squashing innovation, 82 of the 100 largest companies in the United States have embraced it.[40] The main goal of Six Sigma is defect reduction. Lower defects should cause an improvement in yields, which should improve customer satisfaction, which should lead to enhanced income. Given that Six Sigma is a metric designed to measure defects, some argue that it is most effective when used in conjunction with the Baldrige Criteria for Excellence or the European Quality Award.[41]

QUALITY STANDARDS

There are three different levels of quality standards: *general, industry-specific,* and *company-specific levels.* The first is a general standard, such as the Deming Award, which is presented to firms that demonstrate excellence in quality, and the Malcolm Baldrige National Quality Award, which is presented annually to companies that demonstrate quality strategies and achievements. However, even more important than awards is certification of quality.

Levels of quality standards:
- General level—ISO 9000, Malcolm Baldrige National Quality Award
- Industry-specific level
- Company level

General-Level Standards   The **International Organization for Standardization (ISO)** in Geneva was formed in 1947 to facilitate the international coordination and unification of industrial standards. From the beginning, it has partnered with the IEC (International Electrotechnical Commission), which is the originator of global technical standards. It also collaborates with the International Telecommunications Union and the World Trade Organization. The ISO is an NGO and represents a network of standard setters in 158 countries throughout the world. It has established a total of 16,455 international quality standards.[42]

ISO 9000—a global set of quality standards intended to promote quality at every level of an organization.

ISO 9000 and ISO 14000   The International Organization for Standardization has developed over 17,500 international standards, with new ones being published every year. The two main families of standards issued by the ISO are ISO 9000 and ISO 14000. ISO 9000 is concerned with quality management, or "what the organization does to enhance customer satisfaction by meeting customer and applicable regulatory requirements and continually to improve its performance in this regard."[43] ISO 14000 is concerned with environmental management and what the company does to improve its environmental performance.

ISO 14000—a quality standard concerned with environmental management.

ISO 9000 is a set of universal standards for a quality assurance system that is accepted around the world. The standards apply uniformly to companies in any industry and of any size. ISO 9000 is intended to promote the idea of quality at every level of an organization. Initially, it was designed to harmonize technical norms within the EU. Now it is an important part of business operations throughout Europe. These standards are used by over a million organizations in 175 countries.[44] Basically, under ISO 9001:2008, the most recent version, companies must document how workers perform every function that affects quality and install mechanisms to ensure that they follow through on the documented routine. ISO certification entails a complex analysis of management systems and procedures, not just quality-control standards. Rather than judging the quality of a particular product, ISO evaluates the management of the manufacturing process according to standards it has created in 20 domains—from purchasing to design to training. The operation principles of ISO's management-system standards are: plan, do, check, and act (correct and improve plans). A company that wants to be ISO certified must fill out a report and then be certified by a team of independent auditors.[45] The process can be expensive and time consuming. Each site of a company must be separately certified; the certification of one site cannot cover the entire company.

Most MNEs claim ISO certification, but as noted in a humorous way in Figure 17.4, ISO is not the solution to all quality issues. It has also been estimated that in some places, including China, as much as 40 percent of ISO certifications are falsified.[46] However, ISO certification of suppliers will help companies get more business, especially with European companies. When companies are choosing among different suppliers, it would be very beneficial for the supplier to have ISO certification.

U.S. companies that operate in Europe are becoming ISO certified to maintain access to the European market. When DuPont lost a major European contract to an ISO-certified European company, it decided to become certified. By doing so, not only was DuPont able to position itself better in the European market, but it also benefited from the experience of going through ISO certification and focusing on quality in the organization. Some European companies are so committed to ISO certification that they will not do business with a certified supplier if its suppliers are not also ISO certified. They want to be sure that quality flows back to every level of the supply chain.

> Non-European companies operating in Europe need to become ISO certified in order to maintain access to that market.

Industry-Specific Standards In addition to the general standards described earlier, there are industry-specific standards for quality, especially for suppliers to follow. ISO/TS 16946:2002 is derived from ISO 9001, but it is more specific to the auto industry. Under the guidelines, suppliers must adapt their quality systems to meet the expectations of the automakers. Its predecessor, QS9000, was required for any supplier of Ford, General Motors, and Chrysler, but QS9000 was dropped and replaced with the ISO/TS standard.[47]

Company-Specific Standards Individual companies also set their own standards for suppliers to meet if they are going to continue to supply them. A good example is Samsonite's efforts to bring the output of its Eastern European suppliers up to its own quality standards. Toyota is another company that works aggressively with its suppliers to ensure delivery of high-quality parts based on what is acceptable to Toyota.

Case Review Note

FIGURE 17.4 ISO 9000: A Good Reason to Take a Close Look at Your Internal Processes

Source: DILBERT, reprinted by permission of United Feature Syndicate, Inc.

Supplier Networks

Sourcing—the process of a firm having inputs supplied to it from outside suppliers (both domestic and foreign) for the production process.

Global sourcing and production strategies can be better understood by looking at Figure 17.5. **Sourcing** is the firm's process of having inputs (raw materials and parts) supplied to it for the production process. Figure 17.5 illustrates the basic operating-environment choices (the home country or any foreign country) by stage in the production process (sourcing of raw materials and parts and the manufacture and assembly of final products). Global sourcing is the first step in the process of materials management, which includes sourcing, inventory management, and transportation between suppliers, manufacturers, and customers.

From a supplier network perspective, auto companies are good examples. Ford assembles cars in Hermosillo, Mexico, and ships them into the United States for end-use consumers. The cars are designed by Mazda, a Japanese company, and use some Japanese parts. Ford can purchase parts manufactured in Japan and ship them to the United States for final assembly and sale in the U.S. market, or it can have Japanese- and U.S.-made parts shipped to Mexico for final assembly and sale in the United States and Mexico. For Mexican assembly, some of the parts come from the United States, some from Japan, and a small percentage from Mexico.

Case: A Loaf of Whole-Grain White Bread   Although global sourcing is often linked with high-tech and complex products, it is a process that affects even the low-cost products we use and consume every day. A good example of this is U.S.-based Sara Lee's whole-grain white bread. To make the bread, Sara Lee acquires ingredients from a variety of suppliers—nearly a third of them located in foreign countries. For example, it sources guar gum from India. Guar gum is used to keep the bread moist and is a powder that comes from the guar-plant seedpods grown in India. Calcium propionate, a powdery mold inhibitor that is manufactured in several countries, is sourced in the Netherlands. Honey, used as a natural sweetener, is purchased from many suppliers, including from the United States, China, Vietnam, Brazil, Uruguay, India, Canada, Mexico, and Argentina. Sara Lee sources from several different countries, including the United States, because U.S. supply can often run short. Flour enrichments to replenish the vitamins lost in the milling process are sourced in China. Due to consolidation in the industry, there are limited suppliers of flour enrichments. Beta-carotene, an artificial coloring used to provide color to the bread and crust, is sourced in Switzerland, although it is available in many countries. Vitamin D3 is sourced in China, and wheat gluten is sourced from suppliers in several countries, including France, Poland, Russia, the Netherlands, and Australia.[48]

FIGURE 17.5   Global Sourcing and Production Strategy

When a company wants to *source* raw materials, parts, or components as a function of its global strategy, it's faced with some key decisions. It may, for example, decide to source components at home, assemble them abroad, and then export the final product to the home market, to foreign markets, or to both.

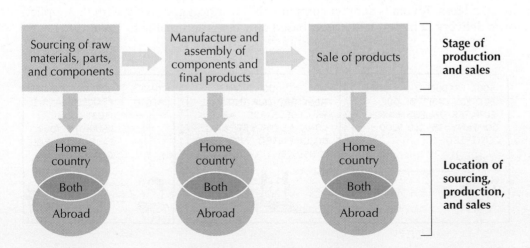

With its sources of ingredients spread all over the globe, Sara Lee must manage its supply chain carefully to ensure timeliness, safety, and quality. To accomplish this, Sara Lee has centralized its global ingredients purchasing, consolidating its previously scattered procurement operations into a single division known as the "nerve center," which is located at company headquarters. Purchasing specialists monitor weather patterns, commodity trends, and energy prices. They also communicate and work closely with Sara Lee's diverse base of suppliers, in some cases even investing money in their suppliers' operations to ensure that they are complying with U.S. food safety standards.[49]

GLOBAL SOURCING

Companies can manufacture parts internally or purchase them from external (unrelated) manufacturers. Companies can also assemble their own products internally or subcontract to external companies; and the manufacture of parts and final assembly may take place in the company's home country, the country in which it is trying to sell the product, or a third country.[50] The term *sourcing* is used in a variety of ways. For example, **outsourcing** refers to the situation when one company externalizes a process or function to another business. This most often occurs with the IT function but is also being used in other areas, such as research, service centers, and even accounting and tax functions. *Offshore manufacturing* was discussed earlier in the chapter. However, another type of offshoring occurs when a company moves part of its business processes outside its home country but internalizes the function rather than outsourcing it to another company. For example, it could set up its own R&D facilities in another country. Outsourcing can be domestic or offshore. For example, if a company hires an HR firm to take care of some of its HR functions rather than having its own HR division, the outsourcing could be domestic, or it could be done offshore by another firm.

> Companies can manufacture parts internally or purchase them from external manufacturers.

Sourcing in the home country enables companies to avoid numerous problems, including those connected with language differences, long distances and lengthy supply lines, exchange-rate fluctuations, wars and insurrections, strikes, politics, tariffs, and complex transportation channels. However, for many companies, domestic sources may be unavailable or may be more expensive than foreign sources. In Japan, foreign procurement is critical, because nearly all of the country's uranium, bauxite, nickel, crude oil, iron ore, copper, and coking coal, and approximately 30 percent of its agricultural products are imported. Japanese trading companies came into being expressly to acquire the raw materials needed to fuel Japan's manufacturing.

> Using domestic sources for raw materials and components allows a company to avoid problems with language differences, distance, currency, politics, and tariffs, as well as other problems.

Procter & Gamble has also found that sourcing chemicals from a variety of suppliers abroad is necessary to provide flexibility in a global environment of volatile energy prices. By diversifying its chemicals supplier base, Procter & Gamble plans on being able to switch procurement between different suppliers as energy prices shift in different regions.[51]

Why Global Sourcing?   Companies pursue global sourcing strategies for a number of reasons:

> Companies outsource abroad to lower costs and improve quality, among other reasons.

- To reduce costs—due to less expensive labor, less restrictive work rules, and lower land and facilities costs
- To improve quality
- To increase exposure to worldwide technology
- To improve the delivery-of-supplies process
- To strengthen the reliability of supply by supplementing domestic with foreign suppliers
- To gain access to materials that are only available abroad, possibly because of technical specifications or product capabilities
- To establish a presence in a foreign market
- To satisfy offset requirements
- To react to competitors' offshore sourcing practices[52]

The reasons given here to engage in global sourcing are similar to the benefits to foreign direct investment discussed in Chapter 14. Whether the suppliers are company-owned or are independent companies, MNEs can take advantage of the location-specific advantages in foreign countries.

In some ways, however, global sourcing is more expensive than domestic sourcing. For example, transportation and communications are more expensive, and companies may have to pay broker and agent fees. Given the longer length of supply lines, it often takes more time to get components from abroad, and lead times are less certain. This problem increases the inventory carrying costs and makes it more difficult to get parts to the production site in a timely manner. If imported components come in with errors and need to be reworked, the cost per unit will rise, and some components may have to be shipped back to the supplier.

Concerns That Come with Global Sourcing   As noted, quality and safety are other concerns with global sourcing. This has been especially evident in the highly publicized recalls of tainted pet food and toothpaste, defective tires, and toys with traces of lead in their paint that were produced in China. Subsequent actions led Chinese regulators and inspectors to close 180 food plants and uncover more than 23,000 food safety violations,[53] forcing the Chinese government to admit that 20 percent of its consumer goods have failed safety inspections. Imagine being a firm that outsourced pet food from Chinese company Xuzhou Anying Biologic Technology Development Company, which resulted in the deaths of several dogs and cats and led to one of the biggest pet-food recalls in U.S. history.[54] A situation like that could have irreversible effects on the image of a company.

In 2008, more than 20 countries banned Chinese dairy products because of contaminated milk that killed four infants and left over 50,000 people sick.[55] A major challenge with these issues is finding the problem. Supply chains have become so long and complex that buyers can't be sure who the original producer is.[56]

China is not the only country producing substandard goods; black pepper with salmonella from India, filthy crabmeat from Mexico, mislabeled candy from Denmark, and produce with traces of illegal pesticides from the Dominican Republic have resulted in thousands of shipments halted by U.S. inspectors.[57] Such incidents have raised concerns over foreign-made products and accusations that quality and safety are being compromised to lower costs. The countries that churn out the cheapest products often lack adequate regulations, enforcement, and logistical infrastructure, leaving it up to the purchasing companies to ensure quality and safety.

MAJOR SOURCING CONFIGURATIONS

Vertical Integration   **Vertical integration** occurs when the company owns the entire supplier network or at least a significant part of it. The company may have to purchase raw materials from outside suppliers, but it produces the most expensive parts itself. By integrating vertically, the company is able to reduce transaction costs (such as finding suppliers, selling output, negotiating contracts, monitoring contracts, and settling disputes with unrelated companies) by internalizing the different levels in the value chain.[58]

Industrial Clusters   Outsourcing through industrial clusters is an alternative way to reduce transportation costs and transaction costs. Under clustering, buyers and suppliers locate in close proximity to each other to facilitate doing business. For example, Dell Computer Corporation established an assembly operation in the Multimedia Supercorridor in Malaysia, where it is close to its key suppliers.

Japanese Keiretsus   Japanese _keiretsus_ are groups of independent companies that work together to manage the flow of goods and services along the entire value chain.[59] Toyota's highly coordinated supplier network is among the most successful and well known of the

Major outsourcing configurations:

- Vertical integration
- Outsourcing through industrial clusters
- Other outsourcing

Concept Check

In discussing "Taking Control: Foreign Direct Investment" in Chapter 14, we define **internalization** as the self-handling of operations (that is, by keeping them _internal_ to the company). We point out the genesis of this concept in _transactions cost theory_, which holds that when there's a decision to be made between handling something internally and contracting with someone else to handle it, companies should opt for the lower-cost alternative. As we suggest later in this chapter, _make-or-buy decisions_ invite the application of this principle.

Japanese keiretsus and a good example of industrial clustering. It almost borders on vertical integration, because parts suppliers tend to set up shop close to Toyota's assembly operations, and Toyota usually has an ownership interest in the suppliers. However, recent changes in its global markets and price pressures resulting from the high cost of steel and the strong yen have caused the company to start looking beyond its closely knit supplier base in Japan. To meet its goal of cutting costs for buying car parts by 30 percent—an objective outlined in its "Construction of Cost Competitiveness for the 21st Century" program—Toyota is putting pressure on its keiretsu suppliers by benchmarking them to China's cheaper suppliers and by courting suppliers outside Japan. These outside suppliers are leaping at the chance of breaking into the supplier network of the world's second-largest automaker.[60]

THE MAKE-OR-BUY DECISION

MNE managers struggle with a dilemma: Which production activities should be performed internally and which ones could be subcontracted to independent companies? That is the *make-or-buy decision.* In the case of subcontracting, companies also need to decide whether the activities should be carried out in the home market or abroad.

In deciding whether to make or buy, MNEs can focus on those parts that are critical to the product and that they are distinctly good at making. They can outsource parts when suppliers have a distinct comparative advantage, such as greater scale, lower cost structure, or stronger performance incentives. They can also use outsourcing as an implied threat to underperforming employees: If they don't improve, companies will move their business elsewhere.[61]

In determining whether to make or buy, the MNE needs to determine the design and manufacturing capabilities of potential suppliers compared to its own capabilities. If the supplier has a clear advantage, management needs to decide what it would cost to catch up to the best suppliers and whether it would make sense to do so.

> Make or buy—outsource or supply parts from internal production.

> **Concept Check**
>
> As we explain in Chapter 14, the **resource-based view** of the firm holds that every company has a unique combination of competencies. Here we suggest that *make-or-buy decisions* may depend on the extent to which a firm embraces this view, which may prompt it to concentrate internally on those activities that best fit its competencies while depending on other firms to supply products, services, or support activities for which it has lesser competency.

> If MNEs outsource parts instead of sourcing them from internal production, they need to determine the degree of involvement with suppliers.

Point ⟩ Counterpoint

Should Firms Outsource Innovation?

Point ⟩ Yes Yes, firms should outsource innovative processes if doing so will allow them to maintain their focus and to position themselves effectively in the increasingly competitive high-tech and electronics industries. Data show that more and more companies are coming to realize the advantages of doing so. Suppliers are taking on such responsibilities as designing and manufacturing prototypes, converting them into workable products, upgrading mature products, conducting quality tests, putting together user manuals, and selecting parts vendors. For example, the designs of 65 percent of PC notebooks and those of 70 percent of PDAs are outsourced. Companies such as Dell, Motorola, and Philips are buying complete designs from Asian developers, and even Boeing is collaborating with an Indian company to develop software for its 787 Dreamliner jet.

Companies willing to outsource some of the R&D and the technological designs of their products can experience enormous cost savings. Although innovation is a key to

Counterpoint ⟩ No No, companies should not outsource their research, design, and development functions. Recent trends have gone beyond outsourcing larger key components to outsourcing the R&D for entire lines of complete products! Many companies insist that although they may outsource some design and development work, they still keep core R&D in-house, but how do they know where to draw the line? How do they determine what is core intellectual property and what is commodity technology?

The truth is that outsourcing turns intellectual property into commodity technology that becomes available to most anyone. By working with South Korean chipmakers to develop its DRAM memory chips, Toshiba allowed the technology behind these components to become commoditized, and it is now struggling to stay ahead of competitors.[63]

A company's competitive advantage often depends on trade secrets that set it apart from its rivals. Outsourcing innovation enhances the risk that a company will pass on these trade secrets and proprietary technologies to suppliers remaining competitive, more and more companies are finding that their internal R&D teams aren't producing results that justify the large amount of investments put into them. Thus, in the face of demanding customers and relentless competition that put pressure on margins, these companies must find a way to reduce their costs or to increase their R&D productivity.

Outsourcing has proven to be a viable solution. Companies can save millions of dollars by simply buying designs rather than developing them in-house. For example, industry estimates indicate that using a predesigned platform for cell phones can reduce the costs of developing them from scratch—which takes approximately $10 million and 150 engineers—by 70 percent! Furthermore, demands by retailers and customers as well as the uncertainty of future market trends require companies to develop a range of product models, which is very costly. Third-party developers are better equipped to handle these costs, because they can spread them over many buyers and because they have the expertise to develop a wide variety of models from a single basic design.

Outsourcing also allows companies to get their products on the market faster, and in the electronics and technology industries, where products become commodities in a matter of months, that speed becomes crucial to maintaining a competitive advantage. Hewlett-Packard claims that by working with partners and suppliers on designs, it now takes 60 percent less time for it to get a new concept to the market. Critics worry that by outsourcing technology, companies are outsourcing their sources of competitive advantage, but outsourcing certain design and development processes allows these companies to better focus on their true core competencies. Few, if any, companies plan on completely eliminating their own R&D forces, and most insist that they will continue with the more proprietary R&D work. By shifting some of the less critical work to outside vendors, they will be able to focus more on the latest innovations and on the next-generation technologies that can truly serve to differentiate them.

No one company can manage everything in-house. Even the chief technology officer of Nokia—a company that once prided itself on developing almost everything on its own—has stated, "Nobody can master it all." In fact, a recent survey of global companies found that almost three-quarters of the respondents believed they could boost innovation dramatically by collaborating with outsiders—even competitors.[62] The companies that are going to survive in the future are those able to control efficiently and effectively a network of partners and suppliers around the world. ▶

and partners, thereby fostering new competitors. Because suppliers rarely cooperate solely with one customer, the R&D they do for one can easily be transferred to another.

Such was the case for Japanese company Sharp, which worked closely with its suppliers to develop a "sixth-generation" plant able to make much larger flat panels for televisions than were "fifth-generation" plants. Unfortunately, its suppliers also work closely with Sharp's rivals, many of them Taiwanese companies, and not long after the completion of the plant, these competitors were constructing their own "sixth-generation" facilities. As a result, Sharp has started to take extra precautions, such as secretly rewriting software on some of the equipment it has purchased and fixing machinery in-house, rather than having suppliers do it, to keep vendors from knowing the problems that may exist in the equipment they have sold to competitors.[64]

There is also the risk that suppliers and partners will take what information and technology have been shared with them and become competitors themselves. After Motorola hired Taiwanese company BenQ Corp. to design and manufacture mobile phones for it, the other company began selling the phones under its own brand name in the highly competitive Chinese market, causing Motorola to terminate the contract.

Perhaps more important than giving rise to new competitors is losing competitive edge and the incentive to invest in new technology. Although some assert that outsourcing certain development and design work allows companies to focus more on new innovative technologies, in actuality, this outsourcing more often prompts companies to decrease the amount they invest in internal R&D and to become lazy in their pursuit of future breakthroughs, relying too much on suppliers to do the work for them. Jim Andrew, senior vice president of Boston Consulting Group, warns, "If the innovation starts residing in the suppliers, you could incrementalize yourself to the point where there isn't much left."

High-tech and electronics companies that outsource their innovative processes risk losing the essence of their actual business, becoming mere marketing fronts for other companies. It also sends a bad message to investors, who might have difficulty finding the intrinsic value in a company that owns little true intellectual property and whose profits from successful products are most likely simply being paid out in licensing fees to the companies that actually developed them.

Although much has been made of the outsourcing of manufacturing in the past few decades, the outsourcing of innovation poses a potentially larger threat to high-tech firms that see it as a shortcut to cost savings. Looking to immediate cost savings as justification for outsourcing technology and innovation is shortsighted, and firms that do so will ultimately damage their competitive positions and lose viability as true players in their industries.[65] ◀

SUPPLIER RELATIONS

Supplier relationships are very important but sometimes complicated, especially for MNEs trying to manage supplier relationships around the world. The CEO of U.S.-based MNE John Deere stated,

> *Our supplier partners have been at the heart of [our] effort to put superior value into our products . . . around the world and throughout the enterprise. Together with our suppliers and dealers, we are enriching the word "value" to include the very best design, quality, delivery, process and the very best cost, all at the same time. We know it has not been easy for suppliers and it still isn't! Following our example, suppliers have had to make major adjustments in how they do business. We've been pretty demanding on ourselves and others, but I'm confident . . . that by working together to aggressively reduce costs, increase quality, and improve delivery time, they've become stronger businesses, as well as stronger Deere suppliers. Like us, they too need a great business in order to sustain long-term success.[66]*

Case: Toyota   If an MNE decides it must outsource rather than integrate vertically, it must determine how to work with suppliers. Toyota pioneered the Toyota Production System to work with unrelated suppliers. Toyota sends a team of manufacturing experts to each of its key suppliers to observe how the supplier organizes its factory and makes its parts. Then the team advises how to cut costs and boost quality. It is also common for Toyota to identify two suppliers for each part and have the suppliers compete aggressively with each other. The supplier that performs the best gets the most business. However, both suppliers know they will have an ongoing relationship with Toyota and will not be dumped easily.[67]

This is a good example of the close relationships that Japanese companies develop with their suppliers. It is very different from the arm's-length relationship that U.S. companies tend to have with their suppliers. Furthermore, Toyota has been able to reduce the number of supplier relationships it develops, which allows it to focus on a few key suppliers, promising to give them a lot of business if they perform up to Toyota standards.

In fact, the relationship between Toyota and its suppliers is often so close that when Toyota opens up production in foreign locations, its suppliers do so as well. One major Toyota supplier, DENSO, invested $1 million to establish a new plant in Tianjin, China, to produce car navigation systems for the Toyota plant located there. It did so partly to follow Toyota there, but also because Toyota made it clear that DENSO had to match Chinese prices or lose their business. The best way for DENSO to protect its market was to move some production to China.

Case: JCPenney   The decision to work closely with suppliers requires a great deal of trust and oftentimes involves making drastic—sometimes risky—changes. However, such changes can provide large strategic advantages. Such is the case for JCPenney and its Hong Kong–based supplier of shirts, TAL Apparel Ltd. The retailer literally allows its supplier to take over some of its own processes. Rather than simply responding to orders sent to it from Penney's, TAL tracks the retailer's sales data directly, running it through its personally designed computer program to determine the number of shirts to make, as well as their sizes, colors, and styles. These shirts are then shipped directly to individual JCPenney stores, completely bypassing the retailer's warehouses.

This cooperation has resulted in quicker merchandise turnovers and an inventory level of virtually zero—a significant improvement over the eight months' worth of inventory the retailer used to keep. TAL has also been allowed to handle market testing and the design of new shirt styles, which has given it the ability to respond more quickly and effectively to customer demands. With the leverage given it, TAL can roll out a new style in just four months.[68]

Not all customer–supplier relationships are as collaborative as those of Toyota and JCPenney, however. Sometimes large customers can use their strong market presence and buying power to place additional demands on suppliers. For many years, General Motors has placed heavy pressure on its U.S. suppliers to lower costs by certain set percentages each year and then to pass those cost savings on to GM via lower prices. As it moved to increase production in China, some suppliers felt pressured to to set up facilities in China to accommodate GM.[69]

The relationships MNEs establish with their suppliers are largely based on their individual competitive strategies, the nature of their products, the competitive environment they are facing, the capabilities of their suppliers, and the level of experience and trust they share with them. MNEs must consider these factors as they determine what kind of supplier relationship will best meet their needs.

THE PURCHASING FUNCTION

The purchasing agent is the link between the company's outsourcing decision and its supplier relationships. Just as companies go through stages of globalization, so does the purchasing agent's scope of responsibilities. Typically, purchasing goes through four phases before becoming "global":

> **Global progression in the purchasing function:**
>
> - Domestic purchasing only
> - Foreign buying based on need
> - Foreign buying as part of a procurement strategy
> - Integration of global procurement strategy

1. Domestic purchasing only
2. Foreign buying based on need
3. Foreign buying as part of procurement strategy
4. Integration of global procurement strategy[70]

Phase 4 occurs when the company realizes the benefits that result from the integration and coordination of purchasing on a global basis and are most applicable to the MNE—as opposed to, say, the exporter.

When purchasing becomes this global, MNEs often face the centralization/decentralization dilemma. Should they allow each subsidiary to make all purchasing decisions, or should they centralize all or some of the purchasing decisions? The primary benefits of decentralization include increased production-facility control over purchases, better responsiveness to facility needs, and more effective use of local suppliers. The primary benefits of centralization are increased leverage with suppliers, getting better prices, eliminating administrative duplication, allowing purchasers to develop specialized knowledge in purchasing techniques, reducing the number of orders processed, and enabling purchasing to build solid supplier relationships.[71]

Case: Electrolux   Swedish appliance manufacturer Electrolux has adopted a global purchasing strategy. Despite the global downturn in 2009, Electrolux had a good second quarter due largely to its cost-reduction efforts. One aspect of the strategy was offshoring production to low-cost countries. Another was the reduction of personnel costs. Still another is the reduction of purchasing and product costs through efficient global purchasing, which reduced the cost of raw materials and components purchases.[72]

> **Sourcing strategies in the global context:**
>
> - Assign domestic buyers for foreign purchasing.
> - Use foreign subsidiaries or business agents.
> - Establish international purchasing offices.
> - Assign the responsibility for global sourcing to a specific business unit or units.
> - Integrate and coordinate worldwide sourcing.

Major Sourcing Strategies   Companies pursue five major sourcing strategies as they move into phases 3 and 4 in the preceding list (foreign buying as part of procurement strategy and integration of global procurement strategy):

1. Assigning domestic buyer(s) for international purchasing
2. Using foreign subsidiaries or business agents
3. Establishing international purchasing offices

4. Assigning the responsibility for global sourcing to a specific business unit or units

5. Integrating and coordinating global sourcing[73]

These strategies move from the simple to the more complex. Companies start by using a domestic buyer and progress all the way to integrating and coordinating worldwide sourcing into the company's purchasing decisions so that there is no difference between domestic and foreign sources.

Some companies are going even further than the last step and coordinating worldwide purchasing with competitor companies. Two automakers, Nissan and Renault, have been able to save millions of dollars in production costs by entering into joint purchasing agreements with each other. Approximately 40 percent of the parts the companies use in their vehicles are the same, and the two are looking to increase this amount to 70 percent to achieve further cost reductions.[74]

Figure 17.6 summarizes some of the key concepts in the preceding discussion in terms of selecting the best supplier. The key is for managers to select the best supplier, establish a solid relationship, and continuously evaluate the supplier's performance to ensure the best price, quality, and on-time delivery possible.

FIGURE 17.6 Global Sourcing: Assessing Your Strategy and Weighing Your Options

Source: Stanley E. Fawcett, "The Globalization of the Supply Environment," *The Supply Management Environment*, Vol. 2 (Tempe, AZ: Institute for Supply Management, 2000): 53. Reprinted by permission of the publisher.

STEPS IN GLOBAL SOURCING PROCESS	QUESTIONS ANSWERED AT EACH STEP
Evaluate operating and competitive environments.	Is global sourcing a valuable competitive option? Can global sourcing help us better meet customers' real needs?
Define scope of international purchasing effort.	How intensive and extensive does the global sourcing effort need to be? • What items should we source globally? • What structure and infrastructure are needed? • What skills will our purchasers need? • Does a cost-benefit analysis support the selected scope?
Identify and evaluate potential suppliers worldwide.	Who are the best suppliers for each item? Where are they located worldwide? Can they provide world-class support to our global operations? What is their total order performance? • Total cost • Delivery • Quality • Innovation • Responsiveness
Determine appropriate nature of buyer-supplier relationship.	Given our needs, the supplier's location and capabilities, and the channel's logistical challenges, what type of buyer-supplier relationship should we establish?
Request/evaluate proposals from suppliers.	Are the proposals truly comparable at the total-ownership level? Who is the best supplier in the short term? Long term?
Select "best" supplier, establish contract terms and conditions, and build desired relationship.	Is future negotiation needed? Are roles and responsibilities clearly understood? Are performance expectations clearly stated and understood? How are resources, risks, and rewards going to be shared?
Continual reevaluation of implementation status, requirements, and capabilities.	Is the buyer-supplier relationship fully established? Effective? Is the selected supplier performing at world-class standards? Based on changes in our own operations, our competitive requirements, and our customers' needs, does this relationship still make sense?

Inventory Management

Whether a company decides to source parts from inside or outside the company or from domestic or foreign sources, it needs to manage the flow and storage of inventory. This is true of raw materials and parts sourced from suppliers, work-in-process and finished-goods inventory inside the manufacturing plant, and finished goods stored at a distribution center (such as the centralized European warehouse for Samsonite).

LEAN MANUFACTURING AND JUST-IN-TIME SYSTEMS

One reason why companies might hesitate when considering whether to source parts from foreign suppliers is because of *lean manufacturing* systems, "a productive system whose focus is on optimizing processes through the philosophy of continual improvement." It embodies the ideas of waste reduction and optimizing quality processes.[75] Because it relies on the efficiencies gained by reducing waste and defects, lean manufacturing is also closely tied to quality management.

An important element of lean manufacturing is the just-in-time (JIT) inventory management. "JIT systems focus on reducing inefficiency and unproductive time in the production process to improve continuously the process and the quality of the product or service."[76] The JIT system gets raw materials, parts, and components to the buyer "just in time" for use, sparing companies the cost of storing large inventories.

That is what Dell hoped to accomplish in its Irish plant by having parts delivered just as they were to enter the production process and then go out the door to the consumers as soon as the computers were built. However, the use of JIT means that parts must have few defects and must arrive on time. That is why companies need to develop solid supplier relationships to ensure good quality and delivery times if JIT is to work and why industrial clustering is a popular way of linking more closely with suppliers.

Risks in Foreign Sourcing   Foreign sourcing can create big risks for companies that use lean manufacturing and JIT, because interruptions in the supply line can cause havoc. Foreign companies are becoming experts at meeting the requirements of JIT—ships that take two weeks to cross the Pacific dock within an hour of scheduled arrival, and factories that are able to more easily fill small orders. However, because of distances alone, the supply chain is open to more problems and delays.[77]

As we mentioned earlier in the chapter, companies such as Toyota that have set up manufacturing and assembly facilities overseas to service local markets have practically forced their domestic parts suppliers to move overseas as well to allow the companies to continue with JIT manufacturing. That is why so many Japanese parts suppliers have moved to the United States and Mexico to be near their major customers.

A company's inventory management strategy—especially in terms of stock sizes and whether JIT will be used—determines the frequency of needed shipments. The less frequent the delivery, the more likely the need to store inventory somewhere. Because JIT requires delivery just as the inventory is to be used, some concession must be made for inventory arriving from foreign suppliers. Sometimes that means adjusting the arrival time to a few days before use rather than a few hours. Kawasaki Motors Corp., U.S.A., carries a minimum of three days' inventory on parts coming from Japan, with an average inventory of five days.[78]

The Kanban System   One system pioneered by Toyota to facilitate its JIT strategies is the *kanban system. Kanban* literally means "card" or "visible record" in Japanese. Kanban cards are used to control the flow of production through a factory. In the kanban system used by Toyota, components are shipped to a plant just before they need to go into production. They are kept in a bin that has a card attached to it identifying the quantity of items in the bin. When the assembly process begins, a production-order card signifies that a bin needs to be moved to the assembly line. When the bin is emptied, it is moved to a storage area and replaced with a full bin. The kanban card is then removed from the empty bin and is used to order a replacement from the supplier.

FOREIGN TRADE ZONES

In recent years, **foreign trade zones (FTZs)** have become more popular as an intermediate step in the process between import and final use. FTZs are areas in which domestic and imported merchandise can be stored, inspected, and manufactured free from formal customs procedures until the goods leave the zones. The zones are intended to encourage companies to locate in the country by allowing them to defer duties, pay fewer duties, or avoid certain duties completely. Sometimes inventory is stored in an FTZ until it needs to be used for domestic manufacture. As noted earlier, one of the problems with JIT is the length of the supply line when relying on global sourcing, possibly causing either the buyer or the supplier to stockpile inventory somewhere until it is needed in the manufacturing process. One place to stockpile inventory is in a warehouse in an FTZ.

> Foreign trade zones (FTZs)—special locations for storing domestic and imported inventory in order to avoid paying duties until the inventory is used in production or sold.

General-Purpose Zones and Subzones

FTZs can be general-purpose zones or subzones. A general-purpose zone is usually established near a port of entry, such as a shipping port, a border crossing, or an airport, and it usually consists of a distribution facility or an industrial park. It is used primarily for warehousing and distribution. A subzone is usually physically separate from a general-purpose zone but under the same administrative structure, usually located at a manufacturing facility. Since 1982, the major growth in FTZs has been in subzones rather than in general-purpose zones, because companies have sought to defer duties on parts that are foreign sourced until they need to be used in the production process.

The major growth in subzones in the United States has been in the automobile industry, especially in the Midwest. Subzone activity is spreading to other industries, especially to shipbuilding, pharmaceuticals, and home appliances, and it is becoming more heavily oriented to manufacturing and assembly than was originally envisioned. Merchandise in U.S. FTZs may be assembled, exhibited, cleaned, manipulated, manufactured, mixed, processed, relabeled, repackaged, repaired, salvaged, sampled, stored, tested, displayed, and destroyed.[79]

In the United States, there are about 250 general-purpose zones and over 450 subzones in all 50 states and Puerto Rico. Over $300 billion a year in merchandise is handled in FTZs, and $19 billion is exported from FTZs each year.[80] FTZs in the United States have been used primarily as a means of providing greater flexibility as to when and how customs duties are paid. However, their use in the export business has been expanding.

The benefits to a zone user are:

- No duties on or quota charges on goods imported into a zone and rexported.
- Customs duties and federal excise tax are deferred on imports until taken from the zone and used in the domestic market.
- Duties can be reduced if foreign inputs that come into the zone at one duty are higher than the duty would have been on the finished product as it leaves the zone for domestic sales (called an inverted tariff).
- Steamlined customs procedures.
- Elimination of state and local inventory taxes if the goods are held in the zone for export.[81]

TRANSPORTATION NETWORKS

For a firm, the transportation of goods in an international context is extremely complicated in terms of documentation, choice of carrier (air or ocean), and the decision whether to establish its own transportation department or outsource to a third-party intermediary.

> Transportation links together suppliers, companies, and customers.

India, and other locations in order to cut costs, enhance quality, and remain competitive on a global basis.

Moreover, Ventus has smartly leveraged the resources of the PLDT group of companies. These include telecom connectivity, redeploying underutilized PLDT assets (e.g., buildings and other physical facilities), and the use of shared services. In this way, Ventus has been able to employ a "model of building to market and to customer specifications" at a relatively faster speed and lower cost than its competitors. On average, Ventus can build, fit, and customize call-center operations for customers within three to six months.

Ventus has also successfully capitalized on its position as a member company of PLDT—the most profitable company in the Philippines—to attract employees to work for its call centers. Although Ventus does not pay the top wage rates in the industry, employees regard the company as a stable and prestigious employer. Employees also enjoy the benefits of working for a large employer, including excellent health benefits, pensions, performance bonuses, and profit sharing for management positions.

The company has also benefited from a strong and stable leadership team. ePLDT Ventus president Ray Espinosa, Ventus CEO Helen Marquez, operations VP Albert Santos, and business development VP Ken Lamzon have created a culture that stresses professionalism, high-quality service, attention to customer needs, and a strong camaraderie among employees. The company has spared no expense on training and in building world-class facilities that provide customer-service representatives an excellent work environment. As a case in point, the company commissioned English as a Second Language (ESL) teachers at a major California university to customize an "English for Filipinos" training module exclusively for Ventus's customer-service representatives.

The partnerships that Ventus has established with major U.S. clients and global third-party providers have been very instrumental in the company's recent success. These successful partnerships have given Ventus credibility and visibility as a global provider of international outsourcing services. In addition, Ventus has used the knowledge gained from these partnerships to build a strong and globally competitive company.

The Impact of the Global Financial Crisis on Outsourcing

The global financial crisis has caused major headwinds for the growth of Ventus and the Philippine BPO industry in 2009. More specifically, it has posed four challenges for Ventus and other BPO providers in the Philippines.

First, the U.S. recession impacted companies that have traditionally fueled the growth of the BPO and call-center industries in the Philippines. The hardest-hit sectors include outsourcing providers to banks and financial-service firms, retailers, and travel and leisure firms. Second, a number of companies with outsourcing plans prior to the financial crisis had to cancel programs or put them on hold due to funding difficulties, management turnover, or lack of business visibility.

Third, consolidation in industries, such as in banking and finance, has resulted in loss of business for a number of BPO providers. A growing number of customers are consolidating their global service supply chains to fewer locations or selling off their captive operations to other providers. Interestingly, the Philippines has emerged as a primary beneficiary of this consolidation as more companies select it as a global hub for their voice-based contact-center facilities.

Finally, mounting U.S. unemployment has changed the labor-cost arbitrage dynamics of international outsourcing. Some outsourcers are responding to this change by repatriating work back to the United States, demanding price concessions from offshore providers, or increasing service-level requirements.

While the growth of Ventus and the Philippine BPO industry will continue, it will be moderated by the above challenges. It is not likely that the Philippines will attain the ambitious targets projected by the Business Process Association/Philippines anytime before the U.S. economy recovers fully from the recession and global financial crisis.

Meeting the Challenges from the Crisis

Even before the global financial crisis, Ventus had diversified its customer base by reaching out to domestic clients. Foremost among these are other PLDT companies (such as SMART, the Philippines' largest provider of mobile communications) and Maynilad (a major water utility company), as well as external clients. This domestic diversification has helped Ventus grow and has cushioned the impact of the financial crisis on its business.

The company's management has been contemplating a path that will address the near-term challenges from the global economic crisis but at the same time sustain Ventus's long-term growth and profitability.

In this regard, the company has to address three key issues.

Expansion into the Data Segment

BPA/P projects the data segment of business-process outsourcing to grow annually by over 50 percent and reach 300,000 employees in 2010. These include back-office transactions (e.g., finance/accounting/HR services), medical and legal transcription, animation, engineering design, software development, and digital-content development and support.

As competition becomes more crowded and pricing pressures become more intense in the call-center space, Ventus and PLDT's management have been looking for ways to provide higher-value added services that will continue to differentiate their company from competitors and accelerate the company's growth.

Expanding the company's presence into the data segment of BPO is one option on the table; however, this could prove to be a double-edged sword. On the one hand, it provides Ventus with a platform for tapping into a fast-growing segment of outsourcing and gives the company an expanded suite of services that it could offer to customers who wish to outsource both voice and data services. On the other hand, running a data-based BPO is different from operating call centers, as this requires different customer-service specializations and entails a different economics (e.g., cost and pricing).

In 2006, PLDT acquired SPi Technologies, a leading global provider of medical and legal transcription and publishing services. Although PLDT has no immediate plans of combining Ventus and SPi, Ray Espinosa, ePLDT's president, has been eager to create synergies between the two companies and to maximize PLDT's voice and data outsourcing capabilities.

Market, Customer, and Geographic Diversification

Shortly after it commenced commercial operations, Ventus signed a marquee client, a major U.S. satellite provider. The client has been a driving force behind Ventus's early growth and to date accounts for the lion's share of the number of call-center seats held by Ventus.

Like many Philippine-based call-center providers, however, Ventus has been largely opportunistic with customer acquisitions. The company's sales presence in the United States has been minimal, and it has relied primarily on networking and customer inquiries and referrals. Ventus realized that it would be difficult to continue generating sales in this manner in light of the U.S. economic slowdown. Ventus's response to this issue is to look into strengthening its sales presence in the United States, including the deployment of one of its key managers to the U.S. and the formation of a sales team that will cover various geographic and industry segments in the U.S.

The focus of the company's business is on inbound calls (customer service, technical support, and sales). The company serves a broad array of industry verticals, including satellite TV, electronics, retail, financial services, flower wire order, technology distribution, and others. Unlike other providers that have been seriously hurt by the downturn in the banking and financial services industry, Ventus is fortunate to have limited exposure to this sector. On the other hand, some of Ventus's business-to-consumer (B-C) retail customers have been significantly hurt by the U.S. recession.

Ventus remains committed to the U.S. market and its current customers. However, it realized that the company would have to build a diversified customer base in order to counter the negative impacts of the financial crisis. These are some of the issues the company is grappling with:

1. How can the company have a better mix between business-to-consumer (B-C) and business-to-business (B-B) customers, particularly since the latter segment has been more resilient to the U.S. recession than the former?

2. How can Ventus tap into telecommunications and other sectors that continue to grow despite the financial crisis? How can Ventus generate business from emerging companies and industries (e.g., smart mobile devices, social-networking space, health-care services)?

3. How can Ventus continue to grow its domestic business—particularly those concerns outside the PLDT group of companies? How can Ventus leverage its expertise in B-C and industry verticals where it has key competencies to serve domestic clients?

4. As new markets emerge and grow, such as the Hispanic market in the United States and multinationals in China, should the company focus on these markets and customer segments? If so, should Ventus build new facilities or acquire or partner with companies near the United States, such as in Mexico or Costa Rica?

Supporting Current Customers

Although Ventus's management has set its sights on addressing issues related to the future growth of the business, the company continues to have one eye keenly set on how it can help current customers weather the challenging global business environment. To this end, Ventus has worked closely with customers to cut costs, improve processes, and increase service-level requirements.

A major priority for Ventus is to further enhance its reputation as an employer of choice in the call-center industry and continue to attract and retain high-quality service representatives. The company has addressed this by locating new facilities in second- or third-tier locations in the Philippines; solidifying relations with colleges and universities in Manila and the provinces; and strengthening Ventus's human resource team. The company has also worked with a major customer to improve recruitment and job-performance standards while enhancing the total pay of successful customer-service representatives. This program has proven to be beneficial to customer-service attraction and retention.

If there is a silver lining to the global financial crisis and the resulting moderate growth in the BPO industry in the Philippines, it is that the slowdown has provided a needed pause for Ventus to implement its programs to attract and retain high-quality customer-service representatives. ∎

QUESTIONS

1. What factors explain the growth of the Philippine call-center industry in general and of ePLDT Ventus in particular? What current role(s) do business-process outsourcers—including call centers like Ventus—play in the global supply chain for services? What additional roles can these outsourcers play in the future?

2. What will be the best path for growth for Ventus? Evaluate the various options discussed in the case. What path would you recommend that Ventus take? Why?

3. How should Ventus address the emerging challenges that could potentially derail its growth? What other challenges are likely to emerge? How should Ventus deal with these additional challenges? It would be helpful to use the five-forces model discussed in Chapter 11 to analyze Ventus's strengths and weaknesses.

SUMMARY

- A company's supply chain encompasses the coordination of materials, information, and funds from the initial raw-materials supplier to the ultimate customer.

- Logistics, or materials management, is that part of the supply-chain process that plans, implements, and controls the efficient, effective flow and storage of goods, services, and related information from the point of origin to the point of consumption to meet customers' requirements.

- The success of a global manufacturing strategy depends on compatibility, configuration, coordination, and control.

- Cost-minimization strategies and the drive for global efficiencies often force MNEs offshore to low-cost manufacturing areas, especially in Asia and Eastern Europe.

- Three broad categories of manufacturing configuration are one centralized facility, regional facilities, and multidomestic facilities.

- The key to making a global supply-chain system work is information. Companies are rapidly turning to the Internet as a way to link suppliers with manufacturing and eventually with end-use customers.

- Quality is defined as meeting or exceeding the expectations of customers. Quality standards can be general level (ISO 9000), industry specific, or company specific (AQL, zero defects, TQM, and Six Sigma).

- Total quality management (TQM) is a process that stresses customer satisfaction, employee involvement, and continuous improvements in quality while aiming for zero defects.

- Global sourcing is the process of a firm having raw materials and parts supplied to it from domestic and foreign sources.

- Domestic sourcing allows the company to avoid problems related to language, culture, currency, tariffs, and so forth. Foreign sourcing allows the company to reduce costs and improve quality, among other things.

- Under the make-or-buy decision, companies have to decide if they will make their own parts or buy them from an independent company.

- Companies go through different purchasing phases as they become more committed to global sourcing.

- When a company sources parts from suppliers around the world, distance, time, and the uncertainty of the international political and economic environment can make it difficult for managers to manage inventory flows accurately.

- Lean manufacturing and just-in-time systems focus on reducing inefficiency and unproductive time in the production process to continuously improve the process and quality of the product or service.

- The transportation system links together suppliers with manufacturers and manufacturers with customers.

KEY TERMS

acceptable quality level (AQL) (p. 686)
e-commerce (p. 684)
electronic data interchange
  (EDI) (p. 683)
enterprise resource planning
  (ERP) (p. 683)
extranet (p. 685)
foreign trade zones (FTZs) (p. 699)
International Organization for
  Standardization (ISO) (p. 688)

intranet (p. 685)
logistics (or materials management)
  (p. 678)
offshore manufacturing (p. 679)
outsourcing (p. 691)
private technology exchange
  (PTX) (p. 685)
quality (p. 685)
Six Sigma (p. 688)

sourcing (p. 690)
supply chain (p. 678)
total quality management
  (TQM) (p. 687)
vertical integration (p. 692)
zero defects (p. 686)

ENDNOTES

1 *Sources include the following:* F. De Beule and D. Van Den Bulcke, "The International Supply Chain Management of Samsonite Europe," Discussion Paper No. 1998/E/34, Centre for International Management and Development, University of Antwerp (1998); "About Samsonite: History," at www.corporate.samsonite.com/samsonite/about/history (accessed October 15, 2009); "Company Briefing Book," *Wall Street Journal*, www.wsj.com (accessed January 27, 2000); *Samsonite Quarterly Report*, SEC Form 10-Q, 2002; "Samsonite to Be Sold," *New York Times* (July 6, 2007): C4; "Samsonite Fiscal Year 2007 Annual 10-K," Samsonite (January 31, 2007); "Samsonite Introduces POINT A Franchise Concept," *Samsonite: Life's a Journey*

(October 1, 2002), at www.samsonite.com/samsonite/?404=http://www.samsonite.com/global/globl_pressrelease_europ5.jsp; Helia Ebrahimi, "Samsonite Bags Debt-for-Equity Rescue Deal," *Sunday Telegraph* (May 31, 2009); Godfrey Deeny, "Y-3 Seals Luggage License with Samsonite," *Fashion Wire Daily* (May 7, 2009); Samsonite Corporation, *Hoover's Company Records,* 40046 (retrieved July 30, 2009), from *Entrepreneurship* (Document ID 168172041).

2 "The Fourth Annual Global Survey of Supply Chain Progress," Computer Sciences Corporation (CSC) and *Supply Chain Management Review* (2006); Darrell Rigby, "Management Tools 2005," *Bain & Company* (2005): 58.

3 Deloitte & Touche, "Energizing the Supply Chain," *The Review* (January 17, 2000): 1.

4 Stanley Fawcett, "Supply Chain Management: Competing through Integration," in Tom L. Beauchamp and Norman E. Bowie (eds.), *Ethical Theory and Business* (Upper Saddle River, NJ: Prentice Hall, 1993): 514.

5 Council of Supply Chain Management Professionals, "Supply Chain Management/Logistics Management Definitions" (2007), at www.cscmp.org/AboutCSCMP/Definitions/Definitions.asp (accessed August 28, 2007).

6 Kevin Reilly, "AMR Research Announces the 2007 Supply Chain Top 25," *AMR Research* (2007), at www.amrresearch.com/Content/View.asp?pmillid=20450 (accessed May 31, 2007).

7 Homin Chen and Tain-Jy Chen, "Network Linkages and Location Choice in Foreign Direct Investment," *Journal of International Business Studies* 29:3 (1998): 447.

8 For a discussion of firm-specific advantages, location-specific advantages, and internalization, see John H. Dunning, *International Production and the Multinational Enterprise* (London: Allen & Unwin, 1981); Peter Buckley and Mark Casson, *The Future of the Multinational Enterprise* (London: Macmillan Press, 1976); Peter Caves, "International Corporations: The Industrial Economics of Foreign Investment," *Economica* 56 (1971): 279–93.

9 Stanley E. Fawcett and Anthony S. Roath, "The Viability of Mexican Production Sharing: Assessing the Four Cs of Strategic Fit," *Urbana* 3:1 (1996): 29.

10 See S. C. Wheelwright, "Reflecting Corporate Strategy in Manufacturing Decisions," *Business Horizons* p. 21 (1978); S. C. Wheelwright, "Manufacturing Strategy: Defining the Missing Link," *Strategic Management Journal* 5 (1984): pp. 77–91; Frank DuBois, Brian Toyne, and Michael D. Oliff, "International Manufacturing Strategies of U.S. Multinationals: A Conceptual Framework Based on a Four-Industry Study," *Journal of International Business Studies* 24:2 (1993): 313–14; Robert H. Hayes, Steven C. Wheelwright, and Kim B. Clark, *Dynamic Manufacturing* (New York: Free Press, 1988), 10–11.

11 Karby Leggett and Peter Wonacott, "Surge in Exports from China Gives a Jolt to Global Industry," *Wall Street Journal,* www.wsj.com (accessed October 10, 2002).

12 Jim Hemerling, "China: Ready for the Next Sourcing Wave?" *Business Week* (April 4, 2007), 1.

13 See James P. Womack and Daniel T. Jones, "Lean Consumption: Locating for Lean Provision," *Harvard Business Review* (March 2005): 66–67.

14 Palu W. Beamish, "The High Cost of Cheap Chinese Labor," *Harvard Business Review* (June 2006): 23.

15 Yuka Hayashi, "Japan Adds Factories at Home," *Wall Street Journal* (June 12, 2007): A8.

16 Interview by author of Wall's Unilever personnel in Beijing, China (June 2006).

17 Jack Ewing, "Why Nokia Is Leaving Moto in the Dust," *Business Week* (July 19, 2007), at www.businessweek.com/globalbiz/content/jul2007/gb20070719_088898.htm (accessed November 9, 2007), 1.

18 Norihiko Shirouzu and Jathon Sapsford, "Heavy Load—For Toyota, a New Small Truck Carries Hopes for Topping GM," *Wall Street Journal* (May 12, 2005): A1.

19 Michael E. McGrath and Richard W. Hoole, "Manufacturing's New Economies of Scale," *Harvard Business Review* (May–June 1992): 94.

20 Fawcett and Roath, "The Viability of Mexican Production Sharing," 29.

21 Richard Karpinski, "Wal-Mart Mandates Secure, Internet-Based EDI for Suppliers," Internetweek.com (September 12, 2002), at www.internetweek.com/supplyChain/INW20020912S0011 (accessed October 1, 2002).

22 R. Sridharan and Shamni Pande, "Surviving Wal-Mart," *Business Today* (July 29, 2007): 166.

23 "You'll Never Walk Alone," in "Business and the Internet: A Survey," *The Economist* (June 26, 1999): 11–12.

24 Vlad Krotov and Iris Junglas, "RFID as a Disruptive Innovation," *Journal of Theoretical and Applied Electronic Commerce Research* 3:2 (August 2008): 44.

25 Scott McCartney, "A New Way to Prevent Lost Luggage," *Wall Street Journal* (February 27, 2007): D1.

26 Karpinski, "Wal-Mart Mandates Secure, Internet-Based EDI for Suppliers."

27 "Worldwide Internet Users Top 1 Billion in 2005," *Computer Industry Almanac Inc.* (January 4, 2006), at www.c-i-a.com/pr0106.htm (accessed November 9, 2007).

28 Check the Dell *Annual Report* for 2002 at www.dell.com (accessed April 20, 2002) and as updated in subsequent *Reports,* (accessed October 15, 2009). Go to "About Dell" at the bottom of the Web page, select "Investors," and search under "Year" to access annual reports.

29 "You'll Never Walk Alone," 17.

30 Jeremy Wagstaff, "Digital Deliverance; Asia's Technology Conundrum," *Asian Wall Street Journal* (July 27, 2007): W8.

31 Lee J. Krajewski and Larry P. Ritzman, *Operations Management: Strategy and Analysis,* 4th ed. (Reading, MA: Addison-Wesley, 1996): 141–42.

32 See "Detroit Is Cruising for Quality," *Business Week* (September 3, 2001), at www.businessweek.com/magazine/content/01_36/b3747098.htm (accessed November 9, 2007); Todd Zaun et al., "Auto Makers Get More Mileage from Low-Cost Plants Abroad," *Wall Street Journal* (July 31, 2002), www.wsj.com (accessed October 16, 2009).

33 J.D. Power & Associates Press Releases, "2009 Vehicle Dependability Study," at www.jdpower.com/autos/car-ratings (accessed July 30, 2009).

34 Hayes, Wheelwright, and Clark, *Dynamic Manufacturing,* 17.

35 S. Thomas Foster, *Managing Quality: Integrating the Supply Chain,* 3rd ed. (Upper Saddle River, NJ: Prentice Hall, 2007): 36–38.

36 Foster, *Managing Quality,* 70–90.

37 Krajewski and Ritzman, *Operations Management,* 140.

38 Krajewski and Ritzman, *Operations Management,* 156.

39 "Six Sigma Definition," at www.sixsigmasurvival.com/SixSigmaDefinition.html (accessed November 9, 2007).

40 Brian Hindo and Brian Grow, "Six Sigma: So Yesterday?" *Business Week* (June 11, 2007): 11.

41 Robert McClusky, "The Rise, Fall and Revival of Six Sigma Quality," *Quality Focus* 4:2 (2000): 6.

42 International Organization for Standardization, "ISO in Figures for the Year 2006" (December 31, 2006), at www.iso.org/iso/en/aboutiso/isoinfigures/January2007-p2.html (accessed July 31, 2007).

43 International Organization for Standardization, "What Makes ISO 9000 and ISO 14000 So Special," www.iso.org/iso/en/aboutiso/introduction/index.html#twentytwo (accessed July 31, 2007).

44 International Organization for Standardization, "ISO 9000 and ISO 14000," http://www.iso.org/iso/iso_catalogue/management_standards/iso_9000_iso_14000.htm (accessed July 30, 2009).

45 See Jonathan B. Levine, "Want EC Business? You Have Two Choices," *Business Week* (October 19, 1992): 58; International Organization for Standardization, "ISO 9000:2000" (2007), at www.iso.org/iso/catalogue_detail?csnumber=21823 (accessed November 9, 2007).

46 Foster, *Managing Quality.*

47 International Organization for Standardization, "ISO/TS 16949:2002," http://www.iso.org/iso/catalogue_detail?csnumber=36155 (accessed July 30, 2009).

48 Amy Schoenfeld, "A Multinational Loaf," *New York Times* (June 20, 2007), at www.nytimes.com/imagepages/2007/06/15/business/20070616_FOOD_GRAPHIC.html (accessed November 9, 2007).

49 Alexei Barrionuevo, "Globalization in Every Loaf," *New York Times* (June 16, 2007), at www.nytimes.com/2007/06/16/business/worldbusiness/16food.html?partner=rssnyt&emc=rss (accessed November 9, 2007).

50 Masaaki Kotabe and Glen S. Omura, "Sourcing Strategies of European and Japanese Multinationals: A Comparison," *Journal of International Business Studies* (Spring 1989): 120–22.

51 David Hannon, "Procter & Gamble Puts a New Spin on Global Chemicals Sourcing," *Purchasing* (February 15, 2007): 32C5.

52 Robert M. Monczka and Robert J. Trent, "Global Sourcing: A Development Approach," *International Journal of Purchasing and Materials Management* (Spring 1991): 3.

53 David Barboza, "Food-Safety Crackdown in China," *New York Times* (June 28, 2007): C1.

54 David Bardoza, "China Makes Arrest in Pet Food Case," *New York Times* (May 4, 2007): C2.

55 Chi-Chu Tschang, "How China's Farmers Spoiled the Milk," *Business Week* (October 13, 2008): 84.

56 Nicholas Zamiska and David Kesmodel, "Tainted Ginger's Long Trip from China to U.S. Stores," *Wall Street Journal* (November 19, 2007): A1.

57 Andrew Martin and Griff Palmer, "China Not Sole Source of Dubious Food," *New York Times* (July 12, 2007): C1.

58 R. D'Aveni and D. Ravenscraft, "Economies of Integration versus Bureaucracy Costs: Does Vertical Integration Improve Performance?" *Academy of Management Journal* 37:5 (1994): 1167–206; O. Williamson, "Vertical Integration and Related Variations on a Transaction-Cost Theme," in J. Stiglitz and G. Mathewson (eds.), *New Developments in the Analysis of Market Structure* (Cambridge, MA: MIT Press, 1986); O. Williamson, *The Economic Institutions of Capitalism* (New York: The Free Press, 1985).

59 Russell Johnston and Paul R. Lawrence, "Beyond Vertical Integration—The Rise of the Value-Adding Partnership," *Harvard Business Review* (July–August 1988): 98.

60 Chester Dawson, "A 'China Price' for Toyota," *Business Week* (February 21, 2005): 50–51.

61 John McMillan, "Managing Suppliers: Incentive Systems in Japanese and U.S. Industry," *California Management Review* (Summer 1990): 38.

62 Rigby, "Management Tools 2005."

63 "Still Made in Japan," Economist.com (April 7, 2004), at www.economist.com/printedition/displayStory. cfm?Story_id=2571689 (accessed November 9, 2007).

64 "Still Made in Japan," Economist.com.

65 Adapted from Pete Engardio and Bruce Einhorn, "Outsourcing Innovation," *Business Week* (March 21, 2005): 84–94.

66 Robert W. Lane, "Competing Globally, Winning Locally," speech to the Waterloo Chamber of Commerce, at www.deere.com/en_US/compinfo/speeches/2004/040819_lane.html (accessed August 19, 2004).

67 Joseph B. White, "Japanese Auto Makers Help Parts Suppliers Become More Efficient," *Wall Street Journal* (September 10, 1991): 1.

68 Gabriel Kahn, "Invisible Supplier Has Penney's Shirts All Buttoned Up," *Wall Street Journal* (September 11, 2003): A1.

69 Lee Hawkins Jr., "GM Is Pushing Its U.S. Suppliers to Reduce Prices," *Wall Street Journal* (April 7, 2005): A2.

70 Monczka and Trent, "Global Sourcing: A Development Approach," 4–5.

71 Stanley E. Fawcett, "The Globalization of the Supply Environment," *The Supply Environment* 2 (Tempe, AZ: NAPM, 2000).

72 "Electrolux Delivers Strong Results in a Very Tough Market," *National Post* (June 25, 2009): FP 9.

73 Monczka and Trent, "Worldwide Sourcing," 17–18.

74 Guy Anderson, "Nissan Gearing Up for a Partnership," *Wall Street Journal* (December 8, 2004): 42.

75 Foster, *Managing Quality,* 87.

76 Krajewski and Ritzman, *Operations Management,* 732.

77 Gabriel Kahn, Trish Saywell, and Quenna Sook Kim, "Backlog at West Coast Docks Keeps Christmas Toys at Sea," *Wall Street Journal* (October 21, 2002), www.wsj.com (accessed October 25, 2002).

78 Shawnee K. Vickery, "International Sourcing: Implications for Just-in-Time Manufacturing," *Production and Inventory Management Journal* (1989): 67.

79 International Trade Administration, "What Activity Is Permitted in Zones?" at http://ia.ita.doc.gov/ftzpage/index.html (accessed August 28, 2007).

80 Foreign-Trade Zones Board, "How Many Zones Exist Now?" under FAQ at http://ia.ita.doc.gov/ftzpage/info/zonestats.html (accessed October 15, 2009).

81 Foreign-Trade Zones Board, "What Are the Benefits to a Zone User," under FAQ at http://ia.ita.doc.gov/ftzpage/info/ftzstart.html (accessed October 15, 2009).

82 Panalpina, www.panalpina.com, various pages (accessed October 15, 2009).

83 Panalpina, "Transporting IBM Products to Latin America" (2005), www.panalpina.com/press/casestudies (accessed June 15, 2007).

84 Fawcett, "The Globalization of the Supply Environment," 11.

85 *Sources include the following:* The Business Processing Association/Philippines and presentations by Mitch Locsin, executive secretary, 2006/2007; A.T. Kearney, *Global Services Location Index,* 2005 and 2009; Trade Union Congress of the Philippines, "Philippines Climbs Up a Notch in Global Offshoring Survey" (May 20, 2009); James Hookway and Josephine Cuneta, "Philippine Call Centers Ring Up Business,"

Wall Street Journal (May 30, 2009), A14; Friedman, Billings, Ramsey & Co. Inc., Offshore Business Services Report, 2008. The information on ePLDT Ventus and Philippine Long Distance Telephone Company is from the author's personal interviews and company sources and references. Personal interviews with Manuel Pangilinan, Chairman, PLDT, January 2007; Ray Espinoza, ePLDT CEO, January 2007/January 2009; Helen Marquez, Ventus CEO, April and July 2009; Rose Montenegro, Ventus CEO (retired), January 2007; Albert Santos, Ventus Vice President, March 2009, January 2007. We would like to acknowledge Professor Manuel Serapio, Director of the Master of Science in International Business Program and Faculty Director of the Center for International Business Education and Research at the University of Colorado Denver, for writing the case.

eighteen

International Accounting Issues

Objectives

- To examine the major factors influencing the development of accounting practices in different countries

- To examine the global convergence of accounting standards

- To explain how companies account for foreign-currency transactions and translate foreign-currency financial statements

- To discuss different forms of performance evaluation of foreign operations and how foreign exchange can complicate the budget process

- To explain how arbitrary transfer pricing can complicate performance evaluation and control

- To introduce the balanced scorecard as an approach to evaluating performance

> *Even between parents and children, money matters make strangers.*
>
> —*Japanese proverb*

711

In January 2002, a European magazine published an article titled "Enron: Could It Happen Here?" At the time the article was published, perhaps most people outside the United States would have answered "no" to that question.[1] In the wake of massive corporate frauds at Enron and WorldCom, there was a feeling outside the United States that such scandals were "an American problem" caused by the more aggressive business environment and practices there. However, a family-owned Italian firm was about to show the world that massive corporate scandals can happen anywhere.

A BRIEF BACKGROUND CHECK

After Calisto Tanzi inherited his father's company at age 22, he directed it into the production of dairy products in 1961 and created the Parmalat brand in 1963. Parmalat was the first Italian manufacturer of branded milk. In 1966, using packaging technology from Tetra Pak, Parmalat created its signature product: milk pasteurized at ultra high temperatures (UHT), giving milk a shelf life of over six months. UHT milk provided Parmalat with a technological competitiveness in the milk industry, placing Parmalat ahead of its competition. In 1970, the law permitted the sale of whole milk in grocery stores, removing the limitation of specialty milk shops. Parmalat quickly became the dominant milk supplier of Italy.

The "Champion's Milk"

Parmalat became known as the "champion's milk" after sponsoring the Ski World Cup and world-champion Formula One race-car driver Nicki Lauda in the 1970s. The company moved into new markets with the production of cheese, butter, and a variety of desserts near the end of the decade. As it increased in popularity, Parmalat also began international expansion through acquisitions in Germany and France, which marked the beginning of a global dairy empire.

The Pious Pioneer Sports Marketer

Calisto Tanzi, an almost legendary figure in Italy, was the author of such growth. It was he who discovered the power of sports marketing to make Parmalat a famous brand. He had friends in important government positions who helped pass laws favoring Parmalat. A pious Catholic, Tanzi was a generous benefactor who sponsored the restoration of Parma's eleventh-century basilica and funded its professional soccer team. And he seemed modest about his achievements. He didn't smoke, drank little, and drove his own Lexus. Throughout Parmalat's expansion, Tanzi maintained a paternalistic approach to the business. "He would stand, for example, at the plant, spoon in hand, ready to taste the first sample each time a new yoghurt [flavor] was launched."

Going Public and Going Global

In 1989, the firm was acquired by a holding company and changed its name to Parmalat Finanziaria SpA. The milk giant showed healthy profits every year, and its balance sheet appeared strong, with large amounts of cash on hand. This allowed Parmalat to go public in Italy and raise capital in the United States and other countries by selling shares and issuing bonds. The company used this new capital to expand into Latin America, where it dominated the dairy markets in Brazil, Argentina, Venezuela, and several other countries.

By the early 1990s, Parmalat was popular not only among grocery shoppers, but investors and creditors deemed the firm a profitable business partner. Large international banks collected hefty fees by helping the company issue bonds, list stock in foreign markets, and raise capital to fund international acquisitions. As CFO Alberto Ferraris put it, "Outside my office, there was always a line of bankers, asking about new business." There was only one problem: The profits that Parmalat reported were only an illusion created by a set of accounting manipulations.

ACCOUNTING ISSUES

One of the most interesting aspects of Parmalat's case is the simplicity of its fraudulent accounting (which was not *quite* as simple as the scheme suggested in Figure 18.1). The purpose of the fraud was straightforward: to hide operating losses so as not to disappoint investors and creditors. The core of the scheme was double billing to Italian supermarkets and other retailers. By standard accounting procedures, every time product is shipped to a customer, a company records a receivable that it later expects to collect as cash. Because receivables count as sales revenue, Parmalat billed customers twice for each shipment, thus greatly enlarging its sales. The company used these inflated revenues as a means of securing loans from several international banks.

"Off-Balance-Sheet Financing"

By 1995, Parmalat was losing more than $300 million annually in Latin America alone. These continued operating losses

"Play around with these figures, Harry. I've given you the total I want them to add up to."

FIGURE 18.1 Top-Down Accounting

Source: www.businesscartoons.co.uk

caused company executives to search for more complex ways of masking the firm's true performance. Using a trick called "off-balance-sheet financing," executives set up three shell companies based in the Caribbean. These firms pretended to sell Parmalat products, and Parmalat would send them fake invoices and charge costs and fees to make the "sales" look legitimate. Then Parmalat would write out a credit note for the amount the subsidiaries supposedly owed it and take that to banks to raise money.

Off-balance-sheet financing was also used to hide debts. The company transferred over half of its liabilities to the books of small subsidiaries based in offshore tax havens such as the Cayman Islands. This allowed Parmalat to present a "healthy" balance sheet and a profitable income statement to investors and creditors by hiding large amounts of debt and overstating sales revenue. In 2002, Parmalat reported liabilities of close to $8 billion on its consolidated balance sheet. In reality, the company had roughly $14 billion in debt.

The Art of Milking Growth

Taking advantage of its image, Parmalat issued bonds in the United States and Europe, which were backed up by falsified assets, especially cash. "It was a reversal of logic," said the chief investigating magistrate after the scheme was discovered. Usually, companies take on debt to grow. But in Parmalat's case, "they had to grow to hide the debt." In other words, the company would obtain loans to pay off previous loans. Investigators report that without the accounting manipulations, the company would have reported operating losses every year between 1990 and 2003.

The circle of hiding operating losses by incurring increasingly larger amounts of debt eventually became hard to sustain. To perpetuate the fraud, Parmalat needed to continue incurring debt, paying interest on old debts with no real cash of its own and finding new ways to create false sales. Alberto Ferraris, who was appointed CFO in March 2003, mentioned that "he couldn't understand why the company was paying so much to service its debt; the interest payments seemed far higher than warranted for the €5.4 billion in debt on the books."

By the late 1990s, auditors in Argentina and Brazil raised several red flags that pointed to problems with Parmalat's accounting. In early December 2003, the company failed to make a €150 million bond payment. This puzzled those familiar with the company because, according to the 2002 financial statements, Parmalat had plenty of cash on hand.

The fraud became public on December 19, 2003, when Grant Thornton, the company's auditor, made a startling discovery. While auditing Bonlat, a fully owned subsidiary of Parmalat based in the Cayman

Islands, the auditors contacted Bank of America to confirm a letter held by Bonlat in which Bank of America allegedly certified that the company had €3.95 billion in cash. Bank of America responded that such an account didn't exist. This resulted in investigators swooping into Parmalat's headquarters to confiscate documents and computer hard drives, which uncovered the accounting tricks. On one computer hard drive, prosecutors found clues to the deception: They found "Account 999," which contained details of secret transactions amounting to more than €8 billion.

THE CONSEQUENCES

Parmalat filed for bankruptcy protection on December 24, 2003. CEO Calisto Tanzi resigned and was detained by Italian authorities three days later and sent to prison. He was subsequently confined to house arrest until September 27, 2004. Also accused of wrongdoing were Fausto Tonna, CFO during most of the period under investigation; Giovanni, Stefano, and Francesca Tanzi, brother, son, and daughter of Calisto Tanzi; and other key employees believed to have been involved in the scheme.

"If Convicted..."

Initially, it was thought that misstatements were created only to hide operating losses; however, prosecutors demonstrated that the Tanzi family financially benefited from the fraud. For example, Calisto Tanzi revealed that $638 million was moved to "a family-owned tourism business." In December 2008, Calisto was finally sentenced to 10 years in jail for market rigging. Others have served or are serving jail time, and Stefano, Calisto's son, is being tried in Switzerland on fraud and money-laundering charges.

Enrico Bondi was appointed by the government as CEO of Parmalat to direct recovery efforts. As part of his campaign, he has brought lawsuits against Grant Thornton and Deloitte, the auditors, for not performing the audit with proper care and not bringing their suspicions to the attention of management. Grant Thornton cut ties with its Italian practice after Parmalat's problems surfaced. In addition, Bondi is suing major international banks, such as Bank of America, Credit Suisse First Boston, Citigroup, and Deutsche Bank.

Lawsuits, Rounds I and II

The lawsuits accuse the banks of ignoring the fraud to obtain fees from doing business with Parmalat. As mentioned earlier, these banks were instrumental in helping the company raise capital to fund its international expansion. The banks and the auditors deny any wrongdoing and claim they were victims of the scheme. Citigroup Inc., UBS AG, Deutsche Bank AG, and Morgan Stanley will be involved in the Milan trial for "failing to have procedures that would have prevented crimes that contributed to" Parmalat's failure. As of mid-June 2007, Bondi has collected almost $900 million in settlements in Italy and the United States, but Parmalat lost its case against Citigroup and actually had to pay them damages.

Parmalat, in turn, has been sued by investors, banks, and other organizations. In the United States, the SEC filed a complaint against Parmalat on December 29, 2003, alleging that the company fraudulently raised money through bonds in the United States by overstating assets and understating liabilities. On July 30, 2004, Parmalat agreed to settle with the SEC without admitting or denying the claims. Parmalat won't be fined but has agreed to make changes to strengthen its board of directors and improve governance.

Restructuring

Besides the legal battles that have resulted from the fraud, Bondi's restructuring campaign calls for aggressive changes in Parmalat's organization. On March 29, 2004, the company announced it would narrow its focus in markets in Italy, Canada, Australia, South Africa, Spain, Portugal, Russia, and Romania and would pull out of other regions. However, in May 2007, "Parmalat . . . agreed to sell its Spanish assets to Lacteos Siglo XXI." Latin American countries "with strong and profitable positions," such as Colombia, Nicaragua, and Venezuela, would be retained. In addition, Parmalat would cut its workforce from 32,000 to less than 17,000, slash the number of brands from 120 to 30, and concentrate on "healthy lifestyle" products.

SO, WHAT'S THE BOTTOM LINE?

In Europe, the Parmalat scandal created deep concern among authorities. The European Commission suggested that it would like to strengthen auditing standards by insisting that member countries introduce accounting-oversight boards similar to those in the United States. Many organizations have proposed reforms to prevent another scandal of such magnitude. One of the areas of reform considered was more transparency in the bond market in Europe; in other words, bond-price disclosure. However, "the [European Commission] has indicated that it will allow traders to police themselves instead of requiring the same data about bonds as for stocks."

From an accounting perspective, Parmalat joined the ranks of other European companies by adopting International Financial Reporting Standards published by the International Accounting Standards Board and adopted by the European Commission for their consolidated financial statements. In addition, Parmalat's independent auditors are now global auditing firm PricewaterhouseCoopers. The hope is that these two moves will help convince investors that Parmalat is moving in the right direction on the accounting side. After the restructuring, Parmalat has risen from the ashes, is now listed again on the Milan stock exchange, and is Italy's biggest listed food company. At least it didn't suffer Enron's fate.

Plus a Little Corporate Misgovernance

However, even though these accounting moves were taken to help Parmalat recover, they are not enough. Although the fraud was perpetrated through a set of accounting tricks, several issues converged to allow such manipulations to happen. One of the clearest deficiencies at Parmalat was its corporate governance system. As a family-owned business, the company was tightly controlled by insiders, especially Calisto Tanzi, who held the positions of CEO and chairman of the board of directors.

Most of the other board members were family members or managers of Parmalat. This prevented the company from having a strong, independent voice to stop the actions taken by management. In addition, Italian law allowed Parmalat to have two auditors instead of one. Grant Thornton was the main auditor, but Deloitte audited some of the subsidiaries, including Bonlat, where the fraud was uncovered. This arrangement made it more difficult for the auditors to have one clear, coherent picture of Parmalat's financial condition. As noted, neither of these auditors is used by Parmalat now. Finally, and perhaps most importantly, management integrity failed. In the end, a manager determined to commit fraud will most likely succeed even in a very good governance system.

In the aftermath of Parmalat's fraud, investigators were left wondering how a few accounting numbers could fool so many people. One thing, however, was clear: Europe now had its very own Enron. **CRN**
Case Review Note

Introduction

International business managers cannot make good decisions without relevant and reliable information about accounting—one of the functional areas that is critical for the operations of the MNE. Although accounting and information systems specialists provide such information, managers must also understand which data they need and the problems specialists face in gathering the data from different accounting systems around the world.

THE CROSSROADS OF ACCOUNTING AND FINANCE

The accounting and finance functions are closely related. Each relies on the other to fulfill its own responsibilities. The chief financial officer (CFO) of any company is responsible for procuring and managing the company's financial resources. This individual is usually one of the members of the top management team of a company. The CFO relies on the controller, or chief accountant, to provide the right information for making decisions.

In addition, the internal audit staff ensures that corporate policies and procedures are followed. They and the CFO and controller work closely with the external auditor to try to safeguard the assets of the business. (As you can see from our opening case on the Parmalat scandal, however, things can go wrong, especially when topmost management is willing to shirk its fiduciary responsibility and the external auditor may see a different sort of value in the company's assets.)

The actual and potential flow of assets across national boundaries complicates the finance and accounting functions. The MNE must learn to cope with differing inflation rates, exchange-rate changes, currency controls, expropriation risks, customs duties, tax rates and methods of determining taxable income, levels of sophistication of local accounting personnel, and local as well as home-country reporting requirements.

What Does the Controller Control?   A company's controller collects and analyzes data for internal and external users. The overall objective of **accounting** is to provide information that management can use to make good decisions.

The role of the corporate controller has expanded beyond the traditional roles of management accounting. As Figure 18.2 indicates, the controller is part of the financial function of the firm. Some of the controller's typical responsibilities can be seen in Figure 18.2, although the exact duties and allocation among the finance staff, the controller, and the treasurer vary from company to company.

Today's controller is engaged in a variety of activities outside of the typical accounting and reporting functions that support the general strategy of the firm, such as managing the supply chain, evaluating potential acquisitions abroad, disposing of a subsidiary or a division, managing cash flow, hedging currency and interest-rate risks, tax planning, internal auditing, and helping in the planning of corporate strategy. Today's accountant must have a much broader perspective of business in general—and international business in particular for the purposes of this book—than was the case even as recently as a decade ago (see Figure 18.3).

As noted in Chapter 15 and elaborated on in this chapter, foreign managers and subsidiaries are usually evaluated at headquarters on the basis of data generated in the company's reporting system that is set up and coordinated by the controller's office. The controller generates reports for internal consideration, local government needs, creditors, employees, suppliers, stockholders, and prospective investors. The controller handles the impact of many different currencies and inflation rates on the statements and should be familiar with different countries' accounting systems.

This chapter discusses some key accounting issues facing companies that do business abroad. Initially, we examine how accounting differs around the world and how global capital markets are forcing countries to consider converging their accounting and reporting standards as we attempt to move to one set of globally accepted standards. Then we examine some unique issues facing MNEs, such as accounting for foreign-currency transactions, translating

The accountant is essential in providing information to financial decision makers.

The controller of an international company must be concerned about a range of issues dealing with corporate strategy broader than just accounting issues.

Concept Check

We discuss **foreign currency exchange rates** and the ways in which they affect the operations of an MNE in Chapter 9. Here we explain the responsibilities of the CFO in overseeing a company's closely related financial and **accounting** functions. As we'll see, financial management deals with the effects of exchange rates on such financial-statement items as *receivables* and *payables*.

FIGURE 18.2   What the Controller Controls

We have our controller reporting to either a VP of finance or a chief financial officer. Note that our controller's area of responsibility, like that of many contemporary controllers, is twofold: He or she oversees not only activities in accounting but those in financial management as well.

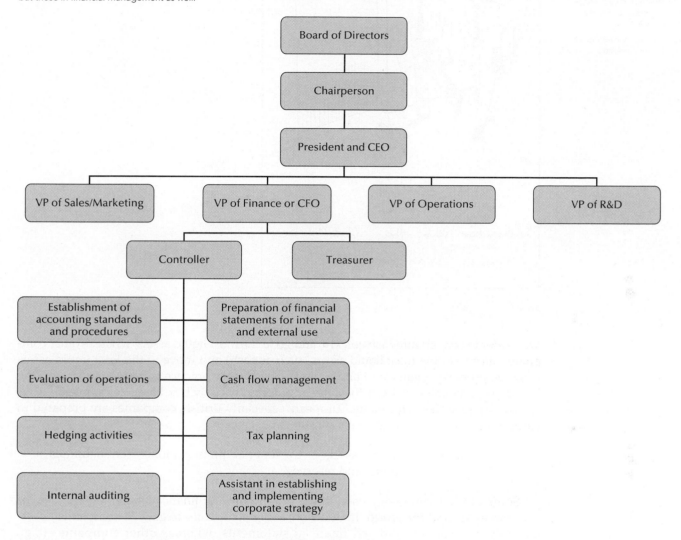

foreign-currency financial statements, reporting on foreign operations to shareholders and potential investors, and evaluating the performance of foreign operations and managers.

Although our focus is on problems of MNEs, many of these issues affect any company doing business overseas, even a small importer or exporter. Foreign-currency transactions, such as denominating a sale or purchase in a foreign currency, must be accounted for in the currency of the parent company, and this is true of both large and small firms, as well as service firms and manufacturing firms.

Accounting for International Differences

One problem an MNE faces is that accounting standards and practices vary around the world. Financial statements in different countries are different in both form (or format) and content (or substance). For example, the balance sheets for U.S. companies are in this format:

$$\text{Assets} = \text{Liabilities} + \text{Shareholders' equity}$$

This format is known as the *balance format*. The balance sheet varies in the order of liquidity of the accounts presented. Some companies start with the least liquid assets (those that

> Both the form and the content of financial statements are different in different countries.

FIGURE 18.3   Accountants Get a Little Semantic Respect

FYI: Properly defined, *haricotology* is "the science, doctrine, or theory of bean pods or seeds."

Source: Wall Street Journal. Reprinted by permission of Cartoon Features Syndicate.

are harder to convert into cash quickly) and go to the most liquid assets, whereas other companies start with the most liquid assets (such as cash) and move to the least liquid assets (such as property, plants, and equipment). The former practice is very common among European companies, whereas the latter approach is used by U.S.-based companies.

The balance sheets for many European, especially British, companies are prepared in a different form known as the analytical format:

$$\text{Fixed assets} + \text{Current assets} - \text{Current liabilities} - \text{Noncurrent liabilities}$$
$$= \text{Capital and reserves}$$

Some of the terminology used in the presentation of financial statements varies for companies around the world. In addition, some companies (e.g., U.S. companies) present only a set of consolidated financial statements, whereas other companies (e.g., European companies) present both parent company and group financial statements. Some observers argue that differences in format are a minor matter, a problem of form rather than substance. In fact, however, the substance also differs, because companies can measure assets and determine income differently in different countries.

ACCOUNTING OBJECTIVES

| The accounting process identifies, records, and interprets economic events.

It's important for the accounting process to identify, record, and interpret economic events. Every country needs to determine the objectives of the accounting system it has put into place. According to the **Financial Accounting Standards Board (FASB)**, the private-sector body that establishes accounting standards in the United States, financial reporting—the external reporting of accounting information—should provide information for three purposes:

| The Financial Accounting Standards Board (FASB) sets accounting standards in the United States.

- Investment and credit decisions
- Assessment of cash-flow prospects
- Evaluation of enterprise resources, claims to those resources, and changes in them[2]

| The International Accounting Standards Board (IASB) is an international private-sector organization that sets accounting standards.

Who Uses Accounting Information?   To establish objectives, managers have to identify the major users of financial information. The **International Accounting Standards Board (IASB)**,

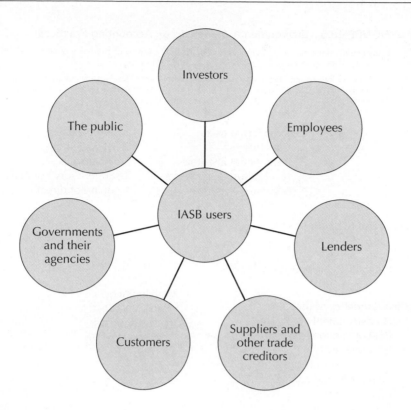

FIGURE 18.4 Who Uses Accounting Information?

Interestingly, key users differ from country to country. In Germany, the key readership of financial statements consists of bankers, who are interested primarily in asset valuation. In the United States, the key readership consists of investors, who want to know primarily how profitable a company is.

Source: Data from International Accounting Standards Committee Foundation, *A Guide through International Financial Reporting Standards (IFRSs®)* (London: IASCF, 2007): 15, paragraph 9.

an international charged with setting accounting standards that can be used worldwide, identifies the key users of accounting information represented in Figure 18.4.

It's important to identify users, because a focus on different users might result in different financial information being reported. For example, because Germany's major users have historically been banks, accounting has focused more on the balance sheet, which contains a description of the company's assets. In the United States, however, because the major users are investors, accounting has focused more on the income statement. Investors see the income statement as an indication of the future success of the company, which affects the company's stock price (or share price) and its flow of dividends.

There is no consensus on whether there should be a uniform set of accounting standards and practices for all classes of users worldwide, but the general movement toward the development of accounting standards and practices is focused on financial information for investors.

Critical users of accounting information are investors, employees, lenders, suppliers and other trade creditors, customers, governments and their agencies, and the public.

FACTORS IN INTERNATIONAL ACCOUNTING PRACTICES

In Figure 18.5, we identify some of the forces leading to the development of international accounting standards and practices. Although all of the factors shown in the figure are significant, their importance varies by country. For example, investors are influential in the United States and the United Kingdom, but creditors—primarily banks—have traditionally been more influential in Germany and Switzerland. Figure 18.5 is comprehensive, because it focuses on *all* elements of the accounting process: national and international influences, users, regulators, auditors, and educators.

Taxation has a big influence on accounting standards and practices in Japan and France, but it is less important in the United States. Cultural issues cut across all countries and strongly influence the development of accounting. Certain international factors also have weight, such as former colonial influence and foreign investment. For example, most countries that are current or former members of the British Commonwealth have accounting systems similar to the United Kingdom's. Former French colonies use the French model, and so forth. Thus companies from those countries use standards and practices that are similar to companies from other countries in the same group. As will be shown later, however, the convergence of accounting standards being led by the IASB will eventually reduce many of these differences.

Concept Check

In discussing "Legal Issues in International Business" in Chapter 3, we survey the various ways in which local legal standards can affect foreign firms in *operational concerns*—in the ways in which they function on a day-to-day basis. Naturally, these standards include **accounting** standards, and here we emphasize that attitudes toward—and, more importantly, regulations concerning—accounting practices vary widely from country to country. Remember, too, that although standard-setting bodies may be public or private organizations, policies such as those pertaining to **FASB** and **GAAP** are strongly influenced by local governments.

FIGURE 18.5 Environmental Influences on Accounting Practices

Every aspect of the accounting process is influenced by a variety of internal and external factors, and they're all potentially important. Degree of importance will vary by country.

Source: Lee H. Radebaugh, "Environmental Factors Influencing the Development of Accounting Objectives, Standards and Practices—The Peruvian Case," *The International Journal of Accounting* 10:3 (1975): 41. © 1975, Lee H. Radebaugh. Reprinted by permission of Elsevier Science.

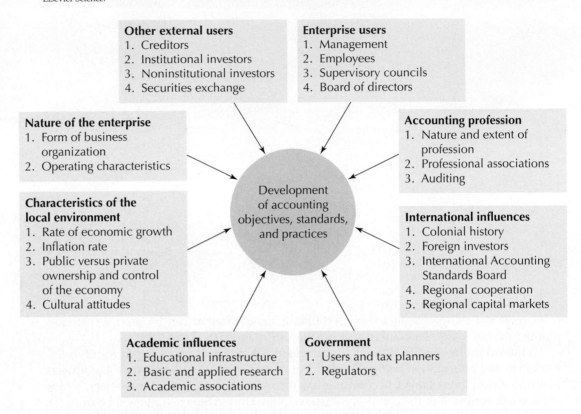

The international public accounting firms, such as KPMG, Deloitte, PricewaterhouseCoopers, and Ernst & Young, are also important sources of influence because they transfer high levels of auditing practices worldwide. As we observe in our opening case on the Parmalat matter, public accounting firms are also responsible for ensuring that proper accounting practices are followed and that publicly released financial statements accurately represent a firm's financial position.

The Emergence of Convergence   These differences in accounting influences have resulted in differences in accounting standards and practices. However, the major development in accounting worldwide is now the issue of **convergence**, which implies that, through negotiations between the IASB and national standards setters (such as the FASB in the United States), we are moving closer to having the *International Financial Reporting Standards (IFRS)* of the IASB as the one set of accounting standards that can be used in capital markets. Before understanding the issue of convergence, however, we need to understand the underlying differences among countries, and culture is a key force.

CULTURAL DIFFERENCES IN ACCOUNTING

A major source of influence on accounting standards and practices is culture. Of special interest to international investors are the differences in measurement and disclosure practices among countries—*measurement* meaning how companies value assets, including

Equity markets are an important source of influence on accounting in the United States and the United Kingdom. Banks are influential in Germany and Switzerland, and taxation is a major influence in Japan and France.

inventory and fixed assets, and *disclosure* meaning how and what information companies provide and discuss in their annual and interim reports for external users of financial data.

Much of the work on culture and accounting is initially based on Hofstede's research on the structural elements of culture, particularly those that most strongly affect behavior in the work situations of organizations and institutions.[3] Hofstede's work was then extended into the accounting area by Gray,[4] which resulted in classifying countries according to disclosure and measurement principles, specifically secrecy/transparency and optimism/conservatism.

The Secrecy–Transparency/Optimism–Conservatism Matrix   Figure 18.6 depicts the accounting practices of various groupings of countries within a matrix of the cultural values of secrecy–transparency and optimism–conservatism. With respect to accounting, secrecy and transparency indicate the degree to which companies disclose information to the public. Countries such as Germany, Switzerland, and Japan tend to have less disclosure (illustrating the cultural value of secrecy) than do the United States and the United Kingdom (Anglo-American countries, which are more transparent or open with respect to disclosure). By the same token, our opening case on the Parmalat scandal demonstrates that even companies that list on global exchanges, borrow money from the largest banks in the world, and turn their financial statements over to the best auditing firms in the world can have secretive corporate cultures.

Generally Accepted Accounting Principles   In addition, as companies from the upper-right quadrant of secrecy and conservatism utilize capital markets more extensively, they move closer to the Anglo-American mode. This is especially true of companies like Deutsche Bank and DaimlerChrysler, which adopted U.S. **Generally Accepted Accounting Principles (GAAP)** for reporting purposes, as allowed under German law, before moving to IFRS. As companies headquartered in the European Union and other countries throughout the world adopt International Financial Reporting Standards issued by the IASB, they should become more transparent and optimistic.

Optimism and conservatism (in an accounting, not a political, sense) are the degree of caution companies exhibit in valuing assets and recognizing income—an illustration of the measurement issues mentioned earlier. Countries more conservative from an accounting point of view tend to understate assets and income, whereas optimistic countries tend to be more liberal in their recognition of income. Banks primarily fund French companies, as they do in Germany and Japan, and banks are concerned with liquidity. So French companies

Concept Check

Chapter 2 is devoted to illustrating the many ways in which local culture shapes the environment in which international business is conducted from country to country. Here we point out that culture also affects differences in approaches to **accounting** systems and policies. In Chapter 2, we cite Geert Hofstede among the researchers who've studied national differences in managerial attitudes and preferences, and here we use applications of Hofstede's findings to studies of work-situation behavior as a means of shedding light on the effect of cultural differences on accounting standards and practices.

Case Review Note

Culture influences measurement and disclosure practices:

- Measurement—how to value assets.
- Disclosure—the presentation of information and discussion of results.

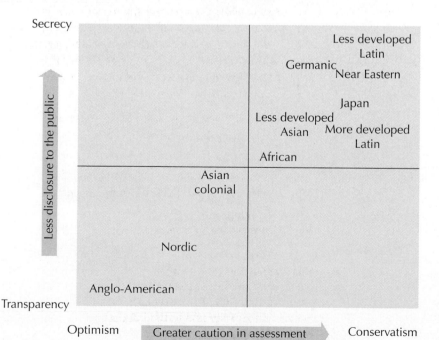

FIGURE 18.6   A Disclosure/Assessment Matrix for National Accounting Systems

The vertical axis reflects practices according to *transparency–secrecy* (the extent to which companies in a country disclose information to the public). The horizontal axis reflects practices according to *optimism–conservatism* (the degree of *caution* taken by companies when it comes to valuing assets and recognizing income). Note that, not surprisingly, transparency and optimism tend to go hand in hand, as do secrecy and conservatism.

Source: Lee H. Radebaugh and Sidney J. Gray, *International Accounting and Multinational Enterprises,* 5th ed. (New York: John Wiley & Sons, 2002). © 2002. Reprinted by permission of John Wiley & Sons.

Secrecy and transparency refer to the degree to which corporations disclose information to the public. Optimism and conservatism refer to the degree of caution companies display in valuing assets and recognizing income.

British companies are optimistic when recognizing income. U.S. companies are slightly less optimistic. Japanese and continental European companies are even less optimistic than U.S. companies.

Macro-uniform accounting systems are shaped more by government influence, whereas micro-based systems rely on pragmatic business practice.

tend to be very conservative both when recording profits that keep them from paying taxes and when declaring dividends to pile up cash reserves to service their bank debts.

In contrast, U.S. companies want to show earning power to impress and attract investors. British companies tend to be more optimistic in earnings recognition than U.S. companies, but U.S. companies are much more optimistic than continental European and Japanese companies.

CLASSIFYING ACCOUNTING SYSTEMS

Although accounting standards and practices differ significantly worldwide, we can still group systems used in various countries according to common characteristics. Figure 18.7 illustrates one approach to classifying accounting systems. It does not attempt to classify all countries, but it simply illustrates the concept using several developed Western countries. Although all major developed countries are moving to an accounting model that favors investors and thus is more similar to the micro-based countries at the bottom of Figure 18.7, understanding the macro tradition is essential for realizing how difficult it is to converge accounting standards from different parts of the world.

From Macro-Uniform to Micro-Based Systems   The creators of Figure 18.7 have used the concept of natural science to classify countries. As you move from left to right, you move from the general to the specific. Macro-uniform systems are shaped more by government influence than are micro-based systems. The major accounting influences on countries that fit into the macro-uniform category are a strong legal system—especially a codified legal

FIGURE 18.7   Development of Accounting Systems in the West

As a class, *macro-uniform accounting systems* have developed in countries with strong, codified legal systems. They're also shaped more heavily by government influences than are *micro-based accounting systems*, which, as a class, prevail in countries where accounting practices have developed in response to pragmatic business needs.

Source: From C. W. Nobes, "A Judgmental International Classification of Financial Reporting Practices," *Journal of Business Finance and Accounting* (Spring 1983). Reprinted by permission of Blackwell Publishing Ltd.

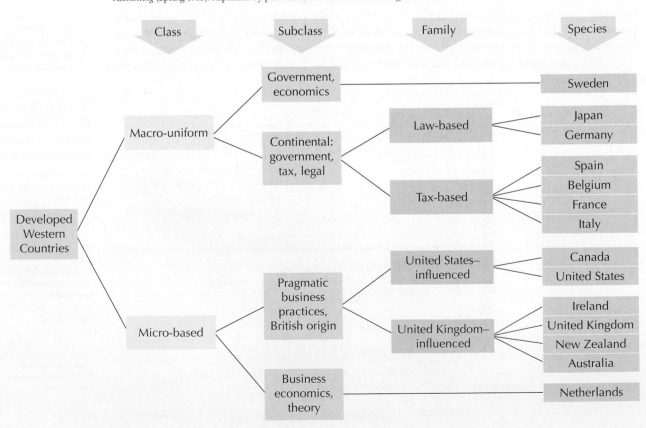

system rather than a common law system—and tax law. Tax law is the most important element, because tax authorities use the statutory financial statements prepared according to local accounting standards to determine tax liability. Thus accounting standards are tax-based, and it is required by law that they be followed. Unlike in the United States, statutory financial statements are based on individual entities, not consolidated entities. These systems also tend to be more conservative and secretive about disclosure. Japan and Germany are legal-based systems, and Spain and France are tax-based systems. The former Soviet-bloc countries and China would also fit in the macro category.

Note that Figure 18.7 identifies the traditions from which countries come, even though their measurement and disclosure practices are moving closer to the micro-based categories. These traditions are very much culturally and institutionally based and are slow to change.

Micro-based systems include features that support pragmatic business practice and have evolved from the British system. The United States is an example of a country that fits in the micro category. It exhibits more optimism and transparency than countries in the macro category, and it also relies less on legal and tax requirements than Germany, France, and Japan. The focus tends to be more on capital markets and less on banks and tax authorities. That is not to say that taxes are unimportant, but there is a separation in most cases between tax income and income provided to the capital markets.

Other countries that closely model the United States are Mexico and Canada, two members of NAFTA, although Mexico also comes from a strong legal and tax tradition inherited from its Spanish roots. The British model is also a micro-based model, but it relies even less on legal and tax influences than the United States. Current and former members of the British Commonwealth, such as the Bahamas, Australia, and New Zealand, also fit into this category.[5]

Strong versus Weak Equity Markets Another approach is to classify countries according to equity markets, as *strong versus weak equity markets* (see Figure 18.8).

> **Concept Check**
>
> In discussing "Regional Economic Integration" in Chapter 8, we observe that the momentum toward cooperation in such blocs as the EU and NAFTA has spilled over into areas of international business that lie beyond the originally targeted terrain of trade and tariffs. Here we cite developments in such areas as accounting **convergence**— especially in the case of the EU—as particularly good examples of this phenomenon.

FIGURE 18.8 Classifying Accounting Systems According to Equity Market Strength

An *equity market* is pretty much the same thing as a *stock market*—a marketplace in which *financial instruments* such as stocks and bonds are traded. An equity market is *strong* when companies can rely on equity instruments to increase their capital bases. This version of accounting-system schemes divides systems into two classes: those that have developed in nations where equity markets are strong and those that have developed in nations where equity markets are weak.

Source: Christopher Nobes and Robert Parker, *Comparative International Accounting*, 7th ed. (Harlow, England: FT Prentice Hall, 2002): 67.

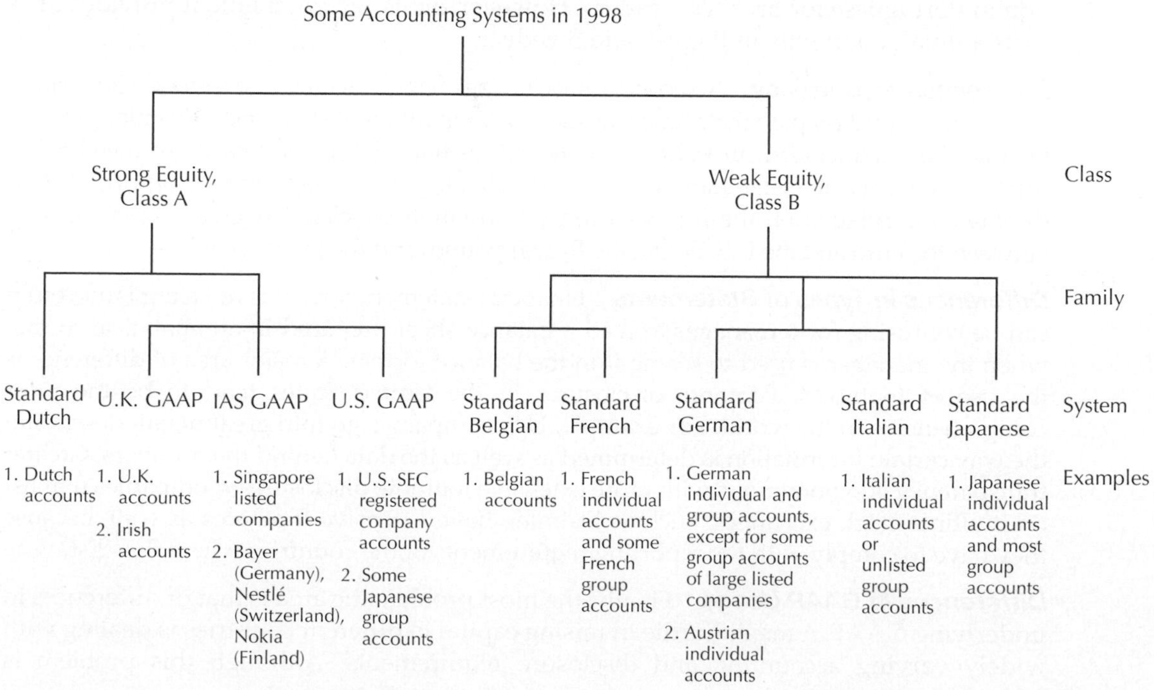

This incorporates changes that are taking place internationally, where some companies in countries such as Germany generate financial statements consistent with U.S. GAAP and IFRS.[6]

The shortcoming of both Figures 18.7 and 18.8 is that they do not include a large part of the world. However, companies from countries that have weak equity markets—true of most countries in Latin America, Asia, and Africa—tend to be more tax and legal oriented and fit in the weak equity part of Figure 18.8. Some companies from the developing countries list on a global stock market, such as the New York Stock Exchange, and they will be much more optimistic and transparent than if they had decided to stay in their local markets to raise capital.

Differences in Financial Statements   The bottom line is that MNEs need to adjust to different accounting systems around the world, thus making the accounting function more complex and costly. The financial statements of a company, for example, include not only the statements themselves but also the accompanying footnotes. Companies that list on stock exchanges usually provide an income statement, a balance sheet, a statement of stockholder equity, a cash-flow statement, and detailed footnotes as an important part of their annual report.

The financial statements of one country differ from those in another country in four major ways:

1. Language
2. Currency
3. Type of statements (including format and extent of footnote disclosure)
4. Underlying GAAP on which the financial statements are based

Differences in Language   As far as language goes, English tends to be the first choice of companies choosing to raise capital abroad. For example, German company Daimler issues financial statements in both German and English. Swedish telecommunications company Ericsson provides its annual reports in Swedish and English.

Many companies also provide a significant amount of information on their home pages on the Internet in different languages. Managers can just click on the desired language button, and all the information is provided in that language. For example, Ericsson has a home page full of information for people all over the world. The company even has a link, www.ericsson.com.br, which gives financial as well as general information in Portuguese for Brazilian readers. However, on its Brazilian link, it provides links to its annual report only in English and Swedish.

Differences in Currency   A second issue in classifying systems is currency. Companies around the world prepare their financial statements in different currencies. Daimler presents its financial statements in euros. Ericsson presents its financial statements in Swedish kronor. Intel presents its financial statements in U.S. dollars. In its 2008 annual report, Adidas discloses information on the firm's currency-translation policies and gives exchange rates between the euro and the U.S. dollar, the British pound, and the Japanese yen.[7]

Differences in Types of Statements   Financial-statement format is not a big issue, but it can be confusing for a manager to read a balance sheet prepared in an analytical format when the manager is used to seeing it in the balance format. A major area of difference is the use of footnotes. Footnote disclosures in the United States tend to be the most comprehensive in the world. For example, U.S. companies go into great detail, describing the way certain information is determined as well as the data behind the numbers. Greater transparency is synonymous with more extensive footnote disclosures. Companies that list on multiple stock exchanges, such as Daimler, have extensive footnotes as well, because they have to comply with the reporting requirements of the countries where they list.

Differences in GAAP Usage   Finally, the most problematic area is that of differences in underlying GAAP. A major hurdle in raising capital in different countries is dealing with widely varying accounting and disclosure requirements. Although this problem is

---

Countries can be distinguished between those with strong and weak equity-market and shareholder orientations.

Major reporting issues:
- *Language*
- *Currency*
- *Type of statements*
- *Financial statement format*
- *Extent of footnote disclosures*
- *Underlying GAAP on which the financial statements are based*

decreasing as more stock exchanges and countries allow the use of International Financial Reporting Standards, some countries care more about those differences than others. In addition, most countries may apply one set of accounting standards for consolidated groups, whereas they use another set for the individual companies in the group. For example, Adidas, the German company, has three distinct companies as part of its group—Adidas, Reebok, and TaylorMade. Consolidated financial statements would combine the results of all three companies into one set of consolidated financial statements. In this situation, individual companies in a group must use local accounting standards that are usually tied to legal requirements and are the basis for tax accounting. Consolidated financial statements, which are used for capital markets and not for tax purposes, are prepared by a different set of standards, such as IFRS. U.S. companies do not have the same situation. They disclose only consolidated financial statements, not individual company financial statements. There are some differences for tax accounting, but those differences are reconciled in the financial statements rather than as separate financial statements for each company in a group.

MUTUAL RECOGNITION VERSUS RECONCILIATION   Before the rise in importance of global capital markets, it was common for most countries to apply the principle of **mutual recognition**. That means that a regulator, such as the German stock exchange, would accept financial statements provided in the GAAP of a foreign issuer, such as U.S. GAAP by a U.S. company wanting to list securities in Germany. The U.S. uses two approaches: adoption of U.S. standards or reconciliation. Prior to the requirement in 2005 that EU companies provide financial statements prepared according to IFRS, some German companies such as Daimler and Deutsche Bank prepared their consolidated financial statements according to U.S. GAAP, as permitted at the time by German law. This made it easier for them to list on the New York Stock Exchange. However, German companies dropped this practice and moved to IFRS in 2007 (they were given a special exemption to delay implementation until 2007 rather than comply in 2005).

The second approach is reconciliation, where a company can list American Depositary Receipts on a U.S. exchange and then reconcile its home-country GAAP with U.S. GAAP in a special statement called Form 20-F on net income and shareholders' equity. This is the approach that Daimler used before it adopted U.S. GAAP for its consolidated financial statements. Since 2007, however, the SEC permits foreign issuers to list without a reconciliation statement as long as their financial statements are prepared in accordance with full IFRS. The EU was going to require U.S. firms that want to list on European exchanges to list in accordance with IFRS. However, the EU announced in 2008 that it would allow U.S. firms to continue to list on EU markets using U.S. GAAP, given the progress of convergence and the fact that U.S. GAAP and IFRS are essentially equivalent. In addition, the dropping by the SEC of the 20-F reconciliation for European firms using IFRS was a contributing factor.[8]

> Major approaches to dealing with accounting and reporting differences:
>
> - Mutual recognition
> - Reconciliation to local GAAP
> - Recasting of financial statements in terms of local GAAP

INTERNATIONAL STANDARDS AND GLOBAL CONVERGENCE

Historically, U.S. GAAP has been the international standard because of the size of the major capital markets in the United States and the need for companies in locations all over the world to list on these exchanges to raise capital. That forced foreign issuers to either adopt U.S. GAAP or reconcile their financial statements to U.S. GAAP on Form 20-F.

Despite the many differences in accounting standards and practices around the world, a number of forces are leading to convergence:

- A movement to provide information compatible with the needs of investors

- The global integration of capital markets, which means that investors have easier and faster access to investment opportunities around the world and, therefore, need financial information that is more comparable

> Convergence is the process of bringing different national Generally Accepted Accounting Principles (GAAP) into line with International Financial Reporting Standards (IFRS) issued by the IASB.

- The need of MNEs to raise capital outside their home-country capital markets while generating as few different financial statements as possible
- Regional political and economic harmonization, such as the efforts of the EU, which affect accounting as well as trade and investment issues
- Pressure from MNEs for more uniform standards to allow greater ease and reduced costs in general reporting in each country

The First Steps in Convergence   The International Accounting Standards Committee (IASC), the forerunner of the International Accounting Standards Board (IASB), was established in 1973 and began working toward harmonizing accounting standards by issuing a set of International Accounting Standards (IAS).

Its original standards had a strong capital-markets focus, which is to be expected because it wanted to issue standards that could be used worldwide to facilitate the free flow of capital. With such a goal, it tended to lean more toward the traditions of the United States and the United Kingdom, which were very capital-markets focused, rather than traditions in legal- and tax-based systems such as in Germany and France, where funding was more the domain of banks than broadly based capital markets. This engendered some hostility in other countries, where it was felt that the international standards were too much like U.S. standards. In addition, these were often very light, with too many options to capture the support of everyone.

The turning point in the significance of IAS came in 1995, when the **International Organization of Securities Commissions (IOSCO)** announced publicly it would endorse IAS if the IASC developed a set of core standards acceptable to it. IOSCO is significant because it is composed of the stock market regulators of most of the stock markets in the world, including the SEC in the United States. In May 2000, the IASC completed a core set of standards acceptable to IOSCO, and securities market regulators began the process of convincing their standards setters to adopt IFRS.

THE INTERNATIONAL ACCOUNTING STANDARDS BOARD

In March 2001, the IASC was reorganized into the International Accounting Standards Committee Foundation and the International Accounting Standards Board. The new IASCF is the parent entity of the IASB, which assumed the major standards-setting functions of the old IASC.[9] Figure 18.9 illustrates the new organization and shows how new standards are set.

Trustees for the IASC foundation search for and appoint members of the IASB. The trustees come from countries all over the world, although the developing countries had not been as represented as the developed countries earlier on. However, of the 22 trustees in place as of August 2009, four were from Brazil, India, China, and Poland. The trustees serve for three years.[10]

International Financial Reporting Standards (IFRS)   When the IASB was organized, all of the old International Accounting Standards from the IASC were adopted, and the board began to go through each standard to upgrade them. Then the board began to issue new standards, called **International Financial Reporting Standards (IFRS)**. Thus, when we use the term *IFRS*, we refer to the new standards as well as the old IAS.

According to the IASB itself, its objectives are fourfold:

(a) [T]o develop, in the public interest, a single set of high quality, understandable and enforceable global accounting standards that require high quality, transparent and comparable information in financial statements and other financial reporting to help participants in the world's capital markets and other users make economic decisions; (b) to promote the use and rigorous application of those standards; (c) in fulfilling the

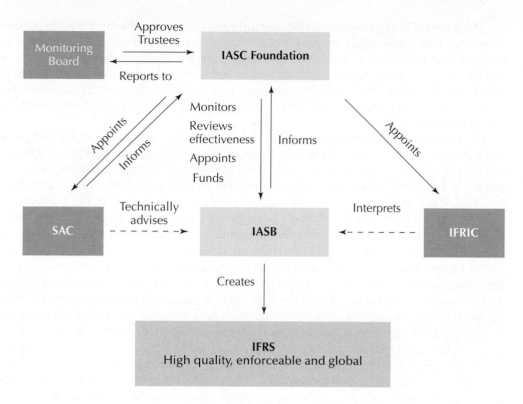

FIGURE 18.9
Organizational Structure of
the IASB

The IASB is an independent
standards-setting board appointed
and overseen by a geographically
and professionally diverse group of
trustees (IASC Foundation) who are
accountable to capital market
authorities (Monitoring Board) and
to public interest. The IASB is
supported by an external standards
advisory council (SAC) and an
interpretations committee (IFRIC) to
offer guidance where divergence in
practice occurs.

Source: http://www.iasplus.com

objectives associated with (a) and (b), to take account of, as appropriate, the special needs of small and medium-sized entities and emerging economies; and (d) to bring about convergence of national accounting standards and International Accounting Standards and International Financial Reporting Standards to high quality solutions.[11]

THE EU AND THE IASCF   Prior to the development of the IASB, the European Union was working to harmonize reporting practices to better coordinate financial markets. To enhance the harmonization process, the EU supported the efforts of the IASB. In the spring of 2002, the EU directed its member countries to adopt International Accounting Standards, as set forth by the IASB, by 2005. The reason for choosing the IASB is that the EU can influence IASB standards, because it is represented on the IASB and not the FASB, and the EU also avoids funding and developing a competing standards-setting body.[12] In addition to the decision by the EU, Australia and New Zealand made the decision at the same time to migrate to IFRS for all publicly listed companies (2005 for Australia and 2007 for New Zealand).

In the case of the EU, this meant that 7,000 publicly listed companies started using IFRS for their consolidated financial statements in 2005.[13]

> The EU and other countries have agreed to require IFRS for publicly listed companies.

THE RELATIONSHIP BETWEEN THE FASB AND THE IASB   In addition, the FASB and the IASB are to adopt a process to achieve a convergence of accounting standards. In the past, the FASB and the IASB have not exactly competed with each other, but they have maintained a professional distance. That is no longer the case. In 2002, the FASB and the IASB reached the Norwalk Agreement. In this agreement, the two boards pledged to use their best efforts to achieve several goals:

> FASB and IASB are trying to converge their standards through a variety of different activities.

1. "To make their existing financial reporting standards fully compatible as soon as is practicable; and

2. To coordinate their future work programmes to ensure that once achieved, compatibility is maintained."[14]

The process to convergence takes several forms. Initially, the two boards identified standards that could easily be converged. Now that the FASB and the IASB have joint projects to establish new standards, they are trying to eliminate existing differences in standards in a short-term convergence project for standards that should be easy to converge, and the FASB is explicitly considering the impact of IFRS on every standard it sets. Some standards are more complicated to converge, and they are part of a long-term convergence process.[15]

However, standard setting in the U.S. depends on the cooperation of the SEC, whose mission is to "protect investors, maintain fair, orderly, and efficient markets, and facilitate capital formation."[16] Although the SEC does not set accounting standards, it gives the power to the FASB to set the standards, because companies—both foreign and domestic—that want to raise capital in the United States must follow the SEC guidelines. As mentioned above, the SEC permitted foreign private issuers that follow IFRS to eliminate providing Form 20-F, which reconciled foreign GAAP to U.S. GAAP. In addition, it proposed the establishment of a Roadmap that could result in U.S. firms being allowed to list in the United States according to IFRS. In the proposal, which was *not* a rule, the SEC identified several milestones that had to be met, including improvements in IFRS and accountability and funding of the IASCF. In 2011, the SEC will meet to determine what to do next. However, the SEC did not identify a "date certain" for the adoption of IFRS. According to the proposed Roadmap, companies could be permitted to issue financial statements in the United States using IFRS as early as 2014 for the largest U.S. companies, followed by another group in 2015, and the final group of smaller companies by 2016.[17] The SEC also proposed a rule for certain U.S. companies meeting certain criteria to adopt IFRS in 2009. However, all of the above are proposals, and until the SEC issues a rule, the proposal has no weight of law.

THE EUROPEAN RESPONSE TO CONVERGENCE The main body of financial reporting requirements for limited liability companies in the EU consists of two directives issued by the European Council. Thus it is important to understand that IFRS and interpretations must be approved by the European Parliament and the European Council and adopted as an official regulation by the European Commission to have legal standing in the EU.[18] This illustrates the importance of the political process in the adoption of IFRS. The EU has adopted most IFRS as written, but they "carved out" or suspended the standard on financial instruments due largely to political pressure from French banks, which has been a problem. The fear is that the EU could end up with its own version of IFRS, resulting from political pressures rather than sound accounting judgment. The convergence process has been very unsettling to some Europeans, especially the French, because they feel the close cooperation of the two boards is making the new IFRS suspiciously similar to standards issued by the FASB. The fact that several Americans are on the IASB is further evidence to them that the board does not have a strong enough European presence and influence.

The IASCF issued a new constitution in 2008 that broadened representation on the board, but the Europeans would like to see the IASB have a distinctly European flavor, to establish standards that are more "European." This is another good example of how culture and tradition come into play, even though the standards are supposed to be for investors worldwide.

Initial reactions of various parties to the adoption of IFRS by European firms have been interesting. Although companies in EU countries adopted IFRS in 2005, various interpretations and applications of IFRS exist. Some companies use wide judgment in applying IFRS, and others use an adapted form of IFRS with changes or alternative interpretations based on individual country accounting treatments.

In addition, the EU's version of IFRS and the IASB's version of IFRS are different from each other. In our closing case, we'll examine the process by which Ericsson, a Swedish telecommunications company, has configured an EU version of IFRS as a means of responding to its particular needs in generating financial statements.

Full application of IFRS in various countries and under various regulatory regimes is difficult to judge. Not all countries require companies to adhere to all IFRS.

Case Review Note

Differences in opinion exist on how IFRS should be applied across borders, even within the European Union. As noted above, the Accounting Regulatory Committee of the European Commission must "recommend endorsement" of the new standards and interpretations, which must then be followed by an adoption of the new standards and interpretations by the European Commission itself.[19]

Concerns have also arisen as to how the new rules will be enforced. If companies disclose that their financial statements have been issued according to IFRS, it is up to the independent external auditors to verify that companies are complying with IFRS. That principle implies that the quality of the auditing profession is the same worldwide—a dubious assumption.

There are differences in Europe as to the relative power of government regulatory bodies and private sector approaches to setting accounting standards. France has the most restrictive/powerful regulatory government body. Differences in regulatory powers and structures may yield differences in the application of the accounting rules (IFRS). It will be interesting to observe just how IFRS are applied and enforced in countries where these standards have been adopted. Also, the adoption of IFRS in the EU is only applicable to companies that are publicly traded. Private companies must still use local GAAP, although the IASB issued a set of standards in 2009 for small- and medium-sized entities, or SMEs.[20]

> Enforcement of IFRS is a major concern.

CONVERGENCE AND MUTUAL RECOGNITION The move to convergence adds an interesting twist to mutual recognition. Today's version of mutual recognition in the United States is that foreign issuers are allowed to list securities using IFRS without reconciliation to U.S. GAAP. However, mutual recognition does not extend to companies that generate financial statements in their home-country GAAP. They are still required to issue Form 20-F. Recently, representatives of the SEC and the U.S. Treasury have made statements that support the mutual recognition of IFRS in the United States. The chairman of the SEC, Christopher Cox, on March 6, 2007, stated that "the Roadmap

> The SEC may soon allow U.S.-listed firms to report financial results using IFRS.

> ... commits us to eliminating the current U.S. GAAP reconciliation requirement, with the result that eligible firms listing on U.S. exchanges could choose whether to report under IFRS or U.S. GAAP. If an issuer chose IFRS, it would not be required to reconcile the differences with GAAP—just as today, issuers reporting under U.S. GAAP aren't required to reconcile the differences with IFRS.[21]

Added then–U.S. treasury secretary Henry M. Paulson:

> U.S. public markets should not be closed off to companies that adhere to high quality internationally accepted accounting standards. The Treasury Department is supportive of the SEC's action to eliminate the U.S. GAAP reconciliation requirement by 2009 [later moved up to 2007] of International Financial Reporting Standards reporting companies and the continued convergence of U.S. GAAP and IFRS.[22]

However, two things have changed the landscape for convergence. The first is the global economic crisis, which diverted attention away from convergence to trying to resolve the credit crisis and the global recession. The second is the election of U.S. president Barack Obama and the selection of a new SEC chairman, Mary Schapiro, who is less inclined to pursue the Roadmap to convergence than her predecessor. In fact, she stated the following in January 2009: "It's critical that these standards are converged in a way that does not kick off a race to the bottom. . . . It is not apparent that the IASB meets those criteria, and I'm not prepared to delegate standard-setting or oversight."[23] Who knows what will happen? As Danish physicist Niels Bohr noted, "prediction is very difficult, especially about the future."

Point ▶ ◀ Counterpoint

Should U.S. Companies Be Allowed to Close the GAAP?

Point **Yes** A major issue for investors around the world is obtaining reliable, comparable financial-statement information for company evaluation and comparison. Investors, as well as creditors and other users, need this information for making well-informed decisions on a global basis. As the business world has shifted from being composed of domestic economies to a global economy, the need for a single set of financial reporting standards has never been greater. In addition, over 100 countries have adopted IFRS, as illustrated on Map 18.1, and more are moving in that direction.

U.S. GAAP and IFRS are the two most recognized sets of standards today, and they are steadily becoming nearly identical to each other. The combined efforts of the IASB and the FASB in their convergence project have brought the gap between IFRS and U.S. GAAP closer than ever before. The SEC should allow foreign firms that list on U.S. exchanges, as well as U.S. firms, to use IFRS for financial reporting. Not only would allowing IFRS to be used by U.S. companies make the United States more a part of the global economy, but it would also allow U.S. firms to raise more capital, because investors in countries that use IFRS would be more familiar and able to keep up with the single international set of standards.

In addition, allowing U.S. companies to use IFRS would benefit U.S. investors: They would become more familiar with the international standards and would feel more apt to invest in international companies. As the gap between IFRS and U.S. GAAP is becoming increasingly small or immaterial, the quality of the financial information presented under IFRS will not be lower than it has been under GAAP.

The "principles-based" approach of IFRS may actually enhance the quality of financial information and help the economy avoid some of the scandals that have occurred due to manipulation of loopholes in the more "rules-based" system that is U.S. GAAP. Principles-based accounting means that the standards setters identify key principles in a conceptual framework used to set standards and then try to establish rules that are simple but conform to the key principles. A rules-based system is very legalistic, with lots of detail and difficulty. Finally, it is important for the U.S. to adopt IFRS, or it runs the risk of being left out of the debate for setting new standards. The rest of the world will be responsible for the development of new standards. ▶

Counterpoint **No** It is unrealistic to assume that IFRS would be appropriate for the unique U.S. economic environment. The U.S. economy is the largest in the world, with the largest and most sophisticated capital market, and thus should have the most stringent financial reporting standards in the world. Many companies around the world continue to prepare their financial information in accordance with U.S. GAAP, because it has historically been the most reliable set of standards in the world, designed to present information that is both relevant and reliable. There are over 25,000 pages of GAAP, compared with 2,500 of IFRS, so there is no way IFRS is as thorough, as broad, or as responsive to issues in the U.S. economy as are U.S. GAAP.

Allowing U.S. companies to use IFRS would impose tremendous costs on the U.S. economy. Publicly traded firms would need trained employees proficient in the application of IFRS. Accounting firms in the United States would be responsible for training their existing auditors in IFRS, hiring new employees and training them in IFRS, or hiring existing experts in IFRS. This training and/or hiring would impose tremendous burdens in both time and money on these important firms, which would still be held responsible for meeting all of the rigorous standards of the Public Company Accounting Oversight Board (PCAOB) and the Sarbanes-Oxley Act of 2002.

The difference between IFRS and U.S. GAAP, although growing more insignificant, still exists. The standards are not directly comparable. This possible lack of comparability between financial statements presented in accordance with IFRS and those presented in accordance with U.S. GAAP could mean trouble for investors, who may have difficulty seeing the difference between the two sets of standards.

In addition, more than one set of IFRS seems to exist: (1) IFRS as issued by the IASB, (2) IFRS as adopted by the EU, and (3) IFRS as applied/adopted on an individual-country basis. How will investors ascertain which set of IFRS are being used by various companies, and how will this information be comparable?

Further, valuable invested money may leave the United States and be invested in foreign corporations not even listed in the country as U.S. investors become more expert in analyzing financial statements prepared in accordance with IFRS. Finally, more accounting scandals could result when U.S. companies use the more "principles-based" IFRS instead of the more "rules-based" U.S. GAAP, because there is more room for interpretation and discretion when applying IFRS. ◀

MAP 18.1   IFRS Adoption as of April 2009: The Global Move toward IFRS

Over 100 countries have adopted IFRS. Note that the U.S. has not yet completely adopted IFRS.

Source: http://www.iasplus.com

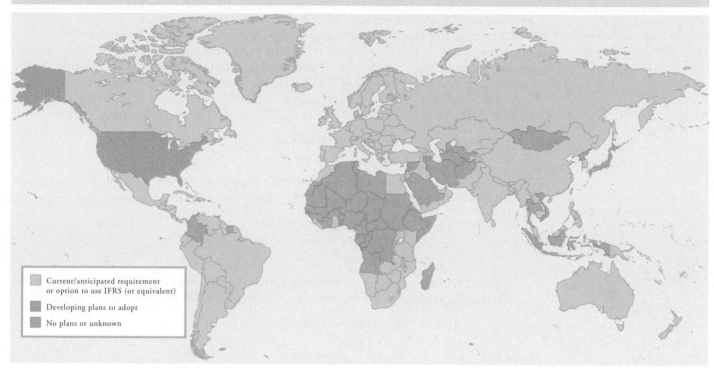

Current/anticipated requirement
or option to use IFRS (or equivalent)

Developing plans to adopt

No plans or unknown

Transactions in Foreign Currencies

When a company operates outside the domestic market, it must concern itself with the proper recording and subsequent accounting of assets, liabilities, revenues, and expenses that are measured or denominated in foreign currencies. These transactions can result from the purchase and sale of goods and services as well as the borrowing and lending of foreign currency.

RECORDING TRANSACTIONS

Any time an importer has to pay for equipment or merchandise in a foreign currency, it must trade its own currency for that of the exporter to make the payment. Assume that Sundance Ski Lodge, a U.S. company, imports skis from a French supplier for 5,000 euros when the exchange rate is $1.4500/euro and agrees to pay in euros. Sundance records the following in its books:

Purchases	7,250	
Accounts payable		7,250
€5,000 @ 1.4500		

If Sundance pays immediately, there's no problem. But what happens if the exporter extends 30 days' credit to Sundance? The original entry would be the same as the one here, but during the next 30 days, anything could happen. If the rate changed to $1.5000/euro by the time the payment was due, Sundance would record a final settlement as:

Accounts payable	7,250	
Foreign-exchange loss	250	
Cash		7,500

The merchandise stays at the original value of $7,250, but there is a difference between the dollar value of the account payable to the exporter ($7,250) and the actual number of dollars the importer must come up with to purchase the euros to pay the exporter ($7,500). The difference between the two accounts ($250) is the loss on foreign exchange and is always recognized in the income statement.

The company that denominates the sale or purchase in the foreign currency (the importer in the current case) must recognize the gains and losses arising from foreign-currency transactions at the end of each accounting period—usually quarterly. In the example here, assume that the end of the quarter has arrived and Sundance has still not paid the French exporter. The skis continue to be valued at $7,250, but the payable has to be updated to the new exchange rate of $1.5000/euro. The journal entry would be:

Foreign-exchange loss	250	
Accounts payable		250

The payable would now be worth $7,500. If settlement was made in the month following the end of the quarter and the exchange rate remained the same, the final entry would be:

Accounts payable	7,500	
Cash		7,500

If the U.S. company were an exporter and anticipated receiving foreign currency, the corresponding entries (using the same information as in the example here) would be:

Accounts receivable	7,250	
Sales		7,250
Cash	7,500	
Foreign-exchange gain		250
Accounts receivable		7,250

In this case, a gain results because the company received more cash than if it had collected its money immediately.

CORRECT PROCEDURES FOR U.S. COMPANIES

The procedures that U.S. companies must follow to account for foreign-currency transactions are found in Financial Accounting Standards Board Statement No. 52, "Foreign Currency Translation." Statement No. 52 requires companies to record the initial transaction at the spot exchange rate in effect on the transaction date and to record receivables and payables on subsequent balance-sheet dates at the spot exchange rate on those dates. Any foreign-exchange gains and losses that arise from carrying receivables or payables during a period in which the exchange rate changes are taken directly to the income statement.[24] This is basically the same procedure required by the IASB as well as in IAS 21.

Translating Foreign-Currency Financial Statements

Even though U.S.-based MNEs receive reports originally developed in a variety of different currencies, they eventually must end up with one set of financial statements in U.S. dollars to help management and investors understand their worldwide activities in a common currency. The process of restating foreign-currency financial statements into U.S. dollars is called **translation**. The combination of all of these translated financial statements into one is **consolidation**. The same concept exists for other countries, such as a British-based MNE that has to come up with a set of financial statements in British pounds. For the sake of illustration, we use a U.S.-based MNE.

Translation in the United States is a two-step process:

1. *Companies recast foreign-currency financial statements into statements consistent with U.S. GAAP.* This occurs because a U.S. company with a subsidiary in Brazil, for example, must keep the books and records in Brazil according to Brazilian GAAP. For consolidation purposes, however, the resulting financial statements have to be issued according to U.S. GAAP in format as well as content. As an example of content, Brazil might require that inventories be valued a certain way. For the U.S. consolidated financial statements, however, inventories must be valued according to U.S., not Brazilian, standards.

2. *Companies translate all foreign-currency amounts into U.S. dollars.* FASB Statement No. 52 describes how companies must translate their foreign-currency financial statements into dollars. All U.S. companies, as well as foreign companies that list on a U.S. exchange, must use Statement No. 52.

> Consolidation—the process of combining the translated financial statements of a parent and its subsidiaries into one set of financial statements.

TRANSLATION METHODS

Statement No. 52 and IAS 21, the relevant translation standards issued by the FASB and the IASB, respectively, are basically the same in how they require MNEs to translate their foreign-currency financial statements into the currency of the parent's country. For simplicity's sake, we continue to use the example of a U.S.-based MNE that must translate its foreign-currency financial statements into dollars. As noted earlier, the same would be true of a British MNE that must translate foreign-currency financial statements into British pounds. In the first case, the U.S.-based MNE would use FASB No. Statement 52, and in the second case, the British-based MNE would use IAS 21. The two standards yield the same result.

Two Methods: Current-Rate and Temporal Methods Both standards allow companies to use either of two methods in the translation process: the **current-rate method** (called the *closing rate method* by the IASB) or the **temporal method**. The method the company chooses depends on the **functional currency** of the foreign operation, which is the currency of the primary economic environment in which that entity operates. Whichever method a company uses, it has to determine the proper exchange rate to translate the foreign-currency balances into U.S. dollars.

> The functional currency is the currency of the primary economic environment in which the entity operates.

◀ A group of visitors looks toward the main floor where stock traders negotiate in the iBovespa future index pit as an electronic board below them shows the value of the real, the Brazilian currency. The real opened on the spot market at 1.97800 real per U.S. dollar at the Mercantile and Futures Exchange (BM&F) in São Paulo, Brazil, on May 29, 2009. The Brazilian government announced that it planned to tax foreign investors in order to keep the real below 2.00 per dollar. This makes it difficult for foreign companies to know if market forces or government intervention will set future rates used to translate their financial statements.

Source: Mauricio Lima/Getty Images, Inc.

FIGURE 18.10 Selecting a Translation Method

When an MNE receives reports from subsidiaries or branches located in different countries, the accounting department is faced with financial figures stated in different currencies. Accountants must *translate* these foreign-currency figures into amounts stated in the currency of the parent's home country. The *functional currency* may be either the currency of the economic environment in which the subsidiary or branch operates or the parent firm's currency, and the choice of functional currency will determine the *translation method* that the company will use.

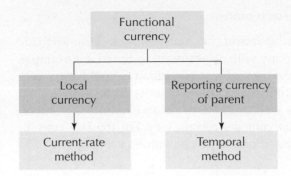

For example, one of Coca-Cola's largest operations outside the United States is in Japan. The primary economic environment of the Japanese subsidiary is Japan, and the functional currency is the Japanese yen. The FASB identifies several factors that can help management determine the functional currency. Among the major factors are cash flows, sales prices, sales market data, expenses, financing, and transactions with other entities within the corporate group. For example, if the cash flows and expenses are primarily in the foreign operation's currency, that is the functional currency. If they are in the parent's currency, that is the functional currency.

| The current-rate method applies when the local currency is the functional currency.

If the functional currency is that of the local operating environment, the company must use the current-rate method. The current-rate method provides that companies translate all assets and liabilities at the current exchange rate, which is the spot exchange rate on the balance-sheet date. All income-statement items are translated at the average exchange rate, and owners' equity is translated at the rates in effect when the company issued capital stock and accumulated retained earnings.

| The temporal method applies when the parent's reporting currency is the functional currency.

If the functional currency is the parent's currency, the MNE must use the temporal method. The temporal method provides that only monetary assets (cash, marketable securities, and receivables) and liabilities are translated at the current exchange rate. The company translates inventory and property, plants, and equipment at the historical exchange rates (or the transaction rate according to IASB terminology), the exchange rates in effect when the assets were acquired. In general, the company translates most income-statement accounts at the average exchange rate, but it translates cost of goods sold and depreciation expense, as well as owners' equity, at the appropriate historical exchange rates.

Because companies can choose the translation method—current-rate or temporal method—that's most appropriate for a particular foreign subsidiary, they don't have to use one or the other for all subsidiaries. Coca-Cola operates in over 200 countries and uses 70 different functional currencies.[25] This practice is typical of many MNEs.

Figure 18.10 summarizes the selection of translation method, depending on the choice of functional currency. As in the preceding explanation, if the functional currency is the currency of the country where the foreign subsidiary is located, the current-rate method applies. If the functional currency is the reporting currency of the parent company, the temporal method applies.

The Translation Process Tables 18.1 and 18.2 show a balance sheet and income statement developed under both approaches, to compare the differences in translation methodologies. The beginning balance in retained earnings for both methods is assumed to be $40,000. If the functional currency is the parent currency, the company uses the temporal method; if it is the local currency, the company uses the current-rate method. The following exchange rates are used to perform the translation process in Tables 18.1 and 18.2.

- $1.5000—Historical exchange rate when fixed assets were acquired and capital stock was issued
- $1.6980—Current exchange rate on December 31, 2009

- $1.5617—Average exchange rate during 2009
- $1.5606—Exchange rate during which the ending inventory was acquired
- $1.5600—Historical exchange rate for cost of goods sold

Because the foreign currency was rising in value (strengthening) between the time when the capital stock was issued ($1.500) and the end of the year ($1.6980), the balance sheet reflects a positive accumulated translation adjustment under the current-rate method. This is consistent with the idea that net assets were gaining value in a strong currency.

Note that under the temporal method, the ending retained earnings balance of $68,652 in Table 18.1 is found by subtracting the translated values of accounts payable, long-term debt, and capital stock from total assets. In Table 18.2, net income is found by subtracting the beginning retained earnings balance ($40,000) from the ending retained earnings balance ($68,652). When translating the income-statement accounts in Table 18.2, however, it is necessary to plug in the translation loss of $9,633 to get the net-income figure of $28,652. In the case of the current-rate method, net income is found in Table 18.2 by subtracting translated expenses from revenues. There is no translation gain or loss on the income statement, as will be explained below. On the balance sheet in Table 18.1, the retained earnings balance of $77,841 is found by adding net income ($37,481) to the beginning retained earnings balance ($40,000). However, total assets must equal total liabilities and owners' equity, so the accumulated translation adjustment of $12,507 must be plugged in to get the right total balance.

> With the current-rate method, the translation gain or loss is recognized in comprehensive income rather than net income, and therefore it goes to owners' equity. With the temporal method, the translation gain or loss is recognized on the income statement.

Disclosing Foreign-Exchange Gains and Losses A major difference between the two translation methods is in the recognition of foreign-exchange gains and losses. Under the current-rate method, the gain or loss is called an *accumulated translation adjustment* and is taken to comprehensive income rather than net income, so it appears as a separate line item in owners' equity. This is important, because the accumulated translation adjustment does not affect earnings per share, a key figure that financial analysts monitor. From a cultural perspective, this points out how important net income is to U.S.-based companies, which rely on the stock market as a major source of funding.

TABLE 18.1 Translating Foreign Currency: The Balance Sheet

	Foreign Currency	Temporal Method Rate	Temporal Method Dollars	Current-Rate Method Rate	Current-Rate Method Dollars
Cash	20,000	1.6980	33,960	1.6980	33,960
Accounts receivable	40,000	1.6980	67,920	1.6980	67,920
Inventories	40,000	1.5606	62,424	1.6980	67,920
Fixed assets	100,000	1.5000	150,000	1.6980	169,800
Accumulated depreciation	(20,000)	1.5000	(30,000)	1.6980	(33,960)
Total Assets	**180,000**		**284,304**		**305,960**
Accounts payable	30,000	1.6980	50,940	1.6980	50,940
Long-term debt	44,000	1.6980	74,712	1.6980	74,712
Capital stock	60,000	1.5000	90,000	1.5000	90,000
Retained earnings	46,000	*	68,652	*	77,481
Accumulated translation adjustment					12,507
Total Liabilities and Owners' Equity	**180,000**		**284,304**		**305,640**

*Retained earnings is the U.S. dollar equivalent of all income earned in prior years retained in the business rather than distributed to shareholders plus this year's income. There is no single exchange rate used to translate retained earnings into dollars.

TABLE 18.2   Translating Foreign Currency: The Income Statement

	Foreign Currency	Temporal Method Rate	Temporal Method Dollars	Current-Rate Method Rate	Current-Rate Method Dollars
Sales	230,000	1.5617	359,191	1.5617	359,191
Expenses:					
Cost of goods sold	(110,000)	1.5600	(171,600)	1.5617	(171,787)
Depreciation	(10,000)	1.5000	(15,000)	1.5617	(15,617)
Other	(80,000)	1.5617	(124,936)	1.5617	(124,936)
Taxes	(6,000)	1.5617	(9,370)	1.5617	(9,370)
Translation gain (loss)	24,000		(9,633)		
Net Income	**24,000**		**28,652**		**37,481**

Under the temporal method, the gain or loss is taken directly to net income and thus affects earnings per share.

Management Accounting Issues

In the prior sections of the chapter, we discuss some important financial accounting issues that relate to preparing financial statements for external users, especially the stock markets. Now we turn to some important management accounting issues that MNEs must deal with, including *performance evaluation and control*, the *impact of transfer pricing on performance evaluation*, and the use of the *balanced scorecard* as a means of broadly evaluating performance.

PERFORMANCE EVALUATION AND CONTROL

Different measures are used to evaluate performance of foreign operations, including ROI, sales, cost reduction, quality targets, market share, profitability, and budget to actual.

In Chapter 15, we discuss the importance of using reports as a part of the control mechanism. The setting of strategic objectives usually requires managers to focus on choosing a suitable numeric target. Objectives can be quantified in terms of a particular budget number or financial ratio, and they seem to vary considerably from country to country. Possible targets include return on investment, sales, cost reduction, quality targets, market share, profitability, and budget to actual. There may also be environmental targets that companies are trying to reach, especially given that many companies must meet Kyoto Protocol goals for reducing greenhouse gas emissions.

The choice of target depends on the company, the home country, and the strategic intent—global versus multidomestic, sales versus cost minimization, and so forth. Sales or market share is particularly relevant for a unit that has no control over its input costs and whose primary purpose is to sell the goods of some other unit. Profitability, measured as a ratio or some other measure, is most appropriate for a fully fledged strategic business unit.

U.S.-based MNEs are more likely to use return on investment (ROI) as the most important measure of performance.[26] In a study of British MNEs, companies tended to use budget versus actual comparisons, followed by some form of ROI.[27] In a study of Japanese MNEs, where the culture is significantly different from what is found in the United States and the United Kingdom, it was found that sales were the most important criterion for performance evaluation.[28] As you can see, there are some major differences in selecting performance-evaluation tools, and most MNEs use a variety of measures, not just one.

Performance Evaluation in the Budgeting Process   A complicating factor for MNEs is setting targets or budgets in different currencies. Either the budget will be set at headquarters in dollars (for a U.S.-based MNE) and then translated into local currency, or it will be set at the foreign location in the local currency and then translated into dollars for use at headquarters. Either way, the MNE must deal with currency in the budgeting process.

There are many different ways that firms can translate the budget from the local currency into the parent currency and then monitor actual performance.[29] Three different exchange rates are used in Table 18.3:

1. The actual exchange rate in effect when the budget was established
2. The rate that was projected at the time the budget was established in the local currency
3. The actual exchange rate in effect when the budgeted period takes place

The attractiveness of the first exchange rate is that it is an objective spot rate that actually exists on a given day. It is a reasonable rate to use in a stable environment, but it may be meaningless in an unstable foreign-exchange environment. The projected rate is an attempt on the part of management to forecast what it thinks the exchange rate will be for the budgeted time period. For example, management might project in November 2010 that the exchange rate between the U.S. dollar and the British pound will be $1.680000 during the first six months of 2011, so that would be the projected exchange rate used in the budgeting process. The actual exchange rate found in cell E-3 is an update of the exchange rate that was in effect when the budget was established. It provides the actual exchange rate in effect when the time period takes place.

These three exchange rates need to be considered for the establishment of the budget as well as the monitoring of performance. In cells A-1, P-2, and E-3, the exchange rate used to establish the budget and monitor performance is the same, so any variances will be due to price and volume, not the exchange rate. The value of P-2 over A-1 and E-3 is that it forces management to think initially of what its performance will be if the forecast is reasonably accurate. A-1 never takes into account what the exchange rate will be, and it does not attempt to reconcile the difference in the budget comparing the original rate with the actual rate. Given the instability in exchange rates, however, some would argue that a forecast exchange rate is no more accurate than any other exchange rate. E-3 does take into consideration what performance is at the actual exchange rate, but it does not force management to be forward thinking during the budget process.

Concept Check

We introduce four "Types of Strategy," including **multidomestic** and **global,** in Chapter 11, explaining that MNEs develop **strategies** by analyzing international markets for growth opportunities, cost reductions, and risk diversification while trying to balance the competing demands of **global integration** and **local responsiveness.** Here we point out that, not surprisingly, *performance evaluation* targets must be consistent with a type of strategy. A firm with a *global strategy,* for example, works to maximize *integration,* centralizes the budgeting process, and probably targets *cost minimization* as one measure of performance.

When using a budget, management must select a currency to set the budget and a currency to evaluate performance.

TABLE 18.3   Exchange Rates and the Budget

The rows identify what exchange rate is used to set the budget. A1 is the actual rate when the budget is set, P1 is a rate projected by management for the period of the budget, and E1 will start off being the same as A1, but with each successive reporting period, it will be updated to reflect the new actual exchange rate. The columns represent the exchange rates used to compare with the initial rates used to establish the budget. Those rates could be the same as when the budget was first established, a projected exchange rate, or the actual exchange rate at the end of the period. Exchange-rate variances occur when a different rate is used to translate final results than was used to establish the initial budget.

Rate Used to Determine Budget	Actual Rate at Time of Budget	Projected Rate at Time of Budget	Actual Rate at End of Period
Actual Rate at Time of Budget	A-1	A-2	A-3
Projected Rate at Time of Budget	P-1	P-2	P-3
Actual Rate at Time of Period End (through updating)	E-1	E-2	E-3

Source: Donald R. Lessard and Peter Lorange, "Currency Changes and Management Control: Resolving the Centralization/Decentralization Dilemma," *Accounting Review* 52 (July 1977): 630.

A-3 and P-3 result in a variance that is a function of operating results and exchange-rate changes. Under A-3, the budget is established at the initial exchange rate, but actual performance is translated at the actual exchange rate. Thus there is an exchange-rate variance that is the difference between the original and the actual rates. P-3 results in a variance that is the difference between what management thought the exchange-rate would be and what it actually was at the end of the operating period. If management's forecast was reasonably accurate, P-3 should result in a very small foreign-exchange variance.

If the exchange rate between the parent and local currency is relatively stable, A-3 should also result in a relatively small foreign-exchange variance. However, it is important to realize that the use of A-3 and P-3 means that someone (usually local management) will be held accountable for exchange-rate variances.

Forecast Rates   As you can see in Table 18.4, the most widely used approaches for taking into consideration foreign exchange when comparing budget with actual performance for a sample of British MNEs are A-1, P-2, and P-3. The use of a *forecast rate* for setting budgets is by far the preferred approach. A forecast is usually made by the economists in the corporate treasury or in consultation with banks.

If the budget process is centralized, corporate treasury probably consults its lead money center bank or a couple of banks to get a consensus forecast of exchange rates. If the process is decentralized, the local operations probably consult one or more local banks for a consensus forecast of exchange rates. Given that most money center banks have operations worldwide, corporate treasury will receive forecasts from their money center bank's subsidiaries in countries where they have operations.

Hedging Strategies   Another interesting twist to using P-2 and P-3 is for companies that extensively use *hedging strategies*. In that case, the company may use a hedge rate instead of a forecast rate for setting budgets. Assume, for example, that a U.S.-based MNE decides to hedge its future balance sheet and income statement in Brazil by entering into forward contracts. Because management knows the forward rate, it could set its budget at the forward rate instead of a forecast rate from a bank. The variance would be the difference between the forward rate and the future spot rate.

TABLE 18.4   Exchange Rates and the British MNE Budget

Note that among British MNEs, using *forecast* rates for setting budgets (P-2 and P-3) is the preferred method. Both methods are also conducive to the use of *hedging strategies*—strategies, such as *forward contracts* and *options*, that allow companies to transfer risk to other parties.

Rate Used to Determine Budget	Rate Used for Performance Evaluation			Total
	Actual Rate at Time of Budget	Projected Rate at Time of Budget	Actual Rate at End of Budget Period	
Actual Rate at Time of Budget	A-1	A-2	A-3	
	10 Firms	0 Firms	4 Firms	**14 Firms**
Projected Rate at Time of Budget	P-1	P-2	P-3	
	0 Firms	16 Firms	11 Firms	**27 Firms**
Actual Rate at End of Budget Period	E-1	E-2	E-3	
	0 Firms	0 Firms	0 Firms	**0 Firms**
Total	**10 Firms**	**16 Firms**	**15 Firms**	

Source: Adapted from S. Demirag and Cristina De Fuentes, "Exchange Rate Fluctuations and Management Control in UK-Based MNCs: An Examination of the Theory and Practice," *European Journal of Finance* 5:3 (1999): 3–28.

TRANSFER PRICING AND PERFORMANCE EVALUATION

One of the additional elements of management of the multinational enterprise is **transfer pricing**. This refers to the pricing of goods and services that are transferred (bought and sold) between members of a corporate family—for example, parent to subsidiaries, between subsidiaries, from subsidiaries to parent, and so on. As such, internal transfers include raw materials, semifinished and finished goods, allocation of fixed costs, loans, fees, royalties for use of trademarks, copyrights, and other factors. In theory, such prices should be based on production costs, but in reality they often are not.

> Transfer pricing refers to prices on intracompany transfers of goods, services, and capital.

One of the important reasons for arbitrarily establishing transfer prices is taxation. However, taxation is only one of a number of reasons why internal transfers may be priced with little consideration for market prices or production costs. Companies may underprice goods sold to foreign affiliates so the affiliates can then sell them at prices that their local competitors cannot match. If tough antidumping laws exist on final products in the affiliate country, a company could underprice components and semifinished products to its affiliates. The affiliates could then assemble or finish the final product at prices that would have been classified as dumping prices had they been imported directly into the country rather than produced domestically.

> There are conflicting reasons for setting transfer prices that make it difficult for top management to select the correct price.

High transfer prices might be used to circumvent or significantly lessen the impact of national controls. A government prohibition on dividend remittances could restrict a firm's ability to maneuver income out of a country. However, overpricing the goods shipped to a subsidiary in such a country would make it possible for funds to be taken out. High transfer prices would also be of considerable value to a firm when it is paid a subsidy or earns a tax credit on the value of goods it exports. The higher the transfer prices on exported goods, the greater the subsidies earned or tax credit received.

High transfer prices on goods shipped to subsidiaries might be desirable when a parent wishes to lower the apparent profitability of its subsidiary. This might be desirable because of the demands of the subsidiary's workers for higher wages or greater participation in company profits; because of political pressures to expropriate high-profit, foreign-owned operations; or because of the possibility that new competitors might be lured into the industry by high profits.

There might also be inducements for having high-priced transfers go to the subsidiary when a local partner is involved, the inducement being that the increase in the parent-company profits will not have to be split with the local partner. High transfer prices may also be desired when increases from existing price controls in the subsidiary's country are based on product costs (including high transfer prices for purchases).

Table 18.5 identifies the conditions in a subsidiary's country inducing either a high or a low transfer price on flows between affiliates and the parent. The challenge with setting an optimal transfer price is that there could be conflicting conditions in the local country. For example, a subsidiary could be in a country with a low corporate income tax rate (which calls for low transfer prices on goods shipped from the parent to the subsidiary to maximize profits at the subsidiary level) but with high political instability (which calls for high transfer prices to get money out of the country as quickly as possible).

THE BALANCED SCORECARD

The concept of the **balanced scorecard (BSC)** is another approach to performance measurement increasingly being used by companies, especially in the United States and Europe. Approximately 50 percent of *Fortune* 1000 companies in North America and about 40 percent in Europe use a version of the BSC, according to a recent survey by Bain & Co.[30] This approach endeavors to link more closely the strategic and financial perspectives of a business and takes a broad view of business performance.[31]

TABLE 18.5   Factors Influencing High and Low Transfer Prices

Members of corporate families are constantly selling goods and services among themselves, and they can sometimes create competitive or financial advantages when determining the prices that they set on internally transferred goods and services. A wide range of factors can influence a parent company's decision to raise or lower prices charged to a subsidiary.

Conditions Conducive to *Low* Transfer Prices *from* Parent Company and *High* Transfer Prices *to* Parent Company	Conditions Conducive to *High* Transfer Prices *from* Parent Company and *Low* Transfer Prices *to* Parent Company
High ad valorem tariffs	Local partners
Corporate income tax rate lower than in parent's country	Pressure from workers to obtain greater share of company profit
Significant competition	Political pressure to nationalize or expropriate high-profit foreign firms
Local loans based on financial appearance of subsidiary	Restrictions on profit or dividend remittances
Export subsidy or tax credit on value of exports	Political instability
Lower inflation rate than in parent's country	Substantial tie-in sales agreements
Restrictions (ceilings) in subsidiary's country on the *value* of products that can be imported	Price of final product controlled by government but based on production cost
	Desire to mask profitability of subsidiary operations to keep competitors out

Source: Jeffrey S. Arpan, *Intracorporate Pricing: Non-American Systems and Views* (New York: Praeger, 1972).

> The balanced scorecard is an approach to performance measurement that closely links the strategic and financial perspectives of a business.

The BSC provides a framework for looking at the strategies giving rise to value creation from the following perspectives:

1. *Financial*—growth, profitability, and risk from the perspective of shareholders
2. *Customer*—value and differentiation from the customer perspective
3. *Internal business processes*—the priorities for various business processes that create customer and shareholder satisfaction
4. *Learning and growth*—the priorities to create a climate supporting organizational change, innovation, and growth

> Using the balanced scorecard helps management avoid using only one measure of performance.

Although the focus is still ultimately on financial performance, the BSC approach reveals the drivers of long-term competitive performance. In simple terms, learning and growth help create more efficient business processes, which create value for customers, who then reward the firm financially. The challenge is to clearly identify these drivers, to agree on relevant measures, and to implement the new system at all levels of the organization. The significant aspect about this measurement approach, however, is that it also creates a focus for the future, because the measures used communicate to managers what is important.

Case: Internal Learning and Growth at IKEA   Although a firm's BSC is a proprietary strategic tool and generally not available to the general public, its principles are evident in the strategic decisions made by MNEs. IKEA, the Swedish firm, is a case in point. With strong roots in the Swedish culture and a centralized operating style, IKEA has grown to become the world's largest furniture retailer. The company uses a global strategy to spread a simple concept: to offer the broadest range of furniture at the lowest price possible.

IKEA's success begins with internal learning and growth by ensuring that all employees are trained in the cost-saving, hands-on, customer-focused mentality. This enables employees to focus on creating efficient processes that keep costs down. For example, the design team is constantly looking for new materials and suppliers to lower the cost of furniture without sacrificing quality.

Since its founding, IKEA has identified a customer base that would find value in low-cost, innovative furniture: young couples looking to furnish their first apartment. This strategic cohesiveness has rewarded the company with phenomenal growth. By August 2009, IKEA operated 301 stores in 37 countries, with sales of €22.5 billion at the end of 2008. In terms of new stores, IKEA was expanding at a rate of about 9.6 percent per year.[32]

Although the BSC offers the advantages of logically connecting financial performance with its nonfinancial drivers, establishing a coherent scorecard for an MNE has its challenges. For example, as IKEA grows, it faces different customer bases in different countries. IKEA must also ensure that its streamlined product line has appeal in its several markets of operation.

The cultural, geographic, and financial complexity of an MNE makes it challenging to establish a set of interrelated cause-and-effect performance measures. This task appears simpler for MNEs with global strategies like IKEA. However, multidomestic MNEs, such as Philips, the Dutch electronics company, have successfully implemented the BSC concept.

Perhaps the BSC helps solve many of the control and evaluation dilemmas presented throughout this chapter. Adequate use of the BSC helps managers avoid using only one measure of performance (such as ROI or sales growth) and forces them to link financial measures with the nonfinancial factors that drive them. In addition, subsidiaries are evaluated based on a coherent set of performance bases instead of just one base that may or may not be directly controlled by that subsidiary. Thus the BSC concept has been refined into a strategic management system, which replaces the traditional focus on the budget as the center of the management process.[33]

The crucial thing is to identify the most essential drivers for success and to look broadly, as recommended in the BSC, rather than focusing on a narrow financial measure. Then management must identify the most important metrics, or set of measurements, to identify how the company is performing.[34] This could be ROI, or it could also be the number of times a company is criticized for using call-center employees who are not fluent in the target language of customers.

Corporate Governance

The work of the controller is an important dimension in the overall corporate governance program that is put into place by a company. Corporate governance refers to the combination of external and internal mechanisms implemented to safeguard the assets of a company and protect the rights of the shareholders. Corporate governance is not a new concept, but corporate scandals in recent years have resulted in increased attention being given to corporate governance. A major problem at Parmalat, for example, was management collusion in diverting corporate resources into private family businesses, thus defrauding investors and creditors by means of improper accounting and reporting. In short, there was very little oversight of Parmalat's operations (and certainly none at the top).

Case Review Note

EXTERNAL CONTROL MECHANISMS: THE LEGAL SYSTEM

An important external mechanism in corporate governance is the legal system. Countries like the United States have a very litigious environment that allows people to sue company management. Countries with a strong legal tradition, such as most developing countries, must have corporate governance practices put into law to ensure that companies will follow the best practices.

Many countries, especially developing countries, have an underdeveloped and poorly functioning legal system that pays scant attention to corporate governance. Other countries have moved forward to institute corporate governance legislation. Mexico, for example, passed a law on corporate governance in 2000 to encourage more accurate financial reporting and more transparent disclosure practices by management.[35] Brazil has increased its corporate governance through the opening of the Novo Mercado (New

Corporate governance is the external and internal factors designed to safeguard the assets of a company and protect the rights of shareholders.

Market) on BM and F BOVESPA, the Brazilian stock exchange. For a firm to list on the Novo Mercado, it must adhere to the highest-possible standards of corporate governance required by the Exchange. Due to this new requirement, some listed Brazilian companies are rated as having the highest levels of corporate governance in Latin America.[36]

The Sarbanes-Oxley Act in the United States   As a result of the corporate scandals in the United States, especially Enron, the U.S. government passed the Sarbanes-Oxley Act of 2002 (SOX), which resulted in strict reporting requirements for public firms in the United States and for foreign firms listing in the United States. In addition to the reporting requirements, SOX required stronger internal controls and tougher oversight on the part of the external auditors.

Satisfying this requirement has proved quite expensive for MNEs, especially those from other countries that list on the New York Stock Exchange (NYSE). However, it also required foreign firms to adopt higher levels of internal control than were required in their home countries, hopefully helping to avoid the types of problems that occurred with Enron and similar corporate scandals. As a result, many foreign MNEs have decided to exit the NYSE as a place to raise capital, and others have decided against listing on the NYSE for the first time. However, some have argued that these decisions were part of an overall cost-benefit analysis of whether to list on the NYSE or NASDAQ, given that other stock markets, especially in Europe, are becoming important places to raise capital and that firms didn't want to go through the rigorous process of registering with the SEC.

INTERNAL CONTROL MECHANISMS

Internal mechanisms refer to the management and ownership structure of the firm as well as the role of the board of directors in overseeing the operations of the firm.[37] Large U.S.-based MNEs rely on the stock market as a major source of financing. Thus the firm's corporate governance system has to take into account how it protects investors and discloses information to the public.

Firms in developing countries tend to be family-controlled, with family members in key management positions and occupying important positions on the boards of directors. This is a major problem that led to Parmalat's fraud. Voting rights for stocks tend to be in the hands of family members instead of outside investors. Thus the rights of minority owners are not protected very much in the absence of legal requirements. Firms from developing countries that list on foreign stock exchanges, however, have to conform more to corporate governance practices in the developed countries.

Boards of directors are now taking a stronger role worldwide, especially in the area of audit. It is more common to have an outside member of the board be responsible for the audit function, which is designed to improve the integrity of the financial reporting of the firm. The implementation of IFRS worldwide is important, but if companies don't implement strong corporate governance practices, investors will still not be safeguarded as much as they need to be.

Looking to the
Future   Will IFRS Become the Global Accounting Standard?

It's quite possible that IFRS will become the global accounting standard. With the adoption of IFRS by the EU, Australia, New Zealand, and others, over 100 countries on six continents will be requiring or permitting the use of IFRS for some or all domestic listed companies. From an accounting standpoint, the key question is this: What will become the Coca-Cola of accounting standards—U.S. GAAP or IFRS? In other words, which will have the most recognized brand name in accounting standards?

IFRS has a lot going for it, and its proponents are working hard to ensure that it is accepted around the world. The IASB reaches through its board members and committees to various regions of the world by assignment to help them with adoption of or convergence with IFRS. The SEC simply sets guidelines and expects companies that wish to list in the United States to abide by these guidelines and laws.

IFRS are being set by collaboration with many of the major countries in the world, so they are the product of a great deal of negotiation, compromise, and broad-based input. They're appealing to the Europeans, because they have a lot of influence in the development of the standards, and the IFRS are free of regulation by the U.S. SEC. In addition, as noted earlier, they have the backing of the EU. Initially, it appeared that by 2009 non-European companies (including U.S. companies) would have to list on European exchanges using IFRS. And if they also wanted to list in the United States, they would have to list according to U.S. GAAP unless they were fully compliant with IFRS. However, at least the new IFRS is modeled after the capital-markets orientation of the United Kingdom and the United States. At some point, it's possible that the United States will simply adopt IFRS, but that is not likely in the near future. The major vote in favor of U.S. GAAP is that half of the world's stock market capitalization is located in the United States, and companies that want access to U.S. capital must play by U.S. rules. People in the United States have always felt that their standards were the best in the world and that it would be unfair for U.S. companies competing for cash in the U.S. market to allow foreign companies to list using IFRS, which is perceived as more flexible and less comprehensive than U.S. GAAP. Foreign companies that want to list outside their national markets typically look to the United States first and thus have to adopt U.S. reporting requirements, although that is shifting rapidly to IFRS. As European stock markets continue to increase in importance, more European companies are choosing to list in Europe instead of the United States. In 2009, about 40 percent of the Global 500 companies listed according to U.S. GAAP, about the same percentage used IFRS, and 20 percent listed in their home markets using home-country GAAP.

An additional complication to combining or converging IFRS and U.S. GAAP is the Sarbanes-Oxley Act of 2002. This act requires companies to establish solid internal controls over financial reporting, limits the types of services that may be performed by primary auditors in addition to the financial-statement audit, and requires the managers of publicly traded companies to assess internal controls and make a statement on this assessment, which must be examined and opined on by external auditors.

All of these requirements add additional costs to those already related to complying with U.S. GAAP. Although perhaps good for companies in the long term, as companies must establish effective controls over financial reporting, the initial costs of complying with the Sarbanes-Oxley Act of 2002 may be too great for some firms to consider listing on U.S. exchanges. In addition, the United States has strict laws on the granting of stock options to managers, and the U.S. market has a heightened sensitivity to wrongdoing because of recent accounting scandals, including Enron and WorldCom.

However, the convergence project between the FASB and IASB may solve some of these problems in the long run. To its credit, the IASB has expanded coverage of key topics and has narrowed the alternatives available to companies. The IASB has sold itself as based on *principles* rather than *rules,* although it is more accurate to say that IFRS are simpler and less comprehensive. Anytime you have a standard, you have to have a rule. It's just that U.S. GAAP is very rule-based and complicated and covers far more topics and industries. However, the FASB and IASB are narrowing the differences in existing standards and developing new standards together. Now they jointly write new standards so that even the wording is the same. In addition, public accounting firms and publicly traded companies have five years of experience in adopting the requirements of Sarbanes-Oxley. Maybe the future of accounting standards will be like a merger of Coca-Cola and Pepsi, but accounting is more complicated than soft drinks. ∎

Ericsson: The Challenges of Listing on Global Capital Markets and the Move to Adopt International Financial Reporting Standards

In 2002, the European Union mandated that its member countries adopt International Financial Reporting Standards (IFRS) as the basis for preparing and issuing consolidated financial statements beginning in 2005.[38] Ericsson, the Swedish MNE that supplies products and services to the world's largest mobile- and fixed-network operators, is a public limited-liability company that must follow the Swedish Companies Act and the listing requirements of the Swedish Stock Exchange. In addition, it must comply with the listing requirements of the London Stock Exchange and NASDAQ in the United States, because it lists securities on both stock exchanges. Given that Sweden is a member of the EU, Ericsson was required to adopt IFRS as of 2005, which is a change from its past practices. However, there are currently two sets of IFRS: (1) EU-approved IFRS and (2) IFRS as issued by the International Accounting Standards Board (IASB).

Should Ericsson adopt the full IFRS or just the more limited EU-approved IFRS? What are the implications of its decision to list on NASDAQ, and what are some of the other issues Ericsson has to face as a result of its decision to raise capital outside of its home market of Sweden?

A Little More about Ericsson

L. M. Ericsson was founded in Sweden in 1876 and is best known to the casual consumer through a Sony Ericsson joint venture that sells cellular handsets worldwide. However, it fits in the broader network of the communications equipment industry. Although Ericsson is known as one of Sweden's premier MNEs, it generates 29 percent of its sales in Western Europe; 28 percent in Central and Eastern Europe, the Middle East, and Africa; and 45 percent in Asia Pacific—but only 9 percent each in Latin America and North America.

It issues stock in three major stock markets: Stockholm, London, and NASDAQ. Thus it raises capital from investors internationally and generates most of its sales outside its native Sweden. In fact, only 3.6 percent of its sales are generated in Sweden, even though 58.4 percent of its assets and 29.9 percent of its employees are located there. Ericsson's major competitors are Nokia, Motorola, Cisco Systems, and Alcatel-Lucent, and it is considered to be the fourth largest company in the industry.

Before the Changeover to IFRS

Prior to the move to IFRS in 2005, Ericsson reported its financial results in compliance with Swedish GAAP—a bit of a mixture between Anglo-American accounting, which is driven by the capital markets, and Germanic accounting, which is driven by bank financing and taxation. Swedish reporting tends to be a little more transparent than German accounting but less transparent than Anglo-American accounting.

Issues of Transparency

One of the reasons why Swedish accounting has been less transparent is its orientation to creditors, government, and tax authorities. However, companies like Ericsson have had to become more transparent because of their desire to raise capital on foreign stock exchanges. In addition, because the Swedish Stock Exchange has become a focal point for listings by Nordic companies, the influential Swedish accounting profession has pushed for consolidated accounts to represent the needs of shareholders, whereas the parent-company accounts have reflected Swedish legal requirements. Swedish accounting tends to be very conservative due to the importance of taxes to fund extensive social welfare programs and the tendency of the Swedish government to use tax policies to influence investment in areas deemed important to the government and its social objectives.

Sweden and the EU

Since Sweden entered the EU, Swedish accounting has evolved to incorporate EU accounting directives and philosophies. The Swedish government established an Accounting Standards Board (BFN) in 1976 to recommend accounting principles that fit within the framework of the Company Law. The Swedish Financial Accounting Council (RR) was established in 1991 to take over the role of the accounting profession in making recommendations on accounting practices, especially with respect to how to prepare an annual report according to the Annual Accounts Act.

The Swedish Stock Exchange has supported the efforts of the Accounting Council and the BFN, even though the recommendations of both bodies are voluntary and subject to the Company Law. However, the decision by the EU to require firms to use IFRS for consolidated financial statements takes precedence over everything for consolidated financial statements.

The Gap between U.S. GAAP and Swedish GAAP

In its 2004 annual report, Ericsson still disclosed information according to the Swedish Company Law, although it knew by then that it would have to adopt IFRS the following year. Because so many IFRS were still being finalized in 2004, it did not "early adopt" the new standards. In its Note on Accounting Policies, Ericsson stated that it prepared its consolidated and parent-company financial statements "in accordance with accounting principles generally accepted in Sweden." However, it also mentioned that "these accounting principles differ in certain respects from generally accepted accounting principles in the United States (US GAAP)" and it gave a description of those differences in a later footnote in the report.

Even though it was trading shares on the London Stock Exchange, it did not make any reference to differences between Swedish GAAP and U.K. GAAP. This is because the London Stock Exchange does not require a reconciliation like the U.S. exchanges do.

Applying the Conservatism Index In its Note to the Financial Statements detailing the differences between Swedish GAAP and U.S. GAAP, Ericsson mentions that the major differences are the treatment of capitalization of development expenses, provisions for restructuring, pension costs, hedge accounting, and goodwill. The overall difference in income is fairly significant. Using *Gray's conservatism index,* we can calculate the degree to which Ericsson's net income in 2004 was more or less conservative compared to U.S. income. We gain this information from Ericsson's Form 20-F, which provides a reconciliation from foreign GAAP to U.S. GAAP required by the SEC for U.S.-listed companies (see Table 18.6).

Given that Sweden is more driven by conservatism and tax issues, one would expect Swedish GAAP income to be more conservative than U.S. GAAP income. Gray's index of conservatism for 2004 is computed as follows:

$$\text{Index} = 1 - \frac{\text{U.S. GAAP earnings} - \text{Swedish GAAP earnings}}{\text{U.S. GAAP earnings}}$$

or

$$\text{Index} = 1 - \frac{(14,386 - 19,024)}{14,386} = 1.3224$$

The result implies that Swedish GAAP income was less conservative than U.S. GAAP income. For example, under U.S. GAAP, the cost of developing new products must be expensed in the period in which it occurs, which lowers net income. In Sweden, development costs can be capitalized, which means they don't show up as expenses for the period, thus resulting in higher income. That was one of the largest adjustments for 2004, so Swedish net income had to be reduced by the amount of development costs amortized to get U.S. GAAP net income.

In addition to these differences, Ericsson mentioned in its report that in 2004 it had adopted a new U.S. accounting standard issued by the FASB (FIN 46R—Consolidation of Variable Interest Entities) and that it planned to adopt two other U.S. standards and pronouncements in 2005 (SFAS 123R—Share Based Payments, and SFAS 151—Inventory Costs). This is interesting, because Ericsson already knew it was going to adopt IFRS the next year. Why, then, did it continue to adopt U.S. standards?

Impact of IFRS on Ericsson's Results

In the Note on Accounting Policies in its 2004 annual report, Ericsson disclosed that from 2005 it would prepare its financial statements according to IFRS. It also mentioned that the IFRS that

TABLE 18.6   Ericsson's Form 20-F: Net Income Reconciliation, 2004

Adjustment of Net Income	2004	2003	2002
Net income as reported per Swedish GAAP	19,024	−10,844	−19,013
U.S. GAAP adjustments before taxes:			
Pensions	−245	−840	412
Pension premium refund	—	—	47
Capital discount on convertible debentures	—	179	124
Goodwill amortization	475	1,636	1,064
Sale-leaseback	352	682	113
Hedging	−2,915	1,603	2,884
Capitalization of development costs for products			
to be sold	−2,606	−4,798	−4,018
for internal use	−131	−355	−922
Restructuring costs	−1,354	1,225	−1,240
Unrealized gains and losses on available-for-sale			
securities	−82	370	−370
Other	37	12	35
Tax effect of U.S. GAAP adjustments	1,831	533	966
Net income in accordance with U.S. GAAP	**14,386**	**−10,597**	**−19,918**
Earnings per share in accordance with U.S. GAAP			
Earnings per share per U.S. GAAP, basic	0.91	−0.68	−1.58
Earnings per share per U.S. GAAP, diluted	0.91	−0.68[*]	−1.58[*]
Average number of shares, basic, per U.S. GAAP (million)	15,829	15,823	12,573
Average number of shares, diluted, per U.S. GAAP (million)	15,855	15,831	12,684

[*]Potential ordinary shares are not considered when their conversion to ordinary shares would increase earnings per share.

Source: Telefonaktiebolaget LM Ericsson, *Ericsson Annual Report on Form 20-F 2004*, www.ericsson.com (accessed May 31, 2007).

were likely to have the greatest impact on income and shareholder equity were standards regarding capitalization of development costs, business combinations, share-based payments, and financial instruments.

Conversion Costs

Ericsson estimated that the conversion to IFRS in 2005 would result in a difference of about 1.5 billion Swedish kronor for 2004 net income and a difference of 5.7 billion kronor for equity as of January 1, 2005. Net income under Swedish GAAP would have been 17,539 million kronor under IFRS, compared with 19,024 million kronor under Swedish GAAP. In addition, the recognition of cash on the balance sheet appears to be quite different under IFRS than it is under Swedish GAAP, with cash under IFRS being SEK46.1 billion less than cash under Swedish GAAP. From Ericsson's Form 20-F report, one can also see that cash at the end of 2004 was the same under U.S. GAAP and IFRS.

Costs of implementing IFRS are difficult to gauge. Many countries implemented national regulations that attempted alignment with IFRS (e.g., Sweden). Thus costs of implementation may have been spread out over several years because companies knew that full IFRS implementation was drawing near. Ericsson's management notes the following in the 2004 annual report:

> Because Swedish GAAP, in recent years, has been adapted to IFRS to a high degree and as the rules for first time adopters allows certain exemptions from full retrospective restatements, the transition from Swedish GAAP to IFRS is expected to have a relatively limited effect on our financial statements. Furthermore, we believe the conversion to IFRS will align our reporting more closely with US GAAP.

After the Changeover to IFRS

As Ericsson studied the transition to IFRS, it had to decide if it wanted to adopt full IFRS or the EU-mandated IFRS, which was more limited in scope. Ericsson stated the following in its 2006 annual report:

> *The consolidated financial reports as at and for the year ended December 31, 2006, have been prepared in accordance with International Financial Reporting Standards as endorsed by the EU, RR 30:05 Additional rules for Group Accounting and related interpretations by the Swedish Financial Accounting Standards Council (Redovisingsrådet) and the Swedish Annual Accounts Act. For the Company there is no difference between IFRS and IFRS endorsed by the EU, nor is RR 30:05 or the Swedish Annual Accounts Act in conflict with IFRS.*

Note P1 to the Parent Company Financial Statements of Ericsson indicates that the parent company generally follows Swedish GAAP, with the following stipulation:

> *The Parent Company, Telefonaktiebolaget LM Ericsson, adopted RR32 'Reporting in separate financial statements' from January 1, 2005. The adoption of RR32 has not had any effect on reported profit or loss for 2004 and 2005. The amended RR32:05 (from 2006) requires the Parent Company to use the same accounting principles as for the Group, i.e. IFRS to the extent allowed by RR32:05.*

The Swedish MNE Electrolux, which lists on the Swedish Stock Exchange and trades in the United States through an American Depositary Receipt, states the following in its 2006 annual report:

> *The consolidated financial statements are prepared in accordance with International Financial Reporting Standards (IFRS) as adopted by the European Union. Some additional information is disclosed based on the standard RR 30:05 from the Swedish Financial Accounting Standards Council. As required by IAS 1, Electrolux companies apply uniform accounting rules, irrespective of national legislation, as defined in the Electrolux Accounting Manual, which is fully compliant with IFRS. . . . The Parent Company's financial statements are prepared in accordance with the Swedish Annual Accounts Act and the standard RR 32:05 from the Swedish Financial Accounting Standards Council.*

A careful reading of these statements indicates two things:

- The consolidated financial statements of some European companies are prepared on a different basis than parent-company financial statements.
- More than one set of IFRS can be used by European companies for their consolidated financial statements: IFRS as adopted by the EU and IFRS as recommended by the IASB.

This dual standard in the EU is disturbing to the IASB.

Future Reconciliation to U.S. GAAP

As we noted in the chapter, companies will not have to file 20-F reports with the SEC in the future if the companies are in compliance with IFRS. Which set of IFRS will the SEC allow registrants to use—the EU version or the version endorsed and issued by the IASB? The EU is not allowing companies to list on European exchanges while preparing financial statements solely in conformance with U.S. GAAP after December 31, 2008. Thus, if firms want to disclose results in U.S. GAAP and list on European exchanges, they will have to report financial results in both U.S. GAAP and IFRS. The cost of using two reporting systems can be large for firms but may not be any larger than the cost currently incurred by firms that reconcile from IFRS to U.S. GAAP and from U.S. GAAP to IFRS today.

Ericsson's shares trade as "pink sheets" (securities traded over the counter (OTC) rather than on an exchange) and on NASDAQ. Because it lists in the United States, Ericsson has to prepare Form 20-F reports with the SEC. Interestingly, however, in its 2006 annual report, no reconciliation to U.S. GAAP is presented, whereas reconciliations were presented in the 2004 annual report. This change in presentation shows that the transition to IFRS is real and that companies in Europe, as well as shareholders, may consider IFRS to be at least as valid as U.S. GAAP.

Even though the reconciliation was not included in the 2006 annual report, Ericsson filed Form 20-F separately with the SEC for 2006. Table 18.7 illustrates that the difference between IFRS net income and U.S. GAAP net income was much less than that between Swedish GAAP net income and U.S. GAAP net income in 2004.

Fast Forward to 2009

Because Ericsson now registers with the SEC using IFRS, it doesn't have to provide a reconciliation report to U.S. GAAP. In the statement on accounting policy, Ericsson discloses the following:

> *The consolidated financial statements for the year ended December 31, 2008, have been prepared in accordance with International Financial Reporting Standards (IFRS) as endorsed by the EU and RFR 1.1 "Additional rules for Group Accounting", related interpretations issued by the Swedish Financial Reporting Board (Rådet för Finansiell Rapportering), and the Swedish Annual Accounts Act. There is no effect on Ericsson's financial reporting 2008 due to differences between IFRS as issued by the IAS B and IFRS as endorsed by the EU, nor is RFR 1.1 or the Swedish Annual Accounts Act in conflict with IFRS.*

TABLE 18.7　Ericsson's Form 20-F: Net Income Reconciliation, 2006

Adjustment of Net Income	2006	2005	2004
Net income attributable to stockholders of the parent company per IFRSs	26,251	24,315	17,539
U.S. GAAP adjustments before taxes:			
Pensions	−439	−64	−245
Sale-leaseback	93	191	352
Hedging	0	408	−2,915
Capitalization of development costs	−37	−78	−76
Restructuring costs	−4	120	−1,354
Unrealized gains and losses on available-for-sale securities	0	0	−82
Reversals of impairment losses	−31	−380	0
Other	93	56	82
Tax effect of U.S. GAAP adjustments	154	−73	1,085
Net income in accordance with U.S. GAAP	**26,080**	**24,495**	**14,386**
Earnings per share in accordance with U.S. GAAP			
Earnings per share per U.S. GAAP, basic	1.64	1.55	0.91
Earnings per share per U.S. GAAP, diluted	1.64	1.54	0.91
Average number of shares, basic, per U.S. GAAP (million)	15,871	15,843	15,829
Average number of shares, diluted, per U.S. GAAP (million)	15,943	15,907	15,855
Net income for the period from continuing operations according to U.S. GAAP	23,260	24,312	14,228
Net income for the period from discontinued operations according to U.S. GAAP	2,820	183	158
Total income for the period according to U.S. GAAP	**26,080**	**24,495**	**14,386**
Earnings per share from continuing operations, basic	1.47	1.53	0.90
Earning per share from discontinued operations, basic	0.17	0.02	0.01
Total earnings per share, basic	**1.64**	**1.55**	**0.91**

Source: Telefonaktiebolaget LM Ericsson, *Ericsson Annual Report on Form 20-F 2006*, www.ericsson.com (accessed July 31, 2007).

As before, Ericsson states that there are no differences between IFRS as issued by the IASB and IFRS as endorsed by the EU. This is an important issue for both the IASB and the SEC. The company also refers to the Swedish Annual Accounts Act, so it is in compliance with Swedish law, and it also mentions a new Swedish Financial Reporting Board, something that was missing in its 2006 annual report. But Ericsson demonstrates that a company can be in compliance with local law, IFRS, EU-sanctioned IFRS, and SEC requirements to raise capital without having to use U.S. GAAP in either its primary financial statements or a reconciliation statement. ■

QUESTIONS

1. What are the major sources of influence on Ericsson's accounting standards and practices?
2. What has been the impact on Ericsson's reporting of its listing on the London Stock Exchange? On NASDAQ?
3. What type of IFRS did Ericsson decide to disclose in its financial statements in 2006?
4. How would the adoption of IFRS affect Ericsson's index of conservatism in 2004? How does that compare with the index for conservatism according to U.S. GAAP? What was the index in 2006 for IFRS GAAP income reported by Ericsson and U.S. GAAP income disclosed to the SEC? What does that tell you about the convergence process?
5. Should Ericsson adopt full IFRS or IFRS as adopted by the EU? What difference does it make?

SUMMARY

- The MNE must learn to cope with differing inflation rates, exchange-rate changes, currency controls, expropriation risks, customs duties, tax rates and methods of determining taxable income, levels of sophistication of local accounting personnel, and local as well as home-country reporting requirements.

- A company's accounting or controllership function is responsible for collecting and analyzing data for internal and external users.

- Culture can have a strong influence on the accounting dimensions of measurement and disclosure. The cultural values of secrecy and transparency refer to the degree of disclosure of information. The cultural values of optimism and conservatism refer to the valuation of assets and the recognition of income. Conservatism results in the undervaluation of both assets and income.

- Financial statements differ in terms of language, currency, type of statements (income statement, balance sheet, etc.), financial-statement format, extent of footnote disclosures, and the underlying GAAP on which the financial statements are based.

- Important users of financial statements that must be considered in determining accounting standards are investors, employees, lenders, suppliers and other trade creditors, customers, governments and their agencies, and the public.

- Some of the most important sources of influence on the development of accounting standards and practices are culture, capital markets, regional and global standards-setting groups, management, and accountants.

- The International Accounting Standards Board (IASB)—an independent, privately funded accounting-standards setter—is charged with developing a single set of high-quality, understandable, and enforceable global accounting standards. Standards developed by the IASB require transparent and comparable information in general-purpose financial statements.

- In cooperation with national accounting-standards setters around the world, especially the Financial Accounting Standards Board (FASB) in the United States, the IASB hopes to achieve convergence in accounting standards.

- The possible elimination of the Form 20-F requirement for foreign companies listing in the United States and different methods of adopting IFRS are major issues that could affect the global convergence of accounting standards.

- When transactions denominated in a foreign currency are translated into dollars, all accounts are recorded initially at the exchange rate in effect at the time of the transaction. At each subsequent balance-sheet date, recorded dollar balances representing amounts owed by or to the company that are denominated in a foreign currency are adjusted to reflect the current rate.

- Companies enter foreign-exchange gains and losses arising from foreign-currency transactions on the income statement during the period in which they occur. Companies enter gains and losses arising from translating financial statements by the current-rate method as a separate component of owners' equity. Companies enter gains and losses arising from translating according to the temporal method directly on the income statement.

- Many different performance evaluation measures are used for global operations, especially return on investment and budget compared with actual performance.

- In comparing budget with actual performance, MNEs need to decide which rate to use to translate the budget into the parent currency and in which currency to monitor results. Then the MNE must decide who is responsible for exchange-rate variances.

- MNEs may set arbitrary transfer prices to take advantage of tax differences between countries or to accomplish other corporate objectives, such as performance evaluation, profit manipulation, and so on.

- The balanced scorecard provides a framework for looking at the strategies giving rise to value creation from the following perspectives: financial, customer, internal business processes, and learning and growth.

- Corporate governance refers to the combination of external and internal mechanisms implemented to safeguard the assets of a company and protect the rights of the shareholders. It involves improved financial disclosures and stronger internal controls, with oversight by an independent board of directors.

KEY TERMS

accounting (p. 716)
balanced scorecard (BSC) (p. 739)
consolidation (p. 732)
convergence (p. 720)
current-rate method (p. 733)
Financial Accounting Standards Board (FASB) (p. 718)

functional currency (p. 733)
Generally Accepted Accounting Principles (GAAP) (p. 721)
International Accounting Standards Board (IASB) (p. 718)
International Financial Reporting Standards (IFRS) (p. 726)

International Organization of Securities Commissions (IOSCO) (p. 726)
mutual recognition (p. 725)
temporal method (p. 733)
transfer pricing (p. 739)
translation (p. 732)

ENDNOTES

1 **Sources include the following:** Vincent Boland, "The Saga of Parmalat's Collapse," FT.com (December 19, 2008); Catherine Boyle, "Parmalat's Founder Is Sentenced to Ten Years' Jail for Market-Rigging," *The Times* (December 19, 2008): 64; Judith Burns, "Parmalat to Settle SEC Charges of Fraud for U.S. Bond Offering," *Wall Street Journal* (Europe) (July 30, 2004), A6; "The Pause after Parmalat," *The Economist* (January 17, 2004), 13; Alessandra Galloni and Yaroslav Trofimov, "Tanzi's Power Games Helped Parmalat Rise, but Didn't Cushion Fall," *Wall Street Journal* (Europe) (March 8, 2004), A1; Mark Tran, "The Milk Sheikh Whose Dream Curdled," *The Guardian* (December 31, 2003), www.guardian.co.uk/business/2003/dec/31/italy.parmalat1 (accessed October 19, 2009); Peter Gumbel, "How It All Went So Sour," *Time* (Europe) (November 29, 2004), 44; Hoover's Online, "Parmalat," at www.hoovers.com (accessed April 19, 2005); Michelle Perry, "Enron: Could It Happen Here?" *Accountancy Age* (January 25, 2004), www.accountancyage.com/accountancyage/analysis/2040660/enron-happen-here (accessed October 19, 2009); David Reilly and Alessandra Galloni, "Spilling Over: Banks Come under Scrutiny for Role in Parmalat Scandal," *Wall Street Journal* (September 28, 2004), A1; David Reilly and Matt Moffett, "Parmalat Inquiry Is Joined by Brazil," *Wall Street Journal* (Europe) (January 7, 2004), A1; Susannah Rodgers and Kenneth Maxwell, "Parmalat Fallout Hits Farmers; Dairies Worry about Their Future as Milk Seller Misses Payments," *Wall Street Journal* (Europe) (January 15, 2004), B6; Securities and Exchange Commission (SEC): Complaint #18527 (December 29, 2003); "Parmalat to Trim Key Operations in 10 Countries," *Wall Street Journal* (Europe) (March 29, 2004), A4; "How Parmalat Differs from U.S. Scandals," Knowledge@Wharton (January 28, 2004), at http://knowledge.wharton.upenn.edu (accessed November 15, 2007); Adrian Michaels, "Parmalat Case Leads to First Jail Sentences," *Financial Times* (June 29, 2005) 28; Bruce Johnston and Caroline Muspratt, "Court Frees Daughter of Parmalat Founder," *The* [London] *Daily Telegraph* (March 9, 2004), 29;

"Daughter of Founder of Parmalat Is Freed," *Wall Street Journal* (Eastern Edition) (March 9, 2004), 1; Eric Sylvers, "In First Trial, Parmalat's Founder Charges That Banks Led Him Astray," *International Herald Tribune* (March 9, 2006), 13; John Hooper, "Parmalat Fraudsters to Avoid Prison," *The Guardian* (June 29, 2005), 18; Giada Zampano and Sabrina Cohen, "Parmalat Trial to Focus on Banks," *Wall Street Journal* (Eastern Edition) (June 14, 2007), C3; "Parmalat Settles Suits with Three Financial Firms," *International Herald Tribune* (June 19, 2007), 16; "Parmalat SpA," *Wall Street Journal* (Europe) (May 18, 2007), 6; Steve Rothwell and Sebastian Boyd, "EU Backing Off Effort on Bond Transparency," *International Herald Tribune* (November 22, 2006), 13.

2 Financial Accounting Standards Board, "Objectives of Financial Reporting by Business Enterprises," *Statement of Financial Accounting Concepts No. 1* (Stamford, CT: FASB, 1979): paragraphs 34–54.

3 Geert Hofstede, *Culture's Consequences: International Differences in Work-Related Values* (Beverly Hills: Sage, 1980); Hofstede and Michael H. Bond, "The Confucius Connection: From Cultural Roots to Economic Growth," *Organizational Dynamics* 16:4 (1988): 4; Hofstede, *Cultures and Organizations* (Maidenhead, England: McGraw-Hill, 1991).

4 Sidney J. Gray, "Towards a Theory of Cultural Influence on the Development of Accounting Systems Internationally," *Abacus* (March 1988): 1.

5 C. W. Nobes and R. H. Parker (eds.), *Comparative International Accounting*, 6th ed. (Upper Saddle River, NJ: Prentice Hall, 2000).

6 Christopher Nobes and Robert Parker, *Comparative International Accounting*, 7th ed. (England: FT Prentice Hall, 2002).

7 Adidas Group, *Annual Report 2008*, at http://www.adidas-group.com/en/investor/_downloads/pdf/annual_reports/2008/GB_2008_En.pdf (accessed July 31, 2009).

8 European Union, "European Commission Grants Equivalence in Relation to Third Country GAAPs," http://europa.eu/rapid/pressReleasesAction.do?reference=IP/08/1962&format=HTML&aged=0&language=EN&guiLanguage=en; the site is located in http://ec.europa.eu/internal_market/accounting/third_countries/index_en.htm (accessed October 20, 2009).

9 International Accounting Standards Committee Foundation, "Revised Constitution" (February 1, 2009). PDF is available at "About the IASC Foundation," www.iasb.org (accessed October 20, 2009).

10 International Accounting Standards Board and International Accounting Standards Committee Foundation, "Who We Are and What We Do," PDF found on http://www.iasb.org/NR/rdonlyres/0A5A767C-E7DE-49E5-8B12-499F62F8870C/0/WhoWeAre_Final12508.pdf (accessed August 3, 2009).

11 International Accounting Standards Committee Foundation, A Guide Through International Financial Reporting Standards (IFRSs®) (London: IASCF, 2007): 1.

12 "Uniform Rules for International Accounting Standards from 2005 Onwards," *European Parliament Daily Notebook*, Report on the Proposal for a European Parliament and Council Regulation on the Application of International Accounting Standards, (COM(2001) 80-C5-0061/2001–2001/004 (COD), Doc.: A5-0070/2002, http://www.europarl.europa.eu/sides/getDoc.do?pubRef=-//EP//TEXT+PRESS+DN-20020312-1+0+DOC+XML+V0//EN&language=EN#SECTION5 (accessed October 21, 2009).

13 "Finance and Economics: Speaking in Tongues," *The Economist* (May 19, 2007): 77–78.

14 Deloitte Touche Tohmatsu, *IFRSs and US GAAP: A Pocket Comparison* (London, 2007): 1.

15 FASB, "Convergence with the International Accounting Standards Board."

16 Securities and Exchange Commission, "About the SEC: What We Do," http://www.sec.gov/about/whatwedo.shtml (accessed October 21, 2009).

17 Floyd Norris, "U.S. Moves Toward International Accounting Rules," *New York Times* (August 28, 2008), www.nytimes.com (accessed October 21, 2009).

18 European Union, "Regulations Adopting IAS," http://ec.europa.eu/internal_market/accounting/legal_framework/regulations_adopting_ias_en.htm (accessed October 21, 2009).

19 International Accounting Standards Board, "IASB Publishes IFRS for SMEs" (July 9, 2009), http://www.iasb.org/News/Press+Releases/IASB+publishes+IFRS+for+SMEs.htm (accessed October 21, 2009).

20 Deloitte Touche Tohmatsu, "IASB Agenda Project" (2007), at www.iasplus.com/agenda/sme.htm (accessed May 29, 2007).

21 Christopher Cox, "Speech by SEC Chairman: Chairman's Address to the SEC Roundtable on International Financial Reporting Standards" (U.S. Securities and Exchange Commission, Washington, DC, March 6, 2007), at www.sec.gov/news/speech/2007/spch030607cc.htm (accessed May 29, 2007).

22 U.S. Department of the Treasury, "Paulson Announces First Stage of Capital Markets Action Plan," HP-408 (May 17, 2007), at www.treas.gov/press/releases/hp408.htm (accessed May 29, 2007).

23 Ian Katz, "New SEC Chief Backs 'Say-on-Pay,'" *Washington Post* (January 24, 2009): D2.

24 FASB, "Foreign Currency Translation," Statement of Financial Accounting Standards No. 52 (Stamford, CT: FASB, December 1981): 6–7.

25 The Coca-Cola Company, Form 10-K (February 26, 2009): 33, 69.

26 S. Robbins and R. Stobaugh, "The Bent Measuring Stick for Foreign Subsidiaries," *Harvard Business Review* (September–October 1973): 80.

27 A. Appleyard, N. Strong, and P. Walton, "Budgetary Control of Foreign Subsidiaries," *Management Accounting* (U.K.) (September 1990): 44–45.

28 M. Shields, C. Chow, Y. Kato, and Y. Nakagawa, "Management Accounting Practices in the U.S. and Japan: Comparative Survey Findings and Research Implications," *Journal of International Financial Management and Accounting* 3:1 (1991): 61–77.

29 Donald Lessard and Peter Lorange, "Currency Changes and Management Control: Resolving the Centralization/Decentralization Dilemma," *Accounting Review* (July 1977): 628.

30 A. Gumbus and B. Lyons, "The Balanced Scorecard at Phillips Electronics," *Strategic Finance* 84:5 (2002): 45–50.

31 R. Kaplan and D. P. Norton, "The Balanced Scorecard—Measures That Drive Performance," *Harvard Business Review* (January–February 1992): 71–79.

32 "About the IKEA Concept and IKEA Franchising," www.ikea.com (accessed August 6, 2009).

33 R. Kaplan and D. P. Norton, *The Strategy-Focused Organization* (Cambridge, MA: Harvard Business School Press, 2001).

34 Mark Hammer, "The 7 Deadly Sins of Performance Measurement and How to Avoid Them," *MIT Sloan Management Review* 40:3 (2007): 19–28.

35 Susan Machuga and Karen Teitel, "The Effects of the Mexican Corporate Governance Code on Quality of Earnings and Its Components," *Journal of International Accounting Research* 6:1 (Spring 2007).

36 Jason Mitchell, "Best Latam Companies 2009: Petrobras Makes the Most of a Special Situation," *Euromoney* (March 2009): 70; "Brazil Extends Governance Lead," *LatinFinance* (June 2008), www.latinfinance.com/ArticleTop100.aspx?ArticleID= 1938037 (accessed October 23, 2009).

37 D. K. Denis and J. J. McConnell, "International Corporate Governance," *Journal of Financial and Quantitative Analysis* 38:1 (2003): 1–36.

38 *Sources include the following:* Telefonaktiebolaget LM Ericsson, *Annual Report 2004* (2005), at www.ericsson.com/ericsson/investors/financial_reports/2004/annual04/ericsson_ar2004_complete_en.pdf (accessed May 31, 2007); Ericsson, Form 20-F (March 23, 2005), at www.ericsson.com/ericsson/investors/financial_reports/2004/20f.pdf (accessed May 31, 2007); Electrolux, "Corporate Information," at www.electrolux.com/ node60.aspx?year=2004 (accessed May 31, 2007); BMW Group, "Investor relations," at www.bmwgroup.com/e/nav/index.html?../0_0_www_bmwgroup_com/home/home.html& source=overview (accessed June 1, 2007); "Finance and Economics: Speaking in Tongues," *The Economist* (May 19, 2007): 77–78; Ericsson, Form 20-F (June 7, 2007), at www.sec.gov/Archives/ edgar/data/717826/000119312507131377/ d20f.htm (accessed July 24, 2007); Ericsson, Form 20-F (June 7, 2007), at www.ericsson .com/ericsson/investors/financial_reports/2006/20f.pdf (accessed July 31, 2007).

nineteen

The Multinational Finance Function

Objectives

- To describe the multinational finance function and how it fits in the MNE's organizational structure

- To show how companies can acquire outside funds for normal operations and expansion, including offshore debt and equity funds

- To explore how offshore financial centers are used to raise funds and manage cash flows

- To explain how companies include international factors in the capital budgeting process

- To discuss the major internal sources of funds available to the MNE and to show how these funds are managed globally

- To describe how companies protect against the major financial risks of inflation and exchange-rate movements

- To highlight some of the tax issues facing MNEs

To have money is a good thing; to have a say over the money is even better.

—*Yiddish proverb*

753

CASE GPS: In the Market for an Effective Hedging Strategy?

On April 10, 2000, U.S.-based Wells Fargo & Company and First Security Corporation announced that they had signed a merger agreement of their banks in San Francisco and Salt Lake City, Utah, respectively.[1] Both banks, located in the West, were clearly positioning themselves to compete with each other, especially in the Utah market, which is composed of individuals, small businesses, middle-market businesses, farmers and ranchers, and a few large corporate customers. Wells Fargo was operating in 22 states, whereas First Security was operating in seven states. Given the overlapping markets and client demographics, it was clear that services would be consolidated over the next several months.

Three key First Security personnel in the international banking area were Ali Manbeian, Jason Langston, and Ryan Gibbons, VP and manager of the Foreign Exchange Department at First Security. On January 31, 2000, Manbeian had been promoted to VP and trade products manager in the International Banking Division, and Langston had been promoted to VP and foreign-exchange trader. All three had significant experience in international banking, and First Security Bank had a trading room where they could provide foreign-exchange services and trade-related collections and payments for clients. With the merger, however, many of the more interesting businesses shifted to San Francisco, and the three could see the writing on the wall.

THE START-UP OF GPS

In 2002, with the help of some key investors, the three entrepreneurs formed GPS Capital Markets Inc. (GPS). They realized that there was a niche market in foreign exchange that was no longer being served in the Intermountain West, and they decided to strike out on their own with a business model they believed could be successful.

Bringing investors on board was essential to their success, because they needed the necessary credit backing and reputation to enter the wholesale market. Without that financial backing, they wouldn't be able to access large clients and brokers. Jason Langston noted that "90 percent of the transactions [we've] done in the past wouldn't have happened without these credible investors."

TARGET MARKET AND CLIENT STRATEGY

To compete effectively in the market, GPS initially decided to target medium-sized companies rather than *Fortune* 500 companies. They focused on serving companies that had significant foreign-exchange needs but didn't have their own foreign-exchange team. With this in mind, they started out by providing the regular services that commercial banks offer. Their feeling was that with their expertise and low overhead, they would be able to outbid the larger banks for their business.

At first, they offered the traditional inbound and outbound payments, areas in which they excelled at First Security Bank. These payments are the basic needs of companies that are going to receive or are required to pay invoices in a different currency.

But GPS was finding it difficult to obtain clients, because companies have strong relationships with the banks where they have accounts. The first choice for most companies when it comes to foreign exchange is to use their commercial bank with which they already have a good relationship and which provides traditional banking services, including the inbound and outbound payments just mentioned. GPS financial advisers have overcome this obstacle with their competitors by visiting potential clients personally and building a relationship. It is more expensive, as they travel to New York, Los Angeles, and other cities outside of the Rocky Mountain region, but it has paid off because they have developed relationships and obtained new clients. Some competitive advantages that GPS has over the commercial banks are lower transaction costs, 100 percent transparency, and customizing solutions to satisfy customer needs.

Commercial banks have so many different departments and services that the foreign-exchange transactions tend to be more expensive to meet the overhead. Also, the banks look at foreign exchange as a potential area to earn a lot of money, so they price aggressively to build their profits. GPS is more specialized in the foreign-exchange market and smaller, so it can keep its costs low and pass on lower prices to companies.

Until the Internet brought more transparency to foreign-exchange markets, companies often didn't know how much banks or brokers were making on foreign-exchange transactions. GPS adopted 100 percent transparency with its clients: GPS shows clients how much it will make on the deal, something the commercial banks hesitate to do. By showing clients the value-added services it is providing, GPS can justify its profits and not hesitate to disclose its model.

GPS has tried to focus on satisfying the foreign-exchange needs of its clients individually, whereas big banks tend to want to sell standardized services—one size fits all. GPS managers sit down with clients and discuss needs and strategies, and they come up with innovative solutions that result in more satisfactory foreign-exchange transactions. These strategies appear to be working, because GPS has grown significantly since its inception.

Reuters and Bloomberg play an important role in the business of GPS. The company uses them because they have the most powerful analytical tools and real-time pricing. In spite of the high cost of subscribing to Reuters's and Bloomberg's services, GPS decided to go with both. In fact, the three partners have different preferences as to which service they like the best. This has generated a friendly rivalry over the merits of Reuters versus Bloomberg. The two services provide real-time market information, analytics, and a trading platform. In addition, the services are essential for trying to price more complex foreign-exchange products such as options.

FUTURE CHALLENGES

Although GPS has never lost a client to another competitor, the future holds a number of challenges. The first challenge faces services. If GPS had stuck with its initial goal of providing traditional foreign-exchange services, it would have opened itself up to significant competition with the banks and other market entrants, such as boutique firms that can focus only on the payments side in the small- and medium-sized market. So the key was to find ways to move its clientele upstream with other value-added services. The problem was to decide what areas it should enter and where to find the expertise. What areas of corporate finance could GPS choose that would leverage its expertise in trading? All three of the founding members had banking backgrounds. Would that be enough as the company moved into new areas?

A second risk has to do with its target market. Given the merger and acquisition activity in the United States, could GPS continue to maintain its client base, or would its clients get bought out by larger firms, just as Wells Fargo snapped up First Security? If that were to happen, GPS would have to figure out how to sell its expertise to larger clients who had no experience or track record with them. A third risk was the potential of unfavorable new regulations. The regulatory environment of the foreign-exchange trade is intense and changes frequently. GPS would have to learn the new laws and regulations and adopt new policies and procedures to work in accordance with any new rules.

THE GLOBAL FINANCIAL CRISIS: CHALLENGES AND OPPORTUNITIES

When the global financial crisis hit, it became obvious that *counterparty risk* was a real issue. Counterparty risk is the risk that the other party to an agreement—in this case a money center bank entering into a foreign-exchange agreement—might default. Many of GPS's clients or potential clients became nervous as one major money center bank after another ran into problems in late 2008. Because GPS was on sound financial footing, many companies flocked to them to handle their foreign-exchange transactions. This caused a large spike in activity. In addition, GPS's lower rates were also more attractive. When the economy was growing rapidly, many companies were not too worried about paying a little more for foreign-exchange transactions with their banks. As the global economy began to contract, however, they realized how important it was to squeeze out any savings they could, and this played right into the hands of GPS.

Just as the crisis dropped a lot of business in GPS's lap, the government bailout pulled it right back. As soon as the U.S. Fed decided to bail out the banks and reduce the counterparty risk, many of GPS's new clients went right back to their banks. Although GPS was able to retain some clients, it lost others. Given how tight credit was, companies realized that they needed to go back to the banks that could help them out.

EXPANDED SERVICES: A KEY TO FUTURE GROWTH

As Manbeian, Langston, and Gibbons looked at their business, they realized that the key to their future was to develop a broader base of services to their clients. As a result, they decided to focus on their strength—corporate foreign exchange—and to provide expanded services in global business risk management. The general idea of trading currencies to satisfy their initial core business of import and export transactions was simple. Some transactions went beyond exports and imports and involved derivatives to protect

Concept Check

We're concerned in this chapter with the *financial* aspects of MNE operations—in particular, with the ways in which MNEs gain access to *capital* in both local and global markets. Recall, however, our introduction of such global information providers as Reuters and Bloomberg in Chapter 9, where we refer to their role in furnishing *money center banks* with the data about **foreign exchange** that the banks pass on to client MNEs. Here, we hasten to reaffirm the importance of information and information flows in making not only **exchange-rate** transactions but a vast range of other decisions as well.

against future risks. With their connection to Bloomberg and Reuters, they had the capabilities necessary to enter into any transaction that the client needed.

But as they began to work with midmarket companies with operations around the world, they realized that many of these companies were spending a lot of money making trades. As they analyzed the cash flows in different currencies, it was easy to see that as their clients' markets and the currencies in which they operated increased, they had to enter into more and more foreign-exchange transactions.

One of their clients, a large technology firm, was expanding internationally so rapidly that the growth was straining the capabilities of its finances to keep up with it. With hundreds of currency pairs and financial statements being generated in many different currencies and using several different functional currencies, the client was having a difficult time keeping on top of the complexities. GPS realized that it could save its client a lot of money by netting its transactions. Instead of having each entity around the world settle its transactions with every other entity, GPS helped the firm set up a system that could reduce the number of times they had to exchange currency. As it did that, it reduced the costs of each transaction—an important source of revenue to the client's bank.

FXpert

GPS developed proprietary software called FXpert to help its clients monitor foreign-exchange flows and determine how to save money on transactions. After identifying the timing and nature of the cash flows through a specialized audit, a GPS financial adviser proposes an effective hedging solution that GPS can provide. The solution might be as simple as reducing the number of foreign-currency transactions or as complex as hedging some of the exposures using forwards, options, or futures contracts. In addition to its software and trading expertise, GPS feels that one of its major strengths is its ability to provide a tailored solution.

The global risk-management business also offers foreign accounts receivable review, global business consultation on global finance methods, dispute resolution in solving payment disputes, international loan packaging, and letters of credit. As it has developed these services, GPS has had to expand its expertise base to include an understanding of complex accounting rules on derivatives, complex financial hedging strategies, and software development.

ADDITIONAL STRATEGIC MOVES

Given the risky foreign-exchange environment, GPS has shifted some of its efforts to work as an agent or broker with their clients' banks instead of being the direct counterparty in foreign-exchange transactions. That allows the company to do what it does best—utilize its proprietary software to find business solutions for clients to reduce foreign-exchange risks and lower the costs of trading foreign exchange. With its knowledge of the markets, GPS is able to negotiate with its clients' banks to get the best possible exchange rate on a transaction and earn a little in the process.

In addition to its technical expertise, GPS has developed a solid marketing strategy. It has segmented its market into SMEs and MNEs. The two different sets of clients, given their size and the nature of their transactions, have different needs, and GPS realizes that it has to sell its services differently to those markets. The initial expansion outside the Utah market was to the West Coast and Intermountain West, but now it is expanding to the East Coast to pick up companies in those important markets.

As GPS expands, the partners need to constantly refine their message. From a sales point of view, what do the CFO and treasurer need to know about GPS and what they have to offer? What is the best way to tell their story, and what materials do they need to provide to potential clients?

Finally, a key aspect of their success is their proprietary software. Given the rapidly changing market and the need to constantly upgrade the quality of what they have to offer, GPS needs to bring its software development in-house. That involves higher costs, but it also results in a better product, and it is essential to control the speed and quality of innovation. Foreign-exchange exposure has provided lots of opportunities, and now GPS needs to keep pushing ahead with its competitive advantage in global **CRN** capital markets.

Case Review Note

Introduction

Why do you need to understand capital markets, cash management, and financial risk? Having a good product idea is not sufficient for success. MNEs need to get access to capital markets in different countries to finance expansion. Indeed, finance is integral to firms' international strategies. The small company involved in international business only tangentially may not be concerned about global capital markets, but it will probably still have to deal in foreign exchange through its commercial bank to settle payments for exports and imports. However, the MNE investing and operating abroad is usually concerned about access to capital in local markets as well as in large global markets.

This chapter examines external sources of debt and equity capital available to companies operating abroad as well as internal sources of funds that arise from intercompany links. The chapter also explores the international dimensions of the capital-investment decision, global cash management, foreign-exchange risk-management strategies, and international tax issues.

The Finance Function

One of the most important people on the management team is the chief financial officer (CFO). This chapter focuses on the CFO's most important global finance-related responsibilities. Figure 19.1 illustrates how the responsibilities of the CFO, controller, and treasurer

Concept Check

It's worthwhile to make a quick comparison between Figure 19.2 and Figure 18.3, which focuses on the twofold responsibility of the company *controller*—overseeing activities in both accounting and financial management. Here we focus on the responsibilities of the *treasurer*—controlling the company's cash payments and related financial functions, both domestic and foreign. As both figures show, the functions of the two offices fall under the overall responsibility of the *CFO* (or VP of Finance).

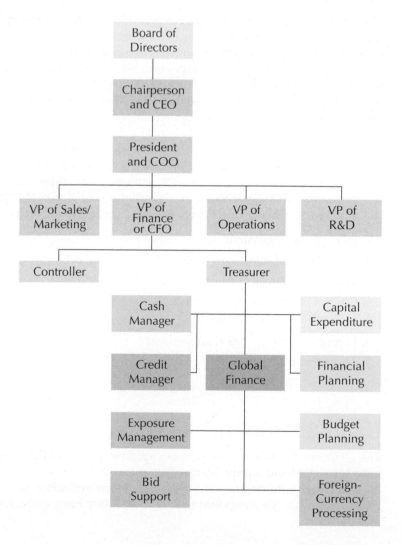

FIGURE 19.1   The Role of the Treasurer in the Financial Function

As a firm's chief accounting officer, the *controller* evaluates the financial results of business operations. The *treasurer* writes the checks—or, more precisely, controls the company's cash payments. The treasurer's department handles both domestic and foreign financial functions, including cash and exposure management, capital expenditure, and foreign-currency processing.

fit into the organizational structure of the firm and especially how global financial management fits into the overall financial function.

The finance function in the firm focuses on cash flows, both short term and long term. The role of financial management is to maintain and create economic value or wealth by maximizing shareholder wealth—the market value of existing shareholders' common stock.[2] The management activities related to cash flows can be divided into these four major areas:

> The corporate finance function acquires and allocates financial resources among the company's activities and projects. Four key functions are
>
> • Capital structure.
> • Long-term financing.
> • Capital budgeting.
> • Working capital management.

- *Capital structure*—determining the proper mix of debt and equity
- *Long-term financing*—selecting, issuing, and managing long-term debt and equity capital, including location (in the company's home country or elsewhere) and currency (the company's home currency or a foreign currency)
- *Capital budgeting*—analyzing investment opportunities
- *Working capital management*—managing the company's currency assets and liabilities (cash, receivables, marketable securities, inventory, trade receivables and payables, short-term bank debt)

In the following sections, we discuss these areas and also the impact of taxation on each of these decisions.[3]

THE ROLE OF THE CFO

The CFO acquires financial resources and allocates them among the company's activities and projects. Acquiring resources (financing) means generating funds either internally (within the company) or from sources external to the company at the lowest possible cost. When GPS began, the founders needed outside investors with significant resources to fund the start-up as well as lend credibility to potential clients. Allocating resources (investing) means increasing stockholders' wealth through the allocation of funds to different projects and investment opportunities.[4]

The CFO's Global Perspective   The CFO's job is more complex in a global environment than in the domestic setting because of forces such as foreign-exchange risk, currency flows and restrictions, political risk, different tax rates and laws pertaining to the determination of taxable income, and regulations on access to capital in different markets. In the remainder of the chapter, we examine the following areas:

1. Overall capital structure
2. Global capital markets
3. Offshore financial centers
4. Capital budgeting in a global context
5. Internal sources of funds
6. Foreign-exchange risk management
7. Taxation of foreign-source income

Capital Structure

The CFO must determine the proper capital structure of the company—the mix between long-term debt and equity. Many companies start off with an initial investment and then grow through internally generated funds. However, when those sources are inadequate to fund continued growth into new markets, they have to decide the proper mix of debt and equity.

LEVERAGING DEBT FINANCING

The degree to which a firm funds the growth of the business by debt is known as **leverage.** The weighted average cost of capital of a company is found as follows:

$$
\begin{bmatrix} Weighted \\ average \ cost \\ of \ capital \end{bmatrix} = \begin{bmatrix} After\text{-}tax & & Proportion \\ cost \ of & \times & of \ debt \\ debt & & financing \end{bmatrix} + \begin{bmatrix} Cost & & Proportion \\ of & \times & of \ equity \\ equity & & financing \end{bmatrix}
$$

Leverage—the degree to which a firm funds the growth of business by debt.

The degree to which companies use leverage instead of *equity capital*—known as stocks or shares—varies from country to country. Country-specific factors are a more important determinant of a company's capital structure than any other factor, because companies tend to follow the financing trends in their own countries and their particular industries within their countries. Japanese companies, for example, are more likely to follow the capital structure of other Japanese companies than they are of U.S. or European companies. Leveraging is often perceived as the most cost-effective route to capitalization, because the interest that companies pay on debt is a tax-deductible expense in most countries, whereas the dividends paid to investors are not.

When Is Leveraging *Not* the Best Option? However, leveraging may not be the best approach in all countries for two major reasons. First, excessive reliance on long-term debt increases financial risk and thus requires a higher return for investors. Second, foreign subsidiaries of an MNE may have limited access to local capital markets, making it difficult for the MNE to rely on debt to fund asset acquisition.[5]

Table 19.1 shows the debt-to-asset ratio on average for companies in a selected group of countries. Note the relatively higher reliance on equity capital by Brazil, Mexico, and Russia. In most emerging markets, there is usually a concentration of wealth in families. So even though there appears to be a heavy reliance on equity, there may only be a few shareholders, whereas in the U.S. and U.K., shares of stock are broadly held. Another interesting dimension of Table 19.1 is the composition of debt—long-term vs. short-term. France, for example, is fairly evenly split between the two, whereas Brazilian firms rely more heavily on long-term debt, and German firms rely more on short-term debt. Recent research has confirmed that country-specific factors are important determinants of the capital structure of firms.[6]

TABLE 19.1 Selected Capital Structures, FY 2007

Because companies tend to follow financing practices that predominate in their own countries, country-specific factors are important in a firm's capital structure. Taxation is among such factors. If in a given country, for example, interest paid on debt is tax deductible and interest paid to shareholders is not, then *leveraging*—funding growth by debt—may be regarded as more cost-effective than *equity financing*.

Country	Equity (%)	Total Debt (%)	Long-Term Debt (%)	Short-Term Debt (%)
Russia	73.8	26.2	13.2	13.1
Mexico	48.7	51.3	31.7	19.6
Brazil	45.7	54.3	32.8	21.4
Japan	44.6	55.4	18.4	37.1
UK	38.0	62.0	32.5	29.4
USA	36.1	63.9	42.8	21.1
France	29.1	70.9	35.6	35.4
Germany	28.2	71.8	32.6	39.2

Source: Data collected by Compustat Global; available at www.wrds.wharton.upenn.edu (accessed July 13, 2009).

FACTORS AFFECTING THE CHOICE OF CAPITAL STRUCTURE

Choice of capital structure depends on tax rates, degree of development of local equity markets, and creditor rights.

Many factors influence the choice of capital structure—both within a country and by MNEs with affiliates in different countries—such as local tax rates, the degree of development of local equity markets, and creditor rights. One study of the capital structure of foreign affiliates of U.S.-based MNEs found that local tax rates influenced the debt-to-equity ratios. Although a U.S.-based MNE, for example, might have a debt-to-equity ratio for the firm as a whole that is based on capital-market expectations in U.S. capital markets, its foreign affiliates have to be sensitive to local conditions.

As noted in the study,

Ten percent higher local tax rates are associated with 2.8 percent higher debt/asset ratios, with internal borrowing particularly sensitive to taxes. Multinational affiliates are financed with less external debt in countries with underdeveloped capital markets or weak creditor rights, reflecting significantly higher local borrowing costs. Instrumental variable analysis indicates that greater borrowing from parent companies substitutes for three-quarters of reduced external borrowing induced by capital market conditions. Multinational firms appear to employ internal capital markets opportunistically to overcome imperfections in external capital markets.[7]

In addition, different tax rates, dividend remission policies, and exchange controls may cause a company to rely more on debt in some situations and more on equity in others. It is important to understand that the different debt and equity markets discussed in this chapter have different levels of importance for companies worldwide.

A major cause of the Asian financial crisis of 1997 was excessive dollar bank debt. This was a contributor to the global financial crisis of 2007–2009, but the issues were more complex, and the crisis was far broader and deeper.

Debt and Exchange Rates   As was the case with the Asian financial crisis of 1997, the global financial crisis of 2007–2009 highlighted foreign-exchange risk. Many individuals, banks, and companies borrowed in dollars or euros leading up to the crisis because of the relatively lower interest rate in the United States and Europe. Although this phenomenon happened around the world, it was especially problematic in Eastern Europe and Iceland. In Iceland, a country with its own currency (the krona, not the euro), the Central Bank kept interest rates high, which attracted lots of foreign investment and kept the krona strong. People's standards of living, among the highest in the world, were supported by the strong currency and the ability to import products. They sustained their high consumption by financing houses and other purchases through borrowing in cheaper currencies. When the financial crisis hit, however, the krona plunged in value, the banks failed, and consumers could not afford to service their debts. The lower foreign interest rates were replaced by exchange-rate risk.[8] One of the major causes of the Asian financial crisis in 1997 was that Asian companies relied too much on debt to fund their growth, especially bank debt. The lack of development of bond and equity markets in those countries forced companies to rely on bank debt for growth. Many of the Asian banks borrowed dollars from international banks and lent the money to local companies in local currencies, not dollars. At the time, many Asian countries pegged their currencies to the U.S. dollar, so the assumption was that if you borrow in dollars, it is the same as borrowing in the local currency. When the Asian currencies fell against the dollar, many of the banks could not service their loans and went into bankruptcy. Asian companies that borrowed directly in dollars suffered the same fate. History tends to repeat itself.

Concept Check

In discussing "Players on the Foreign-Exchange Market" in Chapter 9, we describe the role of *money center banks* (or *reporting dealers*) in making **foreign-exchange** transactions. Here we point out that, as significant players in the *interbank market*—the market for exchanges between dealer banks— money center banks either deal directly with each other or operate through foreign-exchange brokers. They are, in other words, well placed to provide services in **offshore financing.**

DEBT MARKETS AS MEANS OF EXPANSION

An MNE that needs to raise capital through debt markets has a number of options. The local domestic debt market is the first source that a company will tap. This means Japan for Japanese companies, but it could also mean Japan for the Japanese subsidiary of a U.S. company. Nissan is a good example of domestic and foreign borrowing. In its FY 2009 annual report, it listed bonds issued in Japanese yen by domestic and international subsidiaries, and U.S. dollars and Mexican pesos by foreign subsidiaries.[9] A significant amount of the bonds payable are in yen because of low interest rates compared to bond interest rates in other countries.

Here's another example. In the early 1990s, Nu Skin, a direct seller of skin-treatment and personal-care products, embarked upon a program of expansion into Japan. In order to fund a portion of this expansion, the company borrowed capital in yen. As a result, its long-term debt ultimately included the long-term portion of Japanese yen–denominated 10-year notes issued to the Prudential Insurance Company of America in 2000. The notes bear interest at an effective rate of 3 percent per annum and are due October 2010, with annual principal payments that began in October 2004. As of December 31, 2008, the outstanding balance on the notes was 2.8 billion Japanese yen, or $30.6 million, $15.3 million of which was included in the current portion of long-term debt.[10] Since then, Nu Skin has issued more debt in U.S. dollars and Japanese yen. The yen debt has much lower interest rates—ranging from 1.7 to 3.3 percent, compared with U.S. dollar debt ranging from 4.5 to 6.2 percent. The lower-cost Japanese debt is okay as long as the yen remains stable against the dollar. When the yen strengthens against the dollar, however, the dollar equivalent of the debt rises and may wipe out any gains on the lower interest rates. For example, in January 2008, Nu Skin converted $20 million in debt from dollars to yen at an exchange rate of ¥108.5 (an equivalent of ¥2.17 billion). The interest rate dropped from 6.2 to 3.3 percent. By December 31, 2008, the yen had strengthened to 90.38430, and the debt was now worth over $24 million.

MNEs have an advantage because they can tap local debt and equity markets, foreign debt and equity markets (such as the Eurodollar, Eurobond, and Euroequity markets), and internal funds from the corporate family. Most local companies are locked into local debt markets or possibly foreign debt markets, but they may not have the ability to raise funds as extensively as the local affiliates of MNEs do, unless they are MNEs themselves, such as Toyota or Nissan.

> Companies can use local and international debt markets to raise funds.

Global Capital Markets

Companies have many ways of raising capital to fund operations, and their home countries have debt and equity markets, but in this section of the chapter, we look at the role of foreign debt and equity markets as sources of funds for MNEs.

> Two major sources of funds external to the MNE's normal operations are debt markets and equity markets.

EUROCURRENCIES AND THE EUROCURRENCY MARKET

The **Eurocurrency market** is an important source of debt financing for MNEs, to complement what they can find in their domestic markets. A **Eurocurrency** is any currency that is banked outside its country of origin. More specifically, a **Eurodollar** is a certificate of deposit in dollars in a bank outside the United States. Most Eurodollar CDs are held in London, but they could be held anywhere outside the United States. Currencies banked outside their country of origin are also known as *offshore currencies*.

A major advantage of the Eurodollar market is that it is not regulated by the U.S. Federal Reserve Bank, which is a real concern to "the Fed" because the market is off-shore, outside of its control. The same is true for other currencies and their major regulators. The Eurodollar market started with the deposit of U.S. dollars in London banks. As other currencies entered the offshore market, the broader "Eurocurrency" name was adopted for market use, although the market tends to use the name of the specific currency, such as *Euroyen* or *Eurosterling* for offshore Japanese yen and British pounds sterling.

Given the introduction of the euro as the new currency in Europe, the term *Eurocurrency* can be a little confusing, but a euro held outside Europe could be called a *euroeuro* or "offshore euro," similar to Eurodollars or Euroyen. Eurodollars constitute a

> A Eurocurrency is any currency banked outside its country of origin, but it is primarily dollars banked outside the United States.

fairly consistent 65 to 80 percent of the Eurocurrency market. Dollars held by foreigners on deposit in the United States are not Eurodollars, but dollars held at branches of U.S. or other banks outside the United States are.

Major Sources of Eurocurrencies   There are four major sources of Eurocurrencies:

- Foreign governments or individuals who want to hold dollars outside the United States
- Multinational enterprises that have cash in excess of current needs
- European banks with foreign currency in excess of current needs
- Countries such as Germany, Japan, and Taiwan that have large balance-of-trade surpluses held as reserves

The demand for Eurocurrencies comes from sovereign governments, supranational agencies such as the World Bank, companies, and individuals. Eurocurrencies exist partly for the convenience and security of the user and partly because of cheaper lending rates for the borrower and better yield for the lender.

Characteristics of the Eurocurrency Market   Because the Eurocurrency market is a wholesale (companies and other institutions) rather than a retail (individuals) market, transactions are very large. Public borrowers such as governments, central banks, and public-sector corporations are the major players. Although MNEs are involved in the Eurodollar market, the Eurodollar market has historically been an interbank market. Since the late 1990s, however, London banks have shifted to using nonbank customers for Eurodollar transactions. This was partly because of the introduction of the euro, the subsequent fall in foreign transactions, and consolidation in the banking sector.[11]

The Eurocurrency market is both short and medium term. Short-term borrowing is composed of maturities of less than one year. Anything from one to five years is considered a **Eurocredit,** which may be a loan, a line of credit, or another form of medium- and long-term credit, including **syndication,** in which several banks pool resources to extend credit to a borrower and spread the risk. Euro-commercial paper are short-term notes with maturities of less than one year.

Interest Rates in the Eurocurrency Market   A major attraction of the Eurocurrency market is the difference in interest rates compared with those in domestic markets. Of course, the domestic rates vary as well. The prime rate is of particular interest to corporations, because it reflects the interest rates banks charge their prime or best corporate customers. As of July 7, 2009, the prime rate was 3.25 percent in the United States, 1.00 percent in the euro zone, and 1.475 percent in Japan.[12] Other interest rates, such as the Federal Funds Rate in the United States, are good indicators of the future direction of interest rates because they are set daily by the market, whereas the prime rate does not change that often. However, the global economic crisis forced central banks all over the world to drop interest rates in order to stimulate economic growth. When inflation becomes a concern, interest rates will rise again to try to choke off inflation by slowing down economic growth.

London Inter-Bank Offered Rate   Because of the large transactions and the lack of controls and their attendant costs, Eurocurrency deposits tend to yield more than domestic deposits do, and loans tend to be cheaper than they are in domestic markets. Traditionally, loans are made at a certain percentage above the **London Inter-Bank Offered Rate (LIBOR),** which is a short-term interest rate for U.S. dollar loans in London. The LIBOR rates quoted on August 7, 2009, for Eurodollars were 0.27563 percent for one month; 0.46125 percent for three months; 0.90750 percent for six months; and 1.51000 percent for one year. The rate for three-month Euro LIBOR was 0.839, which is higher than the three-month Eurodollar LIBOR rate.

LIBOR is a short-term interest rate for dollars held in the Eurodollar market.

Subprime Loans   Some financial firms lend money at rates above the prime rate—called *subprime loans* because the borrowers are below prime quality. These loans are made and then, at times, sold as securities by lenders to investors.[13] As variable-rate loans are made with rates below prime, problems can arise for debtors and for investors in these subprime loans when variable interest rates rise, as we found in 2007 when the housing market slumped in the United States.[14] Borrowers around the world found that their mortgages were "under water," meaning that the value of their homes was lower than their debt. That has led to default on mortgages and financial problems for institutions that held complex securities made up of subprime mortgages.

The amount of the interest rate above LIBOR that a borrower is charged all depends on the creditworthiness of the customer, and it must be large enough to cover expenses and build reserves against possible losses. Most loans are variable rate, and the rate-fixing period is generally six months, although it may be one or three months.

INTERNATIONAL BONDS

Many countries have active bond markets available to domestic and foreign investors. The United States was the largest market in the world for domestic bonds, accounting for 43 percent of all domestic bonds issued in 2008. Bonds are used by governments, financial institutions, and corporations, with corporate issues being the smallest segment.[15] However, in 2009, there was a significant increase in the issuance of global corporate bonds due to the lack of bank credit.[16] The problem is that the bond market tends to be a little pricier than bank debt, but at least it is available both in the domestic market and offshore.

One of the reasons why the bond (and stock) markets in the United States are so influential is because the companies of continental Europe still rely disproportionately on banks for finance. As noted, however, that began to change in 2009 due to the economic crisis and its impact on the banks. Emerging markets are increasingly turning to the bond market for funding and now constitute about 10 percent of the market worldwide.[17]

Types of International Bonds

Foreign Bonds   There are two types of international bonds: foreign bonds and Eurobonds. Although the international bond market is important, it comprises only 29 percent of the market worldwide, significantly dwarfed by the domestic bond market. **Foreign bonds** are sold outside the borrower's country but denominated in the currency of the country of issue. For example, a French company floating a bond issue in the United States in U.S. dollars would be issuing a foreign bond. They also have creative names, such as Yankee bond (issued in the United States), Samurai bond (issued in Japan), Bulldog bond (issued in England), and Panda bond (issued in China).

A foreign bond is one sold outside the country of the borrower but denominated in the currency of the country of issue. A Eurobond is a bond issue sold in a currency other than that of the country of issue.

Eurobonds   A **Eurobond** is usually underwritten (placed in the market for the borrower) by a syndicate of banks from different countries and sold in a currency other than that of the country of issue. A bond issue floated by a U.S. company in dollars in London, Luxembourg, and Switzerland is a Eurobond. The leading currency in the Eurobond market is the euro, which made up 48 percent of the market in 2008, followed by the dollar, which accounts for 36 percent of international bond issuances. London is the leading center for the issuance of international bonds, with 30 percent of the market, followed by the U.S. with 23 percent of the market.[18]

What's So Attractive about the International Bond Market?   The international bond market is an attractive place to borrow money. For one thing, it allows a company to diversify its funding sources from the local banks and the domestic bond market and borrow in maturities that might not be available in the domestic markets. In addition, the international bond markets tend to be less expensive than local bond markets. However, not all companies are interested in global bonds or Eurobonds. Before the Asian financial crisis hit, Asian companies relied on their domestic banks more because of the ready availability of cheap loans. In addition, the companies and banks tended to develop a cozier relationship than might be the case with Western companies and banks.[19] However, the Asian financial crisis demonstrated the fundamental flaws in this strategy as banks went bankrupt and as companies were forced to face the fact that they couldn't generate enough funds to pay back the loans. The same story was repeated with the global financial crisis of 2007–2009.

Although the Eurobond market is centered in Europe, it has no national boundaries. In contrast to most conventional bonds, Eurobonds are sold simultaneously in several financial centers through multinational underwriting syndicates and are purchased by an international investing public that extends far beyond the confines of the countries of issue.

U.S. companies first issued Eurobonds in 1963 as a means of avoiding U.S. tax and disclosure regulations. They're typically issued in denominations of $5,000 or $10,000, pay interest annually, are held in bearer form, and are traded over the counter (OTC), most frequently in London.[20] Any investor who holds a bearer bond is entitled to receive the principal and interest payments. In contrast, for a registered bond, which is more typical in the United States, the investor is required to be registered as the bond's owner to receive payments. An OTC bond is traded with or through an investment bank rather than on a securities exchange, such as the London Stock Exchange.

Case: Marks & Spencer: How Corporations Use Eurobonds   An example of the use of the Eurobond market is with Gazprombank of Russia. In January 2004, Gazprombank placed a U.S. $300 million Eurobond issue with a maturity of 2008. Seventy percent of the issue went to European investors, 18 percent to offshore structures of investors from the United States, 5 percent to Asians, and 7 percent to other regions. This was one of many Eurobond issues made by Gazprombank, some denominated in dollars and some in euros. The deals were placed by JPMorgan Chase in London.[21]

Occasionally, Eurobonds may provide currency options, which enable the creditor to demand repayment in one of several currencies, thus reducing the exchange risk inherent in single-currency foreign bonds. More frequently, however, both interest and principal on Eurobonds are payable to the creditor in U.S. dollars. It is also possible to issue a Eurobond in one currency—say, the U.S. dollar—and then swap the obligation to another currency. For example, a U.S. company with a subsidiary in Britain would generate large quantities of British pounds through normal operations, and it could use the pounds to pay off a British-pound bond. If the U.S. company had issued Eurobonds in dollars in London, it could enter into a swap agreement through an investment bank to exchange its future dollar obligations with a British-pound obligation and use the pound revenues to pay off the swapped obligation.

EQUITY SECURITIES AND THE EUROEQUITY MARKET

Another source of financing is *equity securities,* whereby an investor takes an ownership position in return for shares of stock in the company and the promises of capital gains—an appreciation in the value of the stock—and maybe dividends.

Access to Equity Capital   One way a company can easily and inexpensively get access to capital is through a private placement with a venture capitalist. In this case, a wealthy venture capitalist (or perhaps a venture-capital firm investing the money of one or several wealthy individuals) invests money in a new venture in exchange for stock.

In addition to private placements, companies can access the *equity-capital market*, more commonly known as the *stock market.* Companies can raise new capital by listing their shares on a stock exchange, and they can list on their home-country exchange or on a foreign exchange. For example, Beijing-based China Techfaith Wireless Communication Technology Limited, a designer and manufacturer of mobile handsets, offered 8.73 million shares on an initial public offering (IPO) on NASDAQ on May 5, 2005. Its underwriters were Merrill Lynch, Lehman Brothers, and CIBC World Markets Corporation. Its shares listed at $16.27, and it raised $141.8 million.

Another example of an international IPO was the listing of Sistema on the London Stock Exchange in 2004. Sistema, the largest private-sector consumer-services company in Russia, issued a U.S. $1.56 billion offering in London, the largest-ever Russian IPO on a public market anywhere. Sistema's offering comprised 1.8 million common shares in the form of 91.6 million Global Depositary Receipts (GDRs), with 50 GDRs representing one common share. (A GDR is listed in several different markets simultaneously.) Sistema needed access to equity dollars, which it was not able to raise inside Russia, so the Euroequity market in London was an obvious site for it to list. The growth in globalization has forced companies to look at equity markets as an alternative to debt markets and banks as a source of funds.

THE SIZE OF GLOBAL STOCK MARKETS

Map 19.1 identifies the 10 largest stock markets in the world and 10 large emerging market stock markets not in the top 10 in terms of **market capitalization**—the total number of shares of stock listed times the market price per share. The global financial crisis has really taken a toll on the global stock markets. Stock market capitalization worldwide dropped by 46.5 percent between the end of 2007 and the end of 2008. It had begun to recover in mid-2009, but the numbers shown in Map 19.1 are quite low compared to even one year earlier. The future of global market capitalization is very uncertain.

The numbers in Map 19.1 represent each specific stock market rather than all of the markets in the country. For example, the NYSE Group as a whole is listed as number one, but that does not include all stock markets in the United States. One interesting trend is the rise in importance of the stock markets in emerging markets, especially China. The Shanghai Stock Exchange was number six, followed by Hong Kong.

> The three largest stock markets in the world are in New York, Tokyo, and London, with the U.S. markets controlling nearly half of the world's stock market capitalization.

Emerging Stock Markets   It's been interesting to track the development of the emerging stock markets. For many years, they were growing fairly rapidly. By 1998, however, the Asian financial crisis had clobbered the emerging stock markets, and they plunged to only 6.9 percent of total. That was followed by crises in Russia and Latin America. However, the emerging markets are growing again and are close to a third of total market capitalization, largely because of the growth of the stock markets in China, India, and Brazil—three of the four BRIC countries.

The Rise of the Euroequity Market   Another significant event in the past decade is the creation of the **Euroequity market,** the market for shares sold outside the boundaries of the issuing company's home country. Prior to 1980, few companies thought about offering stock outside the national boundaries of their headquarters country. Since then,

> Euroequities are shares listed on stock exchanges in countries other than the home country of the issuing company.

Map 19.1   Global Markets: Market Capitalization, 2008

Data reflect domestic *market capitalization*—total number of shares of stock listed multiplied by market price per share.

Source: World Federation of Exchanges, "Equity—1.1 Domestic Market Capitalization," www.world-exchanges.org (accessed July 30, 2009).

Note: Given that this is a Mercator projection, the scale approximates east-west distance at the equator; however, the farther you move from the equator, the more the east-west distance is distorted.

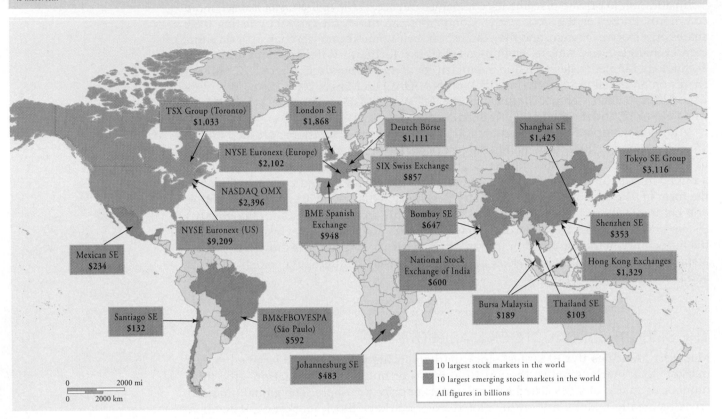

hundreds of companies worldwide have issued stock simultaneously in two or more countries to attract more capital from a wider variety of shareholders. For example, when Daimler and Chrysler merged and issued global shares around the world, the company did so on 21 different markets in eight different countries: Germany, the United States, Austria, Canada, France, Britain, Japan, and Switzerland.

The Trend toward Delisting   However, the trend of listing on more than one exchange, which was popular in the 1990s, is beginning to reverse. More and more companies are reducing the number of exchanges on which their stocks are listed. For example, in March 2005, IBM announced it would remove its shares from the Tokyo Stock Exchange, after already removing its stock from exchanges in Vienna, Frankfurt, and Zurich. Investors are finding that the best price for stocks is usually in the home market of the company in which they are investing.

In addition, companies pay annual fees to list on exchanges, so if trading is light on a certain exchange, they can save money by listing on an exchange with heavier trading volume. Other reasons for delisting shares include weak market returns (fewer investors are putting their money into stocks) and increased regulation, such as the Sarbanes-Oxley Act in the United States. DaimlerChrysler used to list on 15 different stock exchanges in Germany, the United States, France, Japan, and Switzerland; but in 2008, Daimler (no longer DaimlerChrysler) listed only on stock exchanges in

Frankfurt, New York, and Stuttgart, demonstrating the trend to delist on multiple exchanges.

This trend toward delisting has affected even the NYSE. Following its recent corporate governance problems, the NYSE has decreased in popularity. However, it is still one of the most important stock exchanges in the world.[22] The U.S. market is important for U.S. and foreign companies looking for equity capital and is popular for Euroequity issues, partly because of the market size and the speed with which offerings are completed. The large pension funds in the United States can buy big blocks of stock at low transaction costs. Pension fund managers regard foreign stocks as a good form of portfolio diversification. The merger of the NYSE and Euronext has created an even more powerful stock exchange.

AMERICAN DEPOSITARY RECEIPT   The most popular way for a Euroequity to get a listing in the United States is to issue an **American Depositary Receipt (ADR).** An ADR is a negotiable certificate issued by a U.S. bank in the United States to represent the underlying shares of a foreign corporation's stock held in trust at a custodian bank in the foreign country. ADRs are traded like shares of stock, with each one representing some number of shares of the underlying stock. For example, Toyota has listed ADRs on the NYSE since 1999 at a rate of two ADRs per common share of Toyota. They issue through a sponsored ADR facility operated by the Bank of New York as ADRs.

The United States is not the only market for Euroequities. There are also Global Depositary Receipts and European Depositary Receipts, as illustrated in the earlier Sistema example, but the U.S. market dominates the depositary receipt market. However, compared to the NYSE, a much larger percentage of the total shares traded on the London Stock Exchange belongs to foreign companies, even though the total trading volume in the United States is quite large. The creation of NYSE Euronext has complicated the comparisons, because now the merger brings together six cash equities exchanges from five countries.

Many foreign corporations try to raise capital in the United States but don't want to list on an exchange because they don't want to comply with the onerous reporting requirements of the SEC. However, those that do so get access to a large percentage of the world's market capitalization, a fact that is a significant advantage to those with a U.S. listing. Companies generally list on their home country's exchange first and then venture into the international exchanges with depositary receipts.

Offshore Financing and Offshore Financial Centers

Companies can raise debt or equity funds in their domestic markets or offshore. **Offshore financing** is the provision of financial services by banks and other agents to nonresidents. In its simplest form, this involves the borrowing of money from nonresidents and lending to nonresidents.[23] A good example of legitimate offshore financing is the use of the Eurodollar market. A U.S. company can raise Eurodollars in London by working with a bank to issue bonds or syndicate a loan.

WHAT'S AN OFC?

Offshore financial centers (OFCs) are cities or countries that provide large amounts of funds in currencies other than their own and are used as locations in which to raise and accumulate cash. Usually, the financial transactions are conducted in currencies other than the currency of the country and are thus the centers for the Eurocurrency market. An OFC could be defined as any financial center where offshore activity takes place, but a more practical definition of an OFC is a center where the bulk of financial center activity is offshore on both sides of the balance sheet, the transactions are initiated elsewhere, and the majority of the institutions involved are controlled by nonresidents.[24]

Margin notes:

Most foreign companies that list on the U.S. stock exchanges do so through American Depositary Receipts, which are financial documents that represent a share or part of a share of stock in the foreign company.

Offshore financing—the provision of financial services by banks and other agents to nonresidents.

Concept Check

We introduce the *OECD* in discussing the OECD Anti-Bribery Convention in Chapter 5. In addition, the OECD is concerned about a broader range of activities that involve cross-border operations. We also mention the OECD's earlier Guidelines for MNEs, which came out in 1976 and includes a code of conduct for MNEs engaged in cross-border operations. Here we observe that, because **offshore financing** has proved conducive to such misbehavior as tax avoidance, the OECD and several other multilateral organizations have made efforts to strengthen ethical practices in offshore transactions.

Offshore financial centers (OFCs)—cities or countries that provide large amounts of funds in currencies other than their own.

OFCs offer low or zero taxation, moderate or light financial regulation, and banking secrecy and anonymity.

Offshore financial centers can be operational centers or booking centers.

Key offshore financial centers are in the Bahamas, Bahrain, the Caribbean, Hong Kong, Ireland, London, New York, Singapore, and Switzerland, among other locations.

Concept Check

In the section on "Forecasting Exchange-Rate Movements" in Chapter 10, we point out the importance to MNEs of formulating general ideas of the timing, magnitude, and direction of exchange-rate movements. We also describe two approaches that companies can take to forecast exchange rates: **fundamental forecasting** (which bases external or internal decisions on a range of economic variables) and **technical forecasting** (which depends on specialists to analyze trends in exchange rates themselves).

The OECD is trying to eliminate the harmful tax practices in tax-haven countries.

Characteristics of OFCs Generally, the markets in these centers are regulated differently—and usually more flexibly—than domestic markets. The centers provide an alternative, (usually) cheaper source of funding for MNEs so that they don't have to rely strictly on their own national markets. Offshore financial centers have one or more of the following characteristics:

- A large foreign-currency (Eurocurrency) market for deposits and loans (in London, for example)
- A market that functions as a large net supplier of funds to the world financial markets (in Switzerland, for example)
- A market that functions as an intermediary or pass-through for international loan funds (in the Bahamas and the Cayman Islands, for example)
- Economic and political stability
- An efficient and experienced financial community
- Good communications and support services
- An official regulatory climate favorable to the financial industry, in the sense that it protects investors without unduly restricting financial institutions[25]

However, the OECD prefers to differentiate between well and poorly regulated financial centers rather than offshore and onshore.[26]

Operational versus Booking Centers These centers are either *operational centers*, with extensive banking activities involving short-term financial transactions, or *booking centers*, in which little actual banking activity takes place but in which transactions are recorded to take advantage of secrecy and low (or no) tax rates. In the latter case, individuals may deposit money offshore to hide it from their home-country tax authorities, either because the money is earned or to be used illegally—such as in the drug trade or to finance terrorist activities—or because the individual or company does not want to pay tax. London is an example of an operational center; the Cayman Islands is an example of a booking center.

OFCs as "Tax Havens" A major concern with OFCs is the tax avoidance dimension of their activities. The Organization for Economic Cooperation and Development (OECD) has been working closely with the major OFCs to ensure that they are engaged in legal activity. The OECD uses the following key factors in identifying tax havens: (1) no or only nominal taxes, (2) lack of effective exchange of information (especially bank secrecy), (3) lack of transparency, and (4) no substantial activities.[27] Although not trying to tell the sovereign countries what their tax rates should be, the OECD is trying to eliminate harmful tax practices in these four areas:

1. The regime imposes low or no taxes on the relevant income (from geographically mobile financial and other service activities).
2. The regime is ring fenced (i.e., separated) from the domestic economy.
3. The regime lacks transparency; for example, the details of the regime or its application are not apparent or there is inadequate regulatory supervision or financial disclosure.
4. There is no effective exchange of information with respect to the regime.[28]

Obviously, there is a lot of overlap in these definitions. In a 2009 report, the OECD identified 28 tax-haven countries and 10 other financial centers that were moving to adopt their standards for good tax behavior, and they reported that there were no national jurisdictions that had not committed to the internationally accepted tax standard. That is pretty significant progress.[29]

Point ▷ Counterpoint

Should Offshore Financial Centers and Aggressive Tax Practices Be Eliminated?

Point **Yes** The problem with offshore financial centers (OFCs) is that they operate in a shroud of secrecy that allows companies to establish operations there that are used for illegal and unethical behavior. In December 2001, U.S. energy giant Enron filed for bankruptcy, resulting in one of the largest bankruptcies in corporate history. One of the contributors to Enron's problems was the creation of hundreds of subsidiaries in tax havens, including 662 in the Cayman Islands, 119 in Turks and Caicos, 43 in Mauritius, and 8 in Bermuda. The subsidiaries were used to pass off corporate debts, losses, and executive compensation.[30] The fondness of unscrupulous MNEs for OFCs only serves to underscore the unqualified truth voiced in Figure 19.2.

As pointed out in Chapter 18, Parmalat set up three shell companies based in the Caribbean to capture cash. The shell companies allegedly sold Parmalat products, and Parmalat sent them fake invoices and charged costs and fees to make the sales look legitimate. Then Parmalat would write out a credit note for the amount the subsidiaries supposedly owed it and take that to banks to raise money. Given the location of the subsidiaries, you would think that the banks would have been suspicious, but Parmalat got away with these activities.

Off-balance-sheet financing was also used to hide debts. The company transferred over half of its liabilities to the books of small subsidiaries based in offshore tax havens such as the Cayman Islands. This allowed Parmalat to present a healthy balance sheet and a profitable income statement to investors and creditors by hiding large amounts of debt, understating interest expenses (thus overstating income), and overstating revenues for false bookings. Parmalat's actual debt was nearly double the amount disclosed to outsiders.

Terrorists and drug dealers also use OFCs to launder money. When the U.S. government went after the money of Osama bin Laden, it went after OFCs notorious for their secrecy. When a bank in the Bahamas refused to open its books to U.S. government investigators, the United States cut off the bank from the world's wire transfer systems. Within two hours, the bank changed policies.[31] Tax havens have also become a hot political issue, as illustrated in Figure 19.2. ▷

Counterpoint **No** Offshore financial centers are an efficient way for companies to use their financial resources more effectively. They are good locations for companies to establish finance subsidiaries that can raise capital for the parent company or its subsidiaries. They allow the finance subsidiaries to take advantage of lower borrowing costs and tax rates.

This type of activity is not illegal, because the companies are still subject to home- and host-country laws and tax regulations. It is true that some transactions may be illegal, but most are not. The key to policing truly illegal activities, such as hiding drug money or engaging in corporate fraud like the Parmalat case in Chapter 18, is to improve transparency and reporting.

Why shouldn't countries have the opportunity to attract business by offering tax-haven status to MNEs? Many of these countries don't have other visible means of generating resources. They are too small to set up manufacturing operations, don't have a large enough population base to offer low-cost labor, and don't have natural resources they can sell. So what can they do? Companies and individuals need places to bank their wealth or raise capital, so the offshore financial centers have decided to use the theory of factor proportions (discussed in Chapter 6) and develop the banking and financial infrastructure necessary to attract wealth. As long as they establish banking, privacy, and taxation laws that attract money, they should be allowed to do so. The Cayman Islands attracts a lot of tourism, but it is also the world's fifth-biggest financial center and has worked hard to crack down on money laundering so that it can use its financial expertise in legal ways to help companies and individuals.[32]

Offshore financial centers don't rely on taxation to fund huge government expenditures, because they don't have a large military budget or significant welfare costs. Is there anything wrong with not collecting large amounts of taxes? Some countries are upset that offshore financial centers offer a tax-free environment for revenues generated offshore, but that is the business of the countries. Nobody should force them to collect higher taxes just because the high-tax countries are at a disadvantage in attracting banking and other financial transactions. If countries want to charge high taxes on financial transactions, let them do so, but don't force the offshore financial centers to play their game. ◁

Capital Budgeting in a Global Context

The next international dimension of the financial function is the capital budgeting decision whereby the MNE determines which projects and countries will receive its capital investment funds. The parent company must compare the net present value or internal

> Capital budgeting—the process whereby MNEs determine which projects and countries will receive capital investment funds.

FIGURE 19.2   The Classic Lure of Offshore Tax Laxity

Source: John Morris,
www.businesscartoons.co.uk

"Oh, what a tangled web we weave, when first we practise to deceive."

Capital budgeting techniques:
- Payback period.
- Net present value of a project.
- Internal rate of return.

Ugland House, in Georgetown, Grand Cayman, is home to international law firm Maples & Calder, which represents 18,857 separate corporate and individual entities. Maples & Calder of Ugland House is the largest law firm in the Caymans but only one of many to offer services to foreign clients. During the U.S. presidential debates, Senator Barack Obama said that as president he would crack down on corporate loopholes and tax savings, particularly those involving offshore transactions. Obama said, "There's a building in the Cayman Islands [Ugland House] that houses, supposedly, 12,000 U.S.A. based corporations . . . That's either the biggest building in the world or the biggest tax scam in the world. And I think we know which one it is."

Source: Shuma Robbins. *The New York Times*/Redux Pictures

rate of return of a potential foreign project with that of its other projects around the world to determine the best place to invest its resources. The technique used to compare different projects is called *capital budgeting.*

METHODS OF CAPITAL BUDGETING

Payback Period   One approach to capital budgeting is to determine the **payback period** of a project, or the number of years required to recover the initial investment made. That is typically done by estimating the annual after-tax free cash flow from the

investment, determining the present value of the future cash flow for each year, and then determining how many years it will take to recoup the initial investment.

Net Present Value A second approach is to determine the **net present value (NPV)** of a project, which is defined as follows:

$$NPV = \sum_{t=1}^{n} \frac{FCF_t}{(1+k)^t} - IO$$

Where FCF_t = the annual free cash flow in time period t

k = the appropriate discount rate; that is, the required rate of return or cost of capital

IO = the initial cash outlay

n = the project's expected life

The required rate of return is the rate that the company must get from the project to justify the cost of raising the initial investment or at least maintaining the value of its common stock. If the NPV is positive, the project is also considered positive. If the NPV is negative, the company should not enter into the project.

Internal Rate of Return A third approach is to compute the internal rate of return (IRR) of the project and compare it with the required rate of return. The IRR is the rate that equates the present value of future cash flows with the present value of the initial investment. If the IRR is greater than the required rate of return, the investment is considered positive. However, the company then needs to compare the IRR with that of competing projects in other countries.

MNEs need to determine free cash flows based on cash flow estimates and tax rates in different countries and an appropriate required rate of return adjusted for risk.

Several things are common about each of the methods. First, the firm needs to determine the free cash flows, which involves estimating cash flows as well as bringing into the equation different tax rates from different countries. Second, in the case of both NPV and IRR, the company needs to determine what the required rate of return is.

COMPLICATIONS IN CAPITAL BUDGETING

Several aspects of capital budgeting are unique to foreign-project assessment:

- Parent cash flows must be distinguished from project cash flows. *Parent cash flows* refer to cash flows from the project back to the parent in the parent's currency. *Project cash flows* refer to the cash flows in local currency from the sale of goods and services. Will the decision be based on parent cash flows, project cash flows, or both?

- Remittance of funds to the parent, such as dividends, interest on loans, and payment of intracompany receivables and payables, is affected by differing tax systems, legal and political constraints on the movement of funds, local business norms, and differences in how financial markets and institutions function. In addition, tax systems affect free cash flows on the project, irrespective of the remittance issue.

- Differing rates of inflation must be anticipated by both the parent and the subsidiary because of their importance in causing changes in competitive position and in cash flows over time.

- The parent must consider the possibility of unanticipated exchange-rate changes because of both their direct effects on the value of cash flows and their indirect effects on the foreign subsidiary's competitive position.

Concept Check

Later in this chapter, we discuss *hedging strategies*—strategies by which companies can protect themselves from the losses to which they may be exposed in foreign-exchange transactions. Some of these strategies make use of the kinds of *foreign-exchange instruments* that we explain in Chapter 9, such as **forward contracts** (agreeing to exchange currency at a future date), **options** (agreeing to the right to trade currency at a later date), and **futures contract** (agreeing to trade currency at a particular price on a specific date).

- The parent company must evaluate political risk in a target market, because political events can drastically reduce the value or availability of expected cash flows.
- The terminal value (the value of the project at the end of the budgeting period) is difficult to estimate, because potential purchasers from host, home, or third countries—or from the private or public sector—may have widely divergent perspectives on the value of the project. The terminal value is critical in determining the total cash flows from the project. The total cash outlay for the project is partially offset by the terminal value—the amount of cash the parent company can get from the subsidiary or project if it eventually sells it.[33]

Because of all the forces listed here, it's very difficult to estimate future cash flows, both to the subsidiary and to the parent company. There are two ways to deal with the variations in future cash flows. One is to determine several different scenarios and then determine the payback period, net present value, or internal rate of return of the project. The other is to adjust the hurdle rate, which is the minimum required rate of return that the project must achieve for it to receive capital. The adjustment is usually made by increasing the hurdle rate above its minimal level.

> Determine different cash flow scenarios or adjust the hurdle rate (the minimum required rate of return for a project).

Once the budget is complete, the MNE must examine both the return in local currency and the return to the parent in dollars from cash flows. Examining the return in local currency will give management a chance to compare the project with other investment alternatives in the country. However, cash flows to the parent are important, because it is from these cash flows that dividends are paid to shareholders. If the MNE cannot generate a sufficient return to the parent in the parent's currency, it will eventually fall behind in its ability to pay shareholders and pay off corporate debt. Finally, the decision must be made in the strategic context of the investment, not just the financial context.

Internal Sources of Funds

> Funds are working capital, or current assets minus current liabilities.

Although the term *funds* usually means "cash," it is used in a much broader sense in business and generally refers to working capital—that is, the difference between current assets and current liabilities. From a general perspective, funds come from the normal operations of a business (selling merchandise or services) as well as from financing activities, such as borrowing money, issuing bonds, or issuing shares. Uses of funds are for the purchase of fixed assets, paying employees and purchasing materials and supplies, and investing in marketable securities or long-term investments.

Cash Flows and the MNE   Cash flows in an MNE are significantly more complex than for a company that operates in a strictly domestic environment. An MNE that wants to expand operations or needs additional capital can look not only to the domestic and international debt and equity markets but also to sources within itself. For an MNE, the complexity of internal sources is magnified because of the number of its subsidiaries and the diverse environments in which they operate.

> Sources of internal funds are
> - Loans.
> - Investments through equity capital.
> - Intercompany receivables and payables.
> - Dividends.

Figure 19.3 shows a parent company that has two foreign subsidiaries. The parent, as well as the two subsidiaries, may be increasing funds through normal operations. These funds may be used on a company-wide basis, perhaps through loans. The parent can loan funds directly to one subsidiary or guarantee an outside loan to the other. Equity capital from the parent is another source of funds for the subsidiary.

Funds can also go from subsidiary to parent. The subsidiary could declare a dividend to the parent as a return on capital, or it could loan cash directly to the parent. If the subsidiary declared a dividend to the parent, the parent could lend the funds back to the subsidiary. The dividend would not be tax deductible to the subsidiary, but it would be included as income to the parent, and the parent would have to pay tax on the dividend. If the subsidiary loaned money to the parent, the interest paid by the parent would be tax deductible to the parent and would be taxable income to the subsidiary.

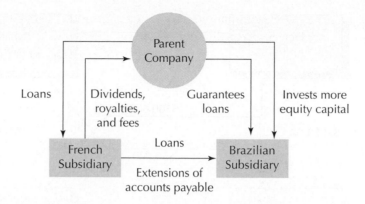

FIGURE 19.3   How the MNE Handles Its Funds (I): Internal Funds

Funds consist of *working capital* that comes from normal business operations and that may be used to purchase assets and materials, to pay employees, and to make investments. If the company is an MNE, funds may come from either parent or subsidiary operations, or both, and can be used by the parent to support either its own operations or those of its subsidiaries.

Merchandise, people (in the case of MNEs involved in services), and financial flows can travel between subsidiaries, giving rise to receivables and payables. Companies can move money between and among related entities by paying quickly, or they can accumulate funds by deferring payment. They can also adjust the size of the payment by arbitrarily raising or lowering the price of intercompany transactions in comparison with the market price—a transfer pricing strategy.

GLOBAL CASH MANAGEMENT

Effective cash management is a chief concern of the CFO, who must answer the following three questions to ensure effective cash management:

1. What are the local and corporate system needs for cash?
2. How can the cash be withdrawn from subsidiaries and centralized?
3. Once the cash has been centralized, what should be done with it?

The cash manager, who reports to the treasurer (as illustrated in Figure 19.1), must collect and pay cash in the company's normal operational cycle and then must deal with financial institutions, such as commercial and investment banks, when generating and investing cash. Before the cash manager remits any cash into the MNE's control center—whether at regional or headquarters level—he or she must first assess local cash needs through cash budgets and forecasts. Because the cash forecast projects the excess cash that will be available, the cash manager will know how much cash can be invested for short-term profits.

Once local cash needs are met, the cash manager must decide whether to allow the local manager to invest any excess cash or have it remitted to a central cash pool. If the cash is centralized, the manager must find a way of making the transfer. A cash dividend is the easiest way to distribute cash, but government restrictions may interfere. For example, foreign-exchange controls may prevent the company from remitting as large a dividend as it would like. Cash can also be remitted through royalties, management fees, and repayment of principal and interest on loans.

Multilateral Netting   An important cash-management strategy is **netting** cash flows internationally. For example, an MNE with operations in four European countries could have several different intercompany cash transfers resulting from loans, the sale of goods, licensing agreements, and so forth. In the illustration in Figure 19.4, for example, there are no fewer than seven different transfers among four subsidiaries. Among its special services, GPS Capital Inc., the foreign-exchange company profiled in our opening case, helps clients determine their foreign-currency cash flows and assists them in developing strategies to net cash flows by minimizing the number of their foreign-currency transactions.

> Cash budgets and forecasts are essential in assessing a company's cash needs.

> Dividends are a good source of intercompany transfers, but governments often restrict their free movement.

> Multilateral netting—the process of coordinating cash inflows and outflows among subsidiaries so that only net cash is transferred, reducing transaction costs.

CRN
Case Review Note

FIGURE 19.4 How the MNE Handles Its Funds (II): Multilateral Cash Flows

As the various subsidiaries of the MNE go about their business, cash can be transferred among them for a variety of reasons (e.g., in the form of loans or as proceeds from the sale of goods). Cash, of course, can flow in any direction, and if the MNE doesn't maintain some kind of cash-management center, each subsidiary must settle its accounts (receivables, payables, etc.) independently.

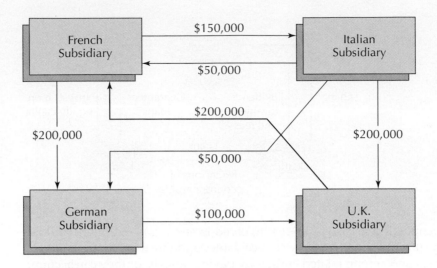

Netting requires sophisticated software and good banking relationships in different countries.

Table 19.2 identifies the total receivables, payables, and net position for each subsidiary. Rather than have each subsidiary settle its accounts independently with subsidiaries in other countries, many MNEs are establishing cash-management centers in one city (such as Brussels) to coordinate cash flows among subsidiaries from several countries.

Figure 19.5 illustrates how each subsidiary in a net payable position transfers funds to the central clearing account. The manager of the clearing account then transfers funds to the accounts of the net receiver subsidiaries. In this example, only four transfers need to take place. The clearing account manager receives transaction information and computes the net position of each subsidiary at least monthly. Then the manager orchestrates the settlement process. The transfers take place in the payor's currency, and the foreign-exchange conversion takes place centrally. For netting to work, the company needs to match its cash needs with software that can keep track of and transfer funds and with banking relationships that allow money to be moved among corporate entities.

Foreign-Exchange Risk Management

As illustrated earlier, global cash-management strategy focuses on the flow of money for specific operating objectives. Another important objective of an MNE's financial strategy is to protect against the foreign-exchange risks of investing abroad. The strategies that an MNE adopts to do this may mean the internal movement of funds as well as the use of one or more of the foreign-exchange instruments described in Chapter 9, such as options and forward contracts.

Concept Check

In Chapter 10, we explain why it's important for MNEs to anticipate exchange-rate changes and make decisions about business activities that may be sensitive to those changes—decisions, for instance, about the sourcing of raw materials and components or the location of manufacturing and assembly facilities. We take up the same theme in Chapter 12, where we cite exchange-rate movement as just one factor that can affect wages in a particular country—and thus any advantage in labor-cost differences that a company might hope to gain from locating operations in that country.

TABLE 19.2 How the MNE Handles Its Funds (III): Net Positions

Assume that these data are from the same MNE as the one introduced in Figure 19.4. Because the company has no cash-management center, *net positions*—the difference between *total receivables* and *total payables*—must be determined on a subsidiary-by-subsidiary basis.

Subsidiary	Total Receivables	Total Payables	Net Position
French	250,000	350,000	(100,000)
German	250,000	100,000	150,000
Italian	150,000	300,000	(150,000)
U.K.	300,000	200,000	100,000

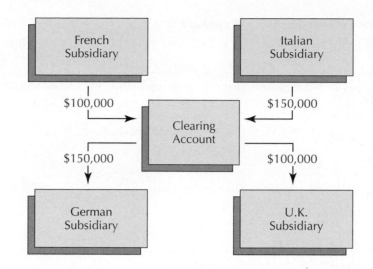

FIGURE 19.5   How the
MNE Handles Its Funds (IV):
Multilateral Netting

Dissatisfied with the process
represented in Figure 19.4, our MNE
has now established a cash-
management center—a *clearing
account*—into which each subsidiary
transfers its net cash. Naturally, the
MNE may in turn distribute the total
to support subsidiary operations.

TYPES OF EXPOSURE

If all exchange rates were fixed in relation to one another, there would be no foreign-exchange risk. However, rates are not fixed, and currency values change frequently. Instead of infrequent, one-way changes, currencies fluctuate often and both up and down. A change in the exchange rate can result in three different exposures for a company: *translation exposure, transaction exposure,* and *economic* or *operational exposure.*

Three types of foreign-exchange exposure: translation, transaction, economic or operational.

Translation Exposure   Foreign-currency financial statements are translated into the reporting currency of the parent company (assumed to be U.S. dollars for U.S. companies) so they can be combined with financial statements of other companies in the corporate group to form the consolidated financial statements. **Translation exposure** occurs because exposed accounts—those translated at the balance-sheet rate or current exchange rate—either gain or lose value in dollars when the exchange rate changes.

Translation exposure arises because the dollar value of the exposed asset or liability changes as the exchange rate changes.

Consider the translation exposure example in Table 19.3 (Panel A) of a U.S. company with a subsidiary in Mexico. In this example, the Mexican subsidiary has 900,000 pesos in the bank. This is the question: What is the value of the cash *after* the exchange rate changes? The subsidiary still has pesos in the bank account; it's just that the dollar equivalent of the pesos has fallen, resulting in a loss. The gain or loss does not represent an actual cash flow effect because the pesos are only translated, not converted, into dollars. In addition, reported earnings can either rise or fall against the dollar because of the translation effect, and this can affect earnings per share and stock prices.

Transaction Exposure   Denominating a transaction in a foreign currency gives rise to **transaction exposure,** because the company has accounts receivable or payable in foreign currency that must be settled eventually. Consider the transaction-exposure example in Table 19.3 (Panel B) of a U.S. exporter delivering merchandise to a British importer. If the exporter were to receive payment in dollars, there would be no immediate impact on the exporter if the dollar/pound exchange rate changed. If payment were to be received in pounds, however, the exporter might incur a foreign-exchange gain or loss. In this case, because the pound is falling in value, the exporter would receive fewer dollars from the sale after the change in the exchange rate. This would be an actual cash flow gain or loss to the exporter.

Transaction exposure arises when a transaction is denominated in a foreign currency and where the settlement gives rises to a cash flow gain or loss.

Economic, or operating, exposure arises from the effects of exchange-rate changes on

- *Future cash flows.*
- *The sourcing of parts and components.*
- *The location of investments.*
- *The competitive position of the company in different markets.*

Economic (or Operating) Exposure   **Economic exposure,** also known as **operating exposure,** is the potential for change in expected cash flows. Economic exposure arises

TABLE 19.3 The Effects of Foreign-Exchange Exposure

Panel A—Translation Exposure

A Mexican subsidiary reports cash in the bank of 900,000 pesos at a time when 9.5 pesos will buy U.S. $1; thus its U.S. parent translates the net in pesos into U.S. $94,737. When the exchange rate changes, however, and 10 pesos are required to buy U.S. $1, the total of 900,000 pesos must be retranslated from U.S. $94,737 into U.S. $90,000.

U.S. Company Bank Account in Mexico	900,000 pesos
Initial Exchange Rate	9.5 pesos/$
Initial Bank Account Worth	$94,737
Calculation: 900,000/9.5 = $94,737	
Subsequent Exchange Rate	10 pesos/$
Subsequent Bank Account Worth	$90,000
Calculation: 900,000/10 = $90,000	

Panel B—Transaction Exposure

If a U.S. company denominates its sales in dollars, it has no transaction exposure. If it denominates the sale in British pounds, the dollar value of the receivable rises or falls as the exchange rate changes, as illustrated below.

Total Price of Merchandise on Exporter's Books	$500,000
Initial Exchange Rate	1.9000 $/£
Initial Underlying Value of Sale	£263,158
Calculation: $500,000/1.9000 = £263,158	
Amount Received by Exporter	£263,158
Subsequent Exchange Rate	1.8800 $/£
Subsequent Payment Value of Collected Receivable	$494,737
Calculation: £263,158 × 1.8800 = $494,737	
Loss to the Exporter	$5,263
Calculation: $500,000 − $494,737 = $5,263	

PANEL B—Transaction Exposure When a U.S. company exports books worth U.S. $500,000 to an importer in the U.K., it's paid with £263,158—the equivalent in U.K. pounds of U.S. $500,000 at an exchange rate of 1.9000 $/£. Subsequently, however, when the value of the U.K. pound falls to a rate of 1.8800 $/£, the value of the U.S. firm's holding in pounds declines from U.S. $500,000 to U.S. $494,737.

Panel C—Economic (or Operating) Exposure

The transaction is the same as in Panel B, but this time the British importer must pay the U.S. exporter in dollars. The first calculation shows how many British pounds the importer must come up with to convert to dollars to pay the exporter. That amount is then marked up 10 percent for sale in the United Kingdom. The next calculation assumes that the British pound weakens to $1.8800 per pound, meaning that the importer has to come up with more pounds to convert to dollars to pay the exporter. The higher amount is then marked up by 10 percent, and we show how much more the importer would have to charge in the market and how much the importer's profit margin would be at the higher price. However, the economic exposure is that the importer may not be able to sell the products at a higher price, so there are two options. One is for the importer to sell the product for the same price as before and accept a lower profit margin (£23,517). The second is for the exporter to charge only $494,737, which would allow the importer to pay the same amount in British pounds as before the exchange-rate change and still be able to keep the price the same in the United Kingdom and earn the same profit margin as before. The difference between the last two calculations is that the importer suffers a drop in profits in the first case and the exporter suffers a drop in profits in the second case.

Total Price of Merchandise on Exporter's Books	$500,000
Initial Exchange Rate	1.9000 $/£
Initial Underlying Value of Sale	£263,158
Calculation: $500,000/1.9000 = £263,158	
Amount Charged by Importer after 10% Markup	£289,474
Subsequent Exchange Rate	1.8800 $/£
Subsequent Underlying Value of Sale	£265,957
Calculation: $500,000/1.8800 = £265,957	
Amount Charged by Importer after 10% Markup	£292,553
Difference in Sales Price before and after Rate Change	£3,079
Profit to Importer If Importer Charges Higher Price	£26,596
Calculation: £292,553 − £265,957 = £26,596	
Profit to Importer If Importer Absorbs Cost Increase	£23,517
Calculation: £289,474 − £265,957 = £23,517	
Price Charged by Exporter for Constant Cost to Importer	$494,737
Calculation: £263,158 × 1.8800 = $494,737	

from the pricing of products, the sourcing and cost of inputs, and the location of investments. Pricing strategies have both an immediate and a long-term impact on cash flows. Consider the economic exposure example from Table 19.3 (Panel C) of the U.S. exporter and the British importer. The first part of Panel C shows what happens if the importer has to pay the exporter $500,000 for the merchandise. Because the pound is falling in value, the importer will have to convert more pounds into dollars to pay the exporter. Now, the *importer* can either sell the product at the original price and not earn as much profit, or it can raise the price and hope that consumers will be willing to pay the higher price. The *exporter,* however, also has two choices. It can continue to sell the merchandise at the same price, or it can lower the price. If it lowers the price, it will incur a lower profit margin. If it continues to sell at the same price, the importer will have to pay more for the merchandise. Then the importer will have to decide what to do.

Another economic-exposure decision involves how to make investment decisions. After three years of the euro strengthening against the dollar, BMW found itself in a very difficult situation in 2005, because its costs were generated in euros (most of its manufacturing facilities were in Europe), whereas its revenues in the United States were in dollars. Thus it was generating revenues in a weak currency and costs in a strong currency, severely affecting earnings. One of its economic solutions was to expand manufacturing operations in the United States to balance its revenues and expenses in the same currency.[34]

EXPOSURE-MANAGEMENT STRATEGY

To adequately protect assets against the risks from translation, transaction, and economic exposure to exchange-rate fluctuations, management must do the following:

- Define and measure exposure
- Organize and implement a reporting system that monitors exposure and exchange-rate movements
- Adopt a policy assigning responsibility for minimizing—or hedging—exposure
- Formulate strategies for hedging exposure

Defining and Measuring Exposure Most MNEs see all three types of exposure: translation, transaction, and economic. To develop a viable hedging strategy, an MNE must forecast the degree of exposure in each major currency in which it operates. Because the types of exposure differ, the actual exposure by currency must be tracked separately. For example, the translation exposure in Brazilian reais should be kept track of separately from the transaction exposure, because the transaction exposure will result in an actual cash flow, whereas the translation exposure may not. Thus the company generates one report on translation exposure and another on transaction exposure. The company may adopt different hedging strategies for the different types of exposure. Recall from our opening case that GPS developed proprietary software, called FXpert, which not only conducts specialized audits of clients' foreign-exchange cash flows but proposes effective hedging strategies for improving them. Solutions may include such well-known hedging strategies as forwards, options, and futures contracts, but GPS has designed FXpert to tailor strategies to clients' specific needs.

A key aspect of measuring exposure is forecasting exchange rates. A company should estimate and use ranges within which it expects a currency to vary over the forecasting period by developing in-house capabilities to monitor exchange rates or using economists who also try to obtain a consensus of exchange-rate movements from the banks they deal with. Their concern is to forecast the direction, magnitude, and timing of an exchange-rate change. As we note in Chapter 10, however, forecasting is imprecise.

Creating a Reporting System Once the company has decided how to define and measure exposure and estimate future exchange rates, it must create a reporting system

To protect assets from exchange-rate risk, management needs to
- Define and measure exposure.
- Establish a reporting system.
- Adopt an overall policy on exposure management.
- Formulate hedging strategies.

All three types of exposure must be monitored and measured separately.

Case Review Note

Exchange-rate movements are forecast using in-house or external experts.

The reporting system should use both central control and input from foreign operations.

Case Review Note

that will assist in protecting it against risk. To achieve this goal, substantial participation from foreign operations must be combined with effective central control. Foreign input is important to ensure that the information the company uses in forecasting is effective. As we'll see in our closing case, for example, Middle Eastern airline Etihad developed a five-step hedging program jointly with outside consultants, who worked alongside its existing team at its corporate headquarters in Dubai.

Because exchange rates move frequently, the company must obtain input from those who are attuned to the foreign country's economy. Central control of exposure protects resources more efficiently than letting each subsidiary and branch manage its own exposure. Each organizational unit may be able to define its own exposure, but the company also has an overall exposure. To set hedging policies on a separate-entity basis might not take into account the fact that exposures of several entities (that is, branches, subsidiaries, affiliates, and so on) could offset one another.

Once each basic reporting unit has identified its exposure, the data should be sent to the next organizational level for preliminary consolidation. The preliminary consolidation enables the region or division to determine exposure by account and by currency for each time period. The resulting reports should be routine, periodic, and standardized to ensure comparability and timeliness in formulating strategies. Final reporting should be at the corporate level, where top management can see the amount of foreign-exchange exposure. Specific hedging strategies can be taken at any level, but each level of management must be aware of the size of the exposure and the potential impact on the company.

Hedging strategies can be operational or financial.

Formulating Hedging Strategies   Once a company has identified its level of exposure and determined which exposure is critical, it can hedge its position by adopting operational and/or financial strategies, each with cost-benefit as well as operational implications. The safest position is a balanced one in which exposed assets equal exposed liabilities.

| Operational strategies include
• Using local debt to balance local assets.
• Taking advantage of leads and lags for intercompany payments. |
|---|

Operational Hedging Strategies   The use of debt to balance exposure is an interesting strategy. Many companies "borrow locally," especially in weak-currency countries, because that helps them avoid foreign-exchange risk from borrowing in a foreign currency and also balances off their exposed position in assets and earnings. One problem with this strategy is that, because interest rates in weak-currency countries tend to be high, there must be a trade-off between the cost of borrowing and the potential loss from exchange-rate variations.

Protecting against loss from transaction exposure becomes complex. In dealing with foreign customers, it is always safest for the company to denominate the transaction in its own currency to avoid any foreign-exchange exposure. The risk shifts to the foreign customer that has to come up with your currency. Or the company could denominate purchases in a weaker currency and sales in a stronger currency. If forced to make purchases in a strong currency and sales in a weak currency, it could resort to contractual measures such as forward contracts or options, or it could try to balance its inflows and outflows through astute sales and purchasing strategies.

A lead strategy means collecting or paying early. A lag strategy means collecting or paying late.

LEADS AND LAGS   Other operational strategies—leads and lags—protect cash flows among related entities, such as a parent and subsidiaries. A **lead strategy** means either collecting foreign-currency receivables before they are due when the foreign currency is expected to weaken or paying foreign-currency payables before they are due when the foreign currency is expected to strengthen. With a **lag strategy,** a company either delays collection of foreign-currency receivables if that currency is expected to strengthen or delays payables when the currency is expected to weaken. In other words, a company usually leads into and lags out of a hard currency and leads out of and lags into a weak currency.

Sometimes an operational strategy means shifting assets overseas to take advantage of currency changes. As mentioned above, when the euro strengthened against the U.S. dollar, BMW shifted some of its manufacturing to the United States.

Using Derivatives to Hedge Foreign-Exchange Risk In addition to the operational strategies just mentioned, a company may hedge exposure through *derivative* financial contracts such as forward contracts and options, with the most common hedge being a forward contract.

Consider a U.S. exporter selling goods to a British manufacturer for £1 million when the exchange rate is $1.9000/£. If the exporter could collect the money right away and convert it into dollars, it would receive $1.9 million. However, if the exporter was not expected to receive payment for 90 days, it would be exposed to an exchange-rate change. One way to protect from this is to enter into a forward contract with a bank to deliver pounds and receive dollars at the forward rate of, say, $1.8500. In 90 days, the exporter would convert the pounds into dollars at $1.8500 and receive $1,850,000, which is less than it would have received at the initial spot rate. But if the pound had deteriorated even more in value, the exporter would still receive the $1.85 million, which is not a bad deal.

A foreign-currency option is more flexible than a forward contract because it gives its purchaser the right, but not the obligation, to buy or sell a certain amount of foreign currency at a set exchange rate within a specified amount of time. In the same situation described above, the exporter would enter into an option contract with a trader to convert pounds into dollars at a certain exchange rate. For the cost of protection, the exporter pays a premium to the trader, which is like insurance. When the exporter receives the cash from the importer, it can decide whether to exercise the option. If the option gives it more money than the spot rate, the exporter will exercise the option. If not, it won't.

Forward contracts can establish a fixed exchange rate for future transactions. Currency options can ensure access to foreign currency at a fixed exchange rate for a specific period of time.

Taxation of Foreign-Source Income

Tax planning is a crucial responsibility for the CFO, because taxes can profoundly affect profitability and cash flow. This is especially true in international business. As complex as domestic taxation seems, it is simple compared to the intricacies of international taxation. The international tax specialist must be familiar with both the home country's tax policy on foreign operations and the tax laws of each country in which the international company operates.

Tax planning influences profitability and cash flow.

Taxation has a strong impact on several choices:

- Location of operations
- Choice of operating form, such as export or import, licensing agreement, or overseas investment
- Legal form of the new enterprise, such as branch or subsidiary
- Possible facilities in tax-haven countries to raise capital and manage cash
- Method of financing, such as internal or external sourcing and debt or equity
- Capital budgeting decisions
- Method of setting transfer prices

INTERNATIONAL TAX PRACTICES

Differences in Tax Practices Differences in tax practices around the world often cause problems for MNEs. Lack of familiarity with laws and customs can create confusion. In some countries, tax laws are loosely enforced. In others, taxes may generally be negotiated between the tax collector and the taxpayer—if they are ever paid at all. In still others, they have to be rigidly followed.

Problems with different countries' tax practices arise from
- *Lack of familiarity with laws.*
- *Loose enforcement.*

Differences in Types of Taxes Countries differ in terms of the types of taxes they have (income versus excise), the tax rates applied to income, the determination of taxable income, and the treatment of foreign-source income. Although we focus in this section on

With a value-added tax, each company pays a percentage of the value added to a product at each stage of the business process.

corporate income tax, excise taxes are another important source of income to governments. The value-added tax is an example of an excise tax used in Europe. It is a percentage levied on products at the point of sale in every stage of the value chain, and it is included in the final price of the product rather than added to the price, as is the case with the sales tax in the United States. There are many other excise taxes, and the large number of taxes in some countries, like Brazil, is very confusing to both local and foreign investors.

Differences in GAAP   Variations among countries in GAAP can lead to differences in the determination of taxable income. In countries where tax laws allow companies to depreciate assets faster than accounting standards allow but where companies must use the same standards for tax and book accounting, higher depreciation expenses result in lower income and therefore lower taxes. Revenue recognition is also an important issue. Some countries tax income from worldwide revenues of MNEs, whereas others only recognize income from revenues generated in the domestic environment.

Corporate tax rates vary from country to country.

Differences in Tax Rates   Corporate tax rates also vary from country to country. Table 19.4 identifies the corporate tax rates of OECD member countries. In OECD countries, central-government corporate income-tax rates range from a low of 8.5 percent in Switzerland to a high of 35 percent in the United States. However, the total corporate income tax burden includes subcentral government taxes (such as provincial or state and local taxes) as well as the central-government corporate income tax. In this case, the combined rate ranges from a low of 12.5 percent in Ireland to a high of 39.54 percent in Japan and 39.1 percent n the United States.[35]

Two Approaches to Corporate Taxation   Taxation of corporate income is accomplished through one of two approaches in most countries: the *separate entity approach* (also known as the *classical approach*) or the *integrated system approach*.

In the separate entity approach, governments tax each taxable entity when it earns income.

Separate Entity Approach   In the separate entity approach, which the United States uses, each separate unit—company or individual—is taxed when it earns income. For example, a corporation is taxed on its earnings, and stockholders are taxed on the distribution of earnings (dividends). The result can be double taxation.

Integrated System Approach   Many other developed countries use an integrated system to eliminate double taxation. For example, Australia and New Zealand give a

TABLE 19.4   Controlled Foreign Corporations

To qualify as a *controlled foreign corporation (CFC)*, more than 50 percent of a company's voting shares must be held by U.S. shareholders. A *U.S. shareholder* must be a U.S. person or company holding at least 10 percent of the corporation's voting shares. Foreign Corporation B qualifies as a CFC, because the combined shares of U.S. Persons V, W, and X (each consisting of at least 10 percent) add up to 75 percent of the total.

	Percentages of the Voting Stock		
Shareholder	**Foreign Corporation A**	**Foreign Corporation B**	**Foreign Corporation C**
U.S. Person V	100%	45%	30%
U.S. Person W		10	10
U.S. Person X		20	8
U.S. Person Y		25	8
Foreign Person Z			44
Total	**100%**	**100%**	**100%**

dividend credit to shareholders to shelter them from double taxation. This means that when shareholders report the dividends in their taxable income, they also get a credit for taxes paid on that income by the company that issued the dividend. That keeps the shareholders from paying tax on the dividend, because the company has already paid a tax on it.

Germany used to have a split-rate system with two different tax rates on corporate earnings—one on retained earnings and one on distributed earnings. However, they abolished the split-rate system in 2001 and adopted a classical system with an overall lower corporate tax rate on earnings of 15 percent plus a 5.5 percent solidarity surcharge (to help in the reunification with East Germany), resulting in a combined rate of 15.8 percent.[36] Taxation of foreign-source income depends on the country where the parent company is domiciled. It is common for most developed countries to tax companies on their worldwide income and give them a credit for foreign corporate income taxes paid. That is not true everywhere, however. Hong Kong companies, for example, pay tax only on Hong Kong–source income, even if remitted to Hong Kong, and their corporate tax rate is only 16.5 percent.[37]

> An integrated system tries to avoid double taxation of corporate income through split tax rates or tax credits.

TAXING BRANCHES AND SUBSIDIARIES

To illustrate the complexities of taxing foreign-source income, let's look at how U.S.-based companies tax earnings from a *foreign branch* and a *foreign subsidiary*.

The Foreign Branch   A foreign branch is an extension of the parent company rather than an enterprise incorporated in a foreign country. Any income the branch generates is taxable immediately to the parent, whether or not cash is remitted by the branch to the parent as a distribution of earnings. However, if the branch suffers a loss, the parent is allowed to deduct that loss from its taxable income, reducing its overall tax liability.

> Foreign branch income (or loss) is directly included in the parent's taxable income.

The Foreign Subsidiary   Whereas a branch is a legal extension of a parent company, a foreign corporation is an independent legal entity set up in a country (incorporated) according to the laws of incorporation of that country. When an MNE purchases a foreign corporation or sets up a new corporation in a foreign country, that corporation is called a *subsidiary* of the parent. Income earned by the subsidiary is either reinvested in the subsidiary or remitted as a dividend to the parent company.

Subsidiary income is either taxable to the parent or tax deferred—that is, it is not taxed until it is remitted as a dividend to the parent. Which tax status applies depends on whether the foreign subsidiary is a *controlled foreign corporation (CFC)*—a technical term in the U.S. tax code—and whether the income is active or passive.

> Tax deferral means that income is not taxed until it is remitted to the parent company as a dividend.

The Controlled Foreign Corporation   A **controlled foreign corporation (CFC),** from the standpoint of the U.S. tax code, is any foreign corporation that meets the following condition: More than 50 percent of its voting stock is held by "U.S. shareholders." A U.S. shareholder is any U.S. person or company that holds 10 percent or more of the CFC's voting stock. Any foreign subsidiary of an MNE would automatically be considered a CFC from the standpoint of the tax code. However, a joint-venture company abroad that is partly owned by the U.S.-based MNE and partly by local investors might not be a CFC if the U.S. MNE does not own more than 50 percent of the stock of the joint-venture company.

> In a CFC, U.S. shareholders hold more than 50 percent of the voting stock.

Table 19.4 shows how this might work. Foreign Corporation A is a CFC, because it is a wholly owned subsidiary of a U.S. parent company (U.S. Person V). Foreign Corporation B also is a CFC, because U.S. Persons V, W, and X each own 10 percent or more of the voting stock, which means they qualify as U.S. shareholders and their combined voting stock is more than 50 percent of the total. This situation might exist if three U.S. companies partnered together with a foreign partner to establish a joint venture overseas.

Such collaborative arrangements are not uncommon, especially in telecommunications and high-tech industries. Foreign Corporation C is not a CFC, because even though U.S. Persons V and W qualify as U.S. shareholders, their combined stock ownership is only 40 percent. U.S. Persons X and Y do not qualify as U.S. shareholders, because their individual ownership shares are only 8 percent each. When Enron set up its shell companies in tax-haven countries, it was careful not to own more than 50 percent of the stock so that it could avoid having to include the debt in those operations in its consolidated income.[38]

> Active income is derived from the direct conduct of a trade or business. Passive income (also called Subpart F income) is usually derived from operations in a tax-haven country.

Active versus Passive Income   If a foreign subsidiary qualifies as a CFC, the U.S. tax law requires the U.S. investor to classify the foreign-source income as *active* or *Subpart F* (or *passive*) *income*. **Active income** is derived from the direct conduct of a trade or business, such as from sales of products manufactured in the foreign country. **Subpart F income,** or **passive income,** which is specifically defined in Subpart F of the U.S. Internal Revenue Code, comes from sources other than those connected with the direct conduct of a trade or business, generally in tax-haven countries. Subpart F income includes the following:

- *Holding company income*—income primarily from dividends, interest, rents, royalties, and gains on sale of stocks.

- *Sales income*—income from foreign sales corporations that are separately incorporated from their manufacturing operations. The product of such entities is manufactured outside and sold for use outside the CFC's country of incorporation, and the CFC has not performed significant operations on the product.

- *Service income*—income from the performance of technical, managerial, or similar services for a company in the same corporate family as the CFC and outside the country in which the CFC resides.

Subpart F income usually derives from the activities of subsidiaries in tax-haven countries such as the Bahamas, the Netherlands Antilles, Panama, and Switzerland. The tax-haven subsidiary may act as an investment company, a sales agent or distributor, an agent for the parent in licensing agreements, or a holding company of stock in other foreign subsidiaries that are called *grandchild*—or *second-tier—subsidiaries*. This setup is illustrated in Figure 19.6. In the role of a holding company, its purpose is to concentrate cash from the parent's foreign operations into the low-tax country and to use the cash for global expansion.

> Different rules regarding the tax status and deferability of income are in effect for non-CFCs, CFCs, and foreign branches.

Determining a Subsidiary's Income   Figure 19.7 illustrates how the tax status of a subsidiary's income is determined. All non-CFC income—active and Subpart F—earned by the foreign corporation is deferred until remitted as a dividend to the U.S.

FIGURE 19.6   The Tax-Haven Subsidiary as Holding Company

A U.S. company has established a *tax-haven subsidiary* as a *holding company* in an offshore location. As such, the offshore subsidiary owns shares in three foreign subsidiaries called *grandchild subsidiaries*. The offshore holding company generates *holding company income*, which is recorded by the U.S. parent company as *Subpart F income*.

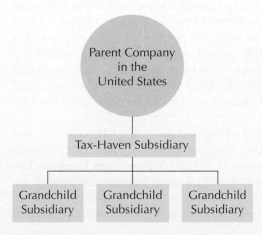

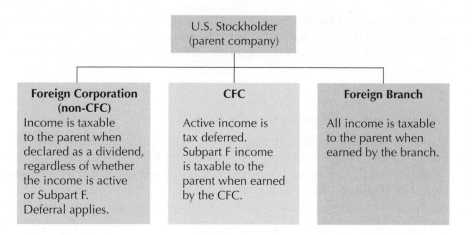

FIGURE 19.7 The Tax Status of U.S.-Owned Foreign Subsidiaries

Both CFC and Subpart F provisions are designed to prevent U.S. firms from establishing tax-haven subsidiaries for the purpose of investing *passive income* indefinitely—and thus earning tax-free income. Basically, these provisions treat tax income just as if it had been remitted to the U.S. parent at the time when it was earned.

shareholder (the parent company in this example). In contrast, a CFC's active income is tax deferred to the parent, but its Subpart F income is taxable immediately to the parent as soon as the CFC earns it, subject to some limitations and exceptions. If a foreign branch earns income, it is immediately taxable to the parent company, whether it is active or Subpart F income.

TRANSFER PRICES

As noted in Chapter 18, a major tax challenge as well as an impediment to performance evaluation is the extensive use of transfer pricing in international operations. Because the price is between related entities, it is not necessarily an **arm's-length price**—that is, a price between two companies that do not have an ownership interest in each other. The assumption is that an arm's-length price is more likely than a transfer price to reflect the market accurately.

A transfer price is a price on goods and services one member of a corporate family sells to another.

Transfer Prices and Taxation   Companies establish arbitrary transfer prices primarily because of differences in taxation between countries. For example, if the corporate tax rate is higher in the parent company's country than in the subsidiary's country, the parent could set a low transfer price on products it sells the subsidiary to keep taxable profits low in its country and high in the subsidiary's country. The parent also could set a high transfer price on products sold to it by the subsidiary.

The OECD is very concerned about the ways in which companies manipulate transfer prices to minimize their tax liability worldwide. Its recommendation is that to determine the tax liability in each country, an arm's-length price should be applied, and it has issued guidelines on the matter. The OECD Centre for Tax Policy and Administration meets periodically to discuss a wide range of tax issues, including the adoption of sound transfer pricing policies. The OECD issued guidelines on transfer pricing in 1979 and updated the policies in 1995 to give guidance on how to tell if a transfer between independent firms is similar to a transfer within a group and on different transfer pricing methods that could be used. Additional revisions have been published since 1995 and are published periodically.[39]

Companies can get into disputes with different tax jurisdictions over transfer pricing policies. GlaxoSmithKline (GSK), the British pharmaceutical company, settled a transfer pricing dispute with the U.S. Internal Revenue Service (IRS) in 2006 by paying $3.1 billion in federal, state, and local taxes and interest—slightly less than the $5 billion the IRS was seeking and nearly half of GSK's operating cash flow. The IRS contends that GSK charged its U.S. affiliate too little for marketing services provided by the affiliate, which meant that U.S. earnings were low, resulting in lower taxes collected in the United States.

The dispute arose over whether GSK should have paid for the marketing services at cost or at the price it would have paid an independent third party. These are complex issues that leave companies open to significant financial risks if they don't price services or products correctly.[40]

DOUBLE TAXATION AND TAX CREDIT

Every country has a sovereign right to levy taxes on all income generated within its borders. However, MNEs run into problems when they earn income taxed in the country where the income is earned and where it might also be taxed in the parent country as well. This could result in double taxation.

> The IRS allows a tax credit for corporate income tax U.S. companies pay to another country. A tax credit is a dollar-for-dollar reduction of tax liability and must coincide with the recognition of income.

In U.S. tax law, a U.S. MNE gets a credit for income taxes paid to a foreign government. For example, when a U.S. parent recognizes foreign-source income (such as a dividend from a foreign subsidiary) in its taxable income, it must pay U.S. tax on that income. However, the U.S. IRS allows the parent company to reduce its tax liability by the amount of foreign income tax already paid. It is limited by the amount it would have had to pay in the United States on that income.

Assume, for example, that U.S. MNE A earns $100,000 of foreign-source income on which it paid $40,000 (40 percent tax rate) on that income in the foreign jurisdiction. If that income is considered taxable in the United States, Company A would have to pay $35,000 in income taxes (35 percent tax rate). In the absence of a tax credit, Company A would have paid a total of $75,000 in income tax on the $100,000 of income, a 75 percent tax rate.

The IRS, however, allows Company A to reduce its U.S. tax liability by a maximum of $35,000—what it would have paid in the United States if the income had been earned there. If Company A's subsidiary had paid $20,000 in foreign income tax (a 20 percent tax rate), it would be able to claim the entire $20,000 as a credit because it was less than the U.S. liability of $35,000. Company A will pay a total of $35,000 in corporate income tax on its foreign-source income—$20,000 to the foreign government and $15,000 to the U.S. government.

> The purpose of tax treaties is to prevent double taxation or to provide remedies when it occurs.

Tax Treaties: Eliminating Double Taxation   The primary purpose of tax treaties is to prevent international double taxation or to provide remedies when it occurs. The United States is an active participant in 65 different tax treaties.[41] The general pattern between two treaty countries is to grant reciprocal deductions on dividend withholding and to exempt royalties—and sometimes interest payments—from any withholding tax.

The United States has a withholding tax of 30 percent for owners (individuals and corporations) of U.S. securities issued in countries with which it has no tax treaty. However, interest on portfolio obligations and on bank deposits is normally exempted from withholding. When a tax treaty is in effect, the U.S. rate on dividends is generally reduced to 5 to 15 percent, and the tax on interest and royalties is either eliminated or reduced to 5 to 10 percent.

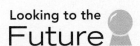

Looking to the Future   Technology and Cash Flows

As companies drive down costs to increase their profitability and market value, they will need to reduce borrowing costs. Greater emphasis will be placed on moving corporate cash worldwide to take advantage of differing rates of return. In addition, companies will need to perfect their strategies for issuing bonds at the cheapest price possible and minimizing their tax bills worldwide.

However, the United States has been clamping down on tax minimization schemes and attacking the providers of such schemes (such as law firms and public accounting firms), as well as going after the corporate clients that are adopting such schemes. In addition, they and other OECD countries are going after tax-haven countries and trying to break down the barriers to bank secrecy so that they can get access to the records of individuals and companies who they suspect are illegally avoiding taxes. As companies establish strategies to take advantage of tax havens, they need to make sure that they are very careful to avoid strategies that will turn them into the next Enron or Parmalat. The move to drive down costs can't come at the expense of the future viability of the company.

The explosion of information and technology and the growing number and sophistication of hedging instruments (financial derivatives such as options and forwards) will significantly influence the cash-management and hedging strategies of MNEs in the future. Advances in information systems will continue to enable companies to get information more quickly and cheaply.

In addition, electronic data interchange (EDI) will allow them to transfer information and money instantaneously worldwide. Companies will significantly reduce paper flow and increase the speed of delivery of information and funds, enabling them to manage cash and use intercompany resources much more

effectively than before. Consequently, companies will reduce not only the cost of producing information but also interest and other borrowing costs.

Investment and commercial banks will continue to develop new derivative instruments that will help companies hedge their currency and interest-rate exposures in the short and long term. However, new standards in accounting for derivative financial instruments by the FASB and IASB will force companies to mark most derivatives to market and recognize gains and losses in income. Despite of the tightening of accounting standards, derivatives will be a big help to companies as they attempt to hedge their cash flows and protect against the erosion of earnings in an unstable financial environment.

The OECD, the IMF, and the EU are three institutions that will help countries narrow their tax differences and crack down on the transfer of money for illegal purposes. Although illegal financial transfers have occurred for years, especially due to drug trafficking, the attacks on 9/11 and subsequent moves to track down money laundering by Osama bin Laden and other terrorists have created a more urgent need to reform the global financial system. This will continue to narrow the options of companies to move funds, but that isn't a bad idea. ■

Etihad—A New Airline Hedging Bets on Profitability

In 2009, fuel hedging for airlines became the topic of the moment for an industry struggling to cope with rising fuel prices and a worldwide economic downturn that has seen passengers substantially cut down in international travel. For those airline executives who kept their feet on the ground and implemented fuel hedging strategies back when fuel prices were at manageable levels, the outlook was good. But for others who took the gamble that oil prices could not possibly go up any further and therefore decided not to hedge, it turned out to be very costly indeed.

Even those that did embrace seemingly successful hedging strategies have been caught out. Dubai's flagship airline Emirates was much vaunted in the press and in the financial markets after managing to reduce its fuel costs by $1 billion between 2000 and 2007. It was a significant savings in an industry where fuel can represent up to 40 per cent of costs. However, in June 2009, Emirates was forced to write down fuel hedging losses of $428 million for its previous financial year. The airline had signed large fuel contracts before the global economic crisis came to a head in October 2008 and oil prices were sent tumbling down to below $40 a barrel. Emirates had purchased much of its fuel needs when oil was between $70 and $80 a barrel.

Rival Middle Eastern airline Etihad, which launched in November 2003, credits its rapid growth to an aggressive fuel-hedging program. The Abu Dhabi-based airline, which in July 2008 placed orders worth £20 billion with Boeing and Airbus for 100 fuel-efficient jets, plans to break even by 2010. Yet the target is only achievable if fuel costs keep going down, making the airline's hedging strategy vital for its future. Etihad's chief executive James Hogan readily admits that fuel is the airline's main challenge, but how is he planning to tackle it?

A Little Background

Etihad was established by the Abu Dhabi government in 2003, with a mandate to become the national airline of the United Arab Emirates. Launched with capital of $136 million, its first commercial service was to Beirut. From then on, nearly one route was added a month, and the company doubled in size every six months for its first four years. Just seven months after its launch, Etihad made its first direct flight from the UAE to Geneva, followed by service to Brussels and Toronto. By 2008—by now doubling in size every year—the airline was carrying 6 million passengers on a fleet of 42 aircraft to over 50 destinations worldwide. Almost overnight, Etihad had become one of the fastest-growing airlines in the world.

The airline credits much of its success to its focus on the customer—particularly at the premium end of the market. Its premium tickets sell out far faster than its economy ones, when it is the other way around with most airlines. Etihad achieves this with touches such as employing outside experts from the hospitality industry to help make passengers' experience as comfortable and luxurious as possible. Etihad's Inspired Service, for example, offers passengers a menu to choose from, and the quality and flavor of the meals are said to be on a par with those of some of the best restaurants in the world. Indeed, the airline has won more than 30 awards for its food and service.

Etihad's main investor, the government of Abu Dhabi, presides over the richest and largest of the Emirates, with oil as its natural resource. The Abu Dhabi government is currently in the process of introducing a wide range of programs in tourism, real estate, hospitals, and other services to help move away from the total reliance on the oil-related industries of the past. With an excess of $200 billion to be invested in the next ten years to drive that activity, the government is particularly keen and committed to building the Etihad business. In 2005, to reinforce this aim, it withdrew as a shareholder of rival Middle East carrier Gulf Air, in order to concentrate more fully on developing Etihad. As a part of this strategy, new terminals are under construction at Abu Dhabi International Airport. These terminals will have an approximate capacity of 12 million passengers a year, and there is a new terminal called Midfield that is being developed exclusively for Etihad. Once this is completed, the airport's capacity will then exceed 20 million passengers a year.

However, despite all the support and development and the fact that Etihad operates in an oil-producing company, the airline does not have access to free fuel. It—like all other airlines—has to operate in the free market, and that means that it has had to consider the risk-mitigation advantages of hedging strategies for fuel.

Building a Hedging Strategy

The reasons for hedging commodity risk for airlines are compelling, particularly when considering the relative volatilities of the respective asset classes. Interest rates, for example, have volatilities of around 10 percent, and foreign-exchange rates have volatilities of around 15 to 20 percent. In contrast, crude oil has volatilities of between 50 to 60 percent.

Exposure to this level of volatility can have, and indeed has, a significant impact on the revenue of airlines and their share prices. As well as affecting profitability, it also has an affect on the price that is passed on to passengers.

However, while there is a strong case for hedging fuel costs to achieve greater stability in cash flows, the outcome is by no means guaranteed. A badly managed hedging program could easily make a bad situation far worse.

It is an issue that James Hogan and his team at Etihad considered carefully. The airline's strategy dictated a need for rapid growth towards profitability, but it could not be at all costs. There was a need for a carefully managed and monitored hedging program, and, using outside consultants, the team developed a five-step hedging program that analyzes the risk levels in the jet-fuel markets.

Step 1: Defining Objectives

In arguably the most important step in a hedging strategy, Etihad's management had to clearly define the objectives of their hedging program and put processes in to measure its success. Without clearly defined, quantifiable objectives, it is impossible to define the outcome of the strategy as successful or unsuccessful.

Thus, the main objective of the hedging strategy was agreed to be that of ensuring that the cost of jet fuel did not exceed 30 percent of the airline's annual revenues. Etihad also declared that it wanted to achieve cost certainty, while protecting business-plan fuel rates and managing seasonal risk, to maximize the impact of fuel volatility on the airline's earnings.

One note of caution is needed here. While it is perfectly acceptable to make losses on hedges—and is indeed likely, which is fine as long as these are offset through gains on the underlying commodity exposure—the objective should not be to make a profit. If a company's hedging program is expected to make a profit, then it is no longer hedging—it is speculating on commodity-price movements, which can create even greater volatility in earnings.

Step 2: Devising a Strategy

There are two key considerations when devising a fuel hedging strategy: how much of the commodity exposure to hedge, allowing for a predetermined level of flexibility, and which instruments and markets the company should use. Etihad used proprietary cash-flow-at-risk modeling technology to simulate how different hedging strategies might perform under differing scenarios and to identify the most favorable hedging ratios. The idea behind this is to ensure that the airline meets its hedging objectives, even in the worst-case scenario.

Step 3: Executing the Strategy

Commodity hedges are usually executed as OTC transactions with banks, in order that corporations can get a tailored product that matches their underlying exposure and minimizes risk. However, these trades can be difficult, due to lack of relevant market data, and it is therefore usual practice to use a dealer in order to get a fair market price. Clearly, overpaying for hedges would have a negative impact on a company's earnings and negate the point of following such a strategy in the first place.

Etihad decided to mitigate the risks by calculating the fair value for the jet-fuel hedges itself, rather than using a dealer. It does this by buying independent market data and employing a team of dedicated specialists. The airline then conducts the OTC transactions independently.

Step 4: Monitoring

It is important to revalue trades, track P&L, and monitor risk throughout the life of a hedge to make sure it remains effective versus the underlying exposure. This also serves the purpose of monitoring performance versus using a dealer-led transaction.

Etihad updates its hedging decisions in real time, constantly tracking their progress and checking them against the objectives in order to control and monitor risk.

A good hedge program is not a static process, and the company executing such a strategy must have the ability to see how the commodity's risks are changing, see how that impacts the business plan, and be able to update the strategy accordingly.

Step 5: Evaluation

Once the hedged trades are complete, the final step is to evaluate the result, netting the realized cash flows from the derivative hedge trades against the actual commodity sale price. This provides a net commodity cost to the business and means that Etihad's management can analyze whether the hedging strategy was a success compared to the original objectives. The airline can quantify the realized amount paid for jet fuel and then easily determine what proportion of fair value should be posted on the balance sheet under hedge accounting rules.

How Much to Hedge?

Getting the right balance of how much fuel to hedge is a question of risk management, and while it may not be prudent to be unhedged, airlines should never completely hedge all of their fuel needs.

Etihad's strategy is to hedge on a rolling basis over three years. Thus, Etihad hedged 70 percent of its fuel costs in 2007, 82 percent in 2008, and 41 percent in 2009. It is "slightly hedged" for 2010 and has hedging transactions in place for 2011, but figures are not yet available. Its hedging team continues to follow the fluctuating oil price hour by hour, and, if the company feels confident enough to hedge more going forward, it will do so.

The Future

There is currently much discussion and debate about fuel hedging in the airline industry. Many companies are fearful that, in the future, hedging will become more expensive than it was (due to the volatility of the market) and may even present a more marginal benefit than it has done in the past because the hedges available will be at higher prices. However, at the present time, more airlines than ever are considering hedging strategies as a way of protecting themselves against the uncertain climate.

Etihad's fuel hedging strategy is vital to the airline's rapid-growth strategy. The $20 billion order for 100 jets in July 2008, was one of the largest deals in aviation history, and Etihad has another 105 options for purchase rights in order to meet its strategic network plan out to 2030.

While many other airlines have declared that they will not be making any orders for a while to slow down their pace of growth in the uncertain economic climate, Etihad will be introducing a substantial amount of new aircraft every year starting in 2011.

For Etihad, fuel hedging is not just an insurance policy that enables them to foresee exactly what they will be paying for fuel, therefore avoiding any nasty shocks. It is a key part of the airline's declared strategy to break even by 2010 and stay profitable beyond that. Although it has received substantial funding, Etihad has been given no guarantees from the government and has had to go out into the market, raise debt, and manage with the funds available as any business would.

In November 2009, it emerged that Etihad had not, in fact, managed to meet its target, although revenues would exceed $3 billion that year. Hogan announced that, thanks to the extreme global downturn coupled with a further fall in passengers as a result of the flu epidemic, Etihad would push back its profitability targets by one year. However, he added, it would indeed post its first profit in 2011, due in a great part to the success of its aggressive hedging strategy.[42] ∎

QUESTIONS

1. How would a sharp fall in the price of a barrel of oil affect Etihad's financial statements? What about a substantial rise?
2. Etihad's fuel hedges have ranged between 40 to 82 percent. Why does this exposure vary? When is it prudent to reduce its exposure?
3. Describe and evaluate Etihad's exposure-management strategy.
4. Are there any other hedging strategies that Etihad's management should consider implementing to help the airline meet its financial goals?

SUMMARY

- The corporate finance function deals with the acquisition of financial resources and their allocation among the company's present and potential activities and projects.

- CFOs need to be concerned with the international dimensions of the company's capital structure, capital budgeting decisions, long-term financing, and working capital management.

- Country-specific factors are the most important determination of a company's capital structure.

- Two major sources of funds external to the MNE's normal operations are debt markets and equity markets.

- A Eurocurrency is any currency banked outside its country of origin, but it is primarily dollars banked outside the United States.

- A foreign bond is one sold outside the country of the borrower but denominated in the currency of the country of issue. A Eurobond is a bond issue sold in a currency other than that of the country of issue.

- Euroequities are shares listed on stock exchanges in countries other than the home country of the issuing company. Most foreign companies that list on the U.S. stock exchanges do so through American Depositary Receipts (ADRs), which are financial documents that represent a share or part of a share of stock in the foreign company. ADRs are easier to trade on the U.S. exchanges than are foreign shares.

- Offshore financial centers such as Bahrain, the Caribbean, Hong Kong, London, New York, Singapore, and Switzerland deal in large amounts of foreign currency and enable companies to take advantage of favorable tax rates.

- When deciding to invest abroad, MNE management must evaluate the cash flows from the local operation as well as the cash flows from the project to the parent. The former allows management to determine how the project stacks up with other opportunities in the foreign country, and the latter allows management to compare projects from different countries.

- The major sources of internal funds for an MNE are dividends, royalties, management fees, loans from parent to subsidiaries and vice versa, purchases and sales of inventory, and equity flows from parent to subsidiaries.

- Global cash management is complicated by differing inflation rates, changes in exchange rates, and government restrictions on the flow of funds. A sound cash-management system for an MNE requires timely reports from affiliates worldwide.

- Management must protect corporate assets from losses due to exchange-rate changes. Exchange rates can influence the dollar equivalent of foreign-currency financial statements, the amount of cash that can be earned from foreign-currency transactions, and a company's production and marketing decisions.

- Foreign-exchange risk management involves defining and measuring exposure, setting up a good monitoring and reporting system, adopting a policy to assign responsibility for exposure management, and formulating strategies for hedging exposure.

- Companies can enter into operational or financial strategies for hedging exposures. Operational strategies include balancing exposed assets with exposed liabilities, using leads and lags in cash flows, and balancing revenues in one currency with expenses in the same currency. Financial strategies involve using forward contracts, options, or other financial instruments to hedge an exposed position.

- International tax planning has a strong impact on the choice of location for the initial investment, the legal form of the new enterprise, the method of financing, and the method of setting transfer prices.

- Countries differ in terms of the types of taxes they have (income versus excise), the tax rates applied to income, the determination of taxable income, and the treatment of foreign-source income.

- Tax deferral means that the income a foreign subsidiary earns is taxed only when it is remitted to the parent as a dividend, not when it is earned.

- A controlled foreign corporation (CFC) must declare its Subpart F income as taxable to the parent in the year it is earned, whether or not it is remitted as a dividend.

- A tax credit allows a parent company to reduce its tax liability by the direct amount its subsidiary pays a foreign government on income that must be taxed by the parent company's government.

- The purpose of tax treaties is to prevent international double taxation or to provide remedies when it occurs.

KEY TERMS

active income (p. 782)
American Depositary Receipt (ADR) (p. 767)
arm's-length price (p. 783)
controlled foreign corporation (CFC) (p. 781)
economic (or operating) exposure (p. 775)
Eurobond (p. 763)
Eurocredit (p. 762)
Eurocurrency (p. 761)

Eurocurrency market (p. 761)
Eurodollar (p. 761)
Euroequity market (p. 765)
foreign bonds (p. 763)
lag strategy (p. 778)
lead strategy (p. 778)
leverage (p. 759)
London Inter-Bank Offered Rate (LIBOR) (p. 762)
market capitalization (p. 765)
net present value (NPV) (p. 771)

netting (p. 773)
offshore financial centers (p. 767)
offshore financing (p. 767)
payback period (p. 770)
Subpart F (or passive) income (p. 782)
syndication (p. 762)
transaction exposure (p. 775)
translation exposure (p. 775)

ENDNOTES

1 *Sources include the following:* "People on the Move," *Deseret News* (January 31, 1999): M02; Wells Fargo News Release, "Wells Fargo & Company and First Security Corporation Agree to Merge" (April 10, 2000), at www.wellsfargo.com/press/firstsec20000410?year= 2000 (accessed November 20, 2007); interviews with Ali Manbeian and Jason Langston; Wells Fargo company literature.

2 Arthur J. Keown, John D. Martin, J. William Petty, and David F. Scott Jr., *Financial Management,* 10th ed. (Upper Saddle River, NJ: Pearson Prentice Hall, 2005): 5.

3 Based on David K. Eiteman, Arthur I. Stonehill, and Michael H. Moffett, *Multinational Business Finance,* 12th ed. (Reading, MA: Addison-Wesley, 2010): 3.

4 Keown et al., *Financial Management,* 290.

5 "Theory versus the Real World," *Finance & Treasury* (April 26, 1993): 1.

6 Abe de Jong, Rezaul Kabir, and Thuy Thu Nguyen, "Capital Structure around the World: The Roles of Firm- and Country-Specific Determinants" (November 2006); EFA 2006 Zurich Meetings, at SSRN, http://ssrn.com/abstract=890525 (accessed November 20, 2007).

7 De Jong et al., "Capital Structure around the World."

8 Charles Forelle, "The Isle That Rattled the World—Tiny Iceland Created a Vast Bubble, Leaving Wreckage Everywhere When It Popped," *Wall Street Journal* (December 27, 2008): A1.

9 Nissan, "Schedule of Bonds Payable," *Nissan Annual Report* (2008): 115, at http://www.nissan-global.com/EN/DOCUMENT/PDF/FR/2008/fr2008.pdf (accessed September 1, 2009).

10 Nu Skin Enterprises Inc., *Nu Skin Form 10-K* (2008): 57–58.

11 Patrick McGuire, "A Shift in London's Eurodollar Market," *BIS Quarterly Review* (September 2004): 67.

12 "International Rates," *Wall Street Journal Online* at www.wsj.com (accessed July 7, 2009).

13 Ben White and Victoria Kim, "Lehman to Shut Down Subprime Unit," *Financial Times* (August 22, 2007), at www.ft.com/cms/s/2caa76fa-50de-11dc-8e9d-0000779fd2ac,dwp_uuid=d355f29c-d238-11db-a7c0-000b5df10621.html (accessed August 27, 2007).

14 "U.S. Senator Sees Sub-Prime Crisis Getting Worse before Better," *Yahoo! News,* at http://news.yahoo.com/s/afp/20070820/pl_afp/marketsfinanceus (accessed August 27, 2007), 1.

15 IFSL Research, *Bond Markets 2009* (International Financial Services London, July 2009), www.ifsl.org.uk, found on the International Capital Market Association Web site, http://www.icmagroup.org (accessed September 1, 2009).

16 International Monetary Fund, "IMF Global Financial Stability Report, 2009," 28 (April 2009), http://www.imf.org/external/pubs/ft/gfsr/2009/01 (accessed September 1, 2009).

17 "IMF Global Stability Report, 2009," 177.

18 IFSL Research, *Bond Markets 2009,* 4.

19 "An Offer They Can Refuse," *Euromoney* (February 1995): 76.

20 Anant Sundaram, "International Financial Markets," in Dennis E. Logue (ed.), *Handbook of Modern Finance* (New York: Warren, Gorham, Lamont, 1994): F3–F4.

21 "Gazprombanks's Eurobonds," at www.gazprombank.ru/eng/corporate/securities/eurobonds/ index.wbp (accessed May 24, 2005).

22 Aaron Lucchetti and Craig Karmin, "Intensity to Be a 'Global' Stock Has Waned," *Wall Street Journal* (May 10, 2005): C1.

23 IMF Monetary and Exchange Affairs Department, "IMF Background Paper: Offshore Financial Centers" (June 23, 2000).

24 "IMF Background Paper: Offshore Financial Centers."

25 "How the Heavyweights Shape Up," *Euromoney* (May 1990): 56.

26 "On or Off? It's a Matter of Degree," in "Places in the Sun: A Special Report on Offshore Finance," *The Economist* (February 24, 2007): 7.

27 OECD, *Harmful Tax Competition: An Emerging Global Issue* (Paris: OECD, 1998): 23.

28 OECD, *Harmful Tax Competition: An Emerging Global Issue,* 27.

29 OECD, *Overview or the OECD's Work on Countering International Tax Evasion* (Paris: OECD, August 11, 2009): 8, http://www.oecd.org/dataoecd/32/45/42356522.pdf (accessed October 23, 2009).

30 David Cay Johnston, " Enron Avoided Income Taxes in 4 of 5 Years," *New York Times (Late Edition (East Coast))* (January 17, 2002): A1.

31 Lucy Komisar, "Funny Money," *Metroactive News & Issues* (January 24, 2002), at www.metroactive.com/papers/sonoma/01.24.02/offshorebanking-0204.html (accessed June 7, 2005).

32 Nick Davis, "Tax Spotlight Worries Cayman Islands," *BBC News* (March 31, 2009), http://news.bbc.co.uk/go/pr/fr/-/2/hi/americas/7972695.stm (accessed October 23, 2009).

33 Eiteman et al., *Multinational Business Finance.*

34 Stephen Power, "BMW's Profit Softened in Quarter," *Wall Street Journal* (May 4, 2005): A12.

35 OECD, "Taxation of Corporate and Capital Income, Table II.1," *OECD Tax Database* (2009), www.oecd.org/ctp/taxdatabase (accessed October 23, 2009).

36 Deloitte, "International Tax and Business Guide: Germany" (2009), at www.deloitte.com/view/en_GX/global/services/tax/international-tax/international-tax-and-business-guides/article/d7c2a6c82b10e110VgnVCM100000ba42f00aRCRD.htm (accessed October 23, 2009).

37 Deloitte, "International Tax and Business Guide: Hong Kong" (2009), at www.deloitte.com/view/en_GX/global/services/tax/international-tax/international-tax-and-business-guides/article/3872a9fd91ffd110VgnVCM100000ba42f00aRCRD.htm (accessed October 23, 2009).

38 Johnston, "How Offshore Havens Helped Enron Escape Taxes."

39 OECD, *Transfer Pricing Guidelines for Multinational Enterprises and Tax Administrations* (Paris: OECD Publishing, August 11, 2009), http://www.oecd.org/document/34/0,3343,en_2649_33753_1915490_1_1_1_1,00.html (accessed October 23, 2009).

40 Ronald Fink, "Haven or Hell," *CFO Magazine* (March 2004), www.cfo.com/article.cfm/3012017 (accessed October 23, 2009); Helen Shaw, "Transfer Students," *CFO Magazine* (April 2007), at www.cfo.com/article.cfm/8885626/c_8910395?f=insidecfo (accessed August 30, 2007).

41 Deloitte, "International Tax and Business Guide: United States" (2009), at www.deloitte.com/view/en_GX/global/services/tax/international-tax/international-tax-and-business-guides/article/1ad803082e10e110VgnVCM100000ba42f00aRCRD.htm (accessed October 23, 2009), 7–9.

42 *Sources include the following:* "Abu Dhabi Withdraws Support for Gulf Air," *Financial Times* (September 13, 2005); "Emirates Saves £1 Billion by Hedging Fuel Contracts," www.iag-inc.com (January 24, 2008); "Etihad Bullish As Rivals Scale Down Operations," *CNN* (July 18, 2008); "Air Transport Fuel Hedging Strategies," *FlightGlobal* (August 20, 2008); "James Hogan: Full Steam Ahead at Etihad," *FlightGlobal* (September 23, 2008); "Emirates Writes Down Dh1.5bn in Fuel Hedge Losses," *The National* (June 1, 2009); Peter Baumgartner, "Etihad," *Daily Times Pakistan* (March 1, 2009); "Etihad Expects $3 Billion Revenues in 2009 – CEO" (November 16, 2009), at www.arabianbusiness.com

twenty
Human Resource Management

Objectives

- To discuss the importance of human resource management

- To profile the staffing frameworks used by MNEs

- To explain the types and competencies of expatriates

- To examine how MNEs select, prepare, compensate, and retain expatriates

- To profile MNEs' relations with organized labor

Excellent people are honored wherever they go.

—*Tibetan proverb*

International companies have been moving people around for centuries, seeking to capture the benefits that follow from putting the right person into the right job at the right place at the right time at the right pay. Now, more than ever, companies engaged in international business must do so. Globalization, by spurring trade, capital, and investment flows across nations, has created many operating units worldwide. An interconnected market means economic patterns and business practices in one area influence the fate of a company in another. Collectively, they indicate that if you are going to be successful, you have to be global.

Increasingly, being a corporate leader demands an international background. "You have to have an intuitive sense of how the world works and how people behave. . . . There is no substitute for personal experience," says Paul Laudicina, vice president of A.T. Kearney. Daniel Meiland, executive chairperson of Egon Zehender International, a large international executive search firm, offers this assessment:

> [T]he world is getting smaller, and markets are getting bigger. In my more than 25 years in the executive search profession, we've always talked about the global executive, but the need to find managers who can be effective in many different settings is growing ever more urgent. In addition to looking for intelligence, specific skills, and technical insights, companies are also looking for executives who are comfortable on the world stage.

The Expatriate Manager

International companies often use expatriates (employees sent by their companies from the employees' home countries to live and work in other countries) to run their foreign operations. Some MNEs, such as FedEx and Johnson & Johnson, use few expatriates; others, like Royal Dutch Shell and Wipro, use many. Unfortunately, little guidance is available for MNEs that must deal with a multitude of human resource management issues. The most fundamental of these are why, when, and where we should use expatriates. Others include selecting the right expatriate, making sure the employee gets the right predeparture preparation, designing the right compensation package to motivate performance, and moving people upward and onward when done overseas.

The benefits of overseas success and the costs of overseas failure move companies like Honeywell to identify and develop potential candidates years before their possible assignment. Honeywell briefs candidates on their cross-cultural skills and prescribes training paths that deal with possible points of culture shock. Manfred Fiedler, vice president of human resources, describes the process: "We give them a horizon, a perspective and, gradually, we tell them they are potentially on an international path. . . . We want them to develop a cross-cultural intellect, what we call 'strategic accountability.'" To this end, Honeywell might advise an executive to network with people who have already worked abroad, study another language, or explore areas where he or she might struggle while living abroad. The pace of globalization accelerates this process; companies begin slotting people for international assignments early on in their careers. Sanjay Joshi, chief executive of global programs at Wipro Technologies, an Indian MNE, notes that "A big part of our recruiting is telling people that they will get a chance to work abroad." This appoach, he believes, improves the quality of new hires as well as fortifies the company's growing cadre of expatriates.[2]

Building Skills, Finding Opportunities

Laying the foundation for an international business career takes time. One must considers many factors, from developing the best skills, managing career progression, and preparing for living outside one's comfort zone. Regarding the latter, for example, people who have worked overseas note that challenges pushed them to look at situations differently. Explained Galina Naumenko of PricewaterhouseCoopers Russia, international assignments "spurs global networking among employees, gives them an understanding of different cultures and gets them thinking about alternative ways of approaching problems and solving them." Similarly, "You get very different thinking if you sit in Shanghai or São Paulo or Dubai than if you sit in New York," noted Michael Cannon-Brookes, head of strategy for IBM's "growth markets" division.[3]

Which Skills Where? Working internationally compels employees to develop richer management repertoires. Consider Joan Pattle, a Microsoft marketing manager who worked at headquarters in Seattle before accepting a post as product manager in Britain. Her U.K. job came with much wider responsibilities: "At home, my job was very strictly defined. I basically had to know everything about managing a database. But when I got to London, I was also in charge of direct marketing and press relations. I was exposed to a much broader set of experiences." Similarly, Laura Anderson, a spokesperson for Intel Corp., explained that her assignments in Hong Kong exposed her to a side of the company's business she had never experienced. In China, a flashy fashion show helped highlight Intel technology, and the press responded with strong coverage. That, and several other Asian media relations encounters, opened Anderson's eyes during her short-term Hong Kong assignments. "For me," she says, "it was a tremendous growth experience."

Mindsets and Sightlines   Along these lines, McKinsey & Company, a global management consulting firm, found that an expatriate who has technical competence is now a given but

> [g]lobal market pioneers must have a particular mind-set. . . . When you look behind the success stories of leading globalizers, you find companies that have learned how to think differently from the herd. They seek out different information, process it in a different way, come to different conclusions, and make different decisions. Where others see threats and complexity, they see opportunity. Where others see a barren landscape, they see a cornucopia of choices.

An international assignment is risky for managers. For many executives, cultural clashes, language difficulties, murky business practices, and harsh environments rule out anything beyond a short-term assignment. Other problems arise when a company asks an executive to transfer to second- or third-tier cities in less preferred countries. The gap between life at home versus "over there" can create professional, family, and personal problems. Well-paid foreigners often produce jealousy in their local colleagues. Despite their best intentions, many people assigned to work in foreign companies struggle with foreign cultures. This difficulty can lead to the expensive problem of expatriate failure.

Coming Home   Eventually, most managers return home. One would think this would be a snap—pack the bags, bid adieu to colleagues, board the plane, and return to a hero's welcome. In many cases, everything but the hero's welcome happens. Tom Schiro of Deloitte & Touche observed, "some companies just send somebody overseas and forget about them for two years." Communication with the home unit is essential to preempt this problem.

Likewise, careful career planning can make a world of difference when it is time to return home. For example, following a four-year assignment in Tokyo, Bryan Krueger returned to a promotion to president of Baxter Fenwal North America. When he had left for Tokyo, his company did not guarantee him a promotion upon his return. So, while away, he kept up-to-date with the goings-on at headquarters. Krueger credited his smooth return to his intensive networking. During his stint in Tokyo, he returned to the United States four to five times a year to visit colleagues. As he explains, "I was definitely proactive. Anyone who is not is doing himself a disservice. I made a conscious effort to stay in touch, and it paid off."

On the other hand, companies may be unable to entice some expatriates to return home. While overseas, an expatriate can achieve remarkable levels of compensation, responsibility, and prestige. A penchant for living abroad creates global nomads who travel from one country to the next for their company. For example, after stints in Singapore and London, a Morgan Stanley expatriate in India muses, "I still don't want to go back to the United States. It's a big world—lots of things to see." Nevertheless, he goes on to say that international business travel "is perhaps the most dangerous form of travel. Tourists wouldn't consider flying into a Colombian war zone for a week, yet folks from oil, computer, pharmaceutical, agricultural and telecom companies do it regularly." Once there, just frequenting good hotels and restaurants with colleagues can make one a prime targets.

INTERNATIONAL EXPERIENCE AND YOUR CAREER TRAJECTORY

The impact of an overseas assignment on one's career trajectory may be positive, neutral, or negative. Companies tout foreign assignments as meaningful development experiences that prepare managers for greater responsibilities. An international assignment accelerates career progression, improves skills and expertise, fosters cultural awareness, increases confidence in overcoming challenges, and enhances creativity through exposure to new ways of doing things. Historically, however, the odds have been on a neutral or negative career outcome. Notwithstanding the rhetoric, companies were slow to reward a manager's successful international experience with expanded leadership responsibilities.

Globalization has changed this situation. Already, globalization has led to shortages of talented executives. Companies worldwide report difficulty finding skilled candidates, significant time and effort spent on interviewing and hiring, and escalating anxiety about losing top talent to rivals. Globalization also changes the standards of evaluation. More CEOs assert that international experience is an essential feature of a high-performance career. At Procter & Gamble, for example, 39 of the company's top 44 global officers have had an international assignment, and 22 were born outside the United States. Giorgio Siracusa, HR director at Procter & Gamble, believes that global awareness and experience are "ingredient[s] you must have if you aspire to be a global player in the long term." Globalization has spurred MNEs like Samsung, Infosys, AstraZeneca, Wipro, and Dow Chemical to see multinational experience as being just as essential as multifunctional and multiproduct experiences in reaching the upper echelons of the company. Data confirm this trend; for example, 80 percent of FTSE 100 CEOs reported international assignments.[4]

CRN
Case Review Note

Introduction

People manage organizations. Granted, successful companies have insightful strategies, efficient supply chains, sharp financial systems, and the like. Ultimately, though, success is a function of the people who start and sustain the organization. The challenge of putting the right person into the right job in the right place at the right time for the right compensation takes us to the front lines of international business. From opening markets to returning home, international business careers take any number of directions. At the center is the individual facing challenges that often lead to surprising opportunities. Indeed, the contest between challenges and opportunities is the spirit of a career in international business.[5] This chapter looks at the role of the individual in international business, profiling key facets of human resource management in the MNE.

WHAT IS HRM?

Human resource management
refers to activities that staff the
organization.

Human resource management (HRM) is the approach a company takes to manage its most valued assets—the people who implement its strategy. Opening and operating a business, no matter if it is a micronational or multinational, requires planning human resource needs, finding people to meet those needs, motivating them to perform well, upgrading their skills so they can move on to more challenging tasks, and, ultimately, retaining them.[6]

This chapter builds on the themes introduced in Chapter 11 and applied since to various value-chain activities. That is, it looks at HRM from the perspective that the successful company staffs its operations with people who leverage its core competencies while resolving pressures for local responsiveness and global integration. This perspective emphasizes that HRM activities, perform best when managers link them to the strategy of the firm (see Figure 20.1).

HRM and the Global Company   HRM is more difficult for the international company than for its domestic counterparts. The international company, besides dealing with situations in its home market, adjusts HRM practices for the political, cultural, legal, and economic differences between countries. For example, leadership styles and management practices vary from country to country.[7] These differences can cause difficulties between people at different units—say, headquarters in Beijing and a local subsidiary in Paris. These differences can turn great managers at home into ineffective ones in foreign markets, as the struggle to adapt erodes the effectiveness of performance. Similarly, labor markets vary in the mix of workers, costs, and productivity. Local labor laws often require a company change its workplace standards and hiring practices.

FIGURE 20.1   Factors Influencing HRM in International Business

Successful companies consistently demonstrate that managing their human resources, like managing their finances, marketing efforts, and supply chain, is best based on the requirements of their strategy. In this case, it's a matter of putting the right person in the right job in the right place at the right time for the right compensation—with the standard of "right" determined by the specifics of the company's strategy.

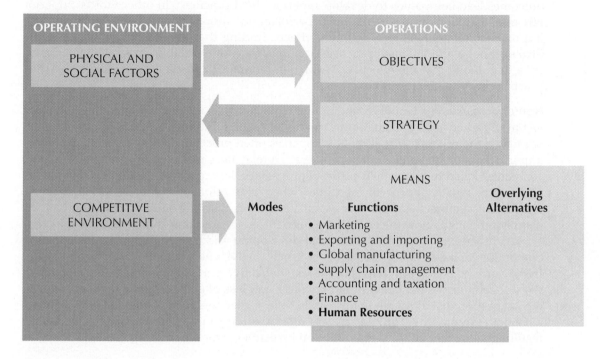

Adjusting labor-management complicates decision making. Lastly, dual career constraints and family obligations make it tough to convince executives to take international assignments. Hence, MNEs must devise and fine tune the best mix of recruitment, training, compensation, transfer, and retention programs to persuade and prepare executives to work abroad.

Global HRM as Competitive Advantage   One may wonder why companies and people put up with these difficulties. The short answer is that, in the face of globalization, they must. The long answer is that in the face of globalization, successfully dealing with these difficulties creates competitive advantages. Both answers highlight the mandate for HRM: Develop the means and methods to build, develop, and retain the cadre of managers that will improve an international company's performance.

This chapter discusses how international companies use HRM processes to meet this mandate. We begin by discussing the role that HRM plays in supporting the strategy the MNE has chosen to create value.[8] We then profile HRM activities that move the company's personnel plans from ambition to action—namely, the selection, development, compensation, and retention of international managers.[9] We conclude with a look at the relationship between the MNE and labor, examining the linkages among international labor relations, management action, and firm strategy.

> HRM is more difficult for the international company than its domestic counterpart due to
>
> - Environmental differences.
> - Organizational challenges.

The Strategic Function of International HRM

The effectiveness of HRM affects firm performance. No matter the scale or scope of the international operations, superior human resources sustain high productivity, competitive advantage, and value creation. The Human Capital Index, synthesized from the practices of 2,000 companies in Asia, Europe, and the United States, found that superior HRM positively correlated with a firm's financial returns.[10] Companies with superior human capital practices, on average, created more shareholder value than those with average practices.

Analysis revealed an intriguing pattern of causality: Superior HRM was a key determinant of a firm's financial performance, in contrast to the thesis that superior financial outcomes lead companies to develop superior HRM practices. In other words, superior HR management improves financial performance more than financial performance improves HRM. Others report similar effects, finding that the interaction between the firm's strategy and its HRM practices accounts for more variation in strategic performance than looking at the effects of HRM.[11] In summary, companies that improve HRM practices improve performance.[12]

Rhetoric vs. Reality Notwithstanding this explicit relationship, good intentions often fall victim to bad actions. Systematic and anecdotal reports find international companies may not match rhetoric to reality. That is, companies often proclaim, "Our people are our most important asset." More than a few workers can relay tales that when push came to shove, companies failed to honor their pledge. For instance, later parts of the chapter discuss the odd fact of what happens to executives when they return home from their expatriate assignments—more than half leave their companies within a year or two due to their dissatisfaction with how their companies recognized their accomplishments.

In a further irony, studies report that developing and managing human resources is one of the weakest capabilities in most firms.[13] MNEs note ongoing battles on several fronts, such as struggling with poor hires, ineffective performance management, teamwork shortfalls, wasted benefits and rewards, and loss of good employees. There is even the suggestion that although many MNEs believe they understand the cost of their international assignments, "only a few are in a position to measure the specific expense, resulting value, and, ultimately, return on investment from such postings."[14]

STRATEGIZING HRM

The relationship between superior HRM and high productivity, competitive advantage, and shareholder value confirms the value of people to performance. The power of this relationship has transformed HRM. No longer is HRM simply personnel management, concerned with administering routine employee processes and setting short-term employment policies. Now, companies see HRM as a driver of company strategy, responsible for providing the people who can leverage the firm's core competencies across the global market. Now, HRM in the MNE has a direct mission: Staff the right person in the right job in the right place at the right time for the right salary.

| Company and HRM are directly linked; one cannot work without the other.

Our earlier look at the strategies that international businesses follow elaborates this view. Chapter 11 profiles four strategies pursued by an MNE: The *international strategy* and its quest to leverage core competencies abroad, the *multidomestic strategy* and its quest to maximize the local responsiveness of foreign operations, the *global strategy* and its quest to maximize global integration, and the *transnational strategy* and its quest to optimize all three tasks. Each strategy sets difficult standards for configuring and coordinating value activities. Hence, each strategy calls upon HRM to develop executives who command the necessary skills.

Looking at the role of HRM in the context of the transnational strategy at GE elaborates these ideas. GE's move to a transnational strategy has spanned two decades. Beginning in the 1980s, GE focused on globalizing its markets by selling existing products abroad (the international strategy). In the late 1980s, the company began globalizing its material sources to get higher-quality inputs for lower prices in the quest to minimize costs (the global strategy). In the mid-1990s, GE began globalizing its intellect—seeking, learning, and transferring ideas throughout operations (the transnational strategy).

Each stop along the evolution to its transnational strategy saw GE resetting its HRM philosophy and practices to develop the required human capital. The key to its international strategy was staffing people who could develop foreign markets based on existing core competencies; the key to its global strategy was staffing people who could optimize location economics and manage global supply chains; and the key to its transnational strategy has been staffing people around the world who can develop, transfer, and engage ideas no matter the business function or market source. At each stage in GE's evolution, its HRM aligned the processes of employee selection, development, and compensation policies to support the company's strategy.

A vital part of GE's HRM evolution has been its use and expectations of expatriates to power its strategy. The role of expatriates at GE has evolved in tandem with its prevailing strategy. CEO Jeffrey Immelt explains, "When I first joined General Electric [in 1982], globalization meant training the Americans to be global thinkers. So Americans got the expat assignments. We still have many Americans living around the world, and that's good, but we shifted our emphasis in the late 1990s to getting overseas assignments for non-Americans. Now you see non-Americans doing new jobs, big jobs, important jobs at every level and in every country." Today, GE commands a powerful competency. It has a cadre of international managers with the expertise to leverage its core competencies in developing and diffusing ideas around the world.

In summary, GE's success in international business—like that of other companies we profile throughout this chapter—highlights the standard for HRM in an MNE: staffing the manager with the necessary qualifications to the job that best supports and sustains the company's strategy. Done well, companies translate HRM into higher management productivity, stronger strategic performance, and improving profitability. Done poorly, people problems create frustrations that ruin careers and undermine company performance.

THE PERSPECTIVE OF THE EXPATRIATE

One can evaluate HRM in the MNE from many perspectives. We apply an executive perspective. Two reasons motivate this choice. One, in the MNE, the tip of the operational spear is the executive developing international operations. Surveys report that expatriates drive the most critical tasks of the company's strategy; they launch new ventures, build management expertise, fill skills gaps, transfer technology, and diffuse the corporate culture. Two, an executive's perspectives speak to your interest in a possible career in international business. As teachers, students ask us about the why, how, when, where, and what of international careers. This chapter provides some guidelines, suggestions, and insights on your career ambitions. Together, these viewpoints direct our attention to the principles and practices that HRM applies to specify the selection, role, responsibility, development, compensation, and retention of the expatriate manager.

First, though, some helpful definition of who is who. Executives in the MNE belong to one of three classes: *locals, citizens of the countries in which they're working,* or *expatriates.* A local is hired by the MNE in his or her home country to staff the local operations; no special provisions, other than those general to the company, apply to his or her work contract. An **expatriate** (or *expat*) is temporarily sent to work in a country other than his or her legal residence. There are two types of expatriates. One type is a **home-country national:** a citizen of the country where the company is headquartered, such as a Brazilian national running the German operations of his Brazilian company. The other type of expatriate is a **third-country national:** a citizen of neither the country where he or she works nor the headquarters country, but a third country, such as a Swedish citizen running the Egyptian operation for an Australian company.

> An expatriate is an employee who leaves her or his native country to live and work in another.

> A third-country national is an employee who is a citizen of neither the home nor the host country.

Trends in Expatriate Assignments There has been a burst in worldwide demand for expatriates.[15] Growing demand follows from the emergence of developing countries as high-growth markets, coupled with difficulty finding skilled locals for start-up operations or in replacing expatriates in existing units. Staffing globalization, so to speak, has led to redefining the mechanics of expatriate assignments.

Traditionally, the idea of an expatriate is someone who leaves his or her home country to work abroad. However, precise classification of an expatriate, like the sort we note

Short-term expatriate assignments—those lasting a year or less—are far more common today than a decade ago.

above, is no longer quite so straightforward. Historically, an expatriate was posted to a particular host country for a three- to five-year assignment, with the ultimate plan of returning to the home country. Now, surveys report that most international assignments are much shorter. A decade ago, little more than 10 percent of international assignments were scheduled for one year or less; today, 80 percent or more run that short.[16] "Short-term assignments are popular because they are more cost-effective than long-term assignments and they allow companies to transfer skill sets quickly and easily," said one analyst.[17]

Short-term expatriate assignments—those lasting a year or less—are far more common today than a decade ago.

Changing markets, growing cost consciousness, and evolving strategies are resetting notions of who is an expatriate—now, we see growing interest in the young and old, not just the midlevel executive.

The Young, the Old, and the Restless   Traditionally, expatriates were midlevel executives being developed for greater responsibilities. As such, companies saw an international assignment as a midcareer stepping-stone for its future executive leadership. Now, companies are changing their traditional profile of an expatriate in terms of age—HRM now looks toward older employees whose children have grown and whose partners may be more willing to move, or younger employees who are single, more mobile, and less resistant to change.

In terms of posting younger managers to international assignments, companies are willing to trade performance track records for long-term potential. For example, PricewaterhouseCoopers (PwC, a global accounting and auditing firm) offers its Early PwC International Challenge (EPIC) program to accelerate international assignments for its younger employees. EPIC identifies promising workers who are interested in living abroad and have been at the firm for three or four years (interested candidates can jumpstart the process by completing an online assessment and consulting the company's careers pages for opportunities). EPIC encouarges people to choose their preferred destination, then posts them abroad for two-year assigments with the goal of developing them for senior leadership roles.[18]

Women increasingly fill expatriate slots in a variety of international assignments.

Similarly, gender dimensions are evolving. The past few years have seen females increasingly sent on international assignments. In absolute terms, roughly 20 percent of expatriates are female.[19] More significant is the trend. Since 2001, MNEs in Asia-Pacific have seen a 16-fold increase in females on international assignments, MNEs in North America have seen a fourfold rise, and Europe has doubled its count. A survey of more than a thousand MNEs found more than half expect the number of female assignees to continue to increase over the next five years, a third believe the number will hold, and a handful see it decreasing. Noted one observer, "Going on expatriate placements can be an important step on the career ladder, and women are increasingly interested in taking these assignments."[20]

Companies are sensitive to the fit between the values held by an employee and those endorsed by its organizational culture.

The changing workplace of globalization also elevates the usefulness of third-country nationals.[21] When companies establish operations abroad, such as the headquarters for a product division, third-country nationals often have the needed outlook and competencies. Moreover, the move toward short-term assignments boosts the appeal of third-country nationals. A banker living in London yet working for a U.S.-headquartered firm, for instance, may spend Monday through Friday working in Zurich and then return home for the weekend.

The rise of emerging markets adds a new twist to our evolving ideas of expatriates. Historically, companies selected expatriates from the pool of executives in richer countries and sent them to staff operations in developing countries. Now, well-educated executives from emerging economies are sent straightaway to the richer ones to develop their skills. Posted to home-country headquarters to learn the ropes, they then return to head operations in their home markets, often replacing expatriates.

Economic pressures and cost concerns spur companies to emphasize more business travel in lieu of an a official international assignment.

Impact of Market Disruption   The fallout of the global credit crisis has moved companies to rethink international assignments. Traditional HRM practices in the MNE are expensive. The quest to reduce expenses turns first to improving candidate assessment and seletion in order to reduce expatriate failure. Once done, companies impose short-term assignments, commuter assignments, and extended business travel in lieu of traditional "permanent assignments." Rather than moving to the foreign markets as they once did, executives are traveling far more often to far more places farther from their home base. Cost sensitivity is accelerating the deployment of third-country nationals in place of executives from the home office; the latter often demand richer compensation packages and impose higher relocation costs.

Cost concerns are leading companies to **"localize"** expatriate assignments—the process whereby an expatriate is offered the option to retain the foreign assignment provided she agrees to forsake the rich expatriate compensation package, accept the status of a local hire and, hence, the host-location salary structure. IBM foreshadows this trend. Its "Project Match" offers employees laid off in North America the option to work for the company in India, China, Brazil, Nigeria, Russia, or several other emerging markets provided they have been "satisfactory performers" and are "willing to work on local terms and conditions."[22] In other words, IBM offers some employees the option to move abroad in order to keep their job but at the price of accepting compensation that, while appropriate to the local market, is lower than the previous salary and far less than traditional expatriate compensation.

An Enduring Constant Change in the global environment—whether due to market opportunities or cost pressures—resets ideas of how to staff international operations. Hence, the types and mechanics of expatriate assignments evolve. Nevertheless, there is an enduring constant: Staffing the hundreds of thousands of plants and offices throughout the world requires that companies find managerial talent. So keen is the demand for qualified expatriates that senior human resource managers report historic shortages of executive talent.[23] Bluntly put, companies around the world struggle to find executives able and willing to run foreign operations.

HRM FRAMEWORKS IN THE MNE

HRM in the typical MNE is a tough task that, when successfully done, drives the company's strategy. When poorly done, it ruins careers and jeopardizes profitability. HRM managers have designed frameworks—conceptual structures used to solve complex issues—to guide decision making. These frameworks direct analysis toward determining the best mix of local workers hired from the host nation, expatriates sent from the home country, or third-country nationals. In broad terms, these frameworks reintroduce earlier ideas on *ethnocentrism, polycentrism,* and *geocentrism.*

Ethnocentric Framework Ethnocentrism occurs when one group places itself at the top of an imagined hierarchy of all groups, thereby seeing other groups as inferior. Hence, an **ethnocentric framework** reflects the belief that the principles and practices used by the home-office country are superior to those used by rivals in other countries. Given the proven success of the company's way of doing things, there is little justification to adapt to foreign markets.[24] This staffing framework leads companies to fill expatriate slots with executives from the home office.

Advantages of the Ethnocentric Framework Table 20.1 lists several benefits of this framework. Notably, MNEs that link firm performance to how well they transfer core competencies abroad typically adopt an ethnocentric approach. Consider that a firm earns success in its home market doing something exceptional. A legacy of success leads the company to see its business methods as the best way to do things. In such situations, companies aim to sustain their success when operating overseas by controlling the transfer and regulating the use of their core competencies.

Wipro, an Indian technology company, highlights the ethnocentric framework. It employs 54,000 people in 35 countries. More than 11,000 of these folks are expatriates of which more than 90 percent are Indian nationals working abroad. Wipro posts these Indian executives abroad—many of which are middle managers directing business

Three perspectives anchor a MNE's staffing policy:

- Ethnocentrism
- Polycentrism
- Geocentrism

Concept Check

In discussing "Company and Management Orientations" in Chapter 2, we introduce *polycentrism, ethnocentrism,* and *geocentrism* as three "attitudes or orientations" that companies and their managers take toward foreign markets. Here, we reintroduce these terms, highlighting the ways these "attitudes or orientations" affect a specific function of a company's global **strategy**, namely its *staffing framework.*

An ethnocentric framework fills key management positions with home-country nationals.

TABLE 20.1   Six Good Reasons to Staff Foreign Operations with Expatriates

Several factors encourage an ethnocentric staffing framework. As we see below, these factors tap competitive, personnel, economic, and leadership concerns. The criterion of evaluation, we note, is the presumption that the means and methods of the home office work well anywhere in the world.

Command and control	Familiarity with the way decisions are made and things get done at headquarters means that expatriates can be counted on to transfer home-country procedures to foreign operations.
Local talent gaps	A shortage of qualified local candidates makes expatriates a direct and immediate solution to staffing shortfalls.
Social integration	Posting expatriates symbolically and operationally diffuses corporate policies and practices. Spreading the faith, so to speak, fortifies the organization's culture internationally.
Local implementation	Expatriates offset the tendency for policies and practices to break down when transferred from the home to host country.
High turnover among locals	Expatriates' lower likelihood of leaving the company to join a local rival reduces the odds of proprietary information leaks.
Management development	The international exposure and experience gained by expatriates boosts a company's knowledge of international business strategies and practices.

development and training local staff—to spread company methods throughout the world. "We sprinkle Indians in new markets to help seed and set up the culture and intensity," says Sanjay Joshi, chief executive of global programs.[25]

Firms that are sensitive to leveraging their core competencies in foreign markets, such as is Wipro, believe an ethnocentric staffing policy works on two levels: transfer and protection. Regarding transfer, staffing overseas operations with people from the home country goes a long way to ensuring that the firm's core competency makes it overseas as planned.[26] This is vital when the core competency is difficult to articulate, specify, or standardize—such as Apple's product-design and media expertise. Posting a home-country manager to foreign operations, therefore, puts the company's core competency under the direction of a battle-tested home-country manager who commands the hands-on knowledge that girds the company's success. The HSBC Group long epitomized this model. For generations, nearly all its top bosses were drawn from a tight-knit cadre of elite expatriates who, in going from one foreign position to another, carried what an executive at HSBC calls "the DNA of the organization."[27]

Regarding protection, a company must safeguard its core competency. With it, the firm prospers; without it, the firm fails. This stark reality leads headquarters to entrust control of the company's "crown jewels" to those who will best protect them: fellow colleagues at headquarters. As we saw in an earlier discussion of intellectual property, safeguards can deter but by no means prevent the theft of corporate assets. The ethnocentric framework fortifies defenses, posting home-country executives who are alert and able to protect corporate assets.

Drawbacks of the Ethnocentric Approach   As the adage goes, "Vices are simply virtues taken to extreme." The same applies to the ethnocentric framework. Force-fitting foreign operations with a standardized staffing policy risks pounding circular pegs into square slots. Certainly, a company can make its foreign operations mirror the outward appearance of the home office. However, assigning home-office executives to foreign operations does not automatically imbue new attitudes. Furthermore, it can create high costs and lost opportunities.

Companies have compelling rationales when asked why they rely on home-country nationals to run international operations. Usually, they note that there is no shortage of brainpower in a particular country, just a shortage of people with the right mix of technical skills, experience with their particular business methods, and professional standards. This limitation can prove detrimental, blinding the company to different, possibly better, business methods.

Ethnocentric staffing policies can also leave local managers unmotivated and demoralized. An assumption of the ethnocentric view—that all the smart, capable people live within a 20-mile radius of headquarters—sends the message to subsidiary personnel that headquarters does not value them. Unless the purpose of the foreign assignment is to develop unique skills, local employees may resent the underqualified expatriate. Unchecked, resentment can lower productivity and increase turnover.

Lastly, an ethnocentric staffing policy can prove impractical. Host governments, alert to the importance of developing and employing the nation's workforce, prefer that foreign subsidiaries hire locals. MNEs' plea that the unique nature of their operations prevents doing so often falls on deaf ears. Governments, if pushed, use immigration laws or workplace regulations to require that the MNEs hire locals.

Polycentric Framework   Polycentrism is the principle of organization around several political, social, or economic centers. Hence, a **polycentric framework** sees the effectiveness of the business practices of foreign "centers" as equivalent to those in the home "center." The fact that the circumstances of the home office as well as those of local subsidiaries differ, coupled with the presumption that neither is intrinsically superior, moves MNEs to adjust staffing policies accordingly. The polycentric framework prompts staffing operations, from headquarters to foreign subsidiaries, with people drawn from the local environment—that is, Chinese run the China operations, Mexicans run the Mexico operations, Austrians run the Austria operations, and so on.

> A polycentric framework uses host-country nationals to manage local subsidiaries.

Advantages of the Polycentric Approach   Staffing foreign operations with locals has several advantages that span economic, political, social, and intellectual concerns (see Table 20.2). J&J, a company that applies the polycentric framework, gives a good sense of these benefits. With few exceptions, each of J&J's international subsidiaries is run by citizens of the host country. J&J lets each foreign unit operate with substantial autonomy, commanding the freedom to act as it sees best, given local market conditions. Each

TABLE 20.2   Six Good Reasons to Staff Foreign Operations with Local Managers

Several factors encourage a polycentric staffing framework. As we see below, these factors tap country, personnel, economic, and leadership concerns. The criterion of evaluation, we note, is the presumption that the means and methods of the home office must be adjusted to reflect national circumstances.

Cost containment	A local hire, given prevailing workplace standards and wage conditions, is typically paid less than the expatriate.
Nationalism	Host countries—especially those that are suspicious of foreign-controlled operations—prefer local managers who presumably are less inclined to emphasize global objectives over local interests.
Management development	Awarding top jobs to local managers makes it far easier to attract, motivate, and retain local employees.
Employee morale	For numerous social and cultural reasons, local workers prefer to work for local managers.
Expatriate failure rates	The failure of some expatriates takes a toll on the company in terms of unsatisfactory performance, sidetracked careers, and deflated morale; *ceteris paribus*, locals are less likely to fail, given their familiarity with the local environment.
Product issues	Sensitivity in interpreting and dealing with local conditions makes many local managers better able than expatriates to adapt global policies and practices.

foreign unit acts as its own small business, entrepreneurial in character and aware that success depends on anticipating local customers' needs and delivering meaningful solutions. The CEO of J&J explained that relying on locals to staff local operations "is a tremendous magnet for talent, because it gives people room to grow and room to explore new ideas, thus developing their own skills and careers."[28]

POLITICAL BENEFITS   Host governments typically see local managers as "better citizens" than expatriates, given the belief that locals will put national interests ahead of global objectives. Besides politically astute choices, hiring local managers in place of foreign expatriates boosts hometown morale.[29] In addition, there are impediments to using expatriates, such as licensing requirements that prevent companies from using expatriate accountants and lawyers. Hiring locals to fill these slots neutralizes these constraints.

ECONOMIC BENEFITS   The economics of staffing international operations is a compelling motivation for a polycentric approach. Hiring local managers eliminates the exorbitant expense of posting expatriates to local slots. A general rule of thumb is that the total cost of an expatriate is, at the minimum, three times the expatriate's annual salary for every year of the assignment; it is difficult to pinpoint total cost due to the range of variables that go into the calculation. Data report that an international assignment costs companies an average of $311,000 per year.[30] Indirect expenses boost this sum; on average, expatriates are supported by twice as many HR professionals (1 HR professional to 37 expats) as staff not on international assignment (1 HR professional to 70 managers).[31] Cost-conscious MNEs respond in kind. For example, HSBC Group had more than 1,000 expats five years ago out of 312,000 worldwide employees. Its concern about the higher costs of expatriates has led to local hires; it now has about 380 expatriates.

Proponents of polycentrism reason that local managers perform better and sooner, given their understanding of local customers, markets, and institutions. When operating outside the United States, for example, Microsoft tries to hire foreign nationals. As its chief operating officer explained: "You want people who know the local situation, its value system, the way work gets done, the way people use technology in that particular country, and who the key competitors are.... If you send someone in fresh from a different region or country, they don't know those things."[32] More philosophically, Bill Gates, chair of Microsoft, reasons that a polycentric policy is a moral obligation of international business, declaring that when staffing an international office, "It sends the wrong message to have a foreigner come over to run things."[33]

Drawbacks to the Polycentric Approach   A polycentric policy requires that companies decentralize authority to locals to run operations. Difficulties arise in terms of accountability and allegiance. Accountability issues emerge when local units evolve into quasi-autonomous operations that depend less and less on the home office for resources. In addition, as local managers develop skills and innovations, they often develop thriving local operations. This success supports resource independence from the home office. Unchecked, powerful local units may then regard the global company as a federation of loosely connected and largely autonomous national operations and pay little mind to headquarters.

Likewise, allegiance issues emerge when host-country nationals in charge of a subsidiary see their commitment to local colleagues and their home country rather than to the faraway headquarters of the company. In theory, local managers balance the competing demands of making sense of events from a local and a home-office view. In practice, however, national concerns often take precedence.[34]

Compounding this situation is a subtle drawback of a polycentric staffing policy—namely, the potential disengagement of local staff from the parent company. By definition and design, a polycentric staffing policy creates few opportunities to work outside

Using host-country managers helps local motivation and morale but at the possible cost of a gap with global operations because of problems with accountability and allegiance.

one's own country; there are few expatriate slots in a polycentric staffing framework. This outcome constrains the international mobility of host-country nationals. As a result, there may be little incentive for local managers to study business and cultural practices in other markets. Unaddressed, these issues can further isolate national subsidiaries.

Geocentric Framework Geocentrism is a "world-oriented" set of attitudes and values that regards humanity as a single entity. The **geocentric framework** does not heed national boundaries and sees the blunt division of home-, host-, and third-country managers as unnecessary. Rather, geocentrism calls upon HRM to develop the best people for key jobs throughout the organization, regardless of their nationality. Jeffrey Immelt of GE elaborates the geocentric framework, noting, "It's more important to find the best people, wherever they may be, and develop them so that they can lead big businesses, wherever those may be."

> A geocentric framework seeks the best people for key jobs throughout the organization, regardless of nationality.

Advantages of the Geocentric Framework A geocentric policy develops international executives who move between countries and cultures without forfeiting their effectiveness.[35] A geocentric staffing policy helps companies pursue a global and, especially, a transnational strategy. Both types of strategies rely on exploiting learning opportunities around the world to generate and leverage ideas. As the CEO of Schering-Plough explains, "Good ideas can come from anywhere... the more places you are, the more ideas you will get. And the more ideas you get, the more places you can sell them and the more competitive you will be. Managing in many places requires a willingness to accept good ideas no matter where they come from—which means having a global attitude."[36]

Many, seeing the power of ideas to create core competencies, adopt this geocentric orientation. For instance, Fujio Mitarai, president of Canon Inc., observes, "Until recently, everything we did overseas was an extension of what we were doing in Japan. From now on, we want to give birth to new value abroad. We want to make the best of the different kinds of expertise available in different countries."

> Economic factors, decision-making routines, and legal contingencies complicate a geocentric framework.

Drawbacks to the Geocentric Framework A geocentric staffing policy is hard to develop and costly to implement. Certainly, the notion of a "world-oriented" set of attitudes and values is intellectually engaging. In addition, the aggressively multinational composition of senior management that results from geocentric staffing policies reduces cultural myopia. Difficulty plagues adoption, however, given the need for executives to retain a sense of identity in the face of empathizing with the views of a diverse range of people.

For example, at one point, J.P. Morgan housed managers of more than 50 nationalities in its London office, reasoning that putting the best people together, regardless of nationality, powered strategic insights.[37] However, research reports—as each of us has likely experienced—that working with groups marked by cultural diversity takes on a different vibe than dealing with groups made up of people of similar ethnicities and nationalities. In the case of the former, the job of making sense of the various outlooks that bear on a decision can prove overwhelming. Like the Tower of Babel, geocentrism can erode the sense of common purpose, as the clarity of the task can get lost in a hodgepodge of different perspectives.

The logistics of the geocentric framework are costly. Exposing people to different ideas in diverse places is expensive. Compensation and relocation costs escalate when transferring high-priced managers from country to country. In addition, the higher pay and prestige enjoyed by those managers in the company's global executive vanguard can trigger resentment. Current cost sensitivities in the face of the global credit crisis further pressure companies to economize the geocentric staffing approach. Presently, companies experiment with short-term engagements, commuter relationships, and extended business travel in lieu of multiyear assignments.

Concept Check

A quick comparison of Table 20.1 (which endorses the *ethnocentric* framework) and Table 20.2 (which endorses the *polycentric* framework) demonstrates a principle that we develop throughout this book: Although most of us are prone to look for a "one best way" of doing things, it's seldom a promising approach in any area, including that of formulating **international business strategy.** We first point out the shortcomings of our three "Staffing Frameworks" when we introduce them in Chapter 2 as three "Company and Management Orientations." We profile **international, multidomestic,** and **global strategies** in Chapter 11.

TABLE 20.3   Comparing Approaches to Staffing Foreign Operations

This chapter provides a summary profile of the assumptions, advantages, drawbacks, and strategic appropriateness of the leading *staffing approaches* used by international companies. The matter of strategic appropriateness follows from our discussion (in Chapter 11) of the generic types of strategies commonly adopted by international companies.

Staffing Approach	General Assumptions	Strategic Appropriateness	Advantages	Drawbacks
Ethnocentric	Presumes that the leadership ideals, management values, and workplace practices of one's company are superior to those in foreign countries Headquarters makes key decisions and foreign subsidiaries follow commands	International	Leverages a company's core competence Gives people a strong point of common perspective Promotes development of the senior management team	Can inspire belief that one's company is intrinsically better at everything Can promote cultural arrogance and illiteracy May blind managers to innovations in other countries
Polycentric	Accepts the importance of adapting to differences, real or presumed, between the home and host countries Headquarters makes broad strategic decisions that local units adapt to their markets	Multidomestic	Helps people see the unique virtues of a particular nation Operationally the least expensive; eases adapting to the local market's workplace norms Placates host governments and promotes local staff development	Complicates value-chain coordination Isolates country operations Reduces incentive to engage an international perspective Potential for quasi-autonomous country operations
Geocentric	All nations are created equal and possess inalienable characteristics that are neither superior nor inferior but simply there Headquarters and subsidiaries collaborate to identify, transfer, and diffuse best practices	Global and Transnational	Adept way to deal with different people in different countries Leverages powerful ideas worldwide Opens learning opportunities	Tough to develop, costly to run, hard to maintain Contrary to many nations' market-development plans Difficult to find qualified expatriates

WHICH FRAMEWORK WHEN?

Table 20.3 summarizes the merits and constraints of the three staffing frameworks. This profile shows that there is no superior approach. Rather, HRM's task is to optimize the staffing policies in terms of the demands of the company's strategy. Earlier, we noted that expatriates drive the critical tasks of the company's strategy; they launch new ventures, build management expertise, fill skills gaps, transfer technology, and diffuse corporate culture. The task of HRM is conceiving the staffing framework that develops the executive resources that can do these jobs.[38] On this point, a survey of worldwide MNEs noted that nearly 90 percent of the companies prepared for global expansion by first determining strategic goals and needs, followed then by identifying the pool of potential expatriates with the requisite outlooks and skills.[39]

Managing Expatriates

Developing a cadre of high-performance expatriates requires MNEs to find those people who are prepared for international assignments, devise ways to motivate them to perform well, and capitalize on their new skills and refined outlook when they are ready for their next job. Therefore, we turn now to the matters of expatriate selection, preparation, compensation, and repatriation.

SELECTING EXPATRIATES

Some people enjoy the thrill of living and working abroad. In our opening case, for example, we heard from a Morgan Stanley expatriate who's worked in Britain, Singapore, and India. He remains excited about the prospect of seeing the "big world." Others, however, prefer not to work in a foreign country. Again, the fellow from Morgan Stanley conceded that international business travel is not always the safest activity. Other executives identify several reasons justifying declining the offer to work abroad or, once overseas, the rationale for returning home before completing the assignment. Consequently, few MNEs have the luxury of a large cadre of mobile, economical, and experienced expatriates to call on. Again, recall our opening case, where we found that maximizing the probability of success and, more often than not, minimizing the odds of failure, Honeywell screens candidates years before they would be posted to an international assignment.

Screening executives to find those with the greatest inclination and highest potential for a foreign assignment is the process of **expatriate selection.** This process, always difficult, is increasingly so given growing concerns about company-wide talent shortages, the difficulty of recruiting future leaders, and the increasing expense of international assignments.[40]

Despite considerable efforts, HRM cannot consult a battery of technical indicators that distinguishes a good versus poor expatriate. Indeed, the selection of people to work abroad often proves arbitrary; in many situations, "there's not a lot of science there at all…people may just get sent because they're willing to go."[41] Nevertheless, the stakes of the decision require assessing a potential expatriate's adaptability to foreign places, people, and processes. Complicating assessment is the fact that career success in one's home country is a necessary but by no means a sufficient basis for career success abroad. Contingencies arise from personality, professional, or family circumstances.

The need for expatriates to run international operations, coupled with the cost of expatriate failure, spurs systematic selection processes. HRM relies on career, cultural, and psychological assessment measures, anchored in the company's staffing framework, to organize the selection process. These measures, applied through both objective evaluations and in-depth interviews, screen expatriate candidates in terms of *technical competence, adaptiveness,* and *leadership ability.*

Technical Competence Corporate managers, expatriates, and local staff agree that technical competence, indicated by past job performance, has been and continues to be the leading determinant of success in foreign assignments.[42] Asked to rank order the most important objectives for an international assignment, HR directors cite the need to fill skills gaps in foreign markets. At the least, then, an expatriate must command the functional skills to do the job and, if necessary, understand how to transfer or tailor them to foreign situations.[43]

Managers often have had several years' worth of work experience before a company sends them abroad. This tendency reflects the fact that expatriate selections are often made by line managers based on the candidate's operational track record. Moreover, many companies translate a record of outstanding technical competence as the self-confidence needed to do well abroad. However, this predisposition is changing. Recall that some companies are seeking younger or older employees to staff international slots. For the former, companies are willing to trade performance records for long-term potential—as we see somewhat to an extreme in Figure 20.2.

Adaptiveness Performance data show that effective expatriates are adaptive; thrust into a new, unusual situation, they develop the outlooks, skills, and poise needed to thrive. MNEs evaluate a possible expatriate in terms of three sets of adaptive characteristics:

Self-Maintenance These qualities, such as personal resourcefulness, are useful because things do not always go as planned. The difficulty of specifying the elements of resourcefulness is evident in companies' struggles to identify candidates commanding

Case Review Note

Concept Check

In Chapters 2, 3, and 4, we analyze the *environments— cultural, political, legal, and economic*—in which **international business** is conducted. In each case, we emphasize that *variability* in these environments prevents setting absolute "standards" for running international operations. Here, we observe that similar differences have similar outcome. With regard to selecting expatriates, general guidelines take the place of absolute standards.

Technical competence often is the leading determinant of who is selected for an international assignment.

Adaptiveness refers to a person's potential for

- Self-maintenance and personal resourcefulness.
- Developing meaningful relationships.
- Interpreting the immediate environment.

*"You'll be perfect for heading up our new push into the global market
place but what's this about you still living at home with your mother?"*

this attribute. Like many MNEs, the selection process at HSBC uses tests, interviews, and
exercises to estimate a candidate's potential. While many are standardized, some assess
intangibles. As its CEO explains, "We don't look so much at what or where people have
studied but rather at their drive, initiative, cultural sensitivity, and readiness to see the
world as their oyster. Whether they've studied classics, economics, history, or languages
is irrelevant. What matters are the skills and qualities necessary to be good, well-
rounded executives in a highly international institution operating in a diverse set of
communities."[44]

Satisfactory Relationships with Host Nationals   Living and working in different
cultures demands flexibility and tolerance. Whether called *cultural empathy* or *others-
orientation,* this outlook enhances an expatriate's ability to interact with different people
in alien settings. Research reports that two factors play vital roles: the ability of an
expatriate to develop sincere, honest friendships with foreign nationals and the
expatriate's willingness to use the host-country language.

Sensitivity to Host Environments   Valuable competencies include the sensitivities
that help one interpret the immediate environment in ways that reject stereotypes,
preconceptions, and unrealistic expectations.[45] As traveling abroad quickly shows, new
situations in new settings challenge one's values and outlooks. Interpreting how
colleagues, customers, and competitors in the local market see events, rather than
criticizing them for dissimilarities, supports strong performance in foreign markets.

Top managers in subsidiaries
usually assume a greater
range of leadership roles and
broader duties than do
managers of similar-size
home-country operations.

Leadership Ability   The precise job descriptions found in the job bank of the home
office often give way to far-broader responsibilities in foreign subsidiaries. Typically, an
expatriate finds himself the senior manager at a foreign subsidiary that lacks the rich
range of resources available at headquarters. The call to do many jobs simultaneously
requires that expatriates find ways to understand cultural differences in problem
solving, motivation, use of power, and consensus building, as well as make sense of
trade rules and regulations, business practices, and joint ventures relations. Companies
expect expatriates to step up to this challenge, developing requisite skills in
communication, motivation, self-reliance, risk-taking, and diplomacy. Consequently,
companies see executive leadership as a key to an expatriate's selection and success; to

that end, increasing an executive's leadership capabilities is a key objective of international assignments.[46]

The track records of successful expatriates show that they often command, in descending order of importance, optimism (believes future challenges can be overcome), drive (has passion to succeed), adaptability (handles ambiguity well), foresight (imagines the future), experience (has seen and done a great deal), resilience (recovers from failure), sensitivity (adjusts management style to cultural differences), and organization (plans ahead, follows through).[47] As we saw in our opening case, Microsoft's Joan Pattle found that working abroad required meeting a host of new work demands. At home, her job in marketing meant working in her department with little responsibility for other business functions. Her expatriate assignment in the United Kingdom pushed her to develop leadership in areas beyond the customary marketing function.

Case Review Note

EXPATRIATE FAILURE

Despite the best-laid plans of mice and men, as the saying goes, things often go awry. MNEs experience this situation when they select their best and brightest managers, send them to a foreign market, pay them well, and watch them fail. **Expatriate failure,** narrowly defined, is a manager's premature return home due to poor job performance; broadly defined, it is the failure of an MNE's selection policies to find individuals who will succeed abroad. However defined, it is an enduring concern among MNEs. In the 1980s, research reported that nearly a third of American managers assigned to developed countries returned early—the failure rate twice that for those sent to developing countries. Today, surveys report that less than 7 to 10 percent of expatriates fail to complete their international assignments.[48]

Expatriate failure is operationally costly and professionally detrimental.

The Costs of Failure   The fall in the rate of expatriate failure testifies to the improving sophistication of selection processes. Still, few see this drop as cause to stop and celebrate. The financial and personal costs of expatriate failure, no matter how infrequent, are destructive. The average cost per failure can be as high as three times the expatriate's annual domestic salary plus the cost of relocation.[49] The direct costs of each failure can reach $1 million when one adds the time and money spent in selection, visits to the location before the executive moves, and the expatriate's lost productivity as things fall apart. Finally, an incalculable cost is the personal implications of professional failure to the formerly high-performing executive's self-confidence and leadership potential. A secondary cost is the disruption of the family, as expatriate failure distorts relationships and creates stress.[50]

Preventing Failure   Sometimes failure is the consequence of poor HRM putting the wrong person in the wrong job at the wrong time with the wrong expectations. Other times, failure is a surprise, as personal circumstances turn a sure thing in the wrong direction. The costs of either situation spur firms to study the causes of expatriate failure and develop preemptive training and preparation programs.

Assessments of expatriate failure have focused on the expatriate's technical expertise and the ability to cope with greater responsibilities overseas, challenges of the new environment, and personal or emotional problems. In addition, MNEs expanded analysis to gauge the ability of the expatriate's spouse and family to adjust to the foreign environment. The growing sophistication of HRM has reduced the rates of expatriate failure due to insufficient technical expertise. Today, rare is the foreign assignment that fails because HRM did not identify the person as technically underqualified prior to departure.

The improving sophistication of selection processes has reduced the rate of expatriate failure.

Dealing with Adjustment and Stress   Other causes of expatriate failure have proven more intractable. Traditionally, attention focused on the expatriate's lack of adjustment to the new environment as a predictor of failure.[51] The inability of an expatriate to adjust to the foreign assignment has consistently been linked to his or her inadequate cultural sensitivities and skills. Hence, the vast majority of MNEs provide cross-cultural preparation.

The central theme to cross-cultural preparation is the idea that the first year or so abroad is especially difficult. Getting ready for the challenge goes a long way toward thriving and, for the unfortunate few, simply surviving the assignment. Surveys report that most MNEs offer cross-cultural training, destination familiarization, and language lessons. Companies increasingly rely on CD-based or Web-based programs to ease preparation. The convenience, efficiency, and lower expense, HRM reasons, provides excellent predeparture preparation as well as in-country reinforcement.

Given that a foreign assignment is usually more stressful for the family than for the expatriate, companies consider the adjustment difficulties for the spouse and family.[52] Expatriates indicate that critical family challenges are children's education, family adjustment, and partner resistance to moving abroad. Difficulties also emerge with respect to location difficulties and general social adjustments. Consequently, the leading cause of expatriate failure is the inability of a spouse and children to adapt to the host nation. More pointedly, "If the family starts to unravel, the employee will at some time start to unravel, too."[53] Abrupt separation from friends, family, and career isolate the spouse and children. In recourse, they often look to the working spouse or parent for companionship and support. Usually, the working spouse has less time because of the new job. This fans family stress, which then affects the expatriate's work performance.

Employers experiment with ways to minimize the risk of family disruption. More executives are sent on short-term or "commuter" assignments for which they need not uproot their families. Also, moves to send younger or older expatriates speak to this threat. The younger are more likely single, while the older have grown children and partners less resistant to change.[54]

PREPARING EXPATRIATES

Companies recognize the need to prepare expatriates for their international assignments. Nevertheless, companies struggle to manage these issues systematically. HRM departments have lots of employee data that monitor employees' technical capabilities and accomplishments. Far less data profile their adaptive capabilities, willingness to accept foreign assignments, international orientation and outlook, or geographic preferences.[55]

Focusing on Adaptiveness and Related Characteristics   This data gap reflects the MNE's historic preoccupation with linking expatriate selection to technical competence. This bias led MNEs to direct training efforts toward improving technical skills and administrative competencies. The issue of adaptiveness was left to the individual, the thinking being that managers interested in international careers would find ways to travel abroad, monitor world events, and socialize with people of different ethnicities, cultures, and nationalities.[56] When posted as expatriates, executives commanding these outlooks performed well.

Performance variability, by highlighting gaps in predeparture training, encouraged companies to absorb this responsibility and move adaptiveness preparation in-house. Now, companies apply development programs geared toward raising expatriates' cross-cultural IQ and sensitivity. Many MNEs prepare potential expatriates by developing their understanding of a country, cultural sensitivity, and practical skills prior to their departure. As we observed in our opening case, for instance, Wipro and Honeywell begins training potential expatriates early and focuses on cross-cultural skills, including those necessary for dealing with culture shock.

General Country Understanding   The most common predeparture training consists of an informational briefing about the way things work in the host country. Topics include

politics, economics, features of the workplace, logistics options, and social situations.[57] Some companies refresh this training, oftentimes through Web-based resources, a few months after the expatriate begins the assignment.

Cultural Sensitivity   Cultural education sensitizes expatriates to see the benefits of working with host-country nationals, encouraging them to keep an open mind to different ideas, attitudes, and beliefs. Developing outlooks to accept different cultures does not always come naturally. Hence, preparing expatriates requires helping them recognize possible prejudices and biases. Early and expansive exposure to aspects of culture, the reasoning goes, is the best medicine to help expatriates withstand **culture shock**—a soon-after-arrival dissatisfaction with the host culture that, if not dealt with, can deteriorate into homesickness, irritability, arrogance, and disdain.

Today, the company that does not offer formal cross-cultural preparation for international assignments is the outlier. Estimates indicate that up to 90 percent of companies—depending on the length of assignment, situation of the employee, job requirements, and destination—provide predeparture preparation.[58] An emerging trend, understandable given the leading cause for expatriate failure, is providing cross-cultural training to the expatriate as well as to his family.

> MNEs usually anchor education programs to transfer specific information about the host country as well as improve the executive's cultural sensitivity.

Practical Skills   Practical training aims to familiarize the expatriate and family with the routines of life in the country of assignment. The sooner the family develops a productive pattern of schooling, socializing, and shopping, the greater the odds that they will withstand culture shock. Expatriates do several things to help themselves adjust to foreign locations, such as socializing with local community groups and joining expatriate associations. In addition, before departing, they consult former expatriates on the successes and struggles of their assignments.

> Key to preempting culture shock is the expatriate's success in developing a productive pattern of schooling, socializing, and shopping.

Two Approaches to Preparation: Specialized Knowledge versus Cultural Sensitivity   MNEs often underprepare potential expatriates for international responsibilities due to uncertainty about the best way to do so. Companies can transfer specific and specialized knowledge about the foreign environments. In contrast, they can develop interpersonal awareness and adaptability in the context of cross-cultural sensitivity training. The former approach tends to reduce some of the fear of dealing with the unknown. The latter approach tends to make people more receptive to and tolerant of foreign environments. However, the awareness of a difference does not imply a willingness to adapt to it, particularly if it is a cultural variation. Although either approach helps a person adjust better than receiving no training, there appears to be no significant difference in their relative effectiveness.[59]

Broader, More Sophisticated Programs   Sophisticated strategies spur MNEs to develop the international competencies of more employees. The need to generate, transfer, and adopt ideas from wherever they originate to wherever they add value—particularly compelling for the MNEs pursuing a global or transnational strategy—calls for preparing employees to do so. In addition, MNEs with an international or multidomestic strategy face pressures, given growing globalization, to help more employees understand worldwide operations.

MNEs use development programs to help employees overcome their hesitancy. MNEs see growing value in adding international business components once reserved for expatriates to company-wide management development programs—irrespective of whether attendees plan to work abroad. Examples include Mattel's and Infosys's regional training centers, where managers from several countries convene to examine specific topics; Procter & Gamble's training on globalization issues; and programs at Honda of America for teaching foreign languages and cultural sensitivity.

> **Concept Check**
>
> In Chapter 11, we explain the concept of "The Firm as Value Chain" and discuss **strategies** by which a company strengthens its competitive position. Here we observe that successful firms show that linking their strategy to expatriate selection boosts performance.

Rhetoric versus Reality   Despite the usefulness of preparation programs, reports suggest that some managers receive little to no predeparture training. Indeed, many expatriates prepare for their assignments on the flights to their new home countries, scanning reports and reviewing resources. Companies blame the urgency of the situation for this deficiency, noting that there is insufficient time for an executive to take a familiarization trip to the host country, let alone a thoughtful course on its history, culture, politics, economy, religion, and business environment. The home office sees the performance of the foreign operations deteriorating or the fading of key opportunities requiring the immediate dispatch of help in the person of the expatriate.

Point ▷ ◁ Counterpoint

Learning a Foreign Language—Still Useful?

Point ▷ **Yes** When asked about the importance of employees' foreign-language needs, human resource managers regularly respond that foreign-language competency adds professional and personal value.[60] Surveys report that managers who learn one or more foreign languages find ways to make innovative contributions to their companies. Even if the expatriate is far from fluent, the willingness to communicate in the language of the host country can help build rapport with local employees, thereby improving the manager's effectiveness. Proponents of language skills also point out that countries have different cultural and business expectations that can only be deciphered through the local language.

Threat of Exclusion   Foreign language aversion, which many extrapolate to general cross-cultural illiteracy, can also lead to exclusion from influential business networks, complicate relations and negotiations with local officials, and make it a struggle to chat with local colleagues.[61] Working abroad is itself a challenge; language limitations make it further isolating.[62] For example, Microsoft's Joan Pattle noted that her inability to speak Turkish made her seven-month stint in Istanbul very lonely. "You can't really mix with the locals... [or] use local transportation because you can't read any of the signs."[63]

Impression Management   Symbolically, the effort to speak the local language, no matter how poorly, sends a subtle but essential cultural message. Says the American Council on the Teaching of Foreign Languages, "[j]ust making an effort to say a few words in the native tongue can make a good impression... [as it] sends a subliminal message that 'we are equal.'"[64] Moreover, as anyone who has struggled to learn a foreign language can attest, unexpected benefits include a good dose of humility and respect for others.

New Perspectives   Against this backdrop, proponents of foreign language competency maintain that one of the central features about learning another language is its potential to be an enriching experience. The study of another culture

Counterpoint ◁ **No** The widespread and growing prevalence of English throughout the world is a sign that learning a foreign language is unnecessary. English performs as the language of world business—it is becoming the *lingua franca* of the world and, for a growing number of people, a practical alternative to their native language. Nearly a quarter of the world's population speaks some English. That includes around 400 million who speak it as their mother tongue and about the same number who speak it as a second language. In general, as shown in Chapter 2, the English language accounts for a much larger share of world output than that represented by the proportion of native speakers in the world. Although English is the first language of 6 percent of the world's population, English speakers generate more than 40 percent of world output.

English Hegemony   Situations in Europe, where more than half the people in the European Union claim to be conversant in English, highlight this trend. Among Europeans born before the Second World War, English, French, and German are equally common. But according to a Eurobarometer survey, 15-to-24-year-old Europeans are five times more likely to speak English as a foreign language than either German or French. Add native speakers to those who have learned it, and some 60 percent of young Europeans speak English "well or very well."[65] Many envision developing their English further; a survey of 16,000 people living in the European Union found that more than 70 percent agreed with the statement "Everybody should speak English." Similar trends show up elsewhere. In 2005, India had the world's largest English-speaking and English-understanding population. It now has the second-largest "fluent" English-speaking population, after the United States. It expects to have the world's largest number of English speakers within a decade.

Global Reach   While English is not an official language in many countries, it is the language most often taught around the world as a second language. In the European Union, often triggers insights and clarifies perspectives of one's own history, society, and values. In addition, an understanding of the local language and culture proves valuable when confronting the consequences of globalization. Growing networks of international cooperation and exchange depend on people who possess foreign-language proficiency.

Evidence suggests that learning a foreign language sharpens your business skills and refines your executive perspective. The process of learning a foreign language teaches us that there are several ways to express a concept, interpret an abstraction, and make sense of a situation. While the various ways are often compatible, occasionally they are not. Hence, managers capture a commanding competitive edge in effectively communicating with foreign suppliers, buyers, officials, and other stakeholders. Certainly, one can rely upon talented interpreters. Still, communicating directly with foreign counterparts creates a relationship that is impossible to achieve through an interpreter.

Competitive Imperative   Moreover, if not for enrichment, some say learning a foreign language will soon be a competitive necessity. The expanding international links and intercultural connections of a globalizing world make linguistic skills crucial for getting a job and accelerating a career. Moreover, in the context of the growing unemployment resulting from the current global economic crisis, any means of differentiating one's competencies, such as that demonstrated by linguistic skills, creates job opportunities.

Some may respond that the growing spread of English competency worldwide means that those who already speak English need not worry. Critics are quick to point out, though, that marketplace trends will punish, not privilege, English-only speakers. Today's English-only speaker will eventually lose the competitive advantage that once came with being among the few native Anglophones who could speak the most useful language of the business world. Now, bilinguals or multilinguals will offer the same abilities that English monoglots can but with richer language skills and broader international perspectives. In some parts of the world, officials have institutionalized incentives to power this movement. For instance, the European Union's official language policy is "mother tongue plus two," in which citizens are encouraged to learn two languages in addition to their own.

Which Languages?   This line of discussion triggers the question: Which foreign language should one study? Growth in expatriate positions is moving from Western Europe and North America to the fast-growing emerging economies. As MNEs struggle to place expatriates in these high-growth markets, for instance, proficiency in these languages will translate into job opportunities and salary premiums. Entrepreneurs may look around their hometowns and go for fast-growing languages such as Spanish, Mandarin, or Arabic. ▶

English is the top foreign language studied by schoolchildren (89 percent), followed by French (32 percent), German (18 percent), and Spanish (8 percent).[66] Nearly 200 million students in China are studying English in school, and more than a fifth of Japanese five-year-olds attend classes in English conversation. Countries from Chile to Mongolia aim to become bilingual in English in the next decade or two. English was added to the Mexican primary-school curriculum in 2006; children there are learning English, along with 200,000 teachers.[67] Collectively, with 2 billion people speaking or studying English today, we are on the verge of a massive diffusion of English competency.[68]

Growing Predominance   The prevalence of English is best seen by the predominance of English on the Internet, in terms of both English language content and the English language itself. Its predominance makes it possible to conduct business all over the world using the English interface of one's preferred browser.[69] Furthermore, reports that more than 80 percent of home pages on the Web are in English reinforce the likelihood of English as a *lingua franca* of the Internet. This trend is accelerating. For example, heavyweight publications around the world such as *Der Spiegel*, a German newsweekly, offer English-language Web sites that list translated news stories and opinion pieces. On a related front, the growing sophistication of translation software makes foreign-language competency a moot point for those who prefer using their local language on the Internet.

Reality vs. Rhetoric   Many managers have responded in kind. *The Economist,* for example, reports that just under half of employers rate language skills as important—a tendency that many link to the laborious struggle to master a foreign language. Others report that language competency ranks well behind technical competencies, and leadership skills, but ahead of motivation for working abroad, previous success abroad, and overall business vision in gauging the suitability of a candidate for international assignments.[70] Operationally, companies act accordingly. English is the working language of a growing number of international companies.

Outlooks, not Languages   Ultimately, language proficiency may be a misleading proxy of an expatriate's cultural sensitivity and general ability to perform in foreign markets. The CEO of Schering-Plough, for example, explains that "I've met many people who speak three or four languages yet still have a very narrow view of the world. At the same time, I've come across people who speak only English but have a real passion and curiosity about the world and who are very effective in different cultures."[71] ◀

COMPENSATING EXPATRIATES

If a U.S. MNE transfers its finance manager who is making $150,000 per year in Philadelphia to Shanghai, where the going rate is $100,000 per year, what should the manager's salary be? Alternatively, if a Chinese finance manager is transferred to the United States, what pay should the company offer? Should it compensate in dollars or yuans? Which set of fringe benefits should apply?

These are a few of the many questions a company faces when it posts people to international assignments. Managing an international workforce requires that HRM deal with differing pay levels, benefits, tax programs, and prerequisites. On the one hand, HRM must prevent the already high costs of an expatriate assignment from spiraling out of control—companies in the United States spend nearly $1.3 million per expatriate during the course of a typical three-year foreign assignment.[72] On the other hand, HRM must pay people enough to motivate them to work hard as well as provide sufficient incentive to the family to move abroad.

The Pay–Performance Link   All things being equal, compensation can determine the likelihood and success of expatriate assignments. Pay too little, and people decline to go or, if they do go, regret it. Pay them too much, then costs escalate, returns fall short, and pay inequities fan dissension. Further complicating the pay–performance link is the weak-to-nonexistent correlation between higher pay and improved performance. Data show that the higher the pay, the longer expatriate assignments tend to last; some managers, quite content to prolong a munificent financial existence abroad, are less eager to return home.[73]

The task facing HRM, then, is straightforward: Devise a compensation package that gets people to go abroad, lets them maintain their standard of living, reflects the responsibility of the foreign assignment, and ensures that after-tax income will not fall because of the foreign assignment. Developing a solution, however, is not quite so straightforward. HRM must balance the financial needs of the company with needs for an attractive salary and benefits package for the expatriate. Also, HRM must ensure that the compensation package preserves pay equity among peers in the company, promotes parity among the various nationalities of expatriates, is competitive with packages offered by industry rivals, and can be easily administered. In the final analysis, therefore, HRM has to balance its responsibility to company goals and individual needs with plans that make the expatriate assignment a win-win situation.

Types of Compensation Plans   Many MNEs, especially in the United States, apply the **balance-sheet approach** to manage expatriate compensation.[74] The approach develops a salary structure that equalizes purchasing power across countries so that expatriates have the same living standard in their foreign posting that they had at home—no matter to which country their assignment takes them.[75] The principle of the balance-sheet approach is equalization; expatriates should neither overly prosper nor unduly suffer because their companies assigned them work abroad. In addition, the balance-sheet approach outlines how the company provides financial incentives that offset qualitative differences between assignment locations.

Three common methods of implementing a balance-sheet compensation plan are:

Home-Based Method   This method bases the expatriate's compensation on the salary of a comparable job in his or her home city. By preserving equity with home-country colleagues, it treats the expatriate's compensation as if the person had never left home. Additionally, it simplifies the expatriate's eventual return. The home-based method is the most prevalent expatriate compensation plan. Most companies use it for both short-term and long-term assignments.

The evolving dynamics of globalization challenges the home-country balance-sheet approach. Initially designed for transferring employees and families from

Western-headquartered companies, this method based its cost-of-living indices and support allowances on transfers from high-cost countries to other countries. Today's global environment is marked by expatriates of many different nationalities, different home and host combinations, different salary levels and transfers to or from headquarters, and growing numbers of transfers between subsidiaries. Hence, companies applying the balance sheet struggle to maintain pay-equity and benefit consistency among their increasingly diverse expatriate populations.

Headquarters-Based Method   A useful way to tweak the home-based method is to set the expatriate's salary in terms of the salary of a comparable job in the city where the MNE has its headquarters. For example, if a Boston-headquartered MNE posted expatriates to its offices in London, Santiago, and Jakarta, it would give each a salary structured in terms of pay rates in Boston. This plan recognizes the disruption of a foreign assignment and ensures an expatriate lives as she had in her home country.

Host-Based Method   Sometimes called *destination pricing* and *localization,* this method provides a way to fine-tune expatriate compensation. The host-based method sets an expatriate's compensation based on the prevailing pay scales in the locale of the foreign assignment. Basically, an expatriate starts with a salary equivalent to that of a local national with similar responsibilities and then adds whatever foreign-service premiums, extra allowances, home-country benefits, and taxation compensation were negotiated. The host-based method pays an expatriate less to reduce tension between the expatriate and his or her colleagues in the host country due to variation in pay for similar jobs as well as to improve the company's return on its investment.

The host-based method is not as lucrative for the expatriate as the home- or headquarters-based methods. PwC, for example, uses this method to set compensation for expatriates involved in its EPIC program. PwC improves the attractiveness of the package, however, by offering other benefits such as assistance with immigration, reimbursement for moving personal effects, reimbursement for relocation travel costs, one home leave per assignment year, and language and intercultural training.

Key Aspects of Expatriate Compensation   Table 20.4 illustrates a typical expatriate compensation package. Expatriates negotiate their compensation packages in terms of a base salary, a foreign-service premium, allowances of various types, fringe benefits, tax differentials, and benefits.[76]

Base Salary   An expatriate's base salary normally falls in the same range as the base salary for the comparable job in the home country. It is paid either in the home-country currency or in the local currency.

Foreign-Service Premium   A *foreign-service premium*, often called a *mobility premium,* is a cash incentive to compensate individuals for the inconveniences of moving to a new country, living away from family and friends, dealing with the day-to-day challenges of a new culture, learning a new language, developing new workplace practices, and preparing for the disruption of eventually returning home. Long-term assignments usually qualify for a mobility premium; few short-term assignments do. Typically, the foreign service premium is expressed as a percentage of annual base salary (between 5 and 15 percent). It varies depending on whether the expatriate assignment requires an intraregional or intercontinental move.

Allowances   Sending an executive on an international assignment creates expensive logistics. Companies adjust the total compensation package with a variety of allowances that help reduce the difficulties the executive and his or her family face.

COST-OF-LIVING ALLOWANCES   Expatriates receive a cost-of-living allowance (sometimes called a *goods-and-services differential*) to nullify the risk that they will suffer a decline in

In designing compensation packages for expatriates, HRM considers the following topics
- Base Salary
- Foreign Service Premium
- Allowances
- Fringe Benefits
- Tax Differentials

Allowances give HRM the flexibility to deal with special situations. Allowances often involve
- Cost-of-Living
- Housing
- Spouse Support
- Hardships

TABLE 20.4   What Does an Expatriate Cost?

Numbers reflect the following scenario: A Seattle-based company will assign a senior executive to run a wholly owned subsidiary in Tokyo. Back in the United States, this executive, who has a working spouse and two children, earns an annual income of $150,000. A quick look at the balance sheet gives us a good idea of the outlay that will be needed to compensate this executive in the overseas posting.

Direct Compensation Costs	
Base salary	$150,000
Foreign-service premium	25,000
Goods-and-services differential	120,000
Housing	97,000
U.S. (hypothetical) taxes	(38,000)
Company-Paid Costs	
Education (schooling for two children)	30,000
Japanese income taxes	115,000
Transfer moving costs	47,000
Miscellaneous costs (e.g., shipping and storage; home sale or property-management fees; cultural, practical, and language training; preassignment orientation trip, destination assistance)	85,000
Working-spouse allowance	75,000
Annual home leave (airfare for four, hotel, and meals)	15,000
Additional health insurance, pension supplements, evacuation coverage	20,000

their standard of living due to the exorbitant expense of a particular city (London or Tokyo) or nation (Switzerland).[77] Some companies reduce the cost-of-living differential over time, reasoning that as expatriates adapt to their environments, they should adopt local purchasing practices—for example, buying vegetables from a neighborhood market instead of using imported packaged goods.[78] MNEs rely on data from firms that specialize in international compensation to estimate cost-of-living differences.[79] Table 20.5 reports the relative cost of living in the world's 20 most expensive cities.

Housing Allowances   A housing allowance ensures that the expatriate will duplicate his or her customary quality of housing—a key concern when asked to move from midpriced Salt Lake City to high-priced Seoul. Housing costs also vary because of crowded conditions that raise land prices, as well as the shortage of homes that are acceptable to expatriates.[80] Westerners pay steep premiums in some parts of Asia to rent accommodations with Western-style bathrooms and kitchens.[81]

Spouse Allowances   A spouse allowance partly funds an expatriate's spouse's effort to find work and take cross-cultural programs. In some cases, this allowance will help offset the loss in income due to the spouse forsaking his or her job.[82] About a quarter of MNEs provide the spouse of an expatriate with job-search assistance, often through networks with other companies.[83]

A spouse allowance also deals with the hardship created by potential changes in total family income and status. In the home country, members of the family may be able to work, whereas when they go abroad, typically only the expatriate has the legal right to do so. Host governments seldom grant permission to work other than to the expatriate. Therefore, the spouse or companion of an expatriate may have to forsake employment or live apart from their partner. Today, about half of large U.S. companies include spouse support in their international assignments policy.

Hardship Allowances   A hardship allowance (sometimes called "combat pay") goes to expatriates assigned to difficult environments or dangerous locations—especially for

MNEs often provide additional compensation or fringe benefits to employees who work in remote or dangerous areas.

TABLE 20.5   Cost of Living in the World's 20 Most Expensive Cities

Base City: New York, U.S. (= 100)

Fair, consistent compensation packages must reflect the expatriate's cost of living in the city of the international assignment. Companies use cost-of-living information, such as that reported below, to make the best determination. These particular data reflect the cost of more than 200 goods and services, including housing, transport, food, clothing, household goods, and entertainment, which are provided by vendors or outlets where expatriates buy products of international quality in the corresponding locale.

Rank, March 2008	City	Country	Cost-of-Living Index, March 2008
1	Moscow	Russia	142.4
2	Tokyo	Japan	127.0
3	London	U.K.	125.0
4	Oslo	Norway	118.3
5	Seoul	South Korea	117.7
6	Hong Kong	China	117.6
7	Copenhagen	Denmark	117.2
8	Geneva	Switzerland	115.8
9	Zurich	Switzerland	112.7
10	Milan	Italy	111.3
11	Osaka	Japan	110.0
12	Paris	France	109.4
13	Singapore	Singapore	109.1
14	Tel Aviv	Israel	105.0
15	Sydney	Australia	104.1
16	Dublin	Ireland	103.9
17	Rome	Italy	103.9
18	St. Petersburg	Russia	103.1
19	Vienna	Austria	102.3
20	Beijing	China	101.9

Source: 2008 Cost of Living survey highlights, Mercer, http://www.mercer.com/costofliving?siteLanguage=100 (accessed June 15, 2009).

long-term assignments. Living conditions in certain settings pose severe hardships, such as harsh climatic or health conditions, or expose the expatriate to security threats.[84] For instance, expatriate personnel of many MNEs, given their high profiles, have been targeted for kidnapping and assault. Companies have had to not only rethink their hardship allowances but also purchase ransom insurance, provide training programs on safety for expatriates and families, pay for home alarm systems and security guards, and assess their legal liability regarding employee safety.[85]

Where conditions are less severe, expatriates may encounter living conditions that are substandard to those at home, thus qualifying for a hardship allowance. Expatriates also receive miscellaneous allowances. Popular ones include a travel allowance that lets an expatriate and his family travel home periodically and an education allowance to finance the expatriate's children's access to a private education in the event that host-country public schools are unsuitable.

TRENDS IN ALLOWANCES   Overall, companies are reducing the range and extent of allowances. Cost pressures imposed by the global credit crisis along with growing job market stresses spur economizing. Foreign-service premiums, for example, if not already eliminated, are being phased out by many MNEs, given people's increased willingness to protect their jobs by working abroad.

Beyond immediate cost concerns, several factors signal fewer allowances. First, more individuals see international assignments as a chance to develop business skills and

Concept Check

Recall our discussion, in Chapter 1, of "The Forces Driving Globalization," in which we identify several factors contributing to the emergence of more and stronger "interdependent relationships" among people from different parts of the world. The convergence of cultures, politics, and markets condense the physical and psychic distances between countries. Here we suggest that this trend has begun to make the prospect of moving from one country to another a more common and attractive career arc (resulting in companies reducing incentives to take overseas assignments).

leadership qualities. These people are more willing to go abroad for less financial reward. In addition, foreign assignments have "gone from being special and unique, with piles of money thrown at them, to being an everyday part of the company."[86] Cost-reduction techniques include dropping benefits and allowances (many companies with operations in Europe now treat the continent as if it were one country) and cutting "hardship" allowances for locales that were once difficult but no longer are, such as a post to Prague or Shanghai. Pressure to reduce pay and perquisites will continue, both for cost control and due to the growing supply of skilled employees from developing countries who are eager to work worldwide.

Fringe Benefits   Firms typically provide expatriates the same level of medical and retirement benefits abroad that they received at home rather than those customarily granted in the host country. However, most companies expand these benefits to deal with local contingencies, such as bearing the cost of transferring ill expatriates or family members to suitable medical facilities.

Tax Differentials   The objective of compensation adjustments is to ensure that expatriates' after-tax income, and presumably their motivation, will not suffer because of the costs created by a foreign assignment. Because taxes are usually assessed on the adjustments that companies make to the expatriate's base salary, companies must adjust it upward if the foreign tax rate is higher than that applied in the home country. Tax equalization has become a costly component of expatriate compensation. If there is no reciprocal tax treaty between the expatriate's home country and host country, then she may be legally obligated to pay income tax to both governments. In such situations, the MNE ordinarily pays the expatriate's tax bill in the host country.

HRM monitors variations in tax codes from nation to nation. Tax authorities regulate issues regarding who must file, filing procedures, tax information to report, and penalties for noncompliance. Unimportant in the context of long-term assignments, tax policy becomes increasingly salient given the time lines of commuter and short-term assignments. For example, Chinese tax authorities stipulate that an expatriate who has spent less than 30 continuous days inside or more than 90 cumulative days outside of China per tax year is not considered a legal resident of China for that tax year. Consequently, executives monitor their time in China, tracking the dates of arrival and departure.

> Companies struggle to determine the proper degree to which they should equalize pay for the same job done in different countries.

Complications Posed by Nationality Differences   In addition to over 1,700 expatriates stationed in more than 50 countries, Unilever has 20,000-plus managers spread over 90 countries.[87] Should Unilever pay executives in different countries according to the prevailing standards in each country, or should it equalize pay for each position on a global basis? Legal, cultural, and regulatory factors complicate how much to pay managers in different countries. As companies employ expatriates from home and third countries, compensation issues grow complicated.

These problems are pressing for companies with a geocentric staffing policy. Both the global and transnational strategies depend on developing a cadre of international managers that includes different nationalities. The issue then emerges as to whether all managers who perform the same job but in different locations should be paid the same salary. For Finnish transnational Nokia, this would require compensating its foreign nationals, no matter where they worked, in terms of Finnish salary levels. If Nokia opts not to develop an equitable standard, it will result in the underpaid members of the expatriate cadre resenting their higher-paid counterparts.

Firms applying ethnocentric or polycentric staffing policies, though largely immune to these distortions, also systematize their compensation programs. If not, then they may pay someone more than necessary to persuade them to go abroad, given unequal cost-of-living conditions among countries. More worrisome, disparities in pay packages for people doing the same jobs can weaken the motivation of home- or host-country managers and impede a sense of unanimity among different parts of global operations. Even though the company with an ethnocentric or polycentric staffing policy may have few expatriates today, growing international activities make it cumbersome to administer foreign compensation packages on a case-by-case basis.

There is little consensus on how to deal with these issues. A decade ago, salaries for similar jobs varied among countries, as did the relationships of salaries within the corporate hierarchy. Today, more MNEs apply a global framework to their pay and benefit programs. Still, they adapt it to regional standards in order to offer consistency in their reward practices worldwide yet differentiate performance-based pay by country and region based on regulatory and cultural differences.

For example, CEOs in the United States enjoy the largest and most comprehensive pay packages, in terms of both base compensation and total remuneration. CEOs in France, Germany, Italy, Switzerland, and the United Kingdom also command higher levels of total compensation than their peers elsewhere. This model inspires emulation; Asian and Latin American companies are instituting similar pay practices, particularly the use of performance-based pay that ties compensation to business results.

> Total compensation as well as forms of compensation vary substantially among countries.

Differences persist. Long-term incentives, such as options on restricted stock, are popular in the United States but not in Germany. However, German managers often receive compensation that U.S. managers do not, such as housing allowances and partial payment of salary outside Germany, neither of which is taxable. Similarly, countries with aggressive personal income tax rates spur employees to ask for pay plans that reduce taxable base salaries in favor of tax-exempt fringe benefits. As companies from more countries become more multinational, they compete globally for executive talent. Likewise, local firms must tailor compensation to retain executives. Therefore, convergence in compensation practices is the order of the day.

REPATRIATING EXPATRIATES

HRM builds a staffing process that creates a cycle of events, beginning with the selection of the right expatriate, the delivery of useful predeparture preparation, the design of a motivating compensation package, and the means of getting one back home and onto the next job in good spirits. The latter task is called **repatriation** and defines the process of reintegrating the expatriate into the home company upon completion of the international assignment. Success at each stage in the cycle, not just the early ones, is vital. Consistent success supports a self-sustaining cycle whereby returning expatriates share their knowledge with colleagues and persuade other high-performing executives, particularly those disinclined, to work abroad.

> Returning home from a foreign assignment, the act of repatriation, is fraught with difficulties.

The repatriation system works—for some. Between a quarter and a third of returning expatriates believe their international experience boosted their career trajectory. Faster promotions and obtaining new positions are commonly cited benefits; nearly one in four expatriates who returns home is promoted in his or her first year of repatriation.

However, some returning executives do not land promotions, and a surprising share of these former high flyers quit. A survey of repatriated executives who had successfully completed their overseas assignments found that more than a third held temporary assignments three months after returning home, nearly 80 percent felt their new job was a demotion from their foreign assignment, and more than 60 percent felt they did not have opportunities to transfer their international expertise to their new jobs.[88] Futhermore, 27 percent of expatriates left the company within one year of returning from their international assignments, with another 25 percent leaving between the first and second year of return.[89] Explanations for this anomaly cite companies' greater concern about preparing and paying workers for the foreign assignment than supporting them upon their return.[90] Although companies see repatriation as important, only 20 percent acknowledge that they manage it effectively.[91] Consequentially, returning home can deteriorate into a disappointing part of the expatriate assignment.

In general, expatriates face repatriation stress in three areas: readjustment to the home-country organization, change in personal finances, and readjusting to life.

Repatriation tends to cause dissonance in many areas, most notably

• Work.
• Financial.
• Social.

Readjustment to Home-Country Organization   Readjusting to the ways of their previous office poses problems on several levels. Returning expatriates may find that their former peers have been promoted above them, enjoy less autonomy as they return to being a "little fish in a big pond," and struggle to rejoin the office network. As a result, they return to a company that does not quite know what to do with them and often views them as having market knowledge and technical skills that are not quite on the cutting edge. In these situations, resentment builds within repatriated executives, as they believe they have grown professionally during their foreign post, worked hard, sacrificed much for the company, and deserve praise and promotion.

More often than not, the opposite happens. One study found that some 60 to 70 percent of repatriated expatriates did not know what their positions would be when they returned home, and more than half said their companies were vague about the repatriation process, their pending jobs, and future career progression. Compounding these tendencies is the fact that, for many expatriates, being out of sight overseas turns out to truly be out of mind back home, amplifying the fear that "companies station people abroad and then forget about them. If anything, advancement is even more difficult for the expat when he returns to headquarters, having missed out on opportunities to network with top management."[92]

The principal cause of repatriation frustrations is finding the right job for the returning expatriate.

MNEs reply that repatriation puts them between a rock and a hard place: An office does not sit vacant while the manager goes abroad; cost cutting, mergers, and acquisitions often mean they cannot be kept on; and permitting the repatriated employee to bump his or her "replacement" upon return is unfair. Still, data indicate that expatriates are likely to stay if the company gives them chances to apply their expertise.[93] Companies push expatriates to take more responsibility for their return. Often, headquarters require that employees take home leave and visit the home office before they finish their international assignments.

Changes in Personal Finances   Changes in personal finances can be dramatic upon returning home. Typically, expatriates receive rich benefits during their foreign assignments; many live in exclusive neighborhoods, send their children to prestigious schools, employ domestic help, socialize with elites, and still save a good amount. Returning home to a reasonable compensation plan with fewer perquisites and privileges is often demoralizing.

Concept Check

In Chapters 3 and 4, we note *political/legal* and *economic* factors that contribute to the changing profile of high-growth markets; in Chapter 17, we discuss new wrinkles in both global manufacturing **strategies** and strategies in **supply chain** management that respond to this changing profile. Here, we suggest that these trends may increase reliance on a particular approach to dealing with the problems not only of repatriation but also of expatriate-staffing policies as a whole: MNEs develop greater confidence in strategies that focus on recruiting *locals* to run local operations.

Readjusting to Life   Readjusting to life at home is stressful.[94] Troubles emerge as returning expatriates and their families experience "reverse culture shock." Upon return, managers and their families need to relearn some of what they once took for granted. Meantime, children may struggle to fit into the local school systems, while spouses may feel isolated or out of touch with the careers or friends they have once again left behind.

Managing Repatriation   Companies are not blind to the problems of repatriation. Moreover, ignoring them is not an option—the greater the difficulties that confront returning expatriates, the greater the difficulty convincing others to accept international assignments. MNEs experiment with a range of remedies. HRM executives advocate providing expatriates with advance notice of when they will return, more information about their possible new jobs, placement in jobs that leverage their foreign experiences, housing assistance, reorientation programs, periodic visits to headquarters while working abroad, and enlisting a formal headquarters mentor to watch over their interests while they are abroad.[95]

Some companies, like Dow Chemical, make written guarantees that repatriated employees will return to jobs at least as good as those they left behind. Other companies integrate foreign assignments into career planning and develop mentoring programs to look after the expatriates' domestic interests. PwC's EPIC program relies on several safety nets, promising participants that "unrivalled support mechanisms" safeguard their careers.[96] Prior to the international assignment, each EPIC participant is linked to a mentor at home and a colleague awaiting his or her arrival overseas. The latter are themselves EPIC graduates who smooth the transition. Together, the mentor at home and partner abroad support the expatriate's career development. Similarly, Avaya charges the manager who sponsored an expatriate with the job of helping his or her protégé find a job upon repatriation. Beside benevolence, cold economics play a part, given Avaya's stand that it has "invested in this person. To leave him overseas or to lose him to another company is a waste of money."[97]

Despite these efforts, statistics show that many expatriates are unhappy upon return. Pressed to pinpoint where repatriation begins to break down, finding the right job for the expatriate to return to is the principal culprit. One report concludes, "People who have spent two years working in different ways across varied markets and cultures are not always happy to return to the same desk and the same prospects. In this vacuum of direction, many have a career 'wobble,' then leave via a recruitment market in which their experience is seen as increasingly valuable."[98]

Personal career management, therefore, is as vital to being selected for a foreign assignment as triumphantly returning home. Recall from our opening case the experience of Bryan Krueger, who accepted a four-year assignment in Tokyo without any guarantees of a promotion when he repatriated. As we saw, Krueger was "proactive," networking avidly, keeping up with events at headquarters, and visiting the home office. The lesson here is that expatriates cannot rely on the company to safeguard their career interests. A passive approach is hazardous given that expatriates often hear too late about possible promotion opportunities back home.[99] Instead they must navigate the repatriation process with a keen sense of its positive and negative aspects.

International Labor Relations

In each country in which an MNE operates, managers deal with groups of workers whose approach to the workplace reflects the local sociopolitical environment. This environment affects whether workers join labor unions, how they collectively bargain, and what they expect from companies. Differences prevail across countries in how labor and management view each other.

When there is little mobility between the two groups (generally, children of laborers become laborers, and children of managers become managers), class differences distinguish the managers who run the MNE and the workers they hire and fire. Labor may perceive itself as being in a class struggle that echoes the divisions of Marx's conception of the proletariat versus the bourgeoisie. Labor–MNE relations in these countries, such as those in Brazil, the United Kingdom, and France, tend to be a zero-sum game—labor wins when the MNE loses and vice versa.

Labor groups in many countries take a less confrontational approach. They are more inclined to follow the advice of their labor leaders and try to negotiate win-win solutions.[100] Unions in these countries often rely on national legislation rather than workplace activism to check MNEs' power. Moreover, labor's agenda may reflect a broader sensitivity to general work conditions in the country—that is, a rising tide lifts all boats—rather than specific conditions at a specific MNE.

The HRM function of an MNE deals with these situations. It takes charge of the company's relations with labor both within a particular country and within the global context. HRM manages workplace issues that fall under the umbrella of international labor relations. HRM integrates its efforts with the standards of how, why, and where organized labor might constrain how the MNE configures or coordinates its value chain.

A labor union is an association of workers who have united to represent their collective views for wages, hours, and working conditions.

HRM then supports the company's leadership in developing options to preempt, neutralize, or resolve these situations.

The intensity of these concerns varies with the type of strategy an MNE pursues. Companies pursuing an international or global strategy, given their heightened sensitivities to exploiting location economies, centralizing decision-making, and protecting the transfer and use of core competencies, are sensitive to labor's actions. Multidomestic and transnational companies, given their greater degrees of local responsiveness, command more flexibility to adapt operations to labor's concerns without sacrificing value-creation capabilities. Still, no matter the strategy of the firm, the strength of organized labor on both a country-to-country basis and internationally spurs MNEs to develop mutually beneficial relations.

We now consider three aspects of international labor relations. First, we discuss how labor represents the motives and means of MNEs, we then turn to the methods and successes of labor's responses to MNEs, and we close with a look at trends that moderate the relationship between MNEs and labor.

HOW LABOR SEES MNES

Labor claims it is disadvantaged in dealing with MNEs because

- It is hard to get comprehensive data on MNEs' global operations.
- MNEs can arbitrage investment incentives.
- MNE can relocate value activities to other countries.
- Ultimate decision making occurs in another country.

Labor criticizes MNEs for shifting work to other countries, leaving behind fewer jobs, lower wages, and grim prospects. An ongoing debate is whether the MNE, through the power of its globally dispersed value chain, weakens labor. Labor argues yes, noting that the multinationality of their product and resource flows MNEs then manipulate markets and governments for gains that labor must bear.

A case in point: When the Disney Company was planning an amusement park for Europe, it began by pitting several countries against each other in an effort to get the best possible investment incentives. It narrowed it down to alternative sites in France and Spain; ultimately, the company chose a site just outside of Paris. Labor's reaction was immediate. A representative of the Confédération Générale du Travail (General Confederation of Labour—CGT) of France contended that the Disney Company had used the threat of locating in Spain to drive a tough bargain with government officials. He asserted that "Disney put Barcelona and the French site in competition and, as a result of this bidding war, the French government won the contract at the expense of many laws and many hard-won social rights."[101]

Concept Check

Chapter 17 profiles the emergence of sophisticated strategies for **supply chain** management that affect wage rates, job creations, and job security in both home- and host-country markets. These developments will likely increase the tension between labor and MNE.

The MNE's Advantages   Once MNEs get their local operations up and running, labor contends that they can outlast workers in resolving a strike. Furthermore, labor contends that MNEs can move value activities from one country to another in an effort to exploit less restrictive labor conditions. Complicating these situations is the complexity of the globally dispersed value chains of MNEs. Labor often lacks the information to verify MNEs' claims about products and profits as well as estimating their capacity to meet workers' demands.

Collective bargaining refers to negotiations between labor union representatives and employers to reach agreement on a work contract.

Product and Resource Flows   Presumably, in the event of a strike in Country X, an MNE can divert output from its facilities in other countries and sell it to the consumers in Country X, thereby reducing the need to settle the strike. Moreover, because each country may comprise a small share of an MNE's worldwide sales, profits, and cash flows, a strike in one country may minimally affect its global performance. Given these circumstances, an MNE faces slight pressure to resolve labor tensions. Therefore, an MNE's ability to threaten dire consequences in the event of a strike, and then hold out longer, gives it a commanding advantage in bargaining with labor.

In their defense, managers explain that an MNE can supply customers in the strike-afflicted country only if it has excess capacity and makes an identical product in more than one country. Even if it meets these preconditions, an MNE still confronts the transport and tariff costs that led it to establish multiple facilities. If the MNE partially owns the struck operation, partners or even minority stockholders may balk at financing a lengthy work stoppage.

If the idle facilities produce components needed for integrated production in other countries, then a strike may have far-reaching effects. For example, a strike at one GM facility in the United States prevented GM's Mexican plants from getting parts needed for assembly operations. Moreover, Mexican laws against layoffs meant GM had to maintain its Mexican workers on the payroll, thus adding pressure on GM to settle.[102] In summary, there appear to be limited advantages of international diversification to enable an MNE to escape conflicts with labor.

Value-Activity Switching   MNEs often threaten to move value activities to other countries to extract wage reductions or work concessions from workers—put bluntly, lower your expectations or lose your job. This tactic presses unions to accept lower compensation, fewer benefits, and poorer workplace conditions in favor of job security. For example, Daimler-Benz's German workers agreed to accept lower wages after the company procured agreements from French, Czech, and British labor to work for less.

Operational Scale and Complexity   Observers claim that it is difficult for labor unions to deal with MNEs because of the global scale of their value chains and the difficulties in interpreting how they coordinate value activities. Both issues are complicated by the difficulty labor has in identifying the location of decision making and interpreting financial data for the typical MNE. These ambiguities mean that labor is often at the mercy of decision makers outside their country. Labor therefore argues that MNEs are more likely to impose arbitrarily stringent anti-labor policies in the event of workplace activism.

Workers and unions examine MNEs' financial reports to determine their ability to meet job demands. Interpreting these data is a difficult task because of disparities among managerial, tax, and disclosure requirements in home and host countries. Moreover, labor has been apprehensive that MNEs might manipulate transfer prices to give the appearance that a given subsidiary cannot meet labor demands.

MNEs reply that these concerns overemphasize their ability to increase compensation and deemphasize the more important issue of prevailing wage rates in both the industry and the geographic area. Although MNEs may report complex data, at least one set of financial statements must satisfy local authorities. By definition, this set should be no more difficult to interpret than that reported by a domestic company. In terms of transfer pricing, the MNE that sets artificial levels to aid in a particular collective-bargaining situation creates distortions and possible problems elsewhere. If an MNE understates profits in one country, it would have to overstate them elsewhere, which would then put it at a disadvantage in collective bargaining in that country.

HOW LABOR RESPONDS TO THE MNE

Workers have responded to the power of the MNEs through several actions. Workers have organized unions to fight, via collective bargaining, for higher pay, better benefits, greater job security, and improved working conditions. Unions' bargaining power follows from their ability to threaten to disrupt production, either by a strike or by some other form of work protest—most commonly through a slowdown in the pace of work or the refusal to work overtime. This threat is credible insofar as management has no alternative but to employ workers who are not union members.

Labor's Options   Unions engage several tactics to counter MNEs' bargaining power. Internationally, unions cooperate in a range of ways, sharing information, assisting bargaining units in other countries, and dealing simultaneously with MNEs.[103] The most

Labor tries to strengthen its bargaining power through cross-national cooperation.

common international cooperation among unions is exchanging information on an MNE's local policies and activities. This sort of collaboration helps determine the validity of the company's local claims and also helps it reference precedents from other countries on bargaining issues.

Exchanging Information International confederations of unions, trade secretariats made up of related unions in a single industry or a complex of related industries, and company councils that include representatives from an MNE's plants around the world can exchange information. A European Work Council (EWC) represents a company's employees throughout the European Union. Through an EWC, a company informs and consults with workers on such issues as its current national, regional, and global performance as well as its strategies so that employees understand staffing, business, and market changes.

Coordinating Activities Labor groups in one country may support their counterparts in other countries, reasoning that coordinating action across countries disrupts the coordination of a MNE's value chain. Popular measures include refusing to work overtime to supply a market served by striking workers' production, sending financial aid to workers in other countries, and disrupting work in their own countries. For example, French workers pledged to disrupt work at Pechiney in support of striking workers in the company's U.S. facilities.

Calling upon Transnational Institutions Labor appeals to transnational institutions to help check the power of MNEs. The International Labor Organization (ILO) was founded in 1919 on the premise that the failure of any country to adopt humane labor conditions impedes other countries' efforts to improve their own conditions. Several associations of unions from different countries endorse similar ideals. These associations include various international trade secretariats representing workers in specific industries—for example, the International Confederation of Free Trade Unions (ICFTU), the World Federation of Trade Unions (WFTU), and the World Confederation of Labour (WCL).

These organizations' activities, along with the general enhancement of worldwide communications, publicize the different labor conditions among countries. Among the newsworthy reports have been legal proscriptions against collective bargaining in Malaysia, wages below minimum standards in Indonesia, and the use of forced labor and child labor in many emerging markets. Upon publicizing such conditions, these organizations then champion economic and political sanctions.[104] Similarly, various codes of conduct on industrial relations, such as those issued by the OECD, ILO, and EU, influence labor practices. Although the codes are voluntary, an MNE's compliance, or lack thereof, has symbolic significance to consumers and governments.

LABOR'S STRUGGLE: BARRIERS TO INTERNATIONAL UNANIMITY

National unions endorse calls for international cooperation with fellow organizations. Offsetting calls for unanimity is a stark reality of globalization—national unions are locked in a zero-sum game of competing with each other to attract investment and jobs. When push comes to shove, there has been little enthusiasm among workers to support their counterparts in other countries.

Different Country-Specific Goals For example, Canada and the United States have long shared a common union membership in the belief that united they stood, divided they fell. Still, there are ongoing moves among Canadian workers to form unions independent of those in the United States given the belief that an American union is not going to fight to protect Canadian jobs at the expense of American jobs. The logic is that

---

Several factors promote global solidarity among unions, including improvements in

- *Exchanging Information*
- *Coordinating Activities*
- *Calling upon Transnational Institutions*

Labor may be at a disadvantage in MNE negotiations because

- *The country bargaining unit is only a small part of the MNE worldwide activities.*
- *The MNE may continue serving customers with foreign production or resources.*

international unions will adopt policies favoring the bulk of their membership, which in any joint Canadian-U.S. relationship is bound to be American.

Even when labor in one country helps labor in another, it likely aims to achieve its own goals. For example, a union representing U.S. tomato pickers helped its Mexican counterpart negotiate a stronger collective agreement that limited the local workplace power of both domestic and foreign companies. This change then dissuaded the Campbell Soup Company from moving operations to Mexico. Competition between national unions weakens solidarity.

Different Structures and Ideals   Impeding international unanimity is the fact that unions have evolved independently in each country. Consequently, the demography, structure, ideals, and goals of unions vary from country to country. For example, the share of workers in unions is much higher in some countries than in others. Some workers in France, Portugal, and Great Britain belong to Communist unions whose view of the intrinsic class conflict of collective bargaining with MNEs clashes with the more moderate views of unions elsewhere, such as in Germany, the Netherlands, Scandinavia, and Switzerland. Cross-national differences in unions' agendas extend to matters like wage rates and workers' preferences. For example, Spanish workers are more willing to work on weekends than their German counterparts.

> Several factors hinder global solidarity among unions, including differences in
> - Country Specific Goals
> - Union Structures and Goals
> - Collective Bargaining Methods
> - Approaches to Deal with Workplace Strife

Different Collective-Bargaining Methods   Unions in different countries prefer different methods of collective bargaining. Therefore, MNEs in a given country may deal with one or several unions that, depending on the situation, represent workers in many industries, in many companies within the same industry, or in just one company. If it represents one company, the union may represent all plants or just one plant. In Sweden, bargaining is centralized; employers from companies across industries unite within a federation of trade unions. In Germany, employers from associations of companies in the same industries bargain jointly with union federations.

Different Approaches to Deal with Workplace Strife   Approaches for reconciling labor tension differ among countries. The use of mediation by an impartial party is mandatory in Israel but voluntary in the United States and the United Kingdom. Among countries that have mediation practices, diverse attitudes prevail. For example, there is much less enthusiasm for it in India than in the United States. Not all differences are settled through changes brought about by legislation or collective bargaining. Labor court and government arbitrators also shape policy. For example, wages in many Austrian industries are arbitrated semiannually. These sorts of ideological and operational gaps have made sustained cross-national cooperation difficult for unions.

Regulatory Access   Organized labor has met with limited success in getting national and international bodies to regulate MNEs. National agencies have helped workers gain better access to the intricacies of the MNEs' decision-making process. Legislation in some countries, particularly in northern Europe, gives labor the legal right to participate in the management of companies. Differences prevail on fundamental standards; for example, the cost, even the option, to fire workers varies enormously across the world. New Zealand, Tonga, and the United States are company-friendly countries, requiring no compensation and imposing no penalty to fire a full-time employee. By contrast, a fired worker in Indonesia is entitled to nearly two years' worth of pay. Venezuela and Bolivia further dramatize the variability—companies there do not have the legal authority to fire workers.[105]

Codetermination   The principle of codetermination emphasizes cooperative decision making within firms that benefits both the workers and the company.[106] Despite some voluntary moves toward codetermination, governments have mandated most instances. Labor has persuaded government officials to require companies to comply with worker-friendly plant closure prenotification requirements. International agencies like the ILO, EU, and OECD have adopted codes of conduct for multinational firms in their relations with labor. These guidelines, from the view of labor, fail to regulate MNEs. For instance, there are examples of workers deterring investment outflows, acquisitions, and plant closures. Still, conduct codes' lack of enforcement capability results in inconsistent regulation of company activity.

Looking to the Future
Which Countries Will Have the Jobs of the Future?

As capital, technology, and information grow more mobile among countries and companies, human resource development explains competitive differences. Companies' access to and retention of more qualified personnel grow more important as they face the challenge of recruiting and retaining skilled workers.

From here on out, worker populations will grow much faster in developing economies (China being the notable exception) than in the wealthier countries. At the same time, the number of retirees as a percentage of the population in the wealthier countries will grow as people live longer and retire earlier. In both types of markets, people will also need to be educated for more years to prepare for higher-paying jobs. These trends suggest that there will be fewer people to do productive work in the wealthier countries. These countries are already trying to adjust, engaging in a range of education and training programs.[107] MNEs must adapt to the social and economic consequences of these programs.

One adjustment in play is wealthier countries encouraging emigration from developing countries that struggle to generate enough jobs for their swelling workforces. In Canada, the United States, and parts of Western Europe, there has been a long-term inward migration, both legally and illegally, of foreign workers from developing economies. These movements generate assimilation costs within wealthier countries and, for developing economies, a brain drain as their qualified people emigrate to other countries. Some, however, suggest that migration—both inward and outward—encourages useful brain circulation among developed and developing economies.[108]

Nationalism   Increasing degrees of unemployment in developed markets, as the fallout from the global economic crisis spread, alters the migration of foreign workers. Concern about creating jobs for locals often devolves into excluding foreigners who aspire to those positions. This situation is glaring in the American high-tech industry, which has relied upon foreign workers to staff operations in the United States. The industry maintains that the United States does not produce enough scientists and engineers to meet its demand; evidence suggests such, given that more than 60 percent of computer-science PhD students in the U.S. are internationals.

Facing outcry from constituents seeking employment as well as nationalistic calls to put Americans to work in America pushed the U.S. Congress to toughen regulation of immigration of foreign workers. Congress reset the rules governing H-1B visas, the necessary permission that allows U.S. employers to employ qualified foreign workers temporarily.[109] Times of economic downturn typically see unemployed workers in struggling countries blaming foreign workers for their plight. Under this scenario, companies will have to spend more time getting work permits and integrating different nationalities into their workforces.

Men or Machines   Another potential adjustment in wealthier countries is the continued push toward adopting robotics and other laborsaving equipment.[110] Although this may help solve labor shortages, it will escalate companies' need for workers who command higher skills. Less-educated members of the workforce will face few prospects for "good jobs," thereby pushing them to compete with immigrants for lower-paying, less appealing jobs. Gaps between haves and have-nots may widen within wealthier countries as well as between those countries and emerging economies. In this scenario, the growing ranks of the have-nots will lobby governments to push companies to shift technological development away from replacing men with machines.

Brains: Drain, Recycle, or Halt?   A third possible adjustment is the acceleration of business migration to developing countries to tap rich supplies of inexpensive, productive labor. At the same time, developing countries may devise ways to support brain circulation or, if unsuccessful, to halt brain drain. Either approach will shift more entry-level production jobs from wealthier countries to their emerging counterparts.[111] If successful, managers who return to their countries will shift many low-skilled jobs to their home markets. Governments in wealthier countries must then deal with the problem of underqualified workers facing deteriorating job prospects.[112] ∎

TABLE 20.6   Trends in Trade Union Membership, 1970–2003

Trade union membership—union membership as a proportion of employed wage and salary earners—is declining in most countries. Note that most of the exceptions are in Scandinavia.

	Percentage of Workforce in Trade Unions					Percentage Change
	1970	**1990**	**1993**	**1998**	**2003**	**1970–2003**
Australia	50	41	38	28	23	−27.3
Austria	63	47	43	38	35*	−27.4
Belgium	42	54	55	55	55*	+13.3
Canada	32	33	33	29	28	−3.2
Denmark	60	75	77	76	70	+10.1
Finland	51	73	81	78	74	+22.8
France	22	10	10	8	8	−13.4
Germany	32	31	32	26	23	−9.4
Ireland	53	51	48	42	35	−17.9
Italy	37	39	39	36	34	−3.3
Japan	35	25	24	23	20	−15.4
Republic of Korea	13	18	15	12	11	−1.4
The Netherlands	37	24	26	25	22	−14.2
New Zealand	55	51	35	22	22*	−33.1
Norway	57	59	58	56	53	−3.5
Spain	N/A	13	18	16	16	N/A
Sweden	68	81	84	82	78	+10.3
Switzerland	29	24	23	22	18**	−11.1
United Kingdom	45	39	36	30	29	−15.5
United States	24	16	15	13	12	−11.1

Note: * = 2002; ** = 2001

Sources: Jelle Visser, "Union Membership Statistics in 24 Countries," *Monthly Labor Review* 129 (2006): 38–49; David G. Blanchflower, "International Patterns of Union Membership," *British Journal of Industrial Relations* 45 (March 2007): 1–28.

TRENDS IN MNE–LABOR RELATIONS

The contentious relationship between labor and MNEs is an enduring facet of international business. Two trends, one from the perspective of labor, the other from MNEs, define the next stage of their relationship.

Table 20.6 shows union membership as a portion of the total workforce has been falling in most countries for the past few decades. Several trends drive this decline.

- *Increase in white-collar workers as a share of total workers.* White-collar workers see themselves more as managers than as laborers, and thus less inclined to join a union.

- *Increase in service employment in relation to manufacturing employment.* The greater variation in service jobs than in manufacturing jobs leads workers to believe their situations differ from those of their coworkers. Weak or absent legacies of unionization in service industries hinders uniting labor.[113]

- *Rising portion of women in the workforce.* Women represent growing shares of the total labor pool in many countries. Social, economic and professional characteristics of female workers makes them less inclined to join unions.

- *Rising portion of part-time and temporary workers.* Short-term workers do not see themselves staying with a job long enough for a union to improve their compensation or work conditions.

Falling union membership in many countries foreshadows lower bargaining power for labor. In contrast, the effort of MNEs to develop integrated labor relations across countries increases their bargaining power.

- *Trend toward smaller average plant size.* Increasingly direct interactions between workers and managers align their respective interests. Proximity often harmonizes outlooks, with labor commonly adopting management's views.

- *Decline in the belief in collectivism among younger workers.* Few of today's younger workers have suffered economic deprivation; hence, many question the value of collective solutions championed by unions.[114]

Decline in union membership is a long-running trend. There are exceptions. Unions in Sweden, for instance, have forged cooperative relationships with flagship companies like Electrolux and Volvo to improve corporate competitiveness and to share the rewards from successes. Developing win-win solutions has improved the work conditions and compensation, thereby fortifying belief in unionization. Outside of these anomalies, union membership declines. The harsh reality is that the power of unions is a function of the size of their membership rolls. Continuing decline in membership foreshadows unions with weaker negotiation positions and less incentive for cooperation with counterparts in other countries.

Currently, collapsing economies has increased unemployment in many countries to levels not seen in decades. History shows that periods of high unemployment are brutal for those seeking work but energizing for the battle for workers' rights. The current crisis in capitalism, union leaders believe, creates a once-in-a-generation, if not lifetime, opportunity to restore solidarity among workers worldwide. Still, unions face immense battles to reverse fortunes. In the United States, union membership has fallen from over 35 percent in the mid-1950s to 8 percent of the workforce in America in 2009.[115] Similar trends, as seen in Table 20.6, play throughout the world.

MNEs: Reaction and Preparation   MNEs develop HRM policies that fortify their bargaining power. Historically, irrespective of the strategy that companies pursued, most MNEs decentralized labor relations responsibilities to HRM managers in foreign subsidiaries. Practicality, rather than bold insight, motivated this policy. Country-to-country

The issue of employment, always a hot-button topic, has become far more controversial given the consequences of the current global economic crisis. Unemployment rates in countries, both rich and poor, are heading to levels not seen since the Great Depression. Presently, companies claim the upper hand in the relationship—people anxious to maintain employment are less prone to challenge authority. Nevertheless, if the economic slowdown drags on, it would be surprising if we do not see increasing protests, of the sort pictured here, calling for greater unionization, sustained job creation, and protection of employment benefits.

Source: Chris Hondros/Getty Images, Inc.

variability in labor laws, union structure, workplace attitudes, and collective-bargaining processes created a complex, changing situation. Most MNEs reasoned that headquarters was poorly positioned to manage worldwide labor relations. Hence, they delegated responsibility to local managers.

This outlook is giving way to a trend toward greater coordination and control of global labor policies by the senior leadership of MNEs. Coordinating globally dispersed value chains spurs headquarters to preempt disruptions caused by sporadic workplace activism in once less but now more interlinked sites around the world. Moreover, companies whose value creation is sensitive to labor costs no longer can delegate labor relations to a series of local managers. Integrating global operations pushes MNEs to integrate labor relations. Growing attention to and integration of their relations creates powerful advantages for MNEs. They translate their understanding of how to use the threat of production switching or resource redirection to strengthen their collective-bargaining positions.

Tel-Comm-Tek (TCT)

CASE

I n May 2010, Mark Hopkins of Tel-Comm-Tek (TCT) India, a company headquartered in the United States, announced his resignation and intention to return to his home in Vermont.[116] At the time, he was the managing director of the Indian subsidiary of TCT. During his tenure, Hopkins oversaw steady growth in market share and profitability of the Indian operation. Upon his announcement, TCT began searching for his replacement.

TCT: A Brief Introduction

TCT manufactures a variety of small office equipment in nine different countries. It distributes and sells products such as copying machines, dictation units, laser printers, and paper shredders worldwide. TCT reported sales in more than 70 countries. TCT has sold and serviced products in India since the early 1980s even though it lacked its own in-country manufacturing facility. Originally, it hired independent importers to sell its products. It soon realized that generating higher sales required setting up its own operations. In 1992, it opened a sales office in New Delhi. Map 20.1 profiles features of India.

Today, TCT is poised to expand its Indian operations. Local sales have been increasing at double-digit rates, powered by a boom in the Indian information-technology sector. Forecasts saw this trend accelerating over the next decade. Headquarters projected TCT India evolving into a key element of its global value chain and, ultimately, the center point of its Asian operations.

India: The Next Economic Juggernaut?

Some see India developing into the world's next big industrial power. This projection has led global companies to increase their local operations. For example, IBM, a longtime customer of TCT, increased its Indian staff from a handful to more than 100,000 employees between the mid-1990s and 2010 through a series of acquisitions and investments. Moreover, internal company analysis indicates that the economic growth rate for the overall economy, along with the sectors that TCT serves, could move total sales of the Indian subsidiary past those in the company's home market.

Expansion: Pros

Improving Infrastructure Shaping TCT India's expansion plans is the ongoing improvement in India's transportation infrastructure. Improvements in highways, railways, and

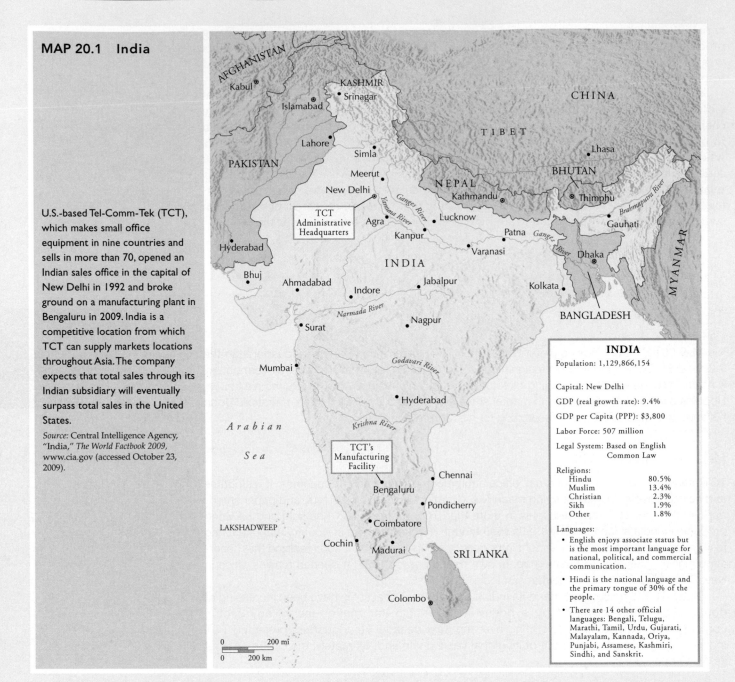

MAP 20.1   India

U.S.-based Tel-Comm-Tek (TCT), which makes small office equipment in nine countries and sells in more than 70, opened an Indian sales office in the capital of New Delhi in 1992 and broke ground on a manufacturing plant in Bengaluru in 2009. India is a competitive location from which TCT can supply markets locations throughout Asia. The company expects that total sales through its Indian subsidiary will eventually surpass total sales in the United States.

Source: Central Intelligence Agency, "India," *The World Factbook 2009,* www.cia.gov (accessed October 23, 2009).

INDIA

Population: 1,129,866,154

Capital: New Delhi

GDP (real growth rate): 9.4%

GDP per Capita (PPP): $3,800

Labor Force: 507 million

Legal System: Based on English Common Law

Religions:
Hindu	80.5%
Muslim	13.4%
Christian	2.3%
Sikh	1.9%
Other	1.8%

Languages:
- English enjoys associate status but is the most important language for national, political, and commercial communication.
- Hindi is the national language and the primary tongue of 30% of the people.
- There are 14 other official languages: Bengali, Telugu, Marathi, Tamil, Urdu, Gujarati, Malayalam, Kannada, Oriya, Punjabi, Assamese, Kashmiri, Sindhi, and Sanskrit.

seaports increase the efficiency of product movement both in and out of the country. Management envisions making the local subsidiary a vital link in TCT's increasingly sophisticated supply chain. Presently, TCT's supply chain integrates input suppliers, production, and wholesalers in the United States and Europe. Long-term plans outlined integrating supply points throughout Asia.

Democratic Norms   India's independence in 1947 institutionalized strong democratic norms of accountability, transparency, and freedom. Progress on the economic front had been even more dynamic. From 1947 through 1990, India's decision to have a centrally planned economy led to the infamous "License Raj," a situation marked by elaborate licenses, regulations, and bureaucracy that were required to open and run a business. In 1991, India began a transition toward a free market economy with the intended demise of the License Raj. This transition, an ongoing process, has helped stabilize the economic environment and boost India's attractiveness as a manufacturing site. Still, India's business environment poses problems.

Expansion: Cons

Problematic Legal Environment   The Indian legal environment, although endorsing the principles of the rule of law, struggles with corruption. The primary driver of corruption, in many observers' eyes, is the country's vast bureaucracy, a legacy of the previous centrally planned economy. Partial success in dismantling the License Raj has resulted in a civil administration that influences many aspects of economic life. Notably, Western high-tech companies run into problems with intellectual property violation. Patent infringement and business-process piracy are not uncommon.

Outmoded Labor Laws   The legal system creates other complications. For example, India's labor laws, little changed since they were enacted after independence in 1947, make it difficult to lay off employees even if a company's fortunes hit hard times or the economy slows. Companies are reluctant to hire workers, given the risk of being unable to fire them if circumstances change. Necessary terminations are difficult to execute and often involve extensive negotiations and settlements. "[C]ompanies think twice, 10 times, before they hire new people," said Sunil Kant Munjal, the chair of the Hero Group, one of the world's largest manufacturers of inexpensive motorcycles.

Anticompetitive Legislation   In addition, Indian laws bar companies with more than 100 employees from competing in many industries. These laws protect small enterprises operating in many villages scattered throughout India, often at the expense of larger-scale operations. Another challenge is high tariffs. These had been put in place to promote domestic production and still apply to many classes of imports, including some that are inputs into products manufactured by TCT. Some of India's labor laws discourage flexibility; for example, some prohibit companies from allowing workers to clock more than 54 hours of overtime in any three-month period, even if workers are willing to do so.

TCT Moves Forward

In late 2009, TCT began building a factory in Bengaluru, the center of India's Silicon Valley (see Map 20.1). The plant will make a full range of laser printers, from entry level to high end. The first production run has been set for June 2010. Logistically, TCT plans to supply the factory with components from its manufacturing facilities in Europe and the United States. Eventually, management plans to find local suppliers or backward integrate into the local production of those components.

The scale of the production operation requires 150 to 200 production workers. TCT anticipates no problems in hiring a skilled labor force, given other companies' success stories. For example, the South Korean conglomerate LG looked to staff 458 assembly-line jobs at its consumer electronics factory opening in India. It required each applicant to have at least 15 years of education—a condition that translates into having both high school and technical college certification. Seeking a young workforce, the company also decided that no more than 50 workers could have prior work experience. Despite these restrictions, 55,000 people qualified for interviews.

TCT enlisted a U.S. engineering firm to supervise construction of its plant in Bengaluru. Upon completion, TCT will "turn over the key" to the on-site factory director, a U.S. expatriate sent to run the operational plant. This director reports to TCT's U.S. headquarters on production and quality-control matters. He or she will report to TCT India's managing director in New Delhi (the position made vacant by Hopkins's retirement) on all other matters, such as accounting, supply-chain logistics, finance, and labor relations. The managing director of TCT India, in turn, will report to the Asian Regional Office at TCT's U.S. headquarters.

Selecting a Managing Director

TCT prefers to fill executive vacancies by promotion from within the company. TCT uses a mix of home-, host-, and third-country nationals. In addition, TCT rotates its managers among its foreign and U.S. locations. Headquarters sees international experience as an important facet of executive leadership.

The Candidates   The Asian Regional Office charged a selection committee to nominate the new managing director for TCT India. The committee identified six candidates:

Tom Wallace   A 30-year TCT veteran, Wallace is experienced in the technical and sales aspects. He has supported some supply-chain initiatives in the U.S. market. Although he has never worked abroad, he has toured the company's foreign operations and always expressed interest in an expatriate position. His superiors rate his performance as proficient. He will retire in about four and a half years. He and his wife speak English. Their children are grown and live with their own families in the United States.

Presently, Wallace supervises a U.S.-based operation that is about the size of that in India. However, the merger of Wallace's unit with another TCT division will eliminate his current position within six months.

Brett Harrison   Harrison, 40, has spent 15 years with TCT, both running line activities and supervising staff. His superiors consider him highly competent and poised to move into upper-level management within the next few years. For the past three years, he has worked in the Asian regional office and has regularly toured TCT's Southeast Asian operations.

Both he and his wife have traveled to India several times in the last 20 years and are well acquainted with its geography, politics, customs, and outlooks. The Harrisons know many U.S. expatriates in the Bengaluru region. Their children, ages 14 and 16, have also vacationed in India with their parents. Mrs. Harrison is a midlevel executive with a multinational pharmaceuticals company that presently does not have an operation in India; there were rumors of a sales office opening in a few years.

Atasi Das   Born in the United States, Das joined TCT 12 years ago after earning her MBA from a university in New England. At 37, she has successfully moved between staff and line positions, with broader responsibilities in strategic planning. For two years, she was the second in command of a product group that was about half the size of the Indian operations. Her performance regularly earns excellent ratings. Currently, she works on a planning-staff team based at TCT headquarters.

When she joined TCT, she noted that her ultimate goal was to be assigned international responsibilities, and she pointed to her undergraduate major in international management as evidence of her long-term plan. She recently reiterated her interest in international responsibilities, seeing it as an essential career step. She speaks Hindi and is unmarried. Her parents, who live in the United States, are first-generation immigrants from India. Several family members and relatives live in Kashmir and Punjab, northern states of India.

Ravi Desai   Desai, 33, is currently an assistant managing director in the larger Asian operation. He helps oversee production and sales for the Southeast Asian markets in Singapore, Malaysia, and China. A citizen of India, he has spent his 10 years with TCT working in operational slots throughout Southeast Asia. He holds an MBA from the prestigious Indian Institute of Management. Some in TCT see him as a candidate to eventually direct the Indian operation. He is married, has four children (ages two to seven), and speaks English and Hindi well. His wife, also a native of India, neither works outside the home nor speaks English.

Jalan Bukit Seng   Seng, 38, is the managing director of TCT's assembly operation in Malaysia. A citizen of Singapore, Seng has worked in either Singapore or Malaysia his entire life. However, he did earn undergraduate and MBA degrees from leading universities in the United States. He is fluent in Singapore's four official languages—Malay, English, Mandarin, and Tamil—and sees himself learning other languages as needed.

His performance reviews, with respect to both the Malaysia plant and other TCT plant operations around the world, have consistently been positive, with an occasional ranking of excellent. Seng is unmarried, but he is close to extended family members who live in Singapore and Malaysia.

Saumitra Chakraborty   At 31, Chakraborty is the assistant to the departing managing director in India. He has held that position since joining TCT upon graduating from a small private university in Europe four years earlier. Unmarried, he consistently earns a job performance rating of competent in operational matters and excellent in customer relationship management. Although he excels in employee relations, he lacks direct-line experience. Still, he has successfully increased TCT India's sales, somewhat owing to his personal connections with prominent Indian families and government officials, along with his skillfulness in the ways of the Indian business environment. Besides speaking India's main languages of English and Hindi fluently, Chakraborty speaks Kannada (the local language of Bengaluru). ■

QUESTIONS

1. Which candidate should the committee nominate for the assignment? Why?
2. What challenges might each candidate encounter in the position?
3. How might TCT go about minimizing the challenges facing each candidate?
4. Should TCT offer all candidates the same compensation package? If not, what factors should influence the features of each package?
5. Returning to material covered in Chapter 15, specifically that dealing with the idea of a matrix organization, do you see any benefit to appointing two of the individuals described here to the post? Operationally, one individual would be in charge of internal affairs, and the other would manage external affairs. What might be the benefits and problems with this arrangement?

SUMMARY

- HRM policies that support the company strategy create superior value. Still, many MNEs struggle to develop effective HRM policies.

- HRM's task is to staff the right person in the right job in the right place at the right time for the right salary.

- Executives in the MNE belong to one of three classes: locals, citizens of the countries in which they are working, or expatriates.

- Three frameworks guide how companies set about staffing their international operations: the ethnocentric, polycentric, and geocentric frameworks.

- Changing markets, growing cost consciousness, and evolving strategies are resetting established notions of who is an expatriate, how he or she should be compensated, and the duration of an international assignment.

- An ethnocentric staffing approach fills foreign management positions with home-country nationals. A polycentric staffing policy uses host-country nationals to manage local subsidiaries. A geocentric staffing policy seeks the best people for key jobs throughout the organization, regardless of nationality.

- Executives transferred from headquarters to local operations are more likely to understand the company's core competencies. However, an ethnocentric framework can result in a narrow perspective in foreign markets.

- MNEs often employ more locals than expatriate managers because the former better understand local operations and demand less compensation.

- Hiring locals rather than expatriates demonstrates that opportunities are available for local citizens, shows consideration for local interests, and is far cheaper.

- The selection of an individual for an expatriate position considers the candidate's technical competence, adaptiveness, and leadership ability.

- MNEs transfer people abroad to infuse technical competence and home-country business practices, control foreign operations, develop managers' business skills, and diffuse the organization culture.

- Training and predeparture preparations often include general country orientation, cultural sensitivity, and practical training.

- Training and predeparture preparations reduce the odds of expatriate failure. Increasingly, preparation activities include the expatriate's spouse and family.

- Expatriate failure, narrowly defined, is the manager's premature return home due to poor performance. Broadly defined, it is the failure of the MNE's selection policies to find individuals who will succeed abroad.

- When transferred abroad, an expatriate's compensation is usually increased because of hardships and differences in the cost of living.

- The compensation of an expatriate must neither overly reward nor unduly punish a person for accepting a foreign assignment. Most MNEs use the balance-sheet approach to manage this dilemma.

- Repatriation, the act of returning home from a foreign assignment, is difficult. Finding the right job for the expatriate to return to is the principal cause of frustration.

- A country's sociopolitical environment shapes the relationship between labor and management and affects the number, representation, and organization of unions.

- International organizations urge companies to follow internationally accepted labor practices wherever they operate, regardless of whether the practices conflict with the norms and laws of the host countries.

- International cooperation among labor groups in a concerted effort to confront MNEs is minimal. Labor groups' initiatives include information exchange, simultaneous negotiations or strikes, and refusals to work overtime.

- Organized labor has, to slight success, formed international labor agreements and strategies that counter MNEs' bargaining power.

- Labor contends that it is disadvantaged in dealing with MNEs because it is hard to get full data on MNEs' global operations, MNEs can manipulate investment incentives, MNEs can move value activities to other countries, and MNEs often make key decisions in another country.

KEY TERMS

balance-sheet approach (p. 812)
culture shock (p. 809)
ethnocentric framework (p. 799)
expatriate (p. 797)
expatriate failure (p. 807)
expatriate selection (p. 805)

geocentric framework
(p. 803)
home-country national
(p. 797)
human resource management
(HRM) (p. 794)

localize (p. 799)
polycentric framework
(p. 801)
repatriation (p. 817)
third-country national
(p. 797)

ENDNOTES

1   *Sources include the following:* "In Search of Global Leaders: View of Jeffery Immelt, Chairman and CEO, General Electric," *Harvard Business Review* (August 1, 2003): 5; Barbara Ettorre, "A Brave New World," *Management Review* 82:4 (1993): 10–16; Mark Larson, "More Employees Go Abroad as International Operations Grow," *Workforce Management* (June 1, 2006): 43; Jane Fraser and Jeremy Oppenheim, "What's New about Globalization?" *McKinsey Quarterly* 2 (1997): 168–79; "Go East, My Son," *The Economist* (August 10, 2006): 12; "China's Recruitment Market Is Booming," *The Economist* (September 21, 2006): 47; Sandra Jones, "Going Stateside: Once the Overseas Hitch Is Over, Homeward-Bound Expats Hit Turbulence," *Crain's Chicago Business* (July 24, 2000): 3; Barry Newman, "Expat Archipelago," *Wall Street Journal* (December 12, 1995): A1; Robert Pelton, *The World's Most Dangerous Places* (New York: Harper Resource, 2003); Joe Sharkey, "Global Economy Is Leading to More Dangerous Places," *New York Times* (April 19, 2005): C-1; Mark Schoeff Jr., "P&G Places a Premium on International Experience," *Workforce Management* (April 10, 2006): 28; Elizabeth Marx, "Route to the Top, 2006," Cranfield University School of Management (2007), at www.som.cranfield.ac.uk/som/news/story.asp?id=329 (accessed July 14, 2008); "In Search of Global Leaders," *Harvard Business Review* (August 1, 2003): 1-11; 2008–2009 Robert Half Global Financial Employment Monitor, at www.rhi.com/OurServices (accessed April 29, 2009); Global

Relocation Trends 2008, *GMAC Global Relocations Services,* www.gmac.com; Early PwC International Challenge (EPIC) programme, www.pwc.com/extweb/career.nsf/docid/9204374F898F3E5A8525748F00741E9D (accessed May 4, 2009).

2   "Staffing Globalisation: Travelling More Lightly," *The Economist* (June 23, 2006): 14.

3   "Globalisation: The Empire Strikes Back," *The Economist* (September 18, 2008): 45.

4   The FTSE 100 Index—also called FTSE 100, FTSE, or, informally, the "footsie"—is a share index of the 100 most highly capitalized UK companies listed on the London Stock Exchange.

5   Paula Caligiuri and Victoria Di Santo, "Global Competence: What Is It, and Can It Be Developed through Global Assignments?" *Human Resource Planning* 24 (September 2001): 27–36; Mark Morgan, "Career-Building Strategies: Are Your Skills Helping You Up the Corporate Ladder?" *Strategic Finance* 83 (June 2002): 38–44.

6   Hoon Park, "Global Human Resource Management: A Synthetic Approach," *Journal of International Business and Economics* 12 (2002): 31.

7   William Judge, "Is a Leader's Character Culture-Bound or Culture-Free? An Empirical Comparison of the Character Traits of American and Taiwanese CEOs," *Journal of Leadership Studies* 8 (Fall 2001): 63–79.

8 Keith Brouthers, "Institutional, Cultural and Transaction Cost Influences on Entry Mode Choice and Performance," *Journal of International Business Studies* 33 (Summer 2002): 203–22.

9 Ben Kedia, Richard Nordtvedt, and Liliana M. Perez, "International Business Strategies, Decision-Making Theories, and Leadership Styles: An Integrated Framework," *Competitiveness Review* 12 (Winter–Spring 2002): 38–53.

10 Watson Wyatt Worldwide, "Human Capital Index: Human Capital as a Lead Indicator of Shareholder Value," at www.watsonwyatt.com/research/resrender.asp?id=w-488&page=1 (accessed November 27, 2007).

11 See, for example, N. Khatri, "Managing Human Resource for Competitive Advantage: A Study of Companies in Singapore," *International Journal of Human Resource Management* 11:2 (2000): 336.

12 "Human Capital: A Key to Higher Market Value," *Business Finance* (December 1999): 15.

13 R. Coleman, "HR Management Lags Behind at World Class Firms," *CMA Management* (July–August, 2002), http://www.entrepreneur.com/tradejournals/article/89156783.html (accessed July 14, 2005).

14 Mercer LLC, "International Assignments Increasing, Mercer Survey Finds" (May 16, 2006), at www.mercerhr. com/summary.jhtml?idContent=1222700 (accessed November 27, 2007).

15 "Travelling More Lightly," *The Economist* (June 22, 2006): 14.

16 Leslie Klaff, "Thinning the Ranks of the Career Expats," *Workforce Management* (October 2004): 84–87.

17 Yvonne Sonsino, reported in "Travelling More Lightly." See also Mercer LLC, "International Assignments Increasing."

18 PwC International Challenge (EPIC) programme, www.pwc.com/extweb/career.nsf/docid/9204374F898F3E5A8525748F00741E9D (accessed May 4, 2009).

19 Global Relocation Trends 2008, *GMAC Global Relocation Services*, www.gmac.com (accessed June 1, 2009).

20 "More Females Sent on International Assignment Than Ever Before, Survey Finds," http://www.mercer.com/pressrelease/details.htm?idContent=1246090 (accessed April 25, 2009).

21 Calvin Reynolds, "Strategic Employment of Third Country Nationals: Keys to Sustaining the Transformation of HR Functions," *Human Resource Planning* 20 (March 1997): 33–50.

22 Karina Frayter, "IBM to Laid-Off: Want a Job in India?" *CNN* (February 5, 2009), http://money.cnn.com/2009/02/05/news/companies/ibm_jobs/ (accessed April 29, 2009).

23 Adrian Wooldridge, "The Battle for the Best," *The Economist: The World in 2007* (Annual Review, 2007): 68.

24 Chi-fai Chan and Neil Holbert, "Marketing Home and Away: Perceptions of Managers in Headquarters and Subsidiaries," *Journal of World Business* 36 (Summer 2001): 205.

25 "Staffing Globalisation: Travelling More Lightly," *The Economist* (June 23, 2006): 14.

26 Tsun-yan Hsieh, Johanne Lavoie, and Robert Samek, "Are You Taking Your Expatriate Talent Seriously?" *McKinsey Quarterly* 3 (Summer 1999): 71.

27 "Staffing Globalisation: Travelling More Lightly," *The Economist* (June 23, 2006): 14.

28 William C. Weldon, "Chairman's Letter: To Our Shareholders," *Annual Report 2006* (Johnson & Johnson, 2007), at http://jnj.v1.papiervirtuel.com/report/2007030901 (accessed November 27, 2007).

29 Vijay Pothukuchi, Fariborz Damanpour, Jaepil Choi, Chao C. Chen, and Seung Ho Park, "National and Organizational Culture Differences and International Joint Venture Performance," *Journal of International Business Studies* 33 (Summer 2002): 243–66.

30 PricewaterhouseCoopers LLP and Cranfield School of Management, "Measuring the Value of International Assignments" (November 9, 2006), at www.som.cranfield.ac.uk/som/news/story.asp?id=329 (accessed June 18, 2009).

31 PricewaterhouseCoopers LLP and Cranfield School of Management, "Measuring the Value of International Assignments."

32 Jeremy Kahn, "The World's Most Admired Companies," *Fortune* (October 11, 1999): 267.

33 Kahn, "The World's Most Admired Companies."

34 David Ahlstrom, Garry Bruton, and Eunice S. Chan, "HRM of Foreign Firms in China: The Challenge of Managing Host Country Personnel," *Business Horizons* 44 (May 2001): 59.

35 "High-Tech Nomads: These Engineers Work as Temps on Wireless Projects All Over the World," *Time* (November 26, 2001): B20; Ben L. Kedia and Ananda Mukherji, "Global Managers: Developing a Mindset for Global Competitiveness," *Journal of World Business* 34 (Fall 1999): 30.

36 "In Search of Global Leaders: View of Fred Hassan, Chairman and CEO, Schering-Plough," *Harvard Business Review* (August 1, 2003): 5.

37 Astrid Wendlandt, "The Name Game Is a Puzzle for Expats at Work," *Financial Times* (August 15, 2000): 3.

38 The type of ownership of its foreign operations influences an MNE's staffing policy. Expatriates transferred abroad to a foreign joint venture, for example, may find themselves in ambiguous situations, unsure of whom they represent and uncertain of whether they report to both partners or to the partner that transferred them. Typically, MNEs insist on using their own executives when they're concerned that local personnel may make decisions in their own interests rather than those of the joint venture.

39 Global Relocation Trends 2008, *GMAC Global Relocation Services*, www.gmac.com.

40 Wooldridge, "The Battle for the Best."

41 View of Yvonne Sonsino, a partner at Mercer, reported in "Staffing Globalisation: Travelling More Lightly," *Economist Intelligence Unit* (June 23, 2006): 14.

42 Susan Schneider and Rosalie Tung, "Introduction to the International Human Resource Management Special Issue," *Journal of World Business* 36 (Winter 2001): 341–46.

43 Caligiuri and Di Santo, "Global Competence"; Hsieh et al., "Are You Taking Your Expatriate Talent Seriously?"

44 "In Search of Global Leaders: View of Stephen Green, Group CEO, HSBC," *Harvard Business Review* (August 1, 2003): 7.

45 Sunkyu Jun, James Gentry, and Yong Hyun, "Cultural Adaptation of Business Expatriates in the Host Marketplace," *Journal of International Business Studies* 32 (Summer 2001): 369; J. Stewart Black and Mark Mendenhall, "Cross-Cultural Training Effectiveness: A Review and a Theoretical Framework for Future Research," *Academy of Management Review* 15 (January 1990): 117.

46 *The New International Executive Business Leadership for the 21st Century* (Boston, MA: Harvard Business School and Amrop International, 1995); Andrew Crisp, "International Careers Made Easy," *The European* (March 24, 1995): 27.

47 Hsieh et al., "Are You Taking Your Expatriate Talent Seriously?"; GMAC Global Relocation Trends, 2008 Survey Report.

48 John D. Daniels and Gary Insch, "Why Are Early Departure Rates from Foreign Assignments Lower than Historically Reported?" *Multinational Business Review* 6:1 (1998): 13–23.

49 Data provided by National Foreign Trade Council. Maria L. Kraimer, Sandy Wayne, and Renata Jaworski, "Sources of Support and Expatriate Performance: The Mediating Role of Expatriate Adjustment," *Personnel Psychology* 54 (Spring 2001): 71.

50 Global Relocation Trends 2008, GMAC Global Relocations Services, www.gmac.com.

51 Margaret Shaffer, David Harrison, K. Matthew Gilley, and Dora Luk, "Struggling for Balance amid Turbulence on International Assignments: Work-Family Conflict, Support and Commitment,"

Journal of Management 27 (January–February 2001): 99; Chris Moss, "Expats: Thinking of Living and Working Abroad?" *The Guardian* (October 19, 2000): 4.

52 "Expat Spouses: It Takes Two," *Financial Times* (March 1, 2002); Staffing Globalisation: Travelling More Lightly," *The Economist* (June 23, 2006): 14.

53 Diane E. Lewis, "Families Make, Break Overseas Moves," *Boston Globe* (October 4, 1998): 5D.

54 Klaff, "Thinning the Ranks of the Career Expats."

55 D. Ones and C. Viswesvaran, "Relative Importance of Personality Dimensions for Expatriate Selection: A Policy Capturing Study," *Human Performance* 12 (1999): 275–94.

56 Chris Brewster, "Making Their Own Way: International Experience through Self-Initiated Foreign Assignments," *Journal of World Business* 35 (Winter 2000): 417; Vesa Suutari, Kerr Inkson, Judith Pringle, Michael B. Arthur, and Sean Barry, "Expatriate Assignment versus Overseas Experience: Contrasting Models of International Human Resource Development," *Journal of World Business* 32 (1997): 351–68.

57 Valerie Frazee, "Send Your Expats Prepared for Success," *Workforce* 78 (March 1999): S6.

58 Larson, "More Employees Go Abroad as International Operations Grow."

59 P. Christopher Earley, "Intercultural Training for Managers: A Comparison of Documentary and Interpersonal Methods," *Academy of Management Journal* 30:4 (1987): 685–98; Sharon Leiba-O'Sullivan, "The Distinction between Stable and Dynamic Cross-Cultural Competencies: Implications for Expatriate Trainability," *Journal of International Business Studies* 30 (Winter 1999): 709.

60 C. Panella, "Meeting the Needs of International Business: A Customer Service-Oriented Business Language Course," *The Journal of Language for International Business* 9:1 (1998): 65–75; Marianne E. Inman, "How Foreign Language Study Can Enhance Career Possibilities" (Washington, DC: ERIC Clearinghouse on Languages and Linguistics, 1987), at www.ericdigests.org/pre-927/career.htm (accessed November 27, 2007); C. Randlesome and A. Myers, "Cultural Fluency: Results from a U.K. and Irish Survey," *Business Communication Quarterly* 60:3 (1997): 9–22.

61 Stephen Baker, "Catching the Continental Drift: These Days, English Will Suffice for Americans Working in Europe," *Business Week* (August 14, 2001): 55.

62 Christopher Cole, "Bridging the Language Gap: Expatriates Find Learning Korean Key to Enjoying a More Satisfying Life," *Korea Herald* (August 16, 2002): 23.

63 Melinda Ligos, "The Foreign Assignment: An Incubator, or Exile?," *New York Times* (October 22, 2000): C-1.

64 Tanya Mohn, "All Aboard the Foreign Language Express," *New York Times* (October 11, 2000): C-3.

65 "English Is Coming: The Adverse Side-Effects of the Growing Dominance of English," *The Economist* (February 14, 2009): 65.

66 European Commission, "Languages of Europe" (July 18, 2007), *Education and Training*, at http://europa.eu. int/comm/education/policies/lang/languages/index_en.html#Most percent20taught percent20languages (accessed November 27, 2007).

67 "They All Speak English," *The Economist* (December 13, 2006): 448.

68 "Global Spread of English Poses Problems for UK," *People's Daily Online* (February 18, 2006): 1.

69 Amy Sitze, "Language of Business: Can E-Learning Help International Companies Speak a Common Language?" *Online Learning* (March 2002): 19–23.

70 PricewaterhouseCoopers, *International Assignments: European Policy and Practice* (1997), at www.pwcglobal.com/extweb/ncsurvres.nsf (accessed July 3, 2002).

71 "In Search of Global Leaders: View of Fred Hassan, Chairman and CEO, Schering-Plough," *Harvard Business Review* (August 1, 2003): 5.

72 Estimate reported in the second annual study of expatriate issues, conducted from January through March 2002, sponsored by CIGNA International Expatriate Benefits; the National Foreign Trade Council, an association of multinational companies that supports open international trade and investment; and WorldatWork, at www.prnewswire.com/micro/CI9 (accessed September 2, 2005).

73 "Measuring the Value of International Assignments."

74 Carolyn Gould, "What's the Latest in Global Compensation?" *Global Workforce* (July 1997): 4.

75 Geoffrey W. Latta, "Expatriate Policy and Practice: A Ten-Year Comparison of Trends," *Compensation and Benefits Review* 31:4 (1999): 35–39, quoting studies by Organization Resources Counselors.

76 "Designing Competitive Expatriate Compensation Packages," Mercer, www.mercer.com/referencecontent.htm?idContent= 1303865 (accessed May 3, 2009).

77 This practice, however, appears to be disappearing, especially for assignments in so-called world capitals like New York, London, and Tokyo, in which many executives are interested and where there is (relatively) little "deprivation." In addition, the number and nature of "hardships" resulting from foreign assignments are in decline, particularly as advances in transportation and communications enable expatriates to keep in closer contact with home countries; the openness of economies allows them to buy familiar goods and services; and the general level of housing, schooling, and medical services increasingly meets their needs.

78 A U.S. family based in China, for example, commonly spends more money to get the same goods than they would back home. Why? Because they simply prefer Western items that must be imported and have thus been subjected to high tariffs. Expatriates often obtain food and housing at rates higher than going local rates because they don't know the language well, where to buy, or how to bargain.

79 Towers Perrin and CIGNA, for example, specialize in international compensation. In addition, companies rely on estimates of cost-of-living differences—even if they're imperfect. MNEs commonly use such sources as the U.S. State Department's cost-of-living index, published yearly in *Labor Developments Abroad,* the UN *Monthly Bulletin of Statistics,* and surveys by the *Financial Times,* P-E International, Business International, and the Staff Papers of the International Monetary Fund.

80 "Home away from Home: Expatriate Housing in Asia," *Korea Herald* (May 2, 2002): 11.

81 "Tokyo Tops in H.K. Survey on Living Cost for Expatriates," *Japan Economic Newswire* (January 24, 2002): 1.

82 Alison Maitland, "A Hard Balancing Act: Management of Dual Careers," *Financial Times* (May 10, 1999): 11.

83 Valerie Frazee, "Expert Help for Dual-Career Spouses," *Workforce* 78 (March 1999): S18.

84 Judy Clark, "Added Global Risks Impact Security Planning for Oil, Gas Expat Workers," *Oil and Gas Journal* (April 2002): 32–37.

85 Roberto Ceniceros, "Precautions, Training Can Lessen Risk of Kidnapping," *Business Insurance* 35 (May 14, 2001): 26.

86 Mercer LLC, "International Assignments Increasing."

87 Gould, "What's the Latest in Global Compensation?"

88 J. S. Black and H. B. Gregersen, "The Right Way to Manage Expats," *Harvard Business Review* (March–April 1999): 52–62.

89 Global Relocation Trends 2008, *GMAC Global Relocation Services,* www.gmac.com.

90 "New Survey Suggests Ways to Maximize Expatriate Performance and Loyalty," *Internet Wire* (March 27, 2001):1. Estimates reported at 2001 National Foreign Trade Council's International HR

Management Symposium; See also Leslie Gross Klaff, "The Right Way to Bring Expats Home," *Workforce* 81 (July 2002): 40–44; Jeff Barbian, "Return to Sender: Companies That Fail to Effectively Manage Employees Returning from a Foreign Assignment May Find Their Investments Permanently Hitting the Road," *Training* 39 (January 2002): 40–43.

91 PricewaterhouseCoopers LLP and Cranfield School of Management, "Understanding and Avoiding Barriers to International Mobility," *Geodesy* (October 2005), at www.pwc.extweb/pwcpublications.nfs/docid/7ACA93FA424E80E88525121E006E82C/$file/geodesy.pdf (accessed November 27, 2007).

92 "In Search of Global Leaders: View of Daniel Meiland, Executive Chairman, Egon Zehender International," *Harvard Business Review* (August 1, 2003):8.

93 Global Relocation Trends 2008, *GMAC Global Relocation Services,* www.gmac.com, (accessed, April 14, 2009).

94 Mila Lazarova and Paula Caligiuri, "Retaining Repatriates: The Role of Organizational Support Practices," *Journal of World Business* 36 (Winter 2001): 389–402.

95 Linda K. Stroh, Hal B. Gregersen, and J. Stewart Black, "Closing the Gap: Expectations Versus Reality Among Repatriates," *Journal of World Business* 33 (1998): 111–124; Klaff, "The Right Way to Bring Expats Home."

96 PwC International Challenge (EPIC) programme, www.pwc.com/extweb/career.nsf/docid/9204374F898F3E5A8525748F00741E9D (accessed May 4, 2009).

97 Klaff, "The Right Way to Bring Expats Home."

98 Abroad but not forgotten: Improving the career management of employees on international assignments, *Human Resource Management International Digest* 15:4 (2007): 29–31.

99 Iris I. Varner and Teresa M. Palmer, "Successful Expatriation and Organizational Strategies," *Review of Business* 23 (Spring 2002): 8–12; Jan Selmer, "Practice Makes Perfect? International Experience and Expatriate Adjustment," *Management International Review* 42 (January 2002): 71–88.

100 Bruce E. Kaufman, "Reflections on Six Decades in Industrial Relations: An Interview with John Dunlop," *Industrial and Labor Relations Review* 55 (January 2002): 324–49.

101 Jean-Louis Chaumet, CGT Labor Representative, "Euro-Disney News Profile," *ABC News* (March 29, 1992):1.

102 Neil Templin, "GM Strike Hits Mexican Output as Talks on Settlement Resume," *Wall Street Journal* (March 20, 1996): A3.

103 Robert A. Senser, "Workers of the World: It's Time to Unite," *Commonweal* (September 22, 2000): 13; Julie Kosterlitz, "Unions of the World Unite: European and American Unions Working Together," *National Journal* 30 (1998): 1134.

104 Ans Kolk and Rob van Tulder, "Child Labor and Multinational Conduct: A Comparison of International Business and Stakeholder Codes," *Journal of Business Ethics* 36 (2002): 291–302.

105 "You're Fired," *The Economist* (September 16, 2008), "Economist.com Daily Chart: What It Costs to Sack a Worker" (accessed October 24, 2009).

106 John Addison, "Nonunion Representation in Germany," *Journal of Labor Research* 20:1 (Winter 1999): 73–91.

107 The Annecy Symposium, "The Future of Work, Employment and Social Protection," *International Labour Review* 140 (Winter 2001): 453–75.

108 Anna Saxenian, "Brain Circulation: How High-Skill Immigration Makes Everyone Better Off," *Brookings Review* 20 (Winter 2002): 28–32; Moises Naim, "The New Diaspora: New Links between Emigrés and Their Home Countries Can Become a Powerful Force for Economic Development," *Foreign Policy* (July–August 2002): 96–98.

109 "H-1B Visas Applications to Decline, Target Existing Workers," *Workforce Management* (Winter 2009): 4.

110 Mark Poster, "Workers as Cyborgs: Labor and Networked Computers," *Journal of Labor Research* 23 (Summer 2002): 339–54.

111 "We Must Halt the Brain-Drain," *Africa News Service* (December 17, 2001): 1.

112 "The Poorest Are Again Losing Ground," *Business Week* (April 23, 2001): 130.

113 Amy Caiazza, "I Knew I Could Do This Work: Seven Strategies That Promote Women's Activism and Leadership in Unions," www.iwpr.org/pdf/I917.pdf (accessed October 23, 2009).

114 Nancy Mills, "New Strategies for Union Survival and Revival," *Journal of Labor Research* 22 (Summer 2001): 599.

115 "Unions: In from the Cold?," *The Economist* (March 12, 2009): 67.

116 *Sources include the following:* Central Intelligence Agency, "India," *The World Factbook 2009,* www.cia.gov/cia/publications/factbook/geos/in.html; Library of Congress (accessed October 15, 2009); "A Country Study: India," *Country Studies,* at http://memory.loc.gov/frd/cs/intoc.html (accessed October 15, 2009); "Country Profile: India," *bbc.co.uk,* news.bbc.co.uk/1/hi/world/south_asia/country_profiles/1154019.stm (July 26, 2009); Keith Bradshers, "A Younger India Is Flexing Its Industrial Brawn," *New York Times* (September 1, 2006): A-1; "Hungry Tiger, Dancing Elephant," *The Economist* (April 4, 2007): 58–61; "Virtual Champions, Survey: Business in India," *The Economist* (June 1, 2006): 34.

glossary

Absolute advantage: A theory first presented by Adam Smith, which holds that because certain countries can produce some goods more efficiently than other countries, they should specialize in and export those things they can produce more efficiently and trade for other things they need.

Acceptable quality level (AQL): A concept of quality control whereby managers are willing to accept a certain level of production defects, which are dealt with through repair facilities and service centers.

Accounting: The process of collecting and analyzing data for internal and external users of information.

Acquired advantage: A form of trade advantage due to technology rather than due to the availability of natural resources, climate, etc.

Acquired group memberships: Affiliations not determined by birth, such as religions, political affiliations, and professional and other associations.

Active income: Income of a CFC that is derived from the active conduct of a trade or business, as specified by the U.S. Internal Revenue Code.

Ad valorem duty: A duty (tariff) assessed as a percentage of the value of the item.

ADR: *See* American Depositary Receipt.

AFTA: *See* ASEAN Free Trade Area.

Agglomeration: A theory that competitive companies may gain efficiencies by locating near each other.

American Depositary Receipt (ADR): A negotiable certificate issued by a U.S. bank in the United States to represent the underlying shares of a foreign corporation's stock held in trust at a custodian bank in the foreign country.

American terms: The practice of using the direct quote for exchange rates.

Andean Community (CAN): A South American form of economic integration involving Bolivia, Colombia, Ecuador, Peru, and Venezuela.

APEC: *See* Asia Pacific Economic Cooperation.

Appropriability theory: The theory that companies will favor foreign direct investment over such nonequity operating forms as licensing arrangements so that potential competitors will be less likely to gain access to proprietary information.

Arbitrage: The process of buying and selling foreign currency at a profit that results from price discrepancies between or among markets.

Arm's-length price: A price between two companies that do not have an ownership interest in each other.

Ascribed group memberships: Affiliations determined by birth, such as those based on gender, family, age, caste, and ethnic, racial, or national origin.

ASEAN: *See* Association of South East Asian Nations.

ASEAN Free Trade Area (AFTA): A free trade area formed by the ASEAN countries on January 1, 1993, with the goal of cutting tariffs on all intrazonal trade to a maximum of 5 percent by January 1, 2008.

Asia Pacific Economic Cooperation (APEC): A cooperation formed by 21 countries that border the Pacific Rim to promote multilateral economic cooperation in trade and investment in the Pacific Rim.

Association of South East Asian Nations (ASEAN): A free trade area involving the Asian countries of Brunei, Indonesia, Malaysia, the Philippines, Singapore, and Thailand.

Authoritarianism: A system of government in which leaders are not subjected to the test of free elections.

Back translation: A method to check the validity of translations by having one person translate to another language and a second person translate it back to the original.

Balance of payments: Statement that summarizes all economic transactions between a country and the rest of the world during a given period of time.

Balance-of-payments deficit: An imbalance of some specific component within the balance of payments, such as merchandise trade or current account, that implies that a country is importing more than it exports.

Balance-of-payments effects: The impact of a foreign direct investment on imports, exports and capital flows.

Balance-of-payments surplus: An imbalance in the balance of payments that exists when a country exports more than it imports.

Balance of trade: The value of a country's exports less the value of its imports

("trade" can be defined as merchandise trade, services, unilateral transfers, or some combination of these three).

Balanced scorecard: An approach to performance measurement that endeavors to more closely link the strategic and financial perspectives of a business and take a broad view of business performance.

Balance sheet approach: Compensation plan that sets expatriate salaries to equallize purchasing power across countries.

Bank for International Settlements (BIS): A bank in Basel, Switzerland, that facilitates transactions among central banks; it is effectively the central banks' central bank.

Bargaining school theory: A theory holding that the negotiated terms for foreign investors depend on how much investors and host countries need each other's assets.

Barriers to entry: Factors that make it difficult or costly for firms to enter an industry or market.

Barter: The exchange of goods for goods or services instead of for money.

Base currency: The currency whose value is implicitly 1 when a quote is made between two currencies; for example, if the Brazilian real is trading at 1.9 reals (reais) per dollar, the dollar is the base currency and the real is the quoted currency.

Bid (buy) rate: The amount a trader is willing to pay for foreign exchange.

Bilateral agreement: An agreement between two countries.

Bilateral integration: A form of integration between two countries in which they decide to cooperate more closely together, usually in the form of tariff reductions.

BIS: *See* Bank for International Settlements.

Black market: The foreign-exchange market that lies outside the official market.

Booking center: An offshore financial center whose main function is to act as an accounting center in order to minimize the payment of taxes.

Born-global company: A company that adopts a global orientation from inception.

Bottom of the Pyramid: The billions of people living on less than a few dollars per day yet who some see as the next market frontier of the global economy.

Boundaries: In terms of political environments, an official or perceived point of separation that defines the boundary of a nation. In terms of organization structure, horizontal constraints that follow from having specific employees only do specific jobs in specific units as well as the vertical constraints that separate employees into specific levels of a precisely stipulated command-and-control hierarchy.

Boundarylessness: State whereby companies build organizations that eliminate the vertical, horizontal, and external boundaries that impede information flows and hinder developing relationship.

Brain drain: A condition where countries lose potentially productive resources when educated people leave.

Bretton Woods Agreement: An agreement among IMF countries to promote exchange-rate stability and to facilitate the international flow of currencies.

Broker (in foreign exchange): Specialists who facilitate transactions in the interbank market.

Bureaucratic control: System whereby an organization uses centralized authority to install rules and procedures to govern activities.

Business environment: The economic, political, legal, and cultural context of business activity.

Buy local legislation: Laws that are intended to favor the purchase of domestically sourced goods or services over imported ones, even though the imports may be a better buy.

CACM: *See* Central American Common Market.

Canada-U.S. Free Trade Agreement: An agreement, enacted in 1989, establishing a free trade area involving the United States and Canada.

Capitalism: An economic system characterized by private ownership, pricing, production, and distribution of goods.

Caribbean Community and Common Market (CARICOM): A customs union in the Caribbean region.

Caribbean Free Trade Association (CARIFTA): *See* Caribbean Community and Common Market.

CARICOM: *See* Caribbean Community and Common Market.

Central American Common Market (CACM): A customs union in Central America.

Central American Free Trade Association-DR (CAFTA-DR): A free trade association between the United States and the CACM countries plus the Dominican Republic.

Central bank: A government institution responsible for setting a country's monetary policy. In the United States, the Federal Reserve Bank is the Central Bank.

Centralization: The degree to which high-level managers, usually above the country level, make strategic dicisions and delegate them to lower levels for implementation.

Centrally planned economy (CPE): *See* Command economy.

Certificate of origin: A shipping document that determines the origin of products and is usually validated by an external source, such as a chamber of commerce; it helps countries determine the specific tariff schedule for imports.

Chaebol: Korean business groups that are similar to *keiretsu* and also contain a trading company as part of the group.

Chicago Mercantile Exchange group: The CME Group is the world's largest derivatives marketplace, dealing in future and options products for a wide variety of asset classes, including foreign exchange.

Civil law system: A legal system based on a very detailed set of laws that are organized into a code; countries with a civil law system, also called a codified legal system, include Germany, France, and Japan.

Civil liberties: The freedom to develop one's own views and attitudes.

Clan control: System whereby an MNE relies on shared values among employees to idealize and enforce preferred behaviors.

Cluster effects: The cluster effect is the effect of buyers and sellers of a particular good or service congregating in a certain place and hence inducing other buyers and sellers to relocate there as well.

Clustering: The location of companies where there are many competitors and suppliers.

Code of conduct: A set of principles guiding the actions of MNEs in their contacts with societies.

Codetermination: A process by which both labor and management participate in the management of a company.

Collaborative arrangement: A formal, long-term contractual agreement among companies.

Collective bargaining: The process of negotiation between employers (or their representatives) and a union on wages and other employment conditions.

Collectivism: Perspective that the needs of the group take precedence over the needs of the individual; Encourages dependence on the organization.

Command economy: An economic system in which the political authorities make major decisions regarding the production and distribution of goods and services.

Commercial bill of exchange: An instrument of payment in international business that instructs the importer to forward payment to the exporter.

Commodity: A product that is difficult to differentiate from those of competitors, such as raw materials and agricultural output.

Common law system: A legal system based on tradition, precedent, and custom and usage, in which the courts interpret the law based on those conventions; found in the United Kingdom and former British colonies.

Common market: A form of regional economic integration in which countries abolish internal tariffs, use a common external tariff, and abolish restrictions on factor mobility.

Communism: A form of totalitarianism initially theorized by Karl Marx in which the political and economic systems are virtually inseparable.

Comparable access argument: Companies and industries often argue that they are entitled to the same access to foreign markets as foreign industries and companies have to their markets.

Comparative advantage: The theory that there is global efficiency gains from trade if a country specializes in those products that it can produce more efficiently than other products regardless of whether other countries can produce those products even more efficiently.

Competitive advantage: The strategies, skills, knowledge, resources or competencies that differentiate a business from its competitors.

Compound duty: A tax placed on goods traded internationally, based on value plus units.

Concentration strategy: A strategy by which an international company builds up operations quickly in one or a few countries before going to another.

Configuration: To set up, arrange, and disperse value activities to the ideal locations around the world so that the company can start and sustain operations.

Confirmed letter of credit: A letter of credit to which a bank in the exporter's country adds its guarantee of payment.

Conservatism: A characteristic of accounting systems that implies that companies are hesitant to disclose high profits or profits that are consistent with their actual operating results; more common in Germanic countries.

Consolidation: An accounting process in which financial statements of related entities, such as a parent and its subsidiaries, are combined to yield a unified set of financial statements; in the process, transactions among the related enterprises are eliminated so that the statements reflect transactions with outside parties.

Consortium: The joining together of several entities, such as companies or governments, in order to strengthen the possibility of achieving some objective.

Constitutional law: Law that is created and changed by the people.

Consumer divergence: Differences in local consumer's preferences due to cultural predisposition, historical legacy, and endemic nationalism.

Consumer price index (CPI): A measure of the cost of typical wage-earner purchases of goods and services expressed as a percentage of the cost of these same goods and services in some base period.

Consumer sovereignty: The freedom of consumers to influence production through the choices they make.

Contract: Formal document that specifies conditions of an exchange and details rights and obligations of involved parties.

Control: The planning, implementation, evaluation, and correction of performance to ensure that organizational objectives are achieved.

Control systems: Process by which managers compare performance to plans, identify differences, and, where found, assess the basis for the gap and implement corrective action; ensure that activities are completed in ways that support the company's strategy.

Contemporary structure: Vertical and horizontal differentiation creates boundaries that constrain how managers coordinate interdependent value activities; contemporary structures eliminate these boundaries.

Controlled foreign corporation (CFC): A foreign corporation of which more than 50 percent of the voting stock is owned by U.S. shareholders (taxable entities that own at least 10 percent of the voting stock of the corporation).

Convergence: Efforts by the FASB and IASC to move toward a common global set of accounting standards.

Coordination: Systems that synchronize the work responsibilities of the value chain so that the company uses its resources efficiently and makes decisions effectively.

Coordination by mutual adjustment: System whereby managers interact extensively with counterparts in setting common goals.

Coordination by plan: System that relies on general goals and detailed objectives to coordinate activities.

Coordination by standardization: System whereby universal rules and procedures that apply to units worldwide, thereby enforcing consistency in the performance of activities in geographically dispersed units.

Core competency: A special outlook, skill, capability, or technology that runs through the firm's operations, weaving together disparate value activities into an integrated value chain.

Corporate culture: The common values shared by employees in a corporation, which form a control mechanism that is implicit and helps enforce other explicit control mechanisms.

Corporate governance: The combination of external and internal mechanisms implemented to safeguard the assets of a company and protect the rights of the shareholders.

Corporate social responsibility: An expression used to describe what some see as a company's obligation to be sensitive to the needs of "all" of its stakeholders in its business operations and produce an overall positive impact on society.

Correspondent (bank): A bank in which funds are kept by another, usually foreign, bank to facilitate check clearing and other business relationships.

Cost-of-living adjustment: An increase in compensation given to an expatriate employee when foreign living costs are more expensive than those in the home country.

Cost leadership: Strategy whereby a firm sells its products at the average industry price to earn a profit higher than that of rivals or below the average industry prices to capture market share.

Cost-plus strategy: The strategy of pricing at a desired margin over cost.

Council of the European Union: One of the five major institutions of the European Union; made up of the heads of state of each of the EU members.

Counterfeiting: The unauthorized copying or imitating of an item which is later passed on as an original.

Countertrade: A requirement that an exporter create value in the importing country, such as by transferring technology or receiving payment in the importing country's merchandise. An umbrella term for several sorts of trade, such as barter or offset, in which the seller accepts goods or services, rather than currency or credit, as payment.

Country of origin: A condition where consumers may prefer to buy goods produced in one country rather than another usually because of quality perceptions or because of nationalism.

Country-similarity theory: The theory that a company will seek to exploit opportunities in those countries most similar to its home country because of the perceived need to make fewer operating adjustments.

Country size theory: The theory that larger countries are generally more self-sufficient than smaller countries.

Creolization: The process by which some, but not all, elements of an outside culture are introduced.

Criminal law: Body of laws dealing with crimes against the public and members of the public.

Cross-licensing: The exchange of technology by different companies.

Cross rate: An exchange rate between two currencies used in the spot market and computed from the exchange rate of each currency in relation to the U.S. dollar.

Cultural collision: A condition that occurs when divergent cultures come in contact with each other.

Cultural diffusion: The cultural changes that occur when different cultures come in contact with each other.

Cultural distance: The degree to which countries differ from each other as measured by different cultural factors; the greater the difference, the greater the distance.

Cultural friction: The result of changes in power relationships and sovereignty when cultures come into contact with each other.

Cultural imperialism: Cultural change by imposition.

Culture: The specific learned norms of a group's attitudes, values, and beliefs.

Culture shock: A generalized trauma one experiences in a new and different culture because of having to learn and cope with a vast array of new cues and expectations.

Currency swaps: The exchange of principal and interest payments.

Current-rate method: A method of translating foreign-currency financial statements that is used when the functional currency is that of the local operating environment.

Custom broker: See Import Broker.

Customary law system: A legal system anchored in the wisdom of daily experience or great spiritual or philosophical traditions.

Customer orientation: A customer orientation asks: What and how can the company sell in country A? In this case, the country is held constant and the product and method of marketing it is varied.

Customs union: A form of regional economic integration that eliminates internal tariffs among member nations and establishes common external tariffs.

Customs valuation: The value of goods on which customs authorities charge tariffs.

Decentralization: The degree to which lower-level managers, usually at or below the country level, make and implement strategic decisions.

Deflation: A decrease in the general price level of goods and services; often caused by a reduction in the supply of money or credit.

Democracy: A political system that relies on citizens' participation in the decision-making process.

Dependencia theory: The theory holding that developing countries have practically no power when dealing with MNEs.

Derivative: A foreign-exchange instrument such as an option or futures contract that derives its value from the underlying currency.

Derivatives market: Market in which forward contracts, futures, options, and swaps are traded in order to hedge or protect foreign-exchange transactions.

Devaluation: A formal reduction in the value of a currency in relation to another currency; the foreign-currency equivalent of the devalued currency falls.

Developed country: High-income country. Also called industrial country.

Developing country: A low-income country, also known as an emerging country.

Diamond of national advantage theory: A theory that says countries usually need four conditions (demand; factors; related and supporting industries; and strategy, structure and rivalry) to develop and sustain a product's competitive advantage.

Differentiation: A business strategy in which a company tries to gain a competitive advantage by providing a unique product or service, or providing a unique brand of customer service.

Digitization: The conversion of paper and other media in existing collections to digital form.

Direct exports: Products sold to an independent party outside of the exporter's home country.

Direct investment: See foreign direct investment.

Direct quote: A quote expressed in terms of the number of units of the domestic currency given for one unit of a foreign currency.

Direct selling: A sale of goods by an exporter directly to distributors or final consumers rather than to trading companies or other intermediaries in order to achieve greater control over the marketing function and to earn higher profits.

Disclosure: The presentation of financial information and discussion of results.

Discount: The difference between the spot and forward exchange rates in the forward market; a foreign currency sells at a discount when the forward rate is less than the spot rate and when the domestic currency is quoted on a direct basis.

Distribution: The physical path or legal title that goods take from production to consumption.

Diversification strategy: A term used in international business to describe a strategy whereby a company moves rapidly into many markets and gradually increases its commitments within each one.

Divesting: Reduction in the amount of investment.

Divisional structures: An organization that contains separate divisions based around individual product lines or based on the geographic areas of the markets served.

Draft: An instrument of payment in international business that instructs the importer to forward payment to the exporter.

Dumping: The underpricing of exports, usually below cost or below the home-country price.

Duty: A government tax (tariff) levied on goods shipped internationally. Also called tariff.

Dynamic effects of integration: The overall growth in the market and the impact on a company of expanding production and achieving greater economies of scale.

EC: *See* European Community.

E-commerce: The use of the Internet to join together suppliers with companies and companies with customers.

Economic Community of West African States (ECOWAS): A form of economic integration among certain countries in West Africa.

Economic exposure (operational exposure): The foreign-exchange risk that international businesses face in the pricing of products, the source and cost of inputs, and the location of investments.

Economic freedom: The absence of government coercion or constraint on the production, distribution, or consumption of goods and services beyond the extent necessary for citizens to protect and maintain liberty.

Economic Freedom Index: The systematic measurement of economic freedom in countries throughout the world. The survey is sponsored by the Heritage Foundation and the *Wall Street Journal*.

Economic integration: The abolition of economic discrimination between national economies, such as within the EU.

Economic system: The system concerned with the allocation of scarce resources.

Economics: A social science concerned chiefly with the description and analysis of the production, distribution, and consumption of goods and services.

Economies of scale: The lowering of cost per unit as output increases because of allocation of fixed costs over more units produced.

Economies of scope: Decreases in average total cost made possible by increasing the range of goods produced.

Effective tariff: The real tariff on the manufactured portion of developing countries' exports, which is higher than indicated by the published rates because the ad valorem tariff is based on the total value of the products, which includes raw materials that would have had duty-free entry.

EFTA: *See* European Free Trade Association.

Electronic data interchange (EDI): The electronic movement of money and information via computers and telecommunications equipment.

Embargo: A specific type of quota that prohibits all trade.

Emerging economy: Countries with developing economies, often experiencing rapid growth and offering lucrative investment opportunities, but also characterized by political instability and high risk.

EMS: *See* European Monetary System.

Enterprise resource planning (ERP): Software that can link information flows from different parts of a business and from different geographic areas.

Equity alliance: A situation in which a cooperating company takes an equity position (almost always a minority) in the company with which it has a collaborative arrangement.

ERP: *See* Enterprise resource planning.

Escalation of commitment: The more time and money companies invest in examining an alternative, the more likely they are to accept it regardless of its merits.

Essential-industry argument: The argument holding that certain domestic industries need protection for national security purposes.

Ethnocentric framework: A staffing approach in which all key management positions, whether in the home country or abroad, are filled by home country nationals.

Ethnocentrism: A belief that one's own group is superior to others; also used to describe a company's belief that what worked at home should work abroad.

Euro: The common currency of the European Union; as of 12/31/09, 16 EU members had adopted the euro, and others were in the process of qualifying for adoption.

Eurobond: A bond sold in a country other than the one in whose currency it is denominated.

Eurocredit: A loan, line of credit, or other form of medium- or long-term credit on the Eurocurrency market that has a maturity of more than one year.

Eurocurrency: Any currency that is banked outside of its country of origin.

Eurocurrency market: An international wholesale market that deals in Eurocurrencies.

Eurodollars: Dollars banked outside of the United States.

Euroequity market: The market for shares sold outside the boundaries of the issuing company's home country.

European Central Bank (ECB): Established July 1, 1998, the ECB is responsible for setting the monetary policy and for managing the exchange-rate system for all of Europe since January 1, 1999.

European Commission: One of the five major institutions of the EU; composed of 27 women and men, one from each EU country. The president is chosen by EU governments and endorsed by the European Parliament. The commissioners do not represent their home country governments, and they serve as an executive branch for the EU.

European Community (EC): The predecessor of the European Union.

European Court of Justice: The court of the European Union. The Court is an appeals court and ensures interpretation and application of EU treaties. One of the five major institutions of the EU; composed of one member from each country in the EU and serves as a supreme appeals court for EU law.

European Economic Community (EEC): The predecessor of the European Community.

European Free Trade Association (EFTA): A free trade area among a group of European countries that are not members of the EU.

European Monetary System (EMS): A cooperative foreign-exchange agreement involving many members of the EU and designed to promote exchange-rate stability within the EU.

European Monetary Union: An agreement by participating European Union member countries that consists of three stages coordinating economic policy and culminating with the adoption of the euro.

European Parliament: One of the five major institutions of the EU; its representatives are elected directly in each member country.

European terms: The practice of using the indirect quote for exchange rates.

European Union (EU): A form of regional economic integration among countries in Europe that involves a free trade area, a customs union, and the free mobility of factors of production that is working toward political and economic union.

Exchange rate: The price of one currency in terms of another currency.

Eximbank: *See* Export-Import Bank.

Exclusive license: The licensor can give rights to no other company for the specified geographic area for a specified period of time.

Expatriate compensation: The process of setting the appropriate level of direct and indirect benefits to motivate someone to accept and perform an international assignment.

Expatriate failure: The premature return of an expatriate manager to the home country.

Expatriates: Noncitizens of the country in which they are working.

Expatriate selection: The process of screening executives to find those with the greatest inclination and highest potential for a foreign assignment.

Experience curve: The relationship of production-cost reductions to increases in output.

Explicit knowledge: Knowledge that can be passed to others through published reports.

Exporting: The sale of goods or services produced by a company based in one country to customers that reside in a different country.

Export intermediaries: Individuals or companies that assume responsibility for different combinations of finding overseas buyers, sourcing and shipping products, and getting paid on the behalf of a manufacturer. The export intermediary may be a commissioned agent, an export

management company (EMC), an export trading company (ETC), an export agent, or a re-marketer.

Export intensity: The fraction of the total output of a firm, or sometimes an industry within a country, that is exported.

Export-led development: An industrialization policy emphasizing industries that will have export capabilities.

Export license: A document that grants a government permission to ship certain products to a specific country.

Export management company (EMC): A company that buys merchandise from manufacturers for international distribution or sometimes acts as an agent for manufacturers.

Export strategy: Specification of the key issues that shape the success of exporting.

Export tariff: A tax on goods leaving a country.

Export trading company (ETC): A form of trading company sanctioned by U.S. law to become involved in international commerce as independent distributors to match up foreign buyers with domestic sellers.

Exports: Goods or services leaving a country for another.

Exposure: A situation in which a foreign-exchange account is subject to a gain or loss if the exchange rate changes.

Expropriation: The taking over of ownership of private property by a country's government.

Extended family: A family situation which includes family members of several generations or family members which stretches out horizontally, including aunts, uncles, cousins, etc.

External debt: Debt owed by a country to non-residents repayable in foreign currency, goods or service.

External environment: The physical, social, and competitive factors in a country that influence a company's international strategy.

Externalities: The impact of an economic activity on someone external to the specific activity, such as the impact of pollution on those not involved in the economic activity that created pollution; the externalities may be positive or negative.

Extranet: The use of the Internet to link a company with outsiders.

Extraterritoriality: The extension by a government of the application of its laws to foreign operations of companies.

Factor-mobility theory: The movement of factors of production such as labor and capital from one location to another.

Factor-proportions theory: The theory that differences in a country's proportionate holdings of factors of production (land, labor, and capital) explain differences in the costs of the factors and that export advantages lie in the production of goods that use the most abundant factors.

Fairness argument: Like the comparable access argument, domestic companies contend that they should have the same access to foreign markets as foreign companies have to their markets.

FASB: *See* Financial Accounting Standards Board.

Fascism: A system of government that promotes extreme nationalism, repression, and anticommunism, and is ruled by a dictator.

Fatalism: A belief that events are fixed in advance and that human beings are powerless to change them.

Favorable balance of trade: An indication that a country is exporting more than it imports.

FCPA: *See* Foreign Corrupt Practices Act.

FDI: *See* Foreign direct investment.

Fees: Payments for services.

Financial Accounting Standards Board (FASB): The private-sector organization that sets financial accounting standards in the United States.

Firm-specific advantage or assets: Advantages or assets that a company can exploit to be effective in global markets.

First-mover advantage: A cost-reduction advantage due to economies of scale attained through moving into a foreign market ahead of competitors.

Fisher Effect: The theory about the relationship between inflation and interest rates; for example, if the nominal interest rate in one country is lower than that in another, the first country's inflation should be lower so that the real interest rates will be equal.

Five-forces model: A framework used to assess industry structure and business strategy in estimating the potential for profitability.

Floating currency: A currency whose value responds to the supply of and demand for that currency.

Floating exchange rate: An exchange rate determined by the laws of supply and demand and with minimal government interference.

Focus strategy: An attempt to sell to a target- rather than a mass-market.

Foreign bond: A bond sold outside of the borrower's country but denominated in the currency of the country of issue.

Foreign Corrupt Practices Act (FCPA): A law that criminalizes certain types of payments by U.S. companies, such as bribes to foreign government officials.

Foreign direct investment (FDI): An investment that gives the investor a controlling interest in a foreign company.

Foreign exchange: Checks and other instruments for making payments in another country's currency.

Foreign-exchange control: A requirement that an individual or company must apply to government authorities for permission to buy foreign currency above some determined threshold amount.

Foreign-exchange market: The market where foreign exchange is traded; usually banks, non-bank financial institutions, and exchanges, such as the CME.

Foreign investment: Direct or portfolio ownership of assets in another country.

Foreign service premium: A cash allowance given to an employee who agrees to transfer to a foreign location. Also called International Adjustment Allowance or International Assignment Premium.

Foreign trade zone (FTZ): A government-designated area in which goods can be stored, inspected, or manufactured without being subject to formal customs procedures until they leave the zone.

Forward contract: A contract between a company or individual and a bank to deliver foreign currency at a specific exchange rate on a future date.

Forward discount: *See* Discount.

Forward premium: *See* Premium.

Forward rate: A contractually established exchange rate between a foreign-exchange trader and the trader's client for delivery of foreign currency on a specific date.

Franchising: A specialized form of licensing in which one party (the franchisor) gives permission to an independent party (the franchisee) the use of a trademark that is an essential asset for the franchisee's business and also gives continual assistance in the operation of the business.

Freedom: The condition of being free; the power to act, speak, and think without externally imposed restraints.

Freedom House: An organization that attempts to classify countries according to political and economic freedom.

Freely convertible currency: *See* Hard currency.

Free trade agreement: An agreement between countries that has the goal of abolishing all tariffs between member countries.

Free trade area (FTA): A form of regional economic integration in which internal tariffs are abolished, but member countries set their own external tariffs.

Free trade theory: This holds that global production will increase if countries do not interfere directly to affect trade.

Freight forwarder: A company that facilitates the movement of goods from one country to another.

FTZ: *See* Foreign trade zone.

Functional currency: The currency of the primary economic environment in which an entity operates; useful in helping a firm determine how to translate its foreign currency financial statements into the current of the parent company.

Functional structure: An organization that is structured according to functional areas of business.

Fundamental forecasting: A forecasting tool that uses trends in economic variables to predict future exchange rates.

Future orientation: An orientation where people invest for the future and delay instant gratification.

Futures contract: An agreement between two parties to buy or sell a particular currency at a particular price on a particular future date, as specified in a standardized contract to all participants in that currency futures exchange.

FX swap: A simultaneous spot and forward transaction in foreign exchange.

G7 countries: *See* Group of 7.

G8 countries: See Group of 8.

G20 Countries: See Group of 20.

GAAP: *See* Generally Accepted Accounting Principles.

Gap analysis: A tool used to discover why a company's sales of a given product are less than the market potential in a country; the reason may be a usage, competition, product line, or distribution gap.

GATT: *See* General Agreement on Tariffs and Trade.

General Agreement on Tariffs and Trade (GATT): A multilateral arrangement aimed at reducing barriers to trade, both tariff and nontariff ones; at the signing of the Uruguay round, the GATT was designated to become the World Trade Organization (WTO).

Generally Accepted Accounting Principles (GAAP): The accounting standards accepted by the accounting profession in each country as required for the preparation of financial statements for external users.

Generic: Any of a class of products, rather than the brand of a particular company; also relates to pharmaceutical products which have lost patent protection and can be sold by any company under a name that is different from the original branded name.

Generic names: Formerly trademarked names that have become part of the public domain.

Geocentric: Operations based on an informed knowledge of both home and host country needs.

Geocentric framework: Staffing perspective that seeks the best people for key jobs throughout the organization, regardless of nationality.

Geographic division structure: An organizational structure in which a company's operations are separated for reporting purposes into regional areas.

Gini coefficient: A measure of the extent to which the distribution of welfare deviates from a perfectly equal distribution.

Global bond: A combination of domestic bond and Eurobond that is issued simultaneously in several markets and that must be registered in each national market according to that market's registration requirements.

Global company: A company that integrates operations located in different countries.

Global integration: The unification of distinct national economic systems into one global market.

Globalization: The broadening set of interdependent relationships among people from different parts of a world that happens to be divided into nations. The term sometimes refers to the integration of world economies through the reduction of barriers to the movement of trade, capital, technology, and people.

Global sourcing: The acquisition on a worldwide basis of raw materials, parts, and subassemblies for the manufacturing process.

Global strategy: A strategy that increases profitability by achieving cost reductions from experience curves and location economies.

Globalization of markets: Thesis that consumers worldwide seek low-cost, high-quality products regardless of country of origin.

Go-no-go decision: A decision is based on a proposal's meeting a specific threshold rather than comparing it with other alternatives.

Gray market: The handling of goods through unofficial distributors.

Green economics: Transdisciplinary field that studies the interdependence and coevolution of human economies and natural ecosystems.

Green GNP: The measurement of national output that attempts to take into account various effects on the environment and natural resources.

Gross domestic product (GDP): The total of all economic activity in a country, regardless of who owns the productive assets.

Gross national income (GNI): Formerly referred to as Gross national product.

Gross national product (GNP): The total of incomes earned by residents of a country, regardless of where the productive assets are located.

Group of 7 (G7): A group of developed countries that periodically meets to make economic decisions; this group consists of Canada, France, Germany, Italy, Japan, the United Kingdom, and the United States.

Group of 8 (G8): The Group of 7 (G7) plus Russia.

Group of 20 (G20): Group of finance ministers and central bank governors from 19 countries plus the European Union.

Hard currency: A currency that is freely traded without many restrictions and for which there is usually strong external demand; often called a freely convertible currency.

Hardship allowance: A supplement to compensate expatriates for working in dangerous or adverse conditions.

Harvesting: Reduction in the amount of investment. Also known as divestment.

Hedge: To attempt to protect foreign-currency holdings against an adverse movement of an exchange rate.

Hedge fund: An investment fund available to a limited number of investors that is managed more aggressively than mutual funds.

Heterarchy: An organizational structure in which management of an alliance of companies is shared by so-called

equals rather than being set up in a superior-subordinate relationship.

Hierarchy of needs theory: A well-known motivation theory stating that there is a hierarchy of needs and that people must fulfill the lower-order needs sufficiently before they will be motivated by the higher-order ones.

High-context culture: A culture in which most people consider that peripheral and indirect information is necessary for decision making because such information bears on the context of the situation.

Home country: The country in which an international company is headquartered.

Home-country nationals: Expatriate employees who are citizens of the country in which the company is headquartered.

Horizontal alliance: An alliance of companies that produce similar products, as opposed to a vertical alliance which links together different elements of the value chain from raw materials to final consumption.

Horizontal differentiation: How the company specifies, divides, and assigns the set of organizational tasks.

Horizontally extended family: Includes aunts, uncles, and cousins.

Host country: Any foreign country in which an international company operates.

Host government policies: The programs put into place by the national government to regulate business activity.

Human development index: A measurement of human progress used by the United Nations Development Programme that combines indicators of purchasing power, education, and health.

Human resource management: The staffing function of the organization; includes the activities of human resources planning, recruitment, selection, performance appraisal, compensation, retention, and labor relations.

Hyperinflation: A rapid increase (at least 1 percent per day) in general price levels for a sustained period of time.

IASB: *See* International Accounting Standards Board.

Idealism: Trying to determine principles before settling small issues.

Ideology: The systematic and integrated body of constructs, theories, and aims that constitute a society.

IFE: *See* International Fisher Effect.

IMF: *See* International Monetary Fund.

Imitation lag: A strategy for exploiting temporary monopoly advantages by moving first to those countries most likely to develop local production.

Import broker: An individual who obtains various government permissions and other clearances before forwarding necessary paperwork to the carrier that will deliver the goods to the importer.

Import documentation: The various categories of documents required in international trade transactions.

Importing: The purchase of products by a company based in one country from sellers that reside in another.

Import or export license: A method of government control of the exchange rate whereby all recipients, exporters, and others who receive foreign exchange are required to sell to the central bank at the official buying rate.

Import strategy: Specification of the key issues that shape the success importing.

Import substitution: An industrialization policy whereby new industrial development emphasizes products that would otherwise be imported.

Imports: Goods or services entering a country from another.

Import tariff: A tax on goods entering a country.

Income distribution: A description of the fractions of a population that are at various levels of income.

Incremental internalization: The view that as a company gains experience, resources, and confidence, it progressively exports to increasingly distant and dissimilar countries.

Indirect exports: Exports that are not handled directly by the manufacturer or producer but through an export agent, freight forwarder, or 3PL.

Indirect quote: An exchange rate given in terms of the number of units of the foreign currency for one unit of the domestic currency.

Indirect selling: A sale of goods by an exporter through another domestic company as an intermediary.

Individualism: An emphasis on the importance of guaranteeing individual freedom and self-expression. Encourages fulfilling leisure time and improving skills outside the organization.

Individualism versus collectivism: A study comparing national preferences toward dependence on the organization for fulfilling leisure time, improving skills, and receiving benefits, along with preferences for personal decision making.

Individualistic paradigm: Minimal government intervention in the economy.

Industrial country: High-income country. Also known as developed country.

Industrial policy: Strong intervention by the government in the nature and direction of the economy.

Industrialization argument: A rationale for protectionism that argues that the development of industrial output should come about even though domestic prices may not become competitive on the world market.

Industry organization paradigm: Field of economics that studies the strategic behavior of firms, the structure of markets, and their interactions.

Industry structure: The makeup of an industry: its number of sellers and their size distribution, the nature of the product, and the extent of barriers to entry.

Infant-industry argument: The position that holds that an emerging industry should be guaranteed a large share of the domestic market until it becomes efficient enough to compete against imports.

Inflation: A general and progressive increase in prices.

Innovation: A new idea, method, or device that, in creating a new product or process, creates competitive advantage.

Integration-responsiveness (IR) grid: Schema that helps managers measure the global and local pressures that influence the configuration and coordination of value chains.

Intellectual property: Property in the form of patents, trademarks, service marks, trade names, trade secrets, and copyrights.

Intellectual property rights: Ownership rights to intangible assets, such as patents, trademarks, copyrights, and know-how.

Interbank market: The market for foreign-exchange transactions among commercial banks.

Interbank transactions: Foreign-exchange transactions that take place between commercial banks.

Interest arbitage: Investing in debt instruments in different countries to take advantage of interest differentials. The investment is "covered" if the investor converts money into foreign exchange at the spot rate, invests it in the foreign market at a higher interest rate, and

enters into a forward contract so that it can convert principle and interest back into the home currency and earn more than if that money had been invested in the home currency.

Intermodal transportation: The transportation of freight in a container or vehicle, using multiple modes of transportation (rail, ocean vessel, and truck), without any handling of the freight itself when changing modes.

Internal debt: Part of a country's debts that is owed to creditors who are citizens of that country.

Internalization: Control through self-handling of foreign operations, primarily because such control is less expensive to deal with in the same corporate family than to contract with an external organization.

International Accounting Standards Board (IASB): The international private-sector organization that sets financial accounting standards for worldwide use.

International business: All commercial transactions involving of two or more countries.

International division structure: A structure whereby the company creates a division that is responsible for its international activities.

International Financial Reporting Standards (IFRS): A set of accounting standards often known by the older name of International Accounting Standards (IAS). They are issued by the International Accounting Standards Board (IASB).

International Fisher Effect (IFE): The theory that the relationship between interest rates and exchange rates implies that the currency of the country with the lower interest rate will strengthen in the future.

Internationalization: The process by which companies gradually increase their commitments to international business.

International law: The regulations resulting from treaties among countries.

International Monetary Fund (IMF): A multigovernmental association organized in 1945 to promote exchange-rate stability and to facilitate the international flow of currencies.

International Organization of Securities Commissions (IOSCO): An international organization of securities regulators that supports the efforts of the IASB to establish comprehensive accounting standards.

International Organization for Standardization (1SO): An international non-governmental organization headquartered in Geneva that publishes industrial and commercial standards.

International strategy: The effort of managers to create value by transferring core competencies from the home market to foreign markets in which local competitors lack those competencies.

Intranet: The use of the Internet to link together the different divisions and functions inside a company.

Invisible hand: The reliance on market forces independent of government policies to allocate resources.

IOSCO: *See* International Organization of Securities Commissions.

Irrevocable letter of credit (L/C): A letter of credit that cannot be canceled or changed without the consent of all parties involved.

Islamic law: A system of theocratic law based on the religious teachings of Islam. Also called Muslim law.

ISO 9000: A quality standard developed by the International Organization for Standardization in Geneva that requires companies to document their commitment to quality at all levels of the organization.

Jamaica Agreement: A 1976 agreement among countries that permitted greater flexibility of exchange rates, basically formalizing the break from fixed exchange rates.

JIT: *See* Just-in-time manufacturing.

Joint venture: An investment in which two or more companies share the ownership.

Just-in-time (JIT) manufacturing system: A system that reduces inventory costs by having components and parts delivered as they are needed in production.

Kaizen: The Japanese process of continuous improvement, the cornerstone of TQM.

Keiretsu: A corporate relationship linking certain Japanese companies, usually involving a noncontrolling interest in each other, strong high-level personal relationships among managers in the different companies, and interlocking directorships.

Key industry: Any industry that might affect a very large segment of a country's economy or population by virtue of its size or influence on other sectors.

Kinesics: Body language; the way people walk, touch, and move their bodies.

Kyoto Protocol: The international agreement among countries to reduce the emission of green house gasses.

Labor union: An association of workers intended to promote and protect the welfare, interests, and rights of its members, primarily by collective bargaining.

LAFTA: *See* Latin American Free Trade Association.

Lag strategy: An operational strategy that involves either delaying collection of foreign-currency receivables if the currency is expected to strengthen or delaying payment of foreign-currency payables when the currency is expected to weaken; the opposite of a lead strategy.

Laissez-faire: The concept of minimal government intervention in a society's economic activity.

Latin American Free Trade Association (LAFTA): A free trade area formed by Mexico and the South American countries in 1960; it was replaced by ALADI in 1980.

Latin American Integration Association (ALADI): A form of regional economic integration involving 12 Latin American countries.

Law: A binding custom or practice of a community.

Lead strategy: An operational strategy that involves either collecting foreign-currency receivables before they are due when the currency is expected to weaken or paying foreign-currency payables before they are due when the currency is expected to strengthen; the opposite of a lag strategy.

Lean manufacturing: A production system whose focus is on optimizing processes through the philosophy of continual improvement.

Learning curve: A concept used to support the infant-industry argument for protection; it assumes that costs will decline as workers and managers gain more experience.

Legal system: The rules that regulate behavior, the processes that enforce the laws of a country, and the procedures used to resolve grievances.

Letter of credit (L/C): A precise document by which the importer's bank extends credit to the importer and agrees to pay the exporter.

Leverage: The amount of debt used to finance a firm's assets.

Liability of foreignness: Foreign companies' lower survival rate in comparison to local companies for many years after they begin operations.

Liberal democracy: A system of government characterized by universal adult suffrage, political equality, majority rule, and constitutionalism.

LIBOR: *See* London Inter-Bank Offered Rate.

License (import or export): Formal or legal permission to do some specified action; a government method of fixing the exchange rate by requiring all recipients, exporters, and others that receive foreign exchange to sell it to the central bank at the official buying rate.

Licensing agreement: Agreement whereby one company gives rights to another for the use, usually for a fee, of such assets as trademarks, patents, copyrights, or other know-how.

Link alliance: An alliance that uses complementary resources to expand into new business areas.

Liquidity preference: A theory that helps explain capital budgeting and, when applied to international operations, means that investors are willing to take less return in order to be able to shift the resources to alternative uses.

Local content: A term used in trade agreements which refers to the percentage of a product which is produced in the member countries to the agreement. Preferential tariff provisions often depend on the amount of local or regional content included in a product.

Localize: Process whereby an expatriate retains a foreign assignment provided she accept the status, and corresponding compensation, of a local hire.

Local responsiveness: The process of disaggregating a standardized whole into differentiated parts to improve responsiveness to local market circumstances.

Locals: Citizens of the country in which they are working.

Location economies: Cost advantages from performing a value activity at the optimal location.

Location-specific advantage: A combination of factor and demand conditions, along with other qualities, that a country has to offer domestic and foreign investors.

Logistics (materials management): That part of the supply chain process that plans, implements, and controls the efficient, effective flow and storage of goods, services, and related information from the point of origin to the point of consumption, to meet customers' requirements; sometimes called materials management.

London Inter-Bank Offered Rate (LIBOR): The interest rate for large interbank loans of Eurocurrencies.

London International Financial Futures Exchange (LIFFE): An exchange dealing in futures contracts for several major currencies. Now part of NYSE Euronext.

London Stock Exchange (LSE): A stock exchange located in London and dealing in Euroequities.

Low-context culture: A culture in which most people consider relevant only information that they receive firsthand and that bears very directly on the decision they need to make.

Maastricht (Treaty of): The treaty approved in December 1991 that was designed to bring the EU to a higher level of integration and is divided into the Economic Monetary Union (EMU) and a political union.

Management contract: An arrangement whereby one company provides management personnel, who perform general or specialized management functions, to another company for a fee.

Maquiladora: An industrial operation, originally developed between the United States and Mexico but now used in other geographic areas, in which components may be shipped duty free, assembled, and then re-exported.

Market capitalization: A common measure of the size of a stock market, which is computed by multiplying the total number of shares of stock listed on the exchange by the market price per share.

Market control: System whereby an MNE uses external market mechanisms to establish internal performance benchmarks and standards.

Market economy: An economic system in which resources are allocated and controlled by consumers who "vote" by buying goods.

Market environment: The environment that involves the interactions between households (or individuals) and companies in the allocation of resources, free from government ownership or control.

Masculinity-femininity index: An index comparing countries' norms on empathy for successful achievers versus the unfortunate, preference for being better than

others versus being on a par with them, belief that it's better "to live to work" versus "to work to live," preference for performance and growth versus quality of life and the environment, and belief that gender roles should be different versus similar.

Master franchise: A franchise agreement that is given to one franchisee in a country to establish franchises in many different areas, possibly the entire country.

Materials management: *See* Logistics.

Matrix structure: An organizational structure in which foreign units report (by product, function, or area) to more than one group, each of which shares responsibility over the foreign unit.

Mercantilism: An economic philosophy based on the beliefs that a country's wealth is dependent on its holdings of treasure, usually in the form of gold, and that countries should export more than they import in order to increase wealth.

Merchandise exports: Goods sent out of a country.

Merchandise imports: Goods brought into a country.

Merchandise trade balance: The part of a country's current account that measures the trade deficit or surplus; its balance is the net of merchandise imports and exports.

MERCOSUR: A major subregional group established by Argentina, Brazil, Paraguay, and Uruguay, which spun off from ALADI in 1991 with the goal of setting up a customs union and common market. Venezuela has applied for membership.

MFN: *See* Most-favored-nation.

Mixed economy: An economic system characterized by some mixture of market and command economies; balances public and private ownership of factors of production.

Mixed legal system: A legal system that emerges when two or more legal systems function in a country.

Mixed structure: A structure that integrates various aspects of other forms of traditional structures.

MNC: See multinational corporation or company.

MNE: *See* Multinational enterprise.

Modes of operations: Different ways of doing business internationally, such as through exports/imports, foreign direct investment, joint ventures, licensing agreements, etc.

Monochronic: A culture in which most people prefer to deal with situations

sequentially (especially those involving other people), such as finishing with one customer before dealing with another.

Most-favored-nation (MFN) clause: A GATT (and now a WTO) requirement that a trade concession that is given to one country must be given to all other countries.

Multidomestic strategy: An approach that emphasizes the need to be responsive to the unique conditions prevailing in different national markets.

Multilateral agreement: An agreement among three or more countries.

Multinational enterprise (MNE): A company that has an integrated global philosophy encompassing both domestic and foreign operations or a company with operations in more than one country; sometimes used simultaneously with multinational corporation or company or transnational corporation.

Multiparty democracy: Multiparty system in which three or more political parties have the capacity to gain control of government separately or in coalition.

Multiple exchange-rate system: A means of foreign-exchange control whereby the government sets different exchange rates for different transactions.

Mutual recognition: The principle that a foreign registrant that wants to list and have its securities traded on a foreign stock exchange need only provide information prepared according to the GAAP of the home country.

National responsiveness: Readiness to implement operating adjustments in foreign countries in order to reach a satisfactory level of performance.

Natural advantage: Climatic conditions, access to certain natural resources, or availability of labor, which gives a country an advantage in producing some product.

Neomercantilism: The approach of countries that apparently try to run favorable balances of trade in an attempt to achieve some social or political objective.

Net present value: The sum of the present values of the annual cash flows minus the initial investment.

Netting: The transfer of funds from subsidiaries in a net payable position to a central clearing account and from there to the accounts of the net receiver subsidiaries.

Network structure: Contemporary structure form whereby a small core organization outsources value activities to linked firms whose core competencies support greater innovation.

Network organization: A situation in which a group of companies is interrelated and in which the management of the interrelation is shared among so-called equals.

Nontariff barriers: Barriers to imports that are not tariffs; examples include administrative controls, "Buy America" policies, and so forth.

Nontradable goods: Products and services that are seldom practical to export, primarily because of high transportation costs.

Normativism: A theory stating that universal standards of behavior (based on people's own values) exist that all cultures should follow, making nonintervention unethical.

North American Free Trade Agreement (NAFTA): A free trade agreement involving the United States, Canada, and Mexico that went into effect on January 1, 1994, and will be phased in over a period of 15 years.

Nuclear family: A family consisting of parents and children.

OAU: *See* Organization of African Unity.

OECD: *See* Organization for Economic Cooperation and Development.

Offer: The amount for which a foreign-exchange trader is willing to sell a currency.

Official reserves: A country's holdings of monetary gold, Special Drawing Rights, and internationally acceptable currencies.

Offsets: A form of countertrade in which an exporter sells goods for cash but then helps businesses in the importing country to find opportunities to earn hard currency.

Offshore financial centers: Cities or countries that provide large amounts of funds in currencies other than their own and are used as locations in which to raise and accumulate cash.

Offshore financing: The provision of financial services by banks and other agents to nonresidents.

Offshoring (offshore manufacturing): The process of shifting production to a foreign country.

Oligopolistic reaction: The process in oligopoly industries for competitors to emulate each other, such as going to the same locations.

OPEC: *See* Organization of Petroleum Exporting Countries.

Operational centers: Offshore financial centers that perform specific functions, such as the sale and servicing of goods.

Operational obstacles: Factors that impede integrating value chain activities.

Opinion leader: One whose acceptance of some concept is apt to be emulated by others.

Opportunity-risk matrix: An investment matrix that compares the opportunities of investing in a country with the risks and is a tool that companies can use to help determine where to invest.

Optimism: A characteristic of an accounting system that implies that companies are more liberal in recognition of income.

Optimum-tariff theory: The argument that a foreign producer will lower its prices if an import tax is placed on its products.

Option: A foreign-exchange instrument that gives the purchaser the right, but not the obligation, to buy or sell a certain amount of foreign currency at a set exchange rate within a specified amount of time.

Organization: The specification of the framework for work, development of the systems that coordinate and control what work is done, and the cultivation of common workplace culture among employees.

Organization of African Unity (OAU): An organization of African nations that is more concerned with political than economic objectives.

Organization culture: The shared meaning and beliefs that shape how employees interpret information, make decisions, and implement actions.

Organization for Economic Cooperation and Development (OECD): A multilateral organization of industrialized and semi-industrialized countries that helps to formulate social and economic policies.

Organization of Petroleum Exporting Countries (OPEC): A producers' alliance among 12 petroleum-exporting countries that attempt to agree on oil production and pricing policies.

Organization structure: The formal arrangement of roles, responsibilities, and relationships within an organization.

Outright forward transaction: A forward contract that is not connected to a spot transaction.

Outsourcing: Where one company contracts with another company to perform certain functions, including manufacturing and back office operations. May be done in or

close to the company's home country (nearshoring) or in another country (offshoring).

Over-the-counter (OTC) market: Trading in stocks, usually of smaller companies, that are not listed on one of the stock exchanges; also refers to how government and corporate bonds are traded, through dealers who quote bids and offers to buy and to sell "over the counter."

Par value: The benchmark value of a currency, originally quoted in terms of gold or the U.S. dollar and now quoted in terms of Special Drawing Rights.

Parliamentary democracy: A system of government where the people exercise their political power by electing representatives to parliament to make laws.

Passive income: Income from investments in tax-haven countries or sales and services income that involves buyers and sellers in other than the tax-haven country, where either the buyer or the seller must be part of the same organizational structure as the corporation that earns the income; also known as Subpart F income.

Patent: A right granted by a sovereign power or state for the protection of an invention or discovery against infringement.

Paternalism: Regulating conduct by satisfying needs of subordinates.

Payback period: The number of years required to recover the initial investment made.

Peg: To fix a currency's exchange rate to some benchmark, such as another currency.

Penetration strategy: A strategy of introducing a product at a low price to induce a maximum number of consumers to try it.

Perfect competition: Industry setting in which there are many firms with small market shares, all firms are price takers, identical products are sold by all firms, companies can freely enter and exit the industry, and there is perfect knowledge.

Piracy: The unauthorized duplication of goods protected by intellectual property law.

PLC: *See* Product life cycle theory.

Pluralism: Belief that there are multiple opinions about an issue, each of which contains part of the truth, but none that contain the entire truth.

Pluralistic societies: Societies in which different ideologies are held by various segments rather than one ideology being adhered to by all.

Political freedom: The right to participate freely in the political process.

Political ideology: The body of constructs (complex ideas), theories, and aims that constitute a sociopolitical program.

Political risk: Potential changes in political conditions that may cause a company's operating positions to deteriorate.

Political science: A discipline that helps explain the patterns of governments and their actions.

Political spectrum: A conceptual structure that specifies various types of political ideologies.

Political system: The system designed to integrate a society into a viable, functioning unit.

Polycentric framework: A staffing policy whereby a company relies on host country nationals to manage operations in their own country, while parent-country nationals staff key positions at corporate headquarters.

Polycentrism: Characteristic of an individual or organization that feels that it should act like locals or local companies.

Polychronic: A culture in which most people are more comfortable dealing simultaneously with multiple situations facing them.

Portfolio investment: An investment in the form of either debt or equity that does not give the investor a controlling interest.

Post-Christian society: A term describing northern European countries that do not adhere strongly to any religion, but which hold strong Christian values because of centuries of profound religious influence.

Power distance: A measurement of preference for consultative versus autocratic styles of management.

PPP: *See* Purchasing power parity.

Pragmatism: Settling small issues before deciding on principles.

Premium (in foreign exchange): The difference between the spot and forward exchange rates in the forward market; a foreign currency sells at a premium when the forward rate exceeds the spot rate and when the domestic currency is quoted on a direct basis.

Primary activities: The steps and sequence of classic business functions that define the value chain of a company.

Principles-based accounting: A system of accounting that identifies key principles in a conceptual framework and establishes simple rules that conform to the key principles.

Private Technology Exchange (PTX): An online collaboration model that brings manufacturers, distributors, value-added resellers, and customers together to execute trading transactions and to share information about demand, production, availability, and more.

Privatization: Selling of government-owned assets to private individuals or companies.

Product diversion: See gray market.

Product division structure: An organizational structure that assigns global responsibilities to each product division.

Productivity: Output per unit of input, usually measured either by labor productivity or by total factor productivity.

Product life cycle (PLC) theory: The theory that certain kinds of products go through a cycle consisting of four stages (introduction, growth, maturity, and decline) and that the location of production will shift internationally depending on the stage of the cycle.

Production orientation: A marketing strategy based on producing products at the lowest cost possible and providing them to consumers everywhere, irrespective of consumer preferences or differences.

Property rights: The legal rights to use goods, services, or resources.

Protectionism: Government restrictions on imports and occasionally on exports that frequently give direct or indirect subsidies to industries to enable them to compete with foreign production either at home or abroad.

Protestant ethic: A theory that there is more economic growth when work is viewed as a means of salvation and when people prefer to transform productivity gains into additional output rather than into additional leisure.

Pull: A promotion strategy that sells consumers before they reach the point of purchase, usually by relying on mass media.

Purchasing power parity (PPP): A theory that explains exchange-rate changes as being based on differences in price levels in different countries. Also, the number of units of a country's currency to buy the same products or services in the domestic market that U.S. $1 would buy in the United States.

Quality: Meeting or exceeding the expectations of a customer.

Quantity controls: Government limitations on the amount of foreign currency that can be used for specific purposes.

Quota: A limit on the quantitative amount of a product allowed to be exported from or imported into a country.

Quoted currency: When dealers quote currencies to their customers, they always quote the base currency first followed by the terms currency. A quote of USD/JPY refers to the number of Japanese yen for one U.S. dollar.

Rationalization: *See* Rationalized production.

Rationalized production: The specialization of production by product or process in different parts of the world to take advantage of varying costs of labor, capital, and raw materials.

Reciprocal quote: One divided by the direct quote in foreign exchange. Also known as the indirect quote.

Regional integration: A form of integration in which a group of countries located in the same geographic proximity decide to cooperate.

Relativism: A theory stating that ethical truths depend on the groups holding them, making intervention by outsiders unethical. The belief that behavior has meaning and can be judged only in its specific cultural context.

Repatriation: An expatriate's return to his or her home country.

Representative democracy: A type of government in which individual citizens elect representatives to make decisions governing the society.

Resource-based view of the firm: A perspective that holds that each company has a unique combination of competencies.

Retaliation: A situation in which one country restricts imports from another country in response to that country's restrictions against its exports.

Revaluation: A formal change in an exchange rate by which the foreign-currency value of the reference currency rises, resulting in a strengthening of the reference currency.

Reverse culture shock: The experience of culture shock when returning to one's own country that is caused by having accepted what was experienced abroad.

Royalty: Payment for the use of intangible assets.

Rule of law: The principle that every member of a society, even a ruler, must follow the laws accepted by society.

Rule of man: Notion that the word and whim of one man are law.

Rules-based accounting: A legalistic accounting system filled with specific details in an attempt to address as many potential contingencies as possible.

Sales orientation: A company tries to sell abroad what it can sell domestically and in the same manner on the assumption that consumers are sufficiently similar globally.

Scale alliance: An alliance where firms aim at providing efficiency through the pooling of similar assets so that partners can carry out business activities in which they already have experience.

Scanning: Examining a variety of variables for different countries that may affect foreign investment alternatives.

SDR: *See* Special Drawing Right.

Secre: A characteristic of an accounting system that implies that companies do not disclose much information about accounting practices; more common historically in Germanic countries.

Secular totalitarianism: A dictatorship not affiliated with a religious group or system of beliefs.

Securities and Exchange Commission (SEC): A U.S. government agency that regulates securities brokers, dealers, and markets.

Separate entity approach: A system for taxation of corporate income in which each unit is taxed when it receives income, with the result being double taxation.

Serendipity: Refers to the trigger of so-called accidental exporters who, responding to happenstance or odd circumstances, enter overseas markets by chance.

Service exports: Internationally paid earnings other than those derived from exporting tangible goods.

Service imports: International payments for imports other than those for tangible goods.

Services: The non-product portion of the economy.

Sight draft: A commercial bill of exchange that requires payment to be made as soon as it is presented to the party obligated to pay.

Silent language: The wide variety of cues other than formal language by which messages can be sent.

Single European Act: A 1987 act of the EU (then the EC) allowing all proposals except those relating to taxation, workers' rights, and immigration to be adopted by a weighted majority of member countries.

Six Sigma: A highly focused system of quality control that uses data and rigorous statistical analysis to identify "defects" in a process or product, reduce variability, and achieve as close to zero defects as possible.

Skimming strategy: Charging a high price for a new product by aiming first at consumers willing to pay that price and then progressively lowering the price.

Small and medium-sized enterprise: Companies whose headcount or sale turnover falls below certain thresholds; in the United States, companies that employ fewer than 500 employees. Commonly expressed as "SME."

Smithsonian Agreement: A 1971 agreement among countries that resulted in the devaluation of the U.S. dollar, revaluation of other world currencies, a widening of exchange-rate flexibility, and a commitment on the part of all participating countries to reduce trade restrictions; superseded by the Jamaica Agreement of 1976.

Social democracy: The political ideology of socialism, including values of a representative government, and private property.

Social stratification: The ranking of individuals in a society.

Socialism: A system based on public ownership of the means of production and distribution of wealth.

Social marketing orientation: Successful international marketing requires serious consideration of potential environmental, health, social, and work-related problems that may arise when selling or making their products abroad.

Society: A broad grouping of people having common traditions, institutions, and collective activities and interests; the term nation-state is often used in international business to denote a society.

Soft currency: *See* Weak currency.

Sogo shosha: Japanese trading companies that import and export merchandise.

Sourcing: The strategy that a company pursues in purchasing materials, components, and final products; sourcing can be from domestic and foreign locations and from inside and outside the company.

Sovereignty: Freedom from external (foreign) control.

Special Drawing Right (SDR): A unit of account issued to countries by the International Monetary Fund to expand their official reserves bases.

Specialization: A result of free trade policies that causes countries to concentrate on producing and exporting those products for which they have the greatest advantage and importing those for which they have less advantage.

Specific duty: A duty (tariff) assessed on a per-unit basis.

Speculation: The buying or selling of foreign currency with the prospect of great risk and high return.

Speculator: A person who takes positions in foreign exchange with the objective of earning a profit.

Spillover effects: Situations in which the marketing program in one country results in awareness of the product in other countries.

Spot market: The market in which an asset is traded for immediate delivery, as opposed to a market for forward or future deliveries.

Spot rate: An exchange rate quoted for immediate delivery of foreign currency, usually within two business days.

Spot transactions: Foreign exchange transactions involving the exchange of currency the second day after the date on which the two foreign-exchange traders agree to the transaction.

Spread: In the forward market, the difference between the spot rate and the forward rate; in the spot market, the difference between the bid (buy) and offer (sell) rates quoted by a foreign-exchange trader.

Stakeholders: The collection of groups, including stockholders, employees, customers, and society at large, that a company must satisfy to survive.

Standardization: The procedure of maintaining methods and equipment as constant as possible.

Static effect: The shifting of resources from inefficient to efficient companies as trade barriers fall.

Stereotype: A standardized and oversimplified mental picture of a group.

Strategic alliance: An agreement between companies that is of strategic importance to one or both companies' competitive viability.

Strategic marketing orientation: Most companies committed to continual rather than sporadic foreign sales adopt a strategy that combines production, sales, and customer orientations.

Strategic trade policy: The identification and development of target industries to be competitive internationally.

Strategy: Management's idea on how to best attract customers, operate efficiently, compete effectively, and create value. Guides managers in building and sustaining the company's competitive position within its industry.

Subpart F income: Income of a CFC that comes from sources other than those connected with the active conduct of a trade or business, such as holding company income.

Subsidiary: A foreign operation that is legally separate from the parent company, even if wholly owned by it.

Subsidies: Direct assistance from governments to companies to make them more competitive.

Supply chain: The coordination of materials, information, and funds from the initial raw material supplier to the ultimate customer.

Support activities: The general infrastructure of the firm that anchors the day-to-day execution of the primary activities of the value chain.

Sustainability: Meeting the needs of the present without compromising the ability of future generations to meet their own needs while taking into account what is best for the people and the environment.

Swap: A simultaneous spot and forward foreign-exchange transaction.

Syndication: Cooperation by a lead bank and several other banks to make a large loan to a public or private organization.

Tacit knowledge: Knowledge imbedded in people, which usually can be transferred only on a person-to-person basis rather than through printed material.

Tariff: A government tax levied on goods, usually imports, shipped internationally.

Tax credit: A dollar-for-dollar reduction of tax liability that must coincide with the recognition of income.

Tax deferral: Income is not taxed until it is remitted to the parent company as a dividend.

Tax-haven countries: Countries with low income taxes or no taxes on foreign-source income.

Tax-haven subsidiary: A subsidiary of a company established in a tax-haven country for the purpose of minimizing income tax.

Tax treaty: A treaty between two countries that generally results in the reciprocal reduction of dividend withholding taxes and the exemption of taxes or royalties and sometimes interest payments.

Technical forecasting: A forecasting tool that uses past trends in exchange rates themselves to spot future trends in rates.

Temporal method: A method of translating foreign-currency financial statements used when the functional currency is that of the parent company.

Terms currency: In a foreign exchange quote, the base currency is 1 and the terms currency gives you the number of units of that currency per one unit of the base currency. If a foreign exchange trader quotes USD/JPY, the dollar is the base currency and the yen is the terms currency. The quote will give you the number of Japanese yen per U.S. dollar. The quote is also shown as USDJPY=X.

Terms of trade: The quantity of imports that can be bought by a given quantity of a country's exports.

Theocratic totalitarianism: A dictatorship led by a religious group.

Theory of country size: See country size theory.

Third wave of democratization: Expression to capture the collective set of nations that moved from nondemocratic to democratic political systems during the 1970s through the 1990s.

Third-country nationals: Expatriate employees who are neither citizens of the country in which they are working nor citizens of the country where the company is headquartered.

Third-party logistics: Agents that develop state-of-the-art technology to help companies understand trade practices, identify opportunities, manage risks, and shepherd exports and imports from buyers to sellers.

Tied aid and loans: Aid and loans given by one government to another on the condition that the recipient country spend the money on products from the donor country.

Time draft: A commercial bill of exchange calling for payment to be made at some time after delivery.

TNC: *See* Transnational company.

Total cost analysis: The process of determining monetary value based on acquisition costs, maintenance costs, and disposal costs.

Total quality management (TQM): The process that a company uses to achieve quality, where the goal is elimination of all defects.

Totalitarian system: A political system characterized by the absence of widespread participation in decision making.

TQM: *See* Total quality management.

Trade creation: Production shifts to more efficient producers for reasons of comparative advantage, allowing consumers access to more goods at a lower price than would have been possible without integration.

Trade deficit: A situation in which a country imports more than it exports.

Trade diversion: A situation in which exports shift to a less efficient producing country because of preferential trade barriers.

Trade Related Aspects of Intellectual Property Rights (TRIPS): A provision from the Uruguay round of trade negotiations requiring countries to agree to enforce procedures under their national laws to protect intellectual property rights.

Trade sanctions: Tariffs and non tariff barriers levied on another country, usually for political reasons.

Trade surplus: A situation in which a country exports more than it imports.

Trademark: A name or logo distinguishing a company or product.

Transaction cost theory: As applied to international business, the choice of operating based on the relative cost of doing business with a company's owned operations versus doing business with an independent company.

Transaction exposure: Foreign-exchange risk arising because a company has outstanding accounts receivable or accounts payable that are denominated in a foreign currency.

Transfer price: A price charged for goods or services between entities that are related to each other through stock ownership, such as between a parent and its subsidiaries or between subsidiaries owned by the same parent.

Transit tariff: A tax placed on goods passing through a country.

Translation: The restatement of foreign-currency financial statements into the currency of the parent company.

Translation exposure: Foreign-exchange risk that occurs because the parent company must translate foreign-currency financial statements into the reporting currency of the parent company.

Transnational: (1) An organization in which different capabilities and contributions among different country-operations are shared and integrated; (2) multinational enterprise; (3) company owned and managed by nationals from different countries.

Transnational company (TNC): Usually used as a term that is synonymous with multinational enterprise.

Transnational strategy: Calls for an MNE to configure a value chain that can exploit location economies as well as coordinate value activities to leverage core competencies while simultaneously responding to local pressures.

Transparency: A characteristic of an accounting system that implies that companies disclose a great deal of information about accounting practices; more common in Anglo-Saxon countries (United States, United Kingdom).

Triad: Refers to the three major economic regions of the world—Europe, North America, and Asia.

TRIPS: *See* Trade Related Aspects of Intellectual Property Rights.

Turnkey operation: An operating facility that is constructed under contract and transferred to the owner when the facility is ready to begin operations.

Uncertainty avoidance: A cultural trait where individuals are uncomfortable with uncertainty and prefer structure to independence.

Underemployed: Those people who are working at less than their capacity.

Unfavorable balance of trade: An indication of a trade deficit—that is, imports are greater than exports. Also called deficit.

United Nations (UN): An international organization of countries formed in 1945 to promote world peace and security.

United Nations Conference on Trade and Development (UNCTAD): A UN body that has been especially active in dealing with the relationships between developing and industrialized countries with respect to trade.

Unity-of-command principle: An unbroken chain of command and communication should flow from the CEO to the entry-level worker.

Value: A measure of a firm's capability to sell what it makes for more than the costs incurred to make it.

Value-added tax (VAT): A tax that is a percentage of the value added to a product at each stage of the business process.

Value chain: The collective activities that occur as a product moves from raw materials through production to final distribution.

VAT: *See* Value-added tax.

VER: See voluntary export control.

Vertical alliance: An alliance that links together elements in the value chain backward and forward, such as back to raw materials and forward to final distribution.

Vertical differentiation: The specification of the degrees of centralization and decentralization of decision-making in an organization.

Vertical integration: The control of the different stages as a product moves from raw materials through production to final distribution.

Vertically extended family: Includes several generations.

Virtual organization: A form of company that acquires strategic capabilities by creating a temporary network of independent companies, suppliers, customers, and even rivals.

Visible exports: *See* Merchandise exports.

Visible imports: *See* Merchandise imports.

Voluntary export restraint (VER): A negotiated limitation of exports between an importing and an exporting country.

Weak (or soft) currency: A currency that is not fully convertible. However, even a hard currency can be weak relative to another currency because of the relative exchange rates over time.

World Bank: A multilateral lending institution that provides investment capital to countries.

World Trade Organization (WTO): A voluntary organization through which groups of countries negotiate trading agreements and which has authority to oversee trade disputes among countries.

WTO: *See* World Trade Organization.

Zero defects: The elimination of defects, which results in the reduction of manufacturing costs and an increase in consumer satisfaction.

company index
and trademarks

Page references with "*f*" refer to figures, page references with "*m*" refer to maps, page references with "t" refer to tables, and page references with "n" refer to endnotes cited by number.

name index

Page references with "*f*" refer to figures, page references with "n" refer to endnotes cited by number, and page references with "*t*" refer to tables.

subject index

Page references with "*f*" refer to figures, page references with "*m*" refer to maps, page references with "*n*" refer to endnotes cited by number, and page references with "*t*" refer to tables.